PATENT LAW

ASPEN TREATISE SERIES

PATENT LAW

Fourth Edition

JANICE M. MUELLER

**Instructor and Co-Founder
Chisum Patent Academy**

Wolters Kluwer
Law & Business

Printed in the United States of America.

1 2 3 4 5 6 7 8 9 0

ISBN 978-1-4548-2244-8

Library of Congress Cataloging-in-Publication Data

Mueller, Janice M., 1963-
    Patent law / Janice M. Mueller. — 4th ed.
        p. cm.
    ISBN 978-1-4548-2244-8
1. Patent laws and legislation — United States. I. Title.

 KF3114.M84 2013

 346.7304'86 — dc23

                                                            2012034434

About Wolters Kluwer Law & Business

Wolters Kluwer Law & Business is a leading global provider of intelligent information and digital solutions for legal and business professionals in key specialty areas, and respected educational resources for professors and law students. Wolters Kluwer Law & Business connects legal and business professionals as well as those in the education market with timely, specialized authoritative content and information-enabled solutions to support success through productivity, accuracy and mobility.

Serving customers worldwide, Wolters Kluwer Law & Business products include those under the Aspen Publishers, CCH, Kluwer Law International, Loislaw, Best Case, ftwilliam.com and MediRegs family of products.

CCH products have been a trusted resource since 1913, and are highly regarded resources for legal, securities, antitrust and trade regulation, government contracting, banking, pension, payroll, employment and labor, and healthcare reimbursement and compliance professionals.

Aspen Publishers products provide essential information to attorneys, business professionals and law students. Written by preeminent authorities, the product line offers analytical and practical information in a range of specialty practice areas from securities law and intellectual property to mergers and acquisitions and pension/benefits. Aspen's trusted legal education resources provide professors and students with high-quality, up-to-date and effective resources for successful instruction and study in all areas of the law.

Kluwer Law International products provide the global business community with reliable international legal information in English. Legal practitioners, corporate counsel and business executives around the world rely on Kluwer Law journals, looseleafs, books, and electronic products for comprehensive information in many areas of international legal practice.

Loislaw is a comprehensive online legal research product providing legal content to law firm practitioners of various specializations. Loislaw provides attorneys with the ability to quickly and efficiently find the necessary legal information they need, when and where they need it, by facilitating access to primary law as well as state-specific law, records, forms and treatises.

Best Case Solutions is the leading bankruptcy software product to the bankruptcy industry. It provides software and workflow tools to flawlessly streamline petition preparation and the electronic filing process, while timely incorporating ever-changing court requirements.

ftwilliam.com offers employee benefits professionals the highest quality plan documents (retirement, welfare and non-qualified) and government forms (5500/ PBGC, 1099 and IRS) software at highly competitive prices.

MediRegs products provide integrated health care compliance content and software solutions for professionals in healthcare, higher education and life sciences, including professionals in accounting, law and consulting.

Wolters Kluwer Law & Business, a division of Wolters Kluwer, is headquartered in New York. Wolters Kluwer is a market-leading global information services company focused on professionals.

This book is dedicated to Judge Giles Sutherland Rich,
1904–1999, the consummate teacher whose passion for patent law
and a life fully lived continues to instruct and inspire us all.

Summary of Contents

Contents

Contents

Contents

Contents

Chapter 8   Correcting and Challenging Issued Patents in the USPTO   401

Contents

Contents

Preface

Preface to the Fourth Edition

One of the wonderful, if sometimes maddening, features of U.S. patent law is the speed at which it evolves. Patent law is never stagnant. Change is driven by scientific and technological progress, public policy debate over the proper role of patents in our free market economy, the burgeoning marketplace for patents as a new class of asset, the rise of "non-practicing entities," a steady stream of precedential decisions from the U.S. Court of Appeals for the Federal Circuit (having nationwide jurisdiction over patent-related appeals), and increasingly frequent course corrections imposed by the U.S. Supreme Court. The extensive new matter added to the fourth edition of *Patent Law* reflects this dynamic milieu.

In the three years following publication of the third edition, the rapidity of change in patent law has, if anything, escalated. After years of conflict between pharmaceutical and technology industry sectors, the America Invents Act (AIA) became law in September 2011. The AIA implements the most significant changes to the U.S. Patent Act since the statute's codification in 1952. Most notably, the AIA shifts the U.S. patent system from its historic first-to-invent priority system to a unique first-inventor-to-file system. The new framework retains the traditional pre-filing "grace period" but limits its protections to inventor-generated or -obtained disclosures. The AIA-implemented first-to-file system also changes the timing for what qualifies as "prior art" and removes geographic limitations. Other AIA amendments expand prior user rights and create new procedures for challenging the validity of issued patents in the USPTO. In these respects, at least, the AIA moves U.S. patent law closer to harmonization with foreign patent systems. Given their complexity, however, it remains to be seen whether the AIA-implemented changes will truly achieve Congress's stated goal of providing greater certainty to inventors regarding the scope of their patent rights.

Importantly, the AIA first-to-file changes are prospective only. Over two million extant patents are not impacted by the AIA. The validity of patents issued from applications filed before March 16, 2013, will continue to be assessed under pre-AIA rules for the remainder of the patents' lives. The upshot is that for the next thirty or more years, the U.S. patent system will operate under a dual system of pre- and post-AIA rules. Students of patent law now need to understand not one but two sets of rules. This text explains both.

Preface

Although the AIA implemented manifold changes, many fundamental aspects of patent law were not impacted by its passage. For example, the AIA did not affect several contentious aspects of patent law practice including patent claim interpretation, standards for nonobviousness, and which types of inventions qualify as patent-eligible subject matter. The courts continue to evolve the law in these areas. Since the third edition of this text, the Supreme Court issued *Bilski v. Kappos*[1] and *Mayo v. Prometheus*,[2] two landmark decisions denying patent-eligibility to inventions deemed "abstract ideas" and "laws of nature." These decisions continue the Court's gradual rebalancing of power away from patent owners and toward those who seek to challenge dubious patents (and/or avoid liability for infringing them).

The composition of the Federal Circuit continues to evolve. The appellate court's newer members bring an impressive array of experience, not only in patent law but in practice areas as diverse as criminal prosecution, labor law, international trade, First Amendment, and war crimes. This variety of perspectives is an undoubtedly healthy input for a specialized court, one increasingly recognizing that "[p]atent law is not an island separated from the main body of American jurisprudence."[3] Since the third edition of this text, the Federal Circuit has acted *en banc* to clarify standards in several areas, including the written description of the invention disclosure requirement, joint or distributed infringement, and the defenses of inequitable conduct and patent misuse. The court has also been active in the realm of patent damages. In other fundamentally important areas such as patent claim interpretation (the single most critical part of a patent infringement lawsuit), the court remains mired in intra-Circuit conflicts.

I am indebted to the many patent law students, academics, and practitioners whose feedback and suggestions for this text have proved invaluable during the revision process. I gratefully acknowledge the astute research assistance of Whitney Waters (University of Kentucky College of Law Class of 2012). Any errors are my own. Comments or questions concerning this text are welcome and should be e-mailed to the author at Janice@chisum.com.

Janice M. Mueller
Lexington, Kentucky

November 2012

---

[1]130 S. Ct. 3218 (2010).

[2]132 S. Ct. 1289 (2012).

[3]Knorr-Bremse Systeme Fuer Nutzfahrzeuge GmbH v. Dana Corp., 383 F.3d 1337, 1351 (Fed. Cir. 2004) (Dyk, J., concurring-in-part and dissenting-in-part).

PATENT LAW

Chapter 1

Foundations of the U.S. Patent System

A. Introduction and Chapter Overview

Readers of this text do not need to be convinced of patent law's importance to the U.S. and international economies. The expanding recognition of patent rights and remedies as issues integral to domestic and global trade policy has brought this once relatively technical and arcane area of the law into the mainstream of legal practice.

This text is written for the many U.S. law students who are discovering, for these and many other reasons, that patent law is one of the most exciting, challenging, and relevant subjects in the law school curriculum. The information presented in this text also will be useful for practicing attorneys trained in general civil litigation and corporate practice who seek a more in-depth understanding of patent law. Engineers and scientists who seek patent protection for their inventions will also benefit. All of these individuals are finding it increasingly necessary to have a working comfort level with the finer points of patent, copyright, trademark, and trade secret (collectively, **intellectual property** or **IP**) law, reflecting the growing prominence of these legal specializations in our legal and economic infrastructure.[1]

After considering why patent law is an important subject for further exploration, the remainder of this chapter will introduce key foundational principles intended to enhance the reader's understanding of the rest of the text. This chapter places patents in context as a powerful form of IP protection that conveys the right to exclude all others from unauthorized imitation or use of a patented invention for a statutorily defined period of time. This chapter also provides the reader with a sample U.S. patent and an explanation of its component parts,

---

[1] U.S. Circuit Judge Richard A. Posner has written that "[l]egal disputes over intellectual property have exploded in recent years. No field of law is in greater ferment." Richard A. Posner, *The Law & Economics of Intellectual Property*, Daedalus, Spring 2002, at 5, *available at* http://www.amacad.org/publications/spring2002/posner.pdf.

emphasizing the importance of patent **claims,** which are meticulously drafted, single-sentence definitions of the patent owner's exclusionary right.[2] The chapter next surveys the fundamental economic theory and philosophical justifications upon which U.S. patent law is based. The various primary sources of U.S. patent law also are considered, including the Constitution, federal statutes and regulations, and common law (i.e., judicial decisions). Chapter 1 next introduces the "players" in the U.S. patent system, namely, the agencies and courts that grant and enforce patents in this country, and explains how these entities interact. Chapter 1 concludes with a summary of patent **prosecution,** the process of obtaining a patent by preparing and filing a patent application and interacting with the U.S. Patent & Trademark Office (USPTO).

B.   Why Study Patent Law?

1.   Rise of the Information-Based Economy

Not long ago, very few U.S. law schools offered many IP courses; most schools offered merely a basic course or two in patent law and copyright law, or perhaps an introductory "IP Survey" course covering patent, copyright, and trademark law. The twenty-first-century legal landscape has shifted dramatically. Many U.S. law schools now offer an impressive array of basic and advanced courses in all aspects of intellectual property,[3] and about 25 schools offer a post-J.D. degree known as the LL.M. (or "master of laws") in intellectual property law.[4]

---

[2]The drafting and interpretation of patent claims are considered in detail in Chapter 2, *infra.*

[3]*See* Kenneth L. Port, *Intellectual Property Curricula in the United States,* 46 IDEA 165, 165, 170 (2005) (reporting findings that 144 U.S. law schools offered an IP Survey course, 139 schools offered Patent Law, and that "[a]ll but seven law schools in America offer at least one course in IP"); Roberta R. Kwall, *The Intellectual Property Curriculum: Findings of Professor and Practitioner Surveys,* 49 J. LEGAL EDUC. 203, 205-216 (1999).

[4]The American Bar Association lists the following U.S. law schools offering an LL.M. degree in IP law: Akron, Albany, Boston Univ., Cardozo (N.Y.), Case Western Reserve, Chicago-Kent, Dayton, DePaul (Chicago), Drake, Fordham (N.Y.), George Mason (Va.), George Washington (D.C.), Golden Gate (San Francisco), Houston, Indiana Univ. (Indianapolis), John Marshall (Chicago), Michigan State, New Hampshire, Univ. of San Francisco, Santa Clara (Cal.), Seton Hall, Thomas M. Cooley (Michigan), Washington Univ. (St. Louis), and Univ. of Washington (Seattle). *See* American Bar Association Section of Legal Education & Admissions to the Bar, *Post J.D. Programs by Category,* http://www.americanbar.org/groups/legal_education/resources/llm-degrees_post_j_d_non_j_d/programs_by_category.html (last visited May 21, 2012). Many other U.S. law schools offer an IP concentration or certificate program for J.D. students.

This increase in IP course offerings reflects dramatic changes in the U.S. and global economies, which have heightened the demand for lawyers trained to assist clients in the creation, protection, and enforcement of **IP rights** (**IPRs**) worldwide. In recent years the United States has seen a dramatic rise in the importance of the "IP industries" (e.g., high technology and entertainment) as a contributor to the nation's gross domestic product.[5] United States exports of the "knowledge goods" produced by these industries—information, entertainment, software, movies, books, and the like—are rapidly growing.[6] Corporations are recognizing and exploiting the potential economic power conveyed by ownership of IP, as reflected by popular books such

---

[5]In 2010 "IP-intensive industries accounted for about $5.06 trillion in value added, or 34.8 percent of U.S. gross domestic product (GDP)." Econ. and Statistics Admin. and U.S. Patent and Trademark Off., *Intellectual Property and the U.S. Economy: Industries in Focus* vii (Mar. 2012) ("ESA Report"), *available at* http://www.esa.doc.gov/sites/default/files/reports/documents/ipandtheuseconomyindustriesinfocus.pdf. The ESA report identified 75 industries (among 313 studied) as "IP-intensive industries" that "directly accounted for 27.1 million American jobs, or 18.8 percent of all employment in the economy, in 2010." *Id.* at vi-vii.

An earlier government report estimated that "[m]ore than half of the U.S. work force is in information-based jobs, and the telecommunications and information sector is growing faster than any other sector of the U.S. economy." Information Infrastructure Task Force, Intellectual Property and the National Information Infrastructure: The Report of the Working Group on Intellectual Property Rights (Sept. 1995), *available at* http://www.uspto.gov/go/com/doc/ipnii/ipnii.pdf. The USPTO reports that

> [t]echnological innovation is linked to three-quarters of America's post–WW II growth rate. Two innovation-linked factors—capital investment and increased efficiency—represent 2.5 percentage points of the 3.4 percent average annual growth rate achieved since the 1940's. Invention, innovation, and diffusion benefit consumers not only through new products and processes that promote efficiency and improve health and lifestyle, but also by providing better, higher-paying jobs. Since 1990, the average compensation per employee in innovation-intensive sectors increased 50 percent—nearly two and one-half times the national average.

United States Patent and Trademark Office, *2010-2015 Strategic Plan* 2 (2010), http:///www.uspto.gov/about/stratplan/USPTO_2010-2015_Strategic_Plan.pdf (footnotes omitted).

[6]*See* Richard A. Posner, *The Law & Economics of Intellectual Property*, DAEDALUS, Spring 2002, at 5, *available at* http://www.amacad.org/publications/spring2002/posner.pdf (stating that "[t]he increase in intellectual property litigation was made inevitable by the rise of the information economy, an economy built on intellectual property—which is now, incidentally, America's largest export"). The World Bank reports that in 2009, about 23 percent of U.S. exports of manufactured goods were "[h]igh-technology exports," which it defines as "products with high R&D intensity, such as aerospace, computers, pharmaceuticals, scientific instruments, and electrical machinery." World Bank, *Data: Indicators: High-Technology Exports (% of Manufactured Exports)*, http://data.worldbank.org/indicator/TX.VAL.TECH.MF.ZS/countries (last visited May 21, 2012).

as *Rembrandts in the Attic.*[7] Many corporations now consider patents and other IP to be the key assets of the corporate balance sheet.

Law students also are drawn to patent law because the field is implicated in so many current issues of public interest and concern. Consider, for example, the controversies raised by patents sought on fragments of the human genome,[8] embryonic stem cells, drug targets, and monoclonal antibodies;[9] by the assertion of U.S. patents directed to

---

[7] KEVIN G. RIVETTE & DAVID KLINE, REMBRANDTS IN THE ATTIC: UNLOCKING THE HIDDEN VALUE OF PATENTS (Harvard Bus. School Press 1999).

[8] Since the 1980s, the USPTO has granted more than 20,000 patents claiming isolated DNA molecules, almost 4,000 of which claim isolated human DNA encoding proteins. *See* Remarks of David Kappos, Under Secretary of Commerce for Intellectual Property and Director of the United States Patent and Trademark Office, BIO International Convention (May 3-6, 2010), *available at* http://www.ipwatchdog.com/2010/05/04/kappos-talks-patent-reform-and-gene-patents-at-bio-convention/id=10382/ (May 4, 2010). Nevertheless, the topic of gene patenting continues to engender heated public debate. For example, a New York federal district court in March 2010 granted summary judgment invalidating a number of biotechnology patents directed to the *BRCA1* and *BRCA2* human breast cancer genes. *See* Ass'n for Molecular Pathology (AMP) v. U.S. Patent and Trademark Office (USPTO) and Myriad Genetics, Inc., 702 F. Supp. 2d 181, 185-186 (S.D.N.Y. 2010) (as amended Apr. 5, 2010) ("[T]he challenged patent claims are directed to (1) isolated DNA containing all or portions of the *BRCA1* and *BRCA2* gene sequence and (2) methods for 'comparing' or 'analyzing' BRCA1 [sic, *BRCA1*] and *BRCA2* gene sequences to identify the presence of mutations correlating with a predisposition to breast or ovarian cancer."). One of the most highly publicized patent disputes in recent memory, the *Myriad* decision pits patient care advocates against the patent-owning biotechnology industry.

In July 2011, the Federal Circuit issued its decision in *Myriad*, generating three separate opinions. *Association for Molecular Pathology v. U.S. Pat. and Trademark Off.*, 653 F.3d 1329 (Fed. Cir. 2011) ("*Myriad*"). In the opinion "for the court" authored by Judge Lourie, the Federal Circuit majority reversed the district court's decision that the claimed isolated DNA molecules were patent-ineligible products of nature under 35 U.S.C. §101. Rather, the molecules qualified as §101 compositions of matter because "the molecules as claimed do not exist in nature." *Myriad,* 653 F.3d at 1334; *see also id.* at 1350 (concluding that "the challenged claims to isolated DNAs, *whether limited to cDNAs or not,* are directed to patent-eligible subject matter under §101") (emphasis added). The Federal Circuit also reversed the district court with regard to Myriad's claim to a method of screening potential cancer therapeutics via changes in cell growth rates; in the appellate court's view, this claim recited a patent-eligible method within §101 rather than a patent-ineligible scientific principle. The Federal Circuit affirmed only one aspect of the district court's decision, agreeing with the lower court that "Myriad's method claims directed to 'comparing' or 'analyzing' DNA sequences are patent ineligible [because] such claims include no transformative steps and cover only patent-ineligible abstract, mental steps." *Myriad,* 653 F.3d at 1334.

As of this writing in mid-2012, the issue of gene patentability remains unresolved. On March 20, 2012, the Supreme Court vacated the Federal Circuit's *Myriad* decision and directed the Circuit to reconsider it in view of the Supreme Court's decision in *Mayo v. Prometheus*, 132 S. Ct. 1289 (2012), discussed *infra* Chapter 7 ("Potentially Patentable Subject Matter (35 U.S.C. §101)").

[9] *See, e.g.,* Eliot Marshall, *Patent on HIV Receptor Provokes an Outcry,* 287 SCIENCE 1375 (2000); Andrew Pollack, *The New High-Tech Battleground,* N.Y. TIMES, July 3,

business methods such as Amazon.com's "One-Click" ordering system;[10] consumer protests and government investigations over the high cost of prescription drugs (many of which are protected by patent);[11] and by the developing world's HIV/AIDS crisis and the corresponding need for low-cost access to patented drugs such as AZT and the "triple cocktail" that are used to treat those diseases.[12]

Students focused on international trade and business law also are finding an understanding of patent law important to their field. Once viewed as a rather specialized and obscure area of international commerce, the transnational aspects of recognizing and enforcing IP rights including patents have taken center stage as an issue of global trade. International intellectual property treaties such as the Trade-Related Aspects of Intellectual Property (TRIPS) Agreement of the World Trade Organization (WTO)[13] continue to spark philosophical and economic debate between the "north" and "south"—pitting the developed, industrialized countries that generally seek strong protection of IP rights against the less- and least-developed countries that have historically opposed strong IP protection because of economic and public health concerns.[14]

The 1995 entry into force of the TRIPS Agreement,[15] to which 155 countries are signatories as of May 2012,[16] was a watershed event

---

1998, at 31 (describing patent battles involving Eli Lilly, Monoclonal Antibodies, Inc., and Abbott Laboratories over use of monoclonal antibodies in diagnostic testing with sandwich immuno-assays).

[10]*See* Patti Waldmeir & Louise Kehoe, *E-Commerce Companies Sue to Protect Patents: Intellectual Rights Given Legal Test*, FINANCIAL TIMES, Oct. 25, 1999, at 16.

[11]*See* Tatiana Boncompagni, *Patently Political*, AMERICAN LAWYER, Sept. 13, 2002, at 96 (describing Federal Trade Commission review of Hatch-Waxman Act litigation settlement practices between brand-name pharmaceutical firms and their generic rivals); Julie Appleby & Jayne O'Donnell, *Consumers Pay as Drug Firms Fight Over Generics*, USA TODAY, June 6, 2002, at A1.

[12]*See* Tina Rosenberg, *Look at Brazil*, N.Y. TIMES, Jan. 28, 2001, §6 (Magazine) at 26 (reporting on HIV/AIDS catastrophe in Africa, differences in pharmaceutical patent protection around the world, challenges in treating patient populations in developing countries, and Brazil's use of compulsory licensing for the manufacture of HIV/AIDS drugs). *See also* A. Samuel Oddi, *Plagues, Pandemics, and Patents: Legality and Morality*, 51 IDEA 1 (2011) (addressing the tension between the need for life-saving medicines for least-developed nations and maintaining incentives for developing these medicines in developed nations).

[13]*See* Agreement on Trade-Related Aspects of Intellectual Property Rights, Marrakesh Agreement Establishing the World Trade Organization, Annex 1C, art. 31(1), Apr. 15, 1994, 1869 U.N.T.S. 299; 33 I.L.M. 1197 (1994) [hereinafter TRIPS].

[14]*See generally* KEITH E. MASKUS, INTELLECTUAL PROPERTY RIGHTS IN THE GLOBAL ECONOMY (Inst. for Int'l Econ. 2000).

[15]The TRIPS Agreement was signed in Marrakesh, Morocco on April 15, 1994. The TRIPS Agreement entered into force on January 1, 1995.

[16]*See* World Trade Organization, *Members and Observers,* http://www.wto.org/english/thewto_e/whatis_e/tif_e/org6_e.htm (last visited May 27, 2012) (stating that the

for the protection of IP worldwide. Countries that are signatories to TRIPS must agree to maintain certain minimum standards of protection for innovation protectable under the law of patents, copyright, trademarks, and trade secrets. They also must commit to instituting minimum acceptable enforcement measures to protect IP rights. Through TRIPS' implementation of the WTO's Dispute Settlement Understanding (DSU), member countries now have a powerful mechanism—the imposition of trade sanctions—for challenging another member country's failure to live up to its obligations under the TRIPS Agreement.[17]

Yet another valuable reason to study patent law is to grasp the complexities of a legal system evolving through significant legislative reform. Discussed in greater detail elsewhere in this text, the America Invents Act of 2011 (AIA) implemented landmark changes to U.S. patent law,[18] probably the most significant since 1952, when the current patent statute was codified at Title 35 of the *United States Code*. For example, the AIA changes the United States practice from its historic first-to-invent **priority system** to a unique first-inventor-to-file system, while retaining some (but not all) aspects of the traditional U.S. pre-filing **grace period**.[19] The first-to-file system and associated changes are prospective, meaning that they apply only to patent applications filed on or after March 16, 2013, and patents issuing therefrom.[20] Patents and applications already existing on March 16, 2013, will continue to be governed by the pre-AIA rules, also detailed in this text. Because a patent's validity may be subject to litigation challenge throughout the patent's lifetime, practitioners of patent law will need to operate in a dual system, understanding and applying both pre- and post-AIA rules, for the next 30 years or more.[21]

WTO had 155 members as of May 10, 2012). All WTO member countries must comply with the WTO's TRIPS Agreement. *See* Scope of the WTO, Apr. 15, 1994, Marrakesh Agreement Establishing the World Trade Organization Art. II(2)—Results of the Uruguay Round, 33 I.L.M. 1125 (1994) (stating that "[t]he agreements and associated legal instruments included in Annexes 1, 2 and 3 . . . are integral parts of this Agreement, binding on all Members"). The referenced "Annex 1" includes the TRIPS Agreement as Annex 1C.

[17]These and other international topics are covered in Chapter 12 ("International Patenting Issues"), *infra*.

[18]Leahy-Smith America Invents Act, Pub. L. No. 112-29 (H.R. 1249), 125 Stat. 284 (2011).

[19]*See* Leahy-Smith America Invents Act, Pub. L. No. 112-29 (H.R. 1249), §3 ("First Inventor to File"), 125 Stat. 284, 285-293 (2011). The concepts of priority and grace period are further explored *infra* Chapter 4 ("Novelty, Loss of Right, and Priority Pre- and Post-America Invents Act of 2011 (35 U.S.C. §102)").

[20]*See* Leahy-Smith America Invents Act, Pub. L. No. 112-29 (H.R. 1249), §3(n) ("Effective Date"), 125 Stat. 284, 293 (2011).

[21]An unfortunate feature of the AIA is that Congress rewrote many critical sections of the Patent Act but retained the original statutory section numbers. Thus, for

2.   Educational Prerequisites

Many law students believe they must have an undergraduate degree in the sciences or engineering disciplines to study patent law. This is incorrect. The study of patent law will entail the application of legal rules to technology, of course, because patents are all about generating and protecting inventions. Although having scientific or technical training may be helpful to a student's understanding of the facts in some cases, it is certainly not a prerequisite for success. Consider that the first time she encounters it, even a nuclear engineer may be mystified by genetic engineering technology. Anyone with a genuine interest and curiosity about inventions and how the law treats them should be able to master patent law. This text endeavors to use straightforward examples of simple inventions to illustrate its points. Technical complexity should not obscure learning about the law.

Only one aspect of patent law practice requires a technical background. In order to sit for the patent bar examination administered by the USPTO, candidates must have an undergraduate degree or equivalent course work in one of the scientific and technical disciplines listed in the USPTO's *General Requirements Bulletin for Admission to the Examination for Registration to Practice in Patent Cases Before the United States Patent and Trademark Office.*[22] Passing the patent bar exam qualifies a person to be a registered patent agent or attorney, who may represent clients before the USPTO in matters such as filing and prosecuting applications for patent.

Many lawyers without a technical background practice in areas of patent law other than patent prosecution. Being a registered patent attorney (i.e., passing the USPTO bar exam) is *not* required to litigate issued patents, to license patents, or to practice other forms of IP law such as trademark, copyright, and trade secret law.

---

example, patent professionals will need to understand and apply the pre-AIA version of 35 U.S.C. §102 as well as the entirely new, post-AIA version of 35 U.S.C. §102. To distinguish between pre- and post-AIA versions of statutory sections, this text will generally use the citation format "35 U.S.C. §102(b) (2006)" or "35 U.S.C. §102(b) (pre-AIA)" when specifically referring to pre-AIA versions of statutory provisions. The statutory provisions amended or created by the AIA will generally be cited with their effective dates, for example, "35 U.S.C. §102(a)(1) (eff. Mar. 16, 2013)."

[22]*Available at* http://www.uspto.gov/ip/boards/oed/GRB_March_2012.pdf (last visited June 13, 2012). Persons who have passed the Fundamentals of Engineering (FE) test, which is administered by individual state boards of engineering examiners, may also qualify to sit for the patent bar exam. *See id.* at 8 ("Category C: Practical Engineering or Scientific Experience").

C.   What Is a Patent?

1.   Patents as a Form of Intellectual Property

Patents, along with copyrights, trademarks, and trade secrets, are a form of legal protection for intellectual property. Ownership of IP represents a proprietary right in intangible products of the human mind. These "knowledge goods" include inventions, ideas, information, artistic creations, music, brand names, celebrity persona, industrial secrets, and customer lists.

2.   The Appropriability Problem of Intellectual Property

Our legal system recognizes separate forms of legal protection for knowledge goods, rather than analyzing them under the same law that applies to real property or tangible objects. Why? As explained below, the fundamentally different nature of knowledge goods dictates this separate structure.

Because they are intangibles, knowledge goods such as information suffer from an "appropriability problem." Knowledge is indivisible, inexhaustible, and nonexcludable. Unlike an item of tangible property, sharing my idea with another person neither splits up nor exhausts my possession of the idea. If I have only one football, giving that football to a friend divests me of its physical possession. But if I invent a way of manufacturing a football out of grooved foam so that it flies higher and farther than existing footballs, I retain possession of that idea even after disclosing it to my friend. As Thomas Jefferson wrote to his colleague Isaac McPherson in 1813, "he who lights his taper at mine, receives light without darkening me. . . . Inventions then cannot, in nature, be a subject of property."[23] After I have disclosed my idea to another, how am I to prevent subsequent uses of the idea? In this sense, knowledge is considered nonexcludable.

Because knowledge goods are inexhaustible and nonexcludable, how then are inventors to profit from the investments made to generate these goods? The key problem with generation of knowledge goods is that the cost of creating knowledge can be very high, but the cost of copying it is often trivial. To see why this is so, consider the discovery of a new drug that cures a life-threatening illness. Many years and millions of dollars of research, development, and testing have gone

---

[23]Graham v. John Deere Co., 383 U.S. 1, 9 n.2 (1966) (quoting 6 Thomas Jefferson, The Writings of Thomas Jefferson 180-181) (H.A. Washington ed., Washington, D.C., Taylor & Maury 1854, 2d ed.)).

into the creation of this drug, but once its chemical structure is known, the drug can be copied for pennies. Because copying is so easy and inexpensive, how, then, do we motivate firms to invest in this technology? How do we encourage innovation in these technologies?

As detailed below, patents are one solution to these quandaries.[24] The ownership of a patent permits the patentee to recoup its investment in discovering and developing the new drug, by conveying a time-limited right to exclude all competitors from the marketplace for that drug. In other words, the patentee will be positioned as the sole source of the patented drug during the life of the patent. This possibility of recouping investment costs by the acquisition of monopoly profits acts as a powerful spur to technical innovation.

3. Public Goods

When adequate incentives for innovation do not exist, the result is underproduction of new inventions. Economists have referred to this "market failure" scenario as a "public goods problem."[25] Besides inventions, other classic examples of public goods include lighthouses and national defense. Consider also the example of a telethon to raise money for a public television station. Each of us watching the telethon on our television has an incentive not to make any donation, that is, to pay less than our pro rata share for these goods, because we know we will benefit (i.e., will be able to watch the station's programming) whether or not we contribute. Absent a mechanism to exclude "free riders"—people who enjoy the benefit of the good without paying for it—these public goods will be underproduced.

To overcome these market failures, society has created systems of intellectual property rights. When the right conveyed is a patent, this means the government conveys to an inventor a time-limited property right in her invention. More specifically, the patent property right is the right to prevent others from making, selling, offering to sell,

---

[24]Alternative proposed solutions to the market failure problem have included government subsidization for research and development, and the grant of prizes or awards for technical achievement (such as the Nobel Prize). *See also* ROBERT P. MERGES ET AL., INTELLECTUAL PROPERTY IN THE NEW TECHNOLOGICAL AGE 13 (5th ed. 2010) (noting that to prevent underproduction of public goods such as national defense and lighthouses, government steps in and pays for them; in contrast, for many forms of information, government has "created intellectual property rights in an effort to give authors and inventors control over the use and distribution of their ideas, thereby encouraging them to invest in the production of new ideas and works of authorship").

[25]*See* ROBERT P. MERGES ET AL., INTELLECTUAL PROPERTY IN THE NEW TECHNOLOGICAL AGE 11-14 (5th ed. 2010) (observing that economists refer to information as a "public good" that may be consumed by many without depletion, and that it is difficult to identify and stop those who use information without paying for it).

importing, or even using the patented invention in the patent-granting country during the term of the patent.[26]

The conveyance of a property right in inventions is by no means a new idea. A right to exclude others from the use of certain worthy inventions was provided in the first known general patent law, enacted by the Venetian Republic in the late fifteenth century.[27] In 1624, England enacted the Statute of Monopolies, which prohibited all monopolies but recognized an exception for "any manner of newe Manufacture within this Realm. . . ."[28] The U.S. patent system owes its origin to these predecessors.

4.   Exception to the General Rule of Competition by Imitation

In a free market economy such as that of the United States, the general rule is that competition through imitation of a competitor's product or service is permitted, so long as that competition is not deemed legally "unfair."[29] Patent rights should be understood as carefully limited exceptions to the general rule of free and open competition through imitation.

Older cases referred to the notion of competition through imitation of others' products or services as the *privilege* to compete, but it is probably more precisely viewed as a *right* to compete, so long as that competition is fair. Although patents are not technically viewed as a subset of unfair competition law,[30] in a larger sense the infringement of another's patent right is a manner of competition that society has decided is wrong and for which it will subject the copier to remedies such as an injunction and damages.[31]

---

[26]35 U.S.C. §154(a)(1); 35 U.S.C. §271(a).

[27]*See* Bruce W. Bugbee, The Genesis of American Patent and Copyright Law 22-23 (Public Affairs Press, Washington, D.C., 1967) (reproducing Venetian enactment of March 19, 1474, which "appearing 150 years before England's Statute of Monopolies, established a legal foundation for the world's first patent system").

[28]*Id.* at 39 (quoting England's Statute of Monopolies (1624)).

[29]*See* 1 J. Thomas McCarthy, McCarthy on Trademarks and Unfair Competition §1.2 (4th ed. 2011) (characterizing public domain as "the rule," and intellectual property as "the exception").

[30]The traditional understanding of "unfair competition law" embraces commercial torts such as trademark infringement, false advertising, and trade secret misappropriation, but not violations of the patent or copyright laws, which are considered separate regimes. *See id.* §1.10 (listing examples of unfair competition).

[31]These remedies for violations of patent laws are explored in greater detail in Chapter 11 ("Remedies for Patent Infringement"), *infra.*

5. The Patent Document and Its Components

The meaning of *patent* can be viewed in at least two senses. One use of "patent" refers to an official document issued by the U.S. government. Figure 1.1 reproduces a typical U.S. patent, directed to an insulating sleeve for a hot beverage cup. Skim over this document and familiarize yourself with its various parts. The entirety of the document is referred to as the patent's **specification,** which is composed of (1) the **written description,** (2) drawings (where necessary, as here in the patent's figures, to fully enable others to make and use the invention), and (3) the claims.

The patent's **claims,** which are the numbered, single-sentence paragraphs found at the very end of the patent document, are its most important part. Although Chapter 2 ("Patent Claims"), *infra,* is devoted to the topic, a brief introduction is helpful here. The claims define the scope of the patent owner's right to exclude others from making, using, selling, offering to sell, or importing her invention, much as a deed to a plot of land defines the geographic boundaries of its owner's right to exclude others from coming onto the land (i.e., trespassing). Patent claims form a sort of lingual fence around an invention. For the patent system to function properly, patent claims must provide clear notice on which marketplace participants can rely.[32] The interpretation and scope of the claims will be the focal point of any litigation involving the patent. The language of the claims is scrutinized intensely in analyzing both the validity of the patent and whether it has been infringed. In determining whether to grant the patent in the first instance, the USPTO will compare the language of the claims with relevant prior technology. This process is described in Section H ("Patent Prosecution Overview"), *infra.*

---

[32]Professors Bessen and Meuer succinctly capture this idea in their book chapter titled "If You Can't Tell the Boundaries, Then It Ain't Property." James Bessen & Michael J. Meurer, Patent Failure: How Judges, Bureaucrats, and Lawyers Put Innovators at Risk 46 (2008). They contend that

> increasingly, patents fail to provide *clear notice* of the scope of patent rights. Thus, innovators find it increasingly difficult to determine whether a technology will infringe upon anyone's patents, giving rise to inadvertent infringement. Similarly, they find it increasingly costly to find and negotiate the necessary patent licenses in advance of their technology development and adoption decisions. Thus, clearance procedures that work well for tangible property are undercut by a profusion of fuzzy patent rights.

Id.

United States Patent [19]

Sorensen

[11]	**Patent Number:** **5,425,497**
[45]	**Date of Patent:** **Jun. 20, 1995**

US005425497A

[54] **CUP HOLDER**

[76] Inventor: **Jay Sorensen,** 3616 NE. Alberta Ct., Portland, Oreg. 97211

[21] Appl. No.: **150,682**

[22] Filed: **Nov. 9, 1993**

[51] Int. Cl.^{6} **B65D 3/22**
[52] U.S. Cl. **220/738;** 220/903; 294/31.2

[58] **Field of Search** .... 294/27.1, 31.2, 33, 294/149, 152; 220/710.5, 753, 758, 759, 412, 738, 739, 903; 229/1.5 B, 1.5 H, 89, 90

[56] **References Cited**

U.S. PATENT DOCUMENTS

1,632,347	6/1927	Pipkin .
1,771,765	7/1930	Benson .
1,866,805	7/1932	Haywood 294/31.2
2,028,566	1/1936	Seipel et al. .
2,266,828	12/1941	Sykes .
2,591,578	4/1952	McNealy et al. .
2,617,549	11/1952	Egger .
2,661,889	12/1953	Phinney .
2,675,954	4/1954	Vogel .
2,853,222	9/1958	Gallagher .
2,979,301	4/1961	Reveal .... 229/1.5 H X

3,049,277	8/1962	Shappell .
3,123,273	3/1964	Miller .... 229/1.5 B
3,157,335	11/1964	Maier .... 229/1.5 B
3,908,523	9/1975	Shikaya .
4,685,583	8/1987	Noon .... 294/31.2 X
5,092,485	3/1992	Lee .
5,145,107	9/1992	Silver et al. .

Primary Examiner—Johnny D. Cherry
Attorney, Agent, or Firm—Kolisch, Hartwell, Dickinson, McCormack & Heuser

[57] **ABSTRACT**

A cup holder is disclosed in the form of a sheet with distal ends. A web is formed in one of the ends, and a corresponding slot is formed in the other end such that the ends interlock. Thus the cup holder is assembled by rolling the sheet and interlocking the ends. The sheet can be an elongate band of pressed material, preferably pressed paper pulp, and is preferably formed with multiple nubbins and depressions. In one embodiment, the sheet has a top and bottom that are arcuate and concentric, and matching webs and cuts are formed in each end of the sheet, with the cuts being perpendicular to the top of the sheet.

6 Claims, 1 Drawing Sheet

Figure 1.1

Java Jacket®
U.S. Patent No. 5,425,497 (issued 1995)

U.S. Patent   June 20, 1995   5,425,497

FIGURE 2

FIGURE 3

FIGURE 1

FIGURE 4

FIGURE 5

Figure 1.1

(Continued)

13

5,425,497

1

CUP HOLDER

FIELD OF THE INVENTION

The present invention relates generally to holders for cups. More particularly, the invention relates to a disposable cup holder that can be stored flat and then assembled by a user to fit around a cup. The resulting cup and holder combination increases the gripability and insulation value of the cup.

BACKGROUND ART

A cup holder is a removable device that encompasses a cup to provide added features to the cup. These features can include gripability, insulation value, and decoration. By gripability it is meant that the cup and holder combination is easier to hold in a human hand. Insulation value is important if the cup is holding hot or cold liquids, particularly if the cup is a thin disposable paper cup which has little inherent insulation value. Decoration can include features that make the cup more appealing, such as texture or color, or features that communicate to the user of the holder, such as advertising or instructions.

A conventional cup holder includes a three-dimensional body into which the cup is inserted. These bodies can be in the shape of an annular ring, such as that shown in U.S. Pat. No. 2,028,566, or in the shape of a cup that is oversized relative to the cup to be held, such as that shown in U.S. Pat. No. 2,617,549. In order to provide insulation value from a material that is thermally conductive, such as paper, the cup holders are usually provided with annular grooves or vertical flutes so that the holder is only in contact with the cup at the valleys in the grooves or flutes. These grooves or flutes provide a structural integrity to the cup holders such that they must be packaged in substantially the same form as they will be used. Thus a significant volume is required to store a quantity of the cup holders. Therefore it is cumbersome for a retailer selling drinks in cups to use the cup holders because a significant amount of shelf space is required just to have a sufficient quantity of cup holders accessible for immediate use.

It is an object of the invention to reduce the volume required to store cup holders.

Conventional cup holders may also require significant amounts of handling and operations to be assembled. It is a further object of this invention to reduce the number of steps involved in making a cup holder ready for ultimate use by the consumer.

An object of the invention is to produce a cup holder by bending a sheet and interlocking the ends.

It is a further object of the invention to improve the gripability of a cup.

Yet another object of the invention is to thermally insulate the hand of a user from the liquid held in a cup.

Another object of the invention is to form a cup holder from a substantially flat sheet of pressed paper pulp.

SUMMARY OF THE INVENTION

The invented cup holder is designed for use with an upright cup. The cup is in turn designed for holding hot or cold liquids, and has an open rim and closed base.

The invented cup holder is formed from a sheet of flat material, preferably pressed paper pulp. The sheet is formed to have a length defined by a first end and a second end. The sheet has a width defined by a top and

2

a bottom. Two cuts are made in the sheet, the first cut extending partially across the width of the sheet and adjacent one end. The second cut also extends partially across the width of the sheet, but is adjacent the end of the sheet opposite from the first cut. Preferably, one of the cuts severs the top of the sheet and the other of the cuts severs the bottom of the sheet. A holder conforming to a cup can then be made by rolling the sheet into a substantially cylindrical shape and interlocking the first end with the second end by interlocking the first cut with the second cut. Once the cylindrically shaped cup holder is made, a cup can be inserted into the cup holder.

The sheet includes a texture to increase the gripability and insulation value of the cup holder. In one embodiment, the texture includes multiple nubbins and depressions interspersed about the sheet, preferably in a uniform repeating geometrical pattern. The depressions can be aligned in rows forming troughs, so that any liquid that should spill on the cup holder will tend to trickle along the troughs.

If the cup holder is to hold a tapered cup, the holder fits the cup better if the top and bottom of the sheet are arcuate and essentially concentric. Preferably, the first cut is substantially non-parallel to the second cut such that the first cut and the second cut extend along lines that are substantially perpendicular to the arcuate top. When a sheet so formed is made into a cup holder, the resulting holder is tapered with a top and bottom that define planes essentially parallel to the planes defined by the rim and base of the cup to be held. The cuts will also be aligned with the taper of the cup when the holder is assembled, that is, the cuts will extend along a line that is substantially perpendicular to the above planes.

Alternatively, the present invention can be viewed as a combination of a cup and a cup holder. The cup holder is an elongate band having ends that detachably interlock. When the ends are so interlocked, the elongate band extends in a continuous loop. One method of interlocking the ends is by forming interlocking slots in the band. Preferably, the band includes a texture to increase the gripability and insulation value of the combination. The texture can include multiple nubbins and depressions interspersed about the band, preferably in a uniform repeating geometrical pattern. If the cup used as part of the combination is tapered, the tipper and lower surfaces of the band can be concentric arcuate shapes so that the continuous loop formed from the band is approximately conformed with the cup.

BRIEF DESCRIPTION OF THE DRAWINGS

FIG. 1 is a perspective view of an assembled cup holder formed in accordance with one embodiment of the present invention, in combination with a cup.

FIG. 2 is a top plan view of the cup holder of the present invention, shown unassembled.

FIG. 3 is a perspective partial view of a stack of the cup holders shown in FIG. 2.

FIG. 4 is a partial front elevation of the combination shown in FIG. 1, shown with liquid spilled on the cup holder.

FIG. 5 is a partial front sectional view of the combination shown in FIG. 4, taken along the line 5—5 shown in FIG. 4.

Figure 1.1

5,425,497

3

DETAILED DESCRIPTION AND BEST MODE OF CARRYING OUT THE INVENTION

Referring to FIG. 1, the cup holder 10 is shown in combination with a cup 12. Cup 12 is usually a tapered paper cup with an open rim 14 and a closed base 16. Cup holder 10 is shown in its assembled state in FIG. 1, and can be described as a continuous loop.

Cup holder 10 is shown unassembled in FIGS. 2 and 3, and is in the form of a sheet 18, also described as an elongate band having distal ends. Sheet 18 has a length 20 defined by a first end 22 and a second end 24. Sheet 18 also has a width 26, defined by a top 28 and a bottom 30. Top 28 and bottom 30 are preferably arcuate in shape. Thus top 28 can be described as an elongate arcuate surface and bottom 30 can also be described as an elongate arcuate surface. Elongate arcuate surface 28 is essentially concentric with elongate arcuate surface 30, such that the radius of surface 28 is longer than the radius of surface 30 by an amount approximately equal to width 26.

A first cut 32 is made in sheet 18 adjacent first end 22. First cut 32 extends partially across width 26, and preferably severs top 28 such that a first tab 34 and first web 36 are formed. A second cut 38 is made in sheet 18 adjacent second end 24. Second cut 38 extends partially across width 26, and preferably severs bottom 30 to form a second tab 40 and second web 42.

When sheet 18 is configured as described above, a cup holder can be assembled as follows. Sheet 18 is rolled into a substantially cylindrical shape, and cuts 32 and 38 are interlocked with webs 42 and 36, respectively, thereby interlocking first end 22 with second end 24. The resulting cup holder forms a continuous loop as shown in FIG. 1, and can hold cup 12 by inserting cup 12 into cup holder 10. Elongate arcuate surface 28 forms an open annular top that is substantially parallel with rim 14 of cup 12. Elongate arcuate surface 30 forms an open annular bottom that is substantially parallel to base 16 of cup 12. Cup 12 extends through the open top and open bottom and, as shown in FIG. 5, encircles cup 12 so that cup holder 10 has an inner surface 58 and an outer surface 60. First cut 32 and second cut 38 extend along a line shown generally at 44. Line 44 is substantially perpendicular to rim 14 of cup 12. Alternatively, line 44 can be described as extending along the taper of cup 12.

As shown in FIGS. 4 and 5, sheet 18 is provided with a texture indicated generally at 46. Texture 46 includes multiple nubbins 48 and oppositely shaped discrete, approximately semi-spherically shaped depressions 50 distributed on substantially the entire inner surface 58 of sheet 18. Nubbins 48 and depressions 50 are arranged in a repeating geometrical pattern. Preferably, depressions 50 are aligned in rows forming troughs indicated generally by line 52 in FIG. 4.

Should liquid spill on cup holder 10, as indicated generally at 54 in FIG. 5, liquid 54 will tend to trickle along troughs 52. When the combination of cup holder 10 and cup 12 is held by a human hand, the hand will tend to be held away from troughs 52 by nubbins 48. Thus the hand will be kept out of contact with liquid 54. Furthermore, as shown in FIG. 4, when cup holder 10 is placed on an upright cup 12, troughs 52 extend along lines that intersect both rim 14 and lines extending along the taper of cup 12 at acute angles. Thus the flow of liquid 54 down cupholder 10 is slowed relative to the flow of liquid down vertically oriented flutes.

4

In addition, texture 46 provides an increased gripability to the cup and cup holder combination. Specifically, nubbins 48 provide a surface texture which is more easily held by a human hand.

Texture 46 also adds an insulation value to the combination because depressions 50 define non-contacting regions 56 of sheet 18, and thus reduce the surface contact between cup holder 10 and the hand of a user and cup 12, respectively. Thus conductive heat transfer is reduced. The insulation value is also increased by air gaps 56 formed by texture 46.

Furthermore, texture 46 is pleasing in appearance, and therefore provides decoration for cup holder 10.

Cup holder 10 as described above and shown in the figures is made from a reversible, two-sided sheet 18. That is, when sheet 18 is rolled to form a continuous loop, either of the textured sides can serve as the outside of cup holder 10. The reversibility of cup holder 10 is particularly evident when, as shown in FIG. 5, inner surface 58 and outer surface 60 are mirrored, that is, when each depression 62 on inner surface 58 defines a nubbine 48 on outer surface 60 and each depression 50 on outer surface 60 defines a nubbin 64 on inner surface 58. Non-reversible cup holders are, however, envisioned within the scope of the present invention.

Alternatively, the present invention can be viewed as a method of making a cup and cup holder combination. The method includes the steps of providing a flat sheet with a texture, forming the flat sheet into an elongate band 18 having a top elongate arcuate surface 28 and a bottom elongate arcuate surface 30. Elongate arcuate surface 28 is severed with a first cut 32 extending partially across elongate band 18. Elongate arcuate surface 30 is severed with a second cut 38 extending partially across elongate band 18. Elongate band 18 is then rolled to form a substantially cylindrical shape, and first cut 32 is interlocked with second cut 38 to form a continuous loop. A cup 12 is then inserted into cup holder 10.

Many materials are envisioned for use in making sheet 10, however pressed paper pulp is preferred. Pressed pulp, similar in properties to that used to make semi-rigid paper products such as egg cartons, is pleasing to the touch, partially absorbent, easily formed and relatively inexpensive.

INDUSTRIAL APPLICABILITY

The invented cup holder and cup and cup holder combination are applicable in any situation where the gripability, insulation value, or decoration of a cup needs to be augmented. It is particularly applicable for a cup holder for holding paper coffee cups.

While a preferred embodiment of the invented cup holder and cup and cup holder combination have been disclosed, changes and modifications can be made without departing from the spirit of the invention.

We claim:

1. A cup and holder combination comprising:
   a cup for holding hot or cold liquids; and
   a holder defined by a band mounted on and encircling the cup, the band having an open top and an open bottom through which the cup extends and an inner surface immediately adjacent the cup with a plurality of discrete, spaced-apart, approximately semi-spherically shaped depressions distributed on substantially the entire inner surface of the band so that each depression defines a non-contacting region of the band creating an air gap between the

Figure 1.1

(Continued)

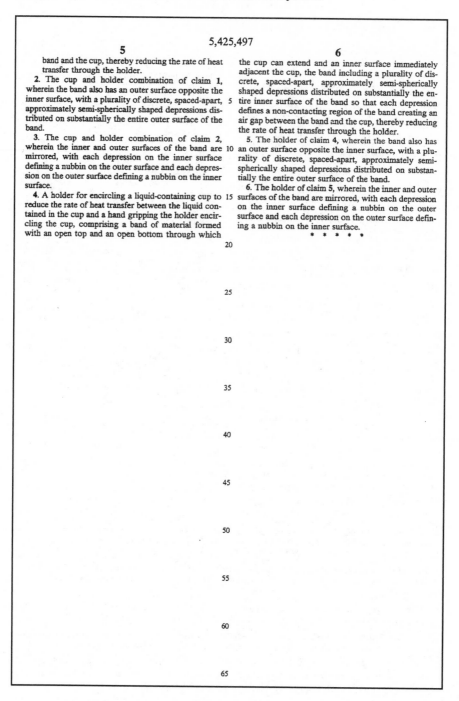

5,425,497

5

band and the cup, thereby reducing the rate of heat transfer through the holder.

2. The cup and holder combination of claim 1, wherein the band also has an outer surface opposite the inner surface, with a plurality of discrete, spaced-apart, approximately semi-spherically shaped depressions distributed on substantially the entire outer surface of the band.

3. The cup and holder combination of claim 2, wherein the inner and outer surfaces of the band are mirrored, with each depression on the inner surface defining a nubbin on the outer surface and each depression on the outer surface defining a nubbin on the inner surface.

4. A holder for encircling a liquid-containing cup to reduce the rate of heat transfer between the liquid contained in the cup and a hand gripping the holder encircling the cup, comprising a band of material formed with an open top and an open bottom through which

6

the cup can extend and an inner surface immediately adjacent the cup, the band including a plurality of discrete, spaced-apart, approximately semi-spherically shaped depressions distributed on substantially the entire inner surface of the band so that each depression defines a non-contacting region of the band creating an air gap between the band and the cup, thereby reducing the rate of heat transfer through the holder.

5. The holder of claim 4, wherein the band also has an outer surface opposite the inner surface, with a plurality of discrete, spaced-apart, approximately semi-spherically shaped depressions distributed on substantially the entire outer surface of the band.

6. The holder of claim 5, wherein the inner and outer surfaces of the band are mirrored, with each depression on the inner surface defining a nubbin on the outer surface and each depression on the outer surface defining a nubbin on the inner surface.

* * * * *

Figure 1.1

6.   The Negative Right to Exclude

A patent, in one sense, is an official government document like the one reproduced at Figure 1.1. More importantly, the patent represents a property right. The paper document is merely a tangible representation of the boundaries of a time-limited property right granted by the U.S. federal government. Importantly, this property right is a *negative* right; that is, a right to exclude others from making, using, selling, offering to sell, or importing the patented invention in the United States during the term of the patent.[33] Much as the owner of real property generally has a right to prevent others from entering onto her land,[34] the owner of a patent can ask a court to enjoin those who make, use, sell, offer to sell, or import her invention into this country without authorization. The patent owner also can grant **licenses** to third parties, authorizing them to make, use, sell, offer to sell, or import the patented invention without fear of being sued for infringement. Licenses are contracts, typically requiring financial payments to the patentee called *royalties*.[35]

Notably, a patent does not convey any *positive* or affirmative right to make, use, sell, offer to sell, or import an invention.[36] Any such positive right to exploit one's own creations arises from the common law, not federal patent law.[37] In fact, there are any number of reasons why one

---

[33]35 U.S.C. §154(a)(1); 35 U.S.C. §271(a).

[34]*See* RESTATEMENT (FIRST) OF PROPERTY §1 cmt. a, illus. 1 (1936) (definition of *right*) (stating that A, the owner of Blackacre, "normally has a right that B [any other person] shall not walk across Blackacre," and that B "normally has a duty not to walk across Blackacre").

[35]*See generally* MICHAEL A. EPSTEIN & FRANK L. POLITANO, DRAFTING LICENSE AGREEMENTS (4th ed. 2011); ROBERT W. GOMULKIEWICZ ET AL., LICENSING INTELLECTUAL PROPERTY: LAW AND APPLICATION (2d ed. 2011).

[36]*See* Leatherman Tool Group Inc. v. Cooper Indus., Inc., 131 F.3d 1011, 1015 (Fed. Cir. 1997) (explaining that "the federal patent laws do not create any affirmative right to make, use, or sell anything. As the Supreme Court has stated, '[t]he franchise which the patent grants, consists altogether in the right to exclude every one from making, using, or vending the thing patented, without the permission of the patentee. This is all that he obtains by the patent.'") (quoting Bloomer v. McQuewan, 55 U.S. 539, 548 (1852)).

[37]*See* Crown Die & Tool Co. v. Nye Tool & Machine Works, 261 U.S. 24, 36 (1923) (noting that "[i]t is the fact that the patentee has invented or discovered something useful[,] and thus has the common-law right to make, use, and vend it himself[,] which induces the government to clothe him with power to exclude every one else from making, using[,] or vending it."). The common law did not provide the inventor with any right to exclude *others*, however. *See* Deepsouth Packing Co. v. Laitram Corp., 406 U.S. 518, 525-526 (1972). The negative right to exclude is provided only through the Patent Act. *See* 406 U.S. at 526 n.8 ("But the right of property which a patentee has in his invention, and his right to its exclusive use, is derived altogether from these statutory provisions; and this court [has] always held that an inventor has no right of property in his invention, upon which he can maintain a suit, unless he obtains a patent for it,

might own a patent and yet not be able to practice (i.e., make or sell) her patented invention. For example, criminal laws may forbid the manufacture of certain patented weapons banned by the government. If the patent is directed to a new medicine or method of treatment, the Food and Drug Administration (FDA) may not yet have granted approval for the sale of the item to U.S. consumers. Under certain narrow circumstances, moreover, the practice of a patent in an anticompetitive manner may result in liability under the antitrust laws.[38]

Yet another situation that may prohibit the practice of a patent involves the issuance of a **blocking patent** to another entity. In this scenario, Inventor A's subservient patent is blocked by a dominant patent owned by Inventor B, even though both A and B independently qualified for patent protection on their respective inventions. Consider an example from the time of cave dwellers, before furniture, at least as we know it today, existed. Assume that the cave dwellers' society has implemented a primitive patent system, and that Inventor A has been issued the first patent claiming a "chair." In her patent, Inventor A discloses only a single embodiment (i.e., one specific example) of a chair, the design of which is a simple straight-backed, four-legged chair of the type seen (in modern times) in classrooms or offices. Because Inventor A is considered a "pioneer," her patent should be entitled to a relatively broad interpretation, so as to offer incentives for the creation of basic inventions such as the first "chair."[39]

Assume further that during the period of time while Inventor A's chair patent is still in force, unrelated Inventor B independently invents a rocking chair. Inventor B obtains what patent attorneys refer to as an "improvement patent" that claims the rocking chair. Inventor B's rocking chair is sufficiently new and nonobvious, as compared to the chair disclosed in A's patent, that B is independently entitled to his own patent. If Inventor B makes or sells his rocking chair in the patent-granting country, however, he will literally infringe Inventor A's patent, which broadly covers all types of chairs.[40]

---

according to the acts of Congress; and that his rights are to be regulated and measured by these laws, and cannot go beyond them.") (quoting Brown v. Duchesne, 60 U.S. (19 How.) 183, 195 (1857)).

[38]See infra Chapter 10 ("Defenses to Patent Infringement"), discussing potential antitrust liability for enforcement of patent rights.

[39]See In re Hogan, 559 F.2d 595, 606 (CCPA 1977) (Markey, C.J.) (contending that if applicants were in fact "pioneers," "they would deserve broad claims to the broad concept," and that to restrict them to claim scope no broader than single disclosed embodiment "is merely to state a policy against broad protection for pioneer inventions, a policy both shortsighted and unsound from the standpoint of promoting progress in the useful arts, the constitutional purpose of the patent laws").

[40]Professor Mark Lemley has noted that "this infringement determination does not take into account the value of the improvement made by the accused infringer," citing as an example Hughes Aircraft Co. v. United States, 717 F.2d 1351 (Fed. Cir. 1983)

Note that although Inventor B obtained his own patent based on his novel and nonobvious improvement invention, nevertheless Inventor B did not receive any *affirmative* right to practice his invention. By the same token, because his patent did give Inventor B a negative right to exclude others from making and selling a rocking chair, Inventor A is now blocked from producing rocking chairs, even though her patent broadly covers any type of chair (including a rocking chair). In other words, if Inventor A wants to manufacture and sell a rocking chair, she must obtain a **license** from Inventor B in order to avoid infringement liability.[41]

In practice, the dilemma of blocking patents in the United States is sometimes resolved by contract; that is, the parties cross-license each other.[42] If the parties are unable to negotiate a solution, however, the public is harmed because no one gets the benefit of the improvement.[43] Alternatively, some foreign patent systems authorize compulsory licensing of a blocking basic patent where the subject matter of the blocked improvement patent qualifies as an "important technical advance of considerable economic significance."[44] The United States has not implemented this type of compulsory licensing.

(holding that government's accused satellite control system, implemented by onboard computers, infringed patent on ground-based analog control system). Mark A. Lemley, *The Economics of Improvement in Intellectual Property Law*, 75 Tex. L. Rev. 989, 1006 (1997).

[41]A license is simply an agreement between the patent owner (licensor) and another party (licensee) that the licensor will not sue the licensee for making, using, selling, offering to sell, or importing the patented invention. The consideration for the licensor's promise not to sue is typically a payment called a royalty, which is computed based on the level of the licensee's use of the invention. *See generally* Michael A. Epstein & Frank L. Politano, Drafting License Agreements (4th ed. 2011); Robert W. Gomulkiewicz et al., Licensing Intellectual Property: Law and Application (2d ed. 2011); *See also infra* Chapter 10 ("Defenses to Patent Infringement"), discussing license defenses.

[42]*See generally* Robert P. Merges, *Intellectual Property Rights and Bargaining Breakdown: The Case of Blocking Patents*, 62 Tenn. L. Rev. 75 (1994).

[43]*See* Mark A. Lemley, *The Economics of Improvement in Intellectual Property Law*, 75 Tex. L. Rev. 989, 1010 (1997). Lemley also notes that, although the defense of the "reverse doctrine of equivalents" is theoretically available to excuse B's infringement, the doctrine has rarely been applied to excuse literal infringement. *See id.* at 1011. For a more optimistic view of the reverse doctrine of equivalents as a solution to the blocking patents problem, *see* Robert P. Merges, *Intellectual Property Rights and Bargaining Breakdown: The Case of Blocking Patents*, 62 Tenn. L. Rev. 75 (1994). The concepts of literal infringement, infringement under the doctrine of equivalents, and the reverse doctrine of equivalents are addressed in further detail *infra* Chapter 9 ("Patent Infringement").

[44]*See* Agreement on Trade-Related Aspects of Intellectual Property Rights [TRIPS], Marrakesh Agreement Establishing the World Trade Organization, Annex 1C, art. 31(l), Apr. 15, 1994, 1869 U.N.T.S. 299; 33 I.L.M. 1197 (1994) (setting forth special criteria for compulsory licensing in the case of blocking patents).

7. The Patent Term

How long does a patent last? The U.S. Constitution specifies that inventors are to be secured exclusive rights to their discoveries "for limited times," but does not specify any particular number of years. The first U.S. patents lasted 14 years from issuance (i.e., the date that the Patent Office issued the patent), based on the **patent term** in England at that time.[45] The U.S. patent term was extended to 17 years from issuance by the Patent Act of 1861.[46] The length of time during which the patent application was pending in the Patent Office before patent issuance was not relevant to the patent's term.[47]

United States law on the term of patents underwent a major change effective June 8, 1995. This change harmonized U.S. law on patent term with that of other countries. It also dramatically reduced incentives to obtain *submarine patents,* the colloquial term for patents that issue after secretly pending in the USPTO for many years.[48] For any patent application filed on or after June 8, 1995, that patent will expire 20 years after the earliest effective U.S. filing date.[49] For patents that were in force on June 8, 1995, or for patent applications

---

[45]Moreover, early U.S. Congresses extended the term of numerous individual patents; the courts saw no "limited times" impediments to these extensions. Eldred v. Ashcroft, 537 U.S. 186, 201-202 (2003).

[46]Act of March 2, 1861, ch. 88, §16, 12 Stat. 246, 249 (1861).

[47]In rare cases, an extended pendency can give rise to a defense against a patent's enforcement. The Federal Circuit has recognized the equitable defense of "prosecution laches," which may be raised as an affirmative defense to charges of infringement even though the patent applicant's delay in issuing its patent was in compliance with the Patent Act and all pertinent USPTO regulations. *See* Cancer Research Tech. Ltd. v. Barr Labs., Inc., 625 F.3d 724, 728 (Fed. Cir. 2010) (recognizing defense but concluding that district court committed legal error in holding patent unenforceable for prosecution laches in the absence of any evidence of intervening rights); Symbol Techs., Inc. v. Lemelson Med., 422 F.3d 1378 (Fed. Cir. 2005); Symbol Techs., Inc. v. Lemelson Med., 277 F.3d 1361 (Fed. Cir. 2002). For discussion of prosecution in further detail, *see infra* Chapter 10 ("Defenses to Patent Infringement").

[48]In Ricoh Co. v. Nashua Corp., No. 97-1344, 1999 U.S. App. LEXIS 2672, at *8 (Fed. Cir. Feb. 18, 1999) (nonprecedential), the Federal Circuit described the legislative change in U.S. patent term as "in effect address[ing] the perceived problem of so-called 'submarine patents,' i.e., the use of continuation applications to claim previously disclosed but unclaimed features of an invention many years after the filing of the original patent application").

[49]35 U.S.C. §154(a)(2). In some cases the 20-year term will be extended by *patent term adjustment. See infra.*

The America Invents Act of 2011 added for the first time to the Patent Act a definition of "effective filing date." *See* Leahy-Smith America Invents Act, Pub. L. No. 112-29 (H.R. 1249), §3(a)(2), 125 Stat. 284, 285 (2011) (adding a new §100(i) to the definitional section 35 U.S.C. §100). The definition provides:

(i)(1) The term "effective filing date" for a claimed invention in a patent or application for patent means—

already pending on that date, the patent will expire on the later of the two dates — either 20 years from filing, or 17 years from issuance, whichever is later.[50]

Although patent attorneys often speak in shorthand of the "20-year patent term," this terminology is not precisely correct. The term, or enforceable life, of a patent does not begin until the date the patent is *issued* (i.e., on the "issue date") by the USPTO. A patent is entirely a creature of statute. While a patent application is still pending, there is no basis for a lawsuit alleging patent infringement, because there is not yet any patent in existence.[51]

The patent term *expires* on the date that is 20 years after the earliest effective U.S. filing date.[52] The application pendency period is subtracted from 20 years to obtain the patent term. Typical U.S. patent application pendencies last about three years, at least for mechanical inventions.[53] Thus, the colloquial "20-year term" is, in reality, usually about 17 years, as illustrated in Figure 1.2.

(A) if subparagraph (B) does not apply, the actual filing date of the patent or the application for the patent containing a claim to the invention; or

(B) the filing date of the earliest application for which the patent or application is entitled, as to such invention, to a right of priority under section 119, 365(a), or 365(b) or to the benefit of an earlier filing date under section 120, 121, or 365(c).

(2) The effective filing date for a claimed invention in an application for reissue or reissued patent shall be determined by deeming the claim to the invention to have been contained in the patent for which reissue was sought.

35 U.S.C. §100 (eff. Mar. 16, 2013).

Note that a U.S. patent's term ends 20 years after its earliest effective *U.S.* filing date, not 20 years from any earlier *foreign* priority date that the applicant may have asserted under 35 U.S.C. §119(a)-(b) or 35 U.S.C. §365(a)-(b) for reasons of patentability (e.g., establishing novelty and/or nonobviousness over prior art). *See* 35 U.S.C. §154(a)(3) ("Priority"). For further discussion of foreign priority, *see infra* Chapter 12 ("International Patenting Issues").

[50]35 U.S.C. §154(c)(1).

[51]The possibility exists of recovering reasonable royalty damages for certain infringements between the date that a patent application was published by the USPTO at 18 months after filing and the date it issued as a patent, but such damages cannot be sought until the patent issues. *See* 35 U.S.C. §154(d) ("Provisional rights").

[52]35 U.S.C. §154(a)(2).

[53]*See* United States Patent and Trademark Office, *Performance and Accountability Report Fiscal Year 2010*, at 128 tbl. 4 (2010), *available at* http://www.uspto.gov/about/stratplan/ar/2010/USPTOFY2010PAR.pdf (listing total average pendency for applications classified in "Tech Center 3700 — Mechanical Engineering, Manufacturing & Products" as 38.4 months). More complicated technologies involve much longer average pendencies. For example, total average pendency for applications classified in "Tech Center 2100 — Computer Architecture, Software & Information Security" is 42.5 months. *Id.*

Chapter 1. Foundations of the U.S. Patent System

Figure 1.2

Typical U.S. Patent Timeline (not to scale)

Because under the current "20-year term" system the term of a patent will be reduced by the period of time in which the application was pending in the USPTO, it is necessary to ensure that patent owners are not penalized for pendency delays caused by the USPTO rather than by the applicants themselves. Accordingly, the 1999 American Inventors Protection Act (AIPA) added to U.S. patent law the concept

---

[54]The **invention date** of a claimed invention is a central concept under pre-AIA novelty and first-to-invent priority rules. (Post-AIA, however, the significance of invention dates is likely limited to derivation proceedings under 35 U.S.C. §135 (eff. Mar. 16, 2013).) For purposes of the example discussed in the text, invention date may be thought of as the date of actual reduction to practice of the invention, that is, the date on which the inventor had constructed a physical embodiment of the invention that worked for its intended purpose. The use of "Yr –X" in Figure 1.2 is intended to indicate that there is no set time period in which a patent application must be filed following the invention date, so long as the invention has not been injected into the public domain in some fashion. *See* 35 U.S.C. §102(b) (2006) (providing one-year grace period for application filing following the first patenting or description of invention in a printed publication anywhere in the world, or the first public use or placement on sale of the invention in the United States). In some cases, the invention date may date back to the date of conception, that is, the date on which the inventor had a complete mental picture of the operative invention, as it was thereafter reduced to practice, if the inventor displayed reasonable diligence in moving from the conception to a reduction to practice. *See* Mahurkar v. C.R. Bard, Inc., 79 F.3d 1572, 1577-1578 (Fed. Cir. 1996). The details of determining an invention date are further addressed *infra* Chapter 4 ("Novelty, Loss of Right, and Priority Pre- and Post-America Invents Act of 2011 (35 U.S.C. §102)").

The AIA transitioned the U.S. patent system away from its historic first-to-invent system, such that for patent applications filed on or after March 16, 2013, the invention date described above is no longer relevant to determining which of two rival claimants for a patent will prevail. Rather, the first inventor to file an application describing the invention generally will obtain the patent. *See infra* Chapter 4, Part III.

Nevertheless, concepts such as invention date, reduction to practice, conception, and diligence remain relevant to patents already in force or already applied for before March 16, 2013. These concepts will also be relevant in derivation proceedings, which replace interference proceedings under the AIA.

[55]The application filing date depicted in this figure refers to the filing date of a nonprovisional application. Non-provisional and provisional applications are explained *infra* Section H of this chapter ("Patent Prosecution Overview").

of *patent term adjustment* for such delays.[56] The statutory provision that governs patent term adjustment is 35 U.S.C. §154(b).[57] Subsection 154(b)(1)(A) concerns prompt USPTO responses. It provides that if the issue of a patent is delayed by certain failures of the USPTO to take timely action during the patent application's pendency, the term of the patent will be extended by one day for each day of such delay. Subsection 154(b)(1)(B) provides a guarantee of no more than a three-year application pendency. If due to certain USPTO delays the patent is not issued within three years after its filing date, the term of the patent will be extended by one day for each day beyond the three-year window. The delay under this subsection does not include time consumed by requests for continued examination (RCEs),[58] by **interferences**, by secrecy orders, by appeals to the Board or the Federal Circuit, or for processing delays requested by the applicant. Moreover, the period of adjustment under this section will be reduced by any delay on the part of the applicant in responding to USPTO actions more than three months after they were transmitted.[59] Section 154(b) (1)(C) provides adjustment for delays due to interferences, secrecy orders, and appeals in which the applicant succeeds in obtaining a reversal of an adverse determination of patentability.

Any period of patent term adjustment resulting from the USPTO delays described above is subject to being reduced by delays that are the fault of the applicant; namely, by any period of time during which the applicant failed to engage in "reasonable efforts to conclude prosecution" of his application.[60] The USPTO will make a determination of any patent term adjustment to which the applicant is entitled and will transmit notice of that determination along with the notice of allowance.[61] A patent applicant who disagrees with the term adjustment determination can request reconsideration by the USPTO[62] or

---

[56]*See* American Inventors Protection Act of 1999, Pub. L. No. 106-113, §4402 ("Patent Term Guarantee Authority"), 113 Stat. 1501 (1999).

[57]The corresponding USPTO rule for patent applications filed on or after May 29, 2000, is 37 C.F.R. §1.702 (2008) ("Grounds for adjustment of patent term due to examination delay under the Patent Term Guarantee Act of 1999 (original applications, other than designs, filed on or after May 29, 2000)"). *See also* 37 C.F.R. §1.703 ("Period of adjustment of patent term due to examination delay"); 37 C.F.R. §1.704 ("Reduction of period of adjustment of patent term"); and 37 C.F.R. §1.705 ("Patent term adjustment determination"). For applications that were filed between June 8, 1995 and May 28, 2000, *see* 37 C.F.R. §1.701 ("Extension of patent term due to examination delay under the Uruguay Round Agreements Act (original applications, other than designs, filed on or after June 8, 1995, and before May 29, 2000)").

[58]*See* 35 U.S.C. §132(b); *infra* Section H ("Patent Prosecution Overview").

[59]*See* 35 U.S.C. §154(b)(2)(C)(ii).

[60]*See* 35 U.S.C. §154(b)(2)(C)(i).

[61]*See* 35 U.S.C. §154(b)(3)(B)(i).

[62]*See* 35 U.S.C. §154(b)(3)(B)(ii).

may seek judicial review by filing a civil action against the USPTO Director in the federal district court.[63]

Patent term adjustment under section 154(b) of the Patent Act should be distinguished from the separate concept of *patent term restoration* under section 156.[64] Section 156 was added to the Patent Act by Title II of the Drug Price Competition and Patent Term Restoration Act of 1984,[65] popularly known as the Hatch-Waxman Act. Pharmaceutical and health care firms often file for and obtain U.S. patents on new drugs and medical devices before they have obtained the requisite final approval of the U.S. FDA to sell these products to the public. To maintain incentives for costly drug and medical device research and development, the Hatch-Waxman legislation provided for limited restoration of patent term that would otherwise be lost due to this delay in pre-market federal regulatory approval. A patent owner seeking extension of the term of its patent under section 156 submits an application therefore to the USPTO Director.[66]

D. Economic Considerations

Patents have been described as "large-scale governmental intrusions into the free-market economy" that "involve manipulating social costs and benefits to increase the national wealth."[67] There is no dispute that patents have a very real impact on domestic and global economics. Patents are valuable government-created property rights with the potential to act as powerful incentives for innovation, affect the supply and prices of goods and services, and impact the flow of commerce across national borders. This section introduces some of the most basic economic theory relevant to patents.[68]

---

[63]*See* 35 U.S.C. §154(b)(4)(A). The America Invents Act of 2011 changed the venue for such actions from the District of Columbia to the Eastern District of Virginia. *See* 35 U.S.C. §154(b)(4)(A) (eff. Sept. 16, 2011).

[64]*See* 35 U.S.C. §156 ("Extension of Patent Term").

[65]Pub. L. No. 98-417, 98 Stat. 1585 (1984).

[66]*See* 35 U.S.C. §156(d)(1).

[67]R. Carl Moy, *The History of the Patent Harmonization Treaty: Economic Self-Interest as an Influence*, 26 JOHN MARSHALL L. REV. 457, 473 (1993).

[68]Those seeking more detailed treatment of the economic impact of the patent system should consult the materials presented during a 2002 series of public hearings on "Competition and Intellectual Property Law and Policy in the Knowledge-Based Economy," jointly sponsored by the U.S. Department of Justice and U.S. Federal Trade Commission. Testimony and presentations delivered on February 20, 25, and 26, 2002, concerning "Economic Perspectives on Intellectual Property, Competition, and Innovation" are available online. Federal Trade Commission, *Schedule of Hearings*, http://www.ftc.gov/opp/intellect/detailsandparticipants.shtm (last visited May 26, 2012) [hereinafter FTC/DOJ HEARINGS]. The final report generated from these hearings is

1. Is a Patent a Monopoly?

Courts and commentators sometimes refer to patents as "monopolies," usually in a pejorative manner to indicate the view that patent rights are being used for anticompetitive purposes.[69] A better way to think of patents is as time-limited government conveyances of *potential* monopoly power, which can be put to "good" or "bad" uses from a societal standpoint.[70]

In the days of Queen Elizabeth I of England, patents were handed out as personal favors to royal cronies.[71] For example, the Queen might award to one royal friend the sole right to sell salt, to another the sole right to sell vinegar, and to yet another the sole right to sell playing cards. These patents were truly "bad" or "odious" monopolies that took from the public what had previously been widely available from multiple suppliers. Because these "staple" articles of commerce were now available from only one source (the patent holder), their prices went up and quantities supplied went down. Such "patents" merely rewarded personal loyalty rather than innovation.

A patent as understood today is very different from the royal privileges conferred by the English monarchy. A modern patent conveys a right to exclude others from making, selling, offering to sell, using, or importing only "novel" and "nonobvious" inventions.[72] Thus a modern patent provides only the right to control new technical contributions, not the ability to extract existing technology from the public domain. Patents do not take from the public any innovations that it already possessed.

Today, the type of harmful patent monopoly with which the law is concerned is the use of patent rights for anticompetitive purposes in a manner that violates the U.S. antitrust laws, including the Sherman

Federal Trade Commission, *To Promote Innovation: The Proper Balance of Competition and Patent Law and Policy* (2003), *available at* http://www.ftc.gov/os/2003/10/innovationrpt.pdf [hereinafter FTC REPORT].

[69]*See, e.g.,* Jamesbury Corp. v. Litton Indus. Prod., Inc., 756 F.2d 1556, 1559 (Fed. Cir. 1985) (admonishing district court that jury instructions that "interject[] language to the effect that the public must be 'protected' against a 'monopoly,' a term found nowhere in the statute, are likely to be prejudicial and should be avoided"), *overruled on other grounds*, A.C. Aukerman Co. v. R.L. Chaides Const. Co., 960 F.2d 1020 (Fed. Cir. 1992); *See also* Schenck v. Nortron Corp., 713 F.2d 782, 786 n.3 (Fed. Cir. 1983) (stating that "[i]t is but an obfuscation to refer to a patent as "the patent monopoly" or to describe a patent as an "exception to the general rule against monopolies").

[70]*See* Giles S. Rich, *Are Letters Patent Grants of Monopoly?*, 15 W. NEW ENG. L. Rev. 239, 251 (1993).

[71]*See id.* at 241-242.

[72]Chapters 4 and 5, *infra*, explore the statutory requirements for novelty and nonobviousness in further detail.

Act.[73] As addressed in further detail in Chapter 10 ("Defenses to Patent Infringement"), *infra,* an antitrust violation must be premised on anticompetitive conduct by a patent owner with "market power" as defined in the antitrust sense. Modern antitrust law recognizes that mere ownership of a patent does not necessarily confer monopoly power of the type necessary to establish a violation of the Sherman Act, however.[74] A number of alternatives to the patented invention may exist that consumers would consider acceptable substitutes. Thus the relevant market for antitrust purposes may be much broader than the market for the claimed invention. For example, if the problem is mouse infestation, the relevant market might be defined as all solutions, including not only a patented, proverbial "better mouse trap" but also all old, non-patented mousetraps as well as cats. Economic, not merely technological, substitutability is the key determiner of relevant market.[75]

2.   Cost/Benefit Analysis for Patents

A government's decision to recognize and enforce patent rights brings with it certain societal costs as well as benefits. Understanding and recognizing both sides of the equation is an essential prerequisite to a thorough understanding of the patent system.[76]

---

[73]15 U.S.C. §§1 *et seq.* Antitrust allegations involving unilateral enforcement of patent rights are premised on Section 2 of the Sherman Act, which criminalizes monopolization and attempted monopolization of "any part of the trade or commerce among the several States, or with foreign nations." 15 U.S.C. §2; *see also infra* Chapter 10, Section F ("Antitrust Counterclaims").

[74]*See* U.S. Dep't of Justice, *Antitrust Guidelines for the Licensing of Intellectual Property* §2.2 (1995), *available at* http://www.usdoj.gov/atr/public/guidelines/0558.pdf. *See also* Richard A. Posner, *Transaction Costs and Antitrust Concerns in the Licensing of Intellectual Property,* 4 J. Marshall Rev. Intell. Prop. L. 325, 329 (2005), http://www.jmripl.com/Publications/Vol4/Issue3/posner.pdf (characterizing patent "monopoly" usage as "unfortunate" because it "confuses an exclusive right with an economic monopoly.").

[75]*See* Unitherm Food Sys., Inc. v. Swift-Eckrich, Inc., 375 F.3d 1341, 1364 (Fed. Cir. 2004), *reversed on other grounds,* 546 U.S. 394 (2006); *see also* Illinois Tool Works Inc. v. Independent Ink, Inc., 547 U.S. 28, 44 (2006) (noting that "the vast majority of academic literature recognizes that a patent does not necessarily confer market power," and rejecting a *per se* presumption of market power for patents involved in tying arrangements).

[76]A classic study of the economic impact of patents is Staff of Subcomm. on Pat. Trademark & Copyright of the Comm. on the Judiciary, 85th Cong., An Economic Review of the Patent System (Comm. Print 1958) (prepared by Fritz Machlup pursuant to S. Res. 236). Other leading works on the economics of patent law include Ward S. Bowman, Jr., Patent and Antitrust Law: A Legal and Economic Appraisal 15-32 (1973), and F.M. Scherer, Industrial Market Structure and Economic Performance 379-399 (1970). More recent scholarly work on the economics of the patent system was

a. *Costs*

Patent systems place a number of short-term costs or burdens on the public. At a microeconomic level, one can see this by comparing a perfectly competitive market[77] for widgets that are not patented with a market in which one person holds a patent on widgets. The introduction of patent rights will result in a reduction in the quantity of widgets supplied, compared with what that quantity would have been in a perfectly competitive market. It will also raise the price of widgets above that which would have been set in a perfectly competitive market.[78]

Creating and maintaining a patent system also entails considerable administrative costs. The U.S. Patent and Trademark Office (USPTO), a bureau of the Department of Commerce, is the federal agency that grants U.S. patents. One of the very oldest federal agencies, the USPTO in fiscal year 2011 employed over 10,000 federal personnel[79] and operated on a budget of over $2.3 billion.[80] To its credit, the USPTO has been fully "user fee-funded" for several years, although Congress has frequently diverted USPTO income to other government entities.[81]

---

presented during a 2002 series of public hearings on "Competition and Intellectual Property Law and Policy in the Knowledge-Based Economy," jointly sponsored by the U.S. Department of Justice and U.S. Federal Trade Commission. *See* Federal Trade Commission, *Schedule of Hearings*, http://www.ftc.gov/opp/intellect/detailsandpartici-pants.shtm (last visited May 26, 2012). A helpful summary of recent empirical work on the patent system's impact on innovation is included in Bronwyn H. Hall, *Testimony for the FTC/DOJ (Antitrust) Hearings on Competition and Intellectual Property Law in the Knowledge-Based Economy* (Feb. 26, 2002), http://www.ftc.gov/opp/intellect/020 226bronwynhhalltext.pdf.

[77]*Perfectly competitive market* refers to the economics concept of a hypothetical market operating at "perfect" competition, in which there are such a large number of firms that no individual firm can influence the market price, and where all parties have "perfect" information. For helpful definitions of these microeconomic terms, *see Economics A-Z: Economic Terms, Topics and Jargon*, ECONOMIST, http://www.economist.com/research/economics/ (last visited May 26, 2012).

[78]For a useful introduction to the microeconomics of patent law, *see* Paul E. Schaafsma, *An Economic Overview of Patents*, 79 J. PAT. & TRADEMARK OFF. SOC'Y 241 (1997).

[79]*See* United States Patent and Trademark Office, *FY 2011 USPTO Performance and Accountability Report* ("Summary of Financial and Performance Highlights"), *available at* http://www.uspto.gov/about/stratplan/ar/2011/par_01.html.

[80]*See* United States Patent and Trademark Office, *FY 2011 USPTO Performance and Accountability Report, available at* http://www.uspto.gov/about/stratplan/ar/2011/ mda_06_01_05.html ("Statement of Budgetary Resources" section including chart depicting "available budgetary resources").

[81]*See* Intellectual Prop. Owners Ass'n, *Background and Status on USPTO Funding, Adequate Funding for the USPTO and Ending Fee Diversion,* http://www.ipo.org/AM/ Template.cfm?Section=Home&Template=/CM/ContentDisplay.cfm&ContentID=3360 (last visited June 16, 2011) (stating that "[s]ince 1990, a total of over $800 Million of USPTO User Fees have been withheld from the agency...").

Another cost of the patent system is duplicative, overlapping expenditures on research and development in the same technical field by different firms. It is not uncommon for multiple firms to focus their research and development efforts on the same or similar technical or scientific problem. If, in so doing, two (or more) entities independently invent the same invention, only one can receive a U.S. patent on the invention.[82] Under the historic U.S. **priority system**, the patent is awarded to the first in time to invent;[83] for patent applications filed on or after March 16, 2013, in accordance with the America Invents Act of 2011, the U.S. patent generally will be awarded to the first inventor to file a patent application describing the invention.[84] In either case, an independent inventor of the same invention, if later in time (later to invent or later to file, respectively, under pre- and post-AIA systems), will not be entitled to the patent, and generally will need a license from the first inventor in order to avoid infringement liability.[85] Thus the research and development work on the invention by the unsuccessful later inventor or filer can be viewed as duplicative and wasteful from an economic standpoint.[86]

The patent system also places costs on society in terms of forgone research and development that is not conducted because of existing patents owned by others. These patents may or may not be valid. Like a "scarecrow," extant patents of questionable validity may dissuade others from doing follow-on work in the same area of the invention. When an invalid patent operates in this manner, society bears the cost

---

[82]*See* 35 U.S.C. §101 (providing that "[w]hoever invents or discovers any new and useful process, machine, manufacture, or composition of matter, or any new and useful improvement thereof, may obtain *a* patent therefor, subject to the conditions and requirements of this title") (emphasis added).

[83]35 U.S.C. §102(g)(1) (2006).

[84]*See* 35 U.S.C. §102(a)(2) (eff. Mar. 16, 2013) (providing that "a person shall be entitled to a patent unless . . . the claimed invention was described in a patent issued under section 151, or in an application for patent published or deemed published under section 122(b), in which the patent or application, as the case may be, names another inventor and was effectively filed before the effective filing date of the claimed invention"); *see also* Leahy-Smith America Invents Act, Pub. L. No. 112-29 (H.R. 1249), §3 ("First Inventor to File"), 125 Stat. 284, 285-293 (2011).

[85]The America Invents Act of 2011 broadened the availability of prior user rights to shield later filers in this scenario who have already made commercial use of their inventions. *See* 35 U.S.C. §273 (eff. Sept. 16, 2011) ("Defense to infringement based on prior commercial use").

[86]The problem of wasteful, duplicative research expenditures was exacerbated by the fact that U.S. patent applications were traditionally maintained in secrecy until they issued as patents. Thus, researchers were unable to discover, at least through the mechanism of patent disclosures, what their competitors were working on until the competitors' patents issued. The secrecy problem has been ameliorated to some degree by the passage of the American Inventors Protection Act of 1999, which enacted 18-month publication for most U.S. patent applications. *See* 35 U.S.C. §122(b); *infra* Section H ("Patent Prosecution Overview").

of losing potentially important innovation that might otherwise have been generated.[87]

Litigation expense represents another cost of the patent system, particularly when infringement is inadvertent.[88] Only a small percentage of issued patents are ever litigated in court, but each such litigation is potentially lengthy and expensive. For example, total litigation costs for a medium-risk patent infringement suit averaged an estimated $2.5 million in 2011.[89]

Policymakers are increasingly concerned about the high costs of patent litigation, which may be a deterrent to patent enforcement by small firms.[90] Although the parties pay attorney fees and litigation

---

[87]A contrary view is the "prospect theory" of patents. *See* Edmund W. Kitch, *The Nature and Function of the Patent System*, 20 J.L. & Econ. 265 (1977). Kitch analogized the grant of patents to the award of mining claims in nineteenth-century America, which reserved for the first claimant to arrive on the scene the exclusive right to mine all territory within the claim. Kitch contended that giving patent rights of broad scope to the first inventor of a particular technological advance would enhance, rather than reduce, incentives for follow-on improvements, and serve the larger social welfare. He described the process of technological innovation as one in which a variety of resources are brought to bear on an array of "prospect[s]," or "particular opportunit[ies] to develop a known technological possibility." *Id.* at 266. Because each prospect can be pursued by multiple firms, the process is efficient only if some system ensures "efficient allocation of the resources among the prospects at an efficient rate and in an efficient amount." *Id.* Kitch contended that the patent system functions in this manner "by awarding exclusive and publicly recorded ownership of a prospect shortly after its discovery." *Id.*

[88]Professors Bessen and Meurer explain that infringement occurs inadvertently when patents fail to provide clear, up-front notice of permitted and non-permitted activity. *See* James Bessen & Michael J. Meurer, Patent Failure: How Judges, Bureaucrats, and Lawyers Put Innovators at Risk 147 (2008) (finding that "inadvertent infringement plays a crucial role in explaining the pattern of litigation over time and . . . across technology. Simply put, notice failure and the resulting inadvertent infringement are central to the failure of patents to provide positive innovation incentives.").

[89]*See* Am. Intellectual Prop. Law Ass'n, Report of the Economic Survey 35 (2011) (reporting survey results for a patent infringement suit with $1 to $25 million at risk). The AIPLA survey lists median litigation costs from the commencement of suit to the "[e]nd of discovery" as $1.5 million, and "[i]nclusive, all costs" as $2.5 million. *Id.* For patent infringement lawsuits with less than $1 million at risk, the median litigation cost figures were $350,000 and $650,000, respectively. *Id.* For patent infringement lawsuits with more than $25 million at risk, the median cost figures were $3 million and $5 million, respectively. *Id.*

[90]*See* Federal Trade Commission, *Schedule of Hearings*, http://www.ftc.gov/opp/intellect/detailsandparticipants.shtm (last visited May 26, 2012), ch. 5, at 3 (stating that "[t]he record is replete with discussion of the cost of litigation and its potential to operate as a drag on the system"); *id.* at 25 (reporting concern of several panelists "that the high cost of litigation may work to the disadvantage of small firms, pressuring them to settle when accused and discouraging them from asserting their own patent rights"). *See also* Federal Trade Commission, *The Evolving IP Marketplace—Aligning Patent Notice and Remedies with Competition* 147 (Mar. 2011), http://www.ftc.gov/os/2011/03/110307patentreport.pdf (recognizing that "[t]he problem of high litigation

expenses, the public also shoulders the costs because taxes support the judicial system. Moreover, as the frequency of patent litigation increases,[91] judicial system resources allocated to protracted patent lawsuits are not available for other types of cases.

b. Benefits

Costs of our patent system must be weighed against the many important benefits that it provides to the public. As Abraham Lincoln famously described it, the patent system "added the fuel of interest to the fire of genius."[92] Patents are fundamentally incentive systems. The time-limited right to exclude others that a patent represents is a powerful incentive for the creation of new innovation from which society benefits.[93]

The specific benefits conferred by the existence and recognition of patents are observable at different stages in the timeline of patent life. When patent applications are published, in most cases 18 months after their effective filing date,[94] the public domain is enhanced by the disclosure of the information in the application. The Patent Act requires that this disclosure be **enabling,** such that it will permit others to make and use the invention (either with the patent owner's authorization during the term of the patent, or after it expires)

costs should be addressed directly. . . . "); Deborah Platt Majoras, Chairman, Federal Trade Commission, *A Government Perspective on IP and Antitrust Law* (June 21, 2006) (transcript available at http://www.ftc.gov/speeches/majoras/060621aai-ip.pdf) (stating that "[e]xpensive and time-consuming litigation to challenge a patent on an obvious technology wastes resources").

[91]Litigants filed more than 3,300 patent infringement actions in 2010. In comparison, only about 800 such suits were brought in 1980. *See Making Sense of Patent Law,* N.Y. Times, Nov. 18, 2011, at B2.

[92]This quote from a speech given by Abraham Lincoln is inscribed over a door of the building that houses the U.S. Department of Commerce in Washington, D.C. The USPTO, a bureau of the Department of Commerce, was once housed in this building, but is currently located in northern Virginia.

[93]Some scholars question the traditional view that the right to exclude conveyed by patent ownership is the "alpha and omega of the private value of patent rights." Clarisa Long, *Patent Signals,* 69 U. Chi. L. Rev. 625, 627 (2002). Professor Long views patents as "a means of credibly publicizing information," which can "reduc[e] informational asymmetries between patentees and observers." *Id.* She contends that the ability of patents to signal information about their owners may be of greater value in some cases than the substance of the exclusionary right. *See id.* at 627-628.

[94]*See* 35 U.S.C. §122(b). Eighteen-month publication was a major change to the U.S. patent system, implemented as part of the American Inventors Protection Act of 1999. Prior to that implementation, pending U.S. patent applications were maintained in secret until they issued as patents. *See infra* Section H ("Patent Prosecution Overview").

without undue experimentation.[95] Patents perform an important role in the dissemination of new technologic information. As soon as the application is published, members of the public can read, study, and learn from the information contained therein. Some may even attempt to "invent around" the patent; that is, they develop alternative devices or methods that accomplish the same purpose as the patented invention but that are sufficiently different to avoid infringement. The U.S. domestic economy also is enhanced when the patent is "practiced" or "worked" in this country, meaning that the patent owner and/or her licensee(s) actually manufactures and sells the patented item in the United States during the term of the patent. This activity generates sales, creates jobs, and spurs investment. Once a patent expires, the invention enters the public domain and is free for all to make and use[96] (assuming that such use is not blocked by another patent, government regulation, or the like).

Utilitarian theory (described below) views the short-term costs of having a patent system as a necessary trade-off to obtain the long-term benefits mentioned above. But determining the precise balance between incentive and reward has eluded economists for centuries.[97] What is the "optimal" level of protection that must be offered, both in terms of patent scope and duration, to call forth the "right" level

---

[95]35 U.S.C. §112, ¶1 (2006); 35 U.S.C. §112(a) (eff. Sept. 16, 2012); *see also* In re Wands, 858 F.2d 731, 737 (Fed. Cir. 1988).

[96]*See* Bonito Boats, Inc. v. Thunder Craft Boats, Inc., 489 U.S. 141, 152 (1989) (stating that "[w]e have long held that after the expiration of a federal patent, the subject matter of the patent passes to the free use of the public as a matter of federal law") (citing Coats v. Merrick Thread Co., 149 U.S. 562, 572 (1893) ("[P]laintiffs' right to the use of the embossed periphery expired with their patent, and the public had the same right to make use of it as if it had never been patented"); Kellogg Co. v. National Biscuit Co., 305 U.S. 111 (1938); Singer Mfg. Co. v. June Mfg. Co., 163 U.S. 169 (1896)).

[97]Johns Hopkins University economist Fritz Machlup authored one of the most important modern studies of the patent system. Staff of Subcomm. on Pat. Trademark & Copyright of the Comm. on the Judiciary, 85th Cong., *An Economic Review of the Patent System* 1-80 (Comm. Print 1958) (prepared by Fritz Machlup pursuant to S. Res. 236), *available at* http://mises.org/etexts/patentsystem.pdf. Machlup's study is famously noted for his lukewarm conclusion about the value of the U.S. patent system:

> If one does not know whether a system "as a whole" (in contrast to certain features of it) is good or bad, the safest "policy conclusion" is to "muddle through"—either with it, if one has long lived with it, or without it, if one has lived without it. If we did not have a patent system, it would be irresponsible, on the basis of our present knowledge of its economic consequences, to recommend instituting one. But since we have had a patent system for a long time, it would be irresponsible, on the basis of our present knowledge, to recommend abolishing it.

Id. at 80.

of innovation? Scholars have long debated this question,[98] and it may never be fully resolved. Most likely the answers will differ depending on the type of technology involved.[99] For example, a longer term of protection is more critical for pharmaceutical innovation than for spurring the development of new computer software products, which typically have a much shorter marketplace life cycle.

E. Philosophical Rationales for Patent Protection

Scholars have identified four primary theories or rationales for the protection of intellectual property, including patents.[100] The "natural rights" and "reward for services rendered" theories are grounded on notions of fundamental fairness and doing justice to individuals who

---

[98]*See, e.g.*, Ted M. Sichelman, *Markets for Patent Scope,* 1 IP THEORY 41 (2010), *available at* http://www.repository.law.indiana.edu/ipt/vol1/iss2/1 (considering the "recurring issue in intellectual property theory is how the scope of patent rights affects invention and commercialization"); Fed. Trade Comm'n, *Ideas Into Action: Implementing Reform of the Patent System: To Promote Innovation: The Proper Balance of Competition and Patent Law and Policy,* 19 BERKELEY TECH. L.J. 861 (2004); Frederic M. Scherer, *Nordhaus' Theory of Optimal Patent Life: A Geometric Reinterpretation*, 62 AM. ECON. REV. 422 (1972); WILLIAM D. NORDHAUS, INVENTION, GROWTH, AND WELFARE: A THEORETICAL TREATMENT OF TECHNOLOGICAL CHANGE (MIT Press 1969).

[99]A Carnegie Mellon survey of R&D laboratories in the U.S. manufacturing sector concluded that patents are far more important for stimulating innovation in the pharmaceutical industry than in any other. Wesley M. Cohen et al., *Protecting Their Intellectual Assets: Appropriability Conditions and Why U.S. Manufacturing Firms Patent (or Not)* (Nat'l Bureau of Econ. Research, Working Paper No. 7522, 2000), *available at* http://www.nber.org/papers/w7552.pdf. The Carnegie Mellon study is summarized at Wesley M. Cohen, *Patents: Their Effectiveness and Role* (Feb. 20, 2002), http://www.ftc.gov/opp/intellect/cohen.pdf [hereinafter Cohen 2002] (prepared for the FTC/DOJ Hearings on Competition and Intellectual Property Law in the Knowledge-Based Economy). Professor Cohen finds that patents are used differently in "[c]omplex product industries," where products (such as computers or communications equipment) are typically protected by numerous (possibly hundreds) of patents, than in "[d]iscrete product industries," where products (such as drugs and chemicals) are protected by relatively few patents. *See id.* at 13. In the complex product industries it is unlikely that any one firm owns all the patent rights in a particular product (such as a computer). Thus, firms are mutually dependent and more likely to use their patents to ensure inclusion in cross-licensing negotiations to gain access to rivals' complementary technology. *Id.* at 14. In discrete product industries, by contrast, patents are used to block substitute products by building "patent fences" rather than to compel cross-licensing. *Id.*

[100]Some of the most important studies of the philosophical foundations of IP law include Edwin C. Hettinger, *Justifying Intellectual Property*, 18 PHIL. & PUB. AFF. 31 (1989); Justin Hughes, *The Philosophy of Intellectual Property*, 77 GEO. L.J. 287 (1988); ROBERT P. MERGES, JUSTIFYING INTELLECTUAL PROPERTY (Harvard Univ. Press 2011); and EDITH TILTON PENROSE, THE ECONOMICS OF THE INTERNATIONAL PATENT SYSTEM (Baltimore: Johns Hopkins Press, 1951).

innovate. In contrast, the "monopoly profits incentive" and "exchange for secrets" rationales are considered "utilitarian," or economically focused, theories. The utilitarian view seeks to maximize the overall happiness of society at large, rather than focusing on rewarding the individual inventor. The utilitarian theories, rather than natural rights–based rationales, are generally considered to be the most aligned with the U.S. patent system.

1.   Natural Rights

The natural rights (or "deontological") justification, which has most strongly influenced the intellectual property systems of continental Europe, is based on the work of John Locke, the seventeenth-century English philosopher who developed a "labor theory" of property.[101] Locke believed that God gave the earth to people "in common," and that all persons have a property interest in their own body and own their own labor. When a person mixes her labor with objects found in the common, she makes it her property. For example, if a person gathers a pile of acorns in a public park, she has mixed her labor with the acorns and by so doing has acquired a property interest in that pile of acorns; if another takes away the acorns without permission, it constitutes stealing. The gatherer in this example must not attempt to appropriate all the available acorns, however; Locke's "proviso" mandates that the right to private ownership is conditional on a person leaving in common "enough and as good" for others. Nor must she take more from the common than she can make use of (i.e., Locke's "nonwaste condition").

Some of the problems with Locke's theory as applied to intellectual property are that it would appear to award property rights that are perpetual, and never permit the intellectual property to pass into the public domain. Natural rights theory does not address the central question of balancing proprietary rights against enhancement of the public domain. The theory also fails to grapple with allocation of efforts by multiple innovators; modern scholars recognize that the process of invention is generally cumulative,[102] meaning

---

[101]John Locke, *Second Treatise of Government*, ch. V, §27 (1690), *available at* http://www.gutenberg.org/files/7370/7370-h/7370-h.htm (last visited May 26, 2012).

[102]*See, e.g.*, Ofer Tur-Sinai, *Cumulative Innovation in Patent Law: Making Sense of Incentives*, 50 Idea 723 (2010); Christopher A. Cotropia, *"After-Arising" Technologies and Narrowing Patent Scope*, 61 N.Y.U. Ann. Surv. Am. L. 151, 178 (2005) (stating that "most inventions build upon earlier inventions"); Arti K. Rai, *Fostering Cumulative Innovation in the Biopharmaceutical Industry: The Role of Patents and Antitrust*, 16 Berkeley Tech. L.J. 813 (2001); Clarisa Long, *Patents and Cumulative Innovation*, 2 Wash. U. J.L. & Pol'y 229 (2000); Suzanne Scotchmer, *Standing on the Shoulders of Giants: Cumulative Research and the Patent Law*, 5 J. Econ. Persp. 29 (1991).

that the work of one inventor typically builds on the work of earlier inventors.[103]

2. Reward for Services Rendered

A second rationale for conveying proprietary rights in intellectual property characterizes these rights as a reward for services rendered. This theory posits that inventors render a useful service to society and that society must reward them for it. An inventor has a right to receive, and therefore society is morally obligated to give, a reward for the inventor's services in proportion to their usefulness to society.

One concern with the reward for services theory is that it does not guide us in rewarding the invention made by accident, rather than conscious effort and hard work. Another problem is that the reward theory assumes that the price a patentee can attain for her invention in the marketplace is the correct measure of its usefulness to society. In reality, however, that price reflects the fact that the patentee is the sole source of the patented invention and can thus set prices without having to meet competition. To see why the price obtained by the patentee for her invention may not always be an accurate reflection of its societal utility, consider inventions created "before their time." Such inventions ultimately become very important to society, but are not recognized as beneficial and in fact are criticized at the time of their introduction to the marketplace on "moral" or other grounds, for example, contraceptives. Conversely, other inventions may be overvalued by the marketplace, well beyond their intrinsic value to society; consider "fad" items such as mood-revealing jewelry or herb gardens grown in clay shaped like animals.[104]

3. Monopoly Profits Incentive

The monopoly profits incentive rationale assumes that innovation is good for society, and that the correct incentive to bring forth the societally optimal level of innovation is the (currently) 20-year period of exclusivity that a patent represents. Economists are divided over whether a 20-year term makes sense. The answer most likely differs

---

[103]Isaac Newton said of his inventive genius that "[i]f I have seen further [than certain other men,] it is by standing on the shoulders of giants." THE COLUMBIA WORLD OF QUOTATIONS No. 41418 (Robert Andrews et al. eds. 1996).

[104]*See* Joseph Enterprises, *Original Chia Pet* (2011), http://www.chia.com/index.php/original-chia-pet.

according to the type of technology involved.[105] While patents of this term are considered essential to the pharmaceutical industry, it is not so clear that 20-year patents are needed to bring forth the optimal level of innovation in computer software or business methods. In many cases, the "first-mover advantage" may be enough to spur innovation in these technological fields. Witness the case of Federal Express, which revolutionized the shipping industry with its new method of overnight package delivery but never sought patent protection.

4.   Exchange for Secrets

The exchange for secrets model assumes that most innovation would remain secret, but for the incentive to disclose that the patent system provides. Seen in this light the patent system often has been described as a *quid pro quo,* or bargain-exchange, in that the inventor is conveyed a time-limited right to exclude others from exploiting her invention, in exchange for disclosing how to make and use the invention in an enabling fashion that will facilitate practice of the invention by all once the patent expires.

One criticism of the exchange for secrets theory is that it fails to account for the "ripeness of time" concept of innovation. This theory posits that multiple inventors are often working simultaneously on the same problem, and that if one of them does not find and disclose her solution, someone else probably will in a relatively short while. For example, the Supreme Court contended in *Kewanee Oil Co. v. Bicron Corp.,*[106] its decision holding that state trade secret laws are not preempted by the federal patent laws, that had Watson and Crick not discovered the doubled-stranded helix structure of DNA, it is very likely that Linus Pauling would have.[107] Thus it is not clear that the

---

[105]*See* Wesley M. Cohen, *Patents: Their Effectiveness and Role* (Feb. 20, 2002), http:// www.ftc.gov/opp/intellect/cohen.pdf [hereinafter Cohen 2002] (prepared for the FTC/ DOJ Hearings on Competition and Intellectual Property Law in the Knowledge-Based Economy); *see also* Bronwyn H. Hall, *The Use and Value of Patent Rights,* at 7, tbl. 2 (2009), *available at* http://www.ipo.gov.uk/ipresearch-useandvalue-200906.pdf (gathering survey results in report to the UK IP Ministerial Forum on the Economic Value of Intellectual Property that present "a rough ranking of the industries in which patents are considered the most important. In almost all cases where it is broken out separately, the pharmaceutical industry ranks at or near the top, followed by specialized machinery and instruments, other chemicals, and occasionally transport equipment including motor vehicles and parts.").

[106]416 U.S. 470 (1974).

[107]*See Kewanee Oil,* 416 U.S. at 491 n.19. More recent scholarship suggests that x-ray crystallographer Rosalind Franklin, a collaborator of James Watson, Francis Crick, and Maurice Wilkins, also played a leading role in the discovery of DNA's double-helix structure, but was never officially credited. *See generally* BRENDA MADDOX, ROSALIND

patent system is needed to guarantee the disclosure of inventions that would otherwise be kept secret.

One response to this criticism of the patent system is that, although the same invention is often being developed in parallel by two or more independent parties, there is nothing that prevents *both* parties from keeping their inventions secret. Absent a patent system, it may make economic sense for *all* parties to maintain the invention in secrecy. Thus, parallel development does not necessarily guarantee disclosure of inventions if maintaining secrecy is a more economically viable option for all. The patent system represents what is, in many cases, a sufficient economic incentive to overcome the attractions of trade secrecy, thus facilitating the disclosure of new inventions in exchange for a time-limited right to exclude others.[108]

F. Primary Sources of U.S. Patent Law

The three primary sources of U.S. patent law are (1) the U.S. Constitution, (2) the federal patent law found in U.S. statutes and regulations, and (3) federal judicial decisions interpreting and applying these statutory and regulatory provisions.[109]

1. The Constitution

Congressional power to establish a patent system derives from the Intellectual Property (IP) Clause of the U.S. Constitution. The IP Clause appears in the Constitution's Article I, section 8 statement of Congress's enumerated powers, which also include the power to collect taxes, provide for the national defense, and the like. In more detailed terms than the other clauses of section 8, the IP Clause provides that Congress shall have the power

---

FRANKLIN: THE DARK LADY of DNA (Harper Collins 2002); ANNE SAYRE, ROSALIND FRANKLIN AND DNA (2d ed., W.W. Norton 2000). Watson, Crick, and Wilkins received a Nobel Prize for the double-helix model of DNA in 1962, four years after Franklin's death at age 37 from ovarian cancer. *See* Merry Maisel & Laura Smart, San Diego Supercomputer Center, *Women in Science: A Selection of 16 Significant Contributors* 3 (1997), http://www.sdsc.edu/ScienceWomen/GWIS.pdf ("Rosalind Elsie Franklin (1920-1958) *Pioneer Molecular Biologist*").

[108]The author thanks Professor Timothy Holbrook for this insight.

[109]In addition to these domestic sources, U.S. patent law is impacted by, and exerts a strong influence on, the patent laws of other countries and on the multinational treaties and agreements that govern patent procurement and enforcement in foreign countries. These international patenting issues are treated separately *infra* Chapter 12.

to promote the Progress of Science and useful Arts by securing for limited Times to Authors and Inventors the exclusive Right to their respective Writings and Discoveries.[110]

The IP Clause (sometimes also referred to as the "Progress Clause") has an interesting parallel structure, for it is really two grants of congressional power rolled into one—the patent power as well as the copyright power. At the time the IP Clause was ratified in 1787, the word "Science" had a much broader connotation than it does today. "Science" then meant knowledge and learning in general.[111] As such, the word "Science" in the IP Clause is viewed as referring to copyrightable subject matter. The phrase "useful Arts" is understood as referring to patentable subject matter, because "Arts" meant "technologies" or "industries." Thus, the portion of the IP Clause pertaining to copyright provides that to promote the progress of "Science," "Authors" shall have a time-limited exclusive right in their "Writings," while the patent portion of the Clause provides that to promote the progress of the "useful Arts," "Inventors" shall have a time-limited exclusive right in their "Discoveries."

Although the IP Clause is a *grant* of congressional power, the Supreme Court also has interpreted it as a *limitation* on Congress's authority to carry out the constitutional goal of "promot[ing] the progress of Science and Useful Arts." Congress may not establish a legal system in which patents can be attained for technology that is already in the public domain, or that is a merely obvious extension thereof. As expressed by the Court in the landmark decision, *Graham v. John Deere Co.*:[112]

> The Congress in the exercise of the patent power may not overreach the restraints imposed by the stated constitutional purpose. Nor may it enlarge the patent monopoly without regard to the innovation, advancement or social benefit gained thereby. Moreover, Congress may not authorize the issuance of patents whose effects are to remove existent knowledge from the public domain, or to restrict free access to materials already available. Innovation, advancement, and things which add to the sum of useful knowledge are inherent requisites in a patent system which by constitutional command must "promote the Progress of . . . useful Arts."[113]

---

[110]U.S. CONST., art. I, §8, cl. 8.

[111]Edward Walterscheid, *The Nature of the Intellectual Property Clause: A Study in Historical Perspective (Part 1)*, 83 J. PAT. & TRADEMARK OFF. SOC'Y 763, 781 (2001); Giles S. Rich, The "Exclusive Right" Since Aristotle, Address at the Foundation for a Creative American Bicentennial Celebration (May 9, 1990), *reprinted in* 14 FED. CIR. B.J. 217 (2004-2005).

[112]383 U.S. 1 (1966). The watershed *Graham* case is explored in greater detail *infra* Chapter 5 ("The Nonobviousness Requirement (35 U.S.C. §103)").

[113]*Graham,* 383 U.S. at 5-6. *See also* Bonito Boats, Inc. v. Thunder Craft Boats, Inc., 489 U.S. 141, 146 (1989) (stating that "the Clause contains both a grant of power and

2. Federal Statutes and Regulations

Pursuant to the constitutional grant, the U.S. Congress enacted the first federal patent statute in 1790.[114] During the first three years after this enactment, patent applications were substantively examined by comparison to earlier-developed technology (i.e., the **prior art**) to determine whether the invention sought to be patented was new and useful. The administrative burden of this on-the-merits examination quickly proved too great, however, and with the Patent Act of 1793, the U.S. patent system became a *pro forma* "registration" system without substantive examination against the prior art. In time, the registration system came under severe criticism for permitting the grant of many invalid patents, and by means of the Patent Act of 1836, Congress reverted to the substantive examination system that we still have today.

The two most important revisions of the U.S. patent statute thereafter were the Patent Act of 1870, which required that patents contain claims, single-sentence definitions of the scope of the patent owner's right to exclude others from her invention,[115] and the Patent Act of 1952, which in amended form is the statute that governs U.S. patent law today. Co-authored by then-attorney and later-judge Giles S. Rich and Pasquale J. Federico, a USPTO official,[116] the Patent Act of 1952 included for the first time the statutory requirement for **nonobviousness,** codified in 35 U.S.C. §103.[117] The 1952 Act also included the first statutory provisions on direct, inducing, and contributory **infringement,** set forth at 35 U.S.C. §271(a)-(c), respectively.[118]

In the twenty-first century, the America Invents Act of 2011 (AIA) implemented what are probably the most significant revisions of the Patent Act since its 1952 codification at Title 35 U.S.C.[119] The AIA

---

certain limitations upon the exercise of that power. Congress may not create patent monopolies of unlimited duration, nor may it 'authorize the issuance of patents whose effects are to remove existent knowledge from the public domain, or to restrict free access to materials already available'") (quoting Graham v. John Deere Co. of Kansas City, 383 U.S. 1, 6 (1966)).

[114]Act of April 10, 1790, ch. 7, 1 Stat. 109.

[115]*See infra* Chapter 2 ("Patent Claims").

[116]Although not officially "legislative history," Federico's *Commentary on the 1952 Patent Act*, 35 U.S.C.A. 1 (1954 ed.), *reprinted at* 75 J. PAT. & TRADEMARK OFF. Soc'y 161 (1993), is considered by the Federal Circuit to be "an invaluable insight into the intentions of the drafters of the Act." Symbol Techs., Inc. v. Lemelson Med., 277 F.3d 1361, 1366 (Fed. Cir. 2002).

[117]The nonobviousness requirement of 35 U.S.C. §103 is the subject of Chapter 5, *infra.*

[118]These theories of patent infringement are discussed in further detail in Chapter 9, *infra.*

[119]Leahy-Smith America Invents Act, Pub. L. No. 112-29 (H.R. 1249), 125 Stat. 284 (2011). A useful resource providing both pre- and post-AIA text of the Patent Act (35

transitioned the U.S. patent system from its historic first-to-invent priority system to a unique first-inventor-to-file regime.[120] The AIA also established a post-grant opposition system, intended to provide a new early-stage means of challenging the validity of issued patents by proceeding in the USPTO rather than federal court.[121] Other notable AIA changes are discussed throughout this text.

U.S.C.) is The New United States Patent Law, Black Line Edition (2011), *available at* www.LegalPub.com.

[120]*See* 35 U.S.C. §102(a)(2) (eff. Mar. 16, 2013) (providing that "a person shall be entitled to a patent unless . . . the claimed invention was described in a patent issued under section 151, or in an application for patent published or deemed published under section 122(b), in which the patent or application, as the case may be, names another inventor and was effectively filed before the effective filing date of the claimed invention"); *see also* Leahy-Smith America Invents Act, Pub. L. No. 112-29 (H.R. 1249), §3 ("First Inventor to File"), 125 Stat. 284, 285-293 (2011); H.R. Rep. No. 112-98 [House Judiciary Comm. Rep. on the America Invents Act], at 53 (2011), which explains that the AIA

> creates a new "first-inventor-to-file" system. This new system provides patent applicants in the United States the efficiency benefits of the first-to-file systems used in the rest of the world by moving the U.S. system much closer to a first-to-file system and making the filing date that which is most relevant in determining whether an application is patentable. The new system continues, however, to provide inventors the benefit of the 1-year grace period. As part of the transition to a simpler, more efficient first-inventor-to-file system, this provision eliminates costly, complex interference proceedings, because priority will be based on the first application. A new administrative proceeding—called a "derivation" proceeding—is created to ensure that the first person to file the application is actually a true inventor. This new proceeding will ensure that a person will not be able to obtain a patent for the invention that he did not actually invent. If a dispute arises as to which of two applicants is a true inventor (as opposed to who invented it first), it will be resolved through an administrative proceeding by the Patent Board. The Act also simplifies how prior art is determined, provides more certainty, and reduces the cost associated with filing and litigating patents.

See also infra Chapter 4 ("Novelty, Loss of Right, and Priority Pre- and Post-America Invents Act of 2011 (35 U.S.C. §102)").

[121]*See* Leahy-Smith America Invents Act, Pub. L. No. 112-29 (H.R. 1249), §6(d), 125 Stat. 284, 305 (2011) (adding to 35 U.S.C. a new Chapter 32 titled "Post-Grant Review"); 35 U.S.C. §§321-329 (eff. Sept. 16, 2012); *see also* H.R. Rep. No. 112-98 [House Judiciary Comm. Rep. on the America Invents Act], at 58 (2011), which explains that the AIA

> creates a new post-grant opposition procedure that can be utilized during the first 12 months after the grant of a patent or issue of a reissue patent. Unlike reexamination proceedings, which provide only a limited basis on which to consider whether a patent should have issued, the post-grant review proceeding permits a challenge on any ground related to invalidity under [35 U.S.C.] section 282. The intent of the post-grant review process is to enable early challenges to patents, while still protecting the rights of inventors and patent owners against new patent challenges unbounded in time and scope. The Committee believes that this new, early-stage process for challenging patent validity and its clear

The statutory provisions of Title 35, U.S.C., governing patentability, which most directly impact the operations of the USPTO, are implemented through the agency's governing regulations. These regulations (sometimes referred to as USPTO "rules"), are found in Title 37 of the Code of Federal Regulations (C.F.R.). The USPTO also publishes the *Manual of Patent Examining Procedure* (MPEP), a detailed internal operating manual for patent examiners.[122] The MPEP is a very useful resource for patent practitioners and courts, but does not have the force and effect of law.[123]

3.   Case Law

Since 1982, the primary source of decisional authority interpreting the patent statute and regulations is the U.S. Court of Appeals for the Federal Circuit. The Federal Circuit (or CAFC) generally hears appeals in patent cases, sitting in panels of three Circuit judges. Prior decisions of Federal Circuit panels are considered binding precedent on later panels, and only the *en banc* court (i.e., all "active" status judges on the CAFC, a maximum of 12) can change the law or overrule existing precedent.[124] The Federal Circuit also has adopted as binding precedent the decisions of its two predecessor courts, the Court of Customs and Patent Appeals (CCPA), which no longer exists, and the appellate decisions of the Court of Claims, which exists today in the form of a specialized trial court called the Court of Federal Claims.[125]

---

procedures for submission of art will make the patent system more efficient and improve the quality of patents and the patent system. This new, but time-limited, post-grant review procedure will provide a meaningful opportunity to improve patent quality and restore confidence in the presumption of validity that comes with issued patents in court.

In the AIA as signed into law, the window for filing a petition for post-grant review was changed from 12 months (as indicated in the House Report above) to 9 months post-issuance. *See* Leahy-Smith America Invents Act, Pub. L. No. 112-29 (H.R. 1249), §6(d), 125 Stat. 284, 305 (2011) (adding new §321(c) to 35 U.S.C.); 35 U.S.C. §321(c) (eff. Sept. 16, 2012).

[122]The MPEP is available electronically. UNITED STATES PATENT AND TRADEMARK OFFICE, MANUAL OF PATENT EXAMINING PROCEDURE (8th ed., Aug. 2001, last rev. July 2010), *available at* http://www.uspto.gov/web/offices/pac/mpep/mpep.htm.

[123]*See* Critikon, Inc. v. Becton Dickinson Vascular Access, Inc., 120 F.3d 1253, 1257 (Fed. Cir. 1997) (observing that "the Manual of Patent Examining Procedure (MPEP), . . . although it does not have the force of law, is well known to those registered to practice in the PTO and reflects the presumptions under which the PTO operates").

[124]*See* Fed. Cir. R. 35(a) (2011), *available at* http://www.cafc.uscourts.gov/images/stories/rules-of-practice/rules.pdf.

[125]*See* South Corp. v. United States, 690 F.2d 1368, 1369 (Fed. Cir. 1982).

F. Primary Sources of U.S. Patent Law

The U.S. Supreme Court infrequently reviews the Federal Circuit's decisions in patent matters. When the Supreme Court does grant writs of *certiorari* from the Federal Circuit, the resulting Supreme Court decisions are very important and, of course, bind the Federal Circuit.[126]

---

[126]Notable U.S. Supreme Court patent decisions since 1996 include: Kappos v. Hyatt, 132 S. Ct. 1690 (2012) (holding that in a civil action to obtain a patent under 35 U.S.C. §145, there are no limitations on a patent applicant's ability to introduce new evidence beyond those already present in the Federal Rules of Evidence and the Federal Rules of Civil Procedure, and that if new evidence is presented on a disputed question of fact the district court must make *de novo* factual findings that take account of both the new evidence and the administrative record before the USPTO); Mayo Collaborative Serv. v. Prometheus Labs., Inc., 132 S. Ct. 1289 (2012) (holding that claimed methods of optimizing therapeutic efficacy for treatment of an immune-mediated gastrointestinal disorder were not patent-eligible subject matter under 35 U.S.C. §101 because claims merely recited "laws of nature" plus additional steps consisting of "well-understood, routine, conventional activity already engaged in by the scientific community"); Global-Tech Appliances Inc., v. SEB S.A., 131 S. Ct. 2060, 2068, 2070-2071 (2011) (holding that to be liable for actively inducing infringement of a patent under 35 U.S.C. §271(b), the inducer must have "knowledge that the induced acts constitute patent infringement," that "willful blindness" may satisfy the knowledge requirement, and that a willfully blind defendant is "one who takes deliberate actions to avoid confirming a high probability of wrongdoing and who can almost be said to have actually known the critical facts"); Microsoft Corp. v. i4i Ltd. P'ship., 131 S. Ct. 2238, 2251, 2252-2253 (2011) (affirming Federal Circuit's interpretation of 35 U.S.C. §282 that invalidity of a patent must be established by clear and convincing evidence, but also stating that "if the PTO did not have all material facts [e.g., prior art] before it, its considered judgment may lose significant force . . . . [a]nd, concomitantly, the challenger's burden to persuade the jury of its invalidity defense by clear and convincing evidence may be easier to sustain."); Bilski v. Kappos, 130 S. Ct. 3218 (2010) (holding that Federal Circuit erred in denominating its "machine-or-transformation test" as the exclusive standard of eligibility for patenting a process under 35 U.S.C. §101, but concluding that Bilski's claims to methods for protecting buyers and sellers against the risk of demand fluctuations in energy markets did not qualify as §101 processes because they attempted to patent an abstract idea); Quanta Comp., Inc. v. LG Elecs., Inc., 553 U.S. 617 (2008) (holding that doctrine of patent exhaustion applies to method patents; Intel's sale of licensed computer microprocessors and chipsets, in which LG's patented methods were "embodied," exhausted LG's right to sue Quanta and other computer manufacturers for infringement based on their combination of the licensed Intel products with non-Intel computer memory and buses); KSR Int'l Co. v. Teleflex, Inc., 550 U.S. 398 (rejecting Federal Circuit's overly rigid application in that case of teaching/suggestion/motivation test for combining references in nonobviousness analysis); Microsoft Corp. v. AT&T Corp., 550 U.S. 437 (2007) (holding that Microsoft's export of "master disk" containing Windows software for copying and installation on foreign-made computers did not trigger infringement liability under 35 U.S.C. §271(f), which prohibits export of a U.S.-patented invention's "component(s)" for "combination" outside U.S.); MedImmune, Inc. v. Genentech, Inc., 549 U.S. 118 (2007) (holding that subject-matter jurisdiction existed over licensee's Declaratory Judgment Act lawsuit challenging validity, enforceability, and infringement of licensed patent; justiciable case, or controversy under U.S. Constitution Art. III existed despite

G. Adjudicatory Forums for Patent Matters

A number of different administrative and judicial entities render decisions in U.S. patent matters. To summarize, the USPTO examines patent applications and grants patents, which are then enforced (or challenged) in the U.S. federal court system. Figure 1.3 below depicts the adjudicatory framework that is further described in the text below.

1. U.S. District Courts

a. *Subject Matter Jurisdiction and Venue*

In accordance with 28 U.S.C. §1338,[127] the U.S. District Courts have original *subject matter jurisdiction*, exclusive of state courts, over cases

---

licensee's payment of royalties under protest); eBay, Inc. v. MercExchange, L.L.C., 547 U.S. 388 (2006) (applying equity courts' traditional four-factor test for determining whether to award permanent injunctive relief in patent infringement dispute; Federal Circuit erred by "categorical[ly]" granting such relief when patents are adjudged valid and infringed); Ill. Tool Works, Inc. v. Indep. Ink, Inc., 547 U.S. 28 (2006) (holding that when a seller conditions its sale of a "tying" product on the purchase of a second, "tied" product, the mere fact that the tying product is patented does not support a presumption that its seller has market power as a matter of antitrust law); Merck KgaA v. Integra Lifesciences I, Ltd., 545 U.S. 193 (2005) (broadly interpreting scope of 35 U.S.C. §271(e)(1) safe harbor for regulatory drug testing); Holmes Group, Inc. v. Vornado Air Circulation Sys., Inc., 535 U.S. 826 (2002) (holding that Federal Circuit's appellate jurisdiction does not extend to cases in which a counterclaim, rather than the well-pleaded complaint, asserts a claim arising under the patent laws); Festo Corp. v. Shoketsu Kinzoku Kogyo Kabushiki Co., 535 U.S. 722 (2002) (rejecting Federal Circuit's "complete bar" rule for prosecution history estoppel; holding that, by amending a claim to narrow a limitation, a patentee presumptively surrenders all equivalents to the limitation, but that the patentee may rebut the presumption by showing that (1) an alleged equivalent was unforeseeable, (2) the rationale underlying the amendment bore no more than a tangential relation to the equivalent in question, or (3) there was some other reason why the patentee could not reasonably have been expected to have literally claimed the equivalent); Dickinson v. Zurko, 527 U.S. 150 (1999) (holding Administrative Procedure Act standards of judicial review applicable to Federal Circuit review of USPTO patentability fact-findings); Pfaff v. Wells Elecs. Inc., 525 U.S. 55 (1998) (announcing "ready for patenting" test as triggering on sale bar under 35 U.S.C. §102(b)); Warner-Jenkinson Co. v. Hilton Davis Chem. Co., 520 U.S. 17 (1997) (reaffirming viability of doctrine of equivalents); Markman v. Westview Instruments, Inc., 517 U.S. 370 (1996) (assigning patent claim interpretational responsibility in jury trials to judges).

[127]28 U.S.C. §1338 (eff. Sept. 16, 2011) provides:

§1338. Patents, plant variety protection, copyrights, mask works, designs, trademarks, and unfair competition

(a) The district courts shall have original jurisdiction of any civil action arising under any Act of Congress relating to patents, plant variety protection,

G. Adjudicatory Forums for Patent Matters

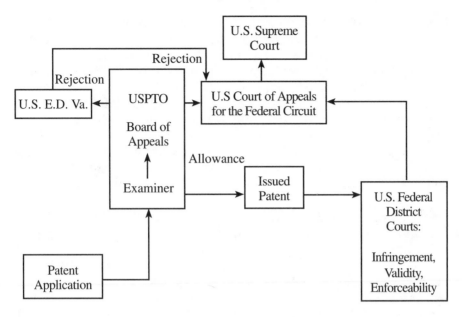

Figure 1.3

**Interaction of USPTO, U.S. Federal District Courts, U.S.
Court of Appeals for the Federal Circuit, and U.S. Supreme
Court in Patent Matters**

---

copyrights and trademarks. No State court shall have jurisdiction over any claim
for relief arising under any Act of Congress relating to patents, plant variety protection, or copyrights. For purposes of this subsection, the term "State" includes
any State of the United States, the District of Columbia, the Commonwealth of
Puerto Rico, the United States Virgin Islands, American Samoa, Guam, and the
Northern Mariana Islands.

(b) The district courts shall have original jurisdiction of any civil action asserting a claim of unfair competition when joined with a substantial and related
claim under the copyright, patent, plant variety protection or trademark laws.

(c) Subsections (a) and (b) apply to exclusive rights in mask works under
chapter 9 of title 17 [17 USCS §§901 et seq.], and to exclusive rights in designs
under chapter 13 of title 17 [17 USCS §§1301 et seq.], to the same extent as such
subsections apply to copyrights.

The pre-AIA version of §1338(a) provided in its second sentence that "such jurisdiction shall be exclusive of the courts of the states in patent, plant variety protection,
and copyright cases." 28 U.S.C. §1338(a) (2006). Section 1338(a), as interpreted by the
Supreme Court in *Holmes Group, Inc. v. Vornado Air Circulation Sys., Inc.*, 535 U.S. 826
(2002), left some ambiguity concerning the power of state courts to assert jurisdiction
over certain patent law–related claims for relief. The AIA deleted the second sentence
of §1338(a) and replaced it with the following text:

No State court shall have jurisdiction over any claim for relief arising under any Act
of Congress relating to patents, plant variety protection, or copyrights. For purposes

that are considered "arising under" the patent laws, in whole or in part. In *Christianson v. Colt Indus. Operating Corp.*,[128] the Supreme Court set forth the "well-pleaded complaint rule," which provides that §1338 "arising under" subject matter jurisdiction extends only to those cases in which a well-pleaded complaint establishes either that (1) federal patent law creates the cause of action, or (2) the plaintiff's right to relief necessarily depends on resolution of a substantial question of federal patent law, in that patent law is a necessary element of one of the well-pleaded claims.[129] Garden-variety patent infringement suits, as well as **declaratory judgment** actions seeking a declaration of non-infringement and/or patent invalidity,[130] fall within category (1) of

---

of this subsection, the term "State" includes any State of the United States, the District of Columbia, the Commonwealth of Puerto Rico, the United States Virgin Islands, American Samoa, Guam, and the Northern Mariana Islands.

Leahy-Smith America Invents Act, Pub. L. No. 112-29 (H.R. 1249), §19(a), 125 Stat. 284, 331 (2011) (titled "State Court Jurisdiction"). The intent of the AIA amendment appears to be "more fully precluding state court jurisdiction over patent legal claims," although the legislative history does not define the phrase "patent legal claims." *See* H.R. Rep. No. 112-98 [House Judiciary Comm. Rep. on the America Invents Act], at 81 (2011) (explaining that "Subsection (a) through (d) [of Section 19 of the AIA] enact the so-called *Holmes Group* fix (H.R. 2955, 109th Congress), which the House Judiciary Committee reported favorably in 2006. The Committee Report accompanying H.R. 2955 (House Rep. 109–407), which we reaffirm, explains the bill's reasons for abrogating *Holmes Group, Inc. v. Vornado Air Circulation Systems, Inc.*, 535 U.S. 826 (2002), *and more fully precluding state court jurisdiction over patent legal claims*.") (emphasis added).

The AIA amendment to 28 U.S.C. §1338 corrected a ten-year aberration in Federal Circuit jurisdiction over cases involving patent issues. In *Holmes Group, Inc. v. Vornado Air Circulation Sys., Inc.*, 535 U.S. 826 (2002), the Supreme Court had very literally interpreted the "arising under" language of 28 U.S.C. §1338(a) (2000) to mean that the Federal Circuit's appellate jurisdiction over patent cases did *not* extend to those cases in which a *counterclaim*, rather than the *complaint*, asserted a patent-based cause of action (e.g., in a lawsuit initially brought on a non-patent basis such as trade dress misappropriation). Assuming such cases were tried in federal district court, *Holmes Group* meant that they would be appealed to the appropriate U.S. Court of Appeals for the regional circuit in which the federal district court was located rather than to the Federal Circuit. For example, an antitrust case litigated in the Northern District of Illinois in which the defendant invoked a patent law–based counterclaim would be appealed to the U.S. Court of Appeals for the Seventh Circuit rather than to the Federal Circuit. Such an outcome was contrary to the policy goals underlying the 1982 formation of the Federal Circuit. *See infra* Section G.2. For critiques of the *Holmes Group* decision, *see* Molly Mosley-Goren, *Jurisdictional Gerrymandering? Responding to Holmes Group v. Vornado Air Circulation Systems*, 36 J. MARSHALL L. REV. 1 (2002); Janice M. Mueller, *"Interpretive Necromancy" or Prudent Patent Policy? The Supreme Court's "Arising Under" Blunder in Holmes Group v. Vornado*, 2 J. MARSHALL REV. INTELL. PROP. L. 57 (2002), http://www.jmripl.com/Publications/Vol2/Issue1/mueller.pdf.

[128]486 U.S. 800 (1988).

[129]*Christianson*, 486 U.S. at 808-809.

[130]Declaratory judgment actions by accused patent infringers are discussed in Chapter 10, Section G, *infra*.

the well-pleaded complaint rule. More problematic are litigations such as *Christianson,* an antitrust lawsuit that raised patent law issues.[131] In such cases, courts must decide whether the dispute falls within category (2), that is, whether the plaintiff's right to relief *necessarily* depends on resolution of a patent law issue, even though the complaint does not assert a patent law cause of action per se.[132]

The issue of *venue* for patent disputes asks *which* U.S. District Court may properly hear the case. Title 28 of the United States Code ("Judiciary and Judicial Procedure") provides that "[a]ny civil action for patent infringement may be brought in the judicial district where the defendant resides, or where the defendant has committed acts of infringement and has a regular and established place of business."[133] For the many defendants that are corporate entities rather than natural persons, the statute provides elsewhere that "[f]or purposes of venue under this chapter, a defendant that is a corporation shall be deemed to reside in any judicial district in which it is subject to personal jurisdiction at the time the action is commenced."[134] In view of Supreme Court precedent governing personal jurisdiction, many corporations will be deemed to reside in any judicial district in which the alleged infringing product can be purchased, e.g., in a local retail outlet.

Given the broad scope of venue choice for plaintiff patent owners, certain U.S. District Courts have become very popular fora in recent years. For example, patent litigation lore suggests that the U.S. District Court for the Eastern District of Texas provides a jury pool tending to award large verdicts to patent owners. Whether or not this belief is borne out by empirical evidence, the Eastern District of Texas in recent years has indisputably attracted a great deal of patent

---

[131]*See Christianson,* 486 U.S. at 804-805 (describing antitrust action by former employee Christianson against patentee Colt, manufacturer of automatic rifles, alleging that Colt drove Christianson out of business by warning former clients against doing business with Christianson because he was allegedly misappropriating Colt's trade secrets).

[132]*See Christianson,* 486 U.S. at 808.

[133]28 U.S.C. §1400(b) (2012).

[134]28 U.S.C. §1391(c) (2010). The Federal Courts Jurisdiction and Venue Clarification Act of 2011, Pub. L. No. 112-63, Title II, §202(1), 125 Stat. 763 (2011), amended this language but did not substantively impact the deemed residence of a corporate defendant. For lawsuits filed on or after January 7, 2012, *see id.* §105 ("Effective Date"), subsection (c) of 28 U.S.C. §1391 now provides that "[f]or all venue purposes—(2) an entity with the capacity to sue and be sued in its common name under applicable law, whether or not incorporated, shall be deemed to reside, if a defendant, in any judicial district in which such defendant is subject to the court's personal jurisdiction with respect to the civil action in question and, if a plaintiff, only in the judicial district in which it maintains its principal place of business. . . . " 35 U.S.C. §1391(c) (eff. Jan. 7, 2012).

litigation.[135] Despite criticism of forum shopping by patentees at the trial court level,[136] the AIA did not change this aspect of the patent venue rules.

b. Civil Actions Against the USPTO Director in the Eastern District of Virginia

Certain U.S. district courts occasionally preside over civil actions to obtain a patent under 35 U.S.C. §145 and civil actions in the case of derivation proceeding under 35 U.S.C. §146 (a proceeding newly created by the AIA).[137] In these proceedings, parties who have had their claims rejected by a USPTO examiner in *ex parte* prosecution and failed to obtain a reversal from the USPTO Patent Trial and Appeal Board (PTAB), or parties who have lost a derivation proceeding before the PTAB, will bring a lawsuit against the Director of the agency in federal district court. Should the plaintiff prevail in the civil action, the District Court will issue an order authorizing the USPTO to issue a patent. If the plaintiff does not prevail, he or she may appeal the District Court's decision to the Federal Circuit.

The America Invents Act of 2011 changed the venue for §145 and §146 actions (and also changed the nature of §146 actions).[138] Prior to the AIA, a civil action to obtain a patent under 35 U.S.C. §145 was

---

[135]*See generally* XIV SMU Sci. & Tech. L. Rev. 191, 191-320 (2011) (symposium issue titled "Emerging Intellectual Property Issues" focusing on Eastern District of Texas). In their symposium article, *Real Reasons the Eastern District of Texas Draws Patent Cases—Beyond Lore and Anecdote*, XIV SMU Sci. & Tech. L. Rev. 299 (2011), attorneys Andrei Iancu and Jay Chung report that the Eastern District of Texas, along with the Central District of California, "is perennially among the busiest patent dockets in the nation, although that that has not always been the case." *Id.* at 299. Based on their statistical analysis, Iancu and Chung disagree with the popular perception that juries in the Eastern District of Texas are "unsophisticated and predisposed to find for plaintiffs." *Id.* at 300. The authors find "little evidence that the District's popularity arises primarily from its jury pool." *Id.* Rather, they contend, a confluence of factors combine "to render a much more satisfactory explanation." *Id.*

[136]*See* Paul M. Janicke, *Venue Transfers from the Eastern District of Texas: Case by Case or an Endemic Problem?,* 2 Landslide 14 (2010) (describing "[a]dverse commentary and congressional proposals to limit patent venue"); *see generally* Kimberly A. Moore, *Forum Shopping in Patent Cases: Does Geographic Choice Affect Innovation?,* 79 N.C. L. Rev. 889 (2001).

[137]*See* 28 U.S.C. §1295(a)(4)(C).

[138]*See* Leahy-Smith America Invents Act, Pub. L. No. 112-29 (H.R. 1249), §9(a), 125 Stat. 284, 316 (2011) ("Technical Amendments Relating to Venue.—Sections 32, *145, 146,* 154(b)(4)(A), and 293 of title 35, United States Code, and section 21(b)(4) of the Trademark Act of 1946 (15 U.S.C. 1071(b)(4)), are each amended by striking 'United States District Court for the District of Columbia' each place that term appears and inserting 'United States District Court for the Eastern District of Virginia.'") (emphasis added); 35 U.S.C. §145 (eff. Sept. 16, 2011); 35 U.S.C. §146 (eff. Sept. 16, 2011).

brought in the U.S. District Court for the District of Columbia.[139] Effective September 16, 2011, §145 actions must be brought in the U.S. District Court for the Eastern District of Virginia. Also prior to the AIA, a civil action could be brought under 35 U.S.C. §146 to contest an adverse USPTO decision in an interference.[140] Such §146 actions could be brought in any U.S. District Court and were not limited to the District of Columbia (unlike a pre-AIA §145 action). The AIA eliminated interferences as well as the §146 civil action in case of interference. The AIA replaced the old §146 civil action in case of interference with a new §146 civil action in case of derivation proceeding. Section 146 derivation actions, like §145 (post-AIA) civil actions to obtain patent, must be brought in the U.S. District Court for the Eastern District of Virginia.

Although this civil action route is generally more expensive and lengthy than a direct appeal from the USPTO to the Federal Circuit under 35 U.S.C. §141, the advantage provided by the civil action is that the plaintiff can put before the federal district court new evidence that was not considered by the USPTO.[141] The civil action is essentially a *trial de novo* of patentability with the opportunity for pre-trial discovery. In contrast, new evidence cannot be presented in a direct appeal from the USPTO to the Federal Circuit because this type of appeal must be "on the record" that was before the agency in accordance with 35 U.S.C. §144.

2. U.S. Court of Appeals for the Federal Circuit

Prior to 1982, appeals of judgments in garden-variety patent infringement cases clearly "arising under" the patent laws were taken

---

[139]Before the AIA, Section 145 actions were filed in the U.S. District Court for the District of Columbia. See 35 U.S.C. §145 (2006) (providing in part that "[a]n applicant dissatisfied with the decision of the Board of Patent Appeals and Interferences in an appeal under section 134(a) of this title may, unless appeal has been taken to the United States Court of Appeals for the Federal Circuit, have remedy by civil action against the Director in the United States District Court for the District of Columbia. . . ."). Pre-AIA, analogous civil actions in the case of interferences could be brought in any U.S. district court in accordance with 35 U.S.C. §146 (2006).

[140]Interferences are *inter partes* proceedings conducted in the USPTO to determine priority of invention between rival claimants under the United States' pre-AIA historic first-to-invent priority system. *See infra* Chapter 4, Section N ("Prior Invention Under 35 U.S.C. §102(g) (Pre-AIA)").

[141]The Supreme Court has confirmed that in a §145 proceeding, introduction of new evidence not previously presented to the USPTO is limited only by the Federal Rules of Evidence and the Federal Rules of Civil Procedure. Kappos v. Hyatt, 132 S. Ct. 1690 (2012). "Moreover, if new evidence is presented on a disputed question of fact, the district court must make *de novo* factual findings that take account of both the new evidence and the administrative record before the PTO." *Id.* at 1701.

to the appropriate federal regional circuit court of appeals for the federal district court in question. For example, if a patent infringement case was tried prior to 1982 in Chicago before the U.S. District Court for the Northern District of Illinois, any appeal would have been taken to the U.S. Court of Appeals for the Seventh Circuit.

Concerns over forum-shopping at the appellate level and lack of national uniformity in patent law prompted Congress to create in 1982 a new appellate court, the U.S. Court of Appeals for the Federal Circuit.[142] The Federal Circuit (or CAFC) has exclusive nationwide jurisdiction over appeals in which the well-pleaded complaint (or a compulsory counterclaim) asserts a cause of action arising under the patent laws. Section 1295 of 28 U.S.C. provides that the Federal Circuit's appellate jurisdiction encompasses all appeals from final decisions of a U.S. district court "in any civil action arising under, or in any civil action in which a party has asserted a compulsory counterclaim arising under, any Act of Congress relating to patents. . . . "[143] Thus, if a patent infringement case is tried today in San Jose before the U.S. District Court for the Northern District of California, any appeal will be taken to the Federal Circuit, not to the U.S. Court of Appeals for the Ninth Circuit.

---

[142]The legislation that created the Federal Circuit is the Federal Courts Improvement Act (FCIA) of 1982, Pub. L. No. 97-164, 96 Stat. 25 (1982). The legislative history for the FCIA is S. Rep. No. 97-275 (Nov. 18, 1981), *reprinted in* 1982 U.S.C.C.A.N. 11. The legislative history states in part:

> The establishment of the Court of Appeals for the Federal Circuit also provides a forum that will increase doctrinal stability in the field of patent law. Based on the evidence it had compiled, the Hruska Commission singled out patent law as an area in which the application of the law to the facts of a case often produces different outcomes in different courtrooms in substantially similar cases. Furthermore, in a Commission survey of practitioners, the patent bar indicated that uncertainty created by the lack of national law precedent was a significant problem, and the Commission singled out patent law as an area in which widespread forum-shopping is particularly acute.

S. Rep. No. 97-275 (1981), at 15 (footnotes omitted).

[143]28 U.S.C. §1295 (eff. Sept. 16, 2011) provides in part:

§1295. Jurisdiction of the United States Court of Appeals for the Federal Circuit

(a) The United States Court of Appeals for the Federal Circuit shall have exclusive jurisdiction—

(1) of an appeal from a final decision of a district court of the United States, the District Court of Guam, the District Court of the Virgin Islands, or the District Court of the Northern Mariana Islands, in any civil action arising under, or in any civil action in which a party has asserted a compulsory counterclaim arising under, any Act of Congress relating to patents or plant variety protection. . . .

G. Adjudicatory Forums for Patent Matters

Although the Federal Circuit has its share of critics,[144] the consensus view is that the CAFC "experiment" has been a success.[145] As a practical matter, the creation of the Federal Circuit has resulted in a single, relatively coherent body of patent case law on which district courts and

---

[144]*See, e.g.,* Lucas S. Osborn, *Instrumentalism at the Federal Circuit*, 56 St. Louis U. L.J. 419, 424 (2012) (concluding that "[r]egardless of the reasons for it, the Federal Circuit's forced formalism tends to lead to opinions lacking full legitimacy and the adoption of sub-optimal legal rules"); Timothy B. Lee, *Bring Appellate Competition Back to Patent Law,* Cato Inst. (July 28, 2008), http://www.cato.org/pub_display.php?pub_id=11455 (stating that "[w]hile the problems of too little uniformity in patent law were obvious in 1982, the policymakers who created the Federal Circuit failed to appreciate that excessive uniformity could be even worse"); Craig A. Nard & John F. Duffy, *Rethinking Patent Law's Uniformity Principle*, 101 Nw. U. L. Rev. 1619 (2007) (reviewing history and criticisms of the Federal Circuit and proposing a decentralized institutional architecture for patent law that would assign appeals from district court patent decisions to at least one other extant U.S. Court of Appeals); Adam B. Jaffe & Joshua Lerner, Innovation and Its Discontents: How Our Broken Patent System Is Endangering Innovation and Progress, and What to Do About It 96-126 (Princeton Univ. Press 2004); Matthew F. Weil & William C. Rooklidge, *Stare Un-Decisis: The Sometimes Rough Treatment of Precedent in Federal Circuit Decision-Making*, 80 J. Pat. & Trademark Off. Soc'y 791 (1998); Allan N. Littman, *Restoring the Balance of Our Patent System*, 37 Idea 545 (1997).

[145]*See, e.g.,* Symposium, *Evolving the Court of Appeals for the Federal Circuit and its Patent Law Jurisprudence*, 76 Mo. L. Rev. 629 (Summer 2011) (stating in Foreword by Professor Dennis Crouch that although the Circuit's evolution in response to questions presented by litigants, external political influences, changing judicial composition, and role of intellectual property in society "alters the law and its practice, it is this evolution that guarantees an ongoing role for the court and satisfies the public demand for a law shaped to fit the needs of society"); Ryan Vacca, *Acting Like an Administrative Agency: The Federal Circuit* En Banc, 76 Mo. L. Rev. 733, 759 (2011) (concluding that "[a]lthough the Federal Circuit's *en banc* practices strongly resemble an agency's procedure for substantive rulemaking, . . . until structural changes are made or enough political will is garnered, the Federal Circuit hearing cases *en banc* is not a bad solution to the ever-present problem of changing circumstances in patent law"); Elizabeth I. Winston, *Differentiating the Federal Circuit*, 76 Mo. L. Rev. 813, 837 (2011) (concluding that "[o]ften referred to as an experiment, the Federal Circuit has flourished. Born again from the ashes of its predecessors, the Phoenix Court continues to grow in significance, stature, and strength."); Paul D. Carrington & Paulina Orchard, *The Federal Circuit: A Model for Reform?*, 78 Geo. Wash. L. Rev. 575 (2010); Symposium, *The U.S. Court of Appeals for the Federal Circuit: Its Critical Role in the Revitalization of U.S. Patent Jurisprudence, Past, Present, and Future*, 43 Loy. L.A. L. Rev. 775 (2010); Daniel J. Meador, *Remarks in the United States Court of Appeals for the Federal Circuit, April 2, 2007*, 17 Fed. Cir. B.J. 125, 126 (2007) ("The beauty of this court's design is that because of the wide-ranging jurisdiction inherited from its predecessor courts, it can secure national uniformity in patent law and other fields without encountering the specialization stigma."); Jonathan Ringel, *A New Order: 20 Years of the Federal Circuit*, IP Worldwide (Dec. 2001), at 40; Victoria Slind-Flor, *Formerly Obscure Court Is in Spotlight*, Nat'l L.J. (Apr. 30, 2001), at B9; Steven Andersen, *Federal Circuit Gets Passing Marks to Date But There's a Lot of Room for Improvement*, Corp. Legal Times (Mar. 2000), at 86; John F. Merz & Nicholas M. Pace, *Trends in Patent Litigation: The Apparent Influence of Strengthened Patents Attributable to the Court of Appeals for the Federal Circuit*, 79 J. Pat. & Trademark Off. Soc'y 579 (1994).

litigants can rely with greater certainty than the disparate decisions reached by the regional circuits in patent cases prior to 1982.[146]

3.   USPTO Patent Trial and Appeal Board

In addition to its jurisdiction to hear appeals from decisions of district courts in litigation involving issued patents, the Federal Circuit

---

[146]A leading study of the Federal Circuit's creation and evolution as a court is Rochelle Cooper Dreyfuss, *The Federal Circuit: A Case Study in Specialized Courts*, 64 N.Y.U. L. REV. 1 (1989). Professor Dreyfuss updated her examination of the Federal Circuit in *In Search of Institutional Identity: The Federal Circuit Comes of Age*, 23 BERKELEY TECH. L.J. 787 (2008). *See also* Rochelle Cooper Dreyfuss, *What the Federal Circuit Can Learn from the Supreme Court—And Vice Versa*, 59 AM. U. L. REV. 787 (2010). Polk Wagner revises and expands upon Dreyfuss's seminal work in R. Polk Wagner, *The Two Federal Circuits*, 43 LOY. L.A. L. REV. 785 (2010) (concluding that "the most important moving part is not so much the specialization of the [Federal Circuit] along subject matter lines but instead the emergence of two distinct understandings of the court's role in patent law [i.e., what Wagner terms its "decisional" versus "managerial" approaches to deciding patent appeals], and how that role should be reflected in its decisions").

A number of patent scholars now use empirical techniques including data gathering and statistical analysis to study the Federal Circuit's performance in several areas of its patent jurisprudence. For example, data on Federal Circuit decision making in validity matters are reported at John R. Allison & Mark A. Lemley, *How Federal Circuit Judges Vote in Patent Validity Cases*, 10 FED. CIR. B.J. 435 (2001). The Federal Circuit's treatment of nonobviousness, the most critical issue within the patentability/validity rubric (*see supra* Chapter 5), is empirically examined in Lee Petherbridge & R. Polk Wagner, *The Federal Circuit and Patentability: An Empirical Assessment of the Law of Obviousness*, 85 TEX. L. REV. 2051 (2007) (presenting data suggesting "that the Federal Circuit has developed a doctrine in this area that is relatively stable and appears reasonably predictable," despite controversy concerning the court's "teaching, suggestion, or motivation" inquiry). The Federal Circuit's oversight of the district courts' patent claim interpretation is analyzed in David L. Schwartz, *Practice Makes Perfect? An Empirical Study of Claim Construction Reversal Rates in Patent Cases*, 107 MICH. L. REV. 223, 267 (2008) (concluding that "the [Federal Circuit's] reversal rate may be essentially constant, regardless of the prior claim construction experience of the district court judge," and identifying three possible reasons for the district courts' lack of improvement: "(1) an indeterminate nature of claim construction; (2) a failure of the Federal Circuit to teach properly how to construe claims; and (3) a failure of district court judges to learn claim construction").

For a compact compendium of Federal Circuit patent decisions, *see* ROBERT L. HARMON, PATENTS AND THE FEDERAL CIRCUIT (10th ed. 2011). Abstracts of all significant Federal Circuit patent decisions appear in the single-volume work DONALD S. CHISUM, PATENT LAW DIGEST (2011 ed.). Chisum reviews all district court, Federal Circuit, and Supreme Court patent cases in the 28-volume treatise DONALD S. CHISUM, CHISUM ON PATENTS (2012), first published in 1978. Another important scholarly treatise is R. CARL MOY, MOY'S WALKER ON PATENTS (4th ed. 2011).

An overview of patent jurisprudence and a look toward the future by a former Chief Judge of the Federal Circuit is available at The Honorable Paul R. Michel, *A Review of Recent Decisions of the United States Court of Appeals for the Federal Circuit: Afterword: Past, Present, and Future in the Life of the U.S. Court of Appeals for the Federal Circuit*, 59 AM. U. L. REV. 1199 (2010).

also hears appeals from decisions of the Patent Trial and Appeal Board (Board or PTAB).[147] The Board is an administrative body within the USPTO that hears appeals from patent examiners' decisions in a variety of USPTO proceedings discussed in later chapters of this text, including refusals to grant patents in *ex parte* patent examination,[148] as well as adverse decisions in **reexamination** (in both its *ex parte*[149] and *inter partes*[150] forms) proceedings[151] as well as **reissue** proceedings.[152] The PTAB also presides over the AIA-implemented "*inter partes* review" and "post-grant review" proceedings.[153] Lastly, the PTAB renders decisions in AIA-implemented "derivation proceedings," which are USPTO *inter partes* proceedings for determining whether one applicant derived her invention from another.[154]

4. U.S. International Trade Commission

Lastly, the International Trade Commission (ITC) has jurisdiction over patent-related matters involving imports under Section 337 of the Tariff Act of 1930, as amended.[155] Section 337 makes it unlawful to import into the U.S. articles that "infringe a valid and enforceable United States patent" or that "are made, produced, processed, or

---

[147]*See* 28 U.S.C. §1295(a)(4)(A); 35 U.S.C. §141. Prior to the America Invents Act of 2011 (AIA), the Board was known as the Board of Patent Appeals and Interferences (BPAI). The AIA changed the Board's name to the Patent Trial and Appeal Board, and broadened the Board's jurisdiction. *See* Leahy-Smith America Invents Act, Pub. L. No. 112-29 (H.R. 1249), §7, 125 Stat. 284, 313 (2011); 35 U.S.C. §6 (eff. Sept. 16, 2012) ("Patent Trial and Appeal Board").

[148]*See* 35 U.S.C. §134(a). *See also infra* Section H ("Patent Prosecution Overview").

[149]*See* 35 U.S.C. §§301-307. Reexamination, a USPTO administrative procedure for reexamining an issued patent based on a substantial new question of patentability, is covered in Chapter 8 ("Correcting and Challenging Issued Patents at the USPTO"), *infra*.

[150]*See* 35 U.S.C. §315. The *inter partes* reexamination proceeding is covered in Chapter 8 ("Correcting and Challenging Issued Patents at the USPTO"), *infra*.

The America Invents Act of 2011 phases out *inter partes* reexamination in favor of a new "*inter partes* review" procedure. *See* Leahy-Smith America Invents Act, Pub. L. No. 112-29 (H.R. 1249), §6(a) (2011); 35 U.S.C. §§311-319 (eff. Sept. 16, 2012).

[151]*See* 35 U.S.C. §134(b).

[152]*See* 35 U.S.C. §251; *id.* §134(a). Reissue, a USPTO administrative procedure for reissuing patents that are defective in certain respects, is covered in Chapter 8 ("Correcting and Challenging Issued Patents at the USPTO"), *infra*.

[153]*See* 35 U.S.C. §§311-319 (eff. Sept. 16, 2012) (*inter partes* review); 35 U.S.C. §§321-329 (eff. Sept. 16, 2012 for applications filed on or afer Mar. 16, 2013) (post-grant review). *Inter partes* review and post-grant review proceedings are covered in Chapter 8 ("Correcting and Challenging Issued Patents at the USPTO"), *infra*.

[154]*See* 35 U.S.C. §135 (eff. Mar. 16, 2013) ("Derivation proceedings"). Before enactment of the AIA, 35 U.S.C. §135 (2006) governed interference proceedings. The AIA discontinues interferences but implements a new derivation proceeding.

[155]*See* 19 U.S.C. §1337 ("Unfair practices in import trade").

mined under, or by means of, a process covered by the claims of a valid and enforceable United States patent."[156] The ITC investigates alleged violations of Section 337, typically at the urging of U.S patent owners.[157] ITC investigations include trial proceedings conducted before an ITC administrative law judge, whose Initial Decision on the merits is reviewed by the Commission.[158]

If it finds patent infringement, the ITC will typically enter an order excluding the infringing articles from entry into the U.S;[159] however, the ITC does not award damages for infringement. Patent litigation conducted before the ITC is resolved much more rapidly than infringement cases in the federal district courts, historically within less than 15 months.[160] For this and other reasons, enforcement at the ITC has become an increasingly attractive option for patent owners.[161] The ITC's Section 337 decisions do not bind the federal district courts, however, and many parties bring actions in both fora.[162]

H.   Patent Prosecution Overview

1.   Introduction

Contrary to its name, patent **prosecution** has nothing to do with criminal law. Rather it refers to the process of preparing and filing a patent application in the USPTO and thereafter interacting with the agency to obtain a U.S. patent. This interaction typically involves a

---

[156] 19 U.S.C. §1337(a)(1)(B). This provision applies "only if an industry in the United States, relating to the articles protected by the patent . . . concerned, exists or is in the process of being established." 19 U.S.C. §1337(a)(2).

[157] See 19 U.S.C. §1337(b) ("Investigation of violations by Commission").

[158] See 19 C.F.R. §§210.43-45 (2010); United States International Trade Commission, USITC—Intellectual Property Infringement and Other Unfair Acts, http://www.usitc.gov/intellectual_property/ (last visited May 26, 2012).

[159] See 19 U.S.C. §1337(d) ("Exclusion of articles from entry"). An exclusion order is the ITC's "primary remedy." United States International Trade Commission, USITC—Intellectual Property Infringement and Other Unfair Acts, http://www.usitc.gov/intellectual_property/ (last visited May 26, 2012).

[160] See United States International Trade Commission, Section 337 Investigations: Answers to Frequently Asked Questions 23 (2009), http://www.usitc.gov/intellectual_property/documents/337_faqs.pdf.

[161] See generally Christopher A. Cotropia, Strength of the International Trade Commission as a Patent Venue, 20 Tex. Intell. Prop. L.J. 1 (2011); id. at 2 (stating that "because of their exclusive jurisdiction over [Section 337] actions, ITC administrative judges are seen by many as patent law savvy and, in turn, patentholder friendly. As a result, the ITC has become a favored jurisdiction for patent infringement disputes, being used more and more by patentees.").

[162] See Colleen V. Chien, Patently Protectionist? An Empirical Analysis of Patent Cases at the International Trade Commission, 50 Wm. & Mary L. Rev. 63, 64 (2008).

multi-year negotiation between the patent applicant and the USPTO examiner over the allowable scope of the patent claims in view of the relevant prior art. Patent prosecution is sometimes referred to as patent solicitation.[163]

2.   Filing the Application

The process begins with the filing of a patent application in the USPTO. A patent applicant can file *pro se* and need not be represented by a patent attorney or agent, but obtaining competent representation is highly recommended in order to minimize the risk of losing important legal rights.[164] Two types of patent applications may be filed: **provisional** applications and **nonprovisional** applications. Provisional applications are the newer option, available for the first time as of June 8, 1995. Prior to that date, only nonprovisional applications (then known simply as "applications") could be filed.[165]

Provisional applications are governed by 35 U.S.C. §111(b), which provides that a provisional application must have a specification (and drawings, if necessary to understand the invention). Unlike a nonprovisional application, however, the provisional application need not include any claims or an oath by the applicant. The provisional patent application has proven very popular as a quick and inexpensive means of establishing an early domestic priority date.[166] Its filing also

---

[163]This discussion of patent prosecution is by necessity a summary overview. Good sources of more detailed guidance on patent application preparation and prosecution include Irah H. Donner, Patent Prosecution: Practice and Procedure Before the U.S. Patent Office (7th ed. BNA 2011); Joshua P. Graham & Thomas G. Marlow, U.S. Patent Prosecutor's Desk Reference (Oxford 2011); James E. Hawes, Patent Application Practice (2d ed. Thomson/West 2008); David Pressman, Patent It Yourself (Nolo 2011); Joseph E. Root, Rules of Patent Drafting (Oxford 2011); Jeffrey G. Sheldon, How to Write a Patent Application (2d ed., PLI 2009); Ronald D. Slusky, Invention Analysis and Claiming: A Patent Lawyer's Guide (Am. Bar Ass'n 2007); Thomas A. Turano, Obtaining Patents (James Pub. 1997). *See also* United States Patent and Trademark Office, Manual of Patent Examining Procedure (8th ed., Aug. 2001, last rev. July 2010), *available at* http://www.uspto.gov/web/offices/pac/mpep/mpep.htm.

[164]Persons who have been admitted to practice before the USPTO can represent inventors before the agency. Attorneys admitted to practice before the USPTO are called "patent attorneys" while non-attorneys admitted to practice before the agency are referred to as "patent agents." For a list of registered patent attorneys and agents, *see* United States Patent & Trademark Office, *Patent Attorney / Agent ZIP File,* https://oedci.uspto.gov/OEDCI/index.jsp (last visited May 26, 2012).

[165]*See* Uruguay Round Agreements Act, Pub. L. No. 103-465, tit. V, subtit. C, §532, 108 Stat. 4983-88 (Dec. 8, 1994) ("Patent Term and Internal Priority").

[166]During fiscal year 2010 approximately 140,000 provisional patent applications were filed with the USPTO, in comparison with the approximately 478,000 nonprovisional utility patent applications filed during the same period. *See* United States Patent & Trademark Office, *Performance and Accountability Report Fiscal Year*

allows the patent applicant to apply the words "patent pending" to her products that embody the invention disclosed in the provisional application.[167] She may also be able to rely on the provisional application as evidence that she had conceived the invention disclosed therein no later than the provisional application's filing date.[168] Lastly, the provisional application filing date may also be relied on as a priority date for the subsequent filing of foreign patent applications on the same invention in accordance with the right of priority of the Paris Convention.[169]

The provisional application is not substantively examined by the USPTO, but rather acts as a sort of placeholder. If the applicant elects to do so, she can file a corresponding nonprovisional application within 12 months of the provisional application's filing date. The nonprovisional ("regular" or "full-service") application will be substantively examined. So long as the invention she claims in the nonprovisional patent application was adequately supported by the disclosure of the provisional application in accordance with 35 U.S.C. §112, ¶1 (renamed §112(a) by the America Invents Act of 2011), the applicant can claim for the later nonprovisional application the benefit of the earlier provisional application's filing date, effectively "backdating" her application by up to 12 months.[170] This benefit means that when the USPTO examiner compares the claims of the nonprovisional application with the prior art for purposes of assessing novelty and nonobviousness, he will consider only that prior art that has an effective date earlier in time than the filing date of the provisional application.

When it is necessary for an applicant to claim the benefit of her earlier provisional filing date, and the examiner determines that the claims in question are adequately supported by the disclosure of the

---

2010 at 112 tbl. 1 (2010), *available at* http://www.uspto.gov/about/stratplan/ar/2010/ USPTOFY2010PAR.pdf. For fiscal year 2011, the filing fee for provisional applications filed by large entities was $380 and by small entities was $190. *See* United States Patent & Trademark Office, *FY 2011 Fee Schedule,* http://www.uspto.gov/web/offices/ac/qs/ope/fee092611.htm (last visited May 26, 2012).

[167]*See* United States Patent & Trademark Office, *Provisional Application for Patent* (2005), *available at* http://www.uspto.gov/web/offices/pac/ProvApp.pdf.

[168]*See* Charles E. Van Horn, *Practicalities and Potential Pitfalls When Using Provisional Patent Applications,* 22 AIPLA Q.J. 259, 299-300 (Summer/Fall 1994). Post-AIA, dates of conception may still be relevant in derivation proceedings under 35 U.S.C. §135 (eff. Mar. 16, 2013).

[169]*See* Charles E. Van Horn, *Practicalities and Potential Pitfalls When Using Provisional Patent Applications,* 22 AIPLA Q.J. 259, 270-273 (Summer/Fall 1994) ("Claiming Benefit Outside the United States"); Paris Convention for the Protection of Industrial Property art. 4(A), *available at* http://www.wipo.int/clea/docs_new/pdf/en/wo/wo020en.pdf. The right of foreign priority is further discussed in Chapter 12, *infra.*

[170]*See* 35 U.S.C. §119(e)(1). For an example of an unsuccessful attempt to claim during litigation the benefit of a provisional application's filing date in order to avoid a 35 U.S.C. §102(b) (pre-AIA) statutory bar, *see* New Railhead Mfg., L.L.C. v. Vermeer Mfg. Co., 298 F.3d 1290 (Fed. Cir. 2002).

provisional application,[171] he will treat the provisional application filing date as either (1) the applicant's presumptive *invention date* for purposes of analyzing novelty, loss of right, and nonobviousness under the pre-AIA version of 35 U.S.C. §102;[172] or (2) the **effective filing date** for analyzing novelty and nonobviousness of the claimed invention(s) in the application if the application has been filed on or after March 16, 2013 (post-AIA).[173] In either case, if someone else filed for a U.S. patent on the same or similar invention during the provisional application's pendency period, or published a description of the invention during that time period, such materials will not count as prior art against the nonprovisional application; the examiner will effectively ignore them.

Moreover, if a patent is ultimately issued from the nonprovisional application, its expiration date will be 20 years after the later nonprovisional application filing date rather than from the earlier provisional application filing date.[174] The up-to-12-month pendency period of the provisional application does not cost the applicant any patent term.[175]

There is certainly no requirement that a patent applicant begin the patent prosecution process by filing a provisional application, however, and many applicants proceed by filing the regular nonprovisional application as their first filing. Section 111(a) of 35 U.S.C. sets forth the requirements for nonprovisional applications. They must include a specification concluding with at least one claim,[176] drawings

---

[171]This means that the disclosure (i.e., written description and drawings) of the provisional application supports the claims of the nonprovisional application in a manner that satisfies the requirements of 35 U.S.C. §112, first paragraph (renamed 35 U.S.C. §112(a) by the AIA (eff. Sept. 16, 2012)).

[172]*See* 35 U.S.C. §102 (2006); UNITED STATES PATENT AND TRADEMARK OFFICE, MANUAL OF PATENT EXAMINING PROCEDURE §201.11.I.A (8th ed., Aug. 2001, last rev. July 2010) (stating that "[i]f the filing date of the earlier provisional application is necessary, for example, in the case of an interference or to overcome a reference, care must be taken to ensure that the disclosure filed as the provisional application adequately provides (1) a written description of the subject matter of the claim(s) at issue in the later filed nonprovisional application, and (2) an enabling disclosure to permit one of ordinary skill in the art to make and use the claimed invention in the later filed nonprovisional application without undue experimentation"). *See also infra* Chapter 3 ("Disclosure Requirements); *infra* Chapter 4 ("Novelty, Loss of Right, and Priority Pre- and Post-America Invents Act of 2011 (35 U.S.C. §102)").

[173]*See* 35 U.S.C. §100(i)(1)(B) (eff. Mar. 16, 2013) (defining "effective filing date" as including "the filing date of the earliest application for which the . . . application is entitled, as to such invention, to a right of priority under section 119 . . ."); 35 U.S.C. §119(e)(1) (domestic priority).

[174]*See* 35 U.S.C. §154(a)(3) (stating that "[p]riority under section 119. . . . shall not be taken into account in determining the term of a patent").

[175]*See* 35 U.S.C. §154(a)(3) (providing that priority under §119 [whether domestic or foreign priority] is not taken into account in determining expiration of 20-year patent term).

[176]*See* 35 U.S.C. §112(b) (eff. Sept. 16, 2012) ("The specification shall conclude with one or more claims particularly pointing out and distinctly claiming the subject matter which the applicant regards as his invention.").

(if necessary to understand the invention),[177] and (subject to certain exceptions) an oath or declaration by each named inventor that she believes herself to be an "original inventor" of the invention she seeks to patent.[178] The nonprovisional application (like the provisional application) must be accompanied by the appropriate fees.[179]

3. Examination by the USPTO

The Patent Act provides that "the Director [of the USPTO] shall cause an examination to be made of the application and the alleged new invention; and if on such examination it appears that the applicant is entitled to a patent under the law, the Director shall issue a patent therefor."[180] A USPTO examiner will be assigned to the application depending upon the type of technology involved. The examiner's job is to determine whether the application and the invention claimed therein satisfy the various statutory requirements for the issuance of a patent; each of these requirements is covered in greater detail in subsequent chapters of this text. To summarize here, however, the examiner will first study the application to understand the claimed invention. He will review the form and content of the application to determine whether it complies with the disclosure and claiming requirements.[181] He will also consider whether the claimed invention falls within one of the permissible categories of potentially patentable subject matter[182] and whether it is useful (i.e., possesses "utility").[183]

---

[177]*See* 35 U.S.C. §113.

[178]*See* 35 U.S.C. §115(a), (b)(2) (eff. Sept. 16, 2012). Prior to the AIA, a patent applicant had to make oath that she believed herself to be "the original and first inventor" of the invention she sought to patent. *See* 35 U.S.C. §115 (2006). The AIA amendments to the Patent Act permit an assignee (that is, a person to whom the inventor has assigned or is under an obligation to assign the invention) to file a patent application under certain circumstances. *See* 35 U.S.C. 118 (eff. Sept. 16, 2012). *See also* United States Patent and Trademark Office, *Final Rule: Changes To Implement the Inventor's Oath or Declaration Provisions of the Leahy-Smith America Invents Act*, 77 FED. REG. 48776 (Aug. 14, 2012).

[179]The current schedule of USPTO fees, revised annually, is *available at* http://www.uspto.gov/web/offices/ac/qs/ope/fee092611.htm (last visited May 26, 2012). In addition to the filing fee, applicants filing nonprovisional applications on or after December 8, 2004, also pay a "search fee" and an "examination fee." All three fees are due at the time of filing. If the applicant is granted a patent, an issue fee is also due. Maintenance fees must be paid during the post-issuance life of the patent in order to keep it in force.

[180]35 U.S.C. §131.

[181]35 U.S.C. §112; *see also infra* Chapter 2 ("Patent Claims") and Chapter 3 ("Disclosure Requirements (35 U.S.C. §112(a))").

[182]35 U.S.C. §101 (defining potentially patentable subject matter as encompassing processes, machines, manufactures, compositions of matter, and improvements thereof); *see also infra* Chapter 7 ("Potentially Patentable Subject Matter (35 U.S.C. §101)").

[183]35 U.S.C. §101; *see also infra* Chapter 6 ("The Utility Requirement (35 U.S.C. §101)").

The examiner's most important and difficult task is to determine whether the invention, as recited by the claims of the patent application, is new ("novel")[184] and "nonobvious."[185] To make this determination the examiner will conduct a search of the prior art, including U.S. and foreign patents and non-patent printed publications, and will compare what is taught by that prior art with what the applicant has claimed as her invention. The examiner will also consider prior art submitted by the applicant (typically accompanying an Information Disclosure Statement).[186] Under certain circumstances, third parties may also submit information they believe relevant to patentability.[187]

Depending upon the results of his search and examination, the examiner may initially "allow" (i.e., approve) certain of the applicant's claims and reject others, or (relatively rarely) may allow all the claims, or (more typically) may reject all the claims. The examiner may also make "objections" to the form of the written description and/or drawings. The examiner will convey all of these determinations (and explanations for them) to the applicant in writing in an official document known as an "examiner's action" or "office action;"[188] subsection H[3][a] of this chapter provides a sample. Due to USPTO backlog and examiner workload, this process does not occur quickly; currently it takes about two years after the filing of her application for the applicant to receive a first office action.[189]

---

[184]35 U.S.C. §102; *see also infra* Chapter 4 ("Novelty, Loss of Right, and Priority Pre- and Post-America Invents Act of 2011 (35 U.S.C. §102)").

[185]35 U.S.C. §103; *see also infra* Chapter 5 ("The Nonobviousness Requirement (35 U.S.C. §103)").

[186] *See* 37 C.F.R. §1.97 ("Filing of Information Disclosure Statement"); *id.* §1.98 ("Content of Information Disclosure Statement").

[187]Before enactment of the AIA, third parties could submit to the USPTO patents or publications they believed relevant to pending patent applications that had been published, but there was no requirement that the examiner consider such submissions. The information would simply be made part of the application file. The submitter could not include any explanation of asserted relevancy. *See* 37 C.F.R. §1.99 (2010).

Effective September 16, 2012, third parties can submit patents or publications of potential relevance to examination "for consideration" (presumably by the USPTO examiner). A description of asserted relevance must accompany any such submission. *See* Leahy-Smith America Invents Act, Pub. L. No. 112-29 (H.R. 1249), §8, 125 Stat. 284, 315-316 (2011) (adding a subsection (e) to 35 U.S.C. §122); *See also* United States Patent & Trademark Office, *Final Rule: Changes To Implement the Preissuance Submissions by Third Parties Provision of the Leahy-Smith America Invents Act*, 77 FED. REG. 42150 (July 17, 2012).

[188]*See* 35 U.S.C. §132(a) (providing in part that "[w]henever, on examination, any claim for a patent is rejected, or any objection or requirement made, the Director shall notify the applicant thereof, stating the reasons for such rejection, or objection or requirement, together with such information and references as may be useful in judging of the propriety of continuing the prosecution of his application . . . ").

[189]In FY 2010, the first office action pendency was about 28 months for mechanical applications, about 26 months for chemical applications, and almost 30 months for

After receiving the first office action, the applicant has a statutorily set period of time (maximum of six months) in which to respond.[190] Failure to make a timely response means that the application will be considered abandoned.[191] Assuming that the applicant decides to go forward with the prosecution rather than abandon her application, she will typically submit a written response to the examiner's rejections.[192] In this response she may make arguments for patentability in an attempt to "traverse" (i.e., overcome) the rejections. She may also submit test data or other evidence in support of her arguments.[193]

Frequently, an applicant will opt to narrow the scope of her claims by amendment in order to avoid the prior art and remove the rejection. Changing the wording of the claims during prosecution of an application (by either narrowing or broadening the claims' scope), or adding new claims, is perfectly proper *if* the application as filed adequately supports the amended or new claims in accordance with 35 U.S.C. §112, ¶1.[194] She may also amend the written description and/or drawings to respond to the examiner's objections thereto, but not in a way that would fundamentally change what she has disclosed as her invention; this would violate the "new matter" prohibition.[195]

After the applicant has responded to the first office action, whether or not she has amended the claims, the application will be reexamined by the USPTO examiner.[196] The examiner will thereafter issue a second

---

software applications. *See* United States Patent & Trademark Office, *Performance and Accountability Report Fiscal Year 2010* at 128 tbl. 4 (2010), *available at* http://www. uspto.gov/about/stratplan/ar/2010/USPTOFY2010PAR.pdf.

[190]*See* 35 U.S.C. §133; 37 C.F.R. §1.134.

[191]*See* 35 U.S.C. §133.

[192]Responses can also be made orally, either in a telephone interview or in person at the USPTO. However, oral responses must be followed up with a written response. *See* 37 C.F.R. §1.133(b).

[193]*See* 37 C.F.R. §1.132 ("Affidavits or declarations traversing rejections or objections").

[194]Renamed 35 U.S.C. §112(a) by the AIA (eff. Sept. 16, 2012). *See* Liebel-Flarsheim Co. v. Medrad, Inc., 358 F.3d 898, 909 n.2 (Fed. Cir. 2004) ("[I]t is not improper for an applicant to broaden his claims during prosecution in order to encompass a competitor's products, as long as the disclosure supports the broadened claims."); Gentry Gallery, Inc. v. Berkline Corp., 134 F.3d 1473, 1479 (Fed. Cir. 1998) ("[O]ne can add claims to a pending application directed to adequately described subject matter.").

Although they may result in allowance of a patent, narrowing claim amendments made during a patent's prosecution may later limit the patentee's ability to rely on the doctrine of equivalents to enforce her patent against competitors. *See infra* Chapter 9, Section D.2 ("Prosecution History Estoppel").

[195]*See* 35 U.S.C. §132(a) ("No amendment shall introduce new matter into the disclosure of the invention.").

[196]*See* 35 U.S.C. §132(a). Note that the word "reexamined" in this context simply means a second examination of the same application, not reexamination of an issued patent under 35 U.S.C. §301 *et seq.* (a separate proceeding). Reexamination proceedings are detailed *infra* Chapter 8 ("Correcting and Challenging Issued Patents at the USPTO").

office action. As in the first action, the examiner in the second action may allow some or all of the claims or may reject some or all of the claims. The examiner's second office action is usually made final.[197]

If in a final action the examiner has maintained rejections with which the applicant disagrees, or has twice rejected any claim, the applicant cannot automatically continue to argue the rejections with the examiner. At this point she must either appeal from the examiner's decision to the USPTO's Patent Trial and Appeal Board,[198] or effectively "buy" more prosecution time. A streamlined way of exercising the latter option, without having to file a new application, is to file a request for continued examination (RCE), an option available since 2000 for nonprovisional applications that were filed on or after June 8, 1995.[199] Alternatively, while her application is still pending an applicant can file a second or "continuing" application that will carry forward the information in the first application and may add additional information thereto. Continuing application practice has its own complexities and is discussed separately *infra*.[200]

The preceding discussion is not intended to suggest that an examiner will always reject all of the applicant's claims. Depending upon the scope of the claims and the state of the prior art, some (or all) claims may be allowed by the examiner immediately (this is called a "first action allowance"). Alternatively, claims that were initially rejected may be allowed in the second office action in light of the applicant's response to the first office action, or after having been amended. Whenever in the process the examiner determines that the applicant is entitled to a patent on some or all of the claims, he will send the applicant a Notice of Allowance so indicating.[201] The applicant must then (within three months) pay an issue fee in order to obtain a pat-

---

[197]*See* 37 C.F.R. §1.113(a).

[198]*See* 35 U.S.C. §134(a) (eff. Sept. 16, 2012) ("Appeal to the Patent Trial and Appeal Board"). Prior to the AIA, the Board was known as the "Board of Patent Appeals and Interferences." *See* 35 U.S.C. §134(a) (2006) ("An applicant for a patent, any of whose claims has been twice rejected, may appeal from the decision of the primary examiner to the Board of Patent Appeals and Interferences, having once paid the fee for such appeal."). For further details on appeals to the Board, *see* United States Patent and Trademark Office, Manual of Patent Examining Procedure ch. 1200 (8th ed., Aug. 2001, last rev. July 2010), *available at* http://www.uspto.gov/web/offices/pac/mpep/mpep.htm.

[199]*See* 35 U.S.C. §132(b) (providing that "[t]he Director shall prescribe regulations to provide for the continued examination of applications for patent at the request of the applicant"); 37 C.F.R. §1.114 ("Request for continued examination"). *See generally* Robert Bahr, *Request for Continued Examination (RCE) Practice*, 82 J. Pat. & Trademark Off. Soc'y 336 (2000).

[200]*See infra* Section H.5 ("Continuing Application Practice"). Yet another option for an applicant faced with a final rejection is to file an "amendment after final" under 37 C.F.R. §1.116.

[201]*See* 35 U.S.C. §151 ("Issue of Patent").

ent encompassing the allowed claims. The USPTO will issue the patent within about three months after the applicant has paid the issue fee.[202] The issue date represents the first date on or after which the patent owner can enforce the patent in U.S. federal court by suing alleged infringers.

a.   Sample Office Action and Applicant's Response

This subsection provides excerpts from a patent's prosecution file history to illustrate some of the basic mechanics of the process.[203] Figure 1.4 reproduces the title page of U.S. Patent No. 7,241,196 ("the '196 patent"), directed to a "Heated Stuffed Animal." The '196 patent was prosecuted in 2005-2007, well before implementation of America Invents Act of 2011 rules.[204]

The invention of the '196 patent modifies a conventional stuffed animal by incorporating a heating source inside the animal's torso. The heated animal provides a means for "warming, comforting and consoling a person embracing the animal."[205] The heating element is programmable such that its temperature and duration can be preselected by the user or a child's parent.

As is typical in patent prosecution practice, the application for the '196 patent was submitted to the USPTO with relatively broad claims. In Application No. 11/096,629, filed April 1, 2005, claim 1 recited:

   1.   A heated stuffed animal comprising:

       a head, limbs and a torso portion;
       a heater means embedded within the torso portion for warming, comforting and consoling a person embracing the animal.

---

[202]*See* Mark Montague et al., *Examination Before the USPTO, in* ADVISING HIGH-TECHNOLOGY COMPANIES §3:5.1[F] (Nathaniel T. Trelease ed., PLI 2004).

[203]Beginning in 2004, members of the public have been able to view prosecution file histories for issued patents and published applications at no charge via the USPTO's Public PAIR (Patent Application and Information Retrieval) system. United States Patent & Trademark Office, *Patent Application Information Retrieval,* http://portal. uspto.gov/external/portal/pair (last visited May 26, 2012). More restricted access to pending application status and history is available to registered users of the Private PAIR system, http://www.uspto.gov/ebc/index.html (follow "Private PAIR" hyperlink) (last visited May 26, 2012).

[204]The first-to-file regime implemented by the AIA takes effect for applications filed on or after March 16, 2013. For more on the distinctions between pre- and post-AIA rules, *see infra* Chapter 4 ("Novelty, Loss of Right, and Priority Pre- and Post-America Invents Act of 2011 (35 U.S.C. §102)").

[205]U.S. Patent No. 7,241,196, col. 2, ll. 57-58 (issued July 10, 2007) (reciting limitation of claim 1).

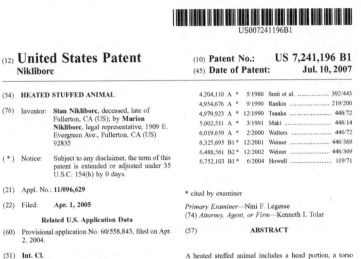

US007241196B1

(12) **United States Patent**
Nikliborc

(10) Patent No.:   **US 7,241,196 B1**
(45) Date of Patent: Jul. 10, 2007

(54)   **HEATED STUFFED ANIMAL**

(76)   Inventor: **Stan Nikliborc**, deceased, late of
Fullerton, CA (US); by **Marion
Nikliborc**, legal representative, 1909 E.
Evergreen Ave., Fullerton, CA (US)
92835

(*)   Notice: Subject to any disclaimer, the term of this
patent is extended or adjusted under 35
U.S.C. 154(b) by 0 days.

(21)   Appl. No.: **11/096,629**

(22)   Filed: **Apr. 1, 2005**

Related U.S. Application Data

(60)   Provisional application No. 60/558,843, filed on Apr.
2, 2004.

(51)   **Int. Cl.**
A63H 3/02   (2006.01)
(52)   **U.S. Cl.** **446/369**; 446/295
(58)   **Field of Classification Search** 446/14,
446/72, 77, 73, 295, 369, 390, 484; 219/200,
219/201, 430, 378, 439, 462, 528, 529, 549
See application file for complete search history.

(56)   **References Cited**

U.S. PATENT DOCUMENTS

1,558,278 A * 10/1925   Phillips 383/96

4,204,110	A	*	5/1980	Smit et al. 392/443
4,954,676	A	*	9/1990	Rankin 219/200
4,979,923	A	*	12/1990	Tanaka 446/72
5,002,511	A	*	3/1991	Maki 446/14
6,019,659	A	*	2/2000	Walters 446/72
6,325,695	B1	*	12/2001	Weiner 446/369
6,488,561	B2	*	12/2002	Weiner 446/369
6,752,103	B1	*	6/2004	Howell 119/71

* cited by examiner

Primary Examiner—Nini F. Legesse
(74) *Attorney, Agent, or Firm*—Kenneth L Tolar

(57)   **ABSTRACT**

A heated stuffed animal includes a head portion, a torso
portion and a plurality of limbs. Embedded within the
animal is a heater assembly including an encircling heating
element extending from a battery casing that is accessible
via a slit on the rear surface of the torso portion. The
operating temperature and duration of the heater assembly
can be selectively programmed with a pair of adjustable
dials positioned on the casing.

6 Claims, 2 Drawing Sheets

Figure 1.4

Various dependent claims recited additional features, such as means for automatically disabling the heater means (claim 3) and means for automatically controlling an operating temperature range of the heater means (claim 4).[206]

In the first office action, the USPTO examiner rejected all the claims as anticipated under 35 U.S.C. §102(b) (2006).[207] The examiner took the position that each feature of the application claims was described in prior art patents that disclosed a heated stuffed animal.[208] Figure 1.5 is an excerpt of the USPTO office action.

In response to the rejection, the applicant effectively narrowed the scope of his claims by canceling the original claims and replacing them with a new set of claims, the broadest of which added features that previously had been recited in dependent claims. After amendment, the broadest application claim recited:

9. (New) A heated stuffed animal comprising:

a head, limbs and a torso portion;
a heater means embedded within the torso portion for warming, comforting and consoling a person embracing the animal;
means for automatically disabling said heater means after a selectively variable duration;
means for automatically controlling an operating temperature range of said heater means.

The applicant's accompanying written remarks to the USPTO emphasized the criticality of the timed disabling means for the heating element as now recited in application claim 9. The child's parent or other user could feel comfortable falling asleep knowing that the heater would be disabled after a set time. The claimed invention was patentable over the prior art heated animals because the latter provided a thermostat but did not provide a timer for automatic shut-off of the heating element after a predetermined time.

These arguments apparently convinced the USPTO examiner that all the amended claims were allowable. After additional communications,

---

[206]Chapter 2 ("Patent Claims"), *infra,* explains the distinction between "independent" and "dependent" patent claims, and the special meaning of the phrase "means for [function]" as used in patent claim drafting.

[207]*See* U.S. Patent Application No. 11/096,629, Office Action Summary (mailed Aug. 3, 2006).

[208]The examiner cited each of U.S. Pat. No. 6,019,659 to Walters and U.S. Pat. No. 6,488,561 to Weiner as anticipatory under 35 U.S.C. §102(b) (pre-AIA). *See* Heated Stuffed Toy, U.S. Patent No. 6,019,659 (issued Feb. 1, 2000); Heated Stuffed Animal, U.S. Patent No. 6,488,561 (issued Dec. 3, 2002). Due to space limitations we do not reproduce the Walters and Weiner patents.

Office Action Summary	Application No.	Applicant(s)
	11/096,629	NIKLIBORC ET AL.
	Examiner	Art Unit
	Nini F. Legesse	3711

-- *The MAILING DATE of this communication appears on the cover sheet with the correspondence address* --

Period for Reply

A SHORTENED STATUTORY PERIOD FOR REPLY IS SET TO EXPIRE <u>3</u> MONTH(S) OR THIRTY (30) DAYS, WHICHEVER IS LONGER, FROM THE MAILING DATE OF THIS COMMUNICATION.
- Extensions of time may be available under the provisions of 37 CFR 1.136(a). In no event, however, may a reply be timely filed after SIX (6) MONTHS from the mailing date of this communication.
- If NO period for reply is specified above, the maximum statutory period will apply and will expire SIX (6) MONTHS from the mailing date of this communication.
- Failure to reply within the set or extended period for reply will, by statute, cause the application to become ABANDONED (35 U.S.C. § 133). Any reply received by the Office later than three months after the mailing date of this communication, even if timely filed, may reduce any earned patent term adjustment. See 37 CFR 1.704(b).

Status

1)☒ Responsive to communication(s) filed on <u>01 April 2005</u>.

2a)☐ This action is **FINAL**.   2b)☒ This action is non-final.

3)☐ Since this application is in condition for allowance except for formal matters, prosecution as to the merits is closed in accordance with the practice under *Ex parte Quayle*, 1935 C.D. 11, 453 O.G. 213.

Disposition of Claims

4)☒ Claim(s) <u>1-8</u> is/are pending in the application.

　　4a) Of the above claim(s) _____ is/are withdrawn from consideration.

5)☐ Claim(s) _____ is/are allowed.

6)☒ Claim(s) <u>1-8</u> is/are rejected.

7)☐ Claim(s) _____ is/are objected to.

8)☐ Claim(s) _____ are subject to restriction and/or election requirement.

Application Papers

9)☐ The specification is objected to by the Examiner.

10)☐ The drawing(s) filed on _____ is/are: a)☐ accepted or b)☐ objected to by the Examiner.

　　Applicant may not request that any objection to the drawing(s) be held in abeyance. See 37 CFR 1.85(a).

　　Replacement drawing sheet(s) including the correction is required if the drawing(s) is objected to. See 37 CFR 1.121(d).

11)☐ The oath or declaration is objected to by the Examiner. Note the attached Office Action or form PTO-152.

Priority under 35 U.S.C. § 119

12)☐ Acknowledgment is made of a claim for foreign priority under 35 U.S.C. § 119(a)-(d) or (f).

　　a)☐ All   b)☐ Some * c)☐ None of:

　　　1.☐ Certified copies of the priority documents have been received.

　　　2.☐ Certified copies of the priority documents have been received in Application No. _____.

　　　3.☐ Copies of the certified copies of the priority documents have been received in this National Stage application from the International Bureau (PCT Rule 17.2(a)).

　　* See the attached detailed Office action for a list of the certified copies not received.

Attachment(s)

1) ☒ Notice of References Cited (PTO-892)
2) ☐ Notice of Draftsperson's Patent Drawing Review (PTO-948)
3) ☐ Information Disclosure Statement(s) (PTO-1449 or PTO/SB/08) Paper No(s)/Mail Date _____.

4) ☐ Interview Summary (PTO-413) Paper No(s)/Mail Date. _____.
5) ☐ Notice of Informal Patent Application (PTO-152)
6) ☐ Other: _____.

U.S. Patent and Trademark Office
PTOL-326 (Rev. 7-05)　　　　　Office Action Summary　　　　　Part of Paper No./Mail Date 20060802
　　　　　　　　　　　　　　　　Page 45 of 80

Figure 1.5

Excerpt of First Office Action

(Continued)

Application/Control Number: 11/096,629
Art Unit: 3711

DETAILED ACTION

Claim Rejections - 35 USC § 102

The following is a quotation of the appropriate paragraphs of 35 U.S.C. 102 that form the basis for the rejections under this section made in this Office action:

A person shall be entitled to a patent unless –

(b) the invention was patented or described in a printed publication in this or a foreign country or in public use or on sale in this country, more than one year prior to the date of application for patent in the United States.

Claims 1-8 are rejected under 35 U.S.C. 102(b) as being anticipated by Walters (US Patent No. 6,019,659).

Walter discloses a heated stuffed animal (see Fig. 1) as claimed comprising a heater means (22) with automatically temperature controlling means (40), and a power source (32) casing as claimed (see Fig. 2).

Claims 1-8 are rejected under 35 U.S.C. 102(b) as being anticipated by Weiner (US Patent No. 6,488,561).

Weiner discloses a heated stuffed animal (see Fig. 1) as claimed comprising a heater means (3) with automatically temperature controlling means (6), and a power source casing as claimed (see Fig. 1).

Conclusion

Any inquiry concerning this communication or earlier communications from the examiner should be directed to Nini F. Legesse whose telephone number is (571) 272-4412. The examiner can normally be reached on 9 AM - 5:30 PM.

Figure 1.5
Excerpt of First Office Action

including a telephone interview, the application issued as U.S. Patent No. 7,241,196 on July 10, 2007.[209]

4. Publication of Pending Patent Applications

Historically, all pending patent applications were maintained in secrecy throughout their pendency by the USPTO. The public did not see the content of the applications unless and until they issued as patents. This led to the problem of so-called "submarine" patents, applications for which would be kept pending in secrecy in the USPTO by their owners for many years through the filing of multiple continuation applications (discussed below). When patents finally issued on these applications, it was often to the great consternation of competitors who had no prior notice and were now suddenly liable as potential infringers.

This state of affairs improved significantly with the implementation of "18-month publication" procedure as part of the American Inventors Protection Act of 1999.[210] Under current law, the default rule is that a nonprovisional (i.e., regular, "full-service") U.S. utility patent application will be automatically published 18 months after its effective filing date.[211] Publication can be avoided by certifying to the USPTO that the applicant has not and will not file any other applications on the same invention in foreign countries or under multinational agreements that would require publication 18 months after filing.[212] In other words,

---

[209]The title page of the patent lists the patent number as "7,241,196 B1." The "B1" notation (or "kind code") is a WIPO (World Intellectual Property Organization) standard code signifying that this document is a patent and is being published for the first time; i.e., there was no pre-issuance publication of this patent. See United States Patent & Trademark Office, *"Kind Codes" Included in USPTO Patent Documents,* http://www.uspto.gov/web/forms/kindcodesum.html (last visited May 27, 2012). Unlike the majority of patents, the applicant for the '196 patent chose to opt-out of automatic publication at 18 months after application filing. He did so by filing during prosecution a document titled "Non-Publication Request Under 35 U.S.C. 122(b)(2)(B)(i)," in which the applicant certified that his invention had not and would not be the subject of an application filed in another country or under a multilateral agreement (such as the Patent Cooperation Treaty) that would require publication at 18 months after filing.

[210]See American Inventors Protection Act of 1999, S. 1948, 106th Cong. tit. IV, §§4501-4502 (1999) ("Domestic Publication of Patent Applications Published Abroad") (as implemented by Pub. L. No. 106-113, 113 Stat. 1501 (1999)). Eighteen-month publication became the default rule for all applications filed on or after the Act's effective date of November 29, 2000. The first applications began to be published around March 2001.

[211]Publication of pending applications is on-line at the USPTO's website. See United States Patent & Trademark Office, *Patent Full-Text Databases (Published Since 15 March 2001),* http://patft.uspto.gov/ (last visited May 27, 2012).

[212]See 35 U.S.C. §122(b)(2)(B)(i).

an application must be purely domestic to avoid 18-month publication.[213] In fiscal year 2011, the USPTO published over 321,000 applications.[214] A government study reported in 2004 that about 85 percent of U.S. patent applications filed by large entities were published at 18 months after filing.[215]

5. Continuing Application Practice

Suppose that an applicant receives from the examiner a final rejection of some of the claims in her application but an allowance of other claims. The applicant would like to obtain a patent (as soon as possible) on the allowed claims, perhaps because of a potential infringer in the marketplace, while at the same time continue prosecuting the rejected claims (rather than appealing their rejection to the Board of Patent Appeals and Interferences). The applicant in this situation has the option of filing what is known as a **continuation application.** Using continuation applications is a way of prolonging the application process; the continuation application extends the patenting transaction that began with the applicant's earlier-filed application.[216]

Currently there is no limit on the number of continuation applications that may be filed,[217] but abuse of the continuation process can

---

[213]Applications subject to a security order and design patent applications are also exempt from 18-month publication. *See* 35 U.S.C. §§122(b)(2)(A)(ii), (iv).

[214]*See* United States Patent & Trademark Office, *Performance and Accountability Report Fiscal Year 2011*, tbl. 1, http://www.uspto.gov/about/stratplan/ar/2011/USPTOFY2011PAR.pdf, at 159 ("Summary of Patent Examining Activities") (reporting that agency published 321,115 applications in FY 2011 pursuant to 18-month publication as provided for by the AIPA, Pub. L. No. 106-113). As a point of reference, the number of nonprovisional utility patent applications *filed* in FY 2009 (two fiscal years earlier) was 458,901. *Id.*

[215]United States General Accounting Office, *Report to Congressional Committees: Patents: Information about the Publication Provisions of the American Inventors Protection Act* 4 (2004), http://www.gao.gov/new.items/d04603.pdf (reporting that for applications received between November 29, 2000, and November 28, 2003, the USPTO "has published or plans to publish applications from about 85 percent of the applicants qualifying as large entities compared with only about 74 percent of those qualifying as small entities").

[216]*See* R. Carl Moy, Moy's Walker on Patents §3:43 (4th ed. 2007).

[217]A federal district court in 2007 preliminarily enjoined the USPTO from implementing new rules that would have limited the number of continuation applications and RCEs that an applicant could file from a given original application. *See* Tafas v. Dudas, 511 F. Supp. 2d 652 (E.D. Va. 2007) (finding that plaintiff/movant Glaxo SmithKline was likely to succeed on the merits of its claims that USPTO lacked authority under 35 U.S.C. §2(b)(2) (2006) to promulgate the new rules and that the rules were contrary to various other provisions of the Patent Act, including §120). After a Federal Circuit panel decision, *Tafas v. Doll*, 559 F.3d 1345 (2009), and a Federal Circuit order granting rehearing *en banc*, 328 Fed. App'x 658 (2009), the USPTO dropped the proposed new

give rise to the defense of "prosecution laches" if and when the patentee later attempts to enforce her patent.[218] Moreover, the longer that the prosecution of the original application is extended through the filing of continuations, the shorter the term of any resulting patent.[219]

The continuation application described in the preceding paragraphs is actually one of three kinds of **continuing applications,** a generic term for a later-filed patent application that contains some or all of the disclosure of that applicant's earlier-filed application (referred to hereafter as the "parent" application) and that names at least one inventor also named in the parent application.[220] The continuing application must be filed while the parent application is still pending (i.e., has not been abandoned or issued as a patent).[221] Procedurally, the pertinent USPTO rule under which an applicant currently may file any type of continuing application is Rule 53(b).[222] The three types of continuing applications are

---

rules limiting the number of continuation applications and RCEs. See 74 FED. REG. 52688 (Oct. 14, 2009).

[218] The defense of prosecution laches is further detailed in Chapter 10 ("Defenses to Patent Infringement"), *infra. See generally* Mark A. Lemley & Kimberly A. Moore, *Ending Abuse of Patent Continuations*, 84 B.U. L. REV. 63 (2004).

[219] *See* 35 U.S.C. §154(a)(2) (providing in part that "such grant shall be for a term beginning on the date on which the patent issues and ending 20 years from the date on which the application for the patent was filed in the United States or, if the application contains a specific reference to an earlier filed application or applications under section 120, 121, or 365(c), from the date on which the earliest such application was filed").

[220] *See* UNITED STATES PATENT AND TRADEMARK OFFICE, MANUAL OF PATENT EXAMINING PROCEDURE §201.11.II.B (8th ed., Aug. 2001, last rev. July 2010), *available at* http://www.uspto.gov/web/offices/pac/mpep/mpep.htm (stating that "[c]ontinuing applications include those applications which are called divisions, continuations, and continuations-in-part"); Transco Prods., Inc. v. Performance Contracting, Inc., 38 F.3d 551, 555 (Fed. Cir. 1994).

[221] *See* 35 U.S.C. §120 ("if filed before the patenting or abandonment of or termination of proceedings on the first application . . . ").

[222] 37 C.F.R. §1.53(b) (2008). Before December 1, 1997, continuing applications could be filed under 37 C.F.R. §1.60 (for continuations or divisionals) and 37 C.F.R. §1.62 ("file wrapper continuing" procedure for continuations, continuations-in-part, or divisionals). Rules 60 and 62 were superseded as of December 1, 1997, however, by the "continued prosecution application" (CPA) procedure of Rule 53(d) [37 C.F.R. §1.53(d)]. From 1997 to 2003, a continuation or divisional application (but not a continuation-in-part application) could be filed as a CPA. Effective July 14, 2003, CPA practice was made inapplicable to utility patent applications. *See* UNITED STATES PATENT AND TRADEMARK OFFICE, MANUAL OF PATENT EXAMINING PROCEDURE §706.07(h), pt. XIII.B (8th ed., 2d rev. 2004) (showing comparison chart), *available at* http://www.uspto.gov/web/offices/pac/mpep/old/E8R2_700.pdf. Currently, CPAs under Rule 53(d) are available only for design patent applications. *See generally* DONALD S. CHISUM, 4A-13 CHISUM on PATENTS §13.03[7] (2008).

1. **Continuation application:** a second application for the same invention claimed in the parent application and filed during the lifetime of the parent application. The continuation application encompasses all the disclosure of the parent application and does not add any new matter to that disclosure. It claims the same invention claimed in the parent application, although there may be some variation in the scope of the subject matter claimed.

2. **Continuation-in-part application:** a second application filed during the lifetime of the parent application that encompasses some substantial portion or all of the disclosure of the parent application and also adds additional matter to that disclosure.[223]

3. **Divisional application:** a second application for an independent and distinct invention, carved out of the parent application during its lifetime and disclosing and claiming only subject matter disclosed in the parent application. A divisional application is appropriate when the parent application claimed more than one invention. A patent may claim only a single invention, so any other invention must be "divided out" and claimed in a separate application. The divisional application is often filed as a result of a **restriction requirement** made by the USPTO examiner.[224]

The statutory bases for continuing application practice are Sections 120 and 121 of the Patent Act. Importantly, §120 provides that to the extent the claims of the continuing application are supported by the disclosure set forth in the parent application in accordance with the requirements of 35 U.S.C. §112, ¶1 (i.e., if the parent application's disclosure satisfies the enablement and written description requirements for the claims of interest in the continuing application),[225] those claims

---

[223]*See* PowerOasis, Inc. v. T-Mobile USA, Inc., 522 F.3d 1299, 1304 n.3 (Fed. Cir. 2008) (noting that "[w]hile the PTO has noted that the expressions 'continuation,' 'divisional,' and 'continuation-in-part' are merely terms used for administrative convenience, . . . the quintessential difference between a continuation and a continuation-in-part is the addition of new matter") (citation omitted).

[224]*See* 35 U.S.C. §121 (providing that "[i]f two or more independent and distinct inventions are claimed in one application, the Director may require the application to be restricted to one of the inventions").

[225]The America Invents Act of 2011 (AIA) deleted the requirement that a parent application provide best mode disclosure support for the claims of a related continuing application. *See* 35 U.S.C. §120 (eff. Sept. 16, 2012) (referring to "[a]n application for patent for an invention disclosed in the manner provided by section 112(a) (other than the requirement to disclose the best mode) in an application previously filed in the United States . . . "). The AIA also renamed 35 U.S.C. §112's first paragraph as 35 U.S.C. §112(a) (eff. Sept. 16, 2012).

are entitled to the benefit of the filing date of the earlier-filed parent application.[226] The *effective filing date* of such claims is the parent application's filing date.[227] Practically speaking, this means that patents and publications of others, describing the same or similar invention but having an effective date in the interim period between the parent application's filing date and the continuing application's filing date, will be ignored. They are not considered prior art against the continuing application claims that are entitled to the parent application's filing date.

In contrast, those claims in a continuing application (namely, a continuation-in-part) that are *not* adequately supported by the disclosure of the parent application will not be entitled to the benefit of the parent application's filing date; rather, they will be considered filed on the continuing application's filing date. Such claims will not relate back to the filing date of the parent application for purposes of avoiding intervening prior art. Thus, patents and publications of others, describing the same invention but having an effective date in the interim period between the parent application's filing date and the continuing application's filing date, *will* be available as prior art against those claims.[228]

---

[226]*See* 35 U.S.C. §120 ("Benefit of Earlier Filing Date in the United States") (eff. Sept. 16, 2012). This rather wordy section provides in part (emphasis added and explanatory references in brackets):

> An [continuing] application for patent for an invention disclosed in the manner provided by section 112(a) (other than the requirement to disclose the best mode) in an [parent] application previously filed in the United States, or as provided by section 363 [35 USC §363] [i.e., an international application designating the U.S. and filed under the Patent Cooperation Treaty (PCT)], which names an inventor or joint inventor in the previously filed [parent] application *shall have the same effect, as to such invention, as though filed on the date of the prior [parent] application*, if filed before the patenting or abandonment of or termination of proceedings on the first [parent] application or on an application similarly entitled to the benefit of the filing date of the first [parent] application and if it [the continuing application] contains or is amended to contain a specific reference to the earlier filed [parent] application.

The key language is "shall have the same effect," which in this context means "shall be entitled to the filing date of" the parent application.

[227]The America Invents Act of 2011 added to the Patent Act a definition of "effective filing date." *See* 35 U.S.C. §100(i)(1)(B) (eff. Mar. 16, 2013) (defining "effective filing date" as including "the filing date of the earliest application for which the . . . application is entitled, as to such invention, . . . to the benefit of an earlier filing date under section 120 . . . "); 35 U.S.C. §120 ("Benefit of earlier filing date in the United States").

[228]*See* PowerOasis, Inc. v. T-Mobile USA, Inc., 522 F.3d 1299, 1301 (Fed. Cir. 2008) (affirming district court's invalidation of two patents on ground that "none of the asserted claims . . . were entitled, under 35 U.S.C. § 120, to the benefit of the filing date of PowerOasis's original application because the earlier application did not provide a

In sum, the claims of a continuing application are entitled to the benefit of the filing date of its parent application only as to commonly disclosed subject matter; claims directed to new matter will not get that benefit.[229]

For example, consider a parent application filed by inventor Jack on January 1, 2005, that disclosed only a widget made of wood and included no broadening language to indicate that the widget could be made of any other material besides wood. Claim 1 of the parent application recited:

1.   A widget formed from wood.

Jack soon thereafter discovered that widgets of his invention could also be made of plastic, metal, or other solid materials. On January 1, 2006, while his parent application was still pending, Jack filed a second application, which he designated as a continuation-in-part (CIP) of the parent application, repeating all the disclosure of his parent application but adding new disclosure concerning the making of widgets from plastic, metal, or other solid materials. Jack's CIP application carried forward and rewrote his original claim 1 in dependent form as claim 2, and added a new, broader claim 1, as follows:

1.   A widget formed from a solid material.
2.   The widget of claim 1 wherein said solid material is wood.

After filing the CIP application, Jack abandoned the parent application.

During subsequent examination of the CIP application, the USPTO examiner's search located a publication authored by independent inventor Jill and published on June 1, 2005, that described identical widgets formed from wood and from metal. As we will see in Chapter 4 *infra,* the teaching of this printed publication would anticipate (i.e., destroy the novelty of) claim 1 of Jack's CIP application under 35 U.S.C. §102(a), because the species of metal widget (and likewise the species of wood widget) described in the publication destroys the novelty of Jack's claimed genus of "solid material" widgets. The printed publication by Jill would be prior art with respect to CIP claim 1 because CIP claim 1 is only entitled to the filing date of the CIP application

---

written description of the invention claimed in the asserted patents, as required by 35 U.S.C. § 112.").

[229]*See Transco,* 38 F.3d at 556.

(January 1, 2006), not to the filing date of the parent application (January 1, 2005).[230]

On the other hand, CIP claim 2 would not be anticipated by the teaching of wood widgets in the printed publication by Jill. This is because CIP claim 2 is entitled to the benefit of the January 1, 2005, filing date of the parent application (because the parent application provided a disclosure of wood widgets that satisfies the enablement, written description, and best mode criteria of 35 U.S.C. §112, ¶1 (2006)). January 1, 2005, is the effective filing date of CIP claim 2. Because Jill's article was published after that date, it is not section 102(a) prior art against CIP claim 2. Disregarding any other potential patentability issues, Jack will receive a patent on CIP claim 2 (but not on CIP claim 1).

In contrast with the claim-by-claim analysis described above for determining benefit of particular claims in a continuing application to a parent application's filing date, the analysis for determining when a patent issued from a continuing application will expire does not distinguish between claims.[231] If we change the facts in the example above and assume that no pertinent prior art was uncovered by the examiner and that Jack's CIP application issued with both claims 1 and 2, both of those claims (along with any other claims in the patent) would expire 20 years after January 1, 2005, Jack's parent application's filing date. It is *not* the case that claim 1 would expire on January 1, 2026, and claim 2 would expire on January 1, 2025.

6. Double Patenting

A patent applicant may obtain only one U.S. patent on a given invention. If a patent applicant is granted a patent on invention X and files another application that again claims invention X (or an obvious variant of invention X), the USPTO examiner will reject the claims of the later application as violating the prohibition on "double

---

[230]The same result would follow under the America Invents Act of 2011 if the applications were governed by the AIA.

[231]In accordance with 35 U.S.C. §154(a)(2), *all* the claims in a designated continuing application will be deemed to expire 20 years after the parent application's filing date, regardless of whether particular claims are supported in the §112 sense by the parent application's disclosure. *See also* United States Patent & Trademark Office, *Changes to Implement 20-Year Patent Term and Provisional Applications*, 60 FED. REG. 20195, 20205 (Apr. 25, 1995) (to be codified at 37 C.F.R. pts. 1, 3) (explaining in response to Comment 5 that "[t]he term of a patent is not based on a claim-by-claim approach"), *available at* http://www.uspto.gov/web/offices/com/doc/uruguay/20_year_term.html (last visited May 26, 2012).

patenting."[232] In the litigation context, double patenting is often charged against pharmaceutical firms allegedly engaged in "evergreening," that is, obtaining a series of patents on closely related drug inventions in an attempt to improperly prolong the patent life of the firm's products.[233]

There are two forms of double patenting. In the example of the preceding paragraph, if the later-filed application claims the *identical* invention as the applicant's patent, the USPTO examiner's rejection will be for "same invention-type" double patenting, which is based on the language of 35 U.S.C. §101 that "[w]hoever invents or discovers any new and useful [invention] may obtain *a* patent therefor . . ." (emphasis added). Same invention-type double patenting is also referred to as "statutory" double patenting. On the other hand, if the later application does not claim the same invention, but rather claims a *merely obvious variant* of it, the rejection will be for "obviousness-type" double patenting. This form of double patenting, which is recognized in judicial decisions but which does not have an explicit basis in the patent statute, is also referred to as "nonstatutory" double patenting.

The policy concern underlying the double patenting doctrine is *not* that an applicant is seeking to patent something that another has already invented.[234] Rather, the primary policy basis underlying the double patenting doctrine is to prevent the same patent owner, through obtaining a second patent on the same invention (or an obvious variant of the same invention) she has already patented, from improperly "extending her monopoly." In other words, the goal is to prevent the patentee from obtaining a second patent that will effectively extend

---

[232]The typical fact situation giving rise to double patenting concerns is one that involves an already issued patent and a pending patent application, both owned by the same entity. However, a double patenting issue may also arise between two or more pending applications or between one or more pending applications and a published application. *See* UNITED STATES PATENT AND TRADEMARK OFFICE, MANUAL OF PATENT EXAMINING PROCEDURE §804 (8th ed., Aug. 2001, last rev. July 2010), *available at* http://www.uspto.gov/web/offices/pac/mpep/mpep.htm.

[233]*See* Rebecca S. Eisenberg, 13 MICH. TELECOMM. & TECH. L. REV. 345, 354 (2007) (commenting that "[i]n recent years drug innovators have sought to prolong their effective periods of patent protection through various 'evergreening' strategies that add new patents to their quivers as old ones expire. Examples include patents on "metabolites" (i.e., the products into which drugs are transformed in a patient's body); patents on intermediate products used in producing drugs; patents on new uses for drugs; and patents on new formulations or preparations.") (footnotes omitted).

[234]Thus, a USPTO rejection of application claims (or a federal court's invalidation of claims in an issued patent) for double patenting is analytically distinct from a rejection (or invalidation) on the grounds of anticipation (*see infra* Chapter 4) or obviousness (*see infra* Chapter 5).

the duration of the right to exclude others from practice of a given invention that was conveyed previously by her first patent.[235]

The scope of the patentee's right to exclude is measured by the language of the patent claims. Therefore, the double patenting analysis necessarily involves comparing the *claims* of the patentee's later-filed application with the *claims* of the patent she has already obtained.[236] As we will see in later chapters, comparing the claims first requires that we understand what the words of the claims mean, and in so doing we may consult the written description and drawings of the corresponding patent or application. However, it is analytically incorrect to view the double patenting analysis as involving the use of the content of the earlier-filed patent as prior art against the later-filed application.[237] Assuming that no statutory bars apply,[238] the earlier-filed patent to the same inventor does not qualify as prior art under

---

[235]*See* In re Zickendraht, 319 F.2d 225, 232 (C.C.P.A. 1963) (Rich, J., concurring) (observing that "[t]he public should . . . be able to act on the assumption that upon the expiration of the patent it will be free to use not only the invention claimed in the patent but also modifications or variants thereof which would have been obvious to those of ordinary skill in the art at the time the invention was made, taking into account the skill in the art and prior art other than the invention claimed in the issued patent").

A second policy concern associated with double patenting is the potential for harassment of an accused infringer by multiple patent owners. *See* In re Van Ornum, 686 F.2d 937, 947 (C.C.P.A. 1982) (Rich, J.) (stating that "extension of monopoly is not the only objection to double patenting" and that "[o]ther[] [objections] include possible harassment by multiple assignees"). If the ownership of two or more patents claiming inventions that are merely obvious variants of one another becomes divided between different owners, a competitor may find itself being sued by all of the patent owners for infringement based on the competitor's single allegedly infringing product or process. The need to alleviate this potential for harassment by multiple patentees has taken on greater significance following the 1994 enactment of the Uruguay Round Amendments Act (URAA) (described *supra* at Section C.7 ("The Patent Term")). This is because many (though not all) obviousness-type double patenting situations stem from the issuance of multiple patents based on a chain of continuing applications (described *supra* at Section H.5 ("Continuing Application Practice"). Although originally owned by the same entity, some of the resulting patents may be sold (i.e., assigned) by the original owner to different entities. Under the URAA-implemented 20-year term, all such patents would expire on the same date. The common expiration date eliminates the policy concern regarding improper extension of monopoly by the patentees, but leaves intact the possibility of harassment by multiple patentees. To respond to the harassment concern, certain provisions must be included in terminal disclaimers, as discussed below, that preclude the original patent owner from dividing ownership of the patents that result from the USPTO's allowance of the two or more patents claiming the obviously variant inventions.

[236]*See* General Foods Corp. v. Studiengesellschaft Kohle mbH, 972 F.2d 1272, 1277 (Fed. Cir. 1992) ("Double patenting is altogether a matter of what is claimed.").

[237]*See* In re Vogel, 422 F.2d 438, 441-442 (CCPA 1970) ("In considering the question [whether any claim in the application defines merely an obvious variation of an invention disclosed and claimed in the patent], the patent disclosure may not be used as prior art.").

[238]*See* 35 U.S.C. §102(b) (2006).

35 U.S.C. §102 (2006) because it does not disclose the invention of "another."[239]

A good case study for double patenting analysis is *In re Vogel*,[240] which involved methods of packaging meat products to prevent spoilage. Vogel initially obtained a patent on his method as applied to pork. Claim 1 of Vogel's patent recited:

> 1. A method of preparing pork products, comprising the steps of: boning a freshly slaughtered carcass while still hot into trimmings; grinding desired carcass trimming while still warm and fluent; mixing the ground trimmings while fluent and above approximately 80 degrees F., mixing to be completed not more than approximately 3 1/2 hours after the carcass has been bled and stuffing the warm and fluent mixed trimmings into air impermeable casings.

Vogel subsequently filed a second patent application that more broadly claimed the method as applied to "meat" generally, and also as applied specifically to beef. Application claim 10 recited:

> 10. A method for prolonging the storage life of packaged meat products comprising the steps of: removing meat from a freshly slaughtered carcass at substantially the body bleeding temperature thereof under ambient temperature conditions; comminuting the meat during an exposure period following slaughter while the meat is at a temperature between said bleeding and ambient temperatures; sealing the comminuted meat within a flexible packaging material having an oxygen permeability ranging from 0.01 x 10(-10) to 0.1 x 10(-10) cc.-mm/sec/cm(2)/cm Hg at 30 degrees C. during said exposure period and before the meat has declined in temperature to the ambient temperature; and rapidly reducing the temperature of the packaged meat to a storage temperature below the ambient temperature immediately following said packaging of the meat.

Application claim 11 depended from claim 10 but was limited to beef. The USPTO rejected Vogel's application claims 10 and 11 as unpatentable in view of claim 1 of Vogel's issued patent (in combination with a reference to one Ellies). The USPTO characterized the rejection as same invention-type double patenting under 35 U.S.C. §101.

In considering whether to affirm the rejection on appeal, the Court of Customs and Patent Appeals (CCPA) set forth the following roadmap for double patenting analysis. The first question to be asked, the court explained, is whether "the same invention [is] being claimed twice?"[241] By "same invention" the court meant "identical subject matter," which

---

[239]*See* 35 U.S.C. §§102(a), (e), (g)(2) (2006).
[240]422 F.2d 438 (C.C.P.A. 1970).
[241]*Vogel*, 422 F.2d at 441.

implies identical claim scope. Thus, "halogen" is not the same invention for double patenting purposes as "chlorine" (a species of the genus halogen), but a widget of length "36 inches" is the same invention as a widget of length "3 feet." The court further instructed that "[a] good test, and probably the only objective test, for 'same invention,' is whether one of the claims could be literally infringed without literally infringing the other. If it could be, the claims do not define identically the same invention."[242] By applying this test the court concluded that same invention-type double patenting did not apply to Vogel's application claims 10 and 11 and that the USPTO had erred in holding to the contrary. Application claims 10 (meat process) and 11 (beef process) did not define the same invention as patent claim 1 (pork process).[243] For example, performing the process of application claims 10 and 11 with beef would literally infringe those claims but would not literally infringe patent claim 1 (pork process).

The *Vogel* court then moved to the second question: "[d]oes any appealed claim define merely an obvious variation of an invention disclosed and claimed in the patent?"[244] With respect to application claim 11 (limited to beef methods), the answer was no. That claim did not define a merely obvious variation of the pork process of patent claim 1. "The specific time and temperature considerations with respect to pork might not be applicable to beef," the court observed. There was "nothing in the record to indicate that the spoliation characteristics of the two meats are similar."[245] Thus, neither same invention-type nor obviousness-type double patenting was implicated by application claim 11, and the USPTO's rejection of application claim 11 on the basis of double patenting was reversed.[246]

The *Vogel* court lastly applied the "mere obvious variation" test to compare patent claim 1 (pork process) and application claim 10 (meat process). This time, obviousness-type double patenting was present. The court explained that "'[m]eat' reads literally on pork. The only limitation appearing in [application] claim 10 which is not disclosed in

---

[242]*Vogel*, 422 F.2d at 441.

[243]*Vogel*, 422 F.2d at 442 (reasoning that "[t]he patent claims are limited to pork. Appealed [application] claims 7 and 10 are limited to meat, which is not the same thing. [Application] Claims 7 and 10 could be infringed by many processes which would not infringe any of the patent claims. [Application] Claim 11 is limited to beef. Beef is not the same thing as pork.").

[244]*Vogel*, 422 F.2d at 442.

[245]*Vogel*, 422 F.2d at 442.

[246]Depending upon the order in which the pertinent patent applications were filed and certain other factors, the USPTO currently applies either a "one-way obviousness" or a "two-way obviousness" test for determining obviousness-type double patenting. For further details, *see* UNITED STATES PATENT AND TRADEMARK OFFICE, MANUAL OF PATENT EXAMINING PROCEDURE §804 (8th ed., Aug. 2001, last rev. July 2010), *available at* http://www.uspto.gov/web/offices/pac/mpep/mpep.htm.

the available portion of the patent disclosure is the permeability range of the packaging material; but this is merely an obvious variation as shown by Ellies." Allowance of application claim 10 for its full term would therefore improperly extend the duration of Vogel's monopoly on the pork process recited in patent claim 1.

Unlike a same invention-type double patenting rejection,[247] an obviousness-type double patenting rejection is not fatal to the applicant's attempt at obtaining a second patent. An obvious-type double patenting rejection can be overcome by the filing of a **terminal disclaimer**, which is authorized by 35 U.S.C. §253.[248] A terminal disclaimer is a document in which the applicant formally agrees that if he is awarded a patent on the application claims that have been rejected for obviousness-type double patenting, that patent will be deemed to expire on the same date as the applicant's first patent (on which the double patenting rejection was based).[249] The terminal disclaimer thus alleviates the concern about extension of monopoly that would otherwise result from granting a patent on the later-filed application. As a result, a patentee may ultimately obtain two (or more) patents claiming inventions that are merely obvious variants of each other, but all of these patents will expire on the same date. In permitting this result the patent system maintains incentives for the patentee to improve his original invention, but does not allow him to extend the period of time in which he can prevent others from practicing the patented invention and its obvious variations.

---

[247]The same invention-type double patenting rejection cannot be overcome by terminal disclaimer because the basis of the rejection is statutory. *See* In re Vogel, 422 F.2d 438, 441 (C.C.P.A. 1970) ("If it is determined that the same invention is being claimed twice, 35 USC 101 forbids the grant of the second patent, regardless of the presence or absence of a terminal disclaimer.").

[248]The second paragraph of 35 U.S.C. §253 (2006) provides that "[i]n like manner any patentee or applicant may disclaim or dedicate to the public the entire term, or any terminal part of the term, of the patent granted or to be granted."

[249]In the terminal disclaimer the applicant must also promise that the ownership of the two (or more) patents at issue will be commonly maintained throughout the term of the patents. *See* 37 C.F.R. §1.321(c)(3) (providing that terminal disclaimer filed to obviate obviousness-type double patenting rejection must "[i]nclude a provision that any patent granted on that application . . . shall be enforceable only for and during such period that said patent is commonly owned with the application or patent which formed the basis for the rejection"). This requirement addresses a second policy concern that would otherwise arise as to harassment of competitors through the filing of multiple lawsuits if ownership of two (or more) patents on obvious variants of the same invention were split up and the two (or more) patentees each sued the same potential infringer.

Patent Claims

A. Introduction

This chapter focuses on **claims,** arguably the most important part
of a patent. A patent claim is a precision-drafted, single-sentence definition of the patent owner's right to exclude others.[1] Every U.S. utility patent must conclude with one or more claims that particularly
point out and distinctly claim the subject matter which the applicant
regards as his invention.[2]

This text addresses claims in Chapter 2 because of their importance to understanding all concepts covered in the remaining chapters. Claims play a central role in all aspects of the U.S. patent system.
The USPTO examines the claims and compares them to the prior art
in order to determine patentability. In federal court litigation involving issued patents, the claims are the central focus of judges and juries
when determining validity and infringement.

The critical threshold step of interpreting the claims—that is,
determining what the words in the claims mean—is quite often dispositive of the issues of infringement and validity. Consequently, the
crafting of patent claims is one of the most challenging and important
drafting tasks in all of legal practice. This chapter therefore covers not
only the legal doctrines pertaining to claim interpretation but also a
number of commonly used drafting techniques and claim formats. In
patent law, "the name of the game is the claim."[3]

1. Historical Development of Patent Claiming

The development of claiming practice in the United States reflects
a shift from a historical **central claiming** regime to the current system of **peripheral claiming.**

---

[1]*See* Chapter 1 ("Foundations of the U.S. Patent System"), *supra,* for further discussion of the nature of the exclusive right conveyed by a patent.

[2]35 U.S.C. §112(b) (eff. Sept. 16, 2012).

[3]Giles S. Rich, *Extent of Protection and Interpretation of Claims—American
Perspectives,* 21 INT'L REV. INDUS. PROP. & COPYRIGHT L. 497, 499 (1990).

The earliest patent claims were written in central claiming style. Central claiming means that the claim recites the preferred embodiment of the invention but is understood to encompass all equivalents. Such claims will typically make an explicit reference to the preceding part of the patent specification. For example, a U.S. patent issued in 1858 included the following claim directed to a writing instrument:

> The combination of the lead and india-rubber or other erasing substance in the holder of a drawing-pencil, the whole being constructed and arranged substantially in the manner and for the purposes set forth.[4]

Claims were first mentioned in the U.S. Patent Act of 1836, but not mandated by statute until 1870. Prior to these enactments, patent applicants disclosed their invention to the world by means of a written description. This description provided a narrative explanation of how to make and use the invention, as well as a statement of how the invention differed from what had come before.[5] If a claim was included in the patent at all, it was something of an afterthought, having no more legal significance than the written description.

In the U.S. Patent Act of 1870, the inclusion of claims became mandatory. From this point on, claiming practice evolved to the peripheral claiming regime we have today in the United States. Peripheral claiming means that the claim recites a precise boundary or periphery of the patentee's property right, which is the patentee's time-limited right to exclude others. The following section elaborates on this idea.

2. Definition of a Patent Claim

A patent claim is a single-sentence definition of the scope of the patent owner's property right—that is, her right to exclude others from making, using, selling, offering to sell, or importing the invention, in this country, during the term of the patent.[6] A common analogy used to explain the concept of patent claiming is that a claim to an invention is like a deed to real property (land): the property description in the deed sets forth the metes and bounds of the plot, but it does not

---

[4]U.S. Patent No. 19,783 (issued Mar. 30, 1858) ("Combination of Lead-Pencil and Eraser").

[5]Evans v. Eaton, 16 U.S. 454, 514-515 (1818).

[6]35 U.S.C. §§154(a)(1); 271(a).

describe the interior of the land (i.e., whether the land is flat, hilly, wooded, boasts structures, or has water running through it).[7]

A patent claim, like a deed to real property, defines the boundaries of the patentee's right to exclude others. It acts as a verbal fence around the patentee's intangible property. But it is equally important to understand what a patent claim does *not* do: a patent claim does not *describe* the invention, in terms of how to make and use it, or its best mode. That is the role of the written description and drawings, parts of the patent document that are distinct from the claims.

In fact, the invention or inventive contribution of the patent applicant is often a far cry from what is ultimately recited in the patent claims. This variance results from the vagaries of patent prosecution: patent applications are typically filed with an array of claims of varying scope, ranging from very broad to very narrow. Over the course of the application's prosecution, as described in Chapter 1, *supra,* the USPTO often will identify prior art that the agency believes would anticipate or render obvious the subject matter of the broadest claims. Unless she believes the rejections are appealable, the patent applicant or her attorney will typically amend the claims so as to narrow them to subject matter that would be novel and nonobvious over the cited prior art.[8] In so doing, the claims, which set forth the literal boundaries of the patentee's right to exclude others, may evolve into something very different from the invention as originally envisioned by the inventor.[9] As expressed by a prominent patent jurist:

> What do we construe claims for, anyway? To find out what the inventor(s) invented? Hardly! Claims are frequently a far cry from what the inventor invented. In a suit, claims are construed to find out what the patentee can exclude the defendant from doing. CLAIMS ARE CONSTRUED TO DETERMINE THE SCOPE OF THE RIGHT TO EXCLUDE, regardless of what the inventor invented. I submit that that is the sole function of patent claims. I think this truism ought to be promoted in every seminar on the subject of claims. . . . Tell [readers] to stop talking about

[7]For example, consider the following property description from a deed to real estate:

Beginning at a point (POB) on the North side of Wells Street 50 feet East from the corner formed by the intersection of the East boundary of Polk Road and the North boundary of Wells Street: thence East 90 degrees 200 feet; thence North 300 feet; thence West 200 feet; thence direct to the POB.

[8]The applicant's ability to amend the claims in this fashion assumes that her application provides adequate support under 35 U.S.C. §112(a) (eff. Sept. 16, 2012) for the amended (narrower) claim(s). *See* Chapter 3 ("Disclosure Requirements (35 U.S.C. §112(a))"), *infra.*

[9]*See, e.g.*, Elekta Instrument S.A. v. O.U.R. Scientific Int'l, Inc., 214 F.3d 1302, 1308 (Fed. Cir. 2000) (concluding that amendments made during prosecution of patent in suit compelled an interpretation of the asserted claim that excluded the preferred and only embodiment of the invention disclosed in the specification).

claims defining the invention. It's a bad habit. And it seems to be almost universal.[10]

Nor do patent claims define a tangible product or thing. Rather, claims may be best understood as *abstractions*. A noted patent law scholar explained:

> The difficulty which American courts [have had in comprehending patent claims] goes back to the primitive thought that an "invention" upon which the patent gives protection is something tangible. The physical embodiment or disclosure, which, in itself is something tangible, is confused with the definition or claim to the inventive novelty, and this definition or claim or monopoly, also sometimes called "invention" in one of that word's meanings, is not something tangible, but is an abstraction. Definitions are always abstractions. This primitive confusion of "invention" in the sense of physical embodiment with "invention" in the sense of definition of the patentable amount of novelty, survives to the present day, not only in the courts, but among some of the examiners in the Patent Office.[11]

Thus, patent claims delineate the patent owner's right to exclude others from practicing the claimed invention, which is intangible. The invention is probably best understood in the form of a physical, tangible embodiment, but that tangible embodiment is not, strictly speaking, what the patent protects.

3.   A Key Reference Work

The leading reference work on U.S. patent claiming practice is Faber's *Mechanics of Patent Claim Drafting.*[12] Much of patent claiming technique has evolved in practice before the USPTO and is governed by convention rather than statute or regulation. Landis's work is an excellent compendium of these practices. All patent attorneys and agents should own, or at least make themselves familiar with, this work.

---

[10]Janice M. Mueller, *A Rich Legacy*, 81 J. Pat. & Trademark Off. Soc'y 755, 758-759 (1999) (quoting remarks of Judge Giles S. Rich).

[11]Emerson Stringham, Double Patenting 209 (1933).

[12]Robert C. Faber, Faber on Mechanics of Patent Claim Drafting (6th ed. 2008), *available at* Westlaw ("PLIREF-PATCLAIM" database). The Faber work (known for many years by the name of its former author, John L. Landis) is an excellent compendium of U.S. patent claim practice.

B. Claim Definiteness Requirement (35 U.S.C. §112(b))

1. Own Lexicographer Rule

The second paragraph of Section 112 of the Patent Act requires that each patent conclude with

> one or more claims particularly pointing out and distinctly claiming the subject matter which the inventor or a joint inventor regards as the invention.[13]

This statutory edict is known to patent lawyers as the claim **definiteness** requirement (although the statute does not use the word "definite").

One might reasonably ask how it is possible to satisfy the claim definiteness requirement, when the invention being claimed may represent novel and nonobvious technology that has never before been known or used or sold. In such a case, sufficient terminology may not even be present in the existing English lexicon to adequately describe the invention. In other cases, the mechanical operation of a more conventional device may be extremely difficult to convey in words. For example, consider the challenge of drafting a claim to the well-known children's SLINKY® toy.[14] Test your claim drafting skill by attempting to write a definite claim to a SLINKY® toy. How would your claim recite its structural features, such as its elongation, and coiled shape? Must the number of twists in the coil be specified? Can the SLINKY® toy be claimed as a spring? Must the material (metal or plastic?) from which the SLINKY® toy is made be specified in the claim?

Fortunately it is possible to write definite claims to novel technology, even if existing words are inadequate, because the patent law permits the applicant to create new words with which to claim her invention. In other words, a patent applicant can be her own lexicographer, meaning that she can make up and define terms to be used in her claims. In this manner the written description portion of a patent operates as a sort of dictionary or concordance that defines and explains terms found in the claims. Each newly created term may be

---

[13]35 U.S.C. §112(b) (eff. Sept. 16, 2012). The America Invents Act of 2011 renamed the second paragraph of 35 U.S.C. §112 (generally referred to as "35 U.S.C. §112, ¶2") as 35 U.S.C. §112(b) and amended its wording. The pre-AIA statutory text required that "[t]he specification shall conclude with one or more claims particularly pointing out and distinctly claiming the subject matter which the applicant regards as his invention." 35 U.S.C. §112, ¶2 (2006).

[14]*See* POOF-Slinky, *Slinky® History*, http://www.poof-slinky.com/check-out-the-on-line-slinky-museum/slinky-history/ (last visited July 9, 2012).

expressly defined (e.g., the written description might state that "as used herein, 'gizmo' means a machine having two lever arms, three pulleys, and four gears, made entirely of aluminum"). In other cases, a claim term may be implicitly defined through consistent use of the term in the written description.[15]

If the applicant chooses *not* to supply definitions for the terms in her claims, either expressly or implicitly, how will they be defined? Case law provides that in the absence of such definitions, terms in patent claims will be given their ordinary and customary meaning to persons of ordinary skill in the art of the invention.[16] This treatment is analogous to the contract law rule of interpreting undefined contractual terms in accordance with "usage in the trade."[17]

2. Definiteness Standards

When the Patent Act requires that claims "particularly point[] out and distinctly claim[] the subject matter which the inventor . . . regards as his invention,"[18] from whose perspective must one determine if the claim language is sufficiently "particular" and "distinct" to satisfy the statute? The proper vantage point is that of the hypothetical **person having ordinary skill in the art (PHOSITA),** whom we will encounter in many other patent law contexts. In other words, we do not interpret patent claims according to what a judge, jury, or scientific experts may understand the terms of the claim to mean.

---

[15]*See* Bell Atlantic Network Servs., Inc. v. Covad Communications Group, Inc., 262 F.3d 1258, 1271 (Fed. Cir. 2001).

[16]*See* Vitronics Corp. v. Conceptronic, Inc., 90 F.3d 1576, 1582 (Fed. Cir. 1996). Following the *Vitronics* decision, the Federal Circuit became increasingly polarized over the use of dictionaries for this purpose rather than reliance on the patent's written description. *See* Section B.4 in Chapter 9 ("Patent Infringement"), *infra*.

[17]*See* U.C.C. §2-202 (2008). Such undefined terms are to be read "on the assumption that . . . the usages of trade were taken for granted when the document was phrased." *Id.* at cmt. 2. Usage of trade is defined in U.C.C. §1-205(2) (2008) as "any practice or method of dealing having such regularity of observance in a place, vocation or trade as to justify an expectation that it will be observed with respect to the transaction in question." As Professor Corbin explains,

> Just as a court would interpret according to the French language a contract written in French by two French speakers, a court will interpret according to trade usage a contract written by two parties familiar with a term common in that trade . . . [t]he law requires the court to put itself as nearly as possible in the position of the parties, with their knowledge and their ignorance, with their language and their usage.

5 A. CORBIN ON CONTRACTS §24.13, at 111 (Joseph M. Perillo ed., LEXIS Publ. 1998) (1952).

[18]35 U.S.C. §112(b) (eff. Sept. 16, 2012).

B. Claim Definiteness Requirement (35 U.S.C. §112(b))

Rather, we must determine whether the claim terms are definite to a PHOSITA, a hypothetical construct that represents the skill and understanding of an "ordinary" person (e.g., whether a scientist, engineer, technician, or other worker) in the particular technology of the claimed invention.[19]

Solomon v. Kimberly-Clark Corp.[20] nicely illustrates this rule. Solomon's patent was directed to a disposable woman's protective undergarment for holding a feminine napkin. The accused infringer, Kimberly-Clark, alleged that the patent was invalid under 35 U.S.C. §112, ¶2, because Solomon failed to claim the subject matter that she regarded as her invention. This argument was based on Solomon's deposition, in which she stated that the "depression" limitation of the claimed invention had a uniform thickness.[21] However, the district court (and on appeal, the Federal Circuit) interpreted the claim language to mean that the depression had a thickness that varied, contrary to Solomon's deposition testimony.

The Federal Circuit rejected Kimberly-Clark's challenge and upheld the validity of the patent claims under §112, ¶2. The definiteness of claims of an issued patent must be evaluated from the perspective of the PHOSITA, the court explained, and not based on evidence extrinsic to the patent such as the inventor's deposition testimony. The inventor's perspective may not be the same as that of the PHOSITA. If the claims of the patent, read in light of the written description, would reasonably give notice to the PHOSITA of the scope of the patentee's right to exclude others, this is all that the definiteness rule of §112, ¶2 requires. After a patent issues, statements by the inventor about what she subjectively intended or understood the claim language to mean are largely irrelevant, the court emphasized. After issuance, the claims must be viewed objectively, from the perspective of the hypothetical PHOSITA.[22]

---

[19]Professor John Golden argues for abandoning the commonly accepted notion that claims should be construed from a PHOSITA's perspective, on the ground that the views of ordinary engineers or scientists may be "too legally ill-informed and idiosyncratic to permit substantial predictability." Golden proposes that a better perspective would be that of "a patent attorney having access to the knowledge of a person of technological skill." Such a perspective would "more generally follow rules and techniques for claim construction that are publicly known and anchored in the practices of an active interpretive community." John M. Golden, *Construing Patent Claims According to Their "Interpretive Community": A Call for an Attorney-Plus-Artisan Perspective*, 21 HARV. J.L. & TECH. 321 (2008).

[20]216 F.3d 1372 (Fed. Cir. 2000).

[21]Kimberly-Clark's invalidity argument also was based on the existence of a prototype of the invention, which depicted an area of uniform thickness in the region where the depression was located.

[22]In contrast, during examination of applications for patent by the USPTO, the examiner will assign the claims their broadest reasonable interpretation consistent

Just how "definite" can the PHOSITA expect a patent claim to be? In *Orthokinetics, Inc. v. Safety Travel Chairs, Inc.,*[23] the patent in suit was directed to a portable folding wheelchair for children that could easily be installed on and removed from the seat of an automobile.[24] A depiction of the portable wheelchair is shown in Figure 2.1. The nature of this invention was such that the dimensions of the chair would need to be altered for a particular make of car. The claim recited "wherein said front leg portion is *so dimensioned* as to be insertable through the space between the doorframe of an automobile and one of the seats thereof."[25] The accused infringer alleged that this variability in dimensions rendered the claim indefinite under 35 U.S.C. §112, ¶2.

The Federal Circuit disagreed. It was not relevant that a particular chair, once constructed, might fit in some cars and not others. The phrase "so dimensioned" was "as accurate as the subject matter permits."[26] "Patent law does not require that all possible lengths corresponding to the spaces in hundreds of different automobiles be listed in the patent, let alone that they be listed in the claims,"[27] the court explained. This would convert a patent into a production specification, which it is not. So long as the PHOSITA could make and use the invention without undue experimentation, the disclosure was enabling,[28] and so long as the PHOSITA could reasonably determine if a particular chair infringed the claim, the claims were sufficiently definite.

The use of adjectives such as "substantially" or "about" to qualify numerical or structural limitations in patent claims does not necessarily render the claims indefinite under 35 U.S.C. §112, ¶2.[29] The patent in *Verve, LLC v. Crane Cams, Inc.,*[30] claimed improved "push rods" for internal combustion engines; the rods actuated "rocker arms" that opened and closed the intake and exhaust valves of engine cylinders. The claimed push rod was made from a single piece of metal in the form

---

with the specification. *See* In re Graves, 69 F.3d 1147, 1152 (Fed. Cir. 1995). Assigning claims a relatively broader interpretation for purposes of examination reduces the possibility that the "claims, finally allowed, will be given broader scope than is justified." In re Yamamoto, 740 F.2d 1569, 1571 (Fed. Cir. 1984). This USPTO practice is not considered unfair to applicants because "before a patent is granted the claims are readily amended as part of the examination process." Burlington Indus., Inc. v. Quigg, 822 F.2d 1581, 1583 (Fed. Cir. 1987).

[23]806 F.2d 1565 (Fed. Cir. 1986).

[24]*See* U.S. Patent No. 3,891,229 (issued June 24, 1975).

[25]*Orthokinetics*, 806 F.2d at 1575.

[26]*Orthokinetics*, 806 F.2d at 1576.

[27]*Orthokinetics*, 806 F.2d at 1576.

[28]For discussion of the enablement requirement of 35 U.S.C. §112(a) (eff. Sept. 16, 2012), *see* Chapter 3 ("Disclosure Requirements (35 U.S.C. §112(a))"), *infra*.

[29]The America Invents Act of 2011 renamed 35 U.S.C. §112, ¶2 as 35 U.S.C. §112(b) (eff. Sept. 16, 2012).

[30]311 F.3d 1116 (Fed. Cir. 2002).

Figure 2.1

Orthokinetics U.S. Patent No. 3,891,229

of an "elongated hollow tube having . . . *substantially* constant wall thickness throughout the length of the tube. . . . "[31] The district court granted summary judgment to the accused infringer on the ground that, *inter alia*, the patent was invalid as indefinite under §112, ¶2 because the meaning of "substantially" was "unclear" from the intrinsic evidence (i.e., the patent document itself and its prosecution history); the district court also found that liability for infringement depended on whether "substantially" embraced the accused push rods.

The Federal Circuit vacated the summary judgment of indefiniteness and remanded the case for further proceedings, concluding that the district court had erred as a matter of law by "requiring that the intrinsic evidence of the specification and prosecution history is the sole source of meaning of words that are used in a technologic context."[32] "[R]esolution of any ambiguity arising from the claims and specification may be aided by extrinsic evidence of usage and meaning of a term in the context of the invention,"[33] the appellate court instructed. A proper analysis would consider whether the word "substantially" as applied to "constant wall thickness" would be understood "by persons experienced in this field of mechanics, upon reading the patent documents."[34] Expressions such as "substantially" are appropriately used in patents when warranted by the nature of the invention, in order to accommodate the minor variations that may be appropriate to secure to the inventor the benefit of her invention. The Federal Circuit concluded that "when the term 'substantially' serves reasonably to describe the subject matter so that its scope would be understood by persons in the field of the invention, and to distinguish the claimed subject matter from the prior art, it is not indefinite."[35]

In contrast to the cases discussed above, the recitation of an "aesthetically pleasing" feature in the claims at issue in *Datamize, LLC v. Plumtree Software, Inc.,*[36] rendered them indefinite under 35 U.S.C. §112, ¶2. Datamize's patent was directed to a software program that allowed a person to customize the user interfaces of electronic kiosks providing information for customers and patrons, such as the kiosk systems that are increasingly seen in museums, airports, banks, hotels, and stores. The claims recited methods for defining custom interface screens for the kiosks in which the screens had an "aesthetically pleasing" look and feel. The Federal Circuit noted at the outset that some ambiguity in a patent claim's wording is not necessarily fatal, and that

---

[31]Verve, LLC v. Crane Cams, Inc., 311 F.3d 1116, 1119 (Fed. Cir. 2002) (emphasis added).

[32]*Verve,* 311 F.3d at 1119.

[33]*Verve,* 311 F.3d at 1119.

[34]*Verve,* 311 F.3d at 1120.

[35]*Verve,* 311 F.3d at 1120.

[36]417 F.3d 1342 (Fed. Cir. 2005).

B. Claim Definiteness Requirement (35 U.S.C. §112(b))

only claims "not amenable to construction" or "insolubly ambiguous" should be held invalid for indefiniteness. In the case at bar, however, the meaning of "aesthetically pleasing" was entirely dependent on the system user's subjective opinion. Thus the claim language was not sufficiently definite to perform its critical notice function. "A purely subjective construction of 'aesthetically pleasing' would not notify the public of the patentee's right to exclude since the meaning of the claim language would depend on the unpredictable vagaries of any one person's opinion of the aesthetics of interface screens. While beauty is in the eye of the beholder, a claim term, to be definite, requires an objective anchor."[37] Here, the patentee failed to provide any reasonable, workable, "objective definition identifying a standard for determining when an interface screen [would be] 'aesthetically pleasing.'"

Patent claims are sometimes rendered indefinite under 35 U.S.C. §112(b) by errors introduced into the claim language during patent prosecution. What appears to be an obvious typographical error can potentially prove fatal to validity, a risk that should reinforce the need for precise, careful drafting and amending of claims. A case in point is *Novo Indus., L.P. v. Micro Molds Corp.*[38] Novo's patent was directed to a carrier assembly that held one of a plurality of vertical slats (or blinds) that covered the interior of a window. The carrier assembly permitted realignment of misaligned slats and included "stop mechanisms" that physically prevented rotation of a support finger when a slat reached an extreme rotational position. During prosecution, the USPTO examiner rejected Novo's application claims 15-17 as obvious under 35 U.S.C. §103.[39] Novo canceled those claims and substituted a new claim 19, which in subparagraphs (a)-(i) incorporated all the limitations of the canceled claims plus one additional limitation; claim 19 was subsequently renumbered and issued as patent claim 13, which read (emphasis added to limitation (g)):

> 13. A carrier assembly for movably supporting one of a plurality of vertical oriented slats in a vertical blind assembly, said carrier assembly comprising:
>> a) a frame . . . ,
>> b) a support finger movably mounted to rotate on said frame . . . ,
>> c) a gear means . . . ,
>> g) stop means formed on *a rotatable with* said support finger and extending outwardly therefrom into engaging relation with one of two spaced apart stop members formed on said frame,

[37]Datamize, LLC v. Plumtree Software, Inc., 417 F.3d 1342, 1350 (Fed. Cir. 2005).

[38] 350 F.3d 1348 (Fed. Cir. 2003).

[39]The nonobviousness requirement of 35 U.S.C. §103 is the subject of Chapter 5, *infra.*

> h) said stop means comprising one outwardly extending protrusion disposed to engage each of said stop members on said frame upon rotation through an arc of substantially 180 degrees, and
>
> i) said drive gear including a substantially round configuration and a plurality of gear teeth formed thereon in spaced relation to one another along an outer periphery of said drive gear to define a circular configuration thereof; . . . .

Notably, the quoted language of limitation (g) of claim 13 was not identical to the wording of the claims Novo had canceled. Rather, it included the additional words "a rotatable with," which did not appear in canceled claim 16. The examiner allowed the claim as written. Novo never sought a certificate of correction from the USPTO.[40]

In subsequent infringement litigation, the parties agreed that issued claim 13 included an error, but disputed whether the error was correctable. While not adopting either party's argument, the district court interpreted the claim so as to correct what it considered "an obvious typographical error." The district court instructed the jury that "a" in limitation (g) of claim 13 should be read as "and." This rendered moot the issue of invalidity for indefiniteness at the district court level. The jury proceeded to find that defendant Micro Molds had literally (and willfully) infringed the patent.

On appeal, the Federal Circuit relied on a 1926 Supreme Court decision, *I.T.S. Rubber Co. v. Essex Rubber Co.,*[41] which held that in a patent infringement suit a court could properly interpret a patent claim to correct an obvious error. In view of subsequent legislative developments codifying the USPTO's certificate of correction procedure, the Federal Circuit concluded that district courts in conjunction with their responsibility to interpret patent claims can correct only *Essex*-type errors. Specifically, a district court can correct a patent "only if (1) the correction is not subject to reasonable debate based on consideration of the claim language and the specification and (2) the prosecution history does not suggest a different interpretation of the claims."[42]

These newly announced criteria were not satisfied in *Novo* because the nature of the error was not evident on the face of the patent. The correct construction had been the subject of considerable debate before the district court. Patentee Novo itself had suggested two different corrections to the district court, which devised a third correction. The correct approach, the Federal Circuit suggested, might be yet a fourth approach, to add a word that was missing, such as "skirt" or "disk."

[40]Certificates of correction are discussed in Chapter 8 ("Correcting and Challenging Issued Patents in the USPTO"), *infra.*
[41]272 U.S. 429 (1926).
[42]*Novo,* 350 F.3d at 1354.

B. Claim Definiteness Requirement (35 U.S.C. §112(b))

Because the Federal Circuit could not discern "what correction [wa]s necessarily appropriate or how the claim should be interpreted," it held claim 13 invalid for indefiniteness under 35 U.S.C. §112, ¶2. The claim was "insolubly ambiguous" and not "amenable to construction" in its present form.

In contrast with *Novo*, the claim error in *Hoffer v. Microsoft Corp.*[43] was correctable by the district court. Claim 22 of Hoffer's patent as written depended from claim 38. In litigation involving the patent a federal district court held claim 22 invalid for indefiniteness because no claim 38 appeared in the issued patent. The error had been introduced into the patent by the USPTO during prosecution when the claims were renumbered and claim 38 was given a different number; the examiner renumbered all claims in preparation for printing the patent but failed to renumber claim 22's internal reference to claim 38. The Federal Circuit disagreed on appeal that the district court was "powerless" to correct the error. In this case the error in dependency of claim 22 was apparent on the face of the printed patent and the correct antecedent claim was apparent from the prosecution history. Citing *Novo*, the Federal Circuit held that "[w]hen a harmless error in a patent is not subject to reasonable debate, it can be corrected by the court, as for other legal documents."[44] The district court's invalidation of claim 22 for indefiniteness was accordingly reversed.

3. Antecedent Basis

The concept of "antecedent basis" is a technique that has developed in patent prosecution practice to aid those who draft patent claims in satisfying the definiteness requirement of 35 U.S.C. §112(b).[45] It helps ensure that "terms and phrases used in the claims . . . find clear support or antecedent basis in the [the application's] description so that the meaning of the terms in the claims may be ascertainable by reference to the description."[46]

Antecedent basis is implemented as follows. The first time a particular element is introduced in a patent claim, it should be preceded or introduced by the indefinite article "a." Thereafter, each time the claims drafter intends to refer back to that same previously introduced element, it is referred to as "said" element or "the" element.

For example, consider the following claim to a toy football:

---

[43]405 F.3d 1326 (Fed. Cir. 2005).
[44]*Hoffer*, 405 F.3d at 1331.
[45]35 U.S.C. §112(b) (eff. Sept. 16, 2012).
[46]37 C.F.R. §1.75(d)(1) (2008).

1. A foam football comprising
    (a) a body having a longitudinal axis and an external surface;
    (b) said external surface comprising a plurality of grooves aligned with said longitudinal axis;
    (c) wherein each of said grooves has a minimum depth of about 0.25 inches and a maximum depth of about 0.5 inches.

The first time that the terms "football," "body," "longitudinal axis," "external surface," and "grooves" are introduced, they are expressed as "*a* foam football," "*a* body," "*a* longitudinal axis," "*an* external surface," and "*a* plurality of grooves."[47] Thereafter, these elements are referred to as "*said* external surface," "*said* longitudinal axis," and "*said* grooves," to indicate that the claims drafter is referring to the same "external surface," the same "longitudinal axis," and the same "grooves" as initially introduced, not some other "longitudinal axis," "external surface," or "grooves."[48]

C. Anatomy of a Patent Claim

Every patent claim has three parts: a preamble, a transition, and a body. As the role of each of these parts is described below, consider the following claim as an example:

1. A widget comprising:

    Part A;
    Part B; and
    Part C, attaching said Part A to said Part B;

wherein said Part A is made of copper and said Part B is made of lead and said Part C is made of gold.

1. Preamble

A preamble is a short and plain expression of what the invention is. In claim 1 above, the words "[a] widget" are the preamble. The preamble need not include an express reference to one of the four statutory classifications of potentially patentable subject matter under 35 U.S.C.

---

[47]A **plurality** is a term of art in patent law, meaning a quantity of two or more.

[48]*See generally* UNITED STATES PATENT AND TRADEMARK OFFICE, MANUAL OF PATENT EXAMINING PROCEDURE (8th ed., 8th rev., 2010), *available at* http://www.uspto.gov/web/offices/pac/mpep/mpep.htm, at §2173.05(e) (discussing basis of rejection for "Lack of Antecedent Basis").

§101 (i.e., process, machine, manufacture, or composition of matter), so long as it is clear from the entirety of the claim that the invention fits within one or more of those classifications. In the above example, it is clear that the claimed widget is either a manufacture or a machine.[49]

Claim preambles are sometimes longer than just one or two words. In such cases, the qualifying language in the preamble is sometimes, but not always, treated as a limitation of the claim. For example, consider the following reformulation of the above claim:

1. A widget for use in marine applications comprising:

    Part A;
    Part B; and
    Part C, attaching said Part A to said Part B;

    wherein said Part A is made of copper and said Part B is made of lead and said Part C is made of gold.

The preamble of this claim is the entire phrase "[a] widget for use in marine applications." The issue here is whether the qualifier "for use in marine applications" represents a limitation of the claim, such that an identical widget, if used on land rather than in the water, would not literally infringe the claim.

The Federal Circuit rule is that, generally, preamble language is considered limiting if the language is necessary to give "life, meaning and vitality" to the claim, or if it recites essential structure or steps.[50] In particular, if the preamble terminology is repeated and referenced in the body of the claim, it is most likely limiting. However, where the body of the claim (i.e., the language following the transition) recites a structurally complete invention and the preamble language only states an intended purpose or use for that invention, the preamble language is generally not limiting.[51]

In the above example, the "marine applications" language is not referred to in the body of the claim, and the body recites a structurally complete invention. The "marine applications" language merely states an intended use for the widget. Thus, it is not likely to be construed as

---

[49]The categories of potentially patentable subject matter are discussed in further detail in Chapter 7, *infra*.

[50]*See* Catalina Marketing Int'l, Inc. v. CoolSavings.com, Inc., 289 F.3d 801, 808 (Fed. Cir. 2002).

[51]*See Catalina Marking*, 289 F.3d at 810 (reversing summary judgment of non-infringement on basis that preamble phrase "located at predesignated sites such as consumer stores," recited in claim to a selection and distribution system for discount coupons, was not a limitation, because "[t]he applicant did not rely on this phrase to define its invention nor is the phrase essential to understand limitations or terms in the claim body," nor did applicant rely on the phrase to distinguish the prior art).

limiting. Unauthorized use of the claimed widget on land would still literally infringe the claim (assuming that all limitations recited in the body of the claim, discussed below, are met).

2. Transition

The transition of the example claim above is the single word "comprising." The transition is a key code word or term of art that affects the scope of the claim. There are three primary claim transitions used in U.S. patent claiming practice: **comprising, consisting of,** and **consisting essentially of.**[52] Each is discussed below.

a. *"Comprising" Transition*

A "comprising" transition means "including" or "containing" the elements listed following the transition. Inclusion in a patent claim of the comprising transition indicates that the claim is open in scope. An "open" claim encompasses or is literally infringed by (or "reads on") another's product that includes each of the explicitly recited elements of the claim, *plus anything else.*

For example, a claim to "a widget comprising A, B, and C" would read on a widget ABC, a widget ABCD, a widget ABCXYZ, and so on.[53] Infringement of a comprising claim cannot be avoided by copying the invention and merely adding on additional elements not recited in the claim.

Use of the "comprising" transition does not broaden a claim to such an extent that it reads on a device containing less (rather than more) than what is expressly recited in the claim, however. In *In re Skvorecz,*[54] a reissue applicant claimed an improved stand for chafing dishes used to keep food warm during serving. The invention's structure allowed multiple stacked stands to be readily separated from one another. The wire legs of the stand included an indent or "offset" located adjacent to the upper ends of the legs, serving to laterally displace each leg relative to its point of attachment to the upper rim of the stand. An embodiment of the claimed invention, including an offset indicated by the number 30 in Fig. 4 of the application drawings, is depicted in Figure 2.2.

---

[52]*See generally* Ex parte Davis, 80 U.S.P.Q. 448, 450 (Bd. Pat. App. & Int. 1948) (discussing these three "code" terms adopted "to aid uniformity of practice").

[53]Every recited element is considered material and must be identically present in the accused device to have **literal infringement.** Another's device that excludes even one element recited in the claim avoids infringement. For example, a widget ACXYZ does not literally infringe the above claim, because it lacks the recited element B.

[54]580 F.3d 1262 (Fed. Cir. 2009).

Figure 2.2

Application Drawings from *In re Skvorecz*

Claim 1 of Skvorecz's reissue application recited:

1. A wire chafing stand comprising a first rim of wire steel which forms a closed geometrical configuration circumscribing a first surface area, having at least two wire legs with each wire leg having two upright sections interconnected to one another in a configuration forming a base support for the stand to rest upon with each upright section extending upwardly from said base support to from [sic, form] an angle equal to or greater than 90° with respect to a horizontal plane through said base support and being affixed to the first rim adjacent one end thereof and further comprising a plurality of offsets located either in said upright sections of said wire legs or in said first rim for laterally displacing each wire leg relative to said first rim to facilitate the nesting of a multiplicity of stands into one another without significant wedging.[55]

The USPTO rejected Skvorecz's claim 1 as anticipated by a prior art structure depicted in a patent to Buff. Notably, the Buff structure did not have an offset located in each wire that served as a leg to support the Buff stand. The USPTO nevertheless took the position that Buff anticipated Skvorecz's claim because of the claim's open-ended "comprising" transition; that is, the claim read on stands having wire legs with offsets, plus anything else—namely, wire legs without such offsets.

The Federal Circuit reversed in *Skvorecz*, concluding that the USPTO had misinterpreted the claim language and therefore had not established anticipation. The USPTO's mandate to give claims their "broadest reasonable interpretation" during examination was not a license to

---

[55]*Skvorecz*, 580 F.3d at 1265.

ignore features required by the claims. "The signal 'comprising' does not render a claim anticipated by a device that contains less (rather th[a]n more) than what is claimed," the Federal Circuit explained.[56] In the case at bar, the USPTO had incorrectly applied the "examination expedient" of "broadest reasonable interpretation" when it construed "comprising" to mean that less than all of the wire legs in the claimed invention needed to have offsets.[57] The Federal Circuit read claim 1 to require that "each wire leg" must have an offset. Accordingly, the claim was not anticipated by a prior art structure made up of some legs with offsets and some legs without offsets.

The Federal Circuit considered whether the linguistically similar phrase "comprised of" should be interpreted differently than the standard "comprising" transition in *CIAS, Inc. v. Alliance Gaming Corp.,*[58] answering the question in the negative. Claim 1 of the patent in suit recited "[a] counterfeit detection system for identifying a counterfeit object from a set of similar authentic objects, each object in said set having unique authorized information associated therewith *comprised of* machine-readable code elements coded according to a detectable series, the system comprising: [various means-plus-function elements]." The Federal Circuit reversed the district court's interpretation of "comprised of" as a closed-ended term that would exclude any elements other than the recited "machine-readable code elements coded according to a detectable series." While recognizing that "comprised of" is less frequently used as a claim transition than "comprising," the Federal Circuit nevertheless concluded that "[t]he usual and generally consistent meaning of 'comprised of,' when it is used as a transition phrase, is, like 'comprising,' that the ensuing elements or steps are not limiting. The conventional usage of 'comprising' generally also applies to 'comprised of.'"[59] The appellate court found support for its holding in several district court cases that followed the "routine construction" of "comprised of" as open-ended, that is, "not of itself exclud[ing] the possible presence of additional elements or steps." The Federal Circuit's construction of "comprised of" as open-ended meant that the district court in *CIAS* had erred in finding no infringement by Alliance's accused code systems, which included elements coded according to a "secret" series as well as the claim-recited "detectable series."

[56]*Skvorecz*, 580 F.3d at 1268.

[57]*See Skvorecz*, 580 F.3d at 1268; *cf.* In re Suitco Surface, Inc., 603 F.3d 1255, 1260 (Fed. Cir. 2010) (stating that "[t]he broadest-construction rubric coupled with the term "comprising" does not give the PTO an unfettered license to interpret claims to embrace anything remotely related to the claimed invention. Rather, claims should always be read in light of the specification and teachings in the underlying patent.").

[58]504 F.3d 1356 (Fed. Cir. 2007).

[59]*CIAS*, 504 F.3d at 1360.

b. *"Consisting of" Transition*

Inclusion in a patent claim of the "consisting of" transition indicates that the claim is closed in scope. A "closed" claim encompasses or is literally infringed by (or "reads on") another's product that includes each of the explicitly recited elements of the claim, *but nothing else* (other than impurities normally associated with the recited elements).[60] For example, a claim to "a widget consisting of A, B, and C" would read on a widget ABC, but not on a widget ABCD or on a widget ABCXYZ.

Thus, a claim that employs a "consisting of" transition is potentially much narrower in scope than a claim that uses a comprising transition. For this reason, patent applicants generally file their applications with comprising claims, and only narrow the claims by amending to a consisting of transition when absolutely necessary for allowance.

c. *"Consisting Essentially of" Transition*

This type of transition is most commonly used when claiming chemical compositions, and can be thought of as creating a partially closed claim. A "consisting essentially of" transition means that the claim is closed, *except for the addition of any elements that do not change the essential function or properties of the composition.*[61]

For example, a claim that recites "an adhesive consisting essentially of A, B, and C" would read on another's adhesive ABC, as well as on an adhesive ABCD if D was merely a dye that made the adhesive a certain color, not impacting its stickiness. This claim would not read on or encompass an adhesive ABCX if the inclusion of X changed the basic nature of the adhesive from one that forms a very strong, permanent bond like SuperGlue® to one that is very tacky and removable, like the repositionable adhesive used with Post-It® notes.[62]

---

[60]A divided panel of the Federal Circuit qualified this understanding of "consisting of" claims. In *Norian Corp. v. Stryker Corp.*, 363 F.3d 1321 (Fed. Cir. 2004), the majority held that a claim to a kit "consisting of" several enumerated chemical components was nevertheless infringed by a kit made up of the same chemical components plus a mechanical component—a spatula. *See id.* at 1331-1332. The dissenting judge charged that the court should not "change the meaning of a well-established phrase to save a patentee from a decision to limit its claims." *Id.* at 1335 (Schall, J., dissenting in part).

[61]*See* PPG Indus. v. Guardian Indus. Corp., 156 F.3d 1351, 1354 (Fed. Cir. 1998).

[62]*See* Ex parte Davis, 80 U.S.P.Q. 448, 450 (Bd. Pat. App. & Int. 1948) (holding that where claim to adhesive composition recited three ingredients and prior art reference disclosed four, the claim's "consisting essentially of" transition excluded the fourth ingredient [thus rendering the claim allowable] because that ingredient "materially changes the fundamental characters of the [claimed] three-ingredient composition . . . . ").

3. Body

The body of a patent claim lists all elements of the invention and should specify how the elements are related to or interact with each other. For example, consider a claim reciting "the widget comprising A, B, and means for attaching A to B." The body of this claim is all the words after the comprising transition. Thus, the body recites three elements: element A, element B, and a "means" element (explained below) that functions to attach element A to element B.

No minimum or maximum number of elements must be included in the body of a patent claim. But in any case, a sufficient number of elements must be included to recite an invention that is novel, non-obvious, and useful. The device as claimed must be operable; that is, it must work. So long as these conditions are met, it is permissible to claim "subcombination" inventions that are some subset of a larger device. For example, automobile carburetors, tires, and headlights are subcombination inventions because they consist of major subassemblies of parts and have their own utility.[63]

Deciding how many elements to include in the body of a patent claim requires a trade-off that balances the patent owner's ability to enforce the claim against infringers versus the likelihood that the claim will withstand a challenge to its validity. Both concepts turn on the scope of the claim. It is axiomatic that the more elements included in a claim, the narrower its scope; the fewer elements included, the broader its scope. For example, a claim reciting "a widget comprising elements A, B, and C" is narrower in scope than a claim reciting "a widget comprising elements A and C."

This difference in scope follows from the **all-elements rule,** which we will study in greater depth in Chapter 9 ("Patent Infringement"), *infra.* In summary, the all-elements rule requires that in order to find that an accused device infringes a particular asserted claim of a patent, every element (more properly, every **limitation**) recited in that claim must be met (i.e., matched) either literally or equivalently in the accused device.[64] Thus, as more elements are added to a claim, it will be progressively more difficult to prove infringement of that claim because each recited element must be present or met in the accused device.

Figure 2.3 illustrates the concept of claim scope by way of a Venn diagram. As depicted in Figure 2.3, the claim to "a widget comprising

---

[63]For further examples of subcombinations, *see* ROBERT C. FABER, LANDIS ON MECHANICS OF PATENT CLAIM DRAFTING §59 (6th ed., Pract. Law Inst. 2008), *available at* Westlaw ("PLIREF-PATCLAIM" database).

[64]The use of "literally or equivalently" here refers to the two theories of infringement we will analyze in Chapter 9, *infra*: (1) literal infringement and (2) infringement under the judicially created doctrine of equivalents.

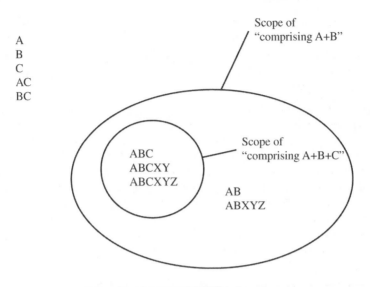

A
B
C
AC
BC

Figure 2.3
Claim Scope

elements A and B," represented by the exterior circle, is literally infringed by (or reads on) an accused widget that has only the two elements AB, or (because of the comprising transition) by an accused widget ABC or by an accused widget ABCXY or by an accused widget ABXYZ. But when an additional element is added so that the claim recites "a widget comprising elements A, B, and C," then in order for the claim to be literally infringed an accused widget must have all three elements ABC (at a minimum). The scope of this claim is represented by the smaller, interior circle. Because the three-element claim uses a comprising transition, it also is infringed by an accused widget ABCXY or by an accused widget ABCXYZ. The accused widgets AB and ABXYZ infringe the former two-element claim but not the latter three-element claim because both accused widgets lack an element C. Because the potential universe of infringing devices is smaller for the three-element claim (as represented by the smaller circular area of the interior circle in Figure 2.3), it is narrower in scope than the two-element claim.

Determining the optimal scope of a claim is a trade-off because its exclusionary scope must be balanced against its sustainable validity. In other words, the scope of a patent claim should not be determined in isolation from consideration of its validity. A claim that is relatively broader in that it is enforceable against a greater number of accused devices is correspondingly easier to invalidate for lack of novelty[65] or for obviousness.[66] For example, the claim to "a widget comprising A and B," represented by the larger circle in Figure 2.3, is more susceptible to invalidation than the claim to "a widget comprising A, B, and C." These relationships lead to the following maxim favored by Judge Giles Rich:

> The strongest claims are the weakest, and the weakest claims the strongest.

This maxim simply means that the claims that are broadest in scope (i.e., the strongest in terms of enforcement against the greatest possible number of accused devices) are also the most vulnerable to invalidation by the prior art, and vice versa.

D. Independent and Dependent Claims

Patent claims are drafted in either independent or dependent form. A dependent claim is one that refers to (or depends from) some other, previously presented claim, while an independent claim stands alone without referring to any other claim. A dependent claim includes (i.e., incorporates by reference) all limitations of the claim from which it depends, and also adds some further limitation(s). Thus, use of the dependent form of claiming is merely a shorthand way of repeating the limitations of some other claim while adding some additional limitation(s).

These claiming principles are governed by the following provisions of 35 U.S.C. §112:

> **(c) Form.**—A claim may be written in independent or, if the nature of the case admits, in dependent or multiple dependent form.
> **(d) Reference in Dependent Forms.**—Subject to subsection (e) [claims in multiple dependent form], a claim in dependent form shall contain a reference to a claim previously set forth and then specify a further limitation of the subject matter claimed. A claim in dependent form shall be construed to incorporate by reference all the limitations of the claim to which it refers. . . .[67]

The important principle of *claim differentiation* provides that the existence of a dependent claim shows that the independent claim from which it depends is not so (thus) limited. For example, if claim 1 of a hypothetical patent recites "a widget comprising A, B, and C," and claim 2 of the patent recites "the widget of claim 1 wherein A is red,"

---

[65]*See* Chapter 4 ("Novelty, Loss of Right, and Priority Pre- and Post-America Invents Act of 2011 (35 U.S.C. §102)"), *infra*.
[66]*See* Chapter 5 ("The Nonobviousness Requirement (35 U.S.C. §103)"), *infra*.
[67]35 U.S.C. §§112(c)-(d) (eff. Sept. 16, 2012).

this means that the widget of claim 2 must comprise a red A, a B (of any color), and a C (of any color). The existence of dependent claim 2 shows that the widget of independent claim 1 is *not* limited to having a red A; rather (barring some sort of limiting language in the written description), the A element in claim 1 can be of any color, whether red or blue or green or anything else. The existence of claim 2 differentiates the widget of claim 2 from the widget of claim 1. Claim 2 in this example also can be thought of as a subset or species of claim 1, which recites a genus of widgets.

For purposes of illustration, consider a hypothetical patent having 20 claims, consisting of 2 independent claims and 18 dependent claims, arranged as shown in Figure 2.4.

Claim 1. A widget comprising A, B, and C.

        [Independent claim (broadest in scope of all 20 claims)]

Claim 2. The widget of claim 1, wherein said A is purple.

        [Dependent claim, narrower in scope than claim 1]

Claim 3. The widget of claim 2, wherein said B is green.

        [Dependent claim, narrower in scope than claim 2]

Claim 4. The widget of claim 3, wherein said C is brown.

        [Dependent claim, narrower in scope than claim 3]

. . .

Claim 10. A widget consisting of A, B, and C.

        [Second independent claim, narrower in scope than the first independent claim, claim 1, because "consisting" transition is used]

Claim 11. The widget of claim 10, wherein said A is purple.

Claim 12. The widget of claim 11, wherein said B is green.

Claim 13. The widget of claim 12, wherein said C is brown.

. . . .

Figure 2.4

Example Claim Groupings (*Continued*)

Claim 20. The widget of claim 19, wherein said A is adjacent to said B.

[Narrowest claim of patent, or "picture" claim— identically covers the product that patentee is selling to the public]

Figure 2.4

Example Claim Groupings

This typical claiming structure can be visualized as two inverted pyramids that represent the variation in scope of the claims from broadest to narrowest, as depicted in Figure 2.5.

Claim 1 (broadest scope)

Claim 9

Claim 10

Claim 20 (narrowest scope)

Figure 2.5

Scope Representation for Example Claim Groupings of Figure 2.4

E.   Specialized Claiming Formats

In addition to the basic claiming techniques mentioned above, U.S. patent claiming practice uses a number of recognized formats. The use of each specialized format is at the option of the claims drafter. Choice of claiming format can significantly impact the interpretation and scope of the claim in both *ex parte* examination and patent infringement litigation. Some of the most commonly used claiming formats are "means-plus-function" claims, "product-by-process" claims, *Jepson* claims, and *Markush* claims. Each format is discussed below.

1. Means-Plus-Function Claim Elements (35 U.S.C. §112(f))

a. *Introduction*

Functional claiming refers to the general notion of claiming an invention by what it does, rather than what it is in terms of physical structure. For example, one might functionally claim a "means for fastening part A to part B" rather than reciting a specific structure such as "a nail."

Section 112(f) of the Patent Act governs a particular type of functional claiming.[68] The statute provides that an element in a claim for a combination (of two or more elements) can be claimed in terms of what the element *does,* rather than what its structure is, by expressing the element as a generic "means" that performs a recited function, without reciting its structure. Although this type of means-plus-function claiming is used more frequently for claiming mechanical or electrical inventions than for chemical or biotechnological inventions, all students of patent law need to understand the origins and operation of means-plus-function claiming.

The U.S. Supreme Court in 1946 prohibited functional claiming at the exact point of novelty in *Halliburton Oil Well Cementing Co. v. Walker.*[69] Congress statutorily overruled the *Halliburton* prohibition by enacting then ¶3 of §112 in the 1952 Patent Act. Today, the means-plus-function claiming provision appears as the sixth and final paragraph of 35 U.S.C. §112:

> **(f) Element in Claim for a Combination.**—An element in a claim for a combination may be expressed as a means or step for performing a specified function without the recital of structure, material, or acts in support thereof, and such claim shall be construed to cover the corresponding structure, material, or acts described in the specification and equivalents thereof.[70]

Because the statute speaks of "[a]n element in a claim *for a combination,*" the use of "single means claims"—that is, claims reciting only a single element expressed in means-plus-function terms—is prohibited. However, claims reciting two or more elements are permitted even though each element may be expressed in means-plus-function format. Thus, a claim to a "widget comprising a means for fastening

---

[68]The America Invents Act of 2011 renamed the sixth paragraph of 35 U.S.C. §112 (generally referred to as "35 U.S.C. §112, ¶6") as 35 U.S.C. §112(f) (eff. Sept. 16, 2012) (titled "Element in Claim for a Combination").

[69]329 U.S. 1 (1946).

[70]35 U.S.C. §112(f) (eff. Sept. 16, 2012).

A to B" is not permitted, but a claim to a "widget comprising A, B, and means for fastening A to B" is. Similarly, a claim reciting a "widget comprising a means for [performing function X] and a means for [performing function Y]" is permissible, because this claim includes more than one means-plus-function element.

More commonly, the claims drafter will use the means-plus-function format to express those elements that can be performed by many different types of structures or devices. All such structures or devices need not be explicitly disclosed in the patent application, so long as at least one "corresponding structure" is clearly identified in the written description.[71] In this manner a claim can cover a relatively large number of possible structures without the patent application becoming excessively detailed.

For example, a claim to an athletic shoe might recite

An athletic shoe comprising:

  (i)   a left upper portion,
  (ii)   a right upper portion,
  (iii) a sole portion integrally connected to said left upper portion and to said right upper portion, and
  (iv)   means for detachably fastening said left upper portion to said right upper portion.

This claim includes four elements. Elements (i) through (iii) are structural elements—they recite physical items. Element (iv) is expressed in means-plus-function form, because it recites a generic "means" for performing a function, in this case the function of "detachably fastening said left upper portion to said right upper portion," without reciting any structure that could be used to perform the fastening function.

b. *Interpreting the Scope of Means-Plus-Function Elements*

If the athletic shoe claim above were construed on its face, without reference to the statutory language of 35 U.S.C. §112(f), one might conclude that the means element would read on (i.e., literally encompass) any and every possible structure in the universe that would perform the recited fastening function. Given the breadth of such a claim, it

---

[71]*See* McGinley v. Franklin Sports, Inc., 262 F.3d 1339, 1347 (Fed. Cir. 2001) (rejecting accused infringer's argument that means-plus-function limitation of asserted claim was not entitled to any range of equivalents as "wholly without merit," and explaining that "[d]rafters of means-plus-function claim limitations are statutorily guaranteed a range of equivalents extending beyond that which is explicitly disclosed in the patent document itself . . . .").

might be attacked as indefinite under 35 U.S.C. §112(b) (and possibly non-enabled under 35 U.S.C. §112(a)). However, because element (iv) is expressed in means-plus-function form, it must be interpreted in accordance with §112(f). Because this section operates to narrow the scope of the claim, as explained below, paragraph (f) saves the claim from indefiniteness.

The last clause of §112(f) mandates that a means element in a patent claim "shall be construed to cover the corresponding structure, material, or acts described in the specification and equivalents thereof." This is mandatory language, which requires that in order to interpret the scope of a means-plus-function element in a claim, reference to the written description must be made. The written description portion of the patent must disclose the "corresponding structure" (or corresponding material or acts) for the means recited in the claim. Failure to do so renders the claim indefinite under §112(b). As explained in *In re Donaldson Co.,*[72]

> [a]lthough paragraph six [of 35 U.S.C. §112] statutorily provides that one may use means-plus-function language in a claim, one is still subject to the requirement [of 35 U.S.C. §112, ¶2] that a claim "particularly point out and distinctly claim" the invention. Therefore, if one employs means-plus-function language in a claim, one must set forth in the specification an adequate disclosure showing what is meant by that language. If an applicant fails to set forth an adequate disclosure, the applicant has in effect failed to particularly point out and distinctly claim the invention as required by the second paragraph of section 112.[73]

As an example of corresponding structure, assume that the written description of the athletic shoe patent in the above example stated that "a pair of shoe laces can be used to detachably fasten the left upper portion of the shoe to the right upper portion," and that the drawings of the patent depicted the use of shoe laces. The recited means for fastening in element (iv) of the claim would be interpreted in accordance with the last clause of §112(f) as reading on the disclosed structure, that is, a pair of shoe laces, as well as any "equivalents thereof." The equivalents thereof, sometimes also referred to as statutory equivalents, need not be (and usually are not) explicitly disclosed in the patent. Determining just what types of items would qualify as equivalents thereof to the shoe laces would likely need to be resolved in litigation. For example, one might conclude that the statutory equivalents of the disclosed shoe laces are buttons, hooks and eyes, and zippers. This is considered a question of fact.[74]

---

[72]16 F.3d 1189 (Fed. Cir. 1994) (*en banc*).

[73]*In re Donaldson Co.*, 16 F.3d at 1195.

[74]*See* In re Hayes Microcomputer Prods., Inc. Patent Litig., 982 F.2d 1527, 1541 (Fed. Cir. 1992) (stating that the "determination of literal infringement (of a §112, ¶6

But suppose that the athletic shoe patent had been granted prior to the invention of Velcro®. Would a later-developed athletic shoe that used a pair of Velcro® tabs as fasteners, instead of shoe laces, literally infringe the patent? The issue raised by this hypothetical is whether the statutory equivalents of a means element must be in existence at the time the patent is granted in order to be considered within the literal scope of the claim. The Federal Circuit answered in the affirmative in *Al-Site Corp. v. VSI Int'l, Inc.,*[75] holding that "an equivalent structure or act under §112 for literal infringement must have been available at the time of patent issuance. . . . "[76] This rule seems correct from the standpoint of preserving the definiteness of the claim under 35 U.S.C. §112(b); it is difficult to see how a claim that literally encompassed technology not yet in existence could satisfy the statutory requirement for claims that "particularly point out and distinctly claim" the subject matter that the applicant regards as his invention.

The threshold determination of whether a claim element should be treated as a means-plus-function element begins with examining the words used to draft the element.[77] The Federal Circuit recognizes a presumption that a claim element using the word "means" will be treated as a means-plus-function element under the sixth paragraph of 35 U.S.C. §112.[78] As explained above, such treatment results in limiting the literal scope of the element to the corresponding structure described in the specification and equivalents thereof.

Even though the word "means" is used in a claim, however, the presumption that §112(f) applies may be rebutted "if the claim limitation itself recites sufficient structure to perform the claimed function in its entirety."[79] For example, the patent in suit in *TI Group Automotive Sys. (N. Am.), Inc. v. VDO N. Am., L.L.C.,*[80] covered an in-tank fuel

---

claim element) is a question of fact").

[75]174 F.3d 1308 (Fed. Cir. 1999).

[76]*Al-Site Corp.*, 174 F.3d at 1320.

[77]The Federal Circuit views the determination of whether certain claim language invokes §112, ¶6 as an exercise in claim construction, and therefore a question of law subject to *de novo* review. Inventio AG v. ThyssenKrupp Elevator Ams. Corp., 649 F.3d 1350, 1356 (Fed. Cir. 2011) (citing Personalized Media Comm., LLC v. ITC, 161 F.3d 696, 702 (Fed. Cir. 1998)).

[78]*See* Rembrandt Data Techs., LP v. AOL, LLC, 641 F.3d 1331, 1340 (Fed. Cir. 2011) (stating that "[a] claim limitation that 'contains the word "means" and recites a function is presumed to be drafted in means-plus-function format under 35 U.S.C. §112, ¶6'") (quoting Net MoneyIN, Inc. v. VeriSign, Inc., 545 F.3d 1359, 1366 (Fed. Cir. 2008)); TriMed, Inc. v. Stryker Corp., 514 F.3d 1256, 1259 (Fed. Cir. 2008) (stating that "[u]se of the word 'means' in claim language creates a presumption that §112 ¶6 applies") (citing Greenberg v. Ethicon Endo-Surgery, Inc., 91 F.3d 1580, 1583 (Fed. Cir. 1996)).

[79]Rembrandt Data Techs., LP v. AOL, LLC, 641 F.3d 1331, 1340 (Fed. Cir. 2011).

[80]375 F.3d 1126 (Fed. Cir. 2004).

assembly for fuel-injected vehicle engines. Independent claim 2 of TI Group's U.S. Patent No. 4,860,714 recited:

> 2. Apparatus for pumping fuel from a fuel tank to an engine comprising: . . . (d) pumping *means* for pumping fuel into the reservoir, said means being located within the reservoir in the region of the opening and including a nozzle and a venturi tube in alignment with the nozzle, the passage of fuel out of the nozzle and through the venturi tube causing fuel to be entrained through the opening into the interior of the reservoir; . . . . [81]

Applying the presumption, a district court interpreted the "pumping means" element as a means-plus-function element under 35 U.S.C. §112, ¶6 (2000).

The Federal Circuit in *TI Group* reversed, because the limitation recited not only the pumping means but also its structure, location, and operation. Specifically, the claim element recited the structure of the pumping means ("including a nozzle and a venturi tube in alignment with the nozzle"), its location ("being located within the reservoir in the region of the opening"), and the manner of its operation ("the passage of fuel out of the nozzle and through the venturi tube causing fuel to be entrained through the opening into the interior of the reservoir"). In this case, the presumption arising from the use of the word "means" was overcome by the recitation in the claim of the structure needed to perform the recited function of "pumping fuel into the reservoir." Moreover, the written description informed and supported the structure recited in the claims by referring to "[j]et pump 30 [which] includes nozzle 54 and venturi tube 58," the numbers corresponding to reference numerals in the patent's drawings.

Conversely, a claim element that does not use the word "means" is presumptively *not* treated as a means-plus-function element.[82] Nevertheless, such "means"-less elements may be interpreted as means-plus-function elements under certain narrow circumstances. For example, the patents in suit in *Welker Bearing Co. v. PHD, Inc.*[83] were directed to pin clamps that held a work piece securely in place during welding and other manufacturing processes. Claim 1 of Welker Bearing's U.S. Patent No. 6,913,254 recited "a locating and clamping assembly . . . characterized by a *mechanism for moving said [clamping] finger along a straight line into and out of said locating pin perpendicular to said axis A in response to said rectilinear movement of said*

---

[81]*TI Group*, 375 F.3d at 1131.

[82]*See* Inventio AG v. ThyssenKrupp Elevator Am. Corp., 649 F.3d 1350, 1356 (Fed. Cir. 2011) (characterizing this presumption as "strong" and "not readily overcome").

[83]550 F.3d 1090 (Fed. Cir. 2008).

locating pin."[84] Notably, the quoted claim limitation did not include the word "means" but rather made use of the similarly generic word "mechanism."

Based on the lack of any structural context for "mechanism" in the language of the claim limitation, the Federal Circuit in *Welker Bearing* affirmed a district court's decision to treat it as a means-plus-function limitation. No adjective provided "mechanism" with a physical or structural component; the claim language merely recited the function of the "mechanism" (i.e., moving the clamping finger in response to movement of the locating pin). One of ordinary skill would have had to consult the specification to find any structural connotation for the recited "mechanism." The appellate court concluded that in the case at bar, "the unadorned term 'mechanism' is 'simply a nonce word or a verbal construct that is not recognized as the name of structure and is simply a substitute for the term "means for.'"[85]

c. *Distinguishing §112(f) Statutory Equivalents and the Doctrine of Equivalents*

A word of caution is in order here about potentially confusing terminology. The *literal* scope of a means-plus-function claim includes the statutory "equivalents thereof." In that sense, at least, the statutory equivalents of 35 U.S.C. §112(f) are not the same animal as the

---

[84]Emphasis added. Claim 1 in its entirety read:

A locating and clamping assembly comprising:
> a body defining an internal cavity and an opening from said cavity to the exterior of said body;
> a locating pin disposed in said cavity and extending along an axis A out of said opening to a distal end;
> an actuator for moving said locating pin rectilinearly along said axis A into and out of said opening;
> at least one finger supported by said locating pin adjacent said distal end;

> said assembly characterized by a mechanism for moving said finger along a straight line into and out of said locating pin perpendicular to said axis A in response to said rectilinear movement of said locating pin.

Welker Bearing, 550 F.3d at 1093-1094 (emphasis added).

[85]*Welker Bearing*, 550 F.3d at 1096 (quoting Lighting World, Inc. v. Birchwood Lighting, Inc., 382 F.3d 1354, 1360 (Fed. Cir. 2004)). The treatment of "mechanism" as a means-plus-function limitation in *Welker Bearing* resulted in a finding of non-infringement. The structure disclosed in the written description that corresponded to the "mechanism" was a rotating central post. The accused device "propel[led] clamping fingers in and out of the locating pin without any rotational movement." Because the patented rotational mechanism and the accused linear-moving mechanism were "substantially different," the Federal Circuit affirmed a district court's judgment that the latter did not literally infringe.

"equivalents" referred to in application of the judicially created **doctrine of equivalents,** which is addressed in a later chapter of this text.[86] As Professor Chisum has explained, "[u]nlike the doctrine of equivalents, which compares a patent *claim* with an accused product or process, Section 112/6 [post-AIA, §112(f)] entails a comparison of one structure, material or act (that in the specification) to another structure, material or act (that in a product or process alleged to be covered by the patent claim)."[87]

Despite these differences, the Federal Circuit has sanctioned the use of the same insubstantial differences test for equivalency under 35 U.S.C. §112, ¶6 as under the doctrine of equivalents.[88] Because one way of establishing insubstantial differences is to apply the classic tripartite "function, way, and result" test,[89] the Federal Circuit also has held that this test collapses to "way" and "result" when applied to §112, ¶6 claim elements.[90] This is because in order to have **literal infringement** of a means-plus-function claim, the function performed by the accused component must be *identical,* not merely insubstantially different, to the function recited in the claim. Thus, the "substantially identical function" part of the function-way-result test is not applicable when determining literal infringement of a means-plus-function claim.

The previous discussion has focused exclusively on the *literal* scope of a means-plus-function element in a claim. Can there be infringement of a claim drafted in means-plus-function format under the judicially created doctrine of equivalents? This is, in a sense, asking if a statutory equivalent can have a judicial equivalent. Some Federal Circuit judges have answered the question in the negative, objecting to the idea of the patentee getting a "second bite at the apple."[91] On the other hand, other opinions of the Federal Circuit recognize the possibility of infringement under the doctrine of equivalents when the

[86]*See* Chapter 9 ("Patent Infringement"), *infra.* The doctrine of equivalents permits a finding of patent infringement liability for accused devices that are not encompassed within the literal scope of a claim, but that differ from the claimed invention in merely insubstantial respects.

[87]5A-18A DONALD S. CHISUM, CHISUM ON PATENTS §18.03 (2008) (citations omitted).

[88]*See* Chiuminatta Concrete Concepts, Inc. v. Cardinal Indus. Co., 145 F.3d 1303, 1309 (Fed. Cir. 1998) (stating that "[t]he proper test is whether the differences between the structure in the accused device and any disclosed in the specification are insubstantial").

[89]*See* Graver Tank & Mfg. Co. v. Linde Air Prods., 339 U.S. 605, 608 (1950).

[90]*See* Al-Site Corp. v. VSI Int'l, Inc., 174 F.3d 1308, 1321 n.2.

[91]*See* Dawn Equip. Co. v. Kentucky Farms, Inc., 140 F.3d 1009, 1022 (Fed. Cir. 1998) (Plager, J., expressing "additional views") (asserting that under a proper understanding of 35 U.S.C. §112, ¶6, "the separate judicially-created doctrine of equivalents would have no application to those limitations drawn in means-plus-function form").

equivalent is after-arising, that is, developed after the patent issued.[92] Yet other opinions recognize that infringement under the doctrine of equivalents also might be possible when the function of the accused component is only insubstantially different, but not identical to, the function recited in the means-plus-function claim element.[93] The case law development in this area is still in flux, and deserves close monitoring by those who draft and/or enforce patents having means-plus-function claims.

2.   Product-by-Process Claims

The "product-by-process" claiming format is used primarily in claiming chemical and biotechnological inventions, although it is not limited to that subject matter. The product-by-process claiming technique was developed in Patent Office practice[94] as a way of claiming a product, such as a composition of matter or an article of manufacture, that could not be adequately identified by its structure (e.g., the structure was unknown and could not be determined). Rather, the only way of identifying the product was through a recitation of the process by which it was made. The rationale for permitting product-by-process claiming was that "the right to a patent on an invention is not to be denied because of the limitations of the English language, and, in a proper case, a product may be defined by the process of making it. . . . [T]he limitations of known technology concerning the subject matter sought to be patented should not arbitrarily defeat the right to a patent on an invention."[95]

In examining claims for patentability (i.e., for novelty[96] and nonobviousness[97]), the USPTO interprets product-by-process claims as drawn

---

[92]*See* NOMOS Corp. v. BrainLAB USA, Inc., 357 F.3d 1364, 1369 (Fed. Cir. 2004) (observing that "[w]hen there is no literal infringement of a means-plus-function claim because the accused device does not use identical or equivalent structure, . . . the doctrine of equivalents might come into play when after-developed technology is involved"); *Chiuminatta*, 145 F.3d at 1310-1311 (holding that where accused device represents technology that predates claimed invention, "a finding of non-equivalence for §112, ¶6, purposes should preclude a contrary finding under the doctrine of equivalents").

[93]*See* Interactive Pictures Corp. v. Infinite Pictures, Inc., 274 F.3d 1371, 1381-1382 (Fed. Cir. 2001) (distinguishing *Chiuminatta* and explaining that "when a finding of noninfringement under 35 U.S.C. §112, paragraph 6, is premised on an absence of identical *function*, then infringement under the doctrine of equivalents is not thereby automatically precluded").

[94]Product-by-process claiming was permitted by the U.S. Patent Office as early as 1891. *See* In re Bridgeford, 357 F.2d 679, 682 (C.C.P.A. 1966).

[95]*In re Bridgeford*, 357 F.2d at 682.

[96]*See* Chapter 4 ("Novelty, Loss of Right, and Priority Pre- and Post-America Invents Act of 2011 (35 U.S.C. §102)"), *infra*.

[97]*See* Chapter 5 ("The Nonobviousness Requirement (35 U.S.C. §103)"), *infra*.

to the product, and not limited by the process steps recited in the claim. The agency effectively ignores the process steps in examining such claims. For example, consider the following product-by-process claim:

A composition of matter X, made by a process comprising the steps of:

(a) obtaining Y,
(b) mixing Y with Z to form a mixture,
(c) heating the mixture to a temperature of 100 degrees C for 30 minutes,
(d) cooling the mixture to form a precipitate,
(e) recovering said precipitate, and
(f) isolating X from said precipitate.

The USPTO's practice in examining this claim for patentability would be to interpret it as a claim to the product X per se, not limited to X made by following the recited process steps (a) through (f). Thus, the USPTO will consider the claim anticipated (i.e., lacking novelty) if the prior art discloses the identical product X made by *any* process, whether that process comprises the steps recited in the claim, uses genetic engineering or nuclear fusion techniques, or employs any other methodology to produce X.

Heated controversy arose within the Federal Circuit in 1992 over the proper interpretation of product-by-process claims in litigation over infringement of issued patents. In 1991, the Federal Circuit held in *Scripps Clinic & Res. Found. v. Genentech, Inc.*[98] that because claims should be treated the same way in determining infringement or validity, a product-by-process claim in an issued patent in litigation should *not* be considered limited by the recited process steps.[99] In other words, according to *Scripps Clinic,* a federal district court should broadly interpret a product-by-process claim in the same manner as the USPTO would, by ignoring the process limitations.

The following year, however, a different panel of the Federal Circuit concluded that the *Scripps* panel had erred.[100] The panel in

---

[98]927 F.2d 1565 (Fed. Cir. 1991). The *Scripps Clinic* opinion was authored for the court by Judge Newman and joined by then–Chief Judge Markey and a federal district court judge sitting by designation.

[99]*See Genentech*, 927 F.2d at 1583 (holding that "[s]ince claims must be construed the same way for validity and for infringement, the correct reading of product-by-process claims is that they are not limited to product prepared by the process set forth in the claims.").

[100]*See* Atlantic Thermoplastics Co. v. Faytex Corp., 970 F.2d 834, 838 n.2 (Fed. Cir. 1992) (asserting that "[a] decision that fails to consider Supreme Court precedent does not control if the court determines that the prior panel would have reached a different

Atlantic Thermoplastics Co. v. Faytex Corp.[101] held that "process terms in product-by-process claims serve as limitations in determining infringement."[102]

Applying the *Atlantic Thermoplastics* rule to the product-by-process claim in the above example means that the claim has a significantly narrower scope and, hence, economic value. The patent owner seeking to establish literal infringement of the claim would need to prove not only that the accused infringer's product X was the same as that recited in the claim but also that the accused product X was made by the same process as that recited in the claim.[103]

Despite the clear conflict between the *Scripps Clinic* and *Atlantic Thermoplastics* decisions, and over the dissents of then–Chief Judge Nies, Judge Rich, Judge Newman, and Judge Lourie,[104] a majority of Federal Circuit judges refused to rehear the *Atlantic Thermoplastics* case *en banc*. While both decisions stood, they generated confusion and uncertainty for those enforcing patents containing product-by-process claims.[105]

The Federal Circuit eventually resolved the conflict in 2009 by deciding *en banc* a portion of its opinion in *Abbott Labs. v. Sandoz, Inc.*[106] Following the *Atlantic Thermoplastics* rule, the *en banc* majority in *Abbott Labs.* held that "process terms in product-by-process claims serve as limitations in determining infringement."[107] Because the accused product was made by a process different from that recited in Abbott's product-by-process claims, the Federal Circuit affirmed a district court's summary judgment of noninfringement.

The patent in suit in *Abbott Labs.* was directed to the antibiotic cefdinir in its crystalline form. Claim 1 of Abbott's U.S. Patent No.

---

conclusion if it had considered controlling precedent," and concluding that *Scripps Clinic* decision was not controlling on this basis).

[101]*Atlantic Thermoplastics Co.*, 970 F.2d at 834. The *Atlantic Thermoplastics* opinion was authored for the court by Judge Rader and joined by Judge Archer and Judge Michel.

[102]*Atlantic Thermoplastics Co.*, 970 F.2d at 846-847.

[103]Whether an accused product X made by any other process would infringe is a question to be resolved under the doctrine of equivalents. *See* Chapter 9 ("Patent Infringement"), *infra*.

[104]*See* Atlantic Thermoplastics Co. v. Faytex Corp., 974 F.2d 1279 (Fed. Cir. 1992) (dissenting opinions from denial of rehearing *en banc*).

[105]*See* Ronald D. Hantman, *Why Not the Statute? Revisited*, 83 J. Pat. & Trademark Off. Soc'y 685, 711 (2001) (describing trial courts' difficulties in determining which decision is controlling).

[106]566 F.3d 1282 (Fed. Cir. 2009) (addressing Part III.A.2 of opinion *en banc*). Then–Chief Judge Michel and Judges Bryson, Gajarsa, Linn, Dyk, Prost, and Moore joined Part III.A.2, which was authored by Judge Rader. Judges Newman and Lourie dissented in separate opinions, with Judges Mayer and Lourie joining in Judge Newman's dissent. Judge Schall did not participate as a member of the *en banc* court.

[107]*Abbott Labs.*, 566 F.3d at 1293.

4,935,507 recited the composition of matter crystalline cefdinir, characterized by a series of peaks at the diffraction angles in its powder X-ray diffraction pattern. Claims 2-5 of the Abbott patent recited the crystalline cefdinir product without any particular peak limitations, but "obtainable" through a series of process steps.[108] As a threshold matter, the Federal Circuit agreed with the district court that claims 2-5 were properly categorized as product-by-process claims.

The Federal Circuit then rejected patentee Abbott's argument that the district court had erred by following *Atlantic Thermoplastics* rather than *Scripps Clinic*. The Federal Circuit reviewed the "extensive support" it found in Supreme Court precedent for the *Atlantic Thermoplastics* rule that process terms limit product-by-process claims. It also cited pre-1982 regional circuit decisions applying the rule. Notably, the *Abbott Labs.* court also relied on the Supreme Court's 1997 watershed decision in *Warner-Jenkinson Co. v. Hilton Davis Chemical Co.*,[109] rendered several years after the Federal Circuit's conflicting decisions in *Scripps Clinic* and *Atlantic Thermoplastics*:

> [T]he Supreme Court has reiterated the broad principle that "[e]ach element contained in a patent claim is deemed material to defining the scope of the patented invention." *Warner-Jenkinson*, 520 U.S. at 19, 117 S. Ct. 1040. Although *Warner-Jenkinson* specifically addressed the doctrine of equivalents, this rule applies to claim construction overall. As applied to product-by-process claims, *Warner-Jenkinson* thus reinforces the basic rule that the process terms limit product-by-process claims. To the extent that *Scripps Clinic* is inconsistent with this rule, this court hereby expressly overrules *Scripps Clinic*.[110]

Responding to the dissenting opinions, the *en banc* majority in *Abbott Labs.* asserted that its decision in no way called into question the right of inventors to include product-by-process claims in their patents.[111] Rather, its decision "merely restate[d] the rule that the

---

[108]For example, claim 5 of Abbott's '507 patent recited:

5. Crystalline 7-[2-(2-aminothiazol-4-yl)-2-hydroxyiminoacetamido]-3-vinyl -3-cephem-4-carboxylic acid (syn isomer) which is obtainable by dissolving 7-[2-(2-aminothiazol-4-yl)-2-hydroxyiminoacetamido]-3-vinyl-3-cephem-4-carboxylic acid (syn isomer) in an alcohol, continuing to stir the solution slowly under warming, then cooling the solution to room temperature and allowing the solution to stand.

Abbott Labs., 566 F.3d at 1286.

[109]520 U.S. 17 (1997).

[110]*Abbott Labs.*, 566 F.3d at 1293.

[111]*See Abbott Labs.*, 566 F.3d at 1293 (stating that "[t]his court's en banc decision in no way abridges an inventor's right to stake claims in product-by-process terms."). The court further opined that "[i]n the modern context . . . if an inventor invents a product whose structure is either not fully known or too complex to analyze (the subject of this case—a product defined by sophisticated PXRD technology—suggests that these

defining limitations of a claim—in this case process terms—are also the terms that show infringement."[112] The majority could not "simply ignore as verbiage the only definition supplied by the inventor."[113]

Because patentee Abbott Laboratories had conceded that its claims 2-5 were not literally infringed by the accused product of generic drug manufacturer Lupin Pharmaceuticals "if the product-by-process analysis is performed pursuant to *Atlantic Thermoplastics*,"[114] the Federal Circuit affirmed the district court's finding of no literal infringement. In view of their prosecution history, the product-by-process claims were not infringed under the doctrine of equivalents, either.[115] Nor was equivalency under the doctrine established by the U.S. Food and Drug Administration's decision that Lupin's generic product was bioequivalent to Abbott's approved drug product.[116]

3. *Jepson* Claims

The *Jepson* claiming format, which takes its name from a 1917 Patent Office decision,[117] is most frequently used in the claiming of mechanical inventions, but is not limited to that subject matter.

---

concerns may no longer in reality exist), this court clarifies that the inventor is absolutely free to use process steps to define this product. The patent will issue subject to the ordinary requirements of patentability. The inventor will not be denied protection." *Id.* at 1294.

[112]*Abbott Labs.*, 566 F.3d at 1293.

[113]*Abbott Labs.*, 566 F.3d at 1294.

[114]*Abbott Labs.*, 566 F.3d at 1296.

[115]Claims 2-5 recited "crystalline" cefdinir made by a particular process. In view of the patent's prosecution history, the meaning of "crystalline" was limited to the "Crystal A" form of cefdinir; the patentee had effectively disclaimed the "Crystal B" form. Lupin's accused cefdinir product, the bulk of which comprised the "Crystal B" form, was outside any permissible scope of equivalents. (Whether the accused Lupin product contained some amount of the Crystal A form of cefdinir was not an issue on appeal.)

[116]*See Abbott Labs.*, 566 F.3d at 1298. The Federal Circuit explained that:

[w]hile bioequivalency may be relevant to the function prong of the function-way-result test, bioequivalency and equivalent infringement are different inquiries. Bioequivalency is a regulatory and medical concern aimed at establishing that two compounds are effectively the same for pharmaceutical purposes. In contrast, equivalency for purposes of patent infringement requires an element-by-element comparison of the patent claim and the accused product, requiring not only equivalent function but also equivalent way and result. Different attributes of a given product may thus be relevant to bioequivalency but not equivalent infringement, and vice versa.

566 F.3d at 1298.

[117]*See* Ex parte Jepson, 1917 Dec. Comm'r Pat. 62, 243 Off. Gaz. Pat. Office 526 (1917).

A *Jepson* claim includes a preamble that begins with the word "in" and ends with the phrase, "an improvement comprising" or "the improvement comprising. . . ." For example, the Federal Circuit considered the following claim, written in *Jepson* format, to a double-walled softball bat:

> *In* a hollow bat having a small-diameter handle portion and a large-diameter impact portion, *an improvement comprising* an internal structural insert defining an annular gap with an inside wall of the impact portion of the bat and the impact portion elastically deflectable to close a portion of the annular gap and operably engage the insert.[118]

Jepson claims are understood to impliedly admit that anything recited in the preamble of the claim is in the prior art.[119] Although preamble language in patent claims is not necessarily limiting, the language in a *Jepson* claim's preamble is generally considered to be limiting.[120] This is because the patentee's choice of a *Jepson* format is seen as an indication of intent to use the preamble to define, in part, the structural features of the claimed invention.

Thus in the above example claim, the applicant is impliedly admitting that a "hollow bat having a small-diameter handle portion and a large-diameter impact portion" is in the prior art. What is novel is the "improvement" portion of the claimed invention, in this case, the "internal structural insert." However, the right to exclude for which the patent is granted is defined by the entirety of the claim, that is, the improvement in combination with the preamble elements.[121] Thus, in order to find infringement of a *Jepson* claim, every limitation of the claim, including the preamble, must be met in the accused device either literally or equivalently.[122]

[118]DeMarini Sports, Inc. v. Worth, Inc., 239 F.3d 1314, 1319 (Fed. Cir. 2001) (emphasis added to indicate *Jepson* claim format).

[119]An exception to this rule applies when the preamble recites the patentee's own prior work. *See* Reading & Bates Constr. Co. v. Baker Energy Res. Corp., 748 F.2d 645, 649-650 (Fed. Cir. 1984).

[120]*See* Epcon Gas Sys., Inc. v. Bauer Compressors, Inc., 279 F.3d 1022, 1029 (Fed. Cir. 2002).

[121]*See* Pentec, Inc. v. Graphic Controls Corp., 776 F.2d 309, 315 (Fed. Cir. 1985) (stating that "[a]lthough a preamble is impliedly admitted to be prior art when a *Jepson* claim is used, . . . the claimed invention consists of the preamble in combination with the improvement").

[122]*See Epcon Gas*, 279 F.3d at 1029.

4. *Markush* Claims

The *Markush* claiming format, which was officially sanctioned at least as early as a 1925 Patent Office decision,[123] is used primarily in claiming chemical and biotechnological inventions, although it is not limited to that subject matter. "*Markush* groups" are used to claim a class of chemical compounds in terms of a structural formula, where a given substituent of the compound can be selected from among a customized list (i.e., an artificial genus) of alternatives, each of which will result in a compound having the same asserted utility.[124]

For example, a *Markush* claim might read as follows:

> A composition of matter comprising C2H5-R, where R is selected from the group consisting of W, X, Y, and Z.

The *Markush* group recited in this claim lists all possible species of R in the claimed composition: W, X, Y, or Z. There is no set number of species that must be included in a *Markush* grouping. Moreover, it is permissible that the various species recited in a *Markush* group have different chemical or physical properties, so long as each one, when substituted in the claimed composition, results in a product having the same asserted utility.

For example, in *In re Harnisch*[125] the CCPA considered *Markush* claims to a class of dyes known as coumarin compounds. The court reversed the USPTO's rejection of the claims as drawn to "improper *Markush* groups" on the ground that the members of the groups were not "functionally equivalent." All of the enumerated compounds were dyes, the court explained, even though some of them were chemical intermediates. The compounds within the *Markush* groups were "not repugnant to scientific classification,"[126] and were all part of a single invention, such that "unity of invention"[127] existed, making the *Markush* groups proper.

---

[123]*See* Ex parte Markush, 1925 Dec. Comm'r Pat. 126, 340 Off. Gaz. Pat. Office 839 (1925).

[124]*See* In re Driscoll, 562 F.2d 1245, 1249 (C.C.P.A. 1977) (explaining that "[i]t is generally understood that in thus describing a class of compounds an applicant is, in effect, asserting that the members of the *Markush* group do not fall within any recognized generic class, but are alternatively usable for the purposes of the invention, and therefore, regardless of which of the alternatives is substituted on the basic structure, the compound as a whole will exhibit the disclosed utility").

[125]631 F.2d 716 (C.C.P.A. 1980).

[126]In re Harnisch, 631 F.2d at 722.

[127]The phrase "unity of invention" has a well-recognized meaning in European patent practice. *See* European Patent Convention (2007), art. 82, *available at* http://www.epo.org/patents/law/legal-texts/html/epc/2000/e/ar82.html (providing that "[t]he European patent application shall relate to one invention only or to a group of inventions so

In some cases of *Markush* claiming, the USPTO may consider the enumerated members of the *Markush* group to be "independent and distinct" inventions. If this is the case, the agency may require that the applicant provisionally elect a single species for purposes of examination.[128]

---

linked as to form a single general inventive concept"). The CCPA in *Harnisch* referred to the "unity of invention" concept because in the court's view, "the term would be more descriptive and more intelligible internationally than is the more esoteric and provincial expression 'Markush practice.'" *Harnisch*, 631 F.2d at 721.

[128]The MPEP provides in pertinent part:

> [Members of a *Markush* group are considered "independent and distinct"] where two or more of the members are so unrelated and diverse that a prior art reference anticipating the claim with respect to one of the members would not render the claim obvious under 35 U.S.C. 103 with respect to the other member(s). In applications containing a Markush-type claim that encompasses at least two independent or distinct inventions, the examiner may require a provisional election of a single species prior to examination on the merits. An examiner should set forth a requirement for election of a single disclosed species in a Markush-type claim. . . . Following election, the Markush-type claim will be examined fully with respect to the elected species and further to the extent necessary to determine patentability. If the Markush-type claim is not allowable, the provisional election will be given effect and examination will be limited to the Markush-type claim and claims to the elected species, with claims drawn to species patentably distinct from the elected species held withdrawn from further consideration.

UNITED STATES PATENT AND TRADEMARK OFFICE, MANUAL OF PATENT EXAMINING PROCEDURE §803.02 (8th ed., 8th rev., 2010), *available at* http://www.uspto.gov/web/offices/pac/mpep/mpep.htm.

Disclosure Requirements (35 U.S.C. §112(a))

A. Introduction

1. The Statutory Framework

The three **disclosure** requirements for a U.S. patent application are found in the first paragraph of 35 U.S.C. §112 (titled "Specification"), which provides

> **(a) In General.**—The specification shall contain a *written description of the invention,* and of the manner and process of making and using it, in such full, clear, concise, and exact terms as to *enable* any person skilled in the art to which it pertains, or with which it is most nearly connected, to make and use the same, and shall set forth the *best mode* contemplated by the inventor or joint inventor of carrying out the invention.[1]

When patent attorneys speak of "the disclosure" or "the teaching" of a patent, they generally are referring to the information provided in the specification other than the claims (i.e., the "written description" portion of the patent, which may include drawings).[2] The italicized terms in the statutory language quoted above are understood as identifying three separate requirements for the disclosure of a patent, each of

---

[1]35 U.S.C. §112(a) (eff. Sept. 16, 2012) (emphases added). Before implementation of the Leahy-Smith America Invents Act of 2011, the individual subparagraphs of 35 U.S.C. §112 were not designated by letter. What is designated as §112(a) after September 15, 2012, was commonly referred to as "§112, ¶1" or "§112, first paragraph" before that date. *See* 35 U.S.C. §112 (2006) (providing that "[t]he specification shall contain a written description of the invention, and of the manner and process of making and using it, in such full, clear, concise, and exact terms as to enable any person skilled in the art to which it pertains, or with which it is most nearly connected, to make and use the same, and shall set forth the best mode contemplated by the inventor of carrying out his invention").

[2]*See* In re Rasmussen, 650 F.2d 1212, 1214 (C.C.P.A. 1981) ("Disclosure is that which is taught, not that which is claimed.").

which is discussed below: (1) **enablement,** (2) **best mode,** and (3) **written description of the invention.**

These disclosure requirements pertain to the informative quality of the patent *application* rather than the technical merits of the claimed invention. Even assuming that the claimed invention is novel,[3] nonobvious,[4] and useful,[5] if the patent application does not satisfy the disclosure requirements of the first paragraph of 35 U.S.C. §112 with respect to that invention, the applicant will not be granted a patent.

For example, the inventor in *In re Glass*[6] filed a patent application directed to methods and apparatus for artificially growing high-strength crystals used to reinforce refractory materials. Although the USPTO did not challenge the novelty or utility of the claimed invention, the Court of Customs and Patent Appeals (CCPA) affirmed the agency's conclusion that the application's disclosure was fatally deficient under the first paragraph of 35 U.S.C. §112. The application did not disclose essential process parameters such as temperature, pressure, and vapor saturation conditions that the inventor had conceded were necessary to form the crystals, either because the applicant was not himself in possession of that information or simply chose to maintain it as a trade secret. In either case, the inventor was not entitled to a patent on his invention because the application did not satisfy the enablement requirement of the first paragraph of 35 U.S.C. §112.[7]

Likewise, an issued patent, although entitled to a rebuttable presumption of validity that includes a presumption of validity under all three requirements of §112(a), may be invalidated in litigation if the challenger can establish, by clear and convincing evidence, that either the enablement requirement[8] or the written description of the invention requirement[9] was not, in fact, complied with.[10]

---

[3]*See* Chapter 4 ("Novelty, Loss of Right, and Priority Pre- and Post-America Invents Act of 2011 (35 U.S.C. §102)"), *infra*.

[4]*See* Chapter 5 ("The Nonobviousness Requirement (35 U.S.C. §103)"), *infra*.

[5]*See* Chapter 6 ("The Utility Requirement (35 U.S.C. §101)"), *infra*.

[6]492 F.2d 1228 (C.C.P.A. 1974).

[7]*See id.* at 1233 (agreeing with USPTO that "the specification leaves too much to conjecture, speculation, and experimentation and is, therefore, insufficient in law to support any of the appealed claims").

[8]*See generally infra* Section B ("The Enablement Requirement").

[9]*See generally infra* Section D ("The Written Description of the Invention Requirement").

[10]*See* 35 U.S.C. §282 ("Presumption of validity; defenses"). The presumption of validity, and the challenger's burden to rebut it, are discussed in further detail in Chapter 10 ("Defenses to Patent Infringement"), *infra*. As discussed later in this chapter, the America Invents Act of 2011 eliminated the possibility of challenging a patent's validity on the ground of failure to satisfy one of the three disclosure requirements, namely, the best mode requirement. *See* 35 U.S.C. §282(b)(3)(A) (eff. Sept. 16, 2011); *see also infra* Section C.1 ("Best Mode Scale-Back by America Invents Act of 2011").

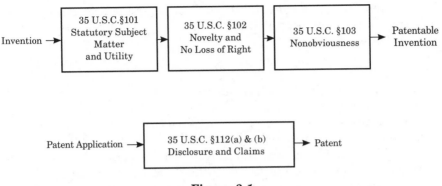

Figure 3.1

Pathway to Patentability

To summarize, obtaining a patent requires not only that the claimed *invention* meets various statutory criteria (detailed in later chapters of this text) but also that the *disclosure* of that invention provided in the patent application satisfies its own statutory criteria. These parallel requirements are depicted in Figure 3.1.

2. Disclosure as *Quid Pro Quo*

The disclosure requirements of 35 U.S.C. §112(a) effectively implement the *quid pro quo* of the patent system. In other words, the statute demands that the applicant's disclosure of her useful, novel, and nonobvious process, machine, manufacture, or composition of matter be of sufficient detail and clarity. In exchange for receiving that disclosure, which will ultimately be disseminated to the public, the U.S. government agrees to convey to the inventor a time-limited right to exclude others from practicing her invention.[11]

Of course, for various strategic and/or economic reasons an inventor may choose not to disclose her invention through patenting and instead maintain it as a trade secret.[12] Trade secret protection is significantly less powerful than patent protection, however, and subject to loss through the inventor's failure to maintain secrecy of the

---

[11]The nature of the "exclusive right," or right to exclude others, that a patent grants is further examined in Chapter 1 ("Foundations of the U.S. Patent System"), *supra*.

[12]*See* United States v. Dubilier Condenser Corp., 289 U.S. 178, 186 (1933) (recognizing that an inventor "may keep his invention secret and reap its fruits indefinitely," but that "[i]n consideration of its disclosure and the consequent benefit to the community, the patent is granted").

information.[13] The stronger rights provided by the patent system help to ensure that innovation is ultimately divulged to the public rather than suppressed.

3.   Timing of Disclosure Compliance

The question whether a patent application satisfies each of the three disclosure requirements of 35 U.S.C. §112(a) (eff. Sept. 16, 2012) (i.e., enablement, best mode, and written description of the invention) is analyzed as of the application's filing date, not at some later date (such as the time of any subsequent infringement litigation in which invalidity under 35 U.S.C. §112(a) might be raised as a counterclaim or affirmative defense[14]). The patent application must comply with the disclosure requirements when it is filed.[15] Its teachings cannot be supplemented with new information (termed **new matter**[16]) after the filing date in order to come into compliance with 35 U.S.C. §112(a).

---

[13]*See* Uniform Trade Secrets Act §1(4) (amended 1985) (defining trade secret as "information . . . that . . . is the subject of efforts that are reasonable under the circumstances to maintain its secrecy").

[14]*See* In re Hogan, 559 F.2d 595, 605-607 (C.C.P.A. 1977) (holding that post-filing date development by third party of novel form of generically claimed polymer did not render original disclosure nonenabling; what counts is whether claimed invention *as it was understood at the filing date* was enabled).

[15]*See* In re Glass, 492 F.2d 1228, 1232 (C.C.P.A. 1974) (holding that "application sufficiency under §112, first paragraph, must be judged as of its filing date").

[16]The addition of "new matter" is prohibited by 35 U.S.C. §132. That section "prohibits addition of new matter to the original disclosure. It is properly employed as a basis for objection to amendments to the abstract, specifications, or drawings attempting to add new disclosure to that originally presented." In re Rasmussen, 650 F.2d 1212, 1214-1215 (C.C.P.A. 1981).

The phrase "new matter" is

> a technical legal term in patent law — a term of art. Its meaning has never been clearly defined for it cannot be. The term is on a par with such terms as infringement, obviousness, priority, abandonment, and the like which express ultimate legal conclusions and are in the nature of labels attached to results after they have been reached by processes of reasoning grounded on analyses of factual situations. In other words, the statute gives us no help in determining what is or is not "new matter." We have to decide on a case-by-case basis what changes are prohibited as "new matter" and what changes are not.

In re Oda, 443 F.2d 1200, 1203 (C.C.P.A. 1971) (Rich, J.). The fundamental principle underlying the new matter prohibition is that "the invention described in the original patent [or application] must not be changed." *Id.* at 1204-1205.

The word "new" as used in "new matter" is not interpreted in its most literal extent. The CCPA explained that "[i]n a sense, anything inserted in a specification that was not there before is *new* to the specification but that does not necessarily mean it is prohibited as 'new matter.'" *Id.* at 1203 (emphasis added). For example, the *Oda* court held that the changing of "nitrous" to "nitric" did not introduce new matter. In preparation

Nor can the applicant rely on information provided by others, published after the application's filing date, to argue that the application's disclosure, supplemented by such publications, suffices to satisfy the statutory requirements by the time the application issues as a patent.[17] This is true even if the information is included in the disclosure of another's earlier-filed but not yet published patent application.[18] If an applicant cannot supply enabling information at the time when she files her patent application, then she is not yet in a position to file.[19]

The USPTO will allow patent applicants to satisfy the disclosure requirements in the first paragraph of 35 U.S.C. §112 by incorporating by reference (i.e., including a cross-reference to but not reproducing the actual text of) "essential material" from certain sources external to the patent application under examination, that is, either (1) a U.S. patent, or (2) a published U.S. patent application.[20] The applicant cannot incorporate essential material through reference to nonpatent publications or foreign patents or foreign patent applications (whether or not published). The intent in forbidding incorporation by reference through documents other than U.S. patents and published U.S. patent applications is to minimize the burden on the public to "search for and

---

for filing in the United States, Oda's Japanese language patent application was translated into English. In so doing the phrase "nitric acid," present in several working examples of the written description, was mistranslated as "nitrous acid." After the patent had issued, Oda filed an application to reissue it in order to correct the translation error. The CCPA reversed the USPTO's rejection of the reissue claims as being based on a specification that contained prohibited new matter. The evidence of record showed that a skilled chemist would have recognized the error and realized that a translation error had occurred. *See id.* at 1206 (concluding that "one skilled in the art would appreciate not only the existence of error in the specification but what the error is . . . [a]s a corollary, it follows that when the nature of this error is known it is also known how to correct it.").

[17]*See Glass*, 492 F.2d at 1232 (citing "new matter" prohibition of 35 U.S.C. §132 and also noting that, in accordance with practice of treating application's filing date as date of constructive reduction to practice of the invention claimed therein, disclosure in application when filed cannot be said to evidence a completed invention if information to be found only in subsequent publications is needed for enablement).

[18]*See id.* at 1231 (affirming USPTO's refusal to allow Glass to rely on contents of four patents issued to others that were filed prior to Glass's filing date; although these patents would have qualified as prior art under 35 U.S.C. §102(e), as of their filing date they did "not show what is known generally to 'any person skilled in the art,' to quote from §112," because their content was not publicly available as of that date).

[19]*Id.* at 1232.

[20]*See* 37 C.F.R. §1.57(c) (2008). The patent or published application that is referred to must not itself incorporate essential material by reference. *See id.* In other words, there can be only one "layer" of incorporation by reference for essential material. "Essential material" includes material that is necessary to satisfy the enablement, best mode, and/or written description requirements of 35 U.S.C. §112(a) (eff. Sept. 16, 2012). *See id.*

obtain copies of documents incorporated by reference which may not be readily available."[21]

When an invention sought to be patented involves biological material (e.g., bacteria, DNA, plant tissue cultures, and seeds), it is customary for the applicant to deposit a sample of the material with a depository such as the American Type Culture Collection (ATCC).[22] Such a deposit is necessary (not optional) if the biological material cannot be sufficiently described in words to satisfy the disclosure requirements in the first paragraph of §112.[23] In *In re Lundak*,[24] the Federal Circuit held that even though Lundak deposited his sample (of a claimed new human cell line) with the ATCC seven days after the filing date of his patent application, he had not violated the new matter prohibition. The court observed that as of his application filing date, Lundak had already deposited samples of his cell line with colleagues at the University of California and elsewhere. This established a constructive reduction to practice of the invention as of the filing date. Had the USPTO needed to examine the cell line during the pendency of Lundak's application, the agency could have requested a sample from Lundak under 35 U.S.C. §114.[25]

The Federal Circuit held that it was "not material whether this request [would be] filled directly by the applicant, or on the instructions of the applicant by a third person to whom the applicant has entrusted the specimen."[26] In sum, the disclosure requirements of §112, ¶1 do "not require the transfer of a sample of the invention to an independent depository prior to the filing date of the patent

---

[21]*See* UNITED STATES PATENT AND TRADEMARK OFFICE, MANUAL OF PATENT EXAMINING PROCEDURE §608.01(p) (8th ed., rev. July 2010), *available at* http://www.uspto.gov/web/offices/pac/mpep/mpep.htm. *See also* In re Hawkins, 486 F.2d 569, 572 (C.C.P.A. 1973) (quoting USPTO Board of Appeals' opinion as stating that "[w]hat is available to a foreign patent office is not necessarily available to the United States Patent Office. It may be that such material may never be made available to the United States Patent Office."). The *Hawkins* court ultimately reversed the USPTO's decision that the applicant's post-filing addition to the application of the information originally incorporated by reference from certain British patent applications was a prohibited addition of "new matter" after the filing date. The court found that "at least so much of the British applications as dealt with the contemplated utility for the present products . . . is *not* new matter within the meaning of 35 U.S.C. 132. It was identified and specifically referred to for that information in the U.S. application *as filed*." *Id.* at 575.

[22]For more information on patent deposits with the ATCC, *see* http://www.atcc.org/DepositServices/PatentDepository/tabid/237/Default.aspx (last visited July 11, 2012).

[23]The USPTO's rules on biological deposits are extensive and beyond the scope of this book. Interested readers should consult 37 C.F.R. §§1.801-1.809.

[24]773 F.2d 1216 (Fed. Cir. 1985).

[25]Section 114 of 35 U.S.C. provides in part that "[w]hen the invention relates to a composition of matter, the Director may require the applicant to furnish specimens or ingredients for the purpose of inspection or experiment."

[26]*Lundak*, 773 F.2d at 1222.

application."[27] Lundak's initial deposit with university colleagues and later deposit with the ATCC satisfied the requirements of USPTO access to a sample of Lundak's cell line throughout his application's pendency.[28]

Under post–America Invents Act of 2011 (AIA) rules, the date at which an application's compliance with the §112 disclosure requirements is measured is the same date as that used for the determination of novelty and nonobviousness, that is, the effective filing date of the claimed invention.[29] Under pre-AIA rules, however, the date at which compliance with the first paragraph of §112 is evaluated may differ from the date on which novelty and nonobviousness are evaluated. Because our pre-AIA rules are based on the United States' historic first-to-invent priority system,[30] the novelty and nonobviousness of an invention are evaluated as of its "invention date."[31] Although the USPTO initially takes the applicant's filing date as the presumptive invention date under a theory of **constructive reduction to practice**,[32] an earlier actual invention date may be established by means of appropriate evidentiary submissions.[33]

---

[27]*Id.*

[28]A second important requirement for deposits of biological materials is that the public be able to access the material after grant of the patent. Lundak's ATCC deposit, properly identified in his specification, met this requirement. More particularly, a biological deposit must be stored under an agreement with a depository which ensures that the material will be "available beyond the enforceable life of the patent for which the deposit was made." 37 C.F.R. §1.806 ("Term of Deposit").

[29]*See* 35 U.S.C. §100(i)(1) (eff. Mar. 16, 2013) (defining term "effective filing date" for a "claimed invention in a patent or application for patent"); *see also* 35 U.S.C. §102 (eff. Mar. 16, 2013) (repeatedly referring to the "effective filing date of the claimed invention"); 35 U.S.C. §103 (eff. Mar. 16, 2013) (referring to the "effective filing date of a claimed invention").

[30]*See generally infra* Chapter 4, Part II ("Novelty, Loss of Right, and Priority Pre- and Post-America Invents Act of 2011").

[31]*See* 35 U.S.C. §§102(a), (e), (g) (2006); 35 U.S.C. §103 (2006). In this sense, "novelty" is distinct from "loss of right" under 35 U.S.C. §102(b) (2006), which evaluates the status of an invention's introduction into the public domain as of a date that is one year before the application filing date. "Invention date" is defined *infra* Chapter 4, Section G.3.

[32]A "constructive reduction to practice" occurs when an inventor files a patent application that discloses his invention in compliance with the first paragraph of 35 U.S.C. §112. The inventor need not have built a prototype or constructed any samples of his invention in order to constructively reduce it to practice, so long as he can provide a sufficient disclosure of the invention in his patent application. In contrast, an **actual reduction to practice** involves constructing a physical embodiment of the invention that works for its intended purpose.

[33]Chapter 4, Section O, *infra*, describes the pre-AIA practice of "antedating" or "swearing behind" a prior art reference by filing an affidavit with the USPTO in accordance with 37 C.F.R. §1.131.

B.   The Enablement Requirement

The enablement requirement is grounded in the Patent Act's mandate that

> The specification shall contain a written description of the invention, and of the manner and process of making and using it, in such full, clear, concise, and exact terms as to *enable* any person skilled in the art to which it pertains, or with which it is most nearly connected, to make and use the same. . . . [34]

Thus, the enablement provision specifies that an inventor must disclose both "how to make" the invention as well as "how to use" it. For example, if the claimed invention is a new chemical compound, the application must include an enabling disclosure of how to synthesize the compound, as well as reveal how the compound is used (e.g., in the form of a therapeutic composition to be administered to humans with a certain disease).

The ultimate goal of the enablement requirement is to put the public in effective "possession" of the invention, by providing to persons of ordinary skill in the art a detailed description of how to make and use the invention. Once the patent expires, and with it the patentee's right to exclude others, these persons should be in a position to make and use the invention without "undue experimentation" (discussed below). The enabling disclosure thus provides a type of a blueprint that such persons can follow once the patent expires, and they are free to make and use the invention without liability.

The "how to use" requirement of 35 U.S.C. §112(a) (eff. Sept. 16, 2012) is closely tied to the utility requirement of 35 U.S.C. §101, discussed later in this text.[35] If an inventor does not know what the utility (or usefulness) of her invention is, then logically she cannot describe how to use the invention.[36]

1.   Undue Experimentation

Case law has engrafted an *undue experimentation* qualifier onto the enablement requirement as set forth in 35 U.S.C. §112(a) (eff. Sept. 16, 2012). A patent application will be considered enabling so long as the disclosure permits the hypothetical person skilled in the

---

[34]35 U.S.C. §112(a) (eff. Sept. 16, 2012) (emphasis added).

[35]*See* Chapter 6 ("The Utility Requirement (35 U.S.C. §101)"), *infra.*

[36]*See* In re Brana, 51 F.3d 1560, 1564 (Fed. Cir. 1995) (noting that "[o]bviously, if a claimed invention does not have utility, the specification cannot enable one to use it.").

art to make and use the invention "without undue experimentation."[37] That the art worker might have to conduct *some* experimentation in order to make and use the invention as broadly as it is claimed is not fatal; only when the degree of experimentation becomes *undue* has the patent application failed to meet the enablement requirement.[38] A patent application need not disclose what is well known in the art;[39] otherwise, patent documents would become product manufacturing specifications, which they are not intended to be.

Whether the degree of experimentation needed to reproduce the claimed invention has become undue, meaning that the enablement requirement has not been satisfied, turns on the application of a number of factors set forth by the Federal Circuit in *In re Wands*,[40] including

(1) the quantity of experimentation necessary;
(2) the amount of direction or guidance presented;
(3) the presence or absence of working examples;
(4) the nature of the invention;
(5) the state of the prior art;
(6) the relative skill of those in the art;
(7) the predictability or unpredictability of the art; and
(8) the breadth of the claims.[41]

Several of these factors are addressed individually below. The *Wands* factors should be analyzed by the USPTO examiner during *ex parte* prosecution of pending patent applications, as well as by the courts in litigation challenging the validity of issued patents on nonenablement grounds. Not every *Wands* factor need be reviewed in every enablement determination, however; the factors are considered "illustrative, not mandatory."[42] Given the facts of a particular case, some factors may be more relevant than others.[43]

[37]*See* In re Wands, 858 F.2d 731, 737 (Fed. Cir. 1988) (recognizing that the phrase "without undue experimentation" is nonstatutory).

[38]*Id*. at 736-737. For example, the quantity of experimentation necessary to carry out the patented numerical control system for machine tools in *White Consol. Indus., Inc. v. Vega Servo-Control, Inc.*, 713 F.2d 788 (Fed. Cir. 1983), was sufficiently high that the Federal Circuit affirmed a district court's holding of invalidity based on noncompliance with the enablement requirement. The record reflected that the claimed system could be carried out only by (1) obtaining access to software maintained as a trade secret, or (2) independently writing software code that would have required 1.5-2 person-years of effort. *See id*. at 790-792.

[39]*Wands*, 858 F.2d at 735.

[40]*Id*. at 731.

[41]*Id*. at 737 (citing In re Forman, 230 U.S.P.Q. 546, 547 (Bd. Pat. App. & Int. 1986)).

[42]Amgen, Inc. v. Chugai Pharm. Co., 927 F.2d 1200, 1213 (Fed. Cir. 1991).

[43]The ultimate question of whether a disclosure is enabling under the first paragraph of 35 U.S.C. §112 is a question of law that the Federal Circuit reviews *de novo*;

2.   *Wands* Factor: Predictable Versus Unpredictable Inventions

The enablement analysis is inherently fact-specific and differs in every case. But one *Wands* factor very often central to the inquiry is whether the invention is considered to be within a "predictable" or "unpredictable" technology.[44] In general, inventions in the mechanical and electrical arts are considered to be predictable. Based on generally well-understood laws of physics, thermodynamics, and other basic scientific principles, if one embodiment of the invention is adequately described, then we can predict fairly easily how other embodiments within the scope of the claimed invention could be made and used.[45]

---

factual findings made on the various underlying *Wands* factors are reviewed in accordance with the "clearly erroneous" standard for bench trials and with the "unsupported by substantial evidence" standard for jury trials.

[44]*See* In re Fisher, 427 F.2d 833 (C.C.P.A. 1970). The CCPA, in an oft-quoted passage from *Fisher*, stated that:

> It is apparent that such an inventor should be allowed to dominate the future patentable inventions of others where those inventions were based in some way on his teachings. Such improvements, while unobvious from his teachings, are still within his contribution, since the improvement was made possible by his work. It is equally apparent, however, that he must not be permitted to achieve this dominance by claims which are insufficiently supported and hence not in compliance with the first paragraph of 35 U.S.C. §112. That paragraph requires that the scope of the claims must bear a *reasonable correlation* to the scope of enablement provided by the specification to persons of ordinary skill in the art. In cases involving *predictable* factors, such as mechanical or electrical elements, a single embodiment provides broad enablement in the sense that, once imagined, other embodiments can be made without difficulty and their performance characteristics predicted by resort to known scientific laws. In cases involving *unpredictable* factors, such as most chemical reactions and physiological activity, the scope of enablement obviously varies inversely with the degree of unpredictability of the factors involved.

Id. at 839 (emphases added).

[45]Exceptions to this general rule exist, even in the mechanical arts. For example, the court in *Liebel-Flarsheim Co. v. Medrad, Inc.*, 481 F.3d 1371 (Fed. Cir. 2007), rejected the patentee's argument that its disclosure of a single embodiment enabled a broader mechanical claim. Two of Liebel's patents in suit were directed to power injectors with replaceable syringes capable of withstanding high pressures for delivering a contrast agent to patients. The as-filed claims required a pressure jacket in front of the opening that received the syringe, but the claims were thereafter amended to remove the pressure jacket limitation. During litigation challenging the validity of the patents, Liebel contended that because it had undisputedly provided an enabling disclosure of its preferred embodiment (i.e., an injector with a pressure jacket), it had sufficiently enabled the full scope of its issued claims (i.e., encompassing injectors both with or without a pressure jacket). Affirming the district court, the Federal Circuit rejected Liebel's argument. The appellate court observed that Liebel's patent specifications depicted only jacketed injectors, and in fact "taught away" from jacketless injectors by characterizing them as "impractical." *See id.* at 1379. The Federal Circuit concluded

For example, consider a mechanical invention claimed as "a widget comprising part A attached to part B by means of a fastener." If the patent application discloses that A can be satisfactorily attached to B by means of a common nail, we can predict that other combinations employing a screw, glue, or Velcro as fasteners would also probably work. At a minimum, a person of ordinary skill in the art of widgets could probably evaluate the feasibility of such alternatives without undue experimentation.

This predictive assumption about alternative embodiments is generally not made in the case of inventions in the chemical and biotechnological arts. In these technologies, at least certain aspects of which are generally considered unpredictable, a minor change in the physical structure of a molecule or compound can result in major changes in properties and functions. In order to be enabling, a patent application directed to these types of inventions must provide a correspondingly greater degree of how-to-make and how-to-use information, in contrast with the disclosure of a simple mechanical device like the widget example above.[46] Exceptions to this rule may be recognized, of course,

---

that undue experimentation would have been required of a person of ordinary skill to make the jacketless injectors, based on testimony by the inventors that their own experiments with such injectors failed. As a result, the inventors deemed a jacketless system "too risky" for further development. Noting the irony of invalidation for non-enablement on the heels of Liebel's earlier, successful argument for a broad claim interpretation, the Federal Circuit repeated the well-known warning "beware of what one asks for."

[46]The Federal Circuit confronted an "unpredictable art" in one of the court's watershed biotechnology cases, *Amgen, Inc. v. Chugai Pharm. Co.*, 927 F.2d 1200 (Fed. Cir. 1991). There the Federal Circuit affirmed the trial court's conclusion that Amgen's generic claims, directed to purified and isolated DNA sequences encoding erythropoietin (EPO, a protein that stimulates the production of red blood cells) and host cells transformed or transfected with a DNA sequence, were invalid because the specification did not provide an enabling disclosure commensurate with the broad scope of the claims. The claims "cover[ed] all possible DNA sequences that will encode any polypeptide having an amino acid sequence 'sufficiently duplicative' of EPO to possess the property of increasing production of red blood cells," *id.* at 1212, and thus, "the number of claimed DNA encoding sequences that can produce an EPO-like product is potentially enormous," the Federal Circuit explained. *Id.* at 1213. Noting the trial court's finding that the technology at issue lacked predictability, *id.*, the Federal Circuit concluded its discussion of enablement as follows:

Considering the structural complexity of the EPO gene, the manifold possibilities for change in its structure, with attendant uncertainty as to what utility will be possessed by these analogs, we consider that more is needed concerning identifying the various analogs that are within the scope of the claim, methods for making them, and structural requirements for producing compounds with EPO-like activity. It is not sufficient, having made the gene and a handful of analogs whose activity has not been clearly ascertained, to claim all possible genetic sequences that have EPO-like activity.

Id. at 1214.

as originally unpredictable technologies mature over time and become better understood and hence more predictable.[47]

Many inventions involve multiple components or factors, some mechanical, some chemical, some physiological, and so on. Consider, for example, the "gene chips" formed by layering DNA nucleotides onto silicon, now being used to screen patients for genetic abnormalities that may indicate a propensity for a certain disease.[48] Certain components of such inventions may be considered within the predictable arts and others not; the inventions do not neatly fall within the mechanical or chemical category. Rather than try to classify the predictability of an invention as a whole, the better approach is to separately consider the nature of each component or factor of the invention. As explained in *In re Cook*,[49] it is preferable to "see [this issue] denominated a dichotomy between predictable and unpredictable factors in any art rather than between 'mechanical cases' and 'chemical cases.'"[50]

3. *Wands* Factor: Scope of the Claims

Another *Wands* factor often of great importance in enablement determinations is the scope of the claims sought by the patent applicant. The degree of enabling disclosure provided by the written description and drawings must bear a "reasonable correlation" to the scope of the claims.[51] In other words, the applicant must seek a right to exclude others from the claimed invention that is reasonably related in scope to the extent of her inventive contribution as disclosed in the patent application.

Deceptively simple on its face, the task of awarding the "right" claim scope for a particular disclosure of a novel and nonobvious invention actually involves a delicate balancing of policy concerns. If an inventor is awarded claims of scope significantly greater than the scope of her enabling disclosure, the public is harmed because subsequent improvers will be blocked unjustly by the original inventor's patent

---

[47]*See* Enzo Biochem, Inc. v. Calgene, Inc., 188 F.3d 1362, 1375 n.10 (Fed. Cir. 1999) (recognizing that "[i]n view of the rapid advances in science, . . . what may be unpredictable at one point in time may become predictable at a later time").

[48]*See, e.g., Using Gene Chips, Scientists Identify Unique Form of Disease*, GENOMICS & GENETICS WKLY. (News RX, Atlanta, Ga.), Dec. 21, 2001, at 6.

[49]439 F.2d 730 (C.C.P.A. 1971).

[50]*Id.* at 734.

[51]*See* In re Fisher, 427 F.2d 833, 839 (C.C.P.A. 1970). *See also* In re Angstadt, 537 F.2d 498, 502 (C.C.P.A. 1976) (summarizing the relevant inquiry in enablement cases as "whether the scope of enablement provided to one of ordinary skill in the art by the disclosure is such as to be commensurate with the scope of protection sought by the claims").

and disinclined to conduct follow-on research in this area. On the other hand, if the patent protection awarded is no broader in scope than the specific embodiments disclosed in the application, the resulting patent is of little economic value.[52] As succinctly stated by Federal Circuit Judge Newman, "[t]he boundary defining the excludable subject matter must be carefully set: it must protect the inventor, so that commercial development is encouraged; but the claims must be commensurate in scope with the inventor's contribution."[53]

The U.S. Supreme Court grappled with these same policy concerns in the infamous case of Samuel Morse, who invented the telegraph but broadly claimed patent rights in "the use of the motive power of the electric or galvanic current, which I call electro-magnetism, however developed, for making or printing intelligible characters, letters, or signs, at any distances. . . . "[54] The Court held Morse's claim invalid as "too broad,"[55] which modern patent law would interpret as meaning "not supported by an enabling disclosure reasonably commensurate with the scope of the claim."

The problem of balancing claim scope against the extent of the disclosure is particularly challenging when a patent applicant claims his invention "generically" and has disclosed one or more "species" that fall within the genus. How many illustrative species must the application disclose in order to satisfy the enablement requirement? For example, in a world without furniture (as hypothesized in Chapter 1 of this text), if an inventor was the first to conceive and reduce to practice a four-legged, straight-back chair, should she be allowed to control all later-developed chairs, no matter how designed? Should she be able to prevent others from making and selling rocking chairs, reclining chairs, and bean-bag chairs, which she herself never actually contemplated? Consider also an applicant who discloses that the

[52]In a leading article on patent scope, Professors Merges and Nelson contend that "[a]t first blush it might seem to make sense to limit the rights of a patentee to only those embodiments of the invention she has disclosed in her specification, i.e., those that she has actually created at the time the patent application is filed. But imitators would soon find some minor variation over the disclosed embodiments; with such an ultra-narrow enablement principle, they would then have a nonenablement defense if the patentee tried to enforce the patent. Such a rule would soon render patents useless." Robert P. Merges & Richard R. Nelson, *On the Complex Economics of Patent Scope*, 90 Colum. L. Rev. 839, 845 (1990).

[53]In re Wands, 858 F.2d 731, 741 (Fed. Cir. 1988) (Newman, J., concurring-in-part and dissenting-in-part).

[54]O'Reilly v. Morse, 56 U.S. 62, 112 (1853) (reproducing eighth claim of Morse's patent); *see id.* at 113 (holding that Morse's eighth claim was "too broad, and not warranted by law," because Morse had "claim[ed] an exclusive right to use a manner and process which he has not described and indeed had not invented, and therefore could not describe when he obtained his patent").

[55]*Id.*

inert gas argon is useful in her invention—a novel method of depositing silicon on a substrate to make semiconductor chips—but generically claims the method as comprising the step of using any noble gas. To what extent should we allow this inventor to exclude others from using embodiments that she has not in fact made or tested?

There is no one-size-fits-all answer to these questions, but the Federal Circuit has instructed as follows:

> It is well settled that patent applicants are not required to disclose every species encompassed by their claims, even in an unpredictable art. However, there must be sufficient disclosure, either through illustrative examples or terminology, to teach those of ordinary skill how to make and use the invention as broadly as it is claimed. . . . [56] The first paragraph of §112 requires nothing more than *objective* enablement. . . . How such a teaching is set forth, either by the use of illustrative examples or by broad terminology, is irrelevant.[57]

4. *Wands* Factor: Working Examples

The "working examples" referred to in *Wands* are commonly included in patent applications to help satisfy the enablement requirement, although examples are not required by statute.[58] Examples that appear in patents are simply specific, illustrative sets of instructions or "recipes" for how to make and/or use the claimed invention. They are less likely to appear in applications directed to fairly simple inventions. For example, the hot beverage cup–insulating sleeve patent reproduced in Chapter 1 of this book does not contain any working examples.[59]

Patent applications may contain two different types of examples.[60] "Working examples" disclose the results of experiments or tests that were actually performed. "Prophetic examples," also referred to as paper examples, suggest how a person of ordinary skill in the art might

[56]In re Vaeck, 947 F.2d 488, 496 & n.23 (Fed. Cir. 1991) (Rich, J.) (citations omitted).

[57]*Id.* at n.23 (citations omitted) (emphasis in original).

[58]*See* In re Borkowski, 422 F.2d 904, 908 (C.C.P.A. 1970) (stating that "a specification need not contain a working example if the invention is otherwise disclosed in such a manner that one skilled in the art will be able to practice it without an undue amount of experimentation").

[59]*See* U.S. Patent No. 5,425,497 (issued June 20, 1995), reproduced in Chapter 1, Section C.5, *supra*.

[60]*See* UNITED STATES PATENT AND TRADEMARK OFFICE, MANUAL OF PATENT EXAMINING PROCEDURE §2164.02 (8th ed., rev. July 2010), *available at* http://www.uspto.gov/web/offices/pac/mpep/mpep.htm ("Working Example").

go about experimenting with or testing the invention in the future.[61] Prophetic examples should be written in the present or future tense, not in the past tense, because they have not actually been conducted.

5.   Nascent and After-Arising Technology

How should courts determine if a patent application's disclosure is enabling when the patent claims are later asserted to cover embodiments of the invention that were not in existence when the patent application was filed? Courts are increasingly likely to confront this issue of "after-arising" or "later-arising" technology when dealing with rapidly advancing scientific disciplines, as aptly illustrated by *Chiron Corp. v. Genentech, Inc.*[62] The Chiron patent in that case issued from a continuation-in-part (CIP) application filed in 1995; it was the last in a chain of CIPs relating back to a 1984 parent application.[63] The asserted claims of the patent were directed to monoclonal antibodies that bind to human c-erbB-2 antigen (HER2) associated with breast cancer cells. Chiron sued Genentech for infringement based on Genentech's sales of Herceptin, a humanized antibody useful for the long-term treatment of breast cancer. A district court broadly interpreted Chiron's claims as encompassing not only monoclonal antibodies made using traditional hybridoma (murine) technology, but also to include those antibodies made using modern genetic engineering techniques. The latter type of antibodies included "chimeric" antibodies that combine DNA encoding regions from more than one type of species, and "humanized" antibodies that comprise DNA encoding regions primarily from humans (i.e., the type of antibodies used in Genentech's accused product). The district court's interpretation was based in part on an express definition included in written description of the 1995 application (but not in earlier applications in the chain) that the term "antibody . . . encompasses . . . chimeric antibodies and humanized antibodies." On appeal, the Federal Circuit accepted this claim interpretation as correct.

The central dispute before the Federal Circuit was whether Chiron's patent applications filed in the 1980s satisfied the enablement requirement of 35 U.S.C. §112, ¶1 for the claims as broadly interpreted in the litigation. The parties had stipulated before trial that if Chiron could not establish entitlement of the claims of the patent in suit to the filing date of any of the earlier 1984, 1985, or 1986 applications in the

---

[61]*See, e.g.,* In re Strahilevitz, 668 F.2d 1229, 1233 (C.C.P.A. 1982) (describing prophetic example 13 detailing method of preparation of matrix with bound antibodies).
[62]363 F.3d 1247 (Fed. Cir. 2004).
[63]Continuation-in-part applications are discussed *supra* Chapter 1, Section H.5.

chain,[64] then the patent would be invalid based on intervening prior art. The jury found against Chiron on this issue, concluding that none of the 1984, 1985, or 1986 applications satisfied *both* the enablement and written description of the invention requirements. The verdict form did not require the jury to specify whether enablement, written description, or both, were not satisfied.

All three Federal Circuit judges on the *Chiron* panel agreed that the *1985* and *1986* applications did not satisfy the enablement requirement with respect to the monoclonal antibodies as claimed in the Chiron patent in suit. The majority opinion authored by Circuit Judge Rader characterized the genetically engineered antibodies (encompassed by the claims as interpreted by the district court) as "nascent" technology in the 1985 and 1986 time period. For such "nascent" technology, Judge Rader wrote, the enabling disclosure must provide a "specific and useful teaching."[65] Judge Rader would locate nascent technology on a "knowledge continuum" somewhere between "routine" technology, which a patentee "preferably omits from the disclosure," and technology that "arises after" the application's filing date, which a "patent document cannot enable. . . . " An enabling disclosure must be provided for nascent technology "because a person of ordinary skill in the art has little or no knowledge independent from the patentee's instruction."

The scientific literature first reported the successful creation of genetically engineered antibodies in May 1984, after the filing date of Chiron's 1984 application but before the filing date of the 1985 and 1986 applications. Nevertheless, the Federal Circuit concluded, the 1985 and 1986 applications did not provide the required specific and useful teaching of the genetically engineered antibodies. Applying the *Wands* factors discussed above, the court concluded that undue experimentation would have been required to make the antibodies, which were "unpredictable" at that early stage in their development. The 1985 and 1986 applications did not provide any disclosure of how to make and use the genetically engineered antibodies or any working examples thereof, experts testified that making chimeric antibodies was "not routine" in 1985 or 1986, and only a few laboratories possessed the required equipment at that time.

Judges Rader and Bryson disagreed, however, with respect to whether the *1984* application satisfied the enablement requirement for the genetically engineered monoclonal antibodies. Writing for the

[64]The entitlement of claims in a later-filed patent application to the benefit of the filing date of a related earlier-filed patent application is governed by 35 U.S.C. §120. *See supra* Chapter 1, Section H.5 ("Continuing Application Practice").

[65]*Chiron*, 363 F.3d at 1254 (citing Genentech, Inc. v. Novo Nordisk, A/S, 108 F.3d 1361, 1368 (Fed. Cir. 1997) (on appeal from grant of preliminary injunction, invalidating Genentech patent as nonenabled)).

majority, Judge Rader concluded that (contrary to the jury's verdict) the 1984 application *did* satisfy the enablement requirement with respect to the claimed antibodies of the patent in suit. The chimeric antibodies (a type of antibody within the scope of claim 1 of the patent in suit) were not known as of the filing date of the 1984 application. Under *In re Hogan,*[66] Judge Rader wrote, there can be no requirement to provide an enabling disclosure of such later-arising technology. Judge Rader would sustain the jury's verdict on the alternative ground of failure to comply with the written description of the invention requirement of 35 U.S.C. §112, ¶1.[67]

Concurring Judge Bryson disagreed with the majority's application of *Hogan,* and would have upheld the jury's [implied] verdict that the 1984 application did not enable the chimeric antibodies now within claim 1 of the patent in suit. Chiron was arguing that its 1984 application provided support for claims covering technology that was not in existence at that time, Judge Bryson observed. In that setting, where the claims are accorded a scope that exceeds the scope of the enablement, Judge Bryson would hold them not entitled to priority as of 1984 because the disclosure of the 1984 application did not enable the asserted claims. The proper approach in Judge Bryson's view would be "to address cases of new technology by construing claims, where possible, as they would have been understood by one of skill in the art at the time of the invention, and not construing them to reach the as-yet-undeveloped technology that the applicant did not enable."[68]

C. The Best Mode Requirement

1. Best Mode Scale-Back by America Invents Act of 2011

The best mode requirement of 35 U.S.C. §112(a) obliges an inventor to disclose the best way known to her on her patent application filing date of "carrying out the invention."[69] The requirement goes beyond

---

[66]559 F.2d 595 (C.C.P.A. 1977).

[67]*See Chiron,* 363 F.3d at 1255 (observing that "[t]he jury may have found that the 1984 application does not provide any support for the new matter, chimeric antibodies, claimed in the [Chiron patent in suit]. Because chimeric antibody technology did not even exist at the time of the 1984 filing, the record conclusively supports that the Chiron scientists did not possess and disclose this technology in the [] 1984 filing.").

[68]*Id.* at 1263 (Bryson, J., concurring).

[69]35 U.S.C. §112(a) (eff. Sept. 16, 2012) (providing that, in addition to an enabling disclosure and a written description of the invention, the specification "shall set forth the best mode contemplated by the inventor or joint inventor of carrying out the invention").

Before enactment of the Leahy-Smith America Invents Act, the individual subparagraphs of 35 U.S.C. §112 were not designated by letter. What is designated as §112(a)

the objective standard of enablement[70] to mandate disclosure of what the inventor believes to be the *best* mode, not just *a* mode, of practicing her invention. Because the best mode is, in part, a subjective inquiry with the potential for significant litigation expenditures to discern what was in the inventor's mind at a particular (sometimes long-past) date, some policymakers objected to the continued presence of a best mode disclosure requirement in U.S. patent law.

In response to these concerns, patent reform legislation enacted in 2011 significantly cabined the scope of the best mode disclosure requirement, although it did not eliminate it.[71] The Leahy-Smith America Invents Act of 2011 (AIA) prohibits asserting best mode noncompliance as grounds for challenging an issued patent's validity or enforceability either in federal court litigation[72] or as part of a post-grant review proceeding in the U.S. Patent and Trademark Office (USPTO).[73] This important change took effect on the AIA's enactment date of September 16, 2011, and applies "to proceedings commenced on or after that date."[74]

Although best mode noncompliance is no longer a basis for challenging an issued patent, pending patent applications remain subject to compliance with the best mode requirement. The first paragraph of 35 U.S.C. §112 was not amended to remove the best mode requirement; the best mode disclosure obligation remains one of three requirements

---

after September 15, 2011, was commonly referred to as "§112, ¶1" or "§112, first paragraph" before that date. *See* 35 U.S.C. §112 (2006).

[70]*See generally supra* Section B ("The Enablement Requirement").

[71]*See* Leahy-Smith America Invents Act, Pub. L. No. 112-29 (H.R. 1249), §15, 125 Stat. 284, 328 (2011); 35 U.S.C. §282(b)(3)(A) (eff. Sept. 16, 2011).

[72]*See* Leahy-Smith America Invents Act, Pub. L. No. 112-29 (H.R. 1249), §15, 125 Stat. 284, 328 (2011). The legislation provides that Section 282 of title 35, United States Code (2006), which enumerates the defenses available in "any action involving the validity or infringement of a patent," is amended in the second undesignated paragraph by striking paragraph (3) and inserting the following:

"(3) Invalidity of the patent or any claim in suit for failure to comply with—

(A) any requirement of section 112, except that the failure to disclose the best mode shall not be a basis on which any claim of a patent may be canceled or held invalid or otherwise unenforceable; or

(B) any requirement of section 251.

[73] *See* 35 U.S.C. 321(b) (eff. Sept. 16, 2012) ("Scope") (providing that "[a] petitioner in a post-grant review may request to cancel as unpatentable 1 or more claims of a patent on any ground that could be raised under paragraph (2) or (3) of section 282(b) (relating to invalidity of the patent or any claim)"). *See also infra* Chapter 8, Section E ("AIA-Implemented Post-Grant Review").

[74]Leahy-Smith America Invents Act, Pub. L. No. 112-29 (H.R. 1249), §15(c), 125 Stat. 284, 328 (2011). This dramatic change means that even if a patent was very likely invalid on September 15, 2011, for failure to satisfy the best mode disclosure requirement, as of September 16, 2011, the patent could no longer be challenged on that basis (so long as litigation was not already underway).

for patent applications.[75] Despite the AIA's enactment, the USPTO retains the ability to reject a pending patent application for failure to identify the best mode.

Historically, however, "such rejections are reported to be rare."[76] Because of the subjective, inventor-centric nature of the best mode disclosure requirement, as well as the USPTO's limited fact-finding resources, a patent applicant's failure to disclose the best mode would be difficult for the agency to discern.

Despite the elimination of best mode noncompliance as a basis for contending that an issued patent is invalid, understanding the best mode requirement remains vital. Importantly, the best mode disclosure obligation continues as a statutory requirement for patent applications, as it has since 1870.[77] Moreover, because the AIA's abrogation of the best mode invalidity defense applies to proceedings commenced on or after September 16, 2011,[78] failure to comply with the best mode disclosure obligation remains available as a defense in any proceeding that was already pending on September 16, 2011.

2. Distinguishing Best Mode from Enablement

The best mode requirement of 35 U.S.C. §112(a) can be thought of as a sort of enablement-plus requirement. Under U.S. patent law, it is not enough that an applicant has merely disclosed *one* way of making and using the invention; he bears a further obligation to disclose the *best* way known to him on the application filing date of "carrying out [the] invention."[79] As explained by the Federal Circuit, the difference between the enablement and best mode requirements is that:

> Enablement looks to placing the subject matter of the claims generally in the possession of the public. If, however, the applicant develops specific instrumentalities or techniques which are recognized at the time of filing as the best way of carrying out the invention, then the best mode

---

[75]*See* 35 U.S.C. §112(a) (eff. Sept. 16, 2011).

[76]Tony Dutra, *House Approves Patent Reform Bill 304-117; Dissent on PTO Funding Change Quelled*, BNA's Pat., Copyright & Trademark J., June 24, 2011.

[77]*See* An Act to revise, consolidate, and amend the Statutes relating to Patents and Copyrights §26, 16 Stat. 198, 201 (1870) (providing that "in case of a machine, he shall explain the principle thereof, and the best mode in which he has contemplated applying that principle so as to distinguish it from other inventions").

[78]Leahy-Smith America Invents Act, Pub. L. No. 112-29 (H.R. 1249), §15(c), 125 Stat. 284, 328 (2011).

[79]35 U.S.C. §112(a) (eff. Sept. 16, 2012) provides that, in addition to an enabling disclosure and a written description of the invention, the specification "shall set forth the best mode contemplated by the inventor of carrying out his invention."

requirement imposes an obligation to disclose that information to the public as well.[80]

3. Policy Rationale

Unlike that of the enablement requirement, the policy rationale for the best mode requirement has never been completely transparent. Although the CCPA explained that "the sole purpose of this [best mode] requirement is to restrain inventors from applying for patents while at the same time concealing from the public preferred embodiments of their inventions which they have in fact conceived,"[81] why is such a requirement necessary *in addition to* the enablement requirement?

Some courts have posited that the underlying goal of the best mode requirement is that when a patent expires, members of the public should not only be able to make and use at least one embodiment of the invention, but rather, through the best mode disclosure, should be put in a *commercially competitive position* with the holder of the expired patent.[82] Although this goal seems laudable on its face, it may be more than is required from patent applicants in order to fulfill the constitutional goal of "promot[ing] the Progress of . . . useful Arts." Some experts advocate abolishment of the best mode requirement, which they view as needlessly exacerbating the already extreme cost and complexity of U.S. patent litigation.[83] These concerns motivated Congress in 2011 to eliminate best mode noncompliance as an invalidity defense, while retaining it as a patentability requirement.[84]

---

[80]Spectra-Physics, Inc. v. Coherent, Inc., 827 F.2d 1524, 1532 (Fed. Cir. 1987).

[81]In re Gay, 309 F.2d 769, 772 (C.C.P.A. 1962).

[82]*See* Christianson v. Colt Indus. Operating Corp., 870 F.2d 1292, 1303 n.8 (7th Cir. 1989) (stating agreement with proposition that "the best mode requirement is intended to allow the public to compete fairly with the patentee following the expiration of the patents"); *contra* 3-7 DONALD S. CHISUM, CHISUM ON PATENTS §7.05 (2008) (disagreeing with Seventh Circuit's view on ground that it "ignores the realities of the patent system and the commercial marketplace" and explaining that "[r]arely will that disclosure [of the best mode known at the time the application was filed] be of competitive interest when the patent expires").

[83]*See* NATIONAL RESEARCH COUNCIL OF THE NATIONAL ACADEMIES, A PATENT SYSTEM FOR THE 21ST CENTURY 82-83 (Stephen A. Merrill et al. eds., 2004) *available at* http://www. nap.edu/html/patentsystem/0309089107.pdf (recommending modification or removal of best mode requirement as a litigation element that depends on a party's state of mind and thus generates high discovery costs and unpredictability of patent infringement litigation outcomes); ADVISORY COMMISSION ON PATENT LAW REFORM: A REPORT TO THE SECRETARY OF COMMERCE 100-103 (1992) (advising under Recommendation V-G(i) that best mode obligation be eliminated).

[84]*See supra* Section C.1 ("Best Mode Scale-Back by America Invents Act of 2011").

Another basis for criticizing the U.S. best mode requirement is the fact that most foreign countries do not have a best mode requirement.[85] Indeed, the absence of a best mode requirement in other countries can disadvantage a foreign national who is applying for a U.S. patent. As discussed in Chapter 12 ("International Patenting Issues"), *infra,* the foreign national may need to rely on the earlier filing date of her home country application in order to avoid prior art cited by the USPTO examiner against her U.S. application. She attempts to do this by claiming the benefit of her foreign filing date under 35 U.S.C. §119, the domestic implementation of the Paris Convention's right of priority.[86]

Under pre-AIA rules, the foreign-filed ("priority") application must satisfy all disclosure requirements in the first paragraph of §112, including best mode, as of the earlier foreign filing date on which the applicant is relying, if it is to be entitled to the benefit of that date under 35 U.S.C. §119.[87] Because it was first filed in a foreign country that does not have a best mode requirement, however, the foreign priority application may not adequately disclose the best mode of carrying out the invention claimed in the corresponding later-filed U.S. application. If this is the case, the applicant will not be able to claim

---

[85]*See* Donald S. Chisum, *Best Mode Concealment and Inequitable Conduct in Patent Procurement: A Nutshell, A Review of Recent Federal Circuit Cases and a Plea for Modest Reform,* 13 SANTA CLARA COMPUTER & HIGH TECH. L.J. 277, 279 (1997) (stating that "[u]nlike other patent law standards, such as novelty and infringement, best mode and inequitable conduct have no counterparts in the major patent systems of Europe, Japan, and elsewhere").

Several developing countries retain a best mode requirement, however, including India and Mexico. *See* India Patents Act 1970 §10(4) (1995) (providing that "[e]very complete specification shall — a. fully and particularly describe the invention and its operation or use and the method by which it is to be performed; b. *disclose the best method of performing the invention which is known to the applicant and for which he is entitled to claim protection*; and c. end with a claim or claims defining the scope of the invention for which protection is claimed") (emphasis added), *available at* http://www.ipindia.nic.in/ipr/patent/patents.htm; Mexico — Ley de Protección a la Propiedad Industrial [LPPI] [Industrial Property Protection Law], *as amended,* art. 47, Diario Oficial de la Federación [DO], 27 de junio de 1991 (Mex.). Other countries requiring best mode disclosure include Australia, Canada, Egypt, Sri Lanka, Pakistan, Thailand, and Honduras. *See* Dale L. Carlson, Katarzyna Przychodzen, & Petra Scamborov, *Patent Linchpin for the 21st Century? Best Mode Revisited,* 45 IDEA 267, 284 (2005). For economic policy reasons, the developing countries require a relatively greater degree of disclosure in exchange for the grant of a patent. *See* Carlson et al., 45 IDEA at 287-289 (arguing that best mode disclosures facilitate technology transfer to developing countries and educate the work force).

[86]*See* Paris Convention for the Protection of Industrial Property art. 4, July 14, 1967, 21 U.S.T. 1983, 828 U.N.T.S. 305 ("Right of Priority"). The right of priority and other aspects of the Paris Convention are discussed in further detail in Chapter 12 ("International Patenting Issues"), *infra.*

[87]*See* In re Gosteli, 872 F.2d 1008, 1010-1011 (Fed. Cir. 1989).

priority back to her home country filing date. The U.S. application filing date will be only the date of actual filing in the United States, and the applicant will not be able to avoid the cited prior art in this fashion.

4. The *Chemcast* Analysis

The Federal Circuit has clearly identified the analysis to be followed when determining whether a patent disclosure satisfies the best mode requirement of the first paragraph of 35 U.S.C. §112. The court outlined a two-step analysis for best mode compliance in *Chemcast Corp. v. Arco Indus. Corp.,*[88] which involved a patent directed to a grommet for sealing openings in sheet metal panels.

a. Step 1: Subjective Inquiry

The first step is a necessarily *subjective* inquiry that focuses on the state of the inventor's mind. Step 1 of the *Chemcast* analysis asks whether, as of the filing date, the inventor considered one particular mode of carrying out his invention to be better than all the others. If so, this mode is the "best mode." For example, the inventor in *Chemcast* considered a certain type of material to be the best mode for making his claimed grommet.[89]

Because of *Chemcast* step 1's focus on the inventor's mind set, it can be said fairly that "the best mode belongs to the inventor."[90] *Glaxo, Inc. v. Novopharm, Ltd.*[91] illustrates this adage. Glaxo's patent claimed a specific crystalline form of ranitidine hydrochloride, a chemical compound useful for treating patients suffering from ulcers; various pharmaceutical compositions and methods of using the compound also were claimed. Unbeknownst to Crookes, the Glaxo scientist who invented the compound, other Glaxo employees subsequently developed a novel azeotroping process that made salts of the compound easier to form into capsules.[92] Glaxo employed this process in the commercial manufacture of its antiulcer product, without any knowledge or further

---

[88]913 F.2d 923 (Fed. Cir. 1990).

[89]*See id.* at 929 (citing district court findings that inventor "selected the material for the locking portion, a rigid polyvinyl chloride (PVC) plastisol composition; knew that the preferred hardness of this material was 75 +/- 5 Shore D; and purchased all of the grommet material under the trade name R-4467 from Reynosol Corporation (Reynosol), which had spent 750 man-hours developing the compound specifically for Chemcast").

[90]Glaxo, Inc. v. Novopharm, Ltd., 52 F.3d 1043, 1049 (Fed. Cir. 1995).

[91]*Id.* at 1043.

[92]*See id.* at 1046.

involvement by Crookes. When Glaxo later sued Novopharm for patent infringement, Novopharm affirmatively defended by asserting that the patent was invalid for failure to satisfy the best mode obligation because it did not disclose the azeotroping process.

The Federal Circuit majority disagreed, holding that the best mode requirement had been satisfied. The court refused to impute Glaxo's corporate knowledge of the azeotroping process to the inventor, Crookes. Congress chose to use the specific term "inventor" in 35 U.S.C. §112, ¶1 (1994), the court noted; had Congress intended the best mode obligation to be broader, it would have drafted the statute accordingly:

> Congress was aware of the differences between inventors and assignees, see 35 U.S.C. §§100(d) and 152, and it specifically limited the best mode required to that contemplated by the inventor. We have no authority to extend the requirement beyond the limits set by Congress.[93]

b. Step 2: Objective Inquiry

The second step of the *Chemcast* best mode inquiry is completely *objective*. Assuming that a best mode exists, step 2 asks whether the application provides an enabling disclosure of this best mode. The second *Chemcast* step, which really merges the enablement and best mode requirements, addresses the *adequacy* of the best mode disclosure, rather than its *necessity*. In contrast with *Chemcast* step 1, the perspective of the second step is that of the hypothetical person of ordinary skill in the art rather than the inventor himself. In other words, the second *Chemcast* step asks the question, "is the hypothetical person skilled in the art enabled by the patent application's disclosure to make and use the best mode of the invention without undue experimentation?"

In the *Chemcast* case, the answer to this question was negative. The Federal Circuit concluded that in light of the specific material that the inventor considered to be the best mode for making his grommet, the patent specification was "manifestly deficient."[94] The patent neither explicitly nor implicitly disclosed how to make and use the claimed grommet with the proprietary R-4467 material that the inventor preferred. Rather, it merely disclosed an open-ended range

---

[93]*Id*. at 1052. Dissenting Judge Mayer decried the majority's narrow interpretation of the best mode obligation as strictly limited to the inventor. He contended that "the court blesses corporate shell games resulting from organizational gerrymandering and willful ignorance by which one can secure the monopoly of a patent while hiding the best mode of practicing the invention the law expects to be made public in return for its protection." *Id*. at 1053.

[94]Chemcast Corp. v. Arco Indus. Corp., 913 F.2d 923, 929 (Fed. Cir. 1990).

for the hardness of the material, broadly stating that "[m]aterials having a durometer hardness reading of 70 Shore A or harder are suitable...."[95] The actual hardness reading of the inventor's preferred material, however, was 70 Shore D; materials of Shore A and Shore D hardnesses are recognized as different types of materials with different classes of physical properties. The Federal Circuit also instructed that because the inventor did not know the proprietary formula, composition, or method of manufacture of his preferred material, R-4467, he was obligated to "disclose the specific supplier and trade name" of the material.[96] Having failed to do so, the inventor had not complied with the best mode disclosure obligation of 35 U.S.C. §112, ¶1 (1988).

When the best mode is properly disclosed, in what manner should that disclosure be made? A common convention in drafting patent applications is to refer to the best mode as the "preferred embodiment" of the invention.[97] Case law indicates that no special labeling of the best mode as such is required in a patent application, however; the application need not expressly state "the best mode of carrying out this invention is X." For example, in *Randomex, Inc. v. Scopus Corp.,*[98] the Federal Circuit determined that the indiscriminate listing of the best mode along with a number of other modes did not violate the best mode disclosure obligation.[99] On the other hand, a scenario in which the best mode is indiscriminately listed among so many other possibilities as to result in "burial" or effective concealment might run afoul of the best mode requirement.[100]

5. Scope of the Best Mode Obligation

Although the *Chemcast* analysis is relatively straightforward, it does not address all aspects of best mode compliance. A still-fuzzy area of best mode analysis concerns the scope of the best mode disclosure obligation vis-à-vis the scope of the claims. Because 35 U.S.C. §112(a) uses the seemingly broad phrase "best mode of *carrying out* the invention," some Federal Circuit decisions suggest that the best

[95]*Id.*

[96]*Id.*

[97]*See* JEFFREY G. SHELDON, HOW TO WRITE A PATENT APPLICATION §14.4.4 (Practising Law Inst. 2001) (explaining that "[t]he best mode may be identified in the specification as a 'particularly preferred," most preferred,' or 'preferred embodiment.'").

[98]849 F.2d 585 (Fed. Cir. 1988).

[99]*See id.* at 589 (holding that "[t]he indiscriminate disclosure in this instance of the preferred cleaning fluid along with one other possible cleaning fluid satisfies the best mode requirement").

[100]*See id.* at 592 (Mayer, J., dissenting) (contending that inventor's "disclosure does not satisfy section 112 because he buried his best mode in a list of less satisfactory ones").

mode obligation may extend to elements of the invention even if those elements are not recited in the claims.

For example, in *Dana Corp. v. IPC Ltd. Partnership*,[101] the Federal Circuit invalidated the patent in suit, which claimed an elastomeric valve stem seal of the type used in automobile engines, because the patent failed to disclose a fluoride surface treatment that the inventor's test reports indicated was "necessary to [the] satisfactory performance of [the] seal."[102] The court held that the best mode obligation had not been satisfied, despite the fact that this fluoride surface treatment was not recited in the claims of the patent, which were directed to the seal itself.

Reliance on these earlier, more expansive best mode decisions should proceed cautiously. More recently, the Federal Circuit has clarified that "an inventor need not disclose a mode for obtaining unclaimed subject matter unless the subject matter is *novel and essential* for carrying out the best mode of the invention."[103]

This more limited disclosure obligation is illustrated by *Eli Lilly & Co. v. Barr Labs., Inc.*,[104] in which the patent in suit claimed the chemical compound fluoxetine hydrochloride and a method of administering the compound to block the uptake of the monoamine serotonin in patients suffering from anxiety or depression. The written description of the patent identified p-trifluoromethylphenol as a starting material from which the claimed compound could be made, but did not disclose the process by which the patentee synthesized this starting material. The Federal Circuit rejected the accused infringer's contention that the patent did not satisfy the best mode requirement because it did not disclose the patentee's method of synthesizing the starting material, a method that the patentee considered proprietary and commercially advantageous. Although the best mode for developing the claimed compound involved the use of this starting material, the Federal Circuit explained, the patent did not "cover" it.[105] Moreover,

---

[101]860 F.2d 415 (Fed. Cir. 1988).

[102]*Id.* at 418.

[103]Eli Lilly & Co. v. Barr Labs., Inc., 251 F.3d 955, 963 (Fed. Cir. 2001) (emphasis added).

[104]*Id.* at 955.

[105]*See id.* at 964, concluding that

> while the best mode for developing fluoxetine hydrochloride involves use of p-trifluoromethylphenol, the claimed inventions do not cover p-trifluoromethylphenol and the patents do not accord Lilly the right to exclude others from practicing Molloy's method for synthesizing p-trifluoromethylphenol. As a result, the best mode requirement does not compel disclosure of Molloy's unclaimed method for synthesizing p-trifluoromethylphenol.

the unclaimed starting material was not itself novel and was available from commercial sources other than the patentee.[106]

The Federal Circuit undertook a comprehensive review of its best mode precedent in the 2002 decision *Bayer AG v. Schein Pharms., Inc.*[107] The Bayer patent in suit claimed as a composition of matter the antibiotic ciprofloxacin, sold as CIPRO®. Accused infringer Schein alleged that the patent was invalid for failure to disclose the best mode of carrying out the claimed invention. Schein singled out Bayer's failure to disclose in the patent the inventor's preferred mode of making a certain novel synthetic compound that he had utilized as a chemical intermediate in his synthesis of the claimed invention, ciprofloxacin. The intermediate was not recited in the claims. Thus, the Federal Circuit was again required to grapple with the extent of the best mode disclosure obligation for elements or materials involved in preparation of the invention but not recited in the patent claims.

The *Bayer* panel majority's opinion noted that the Federal Circuit and its predecessor courts had held claims invalid for failure to satisfy the best mode requirement on only seven occasions. The majority concluded that each of these seven decisions could be grouped within one of two categories: either (1) failure to adequately disclose a preferred embodiment of the invention, or (2) failure to disclose aspects of making or using the claimed invention where the undisclosed matter materially affected the properties of the claimed invention. The second type of alleged failure was at issue in this case. Nevertheless, the Federal Circuit held against Schein, the validity challenger. "[N]ot every preference constitutes a best mode of carrying out the invention," the court observed.[108] Notably, Schein had conceded that the inventor's preferred way of making the intermediate had no material effect on the properties of the claimed ciprofloxacin end product. The facts of *Bayer* were thus distinguishable from the four prior cases in which the Federal Circuit had found a best mode violation where an undisclosed preference clearly had a material effect on the properties of the claimed invention.

---

[106]*See id.* at 964-965. As of this writing, the question of the scope of the best mode obligation with respect to unclaimed subject matter, if any, remains unclear. *See* Bayer AG v. Schein Pharms., Inc., 301 F.3d 1306, 1319-1320 (Fed. Cir. 2002) (summarizing Federal Circuit best mode precedent as requiring "that the best mode of making or using the invention need be disclosed if it materially affects the properties of the claimed invention itself," even if such subject matter is unclaimed); *but see id.* at 1324 (Rader, J., concurring) (criticizing *Bayer* majority for "inexplicably and without support in the statute or case law, . . . widen[ing] its best mode net to capture the properties of the claimed invention and further sweep[ing] in any material effect or impact on those properties").

[107]301 F.3d 1306 (Fed. Cir. 2002).

[108]*Id.* at 1321.

The *Bayer* majority also rejected Schein's argument that because the intermediate at issue was novel, it did not satisfy the standard for best mode compliance that the Federal Circuit had set out one year prior in *Eli Lilly v. Barr Labs.* (discussed above). The *Bayer* majority read *Eli Lilly* as requiring a disclosure of unclaimed but novel starting material only to the extent that the best mode must always be *enabled*:

> We merely acknowledged [in *Eli Lilly*] that when a novel compound is necessary to practice the best mode, one of skill in the art must be able to obtain that compound. In other words, our statements regarding "a method for obtaining that subject matter" and "a mode for obtaining unclaimed subject matter" referred only to the requirement that the best mode be enabled. We were not referring to a best mode disclosure itself.[109]

In his concurring opinion Circuit Judge Rader charged the *Bayer* majority with missing much of the significance of *Eli Lilly*. He viewed *Eli Lilly* as turning on the fact (also present in *Bayer*) that the undisclosed material simply was not covered by the claims, rather than requiring an assessment of the material's effect on the properties of the claimed invention. In Judge Rader's view, the *Bayer* facts "do[] not require creation of a new test for best modes."[110]

D. The Written Description of the Invention Requirement

The last and most obscure of the three disclosure requirements of 35 U.S.C. §112(a) is the requirement that a patent's specification contain a written description of the invention.[111] Before exploring the details of this requirement, it is helpful to understand that patent law uses the phrase "written description" in two ways. In its more commonly used sense, written description refers to a physical part of the patent document. The written description portion of a patent document encompasses all of the patent specification's content other than the claims[112] (i.e., the written description includes those sections of

---

[109]*Id.* at 1322.

[110]*Id.* at 1323.

[111]Part of the material in this section is adapted from Janice M. Mueller, *The Evolving Application of the Written Description Requirement to Biotechnological Inventions*, 13 BERKELEY TECH. L.J. 615 (1998).

[112]*See* 35 U.S.C. §112(a) (eff. Sept. 16, 2012) (mandating that "[t]he specification shall contain a written description of the invention . . . "); *id.* at §112(b) (eff. Sept. 16, 2012) (mandating that "[t]he specification shall conclude with one or more claims . . . ").

the patent specification that are typically labeled "Background of the Invention," "Summary of the Invention," and "Detailed Description of the Invention").

In another sense, the phrase "written description" is a shorthand reference to a *disclosure requirement* that the patent's specification must satisfy in accordance with 35 U.S.C. §112(a). As explained below, the traditional view of the written description disclosure requirement was that the language of patent claims presented or amended after the filing date of the application must find adequate "support" in the written description portion of the patent document. In other words, application of the written description of the invention requirement was understood as limited to policing priority—ensuring that the new claims added post–filing date were entitled to the earlier, original filing date of the application.[113] Starting in 1997, a series of Federal Circuit decisions have expanded the scope of the written description of the invention doctrine well beyond this traditional purview.[114]

In attempting to clearly differentiate these two uses of the phrase "written description," this text will generally refer to the legal requirement by its full statutory identifier as the "written description of the invention" requirement.

1. Timing Mechanism

The written description of the invention requirement can best be understood as a timing or "priority policing" mechanism. As detailed in Chapter 4, *infra,* when operating under pre-AIA rules the USPTO takes the filing date of a patent application as the presumptive or *prima facie* date of invention ("invention date") for the subject matter of the originally filed claims therein.[115] It is quite common for patent

---

[113]Or, for example, ensuring that claims in a continuing application filed in accordance with 35 U.S.C. §120 were entitled to the earlier filing date of the corresponding parent application. *See supra* Chapter 1, Section H.5 ("Continuing Application Practice").

[114]The Federal Circuit's expansion of the written description of the invention requirement has its origins in *Regents of the Univ. of Cal. v. Eli Lilly & Co.,* 119 F.3d 1559 (Fed. Cir. 1997), further examined *infra* Section D.5.

[115]*See* Mahurkar v. C.R. Bard, Inc., 79 F.3d 1572 (Fed. Cir. 1996), in which the court explained that

[i]n *ex parte* patent prosecution, an examiner may refer to a document published within one year before the filing date of a patent application as prior art. However, this label only applies until the inventor comes forward with evidence showing an earlier date of invention. Once the inventor shows an earlier date of invention, the document is no longer prior art under section 102(a).

Id. at 1576. "Invention date" is further defined *infra* Chapter 4, Section G.3.

applicants to submit amendments to a patent application after it has been filed, for the purpose of modifying the originally filed claims or adding one or more new claims. Are these amended or new claims also entitled to the same *prima facie* invention date as the originally filed claims, or merely to the later date on which the new claims were actually presented?

Similarly, the question when one is operating under post-AIA rules is whether the amended or new claims are entitled to the same effective filing date as the other claims of the application.[116] In either case, the answer may determine whether the amended or new claims are patentable, or rather are rendered anticipated or obvious in view of intervening prior art. This is the domain of the written description of the invention requirement.

Satisfaction of the written description of the invention requirement ensures that such subject matter, claimed *after* an application's filing date, was sufficiently disclosed in the application *at the time of its original filing* so that the *prima facie* date of invention for the later-claimed subject matter (or the effective filing date under the AIA) can fairly be held to be the filing date of the application.[117] Without written description of the invention scrutiny, a later-presented or amended claim not truly entitled to the earlier filing date of the application would be improperly examined against a smaller universe of prior art than is legally available. Hence the applicant would unfairly enjoy a windfall vis-à-vis the prior art.

Another way of understanding the written description of the invention requirement is that it functions to ensure that all claims amended or added after the filing date of the application find adequate "support" in the originally filed application. Section 112, first paragraph, requires that claim language be supported in the specification.[118] This can be viewed as a requirement that claim language find "antecedent

---

[116]"Effective filing date" is defined post-AIA at 35 U.S.C. §100(i) (eff. Mar. 16, 2013).

[117]In re Smith, 481 F.2d 910, 914 (C.C.P.A. 1973). The *Smith* court summarized its precedent on the written description of the invention requirement as follows:

> Acknowledgment of that [written description of the invention] requirement evidences appreciation of an important purpose of §112, first paragraph, which is the definition of the attributes which a patent specification must possess as of the filing date to be entitled to that filing date as a *prima facie* date of invention. Satisfaction of the description requirement insures that subject matter presented in the form of a claim subsequent to the filing date of the application was sufficiently disclosed at the time of filing so that the *prima facie* date of invention can fairly be held to be the filing date of the application. . . . Where the claim is an original claim, the underlying concept of insuring disclosure as of the filing date is satisfied, and the description requirement has likewise been held to be satisfied. . . .

Id. (citations omitted).

[118]In re Rasmussen, 650 F.2d 1212, 1214 (C.C.P.A. 1981).

basis" in the specification. The language added to the claims by amendment or introduced in newly presented claims must have previously appeared in the specification, either explicitly or implicitly.[119]

The policy rationale behind the written description of the invention requirement focuses less on the public than on the patent applicant. While the enablement doctrine is concerned with putting the *public* in possession of the invention so that it can be made and used without undue experimentation once the patent expires, the written description of the invention requirement mandates that the *inventor* must have been "in possession" of the claimed invention as of a particular date, that is, the filing date of the application (which under pre-AIA rules is taken by the USPTO as the presumptive invention date of the claimed subject matter). By ensuring that the later-claimed subject matter was in fact within the inventor's original contribution, the written description of the invention requirement guards against unfair "overreaching" by inventors.[120]

2. How an Application Conveys Possession of an Invention

To satisfy the legal requirement for an adequate written description of a claimed invention, the application as originally filed must convey with reasonable clarity to persons of ordinary skill in the art that, as of the application's filing date, the inventor was "in possession" of the subject matter subsequently claimed as her invention.[121]

The precise manner in which a claimed invention is described in a patent is not critical, so long as that description is capable of conveying

---

[119]The support or antecedent basis for the newly added terms need not be verbatim or *in haec verba* (Latin for "in these words"), as the discussion of *In re Smythe, infra*, makes clear.

[120]*See* Vas-Cath, Inc. v. Mahurkar, 935 F.2d 1555, 1561 (Fed. Cir. 1991) (explaining that "[a]dequate description of the invention guards against the inventor's overreaching by insisting that he recount his invention in such detail that his future claims can be determined to be encompassed within his original creation") (quoting Rengo Co. v. Molins Mach. Co., 657 F.2d 535, 551 (3d Cir. 1981)).

[121]Ariad Pharms., Inc. v. Eli Lilly and Co., 598 F.3d 1336, 1351 (Fed. Cir. 2010) (*en banc*) (holding that "the test for sufficiency is whether the disclosure of the application relied upon reasonably conveys to those skilled in the art that the inventor had possession of the claimed subject matter as of the filing date") (citing Vas-Cath Inc. v. Mahurkar, 935 F.2d 1555, 1563 (Fed. Cir. 1991)).

Note the difference between this perspective and that of enablement: the written description inquiry asks whether the *inventor* was in possession at the filing date of the invention she is later claiming, while the enablement inquiry asks whether the patent application would have put the *hypothetical person of ordinary skill in the art* in possession of that invention as of the filing date.

D. The Written Description of the Invention Requirement

to readers of the patent that the inventor had actually invented the claimed subject matter as of the application filing date. Compliance with the written description of the invention requirement should not be so burdensome as to prohibit an applicant from claiming "undisclosed, but obviously art-recognized equivalent[s]"[122] of expressly disclosed aspects of the invention; these "equivalents" are considered within the inventor's possession.

For example, as the CCPA posited in *In re Smythe*,[123] if the original written description of a patent application directed to the "scales of justice" disclosed only a one-pound "lead weight" as a counterbalance to determine the weight of a pound of flesh, the applicant should not be prevented by the written description of the invention requirement from later more broadly claiming the counterbalance as a "metal weight" or even generically as a one-pound "weight." The broader claims should be permitted because the applicant's disclosure of the use and function of the "lead weight" as a counterbalance would immediately convey to others that the applicant had invented a scale with a one-pound counterbalance weight, regardless of what material the weight was made of.[124]

A satisfactory written description of the invention need not even be in words. For example, the medical device patent at issue in *Vas-Cath v. Mahurkar*[125] claimed a catheter having double lumens (tubes) of diameters within a specified range of ratios. The Federal Circuit had to decide whether the *drawings* of Mahurkar's earlier-filed *design* patent application[126] could provide adequate written description support for the diameter range limitations later claimed in Mahurkar's *utility* patent.[127] Even though the design patent application drawings showed

---

[122]In re Smythe, 480 F.2d 1376, 1384 (C.C.P.A. 1973).

[123]*Smythe*, 480 F.2d at 1376.

[124]*Smythe*, 480 F.2d at 1384. *See also* All Dental Prodx, LLC v. Advantage Dental Prods., Inc., 309 F.3d 774, 779 (Fed. Cir. 2002) (reversing summary judgment of invalidity for failure to satisfy the written description of the invention requirement where, even though the disputed language was not a "model of clarity" and was added to the claims during prosecution but did not explicitly appear anywhere in the disclosure, the patent did sufficiently identify what the invention was, and what it was not, to satisfy the statutory requirement).

[125]935 F.2d 1555 (Fed. Cir. 1991) (Rich, J.).

[126]A design patent is available for "any new, original, and ornamental design for an article of manufacture. . . . " 35 U.S.C. §171. A design patent is directed to the appearance of an article of manufacture. If its design is driven primarily by function (i.e., is essential to the use of the article), it cannot be protected with a design patent. *See* L.A. Gear, Inc. v. Thom McAn Shoe Co., 988 F.2d 1117, 1123 (Fed. Cir. 1993). *See also infra* Chapter 7 ("Potentially Patentable Subject Matter (35 U.S.C. §101)") (discussion of design patents).

[127]In order to overcome an intervening §102(b) (pre-AIA) reference that would otherwise have invalidated his utility patent, Mahurkar sought to claim for that patent the benefit of his earlier design application filing date under 35 U.S.C. §120. Entitlement

147

only one particular ratio of diameters falling within the range recited in the utility patent claims, the Federal Circuit concluded that the drawings provided an adequate written description of the invention: "Under proper circumstances, drawings alone may provide a 'written description' of an invention as required by [section] 112."[128] The fact that the drawings did not (and by their nature could not) show every possible embodiment of the claimed catheter within the recited diameter range was not dispositive, in view of expert testimony that persons of skill in the art viewing the drawings would be aware that only certain diameter relationships would produce a physiologically acceptable change in pressure at the transition between catheters.[129]

A Federal Circuit panel in *Enzo Biochem., Inc. v. Gen-Probe, Inc.,*[130] took the extreme view that showing an inventor was in possession of a claimed invention as of the application filing date (e.g., as evidenced by proof of actual reduction to practice) is not necessarily sufficient to satisfy the written description of the invention requirement.[131] The *Enzo* court opined:

> Application of the written description requirement, however, is not subsumed by the "possession" inquiry. A showing of "possession" is ancillary to the *statutory* mandate that "[t]he specification shall contain a written description of the invention," and that requirement is not met if, despite a showing of possession, the specification does not adequately describe the claimed invention.[132]

The court similarly concluded that "proof of a reduction to practice, absent an adequate description in the specification of what is reduced to practice, does not serve to describe or identify the invention for purposes of §112, ¶1."[133]

The *Enzo* court relied solely on its own interpretation of the statutory language and cited no decisional authority for its novel view of the written description of the invention requirement as necessitating more than a showing of possession by the inventor. In the view of this author, the *Enzo* court's elevation of the written description requirement as "the *quid pro quo* of the patent system" confused the

---

to an earlier filing date under 35 U.S.C. §120 (eff. Sept. 16, 2012) requires compliance with the enablement and written description requirements 35 U.S.C. §112(a) (eff. Sept. 16, 2012).

[128]*Vas-Cath*, 935 F.2d at 1565.

[129]*See id*. at 1566-1567.

[130]323 F.3d 956 (Fed. Cir. 2002) (granting petition for rehearing and vacating earlier panel opinion, reported at 285 F.3d 1013 (Fed. Cir. 2002), which erroneously held that biological deposit could not satisfy written description requirement).

[131]*See Enzo Biochem*., 323 F.3d at 969-970.

[132]*Enzo Biochem*., 323 F.3d at 969 (emphasis in original).

[133]*Enzo Biochem*., 323 F.3d at 969.

requirement with enablement. Moreover, the court's assertion that "[t]he appearance of mere *indistinct* words in a specification or a claim, even an original claim, does not necessarily satisfy"[134] the written description of the invention requirement improperly conflates that requirement with the claim definiteness requirement of 35 U.S.C. §112(b).[135]

The Federal Circuit went *en banc* in 2010 to address and resolve questions concerning the written description of the invention requirement. In *Ariad Pharms., Inc. v. Eli Lilly and Co.*,[136] the Federal Circuit conceded the difficulties with its past articulations of the possession test.[137] The *Ariad* court recharacterized the possession test as "possession shown by the disclosure," stating:

> The term "possession" . . . has never been very enlightening. It implies that as long as one can produce records documenting a written description of a claimed invention, one can show possession. But the hallmark of written description is disclosure. Thus, "possession as shown in the disclosure" is a more complete formulation. Yet whatever the specific articulation, the test requires an objective inquiry into the four corners of the specification from the perspective of a person of ordinary skill in the art. Based on that inquiry, the specification must describe an invention understandable to that skilled artisan and show that the inventor actually invented the invention claimed.[138]

That the *Ariad* court's reformulation of the possession test clarified anything is unlikely. The *en banc* court also held that various factors are relevant to the written description inquiry, some of which are *external* to the disclosure of the patent—an approach seemingly at odds with the court's quoted "four corners" directive for evidencing possession of an invention. "Specifically, the level of detail required to satisfy the written description requirement varies depending on the nature and scope of the claims and on the complexity and predictability of the relevant technology."[139] When the claims in dispute are generic claims (a situation that often triggers written description scrutiny), the Federal Circuit will apply "a number of factors for evaluating the adequacy of the disclosure, including 'the existing knowledge in the particular field, the extent and content of the prior art, the

---

[134]*Id.* at 968 (emphasis added).

[135]Effective Sept. 16, 2012. At the time of the 2002 *Enzo* decision, the definiteness requirement was referred to as emanating from 35 U.S.C. §112, ¶2 (2000).

[136]598 F.3d 1336 (Fed. Cir. 2010) (*en banc*).

[137]Other aspects of the important *Ariad* decision are examined in further detail *infra* Section C.5 ("Federal Circuit's Expansion of the Written Description Requirement").

[138]*Ariad,* 598 F.3d at 1351.

[139]*Ariad,* 598 F.3d at 1351.

maturity of the science or technology, [and] the predictability of the aspect at issue.'"[140]

In the view of this author, the Federal Circuit in *Ariad* further complicated the possession test by injecting these external factors into the written description analysis. First, extrinsic evidence going to factors such as predictability or unpredictability of the relevant technology appears inconsistent with a "four corners of the disclosure" rule. More important, the factors identified by the *Ariad* court are also factors traditionally used in the analysis of *enablement* under the first paragraph of 35 U.S.C. §112.[141] Despite the *Ariad* court's emphasis that the written description of the invention requirement is a separate and independent disclosure requirement from the enablement requirement,[142] the overlap in factors identified by the Federal Circuit contradicts that position. The *en banc* decision in *Ariad* heightened, rather than resolved, doctrinal ambiguity in the standard for showing written description "possession" of an invention.

3. Distinguishing Written Description from Enablement

As interpreted and applied by the Federal Circuit, the written description of the invention requirement stands apart from the

---

[140]*Ariad,* 598 F.3d at 1351 (quoting Capon v. Eshhar, 418 F.3d 1349, 1357-1358 (Fed. Cir. 2005)).

[141]*See* In re Wands, 858 F.2d 731, 737 (Fed. Cir. 1988) (listing factors for determining whether the degree of experimentation required of an ordinarily skilled person to make and use a claimed invention would be undue) (citing *In re Forman*, No. 602-90, 230 U.S.P.Q. 546, 547 (Bd. Patent App. & Interferences July 2, 1986)). The *Wands* factors include:

1) the quantity of experimentation necessary;
2) the amount of direction or guidance presented;
3) the presence or absence of working examples;
4) the nature of the invention;
5) the state of the prior art;
6) the relative skill of those in the art;
7) the predictability or unpredictability of the art; and
8) the breadth of the claims.

Wands, 858 F.2d at 737.

[142]*See Ariad*, 593 F.3d at 1343 (stating that "[l]ike [Eli] Lilly, we also read Supreme Court precedent as recognizing a written description requirement separate from an enablement requirement even after the introduction of claims"); *id.*, 593 F.3d at 1347 (stating that "[i]n addition to the statutory language and Supreme Court precedent supporting the existence of a written description requirement separate from enablement, *stare decisis* impels us to uphold it now"); *id.*, 593 F.3d at 1351 (stating that "[s]ince its inception, this court has consistently held that §112, first paragraph, contains a written description requirement separate from enablement").

enablement requirement considered earlier in this chapter.[143] These two requirements have been recognized in the case law as separate and independent legal notions at least since the CCPA's 1967 foundational decision in *In re Ruschig*.[144]

The following simple example helps to clarify the difference between the enablement requirement and the written description of the invention requirement. Assume that a patent application as filed discloses and claims a red widget. No other color of widget is mentioned, nor is any suggestion made in the application that the claimed widget could be any color other than red. Although a person of ordinary skill in the art might arguably be *enabled* by this disclosure to make widgets of other colors (such as blue widgets or yellow widgets), a generic claim later presented during the course of the patent application's prosecution that recited "a widget of a primary color" (i.e., "primary color" meaning blue, red, or yellow) would not be valid under the written description of the invention requirement. This is because the as-filed patent application did not provide a written description of "the invention," as later claimed generically; the application showed only that the inventor was in possession of red widgets when she filed. Thus, the later-filed generic claim would not be entitled to the earlier filing date of the application as the *prima facie* date of invention of the claimed genus of primary color widgets (under pre-AIA rules).

Patent law practitioners might say that in such a situation, the patent's disclosure does not "support" the broader, later-presented claim to "a widget of a primary color." In particular, the disclosure does not support a claim encompassing blue widgets, or yellow widgets, or widgets of any non-primary color.[145] Although the disclosure may well

---

[143]*See Ariad,* 598 F.3d at 1344 (parsing the text of 35 U.S.C. §112, first paragraph, as including a "written description of the invention" separate from the enablement requirement).

[144]379 F.2d 990 (C.C.P.A. 1967). The Federal Circuit's panel opinion in *University of Rochester v. G.D. Searle & Co.*, 358 F.3d 916 (Fed. Cir. 2004) [hereafter *Rochester I*], contends that a written description requirement separate from the enablement requirement was recognized in CCPA decisions even prior to *Ruschig* in 1967. *See Rochester I*, 358 F.3d at 923 (citing Jepson v. Coleman, 314 F.2d 533, 536 (C.C.P.A. 1963); In re Moore, 155 F.2d 379, 382 (C.C.P.A. 1946); In re Sus, 306 F.2d 494, 497 (C.C.P.A. 1962)). *But see* University of Rochester v. G.D. Searle & Co., 375 F.3d 1303, 1311 (Fed. Cir. 2004) [hereafter *Rochester II*] (Rader, J., dissenting from denial of rehearing *en banc*) (discussing *Jepson, Moore,* and *Sus* and concluding that these cases "shed little light on the modern written description requirement.").

[145]The proper basis for rejecting a claim to "a widget of a primary color" in the above hypothetical would be for failure to comply with the written description of the invention requirement of 35 U.S.C. §112(a) (eff. Sept. 16, 2012), *not* as a rejection for new matter under 35 U.S.C. §132(a). The latter section, which states that "[n]o amendment shall introduce new matter into the disclosure of the invention," is "properly employed as a basis for objection to amendments to the abstract, specifications, or drawings attempting to add new disclosure to that originally presented," In re Rasmussen, 650

enable a person having ordinary skill in the art of widgets to make and use widgets of colors other than red, there is no evidence in the application as filed that the inventor was at that time in possession of any invention broader than the red widget.

4.   Typical Fact Scenarios Invoking Written Description Scrutiny

The procedural context of the above example, which involves the presentation of a new claim during ongoing prosecution after the patent application had been filed, is a typical one for written description issues. Written description of the invention issues usually arise in "time gap" situations, when (1) new claims are added to a pending patent application, (2) an originally filed claim is substantively amended during prosecution, (3) an applicant claims the benefit of the earlier filing date of a related domestic patent application[146] or a corresponding foreign-origin patent application,[147] or (4) an interference is declared in which the issue is support for a count in the specification of one or more of the parties.[148] These situations have been referred to as involving "priority policing."[149]

Situation (3), involving claims by patent applicants to the benefit of an earlier domestic or foreign filing date, is of central importance in the post-AIA regime. Written description of the invention compliance often will be at issue. In the post-AIA regime, a great deal turns on

---

F.2d 1212, 1214-1215 (C.C.P.A. 1981), but does not apply to amendments made to patent *claims*.

[146]*See* 35 U.S.C. §119(e) (domestic priority claimed from provisional application); *id.*§120 (domestic priority claimed from parent or earlier-filed continuing application by a later-filed continuing application).

[147]*See* 35 U.S.C. §119(a).

[148]*See* In re Smith, 481 F.2d 910, 914 (C.C.P.A. 1973) (explaining that the written description of the invention "applies whether the case factually arises out of an assertion of entitlement to the filing date of a previously filed application under §120, as was involved, e.g., in *In re Smith* [458 F.2d 1389 (C.C.P.A. 1972)] and *In re Ahlbrecht*, 435 F.2d 908 [C.C.P.A. (1971)], or arises in the interference context wherein the issue is support for a count in the specification of one or more of the parties, e.g., as was the situation in *Fields v. Conover*, 443 F.2d 1386 [C.C.P.A. (1971)], and *Snitzer v. Etzel*, 465 F.2d 899 [C.C.P.A. (1972)], or arises in an *ex parte* case involving a single application, but where the claim at issue was filed subsequent to the filing of the application, e.g. as in *In re Ruschig*, 379 F.2d 990 [C.C.P.A. (1967)], and *In re Welstead*, 463 F.2d 1110 [C.C.P.A. 1972)] (which involved a new matter rejection under §132, but which was resolved on the authority of description requirement cases)").

[149]*See* Anascape, Ltd. v. Nintendo Am., Inc., 601 F.3d 1333, 1341 (Fed. Cir. 2010) (Gajarsa, J., concurring) (writing separately to "highlight the majority's best use of the written description requirement as a priority-policing mechanism in contradistinction to an independent basis for invalidity").

determining the "effective filing date" of a claimed invention. The AIA-implemented definition of "effective filing date" explicitly contemplates that applicants may assert claims to "a right of priority under section 119," which includes domestic priority under 35 U.S.C. §119(e) to the date of an applicant's §111(b) provisional application. The "effective filing date" also explicitly contemplates claims to "the benefit of an earlier filing date" under 35 U.S.C. §120 that seek the filing date of an applicant's earlier-filed co-pending domestic application.[150] In turn, both of these statutory provisions (i.e., 35 U.S.C. §119(e) and §120) explicitly require that the disclosure in the priority document (i.e., the provisional application or the earlier-filed co-pending application) satisfies not only the enablement requirement but also the written description of the invention requirement of 35 U.S.C. §112(a). The written description of the invention requirement must be met for the later-claimed invention as of the earlier effective filing date sought for that invention.[151]

5. Federal Circuit's Expansion of the Written Description Requirement

Beginning in 1997 with *Regents of the Univ. of Cal. v. Eli Lilly & Co.*,[152] the Federal Circuit has expanded written description of the invention analysis to consider the validity of un-amended, originally filed claims (i.e., claims presented in a patent application when it was filed and not amended thereafter).[153] In the view of this author, this is an anomalous application of written description principles, contrary

---

[150]*See* 35 U.S.C. §100(i)(1)(B) (eff. Mar. 16, 2013).

[151]*See* Leahy-Smith America Invents Act, Pub. L. No. 112-29 (H.R. 1249), §15(b), 125 Stat. 284, 328 (2011) ("Conforming Amendment.—Sections 119(e)(1) and 120 of title 35, United States Code, are each amended by striking 'the first paragraph of section 112 of this title' and inserting 'section 112(a) (other than the requirement to disclose the best mode)'"); 35 U.S.C. §119(e)(1) (eff. Sept. 16, 2011); 35 U.S.C. §120 (eff. Sept. 16, 2011).

[152]119 F.3d 1559 (Fed. Cir. 1997).

[153]*See* Ariad Pharms., Inc. v. Eli Lilly and Co., 598 F.3d 1336, 1351 (Fed. Cir. 2010) (*en banc*) (holding that "[n]either the statute nor legal precedent limits the written description requirement to cases of priority or distinguishes between original and amended claims"); Enzo Biochem., Inc. v. Gen-Probe, Inc., 323 F.3d 956, 968 (Fed. Cir. 2002) (rejecting patentee's contention that "the written description requirement for the generic claims is necessarily met as a matter of law because the claim language appears in *ipsis verbis* in the specification" and contending that "[i]f a purported description of an invention does not meet the requirements of the statute, the fact that it appears as an original claim or in the specification does not save it"); Regents of the Univ. of Cal. v. Eli Lilly & Co., 119 F.3d 1559 (Fed. Cir. 1997).

to binding precedent.[154] Nevertheless, the Federal Circuit adopted this view *en banc* in its 2010 *Ariad* decision, so *Ariad* represents the controlling law unless and until the Supreme Court were to overrule it.

In the author's view, originally filed claims constitute their own disclosure, and by their inclusion in the originally filed application clearly signal that the applicant considered herself to be in possession of the claimed subject matter as of the filing date.[155] There is no "time gap" present by which an applicant could unfairly obtain an advantage in terms of the extent of prior art that would be legally available for citation against her originally filed claim.

Although the question whether the patent application provides an *enabling* disclosure having a scope reasonably commensurate with the scope of the originally filed claims may legitimately be at issue in some cases,[156] this is a completely separate inquiry from that of compliance with the written description of the invention requirement. In

---

[154]The inappropriateness of applying written description of the invention analysis to original claims filed with the application was conclusively established in 1973 with *In re Gardner*, 475 F.2d 1389 (C.C.P.A. 1973). Reversing a USPTO Board of Appeals rejection of an original claim under the written description requirement of 35 U.S.C. §112, ¶1, the *Gardner* court explained that "[c]laim 2, which apparently was an original claim, in itself constituted a description in the original disclosure equivalent in scope and identical in language to the total subject matter now being claimed. . . . Nothing more is necessary for compliance with the description requirement. . . ."*Id*. at 1391 (citation omitted). On petition for rehearing, the CCPA rejected the USPTO's argument that an original application claim should not be considered part of the "written description" unless the specification contained or was amended to contain the subject matter of the claim. Whether such amendment should be made was merely an "administrative matter" for the agency rather than a proper basis for the court's decision on description requirement compliance. In re Gardner, 480 F.2d 879 (C.C.P.A. 1973). The CCPA confirmed *Gardner*'s holding that originally filed claims constitute part of the disclosure in *In re Koller*, 613 F.2d 819, 823 (C.C.P.A. 1980) (citing *Gardner* for the proposition that "original claims constitute their own description"). The *Koller* court held that method claims reciting the term "liquid medium," presented in a continuing application, were supported in accordance with §112 of the Patent Act by a grandparent application's claims that used the same terminology. *See id*. (noting that "the term 'liquid medium' is found in both places [and] the two sets of claims are similar in wording").

[155]*See* Janice M. Mueller, *The Evolving Application of the Written Description Requirement to Biotechnological Inventions*, 13 BERKELEY TECH. L.J. 615, 633-639 (1998) (criticizing Federal Circuit's application of written description scrutiny to originally filed claims in *Regents of the Univ. of Cal. v. Eli Lilly & Co.*, 119 F.3d 1559 (Fed. Cir. 1997)).

[156]For example, Circuit Judge Rader views both *Eli Lilly* and *University of Rochester* as invoking enablement issues rather than written description violations. *See* Univ. of Rochester v. G.D. Searle & Co., 375 F.3d 1303, 1312 (Rader, J., dissenting from denial of rehearing *en banc*) (stating that "[i]n both *Eli Lilly* and *Rochester*, for instance, the invention A (rat insulin in *Eli Lilly*; an assay for Cox 1 and 2 in *Rochester*) was enabled and described, but the invention B (human insulin in *Eli Lilly*; a Cox 2 inhibitor in *Rochester*) was not enabled").

D. The Written Description of the Invention Requirement

the author's view, and contrary to the Federal Circuit's *en banc Ariad* decision, the written description of the invention requirement has no applicability to unamended originally filed claims.

In its 1997 decision in *Regents of Univ. of Cal. v. Eli Lilly and Co.* (hereafter *Lilly*),[157] the Federal Circuit for the first time relied on the written description requirement as a general-purpose disclosure doctrine to invalidate un-amended, originally filed claims (i.e., claims presented in a patent application on its filing date and not amended thereafter).[158]

In 1990 the Regents of the University of California (UC) sued Eli Lilly and Company (Lilly) for infringement of UC patents directed to the use of recombinant DNA technology to produce human insulin.[159] The patents were based on UC's successful cloning of the rat insulin gene, a breakthrough development that has been viewed as "open[ing] the way to modern insulin production."[160] Specifically, UC's U.S. Patent

---

[157]119 F.3d 1559 (Fed. Cir. 1997).

[158]*See* Enzo Biochem, Inc. v. Gen-Probe Inc., 323 F.3d 956, 968 (Fed. Cir. 2002) (Lourie, J.) (explaining that "[i]n *Eli Lilly*, we were faced with a set of facts in which the words of the claim alone did not convey an adequate description of the invention... . In such a situation, regardless whether the claim appears in the original specification and is thus supported by the specification as of the filing date, §112, ¶1 is not necessarily met.") (citing Guidelines for Examination of Patent Applications Under the 35 U.S.C. 112, ¶1 "Written Description" Requirement, 66 FED. REG. 1099, 1100 (Jan. 5, 2001) (noting *Eli Lilly*'s clarification of the "original claim" doctrine in situations in which the name of the claimed material does not convey sufficient identifying information)); *see also* Christopher M. Holman, *Is Lilly Written Description a Paper Tiger? A Comprehensive Assessment of the Impact of Eli Lilly and Its Progeny in the Courts and PTO,* 17 ALB. L.J. SCI. & TECH. 1, 14 (2007) (observing that the "biotechnology and patent communities were shocked by *Lilly*, particularly because of the novel manner in which the court applied the written description requirement to originally filed claims, and the stringent disclosure requirements the decision seemed to impose on biotechnology inventors"); Arti K. Rai, *Intellectual Property Rights in Biotechnology: Addressing New Technology,* 34 WAKE FOREST L. REV. 827, 834-835 (1999) (stating that "in [*Lilly*] ... the CAFC broke new ground by applying the written description requirement not only to later-filed claims but also to claims filed in the original patent"); Janice M. Mueller, *The Evolving Application of the Written Description Requirement to Biotechnological Inventions,* 13 BERKELEY TECH. L.J. 615, 617-618 (1998) (contending that "the *Lilly* court improperly diverged from established description doctrine in two significant aspects: first, by utilizing the description requirement to invalidate original application claims; and second, by requiring that a written description of a claim to DNA must set forth the specific nucleotide sequence of that DNA") (footnote omitted).

[159]*See* Regents of Univ. of Cal. v. Eli Lilly and Co., 119 F.3d 1559, 1562 (Fed. Cir. 1997); *see also A Bitter Battle over Insulin Gene,* 277 SCIENCE 1028, 1028 (1997) (describing suit as a "vicious fight [that] centers on a landmark discovery by [University of California at San Francisco] biologists at the dawn of the biotechnology era: the first successful cloning of the rat insulin gene").

[160]*A Bitter Battle over Insulin Gene,* 277 SCIENCE 1028, 1029 (1997) (remarks of William Rutter, former University of California, San Francisco scientist and chair of Chiron Corporation, Emeryville, California). UC's successful isolation of the rat insulin

155

No. 4,652,525 ('525 patent) included claims 1, 2, 4, 6, and 7, which were genus claims that recited complementary DNA (cDNA) encoding vertebrate or mammalian insulin.[161] In contrast, claim 5 of UC's '525 patent specifically recited cDNA encoding human insulin. Claim 3 recited "a nucleotide sequence having the structure of and transcribed from the rat gene for insulin."[162]

Critical to the *Lilly* saga was that as of the 1977 filing date of the application leading to the '525 patent, UC had determined and isolated the preproinsulin (PPI) and proinsulin (PI) cDNA sequences found in rats, but not those in humans.[163] UC included in its patent application a constructive or "prophetic" example describing a method that could be used to obtain the human insulin–encoding cDNA recited in claim 5, as well as the amino acid sequences of human insulin A and B chains.[164] However, UC did not actually isolate and sequence human cDNA until nearly two years after the application's 1977 filing date.[165]

---

gene represented "the first time the entire genetic sequence for an insulin gene had been spelled out. . . . " *Id. See also* Christopher M. Holman, *Is* Lilly *Written Description a Paper Tiger? A Comprehensive Assessment of the Impact of* Eli Lilly *and its Progeny in the Courts and PTO,* 17 ALB. L.J. SCI. & TECH. 1, 13 (2007) (referring to UC's successful cloning of the rat insulin gene as "a technical tour de force").

[161]"Complementary" DNA (cDNA) is a complementary copy or "clone" of messenger RNA (mRNA), made in the laboratory by reverse transcription of mRNA. A cDNA contains only the protein-encoding regions of DNA. *See* In re Deuel, 51 F.3d 1552, 1554 (Fed. Cir. 1995).

[162]The claims of UC's '525 patent read as follows:

1. A recombinant plasmid replicable in procaryotic host containing within its nucleotide sequence a subsequence having the structure of the reverse transcript of an mRNA of a vertebrate, which mRNA encodes insulin.
2. A recombinant procaryotic microorganism modified to contain a nucleotide sequence having the structure of the reverse transcript of an mRNA of a vertebrate, which mRNA encodes insulin.
3. The bacterium Escherichia coli which has been modified to contain a nucleotide sequence having the structure of and transcribed from the rat gene for insulin.
4. A microorganism according to claim 2 wherein the vertebrate is a mammal.
5. A microorganism according to claim 2 wherein the vertebrate is a human.
6. A plasmid according to claim 1 comprising a plasmid containing at least one genetic determinant of col E1.
7. A microorganism according to claim 2 comprising a strain of Escherichia coli.

[163]*See* Regents of Univ. of Cal. v. Eli Lilly and Co., 39 U.S.P.Q.2d (BNA) 1225, 1240 (S.D. Ind. 1995).

[164]*See Lilly,* 119 F.3d at 1567.

[165]*See* Regents of Univ. of Cal. v. Eli Lilly and Co., 39 U.S.P.Q.2d (BNA) 1225, 1240 (S.D. Ind. 1995) (stating that "it was not until nearly two years after the original application for the '525 [patent] was filed that UC inventors actually isolated and characterized human insulin cDNA"); *id.* at 1243 (stating that "UC contends that the [human proinsulin amino acid] sequence was not known until [the September 12, 1979 filing date of UC's U.S. Patent No. 4,431,740 ('740 patent)], at which time inventors of the

D. The Written Description of the Invention Requirement

Accused infringer Lilly did not assert that the '525 patent specification failed to *enable* the human insulin cDNA and vertebrate and mammalian insulin cDNA claims in accordance with §112, ¶1 of the Patent Act.[166] Lilly's decision to forgo a challenge to the '525 patent on enablement grounds was not surprising; UC's isolation of the rat insulin cDNA made the human insulin cDNA "relatively easy" to "fish out" thereafter.[167] Instead, Lilly attacked the validity of the asserted claims on the ground that the '525 patent did not provide an adequate written description of the human, mammalian, and vertebrate cDNA inventions claimed.

The Federal Circuit agreed, affirming a district court's conclusion that all the asserted claims of UC's '525 patent were invalid for failure to comply with the written description of the invention requirement.[168] The appellate court first analyzed species claim 5, which recited human insulin–encoding cDNA, and concluded that the '525 specification was fatally defective for failing to *structurally* describe the claimed cDNA. The human insulin–encoding cDNA of claim 5 was not adequately described, the court held, because the '525 patent's specification lacked a disclosure of that cDNA's "relevant structural or physical characteristics."[169] The court specifically pointed to the absence in the specification of "sequence information indicating which nucleotides constitute human cDNA. . . . "[170] Nor did the '525 specification's provision in Example 6 of a process that could be used to isolate the human cDNA remedy the perceived deficiency of the disclosure; the Federal Circuit concluded that "describing a method of preparing a cDNA or even describing the protein that the cDNA encodes, as the example does, does not necessarily describe the cDNA itself."[171]

The Federal Circuit in *Lilly* then turned to the '525 patent's genus claims 1, 2, 4, 6, and 7, which more broadly recited cDNA encoding vertebrate and mammalian insulin. Like species claim 5, the appellate court held the generic claims invalid as not supported by an adequate

---

'740 patent actually isolated and characterized the human source DNA that codes for proinsulin").

[166]*See* Regents of Univ. of Cal. v. Eli Lilly and Co., 39 U.S.P.Q.2d (BNA) 1225, 1239-1241 (S.D. Ind. 1995) (identifying the "written description requirement" as the only issue of invalidity raised with respect to '525 patent); *see also Federal Circuit Rules It Takes More Than One cDNA Sequence to Claim a Genus*, III INTELL. PROP. LAWCAST (Dec. 29, 1997) (audio interview of UC counsel Harold J. McElhinny) (stating that Lilly never raised non-enablement as a defense to UC's '525 patent).

[167]*A Bitter Battle over Insulin Gene*, 277 SCIENCE 1028, 1029 (1997).

[168]*See* Regents of Univ. of Cal. v. Eli Lilly and Co., 119 F.3d 1559, 1569 (Fed. Cir. 1997).

[169]*See Lilly*, 119 F.3d at 1567.

[170]*See Lilly*, 119 F.3d at 1567 (contrasting the lack of human cDNA sequence data with UC's provision of rat cDNA sequence data in example 5 of the '525 patent).

[171]*Lilly*, 119 F.3d at 1567.

written description.[172] The extent of the written description required to support claims 1, 2, 4, 6, and 7 mirrored, on the genus level, the court's earlier pronouncement that a structural description must be provided to support a claim to a species of cDNA:

> [A] cDNA is not defined or described by the mere name "cDNA," even if accompanied by the name of the protein that it encodes, but requires a kind of specificity usually achieved by means of the recitation of the sequence of nucleotides that make up the cDNA. . . . A description of a genus of cDNAs may be achieved by means of a recitation of a representative number of cDNAs, defined by nucleotide sequence, falling within the scope of the genus or of a recitation of structural features common to the members of the genus, which features constitute a substantial portion of the genus.[173]

In the Federal Circuit's view, a "functional" definition of cDNA was insufficient because it indicated only "what the gene does, rather than what it is."[174] The *Lilly* court viewed such a functional definition as merely a statement of result and observed that "[m]any such genes may achieve that result."[175] Without more, UC's "generic statement[s]" such as "vertebrate insulin cDNA" and "mammalian insulin cDNA" did not constitute an adequate written description of the generic claims because they did "not distinguish the claimed genus from others, except by function."[176]

In the wake of the 1997 *Lilly* decision, Federal Circuit judges continued to debate the proper role of the written description of the invention requirement. The 2002 *Enzo* decision, discussed *supra* Section D.2, is a prime example. In 2004, the *en banc* appellate court declined to rehear the closely watched case of *University of Rochester v. G.D. Searle & Co.*[177] The university's U.S. Patent No. 6,048,850 ('850 patent) claimed methods "for selectively inhibiting PGHS-2 activity in a human host" by "administering a non-steroidal compound that selectively inhibits

---

[172]*Lilly,* 119 F.3d at 1569 (rejecting "UC's argument that the district court clearly erred in finding claims 1, 2, 4, 6 and 7 invalid for failure to provide an adequate written description").

[173]*Lilly,* 119 F.3d at 1568-1569 (citation omitted).

[174]*Lilly,* 119 F.3d at 1568 (citing Fiers v. Revel, 984 F.2d 1164, 1169-1171 (Fed. Cir. 1993)).

[175]*Lilly,* 119 F.3d at 1568.

[176]*Lilly,* 119 F.3d at 1568 (stating further that such generic statement "does not specifically define any of the genes that fall within its definition. It does not define any structural features commonly possessed by members of the genus that distinguish them from others. One skilled in the art therefore cannot, as one can do with a fully described genus, visualize or recognize the identity of the members of the genus. A definition by function . . . does not suffice to define the genus because it is only an indication of what the gene does, rather than what it is.").

[177]358 F.3d 916 (Fed. Cir. 2004).

activity of the PGHS-2 gene product to [or in] a human host in need of such treatment."[178] This invention provided a screening method for use in determining whether a particular drug selectively inhibited the activity of COX-2 so as to reduce inflammation without the gastrointestinal side effects associated with prior art methods that inhibited not only COX-2 but also COX-1, a distinct cyclooxygenase. The university filed its first application directed to the invention in 1992. After filing a series of continuation, continuation-in-part, and divisional applications relating back to the 1992 parent, it received in 1998 Patent No. 5,837,479 ('479 patent) claiming "methods for identifying a compound that inhibits prostaglandin synthesis catalyzed by [PGHS-2]." Rochester's '850 patent in suit issued in 2000 from a related divisional application.

Rochester sued Pfizer in 2000 for infringement of the '850 patent based on Pfizer's sale of its COX-2 inhibitors Celebrex® and Bextra®. The parties disputed whether Rochester was claiming anything new in its '850 patent that it had not already patented in its '479 patent. A district court granted Pfizer's motion for summary judgment of invalidity based on failure to satisfy the written description requirement (as well as lack of enablement), finding that the university's '850 patent failed to describe any "non-steroidal compound that selectively inhibits activity of the PGHS-2 gene," that the university inventors themselves did not know of any such compounds when they filed their application, and that a skilled artisan would have had to engage in undue experimentation in order to deduce the compounds.

The *Rochester* panel affirmed the district court's grant of summary judgment that the university's '850 patent was invalid on written description grounds. The panel rejected the university's argument that no written description requirement exists independent of enablement, stating that "[a]lthough there is often significant overlap between the three requirements [of written description, enablement, and best mode], they are nonetheless independent of each other."[179] In the Federal Circuit's view, the written-description requirement "serves a teaching function" as a "quid pro quo" in which the public is given meaningful disclosure in exchange for being excluded from practice of the invention for a limited time. The court also rejected the university's argument that the written description originally played a public notice function that has been supplanted by the subsequent statutory requirement for claims. "[W]hile the role of the claims is to

---

[178]*Rochester*, 358 F.3d at 918. PGHS-2 is a form of prostaglandin H synthase also known as "COX-2." COX-2 is a type of enzyme known as a cyclooxygenase that is expressed (i.e., produced biologically) in response to inflammatory stimuli and is thought to be associated with arthritis.

[179]*Rochester*, 358 F.3d at 921.

give public notice of the subject matter that is protected, the role of the specification is to teach, both what the invention is (written description) and how to make and use it (enablement)."[180]

The *Rochester* panel also distinguished earlier cases such as *In re Edwards*,[181] in which the court held that the written description requirement was satisfied by a specification that described a claimed compound by the process by which it was made, rather than by its structure. In that case, the Federal Circuit noted, the CCPA found that the application taken as a whole would reasonably lead persons skilled in the art to the claimed compound. Although there is "some flexibility" in the mode of complying with the written description requirement, the specification must set forth enough detail to allow the person of ordinary skill in the art "to understand what is claimed and to recognize that the inventor invented what is claimed." With respect to the Rochester '850 patent in suit, "[t]he only claims that appear to be supported by the specification are claims to assay methods, but those claims were already issued in [Rochester's earlier] '479 patent."[182]

On July 2, 2004, a divided Federal Circuit denied the university's petition for rehearing *en banc*, producing four dissenting votes and five opinions.[183] The lead opinion by Circuit Judge Lourie, author of the *Rochester* panel opinion, concurred in the denial of rehearing largely for the reasons stated in the panel opinion. Circuit Judge Dyk concurred in the decision to deny rehearing *en banc* but noted that his vote "should not be taken as an endorsement" of the court's existing written description jurisprudence. In Judge Dyk's view, the court "ha[s] yet to articulate satisfactory standards that can be applied to all technologies." Circuit Judge Newman dissented from the *en banc* court's decision not to resolve the "burgeoning conflict" of the written description requirement, which she characterized as having been "promoted from simple semantics into a fundamental conflict concerning patent scope and the support needed to claim biological products." Dissenting Circuit Judge Linn, joined by Circuit Judges Rader and Gajarsa, contended that there is no written description requirement divorced from enablement. The patent law "requires a written description of the invention, but the measure of the sufficiency of that written description in meeting the conditions of patentability in paragraph 1 [of section 112] depends solely on whether it enables any person skilled in the art to which the invention pertains to make and use the claimed invention and sets forth the best mode of carrying out

[180]*Rochester,* 358 F.3d at 922 n.5.
[181]568 F.2d 1349 (C.C.P.A. 1978).
[182]*Rochester,* 358 F.3d at 928.
[183]Univ. of Rochester v. G.D. Searle & Co., 375 F.3d 1303 (Fed. Cir. 2004).

D. The Written Description of the Invention Requirement

the invention."[184] "There is simply no reason to interpret section 112 to require applicants for patent to set forth the metes and bounds of the claimed invention in two separate places in the application. That is the exclusive function of the claims."[185] Circuit Judge Rader, joined by Circuit Judges Gajarsa and Linn, provided a lengthy dissenting opinion decrying the court's failure to come to terms with *Eli Lilly* (discussed above), a case in which in 1997 "this court for the first time applied the written description language of 35 U.S.C. §112, ¶1 as a general disclosure requirement in place of enablement, rather than in its traditional role as a doctrine to prevent applicants from adding new inventions to an older disclosure."[186] Judge Rader also noted that "no other patent system in the world has the *Eli Lilly* requirement to this day."[187]

Despite some Federal Circuit judges' clear discomfort with *Eli Lilly*'s expansive formulation of the written description of the invention requirement, the court continued to apply it in its 2008 decision *Carnegie Mellon University v. Hoffmann-La Roche Inc.*[188] The CMU patents in suit were directed to, *inter alia*, recombinant plasmids (small, replicating circular loops of DNA) that contained "*polA*" gene coding regions from bacteria for the expression of large quantities of the enzyme "DNA polymerase I." The *CMU* case did not raise the traditional written description question of support for new claims added after the application filing date. Rather, the issue was support for an originally filed genus claim: the CMU patents (as filed for in 1984) disclosed the *polA* gene from only one type of bacteria (*E. coli*), but the claims were not limited to any particular bacterial species. At the time of the invention, the *polA* gene from *E. coli* was one of only three bacterial *polA* genes that scientists had succeeded in cloning, out of thousands of bacterial species. The Federal Circuit observed that "[t]he narrow specifications of the . . . patents only disclose the *polA* gene coding sequence from one bacterial source, *viz.*, *E. coli*. Significantly, the specification fails to disclose or describe the *polA* gene coding sequence for any other bacterial species."[189] Applying *Eli Lilly,* the court held the challenged claims invalid as not supported by an adequate written description. It rejected the patentee's attempt to distinguish *Eli Lilly* on the ground that the case at bar dealt with a "combination of well known elements that create a generic biological tool," whereas *Eli Lilly* involved a specific cDNA sequence.

---

[184]*Rochester*, 375 F.3d at 1325 (Linn, J., dissenting from denial of rehearing *en banc*).

[185]*Id.* at 1326-1327.

[186]*Id.* at 1307 (Rader, J., dissenting from denial of rehearing *en banc*).

[187]*Id.* at 1312.

[188]541 F.3d 1115 (Fed. Cir. 2008).

[189]*Id.* at 1125.

"[N]othing in *Eli Lilly* indicates that [its] holding was limited to inventions involving novel DNA sequences," the Federal Circuit instructed. The *CMU* court also cited as "accurate" and "persuasive" authority the USPTO's "Guidelines for Examination of Patent Applications under the 35 U.S.C. §112, ¶1, 'Written Description' Requirement,"[190] which state that "[f]or inventions in an unpredictable art, adequate written description of a genus which embraces widely variant species *cannot* be achieved by disclosing only one species within the genus."[191] In sum, the CMU patent specifications failed to show that the inventors possessed enough species to show that they had "invented and disclosed the totality of the genus"[192] that they claimed.

In 2010, the Federal Circuit went *en banc* to resolve its continuing disagreement over the proper role of the written description of the invention requirement.[193] The prevailing party and validity challenger was again the Eli Lilly Corporation. Unless the Supreme Court decides to take up the issue in some future case, the Federal Circuit's *en banc* decision in *Ariad Pharms., Inc. v. Eli Lilly and Co.*[194] establishes that the expansive form of the written description of the invention requirement, as first applied in the 1997 *Lilly* decision as a general-purpose disclosure requirement, is the controlling law for the U.S. patent system. As a long-awaited response by the *en banc* court to the prolonged uncertainty concerning the requirement's scope, the *Ariad* decision mandates careful study.

The *Ariad* case involved a "high-stakes tussle" over the reach of a pioneering biotechnology patent.[195] In the mid-1980s, 13 scientists collaborating at the Massachusetts Institute of Technology (MIT), the Whitehead Institute for Biomedical Research, and Harvard University were the first to identify a protein known as Nuclear Factor Kappa B (NF-κB).[196] Present in the cytoplasm of various types of cells, the

---

[190]66 FED. REG. 1099 (Jan. 5, 2001).

[191]*Id.* at 1106.

[192]*Carnegie Mellon Univ.*, 541 F.3d at 1126.

[193]*See Ariad Pharms., Inc. v. Eli Lilly and Co.*, 598 F.3d 1336, 1342 (Fed. Cir. 2010) (*en banc*) (granting Ariad's petition "[i]n light of the controversy concerning the distinctness and proper role of the written description requirement").

[194]598 F.3d 1336 (Fed. Cir. 2010) (*en banc*).

[195]Ken Garber, *Ariad's NFkB Patent Claims Shot Down on Appeal*, 27 NATURE BIOTECHNOLOGY 494, 494 (2009) (reporting that the *Ariad* case "has embroiled big pharma, several prominent biotech companies and even Nobel Prize winners as courtroom witnesses in a high-stakes tussle over the commercial reach of patents with especially broad claims").

[196]*See* Ariad Pharms., Inc. v. Eli Lilly and Co., 529 F. Supp. 2d 106, 112 (D. Mass. 2007); *see also* Ariad Pharms., Inc. v. Eli Lilly and Co., 598 F.3d 1336, 1340 (Fed. Cir. 2010) (*en banc*). The scientists directing the collaboration were Nobel Laureates Dr. David Baltimore of the Whitehead Institute and Dr. Phillip Sharp of MIT, along with Dr. Thomas Maniatis, the Thomas H. Lee Professor of Molecular and Cellular Biology at Harvard. *See* Complaint at ¶11, Case No. 02 CV 11280RWZ, Ariad Pharms., Inc.

D. The Written Description of the Invention Requirement

NF-κB protein is a transcription factor, that is, a protein that affects gene expression (the process in which a gene's DNA sequence is converted to a protein in a cell).

The scientists were also first to discover the mechanism by which the NF-κB protein activates gene expression underlying the body's immune responses to infection. They found that the NF-κB protein mediates certain intracellular signaling. The inventors postulated that reducing NF-κB activity could reduce the symptoms of diseases including cancer, AIDS, sepsis, and atherosclerosis. They hypothesized that three classes of molecules were capable of reducing NF-κB activity: (1) "specific inhibitors," (2) "dominantly interfering molecules," and (3) "decoy molecules."

The 13 collaborating scientists were named as inventors in a U.S. patent application jointly filed by their institutions in 1986. After a lengthy and complex prosecution, U.S. Patent No. 6,410,516 ('516 patent), titled "Nuclear factors associated with transcriptional regulation," issued in 2002 to the original assignees: MIT, Whitehead Institute, and Harvard. Ariad Pharmaceuticals was the exclusive licensee of the '516 patent.[197]

The relevant claims of the '516 patent are genus claims, encompassing the use of all substances that achieve the desired result of reducing the binding of NF-κB to NF-κB recognition sites.[198] Representative claim 80 (rewritten to include the text of the claim from which it depends) recites:

> 80. [A method for modifying effects of external influences on a eukaryotic cell, which external influences induce NF-κB-mediated intracellular signaling, the method comprising altering NF-κB activity in the cells such that NF-κB-mediated effects of external influences are modified, wherein NF-κB activity in the cell is reduced] wherein reducing NF-κB activity comprises reducing binding of NF-κB to NF-κB recognition sites on genes which are transcriptionally regulated by NF-κB.[199]

---

et al. v. Eli Lilly & Co., No. 02 CV 11280RWZ, 2002 WL 33027597 (D. Mass. June 25, 2002).

[197]*See* Complaint at ¶18, Case No. 02 CV 11280RWZ, Ariad Pharms., Inc. et al. v. Eli Lilly & Co., No. 02 CV 11280RWZ, 2002 WL 33027597 (D. Mass. June 25, 2002).

[198]*Ariad,* 598 F.3d at 1341.

[199]*Ariad,* 598 F.3d at 1340. The district court found that "[t]he allowed claims broadly cover a method of inhibiting the expression of a gene whose transcription is regulated by NF-κB in a eukaryotic cell. The only step required to practice the broadest patented method is to 'reduc[e] NF-κB activity in the cell such that the expression of said gene is inhibited.' No particular agent or substance need be used, nor any particular step(s) performed, to reduce NF-κB activity in order to practice the invention." Ariad Pharms., Inc. v. Eli Lilly and Co., 529 F. Supp. 2d 106, 113-114 (D. Mass. 2007) (footnotes omitted).

The language of the asserted claims, although amended during prosecution, corresponds to language in the original ("priority") application.[200] Thus the *Ariad* case is another in the series of decisions, starting with the 1997 *Lilly* decision, in which the Federal Circuit has applied the written description of the invention requirement to originally filed claims despite the absence of any question regarding priority to an earlier filing date.

When the '516 patent issued in 2002, Ariad and the university assignees (collectively "Ariad") sued Eli Lilly and Co. for infringement. A jury found the asserted claims infringed and not invalid, rejecting Lilly's validity challenges on anticipation, written description, and enablement grounds and awarding damages against Lilly of approximately $65 million.[201] In 2009 a panel of the Federal Circuit overturned the jury verdict on the basis that the claims were invalid under the written description of the invention requirement. The panel noted the "vast scope of these generic claims."[202]

The Federal Circuit thereafter granted Ariad's petition for rehearing *en banc* to resolve much-debated questions concerning the nature and scope of the written description of the invention requirement. The *en banc* court requested briefing on the following two issues:

(1) Whether 35 U.S.C. §112, paragraph 1, contains a written description requirement separate from an enablement requirement?

(2) If a separate written description requirement is set forth in the statute, what is the scope and purpose of that requirement?[203]

In March of 2010, the *en banc* Federal Circuit decided issue (1) in the affirmative, and answered issue (2) as detailed below. The *en banc* opinion for the court was written by Circuit Judge Lourie, who had previously authored the court's written description opinions in *Lilly, Rochester, Enzo,* and *CMU.* The *en banc* opinion for the court in *Ariad* garnered 9 out of 11 possible votes.[204]

---

[200]*Ariad,* 598 F.3d at 1341.

[201]*Ariad Pharms., Inc. v. Eli Lilly and Co.*, 529 F. Supp. 2d 106, 115 (D. Mass. 2007).

[202]*See* Ariad Pharms., Inc. v. Eli Lilly and Co., 560 F.3d 1366, 1376 (Fed. Cir. 2009) (concluding that "[w]hatever thin thread of support a jury might find in the decoy-molecule hypothetical simply cannot bear the weight of the vast scope of these generic claims. . . . Here, the specification at best describes decoy molecule structures and hypothesizes with no accompanying description that they could be used to reduce NF-kB activity. Yet the asserted claims are far broader. We therefore conclude that the jury lacked substantial evidence for its verdict that the asserted claims were supported by adequate written description, and thus hold the asserted claims invalid.").

[203]*Ariad,* 598 F.3d at 1342. In addition to the parties' submissions, the *en banc* court received 25 *amicus curiae* briefs. *Ariad,* 598 F.3d at 1342.

[204]Circuit Judges Rader and Linn each filed dissenting-in-part, concurring-in-part opinions. An "additional views" opinion by Judge Newman and a concurring opinion

D. The Written Description of the Invention Requirement

With respect to *en banc* briefing question (1), the Federal Circuit agreed with Eli Lilly that the text of the first paragraph of 35 U.S.C. §112 requires a written description of the invention requirement separate from the enablement requirement. In other words, the court parsed the statute as requiring that

(1) The specification shall contain a *written description of the invention, and*

(2) The specification shall contain a written description ... of the manner and process of making and using it, in such full, clear, concise, and exact terms as to *enable* any person skilled in the art to which it pertains, or with which it is most nearly connected, to make and use the same.... [205]

In the Federal Circuit's view, the contrary reading urged by Ariad—namely, that the written description requirement exists only to identify the invention that must comply with the enablement requirement—would result in a "surplusage" of the statutory language and contravene its "parallelism."[206]

Policy concerns also supported the existence of a separate written description requirement, which the *en banc* court viewed as "part of the *quid pro quo* of a patent."[207] A patent's written description of a claimed invention serves many important purposes: it "allows the United States Patent and Trademark Office ('PTO') to examine applications effectively; courts to understand the invention, determine compliance with the statute, and to construe the claims; and the public to understand and improve upon the invention and to avoid the claimed boundaries of the patentee's exclusive rights."[208]

The Federal Circuit also cited precedent supporting the independence of the written description requirement from enablement. Among Supreme Court decisions, the *Ariad* court highlighted the 1938 decision in *Schriber-Schroth Co. v. Cleveland Trust Co.*[209] Although the

---

by Judge Gajarsa meant that in total, the *en banc* rehearing of *Ariad* produced five opinions.

[205]*Ariad*, 598 F.3d at 1344 (citing 35 U.S.C. §112, ¶1 (2006)) (emphasis added).

[206]*Ariad*, 598 F.3d at 1344-1345. Dissenting Judge Linn responded on this point that "there is no justification for reading the statute, beyond the priority context suggested by 35 U.S.C. §120, as requiring anything other than a written description sufficient to enable a skilled artisan to make and use the invention particularly pointed out and distinctly recited in the claims." Ariad Pharms., Inc. v. Eli Lilly and Co., 598 F.3d 1336, 1367 (Fed. Cir. 2010) (*en banc*) (Linn, J., dissenting-in-part and concurring-in-part).

[207]*Ariad*, 598 F.3d at 1345.

[208]*Ariad*, 598 F.3d at 1345.

[209]305 U.S. 47 (1938). *Schriber-Schroth* involved *inter alia* a patent to Gulick on pistons used in internal combustion engines. As filed, Gulick's application disclosed "extremely rigid" web elements in the pistons; five years later Gulick copied another's claim to provoke an interference and made corresponding additions to his disclosure to

Court in *Schriber-Schroth* "did not expressly state" that it was applying a written description requirement separate from enablement, the *Ariad* court concluded that "that is exactly what the Court did."[210]

Identifying what particular purpose or role the written description of the invention requirement serves that is not already addressed by the claims of a patent has always been a conceptual challenge.[211] The *Ariad en banc* court held that a separate written description requirement does not conflict with the function of claims. Claims are principally to provide notice of the boundaries of a patentee's right to exclude, the *en banc* court explained; they do not describe the invention (although their original language contributes to the invention's written description and "in certain cases satisfies" the written description of the invention requirement). Rather, patent claims "define and circumscribe." In contrast, the written description "discloses and teaches."[212]

Another conceptual difficulty with an independent written description of the invention requirement is distinguishing its role from the prohibition on "new matter" in 35 U.S.C. §132.[213] The *en banc* court in *Ariad* explained that improperly adding new matter is distinct from a failure to satisfy the written description of the invention requirement because §132 is merely "an examiner's instruction."[214] "[U]nlike §282 of the Patent Act, which makes the failure to comply with §112 a defense

include "flexible" webs. The Supreme Court rejected Gulick's argument that flexibility was an inherent property of the disclosed metal from which the webs were fabricated, and concluded that "the Gulick amendments were . . . new matter beyond the scope of the device described in the application as filed." *Schriber-Schroth*, 305 U.S. at 58.

[210]*Ariad,* 598 F.3d at 1346. Judge Rader's dissenting opinion responded that

> *Schriber-Schroth*, as the court acknowledges, dealt with amended claims, as did *MacKay Radio & Tel. Co. v. Radio Corp. of Am.*, 306 U.S. 86, 59 S. Ct. 427, 83 L. Ed. 506 (1939), and *Gill v. Wells*, 89 U.S. (22 Wall.) 1, 22 L. Ed. 699 (1874). These cases stand only for the unremarkable proposition that an applicant cannot add new matter to an original disclosure. Thus Supreme Court precedent is fully consistent with the logical reading of the statute and impeaches this court's *ultra vires* imposition of a new written description requirement for original claims, an imposition that first arose in *Regents of the University of California v. Eli Lilly & Co.*, 119 F.3d 1559, 1566-69 (Fed. Cir. 1997).

Ariad Pharms., Inc. v. Eli Lilly and Co., 598 F.3d 1336, 1363 (Fed. Cir. 2010) (*en banc*) (Rader, J., dissenting-in-part and concurring-in-part).

[211]*See* Vas-Cath, Inc. v. Mahurkar, 935 F.2d 1555, 1560 (Fed. Cir. 1991) (observing that "[o]ne may wonder what purpose a separate 'written description' requirement serves, when the second paragraph of §112 expressly requires that the applicant conclude his specification 'with one or more claims particularly pointing out and distinctly claiming the subject matter which the applicant regards as his invention'").

[212]*Ariad,* 598 F.3d at 1347.

[213]The Patent Act provides that "[n]o amendment shall introduce new matter into the disclosure of the invention." 35 U.S.C. §132(a) (2006) (last sentence of paragraph).

[214]*Ariad,* 598 F.3d at 1348.

to infringement, §132 provides no statutory penalty for a breach." In contrast, "[e]xpress statutory invalidity defenses carry more weight than examiner's instructions. . . ." In any event, "the prohibition on new matter does not negate the need to provide a written description of one's invention."[215]

In view of the Federal Circuit's 1997 *Lilly* decision and its progeny, it is not surprising that the *Ariad* court firmly rejected the patentee's argument that the written description of the invention requirement should not be applied to original claims, that is, to claims included in an application when it is filed. The argument that such claims should be immune from written description scrutiny is based on the premise that "original claims, as part of the original disclosure, constitute their own written description of the invention."[216] The *Ariad* court rejected this premise, at least in the particular context of genus claims:

> Although many original claims will satisfy the written description requirement, certain claims may not. For example, a generic claim may define the boundaries of a vast genus of chemical compounds, and yet the question may still remain whether the specification, including original claim language, demonstrates that the applicant has invented species sufficient to support a claim to a genus. The problem is especially acute with genus claims that use functional language to define the boundaries of a claimed genus. In such a case, the functional claim may simply claim a desired result, and may do so without describing species that achieve that result. But the specification must demonstrate that the applicant has made a generic invention that achieves the claimed result and do so by showing that the applicant has invented species sufficient to support a claim to the functionally-defined genus.[217]

Repeating the test set forth in its 1997 *Lilly* decision, the *Ariad en banc* court observed that a sufficient description of a claimed genus requires the disclosure of either (1) "a representative number of spe-

---

[215]*Ariad,* 598 F.3d at 1348.

[216]*Ariad,* 598 F.3d at 1349. This position is well supported by precedent. *See* In re Gardner, 475 F.2d 1389, 1391 (C.C.P.A. 1973) (reversing Board's rejection of an original claim under the written description requirement of 35 U.S.C. §112, ¶1 and explaining that "[c]laim 2, which apparently was an original claim, in itself constituted a description in the original disclosure equivalent in scope and identical in language to the total subject matter now being claimed. . . . Nothing more is necessary for compliance with the description requirement. . . .") (citation omitted); In re Koller, 613 F.2d 819, 823 (C.C.P.A. 1980) (citing *Gardner* for the proposition that "original claims constitute their own description"). The *Koller* court held that method claims reciting the phrase "liquid medium," presented in a continuing application, were supported in accordance with §112, ¶1 of the Patent Act by a grandparent application's claims that used the same terminology. *See Koller,* 613 F.2d at 823 (noting that "the term 'liquid medium' is found in both places [and] the two sets of claims are similar in wording").

[217]*Ariad,* 598 F.3d at 1349.

cies falling within the scope of the genus" or (2) "structural features common to the members of the genus so that one of skill in the art can 'visualize or recognize' the members of the genus."[218] Merely "drawing a fence" around the outer limits of a genus is not enough to show "that one has invented a genus and not just a species."[219]

Whether the genus claim in question was an original claim or added by amendment is not relevant. According to the *Ariad* court, "[n]either the statute nor legal precedent limits the written description requirement to cases of priority or distinguishes between original and amended claims."[220]

The *en banc Ariad* court then turned to the "possession" test for written description compliance,[221] candidly admitting that the test "has never been very enlightening."[222] Because "the hallmark of written description is disclosure," the *Ariad* court announced that a more complete formulation of the test is "possession as shown in the disclosure."[223] That test requires an "objective inquiry into the four corners of the specification from the perspective of a person of ordinary skill in the art." The description must be such as to show the hypothetical person that the "inventor actually invented the invention claimed."[224]

Because the written description inquiry is a factual one,[225] certain contextual facts are relevant. The level of detail that the specification must supply "varies depending on the nature and scope of the claims and on the complexity and predictability of the relevant technology." For generic claims, relevant contextual factors include (1) "existing knowledge in the particular field"; (2) the "extent and content of the prior art"; (3) the "maturity of the science or technology"; and (4) the "predictability of the aspect at issue."[226]

Although the application of the written description of the invention requirement may vary in accordance with the different facts and arguments presented to the courts in each case, the *Ariad* court

[218]*Ariad,* 598 F.3d at 1350 (quoting *Lilly,* 119 F.3d at 1568-1569).

[219]*Ariad,* 598 F.3d at 1350. As to the number of constituent species that must be described in order to adequately describe a claimed genus, the court declined to "set out any bright-line rules" because "this number necessarily changes with each invention, and it changes with progress in a field." 598 F.3d at 1351.

[220]*Ariad,* 598 F.3d at 1351.

[221]*See also supra* Section D.2 ("How an Application Conveys Possession of an Invention").

[222]*Ariad,* 598 F.3d at 1351.

[223]*Ariad,* 598 F.3d at 1351.

[224]*Ariad,* 598 F.3d at 1351.

[225]*See Ariad,* 598 F.3d at 1351 (citing Ralston Purina Co. v. Far-Mar-Co, Inc., 772 F.2d 1570, 1575 (Fed. Cir. 1985)).

[226]*Ariad,* 598 F.3d at 1351.

D. The Written Description of the Invention Requirement

explained that there exist "a few broad principles that hold true across all cases."[227] These principles can be summarized as follows:

(1) compliance with the written description of the invention requirement does not require the inclusion of examples in a patent application or proof that the claimed invention has been actually reduced to practice;

(2) a constructive reduction to practice that identifies the claimed invention "in a definite way" can satisfy the requirement;

(3) actual "possession" or reduction to practice outside of the specification is not enough, because the specification itself must demonstrate possession;

(4) compliance with the written description of the invention requirement "does not demand any particular form of disclosure";

(5) compliance with the written description of the invention requirement does not require "that the specification recite the claimed invention *in haec verba*";[228]

(6) a written description that merely renders obvious the claimed invention does not satisfy the written description of the invention requirement;

(7) the written description requirement is not a "super enablement" standard for chemical and biotechnological inventions;

(8) when genetic material is claimed as a genus, the written description of the invention requirement does not mandate that a specification provide a nucleotide-by-nucleotide recitation of the entire genus; and

(9) one may comply with the written description requirement by disclosing structural features common to the members of a claimed genus.[229]

With these principles in hand, the *en banc* court turned to the merits of the *Ariad* dispute. Judge Lourie's opinion for the court tellingly observed that, like the 1997 *Lilly* decision, the case at bar "illustrate[d] the problem of genus claims."[230] Here the claims were to methods encompassing the use of a genus of molecules to achieve a stated useful result (i.e., reducing binding of NF-κB to NF-κB recognition sites).[231] Although the claims were method claims that did not explicitly recite any molecules, the Federal Circuit interpreted the claims as requiring the use of three particular classes of molecules. These classes of molecules had to be sufficiently disclosed:

[227]*Ariad,* 598 F.3d at 1352.
[228]Latin for "in these words."
[229]*Ariad,* 598 F.3d at 1352.
[230]*Ariad,* 598 F.3d at 1350.
[231]*Ariad,* 598 F.3d at 1350.

Regardless whether the asserted claims recite a compound, Ariad still must describe some way of performing the claimed methods, and Ariad admits that the specification suggests only the use of the three classes of molecules to achieve NF-κB reduction [i.e., (1) specific inhibitors, (2) dominantly interfering molecules, and (3) decoy molecules]. Thus, to satisfy the written description requirement for the asserted claims, the specification must demonstrate that Ariad possessed the claimed methods by sufficiently disclosing molecules capable of reducing NF-κB activity so as to "satisfy the inventor's obligation to disclose the technologic knowledge upon which the patent is based, and to demonstrate that the patentee was in possession of the invention that is claimed."[232]

The Federal Circuit treats compliance with the written description of the invention requirement as a question of fact rather than law.[233] Thus the *en banc* court in *Ariad* reviewed the jury's determination that the '516 patent was not invalid for failure to satisfy the written description requirement under the "substantial evidence" standard of review.[234]

To determine whether the jury's verdict upholding validity was supported by substantial evidence, the *en banc* court examined the 1989 patent application's supporting disclosure corresponding to each

----

[232]*Ariad,* 598 F.3d at 1355 (quoting Capon v. Eshhar, 418 F.3d 1349, 1357 (Fed. Cir. 2005)).

[233]*See Ariad,* 598 F.3d at 1351 (citing Ralston Purina Co. v. Far-Mar-Co, Inc., 772 F.2d 1570, 1575 (Fed. Cir. 1985)).

In the author's view, treating written description as a question of fact while treating enablement as a question of law makes little sense. Admittedly, pre-*Ariad* precedent established written description compliance as a question of fact. *See* In re Ruschig, 379 F.2d 990, 9996 (C.C.P.A. 1967) (Rich, J.) (stating that "[t]he issue here is in no wise a question of [the specification's] compliance with section 112, it is a question of fact: Is the compound of claim 13 described therein?"). The *en banc* court in *Ariad* could have exercised its authority to rationalize the law on this point, but chose not to. In his *Ariad* dissent, Judge Rader observed that

> [t]he court makes the subjective/objective nature of the [written description] test even more confusing by perpetuating the test's status as a question of fact. Other, related objective inquiries that focus on the four corners of the specification, such as claim construction and enablement, are questions of law. If the court is right that the written description of the invention test is objective, then either the court misclassifies written description or claim construction and enablement.

Ariad Pharms., Inc. v. Eli Lilly and Co., 598 F.3d 1336, 1366 (Fed. Cir. 2010) (*en banc*) (Rader, J., dissenting-in-part and concurring-in-part).

[234]*See Ariad,* 598 F.3d at 1355 (stating that "'[a] determination that a patent is invalid for failure to meet the written description requirement of 35 U.S.C. §112, ¶1 is a question of fact, and we review a jury's determinations of facts relating to compliance with the written description requirement for substantial evidence.'") (quoting PIN/NIP, Inc. v. Platte Chem. Co., 304 F.3d 1235, 1243 (Fed. Cir. 2002) (citing Vas-Cath Inc. v. Mahurkar, 935 F.2d 1555, 1563 (Fed. Cir. 1991))).

of three types of molecules.[235] Backdropping the court's examination of the record was its observation that as of 1989, the field of Ariad's invention was "particularly unpredictable," and "existing knowledge and prior art [were] scant."[236]

With respect to category (1) molecules, the specification disclosed that "specific inhibitors" are molecules able to reduce or eliminate NF-κB binding to DNA in the nucleus. The specification provided one example, a naturally occurring molecule known as I-κB that holds NF-κB in an inactive state until the cell receives certain external influences. Ariad's expert testified that I-κB existed in 1989 and that an art worker could isolate it through experimentation. Nevertheless, the *Ariad* court concluded that the evidence pertaining to specific inhibitor molecules amounted to merely "a vague functional description and an invitation to further research," not an adequate written description of a specific inhibitor.[237]

The disclosure of the 1989 application with respect to category (2) "dominantly interfering molecules" was more scant than that for category (1). A dominantly interfering molecule is a truncated form of the NF-κB molecule that blocks natural NF-κB from inducing the expression of its target genes. In contrast with category (1) molecules, the 1989 application did not disclose any specific examples of dominantly interfering molecules. The Federal Circuit characterized this fact, coupled with testimony of Ariad's expert, as representing "'just . . . a wish, or arguably a plan' for future research."[238]

The closest question regarding written description compliance in *Ariad* centered on the 1989 application's disclosure of category (3) "decoy molecules." Such molecules are "designed to mimic a region of the gene whose expression would normally be induced by NF-κB"; because NF-κB would bind the decoy, it would not be available to bind its natural target.[239] Unlike the other two categories of useful mol-

---

[235]The jury in *Ariad* found that the priority date of the '516 patent was the April 21, 1989, patent application's filing date, and the parties did not challenge this finding on appeal. *Ariad,* 598 F.3d at 1355.

[236]Ariad Pharms., Inc. v. Eli Lilly and Co., 598 F.3d 1336, 1354 (Fed. Cir. 2010) (*en banc*).

[237]*Ariad,* 598 F.3d at 1356. Another significant problem for Ariad was that the bulk of the evidence it relied on concerning I-κB (including DNA sequence data) was not disclosed until 1991, when Ariad filed a continuation-in-part application claiming priority to its parent 1989 application. The jury found that 1989 was the effective filing date of the '516 patent in suit, and "neither party appealed that determination." *Ariad,* 598 F.3d at 1355. Thus, new matter from the 1991 application was "legally irrelevant" to the written description determination. *Ariad*, 598 F.3d at 1355.

[238]*Ariad,* 598 F.3d at 1357 (quoting Fiers v. Revel, 984 F.2d 1164, 1171 (Fed. Cir. 1993) and also citing Regents of Univ. of Cal. v. Eli Lilly and Co., 119 F.3d 1559, 1567 (Fed. Cir. 1997)).

[239]*Ariad,* 598 F.3d at 1357.

ecules, the 1989 application provided example structures for decoy molecules in the form of specific DNA sequences. But even though the specification adequately described the actual decoy molecules, this did not "answer the question whether the specification adequately describe[d] using those molecules to reduce NF-κB activity."[240]

All that the specification stated with respect to use of the decoy molecules in the claimed methods was that NF-κB "would bind the decoy" and thus "negative regulation can be effected." In the Federal Circuit's view, this disclosure was less a prophetic example than "a mere mention of a desired outcome."[241] The *en banc* court explained that

> [t]he '516 patent discloses no working or even prophetic examples of methods that reduce NF-κB activity, and no completed syntheses of any of the molecules prophesized to be capable of reducing NF-κB activity. The state of the art at the time of filing was primitive and uncertain, leaving Ariad with an insufficient supply of prior art knowledge with which to fill the gaping holes in its disclosure. . . . Whatever thin thread of support a jury might find in the decoy-molecule hypothetical simply cannot bear the weight of the vast scope of these generic claims. . . . Here, the specification at best describes decoy molecule structures and hypothesizes with no accompanying description that they could be used to reduce NF-κB activity. Yet the asserted claims are far broader.[242]

Concluding that the record lacked substantial evidence to support the jury's verdict for the patentee, the Federal Circuit held the asserted claims of Ariad's '516 patent invalid for failure to satisfy the written description of the invention requirement.

---

[240]*Ariad,* 598 F.3d at 1357.
[241]*Ariad,* 598 F.3d at 1357.
[242]*Ariad,* 598 F.3d at 1357-1358 (citations and footnote omitted).

Novelty, Loss of Right, and Priority Pre- and Post-America Invents Act of 2011 (35 U.S.C. §102)

Guide to This Chapter

This chapter is divided into three parts. Its structure has been expanded from earlier editions due to the enactment of the Leahy-Smith America Invents Act (AIA) in late 2011.[1] The AIA fundamentally changed the U.S. Patent Act. The changes are among the most significant since passage of the 1952 Patent Act (which codified the patent laws at Title 35 of the U.S. Code).

This chapter does not cover the entire spectrum of AIA-implemented changes. Rather, the chapter focuses on several fundamental changes relating to novelty and priority of invention, including the switch from the United States' historic first-to-invent priority system to a unique hybrid first-inventor-to-file system. The specific AIA changes covered in this chapter are (1) the determination of novelty and the lack thereof (anticipation) post-AIA, (2) what categories of earlier technology qualify as prior art (and exceptions thereto) under 35 U.S.C. §102 as amended by the AIA, and (3) how the post-AIA patent system handles the question of priority—that is, which of two of more independent inventors who file applications directed to the same invention will receive a patent thereon.

It is important to understand that the AIA changes covered in this chapter generally do *not* impact patents issued or patent applications filed before March 16, 2013. For those patents or applications, the pre-AIA rules will continue to apply throughout their lifespan. Because the AIA is prospective in effect, U.S. patent law will operate on a dual

---

[1]Leahy-Smith America Invents Act, Pub. L. No. 112-29 (H.R. 1249), 125 Stat. 284 (Sept. 16, 2011).

framework of pre- and post-AIA rules for at least 30 years following the AIA's enactment. *Students of patent law now need to understand and apply both sets of rules.*

To facilitate that understanding, Part I of this chapter reviews general concepts of anticipation that remain the same under pre- and post-AIA law. Part II of this chapter explains the pre-AIA framework based on pre-AIA 35 U.S.C. §102. Part III of this chapter explains the post-AIA framework, insofar as it can be understood from the statutory language of post-AIA 35 U.S.C. §102.[2] Because this edition was written in 2012, a few months after enactment of the AIA, there is not yet a body of case law to interpret the AIA and resolve its many ambiguities. Future editions of this text will analyze interpretive precedent as the courts develop it.

Part I: General Principles of Anticipation

The general principles covered in this part of the chapter applied before implementation of the America Invents Act of 2011 and remain applicable thereafter.

A.   The Meaning of Anticipation

The statutory requirement of novelty is "patent-speak" for the bedrock principle that to be patented, an invention must be new (as well as nonobvious and useful). When one or more of the novelty provisions of §102 is triggered, patent attorneys say that the invention has been **anticipated**. When an invention has been anticipated, it is old and thus unpatentable. In other words, anticipation is the opposite, absence, or negation of novelty.

B.   Burden of Proof

The preamble of 35 U.S.C. §102, in both its pre- and post-AIA forms, places a burden of proof on the Patent and Trademark Office (USPTO) to negate a presumption of novelty: "A person *shall* be entitled to a

---

[2]Although Congress radically amended the substance of 35 U.S.C. §102, it unfortunately did not renumber the section. The work of patent practitioners would be much easier for the next 30 or more years if Congress had enacted a newly numbered statutory section addressing novelty and priority post-AIA—numbering it 35 U.S.C. §1002, for example. Congress did not do so, however, and this text will therefore refer to "§102 (pre-AIA)" (or, alternatively, "§102 (2006)") and to "§102 (post-AIA)." The latter statutory section takes effect on March 16, 2013, for applications filed on or after that date and patents issuing therefrom.

patent *unless* . . . . " (emphasis added). The statute is drafted to indicate that the initial burden of disproving novelty during examination of a patent application rests with the government—the USPTO.

To reject an applicant's claim(s) under 35 U.S.C. §102, the agency must show that at least one of the statute's novelty-destroying (or, pre-AIA, loss of right) subsections has been triggered. The USPTO examiner typically rejects an applicant's claims based on the citation of one or more prior art **references,** which are documents such as patents, articles from scientific journals, and other technical literature evidencing the applicability of one or more subsections of §102.[3] Claims also may be rejected under certain subsections of §102 based on events, such as the placing of the invention "on sale" or in "public use" within the meaning of §102(b) (pre-AIA) or §102(a) (post-AIA).

It is therefore helpful to consider 35 U.S.C. §102 as the catalog or universe of prior art that potentially can be cited by the USPTO in rejecting a patent applicant's claims. If a patent, journal article, or other document or event is asserted by the USPTO to be prior art, it must qualify under some subsection of 35 U.S.C. §102. If it does not, then the document or event is not legally available for use as prior art to negate the presumed novelty of the applicant's claimed invention. The same is true in a litigation context, where an issued patent's validity is being challenged.

The introductory phrase of 35 U.S.C. §102 is a bit overstated, of course, because to be "entitled to a patent" one must have an invention that is not only novel, but also in compliance with the Patent Act's additional requirements of statutory subject matter,[4] utility,[5] and nonobviousness,[6] as disclosed and claimed in a patent application that passes muster under the requirements of 35 U.S.C. §112.[7] These additional requirements are detailed elsewhere in this text.

C. The Strict Identity Rule of Anticipation

1. In General

Section 102 uses the word "invention" in two senses: to refer to the anticipatory *prior art invention* and to the *applicant's invention* for

---

[3]*Cf.* In re Hilmer, 359 F.2d 859, 879 (C.C.P.A. 1966) (stating that "[m]uch confused thinking could be avoided by realizing that rejections are based on statutory provisions, not on references, and that the references merely supply the evidence of lack of novelty, obviousness, loss of right or whatever may be the ground of rejection").

[4]*See* Chapter 7 ("Potentially Patentable Subject Matter (35 U.S.C. §101)"), *infra*.

[5]*See* Chapter 6 ("The Utility Requirement (35 U.S.C. §101)"), *infra*.

[6]*See* Chapter 5 ("The Nonobviousness Requirement (35 U.S.C. §103)"), *infra*.

[7]*See* Chapter 3 ("Disclosure Requirements (35 U.S.C. §112(a))"), *supra*.

which a patent is being sought (or in federal district court litigation challenging validity, the invention of the patent in suit). The relationship between these two inventions in an anticipation analysis must be one of **strict identity.** The strict identity rule states that to evidence anticipation of a claimed invention under 35 U.S.C. §102, a single prior art reference must disclose every element of that invention, arranged as in the claim.[8]

For example, consider a patent claim that recites "a widget comprising part A attached to part B by means of part C." The claim is *not* anticipated by a combination of two prior art references (e.g., earlier printed publications or patents) in which one of the references shows a widget having part A attached to part B by means of a part D, and the other reference shows that part D is considered equivalent to or interchangeable with part C by those of ordinary skill in the art of widgets. This combination of prior art references may very well support the position that the claimed widget would have been *obvious* under 35 U.S.C. §103, assuming some motivation to combine the disclosures of the two references, but the claimed widget has not been *anticipated* in this example because the strict identity rule has not been satisfied. Thus, the claimed widget is novel if not, perhaps, nonobvious.[9]

2.   The Special Case of Species/Genus Anticipation

A *genus* is a grouping or category made up of multiple *species* that share some characteristic. For example, the genus of primary colors encompasses the species red, blue, and yellow. Each of these colors is a primary color.

The operation of anticipation under §102 in a genus/species context requires special mention. Genus/species claiming is often, but not exclusively, encountered in chemical and biotechnological patents. For example, a claim that recites "a composition of matter X comprising a halogen" is a genus (or generic) claim in that it encompasses all possible compositions X that include any member of the halogen family (i.e., those elements listed in column VIIA of the periodic table): fluorine, chlorine, bromine, iodine, and so on.[10] Each such composition X can be considered a species falling within the broader genus of claimed compositions.

---

[8]The reference can disclose each element of the invention either explicitly or inherently. For a discussion of anticipation by inherency, *see infra* Section D.

[9]*See* Chapter 5 ("The Nonobviousness Requirement (35 U.S.C. §103)"), *infra*, for further discussion of what is required in order to combine the teachings of multiple prior art references.

[10]*See* Los Alamos National Laboratory's Chemistry Division, *Periodic Table of the Elements, available at* http://periodic.lanl.gov (last visited June 23, 2012).

C. The Strict Identity Rule of Anticipation

A heuristic to keep in mind for anticipation in the species/genus context is that species anticipates genus, but genus does not necessarily anticipate species. To see why this is so, consider a mechanical patent application in which the inventor has claimed "a widget comprising a fastening mechanism." The "fastening mechanism" can be viewed as a generic name for, or genus of, all items that would perform a fastening function. The inventor is therefore claiming a genus of widgets, that is, every widget within the claimed genus of widgets having a fastening mechanism is part of his novel invention.

Now assume that the USPTO examiner finds a prior art reference depicting a widget in which a nail operates as a fastening mechanism. The existence in the prior art of this particular widget species, in which the fastening mechanism is a nail, refutes the inventor's claim that the entirety of his claimed genus of widgets is novel. The genus as a whole cannot be new if one or more of its constituent species is old. Because a species anticipates a genus, the prior art reference is considered anticipatory and prevents the inventor from obtaining his generic claim.[11]

The converse is not necessarily true. Consider a patent application in which the inventor has claimed "a widget comprising a nail," and the USPTO examiner cites against it a prior art reference describing a "widget having a fastening mechanism." So long as the prior art reference does not expressly or inherently[12] disclose that "fastening mechanism" includes "a nail," there is no anticipation. The strict identity rule of anticipation is not met, because each limitation of the

---

[11]*See* In re Ruscetta, 255 F.2d 687, 689-690 (C.C.P.A. 1958) (Rich, J.) (stating that "it is axiomatic that the disclosure of a species in a reference is sufficient to prevent a later applicant from obtaining generic claims, unless the reference can be overcome"). Be aware that this "species anticipates genus" rule does not necessarily follow in the §112, ¶1 disclosure context. *See* In re Lukach, 442 F.2d 967, 970 (C.C.P.A. 1971) (explaining that "the description of a single embodiment of broadly claimed subject matter constitutes a description of the invention for anticipation purposes . . . , whereas the same information in a specification might not alone be enough to provide a description of that invention for purposes of adequate disclosure . . . ") (citations omitted).

[12]To inherently disclose something not expressly stated, a prior art document or event must make clear to the person of ordinary skill that the missing subject matter is "necessarily present" in what is expressly described in or taught by that document or event. Inherency can not be established by mere "probabilities or possibilities." Scaltech, Inc. v. Retec/Tetra, L.L.C., 178 F.3d 1378 (Fed. Cir. 1999). As the court explained,

> The mere fact that a certain thing may result from a given set of circumstances is not sufficient to establish inherency. *See* Continental Can Co. v. Monsanto Co., 948 F.2d 1264, 1269, 20 U.S.P.Q.2d (BNA) 1746, 1749 (Fed. Cir. 1991). However, if the natural result flowing from the operation of the process offered for sale would necessarily result in achievement of each of the claim limitations, then [the] claimed invention was offered for sale. *See id.*

Id. at 1384. For further discussion of anticipation by inherency, *see infra* Section D.

claim has not been *identically* disclosed in a single prior art reference, arranged as in the claim.[13]

Although the patent applicant would not receive an *anticipation* rejection in this situation, it is very likely that the USPTO examiner would make an *obviousness* rejection under 35 U.S.C. §103.[14] The examiner would contend that it would have been obvious for a person of ordinary skill in the art to have selected, from the disclosed prior art genus of widgets having a fastening mechanism, the particular species of interest, that is, a widget having a nail as a fastener, in order to make the claimed invention. This type of obviousness rejection will be more easily overcome if the applicant can show some difference in structure or function of the nail versus the other species within the genus, or some kind of criticality or unexpected result that flows from her selection of the nail species.

D. Anticipation by Inherency

The strict identity rule for anticipation, introduced above, provides that in order to anticipate a claimed invention, a single prior art reference must disclose every element of that invention, arranged as in the claim. A reference's disclosure of individual elements is usually explicit, but case law makes clear that the disclosure can also be *inherent*.[15]

---

[13]*See* Bristol-Myers Squibb Co. v. Ben Venue Labs., Inc., 246 F.3d 1368, 1380 (Fed. Cir. 2001) (vacating district court's grant of summary judgment of invalidity for anticipation where the "Kris [reference] discloses only the use of premedicants generally, not the specific classes of premedicants in those claims: steroids, antihistamines, and H2-receptor antagonists"). One possible exception to the "genus does not necessarily anticipate species" rule is when the genus disclosed in the reference is so small that it effectively describes the claimed species. *See id.* (noting that "the disclosure of a small genus may anticipate the species of that genus even if the species are not themselves recited") (citing In re Petering, 301 F.2d 676, 682 (C.C.P.A. 1962)).

[14]*See, e.g.*, In re Jones, 958 F.2d 347 (Fed. Cir. 1992), in which the court reversed the USPTO's obviousness rejection of a claim to the 2-(2'-aminoethoxy)ethanol salt of dicamba, a type of acid. *Id.* at 348. The prior art Richter reference, "which all agree is the closest prior art, discloses dicamba in free acid, ester, and salt forms, for use as a herbicide. Among the salt forms disclosed are substituted ammonium salts, a genus that admittedly encompasses the claimed salt. Richter does not specifically disclose the claimed 2-(2'-aminoethoxy)ethanol salt, however." *Id.* at 349.

[15]*See* Continental Can Co. USA v. Monsanto Co., 948 F.2d 1264, 1268 (Fed. Cir. 1991) (stating that "[t]o serve as an anticipation when the reference is silent about the asserted inherent characteristic, such gap in the reference may be filled with recourse to extrinsic evidence," and that such evidence "must make clear that the missing descriptive matter is necessarily present in the thing described in the reference, and that it would be so recognized by persons of ordinary skill").

For example, suppose that the USPTO is examining for novelty a claim to "a container structure comprising a plurality of plastic ribs that are hollow." The examiner has located a prior art printed publication showing a container with several plastic ribs. The prior art reference does not explicitly state that the ribs are hollow, but it does indicate that the ribs were formed by conventional blow-molding techniques. If other evidence extrinsic to the reference (e.g., other documents or expert testimony) shows that use of the blow-molding process would *necessarily* have resulted in hollow ribs, then the examiner would be justified in concluding that the reference inherently disclosed the "hollow" feature. Stated another way, practice of the prior art reference would *inevitably* have resulted in the claimed invention. A rejection of the claim as anticipated would be justified under these circumstances.[16]

If, however, the extrinsic evidence presents a legitimate question as to whether the blow-molding process would have resulted in hollow ribs, then anticipation by inherency is not established. If it is to be relied upon to destroy novelty, inherency must be certain:

> Inherency . . . may not be established by probabilities or possibilities. The mere fact that a certain thing may result from a given set of circumstances is not sufficient. [Citations omitted.] If, however, the disclosure is sufficient to show that the natural result flowing from the operation as taught would result in the performance of the questioned function, it seems to be well settled that the disclosure should be regarded as sufficient.[17]

The doctrine of anticipation by inherency should be distinguished from situations in which the claimed invention was *accidentally* made or performed previously by others but not appreciated at the time. For example, the plaintiff in *Tilghman v. Proctor*[18] obtained a patent on a process for separating the component parts of fats and oils. These components included a glycerine base and various "fat acids" such as stearic, margaric, and oleic acids, which were useful in the making of candles and soap. Years before Tilghman's invention, one Perkins had used tallow to lubricate the pistons of his steam engine.[19] The

---

[16]For an argument that reliance on the inherency doctrine should be cabined, and that prior art relied on to show inherent anticipation must satisfy a heightened level of enablement to establish the inevitability of producing the claimed invention, *see* Janice M. Mueller & Donald S. Chisum, *Enabling Patent Law's Inherent Anticipation Doctrine*, 45 HOUSTON L. REV. 1101 (2009), *available at* http://ssrn.com/abstract=1153493.

[17]*Continental Can*, 948 F.2d at 1269 (quoting In re Oelrich, 666 F.2d 578, 581 (C.C.P.A. 1981) (Rich, J.)).

[18]102 U.S. 707 (1880).

[19]For additional background on Perkins' use, *see* Mitchell v. Tilghman, 86 U.S. 287 (1873), *overruled in part by* Tilghman v. Proctor, 102 U.S. 707 (1880).

Supreme Court rejected the argument that this prior use by Perkins invalidated the patent:

> We do not regard the accidental formation of fat acid in Perkins's steam cylinder from the tallow introduced to lubricate the piston (if the scum which rose on the water issuing from the ejection pipe was fat acid) as of any consequence in this inquiry. What the process was by which it was generated or formed was never fully understood. Those engaged in the art of making candles, or in any other art in which fat acids are desirable, certainly never derived the least hint from this accidental phenomenon in regard to any practicable process for manufacturing such acids.[20]

Although older Supreme Court cases such as *Tilghman* might be read to suggest that inherent anticipation requires *recognition* by prior art workers of the fact of the earlier making or performing of the invention,[21] most judges of the Federal Circuit have rejected any contemporaneous recognition requirement. Applied to the container hypothetical above, the question becomes whether it is necessary in order to establish anticipation by inherency that prior artisans who made or used the container described in the prior art reference actually recognized at that time that the ribs of the container were hollow. In *Schering Corp. v. Geneva Pharms., Inc.,*[22] a panel of the court in 2003 flatly rejected "the contention that inherent anticipation requires recognition in the prior art."[23] It distinguished *Tilghman* on the ground that the record in that case "did not show conclusively that the claimed process occurred in the prior art."[24] Two judges of the Federal Circuit filed dissenting opinions to the subsequent denial of rehearing *en banc* in *Schering,* and a third judge voted to rehear the

---

[20]*Tilghman,* 102 U.S. at 711. The Supreme Court continued in the same vein with respect to other prior art of record:

> The accidental effects produced in Daniell's water barometer and in Walther's process for purifying fats and oils preparatory to soap making, are of the same character. They revealed no process for the manufacture of fat acids. If the acids were accidentally and unwittingly produced, whilst the operators were in pursuit of other and different results, without exciting attention and without its even being known what was done or how it had been done, it would be absurd to say that this was an anticipation of Tilghman's discovery.

Id. at 711-712.

[21]*See also* Eibel Process Co. v. Minnesota & Ontario Paper Co., 261 U.S. 45, 66 (1923) ("[A]ccidental results, not intended and not appreciated, do not constitute anticipation.").

[22]339 F.3d 1373 (Fed. Cir. 2003).

[23]*Id.* at 1377.

[24]*Id.* at 1378.

appeal *en banc*.[25] Nevertheless, the clear weight of current Federal Circuit authority is that proof of recognition in the prior art of an inherent characteristic or quality is not necessary.[26]

E. Enablement Standard for Anticipatory Prior Art

We have already established that anticipation requires the description in a single prior art reference of every element of a claimed invention.[27] We must also consider the *quality* of that description. In order to be anticipatory, the prior art reference must describe the claimed invention in an enabling fashion,[28] that is, with sufficient detail that a person of ordinary skill in the art could make what is described in the prior art reference without undue experimentation. For example, if an inventor files a patent application claiming a new chemical compound X, and a prior art reference describes merely the chemical formula of X but does not describe how to make X, the reference would not be adequate to anticipate because it is not enabling.[29]

---

[25]Schering Corp. v. Geneva Pharms., Inc., 348 F.3d 992 (Fed. Cir. 2003) (order denying petition for rehearing *en banc*); *id.* at 993 (Gajarsa, J., voting for rehearing *en banc*); *id.* (Newman, J., dissenting from denial of rehearing *en banc*); *id.* at 995 (Lourie, J., dissenting from denial of rehearing *en banc*).

[26]*See, e.g.,* Leggett & Platt, Inc. v. VUTEk, Inc., 537 F.3d 1349, 1355 (Fed. Cir. 2008) (reaffirming *Schering* panel's rejection of "the contention that inherent anticipation requires recognition in the prior art") (quoting Schering Corp. v. Geneva Pharm., Inc., 339 F.3d 1373, 1377 (Fed. Cir. 2003)); SmithKline Beecham Corp. v. Apotex Corp., 403 F.3d 1331, 1343 (Fed. Cir. 2005) ("inherent anticipation does not require a person of ordinary skill in the art to recognize the inherent disclosure in the prior art at the time the prior art is created"); Toro Co. v. Deere & Co., 355 F.3d 1313, 1321 (Fed. Cir. 2004) ("[T]he fact that a characteristic is a necessary feature or result of a prior art embodiment (that is itself sufficiently described and enabled) is enough for inherent anticipation, even if that fact was unknown at the time of the prior invention.").

[27]*See supra* Section C ("The Strict Identity Rule of Anticipation").

[28]*See* In re Donohue, 766 F.2d 531, 533 (Fed. Cir. 1985) (stating that "[i]t is well settled that prior art under 35 U.S.C. [§102(b)] must sufficiently describe the claimed invention to have placed the public in possession of it. Such possession is effected if one of ordinary skill in the art could have combined the publication's description of the invention with his own knowledge to make the claimed invention. Accordingly, even if the claimed invention is disclosed in a printed publication, that disclosure will not suffice as prior art if it was not enabling. It is not, however, necessary that an invention disclosed in a publication shall have actually been made in order to satisfy the enablement requirement.") (citations omitted).

[29]This assumes that the method of making compound X would not otherwise have been obvious to those of ordinary skill in the art. If it would have been, then the prior art reference would anticipate. *See* In re Le Grice, 301 F.2d 929, 939 (C.C.P.A. 1962) (holding that "the proper test of a description in a publication as a bar to a patent as the clause is used in section 102(b) requires a determination of whether one skilled in the art to which the invention pertains could take the description of the invention in the printed publication and combine it with his own knowledge of the particular art

In Chapter 3, "Disclosure Requirements," this text discussed the enablement requirement as applied to the *applicant's own disclosure.* Thus the inventor seeking a patent in the above example must provide an enabling disclosure of how to make and use the new chemical compound X that he claims. In parallel fashion, the patent law also applies the enablement requirement to the *description in a prior art reference relied on for anticipation.* In other words, the enablement requirement applies to the inventor seeking a patent as well as to the prior artisan whose description is relied on to defeat patentability. In the above example, the author of the prior art reference did not provide an enabling description of X. Thus, the prior art reference does not anticipate and the claimed invention X is novel.[30]

F. What Is a Printed Publication?

Both §102(a) and §102(b) of 35 U.S.C. (pre-AIA) and §102(a) of 35 U.S.C. (post-AIA) indicate that a claimed invention may be rendered unpatentable if it has previously been described in a "printed publication." What counts as a printed publication for prior art purposes? Consider, for example, whether posting a photograph of an invention on the Internet renders that invention anticipated and/or obvious.

A key policy concern expressed by 35 U.S.C. §102 is that we not permit withdrawal by a patent applicant of technology already in the public's possession. Patent law is fairly liberal about what will suffice to put a technology disclosure into the hands of the public (although U.S. patent law is somewhat less expansive in this respect than the

---

and from this combination be put in possession of the invention on which a patent is sought. Unless this condition prevails, the description in the printed publication is inadequate as a statutory bar to patentability under section 102(b).").

A further twist on the requirement that anticipatory prior art references be enabling is the rule that a disclosure of how to *use* (i.e., the utility of) a prior art chemical compound is *not* required for anticipation. *See* In re Hafner, 410 F.2d 1403, 1405 (C.C.P.A. 1969) (observing that "a disclosure lacking a teaching of how to use a fully disclosed compound for a specific, substantial utility or of how to use for such purpose a compound produced by a fully disclosed process is, under the present state of the law, entirely adequate to anticipate a claim to either the product or the process and, at the same time, entirely inadequate to support the allowance of such a claim"). Thus, in the example in the text, if the inventor claiming compound X asserts in his patent application that X has utility in the treatment of cancer, but the prior art description of X says nothing about potential uses for X (in cancer or otherwise), the prior art reference is nevertheless considered anticipatory so long as it teaches X and how to make X (or so long as the method of making X would have been obvious to a person of ordinary skill in the art).

[30]Whether the claimed invention would have been obvious under 35 U.S.C. §103 in view of the description of X in the prior art reference is a separate question. *See* Chapter 5 ("The Nonobviousness Requirement (35 U.S.C. §103)"), *infra.*

laws of foreign countries[31]). Even a drawing without words can qualify (assuming that it is sufficiently enabling under 35 U.S.C. §112(a)).[32] For example, Judge Learned Hand held in *Jockmus v. Leviton*[33] that a patent claim to a candle-shaped light bulb holder was anticipated by a picture of the holder in a third party's French-language catalog. Hand explained that "printed publication" presupposes enough currency to make the work part of the possessions of the art.[34] In other words, the document or drawing will be considered a printed publication if it is sufficiently accessible to the public interested in this particular technology.

In keeping with Learned Hand's definition, the U.S. Court of Appeals for the Federal Circuit has interpreted printed publication so as to

> give effect to ongoing advances in the technologies of data storage, retrieval, and dissemination. Because there are many ways in which a reference may be disseminated to the interested public, "public accessibility" has been called the touchstone in determining whether a reference constitutes a "printed publication" bar under 35 U.S.C. §102(b).[35]

Just *how* accessible is "sufficiently accessible"? A rather extreme illustration is *In re Hall,*[36] in which the Federal Circuit held that a single copy of a doctoral thesis, properly cataloged in the collection of a German university library, qualified as a novelty-destroying §102(b) "printed publication." Based on the facts of the case, which included competent evidence about routine library practices of cataloging and indexing theses from which an approximate time of accessibility could be determined, the court held that the single cataloged thesis in a foreign university's library "could constitute sufficient accessibility to those interested in the art exercising reasonable diligence."[37] In contrast, three student theses listed alphabetically by their authors' names on index cards, kept among 450 index cards in a shoebox in a

---

[31]*See infra* Section I.2 ("Grace Period"). The 2011 enactment of the America Invents Act expands the categories of §102 prior art. *See infra* Sections Q and R.

[32]*See supra* Section E ("Enablement Standard for Anticipatory Prior Art"). The America Invents Act of 2011 renamed §112, ¶1 as §112(a), effective Sept. 16, 2012.

[33]28 F.2d 812 (2d Cir. 1928).

[34]*See Jockmus*, 28 F.2d at 813-814, stating,

> While it is true that the phrase, "printed publication," presupposes enough currency to make the work part of the possessions of the art, it demands no more. A single copy in a library, though more permanent, is far less fitted to inform the craft than a catalogue freely circulated, however ephemeral its existence; for the catalogue goes direct to those whose interests make them likely to observe and remember whatever it may contain that is new and useful.

[35]In re Hall, 781 F.2d 897, 898-899 (Fed. Cir. 1986) (citations omitted).

[36]*Id.* at 897.

[37]*Id.* at 900.

college chemistry department's library, and not otherwise cataloged or indexed by subject, were held not sufficiently accessible to count as printed publications in *In re Cronyn*.[38]

A common source of printed publication prior art is a publication authored by the patent's named inventor(s), particularly in the context of inventions made by scientists and professors who dwell in a "publish or perish" environment. In *In re Klopfenstein*,[39] the court concluded that the inventors' academic conference poster presentation, on display for three days but never reproduced or distributed to any of the conference participants, constituted a "printed publication" that resulted in a pre-AIA §102(b) loss of right to a patent.[40] The court rejected the inventors' argument that the poster display could not qualify as a printed publication because it had never been disseminated by the distribution of reproductions or copies, or by indexing in a library or database. Precedents such as *In re Hall*[41] "do not limit this court to finding something to be a 'printed publication' *only* when there is distribution and/or indexing," the Federal Circuit observed.

Rather, the key inquiry for determining if there has been a printed publication is whether or not a reference has been made "publicly accessible." That determination involves a case-by-case inquiry into the facts and circumstances surrounding the reference's disclosure to members of the public. The *Klopfenstein* court considered the following factors relevant:

- The length of time that the display was exhibited
- The expertise of the target audience
- The existence (or lack thereof) of reasonable expectations that the material displayed would not be copied
- The simplicity or ease with which the material displayed could have been copied

[38]890 F.2d 1158, 1161 (Fed. Cir. 1989) (observing that "the only research aid was the student's name, which, of course, bears no relationship to the subject of the student's thesis"). The dissent argued that indexing is only one factor to be considered in the totality of the circumstances that determine whether a work is sufficiently publicly accessible to count as a printed publication. *See id.* (Mayer, J., dissenting).

[39]380 F.3d 1345 (Fed. Cir. 2004).

[40]Although the Federal Circuit in *Klopfenstein* affirmed the USPTO's denial of patentability under 35 U.S.C. §102(b) (on the ground that the claimed invention had been described in a printed publication more than a year before the patent application's filing date), the determination of what counts as a "printed publication" would have equal relevance in §102(a) situations (i.e., novelty-destroying events, caused by persons other than the inventor, that occurred prior to the invention date of the claimed invention).

[41]781 F.2d 897 (Fed. Cir. 1986) (holding that a single copy of a doctoral thesis, indexed and cataloged in a German university library, was sufficiently publicly accessible to qualify as a §102(b) "printed publication").

Applying these factors, the Federal Circuit cited undisputed facts that the poster presentation (which described methods of preparing foods comprising extruded soy fiber) was "prominently displayed for approximately three cumulative days" to an audience comprising cereal chemists who likely possessed ordinary skill in the art of the invention; that it was displayed "with no stated expectation that the information would not be copied or reproduced by those viewing it"; that the inventors "took no measures to protect the information they displayed," such as by disclaimer discouraging copying; that the professional norms under which the inventors displayed the posters at an academic conference did not entitle them to a reasonable expectation that their display would not be copied; and that the poster display (which comprised four slides of graphs/charts and eight slides of concise bullet points) was relatively simple such that "only a few slides presented would have needed to have been copied by an observer to capture the novel information presented by the slides." Thus, the Federal Circuit concluded, the poster display was made sufficiently accessible to the public to qualify as a "printed publication" under §102(b). The court accordingly affirmed the USPTO's rejection of the Klopfenstein patent application.[42]

New and technology-specific questions of public accessibility arise with regularity in the Internet era. For example, the issue in *SRI Int'l, Inc. v. Internet Sec. Sys., Inc.*[43] was whether an inventor's pre–critical date posting of an otherwise anticipatory paper on the patentee's publicly available FTP ("File Transfer Protocol") server rendered the paper sufficiently accessible to trigger the §102(b) printed publication bar. In response to a call for papers for the 1998 Network and Distributed System Security (NDSS) Symposium, the co-inventor of a network intrusion detection method e-mailed the symposium chair a paper. Titled "Live Traffic Analysis of TCP/IP Gateways," the paper described part of SRI's ongoing "Emerald" research project. Although the call for papers also required a backup submission by postal mail, the inventor opted to post a copy of the paper on SRI's FTP server as the backup copy. The SRI FTP server was publicly accessible and placed no restrictions on access to the "Live Traffic" paper. The inventor also e-mailed the symposium chair the specific FTP address (ftp:// ftp.csl.sri.com/pub/emerald/ndss98.ps) of the paper. The "Live Traffic" paper was posted under the "ndss98.ps" file name for seven days in the SRI FTP server's Emerald subdirectory, which the inventor had

---

[42]The Federal Circuit observed in a footnote that, in contrast to the facts of the case before it, an entirely *oral* presentation that does not include a display of slides or distribution of copies of the presentation would not constitute a "printed publication" under the statute, and that a merely "transient" display of slides accompanying an oral presentation might not either. *See Klopfenstein*, 380 F.3d at 1349 n.4.

[43]511 F.3d 1186 (Fed. Cir. 2008).

previously publicized to other members of the cyber security community as a repository of his research on intrusion detection. A district court granted summary judgment of §102(b) invalidity on the ground that "one of ordinary skill would know that the SRI FTP server contained information on the EMERALD 1997 project and therefore would navigate through the folders [i.e., the server's PUB directory and EMERALD subdirectory] to find the Live Traffic paper."[44]

The Federal Circuit majority disagreed, finding genuine issues of material fact on the public accessibility question that precluded summary judgment. The *SRI* majority viewed the inventor's FTP server posting as a prepublication communication for purposes of peer review; intent to publicize the paper was lacking. The majority considered the "ndss98.ps" file name of the "Live Traffic" paper "relatively obscure" and not reasonably likely to be found by a contemporaneous user skilled in the art.[45] Nor did the FTP server provide an index, catalog, or other meaningful research tool to find the paper, a hallmark of the Federal Circuit's "library cases" such as *In re Hall*.[46] Distinguishing *In re Klopfenstein*,[47] the majority analogized the "Live Traffic" paper to "a poster at an unpublicized conference without a conference index of the location of the various poster presentations."[48]

The dissenting Federal Circuit judge in *SRI* would have upheld the district court's judgment of invalidity, based on the accused infringer's "mountain of evidence" regarding public accessibility and the patentee's failure to raise more than "some metaphysical doubt" about the material facts.[49] The navigable directory of the FTP server represented a research aid or tool that those skilled in the art of cyber detection could have used easily to locate the "Live Traffic" paper. Far from obscure, the paper's "ndss98.ps" file name comprised the initials of the 1998 NDSS Symposium, then in its fifth year and well known to cyber security workers in government, corporations, and academia. In the dissent's view, the facts created an even stronger case for §102(b) invalidity than those of *Klopfenstein* (in which a pre–critical date conference poster display triggered a §102(b) printed publication bar). The "Live Traffic" paper was continuously available on SRI's FTP server for a longer period of time, to any person located anywhere with Internet access. Unlike the presenters in some academic conferences, patentee SRI could have had no expectation of confidentiality for its FTP server; the inventor had affirmatively advertised the Emerald

[44]*Id.* at 1195.
[45]*Id.* at 1197.
[46]781 F.2d 897 (Fed. Cir. 1986).
[47]380 F.3d 1345 (Fed. Cir. 2004).
[48]*SRI Int'l*, 511 F.3d at 1197-1198.
[49]*Id.* at 1198, 1200 (Moore, J., dissenting) (quoting [at 1198] Matsushita Elec. Indus. Co v. Zenith Radio Corp., 475 U.S. 574, 586 (1986)).

subdirectory in e-mails and presentations to persons interested in his research. Lastly, ease of copying was extremely high. Rather than transcribing the text or graphics of posters at a conference, in the case at bar the entire "Live Traffic" paper could have been copied through downloading "at the touch of a button."[50]

Insufficient evidence that a document was publicly accessible via the Internet before the critical date avoided a §102(b) printed publication bar in *In re Lister.*[51] Dr. Lister invented a method of playing golf in which players "were permitted to tee up their balls on every shot except for those taken from designated hazard areas or the putting green."[52] Lister first submitted a manuscript describing his method to the U.S. Copyright Office on July 4, 1994, and the Office issued a certificate of copyright registration for the manuscript later that same month. The manuscript was titled "Advanced Handicap Alternatives for Golf." More than a year later, on August 5, 1996, Lister filed a patent application claiming the golfing method described in the manuscript. The USPTO Board affirmed an examiner's anticipation rejection citing the manuscript as a §102(b) (pre-AIA) printed publication. The commercial databases Westlaw and Dialog included the titles (but not the full texts) of works registered by the Copyright Office. The USPTO took the position that an interested researcher could have found the Lister manuscript by performing a keyword search of the commercial databases using the word "golf" in combination with "handicap."

The Federal Circuit first agreed that a reasonably diligent researcher with access to Westlaw or Dialog would have located the Lister manuscript by performing key word searches using "golf" in combination with "handicap." The court rejected Lister's argument that the word "handicap," though part of his manuscript's title, was not a good descriptor of the claimed invention. "The question is not whether an individual, selecting terms from the claim language, could execute a single keyword search that would yield all relevant references including the anticipatory reference at issue."[53] Rather, a diligent researcher could be expected to have attempted several searches using a variety of keyword combinations. The Federal Circuit concluded that the Lister manuscript was publicly accessible via the keyword search capability of Westlaw or Dialog, as of the date it was included in those databases.

That conclusion did not end Lister's appeal, however. The USPTO had failed to introduce evidence showing *when* the Lister manuscript was included in the commercial databases, and in particular that such

---

[50]*Id.* at 1204 (Moore, J., dissenting).
[51]583 F.3d 1307 (Fed. Cir. 2009).
[52]*Lister*, 583 F.3d at 1309.
[53]*Lister*, 583 F.3d at 1315.

inclusion occurred prior to the §102(b) critical date for Lister's patent application. The Federal Circuit distinguished *In re Hall*,[54] in which the court held that "competent evidence of the general library practice of cataloging and shelving" established that the cited thesis became publicly accessible prior to the applicant's critical date. In the case at bar, the government did not identify any comparable evidence of general practice proving when Westlaw or Dialog would have received and included in their databases the information obtained from the Copyright Office. Absent such evidence, the Federal Circuit in *Lister* had "no basis to conclude that the manuscript was publicly accessible prior to the critical date." Accordingly, the Federal Circuit vacated the USPTO Board's decision that Lister's application claims were barred by a §102(b) printed publication.

Part II: Novelty, Loss of Right, and Priority Pre-America Invents Act of 2011

G. Introduction

1. Statutory Basis

This part of the chapter provides readers with a practical understanding of the multifaceted concepts of **novelty** and **loss of right** as defined by §102 of the U.S. Patent Act prior to the AIA's 2011 enactment.[55] Because the AIA is prospective in effect, these concepts remain applicable to the patentability and validity of any U.S. patent or application filed before March 16, 2013, throughout the life of the patent. Given the possibility of validity-challenging litigation during (and

---

[54]781 F.2d 897 (Fed. Cir. 1986).

[55]Although the requirement that a patentable invention be "new" is stated in 35 U.S.C. §101, novelty, novelty is analyzed under 35 U.S.C. §102 in accordance with long-standing administrative practice. *See* In re Bergy, 596 F.2d 952 (C.C.P.A. 1979) (Rich, J.), *aff'd sub nom.* Diamond v. Chakrabarty, 447 U.S. 303 (1980), in which the court explained,

Of the three requirements *stated* in §101, only two, utility and statutory subject matter, are *applied* under §101. As we shall show, in 1952 Congress voiced its intent to consider the novelty of an invention under §102 where it is first made clear what the statute means by "new", notwithstanding the fact that this requirement is first *named* in §101.

The PTO, in administering the patent laws, has, for the most part, consistently applied §102 in making rejections for lack of novelty. To provide the option of making such a rejection under either §101 or §102 is confusing and therefore bad law. . . .

Id. at 961 (emphases in original).

beyond) the entire term of a patent, the pre-AIA framework regarding novelty and loss of right will remain relevant for 30 years or more following the AIA's 2011 enactment.

The notion that patents are available only for inventions that are truly novel (i.e., new) is a bedrock concept of all patent systems, and continues to govern under the AIA. What is novel, however, is not uniformly defined around the world. Before the AIA's implementation, the United States analyzed novelty quite differently than other countries, in view of its unique pre-AIA "first to invent" system of priority.[56] The pre-AIA statute provided:

35 U.S.C. §102. Conditions for patentability; novelty and loss of right to patent

A person shall be entitled to a patent unless —

(a) the invention was known or used by others in this country, or patented or described in a printed publication in this or a foreign country, before the invention thereof by the applicant for patent, or

(b) the invention was patented or described in a printed publication in this or a foreign country or in public use or on sale in this country, more than one year prior to the date of the application for patent in the United States, or

(c) he has abandoned the invention, or

(d) the invention was first patented or caused to be patented, or was the subject of an inventor's certificate, by the applicant or his legal representatives or assigns in a foreign country prior to the date of the application for patent in this country on an application for patent or inventor's certificate filed more than twelve months before the filing of the application in the United States, or

(e) the invention was described in (1) an application for patent, published under section 122(b), by another filed in the United States before the invention by the applicant for patent or (2) a patent granted on an application for patent by another filed in the United States before the invention by the applicant for patent, except that

---

[56] The first-to-invent principle is most clearly codified in 35 U.S.C. §102(g), as discussed later in this chapter. *See infra* Section N. The United States' historic first-to-invent system differs from the first-to-file system, under which the rest of the world operates. *See infra* Chapter 12 ("International Patenting Issues").

The United States implemented a first-to-invent priority system as early as the late eighteenth century. *See* Edward C. Walterscheid, *Priority of Invention: How the United States Came to Have a "First-to-Invent" System,* 23 AIPLA Q.J. 263, 264 (1995) (explaining that "the initial impetus came from the titanic struggle between John Fitch and James Rumsey for priority of invention with respect to the steamboat during the late eighteenth century, but the actual creation of a true first-to-invent system took almost fifty years").

After many years of debate, the enactment in 2011 of the AIA changed the United States from first-to-invent to a unique first-inventor-to-file system. This landmark change in priority determination governs applications filed on or after March 16, 2013. *See infra* Part III of this chapter.

an international application filed under the treaty defined in section 351(a) shall have the effects for the purposes of this subsection of an application filed in the United States only if the international application designated the United States and was published under Article 21(2) of such treaty in the English language;[57] or

(f) he did not himself invent the subject matter sought to be patented, or

(g) (1) during the course of an interference conducted under section 135 or section 291, another inventor involved therein establishes, to the extent permitted in section 104, that before such person's invention thereof the invention was made by such other inventor and not abandoned, suppressed, or concealed, or (2) before such person's invention thereof, the invention was made in this country by another inventor who had not abandoned, suppressed, or concealed it. In determining priority of invention under this subsection, there shall be considered not only the respective dates of conception and reduction to practice of the invention, but also the reasonable diligence of one who was first to conceive and last to reduce to practice, from a time prior to conception by the other.[58]

Deceptively straightforward at first reading, when applied the seven subsections (a) through (g) of 35 U.S.C. §102 (2006) may seem a rather bewildering Pandora's box of arcane conventions and obscure terms of art. Many students find that mastering §102 is the most conceptually challenging and time-consuming part of a basic patent law course. Fortunately, the complexities of §102 can be mastered by a careful examination of the statutory provisions, a thorough comprehension of fundamental principles and underlying policy concerns, and the precise use of terminology.

First, here are some general recommendations for readers who seek a better understanding of the intricacies of §102. It is important to become comfortable with the statute. Post a copy of 35 U.S.C. §102 on the wall next to your desk or computer and copy its text into your laptop or PDA. Read the language over every day until you know it by heart. In the process, you will begin to understand the statute substantively. Another recommended comfort technique is to diagrammatically analyze all §102 problems on a timeline. (These same recommendations apply to the post-AIA version of §102, discussed in Part III *infra*.)

---

[57]This language represents the text of §102(e) as amended by the Twenty-first Century Department of Justice Appropriations Authorization Act, Pub. L. No. 107-273, §13205, 116 Stat. 1758 (2002) (titled "Domestic Publication of Patent Applications Published Abroad") (amending subtitle E of title IV (the American Inventors Protection Act of 1999) of the Intellectual Property and Communications Omnibus Reform Act of 1999, as enacted by Pub. L. No. 106-113, §1000(a)(9), 113 Stat. 1501 (1999).

[58]35 U.S.C. §102 (2006).

Next, understand that virtually every word in 35 U.S.C. §102 is loaded with meaning. The statute cannot be interpreted in a vacuum; it must be understood in connection with the many judicial decisions and rules of practice that have applied the language of the statute to a multitude of factual situations. Moreover, much (though not all) of the terminology in pre-AIA §102 was carried over to post-AIA §102. Thus, understanding how the courts have interpreted statutory phrases, such as "printed publication" and "public use," that are present in both the pre- and post-AIA versions of §102 is necessary.

After reviewing some key concepts of general applicability to §102 (pre-AIA), this part of this chapter will individually address each subsection of 35 U.S.C. §102 (pre-AIA).

2. Geographic Distinctions

In starting a journey through 35 U.S.C. §102 (pre-AIA) it is helpful to tackle subsections 102(a) and 102(b) together. A common theme of these subsections is the dichotomy between events that will be recognized as triggering the statute only if they occur in the United States, versus those events that will trigger the statute no matter where in the world they take place. For example, under both subsections an invention is not patentable if it was "patented or described in a printed publication" *anywhere in the world,* either before the invention date (per §102(a)) or more than a year before the filing date (per §102(b)). On the other hand, prior "know[ledge] or use[] by others" under §102(a) and "public use[s]" or placing the invention "on sale" under §102(b) count as anticipations or losses of right only if these events took place *in the United States.*

Why are there geographic distinctions? The statute probably reflects a historical notion, translated into an evidentiary presumption, that "personal" activities (such as an individual's knowledge or use or sale of an invention in a foreign country) require greater effort to disseminate to U.S. citizens than do domestic activities. In contrast, we assume that the content of foreign publications and patents is easily transmitted to and obtainable by U.S. citizens. The geographic distinctions in §102 also may reflect a recognition that the search costs of discovering knowledge and use in a foreign country would be unfairly burdensome if placed on U.S. inventors. Whatever its underpinnings, many have criticized the foreign/domestic dichotomy of patentability-defeating events as antiquated and discriminatory against foreign inventors.[59] Nevertheless, the geographic distinctions will remain in

---

[59]For example, consider Inventor A, a Japanese national, who made commercial sales of her invention in Japan more than one year before the U.S. patent application

operation for all pre-AIA applications and patents (throughout their lives). The AIA-implemented removal of geographic limitations on patent-defeating events takes effect prospectively on March 16, 2013, for applications filed on or after that date.

3. Who Is the Actor?

An important distinction between pre-AIA subsections 102(a) and 102(b) of 35 U.S.C. is the identity of the persons who can trigger those subsections and by their actions destroy patentability. Anticipation under 35 U.S.C. §102(a) (pre-AIA) must involve an act by *someone other than the patent applicant,* while loss of right to patent under §102(b) can be the result of acts by *anyone,* including (and in the case of public uses and sales, most often because of) the applicant. The former rule follows from the fact that the novelty-destroying event under §102(a) must have occurred before the applicant's **invention date.**[60] An applicant cannot know, or use, or patent, or describe his invention before he has invented it, so if these events are to anticipate, logically they must have been carried out by others.

Another way of thinking about this is to remember the patent law maxim that "an inventor's own work can only be used against him as prior art if it constitutes a [pre-AIA] §102(b) bar." Thus, if inventor A published a paper describing her invention X on January 1, 2010, and

---

filing date of Inventor B, a U.S. national, claiming the same invention (independently developed by B). Under pre-AIA rules, Inventor A cannot rely on her sales activity in Japan in a defensive manner to prevent Inventor B from obtaining a U.S. patent on the invention. In other words, Inventor A's sales of the invention in Japan do not qualify as §102(b) prior art that would destroy Inventor B's claim to the same invention, as they would have had A's sales been made in the United States.

[60]The *invention date* of a claimed invention is a central concept under pre-AIA novelty and first-to-invent priority rules. (Post-AIA, however, the significance of invention dates is likely limited to derivation proceedings under 35 U.S.C. §135 (eff. Mar. 16, 2013)). Under pre-AIA rules, the invention date of a claimed invention is, at the earliest, the date of **conception.** The conception date is the date on which the inventor had a complete mental picture of the operative invention, as it was thereafter reduced to practice, *so long as* the inventor displayed reasonable **diligence** in moving from the conception to a reduction to practice. *See* Mahurkar v. C.R. Bard, Inc., 79 F.3d 1572, 1577-1578 (Fed. Cir. 1996). Alternatively, the invention date of a claimed invention may be the date of its **actual reduction to practice,** that is, the date on which the inventor had constructed a physical embodiment of the invention that worked for its intended purpose. There is no set time period in which a patent application must be filed following the invention date, so long as the invention has not been injected into the public domain in some fashion. *See* 35 U.S.C. §102(b) (2006) (providing one-year grace period for application filing following the first patenting or description of the invention in a printed publication anywhere in the world, or the first public use or placement on sale of the invention in the United States).

then filed a U.S. patent application claiming X on December 1, 2010, the published paper is *not* §102(a) prior art against the patent application. If the paper had been published on November 1, 2009, however, it would be prior art against the application under §102(b).

4.   Distinguishing Novelty from Loss of Right

Section 102 of 35 U.S.C. (pre-AIA) is really two provisions in one, as reflected by its title: "Conditions for patentability; novelty and loss of right to patent." Subsections (a), (e), and (g) are true novelty provisions, while subsections (b), (c), and (d) concern loss-of-right situations in which the right to a patent may be lost even though the invention is, technically, novel. (Subsection (f), described below, is *sui generis* and does not comfortably fit in either category.)

One of the fundamental differences between the novelty and loss-of-right provisions lies in their respective triggering dates. Novelty provisions §§102(a), (e), and (g) concern (or are triggered by) events taking place "before the invention . . . by the applicant for patent," that is, before the *invention date*.[61] In contrast, the loss-of-right provisions (§§102(b) and (d)) key off of the date that is one year prior to the applicant's filing date, sometimes referred to as the §102(b) **critical date.**

To further complicate matters, it should be understood that under the pre-AIA system, the USPTO presumptively treats the applicant's filing date as her invention date (based on a constructive reduction to practice theory[62]) for purposes of applying pre-AIA §§102(a), (e), and (g), unless and until the applicant proves an earlier actual invention date. In *ex parte* prosecution, the patent applicant may do this by **antedating** or "swearing behind" a §102(a) or §102(e) prior art reference in accordance with applicable USPTO rules.[63] In litigation challenging the validity of an issued patent, a similar procedure is

---

[61]"Invention date" is defined *supra* Section G.3.

[62]As discussed in greater detail later in this chapter, a reduction to practice of an invention may be an "actual" reduction to practice or a "constructive" reduction to practice. An actual reduction to practice generally involves the construction of a physical embodiment of the invention that works for its intended purpose (testing is often involved to verify whether that purpose is met). A constructive reduction to practice means that a patent application claiming the invention has been filed with the USPTO, which application satisfies the disclosure requirements of 35 U.S.C. §112, ¶1 for the claimed invention. *See* Chapter 3 ("Disclosure Requirements (35 U.S.C. §112(a))"), *supra*.

[63]*See* 37 C.F.R. §1.131 ("Affidavit or Declaration of Prior Invention"). Procedures for antedating a reference are further detailed in Section O of this chapter, *infra*.

followed.[64] In a pre-AIA interference proceeding, an earlier invention date is established under §102(g)(1) and §135.[65]

H.   "Known or Used" Under 35 U.S.C. §102(a) (Pre-AIA)

Much controversy and disagreement surrounds the meaning of the statutory phrase "known or used by others" in §102(a). Although some authority exists to support the proposition that prior knowledge or use by even a single person other than the inventor is enough to anticipate, the better view is probably that of Judge Learned Hand, a premier patent jurist.[66] Hand viewed anticipation under §102(a) as requiring that the anticipatory knowledge exist in a manner accessible to the public; that is, it must be "part of the stock of knowledge of the art in question."[67] The current majority rule clearly contemplates that "knowledge and use" under §102(a) must be that which is available to the public.[68]

---

[64]*See* Mahurkar v. C.R. Bard, Inc., 79 F.3d 1572 (Fed. Cir. 1996) (affirming district court's grant of patentee's motion for judgment as a matter of law (JMOL) that patent in suit was not anticipated because accused infringer failed to prove that allegedly anticipatory "Cook catalog" was in fact prior art under 35 U.S.C. §102(a)). The court in *Mahurkar* explained that a patentee such as Mahurkar may seek to establish an actual invention date earlier than the application filing date (i.e., constructive reduction to practice date, taken as presumptive invention date) by analogy to the interference rule of priority of invention:

> In the United States, the person who first reduces an invention to practice is "prima facie the first and true inventor." Christie v. Seybold, 55 F. 69, 76 (6th Cir. 1893) (Taft, J.). However, the person "who first conceives, and, in a mental sense, first invents . . . may date his patentable invention back to the time of its conception, if he connects the conception with its reduction to practice by reasonable diligence on his part, so that they are substantially one continuous act." *Id.*

Mahurkar, 79 F.3d at 1577. In this validity context, the patentee must essentially establish priority vis-à-vis the effective date of a §102(a) prior art reference (rather than another interference party's invention date). Thus, Mahurkar attempted to show an invention date earlier than the Cook catalog publication date in two ways: (1) through evidence showing that he had conceived and reduced to practice his invention before publication of the catalog; and (2) through evidence that he had conceived his invention prior to the date of publication of the Cook catalog and that he proceeded with reasonable diligence from a date just prior to publication of the catalog to his own filing date. *See id.* at 1578. The accused infringer, Bard, failed to carry its burden to rebut this evidence.

[65]*See infra* Section N.2 ("Interference Proceedings Under §102(g)(1)").

[66]*See generally* PAUL H. BLAUSTEIN, LEARNED HAND ON PATENT LAW (Pineridge Pub. 1983).

[67]Picard v. United Aircraft Corp., 128 F.2d 632, 635 (2d Cir. 1942) (L. Hand, J.).

[68]*See* Woodland Trust v. Flowertree Nursery, Inc., 148 F.3d 1368, 1370 (Fed. Cir. 1998); In re Hilmer, 359 F.2d 859, 878 (C.C.P.A. 1966) (observing that §102(a) patent-

Gayler v. Wilder,[69] the "Salamander safe"[70] case, is an important early illustration of the proper interpretation of "known or used by others" as an anticipatory event. The plaintiff, Wilder, owned a patent directed to a fireproof safe, invented by one Fitzgerald. The safe was constructed of inner and outer iron chests, between which Fitzgerald placed an inflammable material such as gypsum or plaster of paris (mineral-based, cement-like substances that do not burn). Thus, the internal fireproofing construction of the Fitzgerald safe, as claimed in the patent, was not visible from its exterior appearance.

Gayler, having been sued by Wilder for infringement of the patent, defended on the ground that it was invalid as anticipated by the prior knowledge or use of the safe by others, before the date of Fitzgerald's invention.[71] Gayler also asserted that because of this earlier use Fitzgerald could not be the "first and original" inventor of the safe.[72] Gayler's invalidity defenses were based on the independent prior invention of the same safe by one Conner, not a party to the law suit. Conner made the safe for his own business use and kept it in the "counting-room" of his foundry, where his employees passed by it on a daily basis.[73]

Nevertheless, the Supreme Court held, because those persons were not aware of the safe's internal construction, they did not possess "knowledge or use of the invention." The Court sustained the validity of the Fitzgerald patent, despite the fact that Fitzgerald was not, literally, the first inventor of the safe:

---

defeating "knowledge" of an invention in this country "had been interpreted, long before the [Patent Act of] 1952 codification, to mean public knowledge"); *id.* (quoting from Federico's *Commentary on the 1952 Patent Act,* 35 U.S.C.A. 1, 18 (1954 ed.), that "[t]he Committee Report both in the general part and in the Revision Notes recognizes that the interpretation of this condition is somewhat more restricted than the actual language, stating 'the interpretation by the courts excludes various kinds of private knowledge not known to the public,' and the narrowing interpretations are not changed [in the 1952 Act codification]"); In re Borst, 345 F.2d 851 (C.C.P.A. 1965).

[69]51 U.S. 477 (1850).

[70]*Gayler,* 51 U.S. at 495. In mythology, the salamander was believed capable of surviving fire. *See* American Heritage Dictionary of the English Language (4th ed. 2000) (entry for salamander).

[71]The language of the Patent Act of 1836 at issue in *Gayler v. Wilder* parallels that of 35 U.S.C. §102(a) (2006). *See Gayler,* 51 U.S. at 496 (stating that "[t]he act of 1836, ch. 357, §6, authorizes a patent where the party has discovered or invented a new and useful improvement, 'not known or used by others before his discovery or invention'").

[72]*See Gayler,* 51 U.S. at 496 (quoting from Patent Act of 1836, "the 15th section [of which] provides that, if it appears on the trial of an action brought for the infringement of a patent that the patentee 'was not the original and first inventor or discoverer of the thing patented,' the verdict shall be for the defendant").

[73]*See Gayler,* 51 U.S. at 512.

In the case thus provided for, the party who invents [Fitzgerald] is not strictly speaking the first and original inventor. The law assumes that the improvement may have been known and used before his discovery [by Conner]. Yet his patent is valid if he discovered it by the efforts of his own genius, and believed himself to be the original inventor. The clause in question qualifies the words before used, and shows that *by knowledge and use the legislature meant knowledge and use existing in a manner accessible to the public*.... It is the inventor here [Fitzgerald] that brings it to them, and places it in their possession. And as he does this by the effort of his own genius, the law regards him as the first and original inventor, and protects his patent, although the improvement had in fact been invented before, and used by others [Conner].[74]

Thus, to anticipate, prior knowledge or use of an invention by others in this country must have been knowledge or use that was accessible to the public. As between the earlier inventor who maintains his invention in secrecy (e.g., Conner), and a later inventor who is first to put the public in possession of the invention by entering into the patenting process (e.g., Fitzgerald), the patent law rewards the latter. Conner's safe, though literally an earlier invention, did not qualify as prior art that could anticipate Fitzgerald's patent because the knowledge or use of it had never been made accessible to the public.[75]

The Federal Circuit considered the quantum of evidence necessary to establish §102(a) prior knowledge or use in *Woodland Trust v. Flowertree Nursery, Inc.*[76] In that case, several witnesses, all of whom were relatives, friends, or business acquaintances of the owner of the accused infringing company, testified that they had observed or made use of the same system (for protecting foliage plants from freeze damage) as that patented by the plaintiff, some 20 or more years before the patent's filing date. Despite the district court's positive assessment of the witnesses' credibility, the Federal Circuit reversed the lower court's judgment of invalidity based on pre-AIA §102(a) prior public knowledge or use. The appellate court required that the witnesses' entirely oral testimony of prior invention be corroborated, relying on the Supreme Court's *Barbed Wire Patent* case.[77] As applied

---

[74]*Id.* at 496-497 (emphasis added).

[75]*Gayler v. Wilder* also can be understood as a case in which Conner's earlier making of the safe in this country would not qualify as prior art under 35 U.S.C. §102(g) (2) (2006) (discussed later in this chapter) because Conner had effectively abandoned, suppressed, or concealed his invention after reducing it to practice.

[76]148 F.3d 1368 (Fed. Cir. 1998).

[77]Washburn & Moen Mfg. Co. v. Beat 'Em All Barbed-Wire Co., 143 U.S. 275 (1892) (hereafter *Barbed Wire Patent*). The Supreme Court in *Barbed Wire Patent* observed that "[i]n view of the unsatisfactory character of testimony, arising from the forgetfulness of witnesses, their liability to mistakes, their proneness to recollect things as the party calling them would have them recollect them, aside from the temptation to actual perjury, courts have not only imposed upon defendants the burden of proving

to the facts of the case at bar, the Supreme Court's guidance in *Barbed Wire Patent* and other cases meant that accused infringer Flowertree Nursery bore a "heavy burden when establishing prior public knowledge and use based on long-past events."[78] Surprisingly, the witnesses for Flowertree were unable to produce a single item of documentary evidence to support their testimony. Given the "ubiquitous paper trail of virtually all commercial activity," it was notable that "some physical record (e.g., a written document such as notes, letters, invoices, notebooks, or a sketch or drawing or photograph showing the device, a model, or some other contemporaneous record) [did] not exist."[79] In view of this lack of corroboration, the Federal Circuit concluded that defendant Flowertree had failed to carry its burden of establishing invalidity by clear and convincing evidence.[80]

I.   The Statutory Bars of 35 U.S.C. §102(b) (Pre-AIA)

1.   Introduction

Recall that 35 U.S.C. §102(b) (2006) is a loss-of-right provision rather than a true novelty provision. Section 102(b) (pre-AIA) lists four different ways in which, even though an invention may have been novel as of its invention date, the right to a patent on that invention nevertheless can be lost or forfeited. These four triggering events, also referred to as **statutory bars,** are as follows: more than one year before the application's filing date, the invention was (1) patented anywhere in the world; (2) described in a printed publication anywhere in the world; (3) in public use in the United States; or (4) on sale in the United States. Patent attorneys refer to the date that is one year prior to the application filing date as the **critical date** for §102(b) purposes. Thus, in order to trigger 35 U.S.C. §102(b), a statutory bar event must have occurred prior to the critical date.

The operation of 35 U.S.C. §102(b) is depicted in timeline format in Figure 4.1. As depicted in Figure 4.1, "§102(a) events" are those that

---

such [earlier-invented] devices, but have required that the proof shall be clear, satisfactory, and beyond a reasonable doubt." *Id.* at 284.

[78] *Woodland Trust*, 148 F.3d at 1373.

[79] *Id.*

[80] Other Federal Circuit cases have clarified that corroboration of oral testimony concerning prior invention is to be evaluated under a "rule of reason" standard that considers all pertinent evidence, which is not necessarily limited to documentary evidence. *See* Loral Fairchild Corp. v. Matsushita Elec. Indus. Co., 266 F.3d 1358, 1364 (Fed. Cir. 2001) (stating that "[u]nder the 'rule of reason,' the [alleged prior] inventor's testimony must be sufficiently corroborated by independent evidence, but not necessarily *documentary* evidence") (emphasis in original).

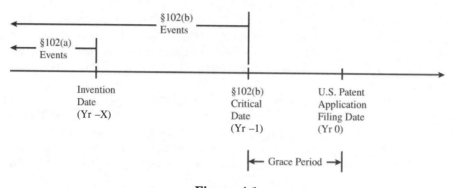

Figure 4.1

35 U.S.C. §102(b) Timeline (Pre-AIA)

occurred prior in time to the invention date,[81] while "§102(b) events" are those that occurred prior in time to the §102(b) critical date. The two relevant time periods overlap for dates prior to the invention date as depicted in Figure 4.1. For example, if we assume that a U.S. patent application as illustrated in Figure 4.1 was filed on January 1, 2005, making the §102(b) critical date January 1, 2004, and assume further that the invention date was sometime in 2002, then a technical article published during 2001 (anywhere in the world and authored by someone other than the application inventor) that identically described the invention claimed in the patent application would qualify as "printed publication" prior art under both §102(a) and §102(b).

Understanding *why* our U.S. patent system includes §102(b) is essential to properly applying this important statutory provision.[82] It has often been said that the statutory bars of 35 U.S.C. §102(b) are, in effect, defined by the policies that underlie the bars.[83] Those policies include the following:[84]

---

[81]As depicted in Figure 4.1, the invention date before which "§102(a) events" occur is the true or actual invention date. Recall that the USPTO in the first instance will treat an applicant's filing date ("Yr 0" in the figure) as her presumptive or *prima facie* invention date, placing the burden on the applicant to establish the actual date of invention through the antedating procedure detailed in Section O, *infra*. Figure 4.1 depicts a scenario in which the applicant has successfully established her actual invention date ("Yr –X" in the figure), thus antedating any *prima facie* §102(a) prior art having an effective date between "Yr –1" and "Yr 0."

[82]The historic origin of 35 U.S.C. §102(b) (2006), and why it stands as a patentability requirement separate and independent from 35 U.S.C. §102(a) (2006), can be traced back to *Pennock v. Dialogue*, 27 U.S. 1 (1829).

[83]*See, e.g.,* Western Marine Elecs., Inc. v. Furuno Elec. Co., 764 F.2d 840, 844 (Fed. Cir. 1985) (on sale bar); TP Labs., Inc. v. Professional Positioners, Inc., 724 F.2d 965, 973 (Fed. Cir. 1984) (public use).

[84]*Cf.* Manville Sales Corp. v. Paramount Sys., Inc., 917 F.2d 544, 549-550 (Fed. Cir. 1990) (stating policies as applied to public use bar of §102(b)); UMC Elecs. Co. v. United

I. The Statutory Bars of 35 U.S.C. §102(b) (Pre-AIA)

1. **Minimize detrimental reliance**—the policy against removing inventions from the public that the public has justifiably come to believe are freely available to all as a consequence of prolonged public use or sales activity.

2. **Encourage prompt dissemination**—the policy favoring prompt and widespread disclosure of new inventions to the public. The inventor is forced to file promptly or risk possible forfeiture of his patent rights due to prior sales or public uses.

3. **Prohibit undue commercial exploitation**—the policy of preventing the inventor from commercially exploiting the exclusivity of his invention substantially beyond the statutorily authorized period (currently about 17-18 years). Section 102(b) forces the inventor to choose between seeking patent protection promptly following sales activity or public use, or taking his chances with his competitors without the benefit of patent protection.

4. **Evaluate marketplace reaction**—the policy of giving the inventor a reasonable amount of time (i.e., the one-year grace period of §102(b)) following sales activity or public uses to determine whether a patent is a worthwhile investment. This benefits the public because it tends to minimize the filing of patent applications of only marginal public interest.

The first three of these four policies primarily benefit the public, while the fourth policy primarily benefits the inventor. Although recent on sale bar decisions of the Federal Circuit eschew the "totality of the circumstances" mantra of the court's earlier §102(b) decisions,[85] in the view of this author the policy underpinnings remain relevant to all §102(b) cases and should not be ignored.[86]

States, 816 F.2d 647, 652 (Fed. Cir. 1987) (stating policies as applied to on sale bar of §102(b)) (citing Gen. Elec. Co. v. United States, 654 F.2d 55, 60-61 (Ct. Cl. 1981) (*en banc*)). In *In re Caveney*, 761 F.2d 671, 676 n.6 (Fed. Cir. 1985), the court noted that the policies had been identified prior to *General Electric* in Barrett, *New Guidelines for Applying the On Sale Bar to Patentability*, 24 STAN. L. REV. 730, 732-735 (1972).

[85]*See* Lacks Indus., Inc. v. McKechnie Vehicle Components USA, Inc., 322 F.3d 1335, 1347 (Fed. Cir. 2003) (defining "totality of the circumstances" test as a flexible analysis in which no single finding or conclusion of law is a *sine qua non* to a holding that a statutory bar has arisen, but characterizing *Pfaff v. Wells Elecs., Inc.*, 525 U.S. 55, 67 (1998), as having "swept away" the totality of the circumstances test); Weatherchem Corp. v. J. L. Clark, Inc., 163 F.3d 1326, 1333 (Fed. Cir. 1998) (stating that Federal Circuit follows the Supreme Court's two-part test [in *Pfaff*] without balancing various policies according to the totality of the circumstances as may have been done in the past").

[86]*Cf.* Bernhardt, L.L.C. v. Collezione Europa USA, Inc., 386 F.3d 1371, 1379 (Fed. Cir. 2004) (applying policies in public use context); Netscape Comm. Corp. v. Konrad, 295 F.3d 1315, 1320 (Fed. Cir. 2002) (same); In re Kollar, 286 F.3d 1326, 1333-1334 (Fed. Cir. 2002) (applying policies in on sale context).

2. Grace Period

Notice in Figure 4.1 that a U.S. patent applicant enjoys a "grace period" or "safe harbor" under 35 U.S.C. §102(b) (2006) comprising the one-year time period between the §102(b) critical date and his application filing date.[87] During this one-year pre–filing date grace period, an invention may be patented, described in a printed publication, in public use, or on sale, all without triggering a §102(b) loss of right. In other words, the one-year pre–filing date grace period that governed before the AIA's March 16, 2013, implementation of first-to-file is a free pass that allows an inventor to test and refine his invention, make sales of it in the marketplace, and evaluate whether the considerable cost of going forward with the patenting process is justified. So long as the patent application is filed within one year of the first instance of the invention being released into the public domain or commercially exploited by patenting, description in a printed publication, public use, or placement of the invention on sale, either by the patent applicant or a third party, the right to a U.S. patent will not be lost under 35 U.S.C. §102(b).[88]

Importantly, countries other than the United States are generally "absolute novelty" systems that do not recognize any pre–filing date grace period (or when they do, the grace period is only for very limited times and purposes such as particularly defined types of international exhibitions). For example, under the European Patent Convention (EPC) Article 54, any activity that makes an invention part of the "state of the art" at any time prior to the filing date of the European patent application will defeat novelty.[89] Thus, when clients want to obtain patent protection in foreign countries as well as in the United States, they should be advised not to make *any* public disclosure of their inventions at any time prior to filing their priority patent application.[90]

[87]Unlike most foreign patent systems, U.S. patent law has long provided patent applicants with a pre-filing grace period. The Patent Act of 1839 instituted a two-year grace period; this was scaled back to one year in 1939.

[88]The America Invents Act of 2011 retained a one-year grace period but only for inventor-generated or inventor-derived disclosures. *See infra* Section S ("Novelty-Preserving Exceptions under Post-AIA 35 U.S.C. §102(b)").

[89]*See* European Patent Convention art. 54(1) (2007) ("An invention shall be considered to be new if it does not form part of the state of the art."), *available at* http://www.epo.org/law-practice/legal-texts/html/epc/2010/e/ar54.html (last visited June 20, 2012); *id.* at art. 54(2) ("The state of the art shall be held to comprise everything made available to the public by means of a written or oral description, by use, or in any other way, before the date of filing of the European patent application.").

[90]*See* Chapter 12 ("International Patenting Issues"), *infra*, for discussion of the right of priority to an earlier foreign filing date under the Paris Convention and the U.S. implementation of the right of priority via 35 U.S.C. §119.

The one-year grace period of the U.S. framework permits us to conceptualize the §102(b) statutory bars in an additional way. The occurrence of any of the four statutory bar events effectively "starts the clock running" against a potential U.S. patent applicant, operating as a sort of statute of limitations.[91] In order not to forfeit the right to a U.S. patent on her invention under §102(b), the inventor must file an application claiming that invention within one year of the first occurrence of any of the four statutory bar events. If she waits to file even a single day beyond the one-year grace period, her right to a patent is lost under 35 U.S.C. §102(b).

3. Section 102(b) Public Use

Because the Patent Act does not define what specific acts will trigger the "public use" or "on sale" statutory bars, we look to the extensive case law on the subject to determine what these terms mean. Broadly speaking, a public use occurs when, prior to the 35 U.S.C. §102(b) critical date, the inventor "releases control" over her invention, effectively dedicating it to the public. The Federal Circuit has defined public use of an invention as any use "by a person other than the inventor who is under no limitation, restriction or obligation of secrecy to the inventor."[92] This definition is overly narrow, because acts by the inventor herself also may (and frequently do) trigger the §102(b) public use bar.

The key criterion of the §102(b) public use bar is whether the inventor kept "control" over the use of her invention. Such "control" does not necessarily require that the inventor kept the invention locked away in secret, however. Rather, the public use bar reflects the traditional case law understanding that patent rights were lost or forfeited when an inventor acted in such a way as to indicate an intent to abandon or otherwise dedicate the invention to the public.[93]

---

[91]See UMC Elecs. v. United States, 816 F.2d 647, 659 (Fed. Cir. 1987) (Smith, J., dissenting) (explaining that "Section 102(b) is in the nature of a statute of limitations, enacted to implement the policy that those who seek the benefits of the patent grant must act promptly after the invention has been placed in possession of the public") (footnote omitted).

[92]In re Smith, 714 F.2d 1127, 1134 (Fed. Cir. 1983).

[93]See, e.g., Pennock v. Dialogue, 27 U.S. 1 (1829), in which the Supreme Court (Story, J.) stated:

It is admitted that the subject is not wholly free from difficulties; but upon most deliberate consideration we are all of opinion, that the true construction of the [Patent Act of 1793] is, that the first inventor cannot acquire a good title to a patent; if he suffers the thing invented to go into public use, or to be publicly sold for use, before he makes application for a patent. His voluntary act or acquiescence

For example, in the oft-cited case of *Egbert v. Lippmann*,[94] the inventor of an improved women's corset[95] gave his "intimate friend," before the critical date, a pair of corset steels that he had made without imposing on his friend any obligation of secrecy or restriction on her use of the steels.[96] The U.S. Supreme Court held that the inventor's acts amounted to a public use that invalidated the corset patent, noting that the inventor's friend "might have exhibited [the steels] to any person, or made other steels of the same kind, and used or sold them without violating any condition or restriction imposed on her by the inventor."[97] The Court concluded that "whether the use of an invention is public or private does not necessarily depend upon the number of persons to whom its use is known. If an inventor, having made his device, gives or sells it to another, to be used by the donee or vendee, without limitation or restriction, or injunction of secrecy, and it is so used, such use is public, even though the use and knowledge of the use may be confined to one person."[98] Figure 4.2 depicts a timeline of events from *Egbert*.

The inventor's relinquishment of control over his invention in *Egbert* is in contrast with the facts of *Moleculon Research Corp. v. CBS, Inc.*[99] Moleculon, assignee of a patent on a three-dimensional, rotating puzzle invented by Nichols, sued CBS (as successor to a toy

---

in the public sale and use is an *abandonment* of his right; or rather creates a disability to comply with the terms and conditions on which alone the secretary of state is authorized to grant him a patent.

Pennock, 27 U.S. at 23-24 (emphasis added).

[94]104 U.S. 333 (1881).

[95]*See generally* VALERIE STEELE, THE CORSET: A CULTURAL HISTORY (Yale Univ. Press 2001); Kara W. Swanson, *Getting a Grip on the Corset: Gender, Sexuality and Patent Law*, 23 YALE J.L. & FEMINISM 57 (2011), *available at* http://ssrn.com/abstract=1753166.

[96]The record also reflected a pre–critical date demonstration of the invention to one Sturgis, a friend of the inventor, without any nondisclosure agreement or obligation of secrecy. *See Egbert*, 104 U.S. at 335.

[97]*Egbert*, 104 U.S. at 337.

[98]*Egbert*, 104 U.S. at 336. This broad statement is in the nature of *dicta*, for the totality of the evidence in *Egbert* showed that many persons besides the inventor had knowledge and use of the corset invention prior to the critical date:

According to the testimony of the complainant, the invention was completed and put into use in 1855. The inventor slept on his rights for eleven years. Letters-patent were not applied for till March, 1866. In the mean time, the invention had found its way into general, and almost universal, use. A great part of the record is taken up with the testimony of the manufacturers and venders of corset-steels, showing that before he applied for letters the principle of his device was almost universally used in the manufacture of corset-steels. It is fair to presume that having learned from this general use that there was some value in his invention, he attempted to resume, by his application, what by his acts he had clearly dedicated to the public.

Egbert, 104 U.S. at 337.

[99]793 F.2d 1261 (Fed. Cir. 1986).

I. The Statutory Bars of 35 U.S.C. §102(b) (Pre-AIA)

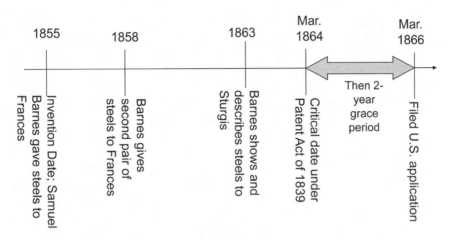

Figure 4.2

Timeline in *Egbert v. Lippmann* (U.S. 1881)

manufacturer) alleging patent infringement by certain of the well-known Rubik's Cube puzzles. CBS answered by alleging that the Nichols patent was invalid for public use of the claimed invention more than a year before the patent application's filing date. The evidence reflected that prior to the §102(b) critical date, Nichols showed paper mockups of the puzzle to his friends at graduate school. When he was later employed by Moleculon as a research scientist, but still prior to the critical date, Nichols brought into his office a working wood-block prototype of the puzzle that he had built at home. Nichols showed the puzzle to Obermayer, the president of Moleculon, and explained its workings. Moleculon thereafter undertook to patent and commercialize the puzzle. The Federal Circuit affirmed the district court's determination that, unlike the inventor in *Egbert,* Nichols had not given over the puzzle invention for free and unrestricted use by others.[100] Rather, based on the personal relationships and surrounding circumstances, Nichols at all times retained control over the puzzle's use and the distribution of information concerning the puzzle. Nichol's use was private and for his own enjoyment; he never used the puzzle or permitted it to be used in a place or time when he did not have a legitimate expectation of privacy and confidentiality. The fact that Nichols allowed Obermayer to briefly use the puzzle without signing a nondisclosure agreement was not determinative, but merely one factor to be considered in the totality of the circumstances.[101]

---

[100]*See id.* at 1266.
[101]*Id.*

Although the inventor in *Egbert* triggered the loss of right to patent by his own actions, §102(b) public use as understood currently is not so limited. Rights to a patent can be lost without the inventor's knowledge or intent or authorization, based on a public use of the same invention by a third party outside of the one-year grace period.[102] The law will not permit an inventor to obtain proprietary rights in an invention that members of the public have come to believe is freely available through prolonged public use before the filing date. Thus the public policy emphasis in statutory bar cases has shifted over time from an "abandonment" rationale to more of a pure "delay" rationale, under which an applicant is penalized for delaying in filing his patent application if he waits more than one year after the first public use of the invention (whether or not he was aware of such public use).

A patent can be invalidated for §102(b) public use even though the claimed invention was used in secret (at least prior to the America Invents Act of 2011). The common thread of the "non-informing public use" cases is the inventor's secret commercialization of the invention outside of the statutory grace period.[103] A classic example is *Metallizing*

---

[102]*See* Lorenz v. Colgate-Palmolive-Peet Co., 167 F.2d 423 (3d Cir. 1948), in which the court held

> The prior public use proviso of R.S. Sec. 4886 [the patent statute then in effect] was enacted by Congress in the public interest. It contains no qualification or exception which limits the nature of the public use. We think that Congress intended that if an inventor does not protect his discovery by an application for a patent within the period prescribed by the Act, and an intervening public use arises from any source whatsoever, the inventor must be barred from a patent or from the fruits of his monopoly, if a patent has issued to him. There is not a single word in the statute which would tend to put an inventor, whose disclosures have been pirated, in any different position from one who has permitted the use of his process.

Id. at 429. The Federal Circuit subsequently cited *Lorenz* with approval in *Evans Cooling Sys. v. General Motors Corp.*, 125 F.3d 1448, 1452 (Fed. Cir. 1997) (refusing to create third-party exception to on sale bar of §102(b) when, as framed by inventor, "a third party surreptitiously steals an invention while it is a trade secret and then, unbeknownst to the inventor, allegedly puts the invention on sale [more than one year] before the inventor files a patent application covering the stolen invention"). *See also* In re Martin, 74 F.2d 951, 955 (C.C.P.A. 1935) (stating court's opinion that "whatever the correct rule may be with respect to a fraudulent use by another of an invention for more than two years prior to the filing of an application for patent therefor, there is no implied exception in the two-year provision removing the bar of the statute where there is a public use of an invention by an innocent user for more than two years prior to the application for patent").

[103]*See* Kinzenbaw v. Deere & Co., 741 F.2d 383, 390 (Fed. Cir. 1984) (observing that "[a] commercial use is a public use even if it is kept secret" and citing authority).

In contrast, the America Invents Act of 2011 does not clearly state whether this type of secret information qualifies as post-AIA prior art. *See infra* Section Q.3 ("Does the AIA Permit Secret Prior Art?").

Engineering Co. v. Kenyon Bearing & Auto Parts Co.[104] There the inventor Meduna obtained a patent on a process of conditioning metal surfaces, useful for building up worn metal machine parts. Prior to the §102(b) critical date Meduna used his process on jobs for numerous commercial customers but without disclosing any details about the process, which also were not discernible from inspecting the finished metal surface.[105] Judge Learned Hand of the Second Circuit reversed a district court decision that had sustained the validity of the patent over a public use challenge; the district court had reasoned that a secret use of a process could never be a public use within the meaning of the statute. In holding that the public use bar can indeed be triggered by secret use that is commercial in nature, Judge Hand overruled his own earlier decision on which the district court had relied:

> [I]t appears that in *Peerless Roll Leaf Co. v. Griffin & Sons,* supra, 2 Cir., 29 F.2d 646, we confused two separate doctrines: (1) The effect upon his right to a patent of the inventor's competitive exploitation of his machine or of his process; (2) the contribution which a prior use by another person makes to the art. Both do indeed come within the phrase, 'prior use'; but the first is a defence for quite different reasons from the second. It had its origin—at least in this country—in the passage we have quoted from *Pennock v. Dialogue,* supra, 2 Pet. 1, 7 L. Ed. 327; i.e., that it is a condition upon an inventor's right to a patent that he shall not exploit his discovery competitively after it is ready for patenting; he must content himself with either secrecy, or legal monopoly. It is true that for the limited period of two years he was allowed to do so, possibly in order to give him time to prepare an application; and even that has been recently cut down by half. But if he goes beyond that period of probation, he forfeits his right regardless of how little the public may have learned about the invention. . . .
>
> It is indeed true that an inventor may continue for more than a year to practice his invention for his private purposes of his own enjoyment and later patent it. But that is, properly considered, not an exception to the doctrine, for he is not then making use of his secret to gain a competitive advantage over others; he does not thereby extend the period of his monopoly.[106]

[104]153 F.2d 516 (2d Cir. 1946).

[105]*See* Metallizing Eng'g Co. v. Kenyon Bearing & Auto Parts Co., 62 F. Supp. 42, 47 (D. Conn. 1945) (finding that "[a]t all times prior to [the critical date of] August 6, 1941, the practice of the process was so guarded as not to come to public knowledge; its nature was disclosed only to a few employees and advisers of the inventor, less than half a dozen in number, in all cases under a promise of confidence which was not abused. . . . [P]rior to August, 1941, the nature of the process could not have been deduced from inspection or physical tests upon specimens of the processed product in the hands of the public. . . . ")

[106]*Metallizing,* 153 F.2d at 519-520.

4.   Section 102(b) on Sale Bar

The "on sale" bar is probably the greatest source of litigation involving 35 U.S.C. §102(b) (2006) challenges to patent validity. Operation of the bar results in a loss of right to a patent when an invention has been sold or offered for sale more than one year before the application filing date (i.e., outside of the one-year pre–filing date grace period). The statutory phrase "on sale" is understood as meaning "placement on sale,"[107] which encompasses offers to sell as well as completed sales. Moreover, a mere offer to sell even a single unit of the invention will trigger the §102(b) clock[108] so long as the offer meets certain "commercialness" requirements established in the on sale bar case law considered below.

The primary public policy rationale underlying the on sale bar is that which prohibits the prolonged commercial exploitation of the invention outside of the statutorily authorized time period of exclusivity.[109] Consider a novel and nonobvious invention first put on the market in the United States, for which a patent application is filed within one year. Although the inventor will have no legal right to exclude others from making, using, or selling the invention unless and until her patent issues, she often benefits from a *de facto* exclusivity of sorts during the time period leading up to issuance of her patent (i.e., during the pre-filing grace period plus the patent application's pendency in the USPTO). This *de facto* exclusivity results simply by virtue of her being first to the marketplace with a (presumably) novel and nonobvious product, and may be facilitated by the inventor's right to mark

---

[107]*See* King Instrument Corp. v. Otari Corp., 767 F.2d 853, 860 (Fed. Cir. 1985) (holding that 35 U.S.C. §102(b) "proscribes not a sale, but a placing 'on sale'") (citing D.L. Auld Co. v. Chroma Graphics Corp., 714 F.2d 1144, 1147 (Fed. Cir. 1984)).

[108]*See* In re Theis, 610 F.2d 786, 791 (C.C.P.A. 1979) (stating that "[e]ven a single, unrestricted sale brings into operation this bar to patentability") (citing Consolidated Fruit-Jar Co. v. Wright, 94 U.S. 92, 94 (1876); In re Blaisdell, 242 F.2d 779, 783 (C.C.P.A. 1957)).

[109]Justice Joseph Story provided the classic expression of this policy rationale:

> If an inventor should be permitted to hold back from the knowledge of the public the secrets of his invention; if he should for a long period of years retain the monopoly, and make, and sell his invention publicly, and thus gather the whole profits of it, relying upon his superior skill and knowledge of the structure; and then, and then only, when the danger of competition should force him to secure the exclusive right, he should be allowed to take out a patent, and thus exclude the public from any farther use than what should be derived under it during his fourteen years [the statutory term at that time]; it would materially retard the progress of science and the useful arts, and give a premium to those who should be least prompt to communicate their discoveries.

Pennock v. Dialogue, 27 U.S. 1, 19 (1829).

her product as "Patent Pending" once she has filed an application.[110] Because the statute provides the patentee with a very powerful right to exclude others generally lasting 17-18 years (20 years less application pendency in the USPTO), the U.S. patent law construes this time period narrowly. No excess time-wise tacking of *de facto* exclusivity onto the initial part of the patent term will be permitted. Thus, offers to sell or sales of an invention outside of the §102(b) grace period will result in a loss of right to patent (if the information is known to the USPTO), or will invalidate an issued patent if the pre–critical date activity does not come to light until the time of subsequent litigation challenging the patent's validity.[111]

A key issue in many on sale bar cases is what state of development the invention must be in before the inventor possesses an "invention" capable of being placed on sale within the meaning of §102(b). For example, an offer of a mere undeveloped "concept" cannot trigger the §102(b) clock.[112] On the other hand, the invention need not necessarily have been actually reduced to practice (i.e., physically constructed and tested) in order to be capable of placement on sale. In a watershed case, the Supreme Court clarified in *Pfaff v. Wells Elec., Inc.,*[113] that in order to be "on sale" within the meaning of 35 U.S.C. §102(b), two conditions must be satisfied before the critical date:

(1) the invention must be the subject of a commercial offer for sale; and
(2) the invention must be ready for patenting.[114]

With respect to prong (1), the Federal Circuit clarified in decisions subsequent to *Pfaff* that a "commercial offer" is one definite enough to qualify as an "offer" in the general contract law sense, as exempli-

---

[110]*See* United States Patent & Trademark Office, *Provisional Application for Patent* (Feb. 2011), http://www.uspto.gov/patents/resources/types/provapp.jsp (noting that filing a provisional patent application "[p]ermits authorized use of 'Patent Pending' notice for 12 months in connection with the description of the invention"). Filing a regular, non-provisional application also permits an applicant to mark products embodying the invention with the words "patent pending." In either case, the words "patent pending" have no enforceable legal effect. They simply provide notice to competitors that the entity marking its products with "patent pending" may eventually obtain a patent on some aspect of the product.

[111]The experimental use doctrine, discussed separately below, may negate what would otherwise appear to be on sale (or public use) activity under 35 U.S.C. §102(b).

[112]*See* UMC Elecs. Co. v. United States, 816 F.2d 647, 656 (Fed. Cir. 1987) (refuting any intention to "sanction attacks on patents on the ground that the inventor or another offered for sale, before the critical date, the mere concept of the invention. Nor should inventors be forced to rush into the Patent and Trademark Office prematurely.").

[113]525 U.S. 55 (1998).

[114]*See Pfaff,* 525 U.S. at 67.

fied by the definition of an "offer" under the Uniform Commercial Code (UCC).[115] "Only an offer which rises to the level of a commercial offer for sale, one which the other party could make into a binding contract by simple acceptance (assuming consideration), constitutes an offer for sale under §102(b)," the Federal Circuit explained.[116]

With respect to prong (2), the Supreme Court in *Pfaff*[117] held that the "ready for patenting" condition can be satisfied in "at least" two ways:[118] (1) the invention may have already been actually reduced to practice,[119] or (2) the invention may have at least been "reduced to drawings," in the sense that drawings or written descriptions of the

---

[115]*See* Group One, Ltd. v. Hallmark Cards, Inc., 254 F.3d 1041, 1047-1048 (Fed. Cir. 2001). In *Group One* the court held that the following language in a letter sent by the patentee Group One to Hallmark, before the §102(b) critical date, did *not* rise to the level of a commercial offer that would trigger the one-year clock of §102(b):

> We have developed a machine which can curl and shred ribbon so that Hallmark can produce the product you see enclosed—a bag of already curled and shredded ribbon. . . . We could provide the machine and/or the technology and work on a license/royalty basis.

Id. at 1044.

[116]*Group One*, 254 F.3d at 1048. The *Group One* court did not offer definitive guidelines for determining when a communication rises to the level of a commercial offer sufficient to trigger the §102(b) clock, but did "note in passing" that

> contract law traditionally recognizes that mere advertising and promoting of a product may be nothing more than an invitation for offers, while responding to such an invitation may itself be an offer. Restatement (Second) of Contracts §26 (1981). In any given circumstance, who is the offeror, and what constitutes a definite offer, requires looking closely at the language of the proposal itself. Language suggesting a legal offer, such as "I offer" or "I promise" can be contrasted with language suggesting more preliminary negotiations, such as "I quote" or "are you interested." Differing phrases are evidence of differing intent, but no one phrase is necessarily controlling. *Id.*§§24, 26. Fortunately, as earlier noted, there is a substantial body of general contract law, widely shared by both state and federal courts, to which courts can resort in making these determinations. *See generally, e.g.*, ARTHUR LINTON CORBIN, CORBIN ON CONTRACTS (1964); JOHN D. CALAMARI & JOSEPH M. PERILLO, THE LAW OF CONTRACTS (4th ed. 1998).

[117]525 U.S. 55 (1998).

[118]*Pfaff*, 525 U.S. at 67. By referring to the "at least" two ways in which an invention can be ready for patenting, the Supreme Court left the door open to additional possibilities for satisfying this condition.

[119]An actual reduction to practice requires the physical construction of an embodiment of the invention that works for its intended purpose, and will usually entail testing. *See Pfaff*, 525 U.S. at 57 n.2 ("A process is reduced to practice when it is successfully performed. A machine is reduced to practice when it is assembled, adjusted and used. A manufacture is reduced to practice when it is completely manufactured. A composition of matter is reduced to practice when it is completely composed.") (quoting Corona Cord Tire Co. v. Dovan Chem. Corp., 276 U.S. 358, 383 (1928)).

invention exist that are sufficiently specific to enable a person having ordinary skill in the art to practice the invention.[120]

The second of these conditions was held satisfied in *Pfaff*. Prior to the critical date, the inventor had offered to sell (and in fact had accepted a purchase order for) 30,100 units of his invention, a simple mechanical socket for holding computer chips during testing, to Texas Instruments for $91,115.[121] Figure 4.3 depicts the socket.

Figure 4.3

Patented Socket from *Pfaff v. Wells* (U.S. 1998)

Despite the fact that at the time of the offer, Pfaff had not actually constructed any of the sockets, the Supreme Court considered the invention ready for patenting such that the §102(b) bar was triggered. Detailed mechanical drawings and descriptions of the sockets existed as of the date that Pfaff accepted the purchase order (prior to the critical date), and the Court considered this information to have been enabling.[122] The Court supported its conclusion by noting that Texas

---

[120]*See Pfaff*, 525 U.S. at 67-68.

[121]*See id.* at 58.

[122]*See Pfaff*, 525 U.S at 63. *See also id.* at 68 (stating that "the second condition of the on sale bar is satisfied because the drawings Pfaff sent to the manufacturer before the critical date fully disclosed the invention"). In the view of this author, a significant concern with the *Pfaff* Court's "ready for patenting" analysis is that it effectively places a burden on the inventor of determining whether or not an enabling disclosure of his invention exists, at a time well prior to the filing of a patent application (or in most cases, even prior to consulting a patent attorney). The decision would seem to prejudice independent inventors without previous experience in the patent system, who cannot

Instruments was able to produce the sockets using Pfaff's drawings and specifications, and that those sockets contained all the elements of the invention as later claimed in Pfaff's patent.[123]

5.   Experimental Use Negation of the §102(b) Bars

The public use and on sale bars of §102(b) (2006) are both subject to "negation"[124] under the judicially developed experimental use doctrine.[125] This doctrine negates or excuses what would otherwise appear to be statutory bar-triggering activity prior to the §102(b) critical date.[126]

In the classic experimental use case, *City of Elizabeth v. American Nicholson Pavement Co.,*[127] the Supreme Court clarified that "[t]he use of an invention by the inventor himself, or of any other person under

---

reasonably be expected to have mastered the finer points of enablement law under 35 U.S.C. §112, ¶1, a subject on which even Federal Circuit judges have been known to disagree.

[123]*See Pfaff,* 525 U.S at 68.

[124]The experimental use doctrine operates as a negation of, rather than an exception to, the statutory bars of 35 U.S.C. §102(b). *See* TP Labs., Inc. v. Professional Positioners, Inc., 724 F.2d 965 (Fed. Cir. 1984), in which the court explained,

> Th[e] difference between "exception" and "negation" is not merely semantic. Under the precedent of this court, the statutory presumption of validity provided in 35 U.S.C. §282 places the burden of proof upon the party attacking the validity of the patent, and that burden of persuasion does not shift at any time to the patent owner. It is constant and remains throughout the suit on the challenger. . . .
>
> Under this analysis, it is incorrect to impose on the patent owner, as the trial court in this case did, the burden of proving that a "public use" was "experimental." These are not two separable issues. It is incorrect to ask: "Was it public use?" and then, "Was it experimental?" Rather, the court is faced with a single issue: Was it public use under §102(b)?
>
> Thus, the [district] court should have looked at all of the evidence put forth by both parties and should have decided whether the entirety of the evidence led to the conclusion that there had been "public use." This does not mean, of course, that the challenger has the burden of proving that the use is not experimental. Nor does it mean that the patent owner is relieved of explanation. It means that if a *prima facie* case is made of public use, the patent owner must be able to point to or must come forward with convincing evidence to counter that showing.

Id. at 971 (citations omitted).

[125]Experimental use negation of the §102(b) statutory bars is an entirely separate doctrine from the experimental (or research) use exemption from patent infringement. The latter is discussed in Chapter 10 ("Defenses to Patent Infringement"), *infra.*

[126]The experimental use doctrine has no relevance to activity *within* the one-year grace period of 35 U.S.C. §102(b). No negation is necessary for public uses or sales activity in this time period; the activity must occur *prior to* the §102(b) critical date in order to trigger a statutory bar.

[127]97 U.S. 126 (1878).

his direction, by way of experiment, and in order to bring the invention to perfection, has never been regarded as [public use within the meaning of the statute]."[128] The Court characterized experimental use as use of an invention "only by way of experiment" that is "pursued with a bona fide intent of testing the qualities" of the invention.[129] So long as the inventor "does not voluntarily allow others to make [the invention] and use it, and so long as it is not on sale for general use, he keeps the invention under his own control, and does not lose his title to a patent."[130]

The inventor/patentee Nicholson in the *City of Elizabeth* case developed a method of paving streets using wooden blocks in a checkerboard arrangement, which he tested by paving a well-traveled section of public carriage road in Boston.[131] Despite the fact that Nicholson did not file a patent application claiming the pavement invention for six years after commencing this testing,[132] the experimental use doctrine preserved his right to a patent. Because its extended durability while exposed to the elements was essential, Nicholson's pavement invention was of the type that could not be satisfactorily tested anywhere other than a public place like the carriage road.[133] Importantly, Nicholson's intent to test his invention was bona fide, and the evidence of record proved that he kept the invention under his control at all times.[134] On these facts, Nicholson's experimental use of his pavement invention, while in a public place, did not amount to a statutory public use that would have otherwise resulted in the invalidation of his patent.[135]

[128]*Id.* at 134.
[129]*Id.* at 135.
[130]*Id.*
[131]Then known as the "mill dam" or "Mill-Dam Avenue," today this road roughly corresponds to Boston's Beacon Street. *See* Neighborhood Association of the Back Bay, *History of Back Bay, available at* http://www.nabbonline.com/about_us/back_bay_history (last visited June 20, 2012).
[132]*See City of Elizabeth*, 97 U.S. at 133 (stating contention of appellants/accused infringers that "the pavement which Nicholson put down by way of experiment, on Mill-dam Avenue in Boston, in 1848, was publicly used for the space of six years before his application for a patent, and that this was a public use within the meaning of the law").
[133]*See id.* at 134, 136.
[134]*See id.* at 133-134 (describing testimony of toll-collector Lang that inventor Nicholson personally examined the pavement on an "almost daily" basis and characterized it to others as "experimental").
[135]For a contrasting example of an inventor's inability to keep his invention under sufficient control, thereby failing to qualify as experimental use that would have negated §102(b) public use, *see* Lough v. Brunswick Corp., 86 F.3d 1113 (Fed. Cir. 1996).

J.   Abandonment Under 35 U.S.C. §102(c) (Pre-AIA)

Judicial decisions invalidating a patent under 35 U.S.C. §102(c) (2006) are rarely seen today. This is because subsection (c) is an anachronism—largely a historic holdover from the time when loss of right to a patent was viewed as being triggered by an inventor's own affirmative act of abandonment or dedication of her invention to the public. The on sale and public use bars as encompassed within 35 U.S.C. §102(b) (2006) initially developed as two specific types of conduct giving rise to a general concept of abandonment, which general concept is still reflected today in §102(c) (2006).[136]

The statutory bars of §102(b) are presently understood as reflecting primarily a delay rationale, and may be triggered by persons other than the inventor, as discussed *supra*. Only an affirmative act of the inventor can trigger an abandonment under §102(c), however. The continued existence of §102(c) most likely indicates that patent rights can theoretically be lost at any time, even within the §102(b) grace period, by the relatively unlikely occurrence of an overt, intentional statement of abandonment of patent rights upon which others are entitled to rely.[137]

Note that what is involved in 35 U.S.C. §102(c) (2006) is not an inventor's abandonment of the affirmative right to practice her invention. Rather, statutory abandonment refers to a waiver or forfeiture of the right to patent protection on (i.e., the right to exclude others from practicing) the invention. As the CCPA explained in *In re Gibbs*,[138]

> We are not at all concerned, therefore, with any abandonment of the invention in the sense of the *thing invented* but only, in the words of the §102 heading, with "loss of right to patent," an inability to obtain that incorporeal property right (35 USC 261) which is the right to exclude others from making, using or selling the invention (35 USC 154).[139]

The *Gibbs* court considered whether abandonment of the right to exclude others may be inferred from an inventor's *failure* to act rather than from some affirmative act, but rejected that notion as applied to

---

[136]*See, e.g.*, Pennock v. Dialogue, 27 U.S. 1, 24 (1829) (explaining that an inventor's "voluntary act or acquiescence in the public sale and use is an abandonment of his right; or rather creates a disability to comply with the terms and conditions on which alone the secretary of state is authorized to grant him a patent.").

[137]*See* City of Elizabeth v. American Nicholson Pavement Co., 97 U.S. 126, 134 (1878) (stating that "[a]n abandonment of an invention to the public may be evinced by the conduct of an inventor at any time, even within the two years named in the law [i.e., the two-year grace period then in effect]").

[138]437 F.2d 486 (C.C.P.A. 1971) (reversing USPTO rejection under 35 U.S.C. §102(c)).

[139]*Id.* at 489 (emphasis in original).

the facts of *Gibbs.* There the CCPA reviewed a USPTO rejection under 35 U.S.C. §102(c) based on the agency's argument that the appellant had forfeited his right to patent protection on an invention that was disclosed but not claimed in his own earlier-issued patent.[140] Within one year of the issuance of that patent, however, the appellant filed another application claiming the subject matter that he had failed to claim in the prior application leading to the patent.[141] The CCPA held that the appellant's claiming of the invention in this fashion overcame any presumption of abandonment for failure to claim it in the first application:

> To return to the present case, assuming, *arguendo,* that appellants' patent contains a disclosure of the invention now being claimed, in an application filed less than one year after the patent issued, the claimed subject matter clearly not being the same,[142] was it "abandoned" by the issuance of the patent? We think not. The determination made below that appellants had abandoned their right to patent the subject matter now claimed is a conclusion of law predicated on a mere inference of dedication drawn from the facts of disclosure and failure to claim. This inference may be rebutted in several ways: by an application for reissue of the patent pursuant to statute, §251, last paragraph, which seems to permit a broadening reissue application to be filed up to two years after the patent issues; it can unquestionably be rebutted by claiming in a copending application before the patent issues[143] and possibly even thereafter. We see no logical reason why it cannot also be rebutted in all cases, as has been held, by the filing of an application within the one-year grace period following the issuance of the patent before the patent has become a statutory bar under §102(b). So far as the statutes are concerned, an inventor clearly has that right.[144]

K.   Foreign Patenting Bar of 35 U.S.C. §102(d) (Pre-AIA)

As with §102(c), invalidation of patents under 35 U.S.C. §102(d) (2006) is today a relatively rare event.[145] Like 35 U.S.C. §102(b) (2006),

---

[140]*See id.* at 486.

[141]Thus, the patent did not become a §102(b) bar against the subsequent application.

[142]Hence, no rejection was made for **double patenting.** *See generally supra* Chapter 1, Section H.6 ("Double Patenting").

[143]This strategy would involve the filing of a continuing application pursuant to 35 U.S.C. §120.

[144]*Gibbs,* 437 F.2d at 494.

[145]*See* Lisa L. Dolak & Michael L. Goldman, *Responding to Prior Art Rejections: An Analytical Framework,* 83 J. Pat. & Trademark Off. Soc'y 5 (2001), explaining that

> [r]ejections under 35 U.S.C. §102(d) are uncommon . . . for several reasons. Patent applicants interested in obtaining the benefit of foreign priority under the Paris

§102(d) (2006) is considered a statutory bar provision, but here the right to a patent is lost by a different sort of delay. Rather than being invoked by domestic activity such as sales or public use in the United States, 35 U.S.C. §102(d) is triggered when an inventor files a patent application in a foreign country, files another application on the same invention in the United States more than one year later, and the inventor's foreign patent has already issued before her U.S. filing.[146]

Thus 35 U.S.C. §102(d) seeks to promote prompt entry into the U.S. patent system once an inventor has commenced obtaining protection on the same invention in other countries.[147] The validity of the corresponding foreign patent is not controlling; what matters is that the foreign patent issued with claims directed to the same invention as the U.S. application.[148]

Convention or Patent Cooperation Treaty must file foreign patent applications within 12 months of the first filing in a convention or treaty member country, and only U.S. applications filed more than twelve months after a foreign filing are potentially vulnerable under Section 102(d). Even in those situations where the U.S. application is filed more than 12 months after a corresponding foreign application, Section 102(d) only applies when the foreign patent also issues before the U.S. filing. Finally, for inventions made in the United States, the patent statute prohibits the filing of patent applications in foreign countries until six months have passed since the filing of the corresponding U.S. application, or until the foreign filing is authorized by a foreign filing license (typically obtained by filing a U.S. application). *See* 35 U.S.C. §184. Accordingly, Section 102(d) has little potential application to U.S. patent applications claiming inventions made in this country.

Id. at 11 n.23 (citations omitted).

[146]Problems under 35 U.S.C. §102(d) (2006) also may arise when a foreign country grants patent-*like* rights. For example, Germany grants exclusive rights against imitation of new and original industrial designs, or *Geschmachmusters. See* In re Talbott, 443 F.2d 1397, 1398 (C.C.P.A. 1971). In *Talbott,* the court concluded that the grant of a German *Geschmachmuster* registration, directed to an automobile rear-view mirror design, triggered the §102(d) bar against the inventor who delayed in seeking U.S. patent protection. The different nature of the rights granted by the German registration and a U.S. patent (i.e., the former being closer to copyright protection than patent) were not viewed as controlling; the court "agree[d] with the [USPTO] board that 'it is sufficient if the inventor receives from the foreign country the exclusive privilege that its laws provide for.'" *Id.* at 1399.

[147]*See* In re Kathawala, 9 F.3d 942, 946 (Fed. Cir. 1993) (stating that policy and purpose behind §102(d) are "to require applicants for patent in the United States to exercise reasonable promptness in filing their applications after they have filed and obtained foreign patents").

[148]*See id.* at 945, stating,

Even assuming that Kathawala's compound, composition, and method of use claims are not enforceable in Greece, a matter on which we will not speculate, the controlling fact for purposes of section 102(d) is that the Greek patent issued containing claims directed to the same invention as that of the U.S. application. When a foreign patent issues with claims directed to the same invention as the U.S. application, the invention is "patented" within the meaning of section

L. Description in Another's Earlier-Filed Patent or Published Patent Application Under 35 U.S.C. §102(e) (Pre-AIA)

Subsection (e) of §102 (2006) involves anticipation through the *description* (though not *claiming*[149]) of the applicant's invention in a patent or published patent application of another, where that "other" filed her application in the United States before the applicant's invention date.[150] This subsection was made a part of the 1952 Patent Act in order to statutorily codify the rule announced by the U.S. Supreme

---

102(d); validity of the foreign claims is irrelevant to the section 102(d) inquiry. This is true irrespective of whether the applicant asserts that the claims in the foreign patent are invalid on grounds of non-statutory subject matter or more conventional patentability reasons such as prior art or inadequate disclosure. . . . The [US]PTO should be able to accept at face value the grant of the Greek patent claiming subject matter corresponding to that claimed in a U.S. application, without engaging in an extensive exploration of fine points of foreign law. The claims appear in the Greek patent because the applicant put them there. He cannot claim exemption from the consequences of his own actions. The Board thus correctly concluded that the validity of the Greek claims is irrelevant for purposes of section 102(d). Accordingly, the Board properly affirmed the examiner's rejection over the Greek patent.

[149]If the reference patent *claims* the same invention, then an interference may be declared under 35 U.S.C. §102(g) *if* the application claims were presented within one year of the issue date of the reference patent. If more than one year has passed, the USPTO may reject the application under 35 U.S.C. §135(b). *See* In re McGrew, 120 F.3d 1236 (Fed. Cir. 1997) (Rich, J.) (affirming USPTO rejection of application claims under §135(b) where "McGrew [] conceded that the claims at issue in the '280 application [on appeal] are for 'the same or substantially the same subject matter' as the claims of the [reference] Takeuchi patent . . . [and] that the claims at issue were first presented more than one year after the Takeuchi patent was granted").

It is theoretically possible that the claims of the reference patent, which are part of the reference patent's specification, *describe* the subject matter claimed by the applicant rather than *claim* that subject matter, and therefore could be relied on as §102(e) prior art. This is because the entirety of a reference patent's disclosure is available as prior art under 35 U.S.C. §102(e), but only as of the U.S. filing date of the reference patent, not any earlier date of conception or actual reduction to practice. *See* Sun Studs, Inc. v. ATA Equip. Leasing, Inc., 872 F.2d 978, 983 (Fed. Cir. 1989) (stating that "[w]hen patents are not in interference, the effective date of a reference United States patent as prior art is its filing date in the United States, as stated in §102(e), not the date of conception or actual reduction to practice of the invention claimed or the subject matter disclosed in the reference patent"); *id.* at 983-984 (stating that "[u]nder 35 U.S.C. §102(e) the entire disclosure of Mouat's [the reference patent] specification is effective as a reference, but only as of Mouat's filing date").

[150]Recall that the USPTO takes the applicant's filing date as her presumptive or *prima facie* invention date based on a constructive reduction to practice theory, and it is up to the applicant to establish an earlier actual invention date if necessary to antedate (i.e., predate or "swear behind") a prior art reference. This may be accomplished through filing an appropriate affidavit or declaration under 37 C.F.R. §1.131 to establish invention of the subject matter of the rejected claim prior to the effective

Court in *Alexander Milburn Co. v. Davis-Bournonville Co.*[151] Distilled to its essence, *Milburn* requires that we treat a prior art U.S. patent as constructively published as soon as it is filed. The patent law engages in the fiction that the contents of the patent's written description instantaneously become available as a printed publication upon filing. Thus, the effective date of the written description portion of a U.S. patent being used as §102(e) prior art is its U.S. filing date.[152]

For example, assume that Andy filed a U.S. patent application claiming a solar-powered toothbrush on January 1, 2005. The USPTO examiner's search of the prior art revealed that Bill had already filed his own U.S. patent application describing (but not claiming) the identical toothbrush on January 1, 2003, and that Bill's application was published 18 months later, on July 1, 2004.[153] The effective date of Bill's application in this example is its U.S. filing date of January 1, 2003, which predates Andy's filing date of January 1, 2005 (i.e., Andy's presumptive invention date). On these facts the examiner would enter a rejection of Andy's claim under 35 U.S.C. §102(e)(1), one of two prongs of §102(e) (pre-AIA), discussed in further detail below.

Unlike the rest of the world, which operates on a first-to-file system, the United States under pre-AIA rules has long awarded patent rights to the first to invent.[154] The policy rationale underlying the

---

date of the reference. Procedures for antedating a reference are detailed in Section O of this chapter, *infra*.

[151]270 U.S. 390 (1926). *See also* P.J. Federico, *Commentary on the New Patent Act*, 35 U.S.C.A. §1 (1954 ed., discontinued in subsequent volumes), *reprinted* at 75 J. PAT. & TRADEMARK OFF. SOC'Y 161, 179 (1993) (explaining that "[p]aragraph (e) is new in the statute and enacts the rule of the decision of the Supreme Court in [*Milburn*] under which a United States patent disclosing an invention dates from the filing of the application for the purpose of anticipating a later inventor, whether or not the invention is claimed in the patent") (citation omitted).

[152]Under the rule of *In re Hilmer*, 359 F.2d 859 (C.C.P.A. 1966), discussed in further detail in Chapter 12 ("International Patenting Issues"), *infra*, the USPTO must ignore any earlier *foreign* filing date, the benefit of which the reference applicant claimed under 35 U.S.C. §119, of a U.S. patent or published application being used as a §102(e) reference. The AIA prospectively eliminated the *Hilmer* rule.

[153]In this hypothetical, for example, Bill might have been claiming a new, compact solar-powered battery and might also have described in his application some specific applications for his invention (e.g., use in a solar-powered toothbrush).

[154]*See* discussion of 35 U.S.C. §102(g), *infra*, and Chapter 12 ("International Patenting Issues"). The United States implemented a first-to-invent priority system as early as the late eighteenth century. *See* Edward C. Walterscheid, *Priority of Invention: How the United States Came to Have a "First-to-Invent" System*, 23 AIPLA Q.J. 263, 264 (1995) (explaining that "the initial impetus came from the titanic struggle between John Fitch and James Rumsey for priority of invention with respect to the steamboat during the late eighteenth century, but the actual creation of a true first-to-invent system took almost fifty years"). The Leahy-Smith America Invents Act of 2011 changed the United States to a first-inventor-to-file priority system. *See infra* Part III of this chapter.

Milburn rule is that the presence of a description of the invention that the applicant is claiming in someone else's earlier-filed patent application evidences that the applicant was *not* in fact the first to invent that subject matter. We may not know the actual identity of the prior inventor when the "someone else" (i.e., the statutory "another" or the "reference patentee") has not *claimed* the invention (and thus presumably did not make it). But based on the existence of the earlier-filed description, the law presumes that the first to invent is someone other than our patent applicant.

Prior to the 1999 enactment of the American Inventors Protection Act (AIPA),[155] which introduced 18-month publication of most pending U.S. patent applications, 35 U.S.C. §102(e) required that an earlier-filed application by "another" had to have already *issued* as a patent before it became available for use by a USPTO examiner as a §102(e) prior art reference. This requirement, which is still reflected in the §102(e)(2) prong of 35 U.S.C. §102(e) (2006) form (i.e., as amended by the AIPA and the Twenty-first Century Department of Justice Appropriations Authorization Act (2002)[156]), guaranteed that the contents of the prior art patent ultimately "saw the light of day" through issuance before that patent could be used as a §102(e) reference. The issuance requirement thus ameliorated the concern that 35 U.S.C. §102(e) (pre-AIA) raises about the use of "secret prior art"—that is, prior art that is used at an effective date (in the case of a §102(e) reference patent, its U.S. filing date) when the applicant against whom it is being asserted cannot have known anything about its contents (because of the pre-AIPA secrecy of all pending patent applications until issuance).[157]

Due to enactment of the AIPA in 1999, the contents of most pending U.S. patent applications are now published automatically at 18 months after the application's filing date.[158] This change means that

---

[155]Pub. L. No. 106-113, 113 Stat. 1501 (enacted Nov. 29, 1999).

[156]As amended in November 2002, subparagraph (e) of 35 U.S.C. §102 provides that a person shall be entitled to a patent unless

> (e) the invention was described in (1) an application for patent, published under section 122(b), by another filed in the United States before the invention by the applicant for patent or (2) a patent granted on an application for patent by another filed in the United States before the invention by the applicant for patent, except that an international application filed under the treaty defined in section 351(a) shall have the effects for the purposes of this subsection of an application filed in the United States only if the international application designated the United States and was published under Article 21(2) of such treaty in the English language. . . .

[157]*See* Sun Studs, Inc. v. ATA Equip. Leasing, Inc., 872 F.2d 978, 983 n.3 (Fed. Cir. 1989) (defining "secret prior art").

[158]With minor exceptions, an inventor can "opt out" of 18-month publication only if she certifies that she is not seeking patent protection on the invention outside of the

the written description of an earlier-filed U.S. patent application is now available for use as a §102(e) prior art reference at an earlier date, that is, at its 18-month publication date rather than at any later issue date. In fact, the §102(e) reference application need never issue as a patent at all, so long as the application is published.[159] An international application filed under the Patent Cooperation Treaty (PCT)[160] also can be relied on by the USPTO as a §102(e)(1) (2006) reference *if* the international application designated the United States *and* was published under the PCT in the English language.[161]

The effective date of a 35 U.S.C. §102(e) reference, whether it is an issued U.S. patent or a published patent application, remains the same in either case, however; the effective date is the U.S. application filing date of the reference patent or application.[162] What has changed is that before the AIPA, the USPTO generally had to wait until the reference application issued as a patent before the agency could rely on its contents as prior art.[163] After the AIPA, that reliance can be made as soon as the reference patent application is published, because at that time it effectively becomes a "printed publication."

United States. *See* 35 U.S.C. §122(b)(2)(B). As of 2004, about 85 percent of U.S. patent applications filed by large entities were published at 18 months after filing. *See* United States General Accounting Office, *Report to Congressional Committees: Patents: Information about the Publication Provisions of the American Inventors Protection Act* 4 (May 2004), *available at* http://www.gao.gov/new.items/d04603.pdf (reporting that for applications received between November 29, 2000, and November 28, 2003, the USPTO "has published or plans to publish applications from about 85 percent of the applicants qualifying as large entities compared with only about 74 percent of those qualifying as small entities").

[159]*See* 35 U.S.C. §102(e)(1) (2006).

[160]The Patent Cooperation Treaty is discussed in greater detail in Chapter 12 ("International Patenting Issues"), *infra*.

[161]*See* 35 U.S.C. §102(e) (2006) (providing in part that "an international application filed under the treaty defined in [35 U.S.C.] section 351(a) [i.e., the Patent Cooperation Treaty] shall have the effects for the purposes of this subsection of an application filed in the United States only if the international application designated the United States and was published under Article 21(2) of such treaty in the English language").

[162]Under the rule of *In re Hilmer*, 359 F.2d 859 (C.C.P.A. 1966), discussed in further detail in Chapter 12 ("International Patenting Issues"), *infra*, the USPTO must ignore any earlier *foreign* filing date, the benefit of which the reference applicant claimed under 35 U.S.C. §119, of a U.S. patent or published application being used as a §102(e) reference. The America Invents Act of 2011 repealed the *Hilmer* rule for applications filed on or after March 16, 2013. *See infra* Section P.3.b ("What Section 3 of the AIA Changed") and *infra* Section R ("Presumptively Novelty-Destroying Events under Post-AIA 35 U.S.C. §102(a)(2) [First-Inventor-To-File Rule])".

[163]The so-called provisional §102(e)-based rejection was an exception to this rule, where the §102(e) reference patent application was commonly owned with the application under examination, and thus could be disclosed to the applicant by the USPTO without violating secrecy obligations. *See* In re Bartfeld, 925 F.2d 1450, 1451 n.5 (Fed. Cir. 1991).

M. Derivation and Inventorship Under 35 U.S.C. §102(f) (Pre-AIA)

Subsection 102(f) is neither an anticipation nor a loss-of-right section; it is *sui generis* in the sense that it reflects the central principle of *originality* or proper inventorship. A person cannot simply copy or steal an invention from another and claim it as his own; the claimed invention must be the original creation of the inventor. Although §102(f) (2006) was eliminated by the AIA, the fundamental concept of originality continues to apply whether one is operating under pre- or post-AIA rules.[164]

Section 102(f) (2006) is implicated in a variety of patent law contexts. For the sake of completeness each is introduced below, although the discussion extends somewhat beyond the scope of this chapter (novelty, loss of right, and priority under 35 U.S.C. §102).

1. Derivation

United States patent law requires that an invention must be the original work of the person(s) named as inventor(s) on the patent application. In other words, Entity A cannot merely copy an invention from Entity B, the true inventor, and claim it as Entity A's own invention.

One particular application of the originality requirement is that an invention is not patentable to an applicant who "derived" it from someone else. **Derivation** in patent law means that another (in the above example, Entity B) conceived the invention and communicated that conception to the person improperly named as the inventor on the patent application at issue (here the "deriver," Entity A).[165]

---

[164]For reasons that are not particularly clear, the AIA eliminated 35 U.S.C. §102(f) (2006), *see* Leahy-Smith America Invents Act, Pub. L. No. 112-29 (H.R. 1249), §3(b)(1), 125 Stat. 284, 285-286 (2011). However, the AIA did not eliminate the requirement of originality. Specifically, the AIA did not change the requirement that, subject to certain exceptions, patent applications shall be made "by the inventor," 35 U.S.C. §111(a)(1) (2006), and the AIA added a definition of "inventor" as "the individual or, if a joint invention, the individuals collectively who invented or discovered the subject matter of the invention." 35 U.S.C. §100(f) (eff. Mar. 16, 2013); Leahy-Smith America Invents Act, Pub. L. No. 112-29 (H.R. 1249), §3(a)(2), 125 Stat. 284, 285 (2011). The AIA also continued the requirement that a patent applicant's oath include a statement that the applicant believes he is an "original" inventor. *See* 35 U.S.C. §115(b)(2) (eff. Mar. 16, 2013) (providing that "[a]n oath or declaration under subsection (a) shall contain statements that . . . such individual believes himself or herself to be the original inventor or an original joint inventor of a claimed invention in the application") (emphases added)

[165]*See* Agawan Co. v. Jordan, 74 U.S. 583, 602-603 (1868) (stating that "[s]uggestions from another, made during the progress of such experiments, in order that they may

Derivation under 35 U.S.C. §102(f) (2006) should be contrasted with a priority determination under 35 U.S.C. §102(g) (2006), discussed below. In the latter, it is assumed that both A and B are original, independent inventors of the same invention; the §102(g) dispute is over which inventor, A or B, was the first to invent.[166]

Note that there are no geographic limitations in §102(f), in contrast with other subsections of 35 U.S.C. §102. Only a true inventor of the claimed subject matter is entitled to patent it, and thus the patent law is not concerned about whether the communication of the conception from Entity B to Entity A occurred in the United States or a foreign country.[167]

2. Who Is an Inventor?

The conception of an invention is the mental part of the inventive act (i.e., the formation in the mind of the inventor(s) of the definite and permanent idea of the invention as it is thereafter reduced to practice). Conception is the touchstone of determining inventorship.[168] For a person to be properly named as an inventor on a patent, he must

---

be sufficient to defeat a patent subsequently issued, must have embraced the plan of the improvement, and must have furnished such information to the person to whom the communication was made that it would have enabled an ordinary mechanic, without the exercise of any ingenuity and special skill on his part, to construct and put the improvement in successful operation"); Gambro Lundia AB v. Baxter Healthcare Corp., 110 F.3d 1573, 1576 (Fed. Cir. 1997) (holding that "[t]o show derivation, the party asserting invalidity must prove both prior conception of the invention by another and communication of that conception to the patentee"); Price v. Symsek, 988 F.2d 1187, 1190 (Fed. Cir. 1993) (stating that "[t]o prove derivation in an interference proceeding, the person attacking the patent must establish prior conception of the claimed subject matter and communication of the conception to the adverse claimant"); DeGroff v. Roth, 412 F.2d 1401, 1405 (C.C.P.A. 1969) (noting in appeal from interference proceeding Board's test that "Roth and Hall [junior party in interference], in order to prevail, must prove by a preponderance of the evidence that they 'had a full concept of the invention encompassed by the counts and this concept was transmitted to DeGroff'").

[166]See Price, 988 F.2d at 1190 (contrasting claim of derivation with claim of priority of invention).

[167]The America Invents Act of 2011 eliminated interferences (proceedings to determine priority under the traditional first-to-invent system) but added a new derivation proceeding. See 35 U.S.C. §135 (eff. Mar. 16, 2013). The AIA derivation proceeding is discussed infra Section S.3.a. Interference cases may no longer be filed after March 15, 2013.

[168]See Sewall v. Walters, 21 F.3d 411, 415 (Fed. Cir. 1994) (explaining that "[d]etermining 'inventorship' is nothing more than determining who conceived the subject matter at issue, whether that subject matter is recited in a claim in an application or in a count in an interference"). Conception of an invention has occurred "when a definite and permanent idea of an operative invention, including every feature of the subject matter sought to be patented, is known." Id.

generally contribute to the conception of the invention.[169] One who derived the invention, rather than contributed to its conception, is not properly named as an inventor.[170]

3. Correction of Inventorship

Section 102(f) is also the pre-AIA vehicle for USPTO rejections on the ground of improper naming of inventors in pending patent applications. In addition, it is the ground on which issued patents may be invalidated based on the improper naming of inventors, whether or not any derivation has occurred.[171] Prior to passage of the 1952 Patent Act, patents were routinely held invalid for failure to correctly name the inventors. Such failures could involve "nonjoinder," which is the failure to name someone who truly is an inventor of the claimed subject matter, or "misjoinder," which is the improper naming of a person as an inventor who is *not* in fact an inventor. For example, assume that both A and B are named as inventors on a patent, but only A invented and B was merely a supervisor or funding source. B is not properly named as a co-inventor (nor, on these facts, is B a deriver).

The risk of invalidation stemming from the improper naming of inventors was significantly lessened with the 1952 Act's enactment of 35 U.S.C. §256, which provides in part that "[t]he error of omitting inventors or naming persons who are not inventors shall not invalidate the patent in which such error occurred if it can be corrected as provided in this section."[172] Under pre-AIA rules, the error to be corrected must be without any deceptive intention on the part of a nonjoined inventor, while the law does not inquire into the intent of a person who was misjoined.[173]

Section 256 further provides that the inventorship of an issued patent may be corrected in two ways. The first paragraph of §256 indicates that if all parties agree on a needed correction, they may

---

[169]*See* Burroughs Wellcome Co. v. Barr Labs., Inc., 40 F.3d 1223, 1227-1228 (Fed. Cir. 1994).

[170]The America Invents Act of 2011 added an explicit, though circularly unhelpful, definition of "inventor." *See* 35 U.S.C. §100(f) (eff. Mar. 16, 2013) (providing that "[t]he term 'inventor' means the individual or, if a joint invention, the individuals collectively who invented or discovered the subject matter of the invention").

[171]Section 102(f) (2006) should be read in tandem with 35 U.S.C. §111 (2006), which requires that patent applications be made "by the inventor," except in situations otherwise provided for (e.g., an inventor who cannot be located or is deceased).

[172]35 U.S.C. §256, ¶2.

[173]*See* Stark v. Advanced Magnetics, Inc., 119 F.3d 1551, 1554 (Fed. Cir. 1997). The America Invents Act of 2011 eliminated the language "and such error arose without any deceptive intention on his part." *See* 35 U.S.C. §256(a) (eff. Sept. 16, 2012).

apply to the Director of the USPTO for that correction. The second paragraph provides that inventorship disputes in which all parties do not agree may be resolved by "the court before which such matter is called in question,"[174] so long as notice and opportunity for a hearing are provided.[175]

4. Joint Inventors

When a pending patent application lists multiple inventors, the USPTO examiner may enter a rejection under 35 U.S.C. §102(f) (2006) if evidence exists suggesting that not all of these individuals contributed to the conception of the invention. The law is quite clear, however, that a patented invention may be the work of multiple inventors (and joint invention is routine).[176]

Section 116 of 35 U.S.C. provides the standard for joint inventions made by two or more persons. Prior to 1984, the law required that to be named as a co-inventor, a person must have contributed to every one of the claims of the application or patent at issue. Section 116 was amended in 1984 so that contribution to the conception of the subject matter recited in every claim is not necessary. Under 35 U.S.C. §116 as it now stands, inventors may apply for a patent jointly even though "each did not make a contribution to the subject matter of every claim of the patent."[177] For example, both A and B are properly named inventors on a patent application comprising 20 claims, even though A contributed to the conception of 19 claims and B contributed to the conception of only 1 claim.[178]

---

[174]Professor Chisum argues that the courts have erred by interpreting the "such matter" language of 35 U.S.C. §256 as creating jurisdiction for an independent cause of action for inventorship correction by omitted inventors. See 1-2 DONALD S. CHISUM, CHISUM ON PATENTS §2.04[7] (2008).

[175]Although 35 U.S.C. §256 governs the correction of inventorship for an issued patent, correction of the inventorship on a still-pending patent application takes place within the USPTO, in accordance with the last paragraph of 35 U.S.C. §116.

[176]The America Invents Act of 2011 added an explicit, though circular, definition of joint inventorship. See 35 U.S.C. §100(g) (eff. Mar. 16, 2013) (providing that "[t]he terms 'joint inventor' and 'coinventor' mean any 1 of the individuals who invented or discovered the subject matter of a joint invention").

[177]35 U.S.C. §116(3).

[178]See Ethicon, Inc. v. United States Surgical Corp., 135 F.3d 1456, 1460 (Fed. Cir. 1998) (stating that "[a] contribution to one claim is enough").

N. Prior Invention Under 35 U.S.C. §102(g) (Pre-AIA)

1. Introduction

Section 102(g) of 35 U.S.C. (2006) is the cornerstone of the historic U.S. first-to-invent priority system. The requirement that patents be granted to the first in time to invent is implemented in two different contexts as indicated by the text of the statutory provision, but the basic concept of first-to-invent informs both situations.[179]

Section 102(g) (2006) comprises two prongs. The first prong, §102(g)(1), deals with pre-AIA priority contests called **interferences** between two or more parties who claim to have made the same invention at about the same time. The interference, an *inter partes* proceeding conducted within the USPTO, will determine which party was first to invent and hence is entitled to the U.S. patent on the invention in question.

The second prong, §102(g)(2), is a basis for proving *anticipation* of the claims of a patent application (in *ex parte* prosecution) or an issued patent (in federal court litigation challenging validity). Anticipation under §102(g)(2) occurs through the act of someone other than the named inventor of the application or patent having made the invention in this country before the invention date of the application or patent.

In both the interference and the anticipation settings, the earlier invention must not have been "abandoned, suppressed, or concealed."[180] The interference and anticipation contexts are discussed separately below, as is the basic rule of time-wise priority that applies in both contexts.

2. Interference Proceedings Under §102(g)(1)

Only one patent can be granted on a particular claimed invention. When two (or more) parties (i.e., inventive entities[181]) apply for a U.S. patent on the same invention, each party having independently made

---

[179]The America Invents Act of 2011 prospectively ended the first-to-invent system and changed the United States to a first-inventor-to-file system. *See infra* Part III.

[180]35 U.S.C. §102(g).

[181]In cases where an invention is made jointly by two or more persons, patent law refers to those persons collectively as the "inventive entity." Consider an invention jointly made by Inventor A and Inventor B. The inventive entity of "A + B" is considered "another" (i.e., a different inventive entity from either A alone or B alone).

the invention (i.e., not copied it), we cannot award both parties their own patents. Rather, the U.S. patent system devised a procedure that has historically awarded the patent (at least theoretically) to the party who was first in time to invent, regardless of the order in which the parties filed their respective patent applications.

The use of "theoretically" in the previous sentence indicates that the process of determining priority of invention does not occur automatically. The competing claimants must participate in an interference proceeding, a pre-AIA *inter partes* adjudicatory proceeding within the USPTO to determine which party invented first.[182] The party who is the last to file her patent application (the "junior party") bears the burden of overcoming a presumption that the first to file (the "senior party") was also the first to invent. Thus, under the historic U.S. priority system the party who was the first to file an application on the invention in question is presumptively entitled to the patent, *unless* the other party can successfully overcome this presumption.

Evidence of earlier invention in an interference proceeding can be based on inventive activity outside the United States in accordance with the pre-AIA version of 35 U.S.C. §104.[183] This section permits the use of evidence of inventive activity (such as conception, diligence, and reduction to practice, as those terms are defined herein) that occurred on or after December 8, 1993, in countries that are signatories to the North American Free Trade Agreement (NAFTA), which currently includes Mexico and Canada in addition to the United States, and on or after January 1, 1996, in countries that are members of the

---

[182]The U.S. patent system developed the interference proceeding as a means of determining priority of invention. Adoption of the first-to-invent principle does not necessarily require interferences, however. Historically, England appears to have used the relative order of filing dates as an irrebuttable presumption of the relative dates of invention, thus avoiding protracted factual disputes over first to invent priority. The author thanks Professor Carl Moy for this observation.

The America Invents Act of 2011 eliminated interferences. *See* Leahy-Smith America Invents Act, Pub. L. No. 112-29 (H.R. 1249) (2011), §§3(i) (amending 35 U.S.C. §135 to eliminate interference proceedings and implement derivation proceedings), 3(j) ("Elimination of References to Interferences") (striking the word "interference" from multiple sections of the Patent Act). Interference cases may no longer be filed after March 15, 2013.

[183]35 U.S.C. §104 (2006) provides in part:

    (a) In general

       (1) Proceedings. In proceedings in the Patent and Trademark Office, in the courts, and before any other competent authority, an applicant for a patent, or a patentee, may not establish a date of invention by reference to knowledge or use thereof, or other activity with respect thereto, in a foreign country other than a NAFTA country or a WTO member country, except as provided in sections 119 and 365 of this title.

World Trade Organization (WTO).[184] Thus, a person who invented in a NAFTA or WTO member country other than the United States and seeks U.S. patent protection on her invention is placed on a more even footing, from an evidentiary standpoint, with a U.S. inventor of the same invention. However, such a person may also be penalized if she fails to disclose evidence of foreign inventive activity in accordance with U.S. discovery norms.[185]

The procedures for conducting interferences are quite complex and beyond the scope of this text.[186] However, the basic rule of time-wise priority set forth in the last sentence of 35 U.S.C. §102(g) (2006) should be mastered by all students of patent law:

> In determining priority of invention under this subsection, there shall be considered not only the respective dates of conception and reduction to practice of the invention, but also the reasonable diligence of one who was first to conceive and last to reduce to practice, from a time prior to conception by the other.[187]

This rule, which applies in both the interference and the anticipation settings, is examined and applied in several examples below.

---

[184]The current membership of the WTO is available at www.wto.org/english/thewto_e/acc_e/members_brief_e.doc (last visited June 22, 2012). As of June 2012, 155 countries were members of the WTO. Countries that were *not* members as of June 2012 include Afghanistan, Bhutan, Bahamas, Iran, and Iraq.

[185]*See* 35 U.S.C. §104(a)(3) (2006), which provides the following:

> (3) Use of information. To the extent that any information in a NAFTA country or a WTO member country concerning knowledge, use, or other activity relevant to proving or disproving a date of invention has not been made available for use in a proceeding in the Patent and Trademark Office, a court, or any other competent authority to the same extent as such information could be made available in the United States, the Director, court, or such other authority shall draw appropriate inferences, or take other action permitted by statute, rule, or regulation, in favor of the party that requested the information in the proceeding.

This portion of 35 U.S.C. §104 imposes "a type of protection for U.S. companies in the form of penalties against foreign parties that do not provide appropriate discovery." Thomas L. Irving & Stacy D. Lewis, *Proving a Date of Invention and Infringement After GATT/TRIPS*, 22 AIPLA Q.J. 309, 318 (1994).

[186]For further guidance on interference law and practice, *see* Practice Before the Board of Patent Appeals and Interferences, 37 C.F.R. §§41.200-41.208 (2010) (titled "Subpart E. Patent Interferences"); United States Patent & Trademark Office, *Interference Proceedings*, MANUAL OF PATENT EXAMINING PROCEDURE §§2301-2309 (8th ed., rev. July 2010); Charles W. Rivise & A.D. Caesar, INTERFERENCE LAW AND PRACTICE (W.S. Hein 2000); Charles L. Gholz, *Interference Practice*, in 6 PATENT PRACTICE 24-1 (Irving Kayton & Karyl S. Kayton eds., 4th ed. 1989). A Federal Circuit judge has described Gholz's work as a "definitive text" on interference practice. *See* Brown v. Barbacid, 276 F.3d 1327, 1340 (Fed. Cir. 2002) (Newman, J., dissenting).

[187]35 U.S.C. §102(g) (2006).

3. Anticipation Under §102(g)(2)

The second subsection of §102(g) (2006) applies not in the interference setting, but rather in either *ex parte* prosecution of a patent
application or in federal court litigation challenging the validity of an
issued patent. In these settings, unlike interferences, there is no rival
party claiming entitlement to a patent on the invention in question.
Rather, a USPTO examiner is asserting under §102(g)(2) (2006) that
some other inventor's earlier making of the invention in this country is
prior art that prevents the grant of a patent on the same invention to
a patent applicant. If in the litigation setting, the challenger of validity (typically an accused infringer) is asserting that some other inventor's earlier making of the invention in this country should invalidate
the patent in suit.

It is analytically helpful to think of §102(g)(2) (2006) as encompassing or subsuming all other novelty-destroying subsections of §102, and
this is why some patent law instructors present §102(g) before covering any other part of the statute. This order of presentation makes a
certain amount of logical sense. Viewed on a timeline, a prior art invention must first be "made" before it can be known or used by others or
patented or described in a printed publication (per §102(a) (2006)), or
put into public use or on sale (per §102(b) (2006)), or described in a
U.S. patent or application (per §102(e) (2006)).

An invention is anticipated under 35 U.S.C. §102(g)(2) (2006) if it
was "made in this country by another inventor" before the applicant's
invention date, and the prior inventor has not subsequently "abandoned, suppressed, or concealed" her invention. Thus, §102(g)(2) is triggered by an earlier "making" of the invention in this country by another
inventor, coupled with some sort of introduction of that invention to
the U.S. public within a reasonable time period thereafter, whether
by patenting, publication, sales, or the like.[188] The prior inventor need
not file a patent application on her invention, but she must take other

---

[188]*See* Int'l Glass Co. v. United States, 408 F.2d 395, 403 (Ct. Cl. 1969) (stating that
"an invention, though completed, is deemed abandoned, suppressed, or concealed if,
within a reasonable time after completion, no steps are taken to make the invention
publicly known"); *id.* (noting that "failure to file a patent application; to describe the
invention in a publicly disseminated document; or to use the invention publicly, have
been held to constitute abandonment, suppression, or concealment") (citations omitted). There is no comparable "introduction" requirement for prior knowledge or use of
an invention under the text of 35 U.S.C. §102(a), but courts have interpreted 35 U.S.C.
§102(a) as requiring that the anticipatory knowledge or use be publicly accessible. *See*
Eolas Techs. Inc. v. Microsoft Corp., 399 F.3d 1325, 1334 (Fed. Cir. 2005); Woodland
Trust v. Flowertree Nursery, Inc., 148 F.3d 1368, 1370 (Fed. Cir. 1998).

action within a reasonable time after her actual reduction to practice to ensure that the public has obtained knowledge of the invention.[189]

In contrast with interferences under 35 U.S.C. §102(g)(1) (2006), the earlier invention that is relied on to anticipate (i.e., destroy novelty) under 35 U.S.C. §102(g)(2) (2006) must have been made in the United States. The provisions of 35 U.S.C. §104 (2006) that speak of events occurring in NAFTA or WTO countries outside the United States do not apply to anticipation under §102(g)(2). In other words, the prior making of an invention relied on to anticipate or invalidate (i.e., defeat patentability) "counts" only if it occurred in the United States. This distinction is reflected in the text of 35 U.S.C. §104, which permits use of evidence of acts abroad only by applicants or patentees who are affirmatively seeking to "establish a date of invention."[190] These persons would include parties in an interference under §102(g)(1) as well as applicants in *ex parte* prosecution who are seeking to antedate §102(a) or §102(e) prior art in accordance with 37 C.F.R. §1.131 by establishing an invention date that predates the effective date of the prior art reference. Both groups of persons are *affirmatively* attempting to establish an invention date, rather than attempting to *defeat* patentability as in §102(g)(2).

Section §102(g)(2) (2006) anticipation rejections are rarely encountered in *ex parte* patent prosecution before the USPTO, because the agency generally does not know (or have the resources to investigate) when the invention *disclosed* in a cited prior art reference was actually *made*.[191] Section 102(g)(2)–based challenges are more typically asserted in the patent litigation context, where accused infringers are more likely to have the strategic incentives and economic resources to investigate the invention date of potentially invalidating prior art inventions.[192]

---

[189]*See* Apotex USA, Inc. v. Merck & Co., 254 F.3d 1031, 1038 (Fed. Cir. 2001). In *Apotex*, even though validity challenger Merck likely suppressed or concealed its admittedly prior invention (of a process for making a blood pressure treatment) by maintaining the process as a trade secret for several years after reducing it to practice, the Federal Circuit held that Merck's later publications and trial testimony disclosing the ingredients and other details of the process, all occurring prior to patentee Apotex's alleged conception date, were sufficient to invalidate the Apotex patents in suit under 35 U.S.C. §102(g)(2). *See Apotex USA*, 254 F.3d at 1040.

[190]35 U.S.C. §104 (2006).

[191]*See* In re Bass, 474 F.2d 1276, 1286 n.7 (C.C.P.A. 1973). *Bass* is discussed in further detail under the heading "Section 102/103 Overlap" in Chapter 5 ("The Nonobviousness Requirement (35 U.S.C. §103)"), *infra*.

[192]*See, e.g.*, Amkor Tech., Inc. v. International Trade Commission, No. 2010–1550, __ F.3d __, 2012 WL 3590825 (Fed. Cir. Aug. 22, 2012) (holding that an oral communication in the United States of a foreign-made invention can qualify as §102(g)(2) patent-defeating prior art); Dow Chem. Co. v. Astro-Valcour Inc., 267 F.3d 1334 (Fed. Cir. 2001); Monsanto Co. v. Mycogen Plant Sci., Inc., 261 F.3d 1356 (Fed. Cir. 2001); Apotex USA, Inc. v. Merck & Co., Inc., 254 F.3d 1031 (Fed. Cir. 2001).

Although it was viewed by the drafters of the 1952 Act as a statute to authorize interferences,[193] our understanding of 35 U.S.C. §102(g) has expanded over time. The section was first recognized as a prior art provision for purposes of the USPTO's *ex parte* examination for obviousness in *In re Bass*,[194] an important case discussed in greater detail in Chapter 5 ("The Nonobviousness Requirement") of this text. Use of §102(g) (2006) prior invention in this manner (as §102(g)(2)/§103 prior art) raises the same concerns about the use of "secret prior art" as when a claim is rejected for anticipation by the disclosure of the invention in another's earlier-filed U.S. patent or published application under 35 U.S.C. §102(e) (2006). However, the requirement of §102(g) that the prior invention not be "abandoned, suppressed, or concealed" injects an analogous "publicness" requirement into the statute that ameliorates the secrecy concern, in much the same way as does the "issued or published" requirement of §102(e).

4.   Applying the Priority Rule of §102(g)

Section 102(g) was amended by the American Inventors Protection Act (AIPA) of 1999 to expressly reflect the modern understanding that the section governs not only interference proceedings, but also anticipation, that is, uses of prior invention as a basis for USPTO rejections in *ex parte* prosecution or as a basis to challenge the validity of an issued patent in federal district court litigation. In all of these settings, the rather cryptic last sentence of §102(g) (2006) applies:

> In determining priority of invention under this subsection, there shall be considered not only the respective dates of conception and reduction to practice of the invention, but also the reasonable diligence of one who was first to conceive and last to reduce to practice, from a time prior to conception by the other.

The quoted statutory provision can be simplified and restated as the following rule for determining time-wise priority of invention:

> *Generally,* **the first to reduce to practice [who thereafter does not abandon, suppress, or conceal] is the first to invent,** *unless* **the last to reduce to practice is also the first to conceive and sufficiently diligent.**

---

[193]*See* Paulik v. Rizkalla, 760 F.2d 1270, 1276-1279 (Fed. Cir. 1985) (*en banc*) (Rich, J., concurring) (detailing history of 35 U.S.C. §102(g)).
[194]474 F.2d 1276 (C.C.P.A. 1973).

Application of this rule, whether in *ex parte* prosecution, validity litigation, or a pre-AIA interference proceeding, requires understanding several important terms of art. The date of **conception** is the date at which there is the "formation in the mind of the inventor, of a definite and permanent idea of the complete and operative invention, as it is hereafter to be applied in practice."[195] A **reduction to practice** is either actual or constructive. An *actual* reduction to practice occurs when a physical embodiment of the invention has been constructed that works for its intended purpose.[196] A *constructive* reduction to practice occurs upon the filing of a patent application that satisfies the disclosure requirements of 35 U.S.C. §112, ¶1 (2006) for the invention claimed therein.[197] Reasonable **diligence** is proved by evidence that the inventor was continuously active in working toward a reduction to practice of the invention she conceived, or that a legitimate excuse exists for any inactivity during the relevant time period.[198]

With these definitions in hand, we can apply the time-wise priority rule to both the §102(g)(1) and §102(g)(2) contexts. First consider the rule as applied in an interference setting involving Inventor A and Inventor B, both claiming to have made the same invention at about the same time. This is an application of 35 U.S.C. §102(g)(1) (2006).

Figure 4.4 illustrates two different applications of the time-wise priority rule in the pre-AIA interference setting under §102 (g)(1) (2006). Inventor A will be awarded priority in the interference if Inventor A reduced the invention to practice before Inventor B did, and did not thereafter abandon, suppress, or conceal it, as in Case 1 in Figure 4.4, *unless* Inventor B conceived the invention before Inventor A did and was diligent in working toward a reduction to practice during a time period from just before Inventor A's conception through to Inventor B's own reduction to practice (as illustrated in Case 2).

Note that the question whether Inventor A was diligent between her conception and reduction to practice dates is not relevant in Case 2; only B's diligence matters in this example. If we are going to award a patent to the later reducer, which means we are accepting a somewhat delayed completion and dissemination of the invention to the

---

[195]Coleman v. Dines, 754 F.2d 353, 359 (Fed. Cir. 1985).

[196]*See* Great Northern Corp. v. Davis Core & Pad Co., 782 F.2d 159, 165 (Fed. Cir. 1986).

[197]*See* Bigham v. Godtfredsen, 857 F.2d 1415, 1417 (Fed. Cir. 1988).

[198]*See* Griffith v. Kanamaru, 816 F.2d 624, 626 (Fed. Cir. 1987) (explaining that "Griffith must account for the entire period from just before Kanamaru's filing date until his reduction to practice"); *see also* Naber v. Cricchi, 567 F.2d 382, 385 n.5 (C.C.P.A. 1977) (explaining that reasonable diligence requirement of §102(g) is founded on public policy that favors the early disclosure of inventions, similar to requirement that there be no unreasonable delay in filing patent application following an actual reduction to practice so as to avoid holding of suppression or concealment).

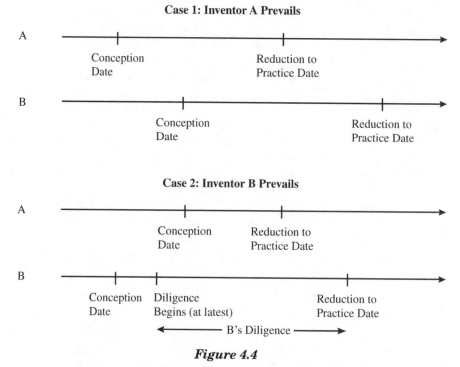

Figure 4.4

**Illustrations of the U.S. Traditional Rule of Time-Wise Priority
Under 35 U.S.C. §102(g) (2006)
in an Interference Setting (Inventor A vs. Inventor B)**

public, we will require that later reducer to have proceeded diligently toward her reduction to practice.

Alternatively, consider the time-wise priority rule as applied in a challenge to the validity of Inventor A's issued patent, raised by accused Infringer X in federal court as an affirmative defense to Inventor A's charge of patent infringement by X. Accused Infringer X may assert that a third party, Inventor B,[199] made the invention in the United

---

[199]Inventor B in this example is not a party to the validity litigation. Rather, evidence of Inventor B's acts is being relied on by the accused Infringer X as prior art to invalidate the patent in suit. Inventor B need not have obtained a patent on the invention, so long as she took other steps to publicize the invention or otherwise bring knowledge of it to the public (e.g., through commercialization) within a reasonable time after completing it. *See* Apotex USA, Inc. v. Merck & Co., Inc., 254 F.3d 1031 (Fed. Cir. 2001) (unpatented prior invention by accused infringer/validity challenger Merck held not to have been suppressed or concealed under §102(g)); Int'l Glass Co. v. United States, 408 F.2d 395, 403 (Ct. Cl. 1969) (unpatented prior invention by third party McDonnell Douglas held to have been suppressed or concealed under §102(g)).

States before Inventor A did, and that Inventor A's patent is therefore invalid under 35 U.S.C. §102(g)(2) (2006).[200] To prevail in this defense, accused Infringer X must establish either (1) that Inventor B reduced the invention to practice before Inventor A and did not thereafter abandon, suppress, or conceal the invention; or (2) that Inventor B conceived the invention before Inventor A and was sufficiently diligent in working toward a reduction to practice of the invention throughout a time period that began just before Inventor A's conception date and ended with Inventor B's own reduction to practice date.[201]

O.   Antedating (or "Swearing Behind") Prior Art (Pre-AIA)

The same traditional first-to-invent principle underlying section 102(g) (2006) is the basis for a procedure used in *ex parte* patent prosecution to antedate (i.e., predate or "swear behind") certain categories of prior art references.[202] Recall that the USPTO will assume that an application's filing date is the applicant's invention date, based on the theory that filing an application that satisfies the disclosure requirements of §112 for the subject matter claimed therein represents a constructive reduction to practice of that subject matter. (Moreover, patent applicants do not typically disclose dates of conception and/or actual reduction to practice in their initial application filings.) If the USPTO examiner locates a §102(a) (2006) or §102(e) (2006) reference that describes the identical invention in an enabling manner and has an effective date earlier than the applicant's filing date, such reference is presumptively anticipatory. The existence of the reference's disclosure, prior to the applicant's presumptive invention date, is inconsistent with the idea that the applicant was first to invent it.

In order to eliminate the cited reference as prior art, the patent applicant must show that she invented the subject matter of the rejected claim(s) prior to the effective date of the reference. In other

---

[200]This theory was successful in Monsanto Co. v. Mycogen Plant Science, Inc., 261 F.3d 1356 (Fed. Cir. 2001). For criticism of the Federal Circuit's refusal in *Monsanto* to adopt a "particularized testimony"/"linking argument" requirement for invalidity defenses litigated in jury trials, *see* Janice M. Mueller, *At Sea in a Black Box: Charting a Clearer Course for Juries Through the Perilous Straits of Patent Invalidity*, 1 J. MARSHALL REV. INTELL. PROP. L. 3 (2001), *available at* http://www.jmripl.com/Publications/Vol1/Issue1/mueller.pdf.

[201]See *Monsanto*, 261 F.3d at 1361-1362, 1362-1363; Mahurkar v. C.R. Bard, Inc., 79 F.3d 1572, 1577 (Fed. Cir. 1996).

[202]There is no antedating under the first-to-file system of the America Invents Act of 2011 for applications filed on or after March 16, 2013, because the AIA eliminated the concept of invention dates.

words, the applicant must show that she, rather than the author of the reference, was the first to invent the claimed subject matter. Although the antedating procedure is not an interference (which is a contest between two or more applicants for patent), antedating can be conceptualized as a "quasi-interference" between the patent applicant and the reference she seeks to eliminate as prior art.

The mechanics of antedating a prior art reference are governed by 37 C.F.R. §1.131 (Rule 131). A patent applicant antedates a §102(a) or §102(e) reference by filing an appropriate affidavit or declaration to establish that she invented the subject matter of her rejected claim(s) prior to the effective date of the reference cited by the USPTO examiner.[203] The showing of facts in the affidavit or declaration must establish either (1) an actual reduction to practice of the invention prior to the effective date of the reference, or (2) conception of the invention prior to the effective date of the reference coupled with due diligence from just prior to that effective date until a subsequent actual reduction to practice date or to the filing date of the patent application.[204]

The antedating procedure of Rule 131 cannot be used to overcome a statutory bar reference, such as a printed publication under 35 U.S.C. §102(b) (2006).[205] This reflects the policy of encouraging prompt filing of patent applications on novel inventions. Nor can antedating be used where the prior art reference is a U.S. patent or published patent application of another that *claims* the same patentable invention. In such a case the basis of the rejection would be 35 U.S.C. §102(g)(1) (2006), and the applicant may suggest an interference.[206] Lastly, although citation by the USPTO of evidence of another's making of the same invention in this country under §102(g)(2) (2006) is rare, if such a rejection was entered the applicant could not overcome it by the Rule 131 antedating procedure. This is because

> subject matter which is available under 35 U.S.C. 102(g) by definition must have been made before the applicant made his or her invention. By contrast, references under 35 U.S.C. 102(a) and (e), for example, merely establish a presumption that their subject matter was made before applicant's invention date. It is this presumption which may be rebutted by evidence submitted under 37 C.F.R. 1.131.[207]

[203]*See* 37 C.F.R. §1.131(a).
[204]*See id.* §1.131(b).
[205]*See id.* §1.131(a)(2).
[206]*See id.* §1.131(a)(1).
[207]United States Patent & Trademark Office, MANUAL OF PATENT EXAMINING PROCEDURE §715(II)(I) (8th ed., rev. July 2010).

Part III: Novelty and Priority Post-America Invents Act of 2011

P.   Introduction

This part of the chapter covers novelty, the definition of prior art, and priority[208] as those topics are defined and analyzed under the Patent Act (35 U.S.C.) as amended by §3 ("First inventor to file") of the Leahy-Smith America Invents Act of 2011 ("AIA").[209] As detailed below, §3 of the AIA rewrote 35 U.S.C. §102 in its entirety. Generally speaking, the new rules implemented by the AIA §3 amendments apply to U.S. patent applications filed on or after March 16, 2013.[210] If patents issuing from such applications are challenged in federal court litigation or in USPTO post-grant review, their validity will be assessed under the post-AIA regime.[211]

---

[208]The word "priority" in this chapter refers to priority as between two (or more) U.S. patent applicants. If each of multiple inventors independently invents the same invention and files his or her own patent application in the USPTO, which inventor/applicant will be awarded the patent? The AIA generally awards the patent to the first inventor *to file* her patent application. *See* 35 U.S.C. 102(a)(2) (eff. Mar. 16, 2013); *see also infra* Section S.3 ("Post-AIA 35 U.S.C. §102(b)(2): Shields Against Post-AIA §102(a)(2) Presumptively Novelty-Destroying Events").

The AIA recognizes significant exceptions to the first-inventor-to-file rule, however. Notably, a second (i.e., later in time) filer will obtain the patent if the second filer had publicly disclosed the invention before the first filer's effective filing date and thereafter files her own (i.e., the second filer's) application in a timely fashion. *See* 35 U.S.C. §102(b)(2)(B) (eff. Mar. 16, 2013); *see also infra* Section S.3 ("Post-AIA §102(b)(2): Shields Against Post-AIA §102(a)(2) Presumptively Novelty-Destroying Events").

[209]Leahy-Smith America Invents Act, Pub. L. No. 112-29 (H.R. 1249), 125 Stat. 284 (Sept. 16, 2011).

For comprehensive overviews of the entire AIA, *see* Robert A. Armitage, *Understanding the America Invents Act and Its Implications for Patenting*, 40 AM. INTELLECTUAL PROP. L. Q.J. 1, 1-133 (Winter 2012); Donald S. Chisum, *America Invents Act of 2011: Analysis and Cross-References* (Dec. 5, 2011), *available at* http://www.chisum.com/wp-content/uploads/AIAOverview.pdf. *See also* Robert P. Merges, *Priority and Novelty under the AIA* (August 15, 2012), *available at* SSRN: http://ssrn.com/abstract=2130209.

[210]*See* Leahy-Smith America Invents Act, Pub. L. No. 112-29 (H.R. 1249), §3(n) ("Effective Date"), 125 Stat. 284, 293 (2011).

[211]Importantly, patents issuing from applications filed *before* the AIA §3 effective date of March 16, 2013, will continue to be litigated under pre-AIA rules. *See supra* Part II. As of the March 16, 2013 implementation date of first-to-file, it is highly probable that more than two million U.S. patents will already be in force. *See* World Intellectual Property Organization, 2011 WORLD INTELLECTUAL PROPERTY INDICATORS 197 (Table P2: Patent grants by office and origin, and patents in force, 2010) (reporting 2,017,318 U.S. patents in force as of 2009). The enforceable life of a U.S. patent can (in theory) run as long as twenty years, and a patent's validity can be challenged by an accused infringer in federal court litigation (potentially involving long-running trial and appeal) throughout that period. Thus for thirty years or more following the AIA's

Chapter 4. Novelty, Loss of Right, and Priority (35 U.S.C. §102)

Because the AIA §3 ("First inventor to file") changes have not taken effect as of the time of this edition's writing (mid-2012), no court decisions are available to interpret the section's many points of ambiguity. Clarification must wait for disputes to work their way through the courts, although some ambiguities will likely be resolved through the implementation of USPTO rules or, perhaps, congressional "clean-up" amendments to the AIA. Thus, this part of the chapter is limited to analyzing the as-enacted text of §3 of the legislation and its legislative history. Later editions of this text will add discussion of new judicial decisions and agency rules that interpret and apply the AIA provisions.[212]

Section 3 of the AIA introduced landmark changes to U.S. patent law.[213] Those changes include redefining what counts as prior art by expanding the 35 U.S.C. §102 categories of novelty-destroying events and removing all prior geographic limitations; altering the date on which novelty is assessed so as to focus on the effective filing date of the application or claim in question rather than the invention date; and switching the United States from its traditional first-to-invent priority system to a unique first-inventor-to-file system (a hybrid of the European first-to-file regime and certain prior art exclusions based on the traditional U.S. pre-filing grace period of 35 U.S.C. §102(b) (pre-AIA).

These §3 AIA changes generally apply to patent applications filed *on or after March 16, 2013*.[214] Critically, the changes do *not* apply to the over two million U.S. patents that will already be in force on March

---

enactment, the pre-AIA version of the Patent Act addressed *supra* in Part II of this chapter will continue to be relevant.

[212]The USPTO issued proposed rules and proposed examination guidelines for implementing the first-inventor-to-file provisions of the AIA in July 2012. The proposed rules and guidelines also address the agency's interpretation of what qualifies as prior art under the post-AIA versions of 35 U.S.C. §§102 and 103 (eff. Mar. 16, 2013). *See* United States Patent & Trademark Office, *Notice of Proposed Rulemaking: Changes To Implement the First Inventor to File Provisions of the Leahy-Smith America Invents Act*, 77 Fed. Reg. 43742 (July 26, 2012) (proposed rules), *available at* http://www.uspto.gov/aia_implementation/first-inventor-to-file_proposed_rules.pdf; United States Patent & Trademark Office, *Request for Comments: Examination Guidelines for Implementing the First-Inventor-to-File Provisions of the Leahy-Smith America Invents Act*, 77 Fed. Reg. 43759 (July 26, 2012) (proposed examination guidelines), *available at* http://www.uspto.gov/aia_implementation/first-inventor-to-file_proposed_examination_guidelines.pdf.

[213]*See generally* Joe Matal, *A Guide to the Legislative History of the America Invents Act: Part I of II*, 21 Fed. Cir. B.J. 435, 449 (2012) (stating that "[n]o part of the AIA is more significant, nor has generated more legislative discussion and debate, than the Act's changes to §102").

[214]*See* Leahy-Smith America Invents Act, Pub. L. No. 112-29 (H.R. 1249), §3(n) ("Effective Date"), 125 Stat. 284, 293 (2011). *See also infra* Section T ("Effective Date for AIA §3 'First Inventor to File' Amendments").

16, 2013,[215] or to pending patent applications filed before March 16, 2013 (or patents issuing therefrom). For decades to come, the pre-AIA version of the Patent Act as addressed in Part II of this chapter and in other chapters of this text will continue to apply to millions of U.S. patents and applications. The practical result of the AIA's framework for implementing the first-inventor-to-file system and associated changes to novelty and prior art is that the U.S. patent system will operate under a dual regime (encompassing both "pre-AIA" and "post-AIA" rules) for 30 years or more following the AIA's September 2011 enactment.

To ensure clarity and demarcation between the "old" and "new" systems, this part of the chapter separately analyzes the AIA-implemented changes pertaining to novelty, prior art, and priority. Part II addressed the issues of novelty, loss of right (i.e., "statutory bars"), and priority between rival inventors as those issues are determined under the pre-AIA regime. That regime is based on the United States' historic first-to-invent priority system.

A most unfortunate aspect of the AIA is that Congress entirely rewrote key statutory provisions of the Patent Act without renumbering many of the statutory sections in Title 35, U.S.C. To maintain clarity and demarcation between old and new versions, citations by this text to the pre-AIA version of the patent statute (in particular, those analyzed in Part II, *supra*) typically will take the form "35 U.S.C. §102(x) (pre-AIA)" or "35 U.S.C. §102(x) (2006)."[216] In contrast, the citations by this text to the patent statute, post-AIA implementation (in particular, those analyzed in this part of the chapter) will take the form "35 U.S.C. §102(x) (post-AIA)" or "35 U.S.C. §102(x) (eff. Mar. 16, 2013)." For shorthand purposes, sections of the Patent Act will sometimes be referred to herein as "post-AIA §102," meaning 35 U.S.C. §102 in the form that takes effect on March 16, 2013.

---

[215]*See* World Intellectual Property Organization, 2011 WORLD INTELLECTUAL PROPERTY INDICATORS 197, tbl. P2 ("Patent grants by office and origin, and patents in force, 2010") (reporting 2,017,318 U.S. patents in force as of 2009).

[216]The America Invents Act (AIA) was signed into law on September 16, 2011. Before that date, the most recent main edition of the official *United States Code*, including the Patent Act at Title 35 U.S.C., was published in 2006. This text will generally follow the citation conventions of *The Bluebook: A Uniform System of Citation* (19th ed. 2010). Bluebook Rule 12.3.2 provides that "[w]hen citing a bound volume of the current official or unofficial code, provide parenthetically the year that appears on the spine of the volume. . . . " At the AIA's enactment in September 2011, the "spine" date of the most recent main edition of 35 U.S.C. was 2006. Therefore, pre-AIA code provisions are generally cited herein as "35 U.S.C. §X (2006)."

1. Statutory Basis

As amended by §3 ("First inventor to file") of the Leahy-Smith America Invents Act of 2011 (AIA),[217] §102 of the U.S. Patent Act (35 U.S.C.) will provide:

§102. Conditions for patentability; novelty

(a) NOVELTY; PRIOR ART.—A person shall be entitled to a patent unless—

   (1) the claimed invention was patented, described in a printed publication, or in public use, on sale, or otherwise available to the public before the effective filing date of the claimed invention; or

   (2) the claimed invention was described in a patent issued under section 151, or in an application for patent published or deemed published under section 122(b), in which the patent or application, as the case may be, names another inventor and was effectively filed before the effective filing date of the claimed invention.

(b) EXCEPTIONS.—

   (1) DISCLOSURES MADE 1 YEAR OR LESS BEFORE THE EFFECTIVE FILING DATE OF THE CLAIMED INVENTION.—A disclosure made 1 year or less before the effective filing date of a claimed invention shall not be prior art to the claimed invention under subsection (a)(1) if—

      (A) the disclosure was made by the inventor or joint inventor or by another who obtained the subject matter disclosed directly or indirectly from the inventor or a joint inventor; or

      (B) the subject matter disclosed had, before such disclosure, been publicly disclosed by the inventor or a joint inventor or another who obtained the subject matter disclosed directly or indirectly from the inventor or a joint inventor.

   (2) DISCLOSURES APPEARING IN APPLICATIONS AND PATENTS.—A disclosure shall not be prior art to a claimed invention under subsection (a)(2) if—

      (A) the subject matter disclosed was obtained directly or indirectly from the inventor or a joint inventor;

      (B) the subject matter disclosed had, before such subject matter was effectively filed under subsection (a)(2), been publicly disclosed by the inventor or a joint inventor or another who obtained the subject matter disclosed directly or indirectly from the inventor or a joint inventor; or

      (C) the subject matter disclosed and the claimed invention, not later than the effective filing date of the claimed invention, were owned by the same person or subject to an obligation of assignment to the same person.

---

[217]*See* Leahy-Smith America Invents Act, Pub. L. No. 112-29 (H.R. 1249), §3(b) (1), 125 Stat. 284, 285-287 (Sept. 16, 2011) ("First Inventor to File—Conditions for Patentability—In General").

(c) COMMON OWNERSHIP UNDER JOINT RESEARCH AGREEMENTS.—Subject matter disclosed and a claimed invention shall be deemed to have been owned by the same person or subject to an obligation of assignment to the same person in applying the provisions of subsection (b)(2)(C) if—

(1) the subject matter disclosed was developed and the claimed invention was made by, or on behalf of, 1 or more parties to a joint research agreement that was in effect on or before the effective filing date of the claimed invention;

(2) the claimed invention was made as a result of activities undertaken within the scope of the joint research agreement; and

(3) the application for patent for the claimed invention discloses or is amended to disclose the names of the parties to the joint research agreement.

(d) PATENTS AND PUBLISHED APPLICATIONS EFFECTIVE AS PRIOR ART.—For purposes of determining whether a patent or application for patent is prior art to a claimed invention under subsection (a)(2), such patent or application shall be considered to have been effectively filed, with respect to any subject matter described in the patent or application—

(1) if paragraph (2) does not apply, as of the actual filing date of the patent or the application for patent; or

(2) if the patent or application for patent is entitled to claim a right of priority under section 119, 365(a), or 365(b), or to claim the benefit of an earlier filing date under section 120, 121, or 365(c), based upon 1 or more prior filed applications for patent, as of the filing date of the earliest such application that describes the subject matter.[218]

Generally speaking, this "post-AIA" version of 35 U.S.C. §102 takes effect on March 16, 2013, for patent applications filed on or after that date.[219] Each of the §102 statutory subsections is separately discussed below.

2.   Sense of Congress and Legislative History

Relevant to interpretation of the amended 35 U.S.C. §102 are two "sense of Congress" provisions included in §3 of the AIA. These provide:

(o) SENSE OF CONGRESS.—It is the sense of the Congress that converting the United States patent system from "first to invent" to a system of "first inventor to file" will promote the progress of science and the useful arts by securing for limited times to inventors the exclusive rights to their discoveries and provide inventors with greater certainty

---

[218]35 U.S.C. §102 (effective Mar. 16, 2013) (subparagraph indenting added for clarity).
[219]*See infra* Section T ("Effective Date for AIA §3 'First Inventor to File' Amendments").

regarding the scope of protection provided by the grant of exclusive rights to their discoveries.

(p) SENSE OF CONGRESS.—It is the sense of the Congress that converting the United States patent system from "first to invent" to a system of "first inventor to file" will improve the United States patent system and promote harmonization of the United States patent system with the patent systems commonly used in nearly all other countries throughout the world with whom the United States conducts trade and thereby promote greater international uniformity and certainty in the procedures used for securing the exclusive rights of inventors to their discoveries.[220]

Although Congress's stated intent of "provid[ing] inventors with greater certainty regarding the scope of protection"[221] provided by patents is laudable, it is not clear that the AIA will actually achieve this goal. The post-AIA version of 35 U.S.C. §102, for example, is just as complicated and riddled with ambiguity (if not more so) than its pre-AIA counterpart. The Byzantine wording of post-AIA §102 stands in sharp contrast to the straightforward manner in which other countries define patentable novelty (viz., the European Patent Convention's streamlined Article 54[222]).

Moreover, although Congress speaks of promoting harmonization between the U.S. patent system and foreign patent systems,[223] it is not clear that the AIA achieves this goal either. As described below, §3 of the AIA did not implement a European-style system of first to file with absolute novelty. Rather, the post-AIA version of §102 puts into place a unique hybrid system that preserves many aspects of the pre-AIA grace period found in 35 U.S.C. §102(b) (2006). Rather than a true first-to-file system, the AIA created what is better described (at least in some circumstances) as a "first inventor to disclose" system.[224]

The two "sense of Congress" provisions quoted above are an explicit part of the AIA's text.[225] In addition, a wealth of potentially relevant legislative history exists to inform interpretation of the

[220]Leahy-Smith America Invents Act, Pub. L. No. 112-29 (H.R. 1249), §3(o)-(p), 125 Stat. 284, 293 (2011).

[221]Leahy-Smith America Invents Act, Pub. L. No. 112-29 (H.R. 1249), §3(o), 125 Stat. 284, 293 (2011).

[222]European Patent Convention art. 54(1), Oct. 5, 1973, *available at* http://www.epo.org/patents/law/legal-texts/html/epc/1973/e/ar54.html ("An invention shall be considered to be new if it does not form part of the state of the art."); *id.* at art. 54(2) ("The state of the art shall be held to comprise everything made available to the public by means of a written or oral description, by use, or in any other way, before the date of filing of the European patent application.").

[223]Leahy-Smith America Invents Act, Pub. L. No. 112-29 (H.R. 1249), §3(p), 125 Stat. 284, 293 (2011).

[224]*See* 35 U.S.C. §§102(b)(1)(B), 102(b)(2)(B) (eff. Mar. 16, 2013); *see also infra* Section S ("Novelty-Preserving Exceptions Under Post-AIA 35 U.S.C. §102(b)").

[225]As such they are likely entitled to greater weight than legislative history.

first-inventor-to-file provisions of the AIA. Such legislative history includes the House Judiciary Committee's report on H.R. 1249,[226] as well as remarks by members of Congress during debates on the floors of the House and Senate.[227]

3.   Comparing Pre- and Post-AIA Frameworks

As amended by the AIA, 35 U.S.C. §102(a) (eff. Mar. 16, 2013) (hereafter "post-AIA §102(a)" or simply "§102(a)") enumerates six types of novelty-destroying events. These events make up the catalog or universe of "prior art" for purposes of analyzing an invention's novelty[228] and/or its nonobviousness.[229]

---

[226]H.R. Rep. No. 112-98 [House Judiciary Comm. Rep. on the America Invents Act] (June 1, 2011).

[227]The U.S. Patent and Trademark Office (USPTO) has compiled a comprehensive collection of AIA legislative history in electronic form. *See* USPTO, *AIA Resources*, http://www.uspto.gov/aia_implementation/resources.jsp (last modified Nov. 22, 2011). *See also* Joe Matal, *A Guide to the Legislative History of the America Invents Act: Part I of II*, 21 FED. CIR. B.J. 435 (2012) (providing "a guide to legislative materials that may be useful to practitioners who are required to understand and construe the [AIA]," authored by Judiciary Committee Counsel to Senator Jon Kyl); Joe Matal, *A Guide to the Legislative History of the America Invents Act: Part II of II*, 21 FED. CIR. B.J. 539 (2012).

[228]*See* 35 U.S.C. §102(a) (eff. Mar. 16, 2013) ("Novelty; Prior Art"); *see also supra* Section B ("Burden of Proof") (stating that "[i]t is therefore helpful to consider 35 U.S.C. §102 as the catalog or universe of prior art that potentially can be cited by the USPTO in rejecting a patent applicant's claims. If a patent, journal article, or other document or event is indicated by the USPTO to be prior art, it must qualify under some subsection of 35 U.S.C. §102. If it does not, then the document or event is not legally available for use as prior art to negate the presumed novelty of the applicant's claimed invention. The same is true in a litigation context, where an issued patent's validity is being challenged.").

[229]*See* 35 U.S.C. §103 (eff. Mar. 16, 2013) ("Conditions for patentability; non-obvious subject matter"); *see also infra* Chapter 5, Section F.3 ("Section 102/103 Overlap") (explaining that §102 can be conceptualized as a catalog of the varieties of information (e.g., documents and events) that may potentially qualify as prior art for §103 purposes. In other words, any reference relied on in determining nonobviousness must first qualify as prior art under one or more subsections of §102 (except that the strict identity rule for anticipation would not be satisfied in the obviousness context). As explained by a co-author of the 1952 Patent Act, "[t]he antecedent of the words 'the prior art' . . . lies in the phrase 'disclosed or described as set forth in Section 102' and hence these words refer to the material specified in Section 102 as the basis for comparison." P.J. Federico, *Commentary on the New Patent Act*, 35 U.S.C.A. §1 (1954 ed., discontinued in subsequent volumes), *reprinted at* 75 J. PAT. & TRADEMARK OFF. SOC'Y 161 (1993). *See also* In re Wertheim, 646 F.2d 527, 532 (C.C.P.A. 1981) (Rich, J.) (quoting Federico's *Commentary* on this point). The requirement that prior art be "analogous" is an additional filter applied to prior art for use in a §103 nonobviousness analysis. *See infra* Chapter 5, Section F.4 ("Analogous Art").

The preamble language of post-AIA §102(a) provides that "[a] person shall be entitled to a patent unless. . . . " This language, carried over from the pre-AIA version of §102, indicates that the initial burden of disproving novelty during examination of a patent application continues to rest with the government—the USPTO.[230]

To establish that novelty of a claimed invention has been destroyed—in other words, that a patent is not available because prior art anticipates the claimed invention—the statute requires that the USPTO establish that before the effective filing date of the claimed invention,[231] the invention was already (1) "patented," (2) "described in a printed publication," (3) "in public use," (4) "on sale," (5) "otherwise available to the public," or (6) described in a U.S. patent or published patent application naming another inventor. Each of these six novelty-destroying events is discussed in further detail below.

The AIA is not absolute in its requirement for novelty as of a claimed invention's effective filing date. The occurrence of any of the six §102(a) events before the effective filing date presumptively destroys novelty (i.e., anticipates the invention, assuming that the strict identity standard for anticipation is satisfied[232]). The claimed invention's novelty nevertheless may be preserved (in other words, the presumptively established §102(a) prior art may be removed) if one of the "exceptions" or shields of 35 U.S.C. §102(b) (eff. Mar. 16, 2013) (hereafter "post-AIA §102(b)" or simply "§102(b)") applies.

The post-AIA §102(b) exceptions are discussed separately below.[233] Very generally, the §102(b) exceptions operate in somewhat analogous fashion to "grace period" events under the pre-AIA regime.[234] Hence

---

[230]See supra Section B ("Burden of Proof").

[231]Although the phrase has long been used by patent practitioners and the USPTO, the AIA for the first time added to the Patent Act an explicit definition of "effective filing date." Subparagraph (2) of §3(a) ("Definitions") of the AIA adds the following definition to 35 U.S.C. §100:

> (i) (1) The term "effective filing date" for a claimed invention in a patent or application for patent means—
> (A) if subparagraph (B) does not apply, the actual filing date of the patent or the application for the patent containing a claim to the invention; or
> (B) the filing date of the earliest application for which the patent or application is entitled, as to such invention, to a right of priority under section 119, 365(a), or 365(b) or to the benefit of an earlier filing date under section 120, 121, or 365(c).
> (2) The effective filing date for a claimed invention in an application for reissue or reissued patent shall be determined by deeming the claim to the invention to have been contained in the patent for which reissue was sought.

[232]See supra Section C ("The Strict Identity Rule of Anticipation").

[233]See infra Section S ("Novelty-Preserving Exceptions under Post-AIA 35 U.S.C. §102(b)").

[234]See H.R. Rep. No. 112-98 [House Judiciary Comm. Rep. on the America Invents Act], at 54 (June 1, 2011) (stating that the AIA "maintains a 1-year grace period for

the post-AIA U.S. Patent Act is not a European-style "absolute novelty" system, despite Congress's stated intent to "promote harmonization of the United States patent system with the patent systems commonly used in nearly all other countries throughout the world with whom the United States conducts trade and thereby promote greater international uniformity and certainty in the procedures used for securing the exclusive rights of inventors to their discoveries."[235] Rather, the post-AIA U.S. Patent Act is a unique hybrid that retains many aspects of the pre-AIA regime but jettisoned many others. The following subsections explore what the AIA kept and what it discarded.

a.   What Section 3 of the AIA Retained

As amended by the AIA, 35 U.S.C. §102(a) (eff. Mar. 16, 2013) (hereafter "§102(a)" or "post-AIA §102(a)") merges into a single statutory subsection several aspects of the pre-AIA versions of 35 U.S.C. §§102(a) and (b). For example, novelty is presumptively destroyed under post-AIA §102(a) if any of the following four events occur before a particular date: the invention was "patented," "described in a printed publication," "in public use," or "on sale." Novelty destruction (i.e., anticipation) based on the invention having previously been "patented" or "described in a printed publication" was recognized in pre-AIA §§102(a) and (b).[236] Loss of right to patent based on the invention having previously been "in public use" or "on sale" was recognized in pre-AIA §102(b).[237]

Moreover, each of these four novelty-destroying events (i.e., "patented," "described in a printed publication," "in public use," and "on sale") has a robust history of case law interpretation.[238] Because Congress used well-recognized, common law–defined terms in drafting the AIA, it is reasonable to assume that Congress intended that those same definitions should continue to govern the analysis of novelty under the post-AIA regime.[239]

U.S. applicants. Applicants' own publication or disclosure that occurs within 1 year prior to filing will not act as prior art against their applications. Similarly, disclosure by others during that time based on information obtained (directly or indirectly) from the inventor will not constitute prior art. This 1-year grace period should continue to give U.S. applicants the time they need to prepare and file their applications."). *See also supra* Section I.2 ("Grace Period").

[235]Leahy-Smith America Invents Act, Pub. L. No. 112-29 (H.R. 1249), §3(p), 125 Stat. 284, 293 (2011) ("Sense of Congress").

[236]*See* 35 U.S.C. §§102(a), (b) (2006).

[237]*See* 35 U.S.C. §102(b) (2006).

[238]For analysis of the pre-AIA case law interpretation of these terms, *see supra* Section I ("The Statutory Bars of 35 U.S.C. §102(b) (Pre-AIA)").

[239]A contrary argument is that the "or otherwise available to the public" language of 35 U.S.C. §102(a)(1) (eff. March 16, 2013) narrowed the meaning of the public use

b. What Section 3 of the AIA Changed

Section 3 of the AIA implemented numerous notable changes in U.S. patent law. Probably the most significant is the manner in which the United States will determine priority between two (or more) rival inventors claiming a given invention. The AIA switched the United States from its historic first-to-invent system[240] to a first-inventor-to-file system (characterized by Congress as more in keeping with international standards[241]). In implementing the change, the AIA eliminated the statutory bases for interference practice, §102(g)(1) and §135 of the pre-AIA Patent Act.[242]

Somewhat ironically (given the importance of this change), post-AIA §102 does not explicitly set forth a first-inventor-to-file standard. Rather, the first-inventor-to-file standard is implicit in the language of post-AIA §102(a)(2).[243] Nor is the first-inventor-to-file standard absolute; it is subject to three important exceptions under post-AIA §102(b)(2) as detailed *infra*.[244]

---

and on sale bars by excluding "secret" prior art such as confidential commercialization of an invention. For further discussion of this debate, *see infra* Section Q.3 ("Does the AIA Permit Secret Prior Art?").

[240]*See supra* Section N ("Prior Invention under 35 U.S.C. §102(g) (pre-AIA))." The United States implemented a first-to-invent priority system as early as the late eighteenth century. *See* Edward C. Walterscheid, *Priority of Invention: How the United States Came to Have a "First-to-Invent" System,* 23 AIPLA Q.J. 263, 264 (1995) (explaining that "the initial impetus came from the titanic struggle between John Fitch and James Rumsey for priority of invention with respect to the steamboat during the late eighteenth century, but the actual creation of a true first-to-invent system took almost fifty years").

[241]Section 3 of the AIA did not implement a European-style system of first to file with absolute novelty. Rather, the post-AIA version of §102 puts into place a unique hybrid system that preserves many aspects of the pre-AIA grace period in 35 U.S.C. §102(b) (2006). In contrast to a true first-to-file system, the AIA created what is better described (at least in some circumstances) as a "first inventor to disclose" system. *See infra* Section S.3 ("Post-AIA 35 U.S.C. §102(b)(2): Shields Against Post-AIA §102(a)(2) Presumptively Novelty-Destroying Events").

[242]*See supra* Section N.2 ("Interference Proceedings under [35 U.S.C.] §102(g)(1) [pre-AIA]").

[243]*See* 35 U.S.C. §102(a)(2) (eff. Mar. 16, 2013) (providing that "[a] person shall be entitled to a patent unless . . . (2) the claimed invention was described in a patent issued under section 151, or in an application for patent published or deemed published under section 122(b), in which the patent or application, as the case may be, names another inventor and was effectively filed before the effective filing date of the claimed invention"). *Compare* the more explicit European approach, which provides that "[i]f two or more persons have made an invention independently of each other, the right to a European patent therefor shall belong to the person whose European patent application has the earliest date of filing, provided that this first application has been published." European Patent Convention art. 60(2) (14th ed. 2010).

[244]*See infra* Section S.3 ("Post-AIA §102(b)(2): Shields Against Post-AIA §102(a)(2) Presumptively Novelty-Destroying Events").

Another AIA change of primary import is the timing for determining novelty. Pursuant to the AIA, the novelty of a claimed invention will be assessed under 35 U.S.C. §102 as of the invention's "effective filing date."[245] Under the pre-AIA §102, novelty was assessed at the time of the invention's "invention date" rather than as of the corresponding patent application's filing date.[246] Nonobviousness of an invention under pre-AIA §103 was likewise assessed "at the time the invention was made."[247]

Although before the AIA, the USPTO treated an applicant's filing date as her presumptive invention date under a constructive reduction to practice theory, the applicant could potentially antedate (or "swear behind") and thereby remove certain prior art references cited by the agency in anticipation and/or obviousness rejections. Antedating a prior art reference required proving an earlier date of invention than the effective date of the reference. In the USPTO, antedating was accomplished in accordance with Rule 131 (i.e., 37 C.F.R. §1.131);[248] in litigation challenging the validity of an issued patent, a similar procedure was followed.[249] Under the AIA, however, antedating or "swearing

---

[245]Although the term has long been used by patent attorneys and the USPTO, the AIA for the first time added to the Patent Act an explicit definition of "effective filing date." Subparagraph (2) of §3(a) ("Definitions") of the AIA adds the following definition to 35 U.S.C. §100:

> (i) (1) The term "effective filing date" for a claimed invention in a patent or application for patent means—
>   (A) if subparagraph (B) does not apply, the actual filing date of the patent or the application for the patent containing a claim to the invention; or
>   (B) the filing date of the earliest application for which the patent or application is entitled, as to such invention, to a right of priority under section 119, 365(a), or 365(b) or to the benefit of an earlier filing date under section 120, 121, or 365(c).
>   (2) The effective filing date for a claimed invention in an application for reissue or reissued patent shall be determined by deeming the claim to the invention to have been contained in the patent for which reissue was sought.

35 U.S.C. §100(i) (eff. Mar. 16, 2013) (subparagraph indenting added for clarity).

[246]*See* 35 U.S.C. §102(a) (2006); 35 U.S.C. §102(e) (2006); 35 U.S.C. §102(g) (2006); *see also supra* Section G.4 ("Distinguishing Novelty from Loss of Right").

[247]35 U.S.C. §103(a) (2006). *See also supra* Chapter 5, Section F.3 ("Section 102/103 Overlap").

[248]*See supra* Section O ("Antedating (or "Swearing Behind") Prior Art (Pre-AIA)").

[249]*See Mahurkar v. C.R. Bard, Inc.*, 79 F.3d 1572 (Fed. Cir. 1996) (affirming district court's grant of patentee's motion for judgment as a matter of law (JMOL) that patent in suit was not anticipated because accused infringer failed to prove that allegedly anticipatory "Cook catalog" was in fact prior art under 35 U.S.C. §102(a)). The court in *Mahurkar* explained that a patentee such as Mahurkar may seek to establish an actual invention date earlier than the application filing date (i.e., constructive reduction to practice date, taken as presumptive invention date) by analogy to the interference rule of priority of invention:

behind" a prior art reference is no longer possible. This is because the concepts of "invention date" and priority based on earlier invention date are not part of the post-AIA 35 U.S.C. §102 framework.

A third AIA-implemented change of much importance is the removal of numerous geographic limitations on §102 prior art. Under the pre-AIA regime, "know[ledge] or use[] by others" of a claimed invention had to have occurred "in this country" to count as novelty-destroying prior art.[250] Placement of an invention "on sale" or "in public use" created a loss of right to patent only if the activity had occurred "in this country."[251] The prior making of an invention counted as novelty-destroying prior art only if the invention had been "made in this country."[252] In contrast, there are no geographic limitations in the post-AIA §102(a)(1).[253] Thus, for example, pre–effective filing date sales of a claimed invention anywhere in the world will potentially destroy novelty.

One geographic limitation is retained by the AIA, however: descriptions of a claimed invention in another's earlier-filed application are prior art only if the "another" ultimately obtains a U.S. patent or the "another's" application is published in accordance with U.S. patent law. Under the pre-AIA regime, descriptions of a claimed invention in another's patent or published application counted as novelty-destroying prior art only if the "another's" patent or published application was "filed in the United States."[254] This domestic connection is effectively retained by the AIA (although stated in different words). Under post-AIA §102, the novelty-destroying description must still appear in "a patent issued under section 151 [of 35 U.S.C.]" or in "an application for patent published or deemed published under section 122(b) [of 35 U.S.C.]."[255]

Although the description being relied on as a prior art reference must ultimately appear in a U.S. patent or application published in accordance with U.S. patent law to qualify as post-AIA §102(a)(2) prior

---

In the United States, the person who first reduces an invention to practice is "prima facie the first and true inventor." Christie v. Seybold, 55 F. 69, 76 (6th Cir. 1893) (Taft, J.). However, the person "who first conceives, and, in a mental sense, first invents . . . may date his patentable invention back to the time of its conception, if he connects the conception with its reduction to practice by reasonable diligence on his part, so that they are substantially one continuous act." *Id.*

[250]35 U.S.C. §102(a) (2006); *see also supra* Section H ("'Known or Used' under 35 U.S.C. §102(a) (Pre-AIA)").

[251]35 U.S.C. §102(b) (2006); *see also supra* Section I ("The Statutory Bars of 35 U.S.C. §102(b) (Pre-AIA)").

[252]35 U.S.C. §102(g)(2) (2006); *see also supra* Section N.3 ("Anticipation Under §102(g)(2) (Pre-AIA)").

[253]*See infra* Section Q ("Presumptively Novelty-Destroying Events Under Post-AIA §102(a)(1)").

[254]35 U.S.C. §102(e) (2006); *see also supra* Section L ("Description in Another's Earlier-Filed Patent or Published Patent Application Under 35 U.S.C. §102(e) (Pre-AIA)").

[255]35 U.S.C. §102(a)(2) (eff. Mar. 16, 2013).

art, there is a different AIA-implemented geographic change of note in this context. Before the AIA's effective date, any earlier foreign filing date to which the U.S. patent or published application being relied on as prior art may have been entitled under the Paris Convention's right of priority was ignored under the judicially created *Hilmer* rule.[256] The AIA repealed the *Hilmer* rule.[257]

To see the impact of abolishing the *Hilmer* rule, consider a hypothetical German inventor who first files a patent application directed to her invention in the German Patent Office in 2014 and within one year files another application for the same invention in the USPTO, properly claiming for her U.S. application the Paris Convention right of foreign priority under 35 U.S.C. §119(a). Assume that the German and U.S. applications are identical in terms of the invention's disclosure (setting aside any language translation issues). The U.S. application is published at 18 months after the 2014 German priority date and thereafter a USPTO examiner cites the U.S. application's description of the invention as prior art against another patent applicant under post-AIA §102(a)(2). The AIA provides that the prior art effective date of the invention's description in the German inventor's published U.S. patent application will be its 2014 German filing date.[258] Pre-AIA, the *Hilmer* rule would have limited the prior art effective date of the published application's description to its later U.S. filing date.[259] Thus, post-AIA, the German inventor of this hypothetical has an enhanced defensive opportunity (sometimes referred to as a "senior right") to prevent others from patenting the invention in the United States.

---

[256]*See In re Hilmer*, 359 F.2d 859 (C.C.P.A. 1966); *see also supra* Section L ("Description in Another's Earlier-Filed Patent or Published Patent Application Under 35 U.S.C. §102(e) (Pre-AIA)").

[257]*See* 35 U.S.C. §102(d) (eff. Mar. 16, 2013), which provides:

(d) PATENTS AND PUBLISHED APPLICATIONS EFFECTIVE AS PRIOR ART.— For purposes of determining whether a patent or application for patent is prior art to a claimed invention under subsection (a)(2), such patent or application shall be considered to have been effectively filed, with respect to any subject matter described in the patent or application—
(1) if paragraph (2) does not apply, as of the actual filing date of the patent or the application for patent; or
(2) if the patent or application for patent is entitled to claim a right of priority under section 119, 365(a), or 365(b), or to claim the benefit of an earlier filing date under section 120, 121, or 365(c), based upon 1 or more prior filed applications for patent, as of the filing date of the earliest such application that describes the subject matter.

Subparagraph (d)(2) repeals the *Hilmer* rule implicitly by including foreign priority under 35 U.S.C. §119 in its scope.

[258]*See* 35 U.S.C. §102(d) (eff. Mar. 16, 2013) (quoted *infra*).

[259]*See supra* Section L ("Description in Another's Earlier-Filed Patent or Published Patent Application Under 35 U.S.C. §102(e) (Pre-AIA)").

Chapter 4. Novelty, Loss of Right, and Priority (35 U.S.C. §102)

The AIA removed geographic limitations in yet another way. Evidence relied on pre-AIA by a U.S. patent applicant attempting to swear behind a prior art reference, or relied on by an interference party seeking to establish time-wise priority of invention, was admissible only if the evidence arose from inventive activities in a NAFTA (North American Free Trade Agreement) or WTO (World Trade Organization) member country. Section 104 of 35 U.S.C., the statutory basis for this limitation on evidence relied on to affirmatively establish an earlier date of invention,[260] was eliminated by the AIA.

The AIA made still more changes to 35 U.S.C. §102. It eliminated subsection (c) of 35 U.S.C §102 (2006), which dealt with abandonment;[261] subsection (d) of 35 U.S.C. §102 (2006), which set forth a rarely invoked form of statutory bar based on foreign patenting;[262] and subsection (f) of 35 U.S.C. §102 (2006), the basis for the requirement of originality. Congress's motivation for eliminating §102(f) is unclear, because other portions of the AIA and the post-AIA Patent Act clarify that originality of invention is still a bedrock requirement. In other words, the law remains that one cannot merely copy another's invention and obtain a patent on it.[263]

In addition to its several deletions from 35 U.S.C. §102, the AIA added a new category of novelty-destroying prior art to §102. Post-AIA, a claimed invention is not novel if it was "otherwise available to the public" before the invention's effective filing date. Congress in the AIA text did not define its "otherwise available to the public" language. As further discussed below, a clear understanding of the new language's meaning and scope will likely require interpretation by the courts.[264]

---

[260]35 U.S.C. §104 (2006) ("Invention made abroad").

[261]*See supra* Section J.

[262]*See supra* Section K.

[263]More specifically, the AIA did not change the requirement that, subject to certain exceptions, patent applications shall be made "by the inventor," 35 U.S.C. §111(a)(1) (2006), and the AIA added a definition of "inventor" as "the individual or, if a joint invention, the individuals collectively who invented or discovered the subject matter of the invention." 35 U.S.C. §100(f) (eff. Mar. 16, 2013); Leahy-Smith America Invents Act, Pub. L. No. 112-29 (H.R. 1249), §3(a)(2), 125 Stat. 284, 285 (2011). The AIA also continued the requirement that a patent applicant's oath include a statement that the applicant believes he is an "original" inventor. *See* 35 U.S.C. §115 (2006) (requiring that "[t]he applicant shall make oath that he believes himself to be the *original* and first inventor of the process, machine, manufacture, or composition of matter, or improvement thereof, for which he solicits a patent") (emphasis added); 35 U.S.C. §115(b)(2) (eff. Mar. 16, 2013) (providing that "[a]n oath or declaration under subsection (a) shall contain statements that . . . such individual believes himself or herself to be the *original* inventor or an *original* joint inventor of a claimed invention in the application") (emphases added).

[264]*See infra* Section Q.3 ("Does the AIA Permit Secret Prior Art?").

Q. Presumptively Novelty-Destroying Events Under Post-AIA 35 U.S.C. §102(a)(1)

Subsection (a)(1) of post-AIA §102 enumerates five categories of novelty-destroying events. Four of the five categories are identified by terminology well established in numerous interpretative judicial decisions. The fifth category is new to U.S. patent law. The operation of these categories is explained and illustrated by hypotheticals below.

1. Invention "Patented, Described in a Printed Publication, or in Public Use, [or] on Sale" Before Effective Filing Date

Section §102(a)(1) of 35 U.S.C. (eff. Mar. 16, 2013) provides in part that "[a] person shall be entitled to a patent unless—(1) the claimed invention was patented, described in a printed publication, or in public use, [or] on sale . . . before the effective filing date of the claimed invention. . . ." A wealth of pre-AIA case law has interpreted and applied the four novelty-destroying events identified in this portion of the statute.[265] Presumably those judicial interpretations continue to control under the post-AIA regime and will not be revisited here.[266] The following hypothetical and accompanying variations illustrate the operation of the first four novelty-destroying events of post-AIA §102(a)(1).

Hypothetical.   Consider U.S. patent applicant Aidan, who invents a widget "X" and thereafter files a non-provisional utility patent application disclosing and claiming widget X in the USPTO on July 1, 2014. Aidan's application is a first-filed application, meaning that it is not entitled to any earlier filing date via a right of foreign or domestic priority under 35 U.S.C. §119, or to the benefit of an earlier-filed co-pending application under 35 U.S.C. §120. Thus, the effective filing date of the claims in Aidan's application is his application's actual USPTO filing date of July 1, 2014.[267]

---

[265]For discussion of the pre-AIA case law interpretation of these terms, *see supra* Part II.

[266]Some question exists concerning the continued viability of so-called secret prior art. For example, long-standing precedent holds that secret offers for sale and "non-informing" public uses count as prior art under 35 U.S.C. §102(b) (2006). Based on certain AIA legislative history, however, a contrary argument can be made that the AIA narrowed the scope of "on sale" and "public use" activity to eliminate secret prior art, and thus limited novelty-destroying "on sale" and "public use" situations to those that are not confidential (i.e., are always "public"). For further discussion of this unresolved issue, *see infra* Section Q.3 ("Does the AIA Permit Secret Prior Art?").

[267]*See* 35 U.S.C. §100(i)(1) (eff. Mar. 16, 2013) (defining "effective filing date").

First Variation. Assume that an identical widget X was patented in Germany on June 30, 2014 (that is, the German patent issued one day before Aidan's effective filing date) by Gertrude, a German national who independently invented widget X.[268] As a result, the novelty of Aidan's claimed widget X has been presumptively destroyed by Gertrude's act of patenting the same widget. In other words, the issuance of Gertrude's patent anticipated Aidan's application claims, and the USPTO will reject them.[269] The date on which Aidan invented his claimed widget X (i.e., his "invention date" in pre-AIA parlance) is not relevant to the analysis, even if earlier in time than Gertrude's invention date.

Second Variation. Alter the facts of the Aidan hypothetical so that the identical widget X was "described in a printed publication" by Eli, a national of Estonia. Assume that Eli independently invented widget X and described it in enabling fashion[270] in an article published in an Estonian newspaper in the Estonian language.[271] The newspaper article was published on June 30, 2014 (one day before Aidan's effective filing date). As a result, the novelty of Aidan's claimed widget X has been presumptively destroyed by Eli's description of the same widget in a printed publication having an effective date before Aidan's effective filing date. Again, the date on which Aidan invented his claimed widget X is not relevant to the analysis, even if earlier in time than Eli's invention date. Nor is the fact that Eli's article was published abroad in a foreign language relevant.[272]

Third Variation. Alter the facts of the Aidan hypothetical so that the identical widget X was in "public use" in Paraguay by independent inventor Pamela on June 30, 2014 (one day before Aidan's effective filing date).[273] Assume that Pamela gave away a dozen widget X's to various persons she encountered on the streets of her Paraguayan hometown, with no restrictions on confidentiality or the recipients' further use of the widgets. As a result, the novelty of Aidan's claimed widget X has been presumptively destroyed by Pamela's act of putting the identical widget into public use before Aidan's effective filing date.

---

[268]Minimal modern precedent exists regarding the meaning of "patenting" in 35 U.S.C. §102(a) (2006) and 35 U.S.C. §102(b) (2006). In actual practice, Gertrude's patent application would be published by the German Patent Office at 18 months after filing and would be available as "printed publication" prior art on the publication date.

[269]In this hypothetical and its variations, novelty is "presumptively" destroyed in the absence of other facts to suggest that one of the prior art–removing exceptions of 35 U.S.C. §102(b)(1) (eff. Mar. 16, 2013) applies.

[270]*See supra* Section E ("Enablement Standard for Anticipatory Prior Art").

[271]For pre-AIA precedent regarding the meaning of "described in a printed publication," *see supra* Section F ("What Is a Printed Publication?").

[272]This fact would not be relevant under pre-AIA law either.

[273]For pre-AIA precedent regarding the meaning of an invention being in "public use," *see supra* Section I.3.

Again, the date on which Aidan invented his claimed widget X is not relevant to the analysis. The fact that Pamela's public use occurred outside the United States is likewise not relevant.

Fourth Variation.   Alter the facts of the Aidan hypothetical so that the identical widget X was placed "on sale" in Hungary by independent inventor Heather on June 30, 2014.[274] On that date Heather sold a dozen widget X's to customers in her retail store in Budapest. As a result, the novelty of Aidan's claimed widget X has been presumptively destroyed by Heather's act of putting the identical widget on sale before Aidan's effective filing date. Again, the date on which Aidan invented his claimed widget X is not relevant to the analysis in this hypothetical. The foreign location of Heather's sales is also not relevant.

2. Invention "Otherwise Available to the Public" Before Effective Filing Date

In addition to the first four presumptively novelty-destroying events discussed in the preceding subsection, §102(a)(1) of 35 U.S.C. (eff. Mar. 16, 2013) provides that "[a] person shall be entitled to a patent unless—the claimed invention was . . . otherwise available to the public before the effective filing date of the claimed invention." This is a newly articulated category of prior art for U.S. patent law. The AIA's text does not provide a definition of "otherwise available to the public."

Examining the meaning of the phrase in the context of the statute suggests that it was intended as catch-all language to cover activity not already falling within the first four §102(a)(1) categories of "patented, described in a printed publication, or in public use, [or] on sale . . . ," so long as the activity is "available to the public." For example, a purely oral disclosure of an invention at a scientific conference of non-restrictive attendance might come within "otherwise available to the public," in a manner analogous to European practice.[275] In contrast, the Federal Circuit observed (in *dicta*) that purely oral divulgations do not qualify as prior art under pre-AIA §102(b).[276]

---

[274]For pre-AIA precedent regarding the meaning of placing an invention "on sale," *see supra* Section I.4.

[275]*See* European Patent Convention art. 54(1) (14th ed. 2010) (providing that "[a]n invention shall be considered to be new if it does not form part of the state of the art"); *id.* art. 54(2) (providing that "[t]he state of the art shall be held to comprise everything *made available to the public* by means of a written or *oral description*, by use, or in any other way, before the date of filing of the European patent application") (emphasis added).

[276]*See In re Klopfenstein*, 380 F.3d 1345, 1349 n.4 (Fed. Cir. 2004) (observing, in contrast to the facts of the case before it, that an entirely *oral* presentation that does not include a display of slides or distribution of copies of the presentation would not

The primary issue left unanswered by Congress's addition of "otherwise available to the public" as a category of prior art is whether the language works any change to the extant case law–based interpretations of "public use" and "on sale" activity. The next subsection addresses the issue.

3.   Does the AIA Permit Secret Prior Art?

For many years before the AIA's enactment, U.S. patent case law recognized that certain "secret" activity can potentially qualify as novelty-destroying prior art. A classic example is a "non-informing public use" involving an inventor's secret commercialization of his invention outside of the pre-AIA statutory grace period.[277]

The leading precedent on point is *Metallizing Engineering Co. v. Kenyon Bearing & Auto Parts Co.*[278] The inventor in *Metallizing* developed and used an industrial process while working for numerous commercial customers more than one year before filing a U.S. patent application claiming the process. Although commercially exploiting his process for an extended period of time, the inventor did not disclose to others any details about the process. Nor were the details discernible from inspecting the finished product of the process.[279]

The revered jurist Learned Hand of the U.S. Court of Appeals for the Second Circuit reversed a district court decision that sustained the validity of the patent over a public use challenge. The district court had reasoned that a secret use of a process could never be a public use within the meaning of the statute. In holding that the public use bar could indeed be triggered by secret use that is commercial in nature,

---

constitute a "printed publication" under 35 U.S.C. §102(b) (2006), and that a merely "transient" display of slides accompanying an oral presentation might not either).

[277]*See* Kinzenbaw v. Deere & Co., 741 F.2d 383, 390 (Fed. Cir. 1984) (observing that "[a] commercial use is a public use even if it is kept secret" and citing authority). *See also* Invitrogen Corp. v. Biocrest Mfg., L.P., 424 F.3d 1374, 1381 n.* (Fed. Cir. 2005) (characterizing *Kinzenbaw*'s statement that "[a] commercial use is a public use even if it is kept secret" as *dicta*, because the court in *Kinzenbaw* did not find it necessary to resolve the question whether the use of the invention was secret, but concluding that *Kinzenbaw* "is consistent with the basic principle that a confidential use is not public under §102(b) unless there is commercial exploitation").

[278]153 F.2d 516 (2d Cir. 1946) (L. Hand, J.).

[279]*See* Metallizing Eng'g Co. v. Kenyon Bearing & Auto Parts Co., 62 F. Supp. 42, 47 (D. Conn. 1945) (finding that "[a]t all times prior to [the critical date of] August 6, 1941, the practice of the process was so guarded as not to come to public knowledge; its nature was disclosed only to a few employees and advisers of the inventor, less than half a dozen in number, in all cases under a promise of confidence which was not abused. . . . [P]rior to August, 1941, the nature of the process could not have been deduced from inspection or physical tests upon specimens of the processed product in the hands of the public. . . . ").

Judge Hand overruled his own earlier decision on which the district court had relied:

> [I]t appears that in *Peerless Roll Leaf Co. v. Griffin & Sons,* supra, 2 Cir., 29 F.2d 646, we confused two separate doctrines: (1) The effect upon his right to a patent of the inventor's competitive exploitation of his machine or of his process; (2) the contribution which a prior use by another person makes to the art. Both do indeed come within the phrase, 'prior use'; but the first is a defence for quite different reasons from the second. It had its origin—at least in this country—in the passage we have quoted from *Pennock v. Dialogue,* supra, 2 Pet. 1, 7 L. Ed. 327; i.e., *that it is a condition upon an inventor's right to a patent that he shall not exploit his discovery competitively after it is ready for patenting; he must content himself with either secrecy, or legal monopoly.* It is true that for the limited period of two years he was allowed to do so, possibly in order to give him time to prepare an application; and even that has been recently cut down by half. But if he goes beyond that period of probation, he forfeits his right *regardless of how little the public may have learned about the invention. . . .* [280]

An argument exists that the addition of the "or otherwise available to the public" language in post-AIA §102(a)(1) means that *all five* of the categories of potentially novelty-destroying prior art enumerated in that subsection must be "available to the public." In other words, the argument is that §102(a)(1) excludes any type of "secret" prior art that is not available to the public. According to Professors Robert Merges and John Duffy, the practical result of accepting this view means that an "inventor's own secret commercial exploitation (possibly for years!) will not bar that inventor from later seeking a patent."[281] This interpretation admittedly finds support from (i) the presence of the word "otherwise" in §102(a)(1) as well as (ii) statements in the legislative history of the AIA.[282]

The better view, however, is that enactment of the AIA did not *sub silentio* overrule the well-established case law interpretations of

---

[280]*Metallizing,* 153 F.2d at 519-520 (emphases added).

[281]Robert Merges & John Duffy, *Leahy-Smith America Invents Act of 2011: Overview* 22 (Sept. 16, 2011), https://docs.google.com/leaf?id=0B1P2D6tikiwFMDliMzhhNWMt N GM3ZC00MDYxLTlmMjEtMjE2YjVkMDUwN2Y1&hl=en_US.

[282]*See, e.g.,* H.R. Rep. No. 112-98 [House Judiciary Comm. Rep. on the America Invents Act], at 54 (June 1, 2011) (stating that §3 of the AIA "also, and necessarily, modifies the prior-art sections of the patent law. Prior art will be measured from the filing date of the application and will typically include all art that *publicly exists* prior to the filing date, other than disclosures by the inventor within 1 year of filing. Prior art also will no longer have any geographic limitations. Thus, in section 102 the "in this country" limitation as applied to "public use" and "on sale" is removed, *and the phrase* "available to the public" *is added to clarify the broad scope of relevant prior art, as well as to emphasize the fact that it must be publicly accessible.*") (emphases added).

"public use" and "on sale" as encompassing certain "secret" activity. As Professors Merges and Duffy point out, to conclude otherwise would "reverse centuries of U.S. patent law, dating back to the decision in *Pennock v. Dialogue,* 27 U.S. 1 (1829)."[283] Merges and Duffy conclude that the AIA did *not* make "such a dramatic shift in U.S. patent policy" for the following four reasons:

(i) well established rules of statutory construction provide that "reenactment of statutory language with a known legal meaning continues the known meaning";

(ii) although one sentence in a Senate colloquy addressing the grace period supports the contrary view, nothing in that colloquy "suggested that Congress wanted to undo a fundamental principle of patent law";

(iii) in construing statutes it is accepted that Congress does not "hide elephants in mouseholes," and "overturning two centuries of consistent law would be a big elephant to hide in a [Senate] colloquy"; and

(iv) "[r]emarks in legislative history are not the statutory text."[284]

Resolution of this debate will likely have to await judicial interpretation of post-AIA §102(a)(1).

R. Presumptively Novelty-Destroying Events Under Post-AIA 35 U.S.C. §102(a)(2)

Section §102(a)(2) of 35 U.S.C. (eff. Mar. 16, 2013) provides that "[a] person shall be entitled to a patent unless—the claimed invention was described in a patent issued under section 151, or in an application for patent published or deemed published under section 122(b), in which the patent or application, as the case may be, names another inventor and was effectively filed before the effective filing date of the claimed invention."

The language of post-AIA §102(a)(2) is the closest the statute comes to expressing a first-inventor-to-file priority principle, and the principle is only implicitly gleaned from the statutory text. The essence of §102(a)(2) is that the novelty of a claimed invention is presumptively destroyed if the same invention was already described in an earlier-filed

---

[283]Robert Merges & John Duffy, *Leahy-Smith America Invents Act of 2011: Overview* 22 (Sept. 16, 2011), https://docs.google.com/leaf?id=0B1P2D6tikiwFMDliMzhhNWMt NGM3ZC00MDYxLTlmMjEtMjE2YjVkMDUwN2Y1&hl=en_US.

[284]Robert Merges & John Duffy, *Leahy-Smith America Invents Act of 2011: Overview* 23-24 (Sept. 16, 2011), https://docs.google.com/leaf?id=0B1P2D6tikiwFMDliMzhhNW Mt NGM3ZC00MDYxLTlmMjEtMjE2YjVkMDUwN2Y1&hl=en_US.

U.S. patent or published patent application naming another inventor. In short, the later filer loses the priority contest (barring an exception under §102(b)(2)). The verbal complexity of §102(a)(2) stands in sharp contrast to the first-to-file principle clearly articulated in the European Patent Convention (EPC).[285]

Section 102(a)(2) is the post-AIA counterpart of pre-AIA 35 U.S.C. §102(e).[286] Codified in the 1952 Patent Act, 35 U.S.C. §102(e) implemented the rule announced in the U.S. Supreme Court's landmark decision *Alexander Milburn Co. v. Davis-Bournonville Co.*[287] The policy rationale underlying *Milburn*, a case decided against the backdrop of the United States' historic first-to-invent priority system, was that the presence of a complete description of an invention claimed by a U.S. patent applicant (or patentee), in someone else's earlier-filed U.S. patent, evidences that the applicant or patentee is *not* in fact the first to invent the claimed subject matter and is thus not entitled to patent it. Distilled to its essence, *Milburn* required that the disclosure of a U.S. patent, when used as prior art, must be treated as constructively published on the date that the application for the patent was filed in the USPTO. The *Milburn* Court engaged in the fiction that the contents of the patent's written description became instantaneously available as a printed publication upon filing, although in fact the description would remain secret to the public until some later date (i.e., issuance of the patent or (via later legislative developments) publication of the pending application). Thus, under *Milburn* and pre-AIA law, the effective date of the written description portion of a U.S. patent or published U.S. patent application being used as §102(e) prior art was its U.S. filing date.[288]

The AIA did not change the basic *Milburn* concept of treating an anticipatory description in another's earlier-filed U.S. patent as

---

[285]Article 60 ("Right to a European Patent") of the EPC provides in pertinent part that "[i]f two or more persons have made an invention independently of each other, the right to a European patent therefor shall belong to the person whose European patent application has the earliest date of filing, provided that this first application has been published." European Patent Convention art. 60(2) (14th ed. 2010).

[286]35 U.S.C. §102(e) (2006).

[287]270 U.S. 390 (1926). *See also* P.J. Federico, *Commentary on the New Patent Act*, 35 U.S.C.A. §1 (1954 ed., discontinued in subsequent volumes), *reprinted at* 75 J. Pat. & Trademark Off. Soc'y 161, 179 (1993) (explaining that "[p]aragraph (e) is new in the statute and enacts the rule of the decision of the Supreme Court in [*Milburn*] under which a United States patent disclosing an invention dates from the filing of the application for the purpose of anticipating a later inventor, whether or not the invention is claimed in the patent") (citation omitted). *See generally supra* Section L ("Description in Another's Earlier-Filed Patent or Published Patent Application Under 35 U.S.C. §102(e) (Pre-AIA)").

[288]*See supra* Section L ("Description in Another's Earlier-Filed Patent or Published Patent Application Under 35 U.S.C. §102(e) (Pre-AIA)").

novelty-destroying prior art. However, the AIA did eliminate the notion of "invention date" from all parts of 35 U.S.C. §102, such that novelty is now assessed as of a claimed invention's effective filing date.[289]

The AIA also added to the Patent Act a new §102(d) defining the effective filing date of §102(a)(2) prior art patents or published applications.[290] In accordance with post-AIA §102(d), a U.S. patent or published (or "deemed published") patent application, the description of which is relied on as prior art under post-AIA §102(a)(2), will be assigned an effective date that is (i) its actual U.S. filing date; (ii) the earlier U.S. filing date of a co-pending application (such as a parent or provisional) to which the prior art patent or published application may be entitled (for example, under 35 U.S.C. §119(e) or 35 U.S.C. §120); or (iii) the earlier foreign priority date to which the prior art patent or printed publication may be entitled under 35 U.S.C. §119(a) in view of the *Hilmer* rule's repeal.[291] Notably, the question of entitlement of the prior art patent or printed publication to either effective date (ii) or (iii) will turn on compliance with the enablement and written description of the invention requirements of 35 U.S.C. §112(a).[292]

---

[289]*See* 35 U.S.C. §102(a) (eff. Mar. 16, 2013); 35 U.S.C. §100(i) (eff. Mar. 16, 2013) (defining "effective filing date" for a claimed invention in a patent or application for patent).

[290]See 35 U.S.C. §102(d) (eff. Mar. 16, 2013) ("Patents and Published Applications Effective as Prior Art").

[291]*See* 35 U.S.C. §102(d) (eff. Mar. 16, 2013), which provides:

(d) PATENTS AND PUBLISHED APPLICATIONS EFFECTIVE AS PRIOR ART.—For purposes of determining whether a patent or application for patent is prior art to a claimed invention under subsection (a)(2), such patent or application shall be considered to have been effectively filed, with respect to any subject matter described in the patent or application—

(1) if paragraph (2) does not apply, as of the actual filing date of the patent or the application for patent; or

(2) if the patent or application for patent is entitled to claim a right of priority under section 119, 365(a), or 365(b), or to claim the benefit of an earlier filing date under section 120, 121, or 365(c), based upon 1 or more prior filed applications for patent, as of the filing date of the earliest such application that describes the subject matter.

Subparagraph (d)(2) implicitly repeals the rule of *In re Hilmer*, 359 F.2d 859 (C.C.P.A. 1966). *See also supra* Section P.3.b ("What Section 3 of the AIA Changed"); *supra* Section L ("Description in Another's Earlier-Filed Patent or Published Patent Application Under 35 U.S.C. §102(e) (Pre-AIA)").

[292]The enablement and written description disclosure requirements of 35 U.S.C. §112(a) (eff. Sept. 16, 2012) are explicitly incorporated into post-AIA 35 U.S.C. §119(e) (1) (domestic priority) and post-AIA 35 U.S.C. §120 ("Benefit of earlier filing date in the United States"); the AIA deleted the best mode disclosure requirement from these statutory provisions. Case law establishes that the "for the same invention" language of 35 U.S.C. §119(a) implicitly invokes the §112 disclosure requirements for foreign priority claims. *See infra* Chapter 12, Section B.4.

R. Presumptively Novelty-Destroying Events Under Post-AIA §102(a)(2)

The following hypotheticals illustrate the operation of post-AIA §102(a)(2).

Hypothetical. Consider U.S. patent applicant Matthew, who invented a widget "X" and thereafter filed a non-provisional utility patent application disclosing and claiming widget X in the USPTO on July 1, 2014. Unbeknownst to Matthew, on June 30, 2014, one day before Matthew's filing date, Neal filed his own non-provisional utility patent application in the USPTO. Neal's application described widget X in complete detail. When the USPTO publishes Neal's application at 18 months after its filing date (or, if it is not published at 18 months, when Neal's application issues as a U.S. patent), the description of widget X in Neal's application will be available for citation by the USPTO as §102(a)(2) prior art against Matthew's application claims to widget X. Under these facts, the effective date of the description in Neal's application, which is being used by the USPTO as prior art, is Neal's actual U.S. filing date of June 30, 2014, one day before Matthew's filing date. The description in Neal's application is anticipatory, preventing Matthew from obtaining a patent claiming widget X (in the absence of any facts suggesting that Neal's disclosure is removed as prior art under a §102(b)(2) exception[293]). Matthew's invention date is not relevant. In accordance with *Milburn,* whether Neal or some third party actually invented the widget X described in Neal's application is not relevant either. Section 102(a)(2) merely requires that Neal be named as an inventor on his application, which he is.

First Variation. Change the facts of the above hypothetical such that Neal filed a first patent application identically describing widget X in an enabling fashion in the Japanese Patent Office on June 30, 2014. On June 29, 2015 (within the Paris Convention 12-month priority period), Neal filed a non-provisional utility patent application in the USPTO having the same description of widget X that appeared in the Japanese application (translated into English). Neal claimed for his U.S. application the right of priority under 35 U.S.C. §119(a) to his Japanese filing date of June 30, 2014. Neal's U.S. application is entitled to his Japanese filing date because the disclosure of the Japanese application satisfies the requirements of 35 U.S.C. §112, first paragraph (i.e., enablement and written description) for the subject matter claimed in Neal's U.S. application.[294] When the USPTO publishes Neal's application on or after December 30, 2015 (generally 18 months

---

[293]*See infra* Section S.3 ("Post-AIA §102(b)(2): Shields Against Post-AIA §102(a)(2) Presumptively Novelty-Destroying Events").

[294]*See infra* Chapter 12, Section B.4. It is presumed that the AIA implicitly removed the best mode requirement from foreign priority claims under 35 U.S.C. §119(a), because it did so explicitly for domestic priority claims under §119(e) and claims to the benefit of an earlier-filed co-pending application under §120.

after his foreign filing date), the description in Neal's application will be available for citation as anticipatory §102(a)(2) prior art by the USPTO against Matthew's application claims to widget X. Under these facts, the effective date of Neal's application, which is being used by the USPTO as prior art, is Neal's foreign priority date of June 30, 2014, which is one day before Matthew's filing date. The *Hilmer* rule no longer prevents assigning the foreign priority date as the prior art effective date of Neal's U.S. patent application.[295] The description in Neal's published application is presumptively novelty-destroying prior art under §102(a)(2), preventing Matthew from obtaining a U.S. patent claiming widget X. It is not relevant that as between Matthew and Neal, Matthew was the first to file an application in the USPTO.

S. Novelty-Preserving Exceptions Under Post-AIA 35 U.S.C. §102(b)

1. Introduction

Novelty (or, more precisely, the lack thereof) is not an absolute concept under the AIA. Even though one (or more) of the presumptively novelty-destroying events enumerated in post-AIA §102(a) has occurred, a claimed invention's novelty nevertheless may be preserved (in other words, the presumptively-established §102(a) prior art may be removed) if one of the "exceptions" or shields of 35 U.S.C. §102(b) (eff. Mar. 16, 2013) (hereafter "§102(b)" or "post-AIA §102(b)") applies. The §102(b) exceptions operate in somewhat analogous fashion to "grace period" events under the pre-AIA regime.[296] Even though significantly amended by the AIA, the resultant U.S. Patent Act does not contain a European-style absolute novelty system. Despite Congress's stated intent to "promote harmonization of the United States patent system with the patent systems commonly used in nearly all other countries throughout the world with whom the United States con-

---

[295]Subparagraph (d)(2) of post-AIA §102 implicitly repeals the rule of *In re Hilmer*, 359 F.2d 859 (C.C.P.A. 1966). *See also supra* Section P.3.b ("What Section 3 of the AIA Changed"). *Compare* Section L ("Description in Another's Earlier-Filed Patent or Published Patent Application Under 35 U.S.C. §102(e) (Pre-AIA)").

[296]*See* H.R. Rep. No. 112-98 [House Judiciary Comm. Rep. on the America Invents Act], at 54 (June 1, 2011) (stating that the AIA "maintains a 1-year grace period for U.S. applicants. Applicants' own publication or disclosure that occurs within 1 year prior to filing will not act as prior art against their applications. Similarly, disclosure by others during that time based on information obtained (directly or indirectly) from the inventor will not constitute prior art. This 1-year grace period should continue to give U.S. applicants the time they need to prepare and file their applications."). *See also supra* Section I.2 ("Grace Period").

ducts trade and thereby promote greater international uniformity and certainty in the procedures used for securing the exclusive rights of inventors to their discoveries,"[297] the AIA did not completely (or even largely) harmonize U.S. patent law with international standards. Rather, the AIA created a U.S. patent statute that is a unique hybrid, retaining many aspects of the pre-AIA regime. The "exceptions" of §102(b) are prime examples.

The following subsections separately discuss the exceptions provided for in post-AIA §102(b)(1) and §102(b)(2).

2. Post-AIA §102(b)(1): Shields Against Post-AIA §102(a)(1) Presumptively Novelty-Destroying Events

Post-AIA §102(b)(1) enumerates two categories of exceptions that represent two different ways to remove what would otherwise be novelty-destroying prior art under post-AIA §102(a)(1). The post-AIA version of 35 U.S.C. §102 provides in pertinent part:

> (b) EXCEPTIONS.—
> (1) DISCLOSURES MADE 1 YEAR OR LESS BEFORE THE EFFECTIVE FILING DATE OF THE CLAIMED INVENTION.—A disclosure made 1 year or less before the effective filing date of a claimed invention shall not be prior art to the claimed invention under subsection (a)(1) if—
>> (A) the disclosure was made by the inventor or joint inventor or by another who obtained the subject matter disclosed directly or indirectly from the inventor or a joint inventor; or
>> (B) the subject matter disclosed had, before such disclosure, been publicly disclosed by the inventor or a joint inventor or another who obtained the subject matter disclosed directly or indirectly from the inventor or a joint inventor.[298]

In the discussion that follows, the two categories of §102(b)(1) exceptions are referred to as "(A)-type" and "(B)-type" exceptions. The (A)-type exceptions are those covered by post-AIA §102(b)(1)(A). The (B)-type exceptions are those covered by post-AIA §102(b)(1)(B).

a. (A)-Type Exceptions

The first, or "(A)-type," exception removes from the prior art certain pre-filing disclosures made by the inventor/patent applicant herself or based on information obtained from the applicant. The pertinent

---

[297] Leahy-Smith America Invents Act, Pub. L. No. 112-29 (H.R. 1249), §3(p), 125 Stat. 284, 293 (2011) ("Sense of Congress").
[298] 35 U.S.C. §102(b)(1) (eff. Mar. 16, 2013).

statutory language provides that "[a] disclosure made 1 year or less before the effective filing date of a claimed invention shall not be prior art to the claimed invention under subsection (a)(1) if . . . (A) the disclosure was made by the inventor or joint inventor or by another who obtained the subject matter disclosed directly or indirectly from the inventor or a joint inventor."[299] Thus, an (A)-type exception is triggered by the inventor, a joint inventor, or an "obtainer."[300]

For example, consider an inventor who makes a "disclosure" of her invention and then files in the USPTO an application seeking to patent the invention within one year (to use pre-AIA parlance, during the one-year pre-filing "grace period"). On its face, the applicant's pre-filing date disclosure would appear to have destroyed novelty under post-AIA §102(a)(1). However, the statutory text explicitly ties together the §102(a)(1) presumptively novelty-destroying events and the §102(b)(1) exceptions. In view of this explicit statutory link, the applicant's pre-filing "disclosure" of her invention (i.e., "[a] disclosure made 1 year or less before the effective filing date of a claimed invention," as referred to in the preamble of §102(b)(1)) presumably took the form of the applicant having performed one (or more) of the five acts enumerated in §102(a)(1)—that is, having "patented [the claimed invention], described[it] in a printed publication, or [placing the invention] in public use, on sale, or otherwise [making the invention] available to the public." The preamble language of §102(b)(1) provides that the §102(b)(1)(A) "disclosure" (by the inventor, joint inventor, or obtainer, within one year of the invention's effective filing date) "shall not be prior art to the claimed invention under subsection (a)(1)." In other words, the statute removes the inventor's §102(a)(1) disclosure as prior art by means of the (A)-type exception of §102(b)(1). Consider this scenario as applied to facts from the hypothetical in Section Q.1 of this chapter, *supra*.

Hypothetical.   Assume that Aidan invents a widget "X." Aidan thereafter discloses the invention by publishing on February 1, 2014, an article in the *International Herald Tribune* newspaper that describes widget X. On July 1, 2014, Aidan files in the USPTO a non-provisional utility patent application disclosing and claiming the identical widget X. Because in this hypothetical Aidan's application is not entitled to any earlier filing date under 35 U.S.C. §§119, §120, or the like, the effective filing date of its claims is Aidan's actual USPTO filing date of July 1, 2014.[301]

---

[299]35 U.S.C. §102(b)(1)(A) (eff. Mar. 16, 2013).

[300]As used herein, "obtainer" refers to the statutory "another who obtained the subject matter disclosed directly or indirectly from the inventor or a joint inventor." *See* 35 U.S.C. §102(b)(1) (eff. Mar. 16, 2013).

[301]*See* 35 U.S.C. §100(i)(1) (eff. March 16, 2013) (defining "effective filing date").

S. Novelty-Preserving Exceptions Under Post-AIA 35 U.S.C. §102(b)

Applying post-AIA §102(a)(1) in isolation, the novelty of Aidan's claimed invention was presumptively destroyed (that is, anticipated) by Aidan's February 1, 2014, "descri[ption] [of the claimed invention] in a printed publication" that occurred "before the effective filing date of the claimed invention." The presumption of anticipation has been overcome, however, because post-AIA §102(b)(1)(A) covers a "disclosure . . . made by the inventor" and post-AIA §102(b)(1)'s preamble provides that Aidan's disclosure "shall not be prior art to the claimed invention." In sum, Aidan will still receive a U.S. patent on widget X despite his disclosure thereof during the one-year grace period before his invention's effective filing date (barring some other ground of non-patentability).[302] The same result would have obtained under the pre-AIA regime.[303] The one-year grace period of U.S. patent law remains in effect for acts during the grace period by the inventor or "obtainer."

First Variation. Section 102(b)(1)(A) removes presumptively novelty-destroying prior art created not only by the inventor/applicant (or a joint inventor) himself but also by an "obtainer;" that is, "by another who obtained the subject matter disclosed directly or indirectly from the inventor. . . . " Vary the facts of the above hypothetical such that Eli, a casual acquaintance of Aidan, stole a notebook that Aidan had created to record information concerning widget X. Using the purloined notebook without Aidan's knowledge or permission, Eli on February 1, 2014, published an article in the *International Herald Tribune* newspaper that described widget X. On July 1, 2014, Aidan filed in the USPTO a non-provisional utility patent application disclosing and claiming the identical widget X. Again, although Eli's published newspaper article presumptively destroyed novelty under §102(a)(1) as a pre–filing date "descri[ption] in a printed publication," the novelty of Aidan's claim to widget X was preserved or restored by means of the §102(b)(1)(A) exception. In this hypothetical, the statutory exception operates to remove the obtainer's (i.e., Eli's) disclosure as prior art against Aidan's application because the inventor (Aidan) filed his patent application within one year or less after the obtainer's disclosure.

Second Variation. The text of §102(b)(1)(A) does not define or explain the limits of the obtainer's act of "obtain[ing] the subject matter

---

[302]If, however, Aidan waits *more than* one year after his February 1, 2014, disclosure to file his application in the USPTO, he will be barred from obtaining a patent. The post-AIA §102(b)(1) exceptions last for only one year. This same result would have followed under the pre-AIA regime; that is, the grace period is one year under both systems.

[303]Aidan should be aware, however, that the patent systems of Europe and most other countries require *absolute* novelty (or offer very limited exceptions thereto). If Aidan desires international patent protection for widget X, he should refrain from making any disclosure of the invention before filing his first patent application on X.

disclosed directly or indirectly from the inventor. . . . " At a minimum, it would seem that the obtainer could obtain the subject matter disclosed by misappropriating or stealing information about the subject matter from the inventor/applicant, as in the first variation above, or by deriving it (in the patent law sense). Derivation occurs in patent law when the true inventor discloses her invention to another (the "deriver"), and the deriver then falsely patents the invention as his own.[304] More specifically, case law instructs that derivation requires proof of "'prior conception of the invention by another [i.e., the true inventor] and communication of that conception to the patentee [i.e., the deriver].'"[305]

Modifying the previous variation to incorporate derivation (in contrast with trade secret misappropriation or the crime of theft), assume that Aidan invented widget X and communicated his conception in an enabling fashion to Eli. Thereafter Eli filed a patent application claiming widget X in the Estonian Patent Office. On February 1, 2014, Eli's application issued as an Estonian patent.[306] On July 1, 2014, Aidan filed an application in the USPTO disclosing and claiming the identical widget X. Eli's act of "patent[ing]" widget X before Aidan's effective filing date of July 1, 2014, would presumptively destroy the novelty of Aidan's claim to widget X under §102(a) (1).[307] However, the novelty of Aidan's claim to widget X is preserved by the §102(b)(1)(A) exception. As a deriver, Eli presumably qualifies as "another who obtained the subject matter disclosed directly or indirectly from the inventor . . . " under §102(b)(1)(A), and the preamble of §102(b)(1) operates to remove Eli's disclosure (i.e., the issuance of Eli's Estonian patent during the one-year grace period preceding Aidan's effective filing date) as prior art against Aidan, the true inventor.

b. (B)-Type Exceptions

The second, or "(B)-type," exception under §102(b)(1) involves two "disclosures" of the same invention. Post-AIA §102(b)(1)(B) provides that "[a] disclosure made 1 year or less before the effective filing date

---

[304]See supra Section M ("Derivation and Inventorship Under 35 U.S.C. §102(f) (Pre-AIA)").

[305]Creative Compounds, LLC v. Starmark Labs., 651 F.3d 1303, 1313 (Fed. Cir. 2011) (quoting Eaton Corp. v. Rockwell Int'l Corp., 323 F.3d 1332, 1334 (Fed. Cir. 2003)).

[306]Assuming that Estonian patent law requires originality, Eli's patent would be invalid, but its issuance rather than its validity is the dispositive event in this hypothetical.

[307]The issuance of the Estonian patent would presumably also qualify as a §102(a) (1) "descri[ption] in a printed publication." The hypothetical does not consider the possibility of 18-month publication of the pending Estonian patent application.

of a claimed invention shall not be prior art to the claimed invention under subsection (a)(1) if . . . (B) the subject matter disclosed had, before such disclosure, been publicly disclosed by the inventor or a joint inventor or another who obtained the subject matter disclosed directly or indirectly from the inventor or a joint inventor." To illustrate, if (i) an inventor "publicly disclose[s]" his invention,[308] (ii) another individual (referred to herein as the "third party") thereafter "disclose[s]" the same invention, and (iii) the inventor/first discloser thereafter files his patent application within one year of his (the inventor/first discloser's) public disclosure, the inventor/first discloser will not be prevented by the third party's disclosure (or by the inventor's own public disclosure) from obtaining a patent.[309] Hence, the (B)-type exception illustrates that the AIA implemented what is, at least in part, a "first to disclose" system.

Hypothetical: Consider Aidan and Eli, each of whom independently invents widget X. On February 1, 2014, Aidan publicly discloses widget X by selling hundreds of items, each embodying widget X, to customers at Aidan's retail store located in China.[310] On March 1, 2014, Eli publishes a complete description of widget X in the *New York Times* newspaper. On July 1, 2014, Aidan files an application in the USPTO describing and claiming the identical widget X. Eli's disclosure on March 1, 2014, is removed as prior art under §102(b)(1)(B), because the "subject matter disclosed [by Eli] had, before such disclosure, been publicly disclosed" by Aidan. Aidan's own public disclosure on February 1, 2014, is removed as prior art by operation of §102(b)(1)(A) because Aidan filed his U.S. application within the one-year grace period starting on February 1, 2014.

---

[308]The public disclosure could also have been made by a joint inventor or an "obtainer." *See* §35 U.S.C. §102(b)(1)(B) (eff. Mar. 16, 2013).

[309]Although both terms are used in post-AIA §102(b)(1)(B), the statute does not define or explain the difference between "disclosed" and "publicly disclosed." The use of "disclosed" both with and without the modifier "publicly" suggests that the unqualified "disclosed" could encompass types of "secret" prior art that are traditionally recognized in U.S. case law but probably not "available to the public" under post-AIA §102(a)(1). *See supra* Section Q.3 ("Does the AIA Permit Secret Prior Art?"). Professor Merges analyzes the distinction between "disclosed" and "publicly disclosed" in Robert P. Merges, *Priority and Novelty under the AIA* (August 15, 2012), *available at* SSRN: http://ssrn.com/abstract=2130209 (Part II.B).

[310]The hypothetical assumes that the sale of the item fully and publicly discloses the features of the claimed invention and as such satisfies the "publicly disclosed" language of post-AIA §102(b)(1)(B). This avoids consideration of the *Metallizing*-type "secret prior art" issue discussed *supra* at Section Q.3 ("Does the AIA Permit Secret Prior Art?").

3.   Post-AIA §102(b)(2): Shields Against Post-AIA §102(a)(2) Presumptively Novelty-Destroying Events

The post-AIA §102(b)(2) exceptions remove presumptively novelty-destroying (i.e., anticipatory) §102(a)(2) prior art taking the form of descriptions in earlier-filed patents and patent applications naming another inventor. The post-AIA version of 35 U.S.C. §102(b) provides in pertinent part:

> (b) EXCEPTIONS.—
> . . .
> (2) DISCLOSURES APPEARING IN APPLICATIONS AND PATENTS.—A disclosure shall not be prior art to a claimed invention under subsection (a)(2) if—
> (A) the subject matter disclosed was obtained directly or indirectly from the inventor or a joint inventor;
> (B) the subject matter disclosed had, before such subject matter was effectively filed under subsection (a)(2), been publicly disclosed by the inventor or a joint inventor or another who obtained the subject matter disclosed directly or indirectly from the inventor or a joint inventor; or
> (C) the subject matter disclosed and the claimed invention, not later than the effective filing date of the claimed invention, were owned by the same person or subject to an obligation of assignment to the same person.

In similar fashion to the prior art–removing exceptions in post-AIA §102(b)(1), both (A)-type and (B)-type exceptions appear in §102(b)(2). A third exception, dealing with commonly owned prior art and discussed *infra*, also forms part of §102(b)(2).[311]

a.   (A)-Type Exceptions

The first, or "(A)-type," exception removes from the prior art a specific type of disclosure—a §102(a)(2) description of the claimed invention in an earlier-filed U.S. patent or published (or "deemed published") patent application naming another inventor—when that disclosure was made by an "obtainer," that is, one who "obtained" the "subject matter disclosed . . . directly or indirectly from the inventor or a joint inventor."[312]

Hypothetical.   Consider U.S. patent applicant Alex, who invented a widget "X." Alex thereafter communicated his conception of widget X to

[311]*See infra* Section U ("Common Ownership Under Joint Research Agreements").
[312]35 U.S.C. §102(b)(2)(A) (eff. Mar. 16, 2013) (providing in full that "[a] disclosure shall not be prior art to a claimed invention under subsection (a)(2) if—(A) the subject matter disclosed was obtained directly or indirectly from the inventor or a joint inventor").

his friend Mona in an enabling fashion. Unbeknownst to Alex, Mona filed a non-provisional utility patent application disclosing widget X in the USPTO on February 1, 2014. On July 1, 2014, Alex filed in the USPTO his own non-provisional utility patent application disclosing and claiming the identical widget X. Assume that the USPTO published the contents of Mona's pending application at 18 months after its filing date, that is, on August 1, 2015. A USPTO examiner thereafter cited the description of widget X in Mona's earlier-filed, now published application as anticipatory prior art against the claims of Alex's pending application.

The description in Mona's published application is presumptively novelty-destroying §102(a)(2) prior art because it has an effective date of February 1, 2014, which predates Alex's filing date of July 1, 2014. In other words, the existence of the description of widget X in Mona's earlier-filed patent application presumptively anticipates Alex's application claims to widget X under post-AIA §102(a)(2). The novelty of Alex's claims is preserved, however, by the §102(b)(2)(A) exception. Because Mona derived the widget X invention from Alex, Mona presumably qualifies as one who "obtained" the "subject matter disclosed" in her application "directly or indirectly" from Alex, the true inventor of widget X.[313] The preamble of §102(b)(2) provides that Mona's "disclosure shall not be prior art" to Alex's claimed invention.

As a practical matter, Alex can seek to prove that Mona derived the widget X invention from him by filing a petition to institute a derivation proceeding in accordance with post-AIA §135.[314] That statute provides that the petition must "set forth with particularity the basis for finding that an inventor named in an earlier application [i.e., Mona in this hypothetical] derived the claimed invention from an inventor named in the petitioner's application [i.e., Alex in this hypothetical] and, without authorization, the earlier application claiming such invention was filed."[315]

Alex can file his petition for a derivation proceeding "only within the 1-year period beginning on the date of the first publication of a claim to an invention that is the same or substantially the same as the earlier application's claim to the invention."[316] Although the statute is less than clear, a reasonable interpretation is that Alex, the second filer, must file his derivation petition no later than one year after the publication of the first filer's application, that is, no later than August 1, 2016,

---

[313]Mona may or may not be an inventor of some other invention claimed in her own application, although she is a deriver of widget X in this hypothetical. The statute requires only that Mona be named as an inventor on her application.

[314] Derivation proceedings under the AIA-amended 35 U.S.C. §135 become available on March 16, 2013.

[315]35 U.S.C. §135(a) (eff. Mar. 16, 2013) ("Institution of Proceeding").

[316]*See* 35 U.S.C. §135(a) (eff. Mar. 16, 2013) ("Institution of Proceeding").

in this hypothetical.[317] Alex's petition "shall be made under oath, and shall be supported by substantial evidence."[318] If the USPTO Director determines that a derivation proceeding should be instituted, the proceeding will be conducted by the Patent Trial and Appeal Board.[319]

b.   (B)-Type Exceptions

Like its counterpart in §102(b)(1), the second, or "(B)-type," exception of §102(b)(2) involves two "disclosures" of the same invention. Post-AIA §102(b)(2)(B) provides that "[a] disclosure shall not be prior art to a claimed invention under subsection (a)(2) if . . . (B) the subject matter disclosed had, before such subject matter was effectively filed under subsection (a)(2), been publicly disclosed by the inventor or a joint inventor or another who obtained the subject matter disclosed directly or indirectly from the inventor or a joint inventor."

To illustrate, if (i) an inventor "publicly disclose[s]" his invention, (ii) another individual (referred to hereafter as the "third party") thereafter "disclose[s]" the same subject matter by filing a patent application in the USPTO that names the third party as an inventor and describes the same invention, and (iii) the inventor/first discloser thereafter files his patent application within one year of his (the inventor/first discloser's) public disclosure, then the inventor/first discloser will not be prevented by the third party's description in the third party's application or patent (or by the inventor's own public disclosure) from obtaining a patent.[320] Again, the (B)-type exception of §102(b)(2) illustrates that the AIA implemented what is, at least in part, a "first to disclose" system.

T.   Effective Date for AIA §3 First-Inventor-to-File Amendments

A critical threshold issue for patent practitioners, particularly those preparing to file or already prosecuting patent applications in the

---

[317]*See* 35 U.S.C. §135(a) (eff. Mar. 16, 2013) ("Institution of Proceeding").

[318]*See* 35 U.S.C. §135(a) (eff. Mar. 16, 2013) ("Institution of Proceeding").

[319]*See* 35 U.S.C. §135(b) (eff. Mar. 16, 2013) ("Determination by Patent Trial and Appeal Board").

[320]Although both terms are used in post-AIA §102(b)(2)(B), the statute does not define or explain the difference between "disclosed" and "publicly disclosed." Logically, the unqualified "disclosed" must include the initially secret/confidential filing in the USPTO of the third party's patent application. *See supra* Section Q.3 ("Does the AIA Permit Secret Prior Art?"). Professor Merges analyzes the distinction between "disclosed" and "publicly disclosed" in Robert P. Merges, *Priority and Novelty under the AIA* (August 15, 2012), *available at* SSRN: http://ssrn.com/abstract=2130209 (Part II.B).

T. Effective Date for AIA §3 First-Inventor-to-File Amendments

USPTO during the transition period from pre- to post-AIA regimes, is whether the AIA §3 amendments apply to their applications. Section 3(n) of the AIA controls the issue. Section 3(n) provides that the first-inventor-to-file system implemented by the AIA (as well as its associated new definitions of "prior art") are strictly prospective.[321]

Notably, the AIA does not incorporate the §3(n) transition provision into the text of the Patent Act. The transition provision reads:

> (n) EFFECTIVE DATE.—
> (1) IN GENERAL.—Except as otherwise provided in this section [AIA §3], the amendments made by this section shall take effect upon the expiration of the 18-month period beginning on the date of the enactment of this Act, and shall apply to any application for patent, and to any patent issuing thereon, that contains or contained at any time—
> (A) a claim to a claimed invention that has an effective filing date as defined in section 100(i) of title 35, United States Code, that is on or after the effective date described in this paragraph; or
> (B) a specific reference under section 120, 121, or 365(c) of title 35, United States Code, to any patent or application that contains or contained at any time such a claim.
> (2) INTERFERING PATENTS. . . .[322]

This text interprets the statutory phrase "shall take effect upon the expiration of the 18-month period beginning on the date of the enactment of this Act" to mean that the AIA §3 amendments take

---

[321]Professor Chisum observes that "[t]he 2011 Act makes the change to 'first to file' strictly prospective. The trigger date is 18 months after enactment. Enactment was on September 16, 2011, making the trigger date March 16, 2013. The changes on first-to-file do not apply to patent claims that rely on filing dates before the trigger date (March 16, 2013)." Donald S. Chisum, *America Invents Act of 2011: Analysis and Cross-References*, at 10 (Dec. 5, 2011), *available at* http://www.chisum.com/wp-content/uploads/AIA Overview.pdf.

[322]Leahy-Smith America Invents Act, Pub. L. No. 112-29 (H.R. 1249), §3(n), 125 Stat. 284, 293 (2011). The remaining portion of §3(n)(2) reads:

> (2) INTERFERING PATENTS.—The provisions of sections 102(g), 135, and 291 of title 35, United States Code, as in effect on the day before the effective date set forth in paragraph (1) of this subsection, shall apply to each claim of an application for patent, and any patent issued thereon, for which the amendments made by this section also apply, if such application or patent contains or contained at any time—
> (A) a claim to an invention having an effective filing date as defined in section 100(i) of title 35, United States Code, that occurs before the effective date set forth in paragraph (1) of this subsection; or
> (B) a specific reference under section 120, 121, or 365(c) of title 35, United States Code, to any patent or application that contains or contained at any time such a claim.

effect on March 16, 2013 (i.e., 18 months after the AIA's September 16, 2011, enactment date). In accordance with the two prongs of §3(n)(1), the AIA §3 first-inventor-to-file amendments (to §102 and other sections of the Patent Act) will apply to a patent or patent application in either of two situations: (1) under §3(n)(1)(A), because the effective filing date of a claim contained (at any time) in the patent or patent application is on or after March 16, 2013; or (2) under §3(n)(1)(B), because the patent or application makes a specific type of reference to another patent or application that contained (at any time) a claim having an effective filing date that is on or after March 16, 2013.

Both prongs of the §3(n)(1) transition provision in turn reference the "effective filing date" of a claimed invention in a patent or patent application. The "effective filing date" phrase is defined in the post-AIA Patent Act. As amended by the AIA, 35 U.S.C. §100 provides in pertinent part:

> (i) (1) The term "effective filing date" for a claimed invention in a patent or application for patent means—
> (A) if subparagraph (B) does not apply, the actual filing date of the patent or the application for the patent containing a claim to the invention; or
> (B) the filing date of the earliest application for which the patent or application is entitled, as to such invention, to a right of priority under section 119, 365(a), or 365(b) or to the benefit of an earlier filing date under section 120, 121, or 365(c).
> (2) The effective filing date for a claimed invention in an application for reissue or reissued patent shall be determined by deeming the claim to the invention to have been contained in the patent for which reissue was sought.[323]

Notably, this "effective filing date" definition is applied to "a claimed invention" in a patent or patent application. It is imprecise to refer to the "effective filing date" of the patent or patent application itself. In other words, "'effective filing date' is defined with respect to each claimed invention, rather than the entire patent application or issued patent."[324]

Although they are worded somewhat similarly, it is important to distinguish AIA §3(n), which governs the *effective date* of the AIA first-to-file *legislation*, from §100(i) of the post-AIA Patent Act,

---

[323]35 U.S.C. §100(i) (eff. Mar. 16, 2013).

[324]Joe Matal, *A Guide to the Legislative History of the America Invents Act: Part I of II*, 21 FED. CIR. B.J. 435, 448 (2012). For example, a single patent application or patent could claim more than one invention. As a practical matter, however, this seems unlikely to occur with much frequency due to restriction requirements under 35 U.S.C. §121.

which governs the *effective filing date* for a *claimed invention* in a patent or patent application. Notably, the former is a transition provision that excludes any mention of priority (domestic or foreign) under 35 U.S.C. §119. In practical terms, this means that when the AIA's §3-implemented first-inventor-to-file system goes into effect, it will not have any direct applicability to then-pending U.S. provisional patent applications (dealt with in 35 U.S.C. §119(e)) or foreign priority applications (dealt with in 35 U.S.C. §119(a)). Rather, "[t]he [§3(n)] transition provisions provide that each *nonprovisional* application (and each of that application's *progeny*, defined as any application that at any time made a claim for the benefit of such nonprovisional patent filing) that contained at any time even a single claim with an effective filing date on or after March 16, 2013 (i.e., the effective date for new [post-AIA] §102) is fully subject to new §102."[325]

U. Common Ownership Under Joint Research Agreements

Section 3 of the AIA preserves pre-AIA exclusions or shields of certain commonly owned (or deemed commonly owned) subject matter from being treated as prior art. The AIA expands the exclusions such that they are applicable to the analysis of novelty under 35 U.S.C. §102 as well as nonobviousness under 35 U.S.C. §103. The AIA's legislative history provides that:

> the intent behind the CREATE Act to promote joint research activities is preserved by including a prior art exception for subject matter invented by parties to a joint research agreement. The Act also provides that its enactment of new section 102(c) of title 35 is done with the same intent to promote joint research activities that was expressed in the Cooperative Research and Technology Enhancement Act of 2004 (Public Law 108-453), and that section 102(c) shall be administered in a manner consistent with such intent.[326]

The following background explains the treatment of CREATE Act subject matter in the AIA.

In 1984 Congress amended the patentability requirement of nonobviousness (35 U.S.C. §103) so as to exclude "commonly owned"

---

[325]Robert A. Armitage, *Understanding the America Invents Act and Its Implications for Patenting*, 40 AM. INTELLECTUAL PROP. L. Q.J. 1, 18 n.62 (Winter 2012) (emphasis added).

[326]H.R. Rep. 112-98, at 54 (June 1, 2011).

inventions from the prior art used in nonobviousness analyses.[327] The intent of the 1984 legislation was to shield commonly owned inventions from being rendered obvious by the prior work of other inventors in the same company or firm. In essence, Congress gave corporations the right to patent obvious variants of in-house efforts qualifying as prior art under 35 U.S.C. §102(f) (1984) or 35 U.S.C. §102(g) (1984). In the American Inventors Protection Act of 1999, Congress further expanded the nonobviousness prior art shield to encompass commonly owned prior art under 35 U.S.C. §102(e) (1994).[328] These prior art shields became subsection (c) of 35 U.S.C. §103.

The Cooperative Research and Technology Enhancement (CREATE) Act of 2004 expanded the §103(c) exclusions even more broadly to encompass §§102(e), (f), and (g) prior art that had been earlier generated by the parties to a "joint research agreement" involving the assignees of inventor(s) named in a patent application.[329] Congress was particularly concerned with removing barriers to patenting for collaborative teams encompassing universities and for-profit corporations of the type encouraged by the Bayh-Dole Act of 1980.[330]

The AIA expands the concepts underlying the CREATE Act prior art shield to encompass prior art used in the analysis of novelty under 35 U.S.C. §102 as well as nonobviousness under 35 U.S.C. §103. More specifically, the 35 U.S.C. §103(c) (2006) exclusion of commonly owned subject matter was removed from §103 and transferred to post-AIA

[327]The Patent Law Amendments Act of 1984, Pub. L. No. 98-622 (H.R. 6286) (Nov. 8, 1984), amended the then-in-effect version of 35 U.S.C. §103 by appending to the statute the following sentence: "Subject matter developed by another person, which qualifies as prior art only under subsection (f) or (g) of section 102 of this title, shall not preclude patentability under this section where the subject matter and the claimed invention were, at the time the invention was made, owned by the same person or subject to an obligation of assignment to the same person."

"Commonly owned" means that legal title in both inventions is in the same person (be it a natural person or a firm such as a corporation), or is at least subject to an obligation to assign ownership to the same "person." See 35 U.S.C. §102(c) (eff. Mar. 16, 2013).

[328]See Pub. L. No. 106-113 (H.R. 3194), §4807 (Nov. 29, 1999) (providing that "section 103(c) of title 35, United States Code, is amended by striking 'subsection (f) or (g)' and inserting 'one or more of subsections (e), (f), and (g)'").

[329]See Pub. L. No. 108-453, §2, 118 Stat. 3596 (2004). The CREATE Act added to the Patent Act a definition of "joint research agreement" as "a written contract, grant, or cooperative agreement entered into by two or more persons or entities for the performance of experimental, developmental, or research work in the field of the claimed invention." 35 U.S.C. §103(c)(3) (2006).

[330]The Bayh-Dole Act is codified at 35 U.S.C. §§200-212 (2006).

§102, which defines prior art for anticipation situations as well as obviousness.[331] Post-AIA §102 provides in pertinent part:

(b)(2) DISCLOSURES APPEARING IN APPLICATIONS AND PATENTS.—A disclosure shall not be prior art to a claimed invention under subsection (a)(2) if . . .
(C) the subject matter disclosed and the claimed invention, not later than the effective filing date of the claimed invention, were owned by the same person or subject to an obligation of assignment to the same person.[332]

Moreover, the 35 U.S.C. §103(c) (2006) exclusion of joint research work was likewise removed from §103 and transferred to post-AIA §102,[333] which provides in pertinent part:

(c) COMMON OWNERSHIP UNDER JOINT RESEARCH AGREEMENTS.—Subject matter disclosed and a claimed invention shall be deemed to have been owned by the same person or subject to an obligation of assignment to the same person in applying the provisions of subsection (b)(2)(C) if—
(1) the subject matter disclosed was developed and the claimed invention was made by, or on behalf of, 1 or more parties to a joint research agreement that was in effect on or before the effective filing date of the claimed invention;
(2) the claimed invention was made as a result of activities undertaken within the scope of the joint research agreement; and
(3) the application for patent for the claimed invention discloses or is amended to disclose the names of the parties to the joint research agreement.[334]

In addition to transferring the CREATE Act language to post-AIA §102 of the Patent Act, §3(b) of the AIA also includes this subparagraph (in the nature of a "sense of Congress" provision):

(2) CONTINUITY OF INTENT UNDER THE CREATE ACT.—The enactment of section 102(c) of title 35, United States Code, under paragraph (1) of this subsection is done with the same intent to promote

---

[331]*See* Leahy-Smith America Invents Act, Pub. L. No. 112-29 (H.R. 1249), §3(b)(1), 125 Stat. 284, 286 (Sept. 16, 2011) (amending Patent Act to add 35 U.S.C. §102(b)(2)(C) (eff. Mar. 16, 2013)); *see also* AIA §3(c) (deleting subsection (c) from 35 U.S.C. §103 (2006)).

[332]35 U.S.C. §102(b)(2)(C) (eff. Mar. 16, 2013).

[333]*See* Leahy-Smith America Invents Act, Pub. L. No. 112-29 (H.R. 1249), §3(b)(1), 125 Stat. 284, 286 (Sept. 16, 2011) (amending Patent Act to add 35 U.S.C. §102(c) (eff. Mar. 16, 2013) ("Common Ownership Under Joint Research Agreements")); *see also* AIA §3(c) (deleting subsection (c) from 35 U.S.C. §103 (2006)).

[334]35 U.S.C. §102(c) (eff. Mar. 16, 2013).

joint research activities that was expressed, including in the legislative history, through the enactment of the Cooperative Research and Technology Enhancement Act of 2004 (Public Law 108-453; the "CREATE Act"), the amendments of which are stricken by subsection (c) of this section. The United States Patent and Trademark Office shall administer section 102(c) of title 35, United States Code, in a manner consistent with the legislative history of the CREATE Act that was relevant to its administration by the United States Patent and Trademark Office.[335]

---

[335]Leahy-Smith America Invents Act, Pub. L. No. 112-29 (H.R. 1249), §3(b)(2), 125 Stat. 284, 287 (Sept. 16, 2011).

Chapter 5

The Nonobviousness Requirement (35 U.S.C. §103)

A. Introduction

This chapter considers the ultimate condition of patentability: the requirement that the invention be **nonobvious.** Although not statutorily codified until §103 was enacted in 35 U.S.C. as part of the 1952 Patent Act, this final condition has been recognized in U.S. patent case law since at least 1851, when the Supreme Court articulated in the famous "doorknob case," *Hotchkiss v. Greenwood,*[1] that patentability requires "something more" than novelty. An invention may be technically novel, such that none of the novelty-destroying or loss-of-right provisions of 35 U.S.C. §102 are triggered.[2] But to be patentable, the invention also must represent enough of a qualitative advance over earlier technology to justify what Thomas Jefferson called

---

[1]52 U.S. 248 (1850).

[2]*See* Chapter 4 ("Novelty, Loss of Right, and Priority Pre- and Post-America Invents Act of 2011 (35 U.S.C. §102)"), *supra.* As Chapter 4 describes, §102 of the Patent Act was entirely revised in the America Invents Act of 2011. *See* Leahy-Smith America Invents Act, Pub. L. No. 112-29 (H.R. 1249), §3(b)(1), 125 Stat. 284, 285-286 (2011). The AIA amendments take effect prospectively for patent applications filed on or after March 16, 2013, but applications filed before that date (and patents issuing therefrom) will continue to be assessed under the pre-AIA statutory framework.

An unfortunate aspect of the AIA is that Congress entirely rewrote key provisions of the Patent Act without renumbering many of the statutory sections in Title 35, U.S.C. To maintain clarity and demarcation between old and new, citations in this text to the pre-AIA version of the patent statute (e.g., to §102) typically will take the form "35 U.S.C. §102(x) (pre-AIA)" or "35 U.S.C. §102(x) (2006)." (The 2006 date is used because as of the AIA's enactment in September 2011, the "spine" date of the most recent main edition of 35 U.S.C. was 2006.) In contrast, citations in this text to the patent statute post–AIA implementation will take the form "35 U.S.C. §102(x) (post-AIA)" or "35 U.S.C. §102(x) (eff. Mar. 16, 2013)." For shorthand purposes, sections of the Patent Act will sometimes be referred to herein as "post-AIA §102," meaning the version of 35 U.S.C. §102 that takes effect on March 16, 2013.

"the embarrassment of an exclusive patent."[3] This determination is ultimately a question of public policy, based on underlying factual inquiries[4]—namely, which inventions should be patented and which should not.[5] Although the America Invents Act of 2011 (AIA) amended and eliminated certain parts of 35 U.S.C. §103,[6] the AIA did not change the fundamental analysis for determining whether a claimed invention would have been obvious as described in this chapter.

The introductory clause of 35 U.S.C. §103(a) (2006) states that "[a] patent may not be obtained though the invention is not identically disclosed or described as set forth in section 102 of this title, if . . . . " This qualifying language indicates that nonobviousness is an additional condition that must be satisfied for patentability, even if the invention is not anticipated under one or more subsections of §102 (as discussed in Chapter 4 of this text). The America Invents Act of 2011 did not change this basic principle.[7] The "identically disclosed or described"

---

[3]Graham v. John Deere Co., 383 U.S. 1, 9 (1966) (quoting letter from Thomas Jefferson to Isaac McPherson (Aug. 13, 1813), VI The Writings of Thomas Jefferson, at 181 (H.A. Washington ed. 1854)).

[4]Giles S. Rich, *The Vague Concept of "Invention" as Replaced by Section 103 of the 1952 Act* [the "Kettering Speech"] in Nonobviousness: The Ultimate Condition of Patentablity 1:401 (John F. Witherspoon ed. 1980).

[5]The determination of nonobviousness has similarly been described as "ultimately one of judgment." In re Lee, 277 F.3d 1338, 1345 (Fed. Cir. 2002).

[6]*See* Leahy-Smith America Invents Act, Pub. L. No. 112-29 (H.R. 1249), §3(c), 125 Stat. 284, 287 (2011) (amending the language of 35 U.S.C. §103(a) (2006) and deleting 35 U.S.C. §103(b) (2006) and 35 U.S.C. §103(c) (2006)). With respect to patent applications filed on or after March 16, 2013 and patents issuing therefrom, the statute will provide as follows:

§103. Conditions for patentability; non-obvious subject matter
  A patent for a claimed invention may not be obtained, notwithstanding that the claimed invention is not identically disclosed as set forth in section 102, if the differences between the claimed invention and the prior art are such that the claimed invention as a whole would have been obvious *before the effective filing date of the claimed invention* to a person having ordinary skill in the art to which the claimed invention pertains. Patentability shall not be negated by the manner in which the invention was made.

35 U.S.C. §103 (eff. Mar. 16, 2013) (emphasis added). The emphasized language highlights the primary substantive difference between pre-AIA §103(a) and post-AIA §103. The AIA changed the date for evaluation of an invention's nonobviousness to the date that is "before the effective filing date of the claimed invention," rather than "at the time the invention was made" (i.e., at the invention date, a pre-AIA concept). The AIA also provided a definition of "effective filing date [for a] claimed invention." *See* 35 U.S.C. §100(i) (eff. Mar. 16, 2013). For additional discussion of the AIA and effective filing date, *see supra* Chapter 4, Part III ("Novelty, Loss of Right, and Priority Post-America Invents Act of 2011").

[7]Although the America Invents Act of 2011 amended 35 U.S.C. §103 in several respects, it did not change the substance of the "notwithstanding" phrase of §103. *See* Leahy-Smith America Invents Act, Pub. L. No. 112-29, §3(c), 125 Stat. 284, 287 (2011)

statutory phrase[8] also reinforces that the test for anticipation under 35 U.S.C. §102 is one of "strict identity"; that is, each and every limitation of the claimed invention must be disclosed in a single prior art reference, in order for it to be considered anticipated under §102.[9]

Analyzing nonobviousness is a challenging but frequently encountered task in U.S. patent law. An understanding of the historical development of the nonobviousness requirement will inform the analysis.

B. Historical Context: The *Hotchkiss* "Ordinary Mechanic" and the Requirement for "Invention"

The patentability requirement for something more than novelty was first recognized by the U.S. Supreme Court in *Hotchkiss v. Greenwood,*[10] which addressed the validity of an issued patent that claimed a mechanical combination of doorknob, shank, and spindle. The novel feature of the device was that the doorknob was formed of clay or porcelain. Prior art doorknobs had been made of wood, which was susceptible to warping and cracking, or of metal, which tended to rust from exposure to the elements. The patentee's substitution of materials resulted in a more attractive doorknob, which also was less expensive to manufacture and more durable than conventional doorknobs.

Despite this seemingly significant and beneficial advance in the manufacture of doorknobs, the *Hotchkiss* majority held the patent invalid on the basis that no patentable "invention" resided in the mere substitution of clay for wood:

> But this [substitution], of itself, can never be the subject of a patent. No one will pretend that a machine, made, in whole or in part, of materials better adapted to the purpose for which it is used than the materials of which the old one is constructed, and for that reason better and cheaper,

---

(amending 35 U.S.C. §103 to provide that "[a] patent for a claimed invention may not be obtained, notwithstanding that the claimed invention is not identically disclosed as set forth in section 102, if . . . "). 35 U.S.C. §103 (eff. Mar. 16, 2013). For additional discussion of section 102, *see supra* Chapter 4 ("Novelty, Loss of Right, and Priority Pre- and Post-America Invents Act of 2011 (35 U.S.C. §102)").

[8]For reasons that are unclear, the AIA retained "disclosed" but deleted "described" from the "notwithstanding" phrase. *See* Leahy-Smith America Invents Act, Pub. L. No. 112-29, §3(c), 125 Stat. 284, 287 (2011) (amending 35 U.S.C. §103 to provide that "[a] patent for a claimed invention may not be obtained, notwithstanding that the claimed invention is not identically disclosed as set forth in section 102, if . . . "). 35 U.S.C. §103 (eff. Mar. 16, 2013).

[9]*See supra* Chapter 4, Section C for details of the strict identity standard for anticipation.

[10]52 U.S. 248 (1850).

can be distinguished from the old one; or, in the sense of the patent law, can entitle the manufacturer to a patent.

The difference is formal, and *destitute of ingenuity or invention.* It may afford evidence of judgment and skill in the selection and adaptation of the materials in the manufacture of the instrument for the purposes intended, but nothing more.[11]

With these words, the Supreme Court's *Hotchkiss* decision gave rise to a vague and ambiguous requirement for "invention," representing some abstract, elusive quality beyond mere novelty. This ill-defined term of art proved incapable of precise application; the Court later observed in circular fashion that "the truth is the word ['invention'] cannot be defined in such manner as to afford any substantial aid in determining whether a particular device involves an exercise of the inventive faculty or not."[12] In short, to be patentable, an invention had to involve invention!

The lower courts, struggling to apply the *Hotchkiss* formulation, devised various tests and rules for what did, and did not, qualify as invention.[13] The nebulous concept of invention became "the plaything of the judiciary."[14] Impractical as the terminology was, it took firm root in the patent law lexicon and was not finally banished for over 100 years following *Hotchkiss.* In the 1952 Act, the notion of invention was finally replaced by the modern concept of nonobviousness, the analysis of which is detailed below.

While the terminology it espoused is now seen as outdated and inaccurate, *Hotchkiss v. Greenwood* nevertheless remains fundamental to our understanding of the *perspective* from which the requirement for nonobviousness is to be judged. The Supreme Court in *Hotchkiss* made clear that an invention created with no more skill or ingenuity than that possessed by an "ordinary mechanic," working in the field of the invention, was not deserving of a patent:

[U]nless more ingenuity and skill in applying the old method of fastening the shank and the knob were required in the application of it to the

---

[11]*Hotchkiss,* 52 U.S. at 266 (emphasis added).

[12]Graham v. John Deere, 383 U.S. 1, 11-12 (1966) (quoting McClain v. Ortmayer, 141 U.S. 419, 427 (1891); Great Atl. & Pac. Tea Co. v. Supermarket Equip. Corp., 340 U.S. 147, 151 (1950)). The great patent jurist Learned Hand observed that the question whether a patentable "invention" exists is "as fugitive, impalpable, wayward, and vague a phantom as exists in the whole paraphernalia of legal concepts." Harries v. Air King Prods. Co., 183 F.2d 158, 162 (2d Cir. 1950) (Hand, C.J.).

[13]*See* 2-5 DONALD S. CHISUM, CHISUM ON PATENTS §5.02 (2008) (summarizing cases that held that neither a "change in form, proportions, or degree," nor "a mere aggregation of elements," could constitute patentable "invention").

[14]Giles S. Rich, *Why and How Section 103 Came to Be, in* NONOBVIOUSNESS: THE ULTIMATE CONDITION OF PATENTABLITY 1:208 (John F. Witherspoon ed., 1980).

clay or porcelain knob than were possessed by *an ordinary mechanic
acquainted with the business,* there was an absence of that degree of skill
and ingenuity which constitute essential elements of every invention. In
other words, the improvement is the work of the skillful mechanic, not
that of the inventor.[15]

The *Hotchkiss* "ordinary mechanic" metaphor proved useful as a
reference point for determining patentability, and can today be understood as the historic ancestor of the latter-day hypothetical **person
having ordinary skill in the art** (PHOSITA) currently reflected
in 35 U.S.C. §103. To qualify for a patent under this statutory provision, an invention must not have been obvious to this hypothetical
person, possessed of "ordinary skill" in the art (i.e., the technology) of
the invention, at a particular past point in time. Under pre-AIA rules,
the date in question is the time that the invention was made[16] (i.e., at
the "invention date"[17]). Under post-AIA rules, the date in question is
"before the effective filing date of the claimed invention."[18]

The PHOSITA perspective ensures that nonobviousness under 35
U.S.C. §103 is not judged from the subjective viewpoint of a judge, jury,
patent attorney, USPTO patent examiner, or the named inventor of
the patent at issue. Rather, the decision maker must step backward
in time, into the shoes (and the mind) of the PHOSITA, and make an
objective decision about patentability based on the prior art available
at that time. The claims of the patent or application under consideration cannot be used as a blueprint that, in hindsight, may make the
solution to the inventor's problem appear trivial. This is an admittedly
challenging mental gymnastics exercise, but §103 and the Supreme
Court's interpretation thereof in the landmark case of *Graham v.
John Deere,*[19] discussed below, provide the analytical roadmap to be
followed.

---

[15]*Hotchkiss*, 52 U.S. at 267 (emphasis added).

[16]*See* 35 U.S.C. §103(a) (2006).

[17]As explained in Part II of Chapter 4 ("Novelty, Loss of Right, and Priority Pre- and
Post-America Invents Act of 2011 (35 U.S.C. §102)"), *supra*, under pre-AIA rules a patent's filing date is presumptively the "invention date" of the subject matter claimed
therein, under a constructive reduction to practice theory. However, an inventor may
establish an invention date earlier than his filing date by establishing either (1) the
date of his actual reduction to practice, assuming he did not thereafter abandon, suppress, or conceal his invention; or (2) the date of his conception, if coupled with sufficient diligence in working toward his eventual reduction to practice. *See* 35 U.S.C.
§102(g) (2006).

Congress removed the concept of invention dates from the text of the post-AIA
Patent Act, although invention date principles such as conception will likely continue
to be relevant in post-AIA derivation proceedings under 35 U.S.C. 135 (eff. Mar. 16,
2013).

[18]35 U.S.C. §103 (eff. Mar. 16, 2013).

[19]383 U.S. 1 (1966).

C. Enactment of §103 of the Patent Act of 1952, Incorporating the Requirement of Nonobviousness

In its pre-AIA form, 35 U.S.C. §103 consists of three subsections. Our primary focus is §103(a) (2006), which applies to all types of inventions.[20] Subsection 103(a) provides,

> A patent may not be obtained though the invention is not identically disclosed or described as set forth in section 102 of this title, if the differences between the subject matter sought to be patented and the prior art are such that the subject matter as a whole would have been obvious at the time the invention was made to a person having ordinary skill in the art to which said subject matter pertains. Patentability shall not be negatived by the manner in which the invention was made.[21]

This statutory language was included in the 1952 Patent Act at the behest of its co-authors, Giles Rich and Pasquale Federico. The language reflects the frustration of the patent bar with the traditional invention standard of *Hotchkiss,* which proved so vague and ambiguous as to be unworkable. Judges in different courts around the United

---

[20]The remaining subsections of 35 U.S.C. §103 (2006) are of more recent vintage, and much more narrow in focus. Subsection 103(b) (2006) concerns biotechnological processes, and §103(c) (2006) addresses the "in-house prior art" problem as well as issues specific to "joint research agreements," both of which are discussed *infra* Section F.3.

[21]35 U.S.C. §103(a) (2006). The America Invents Act of 2011 amended 35 U.S.C. §103 in several respects. *See* Leahy-Smith America Invents Act, Pub. L. No. 112-29, §3(c), 125 Stat. 284, 287 (2011) (amending 35 U.S.C. §103 by, *inter alia*, changing the date on which nonobviousness is evaluated and deleting §§103(b) and (c)). Effective for applications filed on or after March 16, 2013 and patents issuing therefrom, the statute will provide as follows:

§103. Conditions for patentability; non-obvious subject matter

A patent for a claimed invention may not be obtained, notwithstanding that the claimed invention is not identically disclosed as set forth in section 102, if the differences between the claimed invention and the prior art are such that the claimed invention as a whole would have been obvious *before the effective filing date of the claimed invention* to a person having ordinary skill in the art to which the claimed invention pertains. Patentability shall not be negated by the manner in which the invention was made.

35 U.S.C. §103 (eff. Mar. 16, 2013) (emphasis added). The italicized language emphasizes the primary difference between pre-AIA §103(a) and post-AIA §103. The AIA changed the evaluation date for nonobviousness to the date that is "before the effective filing date of the claimed invention," rather than evaluating nonobvious "at the time the invention was made" (i.e., at the invention date, a pre-AIA concept). The "effective filing date [for a] claimed invention" is defined at 35 U.S.C. §100(i) (eff. Mar. 16, 2013). For additional discussion, *see supra* Part III of Chapter 4 ("Novelty, Loss of Right, and Priority Pre- and Post-America Invents Act of 2011 (35 U.S.C. §102)").

States came to treat "invention" somewhat like obscenity, by applying an I-know-it-when-I-see-it type of analysis, devoid of common guidelines or uniform analytical framework. After extensive lobbying Rich, Federico, and others convinced Congress to enact legislation that would effectively abolish invention as a condition of patentability and replace it with a statutory requirement for nonobviousness. Thus, §103 provides the modern-day counterpart to the *Hotchkiss* requirement for invention.

The last sentence of 35 U.S.C. §103(a) (2006) provides that "[p]atentability shall not be negatived by the manner in which the invention was made."[22] This simply means that an invention is no more obvious because it results from painstaking, long-running toil than from a "Eureka!" moment. In other words, the way in which an invention was created cannot negate patentability. The drafters of the 1952 Act included this statutory language with the intent of legislatively overruling earlier statements by the Supreme Court that appeared to require a "flash of genius" for patentability.[23]

D.   The *Graham v. John Deere* Framework for Analyzing Nonobviousness

In 1966, almost 15 years after Congress's enactment of 35 U.S.C. §103, the U.S. Supreme Court for the first time had occasion to interpret and apply the statutory language in the course of deciding two companion cases that involved relatively humble technology. The patent in suit in *Graham v. John Deere Co.*[24] was directed to a type of shock-absorber system for a plow shank, while the patent at issue in *Calmar, Inc. v. Cook Chem. Co.*[25] covered a protective cap for shipping spray bottles containing liquids. After surveying the history of the U.S.

---

[22]For reasons that are unclear, the drafters of the America Invents Act of 2011 changed "negatived" to "negated." *See* Leahy-Smith America Invents Act, Pub. L. No. 112-29, §3(c), 125 Stat. 284, 287 (2011); 35 U.S.C. §103 (eff. Mar. 16, 2013) (stating in last sentence that "[p]atentability shall not be negated by the manner in which the invention was made").

[23]*See* Reviser's Notes, 35 U.S.C.A. §103 (1952) (noting that "[t]he second sentence states that patentability as to this requirement is not to be negatived by the manner in which the invention was made, that is, it is immaterial whether it resulted from long toil and experimentation or from a flash of genius"). The earlier Supreme Court cases of concern to the drafters of the 1952 Act include *Cuno Eng'g Corp. v. Automatic Devices Corp.*, 314 U.S. 84, 91 (1941) (stating that to be patentable, "the new device, however useful it may be, must reveal the flash of creative genius, not merely the skill of the calling"); and *Great Atl. & Pac. Tea Co. v. Supermarket Equip. Corp.*, 340 U.S. 147, 155 n.1 (1950) (citing *Cuno*).

[24]383 U.S. 1 (1966).

[25]*Id.* (companion case).

patent system and its concomitant development of the nonobviousness requirement, the Court held both patents invalid as obvious under §103. The Court's appraisal of the particular technologies involved is ultimately much less important, however, than the *Graham* opinion's generalized analytical guidance for determining the issue of nonobviousness. For this reason *Graham* is a landmark opinion, worthy of close study by all students of patent law.

1.   Constitutionality of 35 U.S.C. §103

With respect to the degree of ingenuity or quality of advance (i.e., in the older terminology, the degree of "invention") required for patentability under §103, the Court in *Graham v. John Deere* held that the statutory enactment did not signal any change in substance from the existing standard. Thus, the statute was constitutional as a permissible application of Congress's power to promote the progress of the "useful arts,"[26] and was not a derogation of that responsibility.

Section 103 was merely intended to "codify judicial precedents embracing the principle long ago announced by this Court in *Hotchkiss v. Greenwood,* 11 How. 248 (1851)...,"[27] the Supreme Court explained. The enactment of §103 represented to the *Graham* Court simply a semantic shift in terms of greater focus on nonobviousness, rather than a change in the "general level of innovation necessary to sustain patentability."[28] The fundamental message of *Hotchkiss*—its functional approach to determining patentability—had not changed:

> The *Hotchkiss* formulation ... lies not in any label, but in its functional approach to questions of patentability. In practice, *Hotchkiss* has required a comparison between the subject matter of the patent, or patent application, and the background skill of the calling. It has been from this comparison that patentability was in each case determined.[29]

The *Graham* Court concluded that §103's "emphasis on nonobviousness is one of inquiry, not quality, and, as such, comports with the constitutional strictures."[30]

---

[26]U.S. CONST., art. I, §8, cl. 8. The *Graham* Court characterized the Intellectual Property Clause of the Constitution as both a grant of power and a limit thereon. Congress cannot establish a legal system in which patents can be attained for technology that is already in the public domain, or that is a merely obvious extension thereof. *See Graham*, 383 U.S. at 1.

[27]383 U.S. at 3-4.

[28]*Id.* at 4.

[29]*Id.* at 12.

[30]*Id.* at 17.

2.   *Graham*'s Analytical Framework for a §103 Analysis

Turning to the details of applying the 35 U.S.C. §103 standard, the Supreme Court in *Graham* explained that nonobviousness is ultimately a question of law, the answer to which depends on several underlying factual inquiries. These factual inquiries, referred to thereafter by patent attorneys as the *Graham* factors, must be answered in any determination of nonobviousness, whether made in the USPTO or by the courts. The classic summation of these factors from the *Graham* decision is as follows:

> While the ultimate question of patent validity is one of law, *Great A. & P. Tea Co. v. Supermarket Equipment Corp.*, . . . , the §103 condition, which is but one of three conditions, each of which must be satisfied, lends itself to several basic factual inquiries. Under §103, the scope and content of the prior art are to be determined; differences between the prior art and the claims at issue are to be ascertained; and the level of ordinary skill in the pertinent art resolved. Against this background, the obviousness or nonobviousness of the subject matter is determined. Such secondary considerations as commercial success, long felt but unsolved needs, failure of others, etc., might be utilized to give light to the circumstances surrounding the origin of the subject matter sought to be patented. As indicia of obviousness or nonobviousness, these inquiries may have relevancy. *See* Note, Subtests of "Nonobviousness": A Nontechnical Approach to Patent Validity, 112 U. Pa. L. Rev. 1169 (1964).[31]

With these words, the Supreme Court gleaned from 35 U.S.C. §103 the following four factors that are essential to every nonobviousness analysis:

(1) level of ordinary skill in the art;
(2) scope and content of the prior art;
(3) differences between the claimed invention and the prior art; and
(4) secondary considerations (i.e., objective indicia of nonobviousness).

Each of these *Graham* factors is discussed separately below.

E.   *Graham* Factor: Level of Ordinary Skill in the Art

In litigation challenging a patent's validity under 35 U.S.C. §103, both parties will typically introduce evidence (often in the form of

---

[31]*Id.* at 17-18 (citation omitted).

expert witness testimony) attempting to establish the level of ordinary skill in the technology of the invention. It is from this perspective and skill set, possessed by the hypothetical PHOSITA, that the question of nonobviousness must be resolved.[32] The proponent of validity usually will attempt to establish as low a level of ordinary skill as possible, such that the invention would have been considered nonobvious by the largest possible number of persons, while the challenger of validity typically will seek to raise that level.[33]

In making a finding on the level of ordinary skill in the art, courts or juries will take into consideration some or all of the following types of evidence:[34]

- education level of the inventor;
- education level of a typical worker in this field (e.g., whether the PHOSITA would have a high school degree, college undergraduate degree, or graduate degree such as a master's or Ph.D.);
- type of problems encountered in this technology and previous solutions to such problems;
- how quickly new innovation occurs in this technology; and
- sophistication of the technology (i.e., is the invention a fishing lure or a method of cloning a gene?).

The educational level and expertise of the *inventor* do not necessarily equate to the level of ordinary skill of a hypothetical PHOSITA, for the inventor may (or may not) be a person of extraordinary skill. Nevertheless, the inventors' qualifications played a central role in the nonobviousness analysis in *Daiichi Sankyo Co. v. Apotex, Inc.*[35] Validity challenger Apotex convinced the Federal Circuit that a district court's

---

[32]*See* Kloster Speedsteel AB v. Crucible, Inc., 793 F.2d 1565, 1574 (Fed. Cir. 1986) (explaining that "[t]he primary value in the requirement that level of skill be found lies in its tendency to focus the mind of the decisionmaker away from what would presently be obvious to that decisionmaker and toward what would, when the invention was made, have been obvious, as the statute requires, 'to one of ordinary skill in the art'").

[33]*See, e.g.*, Ryko Mfg. Co. v. Nu-Star, Inc., 950 F.2d 714, 718 (Fed. Cir. 1991) (noting that "[a]ppellee's [accused infringer's] evidence shows that most of the personnel developing the new activation device for [patentee] Ryko had attained an engineering degree at the minimum. However, appellant's [patentee's] expert vaguely described the level of ordinary skill in the art as being 'low to medium.'"); Stratoflex, Inc. v. Aeroquip Corp., 713 F.2d 1530, 1538 (Fed. Cir. 1983) (rejecting patentee's contention that level of ordinary skill was too high).

[34]*See* Envtl. Designs, Ltd. v. Union Oil Co., 713 F.2d 693, 696 (Fed. Cir. 1983).

[35]501 F.3d 1254 (Fed. Cir. 2007). The *Daiichi* court's emphasis on the skill level of the inventors is difficult to square with the Supreme Court's observation that "[t]he question is not whether [an invention] was obvious to the patentee but whether [the invention] was obvious to a person with ordinary skill in the art." KSR Int'l Co. v. Teleflex Inc., 127 S. Ct. 1727, 1742 (2007).

determination of the level of ordinary skill was too low, and that this error permeated the lower court's ultimate conclusion of nonobviousness. The Federal Circuit's reversal in *Daiichi* turned on its conclusion that the district court had clearly erred in finding too low a level of ordinary skill in the pertinent art.[36] According to the Federal Circuit, that error tainted the entirety of the district court's nonobviousness analysis.[37]

Daiichi's patent addressed the problem of creating a topical antibiotic compound for treatment of ear infections that would not risk damage to the ear.[38] Claim 1 recited "[a] method for treating otopathy which comprises the topical otic administration of an amount of ofloxacin or a salt thereof effective to treat otopathy in a pharmaceutically acceptable carrier to the area affected with otopathy."[39] The district court found that a hypothetical person of ordinary skill in the art pertinent to this invention would have had a medical degree, experience treating patients with ear infections, and basic knowledge about pharmacology and the use of antibiotics. Such a person would have been a pediatrician or general practitioner, doctors who are often the "'first line of defense'" in treating ear infections.[40]

The Federal Circuit disagreed, concluding that the person of ordinary skill in the art would have been a specialist in the treatment of ear disease with advanced knowledge of pharmacology. Deeming the district court's contrary finding clearly erroneous, the Federal Circuit found that "[t]he level of ordinary skill in the art of the [ ] patent is that of a person engaged in developing pharmaceutical formulations and treatment methods for the ear or a specialist in ear treatments such as an otologist, otolaryngologist, or otorhinolaryngologist who also has training in pharmaceutical formulations."[41]

---

[36]The Supreme Court in *Graham v. John Deere*, 383 U.S. 1 (1966), enumerated the "level of ordinary skill in the pertinent art" as one of the four factors underlying an analysis of nonobviousness. *See id.* at 17-18. The Federal Circuit in *Daiichi* initially referred to this factor as "the level of ordinary skill in the *prior* art," 501 F.3d at 1256 (emphasis added), but elsewhere in its opinion referred more generally to "the level of ordinary skill in the art." *See id.* at 1257 (concluding that "the level of ordinary skill in the art of the '741 patent is that of a person engaged in developing pharmaceutical formulations and treatment methods for the ear . . . who also has training in pharmaceutical formulations").

[37]*Id.* at 1257.

[38]*See id. See also* U.S. Patent No. 5,401,741 (issued Mar. 28, 1995).

[39]*Daiichi*, 501 F.3d at 1255-1256. The district court interpreted the claim term "otopathy" as meaning "bacterial ear infection" and the claim phrase "effective to treat" as meaning "safe and efficacious." Daiichi Pharm. Co. v. Apotex, Inc., 441 F. Supp. 2d 672, 677 n.7 (D.N.J. 2006).

[40]*Daiichi*, 501 F.3d at 1256 (quoting district court's Claim Construction Order).

[41]*Id.* at 1257. The Federal Circuit's opinion blurs what should have been a brighter analytical line between inventing a chemical compound and discerning new uses for a known compound. Daiichi's '741 patent in suit claimed a method of treatment using

Chapter 5. The Nonobviousness Requirement (35 U.S.C. §103)

Although the Federal Circuit enumerated several factors relevant to the determination of ordinary level of skill in the art,[42] the dispositive factor in *Daiichi* was the level of skill of the inventors.[43] The patent's inventors were specialists, not generalists: a university professor specializing in otorhinolaryngology plus two Daiichi employees, one a clinical development department manager and another a research scientist.[44] The patent described the inventors' tests of ofloxacin on guinea pigs to ensure that the antibiotic did not cause ear damage; "[s]uch animal testing is traditionally outside the realm of a general practitioner or pediatrician," according to the Federal Circuit.[45]

The Federal Circuit's ultimate conclusion of obviousness in *Daiichi* turned primarily on the disclosure of a prior art reference by Ganz. The Ganz reference was directed to the use of ciprofloxacin, known commercially as CIPRO, in treating ear infections. Ciprofloxacin, like ofloxacin, is a type of gyrase inhibitor.[46] Ganz taught that the use of ciprofloxacin in ear drops was not subject to problems like ototoxicity that normally accompany local treatment of the ear with antibiotics. However, Ganz also referred to gyrase inhibitors (such as ciprofloxacin)

---

the compound ofloxacin, not the compound itself. Daiichi had previously claimed the compound ofloxacin in a separate, already-expired patent. *See* Benzoxazine derivatives, U.S. Patent No. 4,382,892 (issued May 10, 1983). The Federal Circuit's opinion mistakenly refers to the invention of the '741 patent in suit as "the claimed compound." *Daiichi*, 501 F.3d at 1257 (stating that "while a general practitioner or pediatrician could (and would) prescribe the invention of the '741 patent to treat ear infections, he would not have the training or knowledge *to develop the claimed compound* absent some specialty training such as that possessed by the '741 patent's inventors") (emphasis added).

[42]The *Daiichi* court quoted the following passage from *Envtl. Designs, Ltd. v. Union Oil Co.,* 713 F.2d 693 (Fed. Cir. 1983):

Factors that may be considered in determining level of ordinary skill in the art include: (1) the educational level of the inventor; (2) type of problems encountered in the art; (3) prior art solutions to those problems; (4) rapidity with which innovations are made; (5) sophistication of the technology; and (6) educational level of active workers in the field.

Daiichi, 501 F.3d at 1256 (quoting *Envtl. Designs*, 713 F.2d at 696 (citing Orthopedic Equip. Co. v. All Orthopedic Appliances, Inc., 707 F.2d 1376, 1381-1382 (Fed. Cir.1983))). The listed factors are "not exhaustive but are merely a guide to determining the level of ordinary skill in the art." *Daiichi*, 501 F.3d at 1256.

[43]The Federal Circuit also stated that "others working in the same field as the inventors of the [] patent were of the same skill level," *Daiichi*, 501 F.3d at 1257, but the court's support for this finding is slim. It cites only a set of Daiichi conference materials, which stated that "there are many voices among medical persons concerned with otorhinolaryngology for demanding development of an otic solution making use of [ofloxacin]." *Id.*

[44]*Id.* at 1257.

[45]*Id.* The Federal Circuit cited no support for this finding.

[46]*Id.* at 1258.

as "second choice" antibiotics.[47] According to Ganz, gyrase inhibitors should be "used only in difficult cases and exclusively by the otologist."[48] The district court viewed Ganz as teaching away from the claimed invention, as well as a document directed only to specialists rather than general practitioners.[49]

The Federal Circuit determined that the district court's erroneous finding on the level of ordinary skill led it to improperly discount Ganz. The Federal Circuit also rejected the district court's reliance on the testimony of the patentee's expert that it was not safe to extrapolate the safety profile of one antibiotic to another. The Federal Circuit found this testimony "conclusory" and "unsupported," but did not further explain its negative evaluation.

The Federal Circuit first issued *Daiichi* as a non-precedential decision, but reissued it with precedential status in September 2007.[50] Taken in tandem with the Supreme Court's April 2007 exposition on the nonobviousness requirement in *KSR Int'l Co. v. Teleflex, Inc.*,[51] further discussed *infra*,[52] the elevation of *Daiichi* to precedential status suggests that the "level of ordinary skill in the pertinent art" *Graham* factor may henceforth merit a more detailed analysis. The level-of-skill factor is also likely to provide increased fodder for litigation challenging patents for obviousness.[53]

[47]Daiichi Pharm. Co. v. Apotex, Inc., 441 F. Supp. 2d 672, 689 (D.N.J. 2006) (stating that "Ganz also notes, however, that gyrase inhibitors such as [c]iprofloxacin are antibiotics of second choice.").

[48]*Daiichi*, 501 F.3d at 1258.

[49]*Daiichi*, 441 F. Supp. 2d at 689 (stating that "Ganz adds that for local treatment in the ear gyrase inhibitors 'should be used only in difficult cases and exclusively by the otologist.' (*Id.*). Therefore Ganz's disclosure does not support Apotex's argument that a person ordinarily skilled in the art would know that the use of ofloxacin, a gyrase inhibitor, to treat bacterial ear infections topically is both efficacious and safe."). The concept of a prior art reference "teaching away" from a claimed invention is further discussed in Section I.3 of this chapter.

[50]*See Daiichi*, 501 F.3d at 1254 (stating that court's non-precedential opinion issued on July 11, 2007, and its precedential opinion issued on September 12, 2007).

[51]127 S. Ct. 1727 (2007).

[52]*See infra* Section I.2 ("*KSR v. Teleflex*: Combinations, Predictability, and 'Common Sense'").

[53]*See Daiichi*, 501 F.3d at 1257 (describing *Merck & Co. v. Teva Pharm. USA, Inc.*, 347 F.3d 1367 (Fed. Cir. 2003), as a case in which "the level of skill in the art was not disputed by the parties"). The Federal Circuit in *Merck* affirmed a district court's finding that the level of ordinary skill in the art pertinent to a claimed method of treating patients with osteoporosis was that of an M.D. with experience treating such patients. *See Daiichi*, 501 F.3d at 1257. The Federal Circuit faulted the district court in *Daiichi* for relying on *Merck* (the only Federal Circuit decision on point) because "the level of skill in the art was not disputed by the parties in that case." *Id.*

F. *Graham* Factor: Scope and Content of the Prior Art

1. Terminology

A term of art in patent law, the phrase **prior art** can be understood at a very basic level as the legally available technology and information with which the claimed invention will be compared in order to determine whether that invention is patentable. Which categories of technology and information are "legally available" for use as prior art in a §103 analysis is governed by the criteria of 35 U.S.C. §102, as well as the notion of **analogous art.** These concepts are detailed below. Prior art documents such as patents and printed publications are typically referred to as **references.**

2. Sources of Prior Art

In evaluating the "scope and content of the prior art" *Graham* factor, the USPTO and the courts may obtain the prior art from several different sources. In a typical USPTO *ex parte* patent prosecution, the patent applicant will submit relevant prior art of which it is aware in the form of an "Information Disclosure Statement."[54] In addition, the examiner will conduct her own independent search of the prior art accessible to the USPTO. All of this prior art will become part of the official prosecution history file for the patent in question, the contents of which will be publicly available once the patent issues (if not sooner[55]).

If an issued patent's validity is being challenged in federal court, the accused infringer (i.e., the challenger of validity) will introduce into evidence the prior art it seeks to have considered. Typically this prior art will include newly discovered prior art, that is, prior art documents or events that were not known to or considered by the USPTO during the initial examination of the patent application but that have been unearthed through the litigation discovery process. Introduction of such "new" prior art, which may be more pertinent than that considered by the USPTO, does not weaken the patent's presumption of validity. Such introduction can nevertheless facilitate the validity

---

[54]*See* 37 C.F.R. §1.98 (2008) ("Content of Information Disclosure Statement"). Under 37 C.F.R. §1.56 ("Rule 56"), the applicant is obligated to disclose to the USPTO all known information that is material to patentability, as defined by the rule. Failure to do so may result in a finding of inequitable conduct and resulting unenforceability of the patent.

[55]The USPTO now makes copies of the prosecution histories of patent applications available to the public, for a fee, on or after the time when it publishes the applications under 35 U.S.C. §122(b). *See* http://www.uspto.gov/web/offices/dcom/olia/aipa/18monthfaq.htm#ca (last visited Apr. 10, 2008).

challenger's carrying of its burden to prove invalidity by clear and convincing evidence, for it would require the patentee to come forward with countervailing evidence.[56]

3. Section 102/103 Overlap

Section 103 of 35 U.S.C. does not define the meaning of prior art as used in that section. Again, case law and legislative history fill the gap. These sources make clear that 35 U.S.C. §102, the statutory provision that governs novelty, loss of right, and priority,[57] is key to determining the scope of the prior art properly available in a *Graham* analysis under §103. Section 102 can be conceptualized as a catalog of the universe of information that may potentially qualify as prior art for purposes of a §103 nonobviousness analysis. In other words, any reference relied on in determining nonobviousness must qualify as prior art under one or more subsections of §102 (except that the strict identity condition for anticipation[58] is relaxed in the §103 obviousness context). As stated by a co-author of the 1952 Act, "[t]he antecedent of the words 'the prior art,' which here appear in a statute [§103] for the first time, lies in the phrase 'disclosed or described as set forth in section 102' and hence these words refer to material specified in section 102 as the basis for comparison."[59] These principles continue to apply whether nonobviousness is being analyzed under pre– or post–America Invents Act of 2011 rules.[60]

Originally, only §102(a) (2006) prior art (most typically printed publications or patents issued before the applicant's filing date (presumptively the applicant's invention date under pre-AIA rules)) was considered appropriate for use in combination to form §103 obviousness rejections. No concern about the use of "secret" prior art existed because such information would clearly have been published or otherwise available to the PHOSITA on or before her invention date.[61] For

---

[56]Stratoflex, Inc. v. Aeroquip Corp., 713 F.2d 1530, 1534 (Fed. Cir. 1983).

[57]Section 102 is discussed in greater detail in Chapter 4 ("Novelty, Loss of Right, and Priority Pre- and Post-America Invents Act of 2011 (35 U.S.C. §102)"), *supra*.

[58]*See supra* Chapter 4, Section C ("The Strict Identity Rule of Anticipation").

[59]P.J. Federico, *Commentary on the New Patent Act*, 35 U.S.C.A. §1 (1954 ed., discontinued in subsequent volumes), *reprinted in* 75 J. Pat. & Trademark Off. Soc'y 161, 180 (1993).

[60]The post-AIA version of §103 continues to refer to situations in which a claimed invention "is not identically disclosed as set forth in section 102 . . . . " 35 U.S.C. §103 (eff. Mar. 16, 2013).

[61]*See* OddzOn Prods., Inc. v. Just Toys, Inc., 122 F.3d 1396, 1402 (Fed. Cir. 1997) (noting that "[i]t has been a basic principle of patent law, subject to minor exceptions, that prior art is 'technology already available to the public'") (quoting Kimberly-Clark Corp. v. Johnson & Johnson, 745 F.2d 1437, 1453 (Fed. Cir. 1984)).

example, if a patent application claim recited "a gizmo comprising X and Y," the USPTO examiner might enter a §103 obviousness rejection by contending that the PHOSITA would have been motivated to make the claimed invention in view of the combined disclosures of element X in a gizmo depicted in a first §102(a) (2006) printed publication (having an effective date prior to the applicant's invention date, a pre-AIA concept[62]), with element Y in a gizmo described in a second §102(a) (2006) printed publication (also having an effective date prior to the applicant's invention date).

The categories of §102 prior art that are available for use in a §103 obviousness rejection are no longer so limited, however. A series of judicial decisions subsequently held that other categories of §102 prior art beyond §102(a) (2006)—namely information (i.e., documentation or events) qualifying under subsections §102(b) (2006),[63] §102(e) (2006),[64] §102(f) (2006),[65] and §102(g)

---

[62]*See supra* Chapter 4 ("Novelty, Loss of Right, and Priority Pre- and Post-America Invents Act of 2011 (35 U.S.C. §102)") for further discussion of invention dates.

[63]In re Foster, 343 F.2d 980, 988 (C.C.P.A. 1965).

The AIA rewrote §102(b) in its entirety, *see* Leahy-Smith America Invents Act, Pub. L. No. 112-29 (H.R. 1249), §3(b)(1), 125 Stat. 284, 285-286 (2011), but retained "exceptions" that are somewhat similar to the pre-AIA §102(b) grace period. The AIA "exceptions" are limited, however, to disclosures made by the inventor (or one who obtained the disclosed subject matter from the inventor) in the year preceding an invention's effective filing date. *See* 35 U.S.C. §102(b)(1) (eff. Mar. 16, 2013) ("Disclosures Made 1 Year or Less Before the Effective Filing Date of the Claimed Invention"); 35 U.S.C. §102(b)(2) (eff. Mar. 16, 2013) ("Disclosures Appearing in Applications and Patents"). For further discussion, *see infra* Chapter 4, Section S ("Novelty-Preserving Exceptions Under Post-AIA 35 U.S.C. §102(b)").

[64]Hazeltine Research, Inc. v. Brenner, 382 U.S. 252 (1965).

The America Invents Act of 2011 eliminated 35 U.S.C. §102(e) (2006) but retained the concept of prior art including the content of earlier-filed patents or published applications. *See* 35 U.S.C. §102(a)(2) (eff. Mar. 16, 2013). For further discussion, *see supra* Chapter 4, Section R ("Presumptively Novelty-Destroying Events Under Post-AIA 35 U.S.C. §102(a)(2)").

[65]*OddzOn*, 122 F.3d at 1396.

The America Invents Act of 2011 eliminated 35 U.S.C. §102(f) (2006), *see* Leahy-Smith America Invents Act, Pub. L. No. 112-29 (H.R. 1249), §3(b)(1), 125 Stat. 284, 285-286 (2011), but retained the requirement of originality that was reflected by §102(f). Specifically, the AIA did not change the requirement that, subject to certain exceptions, patent applications shall be made "by the inventor," 35 U.S.C. §111(a)(1) (2006), and the AIA added a definition of "inventor" as "the individual or, if a joint invention, the individuals collectively who inventoried or discovered the subject matter of the invention." 35 U.S.C. §100(f) (eff. Mar. 16, 2013); Leahy-Smith America Invents Act, Pub. L. No. 112-29 (H.R. 1249), §3(a)(2), 125 Stat. 284, 285 (2011). The AIA also continued the requirement that a patent applicant's oath include a statement that the applicant believes he is an "original" inventor. *See* 35 U.S.C. §115 (2006) (requiring that "[t]he applicant shall make oath that he believes himself to be the original and first inventor of the process, machine, manufacture, or composition of matter, or improvement thereof, for which he solicits a patent") (emphasis added); 35 U.S.C. §115(b)(2) (eff. Mar. 16, 2013) (providing

(2006)[66] of 35 U.S.C.—are legally available as the prior art that can be combined for purposes of making a §103 obviousness rejection.

For example, consider a third party's sale of a product more than one year before the applicant's filing date, which product was similar to but not anticipatory of (i.e., strictly identical to) the claimed invention. The third party's sale of that product would not result in a loss of right to a patent on the claimed invention under §102(b) (2006), because the strict identity rule of anticipation would not be satisfied. However, if the PHOSITA would have been motivated to make the claimed invention by modifying the features of the sold product, in accordance with *other* knowledge available at that time to the PHOSITA (this other knowledge qualifying under some subsection of §102), then the invention would have been unpatentable as obvious under 35 U.S.C. §103. The third party's sale of the product more than a year before the applicant's filing date, even though of something not identical to the claimed invention, effectively added that product to the universe of prior art available to the PHOSITA confronted with the problem addressed by the invention. This can be conceptualized as a "§102(b) (2006)/§103" theory of unpatentability.

In re Bass[67] is a seminal case in the development of §102/§103 "overlap" jurisprudence. *Bass* concerned the applicability of pre-AIA 35 U.S.C. §102(g)[68] as prior art for purposes of nonobviousness analysis under §103. Prior to the *Bass* decision, the courts viewed 35 U.S.C. §102(g) exclusively as a basis for interference proceedings, which are pre-AIA administrative determinations to determine time-wise priority of invention between two rival claimants for the same invention.[69] The USPTO had not had occasion to rely on the prior making of inventions under §102(g) as prior art for the purposes of forming

---

that "[a]n oath or declaration under subsection (a) shall contain statements that . . . such individual believes himself or herself to be the original inventor or an original joint inventor of a claimed invention in the application") (emphasis added).

It is not entirely clear whether §102(f) (2006)–type secret prior art will continue to count as prior art for use in nonobviousness determinations post-AIA. This is because the post-AIA version of 35 U.S.C. §102 includes the phrase "or otherwise available to the public. . . ." For further discussion, *see supra* Chapter 4, Section Q.3 ("Does the AIA Permit Secret Prior Art?").

[66]In re Bass, 474 F.2d 1276 (C.C.P.A. 1973). The America Invents Act of 2011 eliminated 35 U.S.C. §102(g) (2006). *See* Leahy-Smith America Invents Act, Pub. L. No. 112-29 (H.R. 1249), §3(b)(1), 125 Stat. 284, 285-286 (2011).

[67]474 F.2d 1276 (C.C.P.A. 1973).

[68]Recall from Chapter 4, *supra*, that under pre–America Invents Act of 2011 rules, 35 U.S.C. §102(g) prohibits a patent when another inventor has made the invention in this country before the invention date of the patent applicant, and has not abandoned, suppressed, or concealed that earlier invention. *See* 35 U.S.C. §102(g)(2) (2006).

[69]*See Bass*, 474 F.2d at 1283 (stating that the case was "the first time we have considered combining §102(g) and §103 in the context of an *ex parte* rejection entirely divorced from the award of priority in an interference which established the prior

obviousness rejections in *ex parte* prosecution of patent applications.[70] In *Bass,* the CCPA determined that prior invention by another under §102(g) also could be used for that purpose, even though the prior art invention and the invention of the application on appeal were made by employees of the same corporation. The rather complicated facts of *Bass* can be summarized as follows.

The invention of the application on appeal in *Bass,* invented by a group of co-workers consisting of Bass, Jenkins, and Horvat, was a four-element vacuum system for controlling and collecting waste (e.g., dirt and twigs) on carding machines that are used in forming textile fibers. Before the inventive entity of Bass/Jenkins/Horvat filed a patent application claiming their system, however, a separate patent application had been filed that named Jenkins as the sole inventor of one of the four components of the vacuum system (i.e., a main cylinder screen). The USPTO examiner rejected the vacuum system invention as obvious under §103 in view of a combination of prior art references that included the earlier-filed Jenkins patent.[71]

---

inventorship relied on in rejecting"). Interferences are explained *supra* Chapter 4, Section N ("Prior Invention Under 35 U.S.C. §102(g) (Pre-AIA)").

[70]In a footnote in the *Bass* majority opinion, Judge Rich recognized that

> [i]t may be wondered why, in the twenty years since §102(g) came into effect, there have not been more adjudicated cases reported relying on it to show "prior art" in support of a §103 rejection. The answer probably is that there are many other defenses much easier to establish and it is a rare case where the effort of going back to the date of invention of a prior inventor is worth the cost. In particular, §102(e) makes patents unquestioned prior art for all purposes as of their United States filing dates and the date of invention is usually not enough earlier to make a difference in the result.

Id. at 1286 n.7.

The *Bass* case presented an exception to this "usual" state of affairs, of course, because the USPTO possessed information concerning the invention date of the Jenkins screen, and that date was "enough earlier" than the date of invention for the Bass/Jenkins/Horvat system "to make a difference in the result." In most cases, the USPTO does not have information concerning the invention date of the subject matter of prior art patents. Such information is more likely to be unearthed in the process of conducting discovery in cases litigating the validity of issued patents. This is why §102(g) prior art is more commonly employed in §103 obviousness challenges to the validity of issued patents rather than in §103-based rejections of pending patent application claims in the USPTO.

[71]Because the disclosure of Jenkins' patent *described* the "screen" element of the Bass/Jenkins/Horvat combination system invention without claiming the system invention, and because Jenkins was a separate inventive entity from Bass/Jenkins/Horvat, the Jenkins patent was viewed initially by the USPTO as a §102(e) prior art reference, available for combination with other prior art in the §103 obviousness rejection.

F. *Graham* Factor: Scope and Content of the Prior Art

Bass/Jenkins/Horvat were able to antedate the earlier filing date of Jenkins in accordance with 37 C.F.R. §1.131,[72] thus removing the Jenkins patent's disclosure to the extent that it had been relied on by the USPTO as §102(e) (pre-AIA) prior art available for the §103 obviousness rejection. Because Jenkins claimed the main cylinder screen and evidence existed in the prosecution record of Jenkins' dates of conception and actual reduction to practice, however, the USPTO countered that the fact of Jenkins' earlier *invention* nevertheless could be relied on as §102(g) prior art to maintain the obviousness rejection. The CCPA agreed:

> [W]e . . . rule against appellants [Bass/Jenkins/Horvat] and hold that the use of the prior invention of another who had not abandoned, suppressed, or concealed it under the circumstances of this case which include the disclosure of such invention in an issued patent, is available as "prior art" within the meaning of that term in §103 by virtue of §102(g).[73]

The difficulty with the result in *Bass* is that the "another" was Jenkins, the co-worker of Bass and Horvat. Both the Jenkins screen invention, and the Bass/Jenkins/Horvat system invention of which the Jenkins screen was essentially a subcombination, were owned by the same employer. Yet the earlier Jenkins invention theoretically could be used by the USPTO as prior art to prevent the patenting of the later (and arguably more economically important) system invention of Bass/Jenkins/Horvat.[74]

Congress addressed this problem in 1984, when it amended 35 U.S.C. §103 to add the following language:

> Subject matter developed by another person, which qualifies as prior art only under subsections (f) or (g) of section 102 of this title, shall not preclude patentability under this section where the subject matter and the claimed invention were, at the time the invention was made, owned by the same person or subject to an obligation of assignment to the same person.[75]

---

[72]The pre-AIA Rule 131 procedure for antedating or "swearing behind" the effective date of a prior art reference by showing earlier invention is covered *supra* in Chapter 4, Section O.

[73]*Bass*, 474 F.2d at 1286-1287.

[74]This did not actually occur in *Bass*. The rejections based on a combination of Jenkins and a patent to Bass and Horvat on a nozzle for use in the system were reversed because the court determined that the Bass/Horvat patent was not prior art. In his concurrence, Judge Baldwin argued that the majority's discussion of §102(g) as prior art for obviousness determinations under §103 was unnecessary to the result in *Bass. See Bass,* 474 F.2d at 1291-1292.

[75]35 U.S.C. §103 (1984).

Chapter 5. The Nonobviousness Requirement (35 U.S.C. §103)

This statutory provision, which patent attorneys refer to as the "*Bass* disqualifier," had the effect of shielding commonly owned inventions[76] from being rendered obvious by the prior work of other inventors in the same company or firm. In order to promote shared research and greater communication between co-workers, Congress effectively gave corporations the right to patents on obvious variants of in-house efforts qualifying as prior invention under 35 U.S.C. §102 (f) or (g). Had this statutory provision been in effect at the time of *Bass,* the USPTO examiner could not have cited the commonly owned Jenkins screen invention, which was otherwise §102(g) subject matter, as prior art to establish obviousness of the Bass/Jenkins/Horvat system invention.

As part of the American Inventors Protection Act (AIPA) of 1999, the statutory language was further modified to include commonly owned prior art under §102(e) (pre-AIA) (i.e., disclosures in earlier-filed patents or published patent applications of "another") in the list of categories of prior art that "shall not preclude patentability" under §103.[77] This alleviated the problem seen in cases such as *In re Bartfeld.*[78]

The Cooperative Research and Technology Enhancement (CREATE) Act of 2004[79] expanded the §103(c) (pre-AIA) shield even further. Congress wanted to prevent the use in obviousness determinations of §§102(e), (f), and (g) prior art that had been earlier generated not only by an inventor's colleagues in the same corporation, but also §§102(e), (f), and (g) prior art that had been earlier generated by the parties to a joint research agreement involving the inventor.[80] In particular, Congress was concerned about the impact of the Federal Circuit's 1997 decision in *OddzOn Prods., Inc. v. Just Toys, Inc.,*[81] on collaborative research agreements between universities and for-profit corporations

---

[76]"Commonly owned" means that legal title in both inventions is in the same person (be it a natural person or a firm such as a corporation), or are at least subject to an obligation to assign ownership to the same "person."

[77]*See* 35 U.S.C. §103(c) (2002) (as amended by Pub. L. No. 106-113, §1000(a)(9), based on American Inventors Protection Act of Nov. 29, 1999, S. 1948, 106th Cong, tit. IV, subtit. H, §4807(a)).

[78]925 F.2d 1450 (Fed. Cir. 1991) (affirming §103 rejection of appellant's invention as obvious in view of combination of prior art that included the §102(e) disclosure of a commonly assigned, earlier-filed patent granted to appellant's co-worker). The *Bartfeld* court, deciding the case before it under the pre-1999 version of §103, was compelled to reject the appellant's argument that the rejection on commonly assigned art was contrary to the policy underlying the *Bass* disqualifier amendment of 1984, stating that "[w]e may not disregard the unambiguous exclusion of §102(e) prior art from the statute's purview." *Id.* at 1453.

[79]Pub. L. No. 108-453, §2, 118 Stat. 3596 (2004).

[80]A "joint research agreement" is defined by the CREATE Act amendments to mean "a written contract, grant, or cooperative agreement entered into by two or more persons or entities for the performance of experimental, developmental, or research work in the field of the claimed invention." 35 U.S.C. §103(c)(3).

[81]122 F.3d 1396 (Fed. Cir. 1997).

of the type encouraged by the Bayh-Dole Act of 1980.[82] The Federal Circuit held in *OddzOn* that nonpublic information qualifying under 35 U.S.C. §102(f) (1994) could be relied on as prior art for purposes of assessing obviousness under 35 U.S.C. §103(a).[83] Thus, the CREATE Act's sponsors noted, "some collaborative teams that the Bayh-Dole Act was intended to encourage have been unable to obtain patents for their efforts."[84] In order to fix the problem, the CREATE Act expanded the definition of "owned by the same person or subject to an obligation of assignment to the same person" in 35 U.S.C. §103(c)(1) (2000) as follows:

> (2) For purposes of this subsection [§103(c)], subject matter developed by another person and a claimed invention shall be deemed to have been owned by the same person or subject to an obligation of assignment to the same person if—
> (A) the claimed invention was made by or on behalf of parties to a joint research agreement that was in effect on or before the date the claimed invention was made;
> (B) the claimed invention was made as a result of activities undertaken within the scope of the joint research agreement; and
> (C) the application for patent for the claimed invention discloses or is amended to disclose the names of the parties to the joint research agreement.

The CREATE Act amendments to §103 were prospective in effect; they applied only to patents granted on or after the legislation's enactment date of December 10, 2004.[85]

In the America Invents Act of 2011, Congress expanded the §103(c) (2006) exclusion of commonly owned subject matter, including joint research work, to §102 anticipation situations. That is, Congress deleted the exclusionary provisions from §103 and relocated them in 35 U.S.C. §102.[86]

---

[82]The Bayh-Dole Act is codified at 35 U.S.C. §§200-212.

[83]*See OddzOn*, 122 F.3d at 1403-1404 (holding that "subject matter derived from another not only is itself unpatentable to the party who derived it under §102(f), but, when combined with other prior art, may make a resulting obvious invention unpatentable to that party under a combination of §§102(f) and 103").

[84]150 CONG. REC. S2559 (Mar. 10, 2004) (remarks of Sen. Leahy).

[85]Pub. L. No. 108-453, §3(a), 118 Stat. 3596 (2004). The USPTO published interim rules implementing the CREATE Act amendments in 37 C.F.R. *See* 70 FED. REG. 1818 (Jan. 11, 2005).

[86]The pre-AIA exclusion of commonly owned subject matter found in 35 U.S.C. §103(c)(1) (2006) will appear post-AIA at 35 U.S.C. §102(b)(2)(C) (eff. Mar. 16, 2013). The pre-AIA exclusion of joint research agreement work found in 35 U.S.C. §103(c) (2) (2006) will appear post-AIA at 35 U.S.C. §102(c) (eff. Mar. 16, 2013) ("Common Ownership Under Joint Research Agreements"). *See* Leahy-Smith America Invents

Chapter 5. The Nonobviousness Requirement (35 U.S.C. §103)

The current U.S. law is that all types of §102 prior art are available for purposes of establishing obviousness under §103. This rule applies to pre-AIA situations even though some categories of pre-AIA §102 prior art could not have been known to the PHOSITA at the time of her invention, and were thus temporarily "secret" prior art.[87] For example, consider the written description in another's earlier-filed but not yet published or issued U.S. patent application, which qualifies as prior art under 35 U.S.C. §102(e) (2006).[88] As of the PHOSITA's invention date, she could not have known of the contents of a secretly pending patent application. Likewise, earlier inventions of another that qualify as prior art under 35 U.S.C. §102(g) (2006), such as Jenkins' screen in *In re Bass,* would not be known to the PHOSITA in the absence of publication, patenting, or common assignment (as was the case in *Bass*).[89] Even trade secret communications that qualify as prior art under 35 U.S.C. §102(f) (2006) may be cited in a pre-AIA §103 obviousness rejection.[90]

European patent law, by contrast, does *not* permit the use of the contents of an earlier-filed European patent application to establish lack of inventive step (i.e., the European counterpart to the U.S. nonobviousness requirement).[91] The content of an earlier-filed European patent application is considered "part of the state of the art" only if it is novelty-destroying, that is, anticipatory.[92]

Act, Pub. L. No. 112-29 (H.R. 1249), §3(b)(1), 125 Stat. 284, 285-286 (2011); *id.* at §3(c) (deleting paragraph (c) from 35 U.S.C. §103(2006)).

[87]Although secret information (e.g., a confidential sale of an invention in this country prior to the §102(b) (pre-AIA) critical date) has long been considered available as prior art under pre-AIA rules, as of this writing (in mid-2012) it is not clear that such information will qualify as prior art under post-AIA §102, under which the novelty of a claimed invention is presumptively destroyed if the invention was "otherwise available to the public" before the invention's effective filing date. *See* 35 U.S.C. §102(a)(1) (eff. Mar. 16, 2013); *see also supra* Chapter 4, Section Q.3 ("Does the AIA Permit Secret Prior Art?").

[88]*See supra* Chapter 4, Section L ("Description in Another's Earlier-Filed Patent or Published Patent Application Under 35 U.S.C. §102(e) (Pre-AIA)"), for further explanation of 35 U.S.C. §102(e) prior art.

[89]*See* In re Bass, 474 F.2d 1276 (C.C.P.A. 1973).

[90]*See* OddzOn Prods., Inc. v. Just Toys, Inc., 122 F.3d 1396 (Fed. Cir. 1997).

[91]*See* European Patent Convention (EPC) art. 56 (2007) ("Inventive Step"), *available at* http://www.epo.org/patents/law/legal-texts/html/epc/2000/e/ar56.html (last visited Sept. 15, 2008) (providing in part that "[i]f the state of the art also includes documents within the meaning of Article 54, paragraph 3 [earlier-filed European patent applications], these documents shall not be considered in deciding whether there has been an inventive step").

[92]*See id.* at art. 54(3) ("Novelty"), *available at* http://www.epo.org/patents/law/legal-texts/html/epc/2000/e/ar54.html (last visited Sept. 15, 2008) (providing that "[a]dditionally, the content of European patent applications as filed, the dates of filing of which are prior to the date referred to in paragraph 2 [the filing date of the European

F. *Graham* Factor: Scope and Content of the Prior Art

Unlike the European patent system, in the United States the prior art referred to by 35 U.S.C. §103 (at least in its pre-AIA version) is not limited to information that was "publicly known" at the time the invention was made.[93] The U.S. approach may seem unfair to inventors, but it substantially reduces the possibility of two separate patents issuing on inventions that are different in only obvious respects.

4. Analogous Art

Although 35 U.S.C. §102 provides a catalog of prior art that may be available for a 35 U.S.C. §103 obviousness rejection, *not all* prior art that otherwise qualifies under some subsection of 35 U.S.C. §102 is properly used in a §103 analysis. There is yet another important filter or limitation: in order to be considered in a nonobviousness analysis, prior art references also must be what patent attorneys refer to as **analogous art.**[94]

The characteristic of being analogous is a shorthand way of referring to the prior art that courts deem a PHOSITA would reasonably have consulted in solving the problem addressed by the claimed invention. Whether a reference is analogous art is a question of fact.[95] The law recognizes that the PHOSITA cannot know all prior art in every field, and thus "attempt[s] to more closely approximate the reality of the circumstances surrounding the making of an invention by only presuming knowledge by the inventor [sic, PHOSITA] of prior art in the field of his endeavor and in analogous arts."[96]

The Federal Circuit defines analogous art by seeking to recreate the innovation process of a PHOSITA. When faced with a particular problem, it is reasonable to assume that that person would have consulted the following two categories of information:

---

patent application] and which were published on or after that date, shall be considered as comprised in the state of the art").

[93]*See* Hazeltine Research, Inc. v. Brenner, 382 U.S. 252, 255-256 (1965). As of this writing (in mid-2012) it is not clear that information that is not available to the public will qualify as prior art under post-AIA §102. Under that provision, the novelty of a claimed invention is presumptively destroyed if the invention was "otherwise available to the public" before the invention's effective filing date. *See* 35 U.S.C. §102(a)(1) (eff. Mar. 16, 2013); *see also supra* Chapter 4, Section Q.3 ("Does the AIA Permit Secret Prior Art?").

[94]*See* In re Klein, 647 F.3d 1343 (Fed. Cir. 2011) (stating that "[a] reference qualifies as prior art for an obviousness determination under § 103 only when it is analogous to the claimed invention").

[95]Innovention Toys, LLC v. MGA Entertainment, Inc., 637 F.3d 1314, 1321 (Fed. Cir. 2011).

[96]In re Wood, 599 F.2d 1032, 1036 (C.C.P.A. 1979).

1. prior art within the same field of endeavor as the invention; and
2. prior art from a different field of endeavor, but reasonably pertinent to the same problem as that addressed by the invention.[97]

Thus, analogous art is the §102 prior art that is legally permissible to use in a §103 analysis, and it must arise from the same technological field as the claimed invention or be directed to the same problem even if in a different technological field. To go beyond analogous art in a §103 analysis runs the risk of hindsight reconstruction of a claimed invention by merely finding each of its constituent elements somewhere in the prior art, without concern for whether a PHOSITA would have reasonably considered that art.[98]

Applying the *Wood* formulation, if the invention under consideration is, for example, the shock-absorbing construction of the plow shank in *Graham v. John Deere,* the properly considered analogous art would include:

1. other plow shanks; and
2. shock-absorbing devices, whether part of a plow shank, an automobile, or any other type of mechanical device subjected to physical forces when in motion.

Applying prong 1 of the *Wood* formulation necessarily requires determining the "same field of endeavor" for a given invention. The scope of this phrase is not always self-evident. For example, should a toothbrush be considered within the same field of endeavor as a hair brush? Rather surprisingly, two of three Federal Circuit judges answered affirmatively in *In re Bigio.*[99] The applicant in that case sought to patent an ergonomically designed hair brush. The USPTO rejected his claims as obvious in view of a combination of two prior art patents for toothbrushes, and the Federal Circuit majority affirmed. First, the majority applied the "broadest reasonable interpretation" rule to approve the agency's interpretation of the claim

---

[97]*See id.*

[98]*See* Warren D. Woessner, *Innovation* [sic, *Innovention*] *Toys and Analogous Art—Defender Against Hindsight?* (Mar. 24, 2011), http://www.patents4life.com/2011/03/innovation-toys-and-analogous-art-%E2%80%93-defender-against-hindsight/ (explaining that "if a[] [USPTO] Examiner has to reach outside of the relevant art areas to find elements of the claim, the Examiner may be cueing you to argue 'hindsight reconstruction'—the Examiner is using your client's invention like the picture of the finished puzzle on the box, as a guide to locate and assemble widely scattered pieces. In some cases, the Examiner may have reached into such disparate areas of endeavor that the art is not 'logically combinable' to yield the claimed invention.").

[99]381 F.3d 1320 (Fed. Cir. 2004).

term "hair brush" as encompassing "not only brushes that may be used for human hair on [a] scalp, but also brushes that may be used for hairs [o]n other parts of animal bodies (e.g., human facial hair, human eyebrow hair, or pet hair)." The fact that the "Objects of the Invention" section of Bigio's application referred to an anatomically correct hair brush for brushing scalp hair was not dispositive. Absent claim language carrying a narrow meaning, the majority instructed, the USPTO "should only limit the claim based on the specification or prosecution history when those sources expressly disclaim the broader definition." Second, in view of the broad claim interpretation, toothbrushes fell within the field of endeavor of Bigio's invention—namely, the "field of hand-held brushes having a handle segment and a bristle substrate segment." The Federal Circuit majority disputed Bigio's characterization of the field of endeavor test as wholly subjective and unworkable. Rather, "the examiner and the Board must consider the 'circumstances' of the application—the full disclosure—and weigh those circumstances from the vantage point of the common sense likely to be exerted by one of ordinary skill in the art in assessing the scope of the endeavor."[100] Dissenting Judge Newman found the majority's reasoning lacking in common sense, for "teeth are not bodily hair." According to Judge Newman, the broad claim interpretation in this case simply did not justify "the leap from facial hair to teeth and thereby render the brushing of teeth analogous to the brushing of hair."[101]

Prong 2 of the *Wood* analysis, asking whether the prior art reference in question concerns the same problem as that addressed by the claimed invention, is an inquiry often applied broadly by the Federal Circuit. Consider *Innovention Toys, LLC v. MGA Entertainment, Inc.*,[102] in which the claimed invention was directed to a physical board game involving "a chess-styled playing surface, laser sources positioned to project light beams over the playing surface when 'fired,' mirrored and non-mirrored playing pieces used to direct the lasers' beams, and non-mirrored 'key playing pieces' equivalent to the king pieces in chess." The prior art included printed publications describing *electronic* versions of similar chess games, that is, computer-based, chess-like strategy games. The Federal Circuit vacated a district court's summary judgment that Innovention's board game patent would not have been obvious, concluding that the lower court had erroneously "failed to consider whether a reference disclosing an *electronic*, laser-based strategy game, even if not in the same field of endeavor, would nonetheless have been reasonably pertinent to the problem facing an inventor of

---

[100]*Id.* at 1326.
[101]*Id.* at 1328 (Newman, J., dissenting).
[102]637 F.3d 1314 (Fed. Cir. 2011).

a new, *physical*, laser-based strategy game."[103] Contrary to the district court's reasoning, the electronic game references *were* analogous art because they were directed to the same purpose as the claimed invention: "detailing the specific game elements comprising a chess-like, laser-based strategy game."[104] The references and the claimed invention "relate[d] to the same goal: designing a winnable yet entertaining strategy game." Moreover, the record reflected that inventors on many prior art patents "contemplated the implementation of their strategy games in both physical and electronic formats."[105]

In re Klein provides a contrasting (and relatively rare) illustration of the Federal Circuit reversing a USPTO finding that the prior art cited by the agency was analogous art.[106] The claimed invention in *Klein* involved a mixing device for use in preparing sugar-water nectar for certain bird and butterfly feeders. The claims recited a particular structure having a movable divider that formed compartments for various ratios of sugar and water. In its §103 obviousness rejection, the USPTO cited prior art references pertaining to, *inter alia,* tool trays with movable dividers to hold nuts and bolts as well as a cabinet drawer with removable dividers for separating small household articles such as cosmetics and paper clips. The Federal Circuit held that the cited references were non-analogous, for they pertained to the problem of *separating* solid objects rather than mixing components of a solution. Specifically, the court agreed

> with [the applicant] Mr. Klein that the Board's conclusory finding that [the] Roberts, O'Connor, and Kirkman [prior art references] are analogous is not supported by substantial evidence. The purpose of each of Roberts, O'Connor, or Kirkman is to separate solid objects. An inventor considering the problem of "making a nectar feeder with a movable divider to prepare different ratios of sugar and water for different animals," would not have been motivated to consider any of these references when making his invention, particularly since none of these three references shows a partitioned container that is adapted to receive water or contain it long enough to be able to prepare different ratios in the different compartments.[107]

Notably, in contrast with nonobviousness under 35 U.S.C. §103, there is no analogousness requirement for prior art to qualify as *anticipatory* under 35 U.S.C. §102.[108] All references that qualify as prior art

---

[103]*Innovention Toys*, 637 F.3d at 1321-1322 (emphasis in original).
[104]*Innovention Toys,* 637 F.3d at 1322.
[105]*Innovention Toys,* 637 F.3d at 1323.
[106]647 F.3d 1343 (Fed. Cir. 2011).
[107]*Klein,* 647 F.3d at 1350-1351.
[108]*See* In re Schreiber, 128 F.3d 1473, 1478 (Fed. Cir. 1997) (stating that "the question whether a reference is analogous art is irrelevant to whether that reference

under some subsection of §102, regardless of their relationship to the field of the claimed invention or the problem addressed thereby, are available for an anticipation rejection, so long as the strict identity rule of anticipation is satisfied.[109]

G. *Graham* Factor: Differences Between Claimed Invention and Prior Art

This factor is the heart of a nonobviousness analysis under 35 U.S.C. §103. There must be some identifiable difference(s) between the prior art and the claimed invention; otherwise, the invention would be anticipated under §102. The USPTO should clearly identify these differences in issuing any §103 rejection, as should the courts in evaluating an issued patent for obviousness.

For example, the identifiable differences between the claimed plow shank of the '798 patent at issue in *Graham v. John Deere Co.*[110] and the prior art plow shank (in that case, disclosed in Graham's own earlier '811 patent[111]) included moving the hinge plate from below to above the shank, in order to provide the shank with greater flexing ability. This structural rearrangement is depicted in Figure 5.1.

This *Graham* "differences" factor should not be confused with the ultimate question of nonobviousness. The question to be answered under 35 U.S.C. §103 is not whether *the differences* themselves would have been obvious to the PHOSITA. Rather, §103 asks whether the *subject matter as a whole* (i.e., the claimed invention as a whole) would have been obvious, in view of those differences plus the other factors required by the *Graham* analysis.

H. *Graham* Factor: Secondary Considerations

The so-called secondary considerations pertinent to a nonobviousness analysis under §103, sometimes also referred to as objective

---

anticipates. . . . A reference may be from an entirely different field of endeavor than that of the claimed invention or may be directed to an entirely different problem from the one addressed by the inventor, yet the reference will still anticipate if it explicitly or inherently discloses every limitation recited in the claims.") (citation omitted).

[109]*See supra* Chapter 4, Section C for details of the strict identity standard for anticipation.

[110]383 U.S. 1 (1966).

[111]Graham's '811 patent issued on January 10, 1950, more than one year before Graham filed the application (on August 27, 1951) that led to his '798 patent. Thus, the '811 patent was available as a §102(b) reference for use in a §103 challenge by John Deere Co. to the validity of Graham's '798 patent.

GRAHAM '798 PATENT (IN SUIT)

SHANK

Ⓒ

Ⓑ

Ⓓ

NOTE THAT SHANK FLEXES
AWAY FROM HINGE PLATE
(GREATLY EXAGGERATED)

UPWARD FORCE Ⓐ

GRAHAM '811 PATENT (PRIOR ART)

SHANK

ⓒ

ⓑ

ⓓ

NOTE THAT SHANK TENDS
TO FLEX, BUT IS RESTRAINED
BY HINGE PLATE

UPWARD FORCE ⓐ

Figure 5.1

Differences Between Claimed Invention and Prior Art in
***Graham v. John Deere Co.*, 383 U.S. 1 (1966)**

indicia of nonobviousness, include evidence that focuses on the impact of the claimed invention on the marketplace rather than its technical merits. Thus, this final *Graham* factor is based on economic and motivational facts and data that underlie the making and marketing of the invention. Common types of secondary considerations evidence include evidence showing the failure of others to solve the problem addressed by the invention, the commercial success of the invention, the existence of a long-felt need for the invention,[112] the licensing and

---

[112]The mere fact that no one before the patentee has ever offered the invention in the marketplace is insufficient to establish the existence of a long-felt need for the invention. Absent a showing of long-felt need for the claimed invention, the mere passage

acquiescence of others to the patent at issue, and copying of the invention.[113] Such evidence "may often be the most probative and cogent evidence in the record."[114]

1. The Weight to Be Accorded Secondary Considerations Evidence

Although the Supreme Court in *Graham v. John Deere* suggested that evidence of secondary considerations "*might* be utilized" and "*may* have relevancy,"[115] this form of evidence has taken on greater importance in the era of the Federal Circuit. Today the phrase "secondary considerations" is a misnomer, because such evidence must not

---

of time without the claimed invention does not establish nonobviousness. *See* Iron Grip Barbell Co. v. USA Sports, Inc., 392 F.3d 1317, 1325 (Fed. Cir. 2004). In contrast, the patentee in *Uniroyal, Inc. v. Rudkin-Wiley Corp.*, 837 F.2d 1044 (Fed. Cir. 1988), successfully established a long-felt need for its invention, an air-deflecting device for reducing wind resistance encountered by tractor-trailer combination vehicles. The invention decreased the effective surface area of the vehicle encountering wind resistance and achieved significant fuel savings because of the reduced resistance or drag. For evidence of a long-felt need for the invention, the patentee successfully relied on an extensive study, published in 1953 (ten years before the patentee's invention) by the University of Maryland, which "show[ed] a significant interest in drag reduction techniques long before fuel consumption became a critical concern." *Id.* at 1054.

[113]Copying in this context requires proof of replication of a specific product, not just the making of a product that arguably falls within the scope of the patent's claims. Evidence probative of copying includes internal documents, direct evidence such as the disassembly of an invention in order to reverse engineer a virtually identical replica, and access and substantial similarity to the patented product (rather than the patent itself). *See* Iron Grip Barbell Co. v. USA Sports, Inc., 392 F.3d 1317, 1325 (Fed. Cir. 2004).

The proponent of copying as evidence of nonobviousness must also establish a *nexus* between the copying and the novel aspects of the claimed invention. The patentee failed to do so in *Wm. Wrigley Jr. Co. v. Cadbury Adams USA LLC*, 683 F.3d 1356 (Fed. Cir. 2012) (upholding district court's conclusion that, even in light of evidence of secondary considerations, claim 34 of Wrigley's patent would have been obvious in light of two prior art references). The Wrigley patent's claim 34 was directed to a chewing gum that combined menthol and WS-23, a "cooling sensation" agent. Although Wrigley established through internal documents that accused infringer Cadbury had sought to copy Wrigley's invention in some of its products, Wrigley failed to show evidence "suggesting that 'the novel combination of WS–23 and menthol is what led Cadbury to copy Wrigley's chewing gums.'" *Id.* at 1364. Thus the requisite nexus between the copying and the merits of the claimed invention was lacking.

[114]Stratoflex, Inc. v. Aeroquip Corp., 713 F.2d 1530, 1538 (Fed. Cir. 1983). For an interesting discussion that supports the use of secondary considerations evidence as less susceptible to hindsight bias than evidence introduced under the other *Graham* factors, *see* Jeffrey J. Rachlinski, *A Positive Psychological Theory of Judging in Hindsight*, 65 U. Chi. L. Rev. 571, 613-615 (1998).

[115]*See Graham*, 383 U.S. at 17-18 (emphases added).

be treated as secondary to the evidence underlying the other *Graham* factors. The Federal Circuit has held that where secondary considerations evidence is present in the record, it must be considered in determining nonobviousness.[116]

When a patentee relies on secondary considerations evidence in the form of commercial success in attempting to establish nonobviousness, a court must consider marketplace realities in determining what weight that evidence should be given. Even though commercial success was successfully proven by the patentee in *Merck & Co. v. Teva Pharms. USA, Inc.,*[117] the Federal Circuit held that under the particular facts of that case the commercial success was only minimally probative of nonobviousness. Merck's patent in suit covered a method for treating osteoporosis through a once-weekly dosing regime of a drug it marketed under the brand name Fosamax®. The Federal Circuit instructed that "[c]ommercial success is relevant because the law presumes an idea would successfully have been brought to market sooner, in response to market forces, had the idea been obvious to persons skilled in the art."[118] But that inference was inappropriate in *Merck* because other firms were legally barred from commercially testing the prior art-provided suggestion of once-weekly dosing. Merck had a right to exclude competitors from practicing the claimed weekly dosing method because of (1) a separate Merck-owned dominant patent covering methods of treating osteoporosis; and (2) Merck's exclusive statutory right, which it had obtained in conjunction with Food and Drug Administration marketing approvals of Fosamax, to offer Fosamax at any dosage for a five-year period. The Federal Circuit concluded that "[b]ecause market entry by others was precluded on those bases, the inference of non-obviousness of weekly dosing, from evidence of commercial success, is weak."[119] In view of its minimal weight, the commercial success evidence was not sufficient to establish nonobviousness in view of the prior art of record; the asserted claims of Merck's patent were invalid as obvious. In a subsequent opinion dissenting from denial of rehearing *en banc* in *Merck,* three other Federal Circuit judges charged that

> [commercial success] is not negatived by any inability of others to test various formulations because of the existence of another patent. Success

[116]*See Stratoflex*, 713 F.2d at 1538. *See also* In re Piasecki, 745 F.2d 1468, 1471 (Fed. Cir. 1984) (reversing §103 rejection based on USPTO's failure to give weight to evidence submitted by applicant in rebuttal of *prima facie* case of obviousness, which was primarily "secondary considerations" evidence). The concept of a *prima facie* case is further detailed *infra* Section J.

[117]395 F.3d 1364 (Fed. Cir. 2005).
[118]*Id.* at 1376.
[119]*Id.* at 1377.

is success. The panel's rule is especially unsound in the context of an improvement patent, as here, because it holds in effect that commercial success for an improvement is irrelevant when a prior patent dominates the basic invention.[120]

2. The Nexus Requirement for Evidence of Commercial Success

A patent owner facing a challenge to validity will frequently attempt to introduce into the litigation evidence of the commercial success of the patented invention, such as sales volumes, market share, and similar data of positive marketplace reaction. Such evidence is only probative of the nonobviousness of the invention if a sufficient *nexus,* or causal relationship, exists between the commercial success and features recited in the claims.[121]

For example, suppose that the patentee in *Graham v. John Deere*[122] had introduced evidence showing that the commercial embodiment of his patented invention had captured 50 percent of the U.S. market for plow shanks in each year since the product was introduced into the marketplace. This hypothetical evidence would be probative of nonobviousness only if the patentee could show that his sales success was due to consumer desire for the claimed features of the patented plow shank (i.e., its shock-absorbing design). If farmers bought the patented plow shank only because it was painted purple with green polka dots, the item having become a novelty among farmers for that reason, or because the inventor drastically cut its price to a point far below that of competitors' plow shanks, the alleged commercial success evidence would be rejected as nonprobative of nonobviousness *of the claimed invention.*

In *Iron Grip Barbell Co. v. USA Sports, Inc.,*[123] the owner of a patent on a weight plate for barbells attempted to show commercial success from evidence that three out of six retail competitors selling similar plates had taken licenses under the patent. The Federal Circuit explained that because it is often cheaper to take a license than to defend a patent infringement suit, the court "specifically require[s] affirmative evidence" of nexus in cases where licenses are relied on

---

[120]Merck & Co. v. Teva Pharms. USA, Inc., 405 F.3d 1338, 1339 (Fed. Cir. 2005) (Lourie, J., dissenting from denial of reh'g *en banc,* joined by Michel, C.J., and Newman, J.).

[121]Professor Robert Merges has challenged the legitimacy of commercial success evidence and suggests that evidence of the failure of others is much more probative to the nonobviousness inquiry. *See* Robert P. Merges, *Commercial Success and Patent Standards: Economic Perspectives on Innovation,* 76 Cal. L. Rev. 805 (1988).

[122]383 U.S. 1 (1966).

[123]392 F.3d 1317 (Fed. Cir. 2004).

to establish commercial success.[124] In other words, nexus could not be inferred from the mere existence of the licenses.[125] The patentee in *Iron Grip* did not "explain the terms of the licenses nor the circumstances under which they were granted, except to concede that two were taken in settlement of litigation." Hence, nexus was not established. Without a showing of nexus, whatever "little significance" the licenses might have had was outweighed by the strength of the *prima facie* case of obviousness based on the prior art of record.[126]

I. Combining the Disclosures of Prior Art References to Establish Obviousness

Frequently, a §103-based rejection of pending application claims in the USPTO (or a §103 challenge to the validity of an issued patent) will be founded on the argument that the respective disclosures of two or more prior art references, in combination, would have rendered the claimed invention obvious. In other words, this argument contends that the PHOSITA, deemed to have had access to such references at the time he made his claimed invention, would have been motivated to combine their teachings, and that these combined teachings would have rendered the claimed invention obvious to the PHOSITA. (This "motivation to combine" is a factual inquiry that can be conceptualized as a subset of the first *Graham* factor, scope and content of the prior art, but other factors also may impact the analysis.[127])

1. Teaching, Suggestion, or Motivation to Combine

In order for a "combination of references" type of obviousness argument to be legitimate, there must exist some teaching, suggestion, or motivation (hereinafter TSM) that would have suggested making the claimed combination. It is legal error to merely combine the discrete disclosures of different references without evidence of some reason or motivation for the PHOSITA to have done so. Rigorous attention to the requirement for a TSM guards against the improper use of hindsight

---

[124]*Id.* at 1324.

[125]Ordinarily, the Federal Circuit noted, nexus may be inferred when the patentee shows both that there is commercial success and that the thing (product or method) that is commercially successful is the invention disclosed and claimed in the patent. *Id.*

[126]When *copying* of the claimed invention is asserted as secondary considerations evidence in support of nonobviousness, a nexus must also exist between the copying and the novel features of the claimed invention. *See* Wm. Wrigley Jr. Co. v. Cadbury Adams USA LLC, 683 F.3d 1356 (Fed. Cir. 2012), discussed *supra* in Section H.1.

[127]*See* McGinley v. Franklin Sports, Inc., 262 F.3d 1339, 1351-1352 (Fed. Cir. 2001).

I. Combining the Disclosures of Prior Art References

in a nonobviousness analysis,[128] that is, using the claimed invention as a blueprint or plan and merely lumping together multiple prior art references that each disclose some limitation of the claims. Such hindsight reasoning "discount[s] the value of combining various existing features or principles in a new way to achieve a new result—often the very definition of invention."[129]

For example, suppose that a patent claim recites "a widget comprising a lever arm A, a pulley B, and a spring C." Suppose further that the USPTO examiner has rejected the claim as obvious, based on the combined teachings of prior art Reference 1, which shows a widget having a lever arm A; Reference 2, which shows another sort of device (e.g., a gizmo) having a pulley B; and Reference 3, which shows yet another type of device (e.g., a whatzit) having a spring C. By extracting the relevant parts from each of the three references and combining those parts, the examiner has effectively re-created the patented invention by using the claim as a blueprint. If the references themselves or other prior art do not suggest the viability of making the combination, it is a legally erroneous analysis.

The law is clear that the record must contain adequate evidence of a suggestion to combine the references. In the above hypothetical, an adequate suggestion to combine might exist if, for example, prior art Reference 1 suggested that a widget can advantageously have multiple parts in addition to a lever arm, and References 2 and 3 showed benefits or advantages to including pulleys and springs in mechanical devices generally.

The Federal Circuit has recognized that motivation to combine the teachings of multiple references may stem from the nature of the problem solved by the invention. The patent in suit in *Ruiz v. A.B. Chance Co.*[130] was directed to a method of underpinning the foundation of a building by use of a screw anchor in conjunction with a metal bracket. One prior art reference disclosed the screw anchor component of the claims while another disclosed the metal bracket component. The Federal Circuit upheld the district court's finding of an implied motivation to combine the teachings of the two references in the nature of the problem itself: how to underpin the unstable foundation of an existing building. Particularly with simpler mechanical technologies, the Federal Circuit observed, motivation may be found in the nature of the problem to be solved; the prior art references themselves need not provide an express, written motivation to combine. The district court in this case properly found the motivation to combine from the fact that the two pertinent prior art references "address[ed] precisely

---

[128]*See id.* at 1351.
[129]Ruiz v. A.B. Chance Co., 357 F.3d 1270, 1275 (Fed. Cir. 2004).
[130]357 F.3d 1270 (Fed. Cir. 2004).

the same problem of underpinning existing structural foundations." Sitting as the finder of fact, the district court correctly "weighed the evidence and found that, because the prior art references address the narrow problem of underpinning existing building foundations, a person seeking to solve that exact same problem would consult the references and apply their teachings together."[131]

2. *KSR v. Teleflex*: Combinations, Predictability, and "Common Sense"

In a highly anticipated decision, the U.S. Supreme Court in 2007 revisited fundamental aspects of the nonobviousness requirement of §103 for the first time since its 1966 foundational decision in *Graham v. Deere*.[132] In *KSR Int'l Co. v. Teleflex, Inc.*,[133] the Court examined what constitutes an adequate TSM to combine prior art disclosures. Expanding the universe of sources from which a TSM may be derived, the Supreme Court reversed the Federal Circuit's holding that an electromechanical device patented by Teleflex would not have been obvious. The Federal Circuit had erred by applying the TSM test too narrowly and rigidly, requiring a more precise and explicit statement of a TSM than the prior art references of record provided.

The Supreme Court's *KSR* decision also stressed the role of "common sense" and "predictability" in determining whether an invention would have been obvious, but did not define those terms or clearly explain how they inform the statutory standard of §103. The net effect of the Supreme Court's *KSR* decision appears to be that the USPTO will more routinely establish a *prima facie* case of obviousness, putting a greater burden on patent applicants to refute or rebut such *prima facie* cases.[134] The *KSR* decision also makes it likely that issued patents will be challenged more frequently as claiming obvious subject matter. The *KSR* Court questioned (without deciding the issue)

---

[131]*Id.* at 1277.

[132]*See generally* Business Law Forum, *Nonobviousness: The Shape of Things to Come*, 12 Lewis & Clark L. Rev. 323-598 (2008) (law review issue compiling multiple articles on the impact of *KSR Int'l v. Teleflex, Inc.*).

After *Graham* but before *KSR,* the Supreme Court applied §103 to hold that the invention at issue in *Dann v. Johnston*, 425 U.S. 219 (1976), would have been obvious. *Dann* primarily dealt with the technical merits of the claimed invention, a computer-implemented system for "provid[ing] bank customers with an individualized and categorized breakdown of their transactions" during particular time periods. The *Dann* Court avoided deciding the §101 patentable subject matter issue that had been the primary focus of the case below.

[133]127 S. Ct. 1727 (2007).

[134]The concept of a *prima facie* case of obviousness is further examined *infra* Section J.

the rationale for presuming an issued patent valid when the USPTO's examination did not consider a prior art reference later asserted by an accused infringer as evidence of invalidity.[135] In making obviousness easier to establish, at least *prima facie*, the *KSR* decision is consistent with other contemporaneous Supreme Court decisions that signal questions about the balance of power in the patent system. At least some of the Supreme Court Justices (including Justice Kennedy, author of the *KSR* opinion) appear to be concerned that that balance has shifted too far in favor of patent owners.[136]

---

[135]*See KSR*, 127 S. Ct. at 1745 (noting that the rationale underlying presumption of validity of issued patent, based on USPTO's expertise when approving the patent's claims, seemed "much diminished" when a prior art reference asserted by accused infringer had not been considered by USPTO).

[136]*See* Mayo Collab. Servs. v. Prometheus Labs., Inc., 132 S. Ct. 1289, 1305 (2012) (Breyer, J., for a unanimous Court) (observing that "[p]atent protection is, after all, a two-edged sword. On the one hand, the promise of exclusive rights provides monetary incentives that lead to creation, invention, and discovery. On the other hand, that very exclusivity can impede the flow of information that might permit, indeed spur, invention, by, for example, raising the price of using the patented ideas once created, requiring potential users to conduct costly and time-consuming searches of existing patents and pending patent applications, and requiring the negotiation of complex licensing arrangements."); Bilski v. Kappos, 130 S. Ct. 3218, 3229 (Kennedy, J., joined by Roberts, C.J., Thomas, J., and Alito, J.) (observing that "[t]he Information Age empowers people with new capacities to perform statistical analyses and mathematical calculations with a speed and sophistication that enable the design of protocols for more efficient performance of a vast number of business tasks. If a high enough bar is not set when considering patent applications of this sort, patent examiners and courts could be flooded with claims that would put a chill on creative endeavor and dynamic change."); MedImmune, Inc. v. Genentech, Inc., 127 S. Ct. 764, 777 (2007) (effectively expanding opportunities for challenging patents by holding that "petitioner was not required, insofar as Article III is concerned, to break or terminate its . . . license agreement before seeking a declaratory judgment in federal court that the underlying patent is invalid, unenforceable, or not infringed"); eBay Inc. v. MercExchange, L.L.C., 547 U.S. 388, 397 (2006) (Kennedy, J., concurring) (observing that "injunctive relief may have different consequences for the burgeoning number of patents over business methods, which were not of much economic and legal significance in earlier times. The potential vagueness and suspect validity of some of these patents may affect the calculus under the [equitable] four-factor test [for permanent injunctive relief]."); Lab. Corp. of Am. Holdings v. Metabolite Labs., Inc., 548 U.S. 124, 127, 138 (2006) (Breyer, J., dissenting from dismissal of writ of *certiorari* as improvidently granted) (observing that "[t]he problem arises from the fact that patents do not only encourage research by providing monetary incentives for invention. Sometimes their presence can discourage research by impeding the free exchange of information, for example by forcing researchers to avoid the use of potentially patented ideas, by leading them to conduct costly and time-consuming searches of existing or pending patents, by requiring complex licensing arrangements, and by raising the costs of using the patented information, sometimes prohibitively so. . . . [A] decision from this generalist Court could contribute to the important ongoing debate, among both specialists and generalists, as to whether the patent system, as currently administered and enforced, adequately reflects the 'careful balance' that 'the federal patent laws . . . embod[y]'") (quoting Bonito Boats, Inc. v. Thunder Craft Boats, Inc., 489 U.S. 141, 146 (1989)).

Chapter 5. The Nonobviousness Requirement (35 U.S.C. §103)

The patent in suit in *KSR,* owned by Teleflex, was directed to a "vehicle control pedal apparatus" incorporating an electronic sensor in a vehicle's accelerator pedal.[137] The sensor was capable of changing the pedal's position depending on the height of the vehicle's driver. More specifically, the apparatus combined the electronic sensor with an adjustable automobile pedal so that the pedal's position could be transmitted to a computer controlling the throttle in the car's engine.[138] Figure 5.2 depicts the Teleflex invention.

The primary prior art reference relied on by validity challenger KSR was a U.S. patent to Asano.[139] The Asano patent disclosed an adjustable pedal, in a support structure housing the pedal such that even when adjusted relative to a driver's height, one of the pedal's pivot points would remain fixed.[140] The problem addressed by the Asano invention was a "constant ratio" problem—ensuring that the force required to depress the pedal always remain the same, no matter how the pedal was adjusted. Teleflex argued before the Federal Circuit that the problem its own invention solved was different—to design a smaller, less complex, and cheaper electronic pedal assembly. Teleflex contended that Asano's mechanical linkage-based device was complex, expensive to make, and difficult to package.

Reversing a district court's summary judgment of invalidity under 35 U.S.C. §103, the Federal Circuit agreed with Teleflex that its invention would not have been obvious in view of the disclosures of Asano in combination with other prior art references. The appellate court emphasized that "[w]hen obviousness is based on the teachings of multiple prior art references, the movant [validity challenger] must also establish some 'suggestion, teaching, or motivation' that would have led a person of ordinary skill in the art to combine the relevant prior art teachings *in the manner claimed.*"[141] Combining references without such a TSM "simply takes the inventor's disclosure as a blueprint for piecing together the prior art to defeat patentability—the essence of hindsight."[142] The district court correctly held that a TSM may be found from the nature of the problem to be solved, "leading inventors to look to references relating to possible solutions to that problem."[143]

---

[137]*See* U.S. Patent No. 6,237,565 (issued May 29, 2001).

[138]*KSR*, 127 S. Ct. at 1734.

[139]*See* U.S. Patent No. 5,010,782 (issued Apr. 30, 1991).

[140]Other prior art references taught that the sensor should be located on a fixed part of the pedal assembly rather than the pedal's footpad, and that sensors located on footpads were known to suffer from wire chafing problems when the pedal was depressed and released.

[141]Teleflex, Inc. v. KSR Int'l Co., 119 Fed. App'x 282, 285 (Fed. Cir. 2005) (nonprecedential).

[142]*Id.* (quoting In re Dembiczak, 175 F.3d 994, 999 (Fed. Cir. 1999)).

[143]*Id.* (quoting Ruiz v. A.B. Chance Co., 234 F.3d 654, 665 (Fed. Cir. 2000)).

Figure 5.2

Engelgau '565 Patent (Teleflex)

However, "the test requires that the nature of the problem to be solved be such that it would have led a person of ordinary skill in the art to combine the prior art teachings in the particular manner claimed."[144] In the case at bar, the Federal Circuit observed, Asano did not address the same problem as the patent in suit. "The objective of the [Teleflex] '565 patent was to design a smaller, less complex, and less expensive electronic pedal assembly. The Asano patent, on the other hand, was directed at solving the 'constant ratio problem.'"[145] The Federal Circuit thus held that the required TSM to combine Asano and the other prior art references was lacking, and accordingly vacated the district court's summary judgment of invalidity for obviousness.[146]

The Supreme Court reversed, concluding that the Federal Circuit had applied too rigid an approach to the TSM test, in a manner contrary to Supreme Court patent precedent. Although the TSM test can serve as a "helpful insight" in analyzing nonobviousness,[147] the Federal Circuit's conception of TSM in the case at bar was simply too narrow.[148] Specifically, the appellate court erred by

> holding that courts and patent examiners should look only to the problem the *patentee* was trying to solve. . . . The question is not whether the combination was obvious to the patentee but whether the combination was obvious to a person with ordinary skill in the art. Under the correct analysis, *any need or problem known in the field of endeavor at the time of invention and addressed by the patent* can provide a reason for combining the elements in the manner claimed.[149]

The Supreme Court also emphasized the role of "predictability" as well as "common sense," which teaches "that familiar items may have obvious uses beyond their primary purposes, and in many cases a person of ordinary skill will be able to fit the teachings of multiple patents together like pieces of a puzzle."[150] The Supreme Court rejected

---

[144]*Id.* at 288.

[145]*Id.*

[146]*See id.* at 286.

[147]KSR Int'l Co. v. Teleflex Inc., 127 S. Ct. 1727, 1741 (2007).

[148]*See id.* at 1741-1742. After reviewing its own earlier cases dealing with the nonobviousness requirement, the *KSR* Court observed that "[h]elpful insights . . . need not become rigid and mandatory formulas; and when it is so applied, the TSM test is incompatible with our precedents." *Id.* at 1741.

[149]*Id.* at 1742 (emphases added).

[150]*Id.* The Supreme Court's emphasis in *KSR* on the use of "common sense" in nonobviousness determinations may require the Federal Circuit to revisit its earlier decisions such as *In re Lee*, 277 F.3d 1338, 1341 (Fed. Cir. 2002). The USPTO Board in *Lee* rejected the patent applicant's argument that the prior art provided no teaching or motivation or suggestion to combine the prior art references cited by the examiner, stating that "[t]he conclusion of obviousness may be made from *common knowledge and common sense* of a person of ordinary skill in the art without any specific hint

I. Combining the Disclosures of Prior Art References

Teleflex's contention that a designer hoping to make an adjustable electronic pedal would have ignored the Asano patent because it focused on a different problem; Asano provided an "obvious example" of an adjustable pedal with a fixed pivot point, and other prior art indicated that a fixed pivot point was the ideal location to mount a sensor. "A person of ordinary skill is also a person of ordinary creativity, not an automaton,"[151] the Court observed. Design incentives and market forces can prompt variations of a known item, either in the same field or a different one. "If a person of ordinary skill can implement a *predictable* variation, §103 likely bars its patentability."[152]

---

or suggestion in a particular reference." *Id.* at 1341 (emphasis added). The Federal Circuit in *Lee* vacated the obviousness determination, highlighting the agency's failure to explain the "common knowledge and common sense" on which it relied:

> [W]hen [the Board and examiner] rely on what they assert to be general knowledge to negate patentability, that knowledge must be articulated and placed on the record. The failure to do so is not consistent with either effective administrative procedure or effective judicial review. The board cannot rely on conclusory statements when dealing with particular combinations of prior art and specific claims, but must set forth the rationale on which it relies.

Id. at 1345. One way of rationalizing *Lee* with the Supreme Court's *KSR* decision is to view *Lee* as permitting reliance on "common sense," but nevertheless requiring the government to clearly and precisely explain and "place[] on the record" some evidence of what it asserts to be common sense.

Future Federal Circuit decisions will undoubtedly further explore the meaning and proof of "common sense" in nonobviousness determinations. One example is *Perfect Web Technologies, Inc. v. InfoUSA, Inc.*, 587 F.3d 1324 (Fed. Cir. 2009). Perfect Web's U.S. Patent No. 6,631,400 was directed to methods of distributing bulk e-mail to groups of targeted consumers. The invention involved "comparing the number of successfully delivered e-mail messages in a delivery against a predetermined desired quantity, and if the delivery [did] not reach the desired quantity, repeating the process of selecting and e-mailing a group of customers until the desired number of delivered messages ha[d] been achieved." On motion for summary judgment, a district court invalidated the '400 patent under §103. The district court explained that "'[i]f 100 e-mail deliveries were ordered, and the first transmission delivered only 95, common sense dictates that one should try again. One could do little else.'" *Perfect Web*, 587 F.3d at 1330 (quoting district court's slip opinion). The Federal Circuit affirmed the conclusion of obviousness, holding that "while an analysis of obviousness always depends on evidence that supports the required *Graham* factual findings, it also may include recourse to logic, judgment, and common sense available to the person of ordinary skill that do not necessarily require explication in any reference or expert opinion." *Perfect Web*, 587 F.3d at 1329. In the case at bar, the district court had adequately explained its reliance on "common sense," which was supported by record evidence, "namely the facts that step (D) [of '400 patent claim 1] merely involves repeating earlier steps, and that a marketer could repeat those steps, if desired." *Perfect Web*, 587 F.3d at 1330.

[151] *KSR*, 127 S. Ct. at 1742.

[152] *Id.* at 1740 (emphasis added). Note that the predictability (or nonpredictability) of particular technologies has long been a factor in the analysis of enablement under 35 U.S.C. §112, but before the Supreme Court's *KSR* decision the notion of whether a particular invention would have been "predictable" was not a central inquiry in the

309

The Supreme Court in *KSR* made other important points about the nonobviousness analysis in addition to the TSM test. These include a new interpretation of the "obvious to try" standard, discussed *infra*.

3. Teaching Away

Whether motivation to combine exists also must take into consideration whether any of the references to be combined actually teach away from the claimed invention. To teach away means that a prior art reference's disclosure would discourage or dissuade the PHOSITA from doing what the inventor actually and successfully did. For example, consider again the example of a patent applicant claiming "a widget comprising a lever arm A, a pulley B, and a spring C."[153] The patent applicant faced with the "motivation to combine"–based §103 rejection of that claim might counter with a teaching away argument if prior art Reference 2 stated that a pulley should not be used in combination with a lever arm because of certain harmful effects produced by that combination.

Note that while an argument that a particular prior art reference teaches away from a claimed invention may be relevant to the determination of whether that invention would have been obvious under §103, such a "teaching away" argument is not pertinent to the question of novelty under §102. As discussed in Chapter 4, *supra*, a strict identity test controls anticipation. If a single prior art reference identically discloses every limitation of a claimed invention, arranged as in the claim, then it anticipates, even if the reference disparages the invention or would otherwise discourage a PHOSITA from making the invention.[154]

---

determination of nonobviousness under 35 U.S.C. §103. Post-*KSR*, the Federal Circuit has not hesitated to invalidate patents under §103 for involving "predictable" inventions. *See, e.g.,* Rothman v. Target Corp., 556 F.3d 1310, 1319 (Fed. Cir. 2009) (sustaining jury verdict of §103 invalidity of patent directed to a nursing garment having a smooth external appearance that concealed a fully supportive nursing bra, and opining that the claimed invention "falls into a very predictable field . . . [in which] a trial record may more readily show a motivation to combine known elements to yield a predictable result, thus rendering a claimed invention obvious") (citing *KSR*, 127 S. Ct. at 1731, 1740-1741).

[153]*See* Section I.1, *supra*.

[154]*See* Celeritas Techs. v. Rockwell Int'l Corp., 150 F.3d 1354, 1361 (Fed. Cir. 1998). Celeritas' patent claimed an apparatus that counteracted the adverse effects of the pre-emphasis and limiter circuits found in conventional analog cellular communications systems, by de-emphasizing the data signal before presenting it to the cellular network. *See id.* at 1356. During prosecution of its patent, Celeritas argued to the USPTO that the agency should not consider a prior art reference referred to as "the Telebit article" because Telebit "describes a modem that uses a large number of simultaneous carriers to transmit data in contrast to single carrier modems for which Applicant's

4. "Obvious to Try"

The Supreme Court's 2007 decision in *KSR Int'l Co. v. Teleflex Inc.*[155] gave new credence to "obvious to try" arguments, which traditionally have been most relevant to chemical obviousness cases. Before *KSR,* the Federal Circuit defined an obvious-to-try situation as one in which a prior art disclosure might have piqued a scientist's curiosity enough to merit further investigation, but the disclosure was too general to sufficiently teach how to obtain the desired result or that the claimed invention would be obtained if the prior art's directions were pursued.[156] If a validity challenger charged "obvious to try" when arguing that a PHOSITA would have made a particular combination of or modification to prior art teachings with a "reasonable expectation of success," the Federal Circuit tended to reject the argument. Pre-*KSR,* the Federal Circuit repeatedly held that obvious-to-try was *not* the standard for determining the ultimate question of nonobviousness.[157]

The Supreme Court in *KSR* breathed new life into obvious-to-try arguments by redefining obvious-to-try situations as follows:

> When there is a design need or market pressure to solve a problem and there are a finite number of identified, predictable solutions, a person of ordinary skill has good reason to pursue the known options within his or her technical grasp. If this leads to the anticipated success, it is likely the product not of innovation but of ordinary skill and common sense. *In that instance the fact that a combination was obvious to try might show that it was obvious under §103.*[158]

---

invention is intended, and teaches that the use of de-emphasis would not work for single carrier systems." *Id.* at 1360-1361. Celeritas repeated the argument to a jury during subsequent litigation challenging the validity of its patent. The Federal Circuit held on appeal that Celeritas' teaching away argument was without merit because the Telebit article was anticipatory. It was "beyond dispute that the Telebit article discloses each of the claimed limitations." *Id.* at 1361. The Federal Circuit observed that "[a] reference is no less anticipatory if, after disclosing the invention, the reference then disparages it." *Id.* In this case, "[t]he fact that a modem with a single carrier data signal is shown to be less than optimal does not vitiate the fact that it is disclosed." *Id.* Thus, whether a reference teaches away from a claimed invention is simply "inapplicable to an anticipation analysis." *Id.*

[155]127 S. Ct. 1727 (2007). *See* Section I.2, *supra,* for more discussion of *KSR.*

[156]*See* In re Eli Lilly & Co., 902 F.2d 943, 945 (Fed. Cir. 1990) (defining "obvious to try" as when the prior art gives "only general guidance as to the particular form of the claimed invention or how to achieve it") (citing In re O'Farrell, 853 F.2d 894, 903 (Fed. Cir. 1988)).

[157]*See* In re Deuel, 51 F.3d 1552, 1559 (Fed. Cir. 1995) (stating that "'[o]bvious to try' has long been held not to constitute obviousness") (citing In re O'Farrell, 853 F.2d 894, 903 (Fed. Cir. 1988)).

[158]*KSR*, 127 S. Ct. at 1742 (emphasis added).

This definition reframes the obvious-to-try inquiry. Patent applicants, USPTO examiners, litigants, judges, and juries considering whether a claimed invention would have been obvious must now determine whether the prior art identified "predictable" solutions, and whether such solutions were "finite" in number. When these conditions are satisfied, obvious-to-try evidence may indeed establish the ultimate conclusion of obviousness.[159] In other cases, however, the Federal Circuit has distinguished the Supreme Court's definition, emphasizing the latter's narrow confines.[160]

J. The *Prima Facie* Case of Obviousness

Understanding how the USPTO examines patent application claims for compliance with the nonobviousness requirement mandates familiarity with the concept of a *prima facie* case of obviousness. The *prima facie* case is a rebuttable legal conclusion drawn by the agency that a claimed invention would have been obvious, generally based on the USPTO's findings on the first three *Graham* factors.[161] The *prima facie* case thus represents a rebuttable presumption of obviousness.

In response to the agency's assertion that a *prima facie* case of obviousness has been made out, a patent applicant may attempt to rebut it, for example, by arguing that the examiner has mischaracterized

---

[159]*See, e.g.*, In re Kubin, 561 F.3d 1351 (Fed. Cir. 2009) (sustaining USPTO rejection of claimed genus of isolated nucleic acid molecules on ground that the claimed invention would have been obvious under §103(a) (2006)). The Federal Circuit concluded that "[i]n light of the concrete, specific teachings of [the] Sambrook and Valiante [prior art references], artisans in this field, as found by the Board in its expertise, had every motivation to seek and every reasonable expectation of success in achieving the sequence of the claimed invention. In that sense, the claimed invention was reasonably expected in light of the prior art and [hence] 'obvious to try.'" *Kubin*, 561 F.3d at 1361. The *Kubin* decision signals that "classical" biotechnology inventions (i.e., claims to isolated genes that encode particular proteins) may now routinely be characterized as "obvious to try" in the *KSR* sense, and thus obvious under 35 U.S.C. §103. *See also* Wm. Wrigley Jr. Co. v. Cadbury Adams USA LLC, 683 F.3d 1356, 1365 (Fed. Cir. 2012) (concluding that "[t]his case is . . . one in which a person of ordinary skill in the art would find it 'obvious to try'" the claimed chewing gum that combined menthol with the "cooling sensation" agent "WS-23"); Pfizer, Inc. v. Apotex, Inc., 488 F.3d 1377, 1384 (Fed. Cir. 2007) (Rader, J., dissenting from denial of reh'g *en banc*) (stating that obvious to try "appears to be the basis for [the panel's] decision in this case").

[160]*See* Takeda Chem. Indus., Ltd. v. Alphapharm Pty., Ltd., 492 F.3d 1350, 1359 (Fed. Cir. 2007) (concluding that case at bar "fails to present the type of situation contemplated by the [Supreme] Court when it stated [in *KSR*] that an invention may be deemed obvious if it was 'obvious to try.' The evidence showed that [the claimed invention in *Takeda*] was not obvious to try.").

[161]Recall from Section D.2, *supra*, that these factors are (1) the level of ordinary skill in the art; (2) the scope and content of the prior art; and (3) the differences between the claimed invention and the prior art.

the teaching of the cited references; that the references teach away from the claimed invention; that there is no teaching, suggestion, or motivation for a PHOSITA to have combined the references in the manner claimed; or that the PHOSITA would not have had a reasonable expectation of success in so combining. These types of arguments directly challenge the establishment of a *prima facie* case by attacking the agency's findings on the "scope and content of the prior art" *Graham* factor. Alternatively, the patent applicant may attempt to rebut the USPTO's assertion of a *prima facie* case by submitting evidence of unexpectedly superior results achieved by the claimed invention, or "secondary considerations" evidence (e.g., commercial success or the failure of others) under the fourth and final *Graham* factor. When the applicant comes forward with relevant rebuttal evidence in response to a *prima facie* case, the USPTO must consider that evidence.[162]

The concept of a *prima facie* case implicates burdens of production (i.e., going forward with evidence) as well as the ultimate burden of proof (i.e., persuasion) on the question of nonobviousness. As the CCPA explained in *In re Rinehart*,[163]

> The concept of rebuttable *prima facie* obviousness is well established.... It is not, however, a segmented concept. When *prima facie* obviousness is established and evidence is submitted in rebuttal, the decision-maker must start over. Though the burden of going forward to rebut the *prima facie* case remains with the applicant, the question of whether that burden has been successfully carried requires that the entire path to decision be retraced. An earlier decision should not, as it was here, be considered as set in concrete, and applicant's rebuttal evidence then be evaluated only on its knockdown ability. Analytical fixation on an earlier decision can tend to provide that decision with an undeservedly broadened umbrella effect. *Prima facie* obviousness is a legal conclusion, not a fact. Facts established by rebuttal evidence must be evaluated along with the facts on which the earlier conclusion was reached, not against the conclusion itself. Though the tribunal must begin anew, a final finding of obviousness may of course be reached, but such finding will rest upon evaluation of all facts in evidence, uninfluenced by any earlier conclusion reached by an earlier board upon a different record.[164]

[162]*See* In re Sullivan, 498 F.3d 1345, 1351-1353 (Fed. Cir. 2007) (agreeing that USPTO had established a *prima facie* case of obviousness, but reversing agency for its failure to consider applicant's rebuttal evidence of teaching away and unexpected results). In *Sullivan*, the unexpected result was the unexpected property and use of the claimed antivenom composition to neutralize the lethality of rattlesnake venom while also reducing the adverse immune reactions of human patients to whom the composition was administered. *See id.* at 1353.

[163]531 F.2d 1048 (C.C.P.A. 1976).

[164]*Id.* at 1052 (citations omitted).

In *In re Piasecki*,[165] the Federal Circuit relied on *Rinehart*'s teaching to criticize the USPTO's evidentiary procedure in a case involving the patentability of a lighter-than-air craft. With controls like a helicopter, the craft was useful for lifting very heavy loads. By giving insufficient or no weight to the patent applicants' "secondary considerations" evidence, the USPTO improperly shifted to the applicants the ultimate burden of proof (rather than merely the burden of production) on the issue of nonobviousness:

> In the case at bar appellants submitted extensive evidence of peer recognition, long-felt need, and commercial interest. Yet the Board's treatment of the rebuttal documents impels us to the conclusion that the Board did exactly that which *Rinehart* warns against: they viewed each piece of rebuttal evidence solely "on its knockdown ability." Under the Board's approach the *prima facie* case took on a life of its own, such that each fact presented in rebuttal, when it was evaluated at all, was evaluated against the conclusion itself rather than against the facts on which the conclusion was based. The *prima facie* case remained "set in concrete."[166]

The USPTO Board's error meant that the conclusion of obviousness flowing from it could not stand. Concluding that the totality of the applicants' rebuttal evidence carried "persuasive weight," the Federal Circuit accordingly reversed the Board's decision that the claimed invention would have been obvious.[167]

Although the invention in *Piasecki* involved an electromechanical device, the concept of a *prima facie* case is more routinely encountered in cases involving chemical and biotechnological inventions. *In re Dillon* is one of the foundational cases for understanding what constitutes a *prima facie* case in the chemical arts.[168] Patent applicant

---

[165]745 F.2d 1468 (Fed. Cir. 1984).

[166]*Id.* at 1473.

[167]*See id.* at 1475.

[168]*See* In re Dillon, 919 F.2d 688 (Fed. Cir. 1990) (*en banc*). The Federal Circuit was by no means writing on a clean slate in *Dillon*, however. More than 25 years earlier, the Federal Circuit's predecessor court rejected a more severe position then taken by the USPTO—that a chemical compound's properties and advantages were simply not relevant at all when its chemical structure was similar enough to prior art compounds so as to be considered obvious "beyond doubt" by chemists. *See* In re Papesch, 315 F. 2d 381 (C.C.P.A. 1963) (Rich, J.). Rejecting this position, the *Papesch* court explained in a much-quoted passage that

> [f]rom the standpoint of patent law, a compound and all of its properties are inseparable; they are one and the same thing. The graphic formulae, the chemical nomenclature, the systems of classification and study such as the concepts of homology, isomerism, etc., are mere symbols by which compounds can be identified, classified, and compared. But a formula is not a compound and while it may serve in a claim to identify what is being patented, as the metes and bounds of a

Dillon discovered that adding certain *tetra*-orthoester compounds (i.e., compounds having four orthoester groups attached to a central carbon atom) to hydrocarbon fuel compositions would reduce soot emission when the fuel burned. She claimed a composition comprising a hydrocarbon fuel plus a sufficient amount of the tetra-orthoester to reduce soot (i.e., particulate emissions) during combustion. A prior art patent to Sweeney described compositions of hydrocarbon fuels with *tri*-orthoesters, useful for a different purpose—scavenging water from the fuels. Another prior art patent, to Elliot, evidenced the equivalence of tri- and tetra-orthoesters as water scavengers in hydraulic (i.e., nonhydrocarbon) fluids.

The issue before the *en banc* Federal Circuit was whether the USPTO had properly established a *prima facie* case of obviousness when it rejected Dillon's claims in view of the prior art. Although the tetra-orthoesters in Dillon's claimed compositions were structurally similar to the tri-orthoesters in the prior art compositions, the latter compositions had a different use. Dillon's new use of the tetra-orthoesters for

---

deed identify a plot of land, the thing that is patented is not the formula but the compound identified by it. And the patentability of the thing does not depend on the similarity of its formula to that of another compound but of the similarity of the former compound to the latter. There is no basis in law for ignoring any property in making such a comparison. An assumed similarity based on a comparison of formulae must give way to evidence that the assumption is erroneous.

Id. at 391. In *Papesch* the USPTO's obviousness rejection of claims to a novel chemical compound was grounded on the agency's finding that the compound was structurally similar to its lower homolog, which was in the prior art (i.e., the claimed and prior art compounds differed "only in that where appellant has three ethyl groups the prior art has three methyl groups"). *Id.* at 383. Although Papesch asserted in his patent application that his claimed compound had unexpectedly potent anti-inflammatory activity, and also submitted during prosecution an affidavit of test results showing that the claimed compound was an "active anti-inflammatory agent" whereas the prior art compound was "completely inactive" in reducing inflammation, the USPTO deemed this evidence irrelevant. According to the agency, evidence of a compound's properties should be considered only in cases where there existed some "doubt" as to obviousness. In the case at bar, the USPTO contended, the claimed compound was obvious "without a shadow of a doubt" based on its structural similarity with the prior art. *Id.* at 385-386.

The CCPA disagreed. Reviewing a long line of chemical patent precedents, the CCPA concluded that "[p]atentability has not been determined on the basis of the obviousness of structure alone." *Id.* at 391. The Board was wrong to conclude that a showing of properties should be used "only to resolve doubt." *Id.* In other words, structural similarity with the prior art creates only a *presumption* of obviousness. *See id.* (observing that "presumption is all we have here"). A chemical compound must be viewed, "realistically and legally, [as] a composite of both structure and properties." *Id.* at 392. The Board's failure to consider Papesch's evidence of the anti-inflammatory property of his claimed compound was "contrary to well established law" and thus justified reversal. *Id.* at 392.

the purpose of reducing soot (i.e., particulate emissions) was not shown or suggested by the prior art.[169]

After a panel of the court reversed the USPTO,[170] the Federal Circuit reheard the case *en banc* and affirmed the USPTO's rejection of Dillon's claims for obviousness. The USPTO had properly established a *prima facie* case of obviousness based on the chemical structural similarity between Dillon's compositions and the prior art compositions. Even though "all evidence of the properties of the claimed compositions and the prior art must be considered in determining the ultimate question of patentability," the *en banc* Federal Circuit emphasized that "the discovery that a claimed composition possesses a property not disclosed for the prior art subject matter [] does not by itself defeat a *prima facie* case."[171] In other words, it was "not necessary in order to establish a *prima facie* case of obviousness that both a structural similarity . . . be shown and that there be a suggestion . . . from the *prior art* that the claimed compound or composition will have the same or a similar utility *as one newly discovered by applicant.*"[172] While the prior art did not suggest Dillon's newly discovered use, the Federal Circuit pointed out that her composition claims were not limited to that use.[173]

A *prima facie* case having been properly established by the USPTO, the burden (and opportunity) to rebut it then shifted to applicant Dillon. Such rebuttal might have included, *inter alia*, comparative test data showing that the claimed composition had unexpectedly improved properties compared to the prior art compositions, or that it possessed properties that the prior art lacked.[174] Dillon did not present such data. The Federal Circuit agreed with the Board's finding that Dillon had made "no showing . . . of unexpected results for the claimed compositions compared with the compositions of [the prior art reference] Sweeney."[175] Nor did Dillon "show that the prior art compositions and use were so lacking in significance that there was no motivation for others to make obvious variants."[176] In fact, Dillon's own patent application included data showing that tri- and tetra-orthoesters were

---

[169]*See Dillon*, 919 F.2d at 691.

[170]*See id.* at 690 n.1.

[171]*Id.* at 693.

[172]*Id.* (emphases in original).

[173]*See id.* at 693-694 (stating that the recitation in Dillon's composition claims "that the amount of orthoester must be sufficient to reduce particulate emissions is not a distinguishing limitation of the claims, unless the amount is different from the prior art and critical to the use of the claimed composition"); *id.* at 694 n.4 (pointing out that Dillon's composition claims were "not structurally or physically distinguishable from the prior art compositions by virtue of the recitation of their newly-discovered use").

[174]*See id.* (enumerating the types of evidence and/or arguments that can be used in attempting to rebut a *prima facie* case).

[175]*Id.* at 694.

[176]*Id.*

equally active in reducing particulate emissions.[177] Having concluded that Dillon had failed to rebut the *prima facie* case of obviousness, the Federal Circuit affirmed the USPTO's rejection of her claims.

As *Dillon* illustrates, the concept of a *prima facie* case is often central to patent disputes involving chemical subject matter (although it is not limited to any particular subject matter, viz., *Piasecki*). A line of Federal Circuit decisions considers whether a *prima facie* case of obviousness has been established when a patentee developed a claimed chemical compound by selecting and then modifying an existing "lead compound" rather than synthesizing the claimed compound "from scratch."

For example, the patent in suit in *Otsuka Pharm. Co., Ltd. v. Sandoz, Inc.*[178] claimed the chemical compound aripiprazole, which is the active ingredient in a very commercially successful drug product for the treatment of the mental disorder schizophrenia. Aripiprazole is a "carbostyril derivative" having a chemical structure different from all other "atypical antipsychotics" approved by the Food and Drug Administration.[179] Affirming a district court, the Federal Circuit sustained the Otsuka patent's validity against an obviousness challenge by applicants to the Food and Drug Administration for approval to market a generic equivalent of Otsuka's drug product. In affirming the district court's judgment that the claimed aripiprazole would not have been obvious under §103, the Federal Circuit explained that whether a new chemical compound would have been *prima facie* obvious over particular prior art chemical compounds "ordinarily follows a two-part inquiry." First, a district court "determines whether a chemist of ordinary skill would have selected the asserted prior art compounds as *lead compounds*, or starting points, for further development efforts."[180] This step of the analysis focuses on the lead compounds proposed by the validity challenger as those that a person of ordinary skill in the art "would have had a reason to select from the panoply of known compounds in the prior art." Considerations in

---

[177]The Federal Circuit rejected Dillon's charge that the USPTO had improperly used her own showing of equivalence against her. Rather, in relying on the data in Dillon's application the USPTO was "simply pointing out that [Dillon] did not or apparently could not make a showing of superiority" for her claimed tetra-ester compositions over the tri-ester compositions of the prior art. *See id.*

[178]678 F.3d 1280 (Fed. Cir. 2012).

[179]*See Otsuka*, 678 F.3d at 1284 (explaining that "[e]very FDA-approved atypical antipsychotic has a chemical structure related either to clozapine or risperidone, with the sole exception of aripiprazole—the compound at issue in the present appeal"). A "typical antipsychotic" treats positive but not negative symptoms and involves a number of problematic side effects, although typical antipsychotics are still administered today. *Id.* In contrast, an "atypical antipsychotic" is useful for treating both positive and negative symptoms of schizophrenia and has a diminished propensity to cause problematic "extrapyramidal symptoms." *Id.* The claimed compound aripiprazole is an atypical antipsychotic. *Id.*

[180]*Otsuka*, 678 F.3d at 1291 (emphasis added).

the selection of a lead compound include a prior art compound's properties such as activity, potency, and toxicity. Absent a motivation to modify the prior art compound based on this type of evidence, "mere structural similarity between a prior art compound and the claimed compound does not inform the lead compound selection."[181]

In the second step of the two-part inquiry, the district court must analyze "whether the prior art would have supplied one of ordinary skill in the art with a reason or motivation to modify [the] lead compound[s] to make the claimed compound with a reasonable expectation of success."[182] The validity challenger must establish "'some reason that would have led a chemist to modify a known compound in a particular manner to establish *prima facie* obviousness of a new claimed compound.'"[183] In keeping with the Supreme Court's teachings in *KSR v. Teleflex* (discussed *supra*), "the reason or motivation for modifying a lead compound may come from any number of sources and need not necessarily be explicit in the prior art."[184]

Turning to the merits in *Otsuka*, the Federal Circuit held that the district court correctly rejected the validity challengers' three proposed lead compounds as those that a skilled artisan would have selected for further investigation and modification.[185] Rather, two other prior art compounds (clozapine and risperidone) were the only promising compounds available when the inventors of the claimed compound aripiprazole began their work. But the inventors did not select these two compounds. Importantly, the carbostyril compounds that the inventors actually selected for further research and modification were *not* plausible lead compounds at that time. The selected carbostyril compounds were not marketed as antipsychotics or publicly known to have potent antipsychotic activity with minimal side effects—primary goals of the inventors' effort. Thus, the district court correctly held that the validity challengers failed to prove by clear and convincing evidence that the claims of the Otsuka patent in suit would have been *prima facie* obvious over the prior art compounds asserted by the validity challengers as lead compounds. In unusually frank wording, the Federal Circuit commended the district court's "careful analysis"

---

[181]*Otsuka*, 678 F.3d at 1292.

[182]*Otsuka*, 678 F.3d at 1292.

[183]*Otsuka*, 678 F.3d at 1292 (quoting Takeda Chem. Indus., Ltd. v. Alphapharm Pty., Ltd., 492 F.3d 1350, 1357 (Fed. Cir. 2007)).

[184]*Otsuka*, 678 F.3d at 1292.

[185]The validity challengers (accused technical infringers) proposed three "lead compounds": (1) 7-[4-(4-phenylpiperazinyl)-butoxy]-3,4-dihydrocarbostyril, referred to by the parties as the "unsubstituted butoxy"; (2) 7-{3-[4-(2,3-dichlorophenyl)-1-piperazinyl]-propoxy}3,4-dihydrocarbostyril, referred to by the parties as the "2,3-dichloro propoxy"; and (3) a compound termed "OPC-4392," a carbostyril derivative having a 2,3-dimethyl substituted phenyl ring, a propoxy linker, and a carbostyril ring containing a double bond at the 3,4-position. See *Otsuka*, 678 F.3d at 1286-1289.

for "expos[ing] the Defendants' obviousness case for what it was—a poster child for impermissible hindsight reasoning."[186]

K.   Federal Circuit Standards of Review in §103 Determinations[187]

The Federal Circuit reviews determinations under 35 U.S.C. §103 made by the USPTO in the context of *ex parte* examination of patent applications, and in federal district court litigation over the validity of issued patents. Although ultimately a question of law, the nonobviousness determination of §103 must be based on underlying findings of fact. The Federal Circuit has different standards of review for these factual findings depending on which entity made them.

1.   USPTO

The Federal Circuit hears appeals from obviousness rejections of pending patent applications made by the USPTO. The Circuit is required to give the USPTO considerable deference when the agency makes properly supported factual findings on the *Graham* factors.[188] In accordance with the judicial review provisions of the Administrative Procedure Act, such USPTO findings may be overturned by the Federal Circuit only if "unsupported by substantial evidence."[189] The *substantial evidence* standard, a term of art in administrative law, asks whether a reasonable fact finder could have arrived at the agency's decision.[190] If he or she could have, then the agency's finding will be upheld. The fact that the record contains evidence going both ways on a particular issue is not sufficient to overturn the agency's finding.[191]

[186]*Otsuka*, 678 F.3d at 1296.

[187]For a thorough compendium of all Federal Circuit patent-related standards of review, see Lawrence M. Sung, *Echoes of Scientific Truth in the Halls of Justice: The Standards of Review Applied by the U.S. Court of Appeals for the Federal Circuit in Patent-Related Matters*, 48 Am. U. L. Rev. 1233 (1999).

[188]The Federal Circuit similarly gives considerable deference to the agency's findings concerning whether there existed a motivation or reason for a person of ordinary skill to combine the teachings of prior art references. *See* In re Suong–Hyu Hyon, 679 F.3d 1363, 1365-1366 (Fed. Cir. 2012) (affirming rejection of all claims of Hyon's reissue application because USPTO Board's findings concerning motivation to combine were supported by substantial evidence).

[189]*See* In re Gartside, 203 F.3d 1305, 1315 (Fed. Cir. 2000) (applying substantial evidence standard of review, 5 U.S.C. §706(2)(E), to USPTO patentability fact findings).

[190]*Id.* at 1312.

[191]*See* Consolo v. Fed. Mar. Comm'n, 383 U.S. 607, 620 (1966) (stating that "the possibility of drawing two inconsistent conclusions from the evidence does not prevent an administrative agency's finding from being supported by substantial evidence").

2.   Federal District Court

The Federal Circuit also encounters obviousness when it hears appeals from federal district court decisions on the validity of issued patents. When the Circuit reviews patentability fact findings made by a federal district court sitting without a jury, the standard of review is the clearly erroneous standard of Fed. R. Civ. P. 52. The Federal Circuit will overturn a fact finding under the clearly erroneous standard only if on the entire evidence it is left with a "definite and firm conviction that a mistake [was] committed."[192] The clearly erroneous standard of review is seen as somewhat less deferential to the fact finder than the substantial evidence standard, discussed below.

Juries can render a verdict on the ultimate legal question of nonobviousness, provided they are properly instructed on the law (i.e., the *Graham* factors).[193] If a post-trial motion for judgment as a matter of law (JMOL) is filed by the losing party, patentability fact findings presumably reached[194] by the jury in the course of determining the ultimate question of nonobviousness must be reviewed under the deferential substantial evidence standard.[195] The jury's factual findings only can be vacated if no reasonable jury could have made the findings based on the evidence of record.[196] "When the jury is supplied with sufficient valid factual information to support the verdict it reaches, that is the end of the matter. In such an instance, the jury's factual conclusions may not be set aside by a JMOL order."[197] Thus, findings of fact by a jury are (at least in theory) more difficult to set aside than those made by the district court in a bench trial.[198]

---

[192]Ruiz v. A.B. Chance Co., 234 F.3d 654, 663 (Fed. Cir. 2000).

[193]*See* R.R. Dynamics, Inc. v. A. Stucki Co., 727 F.2d 1506, 1514-1515 (Fed. Cir. 1984).

[194]In the absence of specific interrogatories, the jury is presumed to have found disputed factual issues in favor of the verdict winner. Newell Cos. v. Kenney Mfg. Co., 864 F.2d 757, 767 (Fed. Cir. 1988).

[195]*See* Teleflex, Inc. v. Ficosa N. Am. Corp., 299 F.3d 1313, 1333-1335 (Fed. Cir. 2002).

[196]*See id.* at 1335.

[197]McGinley v. Franklin Sports, Inc., 262 F.3d 1339, 1355 (Fed. Cir. 2001).

[198]*See* Structural Rubber Prods. Co. v. Park Rubber Co., 749 F.2d 707, 719 (Fed. Cir. 1984) (noting that "[o]n appeal . . . [f]indings of fact by the jury are more difficult to set aside (being reviewed only for reasonableness under the substantial evidence test) than those of a trial judge (to which the clearly erroneous rule applies)").

Chapter 6

The Utility Requirement (35 U.S.C. §101)

A. Introduction

United States patent law protects inventions that are novel, non-obvious, and *useful*. In "patent-speak," a useful invention is one that possesses **utility.** This chapter explores the utility requirement, which has its genesis in the constitutional goal of promoting the progress of the *"useful* arts."[1] Although the utility requirement is statutorily implemented through the mandate of 35 U.S.C. §101 that patentable inventions must be (among other things) "new and *useful,"*[2] the statute does not define what useful (or utility) means. Case law fills this gap.

In contrast with the novelty[3] and nonobviousness[4] requirements discussed in earlier chapters of this text, the substantive threshold for satisfying the utility requirement is relatively low.[5] The great majority of inventions are never challenged as lacking utility. The utility disputes that do arise tend to involve inventions in the chemical and biotechnological arts. For example, satisfaction of the utility requirement is a central issue in the controversy over patenting of genetic fragments known as ESTs (expressed sequence tags), discussed below.

---

[1] U.S. CONST., art. I, §8, cl. 8 (emphasis added).

[2] 35 U.S.C. §101 (2012) (emphasis added).

[3] *See* Chapter 4 ("Novelty, Loss of Right, and Priority Pre- and Post-America Invents Act of 2011 (35 U.S.C. §102)"), *supra.*

[4] *See* Chapter 5 ("The Nonobviousness Requirement (35 U.S.C. §103)"), *supra.*

[5] See Juicy Whip, Inc. v. Orange Bang, Inc., 185 F.3d 1364, 1366 (Fed. Cir. 1999) (stating that "[t]he threshold of utility is not high: An invention is useful under section 101 if it is capable of providing some identifiable benefit.").

B. Practical Utility

United States patent law requires that patentable inventions possess "practical utility."[6] In other words, to be patentable an invention must have some real-world use. "Practical" use does not necessarily mean "significant" or "extensive," however. Even a chemical intermediate, which exists only for an instant of time when it is produced during the course of a chemical reaction, is useful because it is a tool that allows researchers to develop other chemicals that have useful therapeutic properties.[7]

Utility is rarely at issue for mechanical or electrical inventions; even novelty items, games, or toys that might be considered trivial or frivolous can satisfy the utility requirement. For example, the drawings from an issued utility patent directed to a hat in the shape of a fried egg are depicted in Figure 6.1. Perhaps anticipating some question as to its usefulness, the written description of the patent affirms that the hat "finds utility, for example, as an attention-getting item in

---

[6]In re Brana, 51 F.3d 1560, 1564 (Fed. Cir. 1995).

[7]*See* In re Nelson, 280 F.2d 172 (C.C.P.A. 1960) (reversing USPTO's rejection of claimed steroid intermediates as lacking utility under §101). The *Nelson* court considered the practical utility of the chemicals in the following manner:

> The Patent Office position seems to have been that there must be a presently existing "practical" usefulness to some undefined class of persons. We have never received a clear answer to the question "Useful to whom and for what?" Surely a new group of steroid intermediates is *useful to chemists doing research* on steroids, and in a "practical" sense too. Such intermediates are "useful" under section 101. They are often actually placed on the market before much, if anything, is known as to what they are "good" for, other than experimentation and the making of other compounds in the important field of research. *Refusal to protect them at this stage would inhibit their wide dissemination, together with the knowledge of them which a patent disclosure conveys, which disclosure the potential protection encourages. This would tend to retard rather than promote progress.*
>
> The new androstenes, being *useful to research chemists* for the purposes disclosed by appellants, are clearly useful to society and their invention contributes to the progress of an art which is of great potential usefulness to mankind. They are new steroids which in known ways can be made into other steroids, thus furthering the development of this useful art.
>
> We conclude that the claimed compounds are "useful" within the meaning of section 101. . . .

Id. at 180-181 (emphasis added in last sentence of first quoted paragraph; other emphases in original).

The Supreme Court later characterized *Nelson* as the start of a CCPA "trend" toward a more liberal interpretation of patent utility in *Brenner v. Manson*, 383 U.S. 519, 530 (1966), discussed later in this chapter. The Court did not, however, state that it was overruling *Nelson*, and the facts of *Manson* are clearly distinguishable from those of *Nelson*.

United States Patent [19]

Kiefer

[11]   Patent Number: 5,457,821

[45]   Date of Patent: Oct. 17, 1995

US005457821A

[54]   HAT SIMULATING A FRIED EGG

[76]   Inventor: Raymond D. Kiefer, 105 Shady La.,
                    Spring City, Pa. 19475

[21]   Appl. No.: 199,950

[22]   Filed: Feb. 22, 1994

[51]   Int. Cl.⁶ A42B 1/00
[52]   U.S. Cl. 2/195.1; 2/171; 2/195.2;
                                                              D2/872
[58]   Field of Search 2/171, 175.1, 195.1,
                    2/195.2, 195.3, 195.4; D2/865, 869, 872,
                    873, 874, 876, 879, 882, 884, 886, 893

[56]   References Cited

               U.S. PATENT DOCUMENTS

       D. 170,061   7/1953   Maxwell et al. D2/886

       D. 267,285 12/1982   Lipschutz D2/872

               FOREIGN PATENT DOCUMENTS

       292451   6/1928   United Kingdom 2/195.3

Primary Examiner—Diana Biefeld
Attorney, Agent, or Firm—Frederick J. Olsson

[57]   ABSTRACT

A novelty hat in the form of a baseball cap has a yellow
colored dome shaped top and a white colored brim, the outer
periphery of which is irregular and part of which projects
outwardly to form a visor. On the head of the wearer the hat
makes the visual impression of a fried egg.

2 Claims, 2 Drawing Sheets

Figure 6.1

Hat in the Shape of a Fried Egg
U.S. Patent No. 5,457,821 (Issued Oct. 17, 1995)

connection with promotional activities at trade shows, conventions, and the like." This is more than sufficient to satisfy the utility requirement of 35 U.S.C. §101.

Why is the utility threshold relatively low, that is, relatively easy to meet? If an invention does not offer much in the way of usefulness to society, the costs temporarily borne by the public because that invention is protected by patent will not be excessive. Inventions that are only minimally useful will most likely be made or sold in very small quantities, either by the patentee or copyists. The patentee's right to exclude all others from making, using, selling, offering to sell, and importing the claimed invention represents a minimal burden on society in this scenario. Thus, the patent law does not attempt to evaluate the degree of utility of an invention, beyond some *de minimis* threshold level. Rather, the marketplace decides which inventions are the most useful, through the price the inventor can command for her patented product.[8]

Lack of utility is rarely raised as a basis for challenging the validity of an issued patent. Practically speaking, if the accused infringer (i.e, the challenger of validity) is producing a copy of an invention that is similar enough to spark litigation, this in itself evidences that the invention has a practical utility. Instead, utility disputes usually arise in the context of *ex parte* patent examination in the United States Patent & Trademark Office (USPTO).

Patentable utility does not require commercial success in the marketplace. Nor does it require that an invention work better than those that came before it. Rather, the utility requirement simply ensures that the invention *works* on some minimal level.

A good illustration of this principle is found in *Bedford v. Hunt,*[9] in which the utility of a patented method for making shoes and boots was challenged on the ground that "the invention was not useful; but upon experience had been found not to answer the purpose expected, and

---

[8]This pragmatic view of the patent utility requirement was expressed in a now-classic dissent from the CCPA era:

> It has been pointed out time and again since the days of Justice Story, as fully discussed in *Nelson* [280 F.2d 172 (C.C.P.A. 1960)], that degree of utility is of no public concern whatsoever. This elementary principle appears not to have gotten through to those who still talk of utility in terms of "quid pro quo" for a patent. The only quid pro quo demanded by statute is full disclosure of a new and unobvious invention which is of some use to someone. If it is of very little use, the patent will correspondingly be of very little value to the patentee, who has never been called on either to know or to explain all potential uses of his invention. The hard fact is he almost never knows the full extent of the utility until years after he makes his invention. Uses evolve after inventions are disclosed.

In re Kirk, 376 F.2d 936, 955 (C.C.P.A. 1967) (Rich, J., dissenting).
[9]3 F. Cas. 37 (C.C. Mass. 1817) (No. 1,217).

that this mode of making boots and shoes had been of late much laid aside."[10] In other words, at least according to the accused infringer, the patented boot-making method did not work very well and was not being used in the marketplace (other than by the accused infringer!).

The noted patent jurist Joseph Story refused to invalidate the patent as lacking utility. Story rejected the notion that the patent law is concerned with the *degree* of utility of an invention:

> By useful invention, in the statute, is meant such a one as may be applied to some beneficial use in society, in contradistinction to an invention, which is injurious to the morals, the health, or the good order of society. It is not necessary to establish, that the invention is of such general utility, as to supersede all other inventions now in practice to accomplish the same purpose. It is sufficient, that it has no obnoxious or mischievous tendency, that it may be applied to practical uses, and that so far as it is applied, it is salutary. If its practical utility be very limited, it will follow, that it will be of little or no profit to the inventor; and if it be trifling, it will sink into utter neglect. *The law, however, does not look to the degree of utility; it simply requires, that it shall be capable of use,* and that the use is such as sound morals and policy do not discountenance or prohibit.[11]

Story's view of utility shaped U.S. patent law. We do not look to how useful an invention is, but simply require that it have some practical use to society.

C. The Supreme Court View: *Brenner v. Manson*

The U.S. Supreme Court most recently addressed the requirement of patentable utility in the 1966 decision *Brenner v. Manson.*[12] The controversial *Manson* decision arguably represents the high-water mark for what is required to satisfy 35 U.S.C. §101.[13]

---

[10]*Id.* at 37.

[11]*Id.* (emphasis added).

[12]383 U.S. 519 (1966).

[13]There is considerable basis for criticism of *Brenner v. Manson*. The Supreme Court's majority opinion evidences a fundamental misconception of the role of patent claims. The opinion's critical reference to the "highly developed art of drafting patent claims so that they disclose as little useful information as possible," *Manson*, 383 U.S. at 534, is misguided because it is not the role of patent claims to "disclose . . . useful information." Patent claims set forth the literal boundaries of the patentee's right to exclude others. Disclosure is found in the written description, which must be enabling and reveal the best mode in accordance with 35 U.S.C. §112(a) (eff. Sept. 16, 2012).The *Manson* majority opinion also mistakenly contends that, until a chemical process has been developed to the point where it produces a product having an identifiable utility, "the metes and bounds of that monopoly are not capable of precise delineation." *Id.*

Chapter 6. The Utility Requirement (35 U.S.C. §101)

The patent applicant, Manson, claimed a new process for making a known steroid, a type of chemical compound. Manson asserted that his process had utility because the steroid it produced was being screened for tumor-inhibiting effects in mice, and the next adjacent homologue[14] of the steroid had already been shown to work for that purpose.

Reversing the Court of Customs and Patent Appeals (CCPA), the Supreme Court held that the claimed process did not satisfy the utility requirement of 35 U.S.C. §101. It viewed Manson's research in steroid chemistry, which it deemed an unpredictable art, as being at too preliminary a stage to merit patent protection, noting that "a patent is not a hunting license" and "not a reward for the search, but compensation for its successful conclusion."[15] Rather, the Court explained, what is required for patentability is "substantial utility." This substantial utility standard could not be achieved, the Court held, until the process was defined and developed to the point that "specific benefit exists in currently available form."[16]

The USPTO in 2001 issued examination guidelines that interpret the *Manson* decision as requiring utility that is "specific, substantial, and credible."[17] Uncertainty about the requirements for fulfilling this standard permeates current attempts to patent genes and gene fragments that code for proteins, the function or therapeutic value of which has not yet been identified.[18]

---

at 534. Determination of whether the claims of a patent, which define the "metes and bounds" of the patentee's right to exclude, are sufficiently definite occurs under 35 U.S.C. §112(b) (eff. Sept. 16, 2012), and is not a function of the utility requirement of 35 U.S.C. §101. For additional criticism of *Manson, see* In re Kirk, 376 F.2d 936, 947-966 (C.C.P.A. 1967) (Rich, J., dissenting).

[14]Homologues are structurally similar chemical compounds that are members of a series, such as the alkanes (i.e., the straight-chain hydrocarbons methane, ethane, propane, butane, etc.). Adjacent homologues within the alkane family would indicate two member compounds that differ by only one carbon atom, such as ethane (C_2H_6) and propane (C_3H_8).

[15]*Manson*, 383 U.S. at 536.

[16]*Id.* at 534-535.

[17]*See* United States Patent & Trademark Office, *Utility Examination Guidelines*, 66 FED. REG. 1092, 1098 (Jan. 5, 2001), *available at* http://www.uspto.gov/web/offices/com/sol/notices/utilexmguide.pdf. The *Guidelines* define "specific and substantial utility" to mean "useful for any particular practical purpose," exclusive of "throw-away," "insubstantial," or "nonspecific" utilities, such as the use of a complex DNA sequence as landfill, or genetically transformed mice as food for rats. *See id*. The utility requirement of §101 also is satisfied, according to the *Guidelines*, if the claimed invention has a "well-established" utility, which exists if a "person of ordinary skill in the art would immediately appreciate why the invention is useful based on the characteristics of the invention (e.g., properties or applications of a product or process). . . ."*Id*.

[18]*See, e.g., id.* at 66 FED. REG. 1094 (stating that "[a]n isolated and purified DNA molecule may meet the statutory utility requirement if, e.g., it can be used to produce a useful protein or it hybridizes near and serves as a marker for a disease gene").

D. The Federal Circuit View

1. Chemical Compounds

The Federal Circuit for many years gave fairly little attention to the Supreme Court's 1966 *Manson* decision. Decisions such as the Federal Circuit's *In re Brana*[19] appeared to lower the bar back toward the more lenient standards of utility espoused pre-*Manson* by the CCPA, one of the Federal Circuit's two predecessor courts.

In re Brana is an important utility case for several reasons. First, *Brana* clarified the procedural burdens borne by the patent applicant and the USPTO during a utility determination. *Brana* holds that the agency bears the initial burden of challenging an applicant's presumptively correct assertion of utility. Only after the USPTO provides evidence showing that a person having ordinary skill in the art (PHOSITA) would reasonably doubt the asserted utility does the burden shift to the patent applicant to prove that utility. Such proof is typically made through submission of test data, experimental results, affidavits of experts, and the like, although it also may be more qualitative in nature.

Most notably, *Brana* demonstrates that a biomedical invention may possess patentable utility even though it is not yet at the stage of development necessary for sales approval by the U.S. Food & Drug Administration (FDA). Brana's claims were directed to certain novel compounds intended for use in chemotherapy. Brana produced evidence before the USPTO showing that the compounds had cytotoxicity against human tumor cells, *in vitro* (i.e., in a test tube), and an efficacy that favorably compared to that of structurally similar prior art compounds tested in mice. Nevertheless, the USPTO rejected Brana's claims on the ground that the claimed compounds had not yet been approved by the FDA for Phase II clinical trials in human subjects.

On appeal, the Federal Circuit held that Brana's evidence satisfied the utility standard and rejected the USPTO's position.[20] Patentable utility can be achieved well before FDA standards are satisfied, the court emphasized:

> FDA approval, however, is not a prerequisite for finding a compound useful within the meaning of the patent laws. Usefulness in patent law, and particularly in the context of pharmaceutical inventions, necessarily

[19]51 F.3d 1560 (Fed. Cir. 1995).

[20]The USPTO rejected Brana's claims on the basis that the application lacked a "how to use" disclosure under 35 U.S.C. §112, ¶1 (1994), but noted that a rejection for lack of utility under 35 U.S.C. §101 also would have been proper. *See Brana*, 51 F.3d at 1564. The Federal Circuit observed that "the rejection appears to be based on the issue of whether the compounds had a practical utility, a §101 issue. . . . " *Id.*

includes the expectation of further research and development. The stage at which an invention in this field becomes useful is well before it is ready to be administered to humans.[21]

Interestingly, the *Brana* opinion did not cite nor even discuss the substantial utility standard previously set forth by the Supreme Court in *Brenner v. Manson*. This silence may have indicated the Federal Circuit's discomfort with some of the more extreme statements in the *Manson* majority opinion.

To support the assertion that Brana's claimed compounds had utility as antitumor substances, Brana supplemented the *in vitro* data included in his application with test data derived *in vivo* (i.e., within a living organism, such as a laboratory mouse). The Federal Circuit permitted Brana to submit the *in vivo* data in a declaration submitted under 37 C.F.R. 1.132 *after* his application filing date. The court explained that "the [] declaration, though dated after applicants' filing date, can be used to substantiate any doubts as to the asserted utility since this pertains to the accuracy of a statement already in the specification. . . . It does not render an insufficient disclosure enabling, but instead goes to prove that the disclosure was in fact enabling when filed (i.e., demonstrated utility).[22]

2.   Methods of Medical Treatment

In contrast to *Brana*, a failure to submit test data to support an asserted utility contributed to the later invalidation of a granted pharmaceutical patent for lack of utility in *In re '318 Patent Litigation*.[23] The patent in that case was directed to a method of treating Alzheimer's disease (rather than a new chemical compound). The Federal Circuit majority in *'318 Patent Litigation* (Judges Dyk and Mayer) observed that "[t]ypically, patent applications claiming new methods of treatment are supported by test results," although the court stopped short of requiring such results in all cases. But their absence in the case at bar proved fatal. Because the *'318 Patent Litigation* decision is decidedly contrary to the tenor of the Federal Circuit's decision in *In re Brana*, it merits close study.

In *'318 Patent Litigation*, *in vivo* test data from experiments with animal models such as mice were not available to support the inventor's

---

[21]*Id.* at 1568 (emphasis added) (citations omitted).

[22]*Brana*, 51 F.3d at 1567 n.19.

[23]583 F.3d 1317 (Fed. Cir. 2009). The *'318 Patent Litigation*, which resulted from the consolidation of the patentee's several lawsuits against various generic drug manufacturers, has also been cited as *Janssen Pharmaceutica N.V. v. Teva Pharms. USA, Inc.*, 583 F.3d 1317 (Fed. Cir. 2009).

asserted utility until after the USPTO had issued the patent. During prosecution in the USPTO, the applicant supported her assertion of utility by reliance on various prior art teachings, as well as a statement to the examiner that experimental data using animal models would be available within a few months. The USPTO did not reject the application for lack of utility, despite the fact that the applicant never submitted the animal model data to the USPTO.

The claimed invention in '318 Patent Litigation was a method of treating Alzheimer's disease by administering an effective amount of the compound galanthamine. Although the USPTO issued the '318 patent in 1987 and the FDA in 2001 approved galanthamine for treatment of moderate Alzheimer's disease, the Federal Circuit in 2009 affirmed a district court's invalidation of the '318 patent[24] for failure to satisfy the enablement requirement on the ground that the patent's application did not establish utility.[25] Citing the Supreme Court's Brenner v. Manson decision, the Federal Circuit majority characterized the '318 patent's claimed method of treatment as a "mere research proposal" or "simply an object of research." Echoing Manson, the appellate court observed that "[a]llowing ideas, research proposals, or objects only of research to be patented has the potential to give priority to the wrong party" and to confer power to block entire areas of scientific development.[26]

The results of the animal tests proposed in the '318 patent's application were not available until after the USPTO had already issued the patent. The Federal Circuit held that patentee could not rely on those post-issuance test results to sustain the patent's validity. Nor had the patentee managed to establish utility through "analytic reasoning" based on the prior art results described in the '318 patent application. Although the patentee's expert testified that the application's disclosure "connected the dots" for use of galanthamine as a potential treatment for Alzheimer's disease, the Federal Circuit majority concluded that such testimony fell "far short of demonstrating that a person of ordinary skill in the art would have recognized that the

---

[24]Although the '318 patent issued in 1987, its term was extended on October 22, 2004, pursuant to 35 U.S.C. §156; the '318 patent expired in December 2008. See In re '318 Patent Infringement Litigation, 578 F. Supp. 2d 711, 723 n.21 (D. Del. 2008).

[25]'318 Patent Litigation, 583 F.3d at 1327. Specifically, the Federal Circuit affirmed a district court's grant of summary judgment that the claims of the '318 patent were invalid for lack of enablement. The Federal Circuit explained that enablement is closely related to utility, in that a claim that fails to meet the utility requirement because it is not useful or inoperative also fails to satisfy the how-to-use prong of the enablement requirement. '318 Patent Litigation, 583 F.3d at 1323-1324.

[26]'318 Patent Litigation, 583 F.3d at 1324. Priority of invention was not in dispute in '318 Patent Litigation; the case did not involve an interference, unlike the Supreme Court's only recent statement on utility, Brenner v. Manson, discussed supra.

specification conveyed the required assertion of a credible utility."[27] The utility requirement could not be satisfied by filing a patent application that, in the Federal Circuit majority's view, did "no more than state a hypothesis and propose testing to determine the accuracy of that hypothesis."[28]

Dissenting in '318 Patent Litigation, Circuit Judge Gajarsa charged that the relevant question on appeal was whether, at the time it was filed, the disclosure of the patent application would have credibly revealed to an ordinarily skilled artisan that galanthamine had utility as a treatment for Alzheimer's disease. In Judge Gajarsa's view, the district court erred by focusing on what the prior art did or did not teach (the focus for determining nonobviousness) while neglecting to determine what the '318 application itself disclosed to a PHOSITA (the focus for determining utility and enablement). The district court's failure to make fact findings about enablement led the Federal Circuit majority to improperly engage in extensive appellate fact finding. According to dissenting Judge Gajarsa, it was "particularly problematic" that the Federal Circuit majority had effectively shifted the burden with respect to validity to the patentee. Because '318 Patent Litigation involved an issued patent, the burden should have remained on the accused infringers to disprove utility by clear and convincing evidence. Instead, the Federal Circuit majority improperly "focuse[d] almost exclusively on the sufficiency of [the patentee's] showing and the merit of [the patentee's] arguments."[29]

3. Genetic Inventions

In the wake of the USPTO's 2001 promulgation of the *Utility Examination Guidelines* discussed above,[30] a test case was brought to clarify the standards for applying the §101 utility requirement to patent claims reciting ESTs (expressed sequence tags). The result in *In re Fisher*[31] was a return by the Federal Circuit in 2005 to the rigorous utility criteria announced almost 40 years earlier by the Supreme Court in *Brenner v. Manson.*[32] It remains to be seen whether this resurrection of *Manson* signals a heightened utility requirement for *all*

---

[27]'318 Patent Litigation, 583 F.3d at 1327.

[28]'318 Patent Litigation, 583 F.3d at 1327.

[29]'318 Patent Litigation, 583 F.3d at 1331 (Gajarsa, J., dissenting).

[30]See United States Patent & Trademark Office, *Utility Examination Guidelines*, 66 FED. REG. 1092, 1098 (Jan. 5, 2001), *available at* http://www.uspto.gov/web/offices/com/sol/notices/utilexmguide.pdf. The guidelines were discussed *supra* in Section C .

[31]421 F.3d 1365 (Fed. Cir. 2005).

[32]383 U.S. 519 (1966).

inventions, or will instead be limited to those inventions involving genetic materials such as ESTs.

ESTs are short nucleotide sequences that represent a fragment of a cDNA (complementary DNA) clone;[33] they are "typically generated by isolating a cDNA clone and sequencing a small number of nucleotides located at the end of one of the two cDNA strands."[34] In *Fisher*,[35] the USPTO Board of Patent Appeals and Interferences[36] in 2004 affirmed an examiner's rejection of application claims to five ESTs encoding proteins and protein fragments in maize plants[37] as lacking utility under 35 U.S.C. §101.[38] The real party in interest, Monsanto Company, contended that the claimed ESTs were useful, *inter alia*, for identifying the presence or absence of polymorphisms (i.e., alternative forms of the recited sequences).[39] According to Monsanto, the ESTs "provide[d] at least one specific benefit to the public, for example the ability to identify the presence or absence of a polymorphism in a population of maize plants." While the Board admitted that using ESTs to determine whether populations share a common genetic heritage may be a "utility," it was not in the agency's view a "substantial utility" as required by *Manson*, that is, one that provides a "specific benefit in

[33]Complementary DNA (cDNA) is "produced synthetically by reverse transcribing mRNA [messenger ribonucleic acid]. . . . Scientists routinely compile cDNA into libraries to study the kinds of genes expressed in a certain tissue at a particular point in time." *Fisher*, 421 F.3d at 1367. Messenger RNA (mRNA) is what results when a gene, made of deoxyribonucleic acid (DNA), is expressed in a cell. "[T]he relevant double-stranded DNA sequence is transcribed into a single strand of messenger ribonucleic acid ("mRNA")." *Id.* "mRNA is released from the nucleus of a cell and used by ribosomes found in the cytoplasm to produce proteins." *Id.*

[34]*Id.*

[35]Ex parte Fisher, 72 U.S.P.Q.2d 1020 (Bd. Pat. App. & Int. 2004) (non-precedential decision).

[36]Renamed the Patent Trial and Appeal Board by the America Invents Act of 2011.

[37]Claim 1 of the Fisher application recited "[a] substantially purified nucleic acid molecule that encodes a maize protein or fragment thereof comprising a nucleic acid sequence selected from the group consisting of SEQ ID NO:1 through SEQ ID NO:5," where "SEQ ID NO:1 through SEQ ID NO:5 consist of 429, 423, 365, 411, and 331 nucleotides, respectively." In re Fisher, 421 F.3d 1365, 1367-1368, (Fed. Cir. 2005).

[38]*See* Ex parte Fisher, 72 U.S.P.Q.2d 1020, 1021 (Bd. Pat. App. & Int. 2004) (non-precedential decision). The "substantially purified" nucleotide sequences claimed in *Fisher* are nucleic acid molecules "separated from substantially all other molecules normally associated with [the claimed molecule] in its native state." *Id.* at 1022.

[39]Monsanto asserted at least the following seven uses for the claimed ESTs: "(1) serving as a molecular marker for mapping the entire maize genome, which consists of ten chromosomes that collectively encompass roughly 50,000 genes; (2) measuring the level of mRNA in a tissue sample via microarray technology to provide information about gene expression; (3) providing a source for primers for use in the polymerase chain reaction ('PCR') process to enable rapid and inexpensive duplication of specific genes; (4) identifying the presence or absence of a polymorphism; (5) isolating promoters via chromosome walking; (6) controlling protein expression; and (7) locating genetic molecules of other plants and organisms." *Fisher*, 421 F.3d at 1368.

currently available form." The Board observed that "[w]ithout knowing any further information in regard to the gene represented by an EST, as here, detection of the presence or absence of a polymorphism provides the barest information in regard to genetic heritage." On the other end of the utility spectrum, the Board suggested, would be "information gleaned from detecting the presence or absence of a polymorphism when it is known what effect the gene from which the EST is derived has in the development and/or phenotype of the plant." The Board concluded that the requisite substantial utility lies somewhere between these two extremes, but had not been approximated in this case of an "insubstantial use."

In the closely watched appeal from the Board's decision, a divided panel of the Federal Circuit affirmed the utility rejection of the *Fisher* EST claims in September 2005.[40] Notably, the *Fisher* majority rejected Justice Story's *de minimis* view of the utility requirement[41] and instead hewed to (and elaborated on) the "specific" and "substantial" utility criteria espoused in *Manson*. The *Fisher* majority held that in order to show a "specific" utility, "an asserted use must . . . show that the claimed invention can be used to provide a well-defined and particular benefit to the public,"[42] and that in order to demonstrate a "substantial" utility, "an asserted use must show that [the] claimed invention has a significant and presently available benefit to the public."[43]

In the *Fisher* majority's view, the claimed ESTs failed to satisfy either of these criteria. Each claimed EST uniquely corresponded to the single (or "underlying") gene from which it was transcribed; yet as of the application's filing date, no function was known for the underlying genes. The claimed ESTs were thus no more than "research intermediates" that were "unable to provide any information about the overall structure let alone [] the function of the underlying gene."[44] Such research use was not substantial in the majority's view. Nor were Fisher's asserted uses for the ESTs specific; "[n]othing about Fisher's [] alleged uses set the five claimed ESTs apart from the more than 32,000 ESTs disclosed in the [] application or indeed from any EST derived from any organism."[45]

---

[40]In re Fisher, 421 F.3d 1365 (Fed. Cir. 2005) (opinion for the court filed by Michel, C.J., and joined by Bryson, J.; dissenting opinion filed by Rader, J.). Eight organizations filed *amicus curiae* briefs in *Fisher*.

[41]*See* Lowell v. Lewis, 15 F. Cas. 1018, 1019 (C.C. Mass. 1817) (No. 8,568) (patentable utility requires only that a claimed invention "not be frivolous, or injurious to the well-being, good policy, or good morals of society").

[42]*Fisher*, 421 F.3d at 1372.

[43]*Id.*

[44]*Id.* at 1373.

[45]*Id.* at 1374.

Granting Fisher a patent on the claimed ESTs would amount to no more than a "hunting license," to use *Manson*'s terminology, because Fisher could not identify the function for the underlying protein-encoding genes. Absent such identification, the *Fisher* majority concluded, "the claimed ESTs have not been researched and understood to the point of providing an immediate, well-defined, real world benefit to the public meriting the grant of a patent."[46]

Federal Circuit Judge Rader vigorously dissented on the basis that the claimed ESTs were patentable research tools of cognizable benefit to society.[47] Much like a microscope, the ESTs take a researcher "one step closer to identifying and understanding a previously unknown and invisible structure." Chiding the *Fisher* majority for being "oblivious to the challenges of complex research," Judge Rader emphasized that science "always advances in small incremental steps." In his view, the USPTO is not capable of knowing which "insubstantial" research step will contribute to a substantial breakthrough in genomic study. According to Judge Rader, the utility requirement of §101 is not the proper tool for rejecting inventions that do not advance the "useful arts" sufficiently to merit a patent; rather, that tool should be the nonobviousness requirement of §103. However, Judge Rader observed, the Federal Circuit's 1995 holding in *In re Deuel*[48] has effectively "deprived the Patent Office of the obviousness requirement for genomic inventions." Rather than distort the utility requirement, Judge Rader urged, the USPTO should "seek ways to apply the correct test" of nonobviousness.[49]

E. Inoperability

If the utility asserted for an invention contravenes generally accepted scientific principles, the USPTO will reject the inventor's

---

[46]*Id.* at 1376.

[47]*Id.* at 1379 (Rader, J., dissenting).

[48]51 F.3d 1552 (Fed. Cir. 1995) (holding that the combination of a prior art reference teaching a method of gene cloning, together with a reference disclosing a partial amino acid sequence of a protein, does not render DNA and cDNA molecules encoding the protein *prima facie* obvious under 35 U.S.C. §103; and stating that "the existence of a general method of isolating cDNA or DNA molecules is essentially irrelevant to the question whether the specific molecules themselves would have been obvious, in the absence of other prior art that suggests the claimed DNAs").

[49]Following the Supreme Court's watershed decision in *KSR Int'l Co. v. Teleflex Inc.*, 550 U.S. 398 (2007), the Federal Circuit raised the bar significantly for nonobviousness of genetic inventions. *See* In re Kubin, 561 F.3d 1351 (Fed. Cir. 2009) (sustaining USPTO rejection of claimed genus of isolated nucleic acid molecules on ground that the claimed invention would have been obvious under §103(a) (2006)). *KSR* and *Kubin* are discussed *supra* Chapter 5 ("The Nonobviousness Requirement (35 U.S.C. §103)").

claims under 35 U.S.C. §101 as drawn to inoperable subject matter. Inoperability is a type of rejection for lack of utility. If an invention does not work as claimed, then it is not considered useful in the patent law sense. Moreover, one cannot logically describe how to use an inoperable invention in accordance with 35 U.S.C. §112(a).[50]

1. Examples of Inoperable Inventions

The inventor in *Newman v. Quigg*[51] claimed an "Energy Generation System Having Higher Energy Output Than Input," which the USPTO characterized as a "perpetual motion machine." After the agency's rejection of his claims under §101, Newman brought a civil action against the USPTO Commissioner pursuant to 35 U.S.C. §145 (1988).[52] The Federal Circuit affirmed the federal district court's conclusion that the invention was "unpatentable under 35 U.S.C. §101 because 'Newman's device lacks utility (in that it does not operate to produce what he claims it does).'" The district court had properly relied on National Bureau of Standards test results proving that Newman's machine did not in fact generate more energy than the amount input, the machine having at most an efficiency of only 77 percent.

The operability of a treatment for hair loss was at issue in *In re Cortright*.[53] There the patent applicant claimed a method of treating baldness by applying Bag Balm® (a commercially available ointment normally used to moisturize the udders of cows) to the head of a human suffering from hair loss. Although the Federal Circuit did not consider the asserted utility of treating baldness to be "inherently suspect" in view of the several hair loss treatments already approved by the FDA, the court nevertheless affirmed the USPTO's rejection of Cortright's claim 15, which recited a method of

---

[50]*See* EMI Group N. Am., Inc. v. Cypress Semiconductor Corp., 268 F.3d 1342, 1348 (Fed. Cir. 2001) (stating that "[a] claimed invention having an inoperable or impossible claim limitation may lack utility under 35 U.S.C. §101 and certainly lacks an enabling disclosure under 35 U.S.C. §112.") (citing Raytheon Co. v. Roper Corp., 724 F.2d 951, 956 (Fed. Cir. 1983)).

[51]877 F.2d 1575 (Fed. Cir. 1989).

[52]This §145 procedure authorizes a trial *de novo* in federal court that is not limited to the record evidence that was before the USPTO. *See* Kappos v. Hyatt, 132 S. Ct. 1690 (2012) (holding that in a civil action to obtain a patent under 35 U.S.C. §145, there are no limitations on a patent applicant's ability to introduce new evidence beyond those already present in the Federal Rules of Evidence and the Federal Rules of Civil Procedure, and that if new evidence is presented on a disputed question of fact the district court must make *de novo* factual findings that take account of both the new evidence and the administrative record before the USPTO). Section 145 actions are further discussed *supra* Chapter 1 ("Foundations of the U.S. Patent System").

[53]165 F.3d 1353 (Fed. Cir. 1999).

offsetting the effects of lower levels of a male hormone being supplied by arteries to the papilla of scalp hair follicles with the active agent 8-hydroxy-quinoline sulfate to cause hair to grow again on the scalp, comprising rubbing into the scalp the ointment having the active agent 8-hydroxy-quinoline sulfate 0.3% carried in a petrolatum and lanolin base so that the active agent reaches the papilla.[54]

In essence, claim 15 recited the particular way in which Cortright believed that her invention worked. Unfortunately, her patent application lacked any information to substantiate that the method actually operated in this manner; that is, she did not demonstrate that the active ingredient reached the papilla or that it actually offset the effects of lower male hormone levels, as the claims recited. Therefore, the Federal Circuit concluded, Cortright's application did not provide a satisfactory description of how to use the invention of claim 15 in accordance with 35 U.S.C. §112, ¶1 (1994).[55]

2. Inoperable Species Within a Genus

Utility issues sometimes arise in the context of a generic claim that includes within it one or more species that are inoperable.[56] For example, consider a patent claim to a composition of matter comprising component X from 20 to 80 weight percent, for which the inventor asserts the utility of shrinking cancer tumors. If it is established that the embodiment of the invention in which X is present at 30 percent does not have any tumor-shrinking effect on cancer cells, this means that at least that particular species within the genus of all compositions having X present at between 20 to 80 percent is inoperable; that is, the X equals 30 percent species does not possess the utility asserted for the genus. Is the claim in its entirety therefore invalid under 35 U.S.C. §101?

As with so many other patent law questions, the answer depends on the facts of the particular case. Federal Circuit law holds that the presence of *some* inoperative embodiments does not necessarily render a claim invalid as lacking utility.[57] Patent claims need not exclude all possibly inoperative embodiments.[58] However, the presence of too

---

[54]*Id*. at 1355.

[55]The *Cortright* court treated the how-to-use rejection under §112 as essentially equatable to a rejection for inoperability under 35 U.S.C. §101. *See id*. at 1356-1357.

[56]Genus and species claims were introduced in Chapter 2 ("Patent Claims"), *supra*.

[57]*See* Atlas Powder Co. v. E.I. du Pont de Nemours & Co., 750 F.2d 1569, 1576-1577 (Fed. Cir. 1984).

[58]*See* In re Anderson, 471 F.2d 1237, 1242 (C.C.P.A. 1973) (noting that "[i]t is always possible to put something into a combination [claim] to render it inoperative," but that

many inoperative species or embodiments may give rise to enablement problems under 35 U.S.C. §112(a).[59] The patent's written description must provide enough information that one of ordinary skill in the art could select or discern which embodiments are operable and which are not, and thus practice the invention, without undue experimentation.[60] If such selection criteria are lacking, the presence of inoperable species in the generic claims could render those claims invalid.[61]

F.   Immoral or Deceptive Inventions

Early U.S. judicial decisions recognized a morality component within the utility requirement. For example, Justice Story defined patentable utility in 1817 as an invention that "may be applied to some beneficial use in society, in contradistinction to an invention, which is injurious to the morals, the health, or the good order of society."[62] Applying this standard, U.S. courts, including the Court of Appeals for the Second Circuit, subsequently invalidated patents directed to artificially spotted tobacco leaves[63] and faux-seamed women's hosiery.[64] These decisions illustrate the difficulty of assigning to judges or USPTO examiners the task of passing judgment on which inventions are moral and which are immoral. Such value-laden judgments are often highly personalized and typically implicate community standards that vary over time.

In 1977 the USPTO issued a decision signaling that the agency would no longer reject inventions on the ground that they might be viewed by some segment of society as immoral. In *Ex parte Murphy*,[65]

"[i]t is not the function of claims to *exclude* all such matters but to point out what the combination is") (emphasis in original).

[59]The America Invents Act of 2011 renamed the first paragraph of 35 U.S.C. §112 (2006) as 35 U.S.C. §112(a) (eff. Sept. 16, 2012).

[60]In re Cook, 439 F.2d 730, 735 (C.C.P.A. 1971).

[61]The inoperability of *some* species or embodiments within a claim should be contrasted with the scenario in which *every* species or embodiment is inoperable. In *EMI Group North America, Inc. v. Cypress Semiconductor Corp.*, 268 F.3d 1342, 1348 (Fed. Cir. 2001), the court confronted a patent in which each asserted claim contained one limitation (among several) that was deemed scientifically "impossible" on the basis of expert testimony. See id. at 1346 (citing testimony of accused infringer's expert witness that "explosion mechanism" recited in the asserted claims to metallic fuses for semiconductor chips was "impossible"); id. at 1349. This rendered all the claims invalid. See id. (stating that "[w]hen a claim itself recites incorrect science in one limitation, the entire claim is invalid, regardless of the combinations of the other limitations recited in the claim").

[62]Bedford v. Hunt, 3 F. Cas. 37 (C.C.D. Mass. 1817) (No. 1,217).

[63]See Rickard v. Du Bon, 103 F. 868 (2d Cir. 1900).

[64]See Scott & Williams, Inc. v. Aristo Hosiery Co., 7 F.2d 1003 (2d Cir. 1925).

[65]200 U.S.P.Q. 801 (Bd. Pat. App. & Int. 1977).

the agency upheld the patentability of a "one-armed bandit" slot machine. The USPTO Board of Appeals explained that "while some may consider gambling to be injurious to the public morals and the good order of society, we cannot find any basis in 35 U.S.C. 101 or related sections which justify a conclusion that inventions which are useful only for gambling *ipso facto* are void of patentable utility."[66] The Board concluded that "this Office should not be the agency which seeks to enforce a standard of morality with respect to gambling, by refusing, on the ground of lack of patentable utility, to grant a patent on a game of chance if the requirements of the Patent Act otherwise have been met."[67]

In 1999 the Federal Circuit affirmed the rationale of *Murphy* in the oddly named case of *Juicy Whip, Inc. v. Orange Bang, Inc.*[68] The patent in suit was directed to a Slurpee®-like beverage dispenser machine that included a transparent display chamber of the dispensed product, permitting consumers to see in advance the drink they believed they were buying. The patented machine is depicted in Figure 6.2. In actuality the product (syrup and water) was mixed just before dispensing, so that the customer was not given what she had seen in the display chamber.[69] The trial court invalidated the patent in suit under §101 on the ground that the invention was "deceptive," relying on the early Second Circuit morality cases discussed above.

The Federal Circuit reversed, rejecting the relevancy of those decisions. The modern standard for utility as understood post–1952 Patent Act does not attempt to judge the morality of an invention, the court declared; the utility standard only requires some minimal real-world value. The USPTO is not the proper arbitrar of whether an invention is moral or deceptive or illegal. This is the realm of other agencies (e.g., the FDA or the Federal Trade Commission), or of Congress if it chooses to legislate that certain subject matter is not patentable.[70] Thus, even an arguably deceptive invention is potentially patentable under the utility requirement of §101.

[66]*Id.* at 802.
[67]*Id.* at 803.
[68]185 F.3d 1364 (Fed. Cir. 1999).
[69]In fact, this "deception" benefited consumers because it decreased the risk of contamination.
[70]In this regard, the decision in *Juicy Whip* harkens back to the Supreme Court's decision in *Diamond v. Chakrabarty*, 447 U.S. 303 (1980), which held that living subject matter such as a genetically engineered bacterium is within the categories of potentially patentable subject matter enumerated in 35 U.S.C. §101. *See* Chapter 7 ("Potentially Patentable Subject Matter (35 U.S.C. §101)"), *infra*. The *Chakrabarty* Court upheld the bacterium's patentability partly because, in its view, the lower courts and the USPTO were not in a position to make such policy judgments by means of cramped interpretations of broad statutory language. Rather, Congress was the proper forum for changing the law.

Figure 6.2

**Post-Mix Beverage Dispenser with an Associated Simulated Visual
Display of Beverage
U.S. Patent No. 5,575,405 (Issued Nov. 19, 1996)**

G. Relationship Between Utility Requirement of §101 and How-to-Use Requirement of §112(a)

If the patent applicant fails to assert a credible utility for her invention, the USPTO will generally make both a §101 rejection for lack of utility of the claimed invention as well as a §112(a) rejection for the failure of the written description of the patent to adequately describe how to use the invention.[71] Both rejections are made because "the how to use prong of section 112 incorporates as a matter of law the requirement of 35 U.S.C. §101 that the specification disclose as a matter of fact a practical utility for the invention."[72] By definition, "if [certain] compositions are in fact useless, appellant's specification cannot have taught how to use them."[73] Thus, a lack of utility can support a rejection both under §101 and under §112(a).

H.   Utility Requirement in Foreign Patent Systems

1.   Industrial Applicability

In foreign patent systems and multinational patent treaties, the U.S. utility requirement roughly corresponds to a mandate that patentable inventions possess "industrial applicability."[74] The European Patent Convention (EPC) further defines "susceptible of industrial application" as whether an invention "can be made or used in any kind of industry, including agriculture."[75] This language is intended to expressly include agricultural inventions within patentable subject matter, but to exclude methods of medically treating humans and animals.[76]

In its first major patent case on the issue of industrial applicability of biotechnological inventions, the Supreme Court of the United Kingdom (formerly the House of Lords) in *Human Genome Sciences, Inc. v. Eli Lilly & Co.* considered the validity of Human Genome

---

[71]Prior to the America Invents Act of 2011, 35 U.S.C. §112(a) (eff. Sept. 16, 2012) was commonly referred to as "§112, ¶1."

[72]In re Cortright, 165 F.3d 1353, 1356 (Fed. Cir. 1999) (quoting In re Ziegler, 992 F.2d 1197, 1200 (Fed. Cir. 1993)).

[73]In re Fouche, 439 F.2d 1237, 1243 (C.C.P.A. 1971).

[74]*See* Agreement on Trade-Related Aspects of Intellectual Property Rights (TRIPS) art. 27.1, Dec. 15, 1993, 33 I.L.M. 81 (1994) (requiring that invention be "capable of industrial application"); *id.* at n.5 (stating that for purposes of article, "capable of industrial application" may be deemed by member countries to be synonymous with "useful"); European Patent Convention art. 52(1) (2010), *available at* http://www.epo.org/law-practice/legal-texts/html/epc/2010/e/ar52.html (stating that European patents shall be granted "for any inventions, in all fields of technology, provided that they are . . . susceptible of industrial application").

[75]European Patent Convention art. 57 (2010), *available at* http://www.epo.org/law-practice/legal-texts/html/epc/2010/e/ar57.html.

[76]*See* W. R. Cornish, Intellectual Property: Patents, Copyright, Trade Marks and Allied Rights §5-53 (4th ed., Sweet & Maxwell 1999).

Sciences' (HGS's) European Patent (UK) 0,939,804.[77] The patent claimed *inter alia* the nucleotide sequence of the gene encoding a novel protein called Neutrokine-α, a member of the TNF ligand superfamily, which HGS asserted as useful in the diagnosis and treatment of B-cell and T-cell lymphomas. After an exhaustive review of European Patent Office (EPO) Technical Board of Appeal jurisprudence,[78] the UK Supreme Court held that HGS's patent satisfied the industrial applicability requirements of EPC Article 57.[79]

2.   Morality Criterion

In contrast with U.S. law, foreign patent codes do speak to the morality of inventions, although they statutorily categorize this as an issue of potentially patentable subject matter rather than of industrial applicability. For example, the EPC provides that European patents shall not be granted in respect of

> (a) inventions the commercial exploitation of which would be contrary to "ordre public" or morality; such exploitation shall not be deemed to be so contrary merely because it is prohibited by law or regulation in some or all of the Contracting States. . . . [80]

This provision permits signatory countries to exclude from patenting those inventions whose commercial exploitation is banned in the respective country, if such exclusion is deemed necessary to protect the interests of "ordre public"[81] or morality.[82] A handful of decisions from the European Patent Office have not yet ratified a single, succinct test for determining what types of inventions violate this morality

---

[77][2012] R.P.C. 6, [2011] U.K.S.C. 51.

[78]Lord Neuberger's opinion helpfully summarizes the EPO Board's approach in relation to the requirements of EPC art. 57 for biological material. *See Human Genome Sci.,* [2012] R.P.C. 6 at para. 107.

[79]*See Human Genome Sci.,* [2012] R.P.C. 6 at para. 129. Lord Neuberger observed that "[j]ust as it would be undesirable to let someone have a monopoly over a particular biological molecule too early, because it risks closing down competition, so it would be wrong to set the hurdle for patentability too high. . . . " *Id.* at para. 130.

[80]European Patent Convention art. 53(a) (2010), *available at* http://www.epo.org/law-practice/legal-texts/html/epc/2010/e/ar53.html.

[81]This French phrase most closely translates as "public policy" or "public interest." *See* Donna M. Gitter, *Led Astray by the Moral Compass: Incorporating Morality into European Union Biotechnology Patent Law*, 19 Berkeley J. Int'l L. 1, 3 n.18 (2001).

[82]See Carlos Correa, *The GATT Agreement on Trade-Related Aspects of Intellectual Property Rights: New Standards for Patent Protection*, 16 Eur. Int. Prop. Rev. 327 (1994).

criterion.[83] The "ordre public" or "morality" language of EPC art. 53(a) is echoed in Article 27.2 of the WTO-administered Agreement on Trade-Related Aspects of Intellectual Property Rights (TRIPS),[84] which gives WTO member countries the option of adopting a similar morality-based exclusion from patenting.[85]

[83]*See* Donna M. Gitter, *Led Astray by the Moral Compass: Incorporating Morality into European Union Biotechnology Patent Law*, 19 BERKELEY J. INT'L L. 1, 17-34 (2001) (discussing four EPO biotechnology decisions that have applied two conflicting morality standards: one a test of "public abhorrence," where patenting is denied when public consensus determines that a patent grant would be abhorrent, and the other test a more stringent criterion of "unacceptability," in which the grant of a patent is deemed unacceptable in view of conventionally accepted standards of European culture). The European debate over the morality of patenting the Harvard University onco-mouse is discussed *infra* Chapter 7, Section D.3 ("Life Forms").

[84]*See* Agreement on Trade-Related Aspects of Intellectual Property Rights, Including Trade in Counterfeit Goods, Dec. 15, 1993, 33 I.L.M. 81 (1994).

[85]The TRIPS Agreement and other multinational intellectual property treaties are discussed in further detail in Chapter 12 ("International Patenting Issues"), *infra*.

Potentially Patentable Subject Matter (35 U.S.C. §101)

A. Introduction

1. The General Nature of §101

This chapter considers the *types* or *categories* of inventions for which utility patents[1] are potentially available under U.S. law. Patent law practitioners typically refer to these "eligible" types of inventions as comprising **statutory subject matter,** referring to the categories of subject matter recited in 35 U.S.C. §101. That statue provides as follows:

§101. Inventions patentable

Whoever invents or discovers any new and useful *process, machine, manufacture,* or *composition of matter,* or any new and useful improvement thereof, may obtain a patent therefor, subject to the conditions and requirements of this title.[2]

In contrast, this book will generally use the phrase "potentially patentable subject matter" to emphasize that even if an invention is of the proper type or category, it is only "potentially" patentable because it must still satisfy the remaining statutory criteria of utility,[3] novelty,[4] and nonobviousness[5] before a patent will be granted. As Judge Giles

---

[1]In addition to utility patents, the subject matter of which is set forth in 35 U.S.C. §101, the U.S. patent system grants *plant patents* and *design patents*. Plant and design patents have separate statutory frameworks. *See infra* Section H ("Patentable Subject Matter Beyond §101: Plant Patents and Design Patents").

[2]35 U.S.C. §101 (2012) (emphases added).

[3]*See* Chapter 6 ("The Utility Requirement (35 U.S.C §101)"), *supra.*

[4]*See* Chapter 4 ("Novelty, Loss of Right, and Priority Pre- and Post-America Invents Act of 2011 (35 U.S.C. §102)"), *supra.*

[5]*See* Chapter 5 ("The Nonobviousness Requirement (35 U.S.C. §103)"), *supra.*

Rich explained in *In re Bergy*,[6] "[a] person may have 'invented' a machine or a manufacture, which may include anything under the sun that is made by man, *but it is not necessarily patentable* under section 101 unless the conditions of the title [35 U.S.C.] are fulfilled."[7]

Satisfying the potentially patentable subject matter threshold of 35 U.S.C. §101 means that an invention has passed through the first of the three doors in Judge Rich's classic "three doors to patentability" metaphor of *Bergy:*

> The first door which must be opened on the difficult path to patentability is §101 (augmented by the §100 definitions). . . . The person approaching that door is an inventor, whether his invention is patentable or not. There is always an inventor; being an inventor might be regarded as a preliminary legal requirement, for if he has not invented something, if he comes with something he knows was invented by someone else, he has no right even to approach the door. Thus, section 101 begins with the words "Whoever invents or discovers," and since 1790 the patent statutes have always said substantially that. Being an inventor or having an invention, however, is no guarantee of opening even the first door. What *kind* of an invention or discovery is it? In dealing with the question of kind, as distinguished from the qualitative conditions which make the invention patentable, §101 is broad and general; its language is: "any . . . process, machine, manufacture, or composition of matter, or any . . . improvement thereof." Section 100(b) further expands "process" to include "art or method, and . . . a new use of a known process, machine, manufacture, composition of matter, or material." If the invention, as the inventor defines it in his claims (pursuant to §112, second paragraph), falls into any one of the named categories, he is allowed to pass through to the second door, which is §102; "novelty and loss of right to patent" is the sign on it. Notwithstanding the words "new and useful" in §101, the invention is not examined under that statute for novelty because that is not the statutory scheme of things or the long-established administrative practice.[8]

Thus, 35 U.S.C. §101 enumerates the *types* of inventions that can be patented in the United States, in contrast with §102 and §103, which establish *qualitative* conditions for patentability.

The legislative history of the 1952 Patent Act expansively states that U.S. patents are available for "anything under the sun that is made by man."[9] Although the courts have generally construed potentially patentable subject matter quite broadly, in accordance with this legislative direction, the case law interpreting 35 U.S.C. §101 provides

[6]596 F.2d 952 (C.C.P.A. 1979) (Rich, J.), *aff'd sub nom.* Diamond v. Chakrabarty, 447 U.S. 303 (1980).

[7]*Id.* at 961.

[8]*Id.* at 960 (footnote omitted).

[9]S. Rep. No. 82-1979, at 5 (1952); H.R. Rep. No. 82-1923, at 6 (1952).

important limits on what can be patented. A number of notable judicial decisions have refined our understanding of these limits, as detailed below.

2. The Statutory Categories of §101

Each of the four statutory categories of 35 U.S.C. §101—process, machine, manufacture, and composition of matter—is discussed in detail below, but some working definitions and a few examples are warranted here:

- A **process,** in patent parlance, is synonymous with a method, and is merely a series of steps for carrying out a given task. Process patents have been granted for a method of making a "stuffed-crust" pizza,[10] and to the Internet bookseller Amazon.com for its method of "one-click" online ordering of merchandise.[11]
- A **machine** is synonymous with an apparatus, and generally has moving parts, such as an internal combustion engine.
- A **composition of matter** includes chemical compositions and mixtures of substances such as metallic alloys.
- Lastly, a **manufacture** is the "catch-all" category for human-made subject matter without moving parts, such as a helically grooved foam football[12] or the Java Jacket® insulating sleeve for hot drink cups.[13]

These categories of potentially patentable subject matter are examined separately below.

3. Claiming the Inventive Concept Within Different Statutory Categories

The claims of a patent need not explicitly recite the category of potentially patentable subject matter to which the invention belongs

---

[10]*See* "Method for making a stuffed pizza crust," U.S. Patent No. 6,048,556 (issued Apr. 11, 2000).

[11]*See* "Method and system for placing a purchase order via a communications network," U.S. Patent No. 5,960,411 (issued Sept. 28, 1999). The Federal Circuit questioned the validity of this patent when it refused to uphold a preliminary injunction against accused infringer Barnes & Noble in *Amazon.com, Inc. v. Barnesandnoble.com, Inc.*, 239 F.3d 1343 (Fed. Cir. 2001).

[12]*See* U.S. Patent No. Re. 33,449 (reissued Nov. 20, 1990).

[13]The Java Jacket® patent, U.S. Patent No. 5,425,497 (issued June 20, 1995), is reproduced in Chapter 1, Section C.5 ("The Patent Document and Its Components"), *supra.*

(although some patent claims do). The proper categorization is usually clear from the face of the claim. For example, a claim that recites "a programmed computer" is understood as directed to the machine category of §101.[14] So long as the claim is sufficiently definite under the second paragraph of 35 U.S.C. §112,[15] such that the USPTO examiner can determine whether the recited subject matter falls within one or more categories of §101, nothing further is required.

The inventive concept to which a given patent is directed may encompass a number of different manifestations. That is to say, the "invention" may be claimed in many different ways, even within a single patent application, and the claims of that application may be drawn to more than one statutory subject matter category under 35 U.S.C. §101. For example, the inventor of a novel and nonobvious drug may file an application claiming the chemical structure of the drug itself as a composition of matter, as well as a method of synthesizing the drug, as well as a method of treating patients suffering from a certain disease, which method comprises administering an effective amount of the drug. All of these claims would be drawn to various aspects of the same "invention" or "inventive concept," broadly understood.

Claims that recite subject matter falling within different statutory categories, such as those of the preceding new drug example, are often filed in the same patent application because they all stem from the same inventive contribution. In some instances, however, the USPTO will require "restriction" of certain groups of claims into separate patent applications, primarily for the administrative convenience of the agency during the examination process.[16] Restriction is appropriate if the claims are directed to "independent and distinct" inventions.[17] For example, the drug inventor in the above example might be required to

---

[14]*See* WMS Gaming, Inc. v. Int'l Game Tech., 184 F.3d 1339, 1348 (Fed. Cir. 1999) (stating that "[a] general purpose computer, or microprocessor, programmed to carry out an algorithm creates 'a new machine, because a general purpose computer in effect becomes a special purpose computer once it is programmed to perform particular functions pursuant to instructions from program software'") (quoting In re Alappat, 33 F.3d 1526, 1545 (Fed. Cir. 1994) (*en banc*)).

[15]The claim definiteness requirement of 35 U.S.C. §112(b) (eff. Sept. 16, 2012) is discussed further in Chapter 2 ("Patent Claims"), *supra*.

[16]*See* 35 U.S.C. §121 (providing in part that "[i]f two or more independent and distinct inventions are claimed in one application, the Director [of the USPTO] may require the application to be restricted to one of the inventions"). *See also* Transco Prods., Inc. v. Performance Contracting, Inc., 38 F.3d 551, 558 (Fed. Cir. 1994) (explaining that "when confronted with an application claiming more than one independent and distinct invention, an examiner often will impose a restriction requirement pursuant to 35 U.S.C. §121 to ease the burden of examining that subject matter, thus forcing an applicant to file one or more divisional applications"). *See also* Section H.5 of Chapter 1 ("Foundations of the U.S. Patent System"), *supra*.

[17]35 U.S.C. §121. The USPTO provides the following guidance on the meaning of "independent" and "related but distinct" (i.e., dependent) inventions:

restrict her original (*parent*) application to only those claims directed to the composition of matter, and to file one or more additional (*divisional*) applications directed to the remaining groups of claims reciting the method of making and the method of treatment.[18]

Sometimes a pioneer invention may represent such an advance over prior innovation as to defy categorization in a single statutory category. For example, the Supreme Court held that the genetically engineered, petroleum-consuming bacterium of *Diamond v. Chakrabarty*[19] could properly be categorized as either a "composition of matter" *or* a "manufacture."[20] For purposes of potential patentability under §101, all that matters is that the invention fall within at least one statutory category. The precise identity of the category is not important, nor need it be explicitly stated in the claim.

The remainder of this chapter addresses the leading judicial decisions interpreting each of the four statutory categories of 35 U.S.C. §101, as well as judicially recognized exceptions from patentability. Patents are not available for certain types of important scientific

---

I. INDEPENDENT

The term "independent" (i.e., unrelated) means that there is no disclosed relationship between the two or more inventions claimed, that is, they are unconnected in design, operation, and effect. For example, a process and an apparatus incapable of being used in practicing the process are independent inventions. . . .

II. RELATED BUT DISTINCT

Two or more inventions are related (i.e., not independent) if they are disclosed as connected in at least one of design (e.g., structure or method of manufacture), operation (e.g., function or method of use), or effect. Examples of related inventions include combination and part (subcombination) thereof, process and apparatus for its practice, process and product made, etc. In this definition the term related is used as an alternative for dependent in referring to inventions other than independent inventions.

Related inventions are distinct if the inventions *as claimed* are not connected in at least one of design, operation, or effect (e.g., can be made by, or used in, a materially different process) and wherein at least one invention is PATENTABLE (novel and nonobvious) OVER THE OTHER (though they may each be unpatentable over the prior art). . . .

It is further noted that the terms "independent" and "distinct" are used in decisions with varying meanings. All decisions should be read carefully to determine the meaning intended.

U.S. Patent and Trademark Office, Manual of Patent Examining Procedure §802.01 (8th ed. 2001, rev. July 2010) (MPEP citations omitted), *available at* http://www.uspto.gov/web/offices/pac/mpep/documents/0800_802_01.htm#sect802.01.

[18]Divisional applications are discussed in further detail at Section H.5 of Chapter 1 ("Foundations of the U.S. Patent System"), *supra*.

[19]447 U.S. 303 (1980).

[20]*See Chakrabarty*, 447 U.S. at 309-310 (stating that "respondent's . . . claim is not to a hitherto unknown natural phenomenon, but to a nonnaturally occurring manufacture or composition of matter—a product of human ingenuity 'having a distinctive name, character [and] use'") (quoting Hartranft v. Wiegmann, 121 U.S. 609, 615 (1887)).

347

advances, such as the discovery of a previously unrecognized law of nature or scientific principle such as gravity or Einstein's theory of relativity, despite the obvious significance of these contributions to our society. This chapter concludes by introducing two additional types of non-utility patent protection that are available in the United States: plant patents and design patents.

B. Section 101 Processes

1. Basic Principles

The patenting of processes is as old as the patent law itself. The first U.S. patent law, the Patent Act of 1790, referred to a process as an "art."[21] The very first U.S. patent was granted for a process of making potash, a chemical compound used chiefly in fertilizers.[22] Today, the U.S. Patent Act provides that the term *process* means "process, art, or method."[23]

A process is synonymous with a method, or a series of steps for accomplishing some result. Often, the process is a novel and nonobvious method of making some end product. For example, a typical process claim might recite a method of making a chemical compound X as follows:

1. A process for making compound X, comprising the steps of
    (1) mixing equal parts Y with Z to form a mixture,
    (2) heating the mixture to a temperature of about 100 degrees Celsius,
    (3) cooling the mixture to a temperature of about 20 degrees Celsius, and
    (4) recovering a precipitate of said compound X from the cooled mixture.

[21]Patent Act of April 10, 1790, ch. 7, §1, 1 Stat. 109 (providing that patent grant requires that "he, she, or they, hath or have invented or discovered any useful art, manufacture, engine, machine, or device, or any improvement therein"). *See also* S. Rep. No. 82-1979 (1952), *as reprinted in* 1952 U.S.C.C.A.N. 2394, 2398 (explaining that replacement of "art" by "process" in the enactment of 35 U.S.C. §101 resulted in no substantive change because art had been "interpreted by the courts to be practically synonymous with process or method").

[22]See David W. Maxey & Samuel Hopkins, *The Holder of the First U.S. Patent: A Study of Failure,* 122 PA. MAG. OF HIST. & BIOGRAPHY 3 (1998); David W. Maxey, *Inventing History: The Holder of the First U.S. Patent,* 80 J. PAT. & TRADEMARK OFF. SOC'Y 155 (1998).

[23]35 U.S.C. §100(b).

Importantly, the end product of the process, in this hypothetical the compound X, need not itself be patentable; in other words, a process claim can be granted for a novel and nonobvious method of making an old product. The Patent Act's definitional section provides that the "term process . . . includes a new use of a known process, machine, manufacture, composition of matter, or material."[24]

The independent patentability of new processes for making known products reflects the importance to society of stimulating new process innovation. Consider, for example, the societal benefit achieved through the invention of new processes to make insulin, a well-known protein needed by people with diabetes. Insulin is now easily obtained in large quantities through DNA cloning techniques. This recombinant process is much more efficient than the conventional method of extracting the insulin from the pancreas of hogs.[25] By providing the incentive of process patent protection, the patent system calls forth new and nonobvious ways to make existing products.

2.   Process Versus Product

Process claims, as in the example above, should be distinguished from product claims, which are typically drawn to compositions of matter or manufactures, discussed separately below. A process claim is generally considered narrower in scope, and hence of less economic value to the patent owner, than a product claim. Why? Consider the above claim to a process comprising steps (1) to (4), performed in the recited order, (1)-(2)-(3)-(4), which produces a given product, compound X. This process claim is relatively narrow in scope because it is literally infringed only by other processes that make X by repeating the identical series of recited steps, (1) to (4), in that sequence. If a competitor can determine how to make the product X by a different process, for example steps (5) to (8), or by performing steps (1) to (4) in a different order, such as (3)-(4)-(1)-(2), then the process claim has not been literally infringed.[26]

On the other hand, if a patent is obtained with a claim to the product X itself, then the making of X by *any* process, whether it comprises steps (1) to (4), (5) to (8), (3)-(4)-(1)-(2), or any other set of steps, literally infringes the claim. In other words, the scope of protection for the product, claimed as a product, is not limited by the process with

---

[24]*Id.*

[25]*See* KARL DRLICA, UNDERSTANDING DNA AND GENE CLONING: A GUIDE FOR THE CURIOUS 14 (4th ed. 2003) (describing the method for expression of human insulin genes in bacteria).

[26]The process claim might nevertheless be infringed under the doctrine of equivalents if the accused process is insubstantially different. The doctrine of equivalents is examined in Chapter 9 ("Patent Infringement"), *infra.*

which it is made. Nor is it relevant whether the product patent owner knew of or described the processes used by the accused infringer to make product X. "[A] patentee is entitled to every use of which his invention is susceptible, whether such use be known or unknown to him."[27] Accordingly, product claims are generally considered far more economically valuable to a patentee than are process claims.

3. Computer-Implemented Processes

Many patented processes or methods are implemented through the use of computers and software. For example, in 1981 the Supreme Court in *Diamond v. Diehr*[28] upheld the patentability under 35 U.S.C. §101 of a computer-controlled process for curing synthetic rubber. By monitoring the real-time conditions inside the mold, the process control system determined when the mold should be opened by performing calculations based on the well-known Arrhenius equation. Representative claim 1 of the Diehr patent provided:

> 1. A method of operating a rubber-molding press for precision molded compounds with the aid of a digital computer, comprising:
> providing said computer with a data base for said press including at least,
> natural logarithm conversion data (ln),
> the activation energy constant (c) unique to each batch of said compound being molded, and
> a constant (x) dependent upon the geometry of the particular mold of the press,
> initiating an interval timer in said computer upon the closure of the press for monitoring the elapsed time of said closure,
> constantly determining the temperature (Z) of the mold at a location closely adjacent to the mold cavity in the press during molding,
> constantly providing the computer with the temperature (Z),
> repetitively calculating in the computer, at frequent intervals during each cure, the Arrhenius equation for reaction time during the cure, which is
> $$\ln v = CZ + x$$
> where v is the total required cure time,
> repetitively comparing in the computer at said frequent intervals during the cure each said calculation of the total required cure time calculated with the Arrhenius equation and said elapsed time, and
> opening the press automatically when a said comparison indicates equivalence.[29]

---

[27]In re Thuau, 135 F.3d 344, 347 (C.C.P.A. 1943).
[28]450 U.S. 175 (1981).
[29]*Id.* at 179 n.5.

Although unapplied mathematical algorithms, formulas, and equations are considered unpatentable abstract ideas, the Supreme Court in *Diehr* made clear that the presence of such mathematical subject matter in a patent claim (such as Diehr's claim 1) does not necessarily deprive the claim of potential patentability under 35 U.S.C. §101. Claims must be analyzed as a whole, not dissected into their component parts, for purposes of determining if an invention falls within one or more of the §101 categories. The presence of a mathematical algorithm or formula in a patent claim does not necessarily render it ineligible for patent protection.

The Supreme Court concluded that, in contrast with the inventors in its previous decisions denying patentability to computer-implemented inventions,[30] Diehr did not seek to patent a mathematical formula per se but rather a process of curing synthetic rubber. That process "admittedly employ[ed] a well-known mathematical equation, but [did] not seek to pre-empt the use of that equation."[31] Rather, Diehr sought only to foreclose others from using the Arrhenius equation in conjunction with all of the other steps recited in the claimed process, that is, installing rubber in a press, closing the mold, constantly determining the temperature of the mold, constantly recalculating the appropriate cure time through the use of the Arrhenius equation and a digital computer, and automatically

---

[30]*Diamond v. Diehr* represents the last of a trilogy of Supreme Court decisions issued between 1972 and 1981 in which the Court struggled with the patentability of computer-implemented inventions. In holding (by a 5-4 margin) that Diehr's claimed process for curing rubber was patentable subject matter within 35 U.S.C. §101, the Diehr majority sought to distinguish the two earlier decisions of the trilogy, *Gottschalk v. Benson*, 409 U.S. 63 (1972), and *Parker v. Flook*, 437 U.S. 584 (1978), as follows:

> In *Benson*, we held unpatentable claims for an algorithm used to convert binary code decimal numbers to equivalent pure binary numbers. The sole practical application of the algorithm was in connection with the programming of a general purpose digital computer. We defined "algorithm" as a "procedure for solving a given type of mathematical problem," and we concluded that such an algorithm, or mathematical formula, is like a law of nature, which cannot be the subject of a patent.
>
> *Parker v. Flook* . . . presented a similar situation. The claims were drawn to a method for computing an "alarm limit." An "alarm limit" is simply a number and the Court concluded that the application sought to protect a formula for computing this number. Using this formula, the updated alarm limit could be calculated if several other variables were known. The application, however, did not purport to explain how these other variables were to be determined, nor did it purport "to contain any disclosure relating to the chemical processes at work, the monitoring of process variables, or the means of setting off an alarm or adjusting an alarm system. All that it provides is a formula for computing an updated alarm limit."

Diehr, 450 U.S. at 185-187 (footnotes and citations omitted).

[31]*Id*. at 187.

opening the press at the proper time. Although a computer is not necessarily needed to cure natural or synthetic rubber, the Court realized that the computer use incorporated into Diehr's process patent significantly lessened the possibility of overcuring or under-curing the rubber, an important and useful result. The process as claimed represented potentially patentable subject matter under 35 U.S.C. §101.

In the aftermath of *Diehr,* some commentators suggested that in order to come within 35 U.S.C. §101, patent claims to a process (or method) comprising a mathematical algorithm had to involve a "phys-ical transformation" of material into a different state or thing, such as the curing of the synthetic rubber in *Diehr.* The Federal Circuit subsequently rejected a blanket "physical transformation" require-ment in *AT&T Corp. v. Excel Communications, Inc.*[32] There the Circuit reversed a district court's summary judgment that AT&T's '184 pat-ent, directed to a method of inserting information called a "primary interexchange carrier (PIC) indicator" into a long-distance telephone call record in order to facilitate differential billing of subscribers (depending on whether the subscriber called someone with the same or different long-distance carrier), was invalid as not falling within §101 subject matter.[33]

Rejecting defendant Excel's reading of *Diehr* as overly limited, the Federal Circuit interpreted *Diehr* as simply standing for the proposition that a "physical transformation" is "not an invariable requirement, but merely one example of how a mathematical algo-rithm may bring about a useful application."[34] The Federal Circuit concluded in *AT&T* that, although the claimed process admittedly applied a simple Boolean principle to determine the value of the PIC indicator, this process produced a "useful, concrete, tangible result" without preempting other uses of the mathematical princi-ple.[35] Thus the claimed process "comfortably" fell within the scope of 35 U.S.C. §101.[36]

4. Business Methods

A process or method of doing business or operating a business is potentially patentable, just as is a method for doing anything else, so

[32]172 F.3d 1352 (Fed. Cir. 1999).
[33]*Id.* at 1353.
[34]*Id.* at 1358-1359.
[35]*Id.* at 1358.
[36]*Id.*

long as the claimed method is not an unapplied, abstract idea or concept. A watershed case on business method patentability is *State St. Bank & Trust Co. v. Signature Fin. Group, Inc.,*[37] which addressed the patentability of Signature's computer-implemented, hub and spoke–configured system for managing a partner-fund financial services configuration. Representative claim 1 provided as follows, with the bracketed language indicating the structure disclosed in the written description as corresponding to each recited "means" in accordance with 35 U.S.C. §112, ¶6 (1994):

1. A data processing system for managing a financial services configuration of a portfolio established as a partnership, each partner being one of a plurality of funds, comprising:

(a) computer processor means [a personal computer including a CPU] for processing data;

(b) storage means [a data disk] for storing data on a storage medium;

(c) first means [an arithmetic logic circuit configured to prepare the data disk to magnetically store selected data] for initializing the storage medium;

(d) second means [an arithmetic logic circuit configured to retrieve information from a specific file, calculate incremental increases or decreases based on specific input, allocate the results on a percentage basis, and store the output in a separate file] for processing data regarding assets in the portfolio and each of the funds from a previous day and data regarding increases or decreases in each of the funds [sic funds'] assets and for allocating the percentage share that each fund holds in the portfolio;

(e) third means [an arithmetic logic circuit configured to retrieve information from a specific file, calculate incremental increases and decreases based on specific input, allocate the results on a percentage basis and store the output in a separate file] for processing data regarding daily incremental income, expenses, and net realized gain or loss for the portfolio and for allocating such data among each fund;

(f) fourth means [an arithmetic logic circuit configured to retrieve information from a specific file, calculate incremental increases and decreases based on specific input, allocate the results on a percentage basis and store the output in a separate file] for processing data regarding daily net unrealized gain or loss for the portfolio and for allocating such data among each fund; and

(g) fifth means [an arithmetic logic circuit configured to retrieve information from specific files, calculate that information on an aggregate basis and store the output in a separate file] for processing data

---

[37]149 F.3d 1368 (Fed. Cir. 1998).

regarding aggregate year-end income, expenses, and capital gain or loss for the portfolio and each of the funds.[38]

On motion for summary judgment by accused infringer State Street, the district court held Signature's patent invalid as claiming subject matter that fell within two judicially recognized exceptions to patentable subject matter under §101: the so-called business method and mathematical algorithm exceptions.

The Federal Circuit reversed, holding the claims at issue were directed to a statutory "machine" under 35 U.S.C. §101, albeit one programmed with "hub and spoke" software. The key question in a §101 determination, the appellate court stressed, is not which of the four statutory categories the claimed invention may fit into (e.g., machine versus process). Rather, attention should focus on the essential characteristics of the invention, namely, its "practical utility."[39] In this case, the Signature system's utility was evidenced by its production of a "useful, concrete, and tangible result,"[40] even though this result was expressed in numerical values (such as a fund share price) rather than something more conventionally physical (e.g., widgets).[41]

The Federal Circuit minced no words in taking the opportunity presented by the *State Street* case "to lay th[e] ill-conceived [business method] exception to rest."[42] A method of doing business should be treated just as any other type of method, the court emphasized. Each of the earlier business method exception cases could have been decided on clearer grounds, the court explained; the results in those cases would have been the same had the inventions been more properly characterized as abstract ideas under the mathematical algorithm exception to patentability.

[38]*Id.* at 1371-1372. For additional detail on the interpretation of means plus function clauses in patent claims, *see* ROBERT C. KAHRL, PATENT CLAIM CONSTRUCTION §§8.01-8.10 (Aspen 2008 Supp.). The America Invents Act of 2011 renamed paragraph 6 of §112 as 35 U.S.C §112(f) (eff. Sept. 16, 2012).

[39]*State Street*, 149 F.3d at 1375.

[40]*Id.*

[41]In *In re Bilski*, 545 F.3d 943 (Fed. Cir. 2008) *(en banc)*, the Federal Circuit characterized *State Street*'s "useful, concrete, and tangible result" language as an inadequate or insufficient test, standing alone, for determining whether claimed subject matter is potentially patentable under 35 U.S.C. §101. *See In re Bilski*, 545 F.3d at 959-960. The Supreme Court thereafter confirmed that "nothing in today's opinion should be read as endorsing interpretations of §101 that the Court of Appeals for the Federal Circuit has used in the past." *Bilski v. Kappos,* 130 S. Ct. 3218, 3231 (citing *State Street*, 149 F.3d at 1373; *AT&T Corp.,* 172 F.3d at 1357). *Bilski* and its treatment of *State Street* are discussed in further detail *infra*.

[42]*State Street*, 149 F.3d at 1375.

Following the Federal Circuit's 1998 decision in *State Street,* the USPTO received a flood of business method patent applications.[43] Although the eligibility of business methods as potentially patentable subject matter under §101 is now settled, it remains to be seen whether many of the claimed business methods will meet the exacting novelty and nonobviousness criteria of §102 and §103, as well as the enablement and written description requirements under §112(a). For example, the Federal Circuit raised serious questions about the nonobviousness of the "one-click" product ordering method patented to much fanfare by the Internet retailer Amazon.com.[44]

Is a business method for conducting mandatory arbitration of legal documents such as wills and contracts within §101 patentable subject matter? To the extent that such a method depends entirely on the use of human intelligence, and does not require a computer or other machine, the Federal Circuit in 2007 answered in the negative.[45] The claimed invention in *In re Comiskey* encompassed a "method for mandatory arbitration resolution regarding one or more unilateral documents," comprising the steps of enrolling a person and his associated documents (such as a will) in the mandatory arbitration system, incorporating arbitration language in the enrolled document, requiring a complainant to submit a request for binding arbitration resolution when a dispute arises concerning interpretation of the document, conducting arbitration resolution, providing support to the arbitration, and determining a final and binding award or decision in the dispute.[46] Other claims recited using the process to resolve disputes over contracts rather than wills.[47] Applicant Comiskey agreed with the USPTO that these process claims did not require the use of a computer or other mechanical device.

The Federal Circuit affirmed the USPTO's rejection of Comiskey's claims as not within §101 patentable subject matter.[48] Comiskey claimed "the use of mental processes to resolve a dispute"; that is, he sought "to patent the use of human intelligence in and of itself."[49] Even

---

[43]*See generally* United States Patent & Trademark Office, *Whitepaper, Automated Financial or Management Data Processing Methods (Business Methods)* 7, *available at* http://www.uspto.gov/web/menu/busmethp/whitepaper.pdf (last visited June 18, 2012).

[44]*See* Amazon.com, Inc. v. Barnesandnoble.com, Inc., 239 F.3d 1343, 1359-1360 (Fed. Cir. 2001) (vacating district court's grant of preliminary injunction against accused infringer Barnesandnoble.com on ground that it had "mounted a serious challenge to the validity of Amazon's patent" under §103).

[45]*See* In re Comiskey, 499 F.3d 1365 (Fed. Cir. 2007).

[46]*See id.* at 1368 n.1 (reproducing text of application claim 1).

[47]*See id.* at 1369 n.2 (reproducing text of application claim 32).

[48]*See id.* at 1381 (affirming rejection of Comiskey's independent claims 1 and 32 and dependent claims 2-14, 16, 33-34, and 45).

[49]*Id.* at 1379.

though Comiskey's process arguably performed a useful, practical service (arbitration of legal disputes), "mental processes—or processes of human thinking—standing alone are not patentable even if they have practical application."[50] The Patent Act "does not allow patents to be issued on particular business systems—such as a particular type of arbitration—that depend entirely on the use of mental processes."[51] The *Comiskey* court concluded that such endeavors were intended "both [by] the framers and Congress . . . to be beyond the reach of patentable subject matter."[52]

Continued controversy over the patenting of business methods,[53] and a perceived lack of clarity in Federal Circuit law over where to draw the line between patentable process inventions within §101 and unpatentable abstract ideas or fundamental principles, led the court in 2007 to grant *en banc* review of these issues in *In re Bilski.*[54] As discussed *infra,* the case would eventually reach the U.S. Supreme Court.[55]

Bilski's claimed invention involved a method of hedging risk in the field of commodities trading.[56] Claim 1 of Bilski's application recited the following:

[50]*Id.* at 1377. *See also* In re Bilski, 545 F.3d 943, 961 n.26 (Fed. Cir. Oct. 30, 2008) (*en banc*) (stating that "a claimed process wherein all of the process steps may be performed entirely in the human mind is obviously not tied to any machine and does not transform any article into a different state or thing. As a result, it would not be patent-eligible under § 101.").

[51]*Comiskey,* 499 F.3d at 1378.

[52]*Id.* at 1378-1379.

[53]*See, e.g.,* eBay, Inc. v. MercExchange, LLC, 547 U.S. 388, 397 (2006) (Kennedy, J., concurring) (referring to the "potential vagueness and suspect validity" of some business method patents).

[54]In re Bilski, 545 F.3d 943 (Fed. Cir. 2008) (*en banc*). As discussed *infra,* the Supreme Court subsequently granted *certiorari* and reviewed the Federal Circuit in *Bilski v. Kappos,* 130 S. Ct. 3218 (2010), a splintered decision that sustained the Federal Circuit on the merits but rejected much of the appellate court's reasoning.

[55]Bilski v. Kappos, 130 S. Ct. 3218 (2010).

[56]The Federal Circuit provided the following example of one implementation of Bilski's invention:

[C]oal power plants (i.e., the "consumers" [of claim 1]) purchase coal to produce electricity and are averse to the risk of a spike in demand for coal since such a spike would increase the price and their costs. Conversely, coal mining companies (i.e., the "market participants") are averse to the risk of a sudden drop in demand for coal since such a drop would reduce their sales and depress prices. The claimed method envisions an intermediary, the "commodity provider," that sells coal to the power plants at a fixed price, thus isolating the power plants from the possibility of a spike in demand increasing the price of coal above the fixed price. The same provider buys coal from mining companies at a second fixed price, thereby isolating the mining companies from the possibility that a drop in demand would lower prices below that fixed price. And the provider has thus hedged its risk; if demand and prices skyrocket, it has sold coal at a

1. A method for managing the consumption risk costs of a commodity sold by a commodity provider at a fixed price comprising the steps of:
    (a) initiating a series of transactions between said commodity provider and consumers of said commodity wherein said consumers purchase said commodity at a fixed rate based upon historical averages, said fixed rate corresponding to a risk position of said consumer;
    (b) identifying market participants for said commodity having a counter-risk position to said consumers; and
    (c) initiating a series of transactions between said commodity provider and said market participants at a second fixed rate such that said series of market participant transactions balances the risk position of said series of consumer transactions.[57]

A USPTO Examiner had rejected Bilski's claims because they were "not implemented on a specific apparatus and merely manipulate[d] [an] abstract idea and solve[d] a purely mathematical problem without any limitation to a practical application."[58] The USPTO Board agreed that the claims were not patentable, but on the grounds that their "transformation of non-physical financial risks and legal liabilities" was not patentable subject matter, that they pre-empted every possible way of performing the claimed process "by human or by any kind of machine," and that they were directed only to an abstract idea.[59]

The Federal Circuit affirmed the USPTO's rejection of Bilski's claims as not being within §101 patentable processes.[60] In reaching its conclusion, the appellate court undertook an extensive review of Supreme Court, CCPA, and Federal Circuit case law addressing the meaning of "process" under 35 U.S.C. §101. The key issues for the Federal Circuit were whether Bilski was "seeking to claim a fundamental principle (such as an abstract idea) or a mental process,"[61] and if so, whether Bilski's claim "would pre-empt substantially all uses of that fundamental principle if allowed."[62]

---

disadvantageous price but has bought coal at an advantageous price, and vice versa if demand and prices fall.

In re Bilski, 545 F.3d at 950. Notably, Bilski's claim 1 was "not limited to transactions involving actual commodities." *Id*. Bilski's application disclosed that the recited transactions might "simply involve options, i.e., rights to purchase or sell the commodity at a particular price within a particular timeframe." *Id*.

[57]*Id*. at 949.
[58]*Id*. at 950.
[59]*See id*.
[60]*Id*. at 965.
[61]*Id*. at 952. The court defined the phrase "fundamental principles" as used in its *Bilski* opinion to encompass "laws of nature, natural phenomena, and abstract ideas." *Id*. at 952 n.5.
[62]*Id*. at 954. Elaborating on how a claim might "pre-empt" all uses of a fundamental principle, the *Bilski* court explained that "pre-emption is merely an indication that a claim seeks to cover a fundamental principle itself rather than only a specific

Admitting that these issues are "hardly straightforward,"[63] the Federal Circuit devised a new test to govern determinations by the USPTO or the courts "as to whether a claim to a process is patentable under §101, or, conversely, is drawn to unpatentable subject matter because it claims only a fundamental principle."[64] The Federal Circuit drew its test primarily from two Supreme Court decisions, *Gottschalk v. Benson*[65] and *Diamond v. Diehr*[66] (the latter, 1981 decision representing the Supreme Court's most recent consideration of the patentability of a process under §101).[67] The *Bilski* court concluded that

> [a] claimed process is surely patent-eligible under § 101 if (1) it is tied to a particular machine or apparatus, *or* (2) it transforms a particular article into a different state or thing. . . . A claimed process involving a fundamental principle that uses a particular machine or apparatus would not pre-empt uses of the principle that do not also use the specified machine or apparatus in the manner claimed. And a claimed process that transforms a particular article to a specified different state or thing by applying a fundamental principle would not pre-empt the use of the principle to transform any other article, to transform the same article but not in a manner not covered by the claim, or to do anything other than transform the specified article.[68]

The "machine or transformation" test announced in *Bilski* left a number of questions unanswered. For example, because Bilski's claim 1 did not require a machine, the Federal Circuit did not elaborate on issues specific to the "process tied to a machine or apparatus" prong (1) of its machine or transformation test. The court explicitly left open the question whether reciting a computer in a process claim will necessarily satisfy prong (1) and thus render that claim potentially patentable subject matter under §101.[69]

---

application of that principle." *Id.* at 957. However, "a claim that is tied to a particular machine or brings about a particular transformation of a particular article does not pre-empt all uses of a fundamental principle in any field but rather is limited to a particular use, a specific application. Therefore, [such a claim] is not drawn to the principle in the abstract." *Id.* For example, recall that even though the synthetic rubber-curing process in *Diamond v. Diehr*, 450 U.S. 175 (1981), involved the use of the well-known Arrhenius equation, the process did not pre-empt all uses of that equation. Instead, Diehr's patent only prevented competitors from using the equation in conjunction with performing all the other steps recited in Diehr's process of operating a rubber-molding press with the aid of a digital computer. For further discussion of *Diehr, see supra* Section B.3 ("Computer-Implemented Processes").

[63]*Bilski*, 545 F.3d at 953.
[64]*Id.*
[65]409 U.S. 63 (1972).
[66]450 U.S. 175 (1981).
[67]*Diehr* is discussed *supra* at Section B.3 ("Computer-Implemented Processes").
[68]*Bilski*, 545 F.3d at 954 (citations omitted).
[69]*See id.* at 951.

More relevant to the case at bar was whether Bilski's claim 1 satisfied the "transform[ation] of a particular article into a different state or thing" prong (2) of the Federal Circuit's new test. Satisfaction of prong (2) in turn depends on what qualifies as an "article." The court explained that "article" in the sense of its transformation test need not be limited to a tangible, physical substance such as the rubber cured in *Diehr.* It recognized that "[t]he raw materials of many information-age processes . . . are electronic signals and electronically-manipulated data."[70]

Rather than set forth an explicit definition of "article," the Federal Circuit in *Bilski* adopted a "measured approach"[71] and provided examples from precedent. Based on its predecessor court's decision in *In re Abele,*[72] the Federal Circuit concluded that "transformation of . . . raw data into a particular visual depiction of a physical object" will result in a §101 patentable process.[73] For example, Abele's invention as recited in certain dependent claims involved the transformation of x-ray attenuation data to represent physical, tangible objects such as the body's bones, organs, and tissues. These dependent claims were allowable,[74] in contrast to Abele's broader (and not allowable) independent claim that recited a process of graphically displaying variances of data from average values.[75] The Federal Circuit in *Bilski* clarified that transformation of data into a visual depiction (as in *Abele*'s dependent claims) is sufficient; §101 process claims are "not required to involve any transformation of the underlying physical object that the data represented."[76] In sum, a process will satisfy the "transformation" prong (2) of the Federal Circuit's *Bilski* test "[s]o long as the claimed process is limited to a practical application of a fundamental principle to transform specific data, and the claim is limited to a visual depiction that represents specific physical objects or substances. . . . "[77] If a process claim is thus limited, "there is no danger that its scope would wholly pre-empt all uses of the principle."[78]

With this understanding of "transformation" in hand, the Federal Circuit returned to an analysis of Bilski's claim 1 and concluded that it did not satisfy the "transformation" prong of the machine or transformation test. Bilski's claimed process for hedging risk in commodities trading involved the "[p]urported transformations or manipulations

---

[70]*Id.* at 961.
[71]*Id.* at 962.
[72]684 F.2d 902 (C.C.P.A. 1982).
[73]*Bilski,* 545 F.3d at 962.
[74]*See id.* at 963; *Abele,* 684 F.2d at 908-909.
[75]*See Bilski,* 545 F.3d at 962; *Abele,* 684 F.2d at 909.
[76]*Bilski,* 545 F.3d at 963.
[77]*Bilski,* 545 F.3d at 963.
[78]*Bilski,* 545 F.3d at 963.

simply of public or private legal obligations relationships, business risks, or other such abstractions."[79] Such "abstractions" cannot satisfy the transformation test "because they are not physical objects or substances [like the rubber cured in *Diehr*], and they are not representative of physical objects or substances [as were the data in the dependent claims of *Abele*]."[80]

The Federal Circuit in *Bilski* admitted that its new machine or transformation test might present "difficult challenges" for "future developments in technology and the sciences."[81] The Supreme Court apparently agreed. As discussed below, the Supreme Court granted *certiorari* and held in its 2010 *Bilski v. Kappos* decision that while the Federal Circuit's machine or transformation (MORT) test may signify an "important clue" to patent eligibility, it is not a satisfactory stand-alone test.[82]

While the weight to be afforded the Federal Circuit's machine or transformation test remains uncertain, it is important to keep in mind those §101 basic principles that the Federal Circuit in *Bilski* did not alter. The appellate court reaffirmed that the question whether subject matter is potentially patentable under §101 is entirely separate from the analysis of whether that subject matter is novel and nonobvious under §102 and §103, respectively.[83] Moreover, identifying the §101 eligibility of a process claim requires analyzing the claim as a whole, rather than dissecting it to consider whether individual process steps or limitations would be unpatentable under §101.[84]

Notably, the Federal Circuit in *Bilski* did not overrule the core holding of *State St. Bank & Trust Co. v. Signature Fin. Group, Inc.,*[85] discussed *supra,* that business methods are potentially patentable subject matter under §101 just like any other type of method or process.[86] Nor did the Federal Circuit adopt a "broad exclusion over software," as some *amici* had urged.[87] Nevertheless, the Federal Circuit in *Bilski* rejected *State Street*'s "useful, concrete, and tangible result" inquiry as an adequate stand-alone test for determining §101 patentability.[88] While the *State Street* inquiry may still be useful in many cases, it is

---

[79]*Bilski*, 545 F.3d at 963.

[80]*Bilski*, 545 F.3d at 945.

[81]*Bilski*, 545 F.3d at 956.

[82]*See Bilski v. Kappos,* 130 S. Ct. 3218 (2010).

[83]*See Bilski*, 545 F.3d at 958.

[84]*See Bilski,* 545 F.3d at 958.

[85]149 F.3d 1368 (Fed. Cir. 1998).

[86]*See Bilski*, 545 F.3d at 960 (citing *State Street*, 149 F.3d at 1375-1376).

[87]*See id.* at n.23.

[88]*See id.* at 959 (explaining that "while looking for 'a useful, concrete and tangible result' may in many instances provide useful indications of whether a claim is drawn to a fundamental principle or a practical application of such a principle, that inquiry is insufficient to determine whether a claim is patent-eligible under §101").

no longer a controlling legal inquiry for patent eligibility of business methods.

Much as the Federal Circuit rejected the "useful, concrete, and tangible result" test it had previously adopted in *State Street*, so too did the Supreme Court reject the "machine or transformation" test announced by the Federal Circuit in *In re Bilski* as *the* controlling test for determining whether a process claim is eligible for patenting under §101. After the Federal Circuit's decision in *In re Bilski*, the Supreme Court in June 2009 granted a petition for *certiorari* filed by patent applicants Bilski and Warsaw.[89] More than a year later, the Court issued its much-anticipated decision in *Bilski v. Kappos*.[90] The Supreme Court produced a complex, fragmented opinion, but ultimately affirmed the Federal Circuit's holding on the merits that Bilski's claimed method was not a patent-eligible "process" within the meaning of 35 U.S.C. §101. Five Justices joined some (but not all) parts of the "opinion of the Court" authored by Justice Kennedy [hereafter "Kennedy majority"].[91] The four other Supreme Court Justices concurred only in the judgment of the Court, in a separate opinion authored by retiring Justice Stevens [hereafter "Stevens minority"].

Most importantly, the Supreme Court's decision in *Bilski v. Kappos* confirmed (by a one-vote margin) that business methods are still potentially patentable as processes under §101. The Kennedy majority did not categorically exclude business methods from §101 as the Stevens minority would have.

But what are the criteria or indicia required for a claimed process or method, particularly a business method, to qualify as potentially patentable under §101? Unhelpfully, the Supreme Court in *Bilski v.*

---

[89]*See* 129 S. Ct. 2735 (2009).

[90]130 S. Ct. 3218 (2010). The June 28, 2010, date of the decision was significant; it marked both the final day for issuance of opinions in cases argued during the October 2009 term and the last day of Justice John Paul Stevens' 34-year tenure on the Supreme Court.

[91]Justice Scalia did not join Parts II.B.2 and II.C.2 of Justice Kennedy's opinion. Thus Parts II.B.2 and II.C.2 of the Kennedy opinion, while of considerable interest, have only "plurality" or four-vote status and do not constitute binding precedent or a judgment of the Court.

Part II.B.2 of the Kennedy plurality opinion can be summarized by quoting Justice Kennedy's own phrase: "times change." Although the Federal Circuit's MORT test may have worked well for evaluating process patent eligibility in the Industrial Age, application of MORT to "Information Age" technologies such as software and advanced medical diagnostic techniques would create unacceptable uncertainty. Bilski v. Kappos, 130 S. Ct. at 3227.

Part II.C.2 of the Kennedy plurality opinion reiterates Justice Kennedy's concerns about business method patents, some of which he believes "raise special problems in terms of vagueness and suspect validity." Bilski v. Kappos, 130 S. Ct. at 3229 (quoting eBay Inc. v. MercExchange, LLC, 547 U.S. 388, 397 (2006) (Kennedy, J., concurring)).

Kappos clarified what would *not* suffice as an acceptable test, but offered little new or illuminating explanation of what *would*.

The Kennedy majority began by describing §101 patent eligibility principles as "broad," but constrained by three "specific exceptions": (1) laws of nature, (2) physical phenomena, and (3) abstract ideas.[92] The last of these exceptions, "abstract ideas," applied to the case before the Court.

The Kennedy majority took pains to avoid defining the precise parameters of an "abstract idea." Indeed, the Stevens minority aptly complained that "[t]he Court . . . never provides a satisfying account of what constitutes an unpatentable abstract idea."[93] Rather, the Kennedy majority clung to the facts of a trilogy of 1970s/1980s decisions in which the Supreme Court for the first time had confronted the patent eligibility of computer-implemented processes. "Rather than adopting categorical rules that might have wide-ranging and unforeseen impacts," the Kennedy majority in *Bilski v. Kappos* chose to resolve the case before it "narrowly on the basis of [the Supreme Court's prior] decisions in *Benson, Flook,* and *Diehr*, which show that petitioners' claims are not patentable processes because they are attempts to patent abstract ideas."

In denying §101 eligibility to Bilski's application claims, the Kennedy majority relied primarily on the first case of the trilogy, the Supreme Court's 1972 decision in *Gottschalk v. Benson*.[94] Justice Kennedy summarized the *Benson* decision as follows:

> In *Benson*, the Court considered whether a patent application for an algorithm to convert binary-coded decimal numerals into pure binary code was a "process" under §101. . . . The Court first explained that "'[a] principle, in the abstract, is a fundamental truth; an original cause; a motive; these cannot be patented, as no one can claim in either of them an exclusive right.'" . . . The Court then held the application at issue was not a "process," but an unpatentable abstract idea. "It is conceded that one may not patent an idea. But in practical effect that would be the result if the formula for converting . . . numerals to pure binary numerals were patented in this case." . . . A contrary holding "would wholly pre-empt the mathematical formula and in practical effect would be a patent on the algorithm itself."[95]

---

[92]Bilski v. Kappos, 130 S. Ct. at 3227.

[93]Bilski v. Kappos, 130 S. Ct. at 3236 (Stevens, J., concurring in the result). The concurring Justices agreed that the majority's "mode of analysis (or lack thereof) may have led to the correct outcome in this case, but it also means that the Court's musings on this issue stand for very little." 130 S. Ct. at 3236.

[94]409 U.S. 63 (1972) (denying §101 eligibility to a claimed process that utilized an algorithm to convert binary-coded decimal numerals into pure binary code).

[95]Bilski v. Kappos, 130 S. Ct. at 3230 (citations omitted).

The Kennedy majority summarily concluded that Bilski's process was an "unpatentable abstract idea, just like the algorithm[] at issue in *Benson*,"[96] but did not explain how or why Bilski's method was at the same level of abstractness as Benson's.[97]

Also relevant as illustrating an unpatentable "abstract idea" was the Supreme Court's 1978 decision in *Parker v. Flook*,[98] the Court's "next logical step after *Benson*."[99] As in *Benson,* the Court in *Flook* denied §101 eligibility for a process. Flook claimed a process control method for use in connection with catalytic conversion in the oil industry. According to the Kennedy majority in *Bilski v. Kappos*, the *Flook* invention's only point of novelty was its "reliance on a mathematical algorithm."

Admittedly, Flook's process was more narrowly claimed than the *Benson* process because the claims in *Flook* were limited to use of the recited process in the petrochemical and oil refining contexts. Thus the *Flook* process would not "pre-empt" the use of the recited mathematical algorithm in *all* fields of endeavor. Nevertheless, the *Flook* process did not qualify within §101 because it added only conventional "postsolution activity" to the algorithm or formula recited in the claims. The Supreme Court in *Flook* instructed that "the prohibition against patenting abstract ideas 'cannot be circumvented by attempting to limit the use of the formula to a particular technological environment' or adding 'insignificant postsolution activity.'"[100]

Based on this summary of its precedent, the Kennedy majority analogized the process claimed in *Bilski v. Kappos* to the processes at issue in *Benson* and *Flook,* and declared Bilski's claims similarly outside the scope of §101 patent-eligible subject matter. In the Kennedy majority's view, claims 1 and 4 of Bilski's patent application "explain[ed] the basic concept of hedging, or protecting against risk," which the majority considered a "fundamental economic practice long prevalent in our system of commerce."[101] The Kennedy majority held that "the concept of hedging, described in claim 1 [of Bilski's application] and reduced to a mathematical formula in claim 4, is an unpatentable abstract idea, just like the algorithms at issue in *Benson* and *Flook*."[102] To allow

---

[96]Bilski v. Kappos, 130 S. Ct. at 3231.

[97]Professor Chisum critiques the *Bilski* Court's reliance on *Benson,* a decision he views as driven not by sound policy but rather by the anti-patent bias prevalent in the 1960s and 1970s. Donald S. Chisum, *Patenting Intangible Methods: Revisiting Benson (1972) After Bilski (2010)* (Oct. 27, 2010), *available at* http://papers.ssrn.com/sol3/papers.cfm?abstract_id=1698724.

[98]437 U.S. 584 (1978).

[99]Bilski v. Kappos, 130 S. Ct. at 3230.

[100]Bilski v. Kappos, 130 S. Ct. at 3230 (quoting Diamond v. Diehr, 450 U.S. 175, 191-192 (1981)).

[101]Bilski v. Kappos, 130 S. Ct. at 3231.

[102]Bilski v. Kappos, 130 S. Ct. at 3231.

Bilski to patent what the majority deemed "risk hedging" would "pre-empt use of this approach in all fields, and would effectively grant a monopoly over an abstract idea."[103]

Thus the Supreme Court in *Bilski v. Kappos* affirmed the Federal Circuit's holding on the merits that Bilski's claimed method was not a patent-eligible "process" within the meaning of 35 U.S.C. §101. All nine Supreme Court Justices agreed on this point; the Kennedy majority opinion confirmed that "all members of the Court agree that the patent application at issue here falls outside of §101 because it claims an abstract idea."[104]

Although Bilski's claimed process would not satisfy §101, the Kennedy majority did not go so far as to categorically exclude *all* business methods from patenting. The Patent Act specifically enumerates a process as potentially patentable subject matter,[105] and nothing in the statute excludes processes used to conduct a business (i.e., "business methods") from the conventional definition of "process." The Kennedy majority explained that the "term 'method,' which is within §100(b)'s definition of 'process,' at least as a textual matter and before consulting other limitations in the Patent Act and this Court's precedents, may include at least some methods of doing business."[106]

Other provisions of the Patent Act supported the Kennedy majority's reluctance to bar all business methods from eligibility under §101. In the version then in effect, §273 of the patent statute provided a limited prior user defense to charges of infringement of a patent claim that recited a method of doing or conducting business.[107] When Congress enacted §273, it explicitly referred to (and thus implicitly acknowledged) the existence of patent claims for business methods. Thus, the Kennedy majority felt it ill advised to interpret §101 in a manner that would categorically exclude all such methods from patentability. In

---

[103]Bilski v. Kappos, 130 S. Ct. at 3231.

[104]Bilski v. Kappos, 130 S. Ct. at 3230.

[105]35 U.S.C. §101.

[106]Bilski v. Kappos, 130 S. Ct. at 3228. The Court also reasoned that "[n]or is it clear how far a prohibition on business method patents would reach, and whether it would exclude technologies for conducting a business more efficiently." 130 S. Ct. at 3228 (citing Bronwyn H. Hall, *Business and Financial Method Patents, Innovation, and Policy*, 56 Scottish J. Pol. Econ. 443, 445 (2009) ("There is no precise definition of . . . business method patents.")).

[107]*See* 35 U.S.C. §§273(a)(3), (b) (2006). The America Invents Act of 2011 significantly broadened the potential applicability of prior user rights to alleged infringements involving much more than business methods. *See* Leahy-Smith America Invents Act, Pub. L. No. 112-29 (H.R. 1249), §5, 125 Stat. 284, 297 (2011) ("Defense to infringement based on prior commercial use"); 35 U.S.C. §273(a) (effective Sept. 16, 2011, for patents issued on or after that date) (providing that prior use defense is potentially available for otherwise infringing acts involving "subject matter consisting of a process, or consisting of a machine, manufacture, or composition of matter used in a manufacturing or other commercial process").

other words, interpreting §101 to bar all business methods would contravene the statutory construction canon that prohibits interpreting one statutory provision in a manner that would render superfluous another provision of the statute.

The four concurring Justices in *Bilski v. Kappos* would have gone considerably beyond the Kennedy majority in restraining the patenting of business methods. Concurring Justice Stevens (writing for himself and Justices Ginsburg, Breyer, and Sotomayor) would have categorically held that business methods are not patentable.[108] Emphasizing policy concerns, the Stevens minority expressed "serious doubts about whether patents are necessary to encourage business innovation," citing as an example Federal Express's unpatented development of overnight delivery.[109] The Stevens minority also offered a detailed historical justification, focusing on the development of English and American patent law, to conclude that a method of doing business should not be considered a "process" within §101.

Nor was the Stevens minority persuaded by the Kennedy majority's reliance on the enactment of 35 U.S.C. §273 as part of the 1999 First Inventor Defense Act. The opinion in 1999 of some members of Congress that patents were potentially available for business methods should not trump the narrower interpretation of earlier Congresses as evidenced by the historical record. In the Stevens minority's view, the §273 argument was simply a "red herring." Rather than affirmatively *endorsing* the grant of business method patents, the 1999 First Inventor Defense Act focused on providing a *defense* to charges of business method patent infringement, "reflect[ing] surprise and perhaps even dismay that business methods might be patented" in the wake of the Federal Circuit's 1998 decision in *State Street Bank*.[110]

Although affirming the Federal Circuit on the merits, holding that Bilski's claim was not a "process" within §101, the Kennedy majority certainly did not embrace all doctrinal aspects of the Federal Circuit's decision. Consistent with its desire to avoid defining any exact parameters of the "abstract idea" exception to patentable subject matter, the Kennedy majority declined to adopt the Federal Circuit's narrow conceptualization of the machine or transformation test as the *sole* test for §101 eligibility of a process. While the Kennedy majority described the machine or transformation test as a "useful and important clue, an investigative tool" for determining what constitutes a statutory process, it rejected the test as the exclusive or exhaustive test.[111] Although the Supreme Court had admittedly adopted a MORT-style

[108]*See* Bilski v. Kappos, 130 S. Ct. at 3232 (Stevens, J., concurring in the judgment).
[109]*See* Bilski v. Kappos, 130 S. Ct. at 3254 (Stevens, J., concurring in the judgment).
[110]*See* Bilski v. Kappos, 130 S. Ct. at 3251 (Stevens, J., concurring in the judgment).
[111]Bilski v. Kappos, 130 S. Ct. at 3227.

test in its nineteenth-century decisions,[112] more recent precedent such as *Gottschalk v. Benson* "rejected the broad implications of this dictum" and demonstrated that a machine or transformation inquiry "was not intended to be an exhaustive or exclusive test."[113]

Thus, the Supreme Court in its 2010 *Bilski v. Kappos* decision held the claimed business method unpatentable under §101 as an "abstract idea," while providing minimal substantive guidance concerning future identification of unpatentable abstract ideas.[114] In 2012 the Supreme Court would decide another §101 case, this time with a more specific (and potentially wider-reaching) refutation of patent eligibility.

5.   Methods of Medical Treatment

The Supreme Court's 2012 decision in *Mayo Collaborative Servs. v. Prometheus Labs. Inc.* held that patent claims directed to certain diagnostic methods used in health care were not patent-eligible under 35 U.S.C. §101.[115] The Supreme Court's *Mayo* decision refutes the idea that methods of medical treatment claims are fundamentally different and inherently more likely to fit comfortably within §101 than business method claims of the type at issue in *Bilski v. Kappos*.[116] The *Mayo* decision has potentially sweeping negative repercussions for the medical research community. But the language of *Mayo* is not limited to medical diagnostic methods. In the long term, *Mayo* may have a far greater impact than *Bilski* on patent eligibility across the board.

The patents at issue in *Mayo,* owned by plaintiff Prometheus Laboratories, Inc., claimed methods for calibrating the proper dosage of a drug for treating autoimmune diseases such as Crohn's disease and ulcerative colitis.[117] The goal of the methods was to determine

[112]*See* Bilski v. Kappos, 130 S. Ct. at 3226 (citing Cochrane v. Deener, 94 U.S. 780, 788 (1877) (explaining that a "process" is "an act, or a series of acts, performed upon the subject-matter to be transformed and reduced to a different state or thing")).

[113]Bilski v. Kappos, 130 S. Ct. at 3227 (holding that "[t]he machine-or-transformation test is not the sole test for deciding whether an invention is a patent-eligible 'process'").

[114]The USPTO issued guidance to its examining corps that characterized *Bilski v. Kappos* as having "refined the abstract idea exception to subject matter that is eligible for patenting." *See* United States Patent & Trademark Office, *Interim Guidance for Determining Subject Matter Eligibility for Process Claims in View of* Bilski v. Kappos, 75 FED. REG. 43922 (July 27, 2010) (stating that "[t]he Office is especially interested in receiving comments regarding the scope and extent of the holding in *Bilski*").

[115]132 S. Ct. 1289 (2012).

[116]The Federal Circuit felt differently, *see* Prometheus Labs., Inc. v. Mayo Collaborative Servs., 628 F.3d 1347, 1356 n.2 (Fed. Cir. 2010) (pointing out that "this case does not involve business method patents"), but the Supreme Court nonetheless reversed.

[117]*See* U.S. Pat. Nos. 6,355,623 and 6,680,302.

a therapeutically optimal drug dosage while minimizing toxic side effects to the patients taking the drug. More particularly, certain of the claimed methods involved the steps of (1) administering to a patient a drug that, in the patient's body, would metabolize to 6-thioguanine ("6-TG"); then (2) determining the level of 6-TG metabolite in a blood sample taken from the patient; and finally, (3) comparing the level determined from the sample against particular pre-determined levels, to warn the patient or indicate a need to adjust the drug dosage administered thereafter. A representative claim recited:

> 1. A method of optimizing therapeutic efficacy for treatment of an immune-mediated gastrointestinal disorder, comprising:
> (a) *administering* a drug providing 6-thioguanine to a subject having said immune-mediated gastrointestinal disorder; and
> (b) *determining* the level of 6-thioguanine in said subject having said immune-mediated gastrointestinal disorder,
> wherein the level of 6-thioguanine less than about 230 pmol per 8 × 10^8 red blood cells *indicates a need* to increase the amount of said drug subsequently administered to said subject and
> wherein the level of 6-thioguanine greater than about 400 pmol per 8 × 10^8 red blood cells indicates a need to decrease the amount of said drug subsequently administered to said subject.[118]

A district court held that Prometheus's claims were not patentable under 35 U.S.C. §101 because the claims were drawn to correlations between metabolite levels and therapeutic efficacy and toxicity. According to the district court, such correlations were unpatentable natural phenomena resulting from a natural body process and hence outside of §101.

The Federal Circuit reversed.[119] The Circuit interpreted Prometheus's patent claims as directed not to a natural phenomenon, but rather to a particular *application* of that phenomenon. Allowing patents on the former would admittedly and entirely pre-empt the use of the correlation, which would contravene the Supreme Court's teachings in *Gottschalk v. Benson*[120] and *Parker v. Flook*.[121] In the case at bar, however, the claims passed muster under the Supreme Court's preemption test because the correlation was put to practical use in a method of medical treatment. According to the Federal Circuit, such particular

[118]*Prometheus,* 628 F.3d at 1350 (quoting '623 patent claim 1) (emphases added by Federal Circuit).
[119]Prometheus Labs., Inc. v. Mayo Collaborative Servs., 628 F.3d 1347 (Fed. Cir. 2010).
[120]409 U.S. 63 (1972), discussed *supra* in Section B.4.
[121]437 U.S. 584 (1978), discussed *supra* in Section B.4.

applications of natural phenomena are patentable in accordance with the Supreme Court's decision in *Diamond v. Diehr*.[122]

Prometheus's claimed methods of medical treatment were also patent-eligible under §101, in the Federal Circuit's view, because the claims satisfied the "transformation" prong of the Federal Circuit's MORT test. Although the Supreme Court in *Bilski v. Kappos* held that the MORT test was not a dispositive inquiry for §101 eligibility, the Court nevertheless described the MORT test as a "useful and important clue, an investigative tool" for determining whether some claimed inventions are processes under §101.[123] Relying on the continued vitality of the MORT test (at least as an "important clue"), the Federal Circuit in *Prometheus* reaffirmed that the claimed treatment methods transform a human body.[124] In particular, "[t]he asserted claims are in effect claims to methods of treatment, which are *always* transformative when one of a defined group of drugs is administered to the body to ameliorate the effects of an undesired condition."[125] That the claimed methods treated the human body was made clear by the patents' disclosure as well as the preambles of the asserted claims. These claims recited, for example, a method of optimizing therapeutic efficacy to treat certain gastrointestinal disorders and a method of reducing the toxicity associated with such treatment.[126]

The Federal Circuit in *Prometheus* conceded that, as the district court had ruled, the final "wherein" clauses of the asserted claims were merely "mental steps." These claim clauses required a comparison of the level of 6-TG determined from sampling the patient against a pre-determined level of 6-TG, so as to provide an indication or warning that the drug dosage thereafter administered would need to be adjusted up or down. Such a mental step, *in isolation*, would not be patent-eligible under §101. But Prometheus's claimed invention was the *entire* recited method, comprising the administering and determining steps as well as the final indicating step. "[W]hen viewed in the proper context, the final step of providing a warning based on the results of the prior steps does not detract from the patentability of

---

[122]*See Prometheus*, 628 F.3d at 1354, 1355 (citing *Diehr*, 450 U.S. 175 (1981)). *Diehr* is discussed *supra* in Section B.4.

[123]*Prometheus*, 628 F.3d at 1352-1353.

[124]*Prometheus*, 628 F.3d at 1355.

[125]*Prometheus*, 628 F.3d at 1356 (emphasis added).

[126]Contrary to validity challenger Mayo's arguments, the Federal Circuit took the position that the "administering" and "determining" steps of Prometheus's claimed methods did not merely involve data gathering for use in the recited correlations. Although these first two steps did gather data, they were part of a larger treatment protocol. The "administering" step provided a drug for treating a disease, and the "determining" step measured the drug's metabolite levels to assess the drug's dosage level during the course of treatment.

Prometheus's claimed methods as a whole."[127] Although the claimed methods did not require a physician to make any adjustment in a patient's drug dosage, the administering and determining steps provided useful information for such adjustments using particular drugs for a particular patient/subject. Hence, the Federal Circuit concluded, the claims satisfied the transformation prong of the MORT test, as well as the Supreme Court's *Bilski* pre-emption test.[128]

In a unanimous decision with potentially vast ramifications for patent eligibility, the Supreme Court in March 2012 roundly rejected the Federal Circuit's reasoning in *Prometheus* and reversed the appellate court's judgment.[129] In the Supreme Court's view, Prometheus's claims did not recite patentable subject matter under 35 U.S.C. §101 because they expressed unpatentable "laws of nature" accompanied merely by "additional steps consist[ing] of well-understood, routine, conventional activity already engaged in by the scientific community."[130] The additional steps "add[ed] nothing significant beyond the sum of their parts taken separately" and were "not sufficient to transform unpatentable natural correlations into patentable applications of those regularities."[131]

The Supreme Court in *Mayo* initially observed that §101 contains "an important implicit exception" providing that "'[l]aws of nature, natural phenomena, and abstract ideas' are not patentable."[132] In the case at bar, the first of these categories—"laws of nature"—encompassed Prometheus's newly discovered "precise correlations" between metabolite levels in a patient's blood[133] and the "likelihood that a particular dosage of a thiopurine drug could cause harm or prove ineffective."[134] The correlations (recited in the "wherein" clauses of representative claim 1 quoted above[135]) were "relationships" that, although triggered

---

[127]*Prometheus,* 628 F.3d at 1358. This is because all asserted claims required all three steps, and contrary to defendant Mayo's assertion, "a physician who only evaluates the result of the claimed methods, without carrying out the administering and/or determining steps that are present in all the claims, cannot infringe any claim that requires such steps." *Id.*

In the author's view, this statement by the *Prometheus* court would seem to ignore the possibility of inducing infringement liability on the part of the physician, as well as the possibility of "joint" infringement by the physician and other actors who are under the common control of a single "mastermind" entity. *See infra* Chapter 9 ("Patent Infringement").

[128]*Prometheus,* 628 F.3d at 1359.

[129]Mayo Collaborative Servs. v. Prometheus Labs., Inc., 132 S. Ct. 1289 (2012).

[130]*Mayo,* 132 S. Ct. at 1298.

[131]*Mayo,* 132 S. Ct. at 1298.

[132]*Mayo,* 132 S. Ct. at 1293 (quoting Diamond v. Diehr, 450 U.S. 175, 185 (1981)).

[133]*Mayo,* 132 S. Ct. at 1295.

[134]*Mayo,* 132 S. Ct. at 1296.

[135]*See supra* (quoting representative claim 1 of Prometheus's U.S. Patent No. 6,355,623). The "wherein" clauses of claim 1 recited as follows:

by human action in the administration of a thiopurine drug, nevertheless "exist[ed] in principle apart from any human action."[136] The correlation or relation was a "consequence of the ways in which [the drugs] are metabolized by the body—entirely natural processes."[137] A patent such as Prometheus's that "simply describes that relation sets forth a natural law,"[138] the Court concluded, even though the "laws of nature" at issue were admittedly "narrow" and likely had "limited applications."[139]

The additional recitation of the "administering" and "determining" steps in Prometheus's method claims was not enough to "transform an unpatentable law of nature into a patent-eligible *application* of such a law."[140] The *Mayo* Court decreed that

> [i]f a law of nature is not patentable, then neither is a process reciting a law of nature, unless that process has additional features that provide practical assurance that the process is more than a drafting effort designed to monopolize the law of nature itself. A patent, for example, could not simply recite a law of nature and then add the instruction "apply the law."[141]

In the case at bar, the "administering" and "determining" steps did not themselves recite laws of nature, but "neither [were] they sufficient to transform the nature of the claim."[142] Both steps were known in the art and represented "well-understood, routine, conventional activity" to scientists in the relevant technology.[143] Taken together with the "wherein" clauses, all the method steps in combination "add[ed] nothing to the laws of nature that is not already present when the steps are considered separately."[144] In the Court's view, the claimed series of steps "simply tell doctors to

wherein the level of 6-thioguanine less than about 230 pmol per 8×10^8 red blood cells indicates a need to increase the amount of said drug subsequently administered to said subject and

wherein the level of 6-thioguanine greater than about 400 pmol per 8×10^8 red blood cells indicates a need to decrease the amount of said drug subsequently administered to said subject.

[136]*Mayo*, 132 S. Ct. at 1297.
[137]*Mayo*, 132 S. Ct. at 1297.
[138]*Mayo*, 132 S. Ct. at 1297.
[139]*Mayo*, 132 S. Ct. at 1302.
[140]*Mayo*, 132 S. Ct. at 1294.
[141]*Mayo*, 132 S. Ct. at 1297.
[142]*Mayo*, 132 S. Ct. at 1297.
[143]*Mayo*, 132 S. Ct. at 1298.
[144]*Mayo*, 132 S. Ct. at 1298.

gather data from which they may draw an inference in light of the correlations."[145]

The Supreme Court supported its decision denying patent eligibility in *Mayo* with citation to precedent and policy. It identified the precedent "most directly on point" as its earlier decisions in *Diamond v. Diehr*[146] and *Parker v. Flook*.[147] As detailed elsewhere in this chapter, *Diehr* and *Flook* both involved the application of mathematical formulae in computer programs used to control industrial processes. The *Mayo* court characterized Prometheus's method claims as "present[ing] a case for patentability that is weaker than the (patent-eligible) claim in *Diehr* and no stronger than the (unpatentable) claim in *Flook*."[148] The *Mayo* Court's characterization of the claimed inventions in *Diehr* and *Flook* as "processes that embodied *the equivalent of natural laws*"[149] demonstrates the wide-ranging applicability of the *Mayo* holding, potentially reaching far beyond medical diagnostic subject matter.

The Supreme Court's *Mayo* opinion observed that in *Diamond v. Diehr*, the Court had previously held that "the basic mathematical equation, like a law of nature, was not patentable."[150] The overall process claimed in *Diehr* was patent-eligible, however, because the combination of process steps in addition to the recited mathematical formula were not "in context obvious, already in use, or purely conventional." Rather, the additional steps in *Diehr* "apparently added to the formula something that in terms of patent law's objectives had significance—they transformed the process into an inventive application of

---

[145]*Mayo*, 132 S. Ct. at 1298. The Court summarized that

the claims inform a relevant audience about certain laws of nature; any additional steps consist of well-understood, routine, conventional activity already engaged in by the scientific community; and those steps, when viewed as a whole, add nothing significant beyond the sum of their parts taken separately. For these reasons we believe that the steps are not sufficient to transform unpatentable natural correlations into patentable applications of those regularities.

Mayo, 132 S. Ct. at 1298.

[146]450 U.S. 175 (1981). *Diehr* is discussed *supra* at Section B.3 ("Computer-Implemented Processes").

[147]437 U.S. 584 (1978). *Flook* is discussed *supra* at Section B.3 ("Computer-Implemented Processes").

[148]*Mayo*, 132 S. Ct. at 1299. The *Mayo* opinion also distinguished the patent-ineligible claims of Prometheus with the patentable process claimed in the English case *Neilson v. Harford*, Webster's Patent Cases 295 (1841). The *Neilson* process for operating a blast furnace applied the "law of nature" that "hot air promotes ignition better than cold air," *Mayo*, 132 S. Ct. at 1300, but added to that principle "several unconventional steps (such as inserting the receptacle, applying heat to the receptacle externally, and blowing the air into the furnace) that confined the claims to a particular, useful application of the principle." *Mayo*, 132 S. Ct. at 1300.

[149]*Mayo*, 132 S. Ct. at 1298 (emphasis added).

[150]*Mayo*, 132 S. Ct. at 1298.

the formula."[151] In contrast, the process steps in *Parker v. Flook* that supplemented the recitation of a mathematical formula for updating alarm limits were "well known," such that there "was no 'inventive concept' in the claimed application of the formula."[152]

The *Mayo* Court also supported its disqualification of Prometheus's method claims from patent eligibility as furthering the public policy that "patent law [should] not inhibit further discovery by improperly tying up the future use of laws of nature."[153] Although the "laws of nature" encompassing Prometheus's correlations were "narrow" and of "limited application[]," the method claims at issue nevertheless implicated this policy concern. By "tell[ing] a treating doctor to measure metabolite levels and to consider the resulting measurements in light of the statistical relationships they describe, [Prometheus's claims] tie up the doctor's subsequent treatment decision whether that treatment does, or does not, change in light of the inference he has drawn using the correlations."[154] Moreover, the claims "threaten to inhibit the development of more refined treatment recommendations (like that embodied in [accused infringer] Mayo's test), that combine Prometheus' correlations with later discovered features of metabolites, human physiology or individual patient characteristics."[155]

The *Mayo* Court skirted arguments of Prometheus and several *amici* that treating the claimed processes as unpatentable "laws of nature" would significantly chill further medical diagnostic research, responding that it would defer to Congress on such issues.[156] Beyond

---

[151]*Mayo*, 132 S. Ct. at 1299. The *Mayo* Court's use of the qualifying adjective "inventive" is a troubling regression to pre-1952 Patent Act terminology that circularly required that patentable inventions involve an ill-defined quality of "invention." *See infra* Chapter 5, Section B ("Historical Context: The *Hotchkiss* 'Ordinary Mechanic' and the Requirement for 'Invention'").

[152]*Mayo*, 132 S. Ct. at 1299 (quoting *Flook*, 437 U.S. at 594). Again, the Court's reliance on the quotation from *Flook* referring to an "inventive concept" as a criterion of §101 patent eligibility is alarming. *See infra* Chapter 5, Section B ("Historical Context: The *Hotchkiss* 'Ordinary Mechanic' and the Requirement for 'Invention'").

[153]*Mayo*, 132 S. Ct. at 1301.

[154]*Mayo*, 132 S. Ct. at 1302.

[155]*Mayo*, 132 S. Ct. at 1302.

[156]*See Mayo*, 132 S. Ct. at 1305 (recognizing "the role of Congress in crafting more finely tailored rules where necessary [citing Plant Patent Act, 35 U.S.C. §§161-164]" and declining to "determine here whether, from a policy perspective, increased protection for discoveries of diagnostic laws of nature is desirable").

The Court also rejected the argument of *amicus* United States that the novelty, nonobviousness, and disclosure requirements of 35 U.S.C. §§102, 103, and 112 act as the primary screening tools for patentability. According to the Court, "[t]his approach . . . would make the 'law of nature' exception to §101 patentability a dead letter." *Mayo*, 132 S. Ct. at 1303. The Court opined, without citation to authority, that "to shift the patent-eligibility inquiry entirely to these later sections risks creating significantly greater legal uncertainty, while assuming that those sections can do work that they are not equipped to do." *Mayo*, 132 S. Ct. at 1304. The Court "decline[d] the Government's diagnostic research, the Court's *Mayo* decision also appears to have implications for Internet-based methods.[157]

C.   Section 101 Machines

A machine (or apparatus) is a human-made device that has moving parts. The only real area of controversy involving the machine category of potentially patentable subject matter is whether programmed computers (i.e., computers operating under the control of computer software programs) qualify as machines within the meaning of §101. Recent case law generally answers this question in the affirmative.

The *en banc* Federal Circuit considered whether a computer-implemented device qualifies as a machine under 35 U.S.C. §101 in *In re Alappat*.[158] Alappat's patent application was directed to a "rasterizer," a device for creating a smooth waveform display in a digital oscilloscope (analogous to creating a clearer picture on a television screen). The only independent claim at issue in the application recited the following:

> A rasterizer for converting vector list data representing sample magnitudes of an input waveform into anti-aliased pixel illumination intensity data to be displayed on a display means comprising:
> (a) means for determining the vertical distance between the endpoints of each of the vectors in the data list;
> (b) means for determining the elevation of a row of pixels that is spanned by the vector;
> (c) means for normalizing the vertical distance and elevation; and
> (d) means for outputting illumination intensity data as a predetermined function of the normalized vertical distance and elevation.[159]

In an unconventional procedure, an "expanded" panel of the USPTO Board of Patent Appeals and Interferences rejected this claim as failing to recite potentially patentable subject matter under §101. The Board refused to construe the recited "means" limitations in accordance with

---

invitation to substitute §§102, 103, and 112 inquiries for the better established inquiry under §101." *Mayo,* 132 S. Ct. at 1304. The Court did not explain why, in its view, the §101 inquiry is "better established" than the analysis under §§102, 103, and 112.

[157]The Supreme Court issued an order in *Wildtangent, Inc. v. Ultramercial, LLC*, No. 11-902, 2012 WL 369157 (U.S. May 21, 2012), vacating the Federal Circuit's judgment and remanding the case back to the Federal Circuit for further consideration in lieu of *Mayo v. Prometheus*. The patented technology in *Wildtangent* involves a method for viewing copyrighted content on the Internet.

[158]33 F.3d 1526 (Fed. Cir. 1994) (*en banc*).

[159]*Id.* at 1538-1539.

35 U.S.C. §112, ¶6 (1988), which would have limited the claim's reach to the "corresponding structure" that the application disclosed as performing each function, and any "equivalents thereof."[160] Rather, the Board interpreted each means limitation as encompassing any and every means for performing the recited function. The Board concluded that the rasterizer claim, thus interpreted, was in reality a claim to a process, and each means clause merely a disguised step in that process. In the Board's view, the resulting process was nothing more than an unpatentable "mathematical algorithm" for computing pixel information, and thus not patentable because unapplied mathematical algorithms are outside the purview of §101.[161]

The *en banc* Federal Circuit majority reversed, admonishing the USPTO that the agency was not exempt from interpreting patent application claims in accordance with 35 U.S.C. §112, ¶6.[162] Properly applying the statute yielded the following claim construction, with the structure disclosed in the written description as corresponding to each recited "means" appearing in brackets:

> A rasterizer [a "machine"] for converting vector list data representing sample magnitudes of an input waveform into anti-aliased pixel illumination intensity data to be displayed on a display means comprising:
> - (a) [an arithmetic logic circuit configured to perform an absolute value function, or an equivalent thereof] for determining the vertical distance between the endpoints of each of the vectors in the data list;
> - (b) [an arithmetic logic circuit configured to perform an absolute value function, or an equivalent thereof] for determining the elevation of a row of pixels that is spanned by the vector;
> - (c) [a pair of barrel shifters, or equivalents thereof] for normalizing the vertical distance and elevation; and

---

[160]*See* Chapter 2 ("Patent Claims"), *supra*, for further discussion of means-plus-function claims and statutory equivalents under 35 U.S.C. §112, ¶6. The America Invents Act of 2011 renamed this statutory provision 35 U.S.C. §112(f) (eff. Sept. 16, 2012).

[161]*See* Diamond v. Diehr, 450 U.S. 175, 187 (1981) ("It is now commonplace that an *application* of a law of nature or mathematical formula to a known structure or process may well be deserving of patent protection."); Gottschalk v. Benson, 409 U.S. 63, 71-72 (1972) (concluding that "[t]he mathematical formula involved here [for converting binary-coded decimal (BCD) numerals to pure binary numerals] has no substantial practical application except in connection with a digital computer, which means that if the judgment below is affirmed, the patent would wholly pre-empt the mathematical formula and in practical effect would be a patent on the algorithm itself").

[162]This ongoing interpretational battle between the Federal Circuit and USPTO seemingly had been resolved in *In re Donaldson Co.*, 16 F.3d 1189, 1194-1195 (Fed. Cir. 1994) (*en banc*) (holding that the "broadest reasonable interpretation" that an examiner may give means-plus-function language when interpreting patent application claims is that statutorily mandated in 35 U.S.C. §112, ¶6 (1988), and that "the PTO may not disregard the structure disclosed in the specification corresponding to such language when rendering a patentability determination").

(d) [a read only memory (ROM) containing illumination intensity data, or an equivalent thereof] for outputting illumination intensity data as a predetermined function of the normalized vertical distance and elevation.[163]

Thus understood, this claim "unquestionably recite[d] a machine, or apparatus, made up of a combination of known electronic circuitry elements,"[164] the Federal Circuit concluded. Although each means element represented circuitry that performed mathematical calculations (essentially true of all digital electrical circuits), the claimed invention as a whole was not a "disembodied mathematical concept." Rather, the claim recited a "specific machine to produce a useful, concrete, and tangible result,"[165] and was thus within §101. The Federal Circuit would later echo the "useful, concrete, and tangible" criteria in the *State Street* case, discussed earlier in this chapter.[166]

D. Section 101 Compositions of Matter

A composition of matter is a mixture of substances such as a chemical composition or metallic alloy. The Supreme Court in *Diamond v. Chakrabarty*[167] summarized its earlier decisions defining the phrase "composition of matter" as "consistent with its common usage to include 'all compositions of two or more substances and . . . all composite articles, whether they be the results of chemical union, or of mechanical mixture, or whether they be gases, fluids, powders or solids.'"[168]

1. Structure Versus Properties

If a composition of matter is claimed as such, it is the physical structure of the composition that must be novel, not merely its properties. The discovery or recognition of a composition's previously unappreciated property (e.g., the ability of aspirin to lessen the risk of heart attacks) will not impart patentability to that composition if its structure is already known. Such a discovery might merit patentability if claimed as a process, but not as a product.

[163]*Alappat*, 33 F.3d at 1541.
[164]*Id.*
[165]*Id.* at 1544.
[166]State St. Bank & Trust Co. v. Signature Fin. Group, Inc., 149 F.3d 1368, 1373-1375 (Fed. Cir. 1998). For further discussion of *State Street, see supra* Section B.4 ("Business Methods").
[167]447 U.S. 303 (1980).
[168]*Id.* at 308 (quoting Shell Dev. Co. v. Watson, 149 F. Supp. 279, 280 (D.D.C. 1957)).

For example, the inventors in *Titanium Metals Corp. v. Banner*[169] discovered that a titanium alloy made up of certain amounts of titanium, nickel, molybdenum, and iron exhibited exceptionally good corrosion resistance. They claimed the alloy as follows:

> 1. A titanium base alloy consisting essentially by weight of about 0.6% to 0.9% nickel, 0.2% to 0.4% molybdenum, up to 0.2% maximum iron, balance titanium, said alloy being characterized by good corrosion resistance in hot brine environments.[170]

The prior art was a Russian printed publication that disclosed a particular alloy falling within the ranges recited in claim 1, but made no mention of any corrosion resistance property.

The Federal Circuit held that the Russian reference anticipated (i.e., negated the novelty of) the claimed alloy, despite the claim's inclusion of the corrosion resistance limitation. Whether or not the corrosion resistance property was inherent in the Russian alloy, and regardless of whether the authors of the Russian reference recognized this property, its recitation in the claim could not impart novelty to what was an otherwise old composition of matter. The applicants might have obtained a patent by claiming a *process* for preventing corrosion in titanium alloys, but as discussed earlier in this chapter such a claim would be much narrower in scope and thus of less economic value than the product claim they sought (i.e., to the alloy itself). Nevertheless, the more limited scope of a process claim more closely corresponds to the inventors' contribution—the recognition of a previously unrecognized property of a known alloy.

2. Purified Forms of Natural Products

The "product of nature" doctrine recognizes that potentially patentable subject matter must be created through human intervention. Patents are not available for the handiwork of nature. Thus, a newly discovered mineral or a plant found in the wild is not patentable subject matter under 35 U.S.C. §101. Those who make such discoveries or findings have certainly made an important contribution to society, but public policy demands that such advances remain freely available for all to use and build upon.

In contrast, so-called purified forms of natural products may be patentable if sufficiently different from the nonpurified (i.e., natural) forms so as to be novel and nonobvious. In fact, the USPTO has a long

---

[169]778 F.2d 775 (Fed. Cir. 1985).
[170]*Id.* at 776.

history of granting patents on purified forms of natural products; for example, the famous scientist Louis Pasteur was awarded a U.S. patent for purified yeast in 1873.[171]

Judge Learned Hand set forth the modern understanding of the patentability of purified forms of natural products in *Parke-Davis & Co. v. H.K. Mulford Co.*[172] The patent in suit in that case was directed to a purified form of adrenaline, a naturally occurring hormone secreted by the suprarenal glands of animals and released into the bloodstream in situations of fear or stress. The inventor Takamine claimed "[a] substance possessing the herein-described physiological characteristics and reactions of the suprarenal glands in a stable and concentrated form, and practically free from inert and associated gland-tissue."[173] Judge Hand rejected the accused infringer's challenge to the claim's validity. "Nor is the patent only for a degree of purity, and therefore not for a new 'composition of matter,'" he observed. Takamine was "the first to make it available for any use by removing it from the other gland-tissue in which it was found."[174] While Hand conceded that it was "of course possible logically to call this a purification of the principle," the claimed composition "became for every practical purpose a new thing commercially and therapeutically." Hand considered that fact "a good ground for a patent."[175]

In re Bergy further illustrates this principle. The patent applicant, Bergy, claimed a biologically pure culture of a microorganism that produced the antibiotic lincomycin.[176] The CCPA reversed the USPTO's rejection of the claim as, among other grounds, a mere product of nature. The court stressed that "[t]he biologically pure culture of claim 5 clearly does not exist in, is not found in, and is not a product of, 'nature.' It is man-made and can be produced only under carefully controlled laboratory conditions."[177] Indeed, "[t]he nature and commercial uses of biologically pure cultures of microorganisms like the one defined in claim 5 are much more akin to inanimate chemical compositions

---

[171]*See Chakrabarty*, 447 U.S. at 314 n.9 (noting that Louis Pasteur in 1873 obtained U.S. Pat. No. 141,072, which contained the following claim: "[Y]east, free from organic germs of disease, as an article of manufacture").

[172]189 F. 95 (S.D.N.Y. 1911) (L. Hand, J.).

[173]U.S. Pat. No. 730,176 (issued June 2, 1903) (claim 1).

[174]*Parke-Davis*, 189 F. at 103.

[175]For a historical investigation concluding that "Hand's now-famous *Parke-Davis* pronouncements on the patentability of isolated products of nature were under-informed *dicta*, which conflicted with existing patent law," *see* Jon M. Harkness, *Dicta on Adrenalin(e): Myriad Problems with Learned Hand's Product-of-Nature Pronouncements in* Parke-Davis v. Mulford, 93 J. Pat. & Trademark Off. Soc'y 363 (2011).

[176]*See* In re Bergy, 596 F.2d 952, 967 (C.C.P.A. 1979) (quoting claim 5 of Bergy's application).

[177]In re Bergy, 563 F.2d 1031, 1035 (C.C.P.A. 1977).

such as reactants, reagents, and catalysts than they are to horses and honeybees or raspberries and roses."[178]

Realizing the limits on the product of nature doctrine helps us understand why some human-based genetic materials have been patented, a point often discounted by persons opposed to the granting of such patents. First, understand that genes[179] *as they exist in the human body* would, indeed, be considered products of nature outside the purview of 35 U.S.C. §101.[180] The discovery of a gene, however, can be the basis for a patent on the gene as "isolated from its natural state and processed through purifying steps that separate the gene from other molecules naturally associated with it."[181] Patent claims directed to such modified genes and gene fragments typically recite "a purified and isolated nucleic acid" comprising a particular nucleic acid sequence set forth in the patent application.[182] The sequence of nucleotides[183] encompassed by the claim

---

[178]*Id.* at 1038.

[179]Genes are chemicals, the "instruction sets" from which the human body produces proteins. More precisely, a gene is "[t]he region of DNA on the chromosome that codes for the sequence of a single polypeptide." In re O'Farrell, 853 F.2d 894, 897 (Fed. Cir. 1988). Proteins, also called polypeptides, are "biological molecules of enormous importance . . . [that] include enzymes that catalyze biochemical reactions, major structural materials of the animal body, and many hormones." *Id.* at 895-896.

[180]Approximately 95 percent of the human genome is considered "junk DNA" that does not code for proteins. *See* AMERICAN HERITAGE DICTIONARY OF THE ENGLISH LANGUAGE (4th ed. 2000) (defining *junk DNA* as "DNA that does not code for proteins or their regulation but constitutes approximately 95 percent of the human genome" and noting that junk DNA is "postulated to be involved in the evolution of new genes and possibly in gene repair").

[181]*See* United States Patent & Trademark Office, *Utility Examination Guidelines*, 66 FED. REG. 1092, 1093 (Jan. 5, 2001), *available at* http://www.uspto.gov/web/offices/com/sol/notices/utilexmguide.pdf.

[182]*See, e.g.,* In re Deuel, 51 F.3d 1552, 1555 (Fed. Cir. 1995) (addressing patentability of claim to "[a] purified and isolated DNA sequence consisting of a sequence encoding human heparin binding growth factor of 168 amino acids having the following amino acid sequence: Met Gln Ala . . . [remainder of 168 amino acid sequence]"); *cf.* Prostate Cancer Gene, U.S. Patent No. 5,945,522 (issued Aug. 31, 1999) (claiming "[a] purified *or* isolated nucleic acid comprising the sequence of SEQ ID NO: 1 or the sequence complementary thereto") (emphasis added).

[183]As the Federal Circuit explained in *In re O'Farrell*, 853 F.2d 894 (Fed. Cir. 1988),

The subunits of the DNA chain are called *nucleotides*. A nucleotide consists of a nitrogen-containing ring compound (called a *base*) linked to a 5-carbon sugar that has a phosphate group attached. DNA is composed of only four nucleotides. They differ from each other in the base region of the molecule. The four bases of these subunits are adenine, guanine, cytosine, and thymine (abbreviated respectively as A, G, C and T). The sequence of these bases along the DNA molecule specifies which amino acids will be inserted in sequence into the polypeptide chain of a protein.

Id. at 896 (footnotes omitted).

D. Section 101 Compositions of Matter

thus represents a significantly different composition or manufacture from the unpurified and unisolated DNA as it exists in the human body.[184] Accordingly, "purified and isolated" DNA is not necessarily excluded from patentability under §101 as a "product of nature."[185]

---

[184]*See generally* Anna E. Morrison, *The U.S. PTO's New Utility Guidelines: Will They Be Enough to Secure Gene Patent Rights?*, 1 J. MARSHALL REV. INTELL. PROP. L. 142 (2001), http://www.jmripl.com/Publications/Vol1/Issue1/morrison.pdf.

[185]In *Association for Molecular Pathology (AMP) v. United States Patent and Trademark Office (USPTO) and Myriad Genetics, Inc.*, 653 F.3d 1329 (Fed Cir. 2011) [hereafter "*Myriad (2011)*"], the Federal Circuit issued three separate opinions concerning the patentability of isolated DNA molecules. In the opinion "for the court" authored by Judge Lourie, the majority reversed the district court's decision and held that isolated DNA molecules qualified as §101 compositions of matter because "the molecules as claimed do not exist in nature." *Myriad (2011)*, 653 F.3d at 1334.

As this edition is written in 2012, the issue of gene patentability remains highly controversial. On March 20, 2012, the Supreme Court vacated the Federal Circuit's decision in *Myriad (2011)* and directed the Circuit to reconsider *Myriad (2011)* in light of the Court's decision in *Mayo v. Prometheus*, 132 S. Ct. 1289 (2012), discussed *supra* Section B. Its remand suggested that the Supreme Court might not agree with the Federal Circuit that gene patents are §101 patent-eligible subject matter.

The Federal Circuit was not deterred by the Supreme Court's remand. In an August 2012 decision following additional briefing and argument, the same divided three-judge panel of the Federal Circuit reached essentially the same result as in *Myriad (2011)*. *See* Association for Molecular Pathology v. United States Patent and Trademark Office and Myriad Genetics, Inc., 689 F.3d 1303 (Fed. Cir. 2012) [hereafter "*Myriad (2012)*"]. Insofar as Myriad's patent claims reciting isolated DNA were concerned, the Supreme Court's intervening decision in *Mayo* was not relevant:

> The principal claims of the patents before us on remand relate to isolated DNA molecules. *Mayo* does not control the question of patent-eligibility of such claims. They are claims to compositions of matter, expressly authorized as suitable patent-eligible subject matter in § 101. As to those claims, the issue of patent-eligibility remains, as it was on the first appeal to this court, whether they claim patent-ineligible products of nature. We hold that they do not. The isolated DNA molecules before us are not found in nature. They are obtained in the laboratory and are man-made, the product of human ingenuity. While they are prepared from products of nature, so is every other composition of matter. All new chemical or biological molecules, whether made by synthesis or decomposition, are made from natural materials. . . .

Myriad (2012), 689 F.3d at 1325 (Lourie, J., "Opinion for the court"). Although "*Mayo* and earlier decisions concerning *method* claim patentability," *id.* at 1326 (emphasis added), offered "valuable insights" and "broad, foundational principles," the controlling precedent was the Supreme Court's earlier decisions in *Diamond v. Chakrabarty*, 447 U.S. 303 (1980), discussed *infra* Section D.3, and *Funk Bros. Seed Co. v. Kalo Inoculant Co.*, 333 U.S. 127 (1948). These decisions, rather than *Mayo*, "set out the primary framework for deciding the patent eligibility of compositions of matter, including isolated DNA molecules." *Myriad (2012)*, 689 F.3d at 1326.

As in *Myriad (2011)*, Circuit Judge Bryson dissented from the majority's holding that Myriad's *BRCA* breast cancer gene claims and its claims to gene fragments were

Is an otherwise patentable composition of matter an unpatentable product of nature when it is capable of being generated by the spontaneous transformation of a different chemical composition? Although there is no binding precedent on the question, at least one member of the Federal Circuit would answer affirmatively. Claim 1 of the patent in suit in *SmithKline Beecham Corp. v. Apotex Corp.*[186] recited in its entirety "crystalline paroxetine hydrochloride hemihydrate." Accused infringer Apotex's manufacture of the prior art product paroxetine hydrochloride (PHC) *anhydrate* resulted in the spontaneous production of trace amounts of the PHC *hemihydrate* patented by SmithKline.[187] Because the Federal Circuit interpreted claim 1 to embrace PHC hemihydrate without further limitation (i.e., to cover PHC hemihydrate in any amount, whether or not commercially significant), Apotex infringed whether it intended to or not. Apotex escaped infringement liability, however, because the Federal Circuit majority invalidated claim 1 of SmithKline's patent on grounds of inherent anticipation under 35 U.S.C. §102(b) (2000).[188]

In a concurring opinion, Federal Circuit Judge Arthur Gajarsa wrote that claim 1 should instead have been invalidated for failure to recite statutory subject matter within 35 U.S.C. §101. He took the position that "patent claims drawn broadly enough to encompass products that spread, appear, and 'reproduce' through natural processes cover subject matter unpatentable under Section 101—and are therefore invalid."[189] The patent law does not sanction the notion of "inevitable infringement," Judge Gajarsa noted. In future cases of this sort, "[i]nventors wishing to claim products that can either be synthesized in laboratories or generated by natural processes may protect themselves by incorporating negative limitation terms like 'non-natural' or 'non-human' into the claims that they submit for examination."[190]

---

patent-eligible under 35 U.S.C. §101. He warned that the majority's decision, "if sustained, will likely have broad consequences, such as preempting methods for whole-genome sequencing, even though Myriad's contribution to the field is not remotely consonant with such effects." *Myriad (2012)*, 689 F.3d at 1348 (Bryson, J., concurring-in-part and dissenting-in-part).

[186]403 F.3d 1331 (Fed. Cir. 2005).

[187]As explained by the *SmithKline* court, "PHC anhydrate comprises crystals of PHC without bound water molecules. PHC hemihydrate comprises PHC crystals with one bound water molecule for every two PHC molecules. PHC hemihydrate proved more stable, and thus more easily packaged and preserved, than PHC anhydrate." *Id.* at 1334.

[188]*See id.* at 1342-1346. Inherent anticipation is further discussed in Section D of Chapter 4 ("Novelty, Loss of Right, and Priority Pre- and Post-America Invents Act of 2011(35 U.S.C. §102)"), *supra.*

[189]*Id.* at 1361 (Gajarsa, J., concurring in the judgment).

[190]*Id.* at 1363.

3.   Life Forms

In *Diamond v. Chakrabarty*,[191] the U.S. Supreme Court confronted what was probably the most controversial issue of patent law to ever reach it: whether living subject matter, such as a genetically engineered organism, is patentable subject matter under 35 U.S.C. §101. Ananda Chakrabarty, then a researcher for General Electric, developed a bacterium that was intended to consume petroleum spills. Chakrabarty custom-designed its genetic material such that the bacterium would digest a variety of different petroleum components, a property that unmodified bacteria found in nature did not possess. The USPTO rejected certain of Chakrabarty's claims as directed to subject matter that was living, which the agency viewed as something that §101 was not intended to cover.

The CCPA reversed the agency's rejection, emphasizing that the issue was not whether the claimed bacterium was living or inanimate, but whether it constituted an invention made by human intervention. In the court's view, the fact that Chakrabarty's bacterium was alive was "without legal significance."[192]

In a landmark 5-4 decision, the U.S. Supreme Court affirmed the CCPA's decision in *Chakrabarty*. Chakrabarty's bacterium was "not nature's handiwork," the Court reasoned, "but his own."[193] The Court relied on the choice by the drafters of the first U.S. patent statute, the Act of 1790, to use very broad, general terminology (i.e., "any," "composition of matter," or "manufacture"), which had scarcely changed in the ensuing 200 years. This selection of broad language suggested that the drafters' goal was to stimulate innovation in a wide variety of then-unknown technologies and scientific fields, a goal that would be frustrated if Congress were repeatedly required to amend the statute so as to explicitly delineate new categories of patentable inventions. Moreover, the Court observed, the legislative history of the 1952 Patent Act states that patentable subject matter includes "anything under the sun that is made by man."[194] To place a narrow interpretation on §101 would be diametrically opposed to this expansive legislative history and to the general notion that the patent system encourages the creation of new, previously unforeseen inventions.

Rather than directly responding to the many ethical and moral criticisms of "patenting life" that the case invoked from many corners, the Supreme Court in *Chakrabarty* refused to engage in speculation

---

[191]447 U.S. 303 (1980).

[192]*Id*. at 306.

[193]*Id*. at 310.

[194]*Id*. at 309 (quoting S. Rep. No. 82-1979, at 5 (1952); H.R. Rep. No. 82-1923, at 6 (1952)).

about the "gruesome parade of horribles" presented by various *amici*.[195] The Court insisted that it lacked the institutional competence required to take on the complex, public policy-based issues raised by the patenting of life forms; this was the realm of Congress and the legislative branch, not the judiciary.

In the aftermath of the Supreme Court's *Chakrabarty* decision, the U.S. biotechnology industry flourished. Today the United States is a world leader in biotechnology-based research, development, and product introduction, and the availability of patent protection has much to do with this.[196] Numerous U.S. patents have been granted on human-made higher life forms such as transgenic mice, fish, and cows.[197]

---

[195]*See id.* at 316 (noting arguments by Nobel laureate scientists and others that "genetic research may pose a serious threat to the human race, or, at the very least, that the dangers are far too substantial to permit such research to proceed apace at this time" and that "genetic research and related technological developments may spread pollution and disease, that it may result in a loss of genetic diversity, and that its practice may tend to depreciate the value of human life").

[196]*See generally* Jasemine Chambers, *Patent Eligibility of Biotechnological Inventions in the United States, Europe, and Japan: How Much Patent Policy Is Public Policy?*, 34 GEO. WASH. INT'L L. Rev. 223 (2002) (emphasizing importance of patenting to U.S. biotechnology industry).

[197]Europe has been far less welcoming toward the patenting of life forms. For example, the transgenic "onco-mouse" developed by Harvard University researchers to have susceptibility to cancer was granted patent protection in the United States in 1988. *See* Transgenic Non-Human Mammals, U.S. Pat. No. 4,736,866. The counterpart application in Europe was not allowed until 1992. *See* In Re President and Fellows of Harvard College, 1992 O.J. EUR. PAT. OFF. 588, *available at* http://archive.epo.org/epo/pubs/oj1992/p557_615.pdf (decision of Examining Division granting European Pat. No. 0 169 672) [hereinafter *Onco-mouse/Harvard*]. Numerous opposition proceedings were thereafter instituted in the European Patent Office (EPO) against the onco-mouse patent. *See generally* Cynthia M. Ho, *Splicing Morality and Patent Law: Issues Arising from Mixing Mice and Men*, 2 WASH. U. J.L. & POL'Y 247, 257-261 (2000).

A central aspect of the debate concerned whether the granting of a European patent on the Harvard onco-mouse would violate Art. 53(a) of the European Patent Convention. That provision states that European patents shall not be granted in respect of "inventions the commercial exploitation of which would be contrary to 'ordre public' or morality; such exploitation shall not be deemed to be so contrary merely because it is prohibited by law or regulation in some or all of the Contracting States." European Patent Convention art. 53(a) (14th ed. 2010), *available at* http://www.epo.org/law-practice/legal-texts/html/epc/2010/e/ar53.html. (The French phrase *ordre public* loosely translates as public policy or public interest.)

In its deliberations the EPO Examining Division considered whether the societal benefit of the invention as a new and improved human anticancer treatment justified the suffering that would be inflicted on the transgenically manipulated mice and the potential risk to the environment in terms of uncontrolled dissemination of unwanted genes. The Examining Division determined that the potential benefits of the invention outweighed the costs, concluding that

the present invention cannot be considered immoral or contrary to public order. The provision of a type of test animal useful in cancer research and giving rise to a reduction in the amount of testing on animals together with a low risk

Although the USPTO views multicellular organisms as potentially patentable subject matter,[198] it has set one important limit: the agency will not grant patents on human beings per se. The USPTO takes the position that "[i]f the broadest reasonable interpretation of the claimed invention as a whole encompasses a human being, then a rejection under 35 U.S.C. §101 must be made indicating that the claimed invention is directed to nonstatutory subject matter."[199]

E.   Section 101 Manufactures

A manufacture in patent law parlance is something of a catch-all category for those inventions that are human-made but do not neatly fall into the other three categories of 35 U.S.C. §101. A manufacture is generally thought of as a human-made item without moving parts, in contrast to a machine. In *Chakrabarty,* the Supreme Court "read the term 'manufacture' in §101 in accordance with its dictionary definition to mean 'the production of articles for use from raw or prepared materials by giving to these materials new forms, qualities, properties, or combinations, whether by hand-labor or by machinery.'"[200]

Recent controversy centers around whether computer software embodied in a particular medium, such as a disk, is a potentially patentable manufacture within the meaning of 35 U.S.C. §101. In *In re Beauregard,* the applicant sought allowance of the following claim to object code on a floppy disk:[201]

---

connected with the handling of the animals by qualified staff can generally be regarded as beneficial to mankind. A patent should therefore not be denied for the present invention on the ground of Article 53(a) EPC.

Onco-mouse / Harvard, at 593 §(v).

[198]*See* Animal Legal Defense Fund v. Quigg, 932 F.2d 920, 923 (Fed. Cir. 1991) (announcing that "the Patent and Trademark Office is now examining claims directed to multicellular living organisms, including animals" and that "[t]o the extent that the claimed subject matter is directed to a non-human 'nonnaturally occurring manufacture or composition of matter—a product of human ingenuity' (*Diamond v. Chakrabarty*), such claims will not be rejected under 35 U.S.C. §101 as being directed to nonstatutory subject matter.") (quoting USPTO, 1077 OFF. GAZ. PAT. & TRADEMARK OFFICE 24 (1987)).

[199]United States Patent & Trademark Office, MANUAL OF PATENT EXAMINING PROCEDURE §2105.01 (8th ed. 2001, rev. July 2010), *available at* http://www.uspto.gov/web/offices/pac/mpep/documents/2100_2105.htm#sect2105 (last para.).

[200]Diamond v. Chakrabarty, 447 U.S. 303, 308 (1980) (quoting Am. Fruit Growers, Inc. v. Brogdex Co., 283 U.S. 1, 11 (1931)).

[201]*See* In re Beauregard, 53 F.3d 1583 (Fed. Cir. 1995); U.S. Patent No. 5,710,578 (issued Jan. 20, 1998).

1. An article of manufacture comprising:

a computer usable medium having computer readable program code means embodied therein for causing a polygon having a boundary definable by a plurality of selectable pels on a graphics display to be filled, the computer readable program code means in said article of manufacture comprising:

computer readable program code means for causing a computer to effect, with respect to one boundary line at a time, a sequential traverse of said plurality of selectable pels of each respective said boundary line;

computer readable program code means for causing the computer to store in an array during said traverse a value of an outer pel of said boundary of said plurality of selectable pels for each one of a plurality of scan lines of said polygon; and

computer readable program code means for causing the computer to draw a fill line, after said traverse, between said outer pels having said stored values, for each said one of said scan lines.

After the USPTO initially rejected this claim as unpatentable under the printed matter doctrine,[202] Beauregard appealed. Before the Federal Circuit heard oral argument in the case, however, the USPTO changed its policy. The agency withdrew its rejection and told the court that "computer programs embodied in a tangible medium, such as floppy diskettes, are patentable subject matter under 35 U.S.C. §101 and must be examined under 35 U.S.C. §§102 and 103."[203] The agency agreed with Beauregard that the printed matter doctrine was therefore inapplicable. Since it no longer had a case or controversy before it, the Federal Circuit did not decide the issue.[204] The Federal Circuit has sustained the patentability (albeit under §103) of related

---

[202]The printed matter rejection originated with pre–1952 Act decisions of the CCPA, which declared that "the mere arrangement of printed matter on a sheet or sheets of paper does not constitute patentable subject matter." In re Sterling, 70 F.2d 910, 912 (C.C.P.A. 1934). More recently, the Federal Circuit considered "printed matter" in the context of a §103 obviousness challenge (§101 was not at issue) and stated that "[w]here the printed matter is not functionally related to the substrate, the printed matter will not distinguish the invention from the prior art in terms of patentability." In re Gulack, 703 F.2d 1381, 1385 (Fed. Cir. 1983).

[203]Beauregard, 53 F.3d at 1583.

[204]More than 15 years after dismissing the appeal in In re Beauregard without deciding its merits, the Federal Circuit issued a decision in Cybersource Corp. v. Retail Decisions, Inc., 654 F.3d 1366 (Fed. Cir. 2011), that called the legitimacy of some Beauregard claims into serious question. The appellate court reasoned in Cybersource that if a claimed method is not patent-eligible because it is merely an abstract idea under the Supreme Court's decision in Bilski v. Kappos, 130 S. Ct. 3218 (2010), then a Beauregard-type claim to a "computer-readable medium" containing computer program instructions to carry out the method is likewise not patent-eligible. The Federal Circuit in Cybersource emphasized that it will look to the nature of the underlying invention, not the literal terminology of the claim at issue.

types of manufactures such as a computer "memory" that stores a "data structure."[205]

Thus, any notion that software is not patentable is no longer accurate, at least in the United States.[206] An unapplied mathematical

---

[205]*See* In re Lowry, 32 F.3d 1579, 1581 (Fed. Cir. 1994). The applicant in *Lowry* presented the following claim, which the Federal Circuit upheld as patentable in the face of a §103 obviousness challenge:

1. A memory for storing data for access by an application program being executed on a data processing system, comprising:
a data structure stored in said memory, said data structure including information resident in a database used by said application program and including: a plurality of attribute data objects stored in said memory, each of said attribute data objects containing different information from said database; a single holder attribute data object for each of said attribute data objects, each of said holder attribute data objects being one of said plurality of attribute data objects, a being-held relationship existing between each attribute data object and its holder attribute data object, and each of said attribute data objects having a being-held relationship with only a single other attribute data object, thereby establishing a hierarchy of said plurality of attribute data objects; a referent attribute data object for at least one of said attribute data objects, said referent attribute data object being nonhierarchically related to a holder attribute data object for the same at least one of said attribute data objects and also being one of said plurality of attribute data objects, attribute data objects for which there exist only holder attribute data objects being called element data objects, and attribute data objects for which there also exist referent attribute data objects being called relation data objects; and an apex data object stored in said memory and having no being-held relationship with any of said attribute data objects, however, at least one of said attribute data objects having a being-held relationship with said apex data object.

[206]European attitudes toward the patentability of computer software have not been as welcoming as those of the United States. The EPC excludes from patentability "programs for computers . . . as such." European Patent Convention art. 52(2)(c), 52(3) (14th ed. 2010), *available at* http://www.epo.org/law-practice/legal-texts/html/epc/2010/e/ar52.html and http://www.epo.org/law-practice/legal-texts/html/epc/2010/e/ar53.html.

Patentability of software-related inventions in the EPO turns on whether the invention supplies a "technical effect." As explained in the EPO's *How to Get A European Patent: Guide for Applicants — Part 1* §B.I.29, *available at* http://www.epo.org/applying/european/Guide-for-applicants/html/e/ga_b_i.htm,

programs for computers . . . are not regarded as inventions if claimed as such. However, a computer program is not excluded from patentability under Article 52 if, when running on a computer, it causes a further technical effect going beyond the "normal" physical interaction between the program (software) and the computer (hardware). An example of a further technical effect is where the program serves to control a technical process or governs the operation of a technical device. The internal functioning of the computer itself under the influence of the program could also bring about such an effect.

If the computer program itself is not excluded, it is immaterial whether the program is claimed by itself, as a data medium storing the program, as a method or as part of a computer system.

Thus computer programs are not automatically excluded from patentability. . . .

algorithm is not potentially patentable subject matter within §101, but the physical embodiment of that algorithm on a floppy disk, claimed as a manufacture, may nevertheless be patentable so long as it does not recite merely an abstract idea under the Supreme Court's decision in *Bilski v. Kappos.*[207] As is the case with claims to business methods discussed *supra,* the most difficult challenges for such patents likely will be whether the claimed software inventions are novel and nonobvious and properly enabled, rather than their threshold qualification within 35 U.S.C. §101.

Does an electronic signal qualify as a potentially patentable "manufacture" under §101? The Federal Circuit held (by 2-1 vote) in *In re Nuijten* that claims covering "transitory electrical and electromagnetic signals propagating through some medium, such as wires, air, or a vacuum" are *not* §101 patentable subject matter.[208] More particularly, Nuijten's electronic signal claims did not qualify as §101 "manufacture[s]."[209]

When a signal such as a digital audio file is watermarked to protect the file against unauthorized copying, encoding the additional watermark data into the signal introduces some degree of distortion. Nuijten's patent application disclosed a technique for reducing this distortion. In addition to claiming his invention as a process, Nuijten claimed the watermarked signal itself. Claim 14 of Nuijten's application recited:

> A signal with embedded supplemental data, the signal being encoded in accordance with a given encoding process and selected samples of the signal representing the supplemental data, and at least one of the

---

[207]130 S. Ct. 3218 (2010). *See also* Cybersource Corp. v. Retail Decisions, Inc., 654 F.3d 1366 (Fed. Cir. 2011) (calling the legitimacy of some *Beauregard*-type claims into question).

A leading case on software patentability in Europe is *In re Vicom,* 1987 O.J. Eur. Pat. Off. 14 (EPO Decision T0208/84-3.5.1). In *Vicom* the EPO Board of Appeals upheld the patentability of "[a] method of digitally processing images in the form of a two-dimensional data array . . . ," which made use of a mathematical method incorporated in a computer program run on a computer to do the processing. The claimed method was held not to be excluded from patentability because it constituted a technical process that was carried out on a physical entity. This entity could include an image stored as an electric signal. Thus the method was neither a mathematical method as such nor a computer program as such under EPC art. 52. *See* In re International Business Machines Corp., 1999 O.J. Eur. Pat. Off. 609 (EPO Decision T 1173/97-3.5.1) (discussing *Vicom*).

[208]500 F.3d 1346, 1352 (Fed. Cir. 2007).

[209]*See Nuijten,* 500 F.3d at 1357 (holding that Nuijten's signals, standing alone, were not "manufacture[s]" within the meaning of §101). *See also* In re Bilski, 545 F.3d 943, 951 n.2 (Fed. Cir. 2008) (*en banc*) (declining to discuss *Nuijten* because primary issue in that case was whether an electronic signal qualified as a §101 "manufacture," whereas issue facing *en banc* court in *Bilski* was the scope of a §101 "process").

samples preceding the selected samples is different from the sample corresponding to the given encoding process.[210]

The claimed signal was admittedly human-made subject matter, because it was "encoded, generated, and transmitted by artificial means."[211] However, such artificiality is not alone sufficient to render something a §101 manufacture, the Federal Circuit held. The *Nuijten* majority specified that a manufacture must be a "tangible article[] or commodit[y]."[212] In the majority's view, an electronic signal or transmission that is transient does not qualify as a manufacture. "[E]nergy embodying the claimed signal is fleeting and is devoid of any semblance of permanence during transmission."[213] Moreover, the fact that electronic signals, which involve photons traveling at the speed of light, behave in some ways like particles, "does not make them tangible articles."[214]

Dissenting Judge Linn contended that a "manufacture" should not be limited to tangible or nontransitory inventions. He observed that an invention should qualify if it lasts long enough to be useful, citing precedent holding that "'transitory, unstable, and non-isolatable'" chemical intermediates are patentable.[215] Among other arguments for patentability of Nuijten's signal, Judge Linn pointed to the Supreme Court's venerable decision in *O'Reilly v. Morse,* which addressed the validity of a patent issued to the inventor of Morse code.[216] Although the Court in that case held invalid Morse's claim 8, for the use of "electromagnetism, however developed for marking or printing intelligible characters, signs, or letters, at any distances,"[217] it upheld the validity of Morse's claim 5. The latter claim, which covered the use of telegraphy to convey Morse code, recited a "'system of signs, consisting of dots and spaces, and of dots, spaces, and horizontal lines, for numerals, letters, words, or sentences, substantially as herein set forth and illustrated, for telegraphic purposes.'"[218] Judge Linn concluded that Morse's claim 5 was "directed to a signal—a particular way of encoding information so that it can be conveyed . . . in a useful manner at a

[210]*Nuijten,* 500 F.3d at 1351.

[211]*Id.* at 1356.

[212]*Id.*

[213]*Id.* The court noted that, in contrast, a signal stored for later use would result in a "storage medium" containing the signal. Because the USPTO had allowed another of Nuijten's claims drawn to a storage medium, the §101 patentability of the storage medium claim was not before the Federal Circuit. *Id.* at 1356 n.6.

[214]*Id.* at 1357 n.8.

[215]*See id.* at 1359 (Linn, J., dissenting-in-part) (quoting In re Breslow, 616 F.2d 516, 519, 521-522 (C.C.P.A. 1980)).

[216]56 U.S. (15 How.) 62 (1853).

[217]*Nuijten,* 500 F.3d at 1368 (quoting *Morse,* 56 U.S. (15 How.) at 112).

[218]*Id.* at 1368-1369 (quoting *Morse,* 56 U.S. (15 How.) at 86).

distance."[219] Both Morse's and Nuijten's signals were new and useful, in Judge Linn's view; both should be patentable.

F. Nonpatentable Subject Matter

Unlike that of other countries,[220] U.S. patent law defines patentable subject matter positively, meaning that 35 U.S.C. §101 expresses what *is* patentable, but does not state what is *not*. In the U.S. patent framework, case law establishes the categories of subject matter that are excluded from patenting.

Judicial decisions have established that the following are *not* potentially patentable subject matter in the United States:

- laws of nature;
- natural phenomena;
- abstract ideas;
- unapplied mathematical algorithms; and
- products of nature.[221]

For example, the law of gravity, or fundamental laws of motion such as F (force) = M (mass) × A (acceleration), or the value of pi (approximately 3.14159), or the Pythagorean Theorem ($a^2 + b^2 = c^2$), or Einstein's special theory of relativity (expressed by the relationship $E = mc^2$), are not considered patentable. *Applications* of these fundamental laws and principles may be patentable if useful, novel, and nonobvious, but the underlying scientific truths are not. As the Supreme Court has explained, "[h]e who discovers a hitherto unknown phenomenon of nature has no claim to a monopoly of it which the law recognizes. If there is to be invention from such a discovery, it must come from the application of the law of nature to a new and useful end."[222]

Clearly the discovery of previously unrecognized scientific principles and fundamental laws of nature potentially bestows a great benefit on

---

[219]*Id.* at 1369.

[220]*See, e.g.*, European Patent Convention art. 52(2) (14th ed. 2010), *available at* http://www.epo.org/law-practice/legal-texts/html/epc/2010/e/ar52.html (stating that the following shall not be regarded as patentable inventions: "(a) discoveries, scientific theories and mathematical methods; (b) aesthetic creations; (c) schemes, rules and methods for performing mental acts, playing games or doing business, and programs for computers; and (d) presentations of information").

[221]*See* Mayo Collaborative Servs. v. Prometheus Labs., Inc., 132 S. Ct. 1289, 1293 (2012) (stating that "[this] Court has long held that [35 U.S.C. §101] contains an important implicit exception. '[L]aws of nature, natural phenomena, and abstract ideas' are not patentable.") (quoting Diamond v. Diehr, 450 U.S. 175, 185 (1981)).

[222]Funk Bros. Seed Co. v. Kalo Inoculant Co., 333 U.S. 127, 130 (1948).

society. So why not reward the discoverers with patent protection, as an incentive for the discovery of even greater numbers of scientific principles and laws of nature? As a matter of public policy, the U.S. law on this point reflects the determination that such fundamental building blocks of science and technology must be left in the public domain, free for all to use and build upon.

European patent lawyers view this as a dividing line between "discovering" and "inventing" and do not consider discoveries to be patentable.[223] This position is at least facially inconsistent with the Intellectual Property Clause of the U.S. Constitution, however. Recall that the Constitution speaks of giving inventors exclusive rights for limited times to "their discoveries."[224] Moreover, the U.S. Patent Act expressly defines "invention" as meaning "invention or discovery."[225]

G.   Medical/Surgical Procedures

Medical and surgical procedures *are* patentable subject matter in the United States as "processes" within 35 U.S.C. §101.[226] In 1996, however, Congress added an obscure provision to the Patent Act that renders some of these patents essentially null and void. The legislation created a remedies exclusion. Under 35 U.S.C. §287(c), a patent on certain medical or surgical procedures, as narrowly defined by the statute, cannot be enforced. The patentee has no remedy against direct or inducing infringement of such a patent because the provisions of 35 U.S.C. §281 (civil action for infringement), §283 (injunction), §284 (damages), and §285 (attorney fees) are not applicable.

This remedies exclusion came about when one U.S. medical doctor sued another for infringement of a patent on a surgical technique for a method of incision of the eye to implant an intraocular lens.[227] Chagrined members of the medical community lobbied Congress for an exclusion from patentability for medical and surgical procedures.

[223]*See* European Patent Convention art. 52(2)(a) (14th ed. 2010), *available at* http:// www.epo.org/law-practice/legal-texts/html/epc/2010/e/ar52.html (stating that discoveries are not to be regarded as inventions).

[224]U.S. CONST., art. I, §8, cl. 8.

[225] 35 U.S.C. §100(a).

[226]This contrasts the views of many foreign countries, which categorically exclude methods of treatment of the human or animal body by surgery or therapy and diagnostic methods from patenting. *See, e.g.*, European Patent Convention art. 52(3) (14th ed. 2010), *available at* http://www.epo.org/law-practice/legal-texts/html/epc/2010/e/ar52. html; Agreement on Trade-Related Aspects of Intellectual Property Rights, including Trade in Counterfeit Goods, art. 27.3(a), Dec. 15, 1993, 33 I.L.M. 81 (1994) (giving member countries the option to deny such patents).

[227]*See* Method of making self-sealing episcleral incision, U.S. Patent No. 5,080,111 (issued Jan. 14, 1992).

In an eleventh-hour compromise, Congress passed a watered-down version of the legislation, codified at 35 U.S.C. §287(c), which does not prevent such procedures from being patented but deprives the patent owner of any remedy for infringement.[228] In practice, the "medical procedures" encompassed by the statute are so narrowly defined[229] that the legislation has had little more than a symbolic impact.

H.   Patentable Subject Matter Beyond §101: Plant Patents and Design Patents

The large majority of all issued U.S. patents are utility patents,[230] which are available for the categories of subject matter enumerated within 35 U.S.C. §101. In addition to utility patents, however, the United States also grants plant patents and design patents. Each is discussed below.

1.   Plant Patents

The subject matter of U.S. plant patents is governed not by 35 U.S.C. §101 but rather by 35 U.S.C. §161. That section provides that plant patents are available for those who

> invent[ ] or discover[ ] and asexually reproduce[] any distinct and new variety of plant, including cultivated sports, mutants, hybrids, and

---

[228]*See generally* Cynthia M. Ho, *Patents, Patients, and Public Policy: An Incomplete Intersection at 35 U.S.C. §287(c)*, 33 U.C. Davis L. Rev. 601 (2000); Richard P. Burgoon, Jr., *Silk Purses, Sows Ears, and Other Nuances Regarding 35 U.S.C. §287(c)*, 4 U. Balt. Intell. Prop. J. 69 (1996).

[229]*See* 35 U.S.C. §287(c)(2)(A) (narrowly defining "medical activity" as "the performance of a medical or surgical procedure on a body, but . . . not . . . (i) the use of a patented machine, manufacture, or composition of matter in violation of such patent, (ii) the practice of a patented use of a composition of matter in violation of such patent, or (iii) the practice of a process in violation of a biotechnology patent").

[230]For example, in the calendar year 2011, the USPTO granted the following numbers and types of patents:

Utility: 224,505;
Design: 21,356;
Plant: 823; and
Reissue: 1,029.

See United States Patent & Trademark Office, *U.S. Patent Statistics, Calendar Years 1963-2011, available at* http://www.uspto.gov/web/offices/ac/ido/oeip/taf/us_stat.pdf (last visited July 16, 2012).

newly found seedlings, other than a tuber propagated plant or a plant found in an uncultivated state. . . . [231]

The hallmark of a plant patent is the "asexual" reproduction of the new plant "variety."[232] To asexually reproduce a plant means to grow a genetically identical copy through budding, grafting, or cutting. In contrast, the reproduction of plants from seed is considered sexual reproduction and is not covered by plant patents under §161. However, a *sui generis* form of protection for sexually reproduced plant varieties, as well as tuber-propagated plants such as potatoes, is available in the United States under the Plant Variety Protection Act (PVPA).[233]

Why are there separate provisions of the Patent Act for plants? The answer is primarily historical. Prior to 1930, the general consensus was that plants could not qualify for patent protection because even those plants bred by humans were believed to be "products of nature." Moreover, plants were thought not amenable to the written description requirement as set forth in the statutory predecessor of what is today 35 U.S.C. §112(a).[234]

As a means of encouraging greater innovation in plant breeding, Congress in 1930 enacted a special statute, the Plant Patent Act, which addressed these concerns. Congress's action represents an acceptance of the modern view that asexually reproduced, distinct, and new plant varieties are not unprotectable "products of nature," but rather exist only through the intervention of humans. The Plant Patent Act also relaxes the written description requirement for plants.[235] The term of a plant patent is the same as that of a utility patent.[236]

---

[231]35 U.S.C. §161.

[232]A variety is a taxonomic rank beneath subspecies. For example, well-known varieties of grapes from which wine is produced include Chardonnay, Pinot Grigio, Cabernet Sauvignon, Merlot, and so on. As a result of selective breeding, each member of a variety possesses certain common characteristics or traits.

[233]*See* 7 U.S.C. §§2401 *et seq.* (Plant Variety Protection Act). The PVPA is administered by the U.S. Department of Agriculture. Certain plant-related inventions that are protectable under the PVPA may also be eligible for protection under 35 U.S.C. §101 as the subject matter of a utility patent, if they meet the substantive requirements of utility, novelty, and nonobviousness. *See* J.E.M. Ag. Supply, Inc. v. Pioneer Hi-Bred Int'l, Inc., 534 U.S. 124 (2001).

[234]*See* Imazio Nursery, Inc. v. Dana Greenhouses, 69 F.3d 1560, 1563 (Fed. Cir. 1995).

[235]*See* 35 U.S.C. §162 (providing that "[n]o plant patent shall be declared invalid for noncompliance with section 112 of this title if the description is as complete as is reasonably possible. The claim in the specification shall be in formal terms to the plant shown and described."). In practice, many plant patent applications include color photographs showing the features of the plant. *See, e.g.*, Chrysanthemum Plant Named Maroon Pride, U.S. Patent No. PP7,269 (issued July 10, 1990, to the Regents of the University of Minnesota).

[236]*See* 35 U.S.C. §161 (stating that "[t]he provisions of this title relating to patents for inventions shall apply to patents for plants, except as otherwise provided").

Importantly, plant patent protection is available only for plants resulting from human creative efforts by the patent applicant, and not for plants merely found by the applicant. The "invents or discovers" language of 35 U.S.C. §161 means that the plant must result from the applicant's own work, rather than resulting from "a 'chance find' or discovery of a plant explorer."[237] This requirement was not satisfied in *In re Beineke*.[238] In that case Walter Beineke noticed desirable genetic traits in two white oak trees, each over 100 years in age, growing in another person's front yard. Thereafter Beineke planted acorns from the oak trees on his own property, observed that the desirable traits were retained by the progeny trees, asexually reproduced the trees, and sought to patent them as new and distinct tree varieties.

The Federal Circuit affirmed the USPTO's rejection of Beineke's plant patent applications. After reviewing the legislative history of the 1930 Plant Patent Act, the court explained that protection under §161 requires, *inter alia*, that "(1) the plant must have been created in its inception by human activity, i.e., it must be the result of plant breeding or other agricultural or horticultural efforts; and (2) the plant must have been created by the 'inventor,' i.e., the person seeking the patent must have contributed to the creation of the plant in addition to having appreciated its uniqueness and asexually reproduced it."[239] Beineke did not satisfy either of these requirements. The oak trees he sought to patent were not in any way the result of Beineke's creative efforts, or of anyone else's efforts for that matter. Thus the court held that the trees did "not fall within the scope of those plants protected by the 1930 Act."[240]

The scope of exclusionary rights afforded by a plant patent is quite narrow. In the leading case of *Imazio Nursery v. Dana Greenhouses*,[241] the Federal Circuit interpreted the Plant Patent Act to conclude that "the scope of a plant patent is the asexual progeny of the patented plant variety."[242] In order to establish infringement of her plant patent, the patentee must therefore establish that the defendant's allegedly infringing plant is the asexually reproduced progeny of the original patented parent plant.[243] An independently developed plant, even if genetically identical to the patented plant, does not infringe.[244]

---

[237]*See* In re Beineke, Nos. 2011–1459, 2011–1460, __ F.3d __, 2012 WL 3156339, at *5 (Fed. Cir. Aug. 6, 2012) (quoting S. Rep. No. 71–315 (1930), at 3–4.)).

[238]Nos. 2011–1459, 2011–1460, __ F.3d __, 2012 WL 3156339 (Fed. Cir. Aug. 6, 2012).

[239]In re Beineke, Nos. 2011–1459, 2011–1460, __ F.3d __, 2012 WL 3156339, at *3 (Fed. Cir. Aug. 6, 2012).

[240]In re Beineke, Nos. 2011–1459, 2011–1460, __ F.3d __, 2012 WL 3156339, at *7 (Fed. Cir. Aug. 6, 2012).

[241] 69 F.3d 1560 (Fed. Cir. 1995).

[242]*Id.* at 1568.

[243]*See id.* at 1569.

[244]*See id.* at 1570.

Although Congress created two specific types of intellectual property protection for plants (i.e., plant patents and Plant Variety Protection Act certificates as discussed above), the existence of these separate statutory schemes does not prevent plant-related subject matter from being claimed in utility patents. Plant-related subject matter can qualify for protection in a utility patent under 35 U.S.C. §101 *if* the claimed subject matter satisfies all other requirements of utility patentability (e.g., novelty and nonobviousness). In *J.E.M. Ag Supply, Inc. v. Pioneer Hi-Bred Int'l, Inc.*[245] the Supreme Court considered the validity of multiple U.S. utility patents obtained by Pioneer Hi-Bred Int'l (Pioneer) to protect the company's inbred and hybrid corn seed products.[246] An accused infringer contended that Pioneer's utility patents were invalid because the Plant Patent Act and the Plant Variety Protection Act set forth the exclusive statutory means for the protection of plant life. The Supreme Court disagreed, holding that neither of these acts foreclosed utility patent protection for plants. "Whatever Congress may have believed about the state of patent law and the science of plant breeding in 1930 [when it passed the Plant Patent Act], plants have always had the *potential* to fall within the general subject matter of §101, which is a dynamic provision designed to encompass new and unforeseen inventions."[247] Denying utility patent protection to plant life under §101 simply because such coverage was thought "technologically infeasible" when Congress passed the Plant Patent Act "would be inconsistent with the forward-looking perspective of the utility patent statute."[248] The Supreme Court observed that it had taken a broad view of §101 subject matter in its landmark 1980 *Chakrabarty* decision,[249] and thus interpreted §101 "clearly includes plants within its subject matter."[250] Of course, obtaining utility patent protection on plant-related subject matter requires that the claimed matter satisfy the rigorous §102 novelty and §103 nonobviousness requirements and that it be disclosed in accordance with the requirements of §112. If these statutory criteria are met, however, §101 does not stand as a threshold bar.

[245]534 U.S. 124 (2001).

[246]Pioneer's utility patents for inbred corn lines claimed both the seeds and plants of the inbred line and the hybrids produced by crossing the protected inbred line with another corn line. The patents for corn hybrid plants claimed the plant, its seeds, variants, mutants, and trivial modifications of the hybrid. *See id.* at 127.

[247]*Id.* at 135 (emphasis in original).

[248]*Id.*

[249]*See supra* Section D.3 ("Life Forms").

[250]*J.E.M. Ag Supply*, 534 U.S. at 144.

2. Design Patents

In addition to utility patents and plant patents, the United States also grants a third type of patent: design patents. Design patent protection is an increasingly important form of intellectual property protection because judicial decisions have made it more difficult to attain trademark protection for product design.[251] Like plant patents, the subject matter of design patents is defined not in 35 U.S.C. §101 but rather in a separate section of the Patent Act for design patents, 35 U.S.C. §171.

a. Criteria for Obtaining Design Patents

A design patent protects the "new, original and ornamental design for an article of manufacture",[252] for example, the unique external appearance of a digital music player,[253] a line of furniture,[254] an automobile fender, or even a roofing shingle. Patentable designs must also satisfy the nonobviousness requirement of 35 U.S.C. §103.[255] Unlike utility

---

[251]*See* Wal-Mart Stores, Inc. v. Samara Bros., Inc., 529 U.S. 205, 212 (2000) (concluding that product design, like color, cannot be inherently distinctive); *id.* at 214 (holding that product design cannot be protected under §43(a) of the Lanham [Trademark] Act without a showing of secondary meaning [i.e., a showing that consumers have come to identify a particular design primarily as an indicator of product source]); *id.* (stating that the "availability of [design patent or copyright] protections greatly reduces any harm to the producer that might ensue from our conclusion that a product design cannot be protected under § 43(a) without a showing of secondary meaning").

[252] 35 U.S.C. §171.

[253]*See, e.g.*, U.S. Patent No. D497,618 (issued Oct. 26, 2004). The '618 patent, owned by Apple Computer, Inc., claims the "ornamental design for a media device." *Id.* The media device in question is the 3G model of Apple's well-known iPod music player.

[254]Furniture designs are currently the most common subject matter of U.S. design patents. See Daniel H. Brean, *Enough Is Enough: Time to Eliminate Design Patents and Rely on More Appropriate Copyright and Trademark Protection for Product Designs,* 16 Tex. Intell. Prop. L.J. 325, 361 (2008); id. at 355 (tbl. 1) (reporting that since 1976, more design patents have issued in the USPTO's "Furnishings" design classification than in any other classification).

[255]*See* 35 U.S.C. § 171 (providing in part that "[t]he provisions of this title relating to patents for inventions shall apply to patents for designs, except as otherwise provided"); Avia Group Int'l, Inc. v. L.A. Gear Cal., Inc., 853 F.2d 1557, 1563 (Fed. Cir. 1998) ("Design patents must meet a nonobviousness requirement identical to that applicable to utility patents."). Whether a design would have been nonobvious is determined in accordance with the *Graham* factors, as applied from the perspective of a "'designer of ordinary capability who designs articles of the type presented in the [design patent] application.'" *Id.* at 1564 (quoting In re Nalbandian, 661 F.2d 1214, 1216 (C.C.P.A. 1981)).

For more on reconceptualizing the nonobviousness requirement in design patents, *see* Janice M. Mueller & Daniel H. Brean, *Overcoming the "Impossible Issue" of Nonobviousness in Design Patents*, 99 Ky. L.J. 419 (2011).

and plant patents, design patents have a term of only 14 years from date of grant,[256] and their content is not published until grant.[257]

The protection afforded by a design patent is limited to the *ornamental* features of a design and cannot encompass features that are primarily functional (i.e., in which the nature of the design contributes to the operation or performance of the article).[258] For example, the existence of a design patent on a golf club would not prevent others from copying features such as the streamlined shape of the club head, if this shape (although pleasing to look at, especially for golf aficionados) also increased the loft and distance of the golf ball. In this respect, design patent law adopts a nonfunctionality criterion analogous to the useful article doctrine of copyright law.[259]

Care must be taken to distinguish the functionality of the underlying article of manufacture from the alleged functionality of its external design. For example, in *Avia Group Int'l, Inc. v. L.A. Gear Cal., Inc.*[260] the Federal Circuit upheld the validity of two athletic-shoe design patents over the arguments of the accused infringer that the designs were primarily functional rather than ornamental as required by 35 U.S.C. §171. The court did not dispute that "shoes are functional and that certain features of the shoe designs in issue perform functions."[261] However, if functionality of the underlying article is not separable from the alleged functionality of its design, "it would not be possible to obtain a design patent on a utilitarian article of manufacture . . . or to obtain both design and utility patents on the same article."[262] Moreover, the patentability of a claimed design must be considered as a whole. The Federal Circuit agreed with the district court that the patented designs in question, directed to the aesthetic aspects of an athletic shoe's outer sole and its upper, were primarily ornamental. The designs encompassed features such as the location and arrangement of perforations and stitching in the shoe upper, and a "swirl effect" around the pivot point on the sole of the shoe, as depicted in Figure 7.1.[263] Moreover, to the extent that the design

---

[256]*See* 35 U.S.C. §173.

[257] 35 U.S.C. §122(b)(2)(A)(iv).

[258]*See* Lee v. Dayton-Hudson Corp., 838 F.2d 1186 (Fed. Cir. 1988).

[259]*See* 17 U.S.C. §101 (2006) (providing that "the design of a useful article, as defined in this section, shall be considered a [copyrightable] pictorial, graphic, or sculptural work only if, and only to the extent that, such design incorporates pictorial, graphic, or sculptural features that can be identified separately from, and are capable of existing independently of, the utilitarian aspects of the article").

[260] 853 F.2d 1557 (Fed. Cir. 1988).

[261]*Id.* at 1563.

[262]*Id.* (citations omitted).

[263]*See id.*

Figure 7.1

U.S. Pat. Des. 287,301 (Dec. 23, 1986)

features performed the functions suggested by the defendants, the Federal Circuit found persuasive the district court's reasoning that all such functions could have been performed by many other possible design choices.[264]

---

[264]*See id.*

b. *Establishing Infringement of Design Patents*

The leading U.S. Supreme Court case on design patents, *Gorham Co. v. White,*[265] established that design patent infringement must be assessed from the perspective of an "ordinary observer." The ordinary observer is not an expert in the manufacture of designs but rather is a hypothetical purchaser or observer "of ordinary acuteness, bringing to the examination of the article upon which the design has been placed that degree of observation which men of ordinary intelligence give. It is persons of the latter class who are the principal purchasers of the articles to which designs have given novel appearances, and if they are misled, and induced to purchase what is not the article they supposed it to be . . . the patentees are injured, and that advantage of a market which the patent was granted to secure is destroyed."[266] The *Gorham* Court accordingly held that the following test governs in determining whether a design patent has been infringed:

> [I]f, in the eye of an ordinary observer, giving such attention as a purchaser usually gives, two designs are substantially the same, if the resemblance is such as to deceive such an observer, inducing him to purchase one supposing it to be the other, the first one patented is infringed by the other.[267]

After the Federal Circuit's creation in 1982, the court expanded the test for design patent infringement by adding a second prong to the *Gorham* test. In addition to satisfying substantial similarity of the claimed and accused designs, the design patent holder also had to establish that the accused design appropriated the novel feature(s) of the patented design.[268] As evolved by a series of Federal Circuit decisions, this additional "point of novelty" component to the design patent infringement analysis was problematic because it mixed concepts of design patent validity with infringement. The point of novelty inquiry effectively required a patentee to affirmatively establish the novelty of its presumptively valid design.

---

[265]81 U.S. 511 (1871).

[266]*See id.* at 527-528.

[267]*Id.* at 528.

[268]*See* Litton Sys., Inc. v. Whirlpool Corp., 728 F.2d 1423, 1444 (Fed. Cir. 1984) (stating that no matter how similar two designs look, the patented design is not infringed unless "the accused device . . . appropriate[s] the novelty in the patented device which distinguishes it from the prior art"). Federal Circuit decisions following *Litton Sys.* interpreted that decision's language as requiring that design patent infringement "consider both the perspective of the ordinary observer and the particular novelty in the claimed design." Egyptian Goddess, Inc. v. Swisa, Inc., 543 F.3d 665, 671 (Fed. Cir. 2008) (*en banc*) (citing Circuit's design patent infringement decisions issued in the time period from 1988 to 2004).

The Federal Circuit in 2008 went *en banc* in *Egyptian Goddess, Inc. v. Swisa, Inc.* to clarify the standard for infringement of design patents.[269] The court in *Egyptian Goddess* rejected a freestanding point of novelty inquiry as a separate part of the standard. Rather, the infringement test should be applied as a single inquiry, that is, whether the *Gorham* ordinary observer would find the claimed and accused designs substantially similar. The Federal Circuit emphasized that the "ordinary observer" test is "the sole test for determining whether a design patent has been infringed."[270] Under that test, "infringement will not be found unless the accused article 'embod[ies] the patented design or any colorable imitation thereof.'"[271]

The *Egyptian Goddess* court explained further that the "ordinary observer" may sometimes be informed by knowledge of the prior art. For example, in cases where the claimed and accused designs do not appear "plainly dissimilar," the question whether an ordinary observer would determine that the two designs are substantially the same will benefit from comparing both designs with the prior art. The Federal Circuit observed that "[w]here there are many examples of similar prior art designs . . . , differences between the claimed and accused designs that might not be noticeable in the abstract can become significant to the hypothetical ordinary observer who is conversant with the prior art."[272] In short, the prior art may provide an important context or frame of reference for assessing how similar the claimed and accused designs truly are.

Although the Federal Circuit's characterization of the "ordinary observer" to include a person aware of the prior art may suggest that the *Egyptian Goddess* test is not so very different from the rejected two-pronged test that included a point of novelty component, an important practical difference exists. Under the test for design patent infringement as formulated in *Egyptian Goddess,* the burden of proof to introduce any prior art that may have relevance to the infringement inquiry is placed on the accused infringer rather than the patentee.[273] This result is consistent with the principle that a design patent, like a utility patent, is presumed novel,[274] and the burden of

---

[269]Egyptian Goddess, Inc. v. Swisa, Inc., 543 F.3d 665 (Fed. Cir. 2008) (*en banc*).

[270]*Id.* at 678.

[271]*Id.* (quoting Goodyear Tire & Rubber Co. v. Hercules Tire & Rubber Co., 162 F.3d 1113, 1116-1117 (Fed. Cir. 1998)).

[272]*Id.*

[273]*See id.* (stating that "if the accused infringer elects to rely on the comparison prior art as part of its defense against the claim of infringement, the burden of production of that prior art is on the accused infringer").

[274]*See* 35 U.S.C. §282; Avia Group Int'l, Inc. v. L.A. Gear Cal., Inc., 853 F.2d 1557, 1562 (Fed. Cir. 1988) (stating, in a case in which validity of a design patent was challenged by accused infringer, that "[a] patent is presumed valid").

invalidating the patent (e.g., on the basis of prior art that would render the claimed design anticipated or obvious) always remains on the accused infringer/validity challenger.

The patented design in *Egyptian Goddess* was that of a four-sided fingernail file or buffer, having a hollow, square cross-section plus raised strips of nail buffing material on three of its four sides. The accused design incorporated buffing material on all four sides of a nail buffer. The prior art buffers (of square and triangular cross-sections) also included buffing material on all sides. Figure 7.2 depicts the claimed and accused buffers along with the closest prior art nail buffer designs.

Figure 7.2

The infringement question for the Federal Circuit was "whether an ordinary observer, familiar with the prior art Falley and Nailco designs, would be deceived into believing the Swisa buffer is the same as the patented buffer."[275] Answering that question in the negative, the Federal Circuit affirmed the district court's entry of summary judgment of no infringement. Although the patented and accused buffers had the same general shape (hollow and square in cross-section), the absence of buffer material on the fourth side of the claimed design could not be considered a minor feature in view of the closest prior art, which featured buffer material on all sides. An ordinary observer would likely regard the accused design as being closer to the prior art than the patented design.[276] The Federal Circuit concluded that

[275]*Egyptian Goddess*, 543 F.3d at 681.
[276]*See id.* at 682 (discussing "problem with" declaration of patentee's expert Eaton).

"[i]n light of the similarity of the prior art buffers to the accused buffer . . . no reasonable fact-finder could find that [the patentee, Egyptian Goddess] met its burden of showing . . . that an ordinary observer, taking into account the prior art, would believe the accused design to be the same as the patented design."[277]

---

[277]*Id.*

Correcting and Challenging Issued Patents in the USPTO

A. Introduction

Even though it has been granted by the USPTO, an issued patent may suffer from certain defects. The defects may be so severe that, at the conclusion of litigation, a federal court will hold the patent invalid and/or unenforceable.[1] In other cases, however, the patent's defects are of a more minor nature and can be corrected through procedures conducted within the USPTO that are generally less expensive and of shorter duration than federal court litigation. This chapter describes several methods by which issued patents can be returned to the USPTO for correction: certificates of correction, reissue, and reexamination. This chapter also describes two procedures, newly implemented via the America Invents Act of 2011, by which persons other than patent owners can challenge the validity of issued patents in the USPTO: *inter partes* review and post-grant review.[2]

---

[1]The presumption of validity for issued patents, *see* 35 U.S.C. §282 (2012), is rebuttable. Based on clear and convincing evidence, a federal court may hold a patent invalid for failure to comply with the statutory requirements for patentability, 35 U.S.C. §101, §102, or §103; or for failure to satisfy the disclosure and/or claim definiteness requirements of 35 U.S.C. §112(a), (b). Alternatively, the patent may be held unenforceable for inequitable conduct or patent misuse.

[2]Yet another method of correcting an issued patent is by filing a disclaimer of a particular claim or claims of the patent. After obtaining his patent, a patent owner may determine that certain of its claims are invalid. Claims stand or fall independently as far as their validity. If certain claims of the patent are invalid without any deceptive invention, the remaining claims are not thereby rendered invalid. 35 U.S.C. §253, ¶1. The patentee may disclaim the invalid claims by filing a written disclaimer and paying the appropriate fee to the USPTO. The Patent Act provides an incentive to do so. The patentee can bring an action for infringement in which he asserts only the valid claims of a patent, even though he believes other claims in the patent to be invalid. However, the patentee will forfeit any potential recovery of costs from the infringement lawsuit *unless* he filed a disclaimer of the invalid claims before commencing the suit. 35 U.S.C. §288.

B. Certificates of Correction

In some cases, minor mistakes in a patent such as misspellings can be corrected by use of a certificate of correction. The opportunity to seek a certificate of correction arises once the patent applicant (or her patent attorney or agent) receives the official "ribbon copy" of her U.S. patent. The patent should be reviewed carefully for typographical accuracy, and the document maintained in a safe place. If mistakes are found, steps should be taken promptly to correct them.[3] The manner in which any minor mistakes in the patent can be remedied depends on the party responsible for the mistake: the USPTO or the applicant.

If minor mistakes in the issued patent are the fault of the USPTO, they can be corrected by seeking a certificate of correction in accordance with 35 U.S.C. §254. Because the mistake in the patent is the fault of the agency, there is no charge to the applicant for certificates of correction issued under 35 U.S.C. §254. This statutory section requires that the mistake in the patent was "incurred through the fault of the Patent and Trademark Office," and was "clearly disclosed by the records of the Office."[4] For example, in *Southwest Software, Inc. v. Harlequin, Inc.*[5] the patent in suit was twice corrected under 35 U.S.C. §254: once to correct the agency's omission of a comma,[6] and a second time to add to the issued patent a missing "Program Printout Appendix" that disclosed software code arguably necessary

---

[3]The patentee in *Southwest Software, Inc. v. Harlequin, Inc.*, 226 F.3d 1280 (Fed. Cir. 2000), learned this lesson the hard way. Not noticing a USPTO-caused mistake in its patent until after the matter was raised by the opposing party in a lawsuit alleging infringement of the patent, the patentee obtained a certificate of correction from the USPTO during the pendency of the infringement action. Although the Federal Circuit determined that the USPTO had validly issued the certificate under 35 U.S.C. §254, it nevertheless held as a matter of statutory interpretation that the certificate was not effective for causes of action, such as the case at bar, that arose prior to the issuance of the certificate. *See id.* at 1295. Thus, the certificate of correction was not effective for the patent in suit, and the case had to be remanded for consideration of whether the patent was valid under 35 U.S.C. §112, ¶1 absent the disclosure in an appendix that the USPTO had neglected to include in the issued patent. *See id.* at 1297. The fault was not entirely that of the agency, however; the Federal Circuit further remarked that

> it does not seem to us to be asking too much to expect a patentee to check a patent when it is issued in order to determine whether it contains any errors that require the issuance of a certificate of correction. In this case, the omission of the Program Printout Appendix from the '257 patent resulted in the absence of approximately 330 pages of text from the specification. It would seem that such an error would be readily apparent.

Id. at 1296.

[4]35 U.S.C. §254.

[5]226 F.3d 1280 (Fed. Cir. 2000).

[6]*See id.* at 1287 n.6.

for enablement and best mode of the claimed method and apparatus for calibrating digital images in desktop publishing.[7] This appendix was submitted by the patent applicant with the originally filed application but was inadvertently excluded from the patent specification when issued by the USPTO.[8]

If the mistake in the patent is the fault of the applicant rather than the USPTO, it may be remediable with a certificate of correction issued in accordance with 35 U.S.C. §255. To qualify under this section, the mistake must have occurred "in good faith," and be of "a clerical or typographical nature, or of minor character."[9] For example, correction under §255 might be appropriate where a patent's written description referred to a certain process temperature in "degrees Celsius," but the claims as presented by the applicant merely recited "degrees."[10] Because the mistake is not the fault of the USPTO, the patent owner will be required to pay a fee for this type of correction.

New matter cannot be added through the certificate of correction procedure, and the correction cannot be of such magnitude as would be addressed in reexamination or reissue proceedings (discussed below). In particular, the proposed correction cannot be one that would change the scope of the patent claims.[11] For example, the patentee in *In re Arnott*[12] was granted a reissue patent directed to an intraocular lens implant. As reissued, a particular dependent claim (claim 8) depended from another claim of the patent (claim 1). The patentee contended that claim 8 should have depended from claim 7, and that his patent counsel's assistant had simply made a typographical error when typing the application from a handwritten draft in which the number 7 looked like the number 1. The USPTO Commissioner denied the patentee's request for correction because changing the claim dependency under these circumstances would have meant changing the scope of claim 8. When claim 8 depended from claim 7, it incorporated a limitation requiring the implant to be made from a particular material, polymethyl methacrylate, which did not appear in claim 1. Therefore

---

[7]*See id.* at 1287.

[8]*Id.* at 1291 (stating that "[t]he PTO determined that the appendix had been filed with the application for the '257 patent and that the separation and loss of the appendix, as well as the failure to print the appendix in the issued patent, were the result of an error on its part"). The Federal Circuit rejected the accused infringer's argument that the omission of the appendix was the fault of the patentee rather than the USPTO and thus that the certificate of correction should not have been issued under §254; the court stated that it "discern[ed] no clear error in the district court's findings and therefore affirm[ed] the ruling that the certificate of correction was not issued in violation of §254." *Id.* at 1293.

[9]35 U.S.C. §255.

[10]*See* In re Arnott, 19 USPQ.2d 1049, 1053 (Comm'r Pat. 1991).

[11]*Id.* at 1052.

[12]19 USPQ.2d 1049 (Comm'r Pat. 1991).

changing the claim dependency as requested by the patentee would have changed the scope of claim 8 and could not be permitted via the certificate of correction procedure.[13]

Whether a certificate of correction is sought under 35 U.S.C. §254 or §255, the USPTO will issue a separate document titled "Certificate of Correction" that operates much like an errata sheet for the patent. The certificate will list specific corrections by the patent's line and column numbers. The certificate is made a part of the official patent documentation, and the patent is treated as if the corrections had been part of the original patent as issued.[14]

C. Reissue

1. Overview

For errors not remediable by a certificate of correction as discussed above, the patentee may need to consider whether to seek reissuance of his patent. Reissue is an administrative procedure conducted within the USPTO for correcting an issued patent that suffers from certain enumerated errors that must have occurred "without any deceptive intention."[15] Reissue involves an offer by the patentee to surrender the original patent,[16] submission of a reissue application with an oath setting forth the asserted errors, and a reprosecution of the patent's claims. During the reprosecution, all claims of the reissue application are subject to rejection on any statutory ground.[17] The possible results of this procedure are reissue of the patent in original or amended form for the remaining term of the original patent, or if no error is found, a refusal by the agency to reissue the patent. Unless and until a reissued patent is granted, the original patent remains in effect.[18]

---

[13]An applicant in this scenario would need to attempt correction by filing an application to reissue the patent, as discussed below.

[14]*But see* Southwest Software, Inc. v. Harlequin, Inc., 226 F.3d 1280 (Fed. Cir. 2000), in which the Federal Circuit held that a certificate of correction issued under 35 U.S.C. §254 was *not* effective for an infringement cause of action that arose prior to the issuance of the certificate.

[15]35 U.S.C. §251 (2006).

[16]*See* 37 C.F.R. §1.178(a) (providing that "[t]he application for reissue of a patent shall constitute an offer to surrender that patent, and the surrender shall take effect upon reissue of the patent").

[17]*See* Hewlett-Packard Co. v. Bausch & Lomb Inc., 882 F.2d 1556, 1563 (Fed. Cir. 1989) (explaining that "[r]eissue is essentially a reprosecution of all claims. For example, original claims which a patentee wants to maintain unchanged may nevertheless be rejected on any statutory ground.").

[18]*See* 37 C.F.R. §1.178(a) (providing that "[u]ntil a reissue application is granted, the original patent shall remain in effect.").

The USPTO assigns reissued patents a new patent number that begins with the abbreviation "Re."—for example, "U.S. Patent No. Re. 40,000." The specification of the reissued patent will be printed by the agency "in such a manner as to show the changes over the original patent text by enclosing any material omitted by the reissue in heavy brackets [ ] and printing material added by the reissue in *italics*."[19] Although it has been corrected in the USPTO, a reissued patent nevertheless remains subject to the possibility of invalidation in federal court litigation, just as an original patent.

2. Historical Development

The practice of reissuing defective patents was first approved by the U.S. Supreme Court in 1832[20] and legislatively codified in the Patent Act of 1836.[21] Reissue was conceived as a validity-saving mechanism, available when by an innocent mistake, "the instrument introduced to secure this privilege [the patentee's right to exclude] fails in its object. . . ."[22] In other words, reissue was available when the patentee had innocently made an inadequate exchange.

The possibility of reissue recognizes the need for fairness to inventors, given the difficulty of drafting patents.[23] As a remedial provi-

---

[19]UNITED STATES PATENT AND TRADEMARK OFFICE, MANUAL OF PATENT EXAMINING PROCEDURE §1455 (8th ed., rev. July 2010), *available at* http://www.uspto.gov/web/offices/pac/mpep/documents/1400_1455.htm#sect1455.

[20]*See* Grant v. Raymond, 31 U.S. (6 Pet.) 218 (1832).

[21]*See* Festo Corp. v. Shoketsu Kinzoku Kogyo Kabushiki Co., 234 F.3d 558, 602 n.3 (Fed. Cir. 2000) (*en banc*) (Michel, J., dissenting) (noting that "[t]he Patent Act of 1836 authorized a patentee to surrender the claims of his original patent and to obtain a reissue patent whenever the patent was 'inoperative, or invalid, by reason of a defective or insufficient description or specification, or by reason of the patentee claiming in his specification as his own invention, more than he had or shall have a right to claim as new.' Patent Act of 1836, Ch. 357, 5 Stat. 117, at §13 (July 4, 1836)."), *vacated on other grounds*, 535 U.S. 722 (2002).

[22]*Grant*, 31 U.S. (6 Pet.) at 244.

[23]*See* Topliff v. Topliff, 145 U.S. 156 (1892), in which the Court observed the following:

> To hold that a patent can never be reissued for an enlarged claim would be not only to override the obvious intent of the statute, but would operate in many cases with great hardship upon the patentee. The specification and claims of a patent, particularly if the invention be at all complicated, constitute one of the most difficult legal instruments to draw with accuracy; and, in view of the fact that valuable inventions are often placed in the hands of inexperienced persons to prepare such specifications and claims, it is no matter of surprise that the latter frequently fail to describe with requisite certainty the exact invention of the patentee, and err either in claiming that which the patentee had not in fact invented, or in omitting some element which was a valuable or essential part of

sion based on fundamental notions of equity and fairness, reissue is intended to "bail applicants out of difficult situations into which they get 'without any deceptive intention.'"[24] Accordingly, the reissue statute "should be construed liberally."[25]

The nineteenth century saw extensive abuses of the reissue procedure.[26] For example, in *Miller v. Brass Co.*,[27] the Supreme Court held that an application for reissue should be denied because the patent owner delayed in seeking to broaden its claims for 15 years after issuance of the original patent. The Court recognized that reissue might be permitted to broaden claims, even though the statute at that time did not expressly provide for broadening reissues, if the reissue was sought within two years of the original grant (two years being the prefiling grace period at that time). But in this case, the patentee's prolonged delay was unreasonable, and permitting reissue would have had unjust consequences: "Every independent inventor, every mechanic, every citizen, is affected by such delay, and by the issue of a new patent with a broader and more comprehensive claim. The granting of a reissue for such a purpose, after an unreasonable delay, is clearly an abuse of the power to grant reissues, and may justly be declared illegal and void."[28]

The reissue provisions of the Patent Act were subsequently amended in the 1952 Act to make explicit that broadening reissues must be sought within a two-year window after the grant of the original patent. This and other amendments, as well as a series of Supreme Court decisions on reissue patents, curbed the earlier abuses. Today, less than 1 percent of the U.S. patents granted annually are reissue patents.[29] Many reissued patents are involved in pending or contemplated litigation over infringement and/or validity.

---

his actual invention. Under such circumstances, it would be manifestly unjust to deny him the benefit of a reissue to secure to him his actual invention, provided it is evident that there has been a mistake, and he has been guilty of no want of reasonable diligence in discovering it, and no third persons have in the meantime acquired the right to manufacture or sell what he had failed to claim. The object of the patent law is to secure to inventors a monopoly of what they have actually invented or discovered, and it ought not to be defeated by a too strict and technical adherence to the letter of the statute, or by the application of artificial rules of interpretation.

Id. at 171.

[24]In re Oda, 443 F.2d 1200, 1203 (C.C.P.A. 1971) (Rich, J.).

[25]In re Weiler, 790 F.2d 1576, 1579 (Fed. Cir. 1986).

[26]*See generally* Kendall J. Dood, *Pursuing the Essence of Inventions: Reissuing Patents in the 19th Century*, 32 Tech. & Culture 999, 999-1017 (1991).

[27]104 U.S. 350 (1881).

[28]*Id.* at 355.

[29]For example, in calendar year 2011, a total of 247,713 U.S. patents (utility, design, plant, and reissue) issued. Of these, only 1,029, or 0.4 percent, were reissue patents.

3. Statutory Basis

The statutory provision governing patent reissues is 35 U.S.C. §251, which provides in part that:

> **(a) In general.**—Whenever any patent is, through error, deemed wholly or partly inoperative or invalid, by reason of a defective specification or drawing, or by reason of the patentee claiming more or less than he had a right to claim in the patent, the Director shall, on the surrender of such patent and the payment of the fee required by law, reissue the patent for the invention disclosed in the original patent, and in accordance with a new and amended application, for the unexpired part of the term of the original patent. No new matter shall be introduced into the application for reissue. . . .
>
> **(d) Reissue patent enlarging scope of claims.**—No reissued patent shall be granted enlarging the scope of the claims of the original patent unless applied for within two years from the grant of the original patent.[30]

The basic criteria for reissue are identified by parsing this statutory text. In order to qualify for reissue, a patent must be "wholly or partly inoperative or invalid," meaning that the patent is "ineffective to protect the invention adequately or it is a nullity. . . ."[31] Importantly, this inoperativeness or invalidity must have been caused by "error." Thus, reissue *cannot* be used to rehabilitate a patent that was procured through inequitable conduct,[32] which by definition involves intent to deceive the USPTO. Types of reissue error specifically mentioned in the statute are "a defective specification or drawing,"[33] or "the patentee claiming more or less than he had a right to claim in the patent."[34]

If the patent is reissued, the reissued patent will expire on the same date that the original patent would have, so that reissue in no way extends the term of the patent. Moreover, no new matter can

---

See United States Patent & Trademark Office, *U.S. Patent Statistics, Calendar Years 1963-2011, available at* http://www.uspto.gov/web/offices/ac/ido/oeip/taf/us_stat.pdf (last visited July 16, 2012).

[30]35 U.S.C. §251 (eff. Sept. 16, 2012) (as amended by the AIA). The pre-AIA version of the first paragraph of 35 U.S.C. §251 required that the error be "without any deceptive intention." The AIA deleted the intent language. *See* Leahy-Smith America Invents Act, Pub. L. No. 112-29 (H.R. 1249), §20(d)(1)(B),125 Stat. 284, 334 (Sept. 16, 2011). This amendment to §251 is effective Sept. 16, 2012, and applies prospectively to "proceedings commenced on or after that effective date." AIA §20(l).

[31]In re Oda, 443 F.2d 1200, 1206 (C.C.P.A. 1971) (Rich, J.).

[32]*See* Hewlett-Packard Co. v. Bausch & Lomb, Inc., 882 F.2d 1556, 1563 n.7 (Fed. Cir. 1989).

[33]35 U.S.C. §251(a) (eff. Sept. 16, 2012).

[34]35 U.S.C. §251(a) (eff. Sept. 16, 2012).

be introduced in a reissue application.[35] Thus, although the scope of claims may be broadened in reissue, this is only possible to the extent that the broadening is supported by the original specification in accordance with 35 U.S.C. §112(a). The reissue must be "for the invention disclosed in the original patent."[36]

4.   Broadening Reissues

A "broadening reissue" is sought when the patentee erred by "claiming less than he had a right to claim in the patent," and wants to obtain claims of broader scope than those that appear in the issued patent. Such broadened claims must nevertheless be supported by the patent's disclosure in accordance with 35 U.S.C. §112(a), because the reissue must be "for the invention disclosed in the original patent."[37] If a broadening reissue is desired, the patentee must file an application to reissue "within two years from the grant of the original patent."[38] This two-year statute of limitations for broadening reissues is based on the two-year prefiling grace period provided by the Patent Act between 1839 and 1939. Courts construed any delay longer than the two-year period as a presumptive abandonment of any described but nonclaimed subject matter.[39]

Case law on what constitutes a broadening reissue applies a "broader in any respect" rule; in other words, if the scope of even a single limitation of a claim is broadened, although other limitations remain unchanged or are even narrowed in scope, this counts as a broadening reissue that must be initiated within the two-year statute of limitations.[40] For example, consider the following claim of an issued patent:

> 1. A ceiling fan comprising a plurality of hollow blades, attached to a rod, attached to a motor.

Assume that the written description supports the modification of claim 1 to read as follows:

> 1. A ceiling fan comprising a plurality of blades, attached to a solid rod, attached to a motor.

---

[35]In interpreting the reissue statutes the Supreme Court has explained that "by 'new matter' we suppose to be meant new substantive matter, such as would have the effect of changing the invention, or of introducing what might be the subject of another application for a patent." Powder Co. v. Powder Works, 98 U.S. 126, 138 (1878).

[36]35 U.S.C. §251(a) (eff. Sept. 16, 2012).

[37]*Id.*

[38]*Id.*

[39]*See* Topliff v. Topliff, 145 U.S. 156, 170-171 (1892); Miller v. Brass Co., 104 U.S. 350, 352 (1881).

[40]*See* Ball Corp. v. United States, 729 F.2d 1429, 1437-1438 (Fed. Cir. 1984).

If the patentee seeks to reissue the patent so as to obtain the modified version of claim 1, he must file his reissue application within two years of the issuance of the original patent. The proposed modification of claim 1 satisfies the "broader in any respect" rule. Even though the rod limitation is now narrower in scope because the qualifier "solid" has been added, the blades limitation has been broadened because the "hollow" qualification for the blade configuration has been removed (i.e., the blades can be hollow or solid or of any other construction).

When considering whether to seek broadening reissue, the patentee should keep in mind that this strategy may give rise to intervening rights in third parties who relied on the narrower version of the claims that issued in the original patent, as discussed further in Section C.7 below.

5. Reissue Error

A number of types of errors in an issued patent may qualify it for reissue. The Patent Act of 1946, which defined reissue error in terms of "inadvertence, accident, mistake," was generally construed rather liberally. Although the 1952 Act implementation of reissue required that the error be committed "without any deceptive intention,"[41] the America Invents Act of 2011 deleted the "without any deceptive intention" language.[42] Post-AIA, reissues must still correct "error" in patents, but the intent of the entity responsible for the error is no longer relevant.

A representative type of reissue error is a translation error in the patent specification that is more severe than the type of typographical error correctable by a certificate of correction. For example, in *In re Oda*,[43] the translating of a Japanese priority application into English resulted in the mistranslation of "nitric acid" as "nitrous acid," two different chemical entities. These mistranslations occurred in several places in the written description of the patent, including a working example, but not in the claims. The USPTO rejected the reissue application as drawn to new matter. The Court of Customs and Patent Appeals (CCPA), one of the Federal Circuit's two predecessor courts, disagreed. The CCPA concluded, based on all evidence of record, that one skilled in the art "would appreciate not only the

---

[41]35 U.S.C. §251 (2006).

[42]*See* Leahy-Smith America Invents Act, Pub. L. No. 112-29 (H.R. 1249), §20(d)(1)(B),125 Stat. 284, 334 (Sept. 16, 2011).This amendment, made to what is now designated 35 U.S.C. §251(a), is effective Sept. 16, 2012, and applies prospectively to "proceedings commenced on or after that effective date." AIA §20(l).

[43]443 F.2d 1200 (C.C.P.A. 1971).

existence of error in the specification but what the error is,"[44] and that from this it followed that "when the nature of this error is known it is also known how to correct it."[45] Thus, the reissue was permissible to change nitrous to nitric in the written description and did not constitute prohibited new matter.

Another type of reissue error occurs when the patentee claimed more or less than she had a right to claim. In *Scripps Clinic & Research Foundation v. Genentech, Inc.,*[46] the inventors asserted that they had erred in claiming less than they had a right to claim. In the original patent, which was directed to highly purified Factor VIII:C protein product, a substance involved in the clotting of blood, the invention was claimed only by means of process and product-by-process claims. The patent did not include product claims (i.e., to Factor VIII:C itself as a composition of matter) because the patent attorney at the time of the original prosecution did not believe that such claims were legally available.

The Federal Circuit held that, in this case, the patent attorney's misunderstanding of the law was the type of error that could be corrected by reissue. "Although attorney error is not an open invitation to reissue in every case in which it may appear,"[47] the court cautioned, here the error was made without deceptive intent, and the reissue application complied with all pertinent statutory and regulatory requirements. Contrary to the district court's view, the reissue applicant need not prove that "no competent attorney or alert inventor could have avoided the error sought to be corrected by reissue."[48]

A reissue applicant must be truthful about the cause of the error(s) sought to be corrected, as illustrated by *Hewlett-Packard Co. v. Bausch & Lomb, Inc.,*[49] a case that highlights the risks involved in attempting to reissue a patent purchased from a third party. After Bausch & Lomb (B&L) purchased a patent directed to an X-Y plotter in an attempt to gain negotiating leverage in an ongoing infringement lawsuit against Hewlett-Packard (HP), B&L filed an application to reissue the patent. The reissue application added new dependent claims specifically targeted at the device being sold by HP, and the accompanying oath asserted reissue error in the failure to include dependent claims of narrower scope. When B&L amended its complaint to assert the reissue patent, HP defended on the ground that the reissue patent was invalid and the district court so held.

---

[44]*Id.* at 1206.
[45]*Id.*
[46]927 F.2d 1565 (Fed. Cir. 1991).
[47]*Id.* at 1575.
[48]*Id.*
[49]882 F.2d 1556 (Fed. Cir. 1989).

On appeal the Federal Circuit agreed, holding that B&L's reissue application was defective and the reissue patent claims invalid. The statutorily required "error" of §251 has two parts, the court explained, both of which the reissue applicant must establish: (1) error (or defect) in the patent, and (2) inadvertent error in conduct.[50] With respect to error (or defect) in the patent, the court did not need to decide whether as a legal matter a failure to file dependent claims constitutes reissue error.[51] With respect to the asserted error in conduct, however, the court concluded that the affidavits of a former B&L patent agent, purporting to explain why narrower claims were not previously included in the patent, were "blatantly inaccurate"[52] and "factually untrue,"[53] and therefore did not support reissue. The patent agent had averred that the failure to include more specific claims was based on his inability to contact the inventor, coupled with his misunderstanding of the invention, when in fact the agent's records, produced in discovery, established that the patent agent and inventor had met and communicated repeatedly and extensively.[54]

6. The Recapture Rule

The recapture rule, which can be thought of as analogous to the doctrine of prosecution history estoppel,[55] provides that a patentee cannot use reissuance of his patent as a means to "recapture" subject matter that he earlier surrendered during prosecution of the original patent in order to gain issuance thereof. Such surrenders are not the kind of error that reissue was intended to correct. The Federal Circuit has explained that "[u]nder the rule against recapture, a patentee's reissue claims are invalid when the patentee broadens the scope of a claim in reissue to cover subject matter that he surrendered during prosecution of the original claims."[56]

For example, the Federal Circuit held in *Mentor Corp. v. Coloplast, Inc.*,[57] that claims 6 to 9 of the reissue patent in suit, directed to a male condom catheter for patients suffering from incontinence, were invalid because they were broader than the corresponding claims of

---

[50]*See id.* at 1564 (citing In re Clark, 522 F.2d 623, 626 (C.C.P.A. 1975)).

[51]*See id.* at 1565.

[52]*Id.* at 1558.

[53]*Id.* at 1566.

[54]*See id.* at 1561.

[55]The doctrine of prosecution history estoppel, which operates as a legal limitation on the availability of the doctrine of equivalents theory of infringement, is detailed in Chapter 9 ("Patent Infringement"), *infra*.

[56]MBO Labs., Inc. v. Becton, Dickinson & Co., 602 F.3d 1306, 1313 (Fed. Cir. 2010).

[57]998 F.2d 992 (Fed. Cir. 1993).

the original patent in a manner directly pertinent to subject matter that had been surrendered during prosecution of the original patent. In order to overcome a §103 obviousness rejection of the claims in its original patent application, Mentor distinguished prior art catheters by arguing to the USPTO examiner that none of them showed transfer of the adhesive from the catheter's outer surface to its inner surface as the sheath is rolled up and then unrolled. After Mentor amended the claims to recite this transfer feature, the patent issued.

Within two years of issuance, Mentor filed an application seeking broadening reissuance of the patent, adding new claims 6 to 9 that deleted the adhesive transfer limitation. Mentor asserted reissuable error in claiming less than it had a right to claim, admitting in its oath that the claims of the original patent did not literally read on a type of catheter (made by Mentor's competitors) in which the adhesive is applied to the inner surface of the sheath before the device is rolled up. Mentor's patent attorney had assumed, incorrectly, that this method of manufacture was too impractical to be commercially feasible.

The Federal Circuit agreed with accused infringer Coloplast that Mentor's "deliberate and intentional" amendment of its claims to recite the adhesive transfer feature, made in order to overcome a §103 obviousness rejection, was not the kind of error that the reissue procedure is intended to correct. The court distinguished cases in which "there is no evidence that amendment of the originally filed claims was in any sense an admission that the scope of that claim was not in fact patentable."[58] As the court explained,

> [e]rror under the reissue statute does not include a deliberate decision to surrender specific subject matter in order to overcome prior art, a decision which in light of subsequent developments in the marketplace might be regretted. It is precisely because the patentee amended his claims to overcome prior art that a member of the public is entitled to occupy the space abandoned by the patent applicant. Thus, the reissue statute cannot be construed in such a way that competitors, properly relying on prosecution history, become patent infringers when they do so. In this case, Mentor narrowed its claims for the purpose of obtaining allowance in the original prosecution and it is now precluded from recapturing what it earlier conceded.[59]

The impact of invoking the recapture rule, as in *Mentor*, should be contrasted with an assertion of intervening rights, discussed in

---

[58]*Id*. at 995 (citing Seattle Box Co. v. Indus. Crating & Packing, Inc., 731 F.2d 818, 826 (Fed. Cir. 1984)).
[59]*Id*. at 996.

the following section. In *Mentor,* application of the recapture rule resulted in invalidation of claims 6 to 9 of the reissue patent. This protected not only the accused infringer Coloplast, but also the public at large—anyone who might have otherwise infringed those claims. In contrast, application of intervening rights would not have invalidated the patent, and would merely have provided Coloplast (but no others) with a defense to infringement.

In *MBO Labs., Inc. v. Becton, Dickinson & Co.,*[60] the Federal Circuit explained that it follows a three-step test in determining whether the rule against recapture has been violated when reissued patents broaden claim scope:

> First, the court construes the reissued claims to "determine whether and in what 'aspect' the reissue claims are broader than the [original] patent claims." . . . Second, if the reissue claims are broader, the court determines whether the patentee surrendered subject matter [in the prosecution of the original patent] and "whether the broader aspects of the reissued claim relate to [the] surrendered subject matter." . . . To determine whether a patentee surrendered subject matter [in the prosecution of the original patent], we ask "whether an objective observer viewing the prosecution history would conclude that the purpose of the patentee's amendment or argument was to overcome prior art and secure the [original] patent." . . . If the patentee surrendered by argument [rather than by explicitly amending the claims], he must clearly and unmistakably argue that his invention does not cover certain subject matter to overcome an examiner's rejection based on prior art. . . . Third, a court must "determine whether the reissued claims were materially narrowed in other respects to avoid the recapture rule."[61]

The parties in *MBO Labs.* disputed the validity of MBO's reissue patent and specifically whether the second step of the above test was met. MBO's patents were directed to hypodermic safety syringes intended to protect health care workers from accidental needle sticks following patient injections. During original prosecution, MBO twice overcame USPTO obviousness rejections by emphasizing that although the prior art disclosed a type of guard that moved relative to a fixed needle, MBO's needle instead moved relative to the guard by "slidably retracting." MBO thereafter obtained a broadening reissue patent in order to "claim a system having 'any relative movement between the needle and the body,' not just a 'system wherein the needle must be bodily moved toward the safety device.'"[62] Affirming a district court's

---

[60]602 F.3d 1306 (Fed. Cir. 2010).
[61]*MBO Labs.,* 602 F.3d at 1314 (citations omitted).
[62]*MBO Labs.,* 602 F.3d at 1311.

invalidation of four claims in MBO's reissue patent, the Federal Circuit concluded that MBO had violated the rule against recapture. During original prosecution, MBO "clearly and unmistakably" surrendered a guard body that moved forward to cover a fixed needle, but then sought to reclaim relative movement in its reissue claims.[63] In so doing MBO had violated the rule against recapture, rendering the challenged reissue patent claims invalid.[64]

7. Effect of Reissue: Intervening Rights

When a patent owner obtains reissue of her patent from the USPTO, her right to exclude under the original patent continues after reissue, for the remainder of the term of the original patent, insofar as the claims of the original and reissue patents are "substantially identical."[65] Thus, although the original patent no longer exists once the reissue patent has been granted (because the original patent has been surrendered upon reissue), the claims of the reissue patent

---

[63]*MBO Labs.*, 602 F.3d at 1313, 1314-1315.

[64]For a decision analyzing the third and final prong of the three-step recapture test, *see* In re Mostafazadeh, 643 F.3d 1353 (Fed. Cir. 2011) (affirming USPTO rejection of reissue application claims that impermissibly attempted to recapture subject matter surrendered during prosecution of the original patent application). The *Mostafazadeh* court explained that in analyzing the third step of the recapture test, one must distinguish between the original claims (i.e., the claims before the surrender), the patented claims (i.e., the claims allowed after surrender), and the reissue claims. Violation of the rule against recapture may be avoided under step 3 of the recapture test "if the reissue claims 'materially narrow' the claims relative to the original claims such that full or substantial recapture of the subject matter surrendered during prosecution is avoided." *Id.* at 1358-1359. The narrowing "must relate to the subject matter surrendered during the original prosecution (i.e., the applicant cannot recapture the full scope of what was surrendered)." *Id.* at 1359. More specifically, a claim limitation that was added during prosecution to distinguish the prior art cannot be entirely eliminated on reissue; doing so would constitute recapture of the surrendered subject matter. *Id.* at 1359. The added claim limitation may be modified, however, "so long as it continues to materially narrow the claim scope relative to the surrendered subject matter such that the surrendered subject matter is not entirely or substantially recaptured." *Id.* at 1359.

The *Mostafazadeh* court rejected the reissue patentee's argument that its recapture was only "partial." The claims (directed to packaging for semiconductors) retained an "attachment pad" limitation that was related to the surrendered subject matter. The claim scope was not *materially* narrowed, however, because the use of an attachment pad was well known in the prior art. *See id.* at 1361. The reissue application claims also included "bus bar" limitations. Although the bus bar limitations narrowed the reissue claims relative to the original claims, that narrowing was related only to the bus bar and not to the circular attachment pad limitation. "In other words, the narrowing limitations [were] unrelated to the surrendered subject matter and thus insufficient to avoid recapture." *Id.* at 1361.

[65]35 U.S.C. §252, ¶1.

"reach back" to the date that the original patent issued if the claims are "substantially identical."[66]

With respect to claims in the reissue patent that are *not* substantially identical, particularly those that have been broadened, the patentee's right to exclude may be limited by the intervening rights of third parties. Recognition of intervening rights represents the patent system's attempt to protect the third party who relied on the notice provided by the claims of the original patent as signaling what subject matter was within the patentee's exclusive right and what was in the public domain, available to all. If the third party commences the manufacture and sale of a product that does not infringe the claims of the original patent, only to later find that the patent has been broadened through reissue such that the same product now infringes the reissue claims, the third party will be permitted to use or sell those already-manufactured items, and may be permitted to continue manufacturing more of the same under certain circumstances.[67] "Recapture through a reissue patent of what is dedicated to the public by omission in the

---

[66]*See* 35 U.S.C. §252 ("Effect of Reissue"), ¶1 (emphasis added):

> The surrender of the original patent shall take effect upon the issue of the reissued patent, and every reissued patent shall have the same effect and operation in law, on the trial of actions for causes thereafter arising, as if the same had been originally granted in such amended form, but in so far as the claims of the original and reissued patents are substantially identical, such surrender shall not affect any action then pending nor abate any cause of action then existing, and the reissued patent, to the extent that its claims are *substantially identical* with the original patent, shall constitute a continuation thereof and have effect continuously from the date of the original patent.

Federal Circuit case law has interpreted "identical" as used in §252 to require that the claims of the reissue patent not be substantively changed in scope from those of the original patent; the reissue claim language need not be literally identical to that of the original claims, however. *See* Slimfold Mfg. Co. v. Kinkead Indus., Inc., 810 F.2d 1113, 1115-1116 (Fed. Cir. 1987).

[67]To be clear, intervening rights are not necessarily limited to reissues or to situation in which a patentee has broadened the scope of its claims. Intervening rights may also arise as a result of reexamination, in which the scope of the claims cannot be broadened. *See* 35 U.S.C. §305 (2012) (claim scope cannot be enlarged via reexamination); 35 U.S.C. §307(b) (2012) (providing that "[a]ny proposed amended or new claim determined to be patentable and incorporated into a patent following [an *ex parte*] reexamination proceeding will have the same effect as that specified in section 252 of this title for reissued patents on the right of any person who made, purchased, or used within the United States, or imported into the United States, anything patented by such proposed amended or new claim, or who made substantial preparation for the same, prior to issuance of a [reexamination] certificate under the provisions of subsection (a) of this section"); 35 U.S.C. §316(b) (2012) (providing same for pre-AIA *inter partes* reexamination). *See also* Marine Polymer Techs., Inc. v. Hemcon, Inc., 672 F.3d 1350, 1362 (Fed. Cir. 2012) (*en banc*) (explaining that although intervening rights doctrine originated as a defense against patents modified through reissue, the doctrine has been extended to the reexamination context).

original patent is permissible under specific conditions, but not at the expense of innocent parties."[68]

Intervening rights are governed by the second paragraph of 35 U.S.C. §252. The text of this rather long-winded paragraph is reproduced below, with the addition of bracketed labels for each sentence and a space between them for readability:

[A] A reissued patent shall not abridge or affect the right of any person or that person's successors in business who, prior to the grant of a reissue, made, purchased, offered to sell, or used within the United States, or imported into the United States, anything patented by the reissued patent, to continue the use of, to offer to sell, or to sell to others to be used, offered for sale, or sold, the specific thing so made, purchased, offered for sale, used, or imported unless the making, using, offering for sale, or selling of such thing infringes a valid claim of the reissued patent which was in the original patent.

[B] The court before which such matter is in question may provide for the continued manufacture, use, offer for sale, or sale of the thing made, purchased, offered for sale, used, or imported as specified, or for the manufacture, use, offer for sale, or sale in the United States of which substantial preparation was made before the grant of the reissue, and the court may also provide for the continued practice of any process patented by the reissue that is practiced, or for the practice of which substantial preparation was made, before the grant of the reissue, to the extent and under such terms as the court deems equitable for the protection of investments made or business commenced before the grant of the reissue.[69]

Sentence [A] of §252, ¶2 gives the third party who made a noninfringing "specific thing" prior to the grant of the reissue, which now infringes the reissue patent, an absolute right to continue to use or to sell that "specific thing."[70] Note that this is an *absolute* right to continue to use or sell, but not to manufacture more of, the "specific thing."[71]

---

[68]Seattle Box Co. v. Indus. Crating & Packing, 756 F.2d 1574, 1579 (Fed. Cir. 1985).
[69]35 U.S.C. §252, ¶2.
[70]*See* Pasquale J. Federico, *Commentary on the New Patent Act*, 35 U.S.C.A. 1 (1954 ed.), *reprinted in* 75 J. Pat. & Trademark Off. Soc'y 161, 207 (1993) (noting that "[t]his absolute protection extends only to the specific objects actually made before the grant of the reissued patent and does not extend to the making of additional objects of identical or like kind. With respect to the latter the court is given discretion to act.").
[71]*See* Marine Polymer Techs., Inc. v. Hemcon, Inc., 672 F.3d 1350, 1361-1362 (Fed. Cir. 2012) (*en banc*) (explaining that "absolute intervening rights" are those that "abrogate liability for infringing claims added to or modified from the original patent if the accused products were made or used before the reissue").

Sentence [B] of §252, ¶2 involves *equitable* rights.[72] The text of sentence [B] gives a federal district court the discretion, to the extent that the court deems necessary to protect business investments made before the reissue, to permit the third party to *continue* to manufacture more of "the thing" made before the grant of the reissue (which "thing" did not infringe the original patent but now infringes the reissue), or to continue the manufacture of that which the patentee made "substantial preparation" to manufacture before the grant of the reissue.[73] This is an exercise of the district court's equitable powers, reviewable by the Federal Circuit for abuse of discretion.

Seattle Box Co. v. Industrial Crating & Packing, Inc.[74] illustrates the application of sentence [B] of 35 U.S.C. §252, ¶2. The original patent of plaintiff Seattle Box, directed to an arrangement for separating oil pipes stacked in a pipe bundle, claimed a double-concave wooden "spacer block" having a height "greater than the diameter of the pipe."[75] After commencing an infringement action against Industrial Crating, Seattle Box applied to reissue the patent, asserting error in claiming less than it had a right to, and broadening the claims to recite a spacer block with height "substantially equal to or greater than" the pipe diameter.[76] Industrial Crating's accused spacer blocks did not literally infringe (and most likely did not equivalently infringe) the claims of the original patent because the blocks were of a height 1/16 of an inch less than the pipe height.[77] The accused blocks did arguably infringe the broadened claims of the reissue patent, however, which the Federal Circuit held to be "substantively different" from the original claims. As of the date that the reissue patent was granted, defendant Industrial Crating had in its inventory the materials necessary to make 224 bundles. The bundles were assembled after the grant of the reissue, however.[78] A district court

---

[72]*See* Marine Polymer Techs., Inc. v. Hemcon, Inc., 672 F.3d 1350, 1362 (Fed. Cir. 2012) (*en banc*) (explaining that "equitable intervening rights" are those that "apply as a matter of judicial discretion to mitigate liability for infringing such claims even as to products made or used after the reissue if the accused infringer made substantial preparations for the infringing activities prior to reissue").

[73]*See* Pasquale J. Federico, *Commentary on the New Patent Act*, 35 U.S.C.A. 1 (1954 ed.), *reprinted in* 75 J. Pat. & Trademark Off. Soc'y 161, 207 (1993) (stating that "[w]hen the specified conditions obtain, the court has the power to permit (1) continuation of the manufacture of things made before the grant of the reissue (that is, the manufacture of additional objects), and their use or sale, (2) the continued manufacture, use or sale when substantial preparation was made before the grant of the reissue, and (3) the continued practice of a process patented by the reissue practiced, or for the practice of which substantial preparation was made, before the grant of the reissue").

[74]756 F.2d 1574 (Fed. Cir. 1985).

[75]*Id.* at 1576.

[76]*Id.*

[77]*See id.* at 1580.

[78]*See id.* at 1577.

denied Industrial Crating the defense of intervening rights for the 224 bundles.

The Federal Circuit held on appeal that sentence [B] of §252, ¶2 applied. Concluding that the district court had abused its discretion in denying intervening rights, the Federal Circuit ruled that defendant Industrial Crating should have been allowed to dispose of the old inventory on hand at the date of reissue, without liability to the patentee.[79] The equities favored Industrial Crating, the Federal Circuit found, because it relied on the advice of counsel in attempting to design around the original patent, and because at the time that the reissue patent was granted it already had pending orders for the 224 spacer blocks in its inventory.[80] The court concluded that "[i]n these circumstances, the new reissue claims in this case present a compelling case for the application of the doctrine of intervening rights because a person should be able to make business decisions secure in the knowledge that those actions which fall outside the original patent claims are protected. . . . Here, the spacer blocks involved were made or acquired, before the reissue, so as not to infringe the then existing [original] patent."[81]

8.   Strategic Considerations for Reissue

The decision to reissue a patent deserves careful consideration. As with most actions taken in regard to an issued patent, substantial risks may be encountered. Various strategic aspects of the reissue procedure will affect the decision.

First, reissue differs from reexamination (discussed below) in that only the patentee can seek reissuance of his patent. There is no means of third-party involvement in reissue.[82] An accused infringer does not have standing to seek reissuance of a patent (unless the accused infringer becomes the owner thereof).

When the AIA-implemented post-grant review procedure becomes available to patent challengers on March 16, 2013, patents will be open to attack in the USPTO by any person on a wide variety of grounds

---

[79]*See id.* at 1581.

[80]*See id.* at 1580.

[81]*Id.* (citations omitted).

[82]However, a reissue application may be subject to a third party's protest under 37 C.F.R. §1.291 ("Protests by the public against pending applications"), as occurred in *In re Hall*, 781 F.2d 897, 897 (Fed. Cir. 1986). *Hall* is better known for its analysis of whether a single copy of a thesis cataloged in a German library qualified as a "printed publication" under 35 U.S.C. §102(b) (1982). This latter aspect of *Hall* is discussed in Chapter 4 ("Novelty, Loss of Right, and Priority Pre- and Post-America Invents Act of 2011 (35 U.S.C. §102)"), *supra*.

during the nine-month window following the patent's issuance.[83] Patent owners will likely have only a single opportunity to amend their claims during the post-grant review.[84] As a result, patentees may increasingly turn to reissue as a means to circumvent the restrictions of post-grant review and gain greater opportunities to control the revision of their claim scope.[85]

Reissue can be highly advantageous to the patent owner because it is generally a far less expensive alternative than litigation for correcting patent defects. Moreover, reissue is conducted in the USPTO, the forum that previously issued the patent and that is presumed to have technical expertise in the subject matter of the invention.

The patentee may use reissue to add new claims to her patent that specifically target a competitor's product, so long as the specification supports these claims in accordance with 35 U.S.C. §112(a). The patentee in some cases also may seek to reissue the patent with claims narrower than those that issued in the original patent, with the intent of avoiding newly discovered prior art that was not before the USPTO during its examination of the original patent.

Reissue also can involve considerable risks for the patent owner. Applying for reissue requires an offer to surrender the original patent, with no guarantee that the patent will be reissued. The presumption of validity that accompanies an issued patent does not continue once an application to reissue the patent has been filed.[86] This makes logical sense because in filing to reissue, the patentee is admitting that its patent may be "wholly or partly inoperative or invalid. . . ."[87] All claims of the reissue application, even claims of the original patent that the patentee wants to carry over unchanged, are subject to examination and rejection on any statutory ground.[88]

---

[83]*See infra* Section E.2 ("Post-Grant Review").

[84]*See* 35 U.S.C. §326(d)(1) (eff. Sept. 16, 2013, for patents having claims with an effective filing date on or after Mar. 16, 2013) (providing that "IN GENERAL.—During a post-grant review instituted under this chapter, the patent owner may file 1 motion to amend the patent in 1 or more of the following ways: (A) Cancel any challenged patent claim. (B) For each challenged claim, propose a reasonable number of substitute claims."). Section 326(d)(2) provides that additional motions to amend a challenged patent may be permitted when they are jointly requested by the post-grant review petitioner and the patentee to materially advance a settlement of the post-grant review, or when requested by the patentee "for good cause shown."

[85]*See* Donald S. Chisum, Reissue: Recent Federal Circuit Decisions (2012).

[86]*See* In re Sneed, 710 F.2d 1544, 1550 n.4 (Fed. Cir. 1983) (noting that "contrary to appellants' argument, claims in a reissue *application* enjoy no presumption of 'validity'") (emphasis in original).

[87]35 U.S.C. §251(a) (eff. Sept. 16, 2012).

[88]*See* Hewlett-Packard v. Bausch & Lomb, 882 F.2d 1556, 1563 (Fed. Cir. 1989) (characterizing reissue as "essentially a reprosecution of all claims").

D. Reexamination

1. Introduction

Reexamination is a much newer administrative procedure in the U.S. patent system than reissue, having been established by legislation enacted in 1980.[89] Reexamination's purpose was to provide a lower-cost alternative to federal court litigation in which to resolve certain questions of validity. Congress was influenced by studies showing that in the 1950s and 1960s, a large portion of the U.S. patents adjudicated invalid by federal courts were invalidated based on newly discovered prior art that had never been considered by the USPTO.[90] Reexamination was seen as creating a relatively low-cost method of obtaining a USPTO examination on this newly discovered prior art. Reexamination represented, if not a copy of, at least the closest parallel in U.S. practice to the well-regarded post-grant opposition procedure of the European patent system.[91]

In practice, reexamination did not prove to be the panacea its proponents hoped for. The reexamination system was criticized as biased in favor of patent owners because of the extremely limited opportunities for third-party participation. Responding to these and other concerns, Congress as part of the American Inventors Protection Act of 1999 enacted a second, *inter partes* form of reexamination (renaming the original form *ex parte* reexamination). Although it offered greater participation for third parties, *inter partes* reexamination suffered from its own shortcomings in terms of a severe estoppel provision

---

[89]*See* Act of Dec. 12, 1980, Pub. L. No. 96-517, 94 Stat. 3015 (codified as amended in scattered sections of 35 U.S.C.).

[90]*See* In re Portola Packaging, Inc., 110 F.3d 786 (Fed. Cir. 1997), stating that:

> Congress recognized that holdings of patent invalidity by courts were mostly based on prior art that was not before the PTO. *Patent Reexamination: Hearings on S. 1679 Before the Senate Comm. on the Judiciary*, 96th Cong. 2 (1980) (opening statement of Senator Birch Bayh) ("All too often, patent holders find themselves in lengthy court proceedings where valuable patents are challenged on the grounds that the patent examiner missed pertinent data during the initial patent search."); *id.* at 14 (testimony of Sydney Diamond, Commissioner, U.S. Patent and Trademark Office) (referring to Gloria K. Koenig, *Patent Validity: A Statistical and Substantive Analysis* §5.05[4] (1974), in which the author found that from 1953 through 1967 "the proportion of invalid patents wherein uncited prior art [i.e., prior art not before the PTO] figured into the result is between 66 and 80 percent").

Id. at 789 (italics added).

[91]*See* European Patent Convention arts. 99-105 (14th ed. 2010), *available at* http://www.epo.org/law-practice/legal-texts/html/epc/2010/e/ma1.html.

and procedural delays.[92] In the America Invents Act of 2011, Congress phased out *inter partes* reexamination and replaced it with a new proceeding called "*inter partes* review" (eff. Sept. 16, 2012).[93]

Both *ex parte* and *inter partes* reexamination are detailed below. The statutes governing *ex parte* reexamination are found at 35 U.S.C. §§301-307 and continue in effect post-AIA. The statutes dealing with *inter partes* reexamination are found at 35 U.S.C. §§311-318 (2006), and will no longer be in effect after September 16, 2012. In order to initiate either type of reexamination, the USPTO must be convinced that a "substantial new question of patentability"[94] arises from the prior art on which the request is based, as discussed below. If a substantial new question of patentability exists, the USPTO will issue an order for reexamination.[95] The reexamination of a patent proceeds in essentially the same manner as an original examination.[96] Reexaminations are decided in the first instance by individual examiners, as in the examination of original applications. The presumption of validity that applies to an issued patent under 35 U.S.C. §282 is no longer applicable once a patent is in reexamination; in rejecting claims during reexamination the USPTO examiner is not required to satisfy the rigorous "clear and convincing" standard that applies in federal court litigation challenging the validity of issued patents.[97]

At the completion of either type of reexamination proceeding, the USPTO will issue a "Reexamination Certificate" that becomes part of the official patent document. The certificate will operate to (1) cancel any claim of the issued patent that is determined to be unpatentable, (2) confirm any claim of the issued patent that is determined to be patentable, and/or (3) incorporate into the issued patent any proposed amended claims or new claims that have been determined to be patentable.[98]

---

[92]USPTO officials admit that "[i]nter partes reexamination has not proven as efficient as was originally intended. It has taken an average of 32 to 38 months to move from filing to issuance of a final reexamination certificate. The time to a final determination within the USPTO is even longer, when you factor in appeals." Teresa Stanek Rea, Deputy Under Secretary of Commerce for Intellectual Property and Deputy Director of the USPTO, *Building a Better Post Grant* (May 15, 2012), *available at* http://www.uspto.gov/blog/director/entry/building_a_better_post_grant.

[93]*See infra* Section E.1 ("*Inter Partes* Review").

[94]35 U.S.C. §§303(a), 304 (*ex parte*); 35 U.S.C. §312(a) (2006) (*inter partes*).

[95]*See* 35 U.S.C. §304 (*ex parte* reexamination order); 35 U.S.C. §313 (2006) (*inter partes* reexamination order).

[96]*See* 35 U.S.C. §305 (conduct of *ex parte* reexamination proceedings); 35 U.S.C. §314 (2006) (conduct of *inter partes* reexamination proceedings). Reexamination proceedings are to be conducted with "special dispatch" within the USPTO. 35 U.S.C. §305; 35 U.S.C. §314(c) (2006).

[97]*See* In re Etter, 756 F.2d 852, 855-859 (Fed. Cir. 1985) (*en banc*).

[98] 35 U.S.C. §307(a).

2. *Ex Parte* Reexamination

a. Who Can Request

The *ex parte* reexamination procedure, the "older" form of reexamination, is governed by 35 U.S.C. §§301-307 and continues to be available post–America Invents Act of 2011. Although the name "ex parte" might suggest otherwise, this form of reexamination can be requested by anyone, not just the patent owner.[99] Even the Director of the USPTO has requested reexamination of patents issued by his own agency.[100] When someone other than the patent owner requests that a patent be reexamined, that person or entity is generally referred to as the "third-party requester." A third-party requester may be anonymous.[101]

The *ex parte* nature of this form of reexamination reflects the very limited opportunities for participation by the third-party requester after it files the request for reexamination. If the USPTO orders reexamination, the patent owner will be permitted to file a responsive statement, which may include a proposed amendment to his claims, or new claims.[102] The third-party requester will receive a copy of this statement and can file a response to it.[103] From that point on, however, the reexamination proceeds much like the initial examination of an original application; the prosecution is conducted entirely between the patent owner and the USPTO, and the administrative records are maintained in secrecy (until application publication or patent issuance).[104]

It is commonly thought that because it has so little opportunity to participate, a third party (who is often in the position of accused or potential infringer of the patent) should request *ex parte* reexamination only if it has "dead-on" prior art that is virtually sure to invalidate the claims. If the third party's attempt does not succeed and the reexamination certificate confirms the patentability of all the claims, the patent may take on a "gold-plated" hue to judges and juries who will understand that the USPTO has twice confirmed its validity.

---

[99]*See* 35 U.S.C. §302 (providing that "[a]ny person at any time may file a request for reexamination").

[100]*See* Peter J. Ayers, *Interpreting* In re Alappat *with an Eye Towards Prosecution*, 76 J. PAT. & TRADEMARK OFF. SOC'Y 741, 744 n.18 (1994).

[101]*See* 35 U.S.C. §301 (providing in part that "[a]t the written request of the person citing the prior art, his or her identity will be excluded from the patent file and kept confidential").

[102]35 U.S.C. §304.

[103]*Id.*

[104]35 U.S.C. §305.

b. *Statutory Grounds for Reexamination*

Sections 301 and 302 of the Patent Act significantly limit the grounds on which reexamination of a patent can be sought. A request for reexamination can be based only on prior art consisting of patents or printed publications,[105] which means that patentability can be challenged in reexamination only under an appropriate portion of 35 U.S.C. §102 (lack of novelty) or under 35 U.S.C. §103 (obviousness).[106] Reexamination cannot be sought to challenge inventorship, or to assert nonstatutory subject matter or lack of utility under 35 U.S.C. §101, or nonenablement or noncompliance with the written description of the invention requirement under 35 U.S.C. §112(a). Under pre-AIA rules, reexamination could not be used to inquire into potentially invalidating on sale or public use bars under 35 U.S.C. §102(b) (2006).

c. *Substantial New Question of Patentability*

Before it will issue an order for reexamination, the USPTO must find that the request raises a "substantial new question of patentability."[107] The purpose of incorporating this threshold requirement into the statute was to prevent abuse of the system and harassment of patentees by third parties making multiple requests for reexamination without a substantial basis.[108] The standard applied by the USPTO for identifying a substantial new question sufficient to support an order for reexamination is that the prior art identified in the request would be considered "important" in deciding patentability to a reasonable

---

[105]*Id.* at §302 (providing that request for reexamination may be filed "on the basis of any prior art cited under the provisions of section 301 of this title").

[106]*See* In re Recreative Techs. Corp., 83 F.3d 1394, 1397 (Fed. Cir. 1996) (stating with respect to reexamination as enacted by Congress in 1980, "[n]o grounds of reexamination were to be permitted other than based on new prior art and sections 102 and 103"); UNITED STATES PATENT AND TRADEMARK OFFICE, MANUAL OF PATENT EXAMINING PROCEDURE §2217 (8th ed., rev. July 2010) (identifying appropriate portions of §102 on which substantial new question of patentability can be based), *available at* http://www.uspto.gov/web/offices/pac/mpep/documents/2200_2217.htm#sect2217.

[107]35 U.S.C. §§303, 304. As discussed *infra,* the threshold standard for the AIA-implemented *inter partes* review is different: whether "the information presented in the request shows that there is a reasonable likelihood that the requester would prevail with respect to at least 1 of the claims challenged in the request." 35 U.S.C. §312(a) (eff. Sept. 16, 2012). The threshold standard for granting the AIA-implemented post-grant review is also different: whether the information in the petition, "if such information is not rebutted, would demonstrate that it is more likely than not that at least 1 of the claims challenged in the petition is unpatentable." 35 U.S.C. §324(a) (eff. Mar. 16, 2013)).

[108]*See* In re Portola Packaging, Inc., 110 F.3d 786, 790 (Fed. Cir. 1997).

examiner, but need not necessarily render the claims *prima facie* unpatentable.[109]

Can a substantial new question of patentability be based on prior art that was known to the USPTO during examination of the original application? The Federal Circuit's 1997 decision in *In re Portola Packaging, Inc.*[110] temporarily eliminated this possibility.[111] The *Portola* court held that the agency cannot make rejections in reexamination based on any combination of prior art references that were previously considered by the USPTO in the prosecution of the original application, even where the claims had been amended during reexamination such that they were not the same as those considered in the original examination.

The facts of *Portola* are these: During examination of the original application, a number of prior art references were cited by the examiner, including the "Hunter" patent and the "Faulstich" patent. Specifically, the examiner rejected certain claims of the original application as anticipated under §102 by Hunter, and other claims as obvious under §103 in view of Faulstich in combination with two other references.[112] The applicant amended the claims in response to the rejections, added new claims, and was ultimately granted a patent, which was assigned to Portola.

A third party subsequently requested reexamination of the Portola patent, and the USPTO so ordered. Following amendments to the claims, the agency rejected them as obvious under §103 in view of the combined teachings of the Hunter and Faulstich patents. On appeal to the Federal Circuit, the patentee Portola contended that the reexamination statute does not permit the USPTO to issue rejections in a reexamination based solely on the same prior art that was previously before the agency. The USPTO responded that because the claims of the original application were never rejected under §103 in view of the combination of Hunter and Faulstich, the rejection was a "new" one that was permitted by statute.

The Federal Circuit sided with Portola. The court expressed great concern about the potential for abuse of the reexamination process based on subjecting a patentee to repeated reexaminations based on the same prior art previously considered by the USPTO.[113] The agency cannot use reexamination as a mechanism to correct an examiner's

---

[109]*See* UNITED STATES PATENT AND TRADEMARK OFFICE, MANUAL OF PATENT EXAMINING PROCEDURE §2242 (8th ed., rev. July 2010), *available at* http://www.uspto.gov/web/offices/pac/mpep/documents/2200_2242.htm#sect2242.

[110]110 F.3d 786 (Fed. Cir. 1997).

[111]In November 2002 the holding of *Portola* was legislatively overruled, as discussed below.

[112]*Portola*, 110 F.3d at 787.

[113]*See id.* at 789-790.

mistakes, such as a failure to make all proper rejections in the initial examination, the court cautioned. Examiners are presumed to have considered all combinations of the cited prior art. The court would not allow the USPTO to use reexamination to second guess itself.[114]

The *Portola* requester's best argument for a substantial new question of patentability was that the patentee had amended the claims during reexamination, such that they were not the same as the claims examined in the original prosecution. By definition, the requester contended, this must present a substantial new question of patentability. The Federal Circuit again disagreed. Claims amended in a reexamination must be narrower in scope than the original claims; unlike reissue, no broadening of claims is permitted in reexamination.[115] Therefore, the court explained, any question of patentability for the narrower reexamination claims was "necessarily" considered by examiner during the original examination.[116]

d.   *Legislative Changes in Response to* Portola

On November 2, 2002, then–President George W. Bush signed into law new legislation that, *inter alia*, overruled the Federal Circuit's holding in *Portola*.[117] The legislation amended the language of 35 U.S.C. §§303(a) ("Determination of issue by Director" in *ex parte* reexamination proceedings) and 312(a) ("Determination of issue by Director" in *inter partes* reexamination proceedings) by adding the following sentence to each section: "The existence of a substantial new question of patentability is not precluded by the fact that a patent or printed publication was previously cited by or to the [U.S. Patent and Trademark] Office or considered by the Office."[118] This change was not retroactive; that is, it was effective only for determinations of a "substantial new question of patentability" made by the USPTO on or after the date of enactment of the Act (i.e., Nov. 2, 2002). The Act also modified the appeal procedures for *inter partes* reexamination to give enhanced appeal rights to third-party requesters.[119]

---

[114]*See id.* at 791 (citing In re Etter, 756 F.2d 852, 865 (Fed. Cir. 1985) (Nies, Smith & Bissell, JJ., concurring) ("Clearly, reexamination was not designed to allow the PTO simply to reconsider and second guess what it has already done.")).

[115]Reexamination is further compared to reissue *infra*.

[116]*See Portola*, at 791 (Fed. Cir. 1997).

[117]*See* Twenty-first Century Department of Justice Appropriations Authorization Act, H.R. 2215, 107th Cong. §13105 (2002) ("Determination of Substantial New Question of Patentability in Reexamination Proceedings") (amending 35 U.S.C. §§303(a), 312(a)), *available at* http://thomas.loc.gov.

[118]*Id.*

[119]*See id.* §13106 ("Appeals in inter partes reexamination proceedings") (amending 35 U.S.C. §§315(b), 134(c), 141).

e. *Reexamination Compared to Reissue*

The reexamination and reissue procedures differ in fundamental respects. Reexamination is narrower than reissue in the sense that reexamination cannot be used to correct defects other than anticipation and obviousness based exclusively on the content of the prior art references.[120] Reexamination is broader than reissue, however, in the sense that anyone can request reexamination,[121] while only the owner of the patent in question can seek to reissue it.[122]

The most important difference between the two procedures is probably the fact that, unlike reissue, reexamination cannot be used to broaden the claims of an issued patent.[123] There is no broadening reexamination. For example, in *Quantum Corp. v. Rodime, PLC*,[124] the accused infringer brought a declaratory judgment action seeking a declaration that a previously reexamined patent, directed to a micro harddisk drive system suitable for use in personal computers, was invalid and not infringed. The validity challenge was based on the facts that as originally issued, the claims of the patent recited a track density of "at least 600 concentric tracks per inch," but that during reexamination, the patentee amended the claims to recite "at least *approximately* 600 concentric tracks per inch," and the USPTO issued a reexamination certificate confirming the patentability of these amended claims. The accused infringer thus contended that the amendments made by

---

[120]*See* 35 U.S.C. §§301, 302.

[121]*See* 35 U.S.C. §302 (providing that "[a]ny person at any time may file a request for reexamination by the Office of any claim of a patent on the basis of any prior art cited under the provisions of section 301 of this title").

[122]*See* 35 U.S.C. §251(a) (eff. Sept. 16, 2012) (requiring "surrender" of the patent to the USPTO in order to reissue it); *id.* (stating that the "provisions of this title relating to applications for patent shall be applicable to applications for reissue of a patent, except that application for reissue may be made and sworn to by the assignee of the entire interest if the application does not seek to enlarge the scope of the claims of the original patent"); 37 C.F.R. §1.172(a) (providing that "[a] reissue oath must be signed and sworn to or declaration made by the inventor or inventors except as otherwise provided (see §§1.42, 1.43, 1.47), and must be accompanied by the written consent of all assignees, if any, owning an undivided interest in the patent, but a reissue oath may be made and sworn to or declaration made by the assignee of the entire interest if the application does not seek to enlarge the scope of the claims of the original patent"). *See also* Baker Hughes, Inc. v. Kirk, 921 F. Supp. 801, 809-810 (D.D.C. 1995) (in case where Baker Hughes and Hydril were both assignees of original patent, holding that USPTO did not have authority under 35 U.S.C. §251 to consider reissue application filed by Hydril only and to which Baker Hughes did not consent, and concluding that "a reissue application, if made by an assignee, must be made by the assignee of the entire interest in the patent").

[123]*See* 35 U.S.C. §305 (providing in part that "[n]o proposed amended or new claim enlarging the scope of a claim of the patent will be permitted in a reexamination proceeding under this chapter").

[124] 65 F.3d 1577 (Fed. Cir. 1995).

the patentee during the reexamination amounted to an impermissible broadening of the claims, as prohibited by 35 U.S.C. §305.

The Federal Circuit agreed, pointing to dictionary definitions of "at least" as meaning "as the minimum," and thus interpreted the original claim language as meaning "600 tpi on up." The addition of the *approximately* qualifier during reexamination eliminated the precise lower limit of the range, the court concluded, and therefore defined an open-ended range starting slightly below 600 tpi. This constituted an impermissible broadening of claim scope in reexamination. The Federal Circuit refused to rewrite the claims back to their original scope. Because the patentee violated the terms of §305, the claims of the reexamined patent could not stand. The reexamined patent was therefore invalid.

Another difference between reexamination and reissue concerns timing. Reexamination may be requested at any time during the life of a patent.[125] In contrast, when a reissue application is filed that seeks to *broaden* the scope of a patent's claims, such application must be filed "within two years from the grant of the original patent."[126]

3.   *Inter Partes* Reexamination (Pre-AIA)

The newer, *inter partes* form of reexamination[127] became available for U.S. patents granted on original applications filed in the USPTO on or after November 29, 1999.[128] Due to dissatisfaction with the

---

[125]*See* 35 U.S.C. §302 (providing that "[a]ny person at any time may file a request for reexamination . . . ").

[126]35 U.S.C. §251(d) (eff. Sept. 16, 2012).

[127]*See generally* Tun-Jen Chiang, *The Advantages of* Inter Partes *Reexamination*, 90 J. Pat. & Trademark Off. Soc'y 579 (2008); Sherry M. Knowles et al., *Inter Partes Patent Reexamination in the United States*, 86 J. Pat. & Trademark Off. Soc'y 611 (2004); Kenneth L. Cage & Lawrence T. Cullen, *An Overview of Inter Partes Reexamination Procedures*, 85 J. Pat. & Trademark Off. Soc'y 931 (2003); Michael L. Goldman & Alice Y. Choi, *The New Optional Inter Partes Reexamination Procedure and Its Strategic Use*, 28 AIPLA Q.J. 307 (2000).

[128]*See* Cooper Techs. Co. v. Dudas, 536 F.3d 1330, 1331 (Fed. Cir. 2008) (stating that "Congress established the *inter partes* reexamination procedure as part of the American Inventors Protection Act of 1999. . . . ('AIPA'). Pursuant to section 4608 of the AIPA, the *inter partes* reexamination procedure is available for 'any patent that issues from an original application filed in the United States on or after' November 29, 1999—the date of the enactment of the AIPA.") (citations omitted). The court in *Cooper* interpreted "original application" to include, *inter alia*, continuation applications. *See id.* at 1343. Thus, *inter partes* reexamination can be sought for patents issuing from applications actually filed on or after November 29, 1999, but claiming priority to a pre–November 19, 1999, filing date. Affirming the USPTO's statutory interpretation, the Federal Circuit concluded that "original application" broadly encompasses "utility, plant and design applications, including first filed applications, continuations,

proceeding,[129] the America Invents Act of 2011 phased out *inter partes* reexamination and replaced it with a new proceeding called *"inter partes* review," discussed separately below. For clarity, this chapter refers to *inter partes* reexamination as *"inter partes* reexamination (pre-AIA)." Petitions for *inter partes* reexamination (pre-AIA) can no longer be filed after September 15, 2012.

The procedures for *inter partes* reexamination (pre-AIA) were governed by 35 U.S.C. §§311-318 (2006). *Inter partes* reexamination (pre-AIA) supplemented, but did not replace, the older *ex parte* reexamination process (discussed above). *Ex parte* reexamination is governed by 35 U.S.C. §§301-307 and continues to be available post-AIA.

As the name "inter partes" suggests, the purpose of creating an alternative form of reexamination was to permit greater participation by third-party requesters. Indeed, only "third party requesters" (i.e., entities other than the patent owner) could file a request for *inter partes* reexamination.[130] Additionally, the third-party requester in *inter partes* reexamination was permitted to file a response to each statement filed by the patentee throughout the entire reexamination process.

When *inter partes* reexamination (pre-AIA) was implemented in late 1999, the atypical appeal provisions of the procedure were subject to much criticism. Although a patent owner could appeal an adverse decision by the examiner in *inter partes* reexamination to the USPTO Board of Patent Appeals and Interferences (BPAI) and, if unsuccessful there, to the Federal Circuit, the third-party requester in *inter partes* reexamination could appeal an adverse decision only as far as the BPAI;[131] no appeal by the third-party requester to the Federal Circuit was permitted. Moreover, if the patentee appealed to the Federal Circuit, the third-party requester was not permitted to participate. Commentators questioned whether these limitations on the

---

divisionals, continuations-in-part, continued prosecution applications and the national stage phase of international applications." *Id.* at 1331.

[129]*See* Teresa Stanek Rea, Deputy Under Secretary of Commerce for Intellectual Property and Deputy Director of the USPTO, *Building a Better Post Grant* (May 15, 2012), *available at* http://www.uspto.gov/blog/director/entry/building_a_better_post_grant (admitting that "[i]nter partes reexamination has not proven as efficient as was originally intended. It has taken an average of 32 to 38 months to move from filing to issuance of a final reexamination certificate. The time to a final determination within the USPTO is even longer, when you factor in appeals.").

[130]35 U.S.C. §311(a) (2006) (providing that "[a]ny third party requester at any time may file a request for inter partes reexamination by the Office of a patent on the basis of any prior art cited under the provisions of section 301 [35 USC § 301]").

[131]*See* 35 U.S.C. §315(b). The America Invents Act of 2011 renamed and expanded the jurisdiction of the Board of Patent Appeals and Interferences (BPAI). The post-AIA administrative tribunal is named the Patent Trial and Appeal Board (PTAB).

third-party requester's appeal rights comported with the Due Process, Takings, or other clauses of the U.S. Constitution.

The issue became moot when the *inter partes* reexamination statutes were amended, effective November 2, 2002, to alleviate the disparity of appeal options between patent owners and third-party requesters.[132] Thereafter, both the patentee and the third-party requester had equal rights to appeal unfavorable decisions to the Federal Circuit and to participate in appeals filed there by the other party.[133]

Although they obtained the same appeal rights as patent owners, third-party requesters remained subject to a rather draconian estoppel provision that operated to prevent them from raising the same validity issues in any subsequent litigation of the patent in federal court.[134] Section 315(c) (2006) of the Patent Act prohibited the third-party requester from

> asserting at a later time, in any civil action arising in whole or in part under section 1338 of title 28 [United States Code], the invalidity of any claim finally determined to be valid and patentable on any ground which the third-party requester *raised or could have raised* during the *inter partes* reexamination proceedings. This subsection does not prevent the assertion of invalidity based on newly discovered prior art unavailable to the third-party requester and the Patent and Trademark Office at the time of the inter partes reexamination proceedings.[135]

Because of the relative severity of this estoppel provision, some commentators predicted that the *inter partes* reexamination procedure would not be used extensively.[136] The predictions were fairly accurate. A study published in 2005 reported that only 65 requests for *inter partes* reexamination had been filed with the USPTO through

---

[132]*See* Twenty-first Century Department of Justice Appropriations Authorization Act, Pub. L. No. 107-273, div. C, tit. III ("Intellectual Property"), subtit. A ("Patent and Trademark Office Authorization"), §13106, subtit. B ("Intellectual Property and High Technology Technical Amendments"), §§13202(a)(4), (c)(1), 116 Stat. 1900, 1901, 1902 (Nov. 2, 2002).

[133]*See* 35 U.S.C. §§315(a) (2006) (patent owner's appeal rights), 315(b) (2006) (third-party requester's appeal rights).

[134]*See* Mark D. Janis, *Inter Partes Reexamination*, 10 FORDHAM INTELL. PROP. MEDIA & ENT. L.J. 481, 492 (2000) (characterizing the *inter partes* reexamination estoppel provisions as "draconian").

[135]35 U.S.C. §315(c) (2006) (emphasis added).

[136]*See* Mark D. Janis, *Inter Partes Reexamination*, 10 FORDHAM INTELL. PROP. MEDIA & ENT. L.J. 481, 498 (2000) (characterizing *inter partes* reexamination as "a dog . . . [of] a proceeding that is likely to confuse and annoy its participants, few though they may be"); Robert P. Merges, *One Hundred Years of Solicitude: Intellectual Property Law, 1900–2000,* 88 CAL. L. REV. 2187, 2232 n.209 (2000) (predicting that "[f]ew patent lawyers will be willing to risk a reexamination request for a client, knowing the client will be precluded from arguing the same factual issues in a patent case in district court").

the end of 2004.[137] Although 374 *inter partes* reexamination requests were filed in fiscal year 2011, this number is considerably lower than the 759 *ex parte* reexamination requests filed in the same time period.[138] The legislative history hints that even the statute's drafters had mixed feelings about the propriety of the estoppel provision.[139]

The *inter partes* reexamination statutes provided an important strategic benefit, however, for the owner of a patent whose validity was concurrently being litigated in federal court. Under 35 U.S.C. §318 (2006), the patentee in *inter partes* reexamination could request a stay of the federal court litigation, which could be denied only if the court "determines that a stay would not serve the interests of justice." The *ex parte* reexamination statutes do not speak of the possibility of a stay of concurrent validity litigation; in such a case, the grant or denial of a stay is entirely at the discretion of the federal district court.[140]

E.   AIA-Implemented Procedures for Challenging Issued Patents

The America Invents Act of 2011 implemented two new primary procedures for challenging the validity of issued patents in the USPTO rather than the federal courts: (1) *inter partes* review, which replaces *inter partes* reexamination, and (2) post-grant review, which is similar (but not identical) to European-style opposition practice.[141]

---

[137]*See* Joseph D. Cohen, *What's Really Happening in Inter Partes Reexamination,* 87 J. Pat. & Trademark Off. Soc'y 207, 213 (2005) (stating that "[r]equesters filed 65 *inter partes* requests through December 23, 2004"); *id.* at 207 n.3 (noting that the first request for *inter partes* reexamination was filed with the USPTO on July 27, 2001); *id.* at 218 (stating that "[o]nly 65 *inter partes* requests have been filed in the last three years").

[138]*See* USPTO, *2011 Performance and Accountability Report, Fiscal Year 2011 USPTO Workload Tables,* tbl. 14A ("Ex Parte Reexamination"), *available at* http://www.uspto.gov/about/stratplan/ar/2011/oai_05_wlt_14a.html; *id.* at tbl. 14B ("Inter Partes Reexamination"), *available at* http://www.uspto.gov/about/stratplan/ar/2011/oai_05_wlt_14b.html.

[139]The Intellectual Property and Communications Omnibus Reform Act of 1999 provided with regard to the estoppel provision of 35 U.S.C. §315 that "if this section is held to be unenforceable, the enforceability of the remainder of this subtitle or of this title shall not be denied as a result." S. 1948, 106th Cong. §4607 (1999) (enacted by Act of Nov. 29, 1999, Pub. L. No. 106-113, §1000(a)(9), 113 Stat. 1536, and effective as provided by S. 1948, §4608, which is set out in 35 U.S.C. §41).

[140]*See* Ethicon, Inc. v. Quigg, 849 F.2d 1422, 1426-1427 (Fed. Cir. 1988); 4-11 Donald S. Chisum, Chisum on Patents §11.07[4][b][iv][B] (2008).

[141]*See* European Patent Convention arts. 99-105 (14th ed. 2010), *available at* http://www.epo.org/law-practice/legal-texts/html/epc/2010/e/ma1.html.

E. AIA-Implemented Procedures for Challenging Issued Patents

Congress terms these proceedings *adjudicative* rather than *examinational*.[142] They can be initiated by anyone who is not an owner of the challenged patent. *Inter partes* review and post-grant review proceedings will be decided in the first instance before panels of three administrative patent judges from the AIA-implemented Patent Trial and Appeal Board (PTAB) rather than a single examiner. Certain forms of pre-trial discovery, including depositions, will also be available.

Inter partes review and post-grant review share a great many procedural and administrative aspects,[143] although substantively the scope of post-grant review is far broader than that of *inter partes* review. On the other hand, post-grant review is available only during the nine months

---

In addition to *inter partes* review and post-grant review, a third adjudicative proceeding implemented by the AIA is the "Transitional Program for Covered Business Method Patents" (TPCBM). The TPCBM review proceeding will operate similarly in many respects to post-grant review, but will apply only to certain business method patents related to financial products or services. Moreover, only entities already sued or charged with infringement of a covered business method patent may petition for TPCBM review. The TPCBM will take effect on September 16, 2012, and is scheduled to sunset on September 16, 2020. *See* Leahy-Smith America Invents Act, Pub. L. No. 112-29 (H.R. 1249), §18,125 Stat. 284, 329 (Sept. 16, 2011). The AIA did not codify the TPCBM review provisions in the Patent Act; thus the proceeding's contours are set forth by the implementing legislation (AIA §18) and USPTO implementing regulations. *See* United States Patent & Trademark Office, *Final Rule: Changes to Implement Inter Partes Review Proceedings, Post-Grant Review Proceedings, and Transitional Program for Covered Business Method Patents*, 77 FED. REG. 48680 (Aug. 14, 2012), *available at* http://www.uspto.gov/aia_implementation/fr_specific_trial.pdf (adding 37 C.F.R. Chapter I, Part 42 ("Trial Practice Before the Patent Trial and Appeal Board"), Subpart D ("Transitional Program for Covered Business Methods"), 37 C.F.R. §§ 42.300-42.304).

[142]*See* H.R. Rep. No. 112-98 [House Judiciary Comm. Rep. on the America Invents Act] (June 1, 2011), at 57 (stating that the AIA "converts inter partes reexamination from an examinational to an adjudicative proceeding, and renames the proceeding 'inter partes review'").

[143]The USPTO has issued a helpful trial practice guide setting forth the procedural aspects for the new AIA-implemented proceedings, including *inter partes* review and post-grant review. *See* United States Patent & Trademark Office, *Office Patent Trial Practice Guide*, 77 FED. REG. 48756 (Aug. 14, 2012), *available at* http://www.uspto.gov/ aia_implementation/trial_practice_guide_48756.pdf (providing "a practice guide for the trial final rules to advise the public on the general framework of the regulations, including the structure and times for taking action in each of the new proceedings [i.e., *inter partes* review, post-grant review, the transitional program for covered business method patents, and derivation proceedings]"). The trial rules themselves are set forth in United States Patent & Trademark Office, *Final Rule: Rules of Practice for Trials Before the Patent Trial and Appeal Board and Judicial Review of Patent Trial and Appeal Board Decisions*, 77 FED. REG. 48612 (Aug. 14, 2012), *available at* http:// www.uspto.gov/aia_implementation/fr_general_trial.pdf (providing a "consolidated set of rules relating to Board trial practice for *inter partes* review, post-grant review, the transitional program for covered business method patents, and derivation proceedings[, as well as] a consolidated set of rules to implement the provisions of the AIA related to seeking judicial review of Board decisions").

following a patent's issuance, while *inter partes* review can be sought once the nine-month window has closed and then throughout the remaining life of a patent. Each proceeding is discussed separately below.

1. *Inter Partes* Review

The AIA-implemented *inter partes* review proceeding replaces and expands *inter partes* reexamination. Sections 311 through 319 of the Patent Act as amended by the AIA govern *inter partes* review.[144] Petitions for *inter partes* review can be filed with the USPTO beginning on September 16, 2012, and such petitions can challenge existing patents. For newly granted patents, a petition for *inter partes* review cannot be filed until nine months after the grant (i.e., not during the nine-month window for filing a petition for post-grant review[145]). If a petition for post-grant review is filed and granted, the post-grant review must be terminated before *inter partes* review can be sought.[146]

Like reexamination, *inter partes* review is limited with respect to the scope of issues that the petitioner can raise. The *inter partes* review petitioner can request to cancel as unpatentable one or more claims of a patent "only on a ground that could be raised under section 102 [novelty] or 103 [nonobviousness] and only on the basis of prior art consisting of patents or printed publications."[147] This significant limitation on the scope of review is a carryover from reexamination,[148] and also represents one of the major distinctions between *inter partes* review and post-grant review, discussed *infra*.[149]

---

[144]*See* 35 U.S.C. §§311-319 (eff. Sept. 16, 2012).

[145]Filing deadlines for post-grant review are discussed *infra* at Section E.2.

[146]More specifically, 35 U.S.C. §311 (eff. Sept. 16, 2012) provides in part:

> (c) FILING DEADLINE.—A petition for inter partes review shall be filed after the later of either—
>> (1) the date that is 9 months after the grant of a patent or issuance of a reissue of a patent; or
>> (2) if a post-grant review is instituted under chapter 32 [35 U.S.C. §§321-329], the date of the termination of such post-grant review.

[147]35 U.S.C. §311(b) (eff. Sept. 16, 2012) ("Scope").

[148]*See* In re Recreative Techs. Corp., 83 F.3d 1394, 1397 (Fed. Cir. 1996) (stating with respect to reexamination as enacted by Congress in 1980, "No grounds of reexamination were to be permitted other than based on new prior art and sections 102 and 103."); UNITED STATES PATENT AND TRADEMARK OFFICE, MANUAL OF PATENT EXAMINING PROCEDURE §2217 (8th ed., rev. July 2010) (identifying appropriate portions of 35 U.S.C. §102 (pre-AIA version) on which substantial new question of patentability can be based), *available at* http://www.uspto.gov/web/offices/pac/mpep/documents/2200_2217.htm#sect2217.

[149]As explained *infra,* a petition for post-grant review can raise "any ground that could be raised under paragraph (2) or (3) of [35 U.S.C.] section 282(b) (relating to invalidity of the patent or any claim)." 35 U.S.C. §321(b) (eff. Sept. 16, 2012, for patents having an effective filing date on or after Mar. 16, 2013) ("Scope").

E. AIA-Implemented Procedures for Challenging Issued Patents

The threshold standard for the grant of a petition for *inter partes* review is no longer a "substantial new question of patentability" as in reexamination. Rather, the USPTO will not institute *inter partes* review unless the petitioner's petition and any response thereto by the patentee "show[] that there is a reasonable likelihood that the petitioner would prevail with respect to at least 1 of the claims challenged in the petition."[150] Whether this new threshold was intended to be a lower or higher threshold than "substantial new question of patentability" is unclear. Given that the AIA provides new ways to challenge the validity of issued patents, however, it is reasonable to interpret the statutory text as lowering the threshold.

Unlike reexaminations, *inter partes* review will be decided in the first instance by a three-member panel of the Patent Trial and Appeal Board (PTAB) rather than a single examiner. Notably, the review proceeding will be conducted expeditiously; the Patent Act requires a final determination within one year of the institution of *inter partes* review, absent a showing of good cause for a six-month extension.[151] The Patent Act also requires the USPTO to issue regulations concerning the conduct of *inter partes* review, including issues such as discovery standards and procedures, protective orders, patent owner response and amendment of claims, and oral hearings.[152] The USPTO issued final regulations on these issues in August 2012.[153]

As discussed *supra,* the estoppel provision for *inter partes* reexamination may have dissuaded some patent challengers from using that form of reexamination.[154] An estoppel provision remains in the statute for *inter partes* review, but its impact may be relatively less draconian. The Patent Act provides that

> [t]he petitioner in an inter partes review of a claim in a patent under this chapter that results in a final written decision under section 318(a), or the real party in interest or privy of the petitioner, may not assert either in a civil action arising in whole or in part under section 1338 of title 28 or in a proceeding before the International Trade Commission under section 337 of the Tariff Act of 1930 that the claim is invalid *on any ground that the petitioner raised or reasonably could have raised during that inter partes review.*[155]

[150]35 U.S.C. §314(a) (eff. Sept. 16, 2012) ("Threshold").

[151]35 U.S.C. §316(a)(11) (eff. Sept. 16, 2012).

[152]35 U.S.C. §316(a)(1)-(13) (eff. Sept. 16, 2012).

[153]*See* United States Patent & Trademark Office, *Final Rule: Changes to Implement Inter Partes Review Proceedings, Post-Grant Review Proceedings, and Transitional Program for Covered Business Method Patents,* 77 FED. REG. 48680 (Aug. 14, 2012), *available at* http://www.uspto.gov/aia_implementation/fr_specific_trial.pdf (adding 37 C.F.R. Chapter I, Part 42 ("Trial Practice Before the Patent Trial and Appeal Board"), Subpart B ("*Inter Partes* Review"), 37 C.F.R. §§ 42.100-42.123).

[154]*See supra* Section D.3.

[155]35 U.S.C. §315(e)(2) (eff. Sept. 16, 2012) ("Civil Actions and Other Proceedings").

In other words, if the petitioner in an *inter partes* review that goes to final determination is thereafter involved in federal court or ITC litigation challenging the patent's validity, the petitioner (and those in privity with the petitioner) are estopped from asserting that the patent is invalid on the same ground(s) that the petitioner raised (or reasonably could have raised) during the *inter partes* review in the USPTO. This statutory language differs from the pre-AIA estoppel provision for *inter partes* reexamination by adding the qualifier "reasonably" to the phrase "could have raised."[156] Moreover, the grounds on which the petitioner will be estopped are only those that were raised (or reasonably could have been raised) *during* the *inter partes* review, and not (apparently) any and all invalidity grounds that might have been considered at a time before the USPTO instituted the *inter partes* review.[157]

Lastly, *inter partes* review cannot be instituted if the would-be petitioner (or real party in interest) has already "filed a civil action challenging the validity of a claim of the patent,"[158] such as a declaratory judgment action seeking from a federal court a declaration that a patent is invalid. Notably, however, if the petitioner first files a petition for *inter partes* review in the USPTO and thereafter the petitioner (or real party in interest) files a civil action in federal court challenging the validity the patent (i.e., a declaratory judgment action), the civil action in federal court will be *automatically stayed*.[159] The automatic stay will continue until one of three things occurs: (1) the patentee moves the court to lift the stay, (2) the patentee files a separate action or a counterclaim alleging that the petitioner (or real party in interest) infringes the patent, or (3) the petitioner (or real party in interest) files a motion to dismiss the civil action.[160]

2.   Post-Grant Review

Responding to high-level calls for a less expensive and more widely available system to challenge the validity of issued patents,[161]

---

[156]*Compare* 35 U.S.C. §315(e)(2) (eff. Sept. 16, 2012) *with* 35 U.S.C. §315(c)(2006).

[157]*Inter partes* review is not "instituted" until the USPTO Director determines that the petition satisfies the threshold standard set out in 35 U.S.C. §314(a) (eff. Sept. 16, 2012). This suggests that the phrase "during that inter partes review" refers only to the time period after the Director granted the petition.

[158]35 U.S.C. §315(a)(1) (eff. Sept. 16, 2012) ("Inter Partes Review Barred by Civil Action").

[159]*See* 35 U.S.C. §315(a)(2) (eff. Sept. 16, 2012) ("Stay of Civil Action").

[160]*See* 35 U.S.C. §315(a)(2)(A)-(C) (eff. Sept. 16, 2012).

[161]For example, the Federal Trade Commission's 2003 comprehensive study of the patent system recommended the enactment of post-grant opposition in the U.S. patent system. *See* FEDERAL TRADE COMMISSION, TO PROMOTE INNOVATION: THE PROPER BALANCE OF COMPETITION AND PATENT LAW AND POLICY 7 (2003), *available at* http://www.ftc.gov/

E. AIA-Implemented Procedures for Challenging Issued Patents

Congress in the America Invents Act of 2011 implemented a new adjudicative proceeding termed "post-grant review." It is similar, but not identical, to the opposition system that has successfully operated for a number of years under the European Patent Convention.[162] Sections 311 through 329 of the Patent Act as amended by the AIA govern post-grant review.[163] Section 326 of the Patent Act requires the USPTO Director to prescribe regulations for the conduct of post-grant review; the agency issued its final rules in August 2012.[164] The AIA-implemented post-grant review proceeding does not replace *ex parte* reexamination but rather exists in addition thereto.[165]

Any person who is not the patent owner can petition the USPTO to authorize its post-grant review, with the petitioner's goal being to invalidate the patent by persuading the USPTO to cancel its claims. The petitioner need not be practicing the patented invention (in other words, need not be a potential infringer). This is a significant difference from the pre-AIA framework under which patent validity challenges were largely limited to expensive, long-running federal court

---

os/2003/10/innovationrpt.pdf [hereinafter FTC Report] (recommending the enactment of legislation to allow post-grant review and opposition to patents). The FTC Report explained that "[e]xisting means for challenging questionable patents are inadequate." *Id.* (discussing limitations of reexamination and high costs and lengthy duration of federal court litigation). Given these drawbacks with the existing methods of challenging issued patents, the FTC Report recommended the creation of "an administrative procedure for post-grant review and opposition that allows for meaningful challenges to patent validity short of federal court litigation." *Id.*

[162]*See* European Patent Convention arts. 99-105 (14th ed. 2010), *available at* http://www.epo.org/law-practice/legal-texts/html/epc/2010/e/ma1.html.

[163]*See* 35 U.S.C. §§321-329 (eff. Sept. 16, 2012, for patent claims having an effective filing date that is on or after Mar. 16, 2013).

[164]*See* United States Patent & Trademark Office, *Final Rule: Changes to Implement Inter Partes Review Proceedings, Post-Grant Review Proceedings, and Transitional Program for Covered Business Method Patents*, 77 Fed. Reg. 48680 (Aug. 14, 2012), *available at* http://www.uspto.gov/aia_implementation/fr_specific_trial.pdf (adding 37 C.F.R. Chapter I, Part 42 ("Trial Practice Before the Patent Trial and Appeal Board"), Subpart C ("Post-Grant Review"), 37 C.F.R. §§ 42.200-42.224).

[165]After the AIA-implemented *inter partes* review proceeding becomes effective on September 16, 2012, reexamination will be limited to the *ex parte* form of reexamination. *Ex parte* reexamination was analyzed at Section D.2, *supra*. *Ex parte* reexamination can be requested by anyone, including the patent owner, throughout the life of a patent. The scope of issues and evidence that can be relied on in *ex parte* reexamination is limited, however, and a "substantial new question of patentability" must be involved. Reexaminations are decided in the first instance by USPTO examiners rather than by the Patent Trial and Appeal Board (PTAB). Reexaminations are a more examinational proceeding than an adjudicative one, *see* H.R. Rep. No. 112-98 [House Judiciary Comm. Rep. on the America Invents Act] (June 1, 2011), at 57 (stating that the AIA "converts inter partes reexamination from an examinational to an adjudicative proceeding, and renames the proceeding "inter partes review"), and do not involve litigation-type procedures such as discovery depositions.

proceedings involving parties who were accused of infringing the patent (or at least in legitimate danger of being sued therefor).[166]

Perhaps the most important *procedural* aspect of post-grant review to understand is that such review may be sought only during the nine-month "window" following the issuance of a patent.[167] Post-grant review is *not* available throughout the life of the patent, in contrast with *ex parte* reexamination and the AIA-implemented *inter partes* review. Other procedural aspects of post-grant review largely track those specified for *inter partes* review.[168]

The most important *substantive* aspect of post-grant review is the broad scope of the review; that is, a petitioner can assert a relatively large number of grounds to establish patent invalidity (in contrast with *ex parte* reexamination and *inter partes* review). Specifically, a petition for post-grant review can raise "any ground that could be raised under paragraph (2) or (3) of [35 U.S.C.] section 282(b) (relating to invalidity of the patent or any claim)."[169] Such grounds include patent-ineligible subject matter or lack of utility under 35 U.S.C. §101; anticipation (i.e., lack of novelty) under 35 U.S.C. §102; obviousness

---

[166]The Supreme Court clarified the jurisdictional prerequisites for actions seeking a declaratory judgment of patent invalidity in *MedImmune, Inc. v. Genentech, Inc.*, 549 U.S. 118 (2007) (holding that subject-matter jurisdiction existed over licensee's Declaratory Judgment Act lawsuit challenging validity, enforceability, and infringement of licensed patent; justiciable case or controversy under U.S. Constitution Art. III existed despite licensee's payment of royalties under protest). *MedImmune* is further analyzed *infra* Chapter 10, Section G.

Even prior to the AIA, federal court litigation such as declaratory judgment actions and invalidity defenses or counterclaims in infringement actions was not the sole means of challenging the validity of issued patents. As discussed *supra, ex parte* reexamination has been available since 1980 and remains available post-AIA, but is limited in scope as outlined above in Section D. Reexamination is considered an "examinatory" proceeding rather than an "adjudicative" one.

[167]*See* 35 U.S.C. §321(c) (eff. Sept. 16, 2012, for patent claims having an effective filing date on or after Mar. 16, 2013).

[168]*See* United States Patent & Trademark Office, *Final Rule: Rules of Practice for Trials Before the Patent Trial and Appeal Board and Judicial Review of Patent Trial and Appeal Board Decisions*, 77 Fed. Reg. 48612 (Aug. 14, 2012), *available at* http://www.uspto.gov/aia_implementation/fr_general_trial.pdf (providing a "consolidated set of rules relating to Board trial practice for *inter partes* review, post-grant review, the transitional program for covered business method patents, and derivation proceedings[, as well as] a consolidated set of rules to implement the provisions of the AIA related to seeking judicial review of Board decisions"); United States Patent & Trademark Office, *Office Patent Trial Practice Guide*, 77 Fed. Reg. 48756 (Aug. 14, 2012), *available at* http://www.uspto.gov/aia_implementation/trial_practice_guide_48756.pdf (providing "a practice guide for the trial final rules to advise the public on the general framework of the regulations, including the structure and times for taking action in each of the new proceedings [i.e., *inter partes* review, post-grant review, the transitional program for covered business method patents, and derivation proceedings]").

[169]35 U.S.C. §321(b) (eff. Sept. 16, 2012, for patent claims having an effective filing date on or after Mar. 16, 2013) ("Scope").

under 35 U.S.C. §103; and non-enablement, failure to satisfy the written description of the invention requirement, and claim indefiniteness under 35 U.S.C. §112. Presumably double patenting can also be asserted as a ground relating to invalidity.[170] Post-grant review *cannot* be used to assert a failure to satisfy the best mode requirement of 35 U.S.C. §112,[171] or the defenses of noninfringement and unenforceability (the latter traditionally viewed as including inequitable conduct and patent misuse).[172]

The threshold standard for the USPTO Director to grant a petition for post-grant review is whether "the information presented in the petition . . . , if not rebutted, would demonstrate that it is more likely than not that at least 1 of the claims challenged in the petition is unpatentable."[173] The USPTO Director may also grant the petition if it "raises a novel or unsettled legal question that is important to other patents or patent applications."[174] These two threshold tests are different from the "reasonable likelihood that the petitioner would prevail" threshold for *inter partes* review. At least the first threshold test, "more likely than not," arguably sets a somewhat higher bar.

With regard to the interaction of post-grant review and civil actions (e.g., federal court litigation) involving patent invalidity, the automatic stay and estoppel provisions for post-grant review operate in the same manner as those described above for *inter partes* review.[175]

Any ambiguities in the procedural or substantive aspects of post-grant review will not be resolved with finality for some time. The first petitions for post-grant review likely will not be received by the USPTO until 2015 or beyond. This means that the Federal Circuit likely will

---

[170]Same invention-type double patenting is viewed as based on the language of 35 U.S.C. §101, although obviousness-type double patenting is a judicially created doctrine and not analytically the same as obviousness under 35 U.S.C. §103. Double patenting is further discussed *supra* Chapter 1, Section H.6.

[171]*See* 35 U.S.C. §282(b)(3) (eff. Sept. 16, 2012) (providing that "[t]he following shall be defenses in any action involving the validity . . . of a patent . . . : any requirement of section 112, *except that the failure to disclose the best mode shall not be a basis on which any claim of a patent may be cancelled* . . . ") (emphasis added).

[172]*See* 35 U.S.C. 282(b)(1) (eff. Sept. 16, 2012). Unenforceability (including inequitable conduct and patent misuse) is analyzed *infra* Chapter 10, Section D.

[173]35 U.S.C. §324(a) (eff. Sept. 16, 2012, for patent claims having an effective filing date on or after Mar. 16, 2013) ("Threshold"). The statutes permit the patent owner to attempt to rebut the information in the petition for post-grant review by filing a "preliminary response" thereto. *See* 35 U.S.C. §323 (eff. Sept. 16, 2012, for patent claims having an effective filing date on or after Mar. 16, 2013) ("Preliminary response to petition").

[174]35 U.S.C. §324(b) (eff. Sept. 16, 2012, for patent claims having an effective filing date on or after Mar. 16, 2013) ("Additional Grounds").

[175]*See* 35 U.S.C. §325 (eff. Sept. 16, 2012, for patent claims having an effective filing date on or after Mar. 16, 2013) ("Relation to other proceedings or actions"). Subsection 325(a)(2) deals with stays of civil actions; subsection 325(e) deals with estoppel. *See also supra* Section E.1 ("*Inter Partes* Review").

not be hearing appeals from USPTO decisions in post-grant reviews before 2016 or beyond. Although the new sections 321 to 329 of the Patent Act that govern post-grant review take effect on September 16, 2012, they "shall apply only to patents described in section 3(n)(1)" of the America Invents Act of 2011.[176] In other words, a patent subject to post-grant review must contain a claim to a claimed invention having an effective filing date on or after March 16, 2013; or, alternatively, the patent must contain a specific reference under 35 U.S.C. §120 (continuation or continuation-in-part application), 35 U.S.C. §121 (divisional application), or 35 U.S.C. §365(c) (international application designating the United States and entitled to benefit of earlier-filed application) to a patent that contains such a claim.[177] With U.S. patent application pendency averaging over two years, few patents subject to challenge via post-grant review will issue before 2015.

[176]Leahy-Smith America Invents Act, Pub. L. No. 112-29 (H.R. 1249), §6(f)(2)(A),125 Stat. 284, 311 (Sept. 16, 2011).

[177]*See* Leahy-Smith America Invents Act, Pub. L. No. 112-29 (H.R. 1249), §3(n)(1), 125 Stat. 284, 293 (Sept. 16, 2011), which provides that

> IN GENERAL.—Except as otherwise provided in this section, the amendments made by this section shall take effect upon the expiration of the 18-month period beginning on the date of the enactment of this Act, and shall apply to any application for patent, and to any patent issuing thereon, that contains or contained at any time—
>
> (A) a claim to a claimed invention that has an effective filing date as defined in section 100(i) of title 35, United States Code, that is on or after the effective date described in this paragraph; or
>
> (B) a specific reference under section 120, 121, or 365(c) of title 35, United States Code, to any patent or application that contains or contained at any time such a claim.

The AIA-amended version of 35 U.S.C. §100 in turn defines "effective filing date" as follows:

> (i) (1) The term "effective filing date" for a claimed invention in a patent or application for patent means—
>
> (A) if subparagraph (B) does not apply, the actual filing date of the patent or the application for the patent containing a claim to the invention; or
>
> (B) the filing date of the earliest application for which the patent or application is entitled, as to such invention, to a right of priority under section 119, 365(a), or 365(b) or to the benefit of an earlier filing date under section 120, 121, or 365(c).
>
> (2) The effective filing date for a claimed invention in an application for reissue or reissued patent shall be determined by deeming the claim to the invention to have been contained in the patent for which reissue was sought.

35 U.S.C. §100 (eff. Mar. 16, 2013).

Chapter 9

Patent Infringement

A. Introduction

Equipped with an understanding of the process for obtaining a U.S. patent, we are now ready to consider how a patent owner enforces her statutory right to exclude others from unauthorized making, using, selling, offering to sell, or importing of the patented invention.[1] Analysis of patent **infringement** in the United States involves the application of governing statutory provisions as well as judicial decisions. Briefly, the U.S. courts recognize two basic forms of infringement, each discussed in detail below: (1) **literal infringement** and (2) infringement under the judicially created **doctrine of equivalents.** Literal infringement means that an accused product or process comes precisely within the terms of an asserted patent claim, while infringement under the doctrine of equivalents recognizes that, in order to adequately protect a patentee, we may sometimes extend the scope of her right to exclude beyond the literal boundaries of the claim. This chapter surveys the essential authority.[2]

1. Statutory Framework

The sections of the U.S. Patent Act, 35 U.S.C., most pertinent to an analysis of patent infringement are these:

§271. Infringement of patent

(a) Except as otherwise provided in this title [35 U.S.C. §§1 *et seq.*], whoever without authority makes, uses, offers to sell, or sells any

---

[1]*See* 35 U.S.C. §271(a) (2012).

[2]For more detailed treatments of patent enforcement, *see* AM. BAR ASS'N: SECTION OF INTELLECTUAL PROPERTY LAW, PATENT LITIGATION STRATEGIES HANDBOOK (Barry L. Grossman & Gary M. Hoffman eds., BNA Books 3d ed. Supp. 2011); PAUL M. JANICKE, MODERN PATENT LITIGATION (Carolina Acad. Press 3d ed. 2012); KIMBERLY A. MOORE, PAUL R. MICHEL, & TIMOTHY HOLBROOK, PATENT LITIGATION AND STRATEGY (ThomsonWest 3d ed. 2008).

patented invention, within the United States or imports into the United States any patented invention during the term of the patent therefor, infringes the patent.

(b) Whoever actively induces infringement of a patent shall be liable as an infringer.

(c) Whoever offers to sell or sells within the United States or imports into the United States a component of a patented machine, manufacture, combination or composition, or a material or apparatus for use in practicing a patented process, constituting a material part of the invention, knowing the same to be especially made or especially adapted for use in an infringement of such patent, and not a staple article or commodity of commerce suitable for substantial noninfringing use, shall be liable as a contributory infringer.

(d) . . . (i) . . . . [3]

§281. Remedy for infringement of patent

A patentee shall have remedy by civil action for infringement of his patent.[4]

Section 271 of 35 U.S.C. does not so much define what constitutes infringement as set forth the categories of acts (i.e., "mak[ing]," "us[ing]," "sell[ing]," and so on) that can create liability for infringement. Case law, discussed below, fleshes out the elements of these acts.

As provided by §281, patent infringement actions are brought in the United States as civil actions. No criminal proceeding is recognized for patent infringement in the United States.

a. Direct Versus Indirect Infringement Under 35 U.S.C. §271

Section 271 of the Patent Act (35 U.S.C.) distinguishes between acts of *direct* infringement and acts of *indirect* infringement. Subsection 271(a) governs *direct* infringement—the unauthorized making, using, selling, offering to sell, or importing[5] of the *entire* claimed invention.

---

[3]35 U.S.C. §271 (2012). Subsection (d) of §271 is discussed in Chapter 10, Section D.2, *infra*. Subsections (e) through (g) of §271 are quoted and discussed in Section E of this chapter, *infra*.

[4]35 U.S.C. §281 (2012).

[5]The "offers to sell" and "imports" provisions of 35 U.S.C. §271(a) became effective January 1, 1996. They were added to the statute by the Uruguay Round Agreements Act, which brought U.S. patent law into compliance with certain provisions of the World Trade Organization–administered Agreement on Trade-Related Aspects of Intellectual Property Rights (TRIPS). For further discussion of TRIPS, *see* Chapter 12, Section D, *infra*. A good resource on the meaning of §271(a)'s "offers to sell" infringement provision is Timothy R. Holbrook, *Liability for the "Threat of a Sale": Assessing*

By application of the **all-limitations rule**, derived from case law as discussed below, the act of "making" the claimed invention under 35 U.S.C. §271(a) requires that an accused infringer has manufactured a device that meets each and every **limitation** of the asserted claim. Generally speaking, this means that if the claimed invention is a combination of elements, the **accused device** must be fully assembled and ready for use.[6]

Notably, 35 U.S.C. §271(a) enumerates the various directly infringing acts in the disjunctive (i.e., using "or"). Thus the act of merely making the claimed invention without authority creates infringement liability, even if the accused infringer thereafter does not sell the infringing device. Likewise, a mere "using" of the claimed invention without authority creates liability even where the accused infringer did not make the infringing device. To see this, consider a scenario in which Accused Infringer 1 manufactures an infringing machine for sowing seeds and sells it to Accused Infringer 2, a farmer who merely uses the infringing machine to plant his crop. Accused Infringer 1 and Accused Infringer 2 are considered jointly and severally liable for patent infringement.[7]

Indirect infringement concerns activity involving *less than* a making of the entire invention, such as assisting one who does or supplying certain required components of the invention. Nevertheless, such indirect activity is considered infringing because it assists or supports another party's direct infringement. The direct infringer and the indirect infringer are considered jointly and severally liable for the infringement under a theory of joint tortfeasance.[8] Another distinction between indirect and direct infringement is that indirect infringement liability requires proof of intent, or *scienter*, while "a direct infringer's knowledge or intent is irrelevant."[9] Forms of indirect infringement under 35 U.S.C. §271(b), which governs inducing infringement, and

---

Patent Infringement for Offering to Sell an Invention and Implications for the On-Sale Patentability Bar and Other Forms of Infringement, 43 Santa Clara L. Rev. 751 (2003).

[6]*But see* Paper Converting Machine Co. v. Magna-Graphics Corp., 745 F.2d 11, 19 (Fed. Cir. 1984) (finding infringement where "significant, unpatented assemblies of elements [were] tested during the patent term, enabling the infringer to deliver the patented combination in parts to the buyer"), *aff'd after remand,* 785 F.2d 1013 (Fed. Cir. 1986).

[7]*See* Birdsell v. Shaliol, 112 U.S. 485, 489 (1884). In practice, a consumer purchaser of an infringing product may be entitled to sue her seller for breach of warranty under the Uniform Commercial Code. *See* U.C.C. §2-312, *available at* http://www.law.cornell.edu/ucc/2/2-312.html (last visited Aug. 12, 2012).

[8]*See* Hewlett-Packard Co. v. Bausch & Lomb, Inc., 909 F.2d 1464, 1469 (Fed. Cir. 1990).

[9]Global-Tech Appliances, Inc. v. SEB S.A., 131 S. Ct. 2060, 2065 n.2 (2011).

§271(c), which governs contributory infringement, are discussed later in this chapter.[10]

b. Joint Direct Infringement by Multiple Parties Under §271(a)

Consider the increasingly common scenario of a patent claiming a business method comprising a number of steps. Depending on the manner in which the method claim is drafted, no single entity may perform all the steps of the method. In other words, a "use" of the patented method would involve acts by multiple entities. These entities may be completely unrelated or nominally related only at arm's length. Is there direct infringement in this scenario?

For example, the patents in suit in *BMC Resources, Inc. v. Paymentech, L.P.*[11] claimed a method for processing debit or credit card transactions without having to enter a personal identification number (PIN). The method allowed a customer to pay her bills by accessing an interface between a standard touch-tone telephone and a debit or credit card network. Performance of the method as claimed required acts by four different entities, each of whom participated in carrying out and authorizing the transaction, that is, the merchant whom the customer sought to pay, an agent of the merchant (such as the patentee BMC Resources), a remote payment network such as an ATM network, and the financial institution that issued the debit or credit card.[12] BMC Resources sued Paymentech, a payment services processor, alleging that Paymentech's PIN-less debit bill payment service directly infringed BMC's patented method claims.[13] Paymentech responded that it could not be a direct infringer because it did not perform all the steps of the claimed process, nor did it perform all the steps "in coordination with its customers and financial institutions." [14]

Recall that §271(a) creates direct infringement liability for "whoever" without authority "uses" a patented invention within the United States during the term of the patent. Thus, the precise issue raised by *BMC Resources* is this: who qualifies as the statutory "whoever"? Must "whoever" be limited to a single entity that performs each and every method step, or can a single entity (e.g., Paymentech, the sole named defendant in *BMC Resources*) be liable for direct infringement

---

[10]*See* Section E, *infra.*

[11]498 F.3d 1373 (Fed. Cir. 2007).

[12]*See id.* at 1375 (describing claimed method); *id.* at 1376-1377 (quoting allegedly infringed claim 7 of BMC's U.S. Patent No. 5,870,456, and allegedly infringed claim 2 of BMC's U.S. Patent No. 5,718,298).

[13]Patentee BMC also asserted that Paymentech was liable for inducing infringement under 35 U.S.C. §271(b). *See id.* at 1376.

[14]*Id.* at 1377.

based on its participation in the combined acts of multiple entities under a theory of "joint infringement"?[15]

The Federal Circuit in *BMC Resources* rejected a mere "participation and combined action" standard,[16] holding instead that direct liability exists in a joint infringement scenario only when the accused infringer is the effective "mastermind" who "controls or directs" all the other entities performing the method steps.[17] For example, if an accused infringer entered into contracts with other entities requiring them to perform steps of a patented process, the accused infringer presumably would be "in control" and liable as a direct infringer; "[a] party cannot avoid infringement . . . simply by contracting out steps of a patented process to another entity."[18] In the case at bar, however, the various entities that carried out the multiple steps of the claimed process were related merely at "arm's length,"[19] and not by contract.[20] The evidence proffered by BMC to establish "some relationship" between Paymentech and the other entities was not sufficient to create a genuine issue of material fact as to whether Paymentech controlled or directed the activity of the other entities. Accordingly, the Federal Circuit affirmed the district court's grant of summary judgment of no infringement.[21] The appellate court concluded that "[i]n this situation, neither the financial institutions, the debit networks, nor the payment services provider, Paymentech, bears responsibility for the actions of the other."[22]

---

[15]This theory has also been referred to as "distributed" infringement or "divided" infringement.

[16]A "participation and combined action" standard for joint infringement was set forth in jury instructions that the Federal Circuit had previously approved in *On Demand Machine Corp. v. Ingram Indus., Inc.*, 442 F.3d 1331 (Fed. Cir. 2006). *See BMC Resources*, 498 F.3d at 1379 (quoting instructions from *On Demand*). However, the Federal Circuit in *BMC Resources* agreed with the district court that that aspect of *On Demand* was merely dictum, not relied on by the *On Demand* court in reaching its decision. *See id.* at 1380 (stating that "*On Demand* did not change this court's precedent with regard to joint infringement").

[17]*See id.* at 1381.

[18]*Id.*

[19]*Id.* at 1380 (quoting with approval statement of district court that "[n]o court has ever found direct infringement based on the type of arms-length business transaction presented here").

[20]*See id.* at 1382 (noting district court's observance that "the record contained no evidence even of a contractual relationship between Paymentech and the financial institutions").

[21]Nor could Paymentech be liable for inducing infringement under 35 U.S.C. §271(b), because the patentee BMC had not established a predicate act of direct infringement. *See id.* at 1379 (stating that "[i]ndirect infringement requires, as a predicate, a finding that some party amongst the accused actors has committed the entire act of direct infringement").

[22]*Id.* at 1382. *Compare* Centillion Data Sys., LLC v. Qwest Comm. Int'l, Inc., 631 F.3d 1279, 1285 (Fed. Cir. 2011) (holding that the customer of accused infringer Qwest

The Federal Circuit soon reconfirmed the *BMC Resources* "control or direction" standard in *Muniauction, Inc. v. Thomson Corp.*, reversing a district court's post-jury trial judgment that had awarded a patentee $77 million in damages.[23] Like *BMC Resources, Muniauction* involved a business method patent. Specifically, Muniauction's patent covered methods for conducting original issuer municipal bond auctions over an electronic network such as the Internet. Advantageously, bond issuers (e.g., municipalities) could run an auction and bidders (e.g., underwriters) could submit bids using a conventional Web browser without requiring other separate, preinstalled software. The *Muniauction* court summarized the standards enunciated in *BMC Resources* as follows:

> [W]here the actions of multiple parties combine to perform every step of a claimed method, the claim is directly infringed only if one party exercises "control or direction" over the entire process such that every step is attributable to the controlling party, i.e., the "mastermind." At the other end of this multi-party spectrum, mere "arms-length cooperation" will not give rise to direct infringement by any party.[24]

Applying the *BMC Resources* standard, the *Muniauction* court concluded that even though accused infringer Thomson "control[led] access to its system and instruct[ed] bidders on its use," these acts were not sufficient to incur liability for direct infringement.[25] Rather, the requisite "control or direction" standard is satisfied "in situations where the law would traditionally hold the accused direct infringer vicariously liable for the acts committed by another party that are required to complete performance of a claimed method."[26] In the case at bar, accused infringer Thomson did not perform all the claim steps when it conducted auctions using its accused BidComp/Parity® system, nor did others (e.g., the bidders) perform those steps on Thomson's behalf. The Federal Circuit concluded that Thomson was not vicariously liable for the actions of the auction bidders.

The take-away message of these joint infringement cases is that those who draft business method claims should strive whenever possible to craft single-user claims. For example, the *BMC Resources* court suggested that the method claims in that case could have been drafted

---

"is a single 'user' of the [on-demand operation of the patented] system [for processing call data and delivering it to customers in a format appropriate for a personal computer] and because there is a single user, there is no need for the vicarious liability analysis from *BMC* [*Resources*] . . .").

[23] 532 F.3d 1318 (Fed. Cir. 2008).

[24] *Id.* at 1329 (citations omitted).

[25] *Id.* at 1330.

[26] *Id.* (citing, *inter alia*, BMC Resources, Inc. v. Paymentech, L.P., 498 F.3d 1373, 1379 (Fed. Cir. 2007)).

to "feature[] references to a single party's supplying or receiving each element of the claimed process."[27] In cases where such drafting strategies are not a feasible way to capture the invention, the patentee will be required to show that the accused infringer satisfies the rigorous "direction and control" standard with respect to the other entities performing the method steps.

As of the writing of this edition in 2012, Federal Circuit judges continue to debate the proper test for liability in joint or distributed infringement situations. Attempting to clarify the issue, the court took two additional distributed infringement cases under *en banc* review.[28] In *Akamai Techs., Inc. v. Limelight Networks, Inc.*,[29] the *en banc* court avoided answering the question "whether direct infringement can be found when no single entity performs all of the claimed steps of the patent."[30] By a 6-5 vote, the *Akamai* majority instead resolved the joint infringement issue in the cases before it under the theory of induced infringement under 35 U.S.C. §271(b).[31] The majority rejected the single entity rule of *BMC Resources* insofar as the rule applied to induced infringement liability.[32] Although "all the steps of a claimed method must be performed in order to find induced infringement," the majority held, "it is not necessary to prove that all the steps were committed by a single entity."[33] As a policy matter, resolving the joint infringement question under the doctrine of induced infringement advantageously protected unsuspecting innocent parties. Because liability for induced infringement (unlike direct infringement) requires "specific intent to cause infringement," "using

[27]*BMC Resources*, 498 F.3d at 1381.
[28]*See* Akamai Techs., Inc. v. MIT, 419 Fed. App'x 989 (Fed. Cir. 2011) (*en banc*) (order granting rehearing *en banc* and vacating panel's opinion in Akamai Techs., Inc. v. Limelight Networks, Inc., 629 F.3d 1311 (Fed. Cir. 2010)); McKesson Techs. Inc. v. Epic Sys. Corp., 463 Fed. App'x 906 (Fed. Cir. 2011) (*en banc*) (order granting rehearing *en banc* and vacating panel's opinion in McKesson Techs., Inc. v. Epic Sys. Corp., No. 2010-1291 (Fed. Cir. Apr. 12, 2011), *available at* http://www.cafc.uscourts.gov/images/stories/opinions-orders/10-1291.pdf.
[29]Nos. 2009–1372 et seq., __ F.3d __, 2012 WL 3764695 (Fed. Cir. Aug. 31, 2012) (*en banc*).
[30]*Akamai Techs.,* __ F.3d __, 2012 WL 3764695 at *1. The majority explained that "[b]ecause the reasoning of our decision today is not predicated on the doctrine of direct infringement, we have no occasion at this time to revisit any of those principles regarding the law of divided infringement as it applies to liability for direct infringement under 35 U.S.C. § 271(a)." *Id.,* 2012 WL 3764695 at *3.
[31]Indirect infringement liability under the theory of induced infringement is analyzed *infra* Section E.1.
[32]*Akamai Techs.,* __ F.3d __, 2012 WL 3764695 at *1 ("[W]e reconsider and overrule the 2007 decision of this court in which we held that in order for a party to be liable for induced infringement, some other single entity must be liable for direct infringement. *BMC Resources, Inc. v. Paymentech, L.P.*, 498 F.3d 1373 (Fed. Cir. 2007).").
[33]*Akamai Techs.,* __ F.3d __, 2012 WL 3764695 at *1.

445

inducement to reach joint infringement does not present the risk of extending liability to persons who may be unaware of the existence of a patent or even unaware that others are practicing some of the steps claimed in the patent."[34]

2. Two-Step Analysis for Patent Infringement

Numerous judicial decisions provide that analyzing patent infringement is a two-step process comprising:

1. Interpretation of the patent claims; and
2. Comparison of the properly interpreted claims with the accused device.[35]

These steps are considered separately in Sections B and C below.

A few words on terminology are appropriate here. Step One of the infringement analysis, interpreting the claims, is sometimes also referred to by patent attorneys as claim construction or as the task of construing the claims. This author prefers to speak of claim interpretation rather than construction, because the notion of construction is somewhat confusingly similar to claim drafting, a related but conceptually distinct task. Step Two of the analysis, comparing the properly interpreted claims with the accused device, is sometimes referred to by patent attorneys as "reading the claims onto the accused device."[36]

---

[34]*Akamai Techs.*, __ F.3d __, 2012 WL 3764695 at *3 n.1.

[35]*See, e.g.,* Cybor Corp. v. FAS Techs., Inc., 138 F.3d 1448, 1454 (Fed. Cir. 1998) (*en banc*) ("First, the court determines the scope and meaning of the patent claims asserted. . . . [Second,] the properly construed claims are compared to the allegedly infringing device.") (citations omitted); Caterpillar Tractor Co. v. Berco, S.p.A., 714 F.2d 1110, 1114 (Fed. Cir. 1983) (citing Autogiro Co. of America v. United States, 384 F.2d 391, 401 (Ct. Cl. 1967)).

In the comparison step (Step Two of the process for analyzing infringement), infringement will be found only if each and every limitation of the claim is met in the accused device, either literally or under the doctrine of equivalents. Infringement cannot be determined by comparing the claimed and accused devices as a whole; the analysis must be performed on a limitation-by-limitation level. This "all-limitations rule," and the meaning of "limitation," are discussed in further detail below.

[36]Patent claims are said to "read on" an accused device when the device would literally infringe the claimed invention (likewise, patent claims are said to "read on" the prior art when that subject matter would anticipate the claimed invention). It is improper to say that a device "reads on" a patent claim, however. Claims "read on" accused or prior art devices, not the other way around.

B. Step One: Patent Claim Interpretation

It cannot be overstated that, in patent law, "the name of the game is the claim."[37] This maxim reflects the prominence of claims in patent litigation. Federal Circuit judges observe that "[c]laim construction is the single most important event in the course of a patent litigation."[38] The manner in which the claims are interpreted is, in many cases, dispositive of literal infringement. In a smaller but growing number of cases, claim interpretation also may effectively decide whether infringement is found under the doctrine of equivalents.[39]

After a review of the central function played by the claims of a patent, the remainder of this section considers three key questions pertaining to patent claim interpretation: Who interprets patent claims? What evidentiary sources are used to interpret patent claims? And last, what are the primary rules (or "canons") of claim interpretation?

1. The Central Role of Claims

Chapter 2 of this text addressed patent claims in detail, and the reader is encouraged to review Chapter 2 prior to consulting this chapter. Some key aspects of patent claims as they impact patent enforcement are repeated here for emphasis.

The claims are the most important part of a patent. A patent claim is a single-sentence definition of the literal boundary of the patent owner's right to exclude. Acting as a sort of verbal fence, the patent claim is intended to provide reasonably clear notice, in advance of

---

[37]Giles S. Rich, *The Extent of the Protection and Interpretation of Claims: American Perspectives,* 21 INT'L REV. INDUS. PROP. & COPYRIGHT L. 497, 499, 501 (1990).

[38]Retractable Techs., Inc. v. Becton, Dickinson and Co., 659 F.3d 1369, 1373 (Fed. Cir. 2011) (Moore, J., joined by Rader, C.J., dissenting from denial of rehearing *en banc*).

[39]Disposing of the doctrine of equivalents infringement question at the completion of the claim interpretation stage is increasingly common as the Federal Circuit develops its jurisprudence concerning "vitiation" of claim limitations. Recall the Supreme Court's guidance in *Warner-Jenkinson Co. v. Hilton Davis Chem. Co.*, 520 U.S. 17 (1997), that various legal limitations on a patentee's ability to rely on the doctrine of equivalents should be decided by the trial court, possibly on pre-trial motion. *See id.* at 39 n.8. For example, "if a theory of equivalence would entirely vitiate a particular claim element, partial or complete judgment should be rendered by the court, as there would be no further material issue for the jury to resolve." *Id.* By "vitiation" the *Warner-Jenkinson* Court referred to a situation in which finding a particular claim limitation infringed under the doctrine of equivalents would be tantamount to ignoring or eliminating that limitation. *See, e.g.,* Asyst Techs., Inc. v. Emtrak, Inc., 402 F.3d 1188, 1195 (Fed. Cir. 2005) (stating that "[t]o hold that 'unmounted' is equivalent to 'mounted' would effectively read the 'mounted on' limitation out of the patent"). Section D.5, *infra*, addresses in greater detail the Federal Circuit's unsettled jurisprudence concerning vitiation as a legal limit on the doctrine of equivalents.

litigation, of just how far the patentee's competitors can proceed in imitating the patented invention without infringing the patent owner's right to exclude.[40]

In emphasizing to students the importance of patent claims, the patent law professor's classic analogy compares a patent claim with a deed to real property. The deed very specifically defines the boundaries of a plot of land, but does not describe what may be located in the interior—buildings, trees, water, and the like. Similarly, a patent claim does not describe the invention to which the patent is directed. Rather, it defines the extent of the patent owner's right to prevent others from exploiting that invention.[41]

The role of describing the patented invention is played not by the patent's claims, but rather by its written description and drawings. In accordance with 35 U.S.C. §112(a) (eff. Sept. 16, 2012), these parts of the patent specification must provide an enabling disclosure of how to make and use the invention without undue experimentation, and also must disclose the best mode of carrying out the invention if such a mode was known to the inventor on the application filing date.[42] Thus, it is legally erroneous to refer to patent claims as *describing* an invention.

During the process of applying for a patent, the claims may be amended (frequently by narrowing) such that their final scope varies from the scope of the inventive concept as described to its fullest extent in the written description and drawings. Thus, what is described in the patent as "the invention" may (and often does) differ in scope from the claims that ultimately issue.

The claims are found at the end of each patent's specification; a patent must conclude with at least one claim,[43] and usually includes 10,

---

[40]As the Supreme Court has observed,

The patent laws "promote the Progress of Science and useful Arts" by rewarding innovation with a temporary monopoly. U.S. Const., Art. I, §8, cl. 8. The monopoly is a property right; and like any property right, its boundaries should be clear. This clarity is essential to promote progress, because it enables efficient investment in innovation. A patent holder should know what he owns, and the public should know what he does not.

Festo Corp. v. Shoketsu Kinzoku Kogyo Kabushiki Co., 535 U.S. 722, 730-731 (2002).

[41]As mentioned in the introduction to this chapter, U.S. patent law recognizes two forms of infringement: (1) literal infringement, and (2) infringement under the doctrine of equivalents. A patent claim recites the boundaries of the patentee's right to exclude others from making, using, selling, offering to sell, or importing products or processes that *literally* infringe the claim. Under the judicially created doctrine of equivalents, however, a patentee's right to exclude may be extended beyond the literal scope of the claims when circumstances warrant.

[42]The requirements of 35 U.S.C. §112(a) are detailed *supra* Chapter 3 ("Disclosure Requirements (35 U.S.C. §112(a))").

[43]35 U.S.C. §112(b) (eff. Sept. 16, 2012).

20, or more claims. The only limits on the number of claims included in a patent are the applicant's willingness to pay additional filing fees, which increase as claims are added,[44] and human resource limitations on the USPTO's ability to examine large numbers of claims, particularly in complex technologies such as biotechnology.

2. Judge or Jury as Interpreter? The *Markman* Revolution

The first question of the three posed above, who interprets patent claims, is particularly important in the context of jury trials. In recent years, more patent infringement cases are being tried to juries than to the courts.[45] In *Markman v. Westview Instruments,*[46] the Supreme Court held that the Seventh Amendment of the U.S. Constitution[47] does not provide a right to a jury trial for the interpretation of patent claims. Rather, policy concerns dictate that the role of claim interpretation is to be performed by the judge instead of the jury in a jury trial. *Markman* was a watershed event in the history of U.S. patent litigation, and thus the details of the case merit considerable attention.

Markman, the plaintiff, owned a patent on a system for tracking articles of clothing in a dry-cleaning process.[48] The claims of Markman's patent required that the system include means to maintain an inventory total, and that the system be able to "detect and localize spurious additions to inventory as well as spurious deletions therefrom."[49] The

---

[44]The USPTO currently charges additional fees for independent claims in excess of 3, and for a total number of claims in excess of 20. *See* United States Patent & Trademark Office, *Patent Application Filing Fees* (eff. Sept. 16, 2011), *available at* http://www.uspto.gov/web/offices/ac/qs/ope/fee092611.htm#patapp. See also 37 C.F.R. §1.16(h) (2011) (independent claims in excess of 3); 37 C.F.R. §1.16(i) (claims in excess of 20).

[45]*See* Admin. Off. U.S. Cts., Jud. Bus. U.S. Cts. 170 tbl. C4 (2007), *available at* http://www.uscourts.gov/judbus2007/JudicialBusinespdfversion.pdf (reporting for 12-month period ending Sept. 30, 2007, that out of 94 patent cases terminated during or after trial in the U.S. District Courts, 63 of the cases (or 67 percent) were tried before juries). This percentage has increased slightly in recent years. *Compare* Kimberly A. Moore, *Judges, Juries, and Patent Cases: An Empirical Peek Inside the Black Box,* 99 Mich. L. Rev. 365, 366 n.7 (2000) (reporting that in 1998, 60 percent of all patent trials (62 out of 103) were tried before juries) (citing Admin. Off. U.S. Cts., Jud. Bus. U.S. Cts. 167 tbl. C4 (1998)). For 1999, the percentage of patent jury trials rose to 62 percent (61 out of 98). *See id.* (citing Admin. Off. U.S. Cts., Jud. Bus. U.S. Cts. 161 tbl. C4 (1999)).

[46]517 U.S. 370 (1996).

[47]The Seventh Amendment provides that "[i]n Suits at common law, where the value in controversy shall exceed twenty dollars, the right of trial by jury shall be preserved. . . . " U.S. Const., amend. VII.

[48]*See* U.S. Pat. No. Re. 33,054.

[49]Markman v. Westview Instruments, Inc., 772 F. Supp. 1535, 1537 (E.D. Pa. 1991).

key claim interpretation dispute concerned the meaning of "inventory." Because the defendant's accused system tracked only cash invoices, not articles of clothing, Markman introduced expert testimony to support his position that "inventory" meant cash invoices. After the jury found for Markman, the district court granted the defendant's motion for judgment of noninfringement as a matter of law. The district court concluded that the intrinsic evidence (the patent itself and its prosecution history) made clear that "inventory" as used in Markman's patent had to include "items of clothing." Because the accused system did not track clothing, there could be no literal infringement.[50]

On appeal, Markman's primary argument was that the Seventh Amendment of the U.S. Constitution guarantees a right to a jury trial on claim interpretation, and that the district court had erred by effectively taking that role away from the jury through the grant of judgment as a matter of law (JMOL). The Federal Circuit rejected this argument, and the Supreme Court affirmed. Applying the "historical" test, the Supreme Court explained that although it is clear that English juries were hearing patent infringement cases in 1791 (when the Seventh Amendment was ratified), there was no clear historical antecedent at that time for the practice of claim interpretation. In fact, patent claims were not mentioned by statute in the United States until the Patent Act of 1836, and were not statutorily required until the Patent Act of 1870.

Because the historical test does not answer the question of whether judge or jury should construe patent claims in a jury trial of patent infringement, the Supreme Court's decision in *Markman* ultimately turned on functional (i.e., public policy) considerations. The Court concluded that judges are simply better equipped than jurors to construe the meaning of claim terms based on documentary evidence, because the bread-and-butter work of the judiciary is to construe the meaning of language in legal documents (e.g., contracts and statutes) upon receipt of evidence. Judges understand that this role must be performed in a manner that comports with a "whole contents" approach, that is, the fundamental interpretive canon that a term or phrase in a document must be construed in such a way as to comport with the document as a whole. In this manner a patent's internal coherence

---

[50]In *Markman* a federal district court construed the patent claims in the context of a post-trial motion for judgment as a matter of law (JMOL). The Federal Circuit and the Supreme Court ostensibly blessed this practice by affirming the trial court's decision in *Markman*; at least those decisions did *not* hold that claim interpretation at the JMOL stage was reversible error. Although many federal district courts now construe the claims of a patent relatively early in the course of a patent litigation (sometimes before the close of discovery), the Federal Circuit has not yet held in any case following *Markman* that it is reversible error to proceed as the *Markman* district court did and postpone claim interpretation until after trial.

is best preserved. Although some cases may arise in which competing interpretations of patent terms by opposing experts would require that judges make credibility determinations, a traditional province of the jury, "in the main" the Court expects that these determinations will be "subsumed within the necessarily sophisticated analysis of the whole document, required by the standard construction rule that a term can be defined only in a way that comports with the instrument as a whole." [51]

The Supreme Court in *Markman* also cited the importance of the uniform interpretation of a given patent as another policy reason why judges are better suited than juries to interpret patent claims. In the Court's view, "[u]niformity would . . . be ill served by submitting issues of document construction to juries."[52] The treatment of claim interpretation as a "purely legal" issue for the court will promote certainty through *stare decisis* principles, the Court declared.[53] Consistent with the common law system's fundamental principle of "standing by the decision," courts should give due weight and consideration to the decisions of other courts who have previously ruled on the same issues, even in cases where the Federal Circuit has not yet blessed a particular claim interpretation or where collateral estoppel would not apply because a defendant did not have a full and fair opportunity to litigate a particular claim interpretation issue in an earlier proceeding involving the same patent.[54]

---

[51]*Markman,* 517 U.S. at 389.

[52]*Id.* at 391.

[53]*Id.*

[54]In order for collateral estoppel to apply against a party, the following elements are required:

   (1) The issues raised in both proceedings must be identical;

   (2) The relevant issue must have actually been litigated and decided in prior proceeding;

   (3) The party to be estopped must have had a full/fair opportunity to litigate the issue in prior proceeding; and

   (4) Resolution of the issue must have been necessary to support a valid and final judgment on the merits.

TM Patents, L.P. v. Int'l Bus. Machs. Corp., 72 F. Supp. 2d 370, 375, 377 (S.D.N.Y. 1999) (holding patent owner estopped from asserting a different claim interpretation in second action asserting infringement of same patent against new defendant, where patentee had full and fair opportunity to litigate claim construction in first proceeding and claim construction decision in first case, rendered following a *Markman* hearing, was sufficiently "final" to satisfy collateral estoppel rule). *See also* Jet, Inc. v. Sewage Aeration Sys., 223 F.3d 1360, 1365-1366 (Fed. Cir. 2000) (identifying four prerequisites to the application of issue preclusion).

   Note that the *TM Patents* case cited above held that the *patent owner* was collaterally estopped. In contrast, under any traditional definition of collateral estoppel an *accused infringer* who was not a party to an earlier infringement litigation concerning the same patent should not be estopped in a later, separate infringement proceeding

3. Evidentiary Sources for Claim Interpretation

In the aftermath of *Markman,* the Federal Circuit has developed a robust jurisprudence addressing what evidentiary sources should be relied on to interpret patent claims. The foundational case here is *Vitronics Corp. v. Conceptronic, Inc.*[55] The Federal Circuit in *Vitronics* established a hierarchy of claim interpretational tools that distinguishes between "intrinsic" and "extrinsic" evidence. *Intrinsic* evidence is that which is part of the public record associated with a patent's issuance: the patent itself and its prosecution history,[56] including the prior art cited therein.[57] Competitors have access to this information as soon as the patent issues, if not before,[58] and it is not considered "litigation-influenced." *Extrinsic* evidence is evidence outside the official

---

from challenging the claim interpretation reached in the earlier proceeding. *Cf.* In re Trans Texas Holdings Corp., 498 F.3d 1290, 1297 (Fed. Cir. 2007) (stating that "[w]e have never applied issue preclusion *against* a non-party to the first action"). The Federal Circuit rejected reexamination applicant Trans Texas's argument that the USPTO should be bound by a federal district court's earlier (and narrower) interpretation of the same disputed claim limitations. Issue preclusion (also known as collateral estoppel) did not apply against the USPTO, which was not a party in the earlier district court proceeding. *See id.* Rather, the USPTO correctly applied a "broadest reasonable interpretation, consistent with the specification" rule in the reexamination proceeding. *See id.* at 1298.

Should it make any difference, in a later proceeding in which a party seeks to apply the claim interpretation from an earlier proceeding against a non-party to that earlier proceeding, if the Federal Circuit has "blessed" (i.e., reviewed and affirmed) the district court's claim interpretation in the earlier proceeding? In other words, should "law of the case" principles be expanded into "law of the patent" rules for patent litigation?

[55]90 F.3d 1576 (Fed. Cir. 1996) (reversing district court's summary judgment of noninfringement, based on an erroneous claim construction that improperly relied on extrinsic evidence to determine meaning of claim term "solder reflow temperature").

[56]The Federal Circuit for the first time as an *en banc* court expressed some reservation about reliance on a patent's prosecution history for claim interpretation purposes in *Phillips v. AWH Corp.*, 415 F.3d 1303 (Fed. Cir. 2005) (*en banc*):

> [B]ecause the prosecution history represents an ongoing negotiation between the PTO and the applicant, rather than the final product of that negotiation, it often lacks the clarity of the specification and thus is less useful for claim construction purposes. Nonetheless, the prosecution history can often inform the meaning of the claim language by demonstrating how the inventor understood the invention and whether the inventor limited the invention in the course of prosecution, making the claim scope narrower than it would otherwise be.

Id. at 1317 (citations omitted).

[57]*Vitronics* is somewhat ambiguous with respect to the status of prior art not cited in the prosecution history. *See* Hon. Paul R. Michel & Lisa A. Schneider, *Side Bar: Vitronics—Some Unanswered Questions, in* Donald S. Chisum et al., Principles of Patent Law, Cases and Materials 870, 871 (2d ed. 2001).

[58]Most pending patent applications are now published 18 months after their earliest effective filing date, in accordance with 35 U.S.C. §122(b).

administrative record of the patent's procurement, such as expert testimony.

Although literally extrinsic to the official administrative record, some Federal Circuit judges questioned whether *dictionaries* are properly classified as extrinsic evidence. The Federal Circuit opined in a 2001 decision that dictionaries hold a "special place" and "may sometimes be considered along with the intrinsic evidence when determining the ordinary meaning of claim terms."[59] In a 2002 decision the court went further, expressing the following view:

> As resources and references to inform and aid courts and judges in the understanding of technology and terminology, it is entirely proper for both trial and appellate judges to consult these materials at any stage of a litigation, regardless of whether they have been offered by a party in evidence or not. Thus, categorizing them as "extrinsic evidence" or even a "special form of extrinsic evidence" is misplaced and does not inform the analysis.[60]

Despite the tenor of these Federal Circuit decisions that dictionaries, encyclopedias, and treatises that were available at the time a patent was procured should be treated as intrinsic evidence, the *en banc* court clarified in 2005 that dictionaries are extrinsic evidence.[61] As such they may be useful construction tools, but they are not assigned primary importance in the evidentiary hierarchy for patent claim interpretation.

Vitronics instructs that, in most cases, the intrinsic evidence alone will be sufficient to resolve any claim interpretation issues. Only when the disputed patent claim terminology is still genuinely ambiguous following review of the public record of the patent may a district court rely on the extrinsic evidence.[62] Although a district court may always admit and use extrinsic evidence for the purpose of *understanding* the invention, it may not rely on the extrinsic evidence to arrive at a claim interpretation that is contrary to that provided by the intrinsic evidence.[63]

---

[59]Bell Atl. Network Servs., Inc. v. Covad Commc'ns Group, Inc., 262 F.3d 1258, 1267 (Fed. Cir. 2001).

[60]Texas Digital Sys., Inc., v. Telegenix, Inc., 308 F.3d 1193, 1203 (Fed. Cir. 2002).

[61]*See* Phillips v. AWH Corp., 415 F.3d 1303, 1318 (Fed. Cir. 2005) (*en banc*) (characterizing dictionaries and treatises as "[w]ithin the class of extrinsic evidence" that "can be useful in claim construction"). *See also* Section B.4 *infra* for further discussion of the use of dictionaries.

[62]*See* Vitronics Corp. v. Conceptronic, Inc., 90 F.3d 1576, 1583 (Fed. Cir. 1996) (stating that "[i]n those cases where the public record unambiguously describes the scope of the patented invention, reliance on any extrinsic evidence is improper").

[63]*See id.* at 1584 (stating that "extrinsic evidence in general, and expert testimony in particular, may be used only to help the court come to the proper understanding

4. The *Phillips* Debate: "Contextualist" Versus "Literalist" Approaches

Decisions of the Federal Circuit issued between 2002 and 2005 demonstrated a sharp divergence in approaches to patent claim interpretation. The Circuit judges appeared to have aligned themselves in two schools of thought on the issue: the "contextualist" and "literalist" viewpoints.[64] This divergence of interpretational methodologies led the court in 2004 to issue an *en banc* referendum on patent claim interpretation.[65] The basis of the dispute can be summarized as follows.

Federal Circuit judges who espoused the contextualist approach[66] seek the "felt meaning" of patent claim terms in the context of the invention described in the patent specification. They view the written description and drawings of the patent as the primary tool for discerning what terms in the patent's claims mean. Contextualist judges

---

of the claims; it may not be used to vary or contradict the claim language"). Federal Circuit Judge Rader has commented that the line between understanding and interpreting is a blurred one in the real world of patent litigation:

> As a matter of logic, this instruction is difficult to grasp. What is the distinction between a trial judge's understanding of the claims and a trial judge's interpretation of the claims to the jury? Don't judges instruct the jury in accordance with their understanding of the claims? In practice, how does this court's lofty appellate logic work? As this court acknowledges, a trial court must often resort to experts to learn complex new technologies. *See, e.g., Markman I,* 52 F.3d at 986. What happens when that learning influences a trial judge's interpretation of the claim terms? Are trial judges supposed to disguise the real reasons for their interpretation? How will this perverse incentive to "hide the ball" improve appellate review?

Cybor Corp. v. FAS Techs., 138 F.3d 1448, 1474-1475 (Fed. Cir. 1998) (*en banc*) (Rader, J., dissenting).

[64]Commentators charged during this era that outcomes in claim interpretation decisions were statistically predictable depending upon the composition of the panel of judges deciding the case. *See* Professor Polk Wagner's claim construction predictor tool ("If you know the panel, we'll predict the result!"), http://predictor.claimconstruction.com/ (last visited Aug. 12, 2012). Due to the subsequent effect of the Federal Circuit's decision in *Phillips v. AWH Corp.,* 415 F.3d 1303 (Fed. Cir. 2005) (*en banc*), discussed *infra,* Professor Wagner cautions that his claim construction predictor tool no longer reliably indicates the court's approach to claim construction. Nevertheless, he maintains the Web site for historical purposes. *See* http://predictor.claimconstruction.com/ (last visited Aug. 12, 2012).

[65]Phillips v. AWH Corp., 376 F.3d 1382 (Fed. Cir. July 21, 2004) (order) (*en banc*).

[66]Judges following the contextualist approach have also been referred to as "holistics" or "pragmatic textualists." *See* R. Polk Wagner & Lee Petherbridge, *Is the Federal Circuit Succeeding? An Empirical Assessment of Judicial Performance,*152 U. Pa. L. Rev. 1105, 1111 (2004) (dividing Federal Circuit into "holistic" and "procedural-ist" methodological approaches for patent claim interpretation); Craig Allen Nard, *A Theory of Claim Interpretation,* 14 Harv. J.L. & Tech. 1, 4-6 (2000) (dividing court into "hypertextualists" and "pragmatic textualists").

"look to the specification 'to ascertain the meaning of a claim term as it is used by the inventor in the context of the entirety of his invention.'"[67] The ordinary meaning of a term in a claim "must be considered in view of the intrinsic evidence: the claims, the specification, and the prosecution history."[68] This is the traditional approach to patent claim interpretation generally followed by the Federal Circuit in its decisions prior to 2002.

In contrast, Federal Circuit judges in the literalist school[69] took as their lodestar the court's 2002 decision in *Texas Digital Sys. v. Telegenix, Inc.*[70] In accordance with that decision, the literalist judges engage in a "heavy presumption" that claim terms carry the "ordinary and customary" meaning that a person having ordinary skill in the art (PHOSITA) would attribute to them. To discern this meaning the literalist judges typically consult definitions in dictionaries, technical treatises, and other evidentiary sources extrinsic to the patent itself.[71] Indeed, *Texas Digital* instructed that in construing patent claims, courts should consult the dictionary before turning to a patent's written description and drawings.[72] The ordinary and customary meaning as gleaned from dictionaries would be trumped only when a patent's written description or its prosecution history showed that the patentee was her "own lexicographer" in providing an explicit definition for a claim term, or had otherwise clearly disclaimed or disavowed the ordinary and customary meaning.

The April 2004 decision of a Federal Circuit panel in *Phillips v. AWH Corp.*[73] exemplifies the burgeoning conflict between the "literalist" and "contextualist" claim interpretation approaches. Phillips' patent was directed to modular, vandalism-resistant wall panels useful in building

[67]*See* Phillips v. AWH Corp., 363 F.3d 1207, 1213 (Fed. Cir. 2004) (Lourie, J.) (quoting Comark Commc'ns v. Harris Corp., 156 F.3d 1182, 1187 (Fed. Cir. 1998)), *vacated*, 376 F.3d 1382 (Fed. Cir. 2004) (order granting rehearing *en banc*).

[68]*See id.* (citing Rexnord Corp. v. Laitram Corp., 274 F.3d 1336, 1342-1343 (Fed. Cir. 2001)).

[69]Literalist judges have also been referred to as "proceduralists" or "hypertextualists." *See* R. Polk Wagner & Lee Petherbridge, *Is the Federal Circuit Succeeding? An Empirical Assessment of Judicial Performance*,152 U. PA. L. REV. 1105 (2004); Craig Allen Nard, *A Theory of Claim Interpretation*, 14 HARV. J.L. & TECH. 1 (2000).

[70]308 F.3d 1193 (Fed. Cir. 2002).

[71]Most often the literalist judges rely on general-usage dictionaries such as WEBSTER'S THIRD NEW INTERNATIONAL DICTIONARY. *See* Joseph Scott Miller & James A. Hilsenteger, *The Proven Key: Roles and Rules for Dictionaries at the Patent Office and the Courts*, 54 AM. U. L. REV. 829 (2005).

[72]The *Texas Digital* court concluded that it is improper to consult "the written description and prosecution history as a threshold step in the claim construction process, before any effort is made to discern the ordinary and customary meanings attributed to the words themselves." *Texas Digital*, 308 F.3d at 1204.

[73] 363 F.3d 1207 (Fed. Cir. Apr. 8, 2004), *vacated*, 376 F.3d 1382 (Fed. Cir. July 21, 2004) (order granting rehearing *en banc*).

prisons and security institutions.[74] The parties disputed the meaning
of "baffle" in the asserted patent claim, which recited in part, "means
disposed inside the [outer] shell for increasing its load bearing capacity comprising internal steel *baffles* extending inwardly from the steel
shell walls." The *Phillips* panel majority affirmed the district court's
reading of "baffle" as limited by the patent's specification to baffles
that are oriented at acute or obtuse angles other than 90 degrees from
the wall face. Such angles were necessary to the invention's purpose
of providing impact or projectile-resistant panels and constituted
the only embodiment of the invention depicted in the patent's figures as shown in Figure 9.1. Because the accused infringer used only
90 degree-angled baffles in its panels, the *Phillips* majority affirmed
the district court's grant of summary judgment of noninfringement.

Figure 9.1

Figures of the *Phillips* Patent Showing Internal Baffles

The dissenting Federal Circuit judge on the *Phillips* panel criticized
the majority for effectively limiting the claim to the preferred embodiment of the invention. The majority's reading was "contrary to the
plain meaning" of "baffle" in the absence of any "suggestion that the
patentee, acting as his own lexicographer, gave a special meaning to
the term baffles."[75] According to the dissent, the ordinary meaning as
set out in the dictionary should control, that is, "baffle" defined as "a
means for obstructing, impeding, or checking the flow of something."

---

[74]*See* Steel shell modules for prisoner detention facilities, U.S. Pat. No. 4,677,798
(issued July 7, 1987).

[75]*Phillips*, 363 F.3d at 1217 (Dyk, J., dissenting-in-part).

Limiting the claim to nonperpendicular (i.e., acute- or obtuse-angled) baffles was not required, because impact resistance/bullet deflection was only one of several objectives identified for the invention. Other objectives included structural stability and sound dampening. In the dissent's view, the assertion that an invention achieves several objectives did not require that the claims be limited to structures capable of achieving all of them.

On July 21, 2004, the *en banc* Federal Circuit vacated the panel decision in *Phillips* and ordered that the case be reheard.[76] One year later, the Federal Circuit announced its *en banc* decision on the merits in *Phillips*.[77] The *en banc* court decreed a return to the traditional contextualist analysis and downgraded the use of dictionaries in interpreting patent claims. Observing that excessive reliance on dictionaries risks claim interpretations that are abstract and divorced from the context of the invention, the *en banc* court explained that

> [t]he main problem with elevating the dictionary to such prominence is that it focuses the inquiry on the abstract meaning of words rather than on the meaning of claim terms within the context of the patent. Properly viewed, the "ordinary meaning" of a claim term is its meaning to the ordinary artisan after reading the entire patent. Yet heavy reliance on the dictionary divorced from the intrinsic evidence risks transforming the meaning of the claim term to the artisan into the meaning of the term in the abstract, out of its particular context, which is the specification.[78]

Thus, the *en banc Phillips* court reaffirmed, a patent's specification, rather than extrinsic evidence such as a dictionary, is "'the primary basis for construing the claims.'"[79]

---

[76]*See* Phillips v. AWH Corp., 376 F.3d 1382 (Fed. Cir. 2004) (order granting rehearing *en banc*). The Federal Circuit sought briefing from the parties and *amici* with respect to an extensive series of questions. *See id.* at 1383. Federal Circuit Judge H. Robert Mayer dissented in a separate opinion, charging that "any attempt to refine the process is futile" so long as the court refuses to reconsider "the fiction that claim construction is a matter of law." *Id.* at 1384.

[77]Phillips v. AWH Corp., 415 F.3d 1303 (Fed. Cir. 2005) (*en banc*).

[78]*Id.* at 1321.

[79]*Id.* at 1315 (quoting Standard Oil Co. v. Am. Cyanamid Co., 774 F.2d 448, 452 (Fed. Cir. 1985) (Rich, J.)). Although the *Phillips en banc* decision downgraded reliance on dictionaries for patent claim interpretation, it did not preclude their use in appropriate circumstances. The *en banc* court reaffirmed the Federal Circuit's earlier pronouncement in *Vitronics Corp. v. Conceptronic, Inc.*, 90 F.3d 1576 (Fed. Cir. 1996), that "judges are free to consult dictionaries and technical treatises 'at any time in order to better understand the underlying technology and may also rely on dictionary definitions when construing claim terms, so long as the dictionary definition does not contradict any definition found in or ascertained by a reading of the patent documents.'" *Phillips*, 415 F.3d at 1322-1323 (quoting *Vitronics*, 90 F.3d at 1584 n.6).

Despite its strong affirmance of the contextualist rationale, the *Phillips en banc* court disagreed with the panel majority on the merits and ultimately adopted the broader definition of a "baffle" as not limited to any particular angle and thus encompassing baffles perpendicular to the shell wall. The *en banc* court relied first on the principle of claim differentiation, noting for example that dependent claim 2 of Phillips' patent recited baffles that were "oriented with the panel sections disposed at angles for deflecting projectiles such as bullets able to penetrate the steel plates." The inclusion of such a specific limitation on the term "baffles" in claim 2 made it likely that the patentee did not contemplate that "baffles" as recited in independent claim 1 already incorporated that limitation.[80] Second, the *en banc* court observed (as the panel dissent had also noted) that the Phillips patent disclosed several functions for the baffles besides that of deflecting bullets, and concluded that claim 1 did not have to be interpreted narrowly so as to encompass each such function: "Although deflecting projectiles is one of the advantages of the baffles of the '798 patent, the patent does not require that the inward extending structures always be capable of performing that function."[81]

Answering some of the other questions posed by the July 2004 order for rehearing *en banc*, the *Phillips en banc* decision also held that the appropriate temporal perspective for assessing the words in a patent claim is their ordinary and customary meaning to a person having ordinary skill in the art in question "at the time of the invention, i.e., as of the effective filing date of the patent application."[82] Moreover, the maxim that claims should be interpreted so as to preserve their validity is of "limited utility" in general, and in any event is not applicable to the facts of *Phillips*.[83] The *en banc* decision did not address

---

[80]*Phillips*, 415 F.3d at 1324.

[81]*Id*. at 1327.

[82]*Id*. at 1313. This statement apparently refers to the concept of a *prima facie* invention date based on construing the patent application's filing date as the invention's constructive reduction to practice date. *See* Chapter 4, Section J, *supra*. The *Phillips en banc* decision does not explain the correct time frame for claim interpretation when the inventor can backdate her invention date from the filing date to her earlier conception date or actual reduction to practice date (assuming that the difference in dates would be material to the meaning of disputed claim terms).

[83]*See Phillips*, 415 F.3d at 1328. Although acknowledging the maxim of construing claims so as to preserve their validity, the *Phillips* court observed that in earlier decisions it had "not applied that principle broadly, and [had] certainly not endorsed a regime in which validity analysis is a regular component of claim construction." *Id*. at 1327. Rather, the relevancy of the doctrine should be limited to cases "in which 'the court concludes, after applying all the available tools of claim construction, that the claim is still ambiguous.'" *Id*. (quoting Liebel-Flarsheim Co. v. Medrad, Inc., 358 F.3d 898, 911 (Fed. Cir. 2004)). In such cases, courts should discern "whether it is reasonable to infer that the PTO would not have issued an invalid patent, and that the ambiguity in the claim language should therefore be resolved in a manner that would preserve

the controversial question of the appropriate standard of appellate review of claim interpretation decisions by district courts, leaving that dispute for another day.[84]

5. *Markman* Hearings

Many district courts now carry out their claim interpretation responsibilities in the context of a separate pre-trial hearing variously referred to as a "claim interpretation hearing" or a *Markman* hearing." District courts around the country vary widely in their approach to *Markman* hearings, and no uniform procedure exists.[85] Some district courts conduct the *Markman* hearing relatively early in a case, perhaps even before the close of discovery. Other courts conduct the *Markman* hearing in the context of a motion for summary judgment of infringement or noninfringement. A 1997 American Bar Association report indicated that 85 percent of *Markman* hearings are conducted prior to trial but after the close of discovery.[86] The federal district court for the Northern District of California, San Jose, was the first U.S.

---

the patent's validity." *Id.* In *Phillips,* however, the term "baffle" was "not ambiguous" and could therefore "be construed without the need to consider whether one possible construction would render the claim invalid while the other would not." *Id.* at 1328.

[84]*See* Section B.6 ("Appellate Review of Claim Interpretation"), *infra,* for more background on this issue. Federal Circuit (and former Chief) Judge H. Robert Mayer, joined by Judge Pauline Newman, wrote a stinging dissent to the *Phillips en banc* majority's failure to address the standard of review question, emphasizing the "futility, indeed the absurdity, of [the] court's persistence in adhering to the falsehood that claim construction is a matter of law devoid of any factual component." *Id.* at 1330.

[85]*See* Committee No. 601—Federal Practice and Procedure, *Reports Considered (Annual Report 2000-01), in* ABA Section of Intellectual Property Law, Annual Reports 1996-2001, *available at* http://www.abanet.org/intelprop/intelprop.pdf, which provides in part:

> As a consequence, *Markman* hearings (as claim construction hearings are known) "run the gamut from mid-trial sidebar conferences that undergird relevance rulings . . . to virtual mini-trials extending over several days and generating extensive evidentiary records." Some courts prefer an early decision, with others warning that claim construction at too early a stage in a case may constitute an unconstitutional advisory opinion. Other courts address the question following discovery. Some favor the combination of claim construction with summary judgment motions, while others warn against it, citing the risk of "erodi[ng] . . . the role of the fact finder in patent litigation." Still other courts defer claim construction until after the close of evidence at trial.

Id. at 615 (footnotes and citations omitted).

[86]*See* Committee No. 601—Federal Practice and Procedure, *Reports Considered (Annual Report 1997-98), in* ABA Section of Intellectual Property Law, Annual Reports 1996-2001, at 2716, *available at* http://www.abanet.org/intelprop/intelprop. pdf (summarizing survey results).

court to adopt a set of local rules that provide a very detailed procedure and timetable for claim interpretation and other pre-trial patent matters.[87]

Following a claim interpretation hearing, a district court will typically issue an order setting forth the manner in which the claims will be construed in the remainder of the case.[88] Although a number of parties have attempted to obtain immediate Federal Circuit review of district court claim interpretations through the vehicle of a certified question for interlocutory appeal under 28 U.S.C. §1292(b), thus far the Federal Circuit has denied all such appeals. Thus, a litigant's chance of getting an early Federal Circuit review of a claim interpretation depends on the grant of a motion for summary judgment on the infringement issue that permits an immediate appeal.[89] Absent the district court granting such a summary judgment, claim interpretations generally will not be reviewed by the Federal Circuit until appeal is taken from a final judgment rendered after the completion of trial.

6. Appellate Review of Claim Interpretation

What standard of review does the Federal Circuit apply to a district court's claim interpretation? The controlling case on this question is *Cybor Corp. v. FAS Techs., Inc.*[90] Recall that in *Markman,* the Supreme Court clearly held that patent claim interpretation is for the court rather than the jury. But by referring to claim interpretation as a "mongrel practice,"[91] the Court left some question as to whether

---

[87]The U.S. District Court for the Northern District of California first promulgated a set of Patent Local Rules effective January 1, 2001. Revised rules are now in effect. *See* Northern Dist. of Cal., *Patent Local Rules* (last rev. Dec. 1, 2009), *available at* http://www.cand.uscourts.gov/localrules/patent.

[88]For a helpful example of a district court's *Markman* order, *see* Neomagic Corp. v. Trident Microsystems, Inc., 98 F. Supp. 2d 538 (D. Del. 2000) (McKelvie, J.) (construing claim terms), *later proceeding,* 129 F. Supp. 2d 689 (D. Del. 2001) (granting defendant's motion for summary judgment of no infringement), *aff'd-in-part, vacated-in-part, and remanded,* 287 F.3d 1062 (Fed. Cir. 2002).

[89]"A substantial majority of patent cases decided by the Federal Circuit are on appeals from summary judgment." University of Houston Law Center—Institute for Intellectual Property and Information Law, *Patstats: U.S. Patent Litigation Statistics,* http://www.patstats.org/Patstats3.html (last visited Nov. 11, 2008). *See also* Nystrom v. TREX Co., 339 F.3d 1347 (Fed. Cir. 2003) (dismissing appeal for lack of jurisdiction where district court granted summary judgment of noninfringement based on its claim construction rulings but stayed counterclaim on invalidity and unenforceability, thereby violating the final judgment rule of 28 U.S.C. §1295).

[90]138 F.3d 1448 (Fed. Cir. 1998) (*en banc*).

[91]Markman v. Westview Instruments, 517 U.S. 370, 378 (1996).

a district court in carrying out its interpretational responsibilities is making an entirely legal determination or instead needs to find facts.

Because of continued disagreement among Federal Circuit judges over this fact-versus-law question, the appellate court went *en banc* to resolve the issue. In *Cybor,* a majority of Federal Circuit judges agreed that claim interpretation is entirely a legal determination.[92] No findings of fact are made by a district court in the construction of claims. Thus, the Federal Circuit reviews a district court's claim interpretation under the *de novo* (i.e., no deference) standard of review.

Supporters of the *Cybor* decision contend that it promotes greater uniformity in the treatment of a given patent. For example, consider a hypothetical in which two different district courts construed the same patent claim, and one court interpreted the disputed language in a manner that rendered the patent invalid while the other court reached a contrary decision and sustained validity. If the Federal Circuit were required to defer to each of these opposing interpretations as factual findings, an unacceptable level of inconsistency would result.

Detractors of *Cybor* point to the dissent of Circuit Judge Rader, who cited a study indicating that approximately 40 percent of the claim interpretation decisions reviewed on appeal by the Federal Circuit are reversed.[93] In Judge Rader's view, shared by many patent litigators, this level of uncertainty renders the patent litigation process little better than a coin toss in terms of predictability of outcome. Former Federal Circuit Chief Judge Mayer charged that the Federal Circuit's continued treatment of claim interpretation as lacking any factual component has resulted in "mayhem," which "seriously undermine[s] the legitimacy of the process, if not the integrity of the institution." [94]

Despite the rather strident tone of the *Cybor* majority opinion that district courts deserve no deference in their claim interpretations because these determinations are entirely legal rather than factual, some members of the Federal Circuit appear to take a more pragmatic, common-sense position. These judges suggest that, despite the "no deference" absolutism of the *Cybor* majority, in practice the Federal Circuit will give weight to a district court's claim interpretation commensurate with the degree of care taken by the district court in its analysis and the informational value of the record that the district court considered.[95]

---

[92]*See Cybor,* 138 F.3d at 1456 (holding that "as a purely legal question, we review claim construction *de novo* on appeal including any allegedly fact-based questions relating to claim construction").

[93]*See id.* at 1476 (Rader, J., dissenting).

[94]Phillips v. AWH Corp., 415 F.3d 1303, 1330 (Fed. Cir. 2005) (Mayer, J., dissenting).

[95]*See Cybor*, 138 F.3d at 1462 (Plager, J., concurring); *id.* at 1463 (Bryson, J., concurring).

This pragmatic approach can be taken only so far. As of the writing of this edition in 2012, Federal Circuit judges continue to sharply disagree on the proper appellate standard of review for district court claim interpretation decisions. A significant number of Federal Circuit judges have repeatedly called for reevaluation of the 1998 *en banc* decision in *Cybor.* For example, in her 2011 dissent from denial of rehearing *en banc* in *Retractable Techs., Inc. v. Becton, Dickinson and Co.,*[96] Judge Moore observed that the Federal Circuit has "waited five years (since *Amgen Inc. v. Hoechst Marion Roussel, Inc.,* 469 F.3d 1039 (Fed. Cir. 2006), where six judges claimed a willingness to review *Cybor*) for that ever-elusive perfect vehicle to review the issue of deference to the district court's claim construction." She urged that it "is time to rethink the deference we give to district court claim constructions and the fallacy that the entire process is one of law."[97] Also dissenting from denial of rehearing *en banc* in *Retractable Techs.,* Judge O'Malley flatly stated that "[i]t is time to revisit and reverse our decision in *Cybor.* . . . That decision was ill considered thirteen years ago and has not proven 'beneficial' to patent jurisprudence 'in the long run.'"[98] Judge O'Malley (the only former federal district court judge serving on the Federal Circuit as of 2012) noted that since the Supreme Court's 1996 *Markman* decision that assigned them the task of patent claim construction,

> district judges have been trained to—and do—engage in detailed and thoughtful analysis of the claim construction issues presented to them. They conduct live hearings with argument and testimony, sometimes covering several days, and certainly always extending beyond the mere minutes that courts of appeals have to devote to live exchanges with counsel. Simply, "the trial court has tools to acquire and evaluate evidence that this court lacks." *Cybor,* 138 F.3d at 1477 (Rader, J., dissenting).[99]

In addition to the standard of review issue, another matter of concern in Federal Circuit review of district court claim interpretations is the Circuit's refusal to accept any interlocutory appeals of these determinations under 28 U.S.C. §1292(b). Although a number

[96]659 F.3d 1369, 1373 (Fed. Cir. 2011) (Moore, J., joined by Rader, C.J., dissenting from denial of rehearing *en banc*).

[97]*Retractable Techs.,* 659 F.3d at 1373 (Moore, J., joined by Rader, C.J., dissenting from denial of rehearing *en banc*).

[98]*Retractable Techs.,* 659 F.3d at 1373-1374 (O'Malley, J., dissenting from denial of rehearing *en banc*) (quoting Cybor Corp. v. FAS Techs., Inc., 138 F.3d 1448, 1463 (Fed. Cir. 1998) (Plager, J., concurring) ("Whether this approach to patent litigation will in the long run prove beneficial remains to be seen.")).

[99]*Retractable Techs.,* 659 F.3d at 1374 (O'Malley, J., dissenting from denial of rehearing *en banc*).

of district courts have certified their claim interpretation determinations as "involv[ing] a controlling question of law as to which there is substantial ground for difference of opinion and that an immediate appeal from the order may materially advance the ultimate termination of the litigation,"[100] the Federal Circuit has thus far exercised its discretion to refuse all such appeals.[101] One can legitimately question whether the Federal Circuit should "have it both ways" in applying a *de novo* standard of review for claim interpretations while refusing to accept any interlocutory appeals from those determinations.[102]

7. Claim Interpretation Canons

A number of rules or "canons" exist for interpreting patent claims, developed primarily through case law. Some of the most important rules to keep in mind are:

- Claim terms are interpreted from the perspective of the hypothetical person having ordinary skill in the art (the PHOSITA), rather than a judge, jury, or technical expert.
- The general rule is that claim terms are assigned their ordinary and customary meaning to the PHOSITA.[103]

[100]28 U.S.C. §1292(b).

[101]*See Cybor*, 138 F.3d at 1479 (Newman, J., stating "additional views") (observing that "[a]lthough the district courts have extended themselves, and so-called '*Markman* hearings' are common, this has not been accompanied by interlocutory review of the trial judge's claim interpretation. The Federal Circuit has thus far declined all such certified questions.").

[102]See Craig Allen Nard, *Intellectual Property Challenges in the Next Century: Process Considerations in the Age of Markman and Mantras*, 2001 U. ILL. L. REV. 355, 357 (2001).

[103]*See* Phillips v. AWH Corp., 415 F.3d 1303, 1312 (Fed. Cir. 2005) (*en banc*) ("We have frequently stated that the words of a claim 'are generally given their ordinary and customary meaning.'") (quoting *Vitronics Corp. v. Conceptronic, Inc.*, 90 F.3d 1576, 1582 (Fed. Cir. 1996)); Bell Atl. Network Servs., Inc. v. Covad Commc'ns Group, Inc., 262 F.3d 1258, 1267 (Fed. Cir. 2001).

A line of Federal Circuit decisions admits only narrow exceptions to the "general" rule. *See, e.g.*, Thorner v. Sony Computer Ent. Am. LLC, 669 F.3d 1362, 1365 (Fed. Cir. 2012), stating:

> The words of a claim are generally given their ordinary and customary meaning as understood by a person of ordinary skill in the art when read in the context of the specification and prosecution history. *See Phillips v. AWH Corp.*, 415 F.3d 1303, 1313 (Fed. Cir. 2005) (*en banc*). There are only two exceptions to this general rule: 1) when a patentee sets out a definition and acts as his own lexicographer, or 2) when the patentee disavows the full scope of a claim term either in the specification or during prosecution. *Vitronics Corp. v. Conceptronic, Inc.*, 90 F.3d 1576, 1580 (Fed. Cir. 1996).

- An important exception to the general rule is that a patentee "may be her own lexicographer." In other words, a patentee may choose to redefine a claim term away from its common, ordinary meaning. Most typically, this will be accomplished through an *express* redefinition, as where a patent's written description expressly states that "as used herein, the term 'primary color' means brown, black, or purple." Less typically, a patentee may be her own lexicographer and redefine a term *implicitly,* by a consistent use of a term in a particular way throughout the written description, even without an express definitional statement of what the term means.[104]
- A fine line often must be drawn between properly interpreting claims in light of the written description, and improperly narrowing the claims by reading in limitations from the written description.[105]
- Courts generally should not adopt a claim interpretation that would exclude the preferred embodiment of an invention, although rare exceptions have been recognized in which a patentee amended the claims during prosecution in such a manner as to exclude the preferred embodiment.[106]
- The principle of *claim differentiation* provides that the existence of a narrower dependent claim shows that the broader claim from which it depends is not so limited.[107] For example, consider the following example in which the patent's written description refers to widgets of a "primary color":

> Claim 1. A widget of a primary color.
> Claim 2. The widget of claim 1 wherein said primary color is blue.

See also Aventis Pharma S.A. v. Hospira, Inc., 675 F.3d 1324, 1330 (Fed. Cir. 2012) (reiterating *Thorner*'s "stringent standard for narrowing a claim term beyond its plain and ordinary meaning").

[104]*See* Bell Atl. Network Servs., Inc. v. Covad Commc'ns Group, Inc., 262 F.3d 1258, 1273 (Fed. Cir. 2001) (concluding that patentee "defined the [claim] term 'mode' by implication, through the term's consistent use throughout the [] patent specification").

[105]*See* Unique Concepts, Inc. v. Brown, 939 F.2d 1558, 1561-1563 (Fed. Cir. 1991).

[106]*See, e.g.,* Elekta Instrument S.A. v. O.U.R. Scientific Int'l, Inc., 214 F.3d 1302 (Fed. Cir. 2000).

[107]More broadly stated, the claim differentiation principle means that when a claim of a patent "does not contain a certain limitation and another claim [of that patent] does, that limitation cannot be read into the former claim in determining either validity or infringement." SRI Int'l v. Matsushita Elec. Corp., 775 F.2d 1107, 1122 (Fed. Cir. 1985) (*en banc*). There are limits, however. *See* O.I. Corp. v. Tekmar Co., 115 F.3d 1576, 1582 (Fed. Cir. 1997) (stating that "the doctrine [of claim differentiation] cannot alter a definition that is otherwise clear from the claim language, description, and prosecution history").

B. Step One: Patent Claim Interpretation

The existence of dependent claim 2 shows that independent claim 1 includes blue widgets but is not limited to blue widgets—claim 1 also literally reads on red widgets and yellow widgets.[108]

[108]A series of 2011-2012 Federal Circuit decisions evidences strong disagreement within the court concerning the relative persuasive weight due the claim differentiation principle as compared with disclosure set forth in a patent's written description and drawings. These decisions suggest that, despite the *en banc* resolution of other claim interpretation issues in the 2005 *Phillips* decision, a claim interpretation schism continues post-*Phillips*. *Compare* Arlington Indus., Inc. v. Bridgeport Fittings, Inc., 632 F.3d 1246, 1253-1256 (Fed. Cir. 2011) (Rader, C.J., joined by Moore, J.) (broadly interpreting "spring metal adaptor" of claimed electrical junction box fitting as simply formed from spring metal and not requiring a split or opening; relying *inter alia* on claim differentiation principle because the limitation "less than a complete circle" was added to independent claim 1 of parent application during its prosecution but not added to independent claim 22 of continuation application that issued as '050 patent in suit) *with* Retractable Techs., Inc. v. Becton, Dickinson and Co., 653 F.3d 1296, 1305 (Fed. Cir. 2011) (Lourie, J., joined by Plager, J.) (narrowly interpreting "body" of safety syringe as limited to one-piece construction because that construction was "required to tether the claims to what the specifications indicate the inventor actually invented"; stating that despite presence of a "one-piece" limitation in dependent claims of patent in suit but not in its independent claims, "any presumption created by the doctrine of claim differentiation [is] 'overcome by a contrary construction dictated by the written description or prosecution history'") (quoting Seachange Int'l, Inc. v. C-COR, Inc., 413 F.3d 1361, 1369 (Fed. Cir. 2005)).

Notably, Judge Lourie, author of the majority opinion in *Retractable Techs.,* dissented in *Arlington Indus.,* and Judge Rader, author of the majority opinion in *Arlington Indus.,* dissented in *Retractable Techs. See Arlington Indus.,* 632 F.3d at 1258 (Lourie, J., concurring-in-part and dissenting-in-part) (stating that "[t]he bottom line of claim construction should be that the claims should not mean more than what the specification indicates, one way or another, the inventors invented"); *id.* at 1257 (stating that "[i]n colloquial terms, 'you should get what you disclose'"); *Retractable Techs.,* 653 F.3d at 1312 (Rader, C.J., dissenting-in-part) (stating that in *Phillips v. AWH Corp.,* 415 F.3d 1303, 1312 (Fed. Cir. 2005) (*en banc*), Federal Circuit recognized as "bedrock principle" that "the claims themselves, not the written description portion of the specification, define the invention"); *id.* (stating that claim differentiation principle is "'especially strong when the limitation in dispute is the only meaningful difference between an independent and dependent claim, and one party is urging that the limitation in the dependent claim should be read into the independent claim'") (quoting SunRace Roots Enter. Co., Ltd. v. SRAM Corp., 336 F.3d 1298, 1303 (Fed. Cir. 2003)).

The debate concerning the proper weight to be given the claim differentiation principle continued (without resolution) in *Marine Polymer Techs., Inc. v. HemCon, Inc.,* 672 F.3d 1350 (Fed. Cir. 2012) (*en banc*). The Federal Circuit in *Marine Polymer* split 5-5 on the claim interpretation issue, thus affirming the district court's interpretation. The claim interpretation dispute concerned the meaning of "biocompatible" for certain claimed "biocompatible" purified compositions of a naturally occurring polymer used to treat traumatic bleeding. Writing for a five-judge plurality, Judge Lourie admitted that accused infringer HemCon's claim construction arguments were "not baseless." *Marine Polymer,* 672 F.3d at 1359. Hemcon's arguments highlighted the inconsistency between the district court's narrow construction of "biocompatible" as permitting "*no detectable biological reactivity as determined by biocompatibility tests,*" *id.* at 1356 (emphasis added), and dependent claims of the patent in suit that required non-zero scores on "elution" tests, one of four types of tests disclosed for testing biocompatibility.

C.   Step Two: Comparing the Properly Interpreted Claims to the Accused Device

The second step of the patent infringement analysis requires that each limitation of the properly interpreted claim be met in the accused device, either literally or equivalently. Although referred to in some earlier decisions as the all-elements rule, this doctrine is more properly termed the all-limitations rule.[109] Infringement cannot be determined by comparing the claimed and accused devices as a whole; the analysis must be performed on a limitation-by-limitation level. Each limitation of a patent claim is material. If even a single limitation is not met in the accused device, there cannot be infringement. For example, if a patent claims "a widget comprising parts A, B, C, D, and E," and an accused widget incorporates parts A, B, C, and E, but lacks a part D (or an equivalent of part D), then the accused widget cannot infringe.

The all-limitations rule incorporates the two basic types of infringement recognized in U.S. patent law: (1) literal infringement and (2) infringement under the judicially created doctrine of equivalents. Each is discussed below.

1.   Literal Infringement

Literal infringement is found where the accused subject matter falls precisely within the express boundaries of the claim. For example, if a claim recites

---

Even if "not baseless," however, Hemcon's arguments "essentially amount[ed] to a conflict between teachings in the specification and the doctrine of claim differentiation. As we have held, claim differentiation is 'not a hard and fast rule and will be overcome by a contrary construction dictated by the written description or prosecution history.'" *Marine Polymer*, 672 F.3d at 1359 (quoting Seachange Int'l, Inc. v. C-COR, Inc., 413 F.3d 1361, 1369 (Fed. Cir. 2005); citing also Laitram Corp. v. Rexnord, Inc., 939 F.2d 1533, 1538 (Fed. Cir. 1991) ("Claim differentiation is a guide, not a rigid rule.")).

Writing for the other five judges on the claim interpretation issue, Judge Dyk countered that "[i]f 'biocompatible' [as present in six independent claims] requires that there be no reactivity, but [six] dependent claims require slight or mild reactivity, they are nullified and become utterly meaningless. . . . Where a particular construction of an independent claim would nullify claims that depend from it, the doctrine of claim differentiation creates a presumption that such a construction is improper." *Marine Polymer*, 672 F.3d at 1368 (citing Liebel-Flarsheim Co. v. Medrad, Inc., 358 F.3d 898, 910 (Fed. Cir. 2004)).

[109]Patent attorneys and Federal Circuit judges sometimes use the words "element" and "limitation" interchangeably. The preferred usage is to speak of limitations of a patent claim and elements of an accused device. *See* Dawn Equip. Co. v. Kentucky Farms Inc., 140 F.3d 1009, 1014 n.1 (Fed. Cir. 1998); Perkin-Elmer Corp. v. Westinghouse Elec. Corp., 822 F.2d 1528, 1533 n.9 (Fed. Cir. 1987).

C. Step Two: Comparing the Properly Interpreted Claims

1. A composition of matter comprising 20-30 percent component X by weight.

and the accused composition includes 25 percent component X, then claim 1 is literally infringed.[110] If the accused composition includes only 15 percent X, however, claim 1 is not literally infringed.[111]

One might expect instances of literal infringement to be relatively rare, assuming that patent claims provide clear, advance notice to competitors of what is and is not permissible imitation. Competitors could reasonably be expected to read the claims and plan their activities accordingly so as to avoid literal infringement. As the Supreme Court has recognized, "[o]utright and forthright duplication is a dull and very rare type of infringement." [112]

In practice, instances of literal infringement are quite common. This follows from the uncertainty of claim interpretation, that is, the pre-litigation ambiguity of the literal scope of the claims. Despite the aspirational goal that patent claims should provide clear, advance notice of the literal scope of the patentee's exclusionary right, as well as the statutory presumption that the claims of an issued patent comply with the definiteness requirement of 35 U.S.C. §112(b) (eff. Sept. 16, 2012), the meaning of one or more terms in the allegedly infringed claim(s) is hotly disputed in practically every patent infringement litigation.[113] An accused infringer may be held to literally infringe a claim that it intended to avoid when that claim is interpreted broadly enough in later litigation to literally read on the accused device. Even technology arising after the patent in suit may literally infringe, if the claims are construed broadly enough (and, of course, are still valid under that broad construction).[114]

---

[110]Note here that because the claim uses an open "comprising" transition, the accused composition may include anything else besides component X but nevertheless still literally infringe.

[111]One might still consider whether the accused composition having 15 percent X infringes under the doctrine of equivalents, although some Federal Circuit decisions applying a theory of "vitiation" of claim limitations would answer in the negative. The court's vitiation jurisprudence remains unsettled. *See* Section D.5, *infra*.

[112]Graver Tank & Mfg. Co. v. Linde Air Prods. Co., 339 U.S. 605, 607 (1950).

[113]*See* University of Houston Law Center—Institute for Intellectual Property and Information Law, *Patstats: U.S. Patent Litigation Statistics*, http://www.patstats.org/Patstats3.html (last visited Nov. 11, 2008) (concluding about patent claim interpretation that "[i]t is safe to say that it is an important contested point in nearly all infringement decisions and some validity rulings.").

[114]*See* Innogenetics, N.V. v. Abbott Labs., 512 F.3d 1363, 1371-1372 (Fed. Cir. 2008). The *Innogenetics* court rejected Abbott's argument that it did not literally infringe because the "Realtime PCR" utilized in Abbott's accused genotyping assay kits was not known to the ordinary artisan when Innogenetics filed the application leading to its '704 patent in suit. *See id.* In so holding the court relied on its earlier decision in *SuperGuide Corp. v. DirecTV Enters., Inc.*, 358 F.3d 870 (Fed. Cir. 2004), in which

2. Infringement Under the Doctrine of Equivalents

United States patent law also recognizes the possibility of "nonliteral" or "nontextual" infringement under the doctrine of equivalents.[115] Notably, the doctrine of equivalents is entirely judge-made law; it does not appear in the Patent Act.[116] Although the Supreme Court has repeatedly reaffirmed the doctrine's viability, it has also pointedly recognized that "Congress can legislate the doctrine of equivalents out of existence any time it chooses." [117]

a. Historical Origins

The doctrine of equivalents has its U.S. genesis in early Supreme Court patent cases such as *Winans v. Denmead*.[118] There the Court found that a patent claiming the configuration of a railroad coal car having a cylindrical, cone-like shape was infringed by an accused car shaped in cross-section like an octagon. *Winans* does not expressly refer to a doctrine of equivalents, but such a doctrine is implied in the result of the case.

Claiming practice at the time of *Winans* (i.e., prior to the Patent Act of 1870) was much more of a **central claiming** regime than the **peripheral claiming** system used today in the United States. Under the central claiming regime, a claim recited the "preferred embodiment" of the invention but was deemed as a matter of law to include

---

it found that the claim limitation "regularly received television signals" was broad enough to literally encompass digital signals, even though no televisions capable of receiving digital signals existed at the time that SuperGuide filed its patent application. *See id.* at 878-880; *Innogenetics*, 512 F.3d at 1371-1372. Note, however, that functional claim limitations drafted in the means-plus-function (MPF) format of 35 U.S.C. §112(f) (eff. Sept. 16, 2012) are treated more narrowly than the non-MPF claim limitations at issue in *Innogenetics* and *SuperGuide*. *See* Al-Site Corp. v. VSI Int'l, Inc., 174 F.3d 1308, 1320 (Fed. Cir. 1999) (holding that "[a]n equivalent structure or act under §112 cannot embrace technology developed after the issuance of the patent because the literal meaning of a claim is fixed upon its issuance").

[115]The proper name of this doctrine is the doctrine of *equivalents,* not the doctrine of *equivalence.*

[116]The doctrine of equivalents should not be confused with the related but separate notion of *statutory* equivalency under 35 U.S.C. §112(f) (eff. Sept. 16, 2012) (referred to pre–America Invents Act of 2011 as "§112, ¶6"). These statutory equivalents are part of the *literal* scope of an MPF claim. *See supra* Chapter 2 ("Patent Claims"); Pennwalt Corp. v. Durand-Wayland, Inc., 833 F.2d 931, 934 (Fed. Cir. 1987) (*en banc*) (explaining that "[s]ection 112, paragraph 6, plays no role in determining whether an equivalent function is performed by the accused device under the doctrine of equivalents").

[117]Warner-Jenkinson Co. v. Hilton Davis Chem. Co., 520 U.S. 17, 28 (1997).

[118]56 U.S. 330 (1853).

all equivalents to (i.e., substantially similar copies of) that preferred embodiment.[119] The *Winans* Court recognized that

> [t]he exclusive right to the thing patented is not secured, if the public are at liberty to make substantial copies of it, varying its form or proportions. And, therefore, the patentee, having described his invention, and shown its principles, and claimed it in that form which most perfectly embodies it, is, in contemplation of law, deemed to claim every form in which his invention may be copied, unless he manifests an intention to disclaim some of those forms.[120]

Thus, the central claiming regime in effect at the time of *Winans* recognized that the patentee's invention was not truly protected unless the patent prohibited not only the unauthorized making of *identical* copies, but also the making of "substantial" copies thereof. As the U.S. patent system eventually transitioned from central claiming to the peripheral claiming system used today, the underlying goal of protecting the patentee to the full extent of her contribution has been maintained and resurrected, so to speak, in the guise of the judicially recognized doctrine of equivalents.

b. *Policy Rationales*

As the Court in *Graver Tank & Mfg. Co. v. Linde Air Prods. Co.*[121] characterized it, the essential thrust of the doctrine of equivalents is that "one may not practice a fraud on a patent."[122] The doctrine of equivalents is a judicial response to the practical reality that if a patent can be avoided by copying the claimed invention while making a minor, insubstantial change of just enough scope to take the copied matter outside of the literal boundaries of the claim, the right to exclude that the patent bestows will not be worth very much. If the value of a patent is lessened by an inability to stop nonliteral copyists, the economic incentive to innovate that the patent represents is likewise diminished and society suffers a resulting impoverishment of new inventions.

In addition to this economic/fairness rationale, the doctrine of equivalents also serves as an important linguistic safety valve. Judicial recognition of the doctrine of equivalents reflects that words are not always the optimal medium for conveying inventive concepts.

---

[119]*Cf. Warner-Jenkinson,* 520 U.S. at 27 n.4 (characterizing central claiming as "describing the core principles of the invention" and peripheral claiming as "describing the outer boundaries of the invention").

[120]*Winans,* 56 U.S. at 343.

[121]339 U.S. 605 (1950).

[122]*Id.* at 608.

Many inventions are best embodied in physical prototypes, mechanical drawings, molecular modeling, or other nonlingual scientific and technical media. Particularly when dealing with "pioneer" inventions involving state-of-the-art technology for which there may not yet exist a recognized, well-established vocabulary, the doctrine of equivalents is an essential tool for conveying to the patent owner the full benefit of her invention.[123]

c. Tension with the Notice Function of Claims

These rationales in support of the doctrine of equivalents admittedly conflict with the principle that claims are intended to provide clear, advance notice to competitors of the scope of the patentee's right to exclude.[124] As the Supreme Court summed it up, "[a] patent holder should know what he owns, and the public should know what he does not."[125] A certain tension arises when courts find liability under the doctrine of equivalents, because they are extending the right to exclude beyond that denoted by the literal boundaries of the patent's claims.[126] How useful is the advance "notice" provided by patent claims if we essentially ignore it for equitable reasons in applying the doctrine of

---

[123]As expressed in a classic passage from *Autogiro Co. of Am. v. United States*, 384 F.2d 391, 397 (Ct. Cl. 1967):

> An invention exists most importantly as a tangible structure or a series of drawings. A verbal portrayal is usually an afterthought written to satisfy the requirements of patent law. This conversion of machine to words allows for unintended idea gaps which cannot be satisfactorily filled. Often the invention is novel and words do not exist to describe it. The dictionary does not always keep abreast of the inventor. It cannot. Things are not made for the sake of words, but words for things.

[124]*See* Festo Corp. v. Shoketsu Kinzoku Kogyo Kabushiki Co., 535 U.S. 722, 727 (2002) (stating that "we appreciate[ ] that by extending protection beyond the literal terms in a patent the doctrine of equivalents can create substantial uncertainty about where the patent monopoly ends. If the range of equivalents is unclear, competitors may be unable to determine what is a permitted alternative to a patented invention and what is an infringing equivalent.") (citations omitted).

[125]*Id.* at 731.

[126]*See* Wilson Sporting Goods Co. v. David Geoffrey & Assocs., 904 F.2d 677 (Fed. Cir. 1990) (Rich, J.):

> To say that the doctrine of equivalents extends or enlarges the *claims* is a contradiction in terms. The claims—i.e., the scope of patent protection as *defined* by the claims—remain the same and application of the doctrine *expands the right to exclude* to "equivalents" of what is claimed. The doctrine of equivalents, by definition, involves going beyond any permissible interpretation of the claim language; i.e., it involves determining whether the accused product is "equivalent" to what is described by the claim language.

Id. at 684 (emphases in original).

equivalents? This undeniable tension has been succinctly described as the "fair protection–certainty conundrum."[127]

d. All-Limitations Rule

In *Warner-Jenkinson Co. v. Hilton Davis Chem. Co.,*[128] the Supreme Court instructed that we can minimize the fair protection–certainty conundrum by vigilant application of the all-elements rule, which requires that the doctrine of equivalents be applied on a claim limitation-by-limitation basis rather than to the "invention as a whole."[129] The Court stated:

> Each element contained in a patent claim is deemed material to defining the scope of the patented invention, and thus the doctrine of equivalents must be applied to individual elements of the claim, not to the invention as a whole. It is important to ensure that the application of the doctrine, even as to an individual element, is not allowed such broad play as to effectively eliminate that element in its entirety.[130]

For example, if a patent claim recites "a widget comprising lever A, pulley B, and spring C," the doctrine of equivalents must be separately applied to determine if (1) lever A of the claimed invention is equivalently met in the accused device; (2) if pulley B of the claimed invention is equivalently met in the accused device; and (3) if spring C of the claimed invention is equivalently met in the accused device. If any of these three limitations is not met equivalently (or literally), there can be no infringement.

e. What Is a Limitation?

Applying the all-limitations rule requires that we first identify each limitation of a claim. Often the task of determining what portion of a patent claim represents a discrete limitation (also sometimes referred to as an element)[131] is not so straightforward. The answer will depend on the level of generality that the court reviewing the matter chooses to adopt.

[127]Donald S. Chisum, *The Scope of Protection For Patents After The Supreme Court's* Warner-Jenkinson *Decision: The Fair Protection–Certainty Conundrum*, 14 SANTA CLARA COMPUTER & HIGH TECH. L.J. 1, 6 (1998).

[128]520 U.S. 17 (1997).

[129]*See id.* at 29.

[130]*Id.*

[131]The preferred usage is to speak of limitations of a patent claim and elements of an accused device. *See* Dawn Equip. Co. v. Kentucky Farms Inc., 140 F.3d 1009, 1014 n.1 (Fed. Cir. 1998); Perkin-Elmer Corp. v. Westinghouse Elec. Corp., 822 F.2d 1528, 1533 n.9 (Fed. Cir. 1987).

For example, consider the interpretation of a patent claim to a widget "having a plastic tube." The district court may consider "plastic" and "tube" to be two separate limitations, such that each limitation would separately need to be met in the accused device in order to find infringement. Thus, if the accused device was a widget that used a steel pipe rather than a plastic tube, the fact finder in the second step of the infringement analysis (whether judge or jury) would need to separately determine (1) whether the steel used in the accused widget's pipe is insubstantially different from the plastic of the claimed tube, and (2) whether the pipe of the accused widget is insubstantially different from the claimed tube. With respect to question (1) the fact finder might evaluate the insubstantiality of the differences by asking whether steel performs the same function in the accused widget's pipe as plastic does in the claimed tube, in substantially the same way, to achieve substantially the same result. Known interchangeability of steel and plastic in widgets also might be relevant to the analysis. For question (2) the fact finder might evaluate the insubstantiality of the differences by asking whether a pipe performs the same function in the accused widget as a tube does in the claimed widget, in substantially the same way, to achieve substantially the same result. Known interchangeability of pipes and tubes in widgets also might be relevant.

Alternatively, the district court interpreting the claim of this example may adopt a higher level of generality and choose to treat the phrase "plastic tube" as one single limitation, rather than two separate limitations. In that case the fact finder would need to determine whether the accused widget's steel pipe is insubstantially different from the claimed widget's plastic tube. In order to analyze the extent of that difference, the fact finder might ask whether the steel pipe performs the same function in the accused widget as the plastic tube does in the claimed widget, in substantially the same way, to achieve substantially the same result. Known interchangeability of steel pipes and plastic tubes in widgets also might be relevant.

As this example attempts to illustrate, the level of generality versus specificity that the district court applies when enumerating the individual limitations of a claim can have a very real impact on the determination of technologic equivalency in the second step of the infringement analysis. Generally speaking, an accused infringer will attempt to establish the greatest possible number of limitations, making more burdensome the patentee's job of having to establish insubstantial differences with respect to each such limitation. In contrast, a patentee generally will seek to minimize the number of limitations so as to lessen her burden.

Determining what the limitations are in a patent claim to biotechnological subject matter may represent an even greater challenge. For example, consider a claim reciting

C. Step Two: Comparing the Properly Interpreted Claims

a purified, isolated DNA molecule comprising the nucleotide sequence AAGGTCAGGTCA.[132]

What are the pertinent limitations of this claim? Is a single nucleotide, A (the base adenine), the relevant limitation to be met in the accused molecule? Or is the pertinent limitation in this example a codon of three nucleotides, AAG (which together form the amino acid lysine)? Or is it an even longer stretch of the recited nucleotide sequence (perhaps the entirety of AAGGTCAGGTCA)? Federal Circuit decisions have not yet clearly answered these questions; the answers are likely to be case-specific.

A foundational Federal Circuit decision dealing with the identification of claim limitations is *Corning Glass Works v. Sumitomo Elec. USA Inc.*[133] Corning's patent in suit was directed to an optical waveguide fiber useful for long-distance telephone transmissions. The fiber was formed from an inner core of fused silica surrounded by an outer cladding; the invention required that the refractive index (RI) of the core be greater than the RI of the cladding. The Corning inventors achieved this RI differential by adding a positive dopant to the core material to increase its RI. Claim 1 recited:

> 1. An optical waveguide comprising
> (a) a cladding layer formed of a material selected from the group consisting of pure fused silica and fused silica to which a dopant material on at least an elemental basis has been added, and
> (b) a core formed of fused silica to which a dopant material on at least an elemental basis has been added to a degree in excess of that of the cladding layer so that the index of refraction thereof is of a value greater than the index of refraction of said cladding layer, said core being formed of at least 85 percent by weight of fused silica and an effective amount up to 15 percent by weight of said dopant material.

In the accused Sumitomo fiber, the RI differential was achieved not by adding a positive dopant to the core but rather by adding a negative dopant to the cladding. Thus, the parties' dispute centered on whether the language of paragraph (b) of claim 1 was met by the accused device (there being no dispute that the language of paragraph (a) was literally met). The Federal Circuit parsed the language of paragraph (b) into discrete limitations. The accused Sumitomo fibers literally met the limitation that the fiber be composed of "a core formed of fused silica," as well as the limitation that "the index of refraction [of the

---

[132]For explanation of basic biotechnological terminology, *see supra* Chapter 7 ("Potentially Patentable Subject Matter (35 U.S.C. §101)") at Section D.2 ("Purified Forms of Natural Products").

[133]868 F.2d 1251 (Fed. Cir. 1989).

core] is of a value greater than the index of refraction of said cladding layer."

The infringement dispute thus centered on the words of the claim following the initial "core" limitation, namely, the limitation "to which a dopant material . . . has been added to a degree in excess of that of the cladding layer." Sumitomo argued that its fibers did not meet this language either literally or equivalently because it did not add any dopant to the core, nor did it add to the core anything equivalent to a dopant.

The Federal Circuit rejected Sumitomo's approach, distinguishing between "components" and "limitations":

> Sumitomo's analysis is faulty in that it would require equivalency in components, that is, the substitution of something in the core for the absent dopant. However, the determination of equivalency is not subject to such a rigid formula. *An equivalent must be found for every limitation of the claim somewhere in an accused device, but not necessarily in a corresponding component, although that is generally the case.*[134]

The Federal Circuit accordingly upheld the district court's finding of infringement under the doctrine of equivalents. Analyzing the equivalency of the disputed limitation, the district court had properly found that "the use of . . . a [negative] dopant in the cladding . . . performs substantially the same function in substantially the same way as the use of a [positive] dopant in the core to produce the same result of creating the refractive index differential between the core and cladding of the fiber which is necessary for the fiber to function as an optical waveguide."[135]

f. Determining Technologic Equivalence

If the doctrine of equivalents applies in a given case to a particular claim limitation, what rules are used to determine whether the limitation is equivalently met in the accused device? This determination is considered a question of fact rather than law.[136] Accordingly, how does

---

[134]*Id.* at 1259 (emphasis added).

[135]*Id.* at 1260.

[136]*See* Graver Tank & Mfg. Co. v. Linde Air Prods. Co., 339 U.S. 605 (1950):

A finding of equivalence is a determination of fact. Proof can be made in any form: through testimony of experts or others versed in the technology; by documents, including texts and treatises; and, of course, by the disclosures of the prior art. Like any other issue of fact, final determination requires a balancing of credibility, persuasiveness and weight of evidence. It is to be decided by the trial court and that court's decision, under general principles of appellate review, should not be disturbed unless clearly erroneous. Particularly is this so in a field where so much depends upon familiarity with specific scientific problems and

C. Step Two: Comparing the Properly Interpreted Claims

the fact finder (whether judge or jury) decide whether an element of the accused device is technologically equivalent to the pertinent claim limitation?

The Supreme Court in *Sanitary Refrigerator Co. v. Winters*[137] indicated that an accused device infringes under the doctrine of equivalents "if it performs substantially the same function in substantially the same way to obtain the same result."[138] This statement sets forth the classic test for infringement under the doctrine of equivalents, which patent attorneys variously refer to as the "function/way/result," "FWR," "triple identity," or "tripartite" test.[139] More recently, the Federal Circuit has explained that function/way/result is merely one way of determining the ultimate equivalency question: Are the differences between the claimed invention and the accused device merely "insubstantial"?[140] If so, the accused device may be found to infringe under the doctrine of equivalents.

---

principles not usually contained in the general storehouse of knowledge and experience.

Id. at 609-610.

[137]280 U.S. 30 (1929).

[138]*Id.* at 42 (citation omitted).

[139]The Supreme Court in *Graver Tank* gave this further guidance on how to apply the function/way/result inquiry:

What constitutes equivalency must be determined against the context of the patent, the prior art, and the particular circumstances of the case. Equivalence, in the patent law, is not the prisoner of a formula and is not an absolute to be considered in a vacuum. It does not require complete identity for every purpose and in every respect. In determining equivalents, things equal to the same thing may not be equal to each other and, by the same token, things for most purposes different may sometimes be equivalents. Consideration must be given to the purpose for which an ingredient is used in a patent, the qualities it has when combined with the other ingredients, and the function which it is intended to perform. An important factor is whether persons reasonably skilled in the art would have known of the interchangeability of an ingredient not contained in the patent with one that was.

Graver Tank, 339 U.S. at 609. The Federal Circuit has emphasized the "known interchangeability" factor of *Graver* as particularly important. *See* Vulcan Eng'g Co. v. FATA Aluminum, Inc., 278 F.3d 1366, 1374 (Fed. Cir. 2002); Interactive Pictures Corp. v. Infinite Pictures, Inc., 274 F.3d 1371, 1383 (Fed. Cir. 2001); Overhead Door Corp. v. Chamberlain Group, Inc., 194 F.3d 1261, 1270 (Fed. Cir. 1999).

[140]Hilton Davis Chem. Co. v. Warner-Jenkinson Co., 62 F.3d 1512, 1517-1518 (Fed. Cir. 1995) (*en banc*). *See also Graver Tank,* 339 U.S. at 610 (characterizing inquiry as to whether the accused infringer's variation, "under the circumstances of this case, and in view of the technology and the prior art, is a change of such substance as to make the doctrine of equivalents inapplicable; or conversely, whether under the circumstances the change was so *insubstantial* that the trial court's invocation of the doctrine of equivalents was justified") (emphasis added).

475

While under current law the degree of substantiality of the differences is the overarching test for infringement under the doctrine of equivalents, it is likely that the Federal Circuit will further refine the inquiry as the court gains experience in applying it to particular technologies. As the Supreme Court in *Warner-Jenkinson* recognized, "[d]ifferent linguistic frameworks may be more suitable to different cases, depending on their particular facts."[141] For example, the classic function/way/result inquiry seems best suited for mechanical inventions but often is not very helpful with respect to biotechnological subject matter.[142] The *Warner-Jenkinson* Court refused to engage in "micromanaging the Federal Circuit's particular word choice for analyzing equivalence,"[143] and chose to leave such decisions up to the Circuit's "sound judgment in this area of its special expertise."[144]

g. *Reverse Doctrine of Equivalents*

The "wholesome realism" [145] of the doctrine of equivalents, as the Supreme Court in *Graver Tank* rather euphemistically termed it, is that the doctrine, which is almost always asserted in its conventional (or "forward") formulation to benefit a patent owner by expanding the scope of exclusive rights beyond those literally encompassed by the patent claims, also can operate (at least theoretically) in "reverse" to assist an accused infringer.

The reverse doctrine of equivalents acts as a defense to a charge of literal infringement. The doctrine absolves an accused infringer from infringement liability where the accused device, although literally falling within the scope of the asserted patent claim, is so far changed in principle from the claimed invention that a finding of liability cannot be justified as a policy matter.[146] The reverse doctrine of equivalents is "equitably applied based upon underlying questions of fact."[147] The doctrine applies "when the accused infringer proves that, despite the

---

[141]Warner-Jenkinson Co. v. Hilton Davis Chem. Co., 520 U.S. 17, 40 (1997).

[142]To see why this is so, consider a claim to "an isolated and purified DNA molecule comprising the nucleotide sequence AAGTCTGGTCCA." Even if we assume that the single nucleotide A is the pertinent limitation, what is the function of that limitation? In what way is that function performed? What is the result?

[143]*Warner-Jenkinson*, 520 U.S. at 40.

[144]*Id.*

[145]*Graver Tank*, 339 U.S. at 608 (stating that "[t]he wholesome realism of this doctrine is not always applied in favor of a patentee but is sometimes used against him").

[146]*See id.* at 608-609; Westinghouse v. Boyden Power Brake Co., 170 U.S. 537, 568 (1898).

[147]*See* Amgen, Inc. v. Hoechst Marion Roussel, Inc., 314 F.3d 1313, 1351 (Fed. Cir. 2003) (citing Scripps Clinic & Res. Found. v. Genentech, Inc., 927 F.2d 1565, 1581 (Fed. Cir. 1991)).

asserted claims literally reading on the accused device, 'it has been so changed that it is no longer the same invention.'"[148]

Despite being the topic of favorable academic attention,[149] the reverse doctrine of equivalents has rarely been applied by the courts to excuse liability.[150] For example, in *Roche Palo Alto LLC v. Apotex, Inc.*, the Federal Circuit observed that application of the doctrine is "rare[]" and emphasized that the Federal Circuit "has never affirmed a finding of non-infringement under the reverse doctrine of equivalents."[151]

D.   Legal Limitations on the Doctrine of Equivalents

1.   Overview

The Supreme Court pointed out in the very important footnote 8 of its 1997 *Warner-Jenkinson* decision that a patentee may not avail itself of the doctrine of equivalents if certain legal limitations preclude it from doing so.[152] If these limitations are triggered, an infringement case may be resolved on summary judgment and the fact question of technologic equivalency may never reach the fact finder.

The primary legal limitations on the doctrine of equivalents that Federal Circuit case law has identified thus far include the following:

- **Prosecution history estoppel:** The doctrine of prosecution history estoppel (PHE) provides that a patentee may not seek

---

[148]*Id.* (quoting Del Mar Avionics, Inc. v. Quinton Instrument Co., 836 F.2d 1320, 1325 (Fed. Cir. 1987)).

[149]*See* Robert P. Merges & Richard R. Nelson, *On the Complex Economics of Patent Scope*, 90 COLUM. L. REV. 839, 862-868 (1990) (advocating reverse doctrine of equivalents as mechanism to limit patent scope in face of significant technological improvement by accused infringer).

[150]*See* Mark A. Lemley, *The Economics of Improvement in Intellectual Property Law*, 75 TEX. L. REV. 989, 1011 (1997). *See also Amgen*, 314 F.3d at 1351-1352 (rejecting defense of noninfringement based on reverse doctrine of equivalents where court was "not persuaded by [accused infringer] TKT that this is a case where equity commands a determination of non-infringement despite its product literally falling within the scope of the asserted claims").

[151]531 F.3d 1372, 1378 (Fed. Cir. 2008). The Federal Circuit has relied on the reverse doctrine of equivalents, however, to vacate a district court's grant of summary judgment of infringement. *See* Scripps Clinic & Res. Found. v. Genentech, Inc., 927 F.2d 1565, 1581 (Fed. Cir. 1991) (finding that accused infringer Genentech had raised genuine issues of scientific and evidentiary fact requiring trial to determine whether Genentech's recombinantly produced version of Factor VIII:C blood-clotting protein literally infringed Scripps' broadly interpreted product patent claim to Factor VIII:C, or instead was so far changed in principle from claimed invention as to be excused from liability under the reverse doctrine of equivalents).

[152]*See* Warner-Jenkinson Co. v. Hilton Davis Chem. Co., 520 U.S. 17, 39 n.8 (1997).

to ensnare under the doctrine of equivalents any subject matter that it surrendered in order to obtain the patent from the USPTO. Prosecution history estoppel is the most frequently encountered legal limitation on the doctrine of equivalents.[153]

- **All-limitations rule:** If even a single claim limitation is not met, either literally or equivalently, in the accused device, there is no infringement. Every limitation of a claim is considered material and must be met in the accused device in order to have infringement.
- **Vitiation of a claim limitation:** The doctrine of equivalents must not be applied so broadly as to entirely vitiate or effectively eliminate a particular claim limitation.[154]
- **Prior art:** A patentee cannot obtain coverage through the doctrine of equivalents over subject matter that it could not have obtained from the USPTO in the first instance. In short, one who merely "practices the prior art" does not infringe under the doctrine of equivalents.[155]
- **Dedication to the public:** The patentee may not attempt to cover through the doctrine of equivalents any subject matter that it disclosed but did not claim in its patent application, thereby avoiding USPTO examination of that subject matter.[156]
- **Foreseeability:** A patentee may not encompass through the doctrine of equivalents reasonably foreseeable alterations to claimed structure, when it had an opportunity to negotiate broader claim coverage in the USPTO but did not do so.[157]

The most frequently encountered of these limitations are discussed in further detail below.

2. Prosecution History Estoppel

a. Definition

Like the doctrine of equivalents, the doctrine of prosecution history estoppel is judge-made law. The most commonly asserted legal limitation on the doctrine of equivalents, prosecution history estoppel

---

[153]*See* Section D.2, *infra.*

[154]*See* Section D.5, *infra.*

[155]The leading case here is *Wilson Sporting Goods Co. v. David Geoffrey & Assocs.*, 904 F.2d 677, 683 (Fed. Cir. 1990). For further discussion, *see* Section D.3, *infra.* Note, however, that the Federal Circuit has rejected the applicability of a "practicing the prior art" defense to allegations of *literal* infringement. *See* Tate Access Floors, Inc. v. Interface Arch. Res., Inc., 279 F.3d 1357, 1365-1366 (Fed. Cir. 2002).

[156]*See* Section D.4, *infra.*

[157]*See* Sage Prods., Inc. v. Devon Indus., Inc., 126 F.3d 1420, 1425 (Fed. Cir. 1997).

is based on the notion that if a patent applicant surrendered certain subject matter in the USPTO in order to obtain its patent (e.g., by narrowing the scope of a claim through amendment in order to distinguish subject matter disclosed in a cited prior art reference), it cannot thereafter rely on the doctrine of equivalents to obtain exclusionary rights over that same subject matter. By reading the patent and its prosecution history in order to determine what the patentee surrendered, competitors should be provided a reasonable degree of certainty that so long as they operate within the confines of the surrendered subject matter, they will not be found to infringe under the doctrine of equivalents.

The most common form of prosecution history estoppel results from narrowing amendments made to the patent application claims during prosecution. For example, the patent allegedly infringed in *Dixie USA, Inc. v. Infab Corp.*[158] was directed to a type of plastic "stretcher" for use in transporting hospital patients. Claim 1 of the issued patent recited the following:

> A patient shifting aid comprising:
> a plastic slab having rounded corners forming a rectangular support surface upon which a patient is adapted [sic] to be placed and having sufficient thickness to support the weight of a patient placed thereon while enabling the obtaining of x-rays through the plastic slab to determine the extent of patient injury without the necessity of additional shifting of the patient;
> a plurality of openings in said slab and disposed adjacent the periphery of said support surface providing means for gripping the plastic slab to effect sliding movement of the plastic slab and the patient support [sic, supported] thereon;
> *said plurality of openings comprising generally rectangular openings having rounded corners and rounded openings for grasping the slab for moving a patient;* ...[159]

Notably, the corresponding claims of the patent application as originally filed did *not* limit the nature of the openings. Rather, the claims merely required that the stretcher comprise "a plurality of openings in said slab and disposed adjacent the periphery of said support surface providing means for gripping the plastic slab to effect sliding movement of the plastic slab and the patient support [sic, supported] thereon."[160]

In due course the USPTO rejected the claims as obvious under 35 U.S.C. §103 in view of several prior art references. The patent applicant responded by amending the claims to add the "rectangular openings"

[158]927 F.2d 584 (Fed. Cir. 1991).
[159]*Id.* at 585-586 (emphasis added).
[160]*Id.* at 585-586.

and "rounded openings" limitation (emphasized above). In remarks accompanying this amendment, the applicant contended that what distinguished the claimed invention from the relevant prior art was the presence of both round *and* rectangular openings, emphasizing to the examiner that "regarding [the amended] claim . . . , none of the cited patents discloses the specific shape and location of the claimed rectangular *and* round openings." [161]

The defendant's accused stretcher did not literally infringe the patent because its handhold openings were all rectangular, not a mixture of rectangular and rounded openings. Because of the described prosecution history, the district court held that prosecution history estoppel precluded the patentee's reliance on the doctrine of equivalents and granted the accused infringer's motion for summary judgment of no infringement.

The Federal Circuit affirmed the district court in *Dixie USA*. Regardless of whether the accused stretcher performed the same function as the claimed invention, in substantially the same way, to achieve substantially the same result (i.e., was technologically equivalent), the patentee in this case was estopped from relying on the doctrine of equivalents to establish infringement liability. The court concluded that "when a patentee, during the prosecution of his application, adds a limitation to rectangular and round openings in response to a rejection based on prior art references describing rectangular openings in an effort to overcome that rejection, the patentee cannot later successfully argue that an accused device that lacks the rectangular and round limitation infringes the patent." [162]

Prosecution history estoppel resulted in *Dixie USA* from the combined effect of the patent applicant's amendment of his claims as well as his legal arguments made to the USPTO in the form of written remarks accompanying the amendment. However, the claims need not be amended at all in order to create prosecution history estoppel. In some cases, the applicant's arguments alone, generally made in the form of the applicant's written "remarks" filed in response to the examiner's rejections, can create estoppel. These arguments may involve characterizations of the claimed invention and/or the prior art, and will typically assert differences between the two that support patentability. Because this type of estoppel, referred to by the Federal Circuit as "argument-based prosecution history estoppel," is not founded on any explicit changes being made to the claims, a "clear and unmistakable surrender of subject matter" is necessary to invoke it. [163]

[161]*Id.* at 588 (emphasis in original).
[162]*Id.* at 587-588.
[163]*See* Conoco, Inc. v. Energy & Env. Int'l, L.C., 460 F.3d 1349, 1364 (Fed. Cir. 2006); Pharmacia & Upjohn Co. v. Mylan Pharms., Inc., 170 F.3d 1373, 1377 (Fed. Cir. 1999).

b. Scope of Estoppel

Assuming that a patentee's actions during prosecution (in the form of claim amendments and/or arguments) triggered prosecution history estoppel, the next step of the analysis is to determine the proper scope of that estoppel. In other words, may the patentee narrow its claim via amendment in response to USPTO rejections and yet still retain some scope of equivalents beyond the literal scope of the amended claim? Consider, for example, a claim reciting "a composition of matter comprising less than 50 percent X by weight." In response to a USPTO rejection based on prior art that taught a composition having 40 percent X, assume that the patent applicant narrowed its claim to recite that the patented composition must comprise "less than 20 percent X by weight."[164] If an accused infringer manufactures and sells a composition having 25 percent X, there is no literal infringement. Nevertheless, could the accused composition still infringe under the doctrine of equivalents?

In its early decisions the Federal Circuit adopted a "flexible" or "spectrum" approach to this question concerning the proper scope of prosecution history estoppel. In frequently quoted language, the court stated in *Hughes Aircraft Co. v. United States*[165] that prosecution history estoppel "may have a limiting effect" on the doctrine of equivalents "within a spectrum ranging from great to small to zero."[166] As discussed below, the Federal Circuit later rejected the flexible approach in favor of an absolute, "complete bar" rule of prosecution history estoppel in its 2000 *en banc* decision in *Festo Corp. v. Shoketsu Kinzoku Kogyo Kabushiki Co.*[167] In 2002 the U.S. Supreme Court vacated the Federal Circuit's decision in *Festo* and announced a new "presumptive bar" rule that lies somewhere between the flexible and complete bar rules. The evolution of the Supreme Court's view of prosecution history estoppel is demonstrated by its 1997 decision in *Warner-Jenkinson* and its 2002 follow-up decision in *Festo,* as discussed in the following section.

The Federal Circuit has explained that, in contrast with amendment-based estoppel, the court will "not presume a patentee's arguments to surrender an entire field of equivalents through simple arguments and explanations to the patent examiner. Though arguments to the examiner may have the same effect, they do not always evidence the same clear disavowal of scope that a formal amendment to the claim would have." *Conoco,* 460 F.3d at 1364.

[164]This assumes that the originally filed patent application provided adequate support for the 20 percent limitation in accordance with 35 U.S.C. §112(a) (eff. Sept. 16, 2012).

[165]717 F.2d 1351 (Fed. Cir. 1983).

[166]*Id.* at 1363.

[167]234 F.3d 558 (Fed. Cir. 2000) (*en banc*).

c. *Presumption of Estoppel Under* Warner-Jenkinson

The Supreme Court in *Warner-Jenkinson Co. v. Hilton Davis Chem., Co.*[168] announced a new presumption with respect to prosecution history estoppel in the case of a silent or unexplained record, where the prosecution history does not reveal the reason for amending the claims.[169] The Court held that in this situation, fairness requires that the burden of establishing a reason for the amendment be placed on the patent owner. Where no explanation is established, a court should "presume that the patent applicant had a substantial reason related to patentability"[170] for making the amendment.

If the patent owner is unable to rebut the presumption that the change was made to the claims for a reason related to patentability, "prosecution history estoppel would bar the application of the doctrine of equivalents as to that element."[171] In other words, an unrebutted presumption of prosecution history estoppel results in a complete bar to the application of the doctrine of equivalents with respect to the disputed claim limitation.

d. *Federal Circuit's Complete Bar Rule of* Festo I

In 2000 the Federal Circuit drastically strengthened the limiting impact of prosecution history estoppel beyond that enunciated in *Warner-Jenkinson* when the *en banc* appellate court decided the long-awaited *Festo Corp. v. Shoketsu Kinzoku Kogyo Kabushiki Co.* [hereinafter *Festo I*].[172] Although the U.S. Supreme Court subsequently

---

[168]520 U.S. 17 (1997).

[169]*See id.* at 33-34. The patent application claims as filed in *Warner-Jenkinson* did not place any limits on the pH range at which the claimed dye purification process operated. The USPTO examiner cited against the claims a prior art reference showing a similar process operating at a pH of above nine (9). *See id.* at 22. In response, the applicant amended its claims to require that the pH parameter of the claimed process fall within a range of "approximately 6.0-9.0." *See id.* Although the reason for the inclusion of pH 9 as the upper limit of this range is obvious (i.e., to distinguish the cited prior art process), the prosecution record was unclear as to why the applicant included pH 6 as a lower limit. *See id.* at 32. Because the prosecution record in *Warner-Jenkinson* did not explain the reason for this aspect of the narrowing claim amendment, a presumption of complete estoppel was triggered as to that limitation of the claim. *See id.* at 33-34.

[170]*Id.* at 33. The Supreme Court did not expressly define what it meant by "reason[s] related to patentability," but provided a number of case law examples that all involved changes made to claims in response to prior art rejections (i.e., based on anticipation under 35 U.S.C. §102 or obviousness under 35 U.S.C. §103). *See id.*

[171]*Id.*

[172]234 F.3d 558 (Fed. Cir. 2000) (*en banc*) (*Festo I*), *vacated and remanded*, Festo Corp. v. Shoketsu Kinzoku Kogyo Kabushiki Co., 535 U.S. 722 (2002) (*Festo II*). The shorthand descriptor "*Festo I*" is used herein for convenience, but is not literally correct; the Federal Circuit first encountered the long-running dispute over infringement of

overturned the *Festo I* decision as described below, a summary of the Federal Circuit's thinking on the matter is important to understanding the current framework for determining prosecution history estoppel.

In *Festo I* a majority of the *en banc* Federal Circuit announced an absolute "bar by amendment" rule that went considerably further than the limited "silent record" presumption announced in *Warner-Jenkinson*. Under the Federal Circuit's *Festo I* rule, *no* scope of equivalents survived for any claim limitation that was narrowed during patent prosecution for any reason related to patentability; such limitations could only be literally infringed. (Thus, the accused composition having 25 percent X from the previous hypothetical would not infringe, either literally or under the doctrine of equivalents.) "Reasons related to patentability" included anything related to the Patent Act, 35 U.S.C., including changes made in response to indefiniteness rejections under the second paragraph of 35 U.S.C. §112. Because at least before *Festo I*, the narrowing of claims by amendment was commonplace practice in the iterative process of patent prosecution, almost all issued patents were impacted and their value significantly reduced by the Federal Circuit's *Festo I* decision.

The *Festo I* majority's policy argument that contracting the doctrine of equivalents would promote innovation by encouraging design-arounds and improvements was certainly valid with respect to follow-on enterprises, but it ignored the dramatic reduction in incentives for "pioneer" innovation and basic research. In *Festo I* the Federal Circuit slashed incentives for the breakthrough inventor because the scope of protection that a patent grant provides had in many cases been narrowed to easily avoided literal infringement.

Especially troubling about the Federal Circuit's decision was the apparently retrospective application of *Festo I*'s absolutism on the approximately 1.2 million U.S. patents then in force. Unlike the Supreme Court in *Warner-Jenkinson,* the Federal Circuit *Festo I* majority showed no sensitivity to reliance interests of patent owners or concern for "chang[ing] so substantially the rules of the game";[173] that is, it did not protect the expectations of those who had procured patents before the Supreme Court in *Warner-Jenkinson* announced its rebuttable presumption of estoppel in certain instances where claim amendments were unexplained. The *Festo I* majority announced a new estoppel framework much more severe than that of *Warner-Jenkinson,* with nonrebuttable, uniform application to all narrowing amendments

---

Festo's magnetic rodless cylinder patents five years earlier. *See* Festo Corp. v. Shoketsu Kinzoku Kogyo Kabushiki Co., 72 F.3d 857 (Fed. Cir. 1995) (affirming district court's grant of summary judgment of infringement of Festo's Carroll patent and affirming judgment of infringement of Festo's Stoll patent following jury trial).

[173]*Warner-Jenkinson,* 520 U.S. at 32 n.6.

made for any reason related to the statutory requirements for obtaining a patent, yet provided no grandfathering for existing patents.

e. *Supreme Court's Presumptive Bar Rule of* Festo II

In a landmark decision issued May 28, 2002, the U.S. Supreme Court vacated the Federal Circuit's decision in *Festo I* and remanded the case to the appellate court.[174] The Supreme Court flatly rejected the Federal Circuit's *per se* rule of complete estoppel (i.e., the "complete bar" approach). The Court agreed that narrowing amendments[175] made for any reason based on the Patent Act, including amendments made in response to rejections under 35 U.S.C. §112, can give rise to estoppel.[176] Rather than apply a *per se* rule that narrowing amendments automatically destroy all possible scope of equivalents, however, an examination of the subject matter surrendered by the narrowing amendment is required.[177]

The Supreme Court in *Festo II* adopted a *rebuttable* presumption that a narrowing amendment surrenders the particular equivalent in question. This can be seen both as an expansion of the "silent record" presumption that the Court had previously announced

[174]Festo Corp. v. Shoketsu Kinzoku Kogyo Kabushiki Co., 535 U.S. 722 (2002) (*Festo II*).

[175]Not every amendment made to patent claims during the prosecution history narrows the scope of the claim. For example, the Federal Circuit held in *Interactive Pictures Corp. v. Infinite Pictures, Inc.*, 274 F.3d 1371 (Fed. Cir. 2001), that a patent applicant's amendment of the phrase "output signals" to read "output transform calculation signals" in a claim directed to an image viewing system was *not* a narrowing amendment that triggered prosecution history estoppel. *See id.* at 1377. The court agreed with the patentee that the amendment was not narrowing because it "merely clarified [the claim] by relabeling the signals without changing their identity or qualities." *Id.* In *Primos, Inc. v. Hunter's Specialties, Inc.*, 451 F.3d 841 (Fed. Cir. 2006), the patentee's amendment of the claim phrase "a plate" to "a plate having a length" did not narrow the scope of the claim because "every physical object has a length." *Id.* at 849.

[176]*See Festo II*, 535 U.S. at 736-737:

Estoppel arises when an amendment is made to secure the patent and the amendment narrows the patent's scope. If a §112 amendment is truly cosmetic, then it would not narrow the patent's scope or raise an estoppel. On the other hand, if a §112 amendment is necessary and narrows the patent's scope—even if only for the purpose of better description—estoppel may apply. A patentee who narrows a claim as a condition for obtaining a patent disavows his claim to the broader subject matter, whether the amendment was made to avoid the prior art or to comply with §112. We must regard the patentee as having conceded an inability to claim the broader subject matter or at least as having abandoned his right to appeal a rejection. In either case estoppel may apply.

[177]*See id.* at 737 (explaining that, "[t]hough prosecution history estoppel can bar a patentee from challenging a wide range of alleged equivalents made or distributed by competitors, its reach requires an examination of the subject matter surrendered by the narrowing amendment").

in *Warner-Jenkinson,*[178] but also as a significant relaxation of the complete bar rule announced in the Federal Circuit's *Festo I* decision. Under the Supreme Court's *Festo II* decision, a patentee can potentially overcome the presumption of estoppel in the following settings:

> There are some cases, however, where the amendment cannot reasonably be viewed as surrendering a particular equivalent. The equivalent may have been *unforeseeable at the time of the application; the rationale underlying the amendment may bear no more than a tangential relation to the equivalent in question; or there may be some other reason suggesting that the patentee could not reasonably be expected to have described the insubstantial substitute in question.* In those cases the patentee can overcome the presumption that prosecution history estoppel bars a finding of equivalence.
>
> This presumption is not, then, just the complete bar by another name. Rather, it reflects the fact that the interpretation of the patent must begin with its literal claims, and the prosecution history is relevant to construing those claims. When the patentee has chosen to narrow a claim, courts may presume the amended text was composed with awareness of this rule and that the territory surrendered is not an equivalent of the territory claimed. In those instances, however, the patentee still might rebut the presumption that estoppel bars a claim of equivalence. *The patentee must show that at the time of the amendment one skilled*

---

[178]The presumption of estoppel announced in *Warner-Jenkinson* appeared to be limited to those amendments made with no explanation in the record of the reasons for the amendments. *See Warner-Jenkinson Co. v. Hilton Davis Chem., Co.,* 520 U.S. 17, 33 (1997) (holding that "[w]here no explanation is established, however, the court should presume that the patent applicant had a substantial reason related to patentability for including the limiting element added by amendment"). Under the Supreme Court's subsequent decision in *Festo II,* the presumption of estoppel applies across the board whenever a "narrowing" amendment has been made, without limitation to amendments made without any accompanying explanation of the reasons therefor:

> When the patentee is unable to explain the reason for amendment, estoppel not only applies but also "bar[s] the application of the doctrine of equivalents as to that element." *Ibid.* These words do not mandate a complete bar; they are limited to the circumstance where "no explanation is established." They do provide, however, that when the court is unable to determine the purpose underlying a narrowing amendment—and hence a rationale for limiting the estoppel to the surrender of particular equivalents—the court should presume that the patentee surrendered all subject matter between the broader and the narrower language.
>
> Just as *Warner-Jenkinson* held that the patentee bears the burden of proving that an amendment was not made for a reason that would give rise to estoppel, we hold here that the patentee should bear the burden of showing that the amendment does not surrender the particular equivalent in question.

Festo II, 535 U.S. at 740.

in the art could not reasonably be expected to have drafted a claim that would have literally encompassed the alleged equivalent.[179]

The Supreme Court's formulation of the prosecution history estoppel test in *Festo II* left a number of important questions unanswered. For example, what will be required to show satisfaction of the "unforeseeability" criterion? Under what circumstances does an amendment bear "no more than a tangential relation" to a particular equivalent that a patentee seeks to encompass through reliance on the doctrine of equivalents? What types of "other reason[s]" would suggest that a "patentee could not reasonably have been expected to have described [sic, claimed] the insubstantial substitute in question"?[180] What is the proper timing for these showings—at the time the application was filed, at the time the amendment in question was made, or the time the patent issued? Who is the "one skilled in the art" for purposes of answering the question whether the claim's author "could not reasonably be expected to have drafted a claim that would have literally encompassed the alleged equivalent"? More specifically, is he/she a person of ordinary skill in the art of the invention in question, or a person of ordinary skill in the art of drafting patent claims?[181] Are each of the above questions to be considered an issue of law or fact? Is there a right to a jury trial on any of these questions?

Before the Federal Circuit could address these questions, some federal district courts began the task, with divergent results.[182]

f. Federal Circuit's Remand Decision in Festo III

The Federal Circuit on September 26, 2003, issued an *en banc* decision[183] from the Supreme Court's remand in *Festo II*. The *Festo III*

---

[179]*Id.* at 740-741 (emphases added).

[180]For example, what if the patentee did not literally claim the alleged insubstantial substitute because of a lack of written description support in the specification? *See* Donald S. Chisum, *The Supreme Court's* Festo *Decision: Implications for Patent Claim Scope and Other Issues* (June 2002), at 16, *available at* http://lexisnexis.com/practiceareas/ip/pdfs/chisumfesto.pdf (last visited Aug. 12, 2012).

[181]Although some inventors are quite sophisticated about the patenting process, in many cases an inventor requires the services of a patent attorney or patent agent who is trained in the law (and lore) of claim drafting.

[182]For example, the following three district court decisions all involve the same patent but reach different conclusions concerning the effect of prosecution history estoppel as resolved in accordance with the Supreme Court's decision in *Festo II*. *See* Glaxo Wellcome, Inc. v. IMPAX Labs., Inc., 220 F. Supp. 2d 1089 (N.D. Cal. 2002); Glaxo Wellcome Inc. v. Eon Labs Mfg., Inc., No. 00 Civ. 9089, 2002 U.S. Dist. LEXIS 14923 (S.D.N.Y. 2002); Smithkline Beecham Corp. v. Excel Pharms., Inc., 214 F. Supp. 2d 581 (E.D. Va. 2002).

[183]Festo Corp. v. Shoketsu Kinzoku Kogyo Kabushiki Co., 344 F.3d 1359 (Fed. Cir. 2003) (*en banc*) [hereinafter *Festo III*].

D. Legal Limitations on the Doctrine of Equivalents

decision set forth a framework for implementing the new presumptive bar regime and answered many, if not all, of the questions raised by *Festo II*. The *Festo III* decision specifically addressed the following four questions on which the Federal Circuit had requested briefing from the parties and *amici*:

1. Whether rebuttal of the presumption of surrender, including issues of foreseeability, tangentialness, or reasonable expectations of those skilled in the art, is a question of law or one of fact; and what role a jury should play in determining whether a patent owner can rebut the presumption.
2. What factors are encompassed by the criteria set forth by the Supreme Court.
3. If a rebuttal determination requires factual findings, then whether, in this case, remand to the district court is necessary to determine whether Festo can rebut the presumption that any narrowing amendment surrendered the equivalent now asserted, or whether the record as it now stands is sufficient to make those determinations.
4. If remand to the district court is not necessary, then whether Festo can rebut the presumption that any narrowing amendment surrendered the equivalent now asserted.[184]

With respect to the first question, concerning the proper role of judge and jury, the *Festo III* court held that whether a patentee has rebutted the presumption that any equivalents to a narrowed claim limitation have been surrendered is a question of law. As such, the question is to be determined by the district court, not a jury, in light of the traditional view of prosecution history estoppel as an equitable determination. Although rebuttal of the presumption may be subject to underlying facts, a district court is to make these factual findings in the course of determining the ultimate issue of law.[185]

The second question addressed by the *Festo III* court was intended to flesh out the three criteria identified by the Supreme Court in *Festo II* for overcoming the presumption of complete estoppel. As discussed in the previous section, those three rebuttal criteria are (1) that the patentee demonstrates that the alleged equivalent would have been unforeseeable at the time of the narrowing amendment, (2) that the rationale underlying the narrowing amendment bears no more than a tangential relation to the equivalent in question, or (3) that there is "some other reason" suggesting that the patentee could not reasonably

[184]Festo Corp. v. Shoketsu Kinzoku Kogyo Kabushiki Co., 304 F.3d 1289, 1290-1291 (Fed. Cir. 2002) (order).
[185]*See Festo III*, 344 F.3d at 1368-1369.

487

have been expected to have drafted a claim encompassing the alleged equivalent at the time the patentee narrowed its claim.

The Federal Circuit in *Festo III* announced that rebuttal criterion (1), "unforeseeability," is an "objective inquiry, asking whether the alleged equivalent would have been unforeseeable to one of ordinary skill in the art at the time of the amendment."[186] Later-developed technology (e.g., transistors in relation to vacuum tubes, or Velcro® in relation to fasteners) generally would not have been foreseeable, while technology known in the art at the time of the patentee's amendment would more likely have been foreseeable. Objective unforeseeability depends on underlying factual issues such as the state of the art and the understanding of a hypothetical person of ordinary skill in the art at the time of the amendment. Thus, district courts may hear expert testimony on these questions and consider other relevant extrinsic evidence.

Rebuttal criterion (2), "mere tangentialness," asks whether the reason for a narrowing amendment was peripheral, not directly relevant, or in other words, unrelated to the alleged equivalent. If a narrowing amendment surrendered the accused equivalent, it cannot be merely tangential: "an amendment made to avoid prior art that contains the equivalent in question is not tangential; it is central to allowance of the claim."[187] The inquiry must focus on the patentee's objectively apparent reason for the narrowing amendment; thus, a district court is limited in answering this question to consideration of the intrinsic evidence. Whether the reason for the amendment was merely tangential to the accused equivalent "is for the court to determine from the prosecution history record without the introduction of additional evidence, except, when necessary, testimony from those skilled in the art as to the interpretation of that record." [188]

Rebuttal criterion (3), that "some other reason" suggests that a patentee could not reasonably have been expected to have claimed the insubstantial substitute in question, is a "narrow" inquiry, but may at least include "the shortcomings of language." Although not definitely ruling out the possibility that extrinsic evidence might be relevant on this point, the *Festo III* court instructed that "[w]hen at all possible, determination of the third rebuttal criterion should also be limited to the prosecution history record,"[189] as is the case with rebuttal criterion (2), mere tangentialness.

Applying the above framework to the parties' arguments and the prosecution history of the Stoll and Carroll patents in suit, the *Festo*

---

[186]*Id.* at 1369.
[187]*Id.*
[188]*Id.* at 1370.
[189]*Id.*

III court determined that patentee Festo could not show that the "magnetizable" and "sealing ring" amendments to the Stoll and Carroll patents were merely "tangential" or were made for "some other reason." However, factual issues relating to the objective unforeseeability of the accused equivalents existed; for example, Festo argued that SMC's accused two-way sealing ring was an inferior and unforeseeable equivalent of the one-way sealing rings located at each end of the piston in the claimed invention. The existence of these fact questions necessitated a remand to the district court to determine whether Festo could successfully rebut the presumption of surrender by demonstrating that the accused elements would have been unforeseeable to a person of ordinary skill in the art at the time of the amendments.[190]

g. *Federal Circuit Decisions Applying the* Festo *Rebuttal Criteria*

Federal Circuit decisions following *Festo III* provide further guidance on application of the three rebuttal criteria. For example, a patentee successfully rebutted the *Festo* presumption of complete estoppel under rebuttal criterion (2) in *Insituform Techs., Inc. v. Cat Contracting, Inc.*[191] Patentee Insituform claimed a process for repairing a broken underground pipe by installing a resin-impregnated liner within the pipe. Although Insituform narrowed its claim during prosecution to recite *inter alia* that the process employed only a single cup for creating a vacuum inside the liner, the Federal Circuit concluded that the rationale underlying that amendment bore "no more than a tangential relation to the equivalent in question," the accused Cat process utilizing multiple vacuum cups. The prosecution history showed that the reason for Insituform's narrowing amendment, which added other limitations to the claim besides the single cup limitation, was

---

[190]Festo did not prevail on remand on the unforeseeability question. *See* Festo Corp. v. Shoketsu Kinzoku Kogyo Kabushiki Co., No. Civ.A. 88-1814-PBS, 2006 WL 47695, *1 (D. Mass. Jan. 10, 2006) (denying Festo's motion under Fed. R. Civ. P. 59(e) to alter or amend the district court's earlier judgment for Shoketsu of noninfringement, finding that "in the context of the very small [magnetic] leakage fields [resulting from Festo's design], the use of an aluminum alloy sleeve (an old technology) instead of a magnetizable one was foreseeable to a person of ordinary skill in the art at the time of the 1981 amendments"). The district court further found that "in the context of the invention, . . . it was objectively foreseeable to one of ordinary skill in the art in 1981 to use one two-way sealing ring, which existed in the prior art, in combination with the guide rings as an equivalent of a sealing ring/guide ring combination at each end of the piston [as recited in Festo's claims]"). *Id.* at *3. As discussed in Section D.2.g, *infra*, the Federal Circuit subsequently affirmed the district court's decision that Festo had not satisfied the unforeseeability rebuttal criterion. *See* Festo Corp. v. Shoketsu Kinzoku Kogyo Kabushiki Co., 493 F.3d 1368 (Fed. Cir. 2007).

[191] 385 F.3d 1360 (Fed. Cir. 2004).

to distinguish a prior art process that disadvantageously employed a large compressor at the end of the liner; limiting the number of vacuum cups was not related to this reason. In other words, Insituform's amendment distinguishing the prior art was based on *where* the vacuum source was located; this was "only tangentially related to an equivalent directed at the *number* of vacuum sources." [192]

The patentee in *Primos, Inc. v. Hunter's Specialties, Inc.* likewise managed to rebut the *Festo* presumption by reliance on rebuttal criterion (2).[193] The patented invention was a game call device used by hunters to emulate the sounds of animals such as turkeys. It featured a moderately curved plate that rose above a flat membrane; the membrane vibrated to produce sound when a hunter used the game call. In response to a USPTO rejection of claim 2 of Primos's '578 patent[194] based on a prior art game call device featuring a shelf-like structure with *no* spacing above the membrane, Primos narrowed the claim to require that its plate be "differentially spaced" above the membrane. Hunter's Specialties' accused product (the "Tone Trough") included a domed structure raised above the membrane, rather than a plate. The Federal Circuit concluded that "[b]ecause the accused device's dome includes the spacing, the amendment was merely tangential to the contested element in the accused device, and thus prosecution history estoppel does not apply to prevent the application of the doctrine of equivalents." [195]

Other Federal Circuit decisions in the wake of *Festo III* illustrate patentee failures to establish any of the three rebuttal criteria and thereby invoke the doctrine of equivalents. For example, the patentee in *Glaxo Wellcome, Inc. v. Impax Labs., Inc.*[196] was unable to rebut the *Festo* presumption under the "unforeseeability" criterion (1). Glaxo's patent was directed to controlled sustained-release tablets containing the antidepressant bupropion hydrochloride, which Glaxo sold commercially under the brand name Wellbutrin® SR for treatment of depression. Specifically, Glaxo's patent claimed a sustained-release tablet containing an admixture of bupropion hydrochloride and hydroxypropyl methylcellulose (HPMC), which extends drug release by transforming into a gel that swells upon ingestion. Rather than

---

[192]Cross Med. Prods., Inc. v. Medtronic Sofamor Danek, Inc., 480 F.3d 1335, 1342 (Fed. Cir. 2007) (citing Biagro W. Sales, Inc. v. Grow More, Inc., 423 F.3d 1296, 1306 (Fed. Cir. 2005)). The amendment and the alleged equivalent in *Insituform* involved "different aspects of the invention—the location of the vacuum source relative to the resin versus the number of vacuum cups." *Biagro,* 423 F.3d at 1306.

[193]*See* Primos, Inc. v. Hunter's Specialties, Inc., 451 F.3d 841, 848-850 (Fed. Cir. 2006).

[194]*See* Game Call Apparatus, U.S. Patent No. 5,415,578 (issued May 16, 1995).

[195]*Primos,* 451 F.3d at 849.

[196] 356 F.3d 1348 (Fed. Cir. 2004).

HPMC, the release agent used in the accused product was hydroxy-propyl cellulose (HPC), a hydrogel-forming compound. The parties did not dispute that HPMC and HPC were technologically equivalent sustained-release agents; nevertheless, accused infringer Impax con-tended that Glaxo was barred by prosecution history estoppel from recourse to the doctrine of equivalents because Glaxo had narrowed its claims by adding a specific recitation of HPMC (as filed, Glaxo's claim did not recite any particular release agent). Glaxo countered that HPC was unforeseeable at the time of its amendment of the disputed claims. Glaxo could not have amended the claims broadly enough to include the accused HPC, it contended, because to do so would have drawn a new matter rejection;[197] its patent application did not reference HPC or any other sustained-release agents beyond HPMC. The Federal Circuit rejected this argument, observing that the "Supreme Court's [discussion of unforeseeability in *Festo II*] addresses the time of amendment only and does not address the instance where the applicant could not properly claim a known equivalent because it had purposely left that known substitute out of its disclosure at the time of filing." The Federal Circuit admitted that at the time Glaxo amended its claims, no known hydrogels other than HPMC had been tested with bupropion hydrochloride to achieve sustained release. Nevertheless, the record contained "considerable evidence" that Glaxo could have described the sustained release compound HPC at the time the '798 patent claims were amended, if not earlier. HPC was then known to Glaxo, the Federal Circuit concluded, at least in view of Glaxo's submission during prosecution of an Information Disclosure Statement that "describe[d] HPC, HPMC, and numerous other poly-meric compounds as extended release drug formulations."[198]

In its most recent (and likely last) decision in the long-running *Festo v. Shoketsu* battle, the Federal Circuit affirmed in 2007 a district court's conclusion that Festo could not rely on "unforeseeabilty" rebut-tal criterion (1) to overcome the presumption of complete estoppel and ensnare Shoketsu's magnetically coupled rodless cylinder having a nonmagnetizable outer sleeve.[199] Reviewing its precedent on applica-tion of the unforeseeability criterion, the court observed that "we have

[197]The prohibition on adding new matter to the disclosure of a pending patent appli-cation is found in 35 U.S.C. §132(a) (stating that "[n]o amendment shall introduce new matter into the disclosure of the invention"). Patent claims and amendments thereto must be supported by the as-filed disclosure (i.e., written description and drawings). *See* USPTO, MANUAL OF PATENT EXAMINING PROCEDURE (8th ed., rev. 2010) §608.01(o) ("Basis for Claim Terminology in Description"), *available at* http://www.uspto.gov/web/offices/pac/mpep/documents/0600_608_01_o.htm#sect608.01o.

[198]*Glaxo Wellcome*, 356 F.3d at 1355.

[199]*See* Festo Corp. v. Shoketsu Kinzoku Kogyo Kabushiki Co., 493 F.3d 1368 (Fed. Cir. 2007).

consistently held that an equivalent is foreseeable when the equivalent is known in the pertinent prior art at the time of amendment."[200] The court rejected Festo's proposed alternative test, which contended that in order to be considered foreseeable an accused equivalent must have satisfied the "function/way/result" or "insubstantial differences" test as of the time of the claim amendment, looking only at information available at that date.[201] The court instructed that the purpose of the function/way/result or insubstantial differences test is to determine whether an accused equivalent is sufficiently close to a claimed feature that the patentee should be able to capture it under the doctrine of equivalents; that test is not designed for the "entirely different context" of determining whether prosecution history estoppel applies because of a patentee's limiting amendment of its claims.[202] In short, the function/way/result or insubstantial differences inquiry is not applicable to the question of foreseeability.[203]

Additionally, the timing of Festo's proposed test for unforeseeability was incorrect. The Federal Circuit explained that "[t]he question is not whether *after* the narrowing amendment the [accused] alternative was a known equivalent, but rather whether it was a known equivalent *before* the narrowing amendment."[204] Applying this understanding, an "equivalent is foreseeable if one skilled in the art would have known that the alternative existed in the field of art as defined by the original claim scope, even if the suitability of the alternative for the particular purposes defined by the amended claim scope were unknown."[205] The Federal Circuit illustrated its rule by positing that "if a claim before amendment broadly claimed a metal filament for a light bulb but was later amended to avoid prior art and to specify metal A because of its longevity, the equivalent metal B, known in the prior art to function as a bulb filament, is not unforeseeable even though its longevity was unknown at the time of amendment." [206]

Other post-*Festo III* decisions have addressed the nature of the amendments that will trigger the *Festo* presumption in the first instance. For example, the Federal Circuit went *en banc* in *Honeywell Int'l Inc. v. Hamilton Sundstrand Corp.*[207] to clarify that "the rewriting of

[200]*Id.* at 1378.
[201]*See id.* at 1378-1379.
[202]*See id.* at 1380.
[203]*See id.* at 1382.
[204]*Id.* at 1381 (emphasis in original).
[205]*Id.* In other words, "an alternative is foreseeable if it is known in the field of the invention as reflected in the claim scope before amendment." *Id.* at 1379. The court did not rule out the possibility of additional formulations for foreseeability, but stated that it had "no occasion here to determine in what other circumstances an equivalent might be foreseeable." *Id.*
[206]*Id.* at 1381.
[207]370 F.3d 1131 (Fed. Cir. 2004) (*en banc*).

dependent claims into independent form coupled with the cancellation of the original independent claims creates a presumption of prosecution history estoppel."[208] This is true even when, as in *Honeywell,* the dependent claim included an additional claim limitation not found in the cancelled independent claim. Honeywell contended that although it had surrendered its broader originally filed independent claims by cancellation, there was no presumption of surrender because the scope of the rewritten claims themselves was not narrowed; they had simply been rewritten in independent form.[209] The Federal Circuit disagreed, because "the proper focus is whether the amendment narrow[ed] the *overall* scope of the claimed subject matter."[210] "[T]he fact that the scope of the rewritten claim has remained unchanged will not preclude the application of prosecution history estoppel if, by canceling the original independent claim and rewriting the dependent claims into independent form, the scope of subject matter claimed in the [original] independent claim has been narrowed to secure the patent."[211]

3. Prior Art (Hypothetical Claim Analysis)

The prior art represents another important legal limitation on a patentee's ability to rely on the doctrine of equivalents to establish infringement. This prior art limitation may be applicable even when no prosecution history estoppel exists, for example, when the patent in suit was allowed on a first Office Action without any claims having been rejected by the USPTO, as was the case in *Wilson Sporting Goods v. David Goeffrey & Associates,*[212] the foundational case in this area.

The distilled essence of the prior art limitation on the doctrine of equivalents is that an accused infringer cannot be liable for infringement under the doctrine if by making the accused device it is merely "practicing the prior art"; that is, the accused infringer is making a device that is already in the public domain.[213] The underlying policy concern is that a patentee should not be able to use the doctrine of

---

[208]*Id.* at 1134.

[209]Independent and dependent claims were introduced *supra* Chapter 2, Section D.

[210]*Honeywell*, 370 F.3d at 1141 (emphasis added).

[211]*Id.* at 1142.

[212] 904 F.2d 677, 680 (Fed. Cir. 1990) (Rich, J.).

[213]*See Wilson,* 904 F.2d at 683 (explaining that accused infringer Dunlop "contends that there is no principled difference between the balls which the jury found to infringe and the prior art Uniroyal ball; thus to allow the patent to reach Dunlop's balls under the doctrine of equivalents would improperly ensnare the prior art Uniroyal ball as well"); *id.* (stating that "there can be no infringement if the asserted scope of equivalency of what is literally claimed would encompass the prior art"). Note that although the "practicing the prior art" defense is available against a charge of infringement under the doctrine of equivalents, the Federal Circuit has rejected its applicability to

equivalents to encompass subject matter over which the patentee could not have obtained exclusionary rights in the first instance from the USPTO by applying for patent protection of that scope.[214] The *Wilson* court observed the following:

> [A] patentee should not be able to obtain, under the doctrine of equivalents, coverage which he could not lawfully have obtained from the PTO by literal claims. The doctrine of equivalents exists to prevent a fraud on a patent, *Graver Tank & Mfg. Co. v. Linde Air Prods. Co.*, 339 U.S. 605, 608, 94 L. Ed. 1097, 70 S. Ct. 854 (1950), *not* to give a patentee something which he could not lawfully have obtained from the PTO had he tried. Thus, since prior art always limits what an inventor could have claimed, it limits the range of permissible equivalents of a claim.[215]

In order to determine whether the prior art operates as a limitation (or defense) to the doctrine of equivalents, it is analytically helpful to construct a "hypothetical claim." The hypothetical claim analysis follows the steps listed in Figure 9.2.[216]

Having performed that analysis, one may ask why, when trying to determine the question of *infringement*, we should expend the analytical effort to construct and evaluate the *patentability* of a hypothetical claim. This task seems all the more unlikely because the patentee does not bear the burden of establishing the *validity* of its issued patent.[217] Simply stated, the hypothetical claim exercise is an effort to put the analysis of whether prior art limits the scope of equivalents on more familiar turf. We understand how to evaluate patent claims for patentability under §102 and §103, because this is what USPTO examiners and patent attorneys do on a regular basis.[218] It is not so easy, however, to determine the patentability of an accused device, for which (in most cases[219]) no "claim" exists. This is why we construct a hypothetical claim, based on the claim assertedly infringed, but amended so as to literally encompass the accused device. As explained by the *Wilson* court, the hypothetical claim analysis "allows use of

allegations of *literal* infringement. *See* Tate Access Floors, Inc. v. Interface Arch. Res., Inc., 279 F.3d 1357, 1365-1366 (Fed. Cir. 2002).

[214]*See Wilson*, 904 F.2d at 684.

[215]*Id.* (emphasis in original).

[216]A straightforward example of the above approach is the hypothetical claim analysis applied by the Federal Circuit in *Abbott Labs. v. Dey, L.P.*, 287 F.3d 1097, 1105 (Fed. Cir. 2002) (stating that "[t]o determine the scope of the doctrine of equivalents in light of the prior art, a court can consider a 'hypothetical claim' that literally recites the range of equivalents asserted to infringe").

[217]*See* 35 U.S.C. §282 (providing that "[a] patent shall be presumed valid").

[218]The analysis is described in detail *supra* Chapter 4 ("Novelty, Loss of Right, and Priority Pre- and Post-America Invents Act of 2011 (35 U.S.C. §102)") and *supra* Chapter 5 ("The Nonobviousness Requirement (35 U.S.C. §103)").

[219]In some cases the accused device may itself be the subject of a patent.

D. Legal Limitations on the Doctrine of Equivalents

1. Begin with the properly interpreted language of the patent claim that is allegedly infringed under the doctrine of equivalents.

↓

2. Amend the claim so that it is just broad enough to literally read on the accused device. This may require broadening only a single limitation, or multiple limitations, depending upon the differences between the claimed invention and the accused device. The claim you have rewritten in this manner is the hypothetical claim.

↓

3. Analyze the patentability of the hypothetical claim for novelty under 35 U.S.C. §102 and nonobviousness under 35 U.S.C. §103 in view of the prior art of record in the litigation. If the hypothetical claim *would* have been allowable (*i.e.,* is not anticipated or rendered obvious by the pertinent prior art), then the prior art does *not* operate as a legal limitation on the doctrine of equivalents. If the hypothetical claim would *not* have been allowable, then the patentee cannot rely on the doctrine of equivalents.

Figure 9.2

Procedure for Analyzing Whether Prior Art Limits the Availability of the Doctrine of Equivalents by Means of a Hypothetical Claim

traditional patentability rules and permits a more precise analysis than determining whether an *accused product* (which has no claim limitations on which to focus) would have been obvious in view of the prior art." [220]

4. Dedication to the Public

A patentee may not rely on the doctrine of equivalents to recapture subject matter that it clearly disclosed in its patent application but failed to claim. Allowing access to the doctrine of equivalents in such circumstances would encourage patent applicants to avoid USPTO examination of disclosed but unclaimed embodiments.[221] For example, the patentee in *Maxwell v. J. Baker, Inc.*[222] disclosed in her application two different embodiments of her inventive concept (a system for

[220]*Wilson,* 904 F.2d at 684 (emphasis in original).

[221]In such situations a patentee may attempt to reissue the patent in order to enlarge the scope of the claims to include the disclosed but previously unclaimed subject matter. A broadening reissue of this nature must be sought within two years from the grant of the original patent, however. *See* 35 U.S.C. §251.

[222]86 F.3d 1098 (Fed. Cir. 1996).

securing together the mates of a pair of shoes sold in retail stores), but claimed only one of the disclosed embodiments. By failing to claim the second embodiment, the USPTO did not have an opportunity to assess its patentability. As a matter of law, the Federal Circuit held, the accused infringer Baker could not infringe "by using an alternate shoe attachment system that Maxwell dedicated to the public." [223]

A later decision, *YBM Magnex, Inc. v. Int'l Trade Comm'n*,[224] appeared to conflict with the holding of *Maxwell*. The Federal Circuit went *en banc* in 2002 to resolve the conflict by deciding *Johnson & Johnston Assocs. v. R.E. Serv. Co.*[225] The J&J patent in suit claimed an assembly that lessened possible handling damage to fragile copper foil layers of printed circuit boards by temporarily adhering the layers to a substrate of aluminum. The patent's written description provided that although aluminum was the preferred substrate material, other metals such as stainless steel could be used. Claim 1 of the patent was limited to aluminum substrates, however; it required "a laminate constructed of a sheet of copper foil which, in a finished printed circuit board, constitutes a functional element and a sheet of *aluminum* which constitutes a discardable element."[226] The laminate made by accused infringer RES joined a layer of *steel* to the copper foil. Reaffirming the rule of *Maxwell v. J. Baker, Inc.*, the *Johnson & Johnston en banc* majority concluded that "when a patent drafter discloses but declines to claim subject matter, . . . this action dedicates that unclaimed subject matter to the public."[227] Because J&J had disclosed the steel substrates without claiming them, the court would not allow it to invoke the doctrine of equivalents to extend its aluminum claim limitation to encompass the accused steel substrate. To the extent that the court's earlier decision in *YBM Magnex* was in conflict, the *en banc* court overruled it.[228]

In *PSC Computer Prods., Inc. v. Foxconn Int'l, Inc.*,[229] the Federal Circuit addressed the level of specificity required of a patentee's disclosure of unclaimed material in order to work a dedication to the public under the *Johnson & Johnston* doctrine. PSC's patent was directed to a heat-sink assembly and retainer clip used to dissipate

---

[223]*Id.* at 1108.

[224]145 F.3d 1317 (Fed. Cir. 1998).

[225]285 F.3d 1046, 1054 (Fed. Cir. 2002) (*en banc*).

[226]*Id.* at 1050 (emphasis added).

[227]*Id.* at 1054.

[228]*See id.* at 1055. A dissenting judge contended that J&J's filing of broader claims reciting "metal" substrate sheets in continuation applications was objective evidence that J&J did not intend to dedicate that broader subject matter to the public. *See id.* at 1067 (Newman, J., dissenting) (citing In re Gibbs, 437 F.2d 486 (C.C.P.A. 1971) (holding that claiming subject matter in a continuing application rebuts any inference that the disclosed but unclaimed subject matter was abandoned)).

[229]355 F.3d 1353 (Fed. Cir. 2004).

heat from an electronic package or semiconductor device. The patent's broadest claim recited clips containing "an elongated, resilient *metal* strap."[230] In discussing the background of the invention, the written description of PSC's patent disclosed that certain "prior art devices use molded *plastic* and/or metal parts that must be cast or forged which again are more expensive metal forming operations."[231] Rejecting PSC's argument that this disclosure was merely "oblique and incidental," the Federal Circuit held it specific enough to have dedicated the unclaimed embodiment, plastic clips, to the public, and therefore to have placed plastic clips beyond any permissible scope of equivalents to the claimed metal clips. The test is whether one of ordinary skill in the art can understand the unclaimed disclosed teaching upon reading the written description, the Federal Circuit instructed. In this case, a reader of ordinary skill in the art "could reasonably conclude from th[e] language in the written description that plastic clip parts could be substituted for metal clip parts."[232] PSC was thus "obliged either to claim plastic parts in addition to metal parts and to submit this broader claim for examination, or to not claim them and dedicate the use of plastic parts to the public."[233] Because PSC chose the latter option, it had thereby dedicated plastic clips to the public.

5. Vitiation of Claim Limitations

The concept of "vitiation" is yet another legal limitation on a patentee's ability to use the doctrine of equivalents. The doctrine of equivalents should not be applied to a particular claim limitation if doing so would eliminate or vitiate that limitation, that is, would effectively read the limitation out of the claim. For example, the court in *Asyst Techs., Inc. v. Emtrak, Inc.* contended that "[t]o hold that 'unmounted' is equivalent to 'mounted' would effectively read the 'mounted on' limitation out of the patent." [234]

---

[230]*Id.* at 1355 (emphasis added).

[231]*Id.* at 1356 (emphasis added).

[232]*Id.* at 1360.

[233]*Id.*

[234]402 F.3d 1188, 1195 (Fed. Cir. 2005). The Asyst patent in suit claimed an information processing system having *inter alia* a "second microcomputer means for receiving and processing digital information communicated with said respective second two-way communication means *mounted on* the respective work station therewith." *Id.* at 1190 (quoting claim 1) (emphasis added). The Federal Circuit agreed with the district court's interpretation of "mounted" as literally limited to securely attached or affixed. The accused IridNet system was unmounted such that it did not literally infringe. Moreover, the Federal Circuit held, "[i]n this case . . . the district court was correct in ruling that the doctrine of equivalents cannot be extended to reach an 'unmounted' system such as the IridNet system without vitiating the 'mounted on' limitation

The vitiation doctrine finds its genesis in *Warner-Jenkinson Co. v. Hilton Davis Chem. Co.,*[235] discussed *supra.* Recall the Supreme Court's caution that in order to reduce the uncertainty inherent in applying the doctrine of equivalents, equivalency must be evaluated between each limitation of a claim and its corresponding element in the accused device, rather than comparing the claimed invention as a whole to the accused device as a whole. The Court emphasized the importance of "ensur[ing] that the application of the doctrine [of equivalents], even as to an individual element, is not allowed such broad play as to effectively eliminate that element in its entirety."[236] If applied within appropriate limits, the Court explained, the doctrine of equivalents will not "vitiate the central functions of the patent claims themselves."[237] The *Warner-Jenkinson* Court further instructed that "under the particular facts of a case, if . . . a theory of equivalence would entirely vitiate a particular claim element, partial or complete judgment should be rendered by the [district] court, as there would be no further material issue for the jury to resolve."[238]

In the view of this author, the conceptual difficulty with the vitiation doctrine is that it currently lacks workable limits. If taken to an extreme, application of the vitiation doctrine itself vitiates the doctrine of equivalents. By definition, application of the doctrine of equivalents contemplates finding infringement liability for accused subject matter that falls outside the literal scope of the claims as construed in step (1) of an infringement analysis. In other words, applying the doctrine of equivalents has always involved a type of "vitiation" of claim limitations. Yet the Supreme Court has consistently reaffirmed the viability of the doctrine of equivalents, despite the uncertainty it creates for those seeking to avoid infringement. Even in *Warner-Jenkinson,* despite the Court's cautionary remarks about vitiating claim limitations, the Court remanded the case to permit further consideration of whether the accused process, operating at a pH of 5, equivalently infringed the patentee's claimed process operating at a pH range of "approximately 6.0-9.0." [239]

---

altogether." *Id.* at 1195. Doing so would have violated the "all elements rule" as well as its corollary, the "specific exclusion" principle, "since the term 'mounted' can fairly be said to specifically exclude objects that are 'unmounted.'" *Id.* (citing SciMed Life Sys. v. Advanced Cardiovascular Sys., 242 F.3d 1337, 1346 (Fed. Cir. 2001) (noting close kinship of the "all elements rule" and the "specific exclusion" principle); Moore U.S.A., Inc. v. Standard Register Co., 229 F.3d 1091, 1106 (Fed. Cir. 2000); Athletic Alternatives, Inc. v. Prince Mfg., Inc., 73 F.3d 1573, 1582 (Fed. Cir. 1996) ("specific exclusion" principle is "a corollary to the 'all limitations' rule")).

[235] 520 U.S. 17 (1997).

[236] *Id.* at 29.

[237] *Id.* at 30-31.

[238] *Id.* at 39 n.8.

[239] *See id.* at 41 (reversing and remanding case for further proceedings).

Federal Circuit jurisprudence has not yet developed a consistent framework for identifying when the vitiation doctrine applies, or when it should be rejected. For example, one of the first cases in which the court applied vitiation is *Moore U.S.A., Inc. v. Standard Register Co.*[240] There the court refused to find infringement under the doctrine of equivalents by an accused envelope having adhesive on 47.8 percent of its length. Recognizing equivalency would have "vitiate[d]" the patent claim limitation that required the adhesive to be applied to a "majority" (50.0 percent or more) of the envelope's length.

Although the *Moore U.S.A.* case arguably involved claims reciting numerical ranges (i.e., if one interprets the word "majority" as meaning from 50 to 100 percent of a given length), other Federal Circuit cases reject application of the vitiation doctrine to numerical limitations. For example, in *Abbott Labs. v. Dey, L.P.,*[241] Abbott's asserted claims required that the overall phospholipid component of a lung surfactant composition be present by dry weight in the range of 68.6–90.7 percent. The Federal Circuit vacated a district court's grant of summary judgment of noninfringement and refused to "preclud[e] Abbott from relying on the doctrine of equivalents simply because [its] claim recites numeric ranges for the components of the claimed surfactant."[242] The Federal Circuit concluded that "[t]he fact that a claim recites numeric ranges does not, by itself, preclude Abbott from relying on the doctrine of equivalents."[243]

E.   Aspects of Infringement Beyond 35 U.S.C. §271(a)

The majority of patent infringement lawsuits center on allegations that the accused infringer directly infringed under 35 U.S.C. §271(a) by making, using, or selling the claimed invention without authority, as detailed above. These are not the only acts that constitute patent infringement, however. The following section analyzes liability under each of remaining subsections (b) through (g) of 35 U.S.C. §271.

1.   Inducing Infringement Under §271(b)

Section 271(b) pertains to the act of inducing infringement, which is analogous to the act of aiding and abetting a crime. Inducing

[240]229 F.3d 1091, 1106 (Fed. Cir. 2000).
[241]287 F.3d 1097 (Fed. Cir. 2002).
[242]*Id.* at 1108.
[243]*Id.* at 1107-1108 (relying on Jeneric/Pentron, Inc. v. Dillon Co., 205 F.3d 1377, 1381, 1384 (Fed. Cir. 2000); and Forest Labs., Inc. v. Abbott Labs., 239 F.3d 1305, 1313 (Fed. Cir. 2001)).

infringement requires that the alleged inducer actively and knowingly aid and abet another's direct infringement.[244] While proof of intent is necessary,[245] direct evidence of that intent is not required; rather, circumstantial evidence may suffice.[246] The inducer must have actual or constructive knowledge of the patent.[247]

Inducement cases under 35 U.S.C. §271(b) typically involve one actor (the inducing infringer) providing another (the direct infringer) with instructions and information about how to make or use the accused device or carry out the accused process.[248] A good example of inducing infringement is presented by *Water Techs. Corp. v. Calco, Ltd.*[249] Water Technologies' patent in suit was directed to improved bactericidal resins used as disinfectants for purifying water; the company incorporated the resins into a drinking cup and other products useful to campers, backpackers, and travelers. Calco, a competitor of Water Technologies, directly infringed by making and selling products formed from the claimed resins. Gartner, a consultant to Calco, provided formulas to Calco, helped the company make the infringing resins, and prepared consumer use instructions. Gartner also owned the trademark POCKET PURIFIER under which Calco's accused

---

[244]*See* Water Techs. Corp. v. Calco, Ltd., 850 F.2d 660, 668 (Fed. Cir. 1998) (explaining that "[a]lthough [35 U.S.C.] section 271(b) does not use the word 'knowing,' the case law and legislative history uniformly assert such a requirement") (citing 4 DONALD S. CHISUM, CHISUM ON PATENTS §§17.04[2], [3] (1984) and cases cited therein).

[245]*See* Hewlett-Packard Co., 909 F.2d at 1469 (noting that although §271(b) does not speak of any intent requirement to actively induce infringement, "we are of the opinion that proof of actual intent to cause the acts which constitute the infringement is a necessary prerequisite to finding active inducement").

[246]*Id.* In *Metro-Goldwyn-Mayer Studios Inc. v. Grokster, Ltd.*, 545 U.S. 913 (2005), the Supreme Court considered whether a software company could face liability for copyright infringement under a theory of inducement when it supplied customers with software that could be used for legitimate noninfringing as well as infringing use (to download copyrighted digital music files). In answering the question affirmatively, the Court adopted and applied the patent law doctrine of inducing infringement under 35 U.S.C. §271(b) to the copyright setting. With respect to proving the intent element of inducing infringement, the Court observed that "[e]vidence of 'active steps . . . taken to encourage direct infringement,' *Oak Industries, Inc. v. Zenith Electronics Corp.*, 697 F. Supp. 988, 992 (ND Ill. 1988), such as advertising an infringing use or instructing how to engage in an infringing use, show an affirmative intent that the [dual use] product be used to infringe, and a showing that infringement was encouraged overcomes the law's reluctance to find liability when a defendant merely sells a commercial product suitable for some lawful use" (citations omitted). *Grokster*, 545 U.S. at 936.

[247]*See* Insituform Techs., Inc. v. CAT Contracting, Inc., 161 F.3d 688, 695 (Fed. Cir. 1998).

[248]Inducing infringement is sometimes also found on the part of corporate officers who actively assist their corporation's direct infringement. Such officers "may be personally liable for inducing infringement regardless of whether the circumstances are such that a court should disregard the corporate entity and pierce the corporate veil." Manville Sales Corp. v. Paramount Sys., Inc., 917 F.2d 544, 553 (Fed. Cir. 1990).

[249]850 F.2d 660 (Fed. Cir. 1988).

products were sold, which gave him a contractual right to approve the construction of the product. The Federal Circuit found that the totality of these acts and circumstances made Gartner liable for inducing infringement under §271(b).[250] Gartner's activities provided sufficient circumstantial evidence to sustain the district court's finding that his inducement was intentional. As a result, Gartner was held jointly and severally liable with Calco for all damages attributable to Calco's direct infringement.[251]

It is well settled that holding an accused infringer liable for inducement under §271(b) also requires proving direct infringement under §271(a). In other words, the activity being induced must itself be infringing; direct infringement is a necessary predicate for the existence of inducing infringement liability.[252] In some cases the accused direct infringer may be a consumer who allegedly directly infringed by following instructions provided by the alleged inducing infringer. Must the patentee in such scenarios proffer an actual consumer who will testify that he or she directly infringed? Not necessarily. In appropriate cases the Federal Circuit has allowed patent owners to establish a consumer's direct infringement by circumstantial (as opposed to direct) evidence. For example, in *Symantec Corp. v. Computer Assocs. Int'l, Inc.,*[253] the patentee Symantec's method claims required that its antivirus program run in conjunction with a consumer/end-user's downloading program (such as an Internet browser). Accused infringer Computer Associates (CA) marketed its own antivirus program. Symantec contended that CA induced its customers to directly infringe because CA's software product manual promoted use of the CA program in an infringing manner, that is, in conjunction with a downloading (browser) program. Symantec further contended that the CA program had no utility other than to work in conjunction with a browser. Although a district court granted CA summary judgment of no inducing infringement based on Symantec's failure to prove that any CA customer directly infringed by actually performing the claimed method, the Federal Circuit reversed. The appellate court concluded that CA's customers could have only used CA's program in an infringing manner; this was "not a case where the customers may be using

[250]*See id.* at 668-669.
[251]*Id.* at 669.
[252]*See* Akamai Techs., Inc. v. Limelight Networks, Inc., Nos. 2009–1372 et seq., __ F.3d __, 2012 WL 3764695, at *4 (Fed. Cir. Aug. 31, 2012) (*en banc*) (explaining that "inducement gives rise to liability only if the inducement leads to actual infringement. That principle, that there can be no indirect infringement without direct infringement, is well settled. . . . The reason for that rule is simple: There is no such thing as attempted patent infringement, so if there is no infringement, there can be no indirect liability for infringement.") (citations omitted).
[253]522 F.3d 1279 (Fed. Cir. 2008).

the product in either an infringing way or a non-infringing way."[254]
Symantec had "produced sufficient *circumstantial* evidence of direct
infringement to create a genuine issue of material fact, even though
Symantec has not produced evidence that *any particular customer* has
directly infringed the patent."[255] Circumstantial evidence, as opposed
to direct evidence, was adequate to establish the direct infringement
predicate for inducing infringement liability in this case.

Federal Circuit case law on inducing infringement under §271(b)
has arguably lacked clarity as to whether an accused inducer must
merely intend to cause the *acts* that induce another's direct infringement, or whether the accused inducer must also know that its acts
would induce what amounts to direct *infringement of a patent.* For
example, would Jack be liable for inducing Jill's direct infringement
if Jack provided Jill with instructions for making device X, but was
not aware that device X was patented or that Jill would infringe the
patent if she followed Jack's directions? In light of a perceived conflict
in its precedent,[256] the Federal Circuit went *en banc* for a portion of
its opinion in *DSU Med. Corp. v. JMS Co., Ltd.* to clarify the requisite level of intent required for inducing infringement under 35 U.S.C.
§271(b).[257]

The DSU patent in suit was directed to a guarded, winged-nee-
dle assembly intended to reduce the risk of accidental needle-stick
injuries to health care workers.[258] Accused infringer JMS (Japanese
Medical Supply) purchased the guards in Malaysia from co-defendant
ITL Corp., an Australian manufacturer, then closed the guards around
needles and imported the completed assemblies into the United
States. A jury found importer JMS and its U.S. distributor/subsidiary,
JMS U.S.A., liable for direct (as well as inducing and contributory)

[254]*Id.* at 1293.

[255]*Id.* (emphasis added).

[256]In *Hewlett-Packard Co. v. Bausch & Lomb*, 909 F.2d 1464 (Fed. Cir. 1990), the
court stated that "proof of actual intent to cause the acts which constitute the infringement is a necessary prerequisite to finding active inducement." *Id.* at 1469. Some read
Hewlett-Packard as signaling that such "intent to cause the acts" is the *only* component of the intent standard for §271(b). This interpretation of *Hewlett-Packard* rendered the case in conflict with the Federal Circuit's decision in *Manville Sales Corp.
v. Paramount Sys., Inc.*, 917 F.2d 544 (Fed. Cir. 1990). The court in *Manville Sales*
held that "[t]he plaintiff has the burden of showing that the alleged infringer's actions
induced infringing acts *and* that he knew or should have known his actions would
induce actual infringements." *Id.* at 553 (emphasis added). Not all judges of the Federal
Circuit agreed with the restricted reading of *Hewlett-Packard. See* DSU Med. Corp. v.
JMS Co., Ltd., 471 F.3d 1293, 1311 (Michel, C.J., and Mayer, J., concurring) (stating
that patentee DSU "misreads *Hewlett-Packard*" and that "[t]here is no actual conflict
between *Hewlett-Packard* and *Manville* . . . ").

[257]471 F.3d 1293 (Fed. Cir. 2006) (Part III.B of opinion issued by court *en banc*).

[258]*See* Guarded Winged Needle Assembly, U.S. Patent No. 5,112,311 (issued May
12, 1992).

infringement, but declined to find ITL liable for either contributory or inducing infringement. Rejecting patentee DSU's appeal, the Federal Circuit sustained the jury verdicts. With respect to ITL's alleged inducement by selling its needle guards to JMS, the fact that this act occurred outside the United States did not itself shield ITL from liability, because "'induced infringement does not require any activity by the indirect infringer in this country, as long as the direct infringement occurs [in the United States].'"[259] The primary issue, therefore, was whether ITL possessed the requisite *intent* required for liability as an inducer.

The Federal Circuit clarified the intent standard for inducement in an *en banc* portion of the *DSU Med.* decision, instructing that

> as was stated in *Manville Sales Corp. v. Paramount Systems, Inc.*, 917 F.2d 544, 554 (Fed. Cir. 1990), "[t]he plaintiff has the burden of showing that the alleged infringer's actions induced infringing acts and that he knew or should have known his actions would induce actual infringements." The requirement that the alleged infringer knew or should have known his actions would induce actual infringement necessarily includes the requirement that he or she knew of the patent.[260]

In the case at bar, sufficient evidence existed to support the finding implied from the jury's noninfringement verdict that ITL lacked the requisite intent insofar as knowing that its acts would induce actual infringement.[261] Although ITL unquestionably was aware of the DSU patent, ITL's Australian attorney concluded that ITL's needle guard would not infringe. ITL thereafter obtained a written opinion of noninfringement from U.S. counsel. A co-owner of ITL who had participated in designing ITL's guard testified before the jury that ITL had no intent to infringe DSU's patent. This record "support[ed] the jury's verdict based on the evidence showing a lack of the necessary specific intent," the Federal Circuit concluded.[262]

The Federal Circuit in 2010 applied its *DSU Med.* standard for intent in a case involving knockoffs of "cool touch" deep fryers for

[259]*DSU Med.*, 471 F.3d at 1305 (quoting district court's jury instruction with approval).

[260]*Id.* at 1304 (*en banc*).

[261]*See id.* at 1306-1307 (describing evidence).

[262]*Id.* at 1307. Questions left open by the *DSU Med.* decision include the scope of the "should have known" component of the inducing intent standard, as well as how the "knowledge of the patent" requirement can be constructively satisfied (a question not at issue in *DSU Med.* because accused inducer ITL had actual knowledge of the patent in suit). In 2011 the Supreme Court addressed the Federal Circuit's "knowledge of the patent" requirement in *Global-Tech Appliances, Inc. v. SEB S.A.*, 131 S. Ct. 2060 (2011). The *Global-Tech* decision is discussed in the text *infra*.

home use. *SEB S.A. v. Montgomery Ward & Co.*[263] involved an accused inducing infringer, Pentalpha (a wholly owned subsidiary of Global-Tech Appliances, Inc.), which manufactured home appliances in Hong Kong. Pentalpha obtained and copied "all but the cosmetic features" of a deep fryer sold in Hong Kong by SEB S.A. (a French appliance manufacturer). SEB's fryer was protected in the United States by SEB's U.S. patent, but the Hong Kong product bore no U.S. patent marking. Pentalpha obtained an attorney opinion letter that its fryer was non-infringing, but did not bother to tell the attorney that its fryer was a copy of SEB's fryer. Nor did the attorney locate SEB's U.S. patent. When Pentalpha thereafter supplied its copied fryers in the United States to SEB's competitors Sunbeam Products, Fingerhut Corp., and Montgomery Ward & Co., SEB sued for infringement. A jury found Pentalpha liable for inducing infringement under §271(b) (as well as direct infringement under §271(a)), and found that the infringement was willful.

On appeal, the Federal Circuit sustained the jury's verdict. Although the record contained no direct evidence that Pentalpha knew of SEB's patent before SEB filed its lawsuit, the Federal Circuit found adequate evidence to satisfy the circuit's *DSU Med.* "knew of the patent" standard. The Federal Circuit found that "Pentalpha deliberately disregarded a known risk that SEB had a protective patent," and concluded that such "deliberate disregard" was "a form of actual knowledge."[264]

The Supreme Court thereafter granted *certiorari* to consider the Federal Circuit's intent standard for inducing infringement under 35 U.S.C. §271(b). In its 2011 decision in *Global-Tech Appliances, Inc. v. SEB S.A.,*[265] the Supreme Court affirmed the Federal Circuit on the merits but rejected the appellate court's "deliberate disregard" standard. As a threshold matter, and consistent with its 1964 contributory infringement decision in *Aro Mfg. Co. v. Convertible Top Replacement Co.,*[266] the Supreme Court in *Global-Tech* first held that "induced infringement under §271(b) requires knowledge that the induced acts constitute patent infringement."[267]

Turning to the Federal Circuit's standard for knowledge of the patent, the *Global-Tech* Court agreed with accused infringer Pentalpha that "deliberate indifference to a known risk that a patent exists is not the appropriate standard under §271(b)." Rather, the Court held that the "willful blindness" doctrine of criminal law should apply in civil lawsuits for induced patent infringement under 35 U.S.C. §271(b).[268]

[263]594 F.3d 1360 (Fed. Cir. 2010).
[264]*See* Global-Tech Appliances, Inc. v. SEB S.A., 131 S. Ct. 2060, 2065 (2011).
[265]131 S. Ct. 2060 (2011).
[266]377 U.S. 476 (1964) ("*Aro II*").
[267]*Global-Tech,* 131 S. Ct. at 2068.
[268]*See Global-Tech,* 131 S. Ct. at 2069.

The willful blindness doctrine has two basic requirements: "(1) the defendant must subjectively believe that there is a high probability that a fact exists, and (2) the defendant must take deliberate actions to avoid learning of that fact."[269] More egregious than a "reckless" or "negligent" defendant, a "willfully blind" defendant "is one who takes deliberate actions to avoid confirming a high probability of wrongdoing and who can almost be said to have actually known the critical facts."[270]

Applying these standards to the case at bar, the *Global-Tech* Court concluded that the evidence before it "was more than sufficient for a jury to find that Pentalpha subjectively believed there was a high probability that SEB's fryer was patented, that Pentalpha took deliberate steps to avoid knowing that fact, and that it therefore willfully blinded itself to the infringing nature of Sunbeam's sales [i.e., the direct infringement]."[271] The jury "could have easily found" that before the lawsuit was filed, Pentalpha had willfully blinded itself to the infringing nature of the sales it induced Sunbeam to make. Pentalpha's CEO, John Sham, himself an inventor, was "well aware that products made for overseas markets usually do not bear U.S. patent markings."[272] Sham admittedly conducted market research and gathered as much information as he could about SEB's fryer. Most telling was Sham's decision not to inform the attorney from whom he requested a right-to-use opinion that Pentalpha's fryer "was simply a knockoff" of SEB's product. Although the Federal Circuit had applied an incorrect standard, this evidence was more than enough to affirm the circuit's judgment sustaining the jury's verdict of Pentalpha's inducing infringement liability under a correct "willfully blind" standard.

2. Contributory Infringement Under §271(c)

Section 271(c) governs contributory infringement, which involves one entity (the contributory infringer) supplying a "nonstaple" component of a claimed invention to another entity (the direct infringer), who makes, uses, or sells the entire invention. A nonstaple component is a component or part of an invention that is not suitable for any substantial use other than in the patented invention.[273] Determining that a supplied component is a nonstaple allows courts to "identify

---

[269]*Global-Tech,* 131 S. Ct. at 2070.

[270]*Global-Tech,* 131 S. Ct. at 2070.

[271]*Global-Tech,* 131 S. Ct. at 2072.

[272]*Global-Tech,* 131 S. Ct. at 2071.

[273]*See* Dawson Chem. Co. v. Rohm & Haas Co., 448 U.S. 176, 184 (1980) (citing Fifth Circuit's definition of a nonstaple article as "one that has no commercial use except in connection with respondent's patented invention").

instances in which it may be presumed from distribution of an article in commerce that the distributor intended the article to be used to infringe another's patent, and so may justly be held liable for that infringement."[274] Where an article is "'good for nothing else' but infringement, there is no legitimate public interest in its unlicensed availability, and there is no injustice in presuming or imputing an intent to infringe."[275]

For example, the accused contributory infringer in *Dawson Chemical Co. v. Rohm & Haas Co.*[276] supplied the herbicide propanil to farmers. By using the propanil to control weeds in their rice crops in accordance with the process claimed in the patent in suit, the farmers became liable as direct infringers (presumably for "using" the patented process without authorization). While not covered by a patent, the herbicide propanil was a qualifying nonstaple commodity that had no use other than in the claimed method.[277]

The staple/nonstaple distinction is the key to contributory infringement. Section 271(c) provides a patent owner with "a limited power to exclude others from competition in nonstaple goods,"[278] but does not permit her to control the supply of staple goods, which could have many noninfringing uses.[279] For example, consider a patented process for making cookies that comprises (among other steps) a step of adding salt to a dough mixture. A party who supplies salt to the accused cookie maker cannot be liable for contributory infringement because salt is a staple that has many uses other than in the claimed cookie-making process.[280]

As is the case for inducing infringement under §271(b), there cannot be contributory infringement liability under §271(c) unless direct infringement is proven under §271(a). In the absence of direct infringement, there is no improper act to which an accused contributory

---

[274]Metro-Goldwyn-Mayer Studios Inc. v. Grokster, Ltd., 545 U.S. 913, 932 (2005).

[275]*Id.* (citations omitted).

[276]448 U.S. 176 (1980).

[277]*Id.* at 199.

[278]*Id.* at 201.

[279]The staple article of commerce doctrine "absolves the equivocal conduct of selling an item with substantial lawful as well as unlawful uses, and limits liability to instances of more acute fault than the mere understanding that some of one's products will be misused. It leaves breathing room for innovation and a vigorous commerce." *Grokster*, 545 U.S. at 932-933 (citations omitted).

[280]*See* Carbice Corp. of Am. v. Am. Patents Dev. Corp., 283 U.S. 27 (1931) (reversing finding that patent directed to "transportation packages" in which solid carbon dioxide was used as a refrigerant was contributorily infringed by defendant supplier of solid carbon dioxide ("dry ice")). It was not relevant that the defendant sold its product "with knowledge that the dioxide is to be used by the purchaser in transportation packages like those described in the patent," *id.* at 30, or that "the unpatented refrigerant [was] one of the necessary elements of the patented product." *Id.* at 33.

infringer can be said to have contributed. When a patentee seeks to establish the §271(a) predicate for §271(c) contributory liability by a component supplier, attention must be given to patent law's distinction between permissible "repair" versus infringing "reconstruction." For example, in *Aro Mfg. Co. v. Convertible Top Replacement Co.,*[281] the patent in suit was directed to a top assembly for convertible cars. The claimed assembly required several different components, one of which was a fabric top.[282] These tops tended to wear out much more rapidly than the other components of the assembly,[283] and consumers purchased replacement fabric tops directly from the defendant supplier. When the patentee sued the supplier for contributory infringement, the Supreme Court held that no such liability existed because no direct infringement had occurred. The replacement of the fabric top was within the consumers' implied right to repair their property; a purchaser is deemed to have obtained an implied license to use the patented device she has purchased, which includes a right to repair it.[284] Replacement of the fabric top did not amount to an infringing reconstruction (i.e., a new making) of the entire claimed assembly.[285] Because the consumer purchasers were not direct infringers, the defendant supplier of the replacement tops could not be liable as a contributory infringer.

Infringement actions asserting contributory liability under 35 U.S.C. §271(c) will sometimes trigger an affirmative defense of patent misuse, as in the *Dawson* case described above and further considered in Chapter 10 ("Defenses to Patent Infringement"), *infra*. In such cases §271(c) must be read in conjunction with 35 U.S.C. §271(d). Rather than affirmatively defining patent misuse, §271(d) enumerates acts that are *not* misuse by listing five specific exceptions or "safe harbors" to patent misuse on which a patentee may rely. Chapter 10 considers in further detail the §271(d) statutory exceptions to patent misuse as well as judicially recognized acts that *will* constitute patent misuse.

[281]365 U.S. 336 (1961) (*Aro I*).

[282]*See id.* at 337 (noting that patent in suit "covers the combination, in an automobile body, of a flexible top fabric, supporting structures, and a mechanism for sealing the fabric against the side of the automobile body in order to keep out the rain").

[283]*See id.* at 337-338 (explaining that "[t]he components of the patented combination, other than the fabric, normally are usable for the lifetime of the car, but the fabric ... usually so suffers from wear and tear, or so deteriorates in appearance, as to become 'spent,' and normally is replaced, after about three years of use").

[284]*See* Aro Mfg. Co. v. Convertible Top Replacement Co., 377 U.S. 476, 484 (1964) (*Aro II*) (stating that "it is fundamental that sale of a patented article by the patentee or under his authority carries with it an 'implied license to use'") (citing Adams v. Burke, 84 U.S. (17 Wall.) 453, 456 (1873)).

[285]*See* Hewlett-Packard Co. v. Repeat-O-Type Stencil Mfg. Corp., 123 F.3d 1445, 1451-1452 (Fed. Cir. 1997).

3. Drug Marketing Application Filings Under §271(e)

Section 271(e) is particularly pertinent to allegations of infringement in the pharmaceutical industry. In recent years, an increasing number of firms that manufacture generic equivalent drugs have sought entry onto the market before the expiration of the patents covering those drugs, which are owned by brand-name pharmaceutical manufacturers.[286] These efforts frequently lead to patent infringement/validity litigation between the brand-name and generic firms, as described below. Such litigation activity has spawned a growing demand for attorneys trained both in patent law and regulatory food and drug law.

Section 271(e) was enacted in 1984 pursuant to the Drug Price Competition and Patent Term Restoration Act of 1984,[287] popularly known as the Hatch-Waxman Act. The legislation added, *inter alia*, §271(e)(1) to the Patent Act, which provides in pertinent part that the use of a patented invention solely for purposes reasonably related to gathering data in support of an application seeking Food and Drug Administration (FDA) approval for the manufacture and sale of a generic version of a previously FDA-approved drug (i.e., an "Abbreviated New Drug Application," or ANDA) is *not* patent infringement.[288] Without such a provision, generic drug manufacturers would have to wait to begin testing of an equivalent drug until after the relevant patent had expired, and the patentee of the branded drug would receive a *de facto* extension of the patent term.[289]

The §271(e)(1) safe harbor is not limited to testing conducted by generic drug manufacturers, however. The Supreme Court interpreted the scope of §271(e)(1) in *Merck KgaA v. Integra Lifesciences I, Ltd.,*[290] and held it broad enough to encompass clinical (human) trials as well

---

[286]*See* Federal Trade Commission, *Generic Drug Entry Prior to Patent Expiration: An FTC Study*, at ii (July 2002), *available at* http://www.ftc.gov/os/2002/07/genericdrugstudy.pdf.

[287]Pub. L. No. 98-417, 98 Stat. 1585 (1984).

[288]Section 271(e)(1) of 35 U.S.C. provides,

It shall not be an act of infringement to make, use, offer to sell, or sell within the United States or import into the United States a patented invention . . . solely for uses reasonably related to the development and submission of information under a Federal law which regulates the manufacture, use, or sale of drugs or veterinary biological products.

[289]The U.S. Supreme Court subsequently interpreted 35 U.S.C. §271(e)(1) as broad enough to encompass not only regulatory data gathering on pharmaceuticals but also the comparable testing of medical devices. *See* Eli Lilly & Co. v. Medtronic, Inc., 496 U.S. 661, 679 (1990) (affirming Federal Circuit's interpretation).

[290]545 U.S. 193 (2005).

as pre-clinical (test tube and laboratory animal) testing activity associated with the development of new (or "pioneer") drugs. The Federal Circuit had erred in excluding Merck KgaA–sponsored testing at the Scripps Research Institute of patented peptides with potential cancer-fighting activity from the statutory safe harbor on the ground that its purpose was to identify the best drug candidate for future clinical testing and was thus too remote from the safe harbor's purview. According to the Supreme Court, the facts that not all data developed during pre-clinical and clinical testing are ultimately submitted to the FDA, and that some testing involves drugs not ultimately the subject of an FDA application, are not determinative of eligibility for the liability shield. Rather, "[p]roperly construed, §271(e)(1) leaves adequate space for experimentation and failure on the road to regulatory approval: At least where a drugmaker has a reasonable basis for believing that a patented compound may work, through a particular biological process, to produce a particular physiological effect, and uses the compound in research that, if successful, would be appropriate to include in a submission to the FDA, that use is 'reasonably related' to the 'development and submission of information under . . . Federal law.' §271(e) (1)."[291] Although broad enough to encompass testing of new drugs as well as generic equivalents, the *Merck KgaA* Court made clear that the statutory safe harbor does have limits; §271(e)(1) is not broad enough to reach back in time to shield "[b]asic scientific research on a particular compound, performed without the intent to develop a particular drug or a reasonable belief that the compound will cause the sort of physiological effect the researcher intends to induce."[292]

Federal Circuit decisions in the wake of *Merck KgaA* continue to explore permutations of the §271(e)(1) safe harbor. For example, the appellate court held in *Amgen, Inc. v. Int'l Trade Comm'n* that the safe harbor shielded imports of the biopharmaceutical erythropoiten (EPO) by intervenor Hoffman-La Roche, because the safe harbor applies to §337 actions at the International Trade Commission (ITC).[293] In contrast, the Federal Circuit distinguished *Merck KgaA* and narrowly interpreted the §271(e)(1) safe harbor in *Proveris Sci. Corp. v. Innovasystems, Inc.*[294] so as to uphold a district court's finding of infringement by Innova's optical spray "Analyzer" device. The Analyzer was not itself subject to FDA approval, but rather was a laboratory tool used exclusively by those preparing FDA regulatory submissions to measure and calibrate physical parameters of aerosol sprays used in devices such as inhalers. The Federal Circuit was

---

[291]*Id.* at 207.
[292]*Id.* at 205-206.
[293]519 F.3d 1343 (Fed. Cir. 2008).
[294]536 F.3d 1256 (Fed. Cir. 2008).

persuaded that because Innova was not itself seeking FDA approval for the Analyzer device and did not face regulatory barriers to market entry after the expiration of competitors' patents (unlike the typical case with drug manufacturers), Innova was not within the scope of intended beneficiaries of the §271(e)(1) safe harbor and did not need that statutory protection.

The Hatch-Waxman Act also added §271(e)(2) to the Patent Act. This subsection provides that it *is* an act of patent infringement to submit an ANDA to the FDA if the generic applicant is seeking approval to engage in the commercial manufacture, use, or sale of a patented drug before the expiration of the patent.[295] The mere act of filing the ANDA is considered an act of infringement, even though the generic firm has not yet engaged in any commercial manufacture or sale of the drug (because it does not yet have FDA approval to do so).[296]

Generic drug manufacturers submitting an ANDA must certify one of four things: (1) that the drug for which the ANDA is submitted has not been patented (a "paragraph I" certification); (2) that any patent on such drug has expired (a "paragraph II" certification); (3) the date on which the patent on such drug will expire, if it has not yet expired (a "paragraph III" certification); or (4) that the patent on such drug "is invalid or that it will not be infringed by the manufacture, use, or sale of the new drug" for which the ANDA is submitted (a "paragraph IV" certification).[297]

Paragraph IV certifications are of the greatest interest here, because they generally trigger patent infringement litigation. A generic firm that submits a paragraph IV certification to the FDA also must give notice to the owner of the relevant patent.[298] This notice triggers a 45-day period in which the patentee can initiate an action against the generic firm for infringement under 35 U.S.C. §271(e)(2). If the patentee does not sue within this period, then approval of the ANDA "shall

[295]Subsection 271(e)(2) of 35 U.S.C. provides,

It shall be an act of infringement to submit—

(A) an application under section 505(j) of the Federal Food, Drug, and Cosmetic Act [21 U.S.C. §355(j)] or described in section 505(b)(2) of such Act [21 U.S.C. §355(b)(2)] for a drug claimed in a patent or the use of which is claimed in a patent,

. . . if the purpose of such submission is to obtain approval under such Act to engage in the commercial manufacture, use, or sale of a drug or veterinary biological product claimed in a patent or the use of which is claimed in a patent before the expiration of such patent.

[296]*See* Yamanouchi Pharm. Co. v. Danbury Pharmacal, Inc., 231 F3d 1339, 1346 (Fed. Cir. 2000).

[297]*See* 21 U.S.C. §355(j)(2)(A)(vii)(I)-(IV).

[298]*See id*. §355(j)(2)(B)(i)(I).

be made effective immediately" (assuming that the ANDA meets all applicable scientific and regulatory requirements).[299]

If, however, the patent owner brings an infringement action under §271(e)(2) within the required time period, the FDA must suspend approval of the ANDA.[300] The suspension continues—and the FDA cannot approve the ANDA—until the earliest of three dates: (1) if the district court hearing the lawsuit decides that the patent is invalid or not infringed, the date of the court's decision; (2) if the court decides that the patent has been infringed, the date that the patent expires; or (3) subject to modification by the court, the date that is 30 months from the date on which the patent owner received notice of the generic firm's paragraph IV certification.[301]

Summarizing the above statutory scheme, the Federal Circuit concluded that

> the Hatch-Waxman Act strikes a balance between the interests of a party seeking approval of an ANDA and the owner of a drug patent. On the one hand, the manufacture, use, or sale of a patented drug is not an act of infringement, to the extent it is necessary for the preparation and submission of an ANDA. On the other hand, once it is clear that a party seeking approval of an ANDA wants to market a patented drug prior to the expiration of the patent, the patent owner can seek to prevent approval of the ANDA by bringing a patent infringement suit. While it is pending, such a suit can have the effect of barring ANDA approval for two and a half years [i.e., 30 months].[302]

Some pharmaceutical industry observers question whether the current statutory framework correctly balances the interests of patent owners, generic drug manufacturers, and consumers. They contend that the regulatory framework permits patent owners to postpone competition from generic manufacturers for too long, to the detriment of the consumers who would otherwise benefit from lower drug prices.

In October 2002, then–President George W. Bush announced proposed changes to the FDA's rules for approval of ANDAs, targeting patent owners whom the government contends have improperly delayed market entry of generic drugs for up to 40 additional months by obtaining multiple 30-month stays of FDA approval of a given ANDA.[303] The

---

[299]*See id.* §355(j)(5)(B)(iii).

[300]*See id.*

[301]*See id.* §355(j)(5)(B)(iii)(I)-(III); 35 U.S.C. §271(e)(4)(A).

[302]Bristol-Myers Squibb Co. v. Royce Labs., Inc., 69 F.3d 1130, 1132 (Fed. Cir. 1995).

[303]*See* Office of the White House Press Secretary, *President Takes Action to Lower Prescription Drug Prices by Improving Access to Generic Drugs* (Oct. 21, 2002), http://www.whitehouse.gov/news/releases/2002/10/20021021-4.html; Federal Trade Commission, *Generic Drug Entry Prior to Patent Expiration: An FTC Study* (July 2002), *available at* http://www.ftc.gov/os/2002/07/generic-drugstudy.pdf. The *FTC*

proposed rules limited patent owners to only one 30-month automatic stay per a given ANDA, which the government contended is an appropriate time period for resolution of the infringement case.[304] The proposed rule was made final and effective as of August 2003.[305]

4.   Component Exports Under §271(f)

Subsection (f) of 35 U.S.C. §271 is a hybrid statutory provision that concerns acts of infringement that are completed outside the geographic borders of the United States, but were begun by inducing or contributory activity within the United States. Thus, §271(f) involves certain extraterritorial activities, but those activities must have a nexus to acts occurring in the United States. Where that nexus is adequately established, §271(f) creates liability as an exception to the "general rule under United States patent law that no infringement occurs when a patented product is made and sold in another country."[306] Section 271(f) provides

> (f) (1) Whoever without authority supplies or causes to be supplied in or from the United States all or a substantial portion of the components of a patented invention, where such components are uncombined in whole or in part, in such manner as to actively induce the combination of such components outside of the United States in a manner that would infringe the patent if such combination occurred within the United States, shall be liable as an infringer.
>
> (2) Whoever without authority supplies or causes to be supplied in or from the United States any component of a patented invention that is especially made or especially adapted for use in the invention and not a staple article or commodity of commerce suitable for substantial noninfringing use, where such component is uncombined in whole or in part,

---

Study explains how patent owners may generate multiple 30-month stays by listing additional patents in the FDA's Orange Book after a given ANDA is filed by a generic firm. The generic firm is required to recertify as to those additionally listed patents, which may trigger the patentee to seek additional 30-month stays by adding those patents to its infringement complaint. *See id.* at iii. The "Orange Book" is the colloquial term for an FDA publication officially titled *Approved Drug Products with Therapeutic Equivalents. Id.* at 5. When a brand-name company seeks FDA approval to market a new drug product, it must list in the Orange Book the patents relevant to that product, including not only any patents on the active ingredient(s) of the drug product but also patents on specific formulations (e.g., a tablet form) and methods of use (e.g., use to treat heartburn in mammals). *See id. See also* U.S. FOOD & DRUG ADMINISTRATION, ELECTRONIC ORANGE BOOK (Sept. 2008), http://www.fda.gov/cder/ob/.

[304]*See* Federal Trade Commission, *Generic Drug Entry Prior to Patent Expiration: An FTC Study* 6-7 (July 2002), *available at* http://www.ftc.gov/os/2002/07/generic-drug-study.pdf.

[305]68 FED. REG. 36676 (June 18, 2003).

[306]Microsoft Corp. v. AT&T Corp., 550 U.S. 437, 127 S. Ct. 1746, 1750 (2007).

knowing that such component is so made or adapted and intending that such component will be combined outside of the United States in a manner that would infringe the patent if such combination occurred within the United States, shall be liable as an infringer.

Section 271(f) can be more easily understood if one is familiar with its history. The section was enacted in 1984 to close a loophole in 35 U.S.C. §271 that came to light with the U.S. Supreme Court's 1972 decision in *Deepsouth Packing Co. v. Laitram Corp.*[307] There the Court was confronted with a case of alleged patent infringement in which the various component parts of a patented shrimp deveining machine were separately sold by a U.S. manufacturer to foreign buyers, who then assembled the deveining machine beyond U.S. borders in countries such as Brazil.[308] Was this offshore assembly actionable as a making of the patented invention under §271(a)? The Court concluded that it was not, because it interpreted "making" to require final assembly or combination of the "operable whole,"[309] and the assembly in question did not occur within U.S. borders.[310] The Court moreover refused to apply U.S. patent laws extraterritorially to make the foreign assembly

---

[307]406 U.S. 518 (1972). *See also* Rotec Indus., Inc. v. Mitsubishi Corp., 215 F.3d 1246, 1258 (Fed. Cir. 2000) (Newman, J., concurring) (explaining that "Congress enacted 35 U.S.C. §271(f), 'respond[ing] to the United States Supreme Court decision in [*Deepsouth*], concerning the need for a legislative solution to close a loophole in patent law.' 130 Cong. Rec. 28,069 (1984). *See also* S. Rep. No. 98-663 at 2 (1984) (describing the legislation as 'reversal of *Deepsouth* decision').").

[308]*Deepsouth*, 406 U.S. at 523 n.5.

[309]*See id.* at 528 (stating that "[w]e cannot endorse the view that the 'substantial manufacture of the constituent parts of [a] machine' constitutes direct infringement when we have so often held that a combination patent protects only against the operable assembly of the whole and not the manufacture of its parts").

[310]The Federal Circuit distinguished *Deepsouth* in a case involving alleged infringement by the Blackberry wireless e-mail device. In *NTP, Inc. v. Research in Motion, Ltd.*, 392 F.3d 1336 (Fed. Cir. 2004), the patent in suit was directed to a system for sending e-mail messages between two subscribers; transmissions were made between an originating processor and a destination processor but passed through an "interface switch." In the accused Blackberry system, the interface switch claim limitation was met by a relay physically housed in Canada; on this basis the alleged infringer argued that under *Deepsouth*, there was no actionable infringement within the United States. The Federal Circuit disagreed, concluding that the location of infringement in this case was within U.S. territory, in contrast with *Deepsouth*. All components of the accused Blackberry system except the relay were located in the United States, and the location of the beneficial use and function of the whole operable system assembly was the United States. Therefore, the situs of the "use" of the accused system for purposes of 35 U.S.C. §271(a) was the United States. *See NTP*, 392 F.3d at 1366-1370 (analogizing case to *Decca Ltd. v. United States*, 544 F.2d 1070 (Ct. Cl. 1976)).

an act of infringement in the United States.[311] Since in the *Deepsouth* Court's view there was no act of direct infringement, the component supplier could not be held liable for contributory infringement under 35 U.S.C. §271(c).[312]

Section 271(f) represents a legislative overruling of the *Deepsouth* decision. The two subparagraphs of §271(f) are structured so as to parallel the inducing and contributory infringement provisions of 35 U.S.C. §§271(b) and (c). More specifically, §271(f)(1) echoes the inducing infringement provisions of §271(b) to render infringing the act of supplying "in or from the United States all or a substantial portion of the components of a patented invention" in such a manner as to "actively induce the combination of such components outside of the United States." Similarly, §271(f)(2) echoes the contributory infringement provisions of §271(c) to render infringing the act of supplying "in or from the United States" a nonstaple component of a patented invention "intending that such component will be combined outside of the United States." [313]

Federal Circuit decisions continue to grapple with the limits of extraterritoriality under 35 U.S.C. §271(f). For example, the potential infringement liability of one who "supplies or causes to be supplied in or from the United States all or a substantial portion of the components of a patented invention" under §271(f)(1) does not extend to the mere supply of instructions or authorization from the United States, according to the Federal Circuit's decision in *Pellegrini v. Analog Devices, Inc.*[314] Pellegrini's patent was directed to brushless motor drive circuits that incorporated integrated circuit chips. The chips fabricated and sold by accused infringer Analog Devices were manufactured

---

[311]*See Deepsouth*, 406 U.S. at 531, stating,

In conclusion, we note that what is at stake here is the right of American companies to compete with an American patent holder in foreign markets. Our patent system makes no claim to extraterritorial effect; "these acts of Congress do not, and were not intended to, operate beyond the limits of the United States," *Brown v. Duchesne,* 19 How., at 195; and we correspondingly reject the claims of others to such control over our markets. *Cf.* Boesch v. Graff, 133 U.S. 697, 703 (1890). To the degree that the inventor needs protection in markets other than those of this country, the wording of 35 U. S. C. §§154 and 271 reveals a congressional intent to have him seek it abroad through patents secured in countries where his goods are being used. Respondent holds foreign patents; it does not adequately explain why it does not avail itself of them.

[312]*See id.* at 526.

[313]The patentee asserting infringement under 35 U.S.C. §271(f)(2) need not show that the final assembly in the foreign country actually occurred, only that the nonstaple component was supplied from the United States with the intent that the final assembly would take place. *See* Waymark Corp. v. Porta Sys. Corp., 245 F.3d 1364 (Fed. Cir. 2001).

[314]375 F.3d 1113 (Fed. Cir. 2004).

entirely outside the United States and shipped only to customers outside the United States. Nevertheless, Pellegrini argued that because Analog's corporate headquarters was located in the United States and instructions for the production and disposition of the chips emanated there, the chips should have been regarded as "supplied or caused to be supplied in or from the United States." The Federal Circuit disagreed, holding that the plain meaning of §271(f)(1) makes it applicable only where components of a patent invention are physically present in the United States and then either sold or exported "in such a manner as to actively induce the combination of such components outside the United States in a manner that would infringe the patent if such combination occurred within the United States." Here, the components (i.e., circuit chips) were not present in the United States prior to their combination offshore. The language "supplying or causing to be supplied" in §271(f)(1) "clearly refers to physical supply of components, not simply to the supply of instructions or corporate oversight," the *Pellegrini* court concluded. "[A]lthough Analog may be giving instructions from the United States that cause the components of the patented invention to be supplied, it is undisputed that those components are not being supplied in or from the United States." [315]

The Federal Circuit distinguished *Pellegrini* in *Eolas Techs., Inc. v. Microsoft Corp.* [316] The patent in suit in *Eolas* claimed a "computer program product" comprising *inter alia* a "computer usable medium having computer readable program code physically embodied therein." The claimed invention allowed a user to employ a Web browser in a fully interactive environment, for example, viewing news clips or playing games across the Internet. Eolas, the exclusive licensee of the patent, alleged that certain aspects of Microsoft's Internet Explorer (IE) browser incorporated the claimed invention. Eolas further contended that under 35 U.S.C. §271(f)(1), Microsoft's foreign sales of its IE browser should have been included in the damages base. The legal dispute centered on whether Microsoft's export to foreign manufacturers of certain "golden master" disks containing software code for the Microsoft Windows operating system (including code for the IE browser) constituted the supply of "components" under the statute. The foreign manufacturers used the golden master disks to replicate the software code onto computer hard drives for sale outside of the United States, but the golden master disks themselves did not become a physical part of any infringing product.

The Federal Circuit rejected accused infringer Microsoft's argument that "components of a patented invention" under §271(f)(1) must be limited to physical or tangible components, as suggested by *Pellegrini*.

---

[315]*Id.* at 1118.
[316]399 F.3d 1325 (Fed. Cir. 2005).

Rather, the *Eolas* court concluded, "every form of invention eligible for patenting falls within the protection of section 271(f)," and "software code claimed in conjunction with a physical structure, such as a disk, fits within . . . the broad statutory label of 'patented invention.'"[317] Exact duplicates of the software code on the golden master disks were incorporated into the ultimate products, and that code was "probably the key part" of the patented invention. The *Eolas* court distinguished *Pellegrini* as requiring only that components be "physically *supplied* from the United States,"[318] not that the components themselves *be* physical. *Pellegrini* did "not impose on section 271(f) a tangibility requirement that does not appear anywhere in the language of that section."[319]

Eolas was not the only patent owner to allege a violation of §271(f) based on Microsoft's distribution of its Windows operating system software to foreign computer manufacturers. When the AT&T Corporation sued Microsoft for infringement under §271(f), the case eventually made its way to the Supreme Court. In *Microsoft Corp. v. AT&T Corp.*,[320] the Court held that Microsoft's export of the golden master disks (or counterpart electronic transmissions) containing Windows software for copying and installation on foreign-made computers did *not* trigger infringement liability under §271(f).

AT&T's patent in suit was directed to apparatus for digitally encoding and compressing recorded speech. Microsoft's Windows operating system admittedly included code that enabled a computer to process speech per AT&T's patent claims. Importantly, however, the AT&T claims were infringed only when the relevant Windows code was *installed* on a computer; infringement of the claims occurred "only when a computer is loaded with Windows and is thereby rendered capable of performing as the patented speech processor."[321] The key facet of Microsoft's distribution scheme that avoided infringement liability was that while Microsoft exported the disks (or sent electronic transmissions) containing the code capable of infringing AT&T's patent, those disks or e-mails were not *themselves* installed on the foreign-made computers. Instead, the foreign computer manufacturers first made *copies* of the Windows software, and then used those foreign-made software copies for installation outside the United States. The Supreme Court held that Microsoft's liability did *not* extend to "computers made in another country when loaded with Windows software *copied abroad* from a master disk or electronic transmission dispatched by Microsoft from the United States."[322] Figure 9.3 depicts Microsoft's distribution scheme.

---

[317] *Id.* at 1339.
[318] *Id.* at 1341 (emphasis in original).
[319] *Id.*
[320] 550 U.S. 437, 127 S. Ct. 1746 (2007).
[321] *Id.*, 127 S. Ct. at 1750.
[322] *Id.* at 1750-1751 (emphasis added).

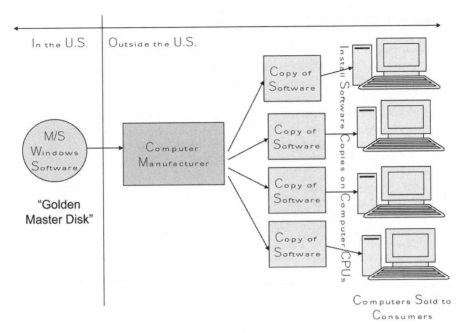

Figure 9.3

Software Distribution Scheme in *AT&T v. Microsoft*

Because Microsoft did not export the software copies actually installed on the foreign-made computers, the *AT&T* Court concluded, Microsoft had not supplied "components" of the claimed invention from the United States "under §271(f) as currently written."[323] The relevant components were the software copies, and those components were supplied from places outside the United States. In its ruling the Supreme Court emphasized the general presumption against extra-territorial application of U.S. laws. The presumption that United States law "does not rule the world" applies "with particular force" in patent law.[324] The Court accordingly "resist[ed] giving the language in which Congress cast §271(f) an expansive interpretation," deferring to "Congress' informed judgment [whether] any adjustment of §271(f) [is] necessary or proper."[325]

[323]*Id.* at 1750.

[324]*Id.* at 1758 (citing 35 U.S.C. §154(a)(1) and Deepsouth Packing Co. v. Laitram Corp., 406 U.S. 518, 531 (1972)).

[325]*Id.* at 1751. Responding to AT&T's argument that denying §271(f) liability in this case creates an easily exploited loophole for software makers, the Supreme Court observed that "Congress is doubtless aware of the ease with which software (and other electronic media) can be copied." *Id.* at 1760 (citing Congress's 1998 enactment of the

517

5.   Importation Under §271(g)

Like §271(f), 35 U.S.C. §271(g) is concerned with acts that take place, in part, outside the geographic borders of the United States. Section 271(g) provides as follows:

> (g) Whoever without authority imports into the United States or offers to sell, sells, or uses within the United States a product which is made by a process patented in the United States shall be liable as an infringer, if the importation, offer to sell, sale, or use of the product occurs during the term of such process patent. In an action for infringement of a process patent, no remedy may be granted for infringement on account of the noncommercial use or retail sale of a product unless there is no adequate remedy under this title for infringement on account of the importation or other use, offer to sell, or sale of that product. A product which is made by a patented process will, for purposes of this title, not be considered to be so made after —
>
> > (1) it is materially changed by subsequent processes; or
> >
> > (2) it becomes a trivial and nonessential component of another product.

Section 271(g) is particularly important for biotechnology firms that own process patents. In many cases such firms may obtain patents on innovative biotech processes for making known products, such as a novel recombinant method for obtaining insulin needed by patients suffering from diabetes. Prior to the enactment of §271(g) in 1988, a U.S. process patent owner had no recourse under the Patent Act[326] against a competitor who carried out the process abroad (where it would not violate the U.S. process patent) and imported the product (which was not protected by U.S. patent) into the United States. By enacting §271(g) in 1988 as part of the Process Patent Amendments Act,[327] Congress closed the loophole and brought this aspect of U.S. patent law into conformity with that of other nations.[328]

Section 271(g) contains certain safeguards. Subsection 271(g)(1) provides that there is no infringement if the imported product of the patented process is "materially changed by subsequent processes"

Digital Millennium Copyright Act, 17 U.S.C. §1201 *et seq.*). If patent law should be adjusted to better account for the realities of software distribution, such alteration "should be made after focused legislative consideration, and not by the Judiciary forecasting Congress' likely disposition." *Id.*

[326]Prior to 1988, the process patent owner's only option was to seek an exclusion order for the imported products from the International Trade Commission under Section 337a of the Tariff Act of 1930, 19 U.S.C. §1337a (1982). *See* Eli Lilly & Co. v. Am. Cyanamid Co., 82 F.3d 1568, 1571-1572 (Fed. Cir. 1996).

[327]Pub. L. No. 100-418, §§9001-9007, 102 Stat. 1107 (Aug. 23, 1988).

[328]*See* Ajinomoto Co. v. Archer-Daniels-Midland Co., 228 F.3d 1338, 1347 (Fed. Cir. 2000).

before the product was imported.[329] The Federal Circuit interpreted the meaning of §271(g)'s "materially changed" clause in *Eli Lilly v. American Cyanamid Co.*[330] Although acknowledging its "considerable appeal," the court ultimately rejected patentee Eli Lilly's argument that "materially changed" must be construed in light of the statute's underlying purpose, which is to protect the economic value of U.S. process patents to their owners. The statutory language focuses on changes to the *product,* the Federal Circuit pointed out, not to the economic value of the process patent to its owner. "In the chemical context," the court noted, "a 'material' change in a compound is most naturally viewed as a significant change in the compound's structure and properties." [331]

In *Eli Lilly,* the compound being imported by the accused infringer was different in four important structural respects from the compound produced by the patented process; these structural differences corresponded to four additional process steps performed abroad by the accused infringer that were not part of the patented process. Although it did not attempt "to define with precision what classes of changes would be material and what would not," the Federal Circuit shared the view of the district court that the changes in chemical structure and properties in the case at bar could not be dismissed as "immaterial."[332] Thus the Federal Circuit concluded that Eli Lilly, which had sought a preliminary injunction below, was not likely to succeed on the merits of its infringement claim under 35 U.S.C. §271(g).

---

[329]*See* Eli Lilly & Co. v. Am. Cyanamid Co., 82 F.3d 1568, 1571 (Fed. Cir. 1996).
[330]*Id.* at 1568.
[331]*Id.* at 1573.
[332]*Id.*

Chapter 10

Defenses to Patent Infringement

A. Introduction

As a practical matter, when sued for patent infringement an **accused infringer** will almost always assert the following two defenses: (1) "my product/process does not infringe"; and (2) "even if my product/process does infringe, your patent is invalid, so I cannot be liable for infringement." In many cases, the accused infringer will add a third defense: "The court should refuse to enforce your patent because you acted inequitably in procuring it."[1]

The statutory basis for these and other defenses is paragraph (b) of 35 U.S.C. §282 (eff. Sept. 16, 2012), which provides that the following defenses can be pleaded in a lawsuit concerning the validity or infringement of a U.S. patent:

(1) Noninfringement, absence of liability for infringement or unenforceability.

(2) Invalidity of the patent or any claim in suit on any ground specified in part II [35 U.S.C. §§100 et seq.] as a condition for patentability.

(3) Invalidity of the patent or any claim in suit for failure to comply with—

　　(A) any requirement of section 112 ["Specification"], except that the failure to disclose the best mode shall not be a basis on which any claim of a patent may be canceled or held invalid or otherwise unenforceable; or

　　(B) any requirement of section 251 ["Reissue of Defective Patents"].

---

[1]A study prepared in the late 1980s estimated that 80 percent of U.S. patent infringement lawsuits included an allegation of inequitable conduct. *See* Therasense, Inc. v. Becton, Dickinson and Co., 649 F.3d 1276, 1289 (Fed. Cir. 2011) (*en banc*) (citing Committee Position Paper, *The Doctrine of Inequitable Conduct and the Duty of Candor in Patent Prosecution: Its Current Adverse Impact on the Operation of the United States Patent System*, 16 AIPLA Q.J. 74, 75 (1988)).

(4) Any other fact or act made a defense by this title.[2]

Several of the defenses enumerated in §282(b) are actually categories that encompass a variety of defensive theories. For example, the defense of unenforceability can be established on the basis of inequitable conduct or patent misuse. The defense of invalidity can be based on a failure of the patent to comply with the requirements of utility, novelty, nonobviousness, enablement, and the like.

Each defense encompassed within §282(b) is discussed below.[3]

B.   Noninfringement

In accordance with 35 U.S.C. §282(b)(1), an accused infringer may assert that it does not infringe the patent in suit either literally or under the doctrine of equivalents. The alleged noninfringement may be based on the failure of the accused device to satisfy one or more limitations of the asserted claims, either literally or equivalently, or the accused infringer may raise a legal limitation to the patentee's reliance on the doctrine of equivalents, such as prosecution history estoppel. The substance of these theories of infringement was discussed in Chapter 9 ("Patent Infringement"), *supra,* and the reader is encouraged to review Chapter 9 before tackling this chapter.

Procedurally, the patent owner bears the burden of proof on infringement. The quantum of evidence required to carry that burden is a preponderance of the evidence (i.e., greater than half of the weight of the evidence of record). If a preponderance of the evidence does not establish infringement, then the patentee has failed to carry its burden and the accused infringer will prevail on the ground of noninfringement.

---

[2]35 U.S.C. §282(b) (eff. Sept. 16, 2012) ("Defenses"). The America Invents Act of 2011 eliminated best mode as an invalidity defense as reflected in the quoted statutory text, effective September 16, 2011. Best mode compliance remains a requirement for obtaining a patent in the first instance, however, under 35 U.S.C. §112(a) (eff. Sept. 16, 2012).

[3]These defensive theories also may be raised as the affirmative allegations of an accused infringer who files a **declaratory judgment action** under 28 U.S.C. §2201. Such an action seeks to obtain a judgment that the putative infringer/declaratory plaintiff is not infringing and/or that the allegedly infringed patent is invalid and/or unenforceable. An important part of patent infringement litigation practice, declaratory judgment actions are considered in further detail in Section G, *infra.*

C. Absence of Liability for Infringement

Asserted in accordance with 35 U.S.C. §282(b)(1) (eff. Sept. 16, 2012), this category of defenses covers situations where there cannot be liability as a matter of law; for example, the patent in suit has been expired for more than six years before the filing of the infringement action.[4] It also can be viewed as encompassing the defenses of license, prior user right, experimental use, laches, equitable estoppel, state sovereign immunity, and temporary presence in U.S. territory. Each is discussed below.

1. License

Absence of liability for infringement under §282(b)(1) encompasses the defense of license. A **license** is simply an agreement or covenant between the patentee and the licensee that the patentee will not sue the licensee for acts that would otherwise constitute infringement; it is not a transfer of ownership of the patent (i.e., an **assignment**). In accordance with the language of 35 U.S.C. §271(a), if an accused infringer believes that it is a licensee, it will assert that it does not infringe because its acts were not "without authority" as required by the statute. In other words, the accused infringer will argue that it acted with the authority or permission of the patentee when it made, used, sold, offered to sell, and/or imported into the United States the patented invention or its substantial equivalent, and therefore cannot be liable for infringement.

Patent licenses may be express or implied. Each type of license is separately considered below.

a. Express License

An express license is formed when the parties agree, either in writing or orally, that the patent owner (licensor) will not sue the other party (licensee) for its acts of using, making, selling, offering to sell, or importing the claimed invention. A license is express if created by the actions of the parties themselves, rather than implied by operation of law.

Express licenses may be exclusive or nonexclusive. An *exclusive* license is one in which the patent owner agrees to grant a license to the licensee only, and to no other third parties. Moreover, an exclusive license usually presumes that the patentee will not compete with

---

[4]*See* 35 U.S.C. §286 (stating six-year limitation on period of time for which damages may be recovered for infringements that occurred prior to filing of lawsuit).

the exclusive licensee in making or selling the licensed product(s).[5] In contrast, a *nonexclusive* license does not give the licensee any right to control competition within the scope of the license; rather, it simply protects the licensee from being sued for infringement.[6]

b. Implied License

The existence of an implied license is a legal conclusion that the patent owner has impliedly waived its statutory right to exclude another from making, using, selling, offering to sell, or importing the claimed invention. The Supreme Court has stated the following with respect to implied licenses:

> No formal granting of a license is necessary in order to give it effect. Any language used by the owner of the patent, or any conduct on his part exhibited to another from which that other may properly infer that the owner consents to his use of the patent in making or using it, or selling it, upon which the other acts, constitutes a license and a defense to an action for a tort. Whether this constitutes a gratuitous [i.e., royalty-free] license, or one for a reasonable compensation, must of course depend upon the circumstances; but the relation between the parties thereafter, in respect of any suit brought, must be held to be contractual and not based on unlawful invasion of the rights of the owner.[7]

The Federal Circuit recognizes that an implied license may arise in at least four different circumstances: by acquiescence, by conduct, by equitable estoppel (i.e., estoppel in pais), or by legal estoppel.[8] *Wang Labs. v. Mitsubishi Elecs. Am.*[9] illustrates a successful assertion of the implied license defense under a theory of equitable estoppel, a recognized but rarely established defense in U.S. patent law.[10] Wang developed Single In-Line Memory Modules (SIMMs) in the 1980s and encouraged Mitsubishi to make 256K chips incorporating the SIMMs. Wang succeeded in its campaign to have an electronics industry standards organization, Joint Electronics Devices Engineering Council (JEDEC), adopt SIMMs as a standard, without informing JEDEC that it was seeking to patent the SIMMs technology.

---

[5]*See* JAY DRATLER, JR., LICENSING OF INTELLECTUAL PROPERTY §8.01 (2008).
[6]*See id.*
[7]De Forest Radio Tel. Co. v. United States, 273 U.S. 236, 241 (1927).
[8]Wang Labs. v. Mitsubishi Elecs. Am., 103 F.3d 1571, 1580 (Fed. Cir. 1997).
[9]*Id.*
[10]*See id.* at 1582; A.C. Aukerman Co. v. R.L. Chaides Construction Co., 960 F.2d 1020, 1041-1044 (Fed. Cir. 1992) (*en banc*) (setting forth elements of equitable estoppel and reversing district court's grant of summary judgment that patentee was equitably estopped to assert patent infringement).

When Wang subsequently sued Mitsubishi for infringement of Wang's SIMMs patent, the Federal Circuit affirmed a district court's holding that Mitsubishi was entitled to an irrevocable, royalty-free implied license based on six years of interaction between the parties that led Mitsubishi to reasonably infer Wang's consent to its use of the invention. Although Wang did not itself make SIMMs and had to buy them from other manufacturers such as Mitsubishi, Wang benefited from Mitsubishi's reliance in the form of lowered prices as the market for SIMMs grew. The Federal Circuit acknowledged its imposition of an implied license in *Wang* was "in the nature of" equitable estoppel, but determined "a formal finding of equitable estoppel [was not required] as a prerequisite to a legal conclusion of implied license."[11]

Another variety of implied license dispute arises when one who has purchased a patented device makes repairs so extensive that the patentee construes them as an infringing **reconstruction** of the claimed invention. As mentioned above, the "use" contemplated by §271(a) as an act of infringement is limited by the statute to use "without authority." By contrast, use of a patented device that has been legally purchased is not infringement. A purchaser is deemed to have obtained an implied license to use the purchased patented device, which includes a right to repair it.[12] When that **repair** expands to become reconstruction or a new making of the patented device, however, such acts are no longer considered within the scope of the purchaser's implied license.[13] Federal Circuit case law has not clearly distinguished between permitted repair and prohibited reconstruction; the cases are by necessity extremely fact-specific and must be carefully scrutinized.[14]

Another variation of an implied license is illustrated by *Anton/Bauer, Inc. v. PAG, Ltd.*[15] The patented invention in that case was a

---

[11]*Wang Labs.,* 103 F.3d at 1581. The implied license was not in the nature of legal estoppel, the Federal Circuit explained, which "refers to a narrower category of conduct encompassing scenarios where a patentee has licensed or assigned a right, received consideration, and then sought to derogate from the right granted." *Id.* (quoting Spindelfabrik v. Schubert, 829 F.2d 1075, 1080 (Fed. Cir. 1987)).

[12]*See* Aro Mfg. Co. v. Convertible Top Replacement Co., 377 U.S. 476, 484 (1964) (stating that "it is fundamental that sale of a patented article by the patentee or under his authority carries with it an 'implied license to use.'") (citing Adams v. Burke, 84 U.S. (17 Wall.) 453, 456 (1873)).

[13]*See* Hewlett-Packard Co. v. Repeat-O-Type Stencil Mfg. Corp., 123 F.3d 1445, 1451-1452 (Fed. Cir. 1997). The issue of permissible repair versus infringing reconstruction often arises in the context of disputes over contributory infringement under 35 U.S.C. §271(c), as further discussed in Chapter 9 ("Patent Infringement"), *supra.*

[14]*Compare* Bottom Line Mgmt., Inc. v. Pan Man, Inc., 228 F.3d 1352 (Fed. Cir. 2000) (affirming district court's conclusion that defendant's refurbishment of platens in hamburger grills was noninfringing repair) *with* Sandvik Aktiebolag v. E.J. Co., 121 F.3d 669 (Fed. Cir. 1997) (reversing district court's conclusion that defendant's retipping of drills was not infringing reconstruction).

[15]329 F.3d 1343 (Fed. Cir. 2003).

battery pack connection that joined a battery pack to a portable television video camera. The patent's claims recited a connection comprising both a male plate and a female plate that would be fitted together
to form a mechanical and electrical connection. Neither the male plate
nor the female plate was separately patented, however. In use, the
female plate would be attached to a television camera or other elec-
trically operated device and the male plate would be attached to the
housing of a battery pack. Notably, the patentee did not sell the patented combination of male and female plates, but rather sold only the
female plates to firms in the portable television video camera industry. These firms in turn sold the cameras with female plates attached
to the public. The accused infringer sold battery packs incorporating
the male plate (only) of the claimed invention. In its infringement suit
the patentee theorized that direct infringement occurred when end-
users connected their video cameras (incorporating the female plate)
with the male plate of the accused battery pack, and that the battery
pack manufacturer had induced or contributed to this infringement
by selling the battery pack for use with the female plate and by urging
end-users to employ it in that fashion.

The Federal Circuit in *Anton/Bauer* rejected the patentee's infringement theory and held that the end-users possessed an implied license
that precluded liability. The court observed that a patentee grants an
implied license to a purchaser when (1) the patentee sells an article
that has no noninfringing uses and (2) the circumstances of the sale
plainly indicate that the grant of a license should be inferred.[16] In the
case at bar, the female plate had no noninfringing uses. The sale by
the patentee of the unpatented female plate as a stand-alone item
effectively extinguished the patentee's right to control the use of the
plate, because the female plate could only be used in the patented
combination and that combination had to be completed by the purchaser.[17] With regard to circumstances of the sale, the Federal Circuit
stressed that the patentee had placed no restrictions on the use of
the female plates it sold.[18] "By the unrestricted sale of the female
plate, [the patentee] grants an implied license to its customers to
employ the combination claimed in the [] patent." Thus there was

[16]*Id.* at 1350 (citing Met-Coil Sys. Corp. v. Korners Unlimited, Inc., 803 F.2d 684,
686 (Fed. Cir. 1986)).

[17]*Id.* at 1351.

[18]*Compare* Mallinckrodt, Inc. v. Medipart, Inc., 976 F.2d 700 (Fed. Cir. 1992) (holding that sale to hospitals of patented nebulizer device for lung therapy with "single use
only" restriction was not a per se antitrust violation nor patent misuse; defendant's
violation of restriction would be remediable by action for patent infringement so long
as sale of the device was "validly conditioned under the applicable law such as the law
governing sales and licenses, and if the restriction on reuse was within the scope of the
patent grant or otherwise justified . . . ").

no direct infringement to support the patentee's claim of inducing and/or contributory infringement by the battery pack manufacturer. The Federal Circuit rejected the patentee's argument that finding an implied license existed would "obviate the applicability of contributory infringement in every case." The key fact here was the involvement of the patentee, the court emphasized; its implied license holding in this case "merely limits a patentee's ability to assert contributory infringement where the patentee has chosen to sell part, but not all, of its patented combination."[19]

In *Zenith Elecs. Corp. v. PDI Commc'n Sys., Inc.*,[20] the Federal Circuit explained that an implied license defense "is typically presented 'when a patentee or its licensee sells an article and the question is whether the sale carries with it a license to engage in conduct that would infringe the patent owner's rights.'"[21] An implied license exists in such a case if two requirements are met: (1) the article involved must not have any noninfringing use, thus making it reasonable to infer that the patentee "relinquish[ed its] monopoly with respect to the article sold";[22] and (2) the circumstances of the sale should plainly indicate that a license should be inferred.[23]

Both prongs of this implied license test were satisfied in *Zenith Elecs.* The '301 patent in suit covered methods of remotely controlling televisions located in hospital rooms.[24] For safety and cost reasons, the remote control devices had to be hard-wired to the televisions. Because they also delivered audio signals to patients via internal speakers, the devices were known as "pillow speakers." The invention of the '301 patent advantageously enabled the transmission of digital (rather than analog) signals from the pillow speaker to the television while using existing wire interfaces already installed in hospital rooms.[25] Patentee Zenith entered into express licenses with three companies

---

[19]*Anton/Bauer*, 329 F.3d at 1353.

[20]522 F.3d 1348 (Fed. Cir. 2008).

[21]*Id.* at 1360 (quoting Jacobs v. Nintendo of Am., Inc., 370 F.3d 1097, 1100 (Fed. Cir. 2004)).

[22]*Id.*

[23]*Id.*

[24]*See* "Three Wire Pillow Speaker with Full Television Remote Control Functions," U.S. Patent No. 5,495,301 (issued Feb. 27, 1996).

[25]Representative claim 1 of Zenith's '301 patent recited

1. A method of operating a television receiver wired to a remote housing including a speaker and a multi function control signal encoder comprising:
    supplying operating power to said multi function control signal encoder from the television receiver over first and second wires;
    supplying audio signals to said speaker from said television receiver over said first wire and a third wire; and
    supplying encoded control signals from said multi function encoder to said television receiver over said first and second wires.

(Curbell, MedTek, and Crest) to make and sell pillow speakers specifically designed to operate Zenith televisions using Zenith control codes. When television manufacturer PDI began to sell a new hospital room television also designed for compatibility with the pillow speakers of the '301 patent (i.e., using Zenith's control codes), Zenith sued for infringement. According to Zenith, PDI directly infringed by operating its televisions with the pillow speakers and indirectly infringed by supplying the televisions and encouraging its customers to operate them using the pillow speakers.

The Federal Circuit agreed with PDI and the district court that an implied license defense shielded PDI from liability for infringement of the '301 patent. First, the pillow speakers in question had no use other than in the method of the '301 patent. Second, there were no restrictions in the express licenses between Zenith and the three pillow speaker manufacturers; for example, nothing required them to affix a "use with Zenith televisions only" label to the pillow speakers they sold. Rather, the express licenses achieved a "clear, broad grant of patent rights" between Zenith and the three companies.[26] The Federal Circuit agreed that "customers who purchase pillow speakers from Curbell, MedTek, and Crest obtain an implied license to use those pillow speakers in combination with any compatible television," not just Zenith televisions, and that the implied license was "derived from the express licenses in place between Zenith and the [pillow speaker] manufacturers."[27] Thus, PDI did not infringe Zenith's patent by making or selling televisions that would work with the pillow speakers sold by the express licensees Curbell, MedTek, and Crest. Accordingly, the Federal Circuit affirmed the district court's summary judgment of no infringement of Zenith's '301 patent on the basis of an implied license.

2. Prior User Rights

The existence of a prior user right represents another, more recently recognized (at least in the United States) instance of an "absence of liability for infringement" under 35 U.S.C. §282(b)(1) (eff. Sept. 16, 2012). A prior user right is a personal defense to a charge of infringement, raised by a person who did not patent the invention herself but rather used it in her business prior to the patent owner's filing of his own application for patent on the same invention, typically maintaining the invention as a trade secret. Because they tend to ameliorate

---

[26]Zenith Elecs. Corp. v. PDI Commc'n Sys., Inc., 522 F.3d 1348, 1362 (Fed. Cir. 2008).

[27]*Id.*

the sometimes harsh results of first-to-file patent systems,[28] prior user rights have long been recognized in Europe.[29] Because recognition of prior user rights reduces the economic value of a patent by abrogating exclusivity, however, the United States historically opposed them.

The U.S. opposition to prior user rights weakened somewhat in 1998 when the Federal Circuit decided *State St. Bank v. Signature Fin. Group, Inc.*,[30] confirming the patentability of business methods. Firms that had long maintained their proprietary business procedures and processes as trade secrets suddenly faced the risk of infringing the exclusive rights of competitors who might legitimately obtain patent protection on the same methods. Responding to these concerns, Congress enacted as part of the American Inventors Protection Act of 1999 (AIPA) a limited form of prior user rights, codified at 35 U.S.C. §273.

The assertion of prior user rights under AIPA 35 U.S.C. §273, inaptly titled "Defense to Infringement Based on Earlier Inventor,"[31] was limited to those cases in which a defendant allegedly infringed a claim that recited a *method,* which the statute further defined as "a method of doing or conducting business."[32] The statute provided that

> [i]t shall be a defense to an action for infringement under section 271 of this title with respect to any subject matter that would otherwise infringe one or more claims for a method in the patent being asserted against a person, if such person had, acting in good faith, actually reduced the subject matter to practice at least 1 year before the effective filing date of such patent, and commercially used the subject matter before the effective filing date of such patent.[33]

Thus, an accused infringer asserting a defense under AIPA §273 had to establish that (1) it was acting in good faith when (2) more

[28]The first-to-file versus first-to-invent debate is discussed in further detail in Chapter 12 ("International Patenting Issues"), *infra.*

[29]*See, e.g.,* Germany Patent Law (as amended by the Law of July 31, 2009) §12(1), *available at* http://www.wipo.int/wipolex/en/text.jsp?file_id=238776 (providing without limitation as to scope of "invention" that "[a] patent shall have no effect against a person who, at the time of the filing of the application, had already begun to use the invention in Germany, or had made the necessary arrangements to do so").

[30]149 F.3d 1368 (Fed. Cir. 1998). The *State Street Bank* decision is further discussed in Chapter 7 ("Potentially Patentable Subject Matter (35 U.S.C. §101)"), *supra.*

[31]Contrary to the title of §273, the party asserting a defense to infringement under that section of the Patent Act is *not* required to prove that it invented before the patent owner in accordance with the criteria of 35 U.S.C. §102(g) (2006). *See* 35 U.S.C. §273(b)(1) (2006) (requiring that defendant show actual reduction to practice more than one year prior to patent's effective filing date but not requiring a showing of prior invention sufficient to satisfy §102(g)).

[32]35 U.S.C. §273(a)(3) (2006).

[33]35 U.S.C. §273(b)(1) (2006).

than one year before the effective filing date of the patent, it actually reduced to practice the subject matter of the asserted claim, and (3) before the effective filing date of the patent, it commercially used that subject matter. The statute defined "commercial use" of the method to mean a "use of a method in the United States, so long as such use is in connection with an internal commercial use or an actual arm's-length sale or other arm's-length commercial transfer of a useful end result, whether or not the subject matter at issue is accessible to or otherwise known to the public. . . ."[34] This definition permitted trade secret users of business methods to avail themselves of the §273 defense; their use of the allegedly infringed method need not have been known to the public, so long as it was used in connection with their business. For example, a mutual fund firm might develop a novel and nonobvious method for maximizing stock market returns and use this method to manage its clients' stock portfolios, but maintain the details of the method as a trade secret.

Because the §273 prior user defense was narrowly defined and largely untested in the federal district courts,[35] the Federal Circuit did

---

[34]*Id.* §273(a)(1).

[35]The district court in *Sabasta v. Buckaroos, Inc.*, 507 F. Supp. 2d 986 (S.D. Iowa 2007), held the §273(b) defense inapplicable to the facts before it. At issue was whether Sabasta's patent in suit claimed a "method" within the meaning of §273(a)(3), which defines "method" as "a method of doing or conducting business." The patent's claims recited an article of manufacture, that is, a "roll bending die for being used with a roll bending machine for producing rib reinforced rolled material," and did not include any method or process claims. *See* "Roll Bending Die," U.S. Patent No. 6,751,995 (issued June 22, 2004). Nevertheless, accused infringer Buckaroos contended that the '995 patent's claims should be construed as method claims because they often referred to the intended use of the recited die. Buckaroos further argued that it should be considered within the protection of §273 because Buckaroos was "in business, and is using a roll-bending process as part of conducting its business." *Sabasta*, 507 F. Supp. 2d at 1002. The district court disagreed. The court noted the lack of any case law directly addressing the scope of §273, but concluded from the section's legislative history that Congress intended "the First Inventor Defense to have a limited scope, that is, the defense is designed to protect small businesses from patent infringement suits for methods of conducting business that use a novel process employing unpatentable subject matter, but that have 'useful, concrete and tangible result[s].'" *Id.* at 1005 (quoting *State St. Bank*, 149 F.3d at 1374). In light of this legislative history and the *State Street* decision, "[t]he fact that Buckaroos is in business and uses a process to manufacture ribbed pipe saddles does not . . . bring it within the intended purview of §273."*Id.*

The §273(b) defense to infringement was also asserted in *Seal-Flex, Inc. v. W.R. Dougherty & Assoc., Inc.*, 179 F. Supp. 2d 735 (E.D. Mich. 2002), a case involving a patented method for manufacturing an all-weather surface for an outdoor running track. Because the district court had previously granted summary judgment to the patentee on the issue of infringement, however, it refused to entertain the §273(b) defense as untimely raised. *Id.* at 742. The court did not discuss the merits of the defense or its potential applicability to the facts of the case.

not address the contours of the defense as implemented by the AIPA of 1999, particularly the question of its limitation to business methods.

The America Invents Act of 2011 significantly broadened the scope of the prior user rights defense to subject matter beyond business methods.[36] Now titled "Defense to infringement based on prior commercial use," the protection of post-AIA 35 U.S.C. §273 is potentially available to alleged infringers practicing "subject matter consisting of a process, or consisting of a machine, manufacture, or composition of matter used in a manufacturing or other commercial process."[37] Thus, post-AIA, the practice of *all* 35 U.S.C. §101 categories of subject matter is potentially shielded by prior user rights so long as the accused infringer was using the allegedly infringing subject matter in a "commercial process" by the requisite date. The defense is no longer limited to those who allegedly infringed patented business methods. The broadened version of the prior user rights defense became available for those accused of infringing patents that issued on or after September 16, 2011.

The post-AIA version of 35 U.S.C. §273 further requires that to assert the prior user rights defense, two primary criteria must be satisfied. First, concerning domestic "commercial use," the accused infringer asserting the §273 defense must have, "acting in good faith, commercially used the subject matter in the United States, either in connection with an internal commercial use or an actual arm's length sale or other arm's length commercial transfer of a useful end result of such commercial use. . . ."[38] Second, concerning timing, the accused infringer's commercial use must have "occurred at least 1 year before the earlier of either—(A) the effective filing date of the claimed invention; or (B) the date on which the claimed invention was disclosed to the public in a manner that qualified for the exception from prior art under [post-AIA 35 U.S.C.] section 102(b) [(eff. Mar. 16, 2013)]."[39]

Essentially carried over from the pre-AIA version of §273, the latter "time gap" requirement that an asserted prior use began at least one year before the patentee's effective filing date represents a significant difference (namely, one favoring patentees) between U.S. and European prior user rights defenses. European countries generally require that the prior use began any time before the patent owner's application

---

[36]*See* Leahy-Smith America Invents Act, Pub. L. No. 112-29 (H.R. 1249), §5, 125 Stat. 284, 297 (Sept. 16, 2011) (titled "Defense to infringement based on prior commercial use") (amending 35 U.S.C. §273 (2006)). The amendment of 35 U.S.C. §273 became effective September 16, 2011, and applies to any patent issued on or after that date.

[37]35 U.S.C. §273(a) (eff. Sept. 16, 2011).

[38]35 U.S.C. §273(a)(1) (eff. Sept. 16, 2011).

[39]35 U.S.C. §273(a)(2) (eff. Sept. 16, 2011).

filing date and do not mandate that the prior use began more than a year before it.[40]

Several aspects of the §273 prior user rights defense remain the same post-AIA as they stood pre-AIA. For example, an accused infringer still bears the burden of establishing the defense by clear and convincing evidence.[41] One major change benefits universities, however. Post-AIA 35 U.S.C. §273 includes a "University Exception" that prohibits an accused infringer from asserting the prior user rights defense if the allegedly infringed subject matter was, "at the time the invention was made, owned or subject to an obligation of assignment to either an institution of higher education . . . or a technology transfer organization whose primary purpose is to facilitate the commercialization of technologies developed by one or more such institutions of higher education."[42]

3.   Experimental Use

Occasionally an accused infringer will assert that it is not liable for infringement because its activities constituted experimental use that should not be considered infringement. As explained below, this defense is construed very narrowly and has rarely succeeded.[43]

---

[40]*See, e.g.*, Germany Patent Law (as amended by the Law of July 31, 2009) §12(1), *available at* http://www.wipo.int/wipolex/en/text.jsp?file_id=238776 (providing that "[a] patent shall have no effect against a person who, *at the time of the filing of the application*, had already begun to use the invention in Germany, or had made the necessary arrangements to do so") (emphasis added); Great Britain Patents Act 1977 (as amended 2004) §§64(1)-(2), *available at* http://www.wipo.int/wipolex/en/text.jsp?file_id=127257 (providing that "[w]here a patent is granted for an invention, a person who in the United Kingdom *before the priority date of the invention* does in good faith an act which would constitute an infringement of the patent if it were in force, or makes in good faith effective and serious preparations to do such an act, shall have the right[] . . . to continue to do or, as the case may be, to do that act himself . . . ") (emphasis added).

[41]35 U.S.C. §273(b) (eff. Sept. 16, 2011).

[42]35 U.S.C. §273(e)(5)(A) (eff. Sept. 16, 2011). The statute defines an "institution of higher education" in accordance with the text of "section 101(a) of the Higher Education Act of 1965 (20 U.S.C. 1001(a))." *Id.*

The AIA's legislative history explains that "Section 5 . . . clarifies that a person may not assert the [prior user] defense if the subject matter of the patent on which the defense is based was developed pursuant to a funding agreement under Chapter 18 of the Patent Act (patent rights in inventions made with Federal assistance) or by a university or a technology transfer organization affiliated with a university that did not receive private business funding in support of the patent's development." H.R. REP. 112-98 (June 1, 2011), at 75.

[43]The foundational article on the U.S. experimental use defense to patent infringement is Rebecca S. Eisenberg, *Patents and the Progress of Science: Exclusive Rights and Experimental Use*, 56 U. CHI. L. REV. 1017 (1989).

C. Absence of Liability for Infringement

A U.S. patent grants its owner the right, *inter alia*, to prevent others from *using* the patented invention, without qualification as to the nature or purpose of the use.[44] Nonconsensual uses of patented inventions that lead to the development of other products may result in patent infringement liability, even though sales of the other products do not involve a making or selling of the patented invention itself. For example, a researcher may infringe if she uses without a license a patented "research tool," such as the biological receptor *Taq*[45] or a transgenic animal model[46] in the research and development of new drugs, therapies, or diagnostic products to be sold commercially.[47] Use liability arises under the U.S. patent laws even though the researcher has not physically incorporated the patented research tool into the new product that is ultimately marketed.[48]

Most of the world's patent systems recognize an exception to patent infringement liability for nonconsensual uses of patented inventions that are for experimental or research purposes, and many countries

---

[44]*See* 35 U.S.C. §154(a)(1) ("Every patent shall contain . . . a grant to the patentee . . . of the right to exclude others from making, using, offering for sale, or selling the invention throughout the United States or importing the invention into the United States. . . ."); 35 U.S.C. §271(a) ("Except as otherwise provided in this title [35 U.S.C. §1 *et seq.*], whoever without authority makes, uses, offers to sell, or sells any patented invention, within the United States or imports into the United States any patented invention during the term of the patent therefore, infringes the patent.").

[45]*Taq* is a shorthand name for the thermostable enzyme *Thermus aquaticus* TY1 DNA polymerase, a widely used biotechnology tool. See PAUL RABINOW, MAKING PCR: A STORY OF BIOTECHNOLOGY 128-132 (1996) (describing identification, purification, and introduction of *Taq*). A receptor is a portion of a cell's surface that binds with specific molecules "like a lock accepting a key." *Human Pheromone Link May Have Been Found*, N.Y. TIMES, Sept. 28, 2000, at A22.

[46]For example, "Transgenic arthritic mice expressing a T-cell receptor transgene," U.S. Patent No. 5,675,060 (issued Oct. 7, 1997), discloses and claims transgenic arthritic mice that are useful as animal models for the evaluation of human arthritogenic and therapeutic anti-arthritic compositions. Genetically altered mice are preferred models for many human diseases because the mouse genome is similar to the human genome. David Malakoff, *The Rise of the Mouse, Biomedicine's Model Mammal*, SCIENCE, Apr. 14, 2000, at 248.

[47]*See* John H. Barton, *Patents and Antitrust: A Rethinking in Light of Patent Breadth and Sequential Innovation*, 65 ANTITRUST L.J. 449, 451 (1997) (suggesting scenario in which firm obtaining patent protection on biological receptor useful in schizophrenia research could preempt others from further research in schizophrenia, without itself having any truly "marketable product"); *see also* Eliot Marshall, *Patent on HIV Receptor Provokes an Outcry*, 287 SCIENCE 1375, 1375-1377 (2000) (describing academic researchers' criticism of patent issued to Human Genome Sciences, Inc. (HGS) on CCR5 cell-surface receptor that HIV uses as cell entry point, and reporting HGS's position that it will enforce patent against "anyone [who] wants to use the receptor to create a drug").

[48]Because the patented research tool is not incorporated into the commercial product, the researcher has not violated the "sells" prohibition of 35 U.S.C. §271(a).

have statutorily implemented such an exception in their patent laws.[49] An experimental use exception to infringement has met with very little success in the United States, however. The only statutory recognition of such a defense in the U.S. Patent Act is a very narrow exception from liability for nonconsensual uses of patented drugs in the preparation of test data to be submitted for regulatory approval by a government agency such as the Food and Drug Administration (FDA).[50] There is no general "fair use" provision in the U.S. Patent Act, in contrast with §107 of the U.S. Copyright Act.

The Federal Circuit has grudgingly recognized the existence of a common law–based experimental use defense, but characterizes it as "truly narrow" and applicable only to trifling, "dilettante affairs."[51] Excluded from the common law–based experimental use doctrine is any activity viewed as "commercialization" or otherwise grounded on profit motive.[52] The Federal Circuit's narrow interpretation of the doctrine virtually assures that it cannot be relied on by the rapidly growing number of university and industry collaborations whose research

---

[49]For example, French law provides that "[a]cts accomplished for personal or domestic purposes or for the purpose of testing the object of the patented invention shall not be considered as affecting the patentee's rights." French Patent Law Including Modifications of 1978, art. 29, reprinted in 2D JOHN P. SINNOTT ET AL., WORLD PATENT LAW AND PRACTICE (1999), at FRANCE-9. Germany provides that the "effects of the patent shall not extend to . . . acts done for experimental purposes relating to the subject matter of the patented invention." German Patent Act of 16 December 1980, §11.2, reprinted in 2D SINNOTT ET AL., supra, at WEST GERMANY-78.22. Great Britain exempts from infringement liability those acts "done privately and for purposes which are not commercial" as well as those acts "done for experimental purposes relating to the subject-matter of the invention." United Kingdom Patent Act 1977, §60(5), reprinted in 2D SINNOTT ET AL., supra, at GREAT BRITAIN-269. The Japanese patent laws provide that "[t]he effects of the patent right shall not extend to the working of the patent right for the purposes of experiment or research." Japanese Patent Law of 1959, as amended through May 6, 1998, effective June 1, 1998, §69(1), reprinted in 2F SINNOTT ET AL., supra, at JAPAN-194.

[50]See 35 U.S.C. §271(e)(1), discussed supra Chapter 9, Section E.3.

[51]Roche Prods. v. Bolar Pharm. Co., 733 F.2d 858, 863 (Fed. Cir. 1984).

[52]E.g., Roche Prods., 733 F.2d at 863 (refusing to adopt broader view of experimental use doctrine that would "allow a violation of the patent laws in the guise of 'scientific inquiry,' when that inquiry has definite, cognizable, and not insubstantial commercial purposes"); Pitcairn v. United States, 547 F.2d 1106, 1125-1126 (Ct. Cl. 1976) (rejecting government's experimental use defense because government's unauthorized use of infringing helicopters for testing, demonstrations, and experiments was "in keeping with the legitimate business of the using agency"); Deuterium Corp. v. United States, 19 Cl. Ct. 624, 633 (1990) (rejecting experimental use defense because government agency's participation in demonstration project with for-profit partner corporation "was not strictly intellectual experimentation, but development of technology and processes for commercial applications").

and development efforts are ultimately targeted at the commercialization of new biomedical products.[53]

Any prospects for a broader recognition of the common law–based experimental use defense were roundly refuted by the Federal Circuit's 2002 decision in *Madey v. Duke Univ.*[54] In that case scientists at Duke University had used laboratory lasers to conduct basic research in nuclear physics without a license from Dr. John Madey, owner of patents on the laser equipment. The Federal Circuit concluded that the district court had erred in excusing the Duke scientists' activity as exempted from patent infringement liability under the experimental use doctrine.[55] The university's nonprofit status was not dispositive, for the university was engaged in its own "legitimate business" of attracting top scholars, students, and funding:

> Our precedent clearly does not immunize use that is in any way commercial in nature. Similarly, our precedent does not immunize any conduct that is in keeping with the alleged infringer's legitimate business, regardless of commercial implications. For example, major research universities, such as Duke, often sanction and fund research projects with arguably no commercial application whatsoever. However, these projects unmistakably further the institution's legitimate business objectives, including educating and enlightening students and faculty participating in these projects. These projects also serve, for example, to increase the status of the institution and lure lucrative research grants, students and faculty.
>
> In short, regardless of whether a particular institution or entity is engaged in an endeavor for commercial gain, so long as the act is in furtherance of the alleged infringer's legitimate business and is not solely for amusement, to satisfy idle curiosity, or for strictly philosophical inquiry, the act does not qualify for the very narrow and strictly limited experimental use defense. Moreover, the profit or non-profit status of the user is not determinative.[56]

In the aftermath of the *Madey* decision, the National Academies of Science (NAS) concluded in an important 2004 report that "most organized research using patented inventions is subject to demands for

[53]For further development of this position, *see* Janice M. Mueller, *No "Dilettante Affair": Rethinking the Experimental Use Exception to Patent Infringement for Biomedical Research Tools*, 76 WASH. L. REV. 1 (2001).

[54]307 F.3d 1351 (Fed. Cir. 2002).

[55]*See id.* at 1352, 1361-1363, 1364.

[56]*Id.* at 1362. For an argument that the Federal Circuit's *Madey* decision fundamentally misapplied the "legitimate business" criterion of an earlier experimental use precedent, *Pitcairn v. United States*, 547 F.2d 1106, 1125 (Ct. Cl. 1977), *see* Janice M. Mueller, *The Evanescent Experimental Use Exemption from United States Patent Infringement Liability: Implications for University and Nonprofit Research and Development*, 56 BAYLOR L. REV. 917 (2004).

licenses and may in some cases be halted by an injunction or assessed money damages for infringement."[57] The NAS report recommended that at least some of these research uses be explicitly shielded from patent infringement liability,[58] but concluded that "[r]ealistically, the likelihood that Congress will pass research-exception legislation in the absence of compelling circumstances is small."[59] The National Academies' prediction has thus far proved correct; neither the 2005 nor the 2007 legislative proposals for U.S. patent law reform,[60] nor the America Invents Act of 2011, codified any experimental use defense.

4. Expiration of Damages Limitation Period of 35 U.S.C. §286

An accused infringer may assert absence of liability for infringement under §282(b)(1) (eff. Sept. 16, 2012) when the alleged infringing activity ended more than six years before the filing of the infringement lawsuit. The defense raised here is not a statute of limitations, but rather is based upon the damages limitation provisions of 35 U.S.C. §286, which operate in a somewhat similar fashion.

Unlike its copyright counterpart,[61] U.S. patent law does not recognize a general statute of limitations in the sense of a statutory provision that bars the maintenance of an infringement suit following a delay in filing the suit for a certain number of years after the patentee had notice of the alleged infringing activity.[62] However, the Patent Act does provide a practical limitation on the time period in which infringement actions seeking the remedy of damages can be brought. Section 286, titled "Time Limitation on Damages," provides that except as otherwise provided by law, "no recovery shall be had for any infringement committed more than six years prior to the filing of the

---

[57]See NATIONAL RESEARCH COUNCIL OF THE NATIONAL ACADEMIES, A PATENT SYSTEM FOR THE 21ST CENTURY 108 (Stephen A. Merrill et al. eds., 2004), available at http://www.nap.edu/html/patentsystem/0309089107.pdf.

[58]See id. at 108-117.

[59]Id. at 115.

[60]See Patent Reform Act of 2007, H.R. 1908, 110th Cong. (2007), available at http://thomas.loc.gov/; S. 1145, 110th Cong. (2007), available at http://thomas.loc.gov/; Patent Reform Act of 2005, H.R. 2795, 109th Cong. (2005), available at http://thomas.loc.gov/.

[61]See 17 U.S.C. §507 (three-year statute of limitations for copyright actions).

[62]The Patent Act includes a statute of limitations for actions seeking the provisional compensation remedy under 35 U.S.C. §154(d), based on infringements that occurred between the time of the publication of a patent application and its issuance as a patent. See 35 U.S.C. §154(d)(3) (providing that "[t]he right under paragraph (1) [of §154(d)] to obtain a reasonable royalty shall be available only in an action brought not later than 6 years after the patent is issued").

complaint or counterclaim for infringement in the action. . . . "[63] Thus, in an infringement action seeking damages (e.g., based on theories of lost profits and/or reasonable royalties),[64] the patent owner's damages recovery period extends retroactively to, at most, six years before the action was filed. This means that even if infringement was ongoing for ten years prior to the filing of suit, §286 provides that only the most recent six years of infringement damages accrued prior to the filing of the lawsuit are recoverable. If the patent expired more than six years prior to the filing of the infringement suit, §286 bars any monetary recovery.[65]

5. Laches and Equitable Estoppel in Initiating Patent Infringement Litigation

a. Introduction

The equitable doctrines of **laches** and **equitable estoppel** also may be asserted by accused infringers as the basis for "absence of liability for infringement" under §282(b)(1) (eff. Sept. 16, 2012). These judicially created doctrines permit the accused infringer to limit or negate its liability when a patentee has unfairly brought suit after an unreasonable delay or after misrepresenting that it would not do so.

The defense of laches targets the plaintiff's unreasonable delay in filing suit. If successfully established, laches does not bar the plaintiff's action in its entirety but rather prevents the recovery of any damages accrued prior to the filing of the action. Equitable estoppel is a separate defense that targets the plaintiff's misleading actions, which led the defendant to believe it would not be sued. If the defense of equitable estoppel is established, then the plaintiff's claim of infringement is entirely barred.

The leading Federal Circuit case addressing the defenses of laches and equitable estoppel is *A.C. Aukerman Co. v. Chaides Constr. Co.*[66] Aukerman, the owner of a U.S. patent on a device and method for forming concrete highway barriers, threatened to sue Chaides for infringement and offered it a license in 1979. Chaides responded that

---

[63]35 U.S.C. §286, ¶1.

[64]*See* Chapter 11 ("Remedies for Patent Infringement"), *infra,* for discussion of theories of monetary recovery for patent infringement.

[65]An infringement suit that seeks only damages can be filed at any time in the six years after the patent expires. No injunctive remedy is available after a patent has expired, however, because the patentee no longer possesses the statutory right to exclude others from manufacture, use, sale, offering to sell, or importation of the invention.

[66]960 F.2d 1020 (Fed. Cir. 1992) (*en banc*).

its alleged infringement was worth only $200 to $300 per year, and that it was not willing to take a license. The patentee Aukerman had no further contact with Chaides for over eight years. During that time, Chaides increased the volume of its business (which employed the allegedly infringing process) twentyfold. When Aukerman finally sued Chaides in 1988, the district court granted summary judgment of nonliability to Chaides on both the defenses of laches and equitable estoppel.

On appeal, the Federal Circuit vacated the summary judgment grant as precluded by unresolved questions of material fact. The court also went *en banc* to clarify and restate the law of laches and equitable estoppel as described below.

b. Laches

First, the *Aukerman* court held that the elements of a laches defense are

1. unreasonable and inexcusable delay by the plaintiff in bringing suit; and
2. the defendant was materially prejudiced due to the plaintiff's delay.[67]

If the plaintiff brings suit *within* six years of learning about the alleged infringement, then the defendant must prove both of these factual elements based on the evidence of record. However, a presumption of laches arises in the defendant's favor in those cases where the plaintiff has delayed in filing suit for *more than* six years after the plaintiff knew or should have known of the alleged infringement. If the presumption is triggered, both of the underlying laches elements of unreasonable delay and material prejudice are presumptively established in the defendant's favor without the need for submission of additional evidence.

Once the laches presumption is triggered, the burden of production (i.e., of going forward with the evidence) then shifts to the plaintiff, who must attempt to rebut the presumption.[68] If the plaintiff establishes facts that create a genuine issue of fact with respect to either one of the two underlying factors, then the laches presumption "bursts"[69] and

---

[67]*See id.* at 1028.

[68]This procedural framework is in accord with Fed. R. Evid. 301. The burden of production, which shifts to the plaintiff when the laches presumption is triggered, should be contrasted with the burden of proof (i.e., persuasion). The defendant always bears the ultimate burden of proof on the defense of laches, and this burden never shifts to the plaintiff.

[69]This is referred to by law professors as the "double bursting bubble" approach to presumptions.

the defendant is "put to its proof," meaning that the defendant must then attempt to establish the existence of both unreasonable delay and material prejudice based on the factual evidence of record.

When attempting to rebut a presumption of laches, the plaintiff patentee may seek to establish a genuine issue of fact with respect to laches element (1), whether the delay in bringing suit was unreasonable, by offering evidence tending to show that its delay was in fact reasonable and justified under the circumstances. Such evidence might include proof of the plaintiff's participation in litigation against other infringers, ongoing negotiations with the defendant, poverty, illness, war, limited extent of infringement, dispute over ownership of the patent, or the like. In *Aukerman,* the plaintiff patentee offered evidence of its participation in other litigation, contending that this represented a legitimate excuse for its delay in suing Chaides. The Federal Circuit agreed that the evidence offered by Aukerman raised at least a genuine factual issue respecting the reasonableness of its conduct, and thus the laches defense needed to be tried rather than resolved prematurely on summary judgment.[70]

With respect to laches element (2), whether the accused infringer was materially prejudiced by the delay, the prejudice may take the form of evidentiary prejudice, such as the loss of documents and the recollections of witnesses over time. The prejudice also may be economic, as where the accused infringer has encountered change in its economic position during the period of the plaintiff's delay. For example, prior to the plaintiff's filing of the infringement suit, the accused infringer may have made substantial investments in manufacturing facilities and capital equipment needed to produce the accused product. In attempting to rebut a presumption of laches, the patentee may attempt to create a genuine issue of fact with respect to element (2) by establishing that the evidence supporting the accused infringer's defenses (such as noninfringement and/or invalidity) remains available, or that the accused infringer has not suffered any substantial economic change during the period of the patentee's delay.

The above discussion sets out the framework for analyzing a laches defense by assuming that the presumption of laches has been triggered, based on a delay in filing suit of more than six years after the patentee first knew or should have known of the alleged infringement. The "should have known" prong of the laches rule incorporates a degree of uncertainty, however. Whether the running of the six-year laches clock has been triggered is not always clear, as illustrated by *Intirtool, Ltd. v. Texar Corp.*[71] There the Federal Circuit reversed a district court's conclusion that laches had presumptively arisen based on a patentee's

---

[70]*Aukerman,* 960 F.2d at 1039.
[71]369 F.3d 1289 (Fed. Cir. 2004).

delay in bringing suit that extended more than six years after a July 1993 conversation between employees of the patentee and the accused infringer. In that conversation, the chief executive officer of accused infringer Texar, a corporation that had previously purchased patented punch pliers from the patentee Intirtool, told an officer of Intirtool that he was "perfectly satisfied" with it as a supplier and "had no real desire to change vendors but [he] was under price pressure."[72] When Intirtool's officer refused to meet the competitive price, Texar stopped ordering from Intirtool and began placing orders with a competing manufacturer of punch pliers. The parties had no further contact after the July 1993 conversation until more than six years later, in April 2000, when the patentee filed its infringement lawsuit.

On these facts, the Federal Circuit held in *Intirtool* that the patentee could not be charged with actual or constructive knowledge of an act of infringement that would trigger the running of the laches clock.[73] At most, the July 1993 conversation may have indicated that accused infringer Texar was considering a change of suppliers; there was no indication that the patentee should have known at any point thereafter that the accused infringer had in fact acted on this plan. A contrary holding would place on the patentee the burden of policing the other party's subsequent conduct because of "speculative comments during a single phone conversation." The Federal Circuit was "unwilling to stretch the concept of due diligence so far."[74]

c. *Equitable Estoppel*

The Federal Circuit in *Aukerman* also considered whether accused infringer Chaides had successfully established the defense of equitable estoppel. As with the laches defense, the court vacated the grant to Chaides of summary judgment of equitable estoppel as precluded by disputed fact issues.

The Federal Circuit explained that equitable estoppel focuses not on the plaintiff's unreasonable delay in suing (i.e., the basis of laches), but rather on the unfairness of the plaintiff's actions in misleading the defendant into believing that it would not be sued and the defendant's detrimental reliance on those actions.[75] The following are required elements of equitable estoppel:

---

[72]*Id.* at 1297.

[73]*See id.* at 1297-1298.

[74]*Id.* at 1298.

[75]The court noted, however, that the patent cases coming before it "involving the issue of a patentee's inequitable delay in suing have almost invariably raised the defense not only of laches but also of equitable estoppel." Aukerman Co. v. Chaides Constr. Co., 960 F.2d 1020, 1042 (Fed. Cir. 1992) (*en banc*). Nevertheless, the elements of the two defenses should not be intertwined. "Delay in filing suit may be evidence

1. the plaintiff misleads the defendant into reasonably infer-
    ring that the plaintiff does not intend to enforce its patent
    against the defendant;
2. the defendant relies on the plaintiff's misleading conduct; and
3. due to its reliance, the defendant will be materially preju-
    diced if the plaintiff is allowed to proceed with its claim.

In contrast with laches, there is no presumption applicable to the
defense of equitable estoppel; a defendant must offer evidence sufficient to prove each of the three factual elements of the equitable
estoppel defense. If the defense of equitable estoppel is sustained, the
result is that the plaintiff's action is completely barred.[76] Thus, the
penalty for equitable estoppel is considerably more severe than for
laches, which limits damages but does not prohibit maintenance of the
infringement suit nor the potential for an injunction against future
infringement.

6. State Sovereign Immunity

Under current Supreme Court authority, state governments (i.e.,
states, instrumentalities thereof such as state universities, and state
employees acting in their official capacity) enjoy constitutional immunity from infringement liability under the U.S. Patent Act.[77] As a general rule, state governments are immune from lawsuits under the
Eleventh Amendment of the U.S. Constitution, which provides that the
"Judicial Power of the United States shall not be construed to extend to
any suit in law or equity, commenced or prosecuted against one of the
United States by Citizens of another State, or by Citizens or subjects

---

which influences the assessment of whether the patentee's conduct is misleading but
it is not a requirement of equitable estoppel. Even where such delay is present, the
concepts of equitable estoppel and laches are distinct from one another." *Id.*

[76]*See* Scholle Corp. v. Blackhawk Molding Co., 133 F.3d 1469, 1473 (Fed. Cir. 1998)
(holding plaintiff equitably estopped from asserting its patent where it had previously
made an accusation of infringement followed by silence after inspection of defendant's
redesigned product); ABB Robotics, Inc. v. GMFanuc Robotics Corp., 52 F.3d 1062, 1064-
1065 (Fed. Cir. 1995) (sustaining equitable estoppel defense where four-and-a-half-
year period of silence by plaintiffs misled defendants into believing plaintiffs would
not enforce their patent rights, emphasizing that "[m]isleading action by the patentee
may be silence, if such silence is accompanied by some other factor indicating that the
silence was sufficiently misleading to amount to bad faith").

[77]Possible exceptions to states' immunity would include state and industry collaborations that are not sufficiently "instrumentalities of the state" to qualify for Eleventh
Amendment immunity, and state officials acting in the scope of their official capacity
who may still be subject to prospective injunctive relief under *Ex parte Young*, 209 U.S.
123, 167-168 (1908).

of any foreign state."[78] Congress in 1992 stripped (i.e., abrogated) the states of their immunity from patent infringement liability by enacting the Patent and Plant Variety Protection Remedy Clarification Act.[79] However, the Supreme Court in *Florida Prepaid Postsecondary Educ. Expense Bd. v. College Savings Bank*[80] subsequently struck down the Patent Remedy Act as unconstitutional based on the following reasoning.

Because Congress could not abrogate the states' Eleventh Amendment sovereign immunity under its Article I powers (which include the power enumerated in the Intellectual Property Clause),[81] the argument in *Florida Prepaid* for constitutionality of the Patent Remedy Act was premised on the Due Process Clause of the Fourteenth Amendment.[82] The petitioner contended that patents are private property and that to allow states to use them without authorization and without remedy was a deprivation of private property without due process. By a 5-4 vote, the Supreme Court rejected the Due Process theory on the grounds that there had not been a sufficient showing that state governments routinely infringe, that such infringement is willful rather than merely negligent or "innocent," or that such infringement results in a property deprivation without due process.[83] In support of its ruling, the Court pointed to the possibility of alternative remedies in state court such as unfair competition causes of action.[84]

Eleventh Amendment immunity as currently construed not only protects states from liability for patent infringement but also shields them from other patent-related causes of action such a suit to correct a patent's inventorship. The Federal Circuit in *Xechem Int'l, Inc. v. Univ. of Texas M.D. Anderson Cancer Ctr.*[85] applied *Florida Prepaid* to

---

[78]U.S. CONST. amend. XI.

[79]Pub. L. No. 102-560, 106 Stat. 4230 (1992) (codified at 35 U.S.C. §§271(h), 296(a) (1994)) (hereafter "Patent Remedy Act"). As codified by the Patent Remedy Act, §296(a) of the Patent Act provides in part that "[a]ny State, any instrumentality of a State, and any officer or employee of a State or instrumentality of a State acting in his official capacity, shall not be immune, under the eleventh amendment of the Constitution of the United States or under any other doctrine of sovereign immunity, from suit in Federal court by any person, including any governmental or nongovernmental entity, for infringement of a patent under section 271, or for any other violation under this title." 35 U.S.C. §296(a).

[80]527 U.S. 627 (1999).

[81]In *Seminole Tribe v. Florida*, 517 U.S. 44 (1996), the Supreme Court held that Congress cannot abrogate the states' Eleventh Amendment sovereign immunity under Congress's Article I powers. *Seminole Tribe* thus foreclosed reliance on congressional authority under the Intellectual Property Clause (or alternatively the Commerce Clause) to sustain the Patent Remedy Act.

[82]*See Florida Prepaid*, 527 U.S. at 636.

[83]*See id*. at 639-646.

[84]*See id*. at 643-644 & nn.8-9.

[85]382 F.3d 1324 (Fed. Cir. 2004).

hold that Eleventh Amendment immunity barred Xechem's claim for correction of inventorship under 35 U.S.C. §256 of two patents owned by the university, an entity of the state of Texas. The patents arose from a collaborative project between the university and Xechem; the sole named inventor on the patents was a university scientist. The Federal Circuit rejected Xechem's various arguments against Eleventh Amendment immunity as contrary to *Florida Prepaid* and its companion case, *College Savings Bank v. Florida Prepaid Postsecondary Educ. Expense Bd.*[86] In particular, the university's entry into commercial relationships and contracts with Xechem did not work a waiver of the university's Eleventh Amendment rights; this activity did not represent the necessary "clear declaration" by the state of its intent to submit to federal jurisdiction. Nor did the university constructively consent to federal jurisdiction by causing its employee (the named inventor) to apply for U.S. patents.

In contrast with *Xechem,* a state university lost its Eleventh Amendment immunity through waiver in *Vas-Cath, Inc. v. Curators of the Univ. of Missouri.*[87] The parties disputed priority of invention with respect to a type of dual lumen catheter. The University of Missouri initiated an interference proceeding in the USPTO between its pending patent application and a patent already issued to Vas-Cath. The university did not assert its Eleventh Amendment immunity at any stage of the proceedings before the USPTO. At the conclusion of the six-year interference, the USPTO awarded priority to the university and revoked Vas-Cath's patent. In accordance with 35 U.S.C. §146 (pre-AIA), Vas-Cath filed a civil action challenging the USPTO's decision in the U.S. District Court for the District of Columbia.[88] After the §146 action was transferred to the U.S. District Court for the Western District of Missouri, the latter court granted the university's motion to dismiss the action on the ground that the university had not waived its Eleventh Amendment immunity.

On appeal, the Federal Circuit reversed and remanded. The appellate court agreed with Vas-Cath that because the university had initiated and prevailed in the interference, it could not thereafter assert immunity from Vas-Cath's §146 action, which was effectively an appeal of the USPTO's decision:

[86]527 U.S. 666 (1999).

[87]473 F.3d 1376 (Fed. Cir. 2007).

[88]Prior to the America Invents Act of 2011, section 146 of the Patent Act provided for a civil action in federal district court against the USPTO Director by a party who had lost an interference in the USPTO. *See* 35 U.S.C. §146 (2006). The AIA eliminated interferences as of March 16, 2013. The post-AIA version of section 146 provides for civil actions against the USPTO Director when a party loses an AIA-implemented derivation proceeding. *See* 35 U.S.C. §146 (eff. Mar. 16, 2013) ("Civil action in case of derivation proceeding"); 35 U.S.C. §135 (eff. Mar. 16, 2013) ("Derivation proceedings").

> [T]he University cannot both retain the fruits of [the interference] and bar the losing party from its statutory right of review, even if that review is conducted in federal court. In the circumstances that here exist, the state's actions with respect to the interference include waiver with respect to the ensuing [§146] civil action. Having waived any potential immunity as to the interference contest in the PTO, we conclude that the University waived any Constitution-based objection to Vas-Cath's statutory right of judicial review.[89]

The Federal Circuit in *Vas-Cath* also distinguished *Xechem,* where no waiver was found. In *Xechem,* "the university . . . did not request the adjudication, did not initiate and participate in a PTO adversarial proceeding, did not engage in litigation like conduct, and there was no contested proceeding in which the university waived immunity and obtained the property of the losing party."[90]

In contrast with state governments, the U.S. *federal* government has expressly waived its sovereign immunity from suit for patent infringement. Such lawsuits against the United States are brought exclusively in the U.S. Court of Federal Claims. The federal government retains the power to use any patented invention without injunction but must pay just compensation for the taking if infringement is proved.[91]

7.   Temporary Presence Exemption

Section 272 of the Patent Act, titled "Temporary Presence in the United States," provides an exemption from patent infringement liability for certain uses of patented inventions in vehicles that temporarily enter United States territory. The statute provides that

> [t]he use of any invention in any vessel, aircraft or vehicle of any country which affords similar privileges to vessels, aircraft or vehicles of the United States, entering the United States temporarily or accidentally, shall not constitute infringement of any patent, if the invention is used exclusively for the needs of the vessel, aircraft or vehicle and is not offered for sale or sold in or used for the manufacture of anything to be sold in or exported from the United States.[92]

In a case of first impression, the Federal Circuit held in *National Steel Car, Ltd. v. Canadian Pac. Ry., Ltd.*[93] that the statutory exemption for "temporarily" entering the United States encompassed a

---

[89]*Vas-Cath, Inc.*, 473 F.3d at 1385.
[90]*Id.* at 1383.
[91]28 U.S.C. §1498(a).
[92]35 U.S.C. §272.
[93]357 F.3d 1319 (Fed. Cir. 2004).

nonpermanent entry of a railroad car engaged in international commerce, even though the car was present in the United States for a majority of its useful life.[94]

National Steel Car's patent in suit was directed to a particular type of railway car used to haul lumber, known as a depressed-center-beam flat car. The Canadian defendant railroad's accused railroad cars, full of lumber, were brought into the United States from Canada on track owned by the defendant, and when that track ran out, the cars were sometimes shifted to locomotives owned by U.S. companies at locations such as Chicago, Illinois. After the lumber was unloaded at its U.S. destination, the accused railroad cars would return (empty) to Canada. A federal district court granted a preliminary injunction against the Canadian railroad, denying it the §272 exemption. In the district court's view, the accused cars' presence could not be "temporary" because the cars were in the United States the majority of the time (i.e., about 57 percent of the useful lifespan of the cars). Moreover, the district court found, this U.S. presence significantly benefited the accused infringer.

On appeal the Federal Circuit vacated the preliminary injunction, concluding that a substantial question existed as to whether the accused rail cars were "temporarily" present. The Federal Circuit first held that as applied to the case at bar, the relevant "vessel" of §272 was an individual accused railroad car. Next, the Federal Circuit rejected both the metrics relied on by the district court—duration and benefit—in determining whether the accused cars were "temporarily" present in the United States. The Federal Circuit instead defined a vehicle entering temporarily as "a vehicle entering the United States for a limited period of time for the sole purpose of engaging in international commerce,"[95] based on the circuit's own interpretation of §272, an issue of first impression.

The Federal Circuit found the language of §272 ambiguous, so it turned to the statute's legislative history. That history reflected that §272 was drafted to codify the Supreme Court's 1856 decision in *Brown v. Duchesne*,[96] and to satisfy the obligations of the United States under the World Intellectual Property Organization (WIPO)–administered Paris Convention for the Protection of Industrial Property. Both of these sources suggested that the word "temporarily" in §272 should be interpreted "in light of a vehicle's purpose to participate in international commerce at the time of entry—namely, a purpose to enter the

---

[94]For a comprehensive study of the *National Steel Car* decision and the growing importance of the §272 temporary presence exemption, *see* Ted. L. Field, *The "Planes, Trains, and Automobiles" Defense to Patent Infringement for Today's Global Economy: Section 272 of the Patent Act*, 12 Boston Univ. J. Sci. & Tech. L. 26 (2006).

[95]*National Steel Car*, 357 F.3d at 1329.

[96]60 U.S. (19 How.) 183 (1856).

United States, engage in international commerce, and then depart."[97] The Federal Circuit explained that in *Brown,* the unauthorized use within U.S. jurisdiction of a patented invention related to the rigging of a French schooner was deemed beyond the scope of the patentee's right to exclude, where the challenged use was limited to the bare essentials of the contact with the United States required to engage in international commerce. Both *Brown* and Article 5*ter* of the Paris Convention[98] demonstrated a concern to leave the vessels and vehicles that pass through channels of international commerce free from the excessive burdens that would result if required to conform to the patent laws of all nations that the vessel or vehicle visited during its lifetime. The Federal Circuit concluded that "[i]f the cars are entering the United States for a limited time—that is, they are not entering permanently—and are entering only for the purpose of engaging in international commerce—that is, they are entering to unload foreign goods and/or to load domestic goods destined for foreign markets—they are entering 'temporarily' for the purposes of section 272 regardless of the length of their stay within the jurisdiction of the United States."[99]

8. Patent Exhaustion

The defense of patent exhaustion prevents a patent owner from getting a "second bite at the apple" once a particular patented device has been sold with the patentee's authority the first time.[100] For example, if a patent owner sells one of its patented widgets to retailer R, thereafter it is not an act of patent infringement for retailer R to resell *that* particular widget to customer C. The patent owner's right to control

---

[97]*National Steel Car,* 357 F.3d at 1330.

[98]Article 5*ter* of the Paris Convention for the Protection of Industrial Property, titled "Patents: Patented Devices Forming Part of Vessels, Aircraft, or Land Vehicles," provides that

> In any country of the Union the following shall not be considered as infringements of the rights of a patentee:
>
> (i) the use on board vessels of other countries of the Union of devices forming the subject of his patent in the body of the vessel, in the machinery, tackle, gear and other accessories, when such vessels temporarily or accidentally enter the waters of the said country, provided that such devices are used there exclusively for the needs of the vessel;
>
> (ii) the use of devices forming the subject of the patent in the construction or operation of aircraft or land vehicles of other countries of the Union, or of accessories of such aircraft or land vehicles, when those aircraft or land vehicles temporarily or accidentally enter the said country.

[99]*National Steel Car,* 357 F.3d 1331.

[100]The copyright law counterpart to patent exhaustion is the "first sale" defense, codified at 17 U.S.C. §109(a).

the disposition of the particular widget in question is said to have been "exhausted" at the time of its first sale, meaning that the patent owner does not have a right to a royalty payment or other monetary tribute for subsequent resales (nor a right to enjoin them).[101] Importantly, the sale of counterfeit or pirated items does not invoke patent exhaustion. Rather, patent exhaustion applies when the first sale of a patented item is authorized; that is, the item is sold by the patent owner or someone acting with the patent owner's permission such as a licensee. Assuming that the first sale was authorized, then the patent owner is viewed as having received its entire reward or "tribute" in the price it obtained for the first sale of the particular patented item.

The U.S. Supreme Court confronted unique permutations of the patent exhaustion defense in *Quanta Computer, Inc. v. LG Elecs., Inc.*[102] The plaintiff LG owned a portfolio of patents on computer systems and methods. LG entered into a license agreement with Intel, the well-known computer chip manufacturer. Under the terms of the license, Intel had permission to make and sell microprocessors and chipsets that were components of the computer systems claimed in LG's patents. A dispute arose when Intel sold its microprocessor and chipset components to third-party computer manufacturers. Defendant Quanta (one of Intel's customers) made its computers by combining the Intel-supplied components with non-Intel components such as computer memory and buses. The claims of LG's patents read on these computers, that is, the overall combination of components assembled and sold by Quanta to consumers practiced LG's patents.

In the ensuing lawsuit between LG and Quanta, LG asserted that Quanta's computer sales infringed LG's patents, while Quanta contended that it was shielded from liability by the patent exhaustion defense. At the heart of the dispute were the terms of the LG-Intel license (even though Intel was not a party to the LG-Quanta lawsuit). The license authorized Intel to make and sell the licensed products (i.e., Intel's microprocessors and chipsets) to third parties, but also stipulated that LG was not granting any license (either express or implied) to any third party that combined the licensed products with non-Intel components. Intel gave written notice of these terms to Quanta, as required by a separate "Master Agreement" between LG and Intel. Nevertheless, Quanta proceeded to make and sell its computers on the theory that it was shielded by the patent exhaustion doctrine. Quanta's view proved correct.

---

[101]The above discussion contemplates sales of patented items within a given country's market. Patent exhaustion in the international context is more complex, as discussed *infra* Chapter 12, Section F.

[102]128 S. Ct. 2109 (2008).

First, the Supreme Court agreed with Quanta that the defense of patent exhaustion can apply to alleged infringements of method claims as well as to apparatus (in this case, system) claims, even though method claims are not linked to a tangible article but rather to a process. "It is true that a patented method may not be sold in the same way as an article or device, but methods nonetheless may be 'embodied' in a product, the sale of which exhausts patent rights."[103]

The more difficult issue in *Quanta Computer* was to what "extent a product must embody a patent in order to trigger exhaustion."[104] The Supreme Court's opinion leaves ample uncertainty on this question. The Court concluded that even though the components sold by Intel to Quanta did not "completely" embody the claimed invention, they "essentially" did so in a manner sufficient to cause exhaustion of LG's patent rights when first sold by Intel to Quanta.[105] The Court reasoned that the Intel microprocessors and chipsets could not function unless connected to computer memory and buses. The only apparent object of Intel's sales was Quanta's combination of the Intel-supplied components with non-Intel computer memory and buses in order to make and sell computers. Moreover, the Intel-supplied components "constitute[d] a material part of the patented invention and all but completely practice[d] the patent." According to the Court, "making a product that substantially embodies a patent is, for exhaustion purposes, no different from making the patented article itself."[106] Neither did Quanta exercise any "creative or inventive" decision making in combining the Intel and non-Intel components; in fact Quanta had no choice but to follow Intel's specifications for incorporating the Intel components because their internal structures were Intel trade secrets.

The Supreme Court in *Quanta Computer* also confirmed that Intel's component sales to Quanta were "authorized" sales, which are required to invoke the patent exhaustion defense as explained above. Nothing in the LG-Intel license restricted Intel's right to sell its chipsets and

---

[103]*Id.* at 2117.

[104]*Id.* at 2119.

[105]In this part of the *Quanta Computer* opinion the Supreme Court relied heavily on its decision in *United States v. Univis Lens Co.*, 316 U.S. 241 (1942). The Court in *Univis Lens* held that the sale of eyeglass lens "blanks" triggered patent exhaustion because the blanks' only reasonable and intended use was to practice the eyeglass lens patent in suit and because the blanks embodied essential features of the patented invention.

[106]It is interesting to contrast the Supreme Court's adoption of an uncertain "substantially embodies" standard in the exhaustion context with its rejection of the Federal Circuit's "substantially complete" standard for triggering the §102(b) on sale bar in *Pfaff v. Wells Elecs., Inc.*, 525 U.S. 59, 65-66 (1998) ("A rule that makes the timeliness of an application depend on the date when an invention is 'substantially complete' seriously undermines the interest in certainty.").

microprocessors to purchasers, even to firms like Quanta that intended to combine them with non-Intel parts. In a much-noted footnote, the Court hinted that patentee LG might have had a claim to breach of contract damages but had no right to patent infringement damages against Quanta.[107] The point was moot, however, because LG's complaint did not include a breach of contract claim.[108]

9.   Plaintiff's Lack of Standing to Sue for Infringement

A lawsuit alleging patent infringement must be brought by the holder of the right to exclude that the patent conveys. The Patent Act provides that "[a] patentee shall have remedy by civil action for infringement of his patent."[109] It further defines "patentee" as "not only the patentee to whom the patent was issued but also the successors in title to the patentee."[110] This statutory definition means that ordinarily, the party bringing an infringement suit must hold legal title in the patent.[111] When the plaintiff filing suit is the record title holder, standing is not a concern.

Questions about standing often arise, however, when a licensee under the patent attempts to file an infringement lawsuit in its own name without the participation of the patent owner/licensor.[112] If the plaintiff/licensee lacks standing, the accused infringer will assert this deficiency as a basis for dismissing the lawsuit. A *nonexclusive* licensee does *not* have standing to sue in its own name for patent infringement.[113] An exclusive licensee *may* have standing to sue in its

---

[107]*Quanta Computer,* 128 S. Ct. at 2122 n.7.

[108]Based in part on footnote 7 of *Quanta,* some observers question whether the Federal Circuit's decision in *Mallinckrodt, Inc. v. Medipart, Inc.*, 976 F.2d 700 (Fed. Cir. 1992), is still good law. The Federal Circuit held in *Mallinckrodt* that a patentee's sale of a medical device bearing a "single use only" label was a permissible post-sale restriction on use of the patented invention, and that only unconditional sales trigger patent exhaustion. The Supreme Court did not cite or discuss *Mallinckrodt* in its *Quanta* decision, so this issue will likely await further Federal Circuit deliberation.

[109]35 U.S.C. §281.

[110]*Id.* at §100(d).

[111]*See* Enzo APA & Son, Inc. v. Geapag, A.G., 134 F.3d 1090, 1093 (Fed. Cir. 1998).

[112]As a practical matter, the patent owner/licensor may not want to be involved in litigation for any number of reasons, for example, not wanting to incur potential liability for counterclaims, an unwillingness to share the potentially high costs of patent litigation, or geographic inconvenience in the case of a patent owner based outside the United States.

[113]*See* Jay Dratler, Jr., Licensing of Intellectual Property §8.06 (2008). Indeed, "[a] nonexclusive license confers no constitutional standing on the licensee to bring suit or even to join a suit with the patentee because a nonexclusive licensee suffers no legal injury from infringement." Sicom Sys., Ltd. v. Agilent Techs., Inc., 427 F.3d 971, 976 (Fed. Cir. 2005).

own name, depending on the terms of the patent license.[114] In particular, the exclusive license must be a "virtual assignment" that confers standing to sue for infringements.[115] The license must transfer "all substantial rights under the patent" and it must be in writing.[116] If the exclusive licensee holds less than all substantial rights, the patentee/licensor must be joined as a party to the lawsuit.[117]

D.   Unenforceability

The defense of unenforceability, asserted under 35 U.S.C. §282(b)(1) (eff. Sept. 16, 2012), has its roots in the equitable doctrine of "unclean hands."[118] In cases where ongoing infringement is alleged and the patent in suit is still in force, the patent owner will seek relief that includes an injunction against any further infringement. Because an injunction is an equitable remedy, however, courts will not grant the patentee an injunction if she has come to the court with unclean hands.

---

[114]See JAY DRATLER, JR., LICENSING OF INTELLECTUAL PROPERTY §8.06 (2008).

[115]See Enzo APA, 134 F.3d at 1093.

[116]See id.

[117]See Sicom Sys., 427 F.3d at 980 (stressing "the principle set forth in Independent Wireless [Tel. Co. v. Radio Corp. of Am., 269 U.S. 459 (1926)] requiring that a patent owner be joined in any infringement suit brought by an exclusive licensee having fewer than all substantial rights. . . . Unlike an assignee who may sue in its own name, an exclusive licensee having fewer than all substantial patent rights and seeking to enforce its rights in a patent generally must sue jointly with the patent owner.") (citations omitted).

AsymmetRx, Inc. v. Biocare Med., LLC, 582 F.3d 1314 (Fed. Cir. 2009), provides a helpful illustration of these standing principles. After summarizing relevant precedent, the Federal Circuit in AsymmetRx concluded that "[a]lthough the AsymmetRx License effected a broad conveyance of rights to [plaintiff] AsymmetRx, [the patent owner, President and Fellows of] Harvard [College] retained substantial interests under the '256 and '227 patents [in suit], including the right to sue for infringement, and AsymmetRx therefore does not have the right to sue for infringement as a 'patentee' under the patent statute." AsymmetRx, 582 F.3d at 1320. Because AsymmetRx had not joined Harvard as a party to the lawsuit, AsymmetRx did not have standing to pursue its action against alleged infringer Biocare.

[118]See Therasense, Inc. v. Becton, Dickinson and Co., 649 F.3d 1276 (Fed. Cir. 2011) (en banc). The en banc court observed that the judge-made doctrine of inequitable conduct, which if established results in the penalty of unenforceability, "evolved from a trio of Supreme Court cases that applied the doctrine of unclean hands to dismiss patent cases involving egregious misconduct: Keystone Driller Co. v. General Excavator Co., 290 U.S. 240, 54 S. Ct. 146, 78 L. Ed. 293 (1933); Hazel–Atlas Glass Co. v. Hartford–Empire Co., 322 U.S. 238, 64 S. Ct. 997, 88 L. Ed. 1250 (1944), overruled on other grounds by Standard Oil Co. v. United States, 429 U.S. 17, 97 S. Ct. 31, 50 L. Ed. 2d 21 (1976); and Precision Instrument Manufacturing Co. v. Automotive Maintenance Machinery Co., 324 U.S. 806, 65 S. Ct. 993, 89 L. Ed. 1381 (1945)." Therasense, 649 F.3d at 1285.

The defense of unenforceability can be based on at least three different equity-based theories: (1) **inequitable conduct,** (2) **patent misuse,** or (3) **prosecution history laches.** Each is discussed separately below. If an equitable defense is successfully established, the result is that the federal district court will enter a judgment of unenforceability, which should be distinguished from a judgment of invalidity. If a patent is held unenforceable, *every* claim of the patent is considered unenforceable. Invalidity, by contrast, is determined on a claim-by-claim basis; some claims of a patent may be held invalid while others are sustained and may still be asserted as the basis for infringement.

Another distinction between unenforceability and invalidity is that the patent misuse form of unenforceability may be purged in some instances, such that the patent may again be enforced once the misuse has been alleviated.[119] In contrast, a judgment of patent invalidity (once affirmed on appeal) is final and cannot be lifted.[120]

1. Inequitable Conduct

The defense of inequitable conduct asserts that a court should refuse to enforce a patent if it was procured through improper conduct before the USPTO. The *ex parte* nature of patent prosecution before the USPTO drives the inequitable conduct defense. The USPTO rules require that all persons substantively involved in the patent application process owe a duty of candor to the agency, which includes a duty to disclose to the agency all known information that is material to patentability.[121] Rigorous compliance with the duty of disclosure may seem contrary to the self-interests of some patent applicants, and the USPTO has limited resources with which to police that compliance. Thus a severe penalty is set for violations of the duty that come to light in subsequent litigation of a patent: if the defense of inequitable conduct is proved, the entire patent (i.e., all claims, regardless of their validity) is rendered unenforceable (a result that courts have termed the "atomic bomb" of patent law).[122]

Because many foreign patent systems have robust opposition procedures allowing challenges to recently granted patents on any statutorily recognized ground of invalidity,[123] the U.S.-based notions of

[119]*See* Morton Salt Co. v. G.S. Suppiger Co., 314 U.S. 488, 493 (1942).
[120]*See* Blonder-Tongue Labs., Inc. v. Univ. of Ill. Found., 402 U.S. 313 (1971), discussed *infra.*
[121]37 C.F.R. §1.56 (2012).
[122]Therasense, Inc. v. Becton, Dickinson and Co., 649 F.3d 1288 (Fed. Cir. 2011) (*en banc*).
[123]*See, e.g.,* European Patent Convention arts. 99-105 (13th ed. 2007), *available at* http://www.epo.org/patents/law/legal-texts/html/epc/2000/e/ma1.html.

a strict duty of disclosure during prosecution and an inequitable conduct defense during litigation are not considered necessary there.[124] In the United States, however, the availability of the inequitable conduct defense is an essential method of ensuring that patent applicants "play by the rules." As a leading U.S. patent scholar observes, "[t]he most cogent practical argument for retaining the inequitable conduct defense is that unless a severe penalty exists for withholding information, practitioners and their clients will not be motivated to help the PTO in its job of examining applications thoroughly and allowing only valid claims."[125]

As with the invalidity defenses discussed below, the quantum of evidence required to satisfy a challenger's burden of establishing inequitable conduct is clear and convincing evidence. More particularly, the proponent of the inequitable conduct defense must prove by clear and convincing evidence each of two underlying factual elements: (1) materiality and (2) intent to deceive the USPTO.[126] Each element is separately discussed below.

a. Materiality

To constitute inequitable conduct, a patent applicant's conduct before the USPTO must involve the nondisclosure or wrongful submission of information that is material to patentability. Such nondisclosure or wrongful submission typically occurs in one of the following three scenarios:

1. failure to disclose to the USPTO information known to the applicant[127] that is material to patentability;

---

[124]See Paul M. Janicke, *Do We Really Need So Many Mental and Emotional States in United States Patent Law?*, 8 TEX. INTELL. PROP. L.J. 279, 292 (2000) (noting that "to date, no other country has adopted a private remedy for deceiving the patent-issuing authorities, with the exception of a German statutory provision whereby the Patent Office can request an applicant to disclose the state of the art truthfully as the applicant knows it"). Professor Janicke suggests that other countries have not adopted the inequitable conduct defense because they consider the possibility of invalidity a sufficient remedy, particularly in those foreign legal systems where the losing party pays the winning party's attorney fees. *Id.*

[125]Paul M. Janicke, *Do We Really Need So Many Mental and Emotional States in United States Patent Law?*, 8 TEX. INTELL. PROP. L.J. 279, 292 (2000).

[126]Dippin' Dots, Inc. v. Mosey, 476 F.3d 1337, 1345 (Fed. Cir. 2007) (stating that "[t]he party urging unenforceability must show by clear and convincing evidence that the [patent] applicant met 'thresholds of both materiality and intent'") (quoting Molins PLC v. Textron, 48 F.3d 1172, 1178 (Fed. Cir. 1995)).

[127]The information must be "known" to the applicant in order for the duty of disclosure to attach. There is no affirmative duty on a patent applicant to conduct a prior art search in order to seek out and find information material to patentability. However, "one should not be able to cultivate ignorance, or disregard numerous warnings that

2. submission to the USPTO of false information that is material to patentability; or
3. affirmative misrepresentations made to the USPTO that are material to patentability.

Thus, inequitable conduct can be based on either a patent applicant's omission (i.e., a failure to act) or commission (i.e., an affirmative act of submitting false information or making a misrepresentation).

The Federal Circuit has grown increasingly concerned about the "plague" of inequitable conduct assertions routinely encountered in patent litigation.[128] In its 2011 decision in *Therasense, Inc. v. Becton, Dickinson and Co.,*[129] a majority of Federal Circuit judges determined *en banc* to "adjust" (that is, make more rigorous) the standard for establishing whether information is material to patentability.[130] The *Therasense en banc* majority read the Supreme Court's 1928 decision in *Corona Cord Tire Co. v. Dovan Chem. Corp.*[131] as supporting a

---

material information or prior art may exist, merely to avoid actual knowledge of that information or prior art. When one does that, the 'should have known' factor becomes operative." FMC Corp. v. Hennessy Indus., Inc., 836 F.2d 521, 526 n.6 (Fed. Cir. 1987).

[128]In *Therasense, Inc. v. Becton, Dickinson and Co.*, 649 F.3d 1276 (Fed. Cir. 2011) (*en banc*), the court observed that

[l]eft unfettered, the inequitable conduct doctrine has plagued not only the courts but also the entire patent system. Because allegations of inequitable conduct are routinely brought on "the slenderest grounds," *Burlington Indus.*, 849 F.2d at 1422, patent prosecutors constantly confront the specter of inequitable conduct charges. With inequitable conduct casting the shadow of a hangman's noose, it is unsurprising that patent prosecutors regularly bury PTO examiners with a deluge of prior art references, most of which have marginal value.

Therasense, 649 F.3d at 1289; *see also* Burlington Indus., Inc. v. Dayco Corp., 849 F.2d 1418, 1422 (Fed. Cir. 1988) (remarking that "the habit of charging inequitable conduct in almost every major patent case has become an absolute plague").

[129]649 F.3d 1276 (Fed. Cir. 2011) (*en banc*).

[130]The *en banc* court in *Therasense* was sharply divided. With 11 Federal Circuit judges participating in *en banc* review, 6 judges signed the opinion for the court (i.e., Rader (author), Newman, Lourie, Linn, Moore, and Reyna). Four judges dissented in full (i.e., Bryson (author), Gajarsa, Dyk, and Prost). Judge O'Malley authored an opinion concurring-in-part and dissenting-in-part. Notably, Judge O'Malley dissented from the materiality portion of the majority's opinion (and the majority's judgment to vacate and remand the district court's decision of inequitable conduct for further inquiry on the materiality determination). Thus, the "but for" materiality standard of *Therasense* became Federal Circuit *en banc* law by a 6-5 vote.

[131]276 U.S. 358, 373-374 (1928). The Supreme Court in *Corona Cord* considered two affidavits falsely stating that the claimed invention of the patent in suit had been used to produce rubber goods, when in fact the invention had been used only to make test slabs of rubber. Although perhaps "reckless," the false affidavits were not essentially material to the issuance of the patent in suit. Hence the *Corona* Court held that they did not destroy the patent's presumption of validity. *Corona Cord*, 276 U.S. at 374. The Federal Circuit majority in *Therasense* relied on the *Corona Cord* Court's

heightened "but-for" materiality standard.[132] Applying this standard to the typical scenario of applicant failure to disclose prior art to the USPTO, the *en banc* Federal Circuit majority held that "prior art is but-for material if the PTO would not have allowed a claim had it been aware of the undisclosed prior art."[133] In other words, when assessing materiality of a withheld reference, "the court must determine whether the PTO would have allowed the claim if it had been aware of the undisclosed information."[134] In so determining, the court should follow the USPTO's "broadest reasonable construction" rule for patent claim interpretation,[135] and impose a "preponderance of the evidence" burden of proof on the question of materiality.

Application of these standards will usually require that in order to reach a conclusion of inequitable conduct, a court must also hold one or more claims of a patent invalid over the withheld reference(s). A judgment of invalidity will not *always* be required for inequitable conduct, however, because the withheld art (although not invalidating under federal court standards) might have prevented patent issuance by the USPTO under the agency's somewhat less rigorous evidentiary and constructional standards (i.e., "preponderance of the evidence"

"unwillingness to extinguish the statutory presumption of validity where the patentee made a misrepresentation to the PTO that did not affect the issuance of the patent," as well as the fact that the "severe remedy of unenforceability for inequitable conduct far exceeds the mere removal of a presumption of validity." *Therasense,* 649 F.3d at 1291.

[132]As a policy matter, the *Therasense* majority opined that "enforcement of an otherwise valid patent does not injure the public merely because of misconduct, lurking somewhere in patent prosecution, that was immaterial to the patent's issuance." *Therasense,* 649 F.3d at 1291. Four judges of the Federal Circuit sharply disputed this reasoning, writing in response to the majority's new "but for" materiality standard that

[i]f a failure to disclose constitutes inequitable conduct only when a proper disclosure would result in rejection of a claim, there will be little incentive for applicants to be candid with the PTO, because in most instances the sanction of inequitable conduct will apply only if the claims that issue are invalid anyway. . . . Even if the nondisclosure or misleading disclosure is later discovered, under the majority's rule the applicant is no worse off, as the patent will be lost only if the claims would otherwise be held invalid. . . . Given the large stakes sometimes at issue in patent prosecutions, a regime that ensures that a dishonest but potentially profitable course of action can be pursued with essentially no marginal added risk is an unwise regime no matter how virtuous its subjects.

Therasense, 649 F.3d at 1305-1306 (Bryson, J., dissenting).

[133]*Therasense,* 649 F.3d at 1291.

[134]*Therasense,* 649 F.3d at 1291.

[135]*Therasense,* 649 F.3d at 1291-1292 (citing UNITED STATES PATENT AND TRADEMARK OFFICE, MANUAL OF PATENT EXAMINING PROCEDURE §§706, 2111 (8th ed. rev. 8, July 2010)).

burden of proof and "broadest reasonable claim construction" rule).[136] In the view of this author, such cases will be few. In most cases, invalidity over the withheld prior art will be a prerequisite to a finding of materiality that supports inequitable conduct.

Though raising the standard for establishing materiality, the *Therasense* majority also recognized an exception to its general rule requiring "but for" proof. Based on the "unclean hands" doctrine of earlier Supreme Court cases, the *en banc* majority in *Therasense* held that the exception is triggered by "affirmative acts of egregious misconduct, such as the filing of an unmistakably false affidavit."[137] In such cases, the misconduct is material regardless of whether the "but for" rule is satisfied. Importantly, the egregious misconduct exception requires an *affirmative* act; neither "mere nondisclosure of prior art references to the USPTO nor failure to mention prior art references in an affidavit" qualifies for the exception (and hence still requires proof of "but for" materiality to establish inequitable conduct).[138]

The facts of *Therasense* concerned Abbott Laboratories' (Abbott's) U.S. Patent No. 5,820,551 ('551 patent), directed to disposable blood glucose test strips used by diabetes patients. The claims recited strips for testing the concentration of a compound such as glucose in a "whole blood" sample (i.e., blood containing all its components, including red blood cells). Notably, the claims required that an "active electrode" on the strip be "configured to be *exposed to said whole*

---

[136]Federal district courts need not apply the USPTO's more expansive "broadest reasonable construction" rule when interpreting patent claims, and the burden of proof to establish invalidity of patent claims before a district court (i.e., clear and convincing evidence) is considered higher than the USPTO's "preponderance of the evidence" burden of proof for rejecting application claims as unpatentable. For more on the "clear and convincing evidence" burden of proof in federal court validity litigation, *see infra* Section E.1 (discussing Microsoft Corp. v. i4i Ltd. P'ship, 131 S. Ct. 2238 (2011)).

[137]*Therasense,* 649 F.3d at 1292.

[138]In the post-*Therasense* decision *Powell v. Home Depot U.S.A., Inc.*, 663 F.3d 1221 (Fed. Cir. 2011), the court rejected an accused infringer's contention that a patentee's failure to update a Petition to Make Special amounted to inequitable conduct. The patentee Powell initially requested expedited prosecution based on a belief that he was obligated to manufacture and supply products embodying his invention to Home Depot. After Powell learned that Home Depot would be procuring the products from another company, he failed to update his Petition to Make Special. The Federal Circuit held that Powell's failure to update did not satisfy the *Therasense* affirmative egregious misconduct exception. "Where, as here, the patent applicant fails to update the record to inform the PTO that the circumstances which support a Petition to Make Special no longer exist—that conduct does not constitute inequitable conduct." *Powell,* 663 F.3d at 1235 (citing *Therasense,* 649 F.3d at 1290). "That is so because Mr. Powell's conduct obviously fails the but-for materiality standard and is not the type of unequivocal act, 'such as the filing of an unmistakably false affidavit,' that would rise to the level of 'affirmative egregious misconduct.'" *Powell,* 663 F.3d at 1235 (quoting *Therasense,* 649 F.3d at 1292–1293).

blood sample without an intervening membrane or other whole blood
filtering member."[139]

A key focus of the '551 patent application's examination in the
USPTO was whether the prior art taught that glucose sensors could
be used to test whole blood without a protective membrane.[140] The
asserted inequitable conduct by Abbott involved taking inconsistent
positions before the USPTO and the European Patent Office (EPO)
without disclosing the inconsistency to the USPTO. Specifically,
Abbott failed to disclose to the USPTO examiner certain briefs that
Abbott had previously submitted to the EPO during prosecution of
the application leading to the European counterpart patent of the '551
patent. During a 13-year prosecution in the USPTO, Abbott submitted (in or after 1997) a sworn declaration from its technical expert
(Abbott's then Director of Research and Development) accompanied
by statements from its patent counsel. These submissions "asserted
unequivocally that one skilled in the art would *not* have read the prior
art to say that use of a protective membrane with whole blood samples
was optional."[141] However, "Abbott [had also] represented [to the EPO
in briefs filed in 1994 and 1995] that it was 'unequivocally clear' that
the same prior art language meant that the protective membrane *was*,
in fact, optional."[142]

Because the district court found inequitable conduct on these
facts but had applied the earlier, less rigorous materiality standard
then codified in the USPTO's Rule 56,[143] the *en banc* Federal Circuit
Therasense majority vacated and remanded the district court's decision for further consideration. On remand, applying the new "but for"
materiality standard announced by the Federal Circuit, the district
court reconfirmed its original determination that Abbott's '551 patent
was unenforceable due to inequitable conduct.[144] The inconsistency of

[139]*Therasense,* 649 F. 3d at 1282 (quoting claim 1 of Abbott's '551 patent) (emphasis added).

[140]*Therasense,* 649 F.3d at 1301 (O'Malley, J., concurring-in-part and dissenting-in-part).

[141]*Id.* (emphasis added).

[142]*Id.* (emphasis added).

[143]The district court applied part of the USPTO materiality definition set forth in 37 C.F.R. §1.56 (1992). The rule provides in pertinent part that information is mate-rial when it is "inconsistent with [] a position that applicant takes in . . . [a]sserting an argument of patentability." 37 C.F.R. 1.56(b)(2)(ii) (1992). *See Therasense,* 659 F.2d at 1312, 1318 (Bryson, J., dissenting).

[144]*See* Therasense, Inc. v. Becton, Dickinson and Co., Nos. Nos. C 04–02123 WHA et seq., 2012 WL 1038715 (N.D. Cal. Mar. 27, 2012) (explaining that "[t]he court of appeals, sitting *en banc*, vacated a finding herein of inequitable conduct and remanded with instructions to redetermine specified questions under a new standard. Using the new standard, this order again comes to the same conclusion that the patent in suit was procured through inequitable conduct.").

Abbott's position concerning what a critical prior art reference taught, or more precisely, Abbott's failure to disclose its inconsistent statements to the USPTO, was information material to patentability.[145]

Prior to its 2011 *Therasense* decision, the Federal Circuit's test for materiality was whether a hypothetical "reasonable examiner" would have considered the information "important" in deciding whether to allow the application to issue as a patent.[146] If that question was answered affirmatively, then the information satisfied the materiality element of the inequitable conduct defense, without regard to a "but for" inquiry. In other words, it was not necessary that the withheld information be invalidating, that is, that the information would have rendered the patent application's claims unallowable if the examiner had been aware of it.[147] A patent might be held unenforceable for inequitable conduct based on the applicant's act of withholding prior art with intent to deceive the USPTO, even though the patent's validity was sustained over that same prior art.[148] In such cases the withheld prior art was not sufficiently relevant to invalidate the claims, but was nevertheless sufficiently material to patentability to form a basis for a judgment of inequitable conduct.

Post-*Therasense,* it remains the law that information is not considered material if it is merely *cumulative* of (i.e., adds nothing new or different to) other information already before the USPTO.[149] Similarly, if an applicant fails to disclose known information but that information

[145]The district court also found that Abbott withheld the EPO briefs with specific intent to deceive the USPTO. *Therasense*, 2012 WL 1038715 at *11 (concluding that Abbott's explanation for not submitting the EPO briefs to the USPTO "simply lacked sufficient coherence and consistency compared to the rest of the record. There is not one shred of documentary evidence to corroborate their testimony that at the time in question they actually believed or documented or discussed the supposed reason for not submitting the EPO briefs. It surfaced for the first time in this litigation.").

[146]*See* Star Scientific, Inc. v. R.J. Reynolds Tobacco Co., 537 F.3d 1357, 1367 (Fed. Cir. 2008); Nilssen v. Osram Sylvania, Inc., 504 F.3d 1223, 1235 (Fed. Cir. 2007) (stating that "[i]nformation is material if there is a substantial likelihood that a reasonable examiner would have considered the information important in deciding whether to allow the application to issue as a patent"); Honeywell Int'l, Inc. v. Universal Avionics Sys. Corp., 488 F.3d 982, 1000 (Fed. Cir. 2007).

[147]*See* Molins PLC v. Textron, Inc., 48 F.3d 1172, 1179-1180 (Fed. Cir. 1995) (stating that "[n]or is a reference immaterial simply because the claims are eventually deemed by an examiner to be patentable thereover" and concluding as to case at bar that "the fact that the examiner did not rely on [the] Wagenseil [reference] to reject the claims . . . is not conclusive concerning whether the reference was material").

[148]*See, e.g.,* Critikon, Inc. v. Becton Dickinson Vascular Access, Inc., 120 F.3d 1253, 1255 (Fed. Cir. 1997) (finding that withheld McDonald prior art patent was material to patentability, but affirming district court's judgment sustaining validity of the patents in suit).

[149]*See Star Scientific,* 537 F.3d at 1367.

is independently discovered by the USPTO examiner, such information is not considered material.[150]

USPTO rules mandate that patent applicants owe the agency a duty of candor and good faith, including a duty to disclose to the USPTO information known to applicants that is material to patentability.[151] The USPTO's definition of materiality has changed over time.[152]

The Federal Circuit's pre-*Therasense* "important to a reasonable examiner" standard for materiality in the inequitable conduct context was linguistically the same as the definition applied by the USPTO in the agency's rules from 1977 to 1992, referred to by patent practitioners as "old Rule 56."[153] Although the USPTO changed its materiality definition in 1992 in an attempt to provide patent practitioners with a standard that was more specific and less open-ended and vague,[154] the Federal Circuit retained the older "important to a reasonable examiner" standard of materiality in its inequitable conduct jurisprudence. The court does not consider itself bound by the USPTO's current definition of materiality as set forth at 37 C.F.R. §1.56(b), referred to by patent practitioners as the "new Rule 56."[155]

---

[150]*See* Eli Lilly & Co. v. Zenith Goldline Pharms., Inc., 471 F.3d 1369, 1383 (Fed. Cir. 2006) (affirming district court's conclusion that patentee's nondisclosure to USPTO of "Chakrabarti 1980a" prior art reference "was neither a material omission nor done with an intent to deceive" in part because "the examiner found and relied on Chakrabarti 1980a during prosecution"); Molins PLC v. Textron, Inc., 48 F.3d 1172, 1185 (Fed. Cir. 1995) (stating that "'[w]hen a reference was before the examiner, whether through the examiner's search or the applicant's disclosure, it cannot be deemed to have been withheld from the examiner'") (quoting Scripps Clinic & Res. Found. v. Genentech, Inc., 927 F.2d 1565, 1582 (Fed. Cir. 1991)); Orthopedic Equip. Co., Inc. v. All Orthopedic Appliances, Inc., 707 F.2d 1376, 1383-1384 (Fed. Cir. 1983) (affirming district court's finding that nondisclosed prior art was not material because "the examiner assigned to prosecution of the patent-in-suit independently ascertained the existence of the undisclosed prior art").

[151]*See* 37 C.F.R. §1.56(a) (2012).

[152]*See* Digital Control Inc. v. The Charles Mach. Works, 437 F.3d 1309, 1314-1316 (Fed. Cir. 2006) (describing history of USPTO changes to its definition of materiality).

[153]*See Digital Control*, 437 F.3d at 1315 (explaining that "in 1977, the PTO amended Rule 56 to clarify the duty of candor and good faith before the PTO. That version of Rule 56 required applicants to disclose 'information they are aware of which is material,' stating that information is material 'where there is a substantial likelihood that a reasonable examiner would consider it important in deciding whether to allow the application to issue as a patent.'") (quoting 37 C.F.R. §1.56 (1977)).

[154]*Cf. Digital Control*, 437 F.3d at 1314 (noting that "in 1992, the PTO amended Rule 56, creating an arguably narrower standard of materiality").

[155]Since 1992, USPTO regulations have defined information material to patentability as information that

is not cumulative to information already of record or being made of record in the application, and
    (1) [i]t establishes, by itself or in combination with other information, a prima facie case of unpatentability of a claim; or

Hence, the Federal Circuit pre-*Therasense* applied its "important to a reasonable examiner" standard of materiality even when USPTO rules would have provided a narrower definition of materiality during the time that the patent application in question was prosecuted.[156] To

---

(2) [i]t refutes, or is inconsistent with, a position the applicant takes in:
    (i) Opposing an argument of unpatentability relied on by the Office, or
    (ii) Asserting an argument of patentability.

A prima facie case of unpatentability is established when the information compels a conclusion that a claim is unpatentable under the preponderance of evidence, burden-of-proof standard, giving each term in the claim its broadest reasonable construction consistent with the specification, and before any consideration is given to evidence which may be submitted in an attempt to establish a contrary conclusion of patentability.

37 C.F.R. §1.56(b) (2008).

In response to the Federal Circuit's *en banc* decision in *Therasense, Inc. v. Becton, Dickinson and Co.*, 649 F.3d 1276 (Fed. Cir. 2011) (*en banc*), the USPTO issued in July 2011 a notice of proposed rulemaking. The agency proposed to change its definition of materiality in 37 C.F.R. §1.56 ("Rule 56") to comport with the "but for" materiality standard announced in *Therasense*. *See* United States Patent & Trademark Office, *Notice of Proposed Rulemaking: Revision of the Materiality to Patentability Standard for the Duty to Disclose Information in Patent Applications*, 76 FED. REG. 43631 (July 21, 2011). The Notice states in part:

Specifically, the Office is proposing to revise the materiality standard for the duty to disclose to match the materiality standard, as defined in *Therasense*, for the inequitable conduct doctrine. While *Therasense* does not require the Office to harmonize the materiality standards underlying the duty of disclosure and the inequitable conduct doctrine, the Office believes that there are important reasons to do so. The materiality standard set forth in *Therasense* should reduce the frequency with which applicants and practitioners are being charged with inequitable conduct, consequently reducing the incentive to submit information disclosure statements containing marginally relevant information and enabling applicants to be more forthcoming and helpful to the Office. At the same time, it should also continue to prevent fraud on the Office and other egregious forms of misconduct. Additionally, harmonization of the materiality standards is simpler for the patent system as a whole.

76 FED. REG. at 43631. As of the writing of this edition in 2012, the USPTO has not implemented the proposed rule.

[156]*See* Digital Control Inc. v. The Charles Mach. Works, 437 F.3d 1309, 1314-1316 (Fed. Cir. 2006) (applying "important to a reasonable examiner" standard of materiality while recognizing that USPTO in 1992 changed its definition of materiality as promulgated in 37 C.F.R. §1.56, and holding that the "reasonable examiner" standard and Federal Circuit's case law interpreting that standard "were not supplanted by the PTO's adoption of a new Rule 56").

The Federal Circuit's position found support in academic commentary. For example, Professor Carl Moy has argued that the USPTO's 1992 revision of Rule 56 was beyond the agency's rulemaking authority. Moy contends that the 1992 version of Rule 56 is merely a "hortatory statement" that the Federal Circuit is not bound to apply in the court's inequitable conduct jurisprudence. *See* R. Carl Moy, *The Effect of New Rule 56 on the Law of Inequitable Conduct*, 74 J. PAT. & TRADEMARK OFF. SOC'Y 257, 277-278 (1992).

the extent that the Federal Circuit's standard was more searching and would have required a patent applicant to submit a greater amount of information than would otherwise satisfy the USPTO definition of materiality, risk-averse patent applicants acted in accordance with the broader Federal Circuit standard of "important to a reasonable examiner." In other words, when in doubt about a prior art reference's materiality, prudence recommends submitting the reference to the USPTO for its consideration.[157]

The facts of *Critikon, Inc. v. Becton Dickinson Vascular Access, Inc.*[158] illustrate another important principle of materiality: what must be disclosed to the USPTO is not merely limited to prior art, but rather includes all *information* known to the applicant that is material to patentability. Critikon sued Becton Dickinson for infringement of Critikon's patents on intravenous (IV) catheters (including the Lemieux patent). During the course of the litigation, the Lemieux patent was reissued; Critikon amended its complaint to assert infringement of certain claims of the reissue patent. Reversing the district court's conclusion of no inequitable conduct, the Federal Circuit found fault not only with Critikon's nondisclosure of a prior art reference (the McDonald patent) that was material to the original and reissue Lemieux patents,[159] but also with Critikon's failure to inform the USPTO reissue examiner that the original Lemieux patent was the subject of concurrent federal court litigation in which Becton Dickinson was challenging its validity and enforceability. The appellate court had "little doubt" that the concurrent litigation involving the Lemieux patent also would be relevant to its reissue proceeding.[160] Given the materiality of the information withheld, together with Critikon's "failure at any point to offer a good faith explanation of the pattern of nondisclosure,"[161] the Federal Circuit was able to infer the patentee's requisite intent to deceive the USPTO. Accordingly, the court held Critikon's patents unenforceable.

A fine line sometimes separates "advantages advocacy" during patent prosecution from a failure to disclose material information to the USPTO, as demonstrated in *Purdue Pharma L.P. v. Endo Pharms.*

---

[157]Patent applicants typically submit prior art references for USPTO consideration by attaching copies of the references to an "Information Disclosure Statement" submitted in accordance with 37 C.F.R. §§1.97-1.98.

[158]120 F.3d 1253 (Fed. Cir. 1997).

[159]It is interesting to note that although the withheld McDonald patent was deemed material to patentability, the Federal Circuit did not reverse that part of the district court's judgment sustaining the validity of the patents in suit. *See id.* at 1255. Thus, *Critikon* is a case in which the withheld prior art was not sufficiently relevant to invalidate the claims, but was nevertheless of sufficient materiality to form a basis for a judgment of inequitable conduct.

[160]*Id.* at 1258.

[161]*Id.* at 1259.

Inc.[162] Purdue's three patents in suit were directed to controlled-release oxycodone medications for pain treatment, sold by Purdue as OxyContin®. In the written description of its patent applications and during prosecution thereof, Purdue repeatedly referred to its "surprising discovery" that its oxycodone formulations controlled pain over a fourfold range of dosages for 90 percent of patients, compared to an eightfold range for prior art opioids such as morphine. The patents also referred to the "clinical significance" of the fourfold dosage range as a more efficient titration process (by which a patient's dosage is adjusted to provide acceptable pain relief without unacceptable side effects). At no time prior to issuance of the patents did Purdue have clinical data to support these assertions, however. While Purdue never stated during prosecution that its discovery had been clinically tested, it discussed the fourfold dosage range under headings containing the phrases "Surprisingly Improved Results" and "Results Obtained." Based on this evidence a federal district court found that Purdue had failed to disclose material information to the USPTO because it did not inform the agency that its discovery was based merely on the inventor's "insight," without scientific proof. Moreover, the district court found, the record as a whole reflected a clear pattern of intentional misrepresentation.[163]

The Federal Circuit affirmed the district court's judgment that Purdue's patents were unenforceable due to inequitable conduct. Although Purdue admittedly had never stated that its discovery of the fourfold dosage range was based on the results of clinical studies, "that conclusion was clearly to be inferred from the language used by Purdue in both the patents and prosecution history,"[164] the court observed. "In the absence of any statements indicating the true origin of its 'surprising discovery,' Purdue's arguments to the PTO provide enough of a suggestion that clinical trials had been performed that failure to tell the PTO the discovery was based on [co-inventor] Dr. Kaiko's insight and not scientific proof was a failure to disclose material information."[165] The Federal Circuit rejected Purdue's argument that the fourfold dosage range was not material because it was simply a benefit of the claimed invention to which the examiner would have given little weight. The court contrasted *CFMT, Inc. v. Yieldup Int'l Corp.*,[166] in which it had held that a patentee did not commit inequitable conduct by setting forth during prosecution a list of advantages of the claimed invention. In *CFMT*, such "'advantages advocacy recited

[162]410 F.3d 690 (Fed. Cir. 2005).
[163]*Id.* at 695.
[164]*Id.* at 698.
[165]*Id.* at 698.
[166]349 F.3d 1333 (Fed. Cir. 2003).

only the natural, expected results of a closed system [for cleaning semi-conductor wafers]."[167] In the case at bar, however, Purdue's assertion concerning the fourfold dosage range was "much more" than advantages advocacy. Rather, it was "one of the key arguments Purdue made consistently and repeatedly during prosecution to overcome prior art cited by the examiner in an obviousness rejection."[168]

b. Intent to Deceive

A breach of a patent applicant's duty of disclosure to the USPTO, without more, does not establish the defense of inequitable conduct. The party asserting the defense also must establish that material information was withheld (or falsely submitted) with a specific intent to deceive the USPTO.[169] Materiality and intent are separate elements of inequitable conduct; materiality does not presume intent.[170] At least a threshold level of each element must be established by clear and convincing evidence.[171] When an inequitable conduct charge is based on an applicant's failure to disclose prior art to the USPTO, "clear and convincing evidence must show that the applicant *made a deliberate decision* to withhold a *known* material reference."[172]

In "tighten[ing] the standards" in order to "redirect" the inequitable conduct doctrine,[173] the *en banc* Federal Circuit majority in *Therasense, Inc. v. Becton, Dickinson and Co.*,[174] discussed *supra*, clarified the intent standard as well as the materiality standard. The "specific intent" called for by the Federal Circuit mandates both knowledge and deliberate action by the patent applicant. When alleged inequitable conduct involves the withholding of prior art from the USPTO, an "accused infringer must prove by clear and convincing evidence that the applicant knew of the reference, knew that it was material, and

---

[167]*Purdue Pharma*, 410 F.3d at 699 (quoting *CFMT*, 349 F.3d at 1342).

[168]*Id.*

[169]*See* Therasense, Inc. v. Becton, Dickinson and Co., 649 F.3d 1290 (Fed. Cir. 2011) (*en banc*) (holding that "[t]o prevail on a claim of inequitable conduct, the accused infringer must prove that the patentee acted with the specific intent to deceive the PTO").

[170]Star Scientific, Inc. v. R.J. Reynolds Tobacco Co., 537 F.3d 1357, 1366 (Fed. Cir. 2008).

[171]*Id.* at 1365.

[172]*Id.* at 1366 (emphasis in original).

[173]*Therasense*, 649 F.3d at 1290. Professor Golden suggests that "[w]ithout a real option of repudiating the [inequitable conduct] defense, the Federal Circuit [in *Therasense*] has instead sought to guide and confine the defense's application in hopes of advancing legitimate aims at acceptable social cost." John M. Golden, *Patent Law's Falstaff: Inequitable Conduct, the Federal Circuit, and* Therasense, 7 Wash. J.L., Tech. & Arts 353 (2012).

[174]649 F.3d 1290 (Fed. Cir. 2011) (*en banc*).

made a deliberate decision to withhold it."[175] It is *not* enough that "the applicant knew of a reference, *should have known* of its materiality, and decided not to submit it to the PTO. . . ."[176]

The Federal Circuit *en banc* majority in *Therasense* also revoked any "sliding scale" analysis for inferring intent.[177] The inequitable conduct elements of materiality and intent must each be independently proved by clear and convincing evidence. Importantly, a district court may not infer intent solely from materiality, nor may a weak showing of intent be rendered sufficient when evidence of materiality is strong. The court "must weigh the evidence of intent to deceive independent of its analysis of materiality."[178]

Because "smoking gun" evidence of intent to deceive rarely exists, intent may be inferred from the circumstances,[179] as in *Critikon*.[180] But inferred evidence of intent nevertheless must satisfy the "clear and convincing" quantum of proof. Moreover, "the inference must not only be based on sufficient evidence and be reasonable in light of that evidence, but it must also be the single most reasonable inference able to be drawn from the evidence to meet the clear and convincing standard."[181] No inference of intent can be drawn if there is no evidence, either direct or indirect, that supports such an inference.[182]

Applying these standards, the Federal Circuit held that a district court had clearly erred in finding intent to deceive the USPTO in *Star Scientific, Inc. v. R.J. Reynolds Tobacco Co.*[183] In that case, accused infringer Reynolds asserted inequitable conduct in the procurement of Star Scientific's '649 patent based on a "quarantine" theory.[184] Reynolds

[175]*Therasense,* 649 F.3d at 1290.

[176]*Therasense,* 649 F.3d at 1290 (emphasis added).

[177]*See Therasense,* 649 F.3d at 1290. Pre-*Therasense* Federal Circuit decisions permitted a sliding-scale approach. Under that approach, "[t]he more material the omission or the misrepresentation, the lower the level of intent required to establish inequitable conduct, and vice versa." Critikon, Inc. v. Becton Dickinson Vascular Access, Inc., 120 F.3d 1253, 1256 (Fed. Cir. 1997). *See also* Honeywell Int'l, Inc. v. Universal Avionics Sys. Corp., 488 F.3d 982, 999 (Fed. Cir. 2007) (stating that "[t]he more material the information misrepresented or withheld by the applicant, the less evidence of intent will be required in order to find inequitable conduct").

[178]*Therasense,* 649 F.3d at 1290.

[179]*See Therasense,* 649 F.3d at 1290 (holding that "[b]ecause direct evidence of deceptive intent is rare, a district court may infer intent from indirect and circumstantial evidence").

[180]For an example of inferred intent post-*Therasense, see* Aventis Pharma S.A. v. Hospira, Inc., 675 F.3d 1324 (Fed. Cir. 2012).

[181]*Star Scientific,* 537 F.3d at 1366.

[182]*Id.* at 1368.

[183]*Id.* at 1365.

[184]Star Scientific's U.S. Patent No. 6,202,649 ('649 patent) was directed to a method for preventing the formation of tobacco-specific nitrosamines (TSNAs), a hazardous chemical present in cured tobacco. *See Star Scientific,* 537 F.3d at 1360-1361.

contended that Star Scientific switched law firms during prosecution of its '649 patent in order to prevent the first law firm from disclosing to the USPTO a potentially damaging letter describing certain prior art, and to purposely keep the second law firm ignorant of the letter.

The Federal Circuit in *Star Scientific* concluded that the accused infringer's quarantine theory of deceptive intent was not supported by clear and convincing evidence. Reynolds' evidence suffered from a "major gap"—no evidence indicated that Star Scientific knew what the letter said before switching law firms, or that the letter was a reason for changing firms.[185] Star Scientific gave two reasons for changing law firms: that a partner at the first firm had recently passed away, and that the inventor had observed unsatisfactory performance by an associate of the same firm in an unrelated patent prosecution. Although the district court found this testimony was not credible, the Federal Circuit emphasized that "even if Star's explanations are not to be believed, it remained [Reynolds'] burden to prove its allegation . . . [Reynolds] cannot carry its burden simply because Star failed to prove a credible alternative explanation."[186] In other words, a patentee "need not offer any good faith explanation unless the accused infringer first carried [its] burden to prove a threshold level of intent to deceive by clear and convincing evidence."[187] It is not incumbent upon a patentee to rebut evidence of deceptive intent by providing a good faith explanation for its alleged misconduct unless and until the accused infringer has met its burden.[188]

The foundational case for understanding the intent requirement for inequitable conduct is *Kingsdown Med. Consultants, Ltd. v. Hollister, Inc.*[189] There the Federal Circuit demonstrated its concern that inequitable conduct has been asserted routinely and virtually automatically in almost every patent infringement litigation. The court went *en banc* to clarify the type of conduct that rises to the level of an intent to deceive. After *Kingsdown,* conduct of the patent applicant characterized as "gross negligence" or "ministerial error" cannot constitute the level of deliberate intent needed to establish inequitable conduct.

Kingsdown filed a U.S. patent application directed to an ostomy appliance for use by patients with openings in their abdominal walls for release of waste. During a lengthy and complex prosecution that lasted more than six years, Kingsdown filed a continuation application in which it carried forward certain claims from its original application. These claims had previously been indicated allowable by the

---

[185]*Id.* at 1368.
[186]*Id.*
[187]*Id.*
[188]*Id.*
[189]863 F.2d 867 (Fed. Cir. 1988) (partially *en banc*).

USPTO examiner after Kingsdown amended them to overcome a §112, ¶2 indefiniteness rejection.[190] In renumbering and carrying forward the claims into the continuation application, Kingsdown's counsel inadvertently copied the earlier, unamended (i.e., broader) version of a certain claim, and the examiner did not notice the mistake before issuing the patent.

The Federal Circuit reversed the district court's decision that Kingsdown's "gross negligence" in not recognizing its mistake rose to the level of an intent to deceive the USPTO:

> [A] transfer of numerous claims *en masse* from a parent to a continuing application, as the district court stated, is a ministerial act. As such, it is more vulnerable to errors which by definition result from inattention, and is less likely to result from the scienter involved in the more egregious acts of omission and commission that have been seen as reflecting the deceitful intent element of inequitable conduct in our cases.[191]

The *Kingsdown* court went *en banc* for a portion of its opinion to conclude that

> "[g]ross negligence" has been used as a label for various patterns of conduct. It is definable, however, only in terms of a particular act or acts viewed in light of all the circumstances. We adopt the view that a finding that particular conduct amounts to "gross negligence" does not of itself justify an inference of intent to deceive; the involved conduct, viewed in light of all the evidence, including evidence indicative of good faith, must indicate sufficient culpability to require a finding of intent to deceive.[192]

Thus, the "intent to deceive" element of the inequitable conduct defense requires a clear and convincing showing of conduct that is culpable, not merely negligent.

c. *Balancing*

Once a patent challenger has established the underlying factual elements of materiality and intent, the district court must engage in an overall balancing of the evidence, including evidence of good faith,[193] to determine as a matter of law whether the scales tilt to a conclusion that inequitable conduct occurred. If they do, the court will hold the patent unenforceable for inequitable conduct.

---

[190]The claim definiteness requirement of 35 U.S.C. §112, ¶2 was discussed *supra* Chapter 2 ("Patent Claims"). Effective September 16, 2012, the America Invents Act of 2011 renamed the second paragraph of §112 as "35 U.S.C. §112(b)."

[191]*Kingsdown*, 863 F.2d at 875.

[192]*Id.* at 876.

[193]*See id.*

Importantly, the balancing step comes only after both underlying elements of materiality and intent have been established by clear and convincing evidence. Once these underlying proofs have been made, "the district court must balance the *substance* of those now-proven facts and all the equities of the case to determine whether the severe penalty of unenforceability should be imposed."[194] This final balancing step is committed to the district court's discretion.[195] In exercising their discretion courts should be mindful that the penalty for inequitable conduct is severe: "the loss of the entire patent even where every claim meets every requirement of patentability."[196] Given this severity, courts must ensure that the underlying factors of materiality and intent have been satisfactorily proven before they exercise their discretion to ultimately determine whether to render a patent unenforceable.[197] The Federal Circuit has cautioned district courts to be "vigilant in not permitting the [inequitable conduct] defense to be applied too lightly."[198] While it is unjust to allow a patentee "who obtained his patent through deliberate misrepresentations or omissions of material information to enforce the patent against others," it is also unfair "to strike down an entire patent where the patentee only committed minor missteps or acted with minimal culpability or in good faith."[199]

d.   *Burden of Proof and Standard of Review*

The party asserting the defense of unenforceability based on inequitable conduct must establish each underlying factor of materiality and intent by clear and convincing evidence, in keeping with the burden of proof for invalidating an issued patent.

Because the overall conclusion of inequitable conduct is an equitable determination within the district court's discretion, the Federal Circuit's standard of review for the ultimate conclusion of inequitable conduct is quite deferential; that is, the Circuit will reverse only if the district court abused its discretion. Assuming that they were found by the district court (the usual case) rather than a jury, each of the underlying factors of materiality and intent is reviewed for clear error

---

[194]Star Scientific, Inc. v. R.J. Reynolds Tobacco Co., 537 F.3d 1357, 1367 (Fed. Cir. 2008) (emphasis in original).

[195]*See id.*

[196]*Id.* at 1365. The penalty may be even more severe in some cases. Through the doctrine of "infectious unenforceability," inequitable conduct that involved one or more patents in a family (e.g., patents issuing from a chain of related continuing applications) can "infect" related applications and render the resulting patents unenforceable. *See* Nilssen v. Osram Sylvania, Inc., 504 F.3d 1223, 1230 (Fed. Cir. 2007).

[197]*See Star Scientific*, 537 F.3d at 1366.

[198]*Id.*

[199]*Id.*

in accordance with Fed. R. Civ. P. 52.[200] If a jury made the findings of materiality and intent, the findings will be upheld so long as they are supported by substantial evidence.[201]

2. Patent Misuse[202]

a. *Introduction*

An accused infringer also may assert a defense of unenforceability under §282(b)(1) (eff. Sept. 16, 2012) on the ground that the patent owner has committed patent misuse. This basis for unenforceability is separate from inequitable conduct. Instead of the patent applicant's conduct before the USPTO, the patent misuse defense focuses on the manner in which the patentee has exploited her issued patent.

Patent misuse is a rather amorphous doctrine,[203] generally understood as a "method of limiting abuse of patent rights separate from the antitrust laws."[204] The misuse doctrine has its origin in judicial decisions that predate any significant development of U.S. antitrust law.[205] Procedurally, patent misuse is asserted as an affirmative defense to an allegation of patent infringement,[206] whereas antitrust violation is asserted by the accused infringer as a counterclaim.[207] Often the same conduct forms the basis for both a patent misuse defense and an antitrust allegation.[208] Substantively, however, different policies ground patent misuse and antitrust doctrine. Misuse focuses primarily on the patentee's behavior in expanding the scope of its rights beyond the

[200]*See* PerSeptive Biosys., Inc. v. Pharmacia Biotech, Inc., 225 F.3d 1315, 1318-1319 (Fed. Cir. 2000).

[201]*See* Juicy Whip, Inc. v. Orange Bang, Inc., 292 F.3d 728, 737 (Fed. Cir. 2002).

[202]Much of the material in this section is based on Janice M. Mueller, *Patent Misuse Through the Capture of Industry Standards,* 17 BERKELEY TECH. L.J. 623 (2002).

[203]Professor Chisum observes in the misuse area "the absence of a clear and general theory for resolving the problem of what practices should be viewed as appropriate exercises of the patent owner's statutory patent rights." 6-19 DONALD S. CHISUM, CHISUM ON PATENTS §19.04 (2008). But given that misuse is a doctrine based in equity, the lack of clarity is hardly surprising. *See* Robert Merges, *Reflections on Current Legislation Affecting Patent Misuse,* 70 J. PAT. & TRADEMARK OFF. SOC'Y 793, 796 (1988) (noting that "[t]he nature of equity is that it is somewhat 'messy'").

[204]B. Braun Med. v. Abbott Labs., 124 F.3d 1419, 1426 (Fed. Cir. 1997).

[205]*See* USM Corp. v. SPS Techs., Inc., 694 F.2d 505, 511 (7th Cir. 1982).

[206]*See* Virginia Panel Corp. v. Mac Panel Co., 133 F.3d 860, 868 (Fed. Cir. 1997); Windsurfing Int'l, Inc. v. AMF, Inc., 782 F.2d 995, 1001 (Fed. Cir. 1986).

[207]Antitrust counterclaims are considered in Section F of this chapter.

[208]However, establishing that a patentee who has committed patent misuse also has violated the antitrust laws requires "much more": in addition to the fact of the misuse, there must be showings of power in the relevant market and anticompetitive effect. *See* Marina Lao, *Unilateral Refusals to Sell or License Intellectual Property and the Antitrust Duty to Deal,* 9 CORNELL J.L. & PUB. POL'Y 193, 207 (1999).

statutory patent grant, whereas antitrust measures the impact of that behavior on the marketplace.[209]

Like inequitable conduct, the roots of patent misuse lie in the equitable doctrine of unclean hands, "whereby a court of equity will not lend its support to enforcement of a patent that has been misused."[210] Application of the misuse doctrine seeks to restrain practices that draw "anticompetitive strength" from the patent right.[211]

Although the patent misuse doctrine has been broadly defined as preventing a patent owner from using its patent in a manner contrary to the public interest, this characterization is too indefinite to provide any meaningful notice to a patentee of the boundaries of prohibited conduct.[212] In practice, determinations of patent misuse have been based on a fairly narrow range of specific practices or acts by the patent owner,[213] often (but not exclusively) in the context of patent licensing.[214] The key inquiry is whether, by imposing a challenged condition (e.g., the imposition of an onerous term in a license granted under the

[209]See Richard Calkins, *Patent Law: The Impact of the 1988 Patent Misuse Reform Act and* Noerr-Pennington *Doctrine on Misuse Defenses and Antitrust Counterclaims*, 38 Drake L. Rev. 175, 187 (1988-1989) (explaining that the antitrust laws are "intended to foreclose unreasonable restraints of trade and illegal monopolies," and consequently bear severe punishments for violators, while patent misuse doctrine, which merely suspends patent owner's right to recover for infringement, "prevent[s] a patentee from projecting the economic effect of his admittedly valid grant beyond the limits of his legal monopoly," which effect can occur "regardless of whether the defendant in a patent infringement action is injured or a monopoly in trade and commerce results") (quoting Panther Pumps & Equip. Co. v. Hydrocraft, Inc., 468 F.2d 225, 231 (7th Cir. 1972)).

[210]B. Braun Med. v. Abbott Labs., 124 F.3d 1419, 1427 (Fed. Cir. 1997).

[211]See Mallinckrodt, Inc. v. Medipart, Inc., 976 F.2d 700, 704 (Fed. Cir. 1992).

[212]See USM Corp. v. SPS Techs., Inc., 694 F.2d 505, 510 (7th Cir. 1982) (asserting that such a vague formulation, if "taken seriously . . . would put all patent rights at hazard").

[213]Id.

[214]See generally 6-19 Donald S. Chisum, Chisum on Patents §19.04[3] (2008) ("Acts of Misuse"). Important guidance on acceptable patent licensing practices is available at United States Department of Justice, *Antitrust Guidelines for the Licensing of Intellectual Property* (1995), *available at* http://www.usdoj.gov/atr/public/guidelines/0558.pdf [hereinafter *Licensing Guidelines*]. The *Licensing Guidelines* provide helpful examples of the application of antitrust principles to particular licensing restraints (such as horizontal restraints, resale price maintenance, tying arrangements, and exclusive dealing) and to arrangements that involve the cross-licensing, pooling, or acquisition of intellectual property. *See id.* at §5. Although the majority of patent misuse cases have examined a patentee's licensing practices, the patent misuse defense also has been raised in a case involving restrictions placed by the patent owner on the conditions of post-sale use of its patented device. *See Mallinckrodt*, 976 F.2d at 709 (Fed. Cir. 1992) (reversing grant of summary judgment of unenforceability based on patent misuse and remanding for determination of whether post-sale restriction was valid under applicable sales law and within scope of patent grant).

patent), the patent owner has "impermissibly broadened the 'physical or temporal scope' of the patent grant with anticompetitive effect."[215]

In its 2010 *en banc* decision *Princo Corp. v. Int'l Trade Comm'n*,[216] the Federal Circuit reconfirmed that the patent misuse doctrine should be construed narrowly. The court observed that patent misuse "is a judge-made doctrine that is in derogation of statutory patent rights against infringement."[217] Even if a patentee has violated the antitrust laws, such conduct does not necessarily establish that it engaged in patent misuse.[218]

At issue in *Princo* was an allegedly anticompetitive agreement between U.S. Philips Corporation (Philips), intervenor in the ITC's case against Princo, and Sony Corporation. Philips and Sony worked together in the 1980s and 1990s to set standards for digital storage recordable and rewritable compact disc technology. The two companies faced a technical problem concerning how to encode position information in the discs. They ultimately chose an analog solution proposed by Philips and covered by Philips's "Raaymakers" patents over a digital solution proposed by Sony and covered by Sony's "Lagadec" patent. The Raaymakers approach was thus incorporated into the technology standard for making the compact discs, published in what was informally known as the "Orange Book." Philips and Sony commercialized their technology by offering "package" licenses for manufacturers of Orange Book–compliant compact discs. Philips, the licensing program administrator, included in the package of licensed patents not only its Raaymakers patents but also Sony's Lagadec patents (and other patents).[219]

Princo was an initial licensee under the package license. When Princo thereafter ceased paying royalties, Philips filed a complaint

---

[215]Windsurfing Int'l, Inc. v. AMF, Inc., 782 F.2d 995, 1001 (Fed. Cir. 1986) (quoting Blonder-Tongue Labs., Inc. v. Univ. of Ill. Found., 402 U.S. 313, 343 (1971)). Commentators have identified *Windsurfing* as a merger by the Federal Circuit of patent misuse and antitrust theories. More specifically, they contend that *Windsurfing's* requirement for an "anticompetitive effect" was a departure from the Supreme Court's decision in *Morton Salt Co. v. G.S. Suppiger Co.*, 314 U.S. 488 (1942), which did not require such a showing in order to establish patent misuse. *See* Robert J. Hoerner, *The Decline (and Fall?) of the Patent Misuse Doctrine in the Federal Circuit*, 69 ANTITRUST L.J. 669, 672-673 (2001) (suggesting that the *Windsurfing* court's citation of *Blonder-Tongue* after the words "with anticompetitive effect" could be regarded as "misleading," for only the phrase "physical or temporal scope" appeared in *Blonder-Tongue*).

[216]616 F.3d 1318 (Fed. Cir. 2010) (*en banc*).

[217]*Princo*, 616 F.3d at 1321.

[218]*Princo*, 616 F.3d at 1329 (stating that "[w]hile proof of an antitrust violation shows that the patentee has committed wrongful conduct having anticompetitive effects, that does not establish misuse of the patent in suit unless the conduct in question restricts the use of that patent and does so in one of the specific ways that have been held to be outside the otherwise broad scope of the patent grant").

[219]*See Princo*, 616 F.3d at 1322.

with the ITC that Princo and other firms were violating the trade laws. Specifically, Philips alleged that Princo was infringing Philips's Raaymakers patents by importing certain compact discs into the United States without Philips' authorization.[220] Princo's answer raised an affirmative defense of patent misuse, contending that Philips had improperly forced Princo (and other licensees), as a condition of licensing patents (e.g., the Raaymakers patents) that were necessary to manufacture the Orange Book–compliant compact discs, to take licenses under other patents (e.g., Sony's Lagadec patent) that were not necessary for such manufacture. Princo further charged that Philips and Sony had agreed to suppress the technology embodied in Sony's Lagadec patent; that is, to anticompetitively eliminate the development of technology alternatives (such as Lagadec) to the Philips-patented Raaymakers approach.

The Federal Circuit rejected Princo's patent misuse argument. Even assuming that Philips and Sony had entered into a horizontal agreement to restrict the availability of Sony's Lagadec patent, Lagadec was an entirely different patent that was never asserted in the infringement action against Princo. These facts presented a "completely different scenario" from the Federal Circuit and Supreme Court precedent finding patent misuse. The *en banc* court in *Princo* held that "[e]ven if [the Philips-Sony] agreement [to suppress technology] were shown to exist, and even if it were shown to have anticompetitive effects, a horizontal agreement restricting the availability of Sony's Lagadec patent would not constitute misuse of Philips's Raaymakers patents or any of Philips's other patents in suit."[221]

The *Princo* court summarized the issue before it as follows: "When a patentee offers to license a patent, does the patentee misuse that patent by inducing a third party not to license its separate, competitive technology?"[222] The Federal Circuit found no authority or underlying policy concerns that would support a holding of patent misuse under the facts before it. "Such an agreement would not have the effect of increasing the physical or temporal scope of the patent in suit," the court concluded, and it "therefore would not fall within the rationale of the patent misuse doctrine as explicated by the Supreme Court and this court."[223]

[220]*See Princo*, 616 F.3d at 1323.
[221]*Princo*, 616 F.3d at 1331.
[222]*Princo*, 616 F.3d at 1331.
[223]*Princo*, 616 F.3d at 1331. Joined by Judge Gajarsa, Federal Circuit Judge Dyk authored an extensive dissenting opinion. Judge Dyk charged that "the relevant Supreme Court cases and congressional legislation . . . support[] a vigorous misuse defense, clearly applicable to agreements to suppress alternative technology. The majority cabins the doctrine in contravention of this Supreme Court authority." *Princo*, 616 F.3d at 1342 (Dyk, J., dissenting).

b. **Morton Salt**

The foundational patent misuse case is *Morton Salt Co. v. G.S. Suppiger Co.*[224] The challenged conduct involved a patentee "tying" the grant of a patent license to the licensee's promise to purchase from the patent owner a nonpatented, staple commodity. The U.S. Supreme Court refused to enforce the patent in suit where the patent owner had conditioned the grant of licenses to use its patented machines, which deposited tablets of salt in a food canning process, on the licensees' purchase of the unpatented salt tablets from the patent owner rather than from any third-party salt supplier.

Although the Supreme Court concluded that this tying constituted patent misuse that justified nonenforcement of the patent,[225] the offense in *Morton Salt* did not necessarily rise to the level of an antitrust violation, because no evidence existed that the patent owner's licensing practice "substantially lessened competition or tended to create a monopoly in salt tablets."[226] Even though the patentee could not enjoin the infringement because of its own misuse, the patentee did not face antitrust remedies such as the imposition of treble damages.[227] Nor was the misused patent held permanently unenforceable, because misuse can be "purged" by alleviating a challenged condition.[228]

Notably, the defendant/accused infringer in *Morton Salt* was not itself a "victim" of the misuse, because it was not a licensee. In the Supreme Court's view, the true victim of the misuse was the public at

[224]314 U.S. 488 (1942).

[225]Older patent misuse precedent such as *Morton Salt* is historically important but should only be relied on today with caution. It is not clear that the patentee in *Morton Salt* would be guilty of patent misuse under current law. As revised by the 1988 Patent Misuse Reform Act, the patent laws now provide that conditioning the grant of a patent license on the licensee's promise to purchase even a staple article (such as salt) from the patentee will *not* be deemed patent misuse *unless* the patent owner has "market power in the relevant market for the patent . . . " 35 U.S.C. §271(d)(5). The §271(d) safe harbors from patent infringement are further discussed in Section D.2.c, *infra*.

[226]*Morton Salt*, 314 U.S. at 490. *See also* Richard Calkins, *Patent Law: The Impact of the 1988 Patent Misuse Reform Act and* Noerr-Pennington *Doctrine on Misuse Defenses and Antitrust Counterclaims*, 38 DRAKE L. REV. 175, 183 (1988-1989) (concluding that "*Morton Salt* reinforced the Court's earlier rulings that the misuse defense was grounded on public policy underlying the patent laws and was not limited to a violation of the antitrust laws").

[227]*See* 15 U.S.C. §15 (§4 Clayton Act) (providing for treble damages recovery in private enforcement action brought by "any person who shall be injured in his business or property by reason of anything forbidden in the antitrust laws").

[228]*See Morton Salt,* 314 U.S. at 493, stating that

[e]quity may rightly withhold its assistance from . . . [a misuse] of the patent by declining to entertain a suit for infringement, and should do so at least until it is made to appear that the improper practice has been abandoned and that the consequences of the misuse of the patent have been dissipated.

large. Despite the defendant's seeming lack of standing to raise a misuse defense, the Court refused to enforce the patent on public policy grounds:

> [T]he public policy which includes inventions within the granted monopoly excludes from it all that is not embraced in the invention. It equally forbids the use of the patent to secure an exclusive right or limited monopoly not granted by the Patent Office and which it is contrary to public policy to grant.[229]

As *Morton Salt* made clear, the importance of preventing a patent owner from exploiting its patent in a way that improperly expands the scope of rights conveyed by the government justifies a liberal interpretation of the standing requirement to raise the misuse defense. Accordingly, an accused infringer need not have been personally impacted by the misuse in order to raise the patent misuse defense.[230]

c.   Limitations on Patent Misuse: §271(d)

Although the courts liberally construe the requirement of standing to assert patent misuse, other components of U.S. patent law provide exceptions or safe harbors that shield certain categories of patent owner activity from patent misuse liability. Section 271(d), added in the 1952 Patent Act and expanded by the 1988 Patent Misuse Reform Act, originated as a legislative attempt to resolve the tension between the defense of patent misuse and a patent owner's right to sue for contributory infringement in accordance with §271(c).[231] The history of

---

[229]*Id. See generally* 6-19 DONALD S. CHISUM, CHISUM ON PATENTS §19.04[4] (2008) ("Purging and Dissipation of Misuse").

Morton Salt, 314 U.S. 492.

[230]Professor Lemley has criticized the lack of a standing requirement in the patent misuse area, asserting that it creates an economic windfall for infringers:

> The lack of an injury requirement often produces situations in which parties who are not injured by misuse are the ones who benefit from the doctrine. Besides annulling any compensatory effect the remedy might have, this undermines the goals of the patent system, since it unnecessarily rewards (and therefore encourages) infringement. Parties unrelated to the patentee's wrongful acts may infringe its patents with impunity, since they are protected from liability by the patent misuse doctrine. Indeed, because the bar on infringement suits continues until the wrongful consequences have been dissipated fully, a finding of misuse essentially gives a green light to infringers of that patent for the foreseeable future.

Mark A. Lemley, *The Economic Irrationality of the Patent Misuse Doctrine,* 78 CALIF. L. REV. 1599, 1618-1619 (1990).

[231]*See* Chapter 9 ("Patent Infringement"), *supra,* for a more detailed treatment of contributory infringement. Briefly, the doctrine of contributory patent infringement, statutorily codified at 35 U.S.C. §271(c) in the 1952 Patent Act, originated in judicial decisions such as *Wallace v. Holmes,* 29 F. Cas. 74 (No. 17,100) (C.C. Conn.

the §271(d) patent misuse limitations shows that they have primarily developed as a counterweight to contributory infringement. An assertion of contributory infringement challenges a defendant's supply of one or more components that make up less than the entirety of a claimed invention. The related patent misuse concern is that through such assertions, the patentee is attempting to expand the scope of its statutorily granted exclusionary right by restraining competition in these components, which are generally nonpatented items.[232]

After the Supreme Court's 1944 *Mercoid* decisions,[233] some courts viewed the very act of bringing a lawsuit that alleged contributory infringement as an act of patent misuse. In response to concerns that patent misuse was eradicating contributory infringement, Congress enacted §271(d) in the 1952 Patent Act.[234] Section 271(d) did not purport to affirmatively define patent misuse, but rather set forth three specific acts which, if the patentee were otherwise entitled to relief for direct or contributory infringement, would not be considered "misuse or illegal extension of the patent right."[235]

Attorney (later Judge) Giles S. Rich and others successfully lobbied for the inclusion of the §271(d) safe harbor provisions as a necessary counterbalance to the contributory infringement provision that had

---

1871). Under a theory of joint tortfeasance, the *Wallace* court held liable for infringement the defendant supplier of a burner, which, when combined by consumers with a chimney, resulted in direct infringement of the plaintiff's patent on the overall lamp device comprising burner and chimney. *See id.* at 79-80; *see also* Tom Arnold & Louis Riley, *Contributory Infringement and Patent Misuse: The Enactment of §271 and Its Subsequent Amendments,* 76 J. PAT. & TRADEMARK OFF. SOC'Y 357, 365 (1994) (discussing view of some courts that after *Mercoid* "the mere act of bringing a contributory infringement action was patent misuse").

[232]*See* Dawson Chem. Co. v. Rohm & Haas Co., 448 U.S. 176, 197 (1980) (noting that "an inevitable concomitant of the right to enjoin another from contributory infringement is the capacity to suppress competition in an unpatented article of commerce").

[233]*See generally* Mercoid Corp. v. Mid-Continent Inv. Co., 320 U.S. 661 (1944); Mercoid Corp. v. Minneapolis-Honeywell Regulator Co., 320 U.S. 680 (1944).

[234]The safe harbors provided in the 1952 Act are those that appear today at 35 U.S.C. §§271(d)(1)-(3) (2008).

[235]*Id.* The three patent misuse safe harbors originally included in the 1952 Patent Act, for which "[n]o patent owner otherwise entitled to relief for infringement or contributory infringement of a patent shall be denied relief or deemed guilty of misuse or illegal extension of the patent right by reason of his having done one or more of the following," were that the patentee had

(1) derived revenue from acts which if performed by another without his consent would constitute contributory infringement of the patent;
(2) licensed or authorized another to perform acts which if performed without his consent would constitute contributory infringement of the patent; and
(3) sought to enforce his patent rights against infringement or contributory infringement.

Act of July 19, 1952, ch. 950, §§1, 66 Stat. 811, codified at 35 U.S.C. §§271(d)(1)-(3) (1952).

been contemporaneously enacted as 35 U.S.C. §271(c). In view of the Supreme Court's *Mercoid* decisions and the lower courts' reaction thereto, Rich and his colleagues believed that having a contributory infringement provision in the Patent Act was meaningless without a counterpart provision to make clear that the assertion of contributory infringement by a patent owner under limited conditions involving a defendant's supply of a nonstaple article should not be regarded as patent misuse. Congress ultimately agreed, enacting §§271(d)(1)-(3) as part of the 1952 Patent Act.

The U.S. Supreme Court did not have occasion to scrutinize the patent misuse safe harbors of 35 U.S.C. §271(d) until 1980. In *Dawson Chem. Co. v. Rohm & Haas Co.*,[236] the Court considered the propriety of a patent owner's refusal to license the defendant and other producers of the nonstaple but unpatented chemical propanil. The propanil was required to perform a patented process for inhibiting the growth of weeds in rice crops. The Court also scrutinized the patent owner's practice of tying the grant of implied licenses to rice farmers for use of the process based on the farmers' purchase of propanil from the patentee, rather than from the patentee's competitors that also manufactured the unpatented chemical. The defendant conceded that its sales of propanil with instructions for use amounted to contributory infringement of the process patent, but asserted the affirmative defense of patent misuse. The defendant argued that the patentee's acts of tying and refusal to license went well outside the three then-existing patent misuse safe harbors of 35 U.S.C. §271(d), and that by virtue of those acts the patentee was excluded from the category of patentees "otherwise entitled to relief" under the prefatory language of §271(d).

By a 5-4 vote, the Supreme Court majority in *Dawson Chem.* rejected the defendant's assertion of patent misuse, concluding that the patentee's acts were "not dissimilar in either nature or effect from the [safe harbor] conduct that is clearly embraced within §271(d)."[237] With respect to the patentee's refusal to license the patented method, the majority provided little analysis except to note that the patentee "does *not* license others to sell propanil, but nothing on the face of the statute requires it to do so."[238] The Court focused much more attention

[236]448 U.S. 176 (1980).

[237]*Id.* at 202, 223.

[238]*Id.* at 202 (emphasis in original). The dissent in *Dawson Chem.* criticized this analysis as simplistic, pointing out that

> Section 271(d) does not define conduct that constitutes patent misuse; rather it simply outlines certain conduct that is not patent misuse. Because the terms of the statute are terms of exception, the absence of any express mention of a licensing requirement does not indicate that respondent's refusal to license others is protected by §271(d).

Id. at 234 (White, J., dissenting).

on the patentee's act of tying than its refusal to license its competitors. The majority held the tying acceptable because the tied product, propanil, was a nonstaple good, one that had "no use except through practice of the patented method."[239] In the majority's view, "the provisions of §271(d) effectively confer upon the patentee, as a lawful adjunct of his patent rights, a limited power to exclude others from competition in nonstaple goods."[240]

Congress in 1988 legislatively codified the holdings of *Dawson Chem.* by adding new subsections (4) and (5) to the three then-existing patent misuse safe harbors of 35 U.S.C. §271(d).[241] The new subsections address refusals to license and tying, respectively:

> No patent owner otherwise entitled to relief for infringement or contributory infringement of a patent shall be denied relief or deemed guilty of misuse or illegal extension of the patent right by reason of his having done one or more of the following:
>
> ...
>
> (4) refused to license or use any rights to the patent; or
> (5) conditioned the license of any rights to the patent or the sale of the patented product on the acquisition of a license to rights in another patent or purchase of a separate product, unless, in view of the circumstances, the patent owner has market power in the relevant market for the patent or patented product on which the license or sale is conditioned.[242]

The language of the tying provision, §271(d)(5), reflects current economic and antitrust law thinking by providing that tying arrangements[243] will not constitute patent misuse or illegal extension of the

---

Contrary to the tenor of the *Dawson Chem.* dissent, and relying in part on the subsequent enactment of 35 U.S.C. §271(d)(4), the Federal Circuit maintains a strong stance against placing on patent owners any affirmative obligations to license their patents. *See* In re Ind. Serv. Orgs. Antitrust Litig. (CSU, L.L.C. v. Xerox Corp.), 203 F.3d 1322, 1326 (Fed. Cir. 2000), discussed in further detail in Section F, *infra*.

[239]*Dawson Chem.*, 448 U.S. at 199.

[240]*Id.* at 201.

[241]Act of Nov. 19, 1988, Title II, Pub. No. 100-703, §201, 102 Stat. 4674; *see also* Robert P. Merges & Richard R. Nelson, *On the Complex Economics of Patent Scope*, 90 COLUM. L. REV. 839, 914 n.347 (1990) (describing legislation as "built on" *Dawson Chem.*). For a detailed description of the passage of the act, see Richard Calkins, *Patent Law: The Impact of the 1988 Patent Misuse Reform Act and* Noerr-Pennington *Doctrine on Misuse Defenses and Antitrust Counterclaims*, 38 DRAKE L. REV. 175, 192-200 (1988-1989).

[242]35 U.S.C. §271(d)(4)-(5) (2008).

[243]"A 'tying' or 'tie-in' or 'tied sale' arrangement has been defined as 'an agreement by a party to sell one product . . . on the condition that the buyer also purchases a different (or tied) product, or at least agrees that he will not purchase that [tied] product from any other supplier.'" United States Department of Justice, *Antitrust Guidelines for the Licensing of Intellectual Property* (1995) §5.3, *available at* http://www.usdoj.gov/

patent right so long as the patentee does not have market power[244] in the relevant market[245] for the tying product.[246]

3.   Prosecution History Laches

A third and more recently recognized basis for asserting the unenforceability of a patent rests on the notion that its owner improperly

---

atr/public/guidelines/0558.pdf (quoting Eastman Kodak Co. v. Image Tech. Servs., Inc., 112 S. Ct. 2072, 2079 (1992)).The Antitrust Division of the U.S. Justice Department (DOJ) and the Federal Trade Commission (FTC) currently take the position that "[a]lthough tying arrangements may result in anticompetitive effects, such arrangements can also result in significant efficiencies and procompetitive benefits." *Id.* The agencies will, in the exercise of their prosecutorial discretion, "consider both the anticompetitive effects and the efficiencies attributable to a tie-in." *Id.*

[244]Market power is "the ability profitably to maintain prices above, or output below, competitive levels for a significant period of time." United States Department of Justice, *Antitrust Guidelines for the Licensing of Intellectual Property* §2.2 (1995), *available at* http://www.usdoj.gov/atr/public/guidelines/0558.pdf. The DOJ and FTC "will not presume that a patent . . . necessarily confers market power upon its owner." *Id.* at §5.3.

[245]"Relevant market" is a term of art in antitrust law. The Federal Circuit has defined it as "the area of effective competition in which competitors generally are willing to compete for the consumer potential." Intergraph Corp. v. Intel Corp., 195 F.3d 1346, 1353 (Fed. Cir. 1999) (citing American Key Corp. v. Cole Nat'l Corp., 762 F.2d 1569, 1581 (11th Cir. 1985)). *The Intergraph* court summarized Supreme Court law on relevant market as follows:

> In *Brown Shoe Co. v. United States,* 370 U.S. 294, 324, 8 L. Ed. 2d 510, 82 S. Ct. 1502 (1962) the Court summarized that the relevant market has two dimensions: first, the relevant product market, which identifies the products or services that compete with each other; and second, the geographic market, which may be relevant when the competition is geographically confined. Thus "the 'market' which one must study to determine when a producer has monopoly power will vary with the part of commerce under consideration." United States v. E. I. du Pont de Nemours & Co., 351 U.S. 377, 404, 76 S. Ct. 994, 100 L. Ed. 1264 (1956).

Id.

[246]*See Indep. Ink, Inc. v. Ill. Tool Works, Inc.*, 396 F.3d 1342, 1349 n.7 (Fed. Cir. 2005) ("Proof of actual market power is required to establish a patent misuse defense based on patent tying."); Virginia Panel Corp. v. MAC Panel Co., 133 F.3d 860, 869 (Fed. Cir. 1997) (characterizing 35 U.S.C. §271(d)(5) as "provid[ing] that . . . in the absence of market power, even a tying arrangement does not constitute patent misuse"). *See also* Robert J. Hoerner, *The Decline (and Fall?) of the Patent Misuse Doctrine in the Federal Circuit,* 69 ANTITRUST L.J. 669, 672-683 (2001) (stating that "[t]ying is not patent 'misuse' or an 'illegal extension of the patent right' unless it meets the 35 U.S.C. §271(d) (5) standard").The government's *Licensing Guidelines* provide that the DOJ and FTC "would be likely to challenge a tying arrangement if: (1) the seller has market power in the tying product, (2) the arrangement has an adverse effect on competition in the relevant market for the tied product, and (3) efficiency justifications for the arrangement do not outweigh the anticompetitive effects." United States Department of Justice, *Antitrust Guidelines for the Licensing of Intellectual Property* §5.3 (1995), *available at* http://www.usdoj.gov/atr/public/guidelines/0558.pdf.

delayed the issuance of the patent by unreasonably extending the time spent prosecuting it through the USPTO. A panel of the Federal Circuit in 2002 gave formal recognition to the defense of **prosecution history laches** in *Symbol Techs., Inc. v. Lemelson Med.*[247] There the patent owner first alleged infringement in 1998 of patents directed to bar code scanning technology, for which it claimed the benefit of the filing dates of two applications filed in 1954 and 1956. The *Symbol Techs.* majority held that as a matter of law, the equitable doctrine of laches may be applied to bar enforcement of a patent that issued after unreasonable and unexplained delay in prosecution, even though the patent applicant complied with all pertinent statutes and rules.[248] The majority found support for a prosecution history laches defense in Supreme Court precedent,[249] and further determined that the 1952 enactment of §§120 and 121 of the Patent Act (which entitle continuation and divisional applications to the filing dates of their parent applications[250]) did not foreclose the application of prosecution history laches to bar enforcement of a patent claim.[251]

Although the defense of prosecution history laches would seem to have fairly limited applicability to so-called "submarine patents" obtained under the pre-TRIPS 17-years-from-issuance patent term,[252] the federal district courts have thus far refused to constrain the

---

[247]277 F.3d 1361 (Fed. Cir. 2002).

[248]The dissent charged that the majority's "judicial creation of a new ground on which to challenge patents that fully comply with the statutory requirements is in direct contravention to the rule that when statutory provisions exist they may be relied on without equitable penalty." *Symbol Techs.*, 277 F.3d at 1369 (Newman, J., dissenting).

[249]The *Symbol Techs.* majority read Supreme Court precedent as having recognized the doctrine of prosecution history laches in at least four decisions, including *General Talking Pictures Corp. v. Western Elec. Co.*, 304 U.S. 175 (1938); *Crown Cork & Seal v. Ferdinand Gutmann Co.*, 304 U.S. 159 (1938); *Webster Elec. Co. v. Splitdorf Elec. Co.*, 264 U.S. 463 (1924); and *Woodbridge v. United States*, 263 U.S. 50 (1923).

[250]*See supra* Chapter 1, Section H.5 ("Continuing Application Practice").

[251]A federal district court subsequently held Lemelson's patents unenforceable on the basis of prosecution history laches. *See* Symbol Techs., Inc. v. Lemelson Med., Educ. & Research Found., 301 F. Supp. 2d 1147, 1155 (D. Nev. 2004) (finding that "Lemelson's 18 to 39 year delay in filing and prosecuting the asserted claims under the fourteen patents-in-suit after they were first purportedly disclosed in the 1954 and 1956 applications was unreasonable and unjustified and that the doctrine of prosecution laches renders the asserted claims unenforceable against [accused infringers] Symbol and Cognex"). The Federal Circuit affirmed. *See* Symbol Techs., Inc. v. Lemelson Med., Educ. & Research Found., LP, 422 F.3d 1378 (Fed. Cir. 2005). Although the extreme facts of the case justified the district court's holding of unenforceability, the Federal Circuit cautioned that the doctrine of prosecution history laches should be "used sparingly lest statutory provisions be unjustifiably vitiated" and "applied only in egregious cases" of misuse of the statutory patent system. *Id.* at 1385.

[252]*See supra* Chapter 1, Section C.7 ("The Patent Term").

defense to that context.[253] Moreover, prosecution history laches is not limited to patent infringement lawsuits in federal court; shortly after *Symbol Techs.* the Federal Circuit held in *In re Bogese* that the USPTO may rely on the doctrine as a basis for rejecting patent applications in appropriate circumstances.[254]

E. Invalidity

Section 282(b)(2) and (b)(3) permit the defense of invalidity of an issued patent to be asserted on the same grounds that could have prohibited patentability in the USPTO, that is, a failure to satisfy one or more of the statutory criteria set forth at 35 U.S.C. §§101, 102, 103, and 112 (with the post-AIA exception of the best mode requirement of 35 U.S.C. §112(a)). Patents reissued in accordance with 35 U.S.C. §251 also are susceptible to invalidation under the same statutory grounds.

1. Burden of Proof

Section 282(a) of the Patent Act, 35 U.S.C., provides that

> **In general.**—A patent shall be presumed valid. Each claim of a patent (whether in independent, dependent, or multiple dependent form) shall be presumed valid independently of the validity of the other claims; dependent or multiple dependent claims shall be presumed valid even though dependent upon an invalid claim. The burden of establishing invalidity of a patent or any claim thereof shall rest on the party asserting such invalidity.[255]

An issued U.S. patent is thus entitled to a presumption of validity in accordance with 35 U.S.C. §282(a). This presumption is based, at least in part, on an assumption of "administrative correctness"—that the USPTO did a thorough, competent job when it examined the patent

---

[253]*See* Cummins-Allison Corp. v. Glory Ltd., 2003 WL 355470, at *41 (N.D. Ill. 2003) (rejecting argument that doctrine of prosecution history laches, as a matter of law, cannot apply to patents filed for after June 8, 1995, GATT TRIPS change to U.S. patent term, in agreement with *Digital Control*); Digital Control, Inc. v. McLaughlin Mfg. Co., 225 F. Supp. 2d 1224, 1226-1228 (W.D. Wash. 2002) (refusing to limit defense of prosecution history laches to patent applications filed before GATT TRIPS change in U.S. patent term).

[254]*See* In re Bogese, 303 F.3d 1362 (Fed. Cir. 2002) (affirming USPTO Board's decision that Bogese had forfeited his right to a patent by filing 12 continuation applications over an eight-year period while failing to substantively advance prosecution when required and given an opportunity to do so by the USPTO).

[255]35 U.S.C. §282(a) (eff. Sept. 16, 2012).

application and decided to issue the patent.[256] Because the patent owner benefits from the presumption of validity, it need not affirmatively establish that its patent is valid in order to bring an infringement lawsuit. Rather, the burden is on the accused infringer to rebut the presumption of validity created by 35 U.S.C. §282(a).

The statute does not specify what evidentiary quantum is needed to satisfy the burden of proof on invalidity. However, judicial decisions make clear that the burden in federal court litigation challenging patent validity is "clear and convincing" evidence, which means that the validity challenger (i.e., the accused infringer) can rebut the presumption only if it establishes invalidity by "clear and convincing" evidence.[257] The quantum of evidence represented by the "clear and convincing" burden is understood to be somewhat more than a mere "preponderance" (or 51 percent) of the evidence, the typical burden of proof in civil litigation, and somewhat less than "beyond a reasonable doubt,"[258] the burden for criminal convictions. The Supreme Court has characterized clear and convincing evidence as "plac[ing] in the ultimate factfinder an abiding conviction that the truth of its factual contentions are 'highly probable.'"[259]

Twenty-first-century patent litigation reflects the growing impact of patent-enforcing "non-practicing entities" (NPEs), sometimes pejoratively referred to as "patent trolls."[260] NPEs own patents but do not manufacture or sell the products covered by the patents and do not compete in the marketplace through such manufacture or sale. The number of infringement lawsuits filed by NPEs rose sharply in the decade of 2000-2010.[261]

---

[256]*See* Applied Materials, Inc. v. Advanced Semiconductor Materials America, Inc., 98 F.3d 1563, 1569 (Fed. Cir. 1996) (explaining that "[t]he presumption of validity is based on the presumption of administrative correctness of actions of the agency charged with examination of patentability"); Interconnect Planning Corp. v. Feil, 774 F.2d 1132, 1139 (Fed. Cir. 1985) (stating that presumption of validity "derives in part from recognition of the technological expertise of the patent examiners").

[257]*See* Microsoft Corp. v. i4i Ltd. P'ship, 131 S. Ct. 2238 (2011), discussed *infra*.

[258]*See* Buildex, Inc. v. Kason Indus., Inc., 849 F.2d 1461, 1463 (Fed. Cir. 1988).

[259]Colorado v. New Mexico, 467 U.S. 310, 316 (1984) (quoting C. McCORMICK, LAW OF EVIDENCE § 320, at 679 (1954)).

[260]*See Intellectual Property: Patent Medicine*, THE ECONOMIST, Aug. 20, 2011, at 50 (referring to "the growing problem of 'patent trolls,' or firms that treat patents as lottery tickets and file expensive, time-consuming lawsuits against companies that have supposedly infringed them"); Ted Sichelman, *Commercializing Patents*, 62 STAN. L. REV. 341, 368 (2010) (stating that "nonpracticing entities (NPEs)—namely, firms that do not commercialize their patented inventions and perform little to no R&D—are often termed 'patent trolls,' because they tend to exploit litigation and licensing market defects to extract unwarranted rents from commercializers, usually on patents that the commercializer was completely unaware of before the NPE's demand for payment").

[261]*See Intellectual-Property Battles: Patent Lather*, THE ECONOMIST, Sept. 4, 2010, at 90 (citing report by PatentFreedom, a body that tracks the activity of NPEs, stating that the number of court cases brought by NPEs rose from 109 in 2001 to 470 in 2009).

Several leading technology companies, including those frequently targeted by NPEs, took the position that the burden of proof to invalidate issued patents should be less than the "clear and convincing" quantum described above. The technology firms contended that accused infringers in infringement actions need only establish the defense of invalidity by a preponderance of the evidence. In particular, the firms asserted that the lesser preponderance standard should apply when an invalidity defense rested on "newly discovered" prior art, that is, evidence of invalidity that was never considered in the first instance by the USPTO during the patent examination process.

The Supreme Court in 2011 rejected this argument in *Microsoft Corp. v. i4i Ltd. P'ship*.[262] The Court in *Microsoft* affirmed the Federal Circuit's interpretation of 35 U.S.C. §282 that invalidity of a patent must be established by clear and convincing evidence. Relying on its earlier decision in *Radio Corp. of America v. Radio Eng'g Labs., Inc.*,[263] the Court reasoned that when Congress stated that a patent is "presumed valid" in §282 of the 1952 Patent Act, it implicitly incorporated the established common law meaning (i.e., as expressed in judicial decisions) of that phrase.[264] By the time of the 1952 Act, the presumption of patent validity had the "settled meaning" that "a defendant raising an invalidity defense bore 'a heavy burden of persuasion,' requiring proof of the defense by clear and convincing evidence."[265] With respect to the argument that the "clear and convincing" burden should not be required when an accused infringer's proffered evidence of invalidity was never considered by the USPTO, the Court responded that if Congress had intended the burden of proof to vary with the facts of every case, it would have said so expressly when enacting §282 (but it did not).

The *Microsoft* Court recognized, however, that a number of appellate decisions predating the 1952 Act characterized the presumption of validity as "weakened" or "dissipated" in cases involving evidence never considered by the USPTO. The Court viewed these decisions as simply "reflect[ing] the same commonsense principle that the Federal Circuit has recognized throughout its existence—namely, that new evidence supporting an invalidity defense may 'carry more weight' in an infringement action than evidence previously considered by the PTO."[266] Accordingly, the *Microsoft* Court observed that "if the PTO

---

[262]131 S. Ct. 2238 (2011) (Sotomayor, J.).

[263]293 U.S. 1 (1934).

[264]*Microsoft*, 131 S. Ct. at 2245 (explaining that "by stating that a patent is 'presumed valid,' [35 U.S.C.] § 282, Congress used a term with a settled meaning in the common law").

[265]*Microsoft*, 131 S. Ct. at 2246.

[266]*Microsoft*, 131 S. Ct. at 2251 (quoting Am. Hoist & Derrick Co. v. Sowa & Sons, Inc., 725 F.2d 1350, 1360 (Fed. Cir. 1984) (Rich, J.)). The Court earlier observed that Judge Rich was "a principal drafter of the 1952 Act. . . ." *Microsoft*, 131 S. Ct. at 2243.

did not have all material facts [e.g., prior art] before it, its considered judgment may lose significant force . . . [a]nd, concomitantly, the challenger's burden to persuade the jury of its invalidity defense by clear and convincing evidence may be easier to sustain."[267]

2. Collateral Estoppel Effect of Invalidity Adjudication

In *Blonder-Tongue Labs., Inc. v. Univ. of Ill. Found.*,[268] the Supreme Court held that once a U.S. patent has been declared invalid by a federal court, the patent owner is collaterally estopped to assert validity of that patent against another accused infringer. In other words, once a U.S. patent has been declared invalid, it is dead and cannot be resuscitated. This rule assumes, of course, that the patentee had a full and fair opportunity to litigate the issue of invalidity in the earlier proceeding and did not obtain a reversal on appeal.

In announcing the rule of collateral estoppel for patent invalidity the Supreme Court in *Blonder-Tongue* specifically rejected the requirement of "mutuality of estoppel" that it had previously espoused in *Triplett v. Lowell*,[269] a decision roundly criticized by other courts and commentators. Continued reliance on the mutuality doctrine would work an economic harm on participants in the patent system, the Court reasoned. Among those who would bear the brunt of this harm were alleged infringers, who would be forced to choose between bearing the high cost of defending against a patent already declared invalid or accepting a license and making royalty payments as a cost

---

[267]*Microsoft,* 131 S. Ct. at 2251. The Court further observed that although it had

> no occasion to endorse any particular formulation, we note that a jury instruction on the effect of new evidence can, and when requested, most often should be given. When warranted, the jury may be instructed to consider that it has heard evidence that the PTO had no opportunity to evaluate before granting the patent. When it is disputed whether the evidence presented to the jury differs from that evaluated by the PTO, the jury may be instructed to consider that question. In either case, the jury may be instructed to evaluate whether the evidence before it is materially new, and if so, to consider that fact when determining whether an invalidity defense has been proved by clear and convincing evidence.

Microsoft, 131 S. Ct. at 2251.

[268]402 U.S. 313 (1971).

[269]297 U.S. 638 (1936). The Court in *Triplett* held that a determination of patent invalidity is not *res judicata* as against the patentee in subsequent litigation against a different defendant. The *Triplett* decision "exemplified the judge-made doctrine of mutuality of estoppel, ordaining that unless both parties (or their privies) in a second action are bound by a judgment in a previous case, neither party (or his privy) in the second action may use the prior judgment as determinative of an issue in the second action." *Blonder-Tongue,* 402 U.S. at 320-321.

of litigation avoidance. In the words of the President's Commission on the Patent System, the Court concluded that the patentee whose patent has been declared invalid has already "had his 'day in court' and should not be allowed to harass others on the basis of an invalid claim."[270]

3.   Statutory Grounds for Invalidity

Section 282(b) (eff. Sept. 16, 2012) provides that invalidity of a patent can be based on "any ground specified in part II [35 U.S.C. §§100 et seq.] as a condition for patentability." These grounds include 35 U.S.C. §101 (patent-eligible subject matter and utility); 35 U.S.C. §102 (novelty); and 35 U.S.C. §103 (nonobviousness). In accordance with §282(b), each of these statutory criteria for patentability (separately discussed in earlier chapters of this text) also can serve as a basis for alleging invalidity of an issued patent. Invalidity also may be based on a "failure to comply with . . . any requirement of section 112" other than failure to disclose the best mode, or "any requirement of section 251."[271] Thus, an issued patent may be held invalid under 35 U.S.C. §112(a) if the specification is nonenabling or fails to provide a written description of the invention, or under 35 U.S.C. §112(b) if the claims are indefinite. A patent reissued in accordance with 35 U.S.C. §251 is subject to the same constraints. A reissued patent is also subject to invalidation if the reissue broadened the claims by means of a reissue application filed more than two years after the original patent issued.[272]

4.   Limits on Accused Infringer's Standing to Assert Invalidity: Licensee Repudiation and Assignor Estoppel

U.S. patent jurisprudence recognizes certain judicially created limitations on an accused infringer's ability to challenge patent validity in

---

[270]*Id.* at 340.

[271]35 U.S.C. §282(b)(3) (eff. Sept. 16, 2012). The AIA abrogated best mode noncompliance as an invalidity defense as of September 16, 2011, while retaining it as a requirement to obtain a patent in the first instance. *See* Leahy-Smith America Invents Act, Pub. L. No. 112-29 (H.R. 1249), §15, 125 Stat. 284, 328 (2011); 35 U.S.C. §282(b) (3)(A) (eff. Sept. 16, 2011). This dramatic change means that even if a patent was very likely invalid on September 15, 2011, for failure to satisfy the best mode disclosure requirement, as of September 16, 2011, the patent could no longer be challenged on that basis (so long as litigation was not already underway).

[272]*See supra* Chapter 8, Section C.4 ("Broadening Reissues").

cases where the accused infringer is or was in a contractual relationship with the patent owner. These limitations have been raised when the accused infringer is or was a licensee under the patent, or was the assignor of the patent (typically an inventor who has transferred title in the patent to her corporate employer). Such cases present the courts with a conflict between enforcement of the defendant's contractual obligations to the patentee under the common law and the federal policy that supports the invalidation of U.S. patents not satisfying the statutory requirements of patentability. Although the courts originally treated licensees and assignors in the same manner, so as to preclude either category of defendant from challenging patent validity, the current state of the law permits licensees to challenge validity in instances where assignors may not. These doctrines, referred to as licensee repudiation and assignor estoppel, are addressed separately below.

a. Licensee Repudiation

Can the licensee of a patent stop paying royalties to the patent owner and challenge the patent's validity if the licensee has a good faith belief that the patent is invalid? The Supreme Court answered affirmatively in *Lear, Inc. v. Adkins.*[273] The Court in *Lear* abrogated the earlier doctrine of licensee estoppel, which had held that in a contract action for unpaid patent royalties the licensee of the patent was estopped from challenging its validity. After *Lear,* licensee repudiation of a license on the ground that the licensed patent is invalid is not only permissible, but perhaps even encouraged.

The facts of *Lear* are as follows. The plaintiff Adkins was a former employee of the Lear Corporation who patented an invention directed to aviation gyroscopes. While Adkins' patent application was pending in the USPTO, he entered into a license agreement with the Lear Corporation. Lear subsequently stopped paying royalties to Adkins, claiming that the invention was anticipated by the prior art. After a lengthy prosecution, the Adkins patent issued. Adkins then sued Lear in California state court for breaching the license agreement. The case eventually progressed to the California Supreme Court, which sided with Adkins and held Lear estopped from challenging validity.

The U.S. Supreme Court reversed, holding that the Lear Corporation could avoid payment of all royalties accruing after Adkins' patent issued in 1960, assuming that Lear could successfully prove invalidity of the patent.[274] The Court recognized the conflict between the

---

[273]395 U.S. 653 (1969).
[274]*Id.* at 674. The question whether the Lear Corporation was nevertheless contractually obligated to pay Adkins royalties for access to his ideas, prior to patent issuance, was a closer call that required remand to the state courts. *See id.* at 674-675.

obligations of contract performance, requiring that a licensee should continue to pay royalties in exchange for the use of a patented invention, and the public's interest in full and free competition in the use of ideas that are in reality part of the public domain. It concluded that the equities favoring the public far outweighed those favoring Adkins, the licensor/patentee. Often the licensee (frequently a marketplace competitor of the patentee) is the only party with sufficient resources and adequate incentives to challenge the patent under which it is licensed. For the sake of the public at large, the law should not prevent such challenges. Particularly in the absence of a robust, European-style opposition procedure,[275] licensee repudiation may be one of the most important vehicles for ensuring that the U.S. public is not burdened by invalid patents.[276]

The policies underlying *Lear* are consistent with the result in the Supreme Court's more recent decision in *MedImmune, Inc. v. Genentech, Inc.*[277] The *MedImmune* Court allowed a *nonrepudiating* licensee (i.e., one who continued to pay royalties to the patentee under protest) to challenge the validity of the licensed patent. In *MedImmune,* however, the licensee's vehicle for challenging validity was its own lawsuit filed under the Declaratory Judgment Act, rather than raising invalidity as a defense to the patentee/licensor's breach of contract action as in *Lear.*[278] The key issue in *MedImmune* was whether a licensee in good standing satisfied the Constitutional "Case[]" or "Controvers[y]" requirement for bringing a lawsuit in federal court, an issue not raised by *Lear*. The *MedImmune* decision and declaratory judgment actions in patent disputes are examined in greater detail later in this chapter.[279]

b. *Assignor Estoppel*

The Supreme Court did not have occasion in *Lear* to address the companion doctrine of assignor estoppel, which operates to estop validity challenges not by a licensee, but rather by the inventor who

---

[275]*See, e.g.,* European Patent Convention arts. 99-105 (13th ed. 2007), *available at* http://www.epo.org/patents/law/legal-texts/html/epc/2000/e/ma1.html.

[276]Not all agree. For cogent criticisms and proposed modifications of *Lear, see* Rochelle Cooper Dreyfuss, *Dethroning Lear: Licensee Estoppel and the Incentive to Innovate,* 72 VA. L. REV. 677 (1986).

[277]549 U.S. 118 (2007).

[278]*See id.* at 145 n.2 (Thomas, J., dissenting) (observing that *Lear* "has little to do with this case. [*Lear*] addressed the propriety and extent of the common-law doctrine of licensee estoppel, and the licensee in *Lear* had ceased making payments under the license agreement—a fact that makes the case singularly inapposite here. *Lear* did not involve the Declaratory Judgment Act because the case was brought as a breach-of-contract action for failure to pay royalties.") (citations omitted).

[279]*See* Section G, *infra.*

has assigned her rights under the patent to another for valuable consideration. In light of different policy concerns that are implicated in the assignment context but absent from mere licensing, the Federal Circuit distinguished *Lear* and upheld the assignor estoppel doctrine in *Diamond Scientific Co. v. Ambico, Inc.*[280]

While an employee of plaintiff Diamond Scientific, Dr. Clarence Welter invented and applied for three patents directed to a vaccine for gastroenteritis in swine. Welter assigned his rights in the patents to Diamond Scientific. When Welter later formed his own company, Ambico, doing business in competition with his former employer, Diamond Scientific sued Welter and Ambico for infringement of the patents. In response to Welter/Ambico's defense that the patents in suit were invalid, Diamond Scientific contended that the doctrine of assignor estoppel prevented Welter and his new company from challenging validity.

The Federal Circuit acknowledged the continuing debate over the vitality of the assignor estoppel doctrine in the aftermath of *Lear*'s renunciation of the "somewhat analogous" doctrine of licensee estoppel, but nevertheless upheld the application of assignor estoppel against Welter as well as Ambico, a party in privity with Welter.[281] In the Circuit's view, the *Lear* public policy favoring a licensee's freedom to contest the validity of a patent under which it had taken a license is not present in the assignment situation. "Unlike the licensee, who, without *Lear* might be forced to continue to pay for a potentially invalid patent, the assignor who would challenge the patent has already been fully paid for the patent rights."[282]

The monetary distinction drawn by the court in *Diamond Scientific* between assignor and licensee is not particularly compelling. Given the public policy of encouraging challenges to invalid patents as expressed in *Lear*, it is difficult to understand why the identity of the party challenging validity—whether licensee or assignor—should matter. The assignor is most likely in the best position to challenge validity, perhaps even to a greater degree than the licensee in *Lear*, because the assignor is the inventor.

The contrary result in *Diamond Scientific* no doubt reflects the Federal Circuit's discomfort with the inequity of allowing a named inventor, who actively participated in the prosecution of the patent, signed an oath (attesting to his belief that he was the first and sole inventor, that the invention was never known or used in the United

---

[280]848 F.2d 1220 (Fed. Cir. 1988).

[281]*Id.* at 1224. The extent to which the assignor's company is in privity and bound by the estoppel depends on how close a relationship exists between the parties, and may vary depending on whether the inventor was a mere employee or the "alter ego" of the corporation.

[282]*Id.*

States before his invention, and that it had not been previously patented or described in a printed publication anywhere),[283] and had been subject to the duty of disclosure while the application was pending, to thereafter attempt to prove that what he attested to and assigned for a valuable consideration was in fact a nullity:[284]

> In other words, it is the implicit representation by the assignor that the patent rights that he is assigning (presumably for value) are not worthless that sets the assignor apart from the rest of the world and can deprive him of the ability to challenge later the validity of the patent. To allow the assignor to make that representation at the time of the assignment (to his advantage) and later to repudiate it (again to his advantage) could work an injustice against the assignee.[285]

Because the equities weighed heavily in favor of Diamond Scientific, the Federal Circuit concluded that the doctrine of assignor estoppel should be applied against Welter and Ambico, even while admitting that "the doctrine of assignor estoppel may no longer be a broad equitable device susceptible of automatic application."[286]

Following *Diamond Scientific*, the Federal Circuit has confronted other assertions of the assignor estoppel doctrine and continues to apply it to preclude challenges to validity by patent assignors, although the court has recognized the possibility of certain narrow exceptions.[287]

---

[283]*Id.* at 1225.

[284]One possible exception to the rule of assignor estoppel might be where the assignee controlled prosecution of the patent application and authorized the amendment of its claims so as to significantly broaden them, without the inventor/assignor's knowledge or participation. *See* Westinghouse Elec. & Mfg. Co. v. Formica Insulation Co., 266 U.S. 342 (1924), in which the Court suggested that

> [w]hen the assignment is made before patent [has been granted], the claims are subject to change by curtailment or enlargement by the Patent Office with the acquiescence or at the instance of the assignee, and the extent of the claims to be allowed may ultimately include more than the assignor [inventor] intended to claim. This difference might justify the view that the range of relevant and competent evidence in fixing the limits of the subsequent estoppel should be more liberal than in the case of an assignment of a granted patent. How this may be, we do not find it necessary to decide.

Id. at 353.

[285]*Diamond Scientific*, 848 F.2d at 1224.

[286]*Id.* at 1225.

[287]*See, e.g.*, Mentor Graphics Corp. v. Quickturn Design Sys., Inc., 150 F.3d 1374, 1378 (Fed. Cir. 1998) (affirming district court's application of assignor estoppel and concluding that exceptional circumstances justifying departure from doctrine, such as an express reservation by assignor of the right to challenge patent's validity or an express waiver by assignee of the right to assert patent's validity, were not present).

F. Antitrust Counterclaims

Section 282(b) of 35 U.S.C. does not speak to the assertion of antitrust liability on the part of the patent owner as a defense to a charge of infringement. Therefore a patent owner's alleged violation of the antitrust laws is not asserted by an accused infringer as an affirmative defense, but rather as the subject of a counterclaim.[288] Nevertheless, antitrust counterclaims in patent infringement cases are included in this chapter because they are the subject of increasing interest among the antitrust bar and Federal Circuit watchers in general.[289]

Antitrust counterclaims in patent cases are most commonly brought under §2 of the Sherman Act, which prohibits acquisition or maintenance of monopoly power through anticompetitive conduct.[290] Patents have been viewed (in somewhat pejorative fashion) as "monopolies," such that accused infringers of patents have asserted (under certain limited circumstances) that patent owners' enforcement of their "monopoly" rights represented a violation of the antitrust laws. The mere assertion of patent rights is certainly not enough to give rise to antitrust liability, however; the party asserting a Sherman Act §2 monopolization must show (1) that the patentee has monopoly power in the relevant market, and (2) that it has acquired or is maintaining that power in an anticompetitive manner.[291] These elements are commonly abbreviated as "market power" and "anticompetitive conduct." Each element is addressed below.

---

[288]*See* Nobelpharma AB v. Implant Innovations, Inc., 141 F.3d 1059, 1067 (Fed. Cir. 1998) (stating that "an antitrust claim premised on stripping a patentee of its immunity from the antitrust laws is typically raised as a counterclaim by a defendant in a patent infringement suit").

[289]A very useful resource on the topic of the patent-antitrust intersection and the Federal Circuit's growing role therein is the collection of articles published at *Symposium: The Federal Circuit and Antitrust,* 69 ANTITRUST L.J. 627-849 (2001).

[290]*See* 15 U.S.C. §2 (providing that "[e]very person who shall monopolize, or attempt to monopolize, or combine or conspire with any other person or persons, to monopolize any part of the trade or commerce among the several States, or with foreign nations, shall be deemed guilty of a felony . . . ")

[291]*See* U.S. Philips Corp. v. Windmere Corp., 861 F.2d 695, 703 (Fed. Cir. 1988) (quoting United States v. Grinnell Corp., 384 U.S. 563, 570-571 (1966)). The Court in *Grinnell* held that

[t]he offense of monopoly under §2 of the Sherman Act has two elements: (1) the possession of monopoly power in the relevant market and (2) the willful acquisition or maintenance of that power as distinguished from growth or development as a consequence of a superior product, business acumen, or historic accident.

Id.

1.   Market Power

In practice, the requirement for a showing of market power[292] excludes much of typical patent owner behavior from antitrust prosecution.[293] The mere fact that a firm owns a patent on a particular invention does not in and of itself demonstrate the requisite market power, because the antitrust law of market definition recognizes the possibility of noninfringing substitutes for the patented technology.[294] Moreover, the successful assertion of an antitrust counterclaim against a patent owner bringing an infringement suit is relatively rare because of certain antitrust protections given to intellectual property holders, discussed below.

The need for rigorous economic analysis of relevant market in patent/antitrust cases was emphasized in *Unitherm Food Sys., Inc. v. Swift-Eckrich, Inc.*[295] There the Federal Circuit vacated the judgment of a district court entered on a jury verdict that had found patent

---

[292]Market power is "the ability profitably to maintain prices above, or output below, competitive levels for a significant period of time." United States Department of Justice, *Antitrust Guidelines for the Licensing of Intellectual Property* §2.2 (1995), *available at* http://www.usdoj.gov/atr/public/guidelines/0558.pdf. The DOJ and FTC "will not presume that a patent . . . necessarily confers market power upon its owner." *Id.* at §5.3.

[293]*See* Robert Merges, *Reflections on Current Legislation Affecting Patent Misuse,* 70 J. Pat. & Trademark Off. Soc'y 793, 793 (1988) (noting that "the often very limited (or 'thin') markets for patented technology make it difficult to apply antitrust law's consumer-demand definition of the relevant market"). *See also* Richard Calkins, *Patent Law: The Impact of the 1988 Patent Misuse Reform Act and* Noerr-Pennington *Doctrine on Misuse Defenses and Antitrust Counterclaims,* 38 Drake L. Rev. 175, 187 (1988-1989) (noting that "[a]s a practical matter, requiring proof of an antitrust violation to check a patentee's economic extension of his patent monopoly may mean that such violations will go unchecked because excessive costs and uncertainty are inherent in proving a rule of reason violation or monopolization charge").

[294]*See* Ill. Tool Works Inc. v. Indep. Ink, Inc., 547 U.S. 28, 45-46 (2006) ("Congress, the antitrust enforcement agencies, and most economists have all reached the conclusion that a patent does not necessarily confer market power upon the patentee. Today, we reach the same conclusion. . . . "); Abbott Labs. v. Brennan, 952 F.2d 1346, 1354-1355 (Fed. Cir. 1991). As Justice O'Connor explained,

> A common misconception has been that a patent or copyright, a high market share, or a unique product that competitors are not able to offer suffices to demonstrate market power. While each of these three factors might help to give market power to a seller, it is also possible that a seller in these situations will have no market power: for example, a patent holder has no market power in any relevant sense if there are close substitutes for the patented product. Similarly, a high market share indicates market power only if the market is properly defined to include all reasonable substitutes for the product. *See generally* Landes & Posner, *Market Power in Antitrust Cases,* 94 HARV. L. REV. 937 (1981).

Jefferson Parish Hospital Dist. No. 2 v. Hyde, 466 U.S. 2, 33 (1984) (O'Connor, J., concurring).

[295]375 F.3d 1341 (Fed. Cir. 2004).

owner Swift-Eckrich (d/b/a ConAgra Refrigerated Foods) liable under the antitrust laws for attempted monopolization in the amount of $18 million in trebled damages. "The district court erred," the Federal Circuit concluded, "in allowing the jury to decide Unitherm's antitrust claims despite the total absence of economic evidence capable of sustaining those claims."[296]

Applying Tenth Circuit law to those antitrust issues not intertwined with patent law, the Federal Circuit in *Unitherm* explained that a relevant product market is composed of "products that have reasonable interchangeability for the purposes for which they are produced."[297] Market definition hinges on economic evidence, the Federal Circuit observed. In this case, Unitherm's expert witness had defined the relevant product market as synonymous with the patented invention, a process for browning pre-cooked meats. The expert identified seven benefits of the patented process that no other similar process possessed and that, in his opinion, made the invention unique. The expert's testimony, "or at least the relevant excerpts in the appellate record, cannot sustain Unitherm's definition of a relevant market," the Federal Circuit concluded. The expert's testimony addressed *technological* substitutability but not *economic* substitutability. Nothing in the record addressed "whether potential customers of the patented process faced with a price increase would shift to other processes offering different combinations of benefits."[298] This determination "lies at the heart of market definition in antitrust analysis." "Not only is economic substitutability critical to market definition," the Federal Circuit explained, but also "it is improper to interpret 'the Sherman Act to require that products be fungible to be considered in the relevant market.'"[299] The minimal economic evidence in the record "suggested strongly" that Unitherm's expert's market definition was incorrect. In particular, the Federal Circuit found ConAgra's inability to attract any licensees indicative of a lack of pricing power—"the single most important element in defining a relevant antitrust market."[300]

Despite its economics-focused treatment of market power in the context of Sherman Act §2 cases such as *Unitherm,* the Federal Circuit in 2005 took a very different approach to market power in another

[296]*Id.* at 1344.

[297]*Id.* at 1363.

[298]*Id.* at 1364.

[299]*Id.* at 1364 (quoting United States v. E. I. Du Pont de Nemours & Co., 351 U.S. 377, 394 (1956), and citing generally U.S. Department of Justice, *Merger Guidelines* (1982), ch. 1.1 (describing the antitrust agencies' approach to product market definition in a merger analysis and the critical rule of economic substitutability)).

[300]*Id.* at 1364.

patent/antitrust context, that of patent tying[301] under Sherman Act §1.[302] In *Indep. Ink, Inc. v. Ill. Tools Works, Inc.*,[303] the appellate court recognized a presumption of market power on the part of the patent owner in a tying case, a presumption rejected shortly thereafter by the Supreme Court as discussed below. Defendant Trident (a wholly owned subsidiary of Illinois Tool Works) held a patent on printheads[304] and sold the printheads as well as ink (unpatented) used in the printheads. Trident's standard form licensing agreements with printer manufacturers (OEMs) granted the OEMs the right to "manufacture, use and sell . . . ink jet printing devices [printheads] supplied by Trident" only "when used in combination with ink and ink supply systems supplied by Trident." Thus, the licenses included an explicit tying provision conditioning the sale of the patented product (the printhead) on the sale of an unpatented product (the ink). Plaintiff Independent Ink, which competed with patent owner Trident in the manufacture and sale of ink, filed suit against Trident seeking a declaratory judgment that Trident's patent was invalid and not infringed. Independent Ink subsequently amended its complaint to allege that Trident had engaged in illegal tying under Sherman Act §1. A federal district court hearing the case rejected the notion of a presumption of market power on the part of a patent owner as contrary to modern economic thinking, and held that an antitrust claimant must affirmatively prove that a patentee has market power. Because antitrust claimant Independent Ink had not submitted any affirmative evidence defining the relevant market nor proving patentee Trident's power within it, the district court granted Trident's motion for summary judgment of no antitrust liability.

The Federal Circuit in *Indep. Ink* reversed the summary judgment for patentee Trident and remanded the case for further proceedings.

---

[301]A tying arrangement is "an agreement by a party to sell one product . . . on the condition that the buyer also purchases a different (or tied) product, or at least agrees that he will not purchase that [tied] product from any other supplier." Eastman Kodak Co. v. Image Tech. Servs., Inc., 504 U.S. 451, 461 (1992).

[302]Section 1 of the Sherman Act declares illegal "[e]very contract, combination in the form of trust or otherwise, or conspiracy, in restraint of trade or commerce among the several States, or with foreign nations." 15 U.S.C. §1. In the patent context, the types of contracts most typically encountered are agreements between patent owners and third-party licensees, or agreements between multiple patent owners to "cross-license" their respective patents or to form patent "pools." Generally such agreements are viewed as procompetitive, but antitrust concerns may arise. Section 1 principles may also be relevant with respect to mergers and acquisitions between patent-owning firms.

[303]396 F.3d 1342 (Fed. Cir. 2005).

[304]A printhead is the component of a printer that controls the flow of ink from the ink cartridge to the paper. The author thanks Neal McFarland of Lexmark for this insight.

After extensively reviewing the Supreme Court's tying jurisprudence, the Federal Circuit concluded that it was bound by the Court's holdings in *Int'l Salt Co. v. United States*[305] and *United States v. Loew's, Inc.*[306] to apply a presumption of market power in patent tying cases. Nor did any of the contrary authority relied on by the district court or Trident constitute an express overruling of the Supreme Court precedent.[307] "Even where a Supreme Court precedent contains many 'infirmities' and rests upon 'wobbly, moth-eaten foundations,'" the Federal Circuit noted, "it remains the 'Court's prerogative alone to overrule one of its precedents.'"[308] The Federal Circuit concluded that although "[t]he time may have come to abandon the doctrine," it is "up to the Congress or the Supreme Court to make this judgment."[309]

[305]332 U.S. 392, 396 (1947) (without making inquiry of the defendant's market power, finding that "the admitted facts left no genuine issue. . . . [T]he tendency of the [patent tying] arrangement to accomplishment of monopoly seems obvious.").

[306]371 U.S. 38, 45 (1962) (stating that "[t]he requisite economic power is presumed when the tying product is patented or copyrighted").

[307]That contrary authority included contrary statements by the Supreme Court in *Walker Process Equip., Inc. v. Food Mach. & Chem. Corp.*, 382 U.S. 172 (1965), a §2 monopolization case discussed above; the statement of Justice O'Connor in her *Jefferson Parish* concurrence (joined by then–Chief Justice Burger, Justice Powell, and Justice Rehnquist) that it is a "common misconception . . . that a patent or copyright . . . suffices to demonstrate market power," 466 U.S. at 37 n.7 (O'Connor, J., concurring); statements by Justices White and Blackmun (both members of the *Jefferson Parish* majority) in their dissent from denial of *certiorari* the following year in *Data General Corp. v. Digidyne Corp.*, 473 U.S. 908, 908 (1985) (White, J., joined by Blackmun, J., dissenting from denial of *certiorari*), noting that that case raised "several substantial questions of antitrust law and policy including . . . what effect should be given to the existence of a copyright or other legal monopoly in determining market power," *id.*; and the antitrust agencies' policy that they will not presume market power in the tying context from the mere fact of patent ownership, United States Department of Justice, *Antitrust Guidelines for the Licensing of Intellectual Property* §5.3 (1995), *available at* http://www.usdoj.gov/atr/public/guidelines/0558.pdf.

[308]*Indep. Ink*, 396 F.3d at 1351 (quoting State Oil Co. v. Khan, 522 U.S. 3, 20 (1997)).

[309]*Id.* In further support of its decision recognizing a presumption of market power in patent tying cases based on the existence of the patent alone, the Federal Circuit in *Indep. Ink* also found it "noteworthy" that "Congress has declined to require a showing of market power for affirmative patent tying claims as opposed to patent misuse defenses based on patent tying," citing 35 U.S.C. §271(d)(5) (2000), which establishes a safe harbor for patentees from a charge of patent misuse "unless, in view of the circumstances, the patent owner has market power in the relevant market for the patent or patented product on which the license or sale is conditioned." The Federal Circuit noted that the version of this statute that originally emerged from the Senate contained language also abrogating the presumption of market power in antitrust patent tying cases, but that this language was removed in a House amendment and does not appear in §271(d)(5) as enacted, "making clear that Congress was not attempting to change existing law in this respect." *Indep. Ink*, 396 F.3d at 1349 n.7.

Not surprisingly, the Supreme Court accepted the Federal Circuit's invitation.[310] In *Ill. Tool Works Inc. v. Indep. Ink, Inc.,*[311] the Court vacated the Federal Circuit's decision and held that "in all cases involving a tying arrangement, the plaintiff must prove that the defendant has market power in the tying product."[312] In other words, market power cannot be presumed from the fact that a patent covers the tying product; the antitrust claimant charging illegal tying must make a satisfactory evidentiary showing of the patent owner's market power based on actual market conditions. The Court characterized the traditional presumption of market power by patent owners as a "vestige of [its] historical distrust of tying arrangements,"[313] which distrust has "substantially diminished" over time.[314] It explained that the presumption of a patentee's market power first arose in the context of the patent misuse doctrine, outside of antitrust law, but later migrated into antitrust jurisprudence. While the presumption's applicability was expanding in the case law, however, Congress began "chipping away at the assumption in the patent misuse context from whence it came."[315] Most notably, Congress in 1988 amended the Patent Act by adding §271(d)(5). This statutory provision eliminated the patent-equals-market-power presumption in the patent misuse context.[316] In view of Congress's judgment, the Supreme Court concluded that tying arrangements involving patented products should no longer be evaluated under the *per se* rule previously applied in cases such as *Loew's* and *Morton Salt Co. v. G.S. Suppiger Co.*[317] While some tying arrangements involving patented products remain unlawful, such as those stemming from a true monopoly or marketwide conspiracy, "that conclusion must be

---

[310]Ill. Tool Works Inc. v. Indep. Ink, Inc., 545 U.S. 1127 (2005) (granting petition for writ of *certiorari*).

[311]547 U.S. 28 (2006).

[312]*Id.* at 46.

[313]*Id.* at 38.

[314]*Id.* at 35.

[315]*Id.* at 41.

[316]Section 271(d)(5) of 35 U.S.C. (2012) provides (emphasis added):

(d) No patent owner otherwise entitled to relief for infringement or contributory infringement of a patent shall be denied relief or deemed guilty of misuse or illegal extension of the patent right by reason of his having done one or more of the following: . . . (5) conditioned the license of any rights to the patent or the sale of the patented product on the acquisition of a license to rights in another patent or purchase of a separate product, *unless, in view of the circumstances, the patent owner has market power in the relevant market for the patent or patented product on which the license or sale is conditioned.*

[317]*See* Morton Salt Co. v. G.S. Suppiger Co., 314 U.S. 488, 490 (1942) (assuming without analyzing actual market conditions that by tying the purchase of unpatented goods to the sale of a patented good, the patentee was "restraining competition").

supported by proof of power in the relevant market rather than by a mere presumption thereof."[318]

The Court also observed that its rejection of the presumption of market power from the existence of a patent "accords with the vast majority of academic literature on the subject."[319] The lesson to be drawn from this literature, as already adopted by Congress and the antitrust enforcement agencies, is that "[m]any tying arrangements, even those involving patents and requirements ties, are fully consistent with a free, competitive market."[320] Hence, the Supreme Court reached the same conclusion: that a patent does not necessarily confer market power on its owner.

2. Anticompetitive Conduct

As applied by the Federal Circuit,[321] the antitrust *Noerr-Pennington* doctrine preserves the patentee's immunity from antitrust liability for asserting its exclusive rights unless the accused infringer establishes that (1) the patent was obtained from the USPTO through knowing and willful fraud within the meaning of *Walker Process Equip., Inc. v. Food Machinery & Chem. Corp.*,[322] (2) the infringement suit is a "mere sham" to cover what is in reality "an attempt to interfere directly with

---

[318]Illinois Tool Works Inc. v. Indep. Ink, Inc., 547 U.S. 28, 42-43 (2006).

[319]*Id.* at 43 n.4.

[320]*Id.* at 45.

[321]*See* Nobelpharma AB v. Implant Innovations, Inc., 141 F.3d 1059, 1068 (Fed. Cir. 1998).

[322]382 U.S. 172, 177 (1965). An antitrust counterclaim to patent infringement asserting "*Walker Process* fraud" is based on the concept of common law fraud as applied to the patentee's conduct before the USPTO. *Walker Process* fraud is more difficult to establish than the affirmative defense of inequitable conduct. The antitrust claimant must show that the patentee acquired the patent by means of either a fraudulent misrepresentation or a fraudulent omission, evidencing a clear intent to deceive the examiner and thereby cause the USPTO to grant an invalid patent, and that the patentee was aware of the fraud when bringing suit to enforce its patent. Moreover, the necessary additional elements of a violation of the antitrust laws (e.g., monopoly power in a relevant market) must be established. *See Nobelpharma AB,* 141 F.3d at 1069-1070. *See generally* Peter M. Boyle et al., *Antitrust Law at the Federal Circuit: Red Light or Green Light at the IP-Antitrust Intersection?,* 69 ANTITRUST L.J. 739, 770-778 (2001) (discussing the proving of *Walker Process* claims under Federal Circuit precedent).

Variations of *Walker Process* antitrust claims have been considered by the Federal Circuit. These include "*Handgards* claims," based on the assertion of a patent allegedly known to be invalid, *see* Bio-Technology Gen. Corp. v. Genentech, Inc., 267 F.3d 1325, 1333 (Fed. Cir. 2001) (concluding that district court's dismissal of *Handgards* claim based on *Noerr-Pennington* immunity was correct), and "*Loctite* claims," based on the assertion of a patent allegedly known not to be infringed. *See* Loctite Corp. v. Ultraseal, Ltd., 781 F.2d 861 (Fed. Cir. 1985), *overruled on other grounds, Nobelpharma AB,* 141 F.3d at 1068.

the business relationships of a competitor,"[323] or (3) the patentee has engaged in illegal tying.[324] Thus, the owner of a patent who seeks to enforce its statutory right to exclude others by bringing suit against an accused infringer is presumptively immune from antitrust liability for bringing the lawsuit, even if maintenance thereof would have an anticompetitive effect. This immunity is only presumptive, however, not absolute; a patentee will be stripped thereof in certain situations. As affirmed by the Federal Circuit, "'[b]eyond the limited monopoly which is granted, the arrangements by which the patent is utilized are subject to general law. . . . The possession of a valid patent or patents does not give the patentee any exemption from the provisions of the Sherman Act beyond the limits of the patent monopoly.'"[325]

One type of anticompetitive conduct potentially resulting in a loss of antitrust immunity for patentees is the knowing enforcement of a patent obtained by common law fraud. In *Walker Process Equip., Inc. v. Food Machinery & Chem. Corp.*,[326] the Supreme Court held that the maintenance and enforcement of a patent obtained by fraud on the USPTO may be the basis of an antitrust action under Sherman Act §2, and therefore subject to a treble damages claim by an injured party under the Clayton Act §4.[327] Permitting such actions, the Court observed, would promote the policies it had earlier articulated in *Precision Instrument Mfg. Co. v. Automotive Maintenance Mach. Co.*:

> A patent by its very nature is affected with a public interest. . . . [It] is an exception to the general rule against monopolies and to the right to access to a free and open market. The far-reaching social and economic

---

[323]*See* In re Independent Serv. Orgs. Antitrust Litigation (CSU, L.L.C. v. Xerox Corp.), 203 F.3d 1322, 1326 (Fed. Cir. 2000). The *Noerr-Pennington* doctrine of antitrust law provides that an attempt to influence the government (e.g., by the filing of a patent infringement lawsuit) is generally protected under the First Amendment and therefore immune from antitrust liability. Eastern R.R. Presidents Conf. v. Noerr Motor Freight, Inc., 365 U.S. 127, 138-139 (1961); United Mine Workers v. Pennington, 381 U.S. 657, 670 (1965). An exception exists to *Noerr-Pennington* antitrust immunity for "sham litigation," where the defendant establishes that the litigation is objectively baseless. *See* Professional Real Estate Investors v. Columbia Pictures Indus., 508 U.S. 49, 60-61 (1993) (discussing the two-part definition of sham litigation). *See also* Filmtec Corp. v. Hydranautics, 67 F.3d 931, 937-938 (Fed. Cir. 1995) (detailing contours of sham litigation exception under *Professional Real Estate Investors* in patent cases); James B. Kobak, Jr., *Professional Real Estate Investors and the Future of Patent-Antitrust Litigation: Walker Process and Handgards Meet Noerr-Pennington*, 63 Antitrust L.J. 185 (1994).

[324]In re Independent Serv. Orgs. Antitrust Litigation (CSU, L.L.C. v. Xerox Corp.), 203 F.3d 1322, 1327-1328 (Fed. Cir. 2000).

[325]*Id.* at 1357 n.4 (quoting United States v. Singer Mfg. Co., 374 U.S. 174, 196-197 (1963)).

[326]382 U.S. 172 (1965).

[327]*Id.* at 176-177.

consequences of a patent, therefore, give the public a paramount interest in seeing that patent monopolies spring from backgrounds free from fraud or other inequitable conduct and that such monopolies are kept within their legitimate scope.[328]

The assertion of what has come to be known among patent lawyers as "*Walker Process* fraud" is based on the concept of common law fraud as applied to the patentee's conduct before the USPTO. The Federal Circuit has stressed that the fraud must be knowing and willful.[329] The antitrust claimant must show that the patent owner acquired the patent by means of either a fraudulent misrepresentation or a fraudulent omission, evidencing a clear intent to deceive the patent examiner and thereby cause the USPTO to grant an invalid patent, and that the patentee was aware of the fraud when bringing suit to enforce its patent.[330]

More recently, the Federal Circuit in *Unitherm Food Sys., Inc. v. Swift-Eckrich, Inc.,*[331] held that *threatened,* if not actually consummated, enforcement of a patent procured by *Walker Process* fraud can also form the predicate for antitrust liability. The putative infringer Unitherm brought a declaratory judgment action[332] against patentee ConAgra, seeking a declaration that its patent was invalid and unenforceable; Unitherm's antitrust claim was an affirmative claim made with its declaratory judgment action (rather than presented as the more typical counterclaim to an allegation of patent infringement). "Strictly speaking," the Federal Circuit observed, "a *Walker Process* claim is premised upon 'the *enforcement* of a patent procured by fraud on the Patent Office.'"[333] However, a party such as Unitherm can bring a declaratory judgment action of patent invalidity even in the absence of overt enforcement actions. A parallel analysis should inform the

---

[328]*Id.* at 177 (quoting Precision Instrument Mfg. Co. v. Automotive Maintenance Mach. Co., 324 U.S. 806, 816 (1945)).

[329]*Walker Process* fraud is considered more difficult to establish than the affirmative defense to patent infringement of inequitable conduct, which requires a showing that the patent owner withheld from the USPTO information known to the patent owner that was material to patentability (or affirmatively submitted false material information), and that the withholding (or submission) was done with intent to deceive the USPTO. For further discussion of the defense of inequitable conduct, *see supra* Section D.1.

[330]*See* Nobelpharma AB v. Implant Innovations, 141 F.3d 1059, 1069-1070 (Fed. Cir. 1998). *See generally* Peter M. Boyle et al., *Antitrust Law at the Federal Circuit: Red Light or Green Light at the IP-Antitrust Intersection?*, 69 ANTITRUST L.J. 739, 770-78 (2001) (discussing the proving of *Walker Process* claims under Federal Circuit precedent).

[331]375 F.3d 1341 (Fed. Cir. 2004).

[332]*See infra* Section G for further discussion of declaratory judgment actions.

[333]*Unitherm,* 375 F.3d at 1357-1358 (quoting Walker Process Equip., Inc. v. Food Machinery & Chem. Corp, 382 U.S. 172, 174 (1965) (emphasis added)).

antitrust claim. "As a matter of Federal Circuit antitrust law," the Federal Circuit concluded, "the standards that we have developed for determining jurisdiction in a Declaratory Judgment Action of patent invalidity also define the minimum level of 'enforcement' necessary to expose the patentee to a *Walker Process* claim for attempted monopolization." Whether sufficiently threatening actions have been taken by the patentee to create a reasonable apprehension of suit in the putative infringer will control. "[I]f the patentee has done nothing but obtain a patent in a manner that the [declaratory judgment] plaintiff believes is fraudulent, the courts lack jurisdiction to entertain either a Declaratory Judgment Action or a *Walker Process* claim."

A second type of anticompetitive conduct potentially resulting in a loss of antitrust immunity for patentees is the enforcement of a patent for "sham" purposes, regardless of the facts of the patent's origin.[334] Sham patent litigation is thus consistent with the "sham litigation" exception to *Noerr-Pennington* antitrust immunity.[335] In order to establish this form of anticompetitive harm, the antitrust challenger must show that the patentee's "infringement suit was 'a mere sham to cover what is actually nothing more than an attempt to interfere directly with the business relationships of a competitor.'"[336] More specifically, the antitrust claimant must establish in accordance with *Prof'l Real Estate Investors, Inc. v. Columbia Pictures Indus., Inc.,*[337] that (1) the lawsuit was "'objectively baseless in the sense that no reasonable litigant could realistically expect success on the merits,'"[338] and (2) that the baseless lawsuit concealed "'an attempt to interfere directly with

---

[334]*See Nobelpharma AB*, 141 F.3d at 1071 (stating that "irrespective of the patent applicant's conduct before the PTO, an antitrust claim can also be based on a *PRE* [*Professional Real Estate Investors*] allegation that a suit is baseless. . . . ").

[335]The *Noerr-Pennington* doctrine of antitrust law provides that an attempt to influence the government (e.g., by the filing of a patent infringement lawsuit) is generally immune from antitrust liability. Eastern R.R. Presidents Conf. v. Noerr Motor Freight, Inc., 365 U.S. 127, 138-139 (1961); United Mine Workers v. Pennington, 381 U.S. 657, 670 (1965). An exception exists to *Noerr-Pennington* antitrust immunity for "sham litigation," where the defendant establishes that the litigation is objectively baseless. *See* Professional Real Estate Investors v. Columbia Pictures Indus., 508 U.S. 49, 60-61 (1993) (discussing the two-part definition of "sham" litigation). *See also* Filmtec Corp. v. Hydranautics, 67 F.3d 931, 937-938 (Fed. Cir. 1995) (detailing contours of "sham litigation" exception under *Professional Real Estate Investors* in patent cases); James B. Kobak, Jr., *Professional Real Estate Investors and the Future of Patent-Antitrust Litigation: Walker Process and Handgards Meet Noerr-Pennington*, 63 Antitrust L.J. 185 (1994).

[336]Nobelpharma AB v. Implant Innovations, 141 F.3d 1059, 1068 (Fed. Cir. 1998) (quoting Eastern R.R. Presidents Conference v. Noerr Motor Freight, Inc., 365 U.S. 172, 177 (1965)).

[337]508 U.S. 49 (1993).

[338]*Nobelpharma AB*, 141 F.3d at 1071 (quoting *Professional Real Estate Investors*, 508 U.S. at 60-61).

the business relationships of a competitor through the use of the governmental process — as opposed to the outcome of that process — as an anticompetitive weapon.'"[339]

A third type of anticompetitive conduct that has been the basis for antitrust claims against patentees involves what antitrust lawyers refer to as "refusals to deal." The essence of a patent as a government-granted property right is the right of its owner to exclude others from practicing the patented innovation during the term of the patent. On the other hand, antitrust law recognizes that a monopolist's refusal to deal with other marketplace actors can be actionable in certain circumstances.[340] Accordingly, patent owners have been charged with anticompetitive conduct in the form of refusing to grant licenses under their patents and/or refusing to sell the patented items. A report by the Antitrust Modernization Commission on intellectual property issues recognizes the existence of "substantial debate over whether and when licensing of intellectual property may appropriately be required under the antitrust laws."[341] The commission's report notes the contrasting approaches of the U.S. Courts of Appeal on this issue. Unlike the First[342] and Ninth[343] Circuits, the Federal Circuit has thus far rejected outright those antitrust claims based on refusal to license.

[339]*Id.*

[340]*See, e.g.,* Aspen Skiing Co. v. Aspen Highlands Skiing Corp., 472 U.S. 585 (1985).

[341]Intellectual Property Working Group, Antitrust Modernization Commission, *Memorandum re Intellectual Property Issues Recommended for Commission Study* (Dec. 21, 2004), *available at* http://govinfo.library.unt.edu/amc/pdf/meetings/IntellectualProperty.pdf (last visited Sept. 7, 2012).

[342]*See* Data General Corp. v. Grumman Sys. Support Corp., 36 F.3d 1147 (1st Cir. 1994) (adopting in a copyright case a rebuttable presumption that an intellectual property holder does not have any obligation to license its intellectual property).

[343]In *Image Tech. Servs. v. Eastman Kodak Co.*, 125 F.3d 1195 (9th Cir. 1997) (*Kodak II*) (appeal after remand in Eastman Kodak Co. v. Image Technical Serv., Inc., 504 U.S. 451 (1992)), the U.S. Court of Appeals for the Ninth Circuit borrowed the First Circuit's *Data General* presumption in a patent case but held that the presumption could be rebutted by evidence of pretext. "Neither the aims of intellectual property law, nor the antitrust laws justify allowing a monopolist to rely upon a pretextual business justification to mask anticompetitive conduct." *Id.* at 1219. The Ninth Circuit rejected Kodak's argument that its subjective motivation for refusing to sell its photocopier parts to the plaintiff independent service organizations was irrelevant. "Evidence regarding the state of mind of Kodak employees may show pretext, when such evidence suggests that the proffered business justification played no part in the decision to act." *Id.* at 1219. The court noted Kodak's "blanket" refusal, including both patent- and copyright-protected products and unprotected products. "Kodak photocopy and micrographics equipment requires thousands of parts, of which only 65 were patented," the Ninth Circuit observed. The trial court's failure to give any weight to Kodak's intellectual property rights in the instructions it had given to the jury was mere harmless error. *Id.* at 1218. Based on the evidence of record, the Ninth Circuit concluded, it was "more probable than not" that even had the instruction been given the jury would have found

The Federal Circuit's negative view of such claims is best illustrated by *CSU, L.L.C. v. Xerox Corp.*,[344] in which the Federal Circuit summarily rejected an accused infringer's assertion that a patent owner's refusal to license or sell its patented products constituted a violation of the antitrust laws (as well as patent misuse). CSU, an independent service organization for photocopiers, sued Xerox for violation of the antitrust laws based on Xerox's refusal to sell it Xerox-patented replacement parts. The district court granted Xerox summary judgment and the Federal Circuit affirmed, concluding that

> [i]n the absence of any indication of illegal tying, fraud in the Patent and Trademark Office, or sham litigation, the patent holder may enforce the statutory right to exclude others from making, using, or selling the claimed invention free from liability under the antitrust laws. We therefore will not inquire into his subjective motivation for exerting his statutory rights, even though his refusal to sell or license his patented invention may have an anticompetitive effect, so long as that anticompetitive effect is not illegally extended beyond the statutory patent grant.[345]

The Federal Circuit's expanding jurisprudence at the intersection of patent law and antitrust, including the court's choice-of-law policy of applying Federal Circuit law to antitrust issues stemming from patent disputes,[346] was the subject of public hearings conducted in 2002 by the U.S. Department of Justice and the Federal Trade Commission.[347] This is an evolving area of Federal Circuit law that patent litigants should monitor closely.

Kodak's presumptively valid business justification rebutted on the grounds of pretext. *Id.* at 1219.

[344]In re Independent Serv. Orgs. Antitrust Litigation (CSU, L.L.C. v. Xerox Corp.), 203 F.3d 1322 (Fed. Cir. 2000).

[345]*Id.* at 1327-1328. For criticism of the *CSU* decision by a former chairman of the Federal Trade Commission, *see* Robert Pitofsky, *Antitrust and Intellectual Property: Unresolved Issues at the Heart of the New Economy,* 16 BERKELEY TECH. L.J. 535, 545-546 (2001) (characterizing Federal Circuit's decision in *CSU* as "[a] striking example of an approach that gives undue weight to intellectual property rights").

[346]*See* Nobelpharma AB v. Implant Innovations, 141 F.3d 1059, 1068 (Fed. Cir. 1998) (holding *en banc* that "whether conduct in procuring or enforcing a patent is sufficient to strip a patentee of its immunity from the antitrust laws is to be decided as a question of Federal Circuit law").

[347]*See* United States Dept. of Justice, Press Release: DOJ/FTC Hearings to Highlight U.S. Court of Appeals for the Federal Circuit Perspectives on the Intersection between Antitrust and Intellectual Property Law and Policy (July 3, 2002), *available at* http://www.usdoj.gov/atr/public/press_releases/2002/11407.pdf. An agenda and some of the materials presented at the FTC/DOJ hearings on July 10-11, 2002, are available at http://www.ftc.gov/opp/intellect/detailsandparticipants.shtm (last visited Sept. 7, 2012).

G. Patent Declaratory Judgment Actions

Although typically asserted as defenses to a patentee's infringement lawsuit, the defensive theories discussed in Sections A through E of this chapter (i.e., noninfringement, absence of liability for infringement, invalidity, and unenforceability) alternatively may be raised as affirmative allegations of a party (such as an accused infringer) who files an action (or counterclaim) under the Declaratory Judgment Act.[348] The plaintiff in a patent declaratory judgment (DJ) action affirmatively seeks a judicial declaration that it is not liable for infringement and/or that the patent in question is invalid and/or unenforceable. A patent DJ action can be thought of as the mirror image of a garden-variety patent infringement suit, because an accused infringer is the typical DJ plaintiff and a patentee is the DJ defendant. In certain circumstances discussed below, the party filing the DJ action may not be a formally "accused infringer" but rather a licensee that has not been explicitly threatened with an infringement action because it is currently paying royalties to the patentee. Nevertheless, the licensee believes that its product is not covered by the licensed patent and/or that the patent is invalid and/or unenforceable.

Because Article III of the U.S. Constitution mandates that federal courts adjudicate only "Cases" and "Controversies,"[349] the Declaratory

---

[348]28 U.S.C. §2201(a). Congress enacted the Declaratory Judgment Act in 1934 "to prevent avoidable damages from being incurred by a person uncertain of his rights and threatened with damage by delayed adjudication." Minn. Mining & Mfg. Co. v. Norton Co., 929 F.2d 670, 673 (Fed. Cir. 1991) (citing EDWIN BORCHARD, DECLARATORY JUDGMENTS 803-804 (2d ed. 1941) [hereinafter Borchard]). Prior to the act's passage, "the patentee was the only one in a position to initiate a suit, usually an action for damages and an accounting, with or without an injunction, against the alleged infringer or his dealers." Borchard at 803. The patentee "could, without actually bringing suit, which might have placed in issue the validity of his patent, publicly and privately charge infringement and threaten to sue the manufacturer or any one who dealt with the product in issue. By continuous threat and coercion, [the patentee] could not only intimidate dealers and customers and gravely injure his competitor's business, but he could often force a settlement, without having risked an adjudication of his possibly unfounded claims of infringement." Id. (citations omitted).

[349]U.S. CONST., art. III, §2, cl. 1 (providing, "The judicial power shall extend to all Cases, in law and equity, arising under this Constitution, the laws of the United States, and treaties made, or which shall be made, under their authority;—to all Cases affecting ambassadors, other public ministers and consuls;—to all Cases of admiralty and maritime jurisdiction;—to Controversies to which the United States shall be a party;—to Controversies between two or more states;—between a state and citizens of another state;—between citizens of different states;—between citizens of the same state claiming lands under grants of different states, and between a state, or the citizens thereof, and foreign states, citizens or subjects.").

Judgment Act requires that a "case of actual controversy" exist.[350] The Supreme Court has upheld the constitutionality of the Declaratory Judgment Act and explained that the act's use of the phrase "case of actual controversy" refers to the types of "Cases" and "Controversies" that are justiciable under Article III.[351] Satisfying the "actual controversy" requirement is thus a jurisdictional prerequisite for filing a declaratory judgment action.

The Federal Circuit's standard for determining the existence of a justiciable actual controversy changed in 2007 when the U.S. Supreme Court decided *MedImmune, Inc. v. Genentech, Inc.*, reversing the circuit.[352] The *MedImmune* decision undoubtedly expands the circumstances under which issued patents may be challenged.[353] "By liberalizing the availability of declaratory judgment relief concerning patent validity and scope, *MedImmune* tilts the patent landscape away from the interests of patent owners and toward those of licensees and other who may be threatened, rightly or wrongly, with the enforcement of patents."[354]

1. Federal Circuit's Pre-*MedImmune* "Reasonable Apprehension" Test

Prior to the Supreme Court's 2007 decision in *MedImmune,* the Federal Circuit considered a sufficient actual controversy to exist if the declaratory plaintiff had a "reasonable apprehension" of being

---

[350]The Declaratory Judgment Act provides in pertinent part:

> In a *case of actual controversy* within its jurisdiction [except with respect to certain tax and trade actions], any court of the United States, upon the filing of an appropriate pleading, may declare the rights and other legal relations of any interested party seeking such declaration, whether or not further relief is or could be sought. Any such declaration shall have the force and effect of a final judgment or decree and shall be reviewable as such.

28 U.S.C. §2201(a) (emphasis added).

[351]*See* MedImmune, Inc. v. Genentech, Inc., 549 U.S. 118, 126-127 (2007) (citing Aetna Life Ins. Co. v. Haworth, 300 U.S. 227, 240 (1937)).

[352]549 U.S. 118 (2007).

[353]*See* Micron Tech., Inc. v. Mosaid Techs., Inc., 518 F.3d 897, 902 (Fed. Cir. 2008) (observing that "[w]hether intended or not, the now more lenient legal standard [set forth by the Supreme Court in *MedImmune*] facilitates or enhances the availability of declaratory judgment jurisdiction in patent cases").

[354]Donald S. Chisum, *Licensee Challenges to Patent Validity After MedImmune* (Feb. 7, 2007), *available at* http://www.chisum.com/MedImmuneWebPost.pdf. *See also* Eric Yeager, *BNA Conference Panelists Examine Pharma Legislation and Declaratory Judgment Trends,* 77 Pat. Trademark & Copyright J. 92 (2008) (noting *MedImmune* decision's "sweeping impact" on declaratory judgment jurisdiction in pharmaceutical cases).

sued for patent infringement. More particularly, the Federal Circuit applied a two-part inquiry for determining the existence of declaratory judgment jurisdiction:

(1) an explicit threat or other action by the patentee which creates a reasonable apprehension on the part of the declaratory judgment plaintiff that it will face an infringement suit; and

(2) present activity by the declaratory judgment plaintiff which could constitute infringement, or concrete steps taken with the intent to conduct such activity.[355]

Prong (1) of this inquiry focused on acts by the patentee; prong (2) examined acts by the DJ plaintiff.

The Federal Circuit clarified that prong (1) required the DJ plaintiff to demonstrate "that it has a reasonable apprehension of *imminent* suit."[356] The requirement of imminence meant that the injury had to be concrete, in other words, "actual or imminent, not conjectural or hypothetical."[357] In many cases, the prong (1) reasonable apprehension of imminent suit arose when the declaratory judgment plaintiff received a "cease and desist" letter or other express threat of suit for infringement from the patentee, although an express threat was not required to create declaratory judgment jurisdiction.[358] No such express threat was involved in *MedImmune*.

2. Supreme Court's Decision in *MedImmune*

The DJ plaintiff in *MedImmune*[359] was not the typical accused infringer that has received a cease-and-desist letter or otherwise been expressly threatened with an infringement suit. Instead, MedImmune manufactured the drug Synagis, for treatment of respiratory disease, under a license agreement with patent owner Genentech. Notably, Synagis accounted for 80 percent of MedImmune's sales revenues. When signed in 1997, the license agreement covered an existing Genentech patent and a then-pending application. When the application issued as the "Cabilly II" patent, Genentech sent MedImmune a letter asserting that Synagis was covered by Cabilly II and that MedImmune would owe Genentech royalties thereunder. MedImmune disagreed, believ-

---

[355]Teva Pharms. USA, Inc. v. Pfizer, Inc., 395 F.3d 1324, 1332 (Fed. Cir. 2005).

[356]*Id.* at 1333 (emphasis in original).

[357]*Id.*

[358]*See* Vanguard Research, Inc. v. PEAT, Inc., 304 F.3d 1249, 1254-1255 (Fed. Cir. 2002).

[359]MedImmune, Inc. v. Genentech, Inc., 549 U.S. 118 (2007).

ing the Cabilly II patent to be invalid and unenforceable, and in any event not infringed by Synagis.

MedImmune was unwilling to risk refusing to pay the royalties demanded, however. MedImmune anticipated that if it refused to pay royalties under the Cabilly II patent, Genentech would terminate the license and sue MedImmune for infringement. Knowing that an infringement lawsuit could potentially result in an injunction against further sales of its primary product, as well as the possibility of liability for enhanced damages and attorney fees, MedImmune paid Genentech the demanded royalties under protest. Thereafter MedImmune filed a DJ action against Genentech. A federal district court dismissed the action for lack of subject matter jurisdiction, and the Federal Circuit affirmed. Dismissal was based on the Circuit's precedent holding that a patent licensee in good standing cannot establish the requisite Article III case or controversy, because the license, "unless materially breached, obliterate[s] any reasonable apprehension" that the licensee will be sued for infringement.[360]

The Supreme Court granted review. By an 8-1 vote, it reversed the Federal Circuit in an opinion authored by Justice Scalia.[361] The Supreme Court agreed that as long as MedImmune continued to make the royalty payments, there was no risk that Genentech would seek to enjoin its sales of Synagis. Thus, the issue for decision was "whether this cause[d] the dispute no longer to be a case or controversy within the meaning of Article III."[362] The Court's earlier decisions required that a justiciable dispute be "'definite and concrete, touching the legal relations of parties having adverse legal interests'; and that it be 'real and substantial' and 'admi[t] of specific relief through a decree of a conclusive character, as distinguished from an opinion advising what the law would be upon a hypothetical state of facts.'"[363] In summary, "'the question in each case is whether the facts alleged, under all the circumstances, show that there is a substantial controversy, between parties having adverse legal interests, of sufficient immediacy and reality to warrant the issuance of a declaratory judgment.'"[364]

After reviewing this and other DJ precedent, which admittedly did "not draw the brightest of lines" between DJ actions that satisfied the case or controversy requirement and those that did not,[365] the Court concluded that the case at bar involved a sufficiently live dispute to establish the district court's jurisdiction over MedImmune's DJ action.

---

[360]Gen-Probe, Inc. v. Vysis, Inc., 359 F.3d 1376, 1381 (Fed. Cir. 2004).

[361]Justice Thomas dissented. *See MedImmune*, 549 U.S. at 137-146.

[362]*Id.* at 128.

[363]*Id.* at 127 (quoting Aetna Life Ins. Co. v. Haworth, 300 U.S. 227, 240-241 (1937)).

[364]*Id.* (quoting Maryland Casualty Co. v. Pacific Coal & Oil Co., 312 U.S. 270, 273 (1941)).

[365]*Id.* at 127.

MedImmune's continued payment of royalties was coerced by the threat of an infringement suit (and the potential negative consequences thereof) if it stopped payment. This coercion was sufficient to create DJ jurisdiction. "The rule that a plaintiff must . . . bet the farm, or (as here) risk treble damages and the loss of 80 percent of its business, before seeking a declaration of its actively contested legal rights finds no support in Article III."[366] The Court rejected Genentech's argument that the license agreement operated as an insurance policy or settlement that precluded MedImmune's challenge; "[p]romising to pay royalties on patents that have not been held invalid does not amount to a promise *not to seek* a holding of their invalidity."[367] The Court concluded that MedImmune "was not required, insofar as Article III is concerned, to break or terminate its . . . license agreement before seeking a declaratory judgment in federal court that the underlying patent is invalid, unenforceable, or not infringed."[368]

In the critical footnote 11 of its decision, the Supreme Court in *MedImmune* effectively overruled the "reasonable apprehension of suit" prong (1) of the Federal Circuit's test for DJ jurisdiction.[369] Several earlier Supreme Court decisions contradicted or conflicted with the Circuit's test,[370] and the test was at least "in tension" with other Supreme Court precedent.[371]

---

[366]*Id.* at 134. Although it held that DJ jurisdiction existed, the Supreme Court did not reach the merits of the dispute or whether the district court should exercise its discretion to dismiss the action. "[I]t would be imprudent for us to decide whether the District Court should, or must, decline to issue the requested declaratory relief. We leave the equitable, prudential, and policy arguments in favor of such a discretionary dismissal for the lower courts' consideration on remand. Similarly available for consideration on remand are any merits-based arguments for denial of declaratory relief." *Id.* at 136-137.

[367]*Id.* at 135 (emphasis in original).

[368]*Id.* at 137.

[369]*Id.* at 132 n.11.

[370]*Id.* (citing Altvater v. Freeman, 319 U.S. 359 (1943) (holding that a licensee's failure to cease its payment of royalties did not render nonjusticiable a dispute over the validity of the patent); Maryland Casualty Co. v. Pacific Coal & Oil Co., 312 U.S. 270, 273 (1941); and Aetna Life Ins. Co. v. Haworth, 300 U.S. 227, 239 (1937)). In contrast with *MedImmune*, however, the licensees in *Altvater* were paying "under protests" royalties "required by an injunction the patentees had obtained in an earlier case." *Id.* at 130. In other words, *Altvater* involved the compulsion of an injunction. Based on this and other factual distinctions, Justice Thomas (as well as the Federal Circuit in *Gen-Probe, Inc. v. Vysis, Inc.*, 359 F.3d 1376 (Fed. Cir. 2004)) considered *Altvater* inapplicable to the *MedImmune* facts. See *MedImmune*, 549 U.S. 143-144 (2007) (Thomas, J., dissenting).

[371]*MedImmune*, 549 U.S. at 132 n.11 (citing Cardinal Chem. Co. v. Morton Int'l, Inc., 508 U.S. 83, 98 (1993) (holding that appellate affirmance of a judgment of noninfringement, eliminating any apprehension of suit, does not moot a declaratory judgment counterclaim of patent invalidity)).

3. Post-*MedImmune* Federal Circuit Decisions

In *Teva Pharms. USA, Inc. v. Novartis Pharms. Corp.*,[372] the Federal Circuit acknowledged that its "reasonable apprehension of suit" test for DJ jurisdiction had been overruled in *MedImmune*'s footnote 11.[373] Henceforth, the Federal Circuit would apply the "all the circumstances" test of *MedImmune,* that is, "whether the facts alleged, under all the circumstances, show that there is a substantial controversy, between the parties having adverse legal interests, of sufficient immediacy and reality to warrant the issuance of a declaratory judgment."[374] In *Caraco Pharm. Labs., Ltd. v. Forest Labs., Inc.*,[375] the Federal Circuit explained that proving a declaratory plaintiff's reasonable apprehension of suit (the Federal Circuit's pre-*MedImmune* test) "is only one of many ways a patentee can satisfy the Supreme Court's more general all-the-circumstances test to establish that an action presents a justiciable Article III controversy."[376] As with any "totality of the circumstances" type of legal standard, each case has to be evaluated on its particular facts, and no bright-line rule exists for determining whether a DJ action satisfies the case or controversy requirement.[377]

A series of post-*MedImmune* Federal Circuit decisions, including *Teva Pharms., Caraco Pharm. Labs.,* and others, have "reshaped the contours of the first prong of [the Federal Circuit's] declaratory judgment jurisprudence."[378] In particular, the Federal Circuit's post-*MedImmune* cases bring additional justiciability doctrines to bear in applying the *MedImmune* test for DJ jurisdiction. In *Caraco,* the Federal Circuit applied *MedImmune*'s all-the-circumstances test by utilizing a three-part framework developed in other Supreme Court cases. This precedent established that an action is justiciable under Article III

> only where (1) the plaintiff has standing, *Lujan v. Defenders of Wildlife,* 504 U.S. 555, 560, 112 S. Ct. 2130, 119 L. Ed. 2d 351 (1992), (2) the issues presented are ripe for judicial review, *Abbott Labs. v. Gardner,* 387 U.S. 136, 149, 87 S. Ct. 1507, 18 L. Ed. 2d 681 (1967), and (3) the case is

[372]482 F.3d 1330 (Fed. Cir. 2007).
[373]*See id.* at 1339.
[374]*Id.* at 1337.
[375]527 F.3d 1278 (Fed. Cir. 2008).
[376]*Id.* at 1291.
[377]*See* Prasco, LLC v. Medicis Pharm. Corp., 537 F.3d 1329, 1336 (Fed. Cir. 2008).
[378]Cat Tech LLC v. Tubemaster, Inc., 528 F.3d 871, 880 (Fed. Cir. 2008). The second prong of the Federal Circuit's pre-*MedImmune* test, that is, whether the DJ plaintiff has already engaged in potentially infringing activity or made meaningful preparation to conduct potentially infringing activity, "remains an important element in the totality of circumstances which must be considered in determining whether a declaratory judgment is appropriate." *Id.*

not rendered moot at any stage of the litigation, *United States Parole Comm'n. v. Geraghty,* 445 U.S. 388, 397, 100 S. Ct. 1202, 63 L. Ed. 2d 479 (1980).[379]

The Federal Circuit has explained that the standing, ripeness, and non-mootness doctrines are "more specific but overlapping doctrines rooted in the same Article III inquiry," and as such they represent "a helpful guide in applying the all-the-circumstances test" of *MedImmune.*[380]

The Federal Circuit applied the standing requirement to affirm a district court's dismissal of a DJ action for want of actual controversy in *Prasco, LLC v. Medicis Pharm. Corp.,*[381] a post-*MedImmune* decision. *Prasco* demonstrates that *MedImmune* did not change the fundamental principle that parties in federal court must have a concrete dispute and not be seeking a mere advisory opinion based on hypothetical facts. The DJ defendant Medicis owned four patents covering a benzoyl peroxide cleansing product. The DJ plaintiff Prasco manufactured a generic benzoyl peroxide cleansing product marketed as OSCION in competition with the patentee's product. Prasco filed its DJ action in 2006, seeking a judicial declaration of noninfringement (it did not assert invalidity) after the following events had occurred: (1) Medicis marked the four patent numbers on its cleansing product in accordance with 35 U.S.C. §287(a); and (2) Medicis sued Prasco in 2005 for infringement of an unrelated patent based on Prasco's sales of a different cleanser product. After Medicis filed a motion to dismiss Prasco's DJ action for lack of a case or controversy, Prasco sent Medicis a sample of OSCION and requested that it sign a covenant not to sue Prasco for infringement under the Medicis patents. Medicis refused to sign the covenant. Based on Medicis' conduct, Prasco alleged that it had suffered an actual harm, namely, "paralyzing uncertainty" from fear that Medicis would sue it again, this time for patent infringement based on Prasco's sales of OSCION.

The Federal Circuit disagreed, affirming the district court's dismissal of Prasco's DJ action. Prasco had failed to allege a controversy of sufficient "immediacy and reality" to create DJ jurisdiction. The Federal Circuit explained that the "immediacy and reality" inquiry can be viewed through the lens of standing, which is satisfied when a DJ plaintiff alleges (1) an "injury-in-fact," meaning a harm that is concrete and actual or imminent, not conjectural or hypothetical; (2) the harm is fairly traceable to the DJ defendant's conduct; and (3) the

[379]Caraco Pharm. Labs., LTD v. Forest Labs., Inc., 527 F.3d 1278, 1291 (Fed. Cir. 2008).

[380]*Prasco,* 537 F.3d at 1336.

[381]537 F.3d 1329 (Fed. Cir. 2008).

harm is redressable by a favorable decision.[382] "Absent an injury-in-fact fairly traceable to the patentee, there can be no immediate and real controversy,"[383] the court explained. Although an injury-in-fact may exist even if the DJ plaintiff does not have a reasonable apprehension of suit (as in *MedImmune*), there must nevertheless exist a "case or controversy . . . based on a *real* and *immediate* injury or threat of future injury that is *caused by the defendants*—an objective standard that cannot be met by a purely subjective or speculative fear of future harm."[384] Generally, some affirmative act by the DJ defendant/patentee will be required to establish a justiciable controversy.

The Federal Circuit concluded in *Prasco* that the evidence was completely lacking as to a "defined, preexisting dispute between the parties concerning OSCION."[385] With respect to patent marking, the court noted that Medicis decided to mark its patent numbers on its cleansing product before it had any knowledge of Prasco's competing OSCION product. With respect to Medicis' 2005 infringement suit against Prasco, the Federal Circuit acknowledged that prior litigious conduct is one factor to be considered in assessing the totality of the circumstances for DJ jurisdiction. In this case, however, the prior lawsuit was entitled to only minimal weight. "[O]ne prior suit concerning different products covered by unrelated patents is not the type of pattern of prior conduct that makes reasonable an assumption that Medicis will also take action against Prasco regarding its new product."[386] With respect to Medicis's refusal to sign the covenant not to sue Prasco, although this too is one factor to be considered in the totality of the circumstances analysis, in this case it was "not sufficient to create an actual controversy—some affirmative actions by the defendant will also generally be necessary."[387] "A patentee has no obligation to spend the time and money to test a competitors' product nor to make a definitive determination, at the time and place of the competitors' choosing, that it will never bring an infringement suit."[388] The Federal Circuit concluded that

> where Prasco has suffered no actual present injury traceable to the defendants, and the defendants have not asserted any rights against Prasco related to the patents nor taken any affirmative actions concerning Prasco's current product, one prior suit concerning unrelated patents and products and the defendants' failure to sign a covenant not

[382]*See id.* at 1338 (citing *Caraco*, 527 F.3d at 1291).
[383]*Id.*
[384]*Id.* at 1339 (emphasis in original).
[385]*Id.* at 1340.
[386]*Id.* at 1341.
[387]*Id.*
[388]*Id.*

606

to sue are simply not sufficient to establish that Prasco is at risk of imminent harm from the defendants and that there is an actual controversy between the parties of sufficient immediacy and reality to warrant declaratory judgment jurisdiction. Although we understand Prasco's desire to have a definitive answer on whether its products infringe defendants' patents, were the district court to reach the merits of this case, it would merely be providing an advisory opinion. This is impermissible under Article III.[389]

Should a patent owner, by promising not to sue an accused infringer, be able to unilaterally divest a federal court's jurisdiction over the accused infringer's counterclaim for a declaratory judgment of patent invalidity? Before *MedImmune*, Federal Circuit precedent answered this question affirmatively.[390] In 2012 the Supreme Court hinted that it may not agree. The Court granted *certiorari* in a trademark case that raises the same issue. The question presented in *Already, LLC v. Nike, Inc.*[391] is:

> Whether a federal district court is divested of Article III jurisdiction over a party's challenge to the validity of a federally registered trademark if the registrant promises not to assert its mark against the party's then-existing commercial activities.

The Supreme Court's decision in *Already, LLC* may have significant consequences for declaratory judgment jurisdiction in patent actions.

---

[389]*Id.* at 1341-1342.

[390]*See* Super Sack Mfg. Corp. v. Chase Packaging Corp., 57 F.3d 1054, 1055, 1059-1060 (Fed. Cir. 1995) (affirming district court's dismissal of case with prejudice for lack of a reasonable apprehension of a future infringement suit because "Super Sack's promise to assert neither U.S. Patent No. 4,143,796 ('796) nor U.S. Patent No. 4,194,652 ('652) against Chase as to any of its past or present products precludes the existence of an actual controversy.").

[391]No. 11-982, __S. Ct. __, 2012 WL 425184 (June 25, 2012) (order granting petition for writ of *certiorari*).

Chapter 11

Remedies for Patent Infringement

A. Introduction

Patent infringement is a tort,[1] for which the patent owner may sue an accused infringer in a civil action.[2] Earlier chapters of this text addressed the substantive law of patent infringement[3] and the defenses that may be raised thereto.[4] This chapter concerns the types of relief that a successful patent owner may obtain if infringement is established and the patent's validity and enforceability are sustained.

To summarize, the available remedies for infringement of a valid, enforceable patent are

- an injunction (preliminary and/or permanent) against future infringement,
- ongoing royalties for future infringement that is not enjoined,
- damages (compensatory and/or enhanced) for past infringements,
- attorney fees,
- costs, and
- prejudgment interest.

In addition, the American Inventors Protection Act of 1999 created a new remedy for violation of a patentee's "provisional rights," which

---

[1]*See* Carbice Corp. v. American Patents Dev. Corp., 283 U.S. 27, 32 (1931) (stating that "infringement . . . , whether direct or contributory, is essentially a tort, and implies invasion of some right of the patentee").

[2]*See* 35 U.S.C. §281 (2012) (providing that "[a] patentee shall have remedy by civil action for infringement of his patent"). The Patent Act does not provide any criminal liability for acts of patent infringement.

[3]*See supra* Chapter 9 ("Patent Infringement").

[4]*See supra* Chapter 10 ("Defenses to Patent Infringement").

attach upon publication of its pending patent application.[5] Each type of remedy is addressed below.

B. Injunctions

An injunction is an order by the court commanding an infringer to cease any further infringement (direct, inducing, or contributory) in the United States during the term of the patent. The Patent Act provides for injunctive relief in §283, which states that

> [t]he several courts having jurisdiction of cases under this title [35 U.S.C.] may grant injunctions in accordance with the principles of equity to prevent the violation of any right secured by patent, on such terms as the court deems reasonable.[6]

In many patent infringement scenarios, the most important remedy for the patent owner is the award of an injunction against future infringement. The importance of injunctive relief reflects the fact that a patent's principal value lies in the right it conveys to exclude others.[7] Without the ability to enjoin infringement, the patentee's exclusivity is abrogated. A defendant's unchecked future infringement may impact the marketplace's perception of the patentee in ways that are never fully compensable by a monetary award;[8] continuing infringement may harm the patentee's reputation and result in loss of the patentee's goodwill if the public develops a mistaken belief that the inferior quality of an accused device is attributable to the patentee. Injunctions also are important for a very practical reason: some accused infringers may be judgment-proof and unable to pay damages. An injunction is the only meaningful remedy available in such cases.

---

[5]*See* 35 U.S.C. §154(d).

[6]35 U.S.C. §283 (2012).

[7]Emphasizing the importance of injunctive remedies in patent cases, the court in *Smith Int'l, Inc. v. Hughes Tool Co.,* 718 F.2d 1573 (Fed. Cir. 1983), observed that without them,

> [t]he patent owner would lack much of the "leverage," afforded by the right to exclude, to enjoy the full value of his invention in the market place. Without the right to obtain an injunction, the right to exclude granted to the patentee would have only a fraction of the value it was intended to have, and would no longer be as great an incentive to engage in the toils of scientific and technological research.

Id. at 1577.

[8]*See* Atlas Powder Co. v. Ireco Chems., 773 F.2d 1230, 1233 (Fed. Cir. 1985) (Rich, J.) (stating that "[t]he patent statute further provides injunctive relief to preserve the legal interests of the parties *against future infringement* which may have market effects never fully compensable in money") (emphasis in original).

Nevertheless, the patent property right should not be viewed as absolute. As further discussed *infra*, the Supreme Court has clarified in *eBay, Inc. v. MercExchange, LLC*[9] that injunctive relief is not automatic even though a patent is adjudged infringed and its validity sustained. As the Court explained, "the creation of a right is distinct from the provision of remedies for violations of that right."[10] The use of the word "may" in 35 U.S.C. §283 makes clear that injunctions are optional, not mandatory, equitable remedies.

Section 283 also provides that the district courts have broad discretion in fashioning injunctions so as to do justice. That discretion is not unfettered, however. In awarding injunctive relief, the courts must comply with the requirements of Fed. R. Civ. P. 65. This rule requires that injunctive orders provide clear notice and specific detail concerning the conduct being enjoined. The rule provides in part,

> (d) Contents and Scope of Every Injunction and Restraining Order.
> (1) *Contents*. Every order granting an injunction and every restraining order must:
> (A) state the reasons why it issued;
> (B) state its terms specifically; and
> (C) describe in reasonable detail--and not by referring to the complaint or other document--the act or acts restrained or required.
> (2) *Persons Bound*. The order binds only the following who receive actual notice of it by personal service or otherwise:
> (A) the parties;
> (B) the parties' officers, agents, servants, employees, and attorneys; and
> (C) other persons who are in active concert or participation with anyone described in Rule 65(d)(2)(A) or (B).[11]

Two types of injunctions are encountered in patent cases: preliminary injunctions and permanent injunctions. Because permanent injunctions are more common, they are addressed first.

1. Permanent Injunctions

A permanent injunction is one that is issued after a final judgment of infringement and no invalidity or unenforceability. Prior to the Supreme Court's decision in *eBay, Inc. v. MercExchange, LLC,*[12] federal courts virtually always granted permanent injunctive relief

---

[9]547 U.S. 388 (2006).
[10] *eBay*, 547 U.S. at 392.
[11]Fed. R. Civ. P. 65(d) (eff. Dec. 1, 2009).
[12]547 U.S. 388 (2006).

as a standard part of the final judgment when patent owners pre-vailed.[13] Such relief permanently enjoined the infringing party from any further infringement during the remaining term of the patent. The Supreme Court's 2006 decision in *eBay* means that permanent injunctions are no longer granted to prevailing patentees on an essentially automatic basis.

Prior to *eBay,* courts refused to enter permanent injunctions against adjudged infringers only in rare cases, such as those clearly impacting the public's health and welfare. For example, the Seventh Circuit in *City of Milwaukee v. Activated Sludge, Inc.*[14] affirmed an award of damages for the city's infringement of a patent on a sewage purification process but refused to permanently enjoin the infringement. Making the injunction permanent "would close the sewage plant, leaving the entire community without any means for the disposal of raw sewage other than running it into Lake Michigan, thereby polluting its waters and endangering the health and lives of that and other adjoining communities."[15]

During patent reform discussions in 2005, a number of technology companies publicly urged that the availability of permanent injunctive relief for patent infringement be limited to those prevailing patent owners that had commercialized their patented inventions. Noncommercializing patentees would be limited to monetary damages.[16] The technology companies, such as Apple, Intel, Microsoft, and Hewlett-Packard, were the targets of patent infringement lawsuits by patent-holding companies or individuals (not infrequently referred to pejoratively as "patent trolls") that acquired patents (sometimes through bankruptcy proceedings) and sued or threatened to sue the technology companies for infringement, but that did not otherwise participate in the marketplace. These patent holders reportedly used the threat of then–virtually automatic injunctive relief to push their targets into settlements. The targeted technology companies contended that courts should consider whether such patent-holding firms would truly suffer irreparable harm in the absence of injunctive relief.[17] Because the 2005 patent reform proposals were never enacted into

---

[13]*See* Richardson v. Suzuki Motor Co., 868 F.2d 1226, 1247 (Fed. Cir. 1989) (observing that "[i]t is the general rule that an injunction will issue when infringement has been adjudged, absent a sound reason for denying it"); *see also* MercExchange, L.L.C. v. eBay, Inc., 401 F.3d 1323, 1338-1339 (Fed. Cir. 2005) (reversing district court's denial of permanent injunction where court failed to "provide any persuasive reason to believe th[e] case [wa]s sufficiently exceptional to justify the denial of a permanent injunction"), *overruled by* eBay, Inc. v. MercExchange LLC, 547 U.S. 388 (2006).

[14]69 F.2d 577 (7th Cir. 1934).

[15]*Activated Sludge, Inc.,* 69 F.2d at 593.

[16]*See infra* Section D ("Damages for Past Infringements").

[17]*See* Brenda Sandburg, *A Modest Proposal,* THE RECORDER (May 9, 2005), *available at* http://www.law.com.

law,[18] concerns remained about the attempted enforcement of patents by holding companies, especially those with patents of questionable validity.[19]

a. *The* eBay v. MercExchange *Standard*

A landmark U.S. Supreme Court decision in 2006 effectively mooted the perceived need for congressional reform of injunctive relief in patent cases. In *eBay, Inc. v. MercExchange, LLC,*[20] the Court announced that a permanent injunction is not to be automatically awarded in every case in which a patent is found infringed and its validity sustained. Rather, a district court's decision to impose or deny a permanent injunction in a patent case should be made after consideration of traditional equitable principles generally applicable to all types of cases. In other words, the equitable considerations for determining whether permanent injunctive relief is warranted should not be applied in a rigid fashion, nor should they be applied differently in patent cases than in nonpatent cases.

Patentee MercExchange, a patent-holding company, licensed its patents but did not manufacture any products. It alleged that the "Buy It Now" feature of eBay's popular online auctions infringed MercExchange's '265 business method patent.[21] After eBay and its

---

[18]The proposed legislation (titled the "Patent Reform Act of 2005") would have added the following language to the end of 35 U.S.C. §283:

> In determining equity, the court shall consider the fairness of the remedy in light of all the facts and the relevant interests of the parties associated with the invention. Unless the injunction is entered pursuant to a nonappealable judgment of infringement, a court shall stay the injunction pending an appeal upon an affirmative showing that the stay would not result in irreparable harm to the owner of the patent and that the balance of hardships from the stay does not favor the owner of the patent.

H.R. 2795, 109th Cong., 1st Sess. §7 (2005).

[19]*See* ADAM B. JAFFE & JOSH LERNER, INNOVATION AND ITS DISCONTENTS: HOW OUR BROKEN PATENT SYSTEM IS ENDANGERING INNOVATION AND PROGRESS, AND WHAT TO DO ABOUT IT 15 (2004) (noting "worrisome development" of individual inventors, who in many cases have received a patent of "dubious validity," attempting to "hold up" established firms in their industries).

[20]547 U.S. 388 (2006).

[21]*See eBay*, 547 U.S. at 390; "Consignment Nodes," U.S. Patent No. 5,845,265 (issued Dec. 1, 1998). The '265 patent is directed to "[a] method and apparatus for creating a computerized market for used and collectible goods by use of a plurality of low cost posting terminals and a market maker computer in a legal framework that establishes a bailee relationship and consignment contract with a purchaser of a good at the market maker computer that allows the purchaser to change the price of the good once the purchaser has purchased the good thereby to allow the purchaser to speculate on the price of collectibles in an electronic market for used goods while assuring the safe and trusted physical possession of a good with a vetted bailee." *Id.* (abstract).

subsidiary Half.com (collectively "eBay") refused to take licenses, MercExchange sued for infringement. A jury sustained the '265 patent's validity, found that eBay infringed, and awarded damages to MercExchange. The district court thereafter denied MercExchange's motion for permanent injunctive relief against eBay, concluding that MercExchange's lack of commercial activity in practicing its patents coupled with its willingness to license them sufficiently established a lack of irreparable harm despite the denial of injunctive relief.[22] The Federal Circuit reversed, applying the appellate court's "general rule" that a permanent injunction should issue once infringement and validity have been adjudged.[23] In the Federal Circuit's view, the district court's citation of growing public concern over the issuance of business method patents was overly general and "not the type of important public need that justifies the *unusual* step of denying injunctive relief."[24]

The Supreme Court in *eBay* vacated the Federal Circuit's judgment, concluding that "[j]ust as the District Court erred in its categorical denial of injunctive relief, the Court of Appeals erred in its categorical grant of such relief."[25] The Court disagreed with the Federal Circuit's assumption that a patent owner's statutory right to exclude others under 35 U.S.C. §154(a)(1) is alone sufficient to justify a general rule favoring injunctive relief against adjudged infringers. The Court observed that "the creation of a right is distinct from the provision of remedies for violations of that right."[26] The Federal Circuit's approach was also contrary to copyright jurisprudence, in which the Supreme Court had "consistently rejected invitations to replace traditional equitable considerations with a rule that an injunction automatically follows a determination that a copyright has been infringed."[27]

Rather than following any general rule or presumption regarding injunctive relief in patent cases, the Supreme Court in *eBay* instructed that courts should instead apply "well established principles of equity."[28] These principles require that a patent owner seeking a permanent injunction must satisfy the following factors:

[22]*See eBay*, 547 U.S. at 393.

[23]MercExchange, LLC v. eBay, Inc., 401 F.3d 1323, 1338 (Fed. Cir. 2005).

[24]*eBay*, 547 U.S. at 1339 (emphasis added). In contrast, some Supreme Court Justices harbored greater concerns about business method patents. *See eBay*, 547 U.S. at 397 (Kennedy, J., concurring) (stating that "injunctive relief may have different consequences for the burgeoning number of patents over business methods, which were not of much economic and legal significance in earlier times. The potential vagueness and suspect validity of some of these patents may affect the calculus under the four-factor test.").

[25]*eBay*, 547 U.S. at 394.

[26]*eBay*, 547 U.S. at 392.

[27]*eBay*, 547 U.S. at 392-393.

[28]*eBay*, 547 U.S. at 391.

(1) that it has suffered an irreparable injury;
(2) that remedies available at law, such as monetary damages, are inadequate to compensate for that injury;
(3) that, considering the balance of hardships between the plaintiff and defendant, a remedy in equity is warranted; and
(4) that the public interest would not be disserved by a permanent injunction.[29]

With respect to the irreparable harm factor, the Supreme Court cautioned courts not to assume that all nonpracticing patentees will be unable to satisfy the four-factor test. The Court observed that "some patent holders, such as university researchers or self-made inventors, might reasonably prefer to license their patents, rather than undertake efforts to secure the financing necessary to bring their works to market themselves. Such patent holders may be able to satisfy the traditional four-factor test, and we see no basis for categorically denying them the opportunity to do so."[30]

Because neither the district court nor the Federal Circuit had correctly applied the traditional four-factor framework governing the award of injunctive relief, the Supreme Court vacated the Circuit's judgment so that the district court could apply the framework in the first instance. The Court took no position on the merits of the case at bar, or on whether permanent injunctions should be awarded in "any number of disputes arising under the Patent Act."[31] It held "only that the decision whether to grant or deny injunctive relief rests within the equitable discretion of the district courts, and that such discretion must be exercised consistent with traditional principles of equity, in patent disputes no less than in other cases governed by such standards."[32]

2. Preliminary Injunctions

A preliminary injunction is "preliminary" because it is entered before trial, that is, before a complete adjudication on the merits of the infringement issue. Preliminary injunctions also are referred to

---

[29]*eBay*, 547 U.S. at 391.

[30]*eBay*, 547 U.S. at 393. Other members of the Court were less willing to contemplate permanent injunctive relief for certain nonpracticing patentees. *See id.* at 396-397 (Kennedy, J., concurring) (stating that "[w]hen the patented invention is but a small component of the product the [accused] companies seek to produce and the threat of an injunction is employed simply for undue leverage in negotiations, legal damages may well be sufficient to compensate for the infringement and an injunction may not serve the public interest").

[31]*eBay*, 547 U.S. at 394.

[32]*eBay*, 547 U.S. at 394.

as interlocutory or *pendente lite* (pending the lawsuit). The goal of a preliminary injunction is to protect the rights of the parties during pendency of the infringement lawsuit, which can take years, by preserving the *status quo* until final disposition of the case.

A preliminary injunction is an extraordinary remedy, not routinely awarded, and will only be granted on a strong showing of the necessary factors by the patentee (the preliminary injunction movant). Federal Circuit case law enumerates the following substantive factors that a district court must consider in evaluating whether to grant a preliminary injunction in a patent case:

   i. A reasonable probability of success on the merits (i.e., the movant will prevail at trial);

  ii. Irreparable harm to the movant if the preliminary injunction is not granted;

 iii. The balance of the hardships tipping in the movant's favor; and

 iv. The impact, if any, of the injunction on the public interest.[33]

The district court must consider the factors and balance all the elements; no one factor is necessarily dispositive.[34] The first two factors are deemed critical, however, such that if a district court finds that the preliminary injunction movant has failed to satisfy either of them, it may deny the injunction without making findings on the third and fourth factors.[35] Each factor is separately discussed below.

Procedurally, the patentee seeking a preliminary injunction against an accused infringer files a motion with the district court.[36] The court will usually hold a hearing with testimony, although the motion is sometimes decided based only on the affidavits and other documentary evidence. In either case, the party sought to be enjoined must be given advance notice. Federal Rule of Civil Procedure 65(a)(1) provides that

---

[33]*See* Nutrition 21 v. United States, 930 F.2d 867, 869 (Fed. Cir. 1991).

[34]*See* Smith Int'l Inc. v. Hughes Tool Co., 718 F.2d 1573, 1579 (Fed. Cir. 1983). *See also* Hybritech, Inc. v. Abbott Labs., 849 F.2d 1446, 1451 (Fed. Cir. 1988) (explaining that the preliminary injunction "factors, taken individually, are not dispositive; rather, the district court must weigh and measure each factor against the other factors and against the form and magnitude of the relief requested").

[35]*See* Reebok Int'l v. J. Baker, Inc., 32 F.3d 1552, 1556 (Fed. Cir. 1994) (stating that "[w]hile a district court must consider all four factors before granting a preliminary injunction to determine whether the moving party has carried its burden of establishing each of the four, we specifically decline today to require a district court to articulate findings on the third and fourth factors when the court denies a preliminary injunction because a party fails to establish either of the two critical factors").

[36]A motion for preliminary injunction in a patent case is sometimes preceded by an application for a temporary restraining order (TRO). *See* Fed. R. Civ. P. 65(b) (eff. Dec. 1, 2009).

"[t]he court may issue a preliminary injunction only on notice to the adverse party." Rule 65(c) further requires that before an injunction is entered, the movant must give security; that is, the movant must post a bond, in an amount that the district court deems proper, for payment of costs and/or damages that could be suffered by the accused infringer if that party is later found to have been wrongfully enjoined.

a. Likelihood of Success on the Merits

This factor is generally considered the most important of the four preliminary injunction factors because if it is "clearly established," the second factor of irreparable harm will be presumed.[37] In order to satisfy the likelihood of success factor, the patentee must show a reasonable probability of success on the merits of infringement as well as validity and enforceability. More specifically, taking into consideration the burdens of proof that will apply at trial, the patentee must show a reasonable probability of success that (1) it will establish infringement by a preponderance of the evidence, and (2) that the accused infringer will not be able to establish invalidity or unenforceability of the patent by clear and convincing evidence.[38] Although a patent owner does not ordinarily bear the burden of proof on validity or enforceability, "at the preliminary injunction stage, because of the extraordinary nature of the relief, the *patentee* carries the burden of showing likelihood of success on the merits with respect to the patent's validity, enforceability, and infringement."[39]

As to infringement, the patentee/preliminary injunction movant will often attempt to establish similarity between the accused product and other products that have previously been adjudicated as infringing the same patent. As to validity, the patentee's chances of success are strengthened if the validity of its patent was previously sustained against a challenge by a different defendant.[40] The patentee also may rely on evidence of public acquiescence in the patent's validity or conclusive direct technical evidence of validity.[41]

---

[37]*Smith Int'l,* 718 F.2d at 1581.

[38]*See* Vehicular Techs. v. Titan Wheel Int'l, Inc., 141 F.3d 1084, 1088 (Fed. Cir. 1998) (stating that "[t]o establish a likelihood of success on the merits, [the patentee] must show that, in light of the presumptions and burdens that will inhere at trial on the merits, (1) it will likely prove that [the accused infringer] infringes the [] patent, and (2) its infringement claim will likely withstand [the accused infringer's] challenges to the validity and enforceability of the [] patent").

[39]Nutrition 21 v. United States, 930 F.2d 867, 869 (Fed. Cir. 1991) (emphasis in original).

[40]The prior adjudication on validity may be given considerable weight, although it does not necessarily bind the district court before whom the preliminary injunction motion is pending. *See* Hybritech, Inc. v. Abbott Labs., 849 F.2d 1446, 1452 (Fed. Cir. 1988).

[41]*See Smith Int'l,* 718 F.2d at 1578.

b. *Irreparable Harm*

Here the patentee must show that it will suffer irreparable harm if the preliminary injunction is not granted. Early cases treated this factor as satisfied only if the accused infringer was likely to be insolvent and/or bankrupt. The modern view does not require that the infringer be unable to pay damages; it recognizes that permitting continued infringement while the litigation is ongoing can also work a harm that is not remediable by money.

In practice, the irreparable harm factor will typically be presumed by the court if the patentee has made a "clear" or "strong" showing on the first factor, probability of success on the merits.[42] Prior to the creation of the Federal Circuit, some courts required patent owners to establish validity and infringement of the patent "beyond question,"[43] a standard rarely satisfied. Most likely this requirement stemmed from the courts' perception of weaknesses in the USPTO's *ex parte* examination system.

An accused infringer may seek to rebut the irreparable harm factor by introducing evidence that it has stopped all infringing activity and has no plans to resume it in the future. A long period of delay by the patentee in moving for a preliminary injunction after learning of the infringement also may refute irreparable harm.[44] Likewise, evidence that the patentee has engaged in a pattern of licensing the patent to

[42]*See Smith Int'l*, 718 F.2d at 1581; *see also* Illinois Tool Works, Inc. v. Grip-Pak, Inc., 906 F.2d 679, 682 (Fed. Cir. 1990).

[43]*See* Atlas Powder Co. v. Ireco Chems., 773 F.2d 1230 (Fed. Cir. 1985) (Rich, J.), in which the court rejected a "beyond question" standard at the preliminary injunction stage:

> The burden upon the movant should be no different in a patent case than for other kinds of intellectual property, where, generally, only a "clear showing" is required. . . . Requiring a "final adjudication," "full trial," or proof "beyond question" would support the issuance of a permanent injunction and nothing would remain to establish the liability of the accused infringer. That is not the situation before us. We are dealing with a provisional remedy which provides equitable preliminary relief. Thus, when a patentee "clearly shows" that his patent is valid and infringed, a court may, after a balance of all of the competing equities, preliminarily enjoin another from violating the rights secured by the patent.

Id. at 1233 (citations omitted) (emphasis in original).

[44]On the other hand,

> The period of delay exercised by a party prior to seeking a preliminary injunction in a case involving intellectual property is but one factor to be considered by a district court in its analysis of irreparable harm. Although a showing of delay may be so significant, in the district court's discretion, as to preclude a determination of irreparable harm, a showing of delay does not preclude, as a matter of law, a determination of irreparable harm. A period of delay is but one circumstance that the district court must consider in the context of the totality of the circumstances.

others, indicating that the receipt of royalties is sufficient remedy for the patentee's surrender of exclusivity, may be grounds for rebuttal of the irreparable harm presumption.[45]

c. Balance of the Hardships Tipping in Movant's Favor

The imposition of a preliminary injunction is a drastic measure. The accused infringer must stop making what may be its primary or only product, with the inevitable loss of assets and jobs that that entails. Some infringers have been forced to declare bankruptcy as a result of a court's injunction against patent infringement.

In the high-profile *Polaroid v. Kodak* instant photography litigation of the 1980s,[46] the accused infringer Kodak asked the district court to stay the entry of an injunction against it pending Kodak's appeal to the Federal Circuit.[47] Kodak contended that entry of the injunction would shut down Kodak's instant photography business, putting over 4,000 employees out of work and would result in lost investments in equipment and facilities of over $200 million.[48] Although admittedly "seductive," Kodak's claims of hardship did not persuade the district court to stay entry of the injunction pending appeal: "[t]o the extent Kodak has purchased [its] success at Polaroid's expense, it has taken a 'calculated risk' that it might infringe existing patents."[49] Thus, the district court found the potential harm to accused infringer Kodak outweighed by the harm that would result to patentee Polaroid had the injunction not been entered.

Because of the potentially significant consequences of its decision, a district court must weigh and balance the equities of the parties' respective positions before granting an injunction. The court must examine the hardships that may ensue if it grants the injunction versus those that will occur if it does not. If an injunction is to be entered,

---

Hybritech, Inc. v. Abbott Labs., 849 F.2d 1446, 1457 (Fed. Cir. 1988) (footnotes omitted) (emphasis in original).

[45]*See* Polymer Techs. v. Bridwell, 103 F.3d 970, 974 (Fed. Cir. 1996).

[46]Kodak ultimately paid Polaroid $925 million to end a "decade-old court battle over Kodak's infringement of instant photography patents held by Polaroid. The $925 million consisted of a patent infringement verdict of $873 million plus $52 million in interest." Shawn K. Baldwin, *"To Promote the Progress of Science and Useful Arts": A Role for Federal Regulation of Intellectual Property as Collateral*, 143 U. Pa. L. Rev. 1701, 1719 n.92 (1995) (citing *Kodak to Pay Polaroid $925 Million to Settle Suit*, Wall St. J., July 16, 1991, at C13).

[47]*See* Polaroid Corp. v. Eastman Kodak Co., 641 F. Supp. 828, 1985 U.S. Dist. LEXIS 15003 (D. Mass. 1985).

[48]*See Polaroid Corp.*, 1985 U.S. Dist. LEXIS 15003 at **5.

[49]*Polaroid Corp.*, 1985 U.S. Dist. LEXIS 15003 at **6 (quoting Smith Int'l, Inc. v. Hughes Tool Co., 718 F.2d 1573, 1581 (Fed. Cir. 1983)) (footnote omitted).

the district court should conclude that the balance of hardships tips in the patentee's favor.

d. Public Interest

Lastly, the district court should consider what, if any, impact the grant of an injunction would have on the public's interest. As with the previous factor, the court must weigh this factor from the perspective of both parties. The public always has an interest in ensuring that valid patents are enforced; this maintains the incentives for innovation that a strong patent system represents. On the other hand, the infringer may be supplying the public with an additional source of a critical product in short supply. For example, consider a breakthrough drug for a potentially fatal disease that a patentee is unable to manufacture in large quantities. Cutting off the infringer as a second source of supply would likely result in price increases and supply constrictions that could mean the difference between life and death to sick patients.

The Seventh Circuit's decision in *City of Milwaukee v. Activated Sludge, Inc.*,[50] discussed above, represents a rare example of a court refusing to enjoin infringement (albeit permanently rather than preliminarily) because of public health concerns. In *Hybritech, Inc. v. Abbott Labs.*,[51] the Federal Circuit affirmed a district court's grant of a preliminary injunction that prevented the alleged infringer Abbott from continuing to sell certain accused products but permitted it to continue selling two others, namely Abbott's cancer test kits and hepatitis test kits. The district court had determined that the public interest was best served by the continued availability of those kits, and the Federal Circuit saw no basis for disturbing that finding.[52]

e. Appellate Standard of Review

The grant or refusal of a preliminary injunction is immediately appealable as an interlocutory order under 28 U.S.C. §1292(a).[53]

---

[50] 69 F.2d 577 (7th Cir. 1934).
[51] 849 F.2d 1446, 1458 (Fed. Cir. 1988).
[52] *See Activated Sludge*, 849 F.2d at 1458.
[53] The statute provides in part:

(a) Except as provided in subsections (c) and (d) of this section, the courts of appeals shall have jurisdiction of appeals from:
(1) Interlocutory orders of the district courts of the United States ... granting, continuing, modifying, refusing or dissolving injunctions, or refusing to dissolve or modify injunctions, except where a direct review may be had in the Supreme Court; ....

28 U.S.C. §1292.

Because the order to grant or refuse the injunction is an equitable decision, the appellate court may overturn it only if the district court abused its discretion. However, the Federal Circuit will not hesitate to vacate the grant of a preliminary injunction where the district court fails to sufficiently explicate its findings on infringement and validity.[54]

C. Ongoing Royalties for Future Infringements

After the Supreme Court's 2006 decision in *eBay, Inc. v. MercExchange, LLC*,[55] district courts in certain cases have denied permanent injunctions (thus allowing ongoing infringement) while requiring that the infringer pay royalties for each infringing sale made during the remaining life of the patent.[56] As one commentator has observed, "while understandably relieved that they may elect to continue their infringing conduct, [such adjudged infringers] are presented with an interesting conundrum if designing around the patent is not possible or practical: continue infringing the patent and risk paying onerous post-verdict ongoing royalties—and possibly enhanced damages—or stop infringing, thereby granting the patentee a de facto injunction."[57]

The Federal Circuit approved the imposition of ongoing royalties in *Paice LLC v. Toyota Motor Corp.*[58] Paice owned and licensed patents directed to drive train technology for hybrid cars but did not manufacture or sell any products.[59] After a jury found that Toyota's

---

[54]*See, e.g.,* Oakley, Inc. v. Int'l Tropic-Cal, Inc., 923 F.2d 167, 168 (Fed. Cir. 1991) (concluding that district court's findings were so limited and conclusory as to make meaningful appellate review impossible).

[55]547 U.S. 388 (2006).

[56]*See, e.g.,* Voda v. Cordis Corp., 536 F.3d 1311, 1329 (Fed. Cir. 2008) (affirming district court's denial of permanent injunction sought by prevailing individual patent owner; rejecting patent owner's argument that denial of permanent injunction would irreparably harm his exclusive licensee); Paice LLC v. Toyota Motor Corp., 504 F.3d 1293, 1313-1315 (Fed. Cir. 2007) (approving denial of permanent injunction but remanding for limited purpose of having district court reevaluate ongoing royalty rate).

[57]Chad S.C. Stover, *When Courts Deny Injunctive Relief Post-eBay: Winning the Injunction Battle but Losing the Ongoing Royalty War*, 79 BNA PAT., TRADEMARK & COPYRIGHT J. 18 (Nov. 6, 2009). Stover contends that the after the Supreme Court's *eBay* decision, the district courts have faced the "complicated, multifaceted" issue of ongoing royalties with "little guidance from the Federal Circuit." *Id.* Stover's article describes and critiques the "distinct" approaches taken by three different federal district courts.

[58]504 F.3d 1293 (Fed. Cir. 2007).

[59]*See Paice LLC.* 504 F.3d at 1302-1303 (discussing Paice's licensing business and noting that "Paice does not actually manufacture any goods").

hybrid vehicles infringed certain claims of Paice's patents under the doctrine of equivalents, a district court denied Paice's motion for a permanent injunction against Toyota. Applying the four-factor test of *eBay*,[60] the district court found that Paice would not be irreparably harmed in its ability to license its patents absent a permanent injunction, that monetary damages were adequate given the relatively small dollar value of the infringing component as a subset of Toyota's entire accused vehicle, and that the balance of hardships favored Toyota.[61] In lieu of imposing a permanent injunction, the district court *sua sponte* imposed an "ongoing royalty" of $25 per infringing vehicle that Toyota would sell during the remaining life of the Paice patent. The court's $25/vehicle ongoing royalty rate was numerically the same as the jury's reasonable royalty award for past infringements.[62]

The Federal Circuit did not reject in principle the district court's imposition of an ongoing royalty, but nevertheless required remand because the district court's order did not explain how it had arrived at the $25/vehicle ongoing royalty. The Federal Circuit observed that awarding an ongoing royalty in lieu of an injunction may be appropriate under some circumstances, including patent infringement or antitrust violations. Such relief should not be awarded "as a matter of course," however.[63] Rather than acting *sua sponte* as in the case at bar, a court "[i]n most cases, whe[n] determin[ing] that a permanent injunction is not warranted, . . . may wish to allow the parties to negotiate a license amongst themselves regarding future use of a patented invention before imposing an ongoing royalty."[64] If the parties fail to

[60]*See eBay*, 547 U.S. at 391 (listing factors that patentee seeking permanent injunction must satisfy as "(1) that it has suffered an irreparable injury; (2) that remedies available at law, such as monetary damages, are inadequate to compensate for that injury; (3) that, considering the balance of hardships between the plaintiff and defendant, a remedy in equity is warranted; and (4) that the public interest would not be disserved by a permanent injunction").

[61]*See Paice LLC*, 504 F.3d at 1302-1303.

[62]*See Paice LLC*, 504 F.3d at 1303 (noting that the reasonable royalty awarded by the jury "amounted to approximately $25 per accused vehicle").

[63]*Paice LLC*, 504 F.3d at 1314-1315.

[64]*Paice LLC*, 504 F.3d at 1315. In *Telcordia Techs., Inc. v. Cisco Sys., Inc.*, 612 F.3d 1365 (Fed. Cir. 2010), the Federal Circuit again affirmed a remedy of ongoing royalties and approved a district court's direction to the parties to negotiate the ongoing royalty rate. *See Telcordia Techs.*, 612 F.3d at 1379 (stating that "after declining [patentee] Telcordia's motion for permanent injunction, the district court directed the parties to negotiate a reasonable royalty for ongoing infringement. An award of an ongoing royalty is appropriate because the record supports the district court's finding that Telcordia has not been compensated for Cisco's continuing infringement. Therefore, the district court did not abuse its discretion by directing the parties to negotiate the terms of the appropriate royalty.").

negotiate a license, however, "the district court could step in to assess a reasonable royalty in light of the ongoing infringement."[65]

Some Federal Circuit judges take the view that an ongoing royalty award of the type imposed in *Paice LLC* should be deemed a "compulsory license," at least when the parties are not afforded a prior opportunity to negotiate the rate of the ongoing royalty. As a general matter, a **compulsory license** is a compelled (rather than voluntary) license, that is, one imposed by the government against the wishes of a patent owner. Historically, the U.S. patent system has strongly disfavored the general availability of compulsory licenses. According to Circuit Judge Rader, for example, "[t]o avoid many of the disruptive implications of a royalty imposed as an alternative to the preferred remedy of exclusion, the trial court's discretion should not reach so far as to deny the parties a formal opportunity to set the terms of a royalty on their own. With such an opportunity in place, an ongoing royalty would be an ongoing royalty, not a compulsory license."[66]

Other Federal Circuit judges disagree, distinguishing an ongoing royalty like that awarded in *Paice LLC* from a compulsory license.[67] While a U.S. federal court may impose ongoing royalty payments on a particular adjudged infringer (e.g., Toyota in *Paice LLC*), a compulsory license as that phrase is understood internationally is potentially available to any applicant meeting applicable statutory or regulatory criteria as determined by a government's patent-granting authority. Unlike the United States, many foreign countries have implemented

[65]*Paice LLC*, 504 F.3d at 1315. In *Amado v. Microsoft Corp.*, 517 F.3d 1353 (Fed. Cir. 2008), the Federal Circuit elaborated that "[t]here is a fundamental difference . . . between a reasonable royalty for pre-verdict infringement and damages for post-verdict infringement. . . . Prior to judgment, liability for infringement, as well as the validity of the patent, is uncertain, and damages are determined in the context of that uncertainty. Once a judgment of validity and infringement has been entered, however, the calculus is markedly different because different economic factors are involved." *Id.* at 1361-1362 (citations omitted).

[66]*Paice LLC*, 504 F.3d at 1316 (Rader, J., concurring). In *Atlas Powder Co. v. Ireco Chems.*, 773 F.2d 1230 (Fed. Cir. 1985) (Rich, J.), the Federal Circuit affirmed a district court's imposition of a preliminary injunction and stated that "[i]f monetary relief were the sole relief afforded by the patent statute then injunctions would be unnecessary and infringers could become compulsory licensees for as long as the litigation lasts." *Id.* at 1233.

[67]*Paice LLC*, 504 F.3d at 1313 n.13 (majority opinion authored by Prost, J.) (using phrase "ongoing royalty" to "distinguish this equitable remedy from a compulsory license"). The *Paice LLC* majority explained that "[t]he term 'compulsory license' implies that anyone who meets certain criteria has congressional authority to use that which is licensed," giving as an example the musical works "mechanical" license codified in U.S. copyright law at 17 U.S.C. §115. *See Paice LLC*, 504 F.3d at 1313 n.13. "By contrast, the ongoing-royalty order at issue here is limited to one particular set of defendants; there is no implied authority in the court's order for any other auto manufacturer to follow in Toyota's footsteps and use the patented invention with the court's imprimatur." *Id.*

statutory frameworks under which domestic manufacturers may apply to their national patent offices for a compulsory patent license on grounds such as a public health crisis.[68] The TRIPS Agreement permits WTO member countries to grant compulsory licenses under specified conditions.[69]

D. Damages for Past Infringements

1. Introduction

In addition to an injunction, the other key form of relief for patent infringement is monetary, in the amount of the damages that the patentee suffered because of the infringement. Section 284 of the Patent Act, titled "Damages," provides,

> Upon finding for the claimant the court shall award the claimant *damages adequate to compensate for the infringement,* but in no event less than a reasonable royalty for the use made of the invention by the infringer, together with interest and costs as fixed by the court.
>
> When the damages are not found by a jury, the court shall assess them. In either event the court may increase the damages up to three times the amount found or assessed. Increased damages under this paragraph shall not apply to provisional rights under section 154(d) [35 USC § 154(d)].
>
> The court may receive expert testimony as an aid to the determination of damages or of what royalty would be reasonable under the circumstances.[70]

The critical language of 35 U.S.C. §284, ¶1, "damages adequate to compensate for the infringement," is the subject of much case law interpretation. The statute does not explain how to determine an "adequate" amount beyond specifying that it must not go below the floor or minimum of a "reasonable royalty" (discussed separately below). Thus, the district courts "have been accorded wide latitude to choose a compensation mode that appears to them to fit the evidence presented."[71] The Federal Circuit has not hesitated to correct what

---

[68]*See, e.g.,* India Patents Act, 1970 (amended 2005) §§83-92A.

[69]*See* TRIPS art. 31. For additional discussion of compulsory licensing, *see infra* Chapter 12, Section D ("The World Trade Organization's Agreement on Trade-Related Aspects of Intellectual Property Rights (TRIPS)").

[70]35 U.S.C. §284 (2012) (emphasis added).

[71]Paul M. Janicke, *Contemporary Issues in Patent Damages,* 42 Am. U. L. Rev. 691, 697 (1993). Professor Janicke's article is a valuable resource on all aspects of patent infringement damages. *See also* Robert S. Frank, Jr. & Denise W. DeFranco, *Patent Infringement Damages: A Brief Summary,* 10 Fed. Cir. B.J. 281 (2000).

it perceives as erroneous economic evaluation, however; since its creation in 1982, the appellate court has developed a detailed jurisprudence on the evaluation of patent infringement damages.

Damage awards may be of two basic types: compensatory and enhanced. Each is discussed below. To summarize, compensatory damages compensate the patentee by trying to approximate the actual monetary loss suffered.[72] Enhanced damages are in the nature of punitive damages and are intended to punish the accused infringer for willful conduct. Enhanced damages cannot be awarded for compensatory purposes; rather, they may be awarded "only as a penalty for an infringer's increased culpability, namely willful infringement or bad faith."[73]

In patent infringement actions, "[d]eciding how much to award as damages is not an exact science, and the methodology of assessing and computing damages is committed to the sound discretion of the district court."[74] The Federal Circuit has taken the position that any doubts as to the amount of a damages award are to be resolved against the infringer as the wrongdoer.[75]

2. Compensatory Damages

Federal Circuit authority expresses the basic goal of compensatory damages: putting the patentee in as good a position as it would have been in had there been no infringement. In the specialized terminology of patent damages, this condition or state is referred to as hypothetically returning the patentee to a "but for world."[76] In other words, U.S.

---

[72]See Birdsall v. Coolidge, 93 U.S. 64, 68-69 (1876) (explaining that when patentee sued for infringement "at law" [before the merger of law and equity in the U.S. courts], "he would be entitled to recover, as damages, compensation for the pecuniary injury he suffered by the infringement, without regard to the question whether the defendant had gained or lost by his unlawful acts,—the measure of damages in such case being not what the defendants had gained, but what the plaintiff had lost") (citing Curtis, Law of Patents §461 (4th ed. 1873); 5 Stat. 123).

[73]See Beatrice Foods Co. v. New England Printing & Lithographing Co., 923 F.2d 1576, 1579 (Fed. Cir. 1991) (stating that "[d]amages cannot be enhanced to award the patentee additional compensation to rectify what the district court views as an inadequacy in the actual damages awarded").

[74]State Indus., Inc. v. Mor-Flo Indus., Inc., 883 F.2d 1573, 1576-1577 (Fed. Cir. 1989).

[75]See Kalman v. Berlyn Corp., 914 F.2d 1473, 1482 (Fed. Cir. 1990).

[76]See Grain Processing Corp. v. American Maize-Prods. Co., 185 F.3d 1341, 1350 (Fed. Cir. 1999) (observing that "trial courts, with this court's approval, consistently permit patentees to present market reconstruction theories showing all of the ways in which they would have been better off in the 'but for world,' and accordingly to recover lost profits in a wide variety of forms").

patent law attempts to restore the patentee to its financial position but for the infringement.[77]

Unlike copyright infringement laws, the patent laws do not provide for an award of "statutory damages" within a specified range of dollars.[78] The amount of the patentee's compensatory damages must be determined based on the facts of each case. There are two primary analytical methods of computing the amount of compensatory damages for infringement of a U.S. utility patent: lost profits and reasonable royalty.[79] Each is discussed separately below.

a. Lost Profits

Damages computed on a theory of lost profits are intended to approximate the profits that the patentee lost because of sales diverted by the presence of the infringing product in the marketplace. The key element that a patentee must prove to attain a lost profits recovery is causation—that the infringement was the cause of the patentee's lost sales rather than some other cause such as the marketplace availability of noninfringing alternatives to the patented item. The patentee

---

[77]*See* Aro Mfg. Co. v. Convertible Top Replacement Co., 377 U.S. 476, 507 (1964) (defining "damages" as the difference between the patentee's pecuniary condition after the infringement and what it would have been had the infringement not occurred).

[78]*Cf.* 17 U.S.C. §504(c) (2012) (providing that copyright owner may elect award of statutory damages of $750 to $30,000 for all infringements in the action (or up to $150,000 if willful infringement) rather than proving amount of its actual damages and profits).

[79]Historically, another method of compensation besides damages applied: an equitable accounting of the infringer's profits, sometimes referred to merely as "profits" but indicating the accused infringer's profits. (Such profits should be distinguished from the lost profits of the patentee, a form of damages. *See infra* Section D.2.a.) An accounting was based on a theory of disgorgement of the profits (i.e., ill-gotten gains) made by the defendant on its infringing sales. Use of this equitable accounting remedy for infringement of utility patents was eliminated by Congress in 1946. *See Aro Mfg.,* 377 U.S. at 505.

Although disgorgement of the defendant's profits is no longer available for infringement of a utility patent, 35 U.S.C. §289 (2012) still provides for recovery of such profits for infringement of a *design* patent:

> Whoever during the term of a patent for a design, without license of the owner, (1) applies the patented design, or any colorable imitation thereof, to any article of manufacture for the purpose of sale, or (2) sells or exposes for sale any article of manufacture to which such design or colorable imitation has been applied shall be liable to the owner to the extent of his total profit, but not less than $250, recoverable in any United States district court having jurisdiction of the parties.
>
> Nothing in this section shall prevent, lessen, or impeach any other remedy which an owner of an infringed patent has under the provisions of this title [35 U.S.C.], but he shall not twice recover the profit made from the infringement.

bears the burden of establishing causation; in other words, the patentee must show that but for the infringement, the patentee would have made the sales for which it seeks lost profits.[80]

To understand the computation of lost profits, consider the following simple example. Assume that it costs a patentee $5 to manufacture a patented widget and that the patentee sells each widget for $25, thus netting a profit of $20 per widget. Assume further that the defendant sold 100 infringing widgets. If the patentee can prove that but for the infringement, it could and would have made those 100 extra widget sales, then the lost profits to be awarded the patentee are computed as $20 × 100, or $2,000.[81]

(1) The Panduit *analysis.* The foundational case of *Panduit Corp. v. Stahlin Bros. Fibre Works, Inc.*[82] set forth the following factors as the elements that a patentee must prove in order to obtain damages based on lost profits:

> To obtain as damages the profits on sales he would have made absent the infringement, i.e., the sales made by the infringer, a patent owner must prove: (1) demand for the patented product, (2) absence of acceptable noninfringing substitutes, (3) his manufacturing and marketing capability to exploit the demand, and (4) the amount of the profit he would have made. . . . [83]

Each factor is separately examined below.

(i) Demand for the patented product. *Panduit* factor (1), demand for the patented product, is usually presumed from the fact of infringement. The Federal Circuit considers "a substantial number of sales" of infringing products containing the patented features to be, itself, "compelling evidence" of the demand for the patented product.[84] Under this analysis, the fact of the infringer's sales necessarily means that there were buyers who wanted the product and were willing to pay the infringer's price.[85]

(ii) Absence of acceptable noninfringing substitutes. *Panduit* factor (2), absence of acceptable noninfringing substitutes, assures

---

[80]*See* Water Techs. Corp. v. Calco, Ltd., 850 F.2d 660, 671 (Fed. Cir. 1988).

[81]A more robust analysis of the patentee's lost profits in this scenario should distinguish between the patentee's fixed and variable costs. As discussed below, lost profits must be computed using an incremental income approach that excludes the patentee's fixed costs, that is, those costs that do not vary with increases in production, such as management salaries, property taxes, and insurance. *See* Paper Converting Mach. Co. v. Magna-Graphics Corp., 745 F.2d 11, 22 (Fed. Cir. 1984).

[82]575 F.2d 1152 (6th Cir. 1978) (Markey, C.J., sitting by designation).

[83]*Panduit Corp.*, 575 F.2d at 1156 (citations omitted).

[84]*See* Gyromat Corp. v. Champion Spark Plug Co., 735 F.2d 549, 552 (Fed. Cir. 1984).

[85]*See Gyromat Corp.*, 735 F.2d at 552.

causation, that is, that the patentee lost its sales because of the defendant's infringement (i.e., the sales that the patentee would have made, but for the infringement, were diverted to the infringer), not because consumers were buying a third party's noninfringing substitute product. An award of lost profits must not be speculative; rather, the patentee's burden is to show a reasonable probability that, absent the infringement, it would have made the infringer's sales.[86] Establishing this under *Panduit* factor (2), and determining what products do or do not qualify as "acceptable substitutes" for the patented product, constitute the major battlegrounds in patent litigation over lost profits damages.

For example, in the long-running *Polaroid v. Kodak* battle over infringement of Polaroid's patents on instant photography,[87] Polaroid sought lost profits damages. The accused infringer Kodak argued that lost profits were not available because conventional (i.e., noninstant) photography represented an acceptable noninfringing substitute. The district court disagreed, finding that instant photography occupied a unique niche in the photography market and that consumers wanted the unique emotional "instant experience" of having the picture developed instantaneously.[88] Thus, *Panduit* factor (2) was satisfied, and lost profits were available.

The Federal Circuit's conception of "acceptable noninfringing substitutes" has evolved over time. Earlier decisions appeared to require that an acceptable noninfringing substitute possess all the advantages or beneficial characteristics of the patented device.[89] It is rather difficult to see how a truly noninfringing device could ever satisfy this condition.

More recently, the Federal Circuit has focused on whether the proffered alternative "competes in the same market for the same customers" as the patented device. This analysis looks at prices as well as product features, and requires careful definition of the "relevant market." The court in *Bic Leisure Prods. v. Windsurfing, Int'l*[90] interpreted *Panduit* factor (2) as follows:

> [T]he second *Panduit* factor—absence of acceptable, noninfringing alternatives—presupposes that the patentee and the infringer sell

---

[86]*See* Bic Leisure Prods., Inc. v. Windsurfing, Int'l, 1 F.3d 1214, 1218 (Fed. Cir. 1993).

[87]*See* Polaroid Corp. v. Eastman Kodak Co., 1990 U.S. Dist. LEXIS 17968, *2 (D. Mass. 1990) (describing parties as "locked in a bitter, unyielding, exhausting and expensive litigation for over fourteen years").

[88]*See Polaroid Corp.,* 1990 U.S. Dist. LEXIS 17968 at *36-*42 (finding that conventional photography was not an acceptable substitute for instant photography during the period of infringement).

[89]*See* TWM Mfg. Co. v. Dura Corp., 789 F.2d 895, 901-902 (Fed. Cir. 1986).

[90]1 F.3d 1214 (Fed. Cir. 1993).

substantially similar products in the same market. To be acceptable to the infringer's customers in an elastic market, the alleged alternative "must not have a disparately higher price than or possess characteristics significantly different from the patented product." Kaufman Co. v. Lantech, Inc., 926 F.2d 1136, 1142 (Fed. Cir. 1991).

In *Kaufman,* for instance, the patent owner and the infringer sold substantially the same product. *Kaufman,* 926 F.2d at 1143. Thus *Panduit*'s second factor, properly applied, ensures that any proffered alternative competes in the same market for the same customers as the infringer's product. *See* Yarway Corp. v. Eur-Control USA, Inc., 775 F.2d 268, 276 (Fed. Cir. 1985) (alternative products did not possess features of the patent owner's and the infringer's products, nor compete in the same "'special niche' or mini-market").[91]

The Federal Circuit has explained that "[c]onsumer demand defines the relevant market and relative substitutability among products therein. . . . Important factors shaping demand may include consumers' intended use for the patentee's product, similarity of physical and functional attributes of the patentee's product to alleged competing products, and price."[92]

Must an acceptable noninfringing substitute be on sale in the marketplace at the time of the infringement? In *Grain Processing Corp. v. American Maize-Prods. Co.*,[93] the Federal Circuit held that it need not be. The court considered an acceptable noninfringing substitute to be "available," despite the fact that it was not actually being made nor offered for sale at the time, where the accused infringer possessed the capability to have made and sold the substitute but chose not to do so for economic reasons.[94] *Grain Processing* thus stands for the proposition that reconstruction of the "but for" world also must consider what the infringer might have offered as a noninfringing substitute, had the infringer known at that time that it was infringing.[95]

[91]*Bic Leisure Prods.*, 1 F.3d at 1219.

[92]Grain Processing Corp. v. American Maize-Prods. Co., 185 F.3d 1341, 1355 (Fed. Cir. 1999).

[93]*Grain Processing Corp.*, 185 F.3d at 1341.

[94]*See Grain Processing Corp.*, 185 F.3d at 1353-1355 (upholding district court's finding that accused infringer "had the necessary chemical materials, the equipment, the know-how and experience, and the economic incentive to produce [the alternative product] throughout the entire accounting period"); *id.* at 1354 (approving trial court's explanation that "sole reason" accused infringer did not use alternative process during accounting period was economic; i.e., alternative was somewhat more expensive than accused product, and accused infringer "reasonably believed it had a noninfringing product").

[95]*See Grain Processing Corp.*, 185 F.3d at 1350-1351 (citations omitted):

By the same token, a fair and accurate reconstruction of the "but for" market also must take into account, where relevant, alternative actions the infringer foreseeably would have undertaken had he not infringed. Without the infringing product, a rational would-be infringer is likely to offer an acceptable noninfringing alternative, if

Although *Grain Processing* seemingly broadened an accused infringer's ability to escape payment of damages based on a theory of lost profits, the availability of acceptable noninfringing substitutes need not prohibit a patentee from *any* recovery of those profits. Although the traditional *Panduit* framework is best suited for two-supplier markets consisting only of the patentee and the infringer (in which it is reasonable to assume that the patentee would have made all the sales diverted by the infringer), subsequent decisions have recognized that the *Panduit* formulation can be modified to fit a multisupplier marketplace involving more sources of supply than just the patentee and the accused infringer. In *State Indus., Inc. v. Mor-Flo Indus., Inc.*,[96] the Federal Circuit approved a "market share" approach that permits a patentee to substitute evidence of its share of a multisupplier market in place of evidence that would satisfy *Panduit* factor (2), the absence of acceptable noninfringing alternatives.[97] Thus, strict application of the *Panduit* formula is not the only way of establishing the amount of lost profits damages.[98]

(iii)   Manufacturing and marketing capability.   With respect to *Panduit* factor (3), capacity to meet the demand, the patentee seeking lost profits must show that it had or could have obtained the manufacturing capacity to make all the sales in question, that is, its own and the infringer's.[99] The patentee can satisfy this factor not only by reliance on its own manufacturing capability but also by evidence of the potential for licensing and contracting for the manufacture.[100]

---

available, to compete with the patent owner rather than leave the market altogether. The competitor in the "but for" marketplace is hardly likely to surrender its complete market share when faced with a patent, if it can compete in some other lawful manner. Moreover, only by comparing the patented invention to its next-best available alternative(s) — regardless of whether the alternative(s) were actually produced and sold during the infringement — can the court discern the market value of the patent owner's exclusive right, and therefore his expected profit or reward, had the infringer's activities not prevented him from taking full economic advantage of this right. . . . Thus, an accurate reconstruction of the hypothetical "but for" market takes into account any alternatives available to the infringer.

[96]883 F.3d 1573 (Fed. Cir. 1989).

[97]*See* Bic Leisure Prods. v. Windsurfing, Int'l, 1 F.3d 1214, 1219 (Fed. Cir. 1993). Under the market share approach, a patentee should be awarded lost profits on its market share percentage of the infringing sales and a reasonable royalty on the remaining infringing sales. *See* Atlantic Thermoplastics Co. v. Faytex Corp., 5 F.3d 1477, 1481 (Fed. Cir. 1993).

[98]*See* Rite-Hite Corp. v. Kelley Co., 56 F.3d 1538, 1545 (Fed. Cir. 1995) (*en banc*).

[99]*See* Datascope Corp. v. SMEC, Inc., 879 F.2d 820, 825 (Fed. Cir. 1989) (stating that "[t]he demand which a patentee must have the capacity to meet is measured by the total sales, by the patentee and the infringer, of the patented product").

[100]*See* Bio-Rad Lab. v. Nicolet Instrument Corp., 739 F.2d 604, 616 (Fed. Cir. 1984); Gyromat Corp. v. Champion Spark Plug Co., 735 F.2d 549, 554 (Fed. Cir. 1984).

(iv)   Amount of profit.   With respect to the final *Panduit* factor, the amount of lost profits must be computed using an incremental income approach that excludes the patentee's fixed costs, that is, those costs that do not vary with increases in production, such as management salaries, property taxes, and insurance.[101] Thus, the precise formula for computing lost profits is

$$\text{Amount of Lost Profits} = \text{Lost Revenues} - \text{Incremental Costs}$$

where

Lost Revenues = the number of additional sales that the patentee would have made but for the infringement, multiplied by the plaintiff's historical prices (i.e., pre-infringement prices, so that the plaintiff is not penalized by any price erosion forced by the defendant's infringement); and

Incremental Costs = variable costs that have already been covered by the plaintiff's own sales (i.e., excluding fixed costs such as management salaries, research and development, and other amounts that would not vary with the extent of infringement).[102]

(2)   *The* Rite-Hite *expansion.*   Since the court's creation in 1982, the trend in Federal Circuit damages jurisprudence has been one of broadening acceptance for new theories of "damages adequate to compensate for the infringement."[103] Emblematic of this expansion is the Federal Circuit's 1995 *en banc* decision in *Rite-Hite Corp. v. Kelley Co.*[104] Prior to *Rite-Hite,* Federal Circuit cases held that lost profits damages were to be based on diverted sales of the product covered by the infringed patent. In other words, the underlying analytical assumption was that each sale by the infringer meant a corresponding lost sale of the plaintiff's patented product. The Federal Circuit in *Rite-Hite* expanded damages law by holding that a patent owner also can potentially recover lost profits on lost sales of *unpatented* products (or products covered by patents other than the one in suit) that compete with the infringing device, so long as the patentee can establish causation.

The facts of *Rite-Hite* are these. Rite-Hite's patent in suit was directed to a manual safety device for securing a truck to a loading dock; it sold the patented device under the name MDL-55 for approximately $500 each. Rite-Hite also sold an automated version of the same device,

[101]*See* Paper Converting Machine Co. v. Magna-Graphics Corp., 745 F.2d 11, 22 (Fed. Cir. 1984).
[102]*See* DONALD S. CHISUM ET AL., PRINCIPLES OF PATENTABILITY 1233 n.8 (2d ed. 2001).
[103]35 U.S.C. §284.
[104]56 F.3d 1538 (Fed. Cir. 1995) (*en banc*).

known as ADL-100, for $1,000 to $1,500 each. Although the ADL was the subject of a U.S. patent, it was not covered by the patent in suit, and thus for purposes of the case was considered "unpatented."[105] The ADL device directly competed with Kelley's accused "Truk Stop" product, however.

Kelley's liability for infringement of Rite-Hite's patent on the manual MDL device had been affirmed on an earlier appeal to the Federal Circuit, and the issue remaining in the bifurcated case was damages. The district court determined that Kelley's sale of 3,825 infringing "Truk Stop" devices caused patentee Rite-Hite to lose the sales of (1) 80 patented, manual MDL-55 devices; (2) 3,243 unpatented APL-100 devices; and (3) 1,692 "dock levelers," unpatented devices frequently sold by Rite-Hite with both the MDL and the APL.[106] The district court awarded Rite-Hite lost profits based on the lost sales of all three products.

On appeal, Kelley argued that even assuming the *Panduit* factors had been met, as a matter of law lost profits must be limited to lost sales of the *patented* device. In other words, Kelley contended, lost profits means that only lost sales of the patented product are compensable.

The Federal Circuit disagreed. A majority of judges affirmed the district court's award of lost profits damages for lost sales of the unpatented automatic APL-100 restraint, even though that device was not covered by the patent in suit.[107] In holding that damages based on lost sales of the APL were recoverable, the appellate court relied on tort-based theories of proximate cause (i.e., "legal" or primary or dominant cause) and reasonable foreseeability.[108] The court expansively held that in patent cases "[i]f a particular injury was or should have been reasonably foreseeable by an infringing competitor in the relevant market, broadly defined, that injury is generally compensable absent a persuasive reason to the contrary."[109]

In the Federal Circuit's view, Kelley's accused device directly competed with the plaintiff's unpatented APL-100 device. In light of this competition in the marketplace, Kelley should have reasonably foreseen that its infringement would cause Rite-Hite not only a loss of the patented MDL device, but also lost sales of the directly competing but unpatented APL-100. The court distinguished those types of losses that are too "remote" to be compensable, such as "a heart attack

---

[105]*See Rite-Hite Corp.*, 56 F.3d at 1543.

[106]While sustaining the award of lost profits damages for lost sales of the ADL device, the Federal Circuit also held that under the "entire market value rule," separately discussed below, Rite-Hite could not recover lost profits damages for lost sales of the dock levelers. *See Rite-Hite Corp.*, 56 F.3d at 1549-1551.

[107]*See Rite-Hite Corp.*, 56 F.3d at 1544-1549.

[108]*See Rite-Hite Corp.*, 56 F.3d at 1546.

[109]*Rite-Hite Corp.*, 56 F.3d at 1546.

of the inventor or loss in value of shares of common stock of a patentee corporation caused indirectly by infringement. . . . [110]

Judge Helen Nies (joined by then–Chief Judge Archer, Judge Mayer, and Senior Judge Smith) offered an extensive dissenting argument that "[t]o constitute legal injury for which lost profits may be awarded, the infringer must interfere with the patentee's property right to an exclusive market in goods embodying the invention of the patent in suit. The patentee's property rights do not extend to its market in other goods unprotected by the litigated patent."[111] She further pointed out that Kelley started selling its Truk Stop device two years before Rite-Hite's patent in suit issued.[112] Thus, there was no way that Kelley could have "foreseen" that it would infringe not-yet-issued claims and that its lawful competition with the ADL would be transformed into compensable injury for infringement of the patent in suit.

b. *Entire Market Value Rule/Convoyed Sales*

Patentees often will seek to recover damages for the lost profits they would have made, but for the infringement, on accessory items that typically would be purchased with the patented item. Such items also are referred to as "tag-along" or "convoyed" sales. For example, a manufacturer of a patented razor might contend that consumers who purchase this particular razor also frequently will buy the razor blades marketed by the patentee to operate with the razor.

In the *Rite-Hite* case discussed above,[113] the Federal Circuit considered whether the patentee could recover lost profits on diverted sales of its "dock levelers," unpatented items frequently sold as accessories with the patentee's MDL and ADL devices.[114] The court analyzed the allowability of such damages under a case law formulation known as the "entire market value rule."[115] Precedent held that damages for component parts used with a patented apparatus were recoverable if the patented apparatus "was of such paramount importance that it substantially created the value of the component parts."[116] Precedent also permitted recovery of damages based on the value of a patentee's entire apparatus containing several features when the patent-related feature was the "basis for customer demand."[117] The court

---

[110]*Rite-Hite Corp.*, 56 F.3d at 1546.

[111]*Rite-Hite Corp.*, 56 F.3d at 1556 (Nies, J., dissenting-in-part).

[112]*Rite-Hite Corp.*, 56 F.3d at 1571.

[113]Rite-Hite Corp. v. Kelley Co., 56 F.3d 1538 (Fed. Cir. 1995) (*en banc*).

[114]The dock levelers were described as "bridging platform[s] sold with the restraints and used to bridge the edges of a vehicle and dock." *Rite-Hite Corp.*, 56 F.3d at 1543.

[115]*Rite-Hite Corp.*, 56 F.3d at 1549.

[116]*Rite-Hite Corp.*, 56 F.3d at 1549.

[117]*Rite-Hite Corp.*, 56 F.3d at 1549.

characterized the entire market value rule as having "typically been applied to include in the compensation base unpatented components of a device when the unpatented and patented components are physically part of the same machine," acknowledging that the rule "has been extended to allow inclusion of physically separate unpatented components normally sold with the patented components."[118] In such cases, the *Rite-Hite* majority concluded, the "unpatented and patented components together were considered to be components of a single assembly or parts of a complete machine, or they together constituted a functional unit."[119]

In view of this authority, the Federal Circuit in *Rite-Hite* summarized the entire market value rule as follows:

> [T]he facts of past cases clearly imply a limitation on damages, when recovery is sought on sales of unpatented components sold with patented components, to the effect that the unpatented components must function together with the patented component in some manner so as to produce a desired end product or result. All the components together must be analogous to components of a single assembly or be parts of a complete machine, or they must constitute a functional unit. Our precedent has not extended liability to include items that have essentially no functional relationship to the patented invention and that may have been sold with an infringing device only as a matter of convenience or business advantage. We are not persuaded that we should extend that liability. Damages on such items would constitute more than what is "adequate to compensate for the infringement."[120]

Under this formulation as applied to the facts of the case, patentee Rite-Hite could not recover damages for diverted sales of its dock levelers.[121] Although the dock levelers may have been used together with Rite-Hite's MDL and ADL restraints, "they did not function together to achieve one result and each could effectively have been used independently of each other."[122] The Federal Circuit concluded that Rite-Hite sold the dock levelers with the restraints "only for marketing reasons, not because they essentially functioned together."[123] Thus, lost profits–based damages were not available for lost sales of the dock levelers.

In contrast with *Rite-Hite*, lost profits were awarded on accessory sales in *Juicy Whip, Inc. v. Orange Bang, Inc.*[124] The claimed invention

---

[118]*Rite-Hite Corp.*, 56 F.3d at 1550.
[119]*Rite-Hite Corp.*, 56 F.3d at 1550.
[120]*Rite-Hite Corp.*, 56 F.3d at 1550.
[121]*See Rite-Hite Corp.*, 56 F.3d at 1551.
[122]*Rite-Hite Corp.*, 56 F.3d at 1551.
[123]*Rite-Hite Corp.*, 56 F.3d at 1551.
[124]382 F.3d 1367 (Fed. Cir. 2004).

was a chilled drink dispenser of the type seen in convenience stores. The Federal Circuit reversed a district court's denial of lost profits on the patentee's asserted lost sales of flavored syrup used in the dispenser. The appellate court observed that the entire market value rule as articulated in *Rite-Hite* permits recovery for lost sales of components that are physically separate from, but which form a "functional unit" with, the patented item. Unlike the dock levelers in *Rite-Hite*, the syrup and dispenser in *Juicy Whip* were not sold together "only as a matter of convenience or business advantage"; rather, "the dispenser needs syrup and the syrup is mixed in a dispenser." The district court had erred in holding that the patented dispenser and the syrup did not share a functional relationship because the dispenser had been sold separately from the syrup on occasion and because other syrups could be used in Juicy Whip's dispenser. The Federal Circuit clarified that "a functional relationship between a patented device and an unpatented material used with it is not precluded by the fact that the device can be used with other materials or that the unpatented material can be used with other devices."[125]

Entire market value analysis can apply in damage computations based on a theory of reasonable royalty rather than lost profits, despite academic criticism of that application.[126] For example, a jury in *Lucent Technologies, Inc. v. Gateway, Inc.*[127] found that use of Microsoft's well-known Outlook software program infringed a Lucent patent. A method claim of Lucent's patent read on the "date picker" tool used in some components of Outlook.[128] The jury awarded Lucent a lump-sum

---

[125]*Juicy Whip, Inc.*, 382 F.3d at 1372.

[126]*See* Lucent Technologies, Inc. v. Gateway, Inc., 580 F.3d 1301 (Fed. Cir. 2009), in which the court responded that such criticisms

> ignore the realities of patent licensing and the flexibility needed in transferring intellectual property rights. The evidence of record in the present dispute illustrates the importance the entire market value may have in reasonable royalty cases. The license agreements admitted into evidence (without objection from [accused infringer] Microsoft, we note) highlight how sophisticated parties routinely enter into license agreements that base the value of the patented inventions as a percentage of the commercial products' sales price. There is nothing inherently wrong with using the market value of the entire product, especially when there is no established market value for the infringing component or feature, so long as the multiplier accounts for the proportion of the base represented by the infringing component or feature.

Lucent, 580 F.3d at 1339.

[127]580 F.3d 1301 (Fed. Cir. 2009).

[128]*See Lucent,* 580 F.3d at 1317 (explaining that "[s]imilar to the number pad tool illustrated in [Lucent's] Day patent, Outlook's calendar date-picker tool enables the user to select a series of numbers, corresponding to the day, month, and year, using graphical controls. This date-picker calendar tool is incorporated in a few of Outlook's features. Microsoft Money and Windows Mobile [products also accused of infringement] have similar functionalities.").

royalty payment of $357,693,056.18 (excluding prejudgment interest). On appeal, the Federal Circuit sustained the jury's verdict that Microsoft had indirectly infringed the Lucent patent and that it had not been proved invalid, but vacated and remanded the damages award as not supported by substantial evidence. The Federal Circuit further held that, to the extent the jury relied on an entire market value calculation to arrive at the $358 million lump-sum damages amount, that award was likewise not supported by substantial evidence and was "against the clear weight of the evidence."[129]

In particular, the patentee Lucent had failed to carry its burden to establish that its patented invention was the basis for consumer demand of Microsoft's overall commercial product, Outlook. In the Federal Circuit's view, the only reasonable interpretation of the evidence was that

> the infringing use of the date-picker tool in Outlook is but a very small component of a much larger software program. The vast majority of the features, when used, do not infringe. The date-picker tool's minor role in the overall program is further confirmed when one considers the relative importance of certain other features, e.g., e-mail. . . . Lucent did not carry its evidentiary burden of proving that anyone purchased Outlook because of the patented method. Indeed, Lucent's damages expert conceded that there was no "evidence that anybody anywhere at any time ever bought Outlook, be it an equipment manufacturer or an individual consumer, . . . because it had a date picker." . . . And when we consider the importance of the many features not covered by the [Lucent] patent compared to the one infringing feature in Outlook, we can only arrive at the unmistakable conclusion that the invention described in claim 19 of the [Lucent] patent is not the reason consumers purchase Outlook.[130]

A second reason for rejecting the jury's apparent application of the entire market value rule in *Lucent* involved the royalty rate testimony of the patentee's licensing expert. The expert told the jury that an 8 percent royalty rate should be applied to a royalty base consisting of sales of the entire Outlook software program. Although "the base used in a running royalty calculation can always be the value of the entire commercial embodiment,"[131] this holds only "as long as the magnitude of the rate is within an acceptable range (as determined by the evidence)."[132] In the case at bar, Lucent's expert had improperly inflated his proposed royalty rate to 8 percent (from 1 percent) after the district court had granted Microsoft's *in limine* motion to exclude

[129]*Lucent,* 580 F.3d at 1324.
[130]*Lucent,* 580 F.3d at 1337-1338.
[131]*Lucent,* 580 F.3d at 1338-1339.
[132]*Lucent,* 580 F.3d at 1339.

from the jury the expert's initial theory that the royalty base should be the value of an *entire computer* running Outlook software.[133] Yet the expert had admitted that "there was no evidence that Microsoft had ever agreed to pay an 8% royalty on an analogous patent."[134] Vacating the damages award, the Federal Circuit concluded that the Lucent expert's approach could "not be an acceptable way to conduct an analysis of what the parties would have agreed to in the hypothetical licensing context."[135]

c. Reasonable Royalty

Where lost profits cannot be proved,[136] the patentee is entitled to an award of damages based on a theory of reasonable royalty. A reasonable royalty has been defined as "an amount 'which a person, desiring to manufacture and sell a patented article, as a business proposition, would be willing to pay as a royalty and yet be able to make and sell the patented article, in the market, at a reasonable profit.'"[137] Recall that §284 of the Patent Act provides that the reasonable royalty is the minimum or floor below which the damages assessment cannot go.[138]

Consider a very simple example of a reasonable royalty–based award. Assume that the standard patent royalty in the widget industry is $5 per each widget sold. If an unlicensed defendant sold 100 infringing widgets, the patentee's reasonable royalty award on the infringing sales would be calculated as $5 × 100, or $500.

(1) Hypothetical negotiation. In the majority of cases, there does not exist an "established royalty" based on an industry standard

---

[133]*See Lucent,* 580 F.3d at 1338 (explaining that "Lucent's expert tried to reach the damages number he would have obtained had he used the price of the entire computer as a royalty base. Being precluded from using the computer as the royalty base, he used the price of the software, but inflated the royalty rate accordingly.").

[134]*Lucent,* 580 F.3d at 1338.

[135]*Lucent,* 580 F.3d at 1338.

[136]Sometimes the patentee will be able to establish the availability of lost profits for some, but not all, of the infringing sales. In such cases the patentee receives a reasonable royalty award for those infringing sales not included in the lost profits computation. *See* State Indus., Inc. v. Mor-Flo Indus., Inc., 883 F.2d 1573, 1577 (Fed. Cir. 1989) (stating that "the award may be split between lost profits as actual damages to the extent they are proven and a reasonable royalty for the remainder").

[137]Panduit Corp. v. Stahlin Bros. Fibre Works, Inc., 575 F.2d 1152, 1157-1158 (6th Cir. 1978) (quoting Goodyear Tire and Rubber Co. v. Overman Cushion Tire Co., 95 F.2d 978, 984 (6th Cir. 1937) (citing Rockwood v. General Fire Extinguisher Co., 37 F.2d 62, 66 (2d Cir. 1930)), *appeal dismissed on motion of counsel for petitioners,* 306 U.S. 665 (1938)).

[138]"Upon finding for the claimant the court shall award the claimant damages adequate to compensate for the infringement, but in no event less than a reasonable royalty for the use made of the invention by the infringer, together with interest and costs as fixed by the court." 35 U.S.C. §284.

rate or extensive prior licensing by the patentee. In such cases the district court must determine what royalty rate would have been "reasonable" in accordance with §284.

The key element in setting a reasonable royalty is to return to the date when the infringement began.[139] The district court must attempt to discern what royalty rate the patentee would have accepted at that time, knowing that the patent was valid and infringed. Courts attempt to do this by positing a "hypothetical negotiation" between a "willing licensor" of the patent and a "willing licensee," and on the basis of that hypothetical negotiation, approximating what royalty the parties would have agreed to.

The hypothetical negotiation is necessarily an exercise in fiction, because in light of the subsequent infringement, the parties, in reality, never entered into a license. As characterized by the court in *Panduit*,

> [t]he setting of a reasonable royalty after infringement cannot be treated . . . as the equivalent of ordinary royalty negotiations among truly "willing" patent owners and licensees. That view would constitute a pretense that the infringement never happened. It would also make an election to infringe a handy means for competitors to impose a "compulsory license" policy upon every patent owner.[140]
>
> . . .
>
> Determination of a "reasonable royalty" after infringement, like many devices in the law, rests on a legal fiction. Created in an effort to "compensate" when profits are not provable, the "reasonable royalty" device conjures a "willing" licensor and licensee, who like Ghosts of Christmas Past, are dimly seen as "negotiating" a "license." There is, of course, no actual willingness on either side, and no license to do anything, the infringer being normally enjoined . . . from further manufacture, use, or sale of the patented product.[141]

Thus, the Federal Circuit characterizes the hypothetical negotiation approach as an attempt to "do justice" to the patentee,[142] and in some cases has affirmed the award of royalty rates significantly above industry norms.[143]

---

[139]*Panduit Corp.*, 575 F.2d at 1158.

[140]*Panduit Corp.*, 575 F.2d at 1158.

[141]*Panduit Corp.*, 575 F.2d at 1159.

[142]*See* TWM Mfg. v. Dura Corp., 789 F.2d 895, 900 (Fed. Cir. 1986) (stating that "[t]he willing licensee/licensor approach must be flexibly applied as a 'device in the aid of justice'") (quoting Cincinnati Car Co. v. New York Rapid Transit Corp., 66 F.2d 592, 595 (2d Cir. 1933)).

[143]*See, e.g.,* Rite-Hite Corp. v. Kelley Co., 56 F.3d 1538, 1554 (Fed. Cir. 1995) (*en banc*) (affirming reasonable royalty rate determination based on approximately 50 percent of patentee's estimated lost profits per unit sold to retailers); Bio-Rad Lab. v. Nicolet Instrument Corp., 739 F.2d 604, 617 (Fed. Cir. 1984) (awarding royalty rate approximating one-third of infringer's sales price where industry rate was only 3 to 10 percent of sales).

D. Damages for Past Infringements

In determining the contours of the hypothetical negotiation, district courts have traditionally considered evidence (typically in the form of testimony by patent licensing experts) on an extensive list of factors as set forth in the leading case of *Georgia Pacific Corp. v. United States Plywood Corp.*[144] A detailed examination of each of the 15

[144]318 F. Supp. 1116 (S.D.N.Y. 1970), *modified by* 446 F.2d 295 (2d Cir. 1971). The *Georgia Pacific* factors are

(1) The royalties received by the patentee for the licensing of the patent in suit, proving or tending to prove an established royalty;

(2) The rates paid by the licensee for the use of other patents comparable to the patent in suit;

(3) The nature and scope of the license, as exclusive or nonexclusive; or as restricted or nonrestricted in terms of territory or with respect to whom the manufactured product may be sold;

(4) The licensor's established policy and marketing program to maintain his patent monopoly by not licensing others to use the invention or by granting licenses under special conditions designed to preserve that monopoly;

(5) The commercial relationship between the licensor and licensee, such as, whether they are competitors in the same territory in the same line of business; or whether they are inventor and promot[e]r;

(6) The effect of selling the patented specialty in promoting sales of other products of the licensee; the existing value of the invention to the licensor as a generator of sales of his nonpatented items; and the extent of such derivative or convoyed sales;

(7) The duration of the patent and the term of the license;

(8) The established profitability of the product made under the patent; its commercial success; and its current popularity;

(9) The utility and advantages of the patent property over the old modes or devices, if any, that had been used for working out similar results;

(10) The nature of the patented invention; the character of the commercial embodiment of it as owned and produced by the licensor; and the benefits to those who have used the invention;

(11) The extent to which the infringer has made use of the invention; and any evidence probative of the value of that use;

(12) The portion of the profit or of the selling price that may be customary in the particular business or in comparable businesses to allow for the use of the invention or analogous inventions;

(13) The portion of the realizable profit that should be credited to the invention as distinguished from nonpatented elements, the manufacturing process, business risks, or significant features or improvements added by the infringer;

(14) The opinion testimony of qualified experts; and

(15) The amount that a licensor (such as the patentee) and a licensee (such as the infringer) would have agreed upon (at the time the infringement began) if both had been reasonably and voluntarily trying to reach an agreement; that is, the amount which a prudent licensee—who desired, as a business proposition, to obtain a license to manufacture and sell a particular article embodying the patented invention—would have been willing to pay as a royalty and yet be able to make a reasonable profit and which amount would have been acceptable by a prudent patentee who was willing to grant a license.

318 F. Supp. at 1120.

Georgia Pacific factors is beyond the scope of this text. Note, however, that *Georgia Pacific* factor (15), the amount of the royalty, essentially subsumes all of the previous 14 factors. In other words, the evidence pertaining to factors (1) through (14) is what supports the ultimate determination of royalty rate in factor (15).

(2)   Analytical approach.   An alternative method of determining the amount of a reasonable royalty has been employed in some cases, referred to as the "analytical method." In this method the court takes an infringer's anticipated net profit margin as the starting point and from this subtracts some "industry standard" or "acceptable" level of profit,[145] so as to leave that amount for the infringer; the remaining portion of the anticipated profit is awarded to the patentee as a reasonable royalty.[146] The analytical approach has been commended by commentators as one that "shifts from the fiction of hypothesizing what would have been negotiated in an imaginary licensing environment to the reality of determining what should be paid as fair compensation for patent infringement."[147]

In a number of cases, litigants and district courts adopted a "25 percent rule of thumb" to "approximate the reasonable royalty rate that the manufacturer of a patented product [i.e., the later-adjudged infringer] would be willing to offer to pay to the patentee during a hypothetical negotiation."[148] Based on empirical studies of actual licenses as well as general licensing practices, the 25 percent rule suggested "that the licensee [would be willing to] pay a royalty rate equivalent to 25 per cent of its expected profits for the product that incorporates the [intellectual property] at issue."[149] Although not without critics, the 25 percent rule was considered by certain organizations at least a valid starting point from which royalty rate could be adjusted up or down in accordance with the *Georgia Pacific* factors (described *supra*).

The Federal Circuit in 2011 roundly rejected the 25 percent rule of thumb in *Uniloc USA, Inc. v. Microsoft Corp.*[150] While admittedly "passively tolerating" the rule's use in earlier decisions, the Federal Circuit in *Uniloc* squarely considered the 25 percent rule of thumb in *Uniloc.* The appellate court concluded that evidence relying on the rule

---

[145]*See TWM Mfg.*, 789 F.2d at 899 (affirming district court's adoption of analytical method in which special master "[s]ubtract[ed] the industry standard net profit of 6.56% to 12.5%" from infringer's anticipated net profit range).

[146]Paul M. Janicke, *Contemporary Issues in Patent Damages,* 42 AM. U. L. REV. 691, 727 (1993).

[147]*Id.*

[148]Robert Goldscheider, John Jarosz & Carla Mulhern, *Use of the 25 Per Cent Rule in Valuing IP,* 37 LES NOUVELLES 123, 123 (Dec. 2002).

[149]*Id.*

[150]632 F.3d 1292, 1315 (Fed. Cir. 2011) (stating that "[t]his court now holds as a matter of Federal Circuit law that the 25 percent rule of thumb is a fundamentally flawed tool for determining a baseline royalty rate in a hypothetical negotiation").

is inadmissible under the leading Supreme Court decision on expert witness testimony, *Daubert v. Merrell Dow Pharmaceuticals, Inc.*,[151] as well as the Federal Rules of Evidence.[152] In a nutshell, the 25 percent rule was not valid because it "fail[ed] to tie a reasonable royalty base to the facts of the case at issue."[153] *Daubert,* subsequent Supreme Court decisions concerning expert testimony, and the Federal Circuit's own prior case law demanded that

> there must be a basis in fact to associate the royalty rates used in prior licenses to the particular hypothetical negotiation at issue in the case. The 25 percent rule of thumb as an abstract and largely theoretical construct fails to satisfy this fundamental requirement. The rule does not say anything about a particular hypothetical negotiation or reasonable royalty involving any particular technology, industry, or party.[154]

Using the 25 percent rule as a starting point for adjustment was not valid, either. "Beginning from a fundamentally flawed premise and adjusting it based on legitimate considerations specific to the facts of the case nevertheless results in a fundamentally flawed conclusion."[155]

d. Price Erosion

In addition to lost profits and reasonable royalties, a third type of compensatory damages available to patent owners is an award of damages for depressed or "eroded" prices due to the infringement.[156] As with lost profits, the patentee seeking price erosion damages must prove causation, that is, that but for the infringement, it would have

---

[151]509 U.S. 579 (1993). In *Daubert,* the Supreme Court assigned to federal district courts the responsibility of ensuring that all expert testimony must pertain to "scientific, technical, or other specialized knowledge" under Federal Rule of Evidence 702. *Id.* at 589. This responsibility required district court judges to determine that the testimony was based on a firm scientific or technical grounding. *Id.* at 589-590.

[152]Titled "Testimony by Expert Witnesses," Rule 702 provides that

> [a] witness who is qualified as an expert by knowledge, skill, experience, training, or education may testify in the form of an opinion or otherwise if:
> (a) the expert's scientific, technical, or other specialized knowledge will help the trier of fact to understand the evidence or to determine a fact in issue;
> (b) the testimony is based on sufficient facts or data;
> (c) the testimony is the product of reliable principles and methods; and
> (d) the expert has reliably applied the principles and methods to the facts of the case.

Fed. R. Evid. 702 (eff. Dec. 1, 2011).

[153]Uniloc USA Inc., v. Microsoft Corp., 632 F.3d 1292, 1315 (Fed. Cir. 2011).

[154]*Uniloc USA Inc.*, 632 F.3d at 1317.

[155]*Uniloc USA Inc.*, 632 F.3d at 1317.

[156]*See* TWM Mfg. v. Dura Corp., 789 F.2d 895, 902 (Fed. Cir. 1986).

sold its patented product at a higher price. A patentee may fail to meet
this burden if the accused infringer can establish that the patentee's
price drop was influenced by factors other than the presence of the
infringer in the marketplace, such as changing consumer preferences
or an influx of foreign products.[157]

3. Enhanced Damages and Willful Infringement

In accordance with 35 U.S.C. §284, a district court has the discretion to increase (or "enhance") damages up to three times the
amount of the compensatory award.[158] "The paramount determination in deciding to grant enhancement and the amount thereof is
the egregiousness of the defendant's conduct. . . ."[159] Enhanced damages are frequently (but not always) awarded when a defendant's
infringement is found to be "willful."[160] As detailed below, the Federal

---

[157]*See* Bic Leisure Prods. v. Windsurfing Int'l, 1 F.3d 1214, 1220 (Fed. Cir. 1993).

[158]35 U.S.C. §284, ¶2 (providing that "[w]hen the damages are not found by a jury,
the court shall assess them. In either event the court may increase the damages up
to three times the amount found or assessed."). The statutory phrase "up to" indicates
that trebling damages is the maximum enhancement. In less egregious cases of willful
infringement, a court may choose to enhance by doubling the compensatory damages
(or by applying some other multiplier less than 3).

[159]Read Corp. v. Portec, Inc., 970 F.2d 816, 826 (Fed. Cir. 1992) (stating that such
egregiousness is to be evaluated based on "all the facts and circumstances," i.e., a total-
ity-of-the-circumstances analysis). The *Read* court enumerated the following factors
"for consideration in determining when an infringer 'acted in [such] bad faith as to
merit an increase in damages awarded against him,' . . . particularly in deciding on the
extent of enhancement":

1. whether the infringer deliberately copied the ideas or design of another;
2. whether the infringer, when he knew of the other's patent protection, investi-
   gated the scope of the patent and formed a good-faith belief that it was invalid
   or that it was not infringed;
3. [the] [infringer's] behavior as a party to the litigation;
4. [the] infringer's size and financial condition; . . .
5. [the] closeness of the case; . . .
6. [the] duration of the defendant's misconduct; . . .
7. remedial action taken by the defendant; . . .
8. [the] defendant's motivation for harm; [and]
9. whether [the] defendant attempted to conceal its misconduct.

Id. at 826-827 (citations omitted). The court observed that using these factors is "in
line with punitive damage considerations in other tort contexts." *Id.* at 827-828.

[160]*See Read Corp.*, at 826 (stating that "[a]n award of enhanced damages for infringement, as well as the extent of the enhancement, is committed to the discretion of the
trial court. . . . [T]his court has approved such awards where the infringer acted in
wanton disregard of the patentee's patent rights, that is, where the infringement is
willful. . . . On the other hand, a finding of willful infringement does not mandate that
damages be enhanced, much less mandate treble damages.") (citations omitted). *See*

Circuit's landmark 2007 decision in *In re Seagate Tech., LLC*[161] required that in order to prove willfulness a patentee must establish that the infringer acted in an objectively reckless manner.[162] The *Seagate* standard significantly raised the bar on willfulness, making it more difficult for a patentee to establish than under the Federal Circuit's previous standard.[163] In practice, it remains to be seen whether *Seagate*'s more rigorous standard has significantly lessened the ability of patentees to obtain verdicts of willful infringement and enhanced damages.[164]

The Federal Circuit's 2007 decision in *Seagate* is best understood in its historical context. After the Federal Circuit was created in 1982, its early decisions emphasized the importance of respecting patent property rights "at a time when widespread disregard of [such] rights was undermining the national innovation incentive."[165] In particular, Federal Circuit decisions during the 1980s established that once a potential infringer became aware of another's patent rights, it had an affirmative duty to proceed with due care to determine whether or not it

---

also In re Seagate Tech., LLC, 497 F.3d 1360, 1368 (Fed. Cir. 2007) *(en banc)* (noting that "a finding of willfulness does not require an award of enhanced damages; it merely permits it").

[161]497 F.3d 1360 (Fed. Cir. 2007) *(en banc)*.

[162]*See Seagate,* 497 F.3d at 1371.

[163]*See* Carl G. Anderson et al., *Willful Patent Infringement: The First Year of the Post-*Seagate *Era*, 20 No. 9 Intell. Prop. & Tech. L.J. 11, 13 (2008) (based on analysis of approximately 40 reported post-*Seagate* district court decisions analyzing willfulness issues, concluding that "*Seagate* has raised the bar with respect to succeeding on a claim of willful infringement"); *cf.* Eric Yeager, *Conferences/Patents: Judge Linn Discusses "Challenges Ahead" for Patentees, PTO at AIPLA Luncheon*, 77 BNA's Pat. Trademark & Copyright J. 12 (2008) (stating that "there is no debate over the fact that patentees can 'no longer bank on a determination of willfulness and enhanced damages merely because infringement was found against an accused who had prior notice of the patent'") (quoting speech by Federal Circuit Judge Richard Linn).

[164]The heightened "objective recklessness" standard of *Seagate*, discussed *infra*, occasioned predictions that the decision would result in far fewer findings of willful infringement and awards of enhanced damages. *See* Christoper B. Seaman, *Willful Patent Infringement and Enhanced Damages After In Re Seagate: An Empirical Study*, 97 Iowa L. Rev. 417 (2012). In an empirical study of district court cases involving willfulness and enhanced damages decided during the six-year time period encompassing three years before the Federal Circuit decided *Seagate* and three years after, Professor Seaman refutes these predictions. He finds that "willfulness was found only about 10% less often after *Seagate*, and this relatively small change was not statistically significant." *Id.* at 402 (footnotes omitted). Moreover, the data showed that judges and juries reached different decisions under the "objective recklessness" standard. "At trial, juries found willful infringement at similar rates both before and after *Seagate*. . . . In contrast, judges found willfulness only a small fraction of the time after *Seagate*, as compared to a majority of the time before *Seagate*." *Id.* (footnotes omitted).

[165]*Seagate*, 497 F.3d at 1369 (citing Dep't of Commerce, Advisory Committee on Industrial Innovation Final Report (Sept. 1979)).

was infringing.[166] That duty required seeking and obtaining competent legal advice *before* initiating any possibly infringing activity.[167]

In decisions such as *Underwater Devices, Inc. v. Morrison-Knudsen Co.*,[168] and *Kloster Speedsteel AB v. Crucible Inc.*,[169] the Federal Circuit went so far as to authorize district courts and juries to draw an "adverse inference" from an accused infringer's failure to produce an exculpatory opinion of counsel in response to a charge of willful infringement. In other words, if no opinion was produced, the fact finder could properly infer that the legal advice given had been negative (i.e., counsel had determined that the client was infringing) and that the accused infringer nevertheless continued to knowingly infringe.

Critics of the adverse inference rule charged that it was in tension with the principle of attorney-client privilege. An accused infringer was effectively forced to choose between producing its opinion of counsel and thereby waiving privilege, or maintaining privilege but being subject to the adverse inference (potentially leading to a finding of willfulness and an award of enhanced damages).

In its 2004 decision in *Knorr-Bremse Sys. v. Dana Corp.*,[170] the *en banc* Federal Circuit eliminated from U.S. patent law the adverse inference that had previously arisen from an accused infringer's failure to produce an exculpatory opinion of counsel. By the time of its decision, the *Knorr-Bremse* court had come to recognize that "the inference that withheld opinions are adverse to the client's actions can distort the attorney-client relationship," and that "a special rule affecting attorney-client relationships in patent cases is not warranted."[171] Thus entering the mainstream of judicial thought on attorney-client privilege, the Federal Circuit appeared to recognize that "patent law is not an island separated from the main body of American jurisprudence."[172]

---

[166]*See* Avia Group Int'l Inc. v. L.A. Gear Cal., Inc., 853 F.2d 1557, 1566 (Fed. Cir. 1988); Underwater Devices, Inc. v. Morrison-Knudsen Co., 717 F.2d 1380, 1389-1390 (Fed. Cir. 1983).

[167]*See Underwater Devices*, 717 F.2d at 1390.

[168]717 F.2d 1380 (Fed. Cir. 1983).

[169]793 F.2d 1565 (Fed. Cir. 1986).

[170]383 F.3d 1337 (Fed. Cir. 2004) (*en banc*).

[171]*Knorr-Bremse Sys.* 383 F.3d at 1344.

[172]*Knorr-Bremse Sys.*, 383 F.3d at 1351 (Dyk, J., concurring-in-part and dissenting-in-part). In his separate opinion Judge Dyk charged that the *en banc Knorr-Bremse* majority had not gone far enough. The majority should also have eliminated the duty of due care, Judge Dyk asserted, which effectively requires an accused infringer to prove a negative; that is, it shifts the burden of proof to the accused infringer to establish that its conduct was not willful. An infringer's failure to proceed with due care, without more, should not be enough to establish willfulness, Judge Dyk contended; rather, a court should require additional "bad acts" such as intentional copying before finding willfulness. In Judge Dyk's view, the *Knorr-Bremse* majority's retention of the duty of due care was inconsistent with Supreme Court decisions indicating that an award of punitive damages not based on truly reprehensible conduct may violate the

In addition to rejecting the adverse inference based on the nonproduction of an opinion of counsel, the *Knorr-Bremse* court also eliminated the drawing of any adverse inference from the fact of an accused infringer's not seeking legal counsel or advice upon notice of potential patent infringement. The *en banc* court left open, however, the question whether the fact finder could be told of the nonrepresentation; this undecided issue has obvious resonance in the jury trial context.[173]

The *Knorr-Bremse* court did not go so far as to hold that the existence of a substantial defense to infringement would negate willfulness, as some *amici* had urged. Rather, the existence of a substantial defense was but one factor to be considered in the multifactor "totality of the circumstances" analysis for willfulness, the standard previously set forth in *Read Corp. v. Portec, Inc.*, discussed *supra*.[174]

In 2007, the Federal Circuit again went *en banc* to consider willfulness. In *In re Seagate Technology, LLC*,[175] the court revisited its willfulness framework in light of the "practical concerns facing litigants under the current regime" as well as guidance from Supreme Court decisions rendered since the Circuit's 1983 decision in *Underwater Devices*.[176] The *Seagate* court announced a substantially heightened burden for a patentee seeking to establish that an accused infringer acted willfully. The court abandoned its earlier imposition of an affirmative duty of due care on accused infringers, rejecting this "negligence"-type standard as "fail[ing] to comport with the general understanding of willfulness in the civil context" and as "allow[ing] for punitive damages in a manner inconsistent with Supreme Court precedent."[177] In its place, the court adopted an objective standard for willfulness that requires "reckless" conduct by an accused infringer, stating

> we overrule the standard set out in *Underwater Devices* and hold that proof of willful infringement permitting enhanced damages requires at least a showing of objective recklessness. Because we abandon the

---

Due Process clause of the Constitution. Three years later, the Federal Circuit adopted Judge Dyk's view by abolishing the affirmative duty of due care in *In re Seagate Tech., LLC*, 497 F.3d 1360 (Fed. Cir. 2007) (*en banc*).

[173] A federal district court has held that even post-*Seagate*, a jury can be told that an accused infringer did not obtain an opinion letter from counsel. *See* Energy Transp. Group, Inc. v. William Demant Holding A/S, C.A. No. 05-422 GMS (D. Del. Jan. 7, 2008), http://65.36.194.206/mnat/documents/010708_Order_DI_493.pdf (rejecting defendant's contention that *Seagate* effected a change in the law such that failure to obtain advice of counsel cannot be considered by the jury, and concluding that "nothing in *Seagate* forbids a jury to consider whether a defendant obtained advice of counsel as part of the totality of the circumstances in determining willfulness").

[174] *See* Read Corp. v. Portec, Inc., 970 F.2d 816, 826-827 (Fed. Cir. 1992).

[175] 497 F.3d 1360 (Fed. Cir. 2007) (*en banc*).

[176] *Seagate*, 497 F.3d at 1370.

[177] *Seagate*, 497 F.3d at 1371 (citations omitted).

affirmative duty of due care, we also reemphasize that there is no affirmative obligation to obtain opinion of counsel.[178]

The *Seagate* court did not attempt to provide a comprehensive definition for objective recklessness, leaving this for further development in the case law. However, relying on the civil law's general definition of "reckless" conduct as acting "in the face of an unjustifiably high risk of harm that is either known or so obvious that it should be known,"[179] the Federal Circuit set forth the following two-part standard:

> [T]o establish willful infringement, a patentee must show by clear and convincing evidence that the infringer acted despite an objectively high likelihood that its actions constituted infringement of a valid patent. *See Safeco* [*Ins. Co. of Am. v. Burr*], 127 S. Ct. [2201,] 2215 ("It is [a] high risk of harm, objectively assessed, that is the essence of recklessness at common law."). The state of mind of the accused infringer is not relevant to this objective inquiry. If this threshold objective standard is satisfied, the patentee must also demonstrate that this objectively-defined risk (determined by the record developed in the infringement proceeding) was either known or so obvious that it should have been known to the accused infringer.[180]

In addition to reframing the standard for willful infringement, the Federal Circuit in *Seagate* considered the appropriate scope of waiver

---

[178]*Seagate*, 497 F.3d at 1371.

[179]*Seagate*, 497 F.3d at 1371 (citing tort law treatises).

[180]*Seagate*, 497 F.3d at 1371. Although the *Seagate* court left it to future cases to "further develop the application of this standard," *id.*, it agreed with the suggestion of concurring Judge Newman that "the standards of commerce would be among the factors a court might consider." *Id.* at 1371 n.5.

In cases after *Seagate,* the Federal Circuit has observed that *Seagate*'s threshold objective prong "'tends not to be met where an accused infringer relies on a reasonable defense to a charge of infringement.'" Advanced Fiber Techs. (AFT) Trust v. J & L Fiber Servs., Inc., 674 F.3d 1365, 1377 (Fed. Cir. 2012) (quoting Spine Solutions, Inc. v. Medtronic Sofamor Danek USA, Inc., 620 F.3d 1305, 1319 (Fed. Cir. 2010)). An example is *Advanced Fiber*, in which the Federal Circuit affirmed a district court's dismissal of patentee AFT's motion for summary judgment that defendant J & L had willfully infringed. The district court's dismissal was properly based on "numerous factors" indicating that the accused infringer's acts were not objectively reckless. *Advanced Fiber,* 674 F.3d at 1377. These factors included "(1) the language of [AFT's] '072 patent [in suit], which 'leaves significant doubt as to the patent's validity'; (2) J & L's 'compelling noninfringement and invalidity arguments'; (3) the PTO's initial 'rejection of [AFT's] reissue application based on it being "structurally indistinguishable" from the Gillespie [prior art patent]'; and (4) the fact that the meaning of certain key claim terms in the '072 patent only became clear through AFT's arguments during reissue prosecution." *Advanced Fiber,* 674 F.3d at 1377 (quoting Advanced Fiber Techs. Trust v. J & L Fiber Servs., Inc., 751 F. Supp. 2d 348, 380-381 (N.D.N.Y. 2010)). "Taken together, these facts show that J & L's assertions of invalidity and noninfringement were, at minimum, objectively reasonable defenses to AFT's charge of infringement." *Advanced Fiber,* 674 F.3d at 1377-1378.

of attorney-client privilege in willfulness cases. When an accused infringer asserts an advice of counsel defense in response to a patentee's charge of willful infringement, the scope of the resulting waiver of attorney-client privilege is typically put at issue. For example, after Convolve, Inc. and the Massachusetts Institute of Technology (collectively "Convolve") accused Seagate of willful infringement, Seagate notified Convolve that it intended to rely on three opinion letters Seagate had obtained concerning the patents in suit. Seagate made its opinion counsel available for deposition and disclosed all of that attorney's work product. In response to Convolve's motion, the district court ruled that the scope of Seagate's waiver extended beyond its communications with its opinion counsel to include all communications between Seagate and *any* counsel, including Seagate's trial counsel and its in-house counsel.[181]

The Federal Circuit rejected as a general matter the broad scope of waiver adopted by the district court in *Seagate*. Opinion counsel and trial counsel serve significantly different functions; the former provides an "objective assessment for making informed business decisions," while the latter develops litigation strategies as part of an adversarial process.[182] Moreover, communications of trial counsel have little relevance to pre-litigation conduct, upon which willfulness depends in ordinary circumstances.[183] Thus, the Federal Circuit held "as a general proposition [] that asserting the advice of counsel defense and disclosing opinions of opinion counsel do not constitute waiver of attorney-client privilege for communications with trial counsel."[184] Similarly, the appellate court held that waiver of opinion counsel's work product does not extend to waiver of trial counsel's work product, "absent exceptional circumstances."[185]

Willfulness was long considered a factual question amenable to jury determination. In 2012 the Federal Circuit concluded that the willfulness inquiry post-*Seagate* had become more complex than a single question of fact. The Federal Circuit held in *Bard Peripheral Vascular, Inc. v. W.L. Gore & Assoc., Inc.*[186] that the threshold objective prong of the willfulness standard enunciated in *Seagate* is a question of law based on underlying mixed questions of law and fact. A district court must determine the threshold objective prong, and its determination

[181]*See Seagate*, 497 F.3d at 1366-1367.
[182]*Seagate*, 497 F.3d at 1373.
[183]*See Seagate*, 497 F.3d at 1374.
[184]*See Seagate*, 497 F.3d at 1374. The Federal Circuit further explained that its announced rule on waiver was not absolute, and that "trial courts remain free to exercise their discretion in unique circumstances to extend waiver to trial counsel, such as if a party or counsel engages in chicanery." *Id.* at 1374-1375.
[185]*See Seagate*, 497 F.3d at 1375-1376.
[186]682 F.3d 1003 (Fed. Cir. 2012).

on that prong is subject to *de novo* review by the Federal Circuit.[187] Thus the *Bard Peripheral* court essentially reallocated the roles of the judge and jury in determining whether or not infringement of a patent is willful. The judge now determines whether a reasonable person would have found there to be a high likelihood of patent infringement.[188] If this threshold objective determination is met, only then does the jury determine the patent infringer's subjective intent.[189]

The America Invents Act of 2011 added a new section to the Patent Act in order to legislatively codify the holdings of *Seagate* and *Knorr-Bremse* regarding an accused infringer's failure to obtain advice of counsel.[190] Section 298 of the Patent Act provides:

§ 298. Advice of counsel

The failure of an infringer to obtain the advice of counsel with respect to any allegedly infringed patent, or the failure of the infringer to present such advice to the court or jury, may not be used to prove that the accused infringer willfully infringed the patent or that the infringer intended to induce infringement of the patent.[191]

The AIA's legislative history explains that the new §298 "is designed to protect attorney-client privilege and to reduce pressure on accused infringers to obtain opinions of counsel for litigation purposes. It reflects a policy choice that the probative value of this type of evidence is outweighed by the harm that coercing a waiver of attorney-client privilege inflicts on the attorney-client relationship."[192]

---

[187]*See Bard,* 682 at 1006-1007 (holding that "the objective determination of recklessness, even though predicated on underlying mixed questions of law and fact, is best decided by the judge as a question of law subject to *de novo* review").

[188]*See Bard,* 682 F.3d at 1008. The court explained that "[i]n considering the objective prong of *Seagate,* the judge may when the defense is a question of fact or a mixed question of law and fact allow the jury to determine the underlying facts relevant to the defense in the first instance, for example, the questions of anticipation or obviousness. But, consistent with this court's holding today, the ultimate legal question of whether a reasonable person would have considered there to be a high likelihood of infringement of a valid patent should always be decided as a matter of law by the judge." *Bard,* 682 F.3d at 1008.

[189]*See Bard,* 682 F.3d at 1008.

[190]*See* Leahy-Smith America Invents Act, Pub. L. No. 112-29 (H.R. 1249), §17, 125 Stat. 284, 329 (Sept. 16, 2011) ("Advice of Counsel") (amending Chapter 29 of 35 U.S.C. by adding at the chapter's end a new section designated §298).

[191]35 U.S.C. §298 (eff. Sept. 16, 2012). *See also* Leahy-Smith America Invents Act, Pub. L. No. 112-29 (H.R. 1249), §35, 125 Stat. 284, 341 (Sept. 16, 2011) ("Effective Date") (providing that "[except as otherwise provided in this Act, the provisions of this Act shall take effect upon the expiration of the 1-year period beginning on the date of the enactment of this Act and shall apply to any patent issued on or after that effective date").

[192]*See* H.R. Rep. No. 112-98 [House Judiciary Comm. Rep. on the America Invents Act], at 63 (June 1, 2011). The legislative history further explains that "Section 298 applies to findings of both willfulness and intent to induce infringement–and thus

E. Attorney Fees

When willful infringement has been found, patentees will frequently seek not only an award of enhanced damages under 35 U.S.C. §284 but also attorney fees under 35 U.S.C. §285. The two types of awards are not necessarily linked, however; the grant of one does not preclude the denial of the other.[193]

Section 285 of the Patent Act, titled "Attorney Fees," provides,

> The court in *exceptional* cases *may* award reasonable attorney fees to the prevailing party.[194]

---

legislatively abrogates the Federal Circuit's decision in *Broadcom Corp. v. Qualcomm Inc.*, 543 F.3d 683, 699 (Fed. Cir. 2008)." *Id.*

In the *Broadcom* litigation referenced by the AIA legislative history, a jury found Qualcomm liable for direct and inducing infringement of Broadcom's patents, and further found that Qualcomm's infringement was willful. *See* Broadcom Corp. v. Qualcomm Inc., 543 F.3d 683 (Fed. Cir. 2008). The jury had been instructed that

> considering whether QUALCOMM acted in good faith, you should consider all the circumstances, including whether or not QUALCOMM obtained and followed the advice of a competent lawyer with regard to infringement. The absence of a lawyer's opinion, by itself, is insufficient to support a finding of willfulness, and *you may not assume that merely because a party did not obtain an opinion of counsel, the opinion would have been unfavorable.* However, you may consider whether QUALCOMM sought a legal opinion as one factor in assessing whether, under the totality of the circumstances, any infringement by QUALCOMM was willful.

Broadcom, 543 F.3d at 698 (emphasis added by the Federal Circuit).

On appeal, accused infringer Qualcomm argued that that the district court erred in allowing the inducing infringement verdicts to stand in light of the quoted jury instruction. Qualcomm asserted that the instruction improperly permitted the jury to consider failure to obtain an opinion of counsel as a factor in determining whether Qualcomm had the requisite level of intent for inducing infringement liability. The Federal Circuit disagreed, approving the jury instruction and sustaining the verdict of inducing infringement. The appellate court held that opinion of counsel evidence remains relevant to establishing the intent element of inducing infringement and that "the failure to procure such an opinion may be probative of intent in this context." *Broadcom,* 543 F.3d at 699. The Federal Circuit reasoned that "[i]t would be manifestly unfair to allow opinion-of-counsel evidence to serve an exculpatory function, as was the case in [the inducing infringement decision, *DSU Med. Corp. v. JMS Co.*, 471 F.3d 1293, 1307 (Fed. Cir. 2006) (*en banc* in relevant part)], and yet not permit patentees to identify failures to procure such advice as circumstantial evidence of intent to infringe." *Broadcom,* 543 F.3d at 699.

By legislatively overruling the *Broadcom* holding, the AIA-implemented §298 of the Patent Act clarifies that an accused infringer's failure to obtain advice of counsel may not be used to establish the intent required for inducing infringement liability. Inducing infringement and its intent requirement are further discussed *supra* Chapter 9, Section E.1 ("Inducing Infringement Under [35 U.S.C.] §271(b)").

[193]*See* Advanced Cardiovascular Sys. v. Medtronic, Inc., 265 F.3d 1294, 1303 (Fed. Cir. 2001) (affirming district court decision in which damages were enhanced based on jury finding of willful infringement but attorney fees were denied).

[194]35 U.S.C. §285 (emphasis added).

A finding by a district court that a case is "exceptional" under §285 may be based on the defendant's willful infringement, which also may support an enhancement of damages under §284. However, an exceptional case determination can be based on conduct other than willful infringement, such as the litigation misconduct of either party, or on the patentee's inequitable conduct in the procurement of the patent in suit,[195] or on "vexatious or unjustified litigation, or a frivolous suit."[196]

Since the statutory language is permissive rather than mandatory, a finding that a case is exceptional need not compel a court to award attorney fees to the prevailing party. However, the Federal Circuit has adopted a general rule that when willful infringement has been found, a district court that decides a case is nevertheless not exceptional under 35 U.S.C. §285 should explain why it is not.[197] Similarly, if the district court concludes that a case is exceptional under §285 but refuses to award attorney fees, it must normally explain that decision as well. The court recognizes an exception to these rules, however, where the record sets forth adequate grounds for affirming the district court's decision making.[198]

Attorney fees can be awarded under 35 U.S.C. §285 only to the "prevailing party." In *Gentry Gallery v. Berkline Corp.*,[199] the Federal Circuit affirmed a district court's ruling that the patent in suit was not infringed, and the accused infringer Berkline Corp. had not proved the patent invalid. Under these circumstances, the patentee Gentry Gallery was not a "prevailing party," and thus did not qualify for an award of attorney fees under §285. Merely overcoming a defense does not elevate a party to prevailing status; the party must obtain some affirmative relief, for example, an injunction or damages for the patentee, in order to be considered prevailing for attorney fee purposes.[200]

F. Prejudgment Interest

Prejudgment interest (sometimes referred to as "delay compensation") is awarded under 35 U.S.C. §284[201] in order to make the patentee

---

[195]*See* A.B. Chance Co. v. RTE Corp., 854 F.2d 1307, 1312 (Fed. Cir. 1988) (stating that patentee's inequitable conduct, either alone or in conjunction with its trial misconduct, may constitute the basis for an award of attorney fees under 35 U.S.C. §285).

[196]Standard Oil Co. v. American Cyanamid Co., 774 F.2d 448, 455 (Fed. Cir. 1985).

[197]*See* Transclean Corp. v. Bridgewood Servs., Inc., 290 F.3d 1364, 1379 (Fed. Cir. 2002).

[198]*See Transclean Corp.*, 290 F.3d at 1379.

[199]134 F.3d 1473 (Fed. Cir. 1998).

[200]*See Gentry Gallery*, 134 F.3d at 1480.

[201]"Upon finding for the claimant the court shall award the claimant damages adequate to compensate for the infringement, . . . , together with *interest* and costs as fixed by the court." 35 U.S.C. §284, ¶1 (emphasis added).

whole, by compensating it for "the forgone use of the money [owed by the infringer to the patentee] between the time of infringement and the date of the judgment."[202] In other words, had the infringer paid the infringement damages (in the form of reasonable royalties or lost profits) to the patentee at the time they were actually incurred (i.e., the time of the infringement), the patentee presumably could have earned interest by investing this money. An award of prejudgment interest attempts to approximate the interest that the patentee would have earned during the period of time between the infringement and the judgment.[203] The U.S. Supreme Court has provided that "pre-judgment interest should ordinarily be awarded."[204]

The Federal Circuit has held that prejudgment interest is available only for that portion of a damages award representing compensatory (actual) damages, not for any portion representing enhanced damages.[205]

In *Sanofi-Aventis v. Apotex Inc.*,[206] the Federal Circuit interpreted a settlement agreement between two parties involved in a long-running Hatch-Waxman dispute over patented clopidogrel bisulfate tablets. The agreement provided that if the U.S. Food and Drug Administration denied generic manufacturer Apotex's Abbreviated New Drug Application (ANDA), the previously stayed litigation between the parties would resume and "[i]f the litigation results in a judgment that [Sanofi's] '265 patent is not invalid or unenforceable, Sanofi agrees that its *actual damages* for any past infringement by Apotex, up to the date on which Apotex is enjoined, *will be 50% of Apotex's net sales* of clopidogrel products."[207] Under the facts of the case and applying New York state contract law, the Federal Circuit concluded that the patentee's agreement to limit itself to "actual damages" foreclosed any award of prejudgment interest. In the Federal Circuit's view, "the parties intended that the phrase 'actual damages' include all dam-

---

[202]General Motors Corp. v. Devex Corp., 461 U.S. 648, 656 (1983).

[203]*See* Whitserve v. Computer Packages, Inc., Nos. 2011–1206, 2011–1261, __ F.3d __, 2012 WL 3573845, at *18 (Fed. Cir. Aug. 7, 2012) ("An award of prejudgment interest carries out Congress's 'overriding purpose of affording patent owners complete compensation' since a patentee's damages also include the 'forgone use of the money between the time of infringement and the date of judgment.'") (quoting *General Motors Corp.*, 461 U.S. at 655–656).

[204]*General Motors Corp*, 461 U.S. at 655. *See also Whitserve*, 2012 WL 3573845 at *18 (holding that when district court judge specifically instructed jury that it could 'not award any interest on any damages,' "[t]he jury's award could not, accordingly, constitute compensation for interest and the trial court abused its discretion in denying prejudgment interest without further analysis or justification").

[205]*See* Underwater Devices, Inc. v. Morrison-Knudsen Co., 717 F.2d 1380, 1389 (Fed. Cir. 1983).

[206]659 F.3d 1171 (Fed. Cir. 2011).

[207]*Sanofi-Aventis,* 659 F.3d at 1177 (emphasis added).

ages necessary to compensate Sanofi for Apotex's infringement."[208] Prejudgment interest is a form of compensatory damages under 35 U.S.C. §284. Hence the "50% of net sales" figure referred to in the agreement was Sanofi's full measure of damages. The Federal Circuit accordingly vacated the district court's award of approximately $108 million in prejudgment interest.[209]

Rather surprisingly, there is no statutorily mandated interest rate for the award of prejudgment interest in U.S. patent cases. The issue of the proper interest rate and method of compounding are separately litigated in each case where interest is awarded. District courts have substantial discretion in determining the interest rate to be applied, as well as whether simple or compounded interest should be awarded.[210]

G. Costs

The availability of "costs" under 35 U.S.C. §284[211] refers to Fed. R. Civ. P. 54(d)(1), which creates a presumption that a prevailing party shall be awarded costs.[212] The types of expenses that a federal court may award as costs under its Rule 54(d)(1) discretionary authority are listed in 28 U.S.C. §1920, and include fees for the court reporter, witnesses, court appointed experts, copying costs, and the like.

The Federal Circuit has adopted a choice-of-law rule in which the court applies its own law, rather than that of the regional circuit for the geographic territory from which a case arose, to define the meaning of prevailing party in the context of an award of costs in patent litigation.[213] In *Manildra Milling Corp. v. Ogilvie Mills, Inc.*,[214] the issue was whether a declaratory judgment plaintiff that "receive[d] no money damages at all but instead 'receive[d] a hard fought declaration that

---

[208]*Sanofi-Aventis*, 659 F.3d at 1178.

[209]*Sanofi-Aventis*, 659 F.3d at 1176. The district court had reached that amount by starting with 50 percent of the patentee's net sales of the patented product over an approximately four-year period during 2006-2010, then computing prejudgment interest on that figure at the average annual prime rate, compounded quarterly. *See id.* at 1176 n.2.

[210]*See* Gyromat Corp. v. Champion Spark Plug Co., 735 F.2d 549, 556-557 (Fed. Cir. 1984).

[211]"Upon finding for the claimant the court shall award the claimant damages adequate to compensate for the infringement, . . . , together with interest and *costs* as fixed by the court." 35 U.S.C. §284, ¶1 (emphasis added).

[212]*See* Manildra Milling Corp. v. Ogilvie Mills, Inc., 76 F.3d 1178 (Fed. Cir. 1996) (holding that declaratory judgment plaintiff that successfully invalidated patent was a prevailing party for purposes of awarding costs in accordance with Fed. R. Civ. P. 54(d) (1), and affirming award of approximately $83,000 in costs).

[213]*See Manildra Milling Corp.*, 76 F.3d at 1181-1182.

[214]76 F.3d 1178 (Fed. Cir. 1996).

its competitor's patents are invalid,' and survive[d] the competitor's counterclaim for $17 million in patent infringement damages,"[215] was a prevailing party for purposes of awarding costs. Although the declaratory judgment plaintiff, Manildra Milling, failed to prevail on its claims under the Sherman (Antitrust) Act, the Lanham (Trademark) Act, and state common law claims, its victory on the patent issues was "complete." In the Federal Circuit's view, such a victory qualified Manildra Milling as a "prevailing party,"[216] entitling it to an award of costs of approximately $83,000.[217]

H. Patent Marking

The U.S. Patent Act strongly encourages (but does not require) patentees and/or those who manufacture, sell, offer to sell, or import patented articles for them to mark the articles with the corresponding U.S. patent number(s).[218] This is why many patented items sold in the marketplace bear a patent number, either on the items themselves or on their packaging. The purpose of the marking provisions of the Patent Act is to provide the public with some degree of notice of patent rights (albeit an imperfect degree, because marking is optional). In order to accomplish this purpose, §287(a) of Title 35 provides that without adequate marking, "no damages shall be recovered by the patentee in any action for infringement, except on proof that the infringer was notified of the infringement and continued to infringe thereafter, in which event damages may be recovered only for infringement occurring after such notice."[219] The filing of the infringement lawsuit

---

[215]*Manildra Milling Corp.*, 76 F.3d at 1182-1183.

[216]*See Manildra Milling Corp.*, 76 F.3d at 1183 (holding that "as a matter of law, a party who has a competitor's patent declared invalid meets the definition of 'prevailing party'").

[217]*See Manildra Milling Corp.*, 76 F.3d at 1180.

[218]The statute provides in part,

Patentees, and persons making, offering for sale, or selling within the United States any patented article for or under them, or importing any patented article into the United States, may give notice to the public that the same is patented, either by fixing thereon the word "patent" or the abbreviation "pat.", together with the number of the patent, or by fixing thereon the word "patent" or the abbreviation "pat." together with an address of a posting on the Internet, accessible to the public without charge for accessing the address, that associates the patented article with the number of the patent, or when, from the character of the article, this cannot be done, by fixing to it, or to the package wherein one or more of them is contained, a label containing a like notice.

35 U.S.C. §287(a) (eff. Sept. 16, 2011).

[219]35 U.S.C. §287(a).

constitutes notice.[220] Thus, notice under §287 can be constructive notice, through marking the patent number on the patented product, or actual notice, through certain communications with the infringer or the actual filing of the lawsuit.[221] In cases where the patented articles were not marked and no other notice was given to the accused infringer, the operation of §287 means that the patentee will not be able to recover any damages for infringements that occurred prior to the filing of the lawsuit.

A number of Federal Circuit decisions address whether particular prefiling communications between patentees and accused infringers established that the "infringer was notified of the infringement" within the meaning of 35 U.S.C. §287(a) so as to start the damages recovery period. The fact that an accused infringer was merely aware of or even possessed a copy of the patent allegedly infringed is not sufficient, without more, to satisfy §287.[222] As the Federal Circuit explained in *Amsted Indus. v. Buckeye Steel Castings Co.*,[223] the determination of notice under 35 U.S.C. §287 "must focus on the action of the patentee, not the knowledge or understanding of the infringer."[224] In order to meet §287's actual notice requirement, an "affirmative communication [to the alleged infringer] of a specific charge of infringement by a specific accused product or device" is required.[225] This standard was not met in *Amsted Indus.* by a letter that notified the entire industry, including the accused infringer, only of the patentee's ownership of the patent and generally advised companies not to infringe.[226]

The §287(a) marking statute does not apply to patents that claim only processes or methods,[227] because in such cases there is usually no tangible article to mark; the marking provisions may be applicable to patents that include both method and apparatus claims, however.[228]

Section 292 of the Patent Act, titled "False Marking," provides that a fine of $500 per offense shall be assessed against those who, without the consent of the patent owner, intentionally mark the patentee's

---

[220]35 U.S.C. §287(a).

[221]*See* Gart v. Logitech, Inc., 254 F.3d 1334, 1345 (Fed. Cir. 2001).

[222]*See* Amsted Indus. v. Buckeye Steel Castings Co., 24 F.3d 178, 187 (Fed. Cir. 1994).

[223]24 F.3d 178 (Fed. Cir. 1994).

[224]*Amsted Indus.*, 24 F.3d at 187.

[225]*Amsted Indus.*, 24 F.3d at 187.

[226]*See Amsted Indus.*, 24 F.3d at 187.

[227]*See* American Med. Sys., Inc. v. Medical Eng'g Corp., 6 F.3d 1523, 1538 (Fed. Cir. 1993).

[228]*See American Med.*, 6 F.3d at 1538 (stating that "[w]here the patent contains both apparatus and method claims, however, to the extent that there is a tangible item to mark by which notice of the asserted method claims can be given, a party is obliged to do so if it intends to avail itself of the constructive notice provisions of section 287(a)").

name or its patent number on their own products.[229] The false marking penalty also applies to those who intentionally mark "patent" or "patent pending" on articles that are not patented or for which no patent application has been filed.[230]

Following a 2009 Federal Circuit decision holding that the $500 fine is assessed for *each article* falsely marked,[231] the federal district courts confronted a surge of false marking *qui tam* actions brought by third parties having no relation to the owners of the patents involved. In many instances, the *qui tam* plaintiffs sued when a patent covering a product expired but the patent owner continued to sell the product without removing the patent number.[232] In the America Invents Act of 2011, Congress amended the false marking statute to eliminate such *qui tam* lawsuits. Effective Sept. 16, 2011, only the United States government, not private individuals, can sue for the false marking penalty.[233]

---

[229]*See* 35 U.S.C. §292(a) ¶1 (2012) (providing that "[w]hoever, without the consent of the patentee, marks upon, or affixes to, or uses in advertising in connection with anything made, used, offered for sale, or sold by such person within the United States, or imported by the person into the United States, the name or any imitation of the name of the patentee, the patent number, or the words 'patent,' 'patentee,' or the like, with the intent of counterfeiting or imitating the mark of the patentee, or of deceiving the public and inducing them to believe that the thing was made, offered for sale, sold, or imported into the United States by or with the consent of the patentee . . . [s]hall be fined not more than $ 500 for every such offense").

[230]*See* 35 U.S.C. §292(a) ¶¶2-3 (2012) (providing that "[w]hoever marks upon, or affixes to, or uses in advertising in connection with any unpatented article, the word 'patent' or any word or number importing that the same is patented, for the purpose of deceiving the public; or [w]hoever marks upon, or affixes to, or uses in advertising in connection with any article, the words 'patent applied for,' 'patent pending,' or any word importing that an application for patent has been made, when no application for patent has been made, or if made, is not pending, for the purpose of deceiving the public — [s]hall be fined not more than $500 for every such offense").

[231]*See* Forest Group, Inc. v. Bon Tool Co., 590 F.3d 1295, 1301 (Fed. Cir. 2009) (concluding that "the statute clearly requires that each article that is falsely marked with intent to deceive constitutes an offense under 35 U.S.C. § 292").

[232]*See* H.R. Rep. No. 112-98 [House Judiciary Comm. Rep. on the America Invents Act], at 62 (June 1, 2011) (observing that "a recent survey of such suits found that a large majority involved valid patents that covered the products in question but had simply expired. For many products, it is difficult and expensive to change a mold or other means by which a product is marked as patented, and marked products continue to circulate in commerce for some period after the patent expires. It is doubtful that the Congress that originally enacted this section anticipated that it would force manufacturers to immediately remove marked products from commerce once the patent expired, given that the expense to manufacturers of doing so will generally greatly outweigh any conceivable harm of allowing such products to continue to circulate in commerce.").

[233]*See* Leahy-Smith America Invents Act, Pub. L. No. 112-29 (H.R. 1249), §16(b) (1), 125 Stat. 284, 329 (Sept. 16, 2011) ("Civil Penalty") (amending 35 U.S.C. §292(a) to add at end of subsection (a) that "[o]nly the United States may sue for the penalty

I. Provisional Compensation Remedy

The American Inventors Protection Act of 1999 (AIPA)[234] created a new remedy for violation of patent-related rights. A U.S. patentee is now entitled to retroactively seek damages for infringement of the claims that appeared in its published patent application,[235] when that infringement occurred on or after the date of publication of the pending application by the USPTO but prior to patent issuance. Pursuant to 35 U.S.C. §154(d), the provisional compensation remedy is limited to a reasonable royalty.

Since passage of the AIPA, U.S. patent applicants have possessed the ability to "opt out" of automatic publication of their applications at 18 months after filing by attesting that they will not seek to patent the same invention in other countries.[236] Some U.S. applicants may want to exercise their option to avoid 18-month publication on the ground that there is no way to *enjoin* another who makes, uses, sells, offers to sell, or imports the subject matter of the published claims before the application has issued as a patent. The provisional compensation remedy creates an alternative remedy—a retroactive right to damages in the form of a reasonable royalty—that is intended to protect patent applicants from unchecked preissuance infringement and to encourage publication of their pending applications.

In order to qualify for the provisional compensation remedy of §154(d), the invention as claimed in the issued patent must be "substantially identical" to the invention as claimed in the published patent

---

authorized by this subsection"). Also permitted are civil actions by persons (such as patent owners) who can prove a "competitive injury" resulting from false marking. *See* Leahy-Smith America Invents Act, Pub. L. No. 112-29 (H.R. 1249), §16(b)(2), 125 Stat. 284, 329 (Sept. 16, 2011) ("Civil Action for Damages") (adding to 35 U.S.C. §292 a new subsection (b) authorizing such suits in federal district courts "for recovery of damages adequate to compensate for the injury"). Lastly, Congress clarified that the false marking statute is not violated by the marking of a product with an expired patent number that once covered the product. *See* Leahy-Smith America Invents Act, Pub. L. No. 112-29 (H.R. 1249), §16(b)(3), 125 Stat. 284, 329 (Sept. 16, 2011) ("Expired Patents") (adding to 35 U.S.C. §292 a new subsection (c) providing that "[t]he marking of a product, in a manner described in subsection (a), with matter relating to a patent that covered that product but has expired is not a violation of this section"). These AIA amendments took effect for "all cases, without exception, that [we]re pending on, or commenced on or after, the date of the enactment of this Act [September 16, 2011]." Leahy-Smith America Invents Act, Pub. L. No. 112-29 (H.R. 1249), §16(b)(4), 125 Stat. 284, 329 (Sept. 16, 2011).

[234]Pub. L. No. 106-113 (Nov. 29, 1999).

[235]Pending U.S. patent applications are now published 18 months after their effective filing dates unless certain exceptions apply. *See* 35 U.S.C. §122(b) (2012).

[236]*See* 35 U.S.C. §122(b)(2)(B).

application.[237] The statute does not define "substantially identical,"[238] but the phrase is a term of art in reissue and reexamination practice,[239] so the courts may look to such cases for guidance in interpreting 35 U.S.C. §154(d). Professor Chisum has observed that

> [t]he "substantially identical" standard will undoubtedly create difficult issues. If prosecution of an application is not substantially complete by the time [of] the publication, the claims in the application may be amended by the addition of narrowing limitations. The claims may also be broadened. To take full advantage of the provisional right, an applicant must take care to include claims of adequate scope in the application as it is published.[240]

Moreover, in order for the patentee to recover a reasonable royalty under §154(d), the alleged infringer must have had "actual notice" of the patentee's published patent application;[241] again, the statute does not define "actual notice," leaving the courts to interpret the phrase based on case law experience.[242]

Compensation for violation of provisional rights cannot be sought unless and until the patent issues. Thus, 35 U.S.C. §154(d) creates a retroactive remedy. The statute also creates a six-year post-issuance limitation on actions to recover damages for violation of provisional rights.[243] This is a true statute of limitations, in contrast with the temporal limitation on recovery of damages under 35 U.S.C. §286.[244]

One of the first court decisions to award reasonable royalties under §154(d) is *Parker-Hannifin Corp. v. Champion Labs., Inc.*[245] The patent in suit covered oil filter assemblies for vehicles, and it was undisputed that the defendant, a former customer of the patentee, sold over 100,000 infringing filters during the provisional compensation right period. At issue was the appropriate reasonable royalty to award the patentee

[237]35 U.S.C. §154(d)(2).

[238]Section 154(d)(2) provides that "[t]he right under paragraph (1) to obtain a reasonable royalty shall not be available under this subsection unless the invention as claimed in the patent is substantially identical to the invention as claimed in the published patent application."

[239]Reexamination and reissue are discussed *supra* Chapter 8 ("Correcting and Challenging Issued Patents in the USPTO").

[240]DONALD S. CHISUM, 4-11 CHISUM ON PATENTS §11.02[4][e] n.145 (2008).

[241]*See* 35 U.S.C. §154(d)(1)(B).

[242]Most likely, the courts will look to the meaning of "notice" as developed in the patent marking cases under 35 U.S.C. §287(a).

[243]*See* 35 U.S.C. §154(d)(3).

[244]Section 286 of 35 U.S.C., titled "Time limitation on damages," provides in part that "[e]xcept as otherwise provided by law, no recovery shall be had for any infringement committed more than six years prior to the filing of the complaint or counterclaim for infringement in the action."

[245]No. 1:06-CV-2616, 2008 WL 3166318 (N.D. Ohio Aug. 4, 2008).

for violation of its provisional compensation right. The district court applied the 15 *Georgia Pacific* factors discussed *supra* to hypothesize a license negotiation between the patentee and the accused infringer.[246] The district court concluded that the parties would have conducted this negotiation at the beginning of the provisional rights period, when the patentee's "rights vested under the Patent Act."[247] The district court did not consider whether any uncertainty at that date concerning whether a patent would ultimately issue (with claims the same or substantially identical to those that had been published) might have impacted the hypothetical license negotiation. The district court also determined that the reasonable royalty for the provisional compensation right period should *not* be capped by the accused infringer's cost of designing around the patent, that is, the cost of implementing its own noninfringing alternative.[248]

[246]*See supra* Section D.2.c.1 ("Hypothetical Negotiation"), discussing factors enumerated in *Georgia Pacific Corp. v. United States Plywood Corp.*, 318 F. Supp. 1116 (S.D.N.Y. 1970).

[247]*See Parker-Hannifin*, 2008 WL 3166318, at *9. The provisional rights period began on June 16, 2005; the USPTO's Notice of Allowance was received on September 12, 2005, and the patent in suit issued on January 10, 2006. The district court rejected the accused infringer's argument that the Notice of Allowance date would have been the proper date for the hypothetical negotiation. *See id.*

[248]On this point the district court relied on *Mars, Inc. v. Coin Acceptors, Inc.*, 527 F.3d 1359, 1373 (Fed. Cir. 2008) (characterizing as "wrong as a matter of law" accused infringer's claim that "reasonable royalty damages are capped at the cost of implementing the cheapest available, acceptable, noninfringing alternative"). *See Parker-Hannifin*, 2008 WL 3166318, at *7-*8.

Chapter 12

International Patenting Issues

A. Introduction

The rise of global commerce requires that U.S. patent attorneys possess not only a thorough understanding of domestic patent law, but also an overall familiarity with the substance and procedure for obtaining and enforcing patent rights worldwide. Many of the fundamental aspects of patentability and infringement previously described in this text are approached differently by foreign patent systems. This chapter introduces the key distinctions. It also summarizes the primary multinational treaties, conventions, and agreements that simplify the task of protecting an invention in multiple countries around the world. The primary provisions of U.S. patent law that implement these treaties will be described. Size constraints limit the scope of this final chapter; however, a number of useful reference works provide a more detailed treatment of international and comparative patent law.[1]

1. Territorial Scope of Patents

Fundamentally, it must be understood that patents are national, not international, in scope. Patents are generally not enforced

---

[1]*See* ARNOLD & SIEDSMA, MANUAL FOR THE HANDLING OF APPLICATIONS FOR PATENTS, DESIGNS AND TRADEMARKS THROUGHOUT THE WORLD (Wolters Kluwer Supp. 2012); J. W. BAXTER & JOHN P. SINNOTT, WORLD PATENT LAW AND PRACTICE (Matthew Bender 1998); GRAEME B. DINWOODIE ET AL., INTERNATIONAL AND COMPARATIVE PATENT LAW (Matthew Bender 2002); PAUL GOLDSTEIN, INTERNATIONAL INTELLECTUAL PROPERTY LAW, CASES AND MATERIALS (Foundation Press 2008); MARSHALL A. LEAFFER, INTERNATIONAL TREATIES ON INTELLECTUAL PROPERTY (BNA 2d ed. 1997); MICHAEL N. MELLER, INTERNATIONAL PATENT LITIGATION: A COUNTRY-BY-COUNTRY ANALYSIS (BNA Supp. 2011); R. Carl Moy, *The History of the Patent Harmonization Treaty: Economic Self-Interest as an Influence*, 26 J. MARSHALL L. REV. 457 (1993); TOSHIKO TAKENAKA, ED., PATENT LAW AND THEORY: A HANDBOOK OF CONTEMPORARY RESEARCH (Edward Elgar 2009).

extraterritorially.[2] This means that the patentee's right to exclude others is extinguished at the geographic borders of the granting country. For example, the owner of a U.S. patent cannot rely on that U.S. patent to stop an unauthorized third party from copying and selling the invention in Japan.[3] Rather, she must obtain a Japanese patent on her invention and enforce the Japanese patent against the infringer, most likely in the courts of Japan.[4]

Consequently, the title of this chapter, which refers to "international patenting," is something of a misnomer. Currently there is no such thing as an international patent, at least in any form other than academic proposals. There are, however, a number of international treaties, conventions, and agreements that make it much easier to obtain patent protection in multiple countries. Understanding the historical background and economic context in which these various agreements were enacted is necessary to understanding the present system of multinational patenting.

---

[2]The negative property right conveyed by a U.S. patent grant is statutorily limited to prohibiting acts of infringement that occur within the United States. See 35 U.S.C. §154(a) (2008) (providing that U.S. patent conveys "the right to exclude others from making, using, offering for sale, or selling the invention *throughout the United States* or importing the invention *into the United States*, and, if the invention is a process, of the right to exclude others from using, offering for sale or selling *throughout the United States*, or importing *into the United States*, products made by that process") (emphases added). For scholarly analysis of territoriality in intellectual property law, *see* Curtis A. Bradley, *Territorial Intellectual Property Rights in an Age of Globalism*, 37 VA. J. INT'L L. 505 (1997).

Given the rise of global commerce and the increasingly complicated and expensive nature of enforcing patent rights to a given invention on a worldwide basis, some scholars have called for a reevaluation of U.S. patent law's traditional territorial view. *See, e.g.,* Timothy R. Holbrook, *Extraterritoriality in U.S. Patent Law*, 49 WM. & MARY L. REV. 2119 (2008) (advocating that U.S. courts consider enforcing U.S. patents extraterritorially if an explicit analysis of a relevant foreign jurisdiction's patent laws indicates that infringement has occurred there and that extraterritorial enforcement of the U.S. patent would not conflict with the foreign jurisdiction's laws).

[3]*See* Microsoft Corp. v. AT&T Corp., 550 U.S. 437, 441 (2007) ("It is the general rule under United States patent law that no infringement occurs when a patented product is made and sold in another country."). Section 271(f) of Title 35, U.S.C., which prohibits the export for assembly abroad of components of an invention patented in the U.S., is an exception to the general rule. *See id.; supra* Chapter 9.E.4 ("Component Exports under 35 U.S.C. §271(f)").

[4]Alternatively, if the patent holder is already litigating infringement of her U.S. patent in a U.S. court, she may request that the U.S. court exercise supplemental jurisdiction under 28 U.S.C. §1367 to adjudicate her claim of infringement of a counterpart Japanese patent. The Federal Circuit has thus far rejected such attempts, however. *See* Section G ("Enforcement of Foreign Patents in U.S. Courts"), *infra*.

2. Obtaining Foreign Patent Protection Prior to the Paris Convention

The Paris Convention for the Protection of Industrial Property (Paris Convention),[5] which entered into force in 1883, was the first truly international agreement concerning industrial property (i.e., patents, trademarks, and industrial designs). The Paris Convention created important rights for nationals[6] of member countries that made it much easier for those persons to obtain patents in multiple countries. The complexities of multinational patenting prior to the Paris Convention's enactment demonstrate why this treaty was such an important advance.

Before the Paris Convention, it was extremely difficult and expensive to obtain patent protection for the same invention in different countries. Some countries (e.g., Country A) considered an application filed on the same invention in another country (e.g., Country B) *even one day* before the filing of the application in Country A to be prior art that would destroy the novelty of the invention under the patent law of Country A. Thus, patent applicants had to arrange to file multiple applications on the same invention in multiple countries *on the same day*. The cost and complexity of accomplishing this, particularly before the invention of the telephone, fax machine, and Internet, are self-evident.

Prior to enactment of the Paris Convention, the various national patent systems differed in some very fundamental aspects of substantive patent law. For example, the United States did not substantively examine patent applications for novelty between 1793 and 1836. France did not do so until the 1960s. Italy, for a time, examined only those patent applications that were related to foods and beverages. Many of the world's developing and least-developed countries refused to grant patents altogether on pharmaceuticals or agricultural inventions.[7]

Procedures for prosecuting patents also varied widely between countries. Patent applications were published at varying times. Some

---

[5]Paris Convention for the Protection of Industrial Property, Mar. 20, 1883, as revised at Stockholm, July 14, 1967, 21 U.S.T. 1583, 828 U.N.T.S. 305, *available at* http://www.wipo.int/treaties/en/ip/paris (as amended Sept. 28, 1979).

[6]In international law terms, a "national" of a country is generally considered to be a natural or legal person who is domiciled or who has a commercial establishment in the country in question (generally referred to as a "state" in international law). Nationality is broader than and should be distinguished from citizenship. "A citizen under national law is generally a national for purposes of international law, but in some states not all nationals are citizens." RESTATEMENT (THIRD) OF THE FOREIGN RELATIONS LAW OF THE UNITED STATES §211, cmt. h (1987).

[7]*See, e.g.*, Janice M. Mueller, *The Tiger Awakens: The Tumultuous Transformation of India's Patent System and the Rise of Indian Pharmaceutical Innovation*, 68 UNIV. PITT. L. REV. 491 (2007).

countries published patent specifications immediately upon the filing of an application, others during the application's pendency, and some countries (such as the United States) did not publish the content of patent applications at all prior to the patent grant.[8]

By the late 1800s, national governments and economists determined that these differences between national patent systems could be used as tools to manipulate national wealth. More specifically, they realized that granting patents to foreign nationals generally results in a net outflow of national wealth.[9]

To understand why this is so, consider the example of a U.S. national who obtains a U.S. patent on her invention, a useful, novel, and nonobvious widget. The price of the widget that the U.S. national can obtain in the marketplace will reflect the fact that the widget is covered by patent, which price we would expect to be higher than if the widget were not patented and could be made and sold by multiple competing parties.[10] In this domestic patenting scenario the link between the costs and benefits of the government's decision to grant patent rights to its own national is relatively tight. Presumably the sales revenues received by the U.S. national will be reinvested domestically, to fund the construction of additional widget factories in the United States or to further U.S.-based research and development in widgets. This business expansion will likely employ other U.S. nationals.

In contrast, when a country makes the decision to grant a patent to a foreign national, the link between cost and benefits is significantly weakened or decoupled. For example, consider a national of Germany who obtains a U.S. patent on her widget. The royalties obtained by the German national from the U.S. sales of her widget will generally be invested not in the U.S. economy but rather in the economy of Germany, the foreign national's home country. Thus, the domestic economy of the granting country generally does not benefit from awarding patent rights to foreign nationals to the same degree that it would have, had patent rights been granted to a national of the granting country.[11]

As national governments realized the economic impact of granting patent protection to foreigners, they began to implement in their laws

---

[8]Historically, the United States did not publish the contents of pending patent applications prior to the patent grant. With the enactment of the American Inventors Protection Act of 1999, however, the majority of patent applications are made public at 18 months after the application's earliest priority date. *See* 35 U.S.C. §122(b).

[9]Much of this section is based on the observations in R. Carl Moy, *The History of the Patent Harmonization Treaty: Economic Self-Interest as an Influence*, 26 J. Marshall L. Rev. 457 (1993).

[10]*See supra* Chapter 1 ("Foundations of the U.S. Patent System") for a general discussion of the economics of patenting.

[11]Of course, the granting country gains some minor economic benefits in the form of the filing and maintenance fees paid to its national patent office and any taxes levied by the granting country on sales of the patented product made in that country.

various protectionist measures that were intended to reduce these costs. Such measures made patenting by foreigners less attractive by decreasing the value of the patents obtained and thus reducing the outflow of national wealth. These measures discriminated against foreign nationals, either expressly or, in some cases, in application even though the provisions were facially neutral.

A pre–America Invents Act of 2011 (AIA) provision of the Patent Act, 35 U.S.C. §104 (2006), is an example of a law that, at least initially, discriminated widely against foreign inventors. Prior to its amendments in connection with U.S. participation in the World Trade Organization (WTO) and the North American Free Trade Agreement (NAFTA), §104 prohibited the admission of evidence into USPTO interference proceedings[12] (and *ex parte* prior art antedating procedures) of inventive activity (such as conception, diligence, reduction to practice) that took place in any foreign country. Under this earlier version of 35 U.S.C. §104, even if a foreign inventor made an invention in her home country before a U.S. inventor independently made the same invention in the United States, the foreign inventor would not be allowed to rely on her earlier home country activity in order to prevail in an interference with the U.S. inventor. As a result, the U.S. inventor would be awarded the patent on the invention, even though the U.S. inventor was not the first to invent on a worldwide basis.[13]

Examples of facially neutral measures that were discriminatory in application included "working requirements." A working requirement mandates that a patentee "work" (or practice) the patent in the granting country; that is, the patentee is obligated to manufacture and/or sell the patented invention in the granting country. While the United States has never implemented working requirements, many

---

[12]As explained in further detail *supra* Chapter 4 ("Novelty, Loss of Right, and Priority Pre- and Post-America Invents Act of 2011 (35 U.S.C. §102)"), interferences are pre-AIA *inter partes* administrative proceedings conducted in the USPTO to determine which of two or more rival claimants was the first to invent a particular claimed invention. The AIA eliminated interference proceedings effective March 16, 2013.

[13]Section 104 of the U.S. Patent Act was amended as a consequence of the U.S. signing of the North American Free Trade Agreement with Mexico and Canada, and the TRIPS Agreement of the World Trade Organization. In accordance with these amendments, inventive activity that occurred on or after December 8, 1993, in the NAFTA countries of Canada and Mexico, or inventive activity that occurred on or after January 1, 1996, in any WTO member country (other than the United States, Canada, and Mexico), was admissible in a U.S. interference proceeding, or in antedating prior art in *ex parte* prosecution, just as if the activity had occurred in the United States. *See* 35 U.S.C. §104 (2006); 37 C.F.R. §1.131 (2008); U.S. PATENT & TRADEMARK OFFICE, MANUAL OF PATENT EXAMINING PROCEDURE §715.07(c) (8th ed., 8th rev. 2010) ("Acts Relied Upon Must Have Been Carried Out in This Country or a NAFTA or WTO Member Country"), *available at* http://www.uspto.gov/web/offices/pac/mpep/mpep.htm.

other countries have.[14] Although such a requirement would be facially neutral because of its applicability to both foreign applicants and nationals of the granting country, the practical reality was that it was much more difficult for a foreign entity to obtain the funding and regulatory permits necessary to set up factories for manufacture of an invention in the granting country than it would be for a domestic entity to do so.

B. The Paris Convention

1. Introduction

The Paris Convention is the oldest body of multinational industrial property[15] law with the widest membership. The Paris Convention first came into force in 1883, and the United States has been a signatory to the Paris Convention since 1903. The Convention has been modified through various revisions; the current version is that which was revised in Stockholm in 1967.[16] The World Intellectual Property Organization (WIPO) in Geneva, a specialized agency of the United Nations, administers the Paris Convention. As of August 2012, 174 countries are signatories to the Paris Convention.[17]

---

[14]For example, the U.S. government in 2001 requested that WTO dispute resolution proceedings be initiated against the government of Brazil, on the ground that Brazil's patent laws violated the TRIPS Agreement by requiring local working of Brazilian patents. Specifically, the United States contended that "Article 68 of Brazil's 1996 industrial property law (Law No. 9,279 of 14 May 1996; effective May 1997), . . . imposes a 'local working' requirement which stipulates that a patent shall be subject to compulsory licensing if the subject matter of the patent is not 'worked' in the territory of Brazil. Specifically, a compulsory license shall be granted on a patent if the patented product is not manufactured in Brazil or if the patented process is not used in Brazil." *Request for the Establishment of a Panel by the United States, Brazil— Measures Affecting Patent Protection*, WT/DS199/3 (Jan. 9, 2001), *available at* http:// docsonline.wto.org. The United States and Brazil later reached agreement on the dispute. *See Notification of Mutually Agreed Solution, Brazil—Measures Affecting Patent Protection*, WT/DS199/4 (July 19, 2001), *available at* http://docsonline.wto.org.

[15]Although the United States refers to "intellectual property" as encompassing the subject matter protected by patent law, trademark law, and copyright law, many foreign jurisdictions prefer the use of the phrase "industrial property" when speaking of the subject matter of patents, trademarks, and industrial designs, and "copyright" when referring to copyrightable subject matter.

[16]*See* Paris Convention for the Protection of Industrial Property, Mar. 20, 1883, as revised at Stockholm, July 14, 1967, 21 U.S.T. 1583, 828 U.N.T.S. 305, *available at* http://www.wipo.int/treaties/en/ip/paris (as amended Sept. 28, 1979).

[17]*See* World Intellectual Property Organization, *Contracting Parties of the Paris Convention*, http://www.wipo.int/treaties/en/ip/paris/index.html (last visited Aug. 2, 2012).

The Paris Convention is the basic international agreement dealing with the treatment of foreigners under national patent laws. It addressed some, but not all, of the obstacles to international patenting discussed above. For example, the Paris Convention did not set up any "substantive minima" for industrial property protection, meaning that it was silent as to the technical criteria for patentability or the types of subject matter for which patents should be available. In fact, a country could be a signatory to the Paris Convention while not granting patents at all; Switzerland and the Netherlands did not have patent systems in the latter part of the nineteenth century, although both countries were signatories to the Paris Convention.[18]

The Paris Convention was fairly silent on the propriety of protectionist measures. For example, the original version of the Paris Convention specifically allowed the continued existence of national working requirements and said nothing at all about **compulsory licensing.** Later versions of the Paris Convention contain only very limited restrictions on the ability of a signatory country to grant compulsory licenses.[19]

Despite the absence of substantive minima and its few limitations on protectionist measures, the Paris Convention did establish two key rights that made it much easier to obtain patent protection in foreign countries than had previously been the case. These rights, which have become cornerstones of all subsequent international patent agreements, are the principles of **national treatment** and the **right of priority.**

2. National Treatment

The national treatment provision is found in Article 2 of the Paris Convention.[20] National treatment simply means that each signatory country to the Paris Convention must treat foreigners seeking

---

[18]*See* ERIC SCHIFF, INDUSTRIALIZATION WITHOUT NATIONAL PATENTS (Princeton 1971). Switzerland and the Netherlands became parties to the Paris Convention in 1884. *See* World Intellectual Property Organization, *Contracting Parties of the Paris Convention*, http://www.wipo.int/treaties/en/ip/paris/index.html (last visited Aug. 2, 2012).

[19]*See* Paris Convention art. 5(A), *available at* http://www.wipo.int/treaties/en/ip/paris/trtdocs_wo020.html#P123_15283.

[20]Article 2, "National Treatment for Nationals of Countries of the Union," provides in part that

(1) Nationals of any country of the [Paris] Union shall, as regards the protection of industrial property, enjoy in all other countries of the Union the advantages that their respective laws now grant, or may hereafter grant, to nationals; all without prejudice to the rights specially provided for by this Convention. Consequently, they shall have the same protection as the latter, and the same legal remedy against any infringement of their rights, provided that the conditions and formalities imposed upon nationals are complied with. . . .

industrial property protection in that country as well as (or, optionally, better than) it treats its own nationals. For example, the national treatment principle prevents the United States from charging U.S. nationals a patent application filing fee of $500 while demanding a filing fee of $1,000 from nationals of other countries. The foreign nationals must be charged the same filing fee of $500 (or, optionally, a lower fee).

The drafters of the Paris Convention chose national treatment over the competing principle of "reciprocity." In a system governed by reciprocity principles, Country A treats foreign nationals of Country B in the same manner as Country B treats the nationals of Country A, regardless of how Country A treats its own nationals (or how it treats the nationals of Country C). For example, if Country B charges nationals of Country A a patent application filing fee of $1,000, then under a reciprocity system Country A will charge the nationals of Country B a patent application filing fee of $1,000 (regardless of whether Country A charges its own nationals only $500 or charges the nationals of Country C a filing fee of $2,000). Implementing a reciprocity-based system imposes significant administrative costs and burdens, because Country A must become intimately familiar with the patent laws and procedures of every other country and vice versa. These heightened burdens led the drafters of the Paris Convention to reject the principle of reciprocity in favor of national treatment.

3. Right of Priority

The other key right established by the Paris Convention is the right of priority, found in Article 4 of the convention.[21] This right greatly

---

Paris Convention art. 2(1), *available at* http://www.wipo.int/treaties/en/ip/paris/trt-docs_wo020.html#P77_5133.

[21] Article 4 of the Paris Convention provides in part:

A. (1) Any person who has duly filed an application for a patent, or for the registration of a utility model, or of an industrial design, or of a trademark, in one of the countries of the Union, or his successor in title, shall enjoy, for the purpose of filing in the other countries, a right of priority during the periods hereinafter fixed.

(2) Any filing that is equivalent to a regular national filing under the domestic legislation of any country of the Union or under bilateral or multilateral treaties concluded between countries of the Union shall be recognized as giving rise to the right of priority.

(3) By a regular national filing is meant any filing that is adequate to establish the date on which the application was filed in the country concerned, whatever may be the subsequent fate of the application.

B. Consequently, any subsequent filing in any of the other countries of the Union before the expiration of the periods referred to above shall not be invalidated by reason of any acts accomplished in the interval, in particular, another simplifies the process of obtaining industrial property protection in multiple signatory countries. By filing a patent application on an invention in a single Paris member country (typically in the inventor's home country, because it is the most convenient), an inventor can obtain the benefit of that same initial filing date (referred to as her *priority date*) in any other Paris Convention signatory countries in which she files additional patent applications on the same invention within the period of time called the *priority period*. For patents, the relevant priority period is 12 months, starting from the date of filing of the first application.[22]

For example, consider an inventor named Mayumi, a Japanese national, who filed a patent application on her invention X in Japan (a signatory to the Paris Convention) on January 1, 2002. On December 15, 2002, Mayumi filed an application for the same invention X in the USPTO. Assume that the Japanese application adequately supports the invention that Mayumi is claiming in her U.S. application in accordance with 35 U.S.C. §112, ¶1 (2000), and that Mayumi makes a formal claim for the benefit of her foreign priority date under 35 U.S.C. §119 (the U.S. implementation of the Paris Convention right of priority, discussed further below). If these criteria are satisfied, the USPTO examiner will treat the U.S. application as if it had been filed on January 1, 2002, for purposes of examining it against the prior art for novelty and nonobviousness. In practical terms this means that the U.S. application will "relate back" to the Japanese filing date; the USPTO will ignore any intervening, potentially patentability-destroying developments that occurred between January 1 and December 15 of 2002. Such developments could include, for example, the publication of a description of the same invention or the filing of another U.S. patent application on the same invention, whether these events were triggered by Mayumi or a third party.

The foreign priority right means that such intervening events are not considered prior art against Mayumi's U.S. application. More specifically, and under pre-AIA rules, Mayumi's January 1, 2002, Japanese filing date would be treated by the USPTO as Mayumi's presumptive invention date in the United States for purposes of applying the novelty provi-

---

filing, the publication or exploitation of the invention, the putting on sale of copies of the design, or the use of the mark, and such acts cannot give rise to any third-party right or any right of personal possession. Rights acquired by third parties before the date of the first application that serves as the basis for the right of priority are reserved in accordance with the domestic legislation of each country of the Union.

Paris Convention art. 4, *available at* http://www.wipo.int/treaties/en/ip/paris/trtdocs_wo020.html#P83_6610.

[22]*See* Paris Convention arts. 4.C(1), 4.C(2).

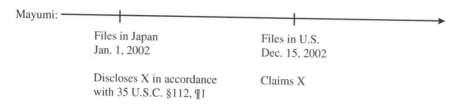

Figure 12.1

Paris Convention Priority Right

sions of 35 U.S.C. §102 (2000) (i.e., §§102(a), (e), and (g))[23] and 35 U.S.C. §103 (2000) (nonobviousness). Figure 12.1 illustrates this practice.

Following implementation of the AIA's first-inventor-to-file system on March 16, 2013,[24] the foreign priority date will be treated as the U.S. application's "effective filing date," assuming all requirements for attaining the foreign priority right are satisfied.[25]

[23]Prior to the AIA, foreign priority under 35 U.S.C. §119 could not be relied on to overcome a loss of right under 35 U.S.C. §102(b) (2000). Thus, in the above example in the text, if Mayumi had placed her invention "on sale" in the United States within the meaning of §102(b) (2000) by making U.S. sales of the invention for commercial purposes beginning in July 2001, then claiming the benefit of her earlier Japanese filing date for her U.S. application filed more than one year after those sales would be of no use. The on sale bar of §102(b) (2000) was considered absolute in the sense that it could not be overcome by relying on foreign priority. *See* 35 U.S.C. §119(a) (2000) ("[B]ut no patent shall be granted on any application for patent for an invention which had been patented or described in a printed publication in any country more than one year before the date of the actual filing of the application in this country, or which had been in public use or on sale in this country more than one year prior to such filing."). The AIA deleted any reference to pre-AIA statutory bars from §119(a). *See* Leahy-Smith America Invents Act, Pub. L. No. 112-29 (H.R. 1249), §3(g)(6),125 Stat. 284, 288 (Sept. 16, 2011); 35 U.S.C. §119(a) (eff. Mar. 16, 2013).

[24]The AIA-implemented first-inventor-to-file priority system is discussed *infra* Section E.1 ("First-to-File Versus First-to-Invent"); *see also supra* Chapter 4, Section R ("Presumptively Novelty-Destroying Events Under Post-AIA 35 U.S.C. §102(a)(2) (First-Inventor-to-File Rule)").

[25]Foreign priority operates in the same manner post-AIA. Assume, for example, that Mayumi files her Japanese priority application on January 1, 2014, and files her U.S. application for the same invention X on December 15, 2014. So long as the requisite formalities are complied with and the disclosure in Mayumi's Japanese application satisfies 35 U.S.C. §112(a) (eff. Sept. 16, 2012) with respect to the claims of her U.S. application, Mayumi's Japanese filing date will be treated as the effective filing date of the claims in her U.S. application under 35 U.S.C. §100(i)(B) (eff. Mar. 16, 2013) for purposes of examination for novelty under 35 U.S.C. §102 (eff. Mar. 16, 2013) and nonobviousness under 35 U.S.C. §103 (eff. Mar. 16, 2013). *See also* 35 U.S.C. §100(i)(B) (eff. Mar. 16, 2013) (defining "effective filing date" for a claimed invention in a patent or patent application to include "the filing date of the earliest application for which the patent or application is entitled, as to such invention, to a *right of priority under*

Thankfully, claiming the benefit of one's Paris Convention priority date does not reduce the term of protection by the length of the priority period.[26] In the above example, Mayumi's U.S. patent would expire 20 years from its earliest effective U.S. filing date, not any earlier foreign priority date. Thus, the U.S. patent would expire on December 15, 2022. Claiming entitlement to the benefit of a Paris Convention foreign priority date is an exclusively positive benefit. Mayumi benefits from being able to avoid any potentially patentability-destroying activity that occurred during the priority period (i.e., events that took place between January 1, 2002, and December 15, 2002), while not facing the start of the 20-year patent term clock until her actual U.S. filing date of December 15, 2002.

The ultimate fate of Mayumi's Japanese application is not relevant to the status of her U.S. application. The Japanese application need not issue as a Japanese patent in order for Mayumi to claim the benefit of its filing date for her U.S. application. All that the Paris Convention requires is that the priority application be "[a]ny filing that is equivalent to a regular national filing under the domestic legislation of any country of the Union or under bilateral or multilateral treaties concluded between countries of the Union. . . . "[27] The convention defines a "regular national filing" as "any filing that is adequate to establish the date on which the application was filed in the country concerned, whatever may be the subsequent fate of the application."[28]

4. U.S. Implementation of the Paris Right of Priority: 35 U.S.C. §119

Section 119(a)-(d) of the U.S. Patent Act is the domestic implementation of the Paris Convention right of priority in patent cases. These

---

section 119, 365(a), or 365(b) or to the benefit of an earlier filing date under section 120, 121, or 365(c)") (emphasis added). The "right of priority under section 119" includes foreign priority under §119(a).

[26]*See* Paris Convention art. 4bis(5) (providing that "[p]atents obtained with the benefit of priority shall, in the various countries of the Union, have a duration equal to that which they would have, had they been applied for or granted without the benefit of priority").

[27]Paris Convention art. 4.A(2).

[28]Paris Convention art. 4.A(3). The USPTO considers a U.S. provisional patent application filed under 35 U.S.C. §111(b) to be a regular national filing under the Paris Convention, such that "an applicant has 12 months from the filing date of a provisional application to file an application abroad or under the PCT to preserve the right to priority under the Paris Convention based on the filing date of the provisional application." Charles E. VanHorn, *Effects of GATT and NAFTA on PTO Practice*, 77 J. PAT. & TRADEMARK OFF. SOC'Y 231, 238, *available at* http://www.uspto.gov/web/offices/com/doc/uruguay/URPAPER.html.

provisions of 35 U.S.C. §119 were added to our patent law by virtue of the 1952 Act, but similar provisions existed in predecessor statutes since 1903.[29]

Section 119 provides in pertinent part that

> (a) An application for patent for an invention filed in this country by any person who has, or whose legal representatives or assigns have, previously regularly filed an application for a patent for the same invention in a foreign country which affords similar privileges in the case of applications filed in the United States or to citizens of the United States, or in a WTO member country, shall have the same effect as the same application would have if filed in this country on the date on which the application for patent for the same invention was first filed in such foreign country, if the application in this country is filed within twelve months from the earliest date on which such foreign application was filed.[30]

This rather complex statutory language can be mastered by understanding a few basic points. Section 119(a) confers an important benefit to U.S. patent applicants who have previously filed a patent application on the same invention in another country. In sum, 35 U.S.C. §119(a) means that if an applicant first files a patent application in a foreign country that is a WTO member or conveys similar privileges to the United States (i.e., in any Paris Convention signatory country or in any of the other countries with which the United States has established bilateral treaties on this point), and then files a second patent application "for the same invention"[31] in the United States within 12 months of the foreign filing date, then the applicant can claim for that

---

[29]*See* In re Hilmer, 359 F.2d 859, 872-876 (C.C.P.A. 1966) (describing history and purpose of §119).

[30]35 U.S.C. §119(a) (eff. Mar. 16, 2013). The AIA deleted the last clause of 35 U.S.C. §119(a) (2006), which had prohibited reliance on foreign priority to overcome statutory bars by including the proviso "but no patent shall be granted on any application for patent for an invention which had been patented or described in a printed publication in any country more than one year before the date of the actual filing of the application in this country, or which had been in public use or on sale in this country more than one year prior to such filing." *See* Leahy-Smith America Invents Act, Pub. L. No. 112-29 (H.R. 1249), §3(g)(6),125 Stat. 284, 288 (Sept. 16, 2011).

[31]Federal Circuit case law has interpreted the meaning of "same invention" as used in §119. The claims set forth in a U.S. patent application are entitled to the benefit of a foreign priority date under §119 to the extent that the corresponding foreign application supports the claims in the manner required by the first paragraph of 35 U.S.C. §112. *See* In re Gosteli, 872 F.2d 1008, 1010 (Fed. Cir. 1989), discussed in the text. Post-AIA, this most likely means that the foreign application must provide an enabling disclosure of the invention as claimed in the U.S. application as well as a written description of that invention. Under pre-AIA rules, the foreign application arguably had to also reveal the best mode of the invention.

U.S. application the benefit of the earlier foreign filing date (foreign priority date).

Obtaining this benefit means that, in the words of the statute, the U.S. application "shall have the same effect" as the same application would have if actually filed in the United States on the foreign filing date. In practice, this means that the USPTO will treat the application as if filed on the foreign priority date for purposes of examining it against the prior art. In other words, the foreign filing date will be taken as the "effective filing date" for purposes of examination for novelty and nonobviousness under post-AIA 35 U.S.C. §102 and 35 U.S.C. §103.[32] Events occurring in the time between the foreign priority date and the U.S. filing date that might otherwise anticipate the claimed invention or render it obvious will not "count" against the application, as explained above.

Although we assumed in the example of the previous section that Mayumi's U.S. application was for the "same invention" as that disclosed in her Japanese application, this is not always the case. Often, an inventor will make improvements over time and claim her invention more broadly in a later-filed application. The Federal Circuit case law has faced this scenario in interpreting the meaning of the phrase *same invention* as used in 35 U.S.C. §119(a). Claims set forth in a U.S. patent application are entitled to the benefit of a foreign priority date under §119(a) to the extent that the disclosure of the corresponding foreign application supports the claims in the manner required by §112, ¶1.[33] This means that the foreign application must provide an **enabling** disclosure of the invention as claimed in the U.S. application and include a **written description of the invention.** In pre-AIA situations, the foreign priority application arguably has to also reveal the **best mode** of carrying out the invention (assuming that a best mode existed).

These requirements were not satisfied in *In re Gosteli,*[34] where the applicant Gosteli first filed a patent application in Luxembourg that disclosed certain species of chemical compounds having antibiotic properties. Within one year, he filed an application in the United States with broader claims to a genus of compounds that encompassed the original species plus other species. In ruling on his priority claim, the USPTO had to determine whether Gosteli's U.S. application claimed the same invention as that disclosed in his earlier Luxembourg application.

---

[32]*See* 35 U.S.C. §100(i)(B) (eff. Mar. 16, 2013) (effective filing date may be based on "a right of priority under section 119"); 35 U.S.C. §102 (eff. Mar. 16, 2013) (novelty); 35 U.S.C. §103 (eff. Mar. 16, 2013) (nonobviousness).

[33]*See Gosteli*, 872 F.2d at 1010 (citing In re Wertheim, 541 F.2d 257, 261-262 (C.C.P.A. 1976)).

[34]872 F.2d 1008 (Fed. Cir. 1989).

On appeal, the Federal Circuit agreed with the agency that it did not. Gosteli was unable to obtain the benefit of his Luxembourg filing date for the genus claims of his U.S. application because the Luxembourg application did not provide a sufficient written description of the invention as claimed generically in the U.S. application. The content of the Luxembourg application did not demonstrate that Gosteli was in possession of the generically claimed invention as of his Luxembourg filing date. Thus, the genus claims of Gosteli's U.S. application would be entitled only to their actual U.S. filing date. Because there was an anticipatory prior art reference (i.e., a 35 U.S.C. §102(e) (1988) reference having an effective date after Gosteli's Luxembourg filing date but before his U.S. filing date), Gosteli's U.S. claims were not allowable.

5.   The *Hilmer* Rule (Pre-America Invents Act of 2011)

The rule of *In re Hilmer*[35] (*Hilmer I*) is a controversial aspect of pre-AIA U.S. patent practice that concerns the effective date of U.S. patents relied on as prior art references. For reasons explained below, the rule was routinely criticized as discriminating against foreign inventors. The America Invents Act of 2011 prospectively repealed the *Hilmer* rule,[36] but it still holds for patents being applied as prior art against claimed inventions in applications and patents having effective dates prior to the AIA's March 16, 2013, first-to-file implementation. Hence, understanding the *Hilmer* rule will remain important for many years to come.

In a nutshell, the *Hilmer* rule states that when a U.S. patent (or published application) is being relied on as a prior art reference under

---

[35]359 F.2d 859 (C.C.P.A. 1966) (Rich, J.) [hereinafter *Hilmer I*].

[36]*See* 35 U.S.C. §102(d) (eff. March 16, 2013), which provides (emphasis added),

> (d) PATENTS AND PUBLISHED APPLICATIONS EFFECTIVE AS PRIOR ART.—For purposes of determining whether a patent or application for patent is prior art to a claimed invention under subsection (a)(2), such patent or application shall be considered to have been effectively filed, with respect to any subject matter described in the patent or application—
>> (1) if paragraph (2) does not apply, as of the actual filing date of the patent or the application for patent; or
>> (2) *if the patent or application for patent is entitled to claim a right of priority under section 119, 365(a), or 365(b), or to claim the benefit of an earlier filing date under section 120, 121, or 365(c), based upon 1 or more prior filed applications for patent, as of the filing date of the earliest such application that describes the subject matter.*

Subparagraph (d)(2) repeals the *Hilmer* rule implicitly by including foreign priority under 35 U.S.C. §119 in its scope.

35 U.S.C. §102(e) (pre-AIA), its effective date is its U.S. filing date, *not* any earlier foreign priority date the benefit of which was claimed in the process of obtaining the reference patent. *Hilmer* requires that we distinguish between patent-obtaining and patent-defeating uses of foreign priority under 35 U.S.C. §119(a), the United States' implementation of the Paris Convention right of priority. Only patent-*obtaining* uses of foreign priority are permitted under the *Hilmer* rule, not patent-*defeating* uses.

The facts of *Hilmer* are illustrative. Two foreign inventors, Hilmer (a German national) and Habicht (a Swiss national), sought a U.S. patent on the same invention. Habicht won an interference against Hilmer; thereafter, Hilmer reentered *ex parte* prosecution claiming a variant of the lost count of the interference. The disclosure of Habicht's patent was cited as a §102(e) reference against Hilmer's application claims, in combination with another prior art reference (Wagner), to form a §103 rejection for obviousness.[37] The timeline in Figure 12.2 depicts the pertinent dates.

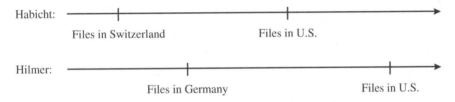

Figure 12.2

Timeline for *In re Hilmer*

Hilmer was able to overcome Habicht's earlier U.S. filing date by claiming the benefit of Hilmer's German priority date in accordance with 35 U.S.C. §119(a). This was a *patent-obtaining* use of foreign priority by Hilmer. The USPTO took the position that Habicht was nevertheless §102(e)/§103 prior art to Hilmer, by virtue of Habicht's earlier Swiss priority date. This was an attempted *patent-defeating* use of

---

[37]Recall that a 35 U.S.C. §102(e) (pre-AIA) rejection relies on subject matter that is *described but not claimed* by the reference patentee. If the reference patent *claims* the same invention as the applicant, an interference may be declared under §102(g) (pre-AIA). In this case, an interference had previously been declared between certain interfering *claims* of Habicht and Hilmer. Habicht prevailed because Hilmer conceded priority to Habicht of the subject matter of what became the interference "count." *See Hilmer*, 359 F.2d at 861. The invention for which Hilmer later sought a patent in *In re Hilmer* was not the same invention as the subject matter of the earlier interference, but rather a variant thereof. *See Hilmer*, 359 F.2d at 862 (quoting Board's statement distinguishing interfering subject matter from Hilmer's appealed application claims 10, 16, and 17, directed to a cyclohexyl substituted compound).

foreign priority by the USPTO. The agency argued that the "shall have the same effect" language of 35 U.S.C. §119(a) should be read broadly as having the "same effect" for all purposes, including that of modifying the "in this country" language of 35 U.S.C. §102(e).

The Court of Customs and Patent Appeals (CCPA) reversed. The effective date of Habicht's disclosure when used as a §102(e) reference in this fashion was Habicht's U.S. filing date, *not* his earlier Swiss filing date. The court read the "filed in the United States" language of 35 U.S.C. §102(e) literally,[38] and refused to impute the patent-obtaining concept of §119(a) into the patent-defeating provision, §102(e). Thus, the *Hilmer* decision means that foreign priority can be used only to affirmatively obtain a patent (in *ex parte* prosecution or an interference), and not for patent-defeating purposes such as dedication of technology to the public through disclosing without claiming it.

The CCPA posited several rationales for the rule it announced in *Hilmer*, but the most compelling was the court's public policy–based refusal to exacerbate the "secret prior art" problem of *Alexander Milburn Co. v. Davis-Bournonville Co.*[39] by pushing back the effective date of a 35 U.S.C. §102(e) reference by up to another year of the foreign priority period. The court viewed §119(a) foreign priority as a benefit, not a burden. It is only a patent-preserving device, while the 35 U.S.C. §102 provisions are patent-defeating. In the view of the CCPA, these statutory provisions were enacted at different times, for very different purposes.

The practical result of the *Hilmer* decision was that Habicht's U.S. patent was rendered considerably less valuable than it might have otherwise been because Hilmer was allowed to obtain his own U.S. patent on an arguably obvious variant of that which Habicht had already patented. Habicht had attempted to dedicate the variant to the public, and thereby prevent others from patenting it, by means of disclosing it in his patent application; under the rule of *Hilmer,* however, Habicht (and the USPTO in its examination of Hilmer's application) were not permitted to rely on Habicht's disclosure in this fashion.[40]

---

[38]At that time, 35 U.S.C. §102(e) provided that a person would be entitled to a patent unless "the invention was described in a patent granted on an application for patent by another filed in the United States before the invention thereof by the applicant for patent.... " *Hilmer*, 359 F.2d at 864.

[39]270 U.S. 390 (1926). The *Milburn* rule, codified as 35 U.S.C. §102(e), is discussed in further detail *supra* Chapter 4 ("Novelty, Loss of Right, and Priority Pre- and Post-America Invents Act of 2011 (35 U.S.C. §102)"), Section L ("Description in Another's Earlier-Filed Patent or Published Patent Application Under 35 U.S.C. §102(e) (Pre-AIA)").

[40]In a subsequent decision involving the same application, *In re Hilmer*, 424 F.2d 1108 (C.C.P.A. 1970) (*Hilmer II*), the court reaffirmed the reasoning of *Hilmer I*, holding that the "shall have the same effect" language of §119 was not intended to modify the "in this country" language of §102(g). The court held that the USPTO cannot treat

The *Hilmer* rule is frequently criticized as protectionist and discriminatory against foreigners because the foreign patentee (e.g., Habicht) is prevented from using his disclosure (as of its foreign priority date) in a defensive manner.[41] Some experts have questioned whether the United States' continued adherence to the *Hilmer* rule is consistent with its national treatment obligations under the Paris Convention and the TRIPS Agreement.[42] In the pre-AIA context, however, the *Hilmer* rule remains the law in the United States.

6. Limitations of the Paris Convention

The primary criticisms of the Paris Convention are (1) that it lacks any substantive minima for patentability, and (2) that it provides no meaningful enforcement mechanism by which to challenge the failure of signatory countries to comply with the standards that are contained in the Convention.[43] By the late 1980s, growing dissatisfaction

---

the foreign filing date of a U.S. patent, when used as a prior art reference, as evidence of a constructive reduction to practice on that date, and thereby convert that foreign filing into a §102(g) event (i.e., the making of the invention in this country by another) to be relied on in a §103 rejection.

[41]To see more clearly the discriminatory effect of the *Hilmer* rule, imagine Hilmer as a U.S. national who first filed in Germany, then (within 12 months) filed in the USPTO. Hilmer (hypothetically the U.S. inventor) is entitled to rely on his German priority date under §119(a) in order to overcome Habicht's U.S. filing date and thereby remove Habicht as §102(e) prior art, but the disclosure in Habicht's Swiss priority application (filed before Hilmer's German priority date) is not recognized as prior art that the USPTO can cite in a §102(e)/§103 rejection against Hilmer's claims.

[42]*See, e.g.*, Heinz Bardehle, *A New Approach to Worldwide Harmonization of Patent Law*, 81 J. PAT. & TRADEMARK OFF. SOC'Y 303, 310 (1999) (suggesting that *Hilmer* rule should be challenged under TRIPS); Harold C. Wegner, *TRIPS Boomerang: Obligations for Domestic Reform*, 29 VAND. J. TRANSNAT'L L. 535, 556 (1996) (stating, "[I]n international circles, the second target after first-to-file has been the elimination of the notorious *Hilmer I* decision, which unfairly denies foreign patentee's their patent-defeating right guaranteed by the Paris Convention."). *See also* TRIPS art. 27.1 (stating that "patents shall be available and *patent rights enjoyable* without discrimination as to the place of invention . . . ") (emphasis added).The *Hilmer* rule may not explicitly violate national treatment obligations because the rule applies to U.S. and foreign patent applicants alike. *See Hilmer*, 359 F.2d 878 n.9 (stating that "[i]t is the first filing in a foreign convention country that creates the priority right, *not the nationality of the applicant*") (emphasis in original). *De facto* discrimination results, however, because many foreign inventors are likely to have first filed in their home country before filing in the United States. Some patent-sophisticated foreign corporations avoid the effects of the *Hilmer* rule by making their first filings in the USPTO.

[43]Theoretically, a Paris Convention signatory country could seek review of another member country's alleged failure to satisfy provisions of the Convention by petitioning the Court of International Justice. However, no country has ever done so. *See* Ralph Oman, *Intellectual Property After the Uruguay Round*, 42 J. COPYRIGHT SOC'Y U.S.A. 18, 26 n.11 (1994).

of Western countries with the WIPO's inability to enforce patent and other intellectual property rights led a number of countries (spearheaded by the United States) to turn to multilateral trade talks, in the form of the Uruguay Round of the General Agreement on Tariffs and Trade (GATT).[44] This round produced the TRIPS Agreement, discussed below, which is administered by the WTO.[45]

Although the WTO, with its elaborate dispute resolution mechanisms and expertise in that area, has come to be viewed as the preferred forum for resolution of country-versus-country disagreements on intellectual property matters, the WTO has not in any way displaced the WIPO's specialized intellectual property expertise. The WIPO remains a central player in the international intellectual property framework, administering many important intellectual property treaties and conventions in addition to the Paris Convention. One of the WIPO's most active and important roles is its administration of the Patent Cooperation Treaty, discussed in the next section.

C. The Patent Cooperation Treaty

The Patent Cooperation Treaty (PCT), which entered into force on January 24, 1978, provides a procedural framework for efficiently exploiting the right of priority created by the Paris Convention. In short, the PCT greatly simplifies the procedures for obtaining patent protection for an invention in multiple countries. The PCT has proven popular; 181,900 international applications were filed in 2011 under the treaty.[46] The PCT, like the Paris Convention, is administered by the WIPO, headquartered in Geneva, Switzerland. The text of the

---

[44]For a firsthand account of the unsuccessful efforts to modernize the Paris Convention in the WIPO during the 1980s and the subsequent shift of U.S. efforts toward including intellectual property in multilateral trade talks, ultimately leading to the TRIPS Agreement, *see* Ralph Oman, *Intellectual Property After the Uruguay Round*, 42 J. COPYRIGHT SOC'Y U.S.A. 18, 26 n.11 (1994).

[45]*See* Agreement on Trade-Related Aspects of Intellectual Property Rights, Apr. 15, 1994, Marrakesh Agreement Establishing the World Trade Organization, Annex 1C, Legal Instruments-Results of the Uruguay Round, 1869 U.N.T.S. 299, 33 I.L.M. 81 (1994), *available at* http://www.wto.org/english/docs_e/legal_e/27-trips.pdf [hereinafter TRIPS Agreement]. The GATT organization, formed in the late 1940s following World War II, was superseded by the WTO, which entered into force on January 1, 1995. The WTO, located in Geneva, Switzerland, administers the TRIPS Agreement.

[46]World Intellectual Property Organization, *PCT Yearly Review, The International Patent System* (2012), *available at* http://www.wipo.int/export/sites/www/freepublications/en/patents/901/wipo_pub_901_2012.pdf.

PCT and a list of PCT contracting states (i.e., signatory countries) are available on the WIPO's Web site.[47]

The PCT created a system of "one-stop shopping" in which an applicant, so long as she is a national or resident of a PCT contracting state, can file a single "international application"[48] with the patent office of her home country (acting as a PCT "receiving office") or with the International Bureau of the WIPO in Geneva. Through designation of any or all of the PCT contracting states, the international application will have the effect of a national patent application in each designated contracting state.[49] The applicant also may claim for the international application the benefit of the filing date (priority date) of an earlier-filed application in a Paris Convention country, if applicable.[50] In such cases, the applicant will file her international application within 12 months of filing an application on the same invention in her home country patent office.

The international application will be searched against the prior art by a PCT international searching authority.[51] A copy of the application, together with the results of the search, will be published at approximately 18 months after the priority date,[52] and these materials will be transmitted by the WIPO's International Bureau to the national patent offices of each designated contracting state.[53] An applicant additionally has the option of requesting an International Preliminary Examination of the application.[54]

---

[47]*See* Patent Cooperation Treaty, June 19, 1970, 28 U.S.T. 7645, 1160 U.N.T.S. 231, *available at* http://www.wipo.int/pct/en/texts/articles/atoc.htm [hereinafter PCT]. The list of PCT contracting states is *available at* http://www.wipo.int/pct/guide/en/gdvol1/annexes/annexa/ax_a.pdf (last visited Aug. 2, 2012). Helpful resources on PCT practice include World Intellectual Property Organization, *The PCT Applicant's Guide* (Jan. 12, 2009), *available at* http://www.wipo.int/pct/en/appguide/index.jsp; World Intellectual Property Organization, *Protecting Your Inventions Abroad: Frequently Asked Questions About the Patent Cooperation Treaty (PCT)* (April 2012), *available at* http://www.wipo.int/export/sites/www/pct/en/basic_facts/faqs_about_the_pct.pdf; World Intellectual Property Organization, *Basic Facts About the Patent Cooperation Treaty (PCT)* (2002).

[48]*See* PCT art. 3.

[49]*See* PCT arts. 4, 11.

[50]*See* PCT art. 8.

[51]*See* PCT arts. 15-18. For international applications filed on or after January 1, 2004, the international searching authority (ISA) also prepares a written opinion (WO) on patentability. *See* World Intellectual Property Organization, *Regulations Under the Patent Cooperation Treaty (as in force from January 1, 2009)*, Rule 43*bis*.1, *available at* http://www.wipo.int/export/sites/www/pct/en/texts/pdf/pct_regs.pdf. The WO will be sent to the PCT applicant but not otherwise published unless and until the applicant enters the national phase. *See id.*, Rules 44.1, 44*ter*.1.

[52]*See* PCT art. 21.

[53]*See* PCT art. 20.

[54]*See* PCT art. 31.

The key cost-saving feature of PCT practice is that the treaty permits the applicant to delay entry into the "national phase," that is, entry into patent prosecution in the national patent office of each designated contracting state, for a considerable period of time: up to 30 months after the priority date in most cases.[55] This ability to delay entry into the national phase gives the patent applicant more time to assess the marketplace for the invention and temporarily postpones incurring the considerable costs of the translations, filing fees, attorney fees, and the like that are required to prosecute patent applications to issuance in each national patent office.

The most important aspect of the PCT to keep in mind is that the PCT procedure results in only a single international application, *not* a single granted patent or even a bundle of national patents (as does the European Patent Convention). The PCT authorities of the WIPO do not issue patents. It is up to the domestic patent systems of the designated PCT contracting states to decide whether to ultimately grant or refuse a national patent based on the PCT international application, the PCT international search report, and (in some cases) the results of the PCT international preliminary examination. These reports are not binding on the national offices.[56]

D. The World Trade Organization's Agreement on Trade-Related Aspects of Intellectual Property Rights (TRIPS)

In the 1980s, the primary forum for legislating multinational intellectual property (IP) agreements shifted from the WIPO, an exclusively IP-focused organization, to the WTO, an independent body with

---

[55]*See* PCT art. 22. The 30-month time limit has been in effect since April 1, 2002. A few countries (specifically Luxembourg, Uganda, and United Republic of Tanzania, as of Apr. 13, 2012) continue to apply the 20-month time limit that was in effect before that date, however. *See* World Intellectual Property Organization, *PCT Reservations, Declarations, Notifications and Incompatibilities* (table), *available at* http://www.wipo.int/pct/en/texts/reservations/res_incomp.pdf (last visited Aug. 2, 2012).

[56]*See* PCT art. 27(5) (providing that "[n]othing in this Treaty and the Regulations is intended to be construed as prescribing anything that would limit the freedom of each Contracting State to prescribe such substantive conditions of patentability as it desires. In particular, any provision in this Treaty and the Regulations concerning the definition of prior art is exclusively for the purposes of the international procedure and, consequently, any Contracting State is free to apply, when determining the patentability of an invention claimed in an international application, the criteria of its national law in respect of prior art and other conditions of patentability not constituting requirements as to the form and contents of applications.").

its roots in post–World War II efforts to reduce trade barriers between nations.[57] The Uruguay Round[58] of GATT brought IP rights (including patents, copyrights, and trademarks) into the GATT WTO system for the first time. The Uruguay Round resulted, *inter alia*, in enactment of the Agreement on Trade-Related Aspects of Intellectual Property Rights (TRIPS Agreement).[59] The TRIPS Agreement entered into force on January 1, 1995.

TRIPS is a landmark agreement for a number of reasons. For example, TRIPS is the first international IP treaty to mandate minimum standards for enforcement of rights by individual IP holders. TRIPS mandates that procedures for enforcing IP rights shall be fair and equitable.[60] Decisions on the merits shall preferably be in writing.[61] Accused

---

[57]The WTO's Web site provides the following overview of the organization's structure:

> The WTO is run by its member governments. All major decisions are made by the membership as a whole, either by ministers (who meet at least once every two years) or by their ambassadors or delegates (who meet regularly in Geneva). Decisions are normally taken by consensus.
>
> In this respect, the WTO is different from some other international organizations such as the World Bank and International Monetary Fund. In the WTO, power is not delegated to a board of directors or the organization's head.
>
> When WTO rules impose disciplines on countries' policies, that is the outcome of negotiations among WTO members. The rules are enforced by the members themselves under agreed procedures that they negotiated, including the possibility of trade sanctions. But those sanctions are imposed by member countries, and authorized by the membership as a whole. This is quite different from other agencies whose bureaucracies can, for example, influence a country's policy by threatening to withhold credit.

World Trade Organization, *The Organization: Whose WTO Is It Anyway?*, http://www.wto.org/english/thewto_e/whatis_e/tif_e/org1_e.htm (last visited Aug. 2, 2012).

[58]The international multilateral trading system in goods and services was developed through a series of trade negotiations, or "rounds," held under the auspices of the General Agreement on Tariffs and Trade. The first GATT rounds dealt mainly with tariff reductions, but later negotiations included other areas such as antidumping and nontariff measures. More recently, the 1986-1994 Uruguay Round led to the WTO's creation and included intellectual property as a trade issue, generating the TRIPS Agreement. *See* World Trade Organization, *The Multilateral Trading System: Past, Present, and Future*, http://www.wto.org/english/thewto_e/whatis_e/inbrief_e/inbr01_e.htm (last visited Aug. 2, 2012).

[59]The Uruguay Round resulted in an umbrella agreement that created the WTO, known as the "Agreement Establishing the World Trade Organization." This umbrella agreement, popularly known as the WTO Agreement, included several "annexed" side agreements. The text of the TRIPS Agreement is officially "Annex 1C" of the WTO Agreement. *See* TRIPS Agreement, *available at* http://www.wto.org/english/docs_e/legal_e/27-trips.pdf.

[60]*See* TRIPS art. 41.2.

[61]*See* TRIPS art. 41.3.

infringers shall have the right to timely and sufficiently detailed notice.[62] Injunctions[63] and damages[64] shall be available.

As part of the WTO Agreement, TRIPS also provides procedures for the settlement of disputes between member countries when one country believes that another's IP laws are not in compliance with the provisions of TRIPS. These procedures involve country-to-country consultations, the establishment of WTO panels to consider disputes and produce written reports, and the possibility of appellate review within the WTO. The considerable details of these dispute settlement procedures are set forth in the Dispute Settlement Understanding (DSU) of the WTO.[65] Thus far the United States has invoked the WTO dispute settlement procedures in patent cases involving such topics as India's "mailbox" rule, "local working" and compulsory licensing in Brazil, and Canada's term of patent protection.[66]

The availability of the DSU procedures puts real "teeth" into TRIPS. If a country is unsuccessful in a WTO dispute proceeding and does not timely bring its intellectual property laws into compliance with the WTO's ruling, trade sanctions (e.g., tariffs, import quotas, and taxes) can potentially be imposed on the offending country's exported products that have nothing to do with the intellectual property dispute at issue. This is known as "cross-sectoral retaliation."[67] For example, consider a hypothetical in which the United States, contending that France is not providing sufficient patent protection for computer software, prevails in a WTO dispute settlement proceeding against France, but France does not subsequently bring its laws into compliance with the decision. The WTO could decide to permit the United States to impose sanctions on France by increasing the tariffs imposed on exports of French wine to the United States. It is irrelevant that computer software and wine are unrelated products and that wine was not the subject of the WTO dispute.

---

[62]*See* TRIPS art. 42.

[63]*See* TRIPS art. 44.

[64]*See* TRIPS art. 45.

[65]*See* Understanding on Rules and Procedures Governing the Settlement of Disputes, Apr. 15, 1994, Marrakesh Agreement Establishing the World Trade Organization, Annex 2, 1869 U.N.T.S. 401, 33 I.L.M. 1226, *available at* http://www.wto.org/english/docs_e/legal_e/28-dsu_e.htm [hereinafter DSU]. For a helpful flowchart of the WTO panel process for settling disputes, *see* World Trade Organization, *The Panel Process*, http://www.wto.org/english/thewto_e/whatis_e/tif_e/disp2_e.htm (last visited Aug. 2, 2012). *See also* TRIPS art. 63 ("Transparency") and art. 64 ("Dispute Settlement").

[66]For the details of these disputes, *see* World Trade Organization, *Index of Disputes Issues,* http://www.wto.org/english/tratop_e/dispu_e/dispu_subjects_index_e.htm (heading "Patents") (last visited Aug. 2, 2012).

[67]*See* DSU art. 22.3 *available at* http://www.wto.org/english/docs_e/legal_e/28-dsu_e.htm.

D. The World Trade Organization's Agreement on TRIPS

TRIPS also is critically important because it is the first international IP treaty to establish "substantive minima" of protection for all types of intellectual property. With respect to patents, TRIPS provides that, subject to certain important exceptions,[68] "[p]atents shall be available for any inventions, whether products or processes, in all fields of technology, provided that they are new, involve an inventive step and are capable of industrial application."[69] This language was targeted at developing and least-developed countries that had previously refused to grant patents on pharmaceuticals and agricultural inventions; if such countries want to become TRIPS signatories, they must bring their national patent laws into compliance with TRIPS within certain designated time periods by providing patent protection (or at least pipeline protection) on this subject matter.[70]

The quoted language of TRIPS Article 27 also establishes three substantive criteria of patentability (novelty, inventive step, and industrial application) that parallel the U.S. criteria of novelty, nonobviousness, and utility. TRIPS does not explicitly define these substantive criteria, however, leaving member countries certain flexibilities in interpretation.

---

[68]The categories of subject matter that member countries may exclude from patentability under the TRIPS Agreement are enumerated in TRIPS Article 27 ("Patentable Subject Matter"). More specifically, Articles 27.2 and 27.3 provide

> 2. Members may exclude from patentability inventions, the prevention within their territory of the commercial exploitation of which is necessary to protect *ordre public* or morality, including to protect human, animal or plant life or health or to avoid serious prejudice to the environment, provided that such exclusion is not made merely because the exploitation is prohibited by their law.
> 3. Members may also exclude from patentability:
> (a) diagnostic, therapeutic and surgical methods for the treatment of humans or animals;
> (b) plants and animals other than micro-organisms, and essentially biological processes for the production of plants or animals other than non-biological and microbiological processes. However, Members shall provide for the protection of plant varieties either by patents or by an effective sui generis system or by any combination thereof. The provisions of this subparagraph shall be reviewed four years after the date of entry into force of the WTO Agreement.

TRIPS art. 27. These optional exclusions from patentability are discussed in further detail in Chapter 6 ("The Utility Requirement (35 U.S.C. §101)"), *supra*, and in Chapter 7 ("Potentially Patentable Subject Matter (35 U.S.C. §101)"), *supra*.

[69]TRIPS art. 27.1.

[70]The "transitional arrangements" provisions of TRIPS give these countries an extended "phase-in" period of time in which to amend their patent laws. *See* TRIPS arts. 65, 66. For example, under TRIPS art. 65.4, India had until January 1, 2005, to begin granting patents on pharmaceutical products. For additional background on the evolution of India's patent system since the nation joined the WTO, *see* Janice M. Mueller, *The Tiger Awakens: The Tumultuous Transformation of India's Patent System and the Rise of Indian Pharmaceutical Innovation*, 68 Univ. Pitt. L. Rev. 491 (2007).

TRIPS also reflects the United States' historic antipathy toward compulsory licensing, which involves a government-compelled grant of a patent license to a third party without the consent of the patent owner. TRIPS permits (but does not require) countries to grant compulsory licenses under patents, but only upon satisfaction of an extensive list of criteria set forth in Article 31. This article requires that unless a national emergency or other extreme circumstance exists, or unless the compulsory use is a public noncommercial use, compulsory licenses cannot be granted before the proposed licensee has attempted but failed to obtain a consensual license from the patent owner on reasonable commercial terms and conditions.[71]

Moreover, the compulsory licensee's use of the patent must be predominantly for the supply of the domestic market of the country granting the compulsory license.[72] This means that, for example, if the Brazilian government granted a compulsory license to a Brazilian domestic drug company to produce and sell an AIDS drug previously patented in Brazil by a U.S.-based pharmaceutical corporation, the Brazilian company must manufacture the drug primarily for the supply of the Brazilian market and not for export to another country (such as South Africa).[73] Responding to concerns of developing and least-developed countries that lack the domestic manufacturing capacity to take advantage of compulsory licensing, the WTO in 2003 implemented a procedure under which the TRIPS Article 31(f) "predominantly for the supply of the domestic market" requirement can be waived in appropriate circumstances. Under this procedure, a country such as Brazil or India could obtain a compulsory license to manufacture and export patented pharmaceuticals to a requesting country such as South Africa, but only in specified amounts and only with appropriate protections against diversion of the pharmaceuticals to non-intended countries.[74]

---

[71]*See* TRIPS art. 31(b).

[72]*See* TRIPS art. 31(f).

[73]Interpretation of the "predominantly for the supply of the domestic market" provision of TRIPS art. 31 was the subject of controversy stemming from the WTO Ministerial Declaration issued at Doha, Qatar, in 2001. *See* Ministerial Conference, *Declaration on the TRIPS Agreement and Public Health,* WT/MIN(01)/DEC/2 (Nov. 20, 2001), *available at* http://www.wto.org/english/thewto_e/minist_e/min01_e/mindecl_trips_e.pdf. Paragraph 6 of the declaration recognizes that "WTO members with insufficient or no manufacturing capacities in the pharmaceutical sector could face difficulties in making effective use of compulsory licensing under the TRIPS Agreement" and "instruct[s] the Council for TRIPS to find an expeditious solution to this problem and to report to the General Council before the end of 2002."*Id.*

[74]*See* WTO General Council, *Implementation of Paragraph 6 of the Doha Declaration on the TRIPS Agreement and Public Health,* WT/L/540 and Corr.1 (Aug. 30, 2003), *available at* http://www.wto.org/english/tratop_e/trips_e/implem_para6_e.htm. The 2003 Implementation Decision will become a permanent part of the TRIPS Agreement

The patent owner who is subject to a compulsory license must be paid "adequate remuneration in the circumstances of each case, taking into account the economic value of the authorization."[75] Decisions to grant compulsory licenses, and those that determine the patentee's remuneration, are subject to judicial review.[76]

E. Patent Harmonization

Efforts to harmonize the world's disparate patent systems have a long history.[77] An important example is WIPO's Patent Law Treaty (PLT), which entered into force on April 28, 2005.[78] The PLT aims to harmonize and streamline formality requirements of national and regional patent procedures, rather than target substantive harmonization issues.[79]

With regard to substantive issues, the international harmonization debate has placed primary focus on two issues: (1) whether timewise priority in patent rights is to be determined under a first-to-file system or a first-to-invent system, and (2) whether the novelty requirement should be "absolute" or "qualified." The priority issue considers whether, in cases of competing claimants to patent the same invention, a patent system should award the patent to the entity who was first in time to invent, or to the entity who was first to file a patent application for the invention. The absolute-versus-qualified novelty issue invokes the question of whether a patent system provides a prefiling grace period. Each of these harmonization topics is addressed below.[80]

(as a new TRIPS art. 31*bis*) if two-thirds of the WTO's members accept the change. The deadline for acceptance is December 31, 2009. *See* Word Trade Organization, *Members Accepting Amendment of the TRIPS Agreement*, http://www.wto.org/english/tratop_e/trips_e/amendment_e.htm (last visited Aug. 2, 2012).

[75]TRIPS art. 31(h).

[76]*See* TRIPS arts. 31(g), (i), (j), and (k).

[77]"Harmonization" should be distinguished from "unification." Harmonization as applied to patent law refers to efforts to bring the patent law systems of different countries into alignment by reducing or eliminating the differences between them. For example, one of the most contentious issues in patent harmonization debates is whether the United States will change from its historic first-to-invent system to the first-to-file system employed by the rest of the world. Harmonization is not unification, which seeks to establish one unified "world patent" system.

[78]The current text of the Patent Law Treaty, June 1, 2000, 28 U.S.T. 7645, 1160 U.N.T.S. 221, is *available at* http://www.wipo.int/treaties/en/ip/plt/trtdocs_wo038.html.

[79]*See* World Intellectual Property Organization, *Patent Law Treaty (PLT)*, http://www.wipo.int/patent-law/en/plt.htm (last visited Aug. 11, 2012).

[80]For a helpful summary of USPTO views on a variety of patent harmonization topics, see USPTO, *Request for Comments on the International Effort to Harmonize the Substantive Requirements of Patent Laws,* 66 Fed. Reg. 15409 (2001), *available at* http://www.uspto.gov/web/offices/com/sol/notices/intpatlaws.pdf.

1. First-to-File Versus First-to-Invent

In the early 1990s the United States announced, after prolonged debate, that it would maintain its unique first-to-invent system.[81] As of this writing, in mid-2012, the United States is the only country in the world that continues to operate under a first-to-invent system. Although first-to-invent is generally thought to be more fair to independent/small entity inventors, it has made U.S. patent law on this point significantly more complex and administratively burdensome than the first-to-file system employed by the rest of the world.

To simplify the U.S. patent system and move toward substantive international harmonization, Congress repeatedly debated switching to a first-to-file system during the first decade of the twenty-first century.[82] After additional years of negotiation aimed at reaching consensus between various industry groups, Congress enacted the Leahy-Smith America Invents Act of 2011 (AIA).[83] The AIA was signed into law by President Obama on September 16, 2011. This landmark legislation transitions the U.S. from its historic first-to-invent priority principle to a unique "first inventor to file" system.[84]

The AIA represents a unique hybrid of (or compromise between) pre-AIA U.S. law and absolute novelty "first to file" European law (described *infra*). The AIA retains a one-year prefiling date grace period, but only for disclosures made by the inventor (or persons directly or indirectly obtaining the invention therefrom), not third parties. The AIA first-inventor-to-file system goes into effect on March 16, 2013 for patent applications filed on or after that date.[85] The mechanics of the post-AIA first-inventor-to-file system are detailed in Chapter 4 of this text.[86]

Critically, the AIA changes concerning first inventor to file are purely *prospective*. This means that for patents or applications already

---

[81]*U.S. Says "Not Now" on First-to-File, Agrees with Japan on Patent Term*, 47 PAT. TRADEMARK & COPYRIGHT J. (BNA) 285 (Jan. 27, 1994).

[82]*See* Patent Reform Act of 2005, H.R. 2795, 109th Cong. (2005); Patent Reform Act of 2007, H.R. 1908, 110th Cong. (2007); S. 1145, 110th Cong. (2007).

[83]Leahy-Smith America Invents Act, Pub. L. No. 112-29 (H.R. 1249), 125 Stat. 284 (Sept. 16, 2011).

[84]The phrase "first inventor to file" simply denotes a first-to-file system named so as to emphasize the requirement of originality; that is, in order to obtain a patent, the invention must be original to the inventor and not copied or derived from another. This originality requirement is not unique to the United States and is part of the first-to-file systems of other countries.

[85]*See* Leahy-Smith America Invents Act, Pub. L. No. 112-29 (H.R. 1249), §3(n) ("Effective Date"), 125 Stat. 284, 293 (2011).

[86]*See supra* Chapter 4 ("Novelty, Loss of Right, and Priority Pre- and Post-America Invents Act of 2011 (35 U.S.C. §102)"), Part III ("Novelty and Priority Post-America Invents Act of 2011").

in existence on March 16, 2013, the traditional pre-AIA framework continues to control throughout the life of the patents or applications. For example, if federal court litigants challenge the validity of patents already issued as of March 16, 2013, they will continue to mount those challenges under pre-AIA rules. Given the 20-year term of a patent,[87] the duration and complexity of patent litigation, and the possibility of appeals to the Federal Circuit and Supreme Court, it will be necessary to know and apply pre-AIA rules for 30 years or more following the AIA's enactment.

Because U.S. patent law will operate on a dual (pre- and post-AIA) system for many years to come, the traditional first-to-invent principles remain relevant and important in the United States.[88] Operating a patent system under a first-to-invent principle means that when two (or more) persons apply for a patent on the same invention, each having independently made the invention (i.e., *not* copied it), the patent will be awarded (at least theoretically) to the person who was first in time to invent, regardless of the order in which the two filed their respective patent applications.

The use of "theoretically" in the previous sentence indicates that the process does not occur automatically. In the USPTO, the competing claimants must participate in an **interference** proceeding, an *inter partes* adjudicatory proceeding within the USPTO to determine which party invented first.[89] Interference proceedings will be available only until March 16, 2013, although first-to-invent priority principles will continue to apply to validity determinations for issued patents for many years beyond that date. In a USPTO interference, the party who is the last to file (the junior party) bears the burden of overcoming a presumption that the first to file (the senior party) also was the first to invent. As discussed in Chapter 4 ("Novelty, Loss of Right, and Priority Pre- and Post-America Invents Act of 2011 (35 U.S.C. §102)"),

[87]This phrase is a shorthand reference to indicate that since June 8, 1995, U.S. patents have a term that expires 20 years after their earliest U.S. filing date. *See infra* Chapter 1, Section C.7 ("The Patent Term").

[88]Moreover, the AIA does not render irrelevant all aspects of the traditional U.S. first-to-invent priority system. For example, the pre-AIA concept of invention dates (including dates of conception) will likely remain relevant to the post-AIA (i.e., AIA-implemented) derivation proceeding under 35 U.S.C. §135 (eff. Mar. 16, 2013). For more on derivation proceedings, *see infra* Chapter 4, Section S.3.a.

[89]The U.S. patent system has developed the interference proceeding as a means of determining priority of invention. *See generally* Edward Walterscheid, *Priority of Invention: How the United States Came to Have a "First-to-Invent" Patent System,* 23 AIPLA Q.J. 263 (1995). Adoption of the first-to-invent principle does not necessarily require interferences, however. Historically, England appears to have used the relative order of filing dates as an irrebuttable presumption of the relative dates of invention, thus avoiding protracted factual disputes over first-to-invent priority. The author thanks Professor Carl Moy for this observation.

supra, the basic statutory provisions that govern interferences are 35 U.S.C. §102(g)(1) (2006) and 35 U.S.C. §135 (2006). The rules and procedures for interferences are quite complex and beyond the scope of this text.[90]

In countries other than the United States, timewise priority has long been established via a first-to-file system. This is much less cumbersome from an administrative standpoint than the United States' historic first-to-invent system. No determination of dates of conception, diligence, and reduction to practice is necessary, as in U.S. interference proceedings; in the event of a conflict, the patent will be awarded to the party that has the earlier filing date. The concept of **invention date** thus has very little meaning in foreign patent systems.

The first-to-file system has been characterized as unfair for prejudicing the independent inventor with fewer resources and limited capacity to win the race to the patent office. This unfairness is ameliorated to some extent, however, by the recognition in many patent systems of "prior user rights."[91]

A prior user right is essentially a defense to infringement. Prior user rights operate as follows: Assume that party A, a German national, obtains a German patent on a process for brewing beer, and sues party B, an unrelated German national, for infringement of A's patent. B determines that she independently developed the same process before A did and began using it in B's beer-brewing business prior to the filing date of A's patent application. Under these facts the German national patent laws will sustain the validity of A's patent but grant B a prior user right,[92] which is essentially a license that permits B to

---

[90]For further guidance on interference law and practice, *see* Practice Before the Board of Patent Appeals and Interferences, 37 C.F.R. §§41.1-41.208 (2008); *Interference Proceedings,* MANUAL OF PATENT EXAMINING PROCEDURE §§2301-2309 (8th ed., 7th rev. 2008); Charles W. Rivise & A.D. Caesar, INTERFERENCE LAW AND PRACTICE (W.S. Hein 2000); Charles L. Gholz, *Interference Practice, in* 5 IRVING KAYTON & KARYL S. KAYTON, PATENT PRACTICE 23.3 (6th ed. 1997).

[91]*See* Gary L. Griswold et al., *Prior User Rights: Neither a Rose Nor a Thorn,* 2 U. BALT. INTELL. PROP. L.J. 233, 236 (1994) (stating that foreign countries that provide defense to infringement based on prior user rights "include our most important trading partners and account for approximately 85% of the world's gross domestic product outside of the United States. (In Europe: France, Germany, Italy, The Netherlands, Spain, the United Kingdom, and 12 other countries. In Asia: China, Hong Kong, Indonesia, Japan, South Korea, Malaysia, the Philippines, Singapore, and Taiwan. In North America: Canada and Mexico. And elsewhere: Australia, Egypt, and Israel).") (footnotes omitted).

[92]The German patent statute provides:

§12. (1) A patent shall have no effect against a person who, at the time of the filing of the application, had already begun to use the invention in Germany, or had made the necessary arrangements for so doing. Said person shall be entitled to use the invention for the needs of his own business in his own workshops or continue using the beer brewing process without liability to A.[93] The license to B is a personal one, such that B cannot transfer the license to third party C, other than in connection with a full, bona fide transfer of B's beer-brewing business.

Prior to 1999, the United States did not recognize prior user rights at all, most likely because they are viewed as reducing the economic value of patents through derogating the patentee's exclusivity. In response to concerns over the rising tide of business method patents, Congress created a very limited prior user right as part of enacting the American Inventor Protection Act of 1999. The misnamed "earlier inventor" defense, codified at 35 U.S.C. §273 (2006), was limited to infringements of claims to methods, which the statute defines as "a method of doing or conducting business."[94] To claim the defense, the prior user must have (1) actually reduced the invention to practice more than one year before the patentee's effective filing date (i.e., U.S. or foreign priority date), and (2) commercially used the invention at any time prior to that same date.[95]

The defense of prior user rights as applicable in U.S. patent litigation was significantly broadened by the America Invents Act of 2011. As described in further detail in Chapter 10 of this text,[96] the protection of the post-AIA version of 35 U.S.C. §273 (eff. Sept. 16, 2011) ("Defense to infringement based on prior commercial use") is potentially available to alleged infringers practicing "subject matter consisting of a process, or consisting of a machine, manufacture, or composition of matter used in a manufacturing or other commercial process."[97] Thus, post-AIA, the practice of *all* 35 U.S.C. §101 categories of subject matter is potentially shielded by prior user rights so long as the accused infringer was using the allegedly infringing subject matter in a "commercial process" by the requisite date. The defense is no longer limited to those who allegedly infringed patented business methods. The broadened version of the prior user rights defense

---

the workshops of others. This right can only be inherited or transferred together with the business. . . .

(2) When the patentee is entitled to a right of priority, the date of the prior application shall be decisive and not the date of the application referred to in subsection (1). However, this provision shall not apply to nationals of a foreign country that does not guarantee reciprocity in this respect, where they claim the priority of a foreign application.

Patentgesetz [Patent Act], Dec. 16, 1980, BGBl.I 1981 at 1, last amended Jul. 31, 2009, BGBl.I at 2030, §12 (F.R.G.), *translated in* http://www.wipo.int/wipolex/en/text.jsp?file_id=238776.

[93]Thus, prior user rights can be viewed as a variety of compulsory licensing.
[94]35 U.S.C. §273(a)(3).
[95]*See* 35 U.S.C. §273(b)(1).
[96]*See supra* Chapter 10, Section C.2.
[97]35 U.S.C. §273(a) (eff. Sept. 16, 2011).

became available for those accused of infringing patents that issued on or after September 16, 2011.

2.   Absolute Versus Qualified Novelty: Grace Period

The second major issue addressed in patent harmonization debates is the need for an internationally recognized prefiling **grace period.** As introduced in Chapter 4, *supra,* a grace period in patent law is a limited period of time prior to the applicant's filing date in which the invention may be commercially exploited or otherwise injected into the public domain without any loss of right to obtain a patent. U.S. patent law has recognized a grace period since 1839.[98] The pre-AIA grace period, as provided for in 35 U.S.C. §102(b) (2006), is one year. During this year-long time period, an invention may be patented, described in a printed publication, in public use, or placed on sale, by the inventor or a third party, all without triggering a §102(b) loss of right. Post-AIA, the one-year grace period continues but in a narrower form. The post-AIA grace period protects inventors only against their own prefiling disclosures (or disclosures made by another who directly or indirectly obtained the invention from the inventor), and not against third-party disclosures.[99]

Countries other than the United States are "absolute novelty" systems, which do not recognize any significant prefiling date grace period (or when they do, the grace period is only for very limited times and purposes, such as particular types of international exhibitions[100]). For example, under the European Patent Convention (EPC) Article 54, any activity that makes the invention part of the "state of the art" at any time prior to the filing of the European patent application will defeat novelty.[101]

---

[98]From 1839 to 1939, U.S. patent law recognized a two-year grace period. In 1939, the grace period was reduced to one year.

[99]*See* 35 U.S.C. §102(b) (1) (eff. Mar. 16, 2013) ("Disclosures Made 1 Year or Less Before the Effective Filing Date of the Claimed Invention"). For further analysis of this provision, *see supra* Chapter 4, Section S ("Novelty-Preserving Exceptions Under Post-AIA 35 U.S.C. §102(b)").

[100]*See, e.g.*, Convention on the Grant of European Patents art. 55 ("Non-prejudicial Disclosures"), Oct. 5, 1973, 13 I.L.M. 268, 2007 O.J. Eur. Pat. Off. (Spec. Ed. 4) 1, 57, *available at* http://www.epo.org/law-practice/legal-texts/html/epc/2010/e/ar55.html [hereinafter European Patent Convention].

[101]*See* European Patent Convention art. 54(1) ("An invention shall be considered to be new if it does not form part of the state of the art."); *id.* at art. 54(2) ("[S]tate of the art shall be held to comprise everything made available to the public by means of a written or oral description, by use, or in any other way, before the date of filing of the European patent application.").

Absolute novelty systems are particularly difficult environments for professors and researchers in the academic community, with its "publish or perish" ethos, who also seek patent protection for their research results. Under an absolute novelty system, the patent application must be filed before any publication of the invention, including oral divulgation, is made.[102]

In previous patent harmonization discussions, the United States proposed that it would consider shifting to first-to-file in exchange for worldwide recognition of a suitable prefiling grace period. Congress passed the AIA in 2011 without the United States having obtained that concession. Independently of U.S. proposals, however, European patent experts continue to press for the international adoption of a grace period.[103]

F. Gray Market Goods and the International Exhaustion Debate[104]

Transborder patent disputes frequently involve "gray market" goods. Such goods, also termed "parallel imports," are not counterfeit, illegal, pirated, or products of the "black market." Rather, gray market goods are legitimate products, manufactured by or under the authority of the patent owner. Whether manufactured domestically or offshore, gray market goods are first sold in a foreign market by the patent owner or its authorized agent, then purchased by third parties for unauthorized importation to the patent owner's home market, where they compete with authorized (and typically higher-priced) channels of distribution. Because these goods are typically sold by the patent owner at discounted prices in foreign markets, they are attractive targets for purchase by gray marketeers, who will import them into the patentee's domestic market to undercut higher prices there.

The divisive legal issue raised by parallel imports is whether the patent owner, having first sold its patented goods outside its domestic market, can prevent their subsequent importation into that market by an unauthorized third party as a violation of the underlying patent right. The patentee's ability to use its patent as a weapon to prevent

---

[102]*See* European Patent Convention art. 54(2).

[103]*See* European Patent Office, Press Release, *The Case For and Against the Introduction of a Grace Period in European Patent Law* (July 25, 2000) (summarizing comments of Mr. Jan Galama and Professor Dr. Joseph Straus). *See also* European Research News Centre, *The Controversial 'Grace Period'* (Aug. 28, 2002), *available at* http://ec.europa.eu/research/news-centre/en/soc/02-07-soc03.html.

[104]Much of this section is based on ideas in Janice Mueller & Jeffery Atik, *New International Dimensions in the Gray Market Goods Debate*, 1 J. MARSHALL CENTER FOR INTELL. PROP. L. NEWS SOURCE 6 (Summer 1999).

competition from gray market goods turns on a legal doctrine rather inaptly named "exhaustion of rights."[105] Three forms of exhaustion should be distinguished: (1) domestic exhaustion, (2) regional exhaustion (e.g., within the European Union), and (3) international exhaustion. Each is discussed below.

1. Domestic Exhaustion

The concept of domestic exhaustion in the patent context is well established in the national laws of all countries and is not directly implicated in parallel imports disputes. Domestic exhaustion simply means that after the first authorized sale of a product in a given domestic market, the owner of the patent right(s) under which that particular item was produced no longer has any enforceable right to control the disposition or profit from the subsequent resale *of that same physical item* within the domestic market.[106]

For example, a consumer who purchases a new Ford automobile in Michigan, which automobile contains one or more internal components covered by Ford patents in the United States, owes no further patent royalty or other remuneration to the Ford Motor Company if and when she resells the same car in California. Ford received full value or "tribute" for the value of its patented automotive inventions

---

[105]The phrase "exhaustion of rights" is something of a misnomer. The intellectual property right itself (e.g., the patent owner's right to exclude others from making, using, selling, offering to sell, or importing the claimed invention) is never exhausted, at least during the term of the patent. Rather, what is exhausted is the IP owner's *right to control the disposition of a particular item* that was originally produced under authority of her patent in a foreign country, but subsequently purchased by a third party and imported without the patent owner's permission into the patent owner's home country.

Judge Giles Rich found the use of exhaustion terminology illogical:

> When the patentee himself makes and sells, he is not exercising his patent rights; in selling, he is, therefore, not exhausting them. It is not a question of control over the thing sold but of control, if any, over the purchaser and others. Having once enjoyed the potential benefit of having made a sale of property without competition, does the statute give the patentee any right whatever to control the purchaser with respect to the property he bought? My answer is "No" and the courts have generally so held, at least for the last half century. They have rationalized the results, however, on the "exhaustion" theory, which is, in my view, logically unjustifiable.

Giles S. Rich, *My Favorite Things*, 35 IDEA 1, 3-4 (1994).

[106]U.S. copyright law implements an analogous domestic exhaustion rule through the "first sale doctrine" of 17 U.S.C. §109(a). The Supreme Court considered domestic patent exhaustion as a defense to patent infringement in *Quanta Computer, Inc. v. LG Elecs., Inc.*, 553 U.S. 617 (2008). For analysis of the *Quanta* decision, *see supra* Chapter 10, Section C.8 ("Patent Exhaustion").

at the time of the first authorized sale of the car, and the purchaser obtained the right to dispose of the car in any manner without having to seek Ford's permission.[107] The principle of domestic exhaustion recognizes that the fundamental legal policy against restraints on alienation of personal property outweighs any patent right of Ford.

2.   Regional (European Community-Wide) Exhaustion

A second variety of exhaustion theory applies within the 27 member countries ("member states") of the European Union (as of the writing of this edition in 2012).[108] The European Court of Justice (ECJ) has adopted a "community-wide exhaustion" approach, which is in essence domestic exhaustion for a marketplace that comprises the entire European Union (EU). In practice, community exhaustion means that once a patented item is put on the market anywhere in the EU with the patent owner's consent, the patent owner cannot thereafter prevent the importation of that patented item into another EU member state.[109] The ECJ's adoption of community exhaustion reflects the Treaty of Rome's bedrock principle of "free movement of goods," which grounds the EU's antipathy toward barriers to trade between EU member states.[110]

---

[107]She did not, however, obtain the right to infringe Ford's patent rights by reconstructing the patented items, effectively "making" the patent items a second time. Infringing **reconstruction** should be distinguished from noninfringing **repair** of a patented item, which is within the purchaser's implied license to use the item she has purchased. *See* Jazz Photo Corp. v. Int'l Trade Comm'n, 264 F.3d 1094, 1105 (Fed. Cir. 2001).

[108]Effective Jan. 1, 2007, the European Union was expanded from 25 to 27 members. *See* http://ec.europa.eu/enlargement/the-policy/from-6-to-27-members/index_en.htm (last visited Aug. 2, 2012).

[109]*See generally* Case 187/80, Merck & Co. v. Stephar BV, 1981 E.C.R. 2063, *available at* http://eur-lex.europa.eu/smartapi/cgi/sga_doc?smartapi!celexplus!prod!CELEX numdoc&numdoc=61980J0187&lg=en.

[110]*See* Consolidated Version of the Treaty Establishing the European Economic Community, 2006 O.J. (C321) E/37, *available at* http://eur-lex.europa.eu/LexUriServ/ LexUriServ.do?uri=OJ:C:2006:321E:0001:0331:EN:pdf [hereinafter Treaty of Rome]. The interface (or tension) between the free movement of goods principle and the territorial nature of intellectual property rights is illustrated by reading Article 28 of the Treaty of Rome in conjunction with Article 30. Article 28 (formerly Article 30) provides that "[q]uantitative restrictions on imports and all measures having equivalent effect shall be prohibited between Member States." However, Article 30 (formerly Article 36) creates a qualified exception for intellectual property rights, providing that (emphasis added)

> [t]he provisions of Article[] 28 . . . shall not preclude prohibitions or restrictions on imports, exports or goods in transit justified on grounds of . . . *the protection of industrial* and commercial *property*. Such prohibitions or restrictions shall not, however, constitute a means of arbitrary discrimination or a disguised restriction on trade between Member States.

3. International Exhaustion

The third and final variety of exhaustion, international exhaustion, is a more complicated and unsettled legal concept than the two previous forms; international exhaustion is directly implicated in parallel imports disputes that span national borders. In contrast with domestic exhaustion, countries do not uniformly agree over whether to adhere to the principle of international exhaustion. Proponents of international exhaustion contend that a patent owner's rights are extinguished at the first authorized sale of a patented item anywhere in the world, and that subsequent importation of that same item into the patentee's home country cannot be a legal wrong. This faction, which includes discount retailers, consumer action groups, and some economists, contends that consumers benefit from the price competition created by parallel imports. Advocates of international free trade and international harmonization of IP rights also favor parallel imports, because permitting entry of gray goods will lessen if not eliminate the patent owner's ability to price-discriminate on an international scale.

International exhaustion is a controversial idea because it flies in the face of traditional thinking that patent rights are merely national, not international, in scope, and that such rights begin and end at national borders. Indeed, the U.S. Patent Act expressly provides that unauthorized importation of goods embodying a patented invention is actionable infringement.[111] Patent owners, particularly in the pharmaceutical industry, contend that sales of their patented product in a foreign market, usually at discounted prices, cannot exhaust their domestic patent rights, which are created by domestic statutes of restricted territorial scope and for which the patentees have not received full value in the lower-priced foreign sales.

Of all forms of IP protection, the complexity of patent law may make it the most territorial, as reflected historically by extensive substantive differences between national patent laws. Indeed, Article 4*bis* of the Paris Convention expressly recognizes the principle of independence of patents obtained for the same invention in different countries. Thus, the Japanese Supreme Court's 1997 decision in *BBS Kraftfahrzeug Technik AG v. Kabushiki Kaisha Racimex Japan and Kabushiki Kaisha JapAuto Prods.*,[112] which adopted and applied the

---

[111]*See* 35 U.S.C. §271(a) (2012) (defining patent infringement as including "import[ation] into the United States" of any patented invention "without authority").

[112]51 Minshu 2299 (Sup. Ct. July 1, 1997), *translated in* http://www.courts.go.jp/english/judgments/text/1997.07.01-1995-O-No.1988.html (last visited Aug. 11, 2012). For additional analysis of *BBS, see* Janice Mueller & Jeffery Atik, *New International Dimensions in the Gray Market Goods Debate*, 1 J. MARSHALL CENTER FOR INTELL. PROP. L. NEWS SOURCE 6 (Summer 1999).

international exhaustion doctrine against a Japanese patent owner, surprised many in the international patent community.

The United States does not (as yet) recognize the principle of international exhaustion with respect to patented items (in contrast with the U.S. courts' treatment of certain categories of copyrighted or trademarked goods[113]). For those novel and nonobvious products that can qualify, protection under U.S. patent laws thus holds the greatest promise for domestic corporations seeking to stop parallel imports.

In its only decision touching on parallel imports of patented goods, the U.S. Supreme Court in *Boesch v. Graff*[114] enjoined the importation of a product covered by U.S. patent and acquired abroad from an authorized German source with prior user rights, broadly asserting that "[t]he sale of articles in the United States under a United States patent cannot be controlled by foreign laws."[115] The Federal Circuit relied on *Boesch*'s rejection of the international exhaustion doctrine in *Jazz Photo Corp. v. U.S. Int'l Trade Commission*,[116] confirming that "United States patent rights are not exhausted by products of foreign provenance" and that for an accused infringer "[t]o invoke the protection of the first sale doctrine, the authorized first sale must have occurred under the United States patent."[117]

G.   Enforcement of Foreign Patents in U.S. Courts

The U.S. Supreme Court's 2007 decision in *Microsoft Corp. v. AT&T Corp.*[118] reinforced a strong presumption against extraterritorial application of U.S. patents.[119] Because a U.S. court is unlikely to hold that

---

[113]*See* Quality King Distributors, Inc. v. L'Anza Res. Int'l, Inc., 523 U.S. 135 (1998) ("round trip" copyrighted goods); K-Mart Corp. v. Cartier, Inc., 486 U.S. 281 (1988) (trademarked goods). The Supreme Court is scheduled to hear oral argument during October 2012 in another important copyright case raising international exhaustion issues. *See* Kirtsaeng v. John Wiley & Sons, Inc., 132 S. Ct. 1905 (*cert. granted* Apr. 16, 2012).

[114]133 U.S. 697 (1890).

[115]Boesch v. Graff, 133 U.S. 697, 703 (1890).

[116]264 F.3d 1094 (Fed. Cir. 2001).

[117]Jazz Photo Corp. v. U.S. Int'l Trade Commission, 264 F.3d 1094, 1105 (Fed. Cir. 2001) (citing *Boesch* for proposition that "a lawful foreign purchase does not obviate the need for license from the United States patentee before importation into and sale in the United States").

[118]550 U.S. 437 (2007).

[119]*See* Microsoft Corp. v. AT&T Corp., 550 U.S. 437, 454-455 (stating that the presumption that United States law "governs domestically but does not rule the world" applied "with particular force in patent law") (citing 35 U.S.C. §154(a)(1), and *Deepsouth Packing Co. v. Laitram Corp.*, 406 U.S. 518, 531 (1972)). The Supreme Court's *Microsoft* decision is examined in further detail *supra* Chapter 9, Section E.4 ("Component Exports Under 35 U.S.C. §271(f)").

acts occurring abroad infringe a U.S. patent, the conventional strategy for combating such acts requires that one has obtained patent protection in foreign countries and thereafter enforces the foreign patents in the courts of the foreign jurisdictions where the acts of infringement allegedly occurred. As commerce expands globally, the expense and complexity of conducting patent litigation in multiple foreign fora loom large.[120]

As a result, U.S. patent holders owning counterpart foreign patents on a particular invention have asked U.S. courts not only to decide the question of domestic infringement but also to exercise supplemental jurisdiction under 28 U.S.C. §1367 in order to decide whether the counterpart foreign patents have been infringed by foreign acts.[121] This strategy has not proved successful thus far, however, because the Federal Circuit continues to reject district court exercises of supplemental jurisdiction over foreign patent issues.[122]

For example, the Federal Circuit held that a district court abused its discretion in exercising supplemental jurisdiction over foreign patent claims in the closely watched *Voda v. Cordis Corp.*[123] The plaintiff Dr. Voda owned U.S. and foreign patents (the latter issuing from the same PCT application) directed to guiding catheters for use in interventional cardiology. Although the parties disputed whether Voda's U.S. and foreign patents differed in any material aspects, the same accused Cordis catheter was sold in the United States as well as France, Germany, the United Kingdom, and Canada. The Federal Circuit discussed but declined to decide under §1367(a) whether Voda's assertion of foreign patent infringement involved a "common nucleus of operative fact" with the question whether Voda's U.S. patent was infringed.[124]

Rather, the Federal Circuit held that the district court had abused its discretion under 28 U.S.C. §1367(c) by not declining to exercise

---

[120]*See* Fairchild Semiconductor Corp. v. Third Dimension (3D) Semiconductor, Inc., 589 F. Supp. 2d 84, 99 (D. Me. 2008) (observing that "[i]n a globalized marketplace, intellectual property disputes can involve many countries' patent laws. Uncertainty and complexity in resolving those disputes can increase the cost of doing business and, as a result, the cost to the consumer.") (footnotes omitted).

[121]Section 1367 ("Supplemental jurisdiction") of 28 U.S.C. provides in part that "[e]xcept as provided in subsections (b) and (c) or as expressly provided otherwise by Federal statute, in any civil action of which the district courts have original jurisdiction, the district courts shall have supplemental jurisdiction over all other claims that are so related to claims in the action within such original jurisdiction that they form part of the same case or controversy under Article III of the United States Constitution." *Id.* at §1367(a).

[122]*See* Voda v. Cordis Corp., 476 F.3d 887 (Fed. Cir. 2007) (vacating district court's acceptance of supplemental jurisdiction); *cf.* Mars, Inc. v. Kabushiki-Kaisha Nippon Conlux, 24 F.3d 1368 (Fed. Cir. 1994) (affirming district court's decision to decline supplemental jurisdiction over claim of infringement of Japanese patent).

[123]476 F.3d 887, 904 (Fed. Cir. 2007).

[124]*See Voda*, 476 F.3d at 896.

supplemental jurisdiction.[125] According to the *Voda* majority, "considerations of comity, judicial economy, convenience, fairness, and other exceptional circumstances constitute compelling reasons to decline jurisdiction . . . in this case."[126] The majority first observed that nothing in the Paris Convention, PCT, or TRIPS Agreement "contemplates or allows one jurisdiction to adjudicate patents of another."[127] With respect to comity, the majority saw "no reason why American courts should supplant British, Canadian, French, or German courts in interpreting and enforcing British, Canadian, European, French, or German patents."[128] Judicial economy would not be realized by the exercise of supplemental jurisdiction because U.S. courts "lack . . . institutional competence in the foreign patent regimes" at issue, and separate trials would likely be required to deal with potential jury confusion in applying the different regimes.[129] The district court had not articulated any analysis regarding factors of convenience.[130] Lastly, the act of state doctrine potentially made the district court's exercise of supplemental jurisdiction over foreign patent claims fundamentally unfair. The doctrine might prevent U.S. courts from inquiring into the validity of foreign patents and might require the courts to adjudicate patent claims regardless of validity or enforceability.[131]

The Federal Circuit concluded by noting that the reasons it had stated as compelling the district court to decline supplemental jurisdiction in *Voda,* namely, limitations imposed by international treaties and considerations of comity, judicial economy, convenience, and fairness, comprised a "non-exhaustive list, not a test, for district courts to consider under §1367(c)."[132] The *Voda* court held out some slight

---

[125]Section 1367(c) provides that "[t]he district courts may decline to exercise supplemental jurisdiction over a claim under subsection (a) if—(1) the claim raises a novel or complex issue of State law, (2) the claim substantially predominates over the claim or claims over which the district court has original jurisdiction, (3) the district court has dismissed all claims over which it has original jurisdiction, or (4) in exceptional circumstances, there are other compelling reasons for declining jurisdiction." The Federal Circuit in *Voda* held that the district court erred by not declining supplemental jurisdiction under subpart (4) of §1367(c), because the case presented "exceptional circumstances" involving "compelling reasons" for declining. *See Voda,* 476 F.3d at 898.

[126]*Voda,* 476 F.3d at 898.

[127]*Voda.* 476 F.3d at 899. The dissent pointed out that none of the treaties affirmatively prohibits resolution by a national court of private disputes that include foreign patent rights. *See id.* at 915 (Newman, J., dissenting).

[128]*Voda,* 476 F.3d at 901.

[129]*See Voda,* 476 F.3d at 903.

[130]*See Voda,* 476 F.3d at 903.

[131]*See Voda,* 476 F.3d at 904. The dissent responded that "the grant of a patent is not an Act of State, whether done by the United States or a foreign country." *Id.* at 914 (Newman, J., dissenting). "Patent validity and infringement are legal and commercial issues, not acts of state." *Id.* at 915 (Newman, J., dissenting).

[132]*Voda,* 476 F.3d at 904-905.

possibility that other cases raising different facts might support the exercise of supplemental jurisdiction over foreign patent claims, "especially if circumstances change, such as if the United States were to enter into a new international patent treaty or if events during litigation alter a district court's conclusions regarding comity, judicial economy, convenience, or fairness."[133] In the case at bar, however, the factors considered by the majority compelled it to conclude that the district court had abused its discretion in exercising supplemental jurisdiction.[134]

---

[133]*Voda*, 476 F.3d at 905.

[134]The dissent in *Voda* observed that, *inter alia*, U.S. courts routinely decide issues of foreign law. The majority's "extreme barrier to exercise of the district court's discretion when foreign patents are involved stands alone among the vast variety of causes in which such determinations have been made." *Id.* at 906 (Newman, J., dissenting). The dissent charged that the majority's ruling "essentially eliminates [the] discretionary option in foreign patent cases." *Id.* at 910. Moreover, it contravened *eBay Inc. v. MercExchange L.L.C.*, 547 U.S. 388 (2006), in which the Supreme Court "discouraged the carving out of an exception uniquely for patent cases, and required that the equitable discretion of the district court be as available in patent cases as in other cases." *Voda*, 476 F.3d at 910 (Newman, J., dissenting).

Echoing the *Voda* dissent, a federal district court has read the *Voda* majority's decision as "seem[ing] vehement that a United States court should almost always decline to hear a dispute about foreign patents, at least if its jurisdiction is discretionary." Fairchild Semiconductor Corp. v. Third Dimension (3D) Semiconductor, Inc., 589 F. Supp. 2d 84, 85 (D. Me. 2008). The district court in *Fairchild* distinguished *Voda*, however, because *Fairchild* involved a licensing dispute in which the parties had agreed to a forum selection clause for resolution of disputes involving the licensed U.S. and Chinese patents. The district court held that its diversity of citizenship jurisdiction (rather than §1367 supplemental jurisdiction) applied to this contractual dispute, and that the court should exercise that jurisdiction even though doing so might require consideration of Chinese patent law. *See Fairchild*, 589 F. Supp. 2d at 98 (concluding that "the concerns expressed in *Voda* do not prevent enforcement of the forum selection clause for this royalty dispute").

Glossary

Accused device, Accused composition of matter, Accused method: The allegedly infringing item (or composition or method) that was made, used, sold, offered for sale, or imported by one accused of infringing a patent (referred to as the **accused infringer**).

All-limitations rule: A doctrine requiring that in order to be found infringing, an accused device must satisfy (i.e., meet or match) each and every limitation of an allegedly infringed patent claim, either literally or under the doctrine of equivalents. The all-limitations rule, sometimes referred to as the all-elements rule, emphasizes that each and every limitation of a patent claim is material.

Analogous art: The prior art permissibly considered in an analysis of nonobviousness under 35 U.S.C. §103; that which, as a matter of law, the person having ordinary skill in the art reasonably would have consulted in attempting to solve the problem addressed by her invention. To be considered analogous to a claimed invention, the prior art in question must be either (1) prior art within the same field of endeavor as the invention, or (2) prior art from a different field of endeavor but reasonably pertinent to the same problem as that addressed by the invention. *See also* **Person having ordinary skill in the art (PHOSITA).**

Antedate: To "swear behind" a prior art **reference**. In accordance with the procedures set forth in 37 C.F.R. §1.131, a patent applicant may establish an **invention date** (pre–America Invents Act of 2011 (AIA)) predating the effective date of a prior art reference that has been cited against his claims in a rejection for lack of novelty under 35 U.S.C. §102(a) or (e) or for obviousness under 35 U.S.C. §103.

Anticipation: The negation (or opposite) of novelty, occurring through the triggering of one or more subsections of 35 U.S.C. §102. When one of the triggering events has occurred, it is said that the claimed invention has been anticipated. The necessary relationship between an anticipatory prior art reference and the claimed invention is one of **strict identity**; that is, in order to evidence anticipation under 35 U.S.C. §102, a single prior art reference must disclose every limitation of the claimed invention, arranged as in the claim. *See also* **Loss of right.**

697

Assignment: A transfer of ownership of a patent, patent application, or any interest therein. *See* 35 U.S.C. §261. *Compare with* **License.**

Best mode: A requirement of 35 U.S.C. §112(a) (eff. Sept. 16, 2012) that an inventor must disclose in a U.S. patent application the best way known to the inventor, as of the application's filing date, of carrying out the invention. The best mode is sometimes designated as the preferred embodiment of the invention. Post-AIA, patent applicants must continue to comply with the best mode disclosure requirement, but failure to satisfy the requirement is no longer a ground for challenging the validity of an issued patent in the federal courts or the USPTO.

Blocking patents: Two or more patents having claim coverage such that the practice of one patent infringes the other and vice versa. Patents are often said to be blocking when one patent issues covering a basic invention, a second patent issues covering an improvement of the basic invention, and the patents are owned by different entities. The blocking patents scenario is traditionally resolved by means of cross-licenses.

Central claiming: A patent claiming regime in which the patent claim recites the preferred embodiment of the invention but is deemed as a matter of law to include all equivalents to (i.e., substantially similar copies of) that preferred embodiment. *Compare with* **Peripheral claiming.**

Claims: Single-sentence definitions of the scope of a patent owner's right to exclude others from making, using, selling, offering to sell, or importing her invention, that appear at the end of the patent's specification. *See* 35 U.S.C. §112(b) (eff. Sept. 16, 2012). The individual elements or components of a patent claim are called **limitations.**

Commercial embodiment: The actual product or process, sold in the marketplace, that corresponds to (i.e., is made in accordance with) the invention as claimed in a patent. For purposes of determining infringement, however, it is improper to compare the commercial embodiment of the patented invention with the accused device. The *patent claims*, rather than the commercial embodiment of the invention, are what must be compared with the accused device in order to find infringement.

Composition of matter: A category of potentially patentable subject matter under 35 U.S.C. §101 that includes chemical compositions and mixtures of substances such as metallic alloys.

Compulsory license: A nonconsensual patent license that a government compels a patent owner to grant to a third party. Signatories to the GATT TRIPS Agreement may implement compulsory licensing systems under the conditions imposed by Article 31. The United States has historically opposed most forms of compulsory licensing.

Conception: The mental part of the act of inventing. Conception involves the formation in the mind of the inventor of the definite and permanent idea of the complete and operative invention, as it is thereafter to be applied in practice. *Compare with* **Reduction to practice.**

Continuation application: A patent application that encompasses all of the disclosure of an earlier (parent or original) application and that does not add any **new matter** to that disclosure. To the extent that it satisfies 35 U.S.C. §120, the continuation application "shall have the same effect" as if it were filed on the filing date of the parent application.

Continuation-in-part (CIP) application: A patent application that encompasses the disclosure of an earlier (parent or original) application and adds **new matter** to that disclosure. For purposes of patentability (i.e., examination for novelty and nonobviousness against the prior art), the claims of the CIP that are directed to common subject matter (i.e., subject matter disclosed in both the parent and the CIP) are entitled to the filing date of the parent, while those claims directed to new matter not disclosed in the parent are entitled only to the actual filing date of the CIP. For purposes of determining a patent's *expiration date*, however, if the patent application contains a specific reference to an earlier-filed application or applications under 35 U.S.C. §120 or §121, all claims of the patent will expire 20 years after the earliest such filing date.

Contributory infringement: A form of indirect infringement. *See* 35 U.S.C. §271(c). Contributory infringement is an act of infringement committed by one who supplies (i.e., sells, offers to sell, or imports into the United States) a nonstaple *component* of a patented invention to another who directly infringes under 35 U.S.C. §271(a) by making, using, selling, offering to sell, or importing the *entire* patented invention. The supplied component must constitute a material part of the invention, and the contributory infringer must know that it is especially made or adapted for use in the infringement. Moreover, the supplied component must not be a staple article or commodity of commerce suitable for substantial noninfringing use. *See also* **Inducing infringement; Infringement.**

Critical date: The date that is one year prior to the date of filing a U.S. patent application. The date is considered critical for purposes of triggering the **statutory bars** of 35 U.S.C. §102(b) (pre-AIA) or the exceptions of 35 U.S.C. §102(b)(1) (post-AIA).

Declaratory judgment action: Under 28 U.S.C. §2201, an accused infringer may initiate a legal action against a patentee, seeking a declaration from a federal district court that he does not infringe the patent in suit and/or that the patent is invalid and/or unenforceable. Before a declaratory judgment action can be filed, an actual controversy must exist between the parties. The accused infringer/declaratory plaintiff (1) must have a reasonable apprehension of being sued for patent infringement, and (2) must be engaging in "present activity which could constitute infringement or [must have taken] concrete steps . . . with the intent to conduct such activity."

Definiteness: Shorthand name for the requirement of 35 U.S.C. §112(b) (eff. Sept. 16, 2012) that patent claims "particularly point[] out and distinctly claim[] the subject matter which the applicant regards as his invention." Claim definiteness is judged from the perspective of a **PHOSITA.**

Derivation: One who derives his invention from another is essentially a copyist, not an inventor, and is not entitled to a patent. Derivation involves the conception of an invention by party A and communication of that conception to party B. Under 35 U.S.C. §102(f) (pre-AIA), party B should not be granted a patent because "he did not himself invent the subject matter sought to be patented." AIA-implemented derivation proceedings are governed by 35 U.S.C. §135 (eff. Mar. 16, 2013).

Diligence: In order to establish a **conception** date as the invention date (an important pre-AIA concept) for a given invention, an inventor must have worked diligently following the conception to reduce the invention to practice (either actually or constructively). In determining priority of invention between two rival claimants for a patent under 35 U.S.C. §102(g) (pre-AIA), the party seeking to establish its conception date as its invention date must show reasonable diligence extending from "a time prior to conception by the other" to the party's own **reduction to practice** date. Reasonable diligence is established by evidence that the inventor was continuously active in working toward a reduction to practice of the invention she conceived, or that a legitimate excuse exists for any inactivity during the relevant time period.

Disclosure: The information included in a patent specification (in the form of text and, in many cases, drawings) in order to satisfy the requirements of 35 U.S.C. §112(a) (eff. Sept. 16, 2012): **enablement, best mode**, and **written description of the invention.**

Divisional application: A patent application that is divided or split from another (parent or original) application. When two or more "independent and distinct" inventions are claimed in a single original application, the USPTO may require that the original application be restricted to one of the inventions in accordance with 35 U.S.C. §121. The applicant may elect to prosecute the claims directed to one of the inventions (the elected claims) in the original application and file a "divisional" application directed to the other, nonelected invention. To the extent that it complies with 35 U.S.C. §120, the divisional application "shall be entitled to the benefit of the filing date of the original application." 35 U.S.C. §120. *See also* **Restriction requirement.**

Doctrine of equivalents: A judicially created theory of nonliteral patent infringement. The doctrine of equivalents extends the scope of the patentee's right to exclude others from making, using, selling, offering to sell, or importing the claimed invention beyond the scope of protection that is literally defined by the patent claims. The doctrine of equivalents evolved as a judicial response to the practical reality that if a party can avoid patent infringement liability by copying the claimed invention while making a minor, insubstantial change of just enough scope to take the copied matter outside of the literal boundaries of the claim, the economic value of the patent is significantly lessened. *See also* **Literal infringement.**

Double patenting: A prohibition against the issuance of more than one U.S. patent on a particular claimed invention. If an applicant attempts to obtain a second patent claiming the same invention or an obvious variant of the invention he has previously patented, he may confront a USPTO rejection of the second application's claims on the basis of double patenting. U.S. patent law recognizes at least two varieties of double patenting: (1) *same invention-type* (or *statutory*) double patenting, which is based on the wording of 35 U.S.C. §101 that "[w]hoever invents or discovers any new and useful process, machine, manufacture, or composition of matter . . . may obtain *a* patent therefor . . . "; and (2) *obviousness-type* double patenting, which is a judicially created doctrine intended to prevent a patentee from effectively extending his patent monopoly by obtaining a second patent on an obvious variant of the invention claimed in a first patent. Unlike same invention-type double patenting rejections, obviousness-type double patenting rejections may be overcome by the filing of a terminal disclaimer in accordance with 35 U.S.C. §253, ¶2. A rejection for double patenting can be conceptualized as the opposite of a

restriction requirement, which is made by the USPTO in response to an applicant's attempted claiming of more than one invention in a single patent application.

Effective filing date (EFD): The effective filing date of a patent application is the filing date of an earlier-filed application, the benefit of which is accorded to the patent application in question under 35 U.S.C. §119 (Right of Priority [from foreign filing date or domestic provisional application filing date]), §120 (Benefit of Earlier U.S. Filing Date), or §121 (Divisional Applications) or, if no such benefit is accorded, the actual filing date of the patent application in question. The AIA added to the Patent Act an explicit definition of the "effective filing date for a claimed invention in a patent or application for patent." *See* 35 U.S.C. §100(i)(1) (eff. Mar. 16, 2013). *See also* **Foreign priority.**

Enablement: The requirement of 35 U.S.C. §112(a) (eff. Sept. 16, 2012) that a patent applicant describe in the **specification** how to make and use the invention claimed therein in such "full, clear, concise, and exact terms" as to permit any person skilled in the art of the invention to do so without undue experimentation.

Equitable estoppel: An equitable defense to a charge of patent infringement. Equitable estoppel is separate and independent from the defense of **laches** (although the two are frequently asserted together). Equitable estoppel targets the plaintiff's misleading actions that led the defendant to believe it would not be sued. If the defense of equitable estoppel is established, then the plaintiff's claim of infringement is entirely barred.

Experimental use: This judicially created doctrine negates (or excuses) certain activity occurring more than one year before a U.S. patent application's filing date that would *prima facie* appear to trigger the on sale or public use bars of 35 U.S.C. §102(b) (pre-AIA). In order to negate a statutory bar, the pre–critical date activity must involve use of the claimed invention "by way of experiment" and be "pursued with a bona fide intent of testing the qualities" of the invention. Presumably the common law-developed doctrine of experimental use remains viable post-AIA. *See also* **Critical date; Statutory bar.**

Foreign priority: A benefit that may be claimed by patent applicants in countries signatory to the Paris Convention for the Protection of Industrial Property, wherein a later-filed application in Country B may be entitled to the benefit of the filing date of an earlier-filed application (i.e., the *priority date*) in Country A for the same invention, so long as the later filing is made during the priority period (i.e., 12 months under the Paris Convention) and all other formalities are complied with. In the U.S. patent system, this right of foreign priority is implemented under 35 U.S.C. §119(a).

Grace period: This term refers to the one-year period of time prior to the filing date of a U.S. patent application, during which the claimed invention may be put on sale or in public use in the United States or patented or described in a printed publication anywhere in the world without triggering a loss of right to a patent under 35 U.S.C. §102(b) (pre-AIA). The AIA retains the one-year pre-filing grace period but narrows it to encompass only those disclosures made by the inventor (or one who obtained the disclosed subject matter from the inventor) under 35 U.S.C. §102(b)(1) (post-AIA). Countries other than the United States generally do not provide such a grace period. *See also* **Critical date; Statutory bar.**

Inducing infringement: A form of indirect infringement. *See* 35 U.S.C. §271(b). Inducing infringement is an act of infringement committed by one who induces (i.e., aids or abets) another to directly infringe under 35 U.S.C. §271(a). *See also* **Contributory infringement; Infringement.**

Inequitable conduct: A defensive theory of patent unenforceability. Under the equitable doctrine of "unclean hands," a court should not come to the aid of a patentee (e.g., by granting an injunction against ongoing infringement) if the patentee acted improperly in procuring his patent from the USPTO. Acts giving rise to inequitable conduct typically involve a violation of a patent applicant's duty of candor to the agency, which encompasses a duty to disclose known information that is material to patentability. Inequitable conduct may be proven by establishing that a patentee withheld known information material to patentability, and did so with a specific intent to deceive the USPTO.

Infringement: A violation of the patentee's right to exclude others. Acts that give rise to liability for infringement are enumerated in 35 U.S.C. §271. *Direct* infringement involves an unauthorized making, using, selling, offering to sell, or importing of the patented invention under 35 U.S.C. §271(a). *Indirect* infringement involves inducing another to directly infringe under 35 U.S.C. §271(b), or contributing to the direct infringement of another under 35 U.S.C. §271(c) by supplying one or more nonstaple components of the invention. *Technical* infringement may occur under 35 U.S.C. §271(e)(2) via the filing of certain applications seeking Food and Drug Administration approval for the manufacture of patented drugs. Certain acts of infringement that involve conduct outside U.S. borders are defined by 35 U.S.C. §271(f) and (g). *See also* **Contributory infringement; Inducing infringement; Literal infringement; Doctrine of equivalents.**

Intellectual property (IP): Intangible products of the human mind, such as inventions, ideas, information, artistic creations, music, brand names, product packaging, product design, celebrity persona, industrial secrets, and customer lists, which are the subject of patent, copyright, trademark, trade secret, or related form(s) of legal protection.

Intellectual property rights (IPRs): A variety of rights arising from patents, copyrights, trademarks, trade secrets, and the like.

Interference: A pre–America Invents Act *inter partes* proceeding conducted in the USPTO to determine which of two (or more) rival claimants was the first to invent a particular claimed invention, and hence entitled to the patent on that invention. The interference proceeding was an essential element of the United States' pre-AIA historic first-to-invent priority system. Interferences were conducted in accordance with the priority rules of 35 U.S.C. §102(g)(1) (2006) and 35 U.S.C. §135 (2006). A losing party in an interference could appeal directly to the U.S. Court of Appeals for the Federal Circuit, or alternatively bring a civil action in case of interference under 35 U.S.C. §146 (2006) in U.S. District Court.

Invention date: The date on which an invention is reduced to practice, either actually or constructively, *unless* the patent applicant can "back date" the invention date to the date on which the invention was conceived through proof of conception coupled with reasonable diligence during the pertinent time period under 35 U.S.C. §102(g) (pre-AIA). For purposes of examining patent applications for novelty under 35 U.S.C. §102(a), (e), and (g), and for nonobviousness under 35 U.S.C. §103, the USPTO when operating under pre-AIA rules takes the application's filing date as the presumptive invention date of the invention claimed therein under a constructive reduction to practice theory. The burden is on the patent applicant to establish any earlier actual invention date, if such proof exists. In *ex parte* patent prosecution this may be accomplished by antedating §102(a) or (e) prior art references in accordance with the procedures set forth in 37 C.F.R. §1.131. In an interference proceeding, an earlier invention date is established under 35 U.S.C. §102(g)(1) and §135. *See also* **Conception; Diligence; Interference; Reduction to practice.**

Inventor: One who substantively contributes to the **conception** of a claimed invention. The inventor is not necessarily the **patentee** or owner of the patent claiming the invention.

Laches: An equitable defense to a charge of patent infringement. Laches targets the plaintiff's unreasonable delay in filing suit after it became (or reasonably should have become) aware of the defendant's alleged infringement. If a patentee delays in filing suit for more than six years after this time, a presumption of laches arises and the burden shifts to the patentee to establish legitimate reasons for the delay (such as involvement in other litigation). If the defense is successfully established, laches does not bar the plaintiff's action in its entirety, but rather prevents the recovery of any damages that accrued prior to the filing of the action. *See also* **Equitable estoppel.**

License: An agreement or covenant between a patentee and a licensee that the patentee will not sue the licensee for acts that would otherwise constitute infringement. The license may be exclusive or nonexclusive, may include up-front lump-sum payments, and may be royalty-bearing or royalty-free. A license conveys lesser rights than an **assignment**, which is a transfer of ownership of the patent.

Limitation: An element or component of an invention as recited in a patent claim.

Literal infringement: One of two varieties of patent infringement (i.e., literal infringement and infringement under the doctrine of equivalents), in which an accused device falls precisely within the express boundaries of the asserted patent claim. *See also* **Doctrine of equivalents.**

Loss of right: The loss of a right to patent what may be an otherwise novel and nonobvious invention by delaying too long in filing a patent application after the invention has entered the public domain and/or been commercially exploited by the inventor. Such loss of right results from actions, either by the patent applicant or third parties, that trigger one or more statutory bar events enumerated in 35 U.S.C. §102(b) (pre-AIA) or §102(d) (pre-AIA). Abandonment of an invention under 35 U.S.C. §102(c) (pre-AIA) also is considered a loss of right. *See also* **Statutory bar.**

Machine: A category of potentially patentable subject matter under 35 U.S.C. §101. Synonymous with an apparatus, a machine generally has moving parts; an example is an internal combustion engine.

Manufacture: A category of potentially patentable subject matter under 35 U.S.C. §101. A manufacture in patent parlance is the "catch-all" category for human-made subject matter without moving parts, such as an insulating sleeve for a coffee cup or a foam football having spiral grooves to enhance flight performance.

National treatment: A principle of international law requiring that a country treat foreign nationals as well as (or better than) its own nationals.

New matter: A term of art representing a prohibition on changing the disclosure of an invention once a patent application has been filed. Under 35 U.S.C. §132, no amendment to a pending patent application shall introduce new matter into the disclosure of the invention. The new matter prohibition is the basis for the USPTO's objection to amendments to the abstract, specifications, or drawings that attempt to add new **disclosure** to that originally presented in the patent application as filed.

Nonobviousness: The ultimate condition or criterion of patentability in the United States. Even though novel, an invention nevertheless may not qualify for patent protection if it does not represent enough of a qualitative advance over the prior art. Pursuant to 35 U.S.C. §103, the nonobviousness of a given invention is evaluated from the perspective of a hypothetical person having ordinary skill in the art (i.e., technical field) to which the invention pertains, at the time the invention was made (pre-AIA) or at its effective filing date (post-AIA). In most foreign patent systems, the counterpart to nonobviousness is inventive step. *See also* **Person having ordinary skill in the art (PHOSITA); Novelty; Prior art.**

Nonprovisional application: A regularly filed (rather than provisionally filed) patent application that has been filed in accordance with the requirements of 35 U.S.C. §111(a).

Novelty: A patent law term of art for the requirement that a patented invention be new as defined by 35 U.S.C. §102.

Patent: A statutorily created, government-granted legal instrument that conveys to its owner a time-limited property right to exclude others from making, using, selling, offering to sell throughout the United States, or importing into the United States the invention recited in the claim(s) of the patent. *See* 35 U.S.C. §154(a)(1). *See also* **Claims.**

Patentee: The owner of a patent; the entity holding legal title in the patent. Patentees include not only the patentee to whom the patent was issued but also the successors in title to that patentee. 35 U.S.C. §100(d). The patentee is not necessarily the same entity as the inventor of the patented invention.

Patent misuse: An affirmative defense to a charge of patent infringement that focuses on the patentee's behavior in improperly expanding the scope of its rights beyond the statutory patent grant. Determinations of patent misuse have been based on a fairly narrow range of specific acts or practices of the patent owner, often (but not exclusively) in the context of patent licensing.

Patent term: The enforceable life of a patent, that is, the period of time between a patent's issue date and its expiration date. For U.S. patent applications filed on or after June 8, 1995, the term of the patent ends on the date that is 20 years after the earliest U.S. effective filing date of the application. *See* 35 U.S.C. §154(a)(2). *See also* **Effective filing date.**

Peripheral claiming: A patent claiming regime in which the claim recites the precise literal boundaries of the patentee's right to exclude others. Accused subject matter falling outside the claim may infringe only the doctrine of equivalents, or not at all. The U.S. patent system presently employs a peripheral claiming regime. *Compare with* **Central claiming**.

Person having ordinary skill in the art (PHOSITA): A hypothetical person from whose perspective the nonobviousness criterion of 35 U.S.C. §103 must be judged. The PHOSITA is understood as the modern-day counterpart of the "ordinary mechanic" described by the Supreme Court in the famous doorknob case *Hotchkiss v. Greenwood*, 52 U.S. 248 (1850). The PHOSITA is presumed to have knowledge of all analogous prior art. *See also* **Analogous art; Nonobviousness; Prior art.**

Plurality: A term of art in patent law indicating a quantity of two or more.

Printed publication: General term for non-patent prior art references, such as treatises, periodicals, catalogs, technical documentation, mechanical drawings, photographs, and the like. To qualify as a printed publication, the content of the reference in question must be sufficiently accessible to that segment of the public interested in the art of which the reference is a part. To anticipate a claimed invention under 35 U.S.C. §102, the teaching of the printed publication also must be enabling in accordance with 35 U.S.C. §112(a) (eff. Sept. 16, 2012). *See also* **Anticipation; Prior art; Reference.**

Prior art: General term for the categories of prior technology or events against which the patentability of a claimed invention is evaluated. What qualifies as prior art in the U.S. system for purposes of novelty is cataloged by the various subcategories of 35 U.S.C. §102. An analysis of nonobviousness under 35 U.S.C. §103 further narrows that universe of prior art to the subject matter that is considered analogous to the claimed invention. *See also* **Analogous art.**

Priority system: Although the term "priority" is used in several different senses in patent law, "priority system" is used in this text to refer to a system for determining time-wise priority of a patent between multiple applicants. Assuming each patent applicant has independently invented the same invention or an obvious variant thereof, only one applicant is entitled to a U.S. patent for the invention. Historically, the U.S. granted the patent to the first in time to *invent*, regardless of the order of filing of a patent application. For applications filed on or after the March 16, 2013, the effective date of §3 of the America Invents Act of 2011, U.S. patent law generally grants the patent to the first inventor to *file* her patent application. There are important exceptions to this general rule, however. *See supra* Chapter 4.

Process: A category of potentially patentable subject matter under 35 U.S.C. §101. Synonymous with a method, a process in patent parlance is a series of steps for carrying out a given task.

Prosecution: The process of obtaining a patent, which involves filing a patent application in the USPTO and responding to any rejections or objections made by the agency. Sometimes referred to as patent solicitation.

Prosecution history estoppel: A judicially created doctrine that operates as a legal limitation on the availability of the doctrine of equivalents. A patentee is estopped from seeking to obtain coverage under the doctrine of equivalents over accused subject matter that the patentee effectively surrendered during prosecution before the USPTO in order to obtain her patent. Sometimes referred to as file wrapper estoppel or file history estoppel. *See also* **Doctrine of equivalents.**

Prosecution history laches: A judicially created equitable doctrine under which a patent may be held unenforceable when it is issued after an unreasonable and unexplained delay in **prosecution,** even though the patent applicant complied with all pertinent statutes and rules. For example, refiling a patent application containing only previously allowed claims for the business purpose of delaying their issuance may trigger the defense of prosecution history laches. Courts should apply the doctrine sparingly, however, and only in egregious cases of misuse of the statutory patent system. Prosecution history laches should be distinguished from the equitable defense of **laches** (or "enforcement laches"), which is based on unreasonable delay in the *enforcement* of an issued patent.

Provisional application: A patent application filed under 35 U.S.C. §111(b), which must have a specification (and drawings, if necessary) but need not include any claims or an oath by the inventor(s). The filing fee for a provisional application is significantly less than that of a **nonprovisional** (i.e., regularly filed) **application** because the former is merely a "place holder" that is not substantively examined for patentability. The value of a provisional application is that it creates an early domestic priority date. If a nonprovisional application is filed under 35 U.S.C. §111(a) within one year of the provisional application's filing date for an invention disclosed in accordance with 35 U.S.C. §112(a) (eff. Sept. 16, 2012) (other than the requirement to disclose the best mode) in the provisional application, the nonprovisional application shall be entitled to the benefit of the provisional application's earlier filing date in accordance with 35 U.S.C. §119(e).

Reduction to practice: The final step in the act of inventing. A reduction to practice of an invention may be an actual reduction to practice or a constructive reduction to practice. An *actual reduction to practice* generally involves the construction of a physical embodiment of the invention that works for its intended purpose (testing is often required to verify whether that purpose is met). A *constructive reduction to practice* means that a patent application claiming the invention has been filed with the USPTO, which application satisfies the disclosure requirements of 35 U.S.C. §112(a) (eff. Sept. 16, 2012) for the claimed invention.

Reference: Term of art for a patent or printed publication that is being relied on as **prior art**.

Reissue: An administrative procedure conducted within the USPTO for correcting an issued patent that suffers from certain errors that render the patent wholly or partly inoperative or invalid. *See* 35 U.S.C. §251. Only the patentee (as opposed to a third party) can seek to reissue her patent.

Repair versus reconstruction: A purchaser of a patented device is deemed to have obtained an implied license to use that device, which includes the right to repair it. Thus, repair is not patent infringement. However, when that repair is so extensive as to be characterized as reconstruction or a new making of the patented device, such an act is no longer considered as being within the scope of the purchaser's implied license. Thus, reconstruction is patent infringement. The line between repair and reconstruction is a fine one and the pertinent cases are extremely fact-specific.

Restriction requirement: A requirement applied by the USPTO when a patent applicant claims two or more "independent and distinct" inventions in a single original application. In accordance with 35 U.S.C. §121, the agency may require that the original application be restricted to one of the inventions. If the applicant does not contest the restriction requirement, she will typically elect a claim (or claims) with which to proceed in the original application while canceling the remaining (nonelected) claims without prejudice to their later refiling in a **divisional application**.

Right of priority: A right provided to inventors in countries signatory to the Paris Convention for the Protection of Industrial Property, which permits them to file a patent application in one signatory country (typically an inventor's home country) and, within one year, file additional applications on the same invention in other countries that are also signatories to the Convention. The applicant exercises her right of priority by making a claim that her later-filed application(s) should be accorded the benefit of the filing date of her earlier-filed (typically home country) application. In the U.S. Patent Act, the Paris Convention right of priority is implemented by 35 U.S.C. §119(a).

Specification: The key documentary part of a patent application (which application under 35 U.S.C. §111(a) also includes an oath by the applicant and drawings if necessary for the understanding of the invention). Under 35 U.S.C. §112(a) (eff. Sept. 16, 2012), the specification must provide a disclosure of the invention that satisfies the requirements of (1) written description of the invention, (2) enablement, and (3) best mode. Under 35 U.S.C. §112(b) (eff. Sept. 16, 2012), the specification must conclude with one or more claims (unless the application is a provisional application, which need not include claims). Thus, the patent's claims are part of the specification. *See also* **Disclosure; Written description of the invention; Enablement; Best mode; Claims; Provisional application.**

Statutory bar: The triggering of a statutory bar means that one (or more) of the four events listed in 35 U.S.C. §102(b) (pre-AIA) has occurred, and will result in a **loss of right** to patent what may be an otherwise novel and nonobvious invention. More specifically, a statutory bar is activated under 35 U.S.C. §102(b) (2006) if, more than one year before the patent application filing date, the claimed invention was (1) patented anywhere in the world, (2) described in a printed publication anywhere in the world, (3) in public use in the United States, or (4) on sale in the United States. Section 102(d) of 35 U.S.C. (pre-AIA), referred to as the foreign patenting bar, is another type of statutory bar.

Statutory subject matter: Subject matter that qualifies as potentially patentable in accordance with 35 U.S.C. §101 under one or more of the following categories: process, machine, manufacture, composition of matter, or improvement thereof. Inventions qualifying under §101 are only potentially patentable because, in addition to falling within a statutory category, they must be useful, novel, and nonobvious. Statutory subject matter is sometimes referred to as "patent-eligible" subject matter.

Strict identity standard: The necessary relationship between an anticipatory prior art reference and a claimed invention; that is, in order to evidence anticipation of a claimed invention under 35 U.S.C. §102, a single prior art reference must disclose each and every limitation of that invention, arranged as in the claim.

Utility: A requirement for patentability under 35 U.S.C. §101. Possessing utility means that an invention is useful in the patent law sense, that is, has some practical utility. Current USPTO guidelines require that a patentable invention have a "specific, substantial, and credible" utility.

Written description: That portion of a patent specification other than the claims, typically including a "background of the invention" section, a "summary of the invention" section, and a "detailed description of the invention" section explaining any drawings present in the patent application.

Written description of the invention: A legal requirement that a patent specification must satisfy under 35 U.S.C. §112(a) (eff. Sept. 16, 2012), recognized as independent from the enablement and best mode requirements. The genesis of this legal requirement is the concept of adequate "support"; that is, the language of patent claims newly presented or amended after the filing date of a patent application must be sufficiently supported in the written description of the patent document so as to be entitled to the application's filing date as the *prima facie* invention date for those claims. A test for compliance with this requirement is whether a PHOSITA reading the patent's specification as it existed on the filing date of the application would reasonably understand that the inventor was at that time in possession of the invention as later claimed. *See also* **Best mode; Enablement; Invention date.**

Table of Cases

Italicized page numbers indicate substantive discussions of cases.

Table of Cases

Table of Cases

Table of Cases

Index

A

Abandonment, 58, 204, 212–213, 246

Abstract ideas, 80, 362–364, 365–366, 388

Accessibility, public. *See* Public accessibility

Accessory items, 634–635

Accidental inventions, 179–180

Accused devices, 441, 466–477, 495

Acquiescence, 524

Actual notice, 657

Actual reduction to practice, 123n32, 192n60, 193n62, 229, 232

Adequate damages, 624, 634, 653

Adjudicatory forums for patent matters, 42–52, 43f. *See also specific courts*

Administrative Procedure Act of 1946, 319

Advantages advocacy, 560–562

Adverse inference rule, 644–645

Affirmative rights. *See* Positive rights

After-arising technology, 108, 131–133, 488

Agents, patent, 53n164

Agreement on Trade-Related Aspects of Intellectual Property Rights (TRIPS)

  compulsory licenses, 624

  entry into force of, 5–6

  foreign patent enforcement, 695

  GATT, 676

  in international patenting system, 678–683

  "local working," 664n14

  morality criterion, 341

  national treatment, 675

  offers to sell, 440n5

Agricultural inventions, 339, 661, 681

AIA. *See* America Invents Act of 2011

AIPA. *See* American Inventors Protection Act of 1999

AIPLA (American Intellectual Property Law Association), 29n89

Algorithms, 351–352, 351n30, 354, 363, 374, 388

All-elements rule, 96, 466, 471, 697. *See also* All-limitations rule

All-limitations rule, 441, 466, 471–474, 478. *See also* All-elements rule

All-the-circumstances test, 604–605. *See also* Totality of circumstances

America Invents Act of 2011 (AIA). *See also* Novelty and priority in America Invents Act of 2011

  advice of counsel, 648, 649n192

  antedating, elimination of, 231n202

  best mode requirement, scale-back of, 133–135, 134n72, 134n74

  challenging patents in USPTO under, 430–438

  citation of Patent Act sections, 235, 235n216, 271n2

  common ownership, 291

  continuing application practice, 68n225

  derivation proceeding, 220n167, 263–264

  effective filing date, 20–21n49, 123, 145, 152–153, 233–234n211, 438n177

  experimental use defense, not implemented, 536

  first-inventor-to-file system, 6, 22n54, 28, 28n84, 39, 39n120, 60n204, 233n208, 242, 684–688

  grace periods, 200n88, 684, 688–689

  Hilmer rule, repeal of, 216n152, 218n162, 245, 254, 256,672, 672n36

Index

Index

Index

Index

In-house prior art, 276*n*20. *See also* Cooperative Research and Technology (CREATE) Act of 2004

Injunctions
appellate standard of review, 620–621
balance of hardships, 615, 616, 619–620, 622
eBay standard, 613–615
irreparable harm, 618–619
merits, success on, 617
permanent, 611–615, 622
preliminary, 615–621
public interest, 620
as remedy for infringement, 609, 610–621

Injury-in-fact, 605–606. *See also* Standing to sue

Innovations, 35, 278, 448*n*40, 483. *See also* Inventions

Inoperability, 333–336, 336*n*61. *See also* Utility

"Instrumentalities of the state," 541*n*77
Insubstantial differences test, 107, 469, 472, 492. *See also* Doctrine of equivalents

Intellectual property (IP)
appropriability problem of, 8–9
industries, 3, 3*n*5
intellectual property rights (IPRs), 3, 9
law schools, 2–3
overview, 1
patents as, 8

Intellectual Property and Communications Omnibus Reform Act of 1999, 190*n*57, 430*n*139

Intellectual Property (IP) Clause (U.S. Constitution), 36–37, 389

Intent to deceive, 552, 562–565

Interferences
burdens of proof, 224
conception, 192*n*60, 229
diligence, 192*n*60, 229
elimination of. *See* America Invents Act of 2011
first-to-invent, 685–686
foreign inventive acts, 224–225

generally, 223–225, 224*n*182
Gholz, Charles L., 225*n*186
parties, 224
"quasi-interference," 232
reduction to practice, 123, 123*n*32, 192*n*60, 193*n*62, 229, 232, 243
rule of timewise priority of invention, 225

Interlocutory injunctions, 615–621

International exhaustion, 692–693

International patenting, 659–696. *See also* European patent law
enforcement in U.S. courts, 693–696, 696*n*134
foreign patent protection, pre-Paris Convention, 661–664. *See also* Foreign patenting
gray market goods and exhaustion, 689–693
domestic exhaustion, 690–691
international exhaustion, 692–693
regional exhaustion, 691
overview, 659–664

Paris Convention, 664–676. *See also* Paris Convention for the Protection of Industrial Property
Hilmer rule, 672–675, 673*f,* 674–675*n*40
limitations of, 675–676
national treatment, 665–666
overview, 664–665
right of priority, 665, 666–667*n*21, 666–672, 668–669*n*25, 668*f*

Patent Cooperation Treaty, 676–678
patent harmonization, 683–689
first-to-file vs. first-to-invent, 684–688
novelty, absolute vs. qualified, 688–689
territorial scope, 659–660

TRIPS Agreement, 678–683. *See also* Agreement on Trade-Related Aspects of Intellectual Property Rights

International Preliminary Examination, 677

International searching authority (ISA), 677, 677*n*51

O

P

Q

R

Index